DIAGNOSTIC AND STATISTICAL MANUAL OF MENTAL DISORDERS

FOURTH EDITION

DSM-IV™

DIAGNOSTIC AND STATISTICAL MANUAL OF MENTAL DISORDERS

FOURTH EDITION

DSM-IV™

AMERICAN PSYCHIATRIC ASSOCIATION · BENJAMIN RUSH · 1844

PUBLISHED BY THE

AMERICAN PSYCHIATRIC ASSOCIATION

WASHINGTON, DC

Manufactured in the United States of America on acid-free paper

American Psychiatric Association
1400 K Street, N.W., Washington, DC   20005

Correspondence regarding copyright permissions should be directed to the Division of Publications and Marketing, American Psychiatric Association, 1400 K Street, N.W., Washington, DC 20005.

The correct citation for this book is American Psychiatric Association: *Diagnostic and Statistical Manual of Mental Disorders,* Fourth Edition. Washington, DC, American Psychiatric Association, 1994.

Library of Congress Cataloging-in-Publication Data
Diagnostic and statistical manual of mental disorders : DSM-IV. — 4th ed.
    p.   cm.
    Prepared by the Task Force on DSM-IV and other committees and work
  groups of the American Psychiatric Association.
    Includes index.
    ISBN 0-89042-061-0 (hard : alk. paper). — ISBN 0-89042-062-9 (paper : alk. paper)
    1. Mental illness—Classification. 2. Mental illness—Diagnosis.
  I. American Psychiatric Association. II. American Psychiatric
  Association. Task Force on DSM-IV. III. Title: DSM-IV.
    [DNLM: 1. Mental Disorders—classification. 2. Mental Disorders—
  diagnosis.   WM 15 D536 1994]
  RC455.2.C4D54   1994
  616.89′075—dc20
  DNLM/DLC
  for Library of Congress   94-6304
                                                                                CIP

British Library Cataloguing in Publication Data
A CIP record is available from the British Library.

First printing, May 1994
Second printing, July 1994
Third printing, August 1994
Fourth printing, January 1995

Text Design—Jane H. Davenport
Manufacturing—R. R. Donnelley & Sons Company

To Melvin Sabshin,
a man for all seasons

Contents

Task Force on DSM-IV

Allen Frances, M.D.
Chairperson

Harold Alan Pincus, M.D.
Vice-Chairperson

Michael B. First, M.D.
Editor, Text and Criteria

Nancy Coover Andreasen, M.D., Ph.D.
David H. Barlow, Ph.D.
Magda Campbell, M.D.
Dennis P. Cantwell, M.D.
Ellen Frank, Ph.D.
Judith H. Gold, M.D.
John Gunderson, M.D.
Robert E. Hales, M.D.
Kenneth S. Kendler, M.D.
David J. Kupfer, M.D.
Michael R. Liebowitz, M.D.
Juan Enrique Mezzich, M.D., Ph.D.
Peter E. Nathan, Ph.D.
Roger Peele, M.D.
Darrel A. Regier, M.D., M.P.H.

A. John Rush, M.D.
Chester W. Schmidt, M.D.
Marc Alan Schuckit, M.D.
David Shaffer, M.D.
Robert L. Spitzer, M.D., *Special Adviser*
Gary J. Tucker, M.D.
B. Timothy Walsh, M.D.
Thomas A. Widiger, Ph.D.,
    Research Coordinator
Janet B. W. Williams, D.S.W.
John C. Urbaitis, M.D., *Assembly Liaison*
James J. Hudziak, M.D.,
    Resident Fellow (1990–1993)
Junius Gonzales, M.D.,
    Resident Fellow (1988–1990)

Ruth Ross, M.A., *Science Editor*
Nancy E. Vettorello, M.U.P., *Administrative Coordinator*
Wendy Wakefield Davis, Ed.M., *Editorial Coordinator*
Cindy D. Jones, *Administrative Assistant*
Nancy Sydnor-Greenberg, M.A., *Administrative Consultant*
Myriam Kline, M.S., *Focused Field Trial Coordinator*
James W. Thompson, M.D., M.P.H., *Videotape Field Trial Coordinator*

Anxiety Disorders Work Group

Michael R. Liebowitz, M.D., *Chairperson*
David H. Barlow, Ph.D., *Vice-Chairperson*
James C. Ballenger, M.D.

Jonathan Davidson, M.D.
Edna Foa, Ph.D.
Abby Fyer, M.D.

Delirium, Dementia, and Amnestic and Other Cognitive Disorders Work Group

Gary J. Tucker, M.D., *Chairperson*
Michael Popkin, M.D., *Vice-Chairperson*
Eric Douglas Caine, M.D.
Marshall Folstein, M.D.

Gary Lloyd Gottlieb, M.D.
Igor Grant, M.D.
Benjamin Liptzin, M.D.

Disorders Usually First Diagnosed During Infancy, Childhood, or Adolescence Work Group

David Shaffer, M.D., *Co-Chairperson*
Magda Campbell, M.D., *Co-Chairperson*
Susan J. Bradley, M.D.
Dennis P. Cantwell, M.D.
Gabrielle A. Carlson, M.D.
Donald Jay Cohen, M.D.
Barry Garfinkel, M.D.
Rachel Klein, Ph.D.

Benjamin Lahey, Ph.D.
Rolf Loeber, Ph.D.
Jeffrey Newcorn, M.D.
Rhea Paul, Ph.D.
Judith H. L. Rapoport, M.D.
Sir Michael Rutter, M.D.
Fred Volkmar, M.D.
John S. Werry, M.D.

Eating Disorders Work Group

B. Timothy Walsh, M.D., *Chairperson*
Paul Garfinkel, M.D.
Katherine A. Halmi, M.D.

James Mitchell, M.D.
G. Terence Wilson, Ph.D.

Mood Disorders Work Group

A. John Rush, M.D., *Chairperson*
Martin B. Keller, M.D., *Vice-Chairperson*
Mark S. Bauer, M.D.

David Dunner, M.D.
Ellen Frank, Ph.D.
Donald F. Klein, M.D.

Multiaxial Issues Work Group

Janet B. W. Williams, D.S.W.,
  Chairperson
Howard H. Goldman, M.D., Ph.D.,
  Vice-Chairperson
Alan M. Gruenberg, M.D.

Juan Enrique Mezzich, M.D., Ph.D.
Roger Peele, M.D.
Stephen Setterberg, M.D.
Andrew Edward Skodol II, M.D.

Personality Disorders Work Group

John Gunderson, M.D., *Chairperson*
Robert M. A. Hirschfeld, M.D.,
  Vice-Chairperson
Roger Blashfield, Ph.D.
Susan Jean Fiester, M.D.

Theodore Millon, Ph.D.
Bruce Pfohl, M.D.
Tracie Shea, Ph.D.
Larry Siever, M.D.
Thomas A. Widiger, Ph.D.

Premenstrual Dysphoric Disorder Work Group

Judith H. Gold, M.D., *Chairperson*
Jean Endicott, Ph.D.
Barbara Parry, M.D.

Sally Severino, M.D.
Nada Logan Stotland, M.D.
Ellen Frank, Ph.D., *Consultant*

Psychiatric Systems Interface Disorders (Adjustment, Dissociative, Factitious, Impulse-Control, and Somatoform Disorders and Psychological Factors Affecting Medical Conditions) Work Group

Robert E. Hales, M.D., *Chairperson*
C. Robert Cloninger, M.D.,
  Vice-Chairperson
Jonathan F. Borus, M.D.
Jack Denning Burke, Jr., M.D., M.P.H.
Joe P. Fagan, M.D.
Steven A. King, M.D.

Ronald L. Martin, M.D.
Katharine Anne Phillips, M.D.
David Spiegel, M.D.
Alan Stoudemire, M.D.
James J. Strain, M.D.
Michael G. Wise, M.D.

Schizophrenia and Other Psychotic Disorders Work Group

Nancy Coover Andreasen, M.D., Ph.D.,
  Chairperson
John M. Kane, M.D., *Vice-Chairperson*

Samuel Keith, M.D.
Kenneth S. Kendler, M.D.
Thomas McGlashan, M.D.

Acknowledgments

DSM-IV is a team effort. More than 1,000 people (and numerous professional organizations) have helped us in the preparation of this document. Members of the Task Force on DSM-IV and DSM-IV Staff are listed on p. ix, members of the DSM-IV Work Groups are listed on pp. x–xii, and a list of other participants is included in Appendix J.

The major responsibility for the content of DSM-IV rests with the Task Force on DSM-IV and members of the DSM-IV Work Groups. They have worked (often much harder than they bargained for) with a dedication and good cheer that has been inspirational to us. Bob Spitzer has our special thanks for his untiring efforts and unique perspective. Norman Sartorius, Darrel Regier, Lewis Judd, Fred Goodwin, and Chuck Kaelber were instrumental in facilitating a mutually productive interchange between the American Psychiatric Association and the World Health Organization that has improved both DSM-IV and ICD-10, and increased their compatibility. We are grateful to Robert Israel, Sue Meads, and Amy Blum at the National Center for Health Statistics and Andrea Albaum-Feinstein at the American Health Information Management Association for suggestions on the DSM-IV coding system. Denis Prager, Peter Nathan, and David Kupfer helped us to develop a novel data reanalysis strategy that has been supported with funding from the John D. and Catherine T. MacArthur Foundation.

Many individuals within the American Psychiatric Association deserve recognition. Mel Sabshin's special wisdom and grace made even the most tedious tasks seem worth doing. The American Psychiatric Association Committee on Psychiatric Diagnosis and Assessment (chaired by Layton McCurdy) provided valuable direction and counsel. We would also like to thank the American Psychiatric Association Presidents (Drs. Fink, Pardes, Benedek, Hartmann, English, and McIntyre) and Assembly Speakers (Drs. Cohen, Flamm, Hanin, Pfaehler, and Shellow) who helped with the planning of our work. Carolyn Robinowitz and Jack White, and their respective staffs in the American Psychiatric Association Medical Director's Office and the Business Administration Office, have provided valuable assistance in the organization of the project.

Several other individuals have our special gratitude. Wendy Davis, Nancy Vettorello, and Nancy Sydnor-Greenberg developed and implemented an organizational structure that has kept this complex project from spinning out of control. We have also been blessed with an unusually able administrative staff, which has included Elisabeth Fitzhugh, Willa Hall, Kelly McKinney, Gloria Miele, Helen Stayna, Sarah Tilly, Nina Rosenthal, Susan Mann, Joanne Mas, and, especially, Cindy Jones. Ruth Ross, our tireless Science Writer, has been responsible for improving the clarity of expression and organization of DSM-IV. Myriam Kline (Research Coordinator for the NIH-funded DSM-IV Focused Field Trials), Jim Thompson (Research Coordinator for the MacArthur Foundation–funded Videotape Field Trial), and Sandy Ferris (Assistant Director for the Office of Research) have made many valuable contributions. We would also like to acknowledge all the other staff persons at the American Psychiatric Association who have helped with this project. Ron McMillen, Claire Reinburg, Pam Harley, and Jane Davenport of American Psychiatric Press have provided expert production assistance.

Allen Frances, M.D.   Harold Alan Pincus, M.D.
Chair, Task Force on DSM-IV   *Vice-Chair, Task Force on DSM-IV*

Michael B. First, M.D.   Thomas A. Widiger, Ph.D.
Editor, DSM-IV Text and Criteria   *Research Coordinator*

Introduction

This is the fourth edition of the American Psychiatric Association's *Diagnostic and Statistical Manual of Mental Disorders,* or DSM-IV. The utility and credibility of DSM-IV require that it focus on its clinical, research, and educational purposes and be supported by an extensive empirical foundation. Our highest priority has been to provide a helpful guide to clinical practice. We hoped to make DSM-IV practical and useful for clinicians by striving for brevity of criteria sets, clarity of language, and explicit statements of the constructs embodied in the diagnostic criteria. An additional goal was to facilitate research and improve communication among clinicians and researchers. We were also mindful of the use of DSM-IV for improving the collection of clinical information and as an educational tool for teaching psychopathology.

An official nomenclature must be applicable in a wide diversity of contexts. DSM-IV is used by clinicians and researchers of many different orientations (e.g., biological, psychodynamic, cognitive, behavioral, interpersonal, family/systems). It is used by psychiatrists, other physicians, psychologists, social workers, nurses, occupational and rehabilitation therapists, counselors, and other health and mental health professionals. DSM-IV must be usable across settings—inpatient, outpatient, partial hospital, consultation-liaison, clinic, private practice, and primary care, and with community populations. It is also a necessary tool for collecting and communicating accurate public health statistics. Fortunately, all these many uses are compatible with one another.

DSM-IV was the product of 13 Work Groups (see Appendix J), each of which had primary responsibility for a section of the manual. This organization was designed to increase participation by experts in each of the respective fields. We took a number of precautions to ensure that the Work Group recommendations would reflect the breadth of available evidence and opinion and not just the views of the specific members. After extensive consultations with experts and clinicians in each field, we selected Work Group members who represented a wide range of perspectives and experiences. Work Group members were instructed that they were to participate as consensus scholars and not as advocates of previously held views. Furthermore, we established a formal evidence-based process for the Work Groups to follow.

The Work Groups reported to the Task Force on DSM-IV (see p. ix), which consisted of 27 members, many of whom also chaired a Work Group. Each of the 13 Work Groups was composed of 5 (or more) members whose reviews were critiqued by between 50 and 100 advisers, who were also chosen to represent diverse clinical and research expertise, disciplines, backgrounds, and settings. The involvement of many international experts ensured that DSM-IV had available the widest pool of information and would be applicable across cultures. Conferences and workshops were held to provide conceptual and methodological guidance for the DSM-IV effort. These included a number of consultations between the developers of DSM-IV and the developers of ICD-10 conducted for the purpose of increasing compatibility between the two systems. Also held were methods conferences that focused on cultural factors in the diagnosis of mental disorder, on geriatric diagnosis, and on psychiatric diagnosis in primary care settings.

To maintain open and extensive lines of communication, the Task Force on DSM-IV established a liaison with many other components within the American Psychiatric Association and with more than 60 organizations and associations interested in the development of DSM-IV (e.g., American Health Information Management Association, American Nurses' Association, American Occupational Therapy Association, American Psychoanalytic Association, American Psychological Association, American Psychological Society, Coalition for the Family, Group for the Advancement of Psychiatry, National Association of Social Workers, National Center for Health Statistics, World Health Organization). We attempted to air issues and empirical evidence early in the process in order to identify potential problems and differences in interpretation. Exchanges of information were also made possible through the distribution of a semiannual newsletter (the *DSM-IV Update*), the publication of a regular column on DSM-IV in *Hospital and Community Psychiatry,* frequent presentations at national and international conferences, and numerous journal articles.

Two years before the publication of DSM-IV, the Task Force published and widely distributed the *DSM-IV Options Book.* This volume presented a comprehensive summary of the alternative proposals that were being considered for inclusion in DSM-IV in order to solicit opinion and additional data for our deliberations. We received extensive correspondence from interested individuals who shared with us additional data and recommendations on the potential impact of the possible changes in DSM-IV on their clinical practice, teaching, research, and administrative work. This breadth of discussion helped us to anticipate problems and to attempt to find the best solution among the various options. One year before the publication of DSM-IV, a near-final draft of the proposed criteria sets was distributed to allow for one last critique.

In arriving at final DSM-IV decisions, the Work Groups and the Task Force reviewed all of the extensive empirical evidence and correspondence that had been gathered. It is our belief that the major innovation of DSM-IV lies not in any of its specific content changes but rather in the systematic and explicit process by which it was constructed and documented. More than any other nomenclature of mental disorders, DSM-IV is grounded in empirical evidence.

Historical Background

The need for a classification of mental disorders has been clear throughout the history of medicine, but there has been little agreement on which disorders should be included and the optimal method for their organization. The many nomenclatures that have been developed during the past two millennia have differed in their relative emphasis on phenomenology, etiology, and course as defining features. Some systems have included only a handful of diagnostic categories; others have included thousands. Moreover, the various systems for categorizing mental disorders have differed with respect to whether their principle objective was for use in clinical, research, or statistical settings. Because the history of classification is too extensive to be summarized here, we focus briefly only on those aspects that have led directly to the development of the *Diagnostic and Statistical Manual of Mental Disorders* (DSM) and to the "Mental Disorders" sections in the various editions of the *International Classification of Diseases* (ICD).

In the United States, the initial impetus for developing a classification of mental disorders was the need to collect statistical information. What might be considered the first official attempt to gather information about mental illness in the United States was the recording of the frequency of one category—"idiocy/insanity" in the 1840 census. By the 1880 census, seven categories of mental illness were distinguished—mania, melancholia, monomania, paresis, dementia, dipsomania, and epilepsy. In 1917, the Committee on Statistics of the American Psychiatric Association (at that time called the American Medico-Psychological Association [the name was changed in 1921]), together with the National Commission on Mental Hygiene, formulated a plan that was adopted by the Bureau of the Census for gathering uniform statistics across mental hospitals. Although this system devoted more attention to clinical utility than did previous systems, it was still primarily a statistical classification. The American Psychiatric Association subsequently collaborated with the New York Academy of Medicine to develop a nationally acceptable psychiatric nomenclature that would be incorporated within the first edition of the American Medical Association's Standard Classified Nomenclature of Disease. This nomenclature was designed primarily for diagnosing inpatients with severe psychiatric and neurological disorders.

A much broader nomenclature was later developed by the U.S. Army (and modified by the Veterans Administration) in order to better incorporate the outpatient presentations of World War II servicemen and veterans (e.g., psychophysiological, personality, and acute disorders). Contemporaneously, the World Health Organization (WHO) published the sixth edition of ICD, which, for the first time, included a section for mental disorders. ICD-6 was heavily influenced by the Veterans Administration nomenclature and included 10 categories for psychoses, 9 for psychoneuroses, and 7 for disorders of character, behavior, and intelligence.

The American Psychiatric Association Committee on Nomenclature and Statistics developed a variant of the ICD-6 that was published in 1952 as the first edition of the *Diagnostic and Statistical Manual: Mental Disorders* (DSM-I). DSM-I contained a glossary of descriptions of the diagnostic categories and was the first official manual of mental disorders to focus on clinical utility. The use of the term *reaction* throughout DSM-I reflected the influence of Adolf Meyer's psychobiological view that mental disorders represented reactions of the personality to psychological, social, and biological factors.

In part because of the lack of widespread acceptance of the mental disorder taxonomy contained in ICD-6 and ICD-7, WHO sponsored a comprehensive review of diagnostic issues that was conducted by the British psychiatrist Stengel. His report can be credited with having inspired many of the recent advances in diagnostic methodology—most especially the need for explicit definitions as a means of promoting reliable clinical diagnoses. However, the next round of diagnostic revision, which led to DSM-II and ICD-8, did not follow Stengel's recommendations to any great degree. DSM-II was similar to DSM-I but eliminated the term *reaction*.

As had been the case for DSM-I and DSM-II, the development of DSM-III was coordinated with the development of the next (ninth) version of ICD, which was published in 1975 and implemented in 1978. Work began on DSM-III in 1974, with publication in 1980. DSM-III introduced a number of important methodological innovations, including explicit diagnostic criteria, a multiaxial system, and a descriptive approach that attempted to be neutral with respect to theories of etiology. This effort was facilitated by the extensive empirical work then under way on the construction and validation of explicit diagnostic criteria and the development of semistructured interviews. ICD-9 did not include diagnostic criteria or a multiaxial system largely because the primary function of this international system was to delineate categories to facilitate the collection of basic health statistics. In contrast, DSM-III was developed with the additional goal of providing a medical nomenclature for clinicians and researchers. Because of dissatisfaction across all of medicine with the lack of specificity in ICD-9, a decision was made to modify it for use in the United States, resulting in ICD-9-CM (for Clinical Modification).

Experience with DSM-III revealed a number of inconsistencies in the system and a number of instances in which the criteria were not entirely clear. Therefore, the American Psychiatric Association appointed a Work Group to Revise DSM-III, which developed the revisions and corrections that led to the publication of DSM-III-R in 1987.

The DSM-IV Revision Process

The third edition of the *Diagnostic and Statistical Manual of Mental Disorders* (DSM-III) represented a major advance in the diagnosis of mental disorders and greatly facilitated empirical research. The development of DSM-IV has benefited from the substantial increase in the research on diagnosis that was generated in part by DSM-III and DSM-III-R. Most diagnoses now have an empirical literature or available data sets that are relevant to decisions regarding the revision of the diagnostic manual. The Task Force on DSM-IV and its Work Groups conducted a three-stage empirical process that included 1) comprehensive and systematic reviews of the published literature, 2) reanalyses of already-collected data sets, and 3) extensive issue-focused field trials.

Literature Reviews

Two methods conferences were sponsored to articulate for all the Work Groups a systematic procedure for finding, extracting, aggregating, and interpreting data in a comprehensive and objective fashion. The initial tasks of each of the DSM-IV Work Groups were to identify the most pertinent issues regarding each diagnosis and to determine the kinds of empirical data relevant to their resolution. A Work Group member or adviser was then assigned the responsibility of conducting a systematic and comprehensive review of the relevant literature that would inform the resolution of the issue and also document the text of DSM-IV. The domains considered in making decisions included clinical utility, reliability, descriptive validity, psychometric performance characteristics of individual criteria, and a number of validating variables.

Each literature review specified 1) the issues or aspects of the text and criteria under consideration and the significance of the issues with respect to DSM-IV; 2) the review method (including the sources for identifying relevant studies, the number of studies considered, the criteria for inclusion and exclusion from the review, and the variables catalogued in each study); 3) the results of the review (including a descriptive summary of the studies with respect to methodology, design, and substantive correlates of the findings, the relevant findings, and the analyses conducted on these findings); and 4) the various options for resolving the issue, the advantages and disadvantages of each option, recommendations, and suggestions for additional research that would be needed to provide a more conclusive resolution.

The goal of the DSM-IV literature reviews was to provide comprehensive and unbiased information and to ensure that DSM-IV reflects the best available clinical and research literature. For this reason, we used systematic computer searches and critical reviews done by large groups of advisers to ensure that the literature coverage was adequate and that the interpretation of the results was justified. Input was solicited especially from those persons likely to be critical of the conclusions of the review. The literature reviews were revised many times to produce as comprehensive and balanced a result as possible. It must be noted that for some issues addressed by the DSM-IV Work Groups, particularly those that were more conceptual in nature or for which there were insufficient data, a review of the empirical literature had limited utility. Despite these limitations, the reviews were helpful in documenting the rationale and empirical support for decisions made by the DSM-IV Work Groups.

Data Reanalyses

When a review of the literature revealed a lack of evidence (or conflicting evidence) for the resolution of an issue, we often made use of two additional resources—data reanalyses and field trials—to help in making final decisions. Analyses of relevant unpublished data sets were supported by a grant to the American Psychiatric Association from the John D. and Catherine T. MacArthur Foundation. Most of the 40 data reanalyses performed for DSM-IV involved the collaboration of several investigators at different sites. These researchers jointly subjected their data to questions posed by the Work Groups concerning the criteria included in DSM-III-R or criteria that might be included in DSM-IV. Data reanalyses also made it possible for Work Groups to generate several criteria sets that were then tested in the DSM-IV field trials. Although, for the most part, the data sets used in the reanalyses had been collected as part of epidemiological studies or treatment or other clinical studies, they were also highly relevant to the nosological questions facing the DSM-IV Work Groups.

Field Trials

Twelve DSM-IV field trials were sponsored by the National Institute of Mental Health (NIMH) in collaboration with the National Institute on Drug Abuse (NIDA) and the National Institute on Alcohol Abuse and Alcoholism (NIAAA). The field trials allowed the DSM-IV Work Groups to compare alternative options and to study the possible impact of suggested changes. Field trials compared DSM-III, DSM-III-R, ICD-10, and proposed DSM-IV criteria sets in 5–10 different sites per field trial, with approximately 100 subjects at each site. Diverse sites, with representative groups of subjects from a range of sociocultural and ethnic backgrounds, were selected to ensure generalizability of field-trial results and to test some of the most difficult questions in differential diagnosis. The 12 field trials included more than 70 sites and evaluated more than 6,000 subjects. The field trials collected information on the reliability and performance characteristics of each criteria set as a whole, as well as of the specific items within each criteria set. The field trials also helped to bridge the boundary between clinical research and clinical practice by determining how well suggestions for change that are derived from clinical research findings apply in clinical practice.

Criteria for Change

Although it was impossible to develop absolute and infallible criteria for when changes should be made, there were some principles that guided our efforts. The threshold for making revisions in DSM-IV was set higher than that for DSM-III and DSM-III-R. Decisions had to be substantiated by explicit statements of rationale and by the systematic review of relevant empirical data. To increase the practicality and clinical utility of DSM-IV, the criteria sets were simplified and clarified when this could be justified by empirical data. An attempt was made to strike an optimal balance in DSM-IV with respect to historical tradition (as embodied in DSM-III and DSM-III-R), compatibility with ICD-10, evidence from reviews of the literature, analyses of unpublished data sets, results of field trials, and consensus of the field. Although the amount of evidence required to support changes was set at a high threshold, it necessarily varied across disorders because the empirical support for the decisions made in DSM-III and DSM-III-R also varied across disorders. Of course, common sense was necessary, and major changes to solve minor problems required more evidence than minor changes to solve major problems.

We received suggestions to include numerous new diagnoses in DSM-IV. The proponents argued that the new diagnoses were necessary to improve the coverage of the system by including a group of individuals that were undiagnosable in DSM-III-R or diagnosable only under the Not Otherwise Specified rubric. We decided that, in general, new diagnoses should be included in the system only after research has established that they should be included rather than being included to stimulate that research. However, diagnoses already included in ICD-10 were given somewhat more consideration than those that were being proposed fresh for DSM-IV. The increased marginal utility, clarity, and coverage provided by each newly proposed diagnosis had to be balanced against the cumulative cumbersomeness imposed on the whole system, the paucity of empirical documentation, and the possible misdiagnosis or misuse that might result. No classification of mental disorders can have a sufficient number of specific categories to encompass every conceivable clinical presentation. The Not Otherwise Specified categories are provided to cover the not infrequent presentations that are at the boundary of specific categorical definitions.

The DSM-IV Sourcebook

Documentation has been the essential foundation of the DSM-IV process. The *DSM-IV Sourcebook*, published in five volumes, is intended to provide a comprehensive and convenient reference record of the clinical and research support for the various decisions reached by the Work Groups and the Task Force. The first three volumes of the *Sourcebook* contain condensed versions of the 150 DSM-IV literature reviews. The fourth volume contains reports of the data reanalyses, and the fifth volume contains reports of the field trials and a final executive summary of the rationale for the decisions made by each Work Group. In addition, many papers were stimulated by the efforts toward empirical documentation in DSM-IV, and these have been published in peer-reviewed journals.

Relation to ICD-10

The tenth revision of the *International Statistical Classification of Diseases and Related Health Problems* (ICD-10), developed by WHO, was published in 1992, but will probably not come into official use in the United States until the late 1990s. Those preparing ICD-10 and DSM-IV have worked closely to coordinate their efforts, resulting in much mutual influence. ICD-10 consists of an official coding system and other related clinical and research documents and instruments. The codes and terms provided in DSM-IV are fully compatible with both ICD-9-CM and ICD-10 (see Appendix H). The clinical and research drafts of ICD-10 were thoroughly reviewed by the DSM-IV Work Groups and suggested important topics for DSM-IV literature reviews and data reanalyses. Draft versions of the ICD-10 Diagnostic Criteria for Research were included as alternatives to be compared with DSM-III, DSM-III-R, and suggested DSM-IV criteria sets in the DSM-IV field trials. The many consultations between the developers of DSM-IV and ICD-10 (which were facilitated by NIMH, NIDA, and NIAAA) were enormously useful in increasing the congruence and reducing meaningless differences in wording between the two systems.

Definition of Mental Disorder

Although this volume is titled the *Diagnostic and Statistical Manual of Mental Disorders,* the term *mental disorder* unfortunately implies a distinction between "mental" disorders and "physical" disorders that is a reductionistic anachronism of mind/body dualism. A compelling literature documents that there is much "physical" in "mental" disorders and much "mental" in "physical" disorders. The problem raised by the term "mental" disorders has been much clearer than its solution, and, unfortunately, the term persists in the title of DSM-IV because we have not found an appropriate substitute.

Moreover, although this manual provides a classification of mental disorders, it must be admitted that no definition adequately specifies precise boundaries for the concept of "mental disorder." The concept of mental disorder, like many other concepts in medicine and science, lacks a consistent operational definition that covers all situations. All medical conditions are defined on various levels of abstraction—for example, structural pathology (e.g., ulcerative colitis), symptom presentation (e.g., migraine), deviance from a physiological norm (e.g., hypertension), and etiology (e.g., pneumococcal pneumonia). Mental disorders have also been defined by a variety of concepts (e.g., distress, dyscontrol, disadvantage, disability, inflexibility, irrationality, syndromal pattern, etiology, and statistical deviation). Each is a useful indicator for a mental disorder, but none is equivalent to the concept, and different situations call for different definitions.

Despite these caveats, the definition of *mental disorder* that was included in DSM-III and DSM-III-R is presented here because it is as useful as any other available definition and has helped to guide decisions regarding which conditions on the boundary between normality and pathology should be included in DSM-IV. In DSM-IV, each of the mental disorders is conceptualized as a clinically significant behavioral or psychological syndrome or pattern that occurs in an individual and that is associated with present distress (e.g., a painful symptom) or disability (i.e., impairment in one or more important areas of functioning) or with a significantly increased risk of suffering death, pain, disability, or an important loss of freedom. In addition, this syndrome or pattern must not be merely an expectable and culturally sanctioned response to a particular event, for example, the death of a loved one. Whatever its original cause, it must currently be considered a manifestation of a behavioral, psychological, or biological dysfunction in the individual. Neither deviant behavior (e.g., political, religious, or sexual) nor conflicts that are primarily between the individual and society are mental disorders unless the deviance or conflict is a symptom of a dysfunction in the individual, as described above.

A common misconception is that a classification of mental disorders classifies people, when actually what are being classified are disorders that people have. For this reason, the text of DSM-IV (as did the text of DSM-III-R) avoids the use of such expressions as "a schizophrenic" or "an alcoholic" and instead uses the more accurate, but admittedly more cumbersome, "an individual with Schizophrenia" or "an individual with Alcohol Dependence."

Issues in the Use of DSM-IV

Limitations of the Categorical Approach

DSM-IV is a categorical classification that divides mental disorders into types based on criteria sets with defining features. This naming of categories is the traditional method of organizing and transmitting information in everyday life and has been the fundamental approach used in all systems of medical diagnosis. A categorical approach to classification works best when all members of a diagnostic class are homogeneous, when there are clear boundaries between classes, and when the different classes are mutually exclusive. Nonetheless, the limitations of the categorical classification system must be recognized.

In DSM-IV, there is no assumption that each category of mental disorder is a completely discrete entity with absolute boundaries dividing it from other mental disorders or from no mental disorder. There is also no assumption that all individuals described as having the same mental disorder are alike in all important ways. The clinician using DSM-IV should therefore consider that individuals sharing a diagnosis are likely to be heterogeneous even in regard to the defining features of the diagnosis and that boundary cases will be difficult to diagnose in any but a probabilistic fashion. This outlook allows greater flexibility in the use of the system, encourages more specific attention to boundary cases, and emphasizes the need to capture additional clinical information that goes beyond diagnosis. In recognition of the heterogeneity of clinical presentations, DSM-IV often includes polythetic criteria sets, in which the individual need only present with a subset of items from a longer list (e.g., the diagnosis of Borderline Personality Disorder requires only five out of nine items).

It was suggested that the DSM-IV Classification be organized following a dimensional model rather than the categorical model used in DSM-III-R. A dimensional system classifies clinical presentations based on quantification of attributes rather than the assignment to categories and works best in describing phenomena that are distributed continuously and that do not have clear boundaries. Although dimensional systems increase reliability and communicate more clinical information (because they report clinical attributes that might be subthreshold in a categorical system), they also have serious limitations and thus far have been less useful than categorical systems in clinical practice and in stimulating research. Numerical dimensional descriptions are much less familiar and vivid than are the categorical names for mental disorders. Moreover, there is as yet no agreement on the choice of the optimal dimensions to be used for classification purposes. Nonetheless, it is possible that the increasing research on, and familiarity with, dimensional systems may eventually result in their greater acceptance both as a method of conveying clinical information and as a research tool.

Use of Clinical Judgment

DSM-IV is a classification of mental disorders that was developed for use in clinical, educational, and research settings. The diagnostic categories, criteria, and textual descriptions are meant to be employed by individuals with appropriate clinical training and experience in diagnosis. It is important that DSM-IV not be applied mechanically by untrained individuals. The specific diagnostic criteria included in DSM-IV are meant to serve as guidelines to be informed by clinical judgment and are not meant to be used in a cookbook fashion. For example, the exercise of clinical judgment may justify giving a certain diagnosis to an individual even though the clinical presentation falls just short of meeting the full criteria for the diagnosis as long as the symptoms that are present are persistent and severe. On the other hand, lack of familiarity with DSM-IV or excessively flexible and idiosyncratic application of DSM-IV criteria or conventions substantially reduces its utility as a common language for communication.

Use of DSM-IV in Forensic Settings

When the DSM-IV categories, criteria, and textual descriptions are employed for forensic purposes, there are significant risks that diagnostic information will be misused or misunderstood. These dangers arise because of the imperfect fit between the questions of ultimate concern to the law and the information contained in a clinical diagnosis. In most situations, the clinical diagnosis of a DSM-IV mental disorder is not sufficient to establish the existence for legal purposes of a "mental disorder," "mental disability," "mental disease," or "mental defect." In determining whether an individual meets a specified legal standard (e.g., for competence, criminal responsibility, or disability), additional information is usually required beyond that contained in the DSM-IV diagnosis. This might include information about the individual's functional impairments and how these impairments affect the particular abilities in question. It is precisely because impairments, abilities, and disabilities vary widely within each diagnostic category that assignment of a particular diagnosis does not imply a specific level of impairment or disability.

Nonclinical decision makers should also be cautioned that a diagnosis does not carry any necessary implications regarding the causes of the individual's mental disorder or its associated impairments. Inclusion of a disorder in the Classification (as in medicine generally) does not require that there be knowledge about its etiology. Moreover, the fact that an individual's presentation meets the criteria for a DSM-IV diagnosis does not carry any necessary implication regarding the individual's degree of control over the behaviors that may be associated with the disorder. Even when diminished control over one's behavior is a feature of the disorder, having the diagnosis in itself does not demonstrate that a particular individual is (or was) unable to control his or her behavior at a particular time.

It must be noted that DSM-IV reflects a consensus about the classification and diagnosis of mental disorders derived at the time of its initial publication. New knowledge generated by research or clinical experience will undoubtedly lead to an increased understanding of the disorders included in DSM-IV, to the identification of new disorders, and to the removal of some disorders in future classifications. The text and criteria sets included in DSM-IV will require reconsideration in light of evolving new information.

The use of DSM-IV in forensic settings should be informed by an awareness of the risks and limitations discussed above. When used appropriately, diagnoses and diagnostic information can assist decision makers in their determinations. For example, when the presence of a mental disorder is the predicate for a subsequent legal determination (e.g., involuntary civil commitment), the use of an established system of diagnosis enhances the value and reliability of the determination. By providing a compendium based on a review of the pertinent clinical and research literature, DSM-IV may facilitate the legal decision makers' understanding of the relevant characteristics of mental disorders. The literature related to diagnoses also serves as a check on ungrounded speculation about mental disorders and about the functioning of a particular individual. Finally, diagnostic information regarding longitudinal course may improve decision making when the legal issue concerns an individual's mental functioning at a past or future point in time.

Ethnic and Cultural Considerations

Special efforts have been made in the preparation of DSM-IV to incorporate an awareness that the manual is used in culturally diverse populations in the United States and internationally. Clinicians are called on to evaluate individuals from numerous different ethnic groups and cultural backgrounds (including many who are recent immigrants). Diagnostic assessment can be especially challenging when a clinician from one ethnic or cultural group uses the DSM-IV Classification to evaluate an individual from a different ethnic or cultural group. A clinician who is unfamiliar with the nuances of an individual's cultural frame of reference may incorrectly judge as psychopathology those normal variations in behavior, belief, or experience that are particular to the individual's culture. For example, certain religious practices or beliefs (e.g., hearing or seeing a deceased relative during bereavement) may be misdiagnosed as manifestations of a Psychotic Disorder. Applying Personality Disorder criteria across cultural settings may be especially difficult because of the wide cultural variation in concepts of self, styles of communication, and coping mechanisms.

DSM-IV includes three types of information specifically related to cultural considerations: 1) a discussion in the text of cultural variations in the clinical presentations of those disorders that have been included in the DSM-IV Classification; 2) a description of culture-bound syndromes that have not been included in the DSM-IV Classification (these are included in Appendix I); and 3) an outline for cultural formulation designed to assist the clinician in systematically evaluating and reporting the impact of the individual's cultural context (also in Appendix I).

The wide international acceptance of DSM suggests that this classification is useful in describing mental disorders as they are experienced by individuals throughout the world. Nonetheless, evidence also suggests that the symptoms and course of a number of DSM-IV disorders are influenced by cultural and ethnic factors. To facilitate its application to individuals from diverse cultural and ethnic settings, DSM-IV includes a new section in the text to cover culture-related features. This section describes the ways in which varied cultural backgrounds affect the content and form of the symptom presentation (e.g., depressive disorders characterized by a preponderance of somatic symptoms rather than sadness in certain cultures), preferred idioms for describing distress, and information on prevalence when it is available.

The second type of cultural information provided pertains to "culture-bound syndromes" that have been described in just one, or a few, of the world's societies. DSM-IV provides two ways of increasing the recognition of culture-bound syndromes:

1) some (e.g., *amok, ataque de nervios*) are included as separate examples in Not Otherwise Specified categories; and 2) an appendix of culture-bound syndromes (Appendix I) has been introduced in DSM-IV that includes the name for the condition, the cultures in which it was first described, and a brief description of the psychopathology.

The provision of a culture-specific section in the DSM-IV text, the inclusion of a glossary of culture-bound syndromes, and the provision of an outline for cultural formulation are designed to enhance the cross-cultural applicability of DSM-IV. It is hoped that these new features will increase sensitivity to variations in how mental disorders may be expressed in different cultures and will reduce the possible effect of unintended bias stemming from the clinician's own cultural background.

Use of DSM-IV in Treatment Planning

Making a DSM-IV diagnosis is only the first step in a comprehensive evaluation. To formulate an adequate treatment plan, the clinician will invariably require considerable additional information about the person being evaluated beyond that required to make a DSM-IV diagnosis.

Distinction Between Mental Disorder and General Medical Condition

The terms *mental disorder* and *general medical condition* are used throughout this manual. The term *mental disorder* is explained above. The term *general medical condition* is used merely as a convenient shorthand to refer to conditions and disorders that are listed outside the "Mental and Behavioural Disorders" chapter of ICD. It should be recognized that these are merely terms of convenience and should not be taken to imply that there is any fundamental distinction between mental disorders and general medical conditions, that mental disorders are unrelated to physical or biological factors or processes, or that general medical conditions are unrelated to behavioral or psychosocial factors or processes.

Organization of the Manual

The manual begins with instructions concerning the use of the manual (p. 1), followed by the DSM-IV Classification (pp. 13–24), which provides a systematic listing of the official codes and categories. Next is a description of the DSM-IV multiaxial system for diagnosis (pp. 25–35). This is followed by the diagnostic criteria for each of the DSM-IV disorders accompanied by descriptive text (pp. 37–687). Finally, DSM-IV includes 10 appendixes.

Cautionary Statement

The specified diagnostic criteria for each mental disorder are offered as guidelines for making diagnoses, because it has been demonstrated that the use of such criteria enhances agreement among clinicians and investigators. The proper use of these criteria requires specialized clinical training that provides both a body of knowledge and clinical skills.

These diagnostic criteria and the DSM-IV Classification of mental disorders reflect a consensus of current formulations of evolving knowledge in our field. They do not encompass, however, all the conditions for which people may be treated or that may be appropriate topics for research efforts.

The purpose of DSM-IV is to provide clear descriptions of diagnostic categories in order to enable clinicians and investigators to diagnose, communicate about, study, and treat people with various mental disorders. It is to be understood that inclusion here, for clinical and research purposes, of a diagnostic category such as Pathological Gambling or Pedophilia does not imply that the condition meets legal or other nonmedical criteria for what constitutes mental disease, mental disorder, or mental disability. The clinical and scientific considerations involved in categorization of these conditions as mental disorders may not be wholly relevant to legal judgments, for example, that take into account such issues as individual responsibility, disability determination, and competency.

Use of the Manual

Coding and Reporting Procedures

Diagnostic Codes

The official coding system in use in the United States as of publication of this manual is the *International Classification of Diseases,* Ninth Revision, Clinical Modification (ICD-9-CM). Most DSM-IV disorders have a numerical ICD-9-CM code that appears several times: 1) preceding the name of the disorder in the Classification (pp. 13–24), 2) at the beginning of the text section for each disorder, and 3) accompanying the criteria set for each disorder. For some diagnoses (e.g., Mental Retardation, Substance-Induced Mood Disorder), the appropriate code depends on further specification and is listed after the text and criteria set for the disorder. The names of some disorders are followed by alternative terms enclosed in parentheses, which, in most cases, were the DSM-III-R names for the disorders.

The use of diagnostic codes is fundamental to medical record keeping. Diagnostic coding facilitates data collection and retrieval and compilation of statistical information. Codes also are often required to report diagnostic data to interested third parties, including governmental agencies, private insurers, and the World Health Organization. For example, in the United States, the use of these codes has been mandated by the Health Care Financing Administration for purposes of reimbursement under the Medicare system.

Subtypes (some of which are coded in the fifth digit) and specifiers are provided for increased specificity. *Subtypes* define mutually exclusive and jointly exhaustive phenomenological subgroupings within a diagnosis and are indicated by the instruction "specify type" in the criteria set. For example, Delusional Disorder is subtyped based on the content of the delusions, with seven subtypes provided: Erotomanic Type, Grandiose Type, Jealous Type, Persecutory Type, Somatic Type, Mixed Type, and Unspecified Type. In contrast, *specifiers* are not intended to be mutually exclusive or jointly exhaustive and are indicated by the instruction "specify" or "specify if" in the criteria set (e.g., for Social Phobia, the instruction notes "Specify if: Generalized"). Specifiers provide an opportunity to define a more homogeneous subgrouping of individuals with the disorder who share certain features (e.g., Major Depressive Disorder, With Melancholic Features). Although a fifth digit is sometimes assigned to code a subtype or specifier (e.g., 290.12 Dementia of the Alzheimer's Type, With Early Onset, With Delusions) or severity (296.21 Major Depressive Disorder, Single Episode, Mild), the majority of subtypes and specifiers included in DSM-IV cannot be coded within the

ICD-9-CM system and are indicated only by including the subtype or specifier after the name of the disorder (e.g., Social Phobia, Generalized).

Severity and Course Specifiers

A DSM-IV diagnosis is usually applied to the individual's current presentation and is not typically used to denote previous diagnoses from which the individual has recovered. The following specifiers indicating severity and course may be listed after the diagnosis: Mild, Moderate, Severe, In Partial Remission, In Full Remission, and Prior History.

The specifiers Mild, Moderate, and Severe should be used only when the full criteria for the disorder are currently met. In deciding whether the presentation should be described as mild, moderate, or severe, the clinician should take into account the number and intensity of the signs and symptoms of the disorder and any resulting impairment in occupational or social functioning. For the majority of disorders, the following guidelines may be used:

> **Mild.** Few, if any, symptoms in excess of those required to make the diagnosis are present, and symptoms result in no more than minor impairment in social or occupational functioning.
> **Moderate.** Symptoms or functional impairment between "mild" and "severe" are present.
> **Severe.** Many symptoms in excess of those required to make the diagnosis, or several symptoms that are particularly severe, are present, or the symptoms result in marked impairment in social or occupational functioning.
> **In Partial Remission.** The full criteria for the disorder were previously met, but currently only some of the symptoms or signs of the disorder remain.
> **In Full Remission.** There are no longer any symptoms or signs of the disorder, but it is still clinically relevant to note the disorder—for example, in an individual with previous episodes of Bipolar Disorder who has been symptom free on lithium for the past 3 years. After a period of time in full remission, the clinician may judge the individual to be recovered and, therefore, would no longer code the disorder as a current diagnosis. The differentiation of In Full Remission from recovered requires consideration of many factors, including the characteristic course of the disorder, the length of time since the last period of disturbance, the total duration of the disturbance, and the need for continued evaluation or prophylactic treatment.
> **Prior History.** For some purposes, it may be useful to note a history of the criteria having been met for a disorder even when the individual is considered to be recovered from it. Such past diagnoses of mental disorder would be indicated by using the specifier Prior History (e.g., Separation Anxiety Disorder, Prior History, for an individual with a history of Separation Anxiety Disorder who has no current disorder or who currently meets criteria for Panic Disorder).

Specific criteria for defining Mild, Moderate, and Severe have been provided for the following: Mental Retardation, Conduct Disorder, Manic Episode, and Major Depressive Episode. Specific criteria for defining In Partial Remission and In Full Remission have been provided for the following: Manic Episode, Major Depressive Episode, and Substance Dependence.

Recurrence

Not infrequently in clinical practice, individuals after a period of time in which the full criteria for the disorder are no longer met (i.e., in partial or full remission or recovery) may develop symptoms that suggest a recurrence of their original disorder but that do not yet meet the full threshold for that disorder as specified in the criteria set. It is a matter of clinical judgment as to how best to indicate the presence of these symptoms. The following options are available:

- If the symptoms are judged to be a new episode of a recurrent condition, the disorder may be diagnosed as current (or provisional) even before the full criteria have been met (e.g., after meeting criteria for a Major Depressive Episode for only 10 days instead of the 14 days usually required).
- If the symptoms are judged to be clinically significant but it is not clear whether they constitute a recurrence of the original disorder, the appropriate Not Otherwise Specified category may be given.
- If it is judged that the symptoms are not clinically significant, no additional current or provisional diagnosis is given, but "Prior History" may be noted (see p. 2).

Principal Diagnosis/Reason for Visit

When more than one diagnosis for an individual is given in an inpatient setting, the *principal diagnosis* is the condition established after study to be chiefly responsible for occasioning the admission of the individual. When more than one diagnosis is given for an individual in an outpatient setting, the *reason for visit* is the condition that is chiefly responsible for the ambulatory care medical services received during the visit. In most cases, the principal diagnosis or the reason for visit is also the main focus of attention or treatment. It is often difficult (and somewhat arbitrary) to determine which diagnosis is the principal diagnosis or the reason for visit, especially in situations of "dual diagnosis" (a substance-related diagnosis like Amphetamine Dependence accompanied by a non-substance-related diagnosis like Schizophrenia). For example, it may be unclear which diagnosis should be considered "principal" for an individual hospitalized with both Schizophrenia and Amphetamine Intoxication, because each condition may have contributed equally to the need for admission and treatment.

Multiple diagnoses can be reported in a multiaxial fashion (see p. 33) or in a nonaxial fashion (see p. 35). When the principal diagnosis is an Axis I disorder, this is indicated by listing it first. The remaining disorders are listed in order of focus of attention and treatment. When a person has both an Axis I and an Axis II diagnosis, the principal diagnosis or the reason for visit will be assumed to be on Axis I unless the Axis II diagnosis is followed by the qualifying phrase "(Principal Diagnosis)" or "(Reason for Visit)."

Provisional Diagnosis

The specifier *provisional* can be used when there is a strong presumption that the full criteria will ultimately be met for a disorder, but not enough information is available to make a firm diagnosis. The clinician can indicate the diagnostic uncertainty by recording "(Provisional)" following the diagnosis. For example, the individual appears to have a Major Depressive Disorder, but is unable to give an adequate history to establish that the full criteria are met. Another use of the term *provisional* is for those situations in which differential diagnosis depends exclusively on the duration of illness. For example, a diagnosis of Schizophreniform Disorder requires a duration of less than 6 months and can only be given provisionally if assigned before remission has occurred.

Use of Not Otherwise Specified Categories

Because of the diversity of clinical presentations, it is impossible for the diagnostic nomenclature to cover every possible situation. For this reason, each diagnostic class has at least one Not Otherwise Specified (NOS) category and some classes have several NOS categories. There are four situations in which an NOS diagnosis may be appropriate:

- The presentation conforms to the general guidelines for a mental disorder in the diagnostic class, but the symptomatic picture does not meet the criteria for any of the specific disorders. This would occur either when the symptoms are below the diagnostic threshold for one of the specific disorders or when there is an atypical or mixed presentation.
- The presentation conforms to a symptom pattern that has not been included in the DSM-IV Classification but that causes clinically significant distress or impairment. Research criteria for some of these symptom patterns have been included in Appendix B ("Criteria Sets and Axes Provided for Further Study"), in which case a page reference to the suggested research criteria set in Appendix B is provided.
- There is uncertainty about etiology (i.e., whether the disorder is due to a general medical condition, is substance induced, or is primary).
- There is insufficient opportunity for complete data collection (e.g., in emergency situations) or inconsistent or contradictory information, but there is enough information to place it within a particular diagnostic class (e.g., the clinician determines that the individual has psychotic symptoms but does not have enough information to diagnose a specific Psychotic Disorder).

Ways of Indicating Diagnostic Uncertainty

The following table indicates the various ways in which a clinician may indicate diagnostic uncertainty:

Term	Examples of clinical situations
V Codes (for Other Conditions That May Be a Focus of Clinical Attention)	Insufficient information to know whether or not a presenting problem is attributable to a mental disorder, e.g., Academic Problem; Adult Antisocial Behavior
799.9 Diagnosis or Condition Deferred on Axis I	Information inadequate to make any diagnostic judgment about an Axis I diagnosis or condition
799.9 Diagnosis Deferred on Axis II	Information inadequate to make any diagnostic judgment about an Axis II diagnosis *(continued)*

Term	Examples of clinical situations
300.9 Unspecified Mental Disorder (nonpsychotic)	Enough information available to rule out a Psychotic Disorder, but further specification is not possible
298.9 Psychotic Disorder Not Otherwise Specified	Enough information available to determine the presence of a Psychotic Disorder, but further specification is not possible
[Class of disorder] Not Otherwise Specified e.g., Depressive Disorder Not Otherwise Specified	Enough information available to indicate the class of disorder that is present, but further specification is not possible, either because there is not sufficient information to make a more specific diagnosis or because the clinical features of the disorder do not meet the criteria for any of the specific categories in that class
[Specific diagnosis] (Provisional) e.g., Schizophreniform Disorder (Provisional)	Enough information available to make a "working" diagnosis, but the clinician wishes to indicate a significant degree of diagnostic uncertainty

Frequently Used Criteria

Criteria Used to Exclude Other Diagnoses and to Suggest Differential Diagnoses

Most of the criteria sets presented in this manual include exclusion criteria that are necessary to establish boundaries between disorders and to clarify differential diagnoses. The several different wordings of exclusion criteria in the criteria sets throughout DSM-IV reflect the different types of possible relationships among disorders:

- **"Criteria have never been met for . . ."** This exclusion criterion is used to define a lifetime hierarchy between disorders. For example, a diagnosis of Major Depressive Disorder can no longer be given once a Manic Episode has occurred and must be changed to a diagnosis of Bipolar I Disorder.
- **"Criteria are not met for . . ."** This exclusion criterion is used to establish a hierarchy between disorders (or subtypes) defined cross-sectionally. For example, the specifier With Melancholic Features takes precedence over With Atypical Features for describing the current Major Depressive Episode.
- **"does not occur exclusively during the course of . . ."** This exclusion criterion prevents a disorder from being diagnosed when its symptom presentation occurs only during the course of another disorder. For example, dementia is not diagnosed separately if it occurs only during delirium; Conversion Disorder is not diagnosed separately if it occurs only during Somatization Disorder; Bulimia Nervosa is not diagnosed separately if it occurs only during episodes of Anorexia Nervosa. This exclusion criterion is typically used in situations in which the symptoms of one disorder are associated features or a subset of the symptoms of the preempting disorder. The clinician should consider periods of partial remission as part of the "course of another disorder." It should be noted that the

excluded diagnosis can be given at times when it occurs independently (e.g., when the excluding disorder is in full remission).

- **"not due to the direct physiological effects of a substance (e.g., a drug of abuse, a medication) or a general medical condition."** This exclusion criterion is used to indicate that a substance-induced and general medical etiology must be considered and ruled out before the disorder can be diagnosed (e.g., Major Depressive Disorder can be diagnosed only after etiologies based on substance use and a general medical condition have been ruled out).
- **"not better accounted for by . . ."** This exclusion criterion is used to indicate that the disorders mentioned in the criterion must be considered in the differential diagnosis of the presenting psychopathology and that, in boundary cases, clinical judgment will be necessary to determine which disorder provides the most appropriate diagnosis. In such cases, the "Differential Diagnosis" section of the text for the disorders should be consulted for guidance.

The general convention in DSM-IV is to allow multiple diagnoses to be assigned for those presentations that meet criteria for more than one DSM-IV disorder. There are three situations in which the above-mentioned exclusion criteria help to establish a diagnostic hierarchy (and thus prevent multiple diagnoses) or to highlight differential diagnostic considerations (and thus discourage multiple diagnoses):

- When a Mental Disorder Due to a General Medical Condition or a Substance-Induced Disorder is responsible for the symptoms, it preempts the diagnosis of the corresponding primary disorder with the same symptoms (e.g., Cocaine-Induced Mood Disorder preempts Major Depressive Disorder). In such cases, an exclusion criterion containing the phrase "not due to the direct physiological effects of . . ." is included in the criteria set for the primary disorder.
- When a more pervasive disorder (e.g., Schizophrenia) has among its defining symptoms (or associated symptoms) what are the defining symptoms of a less pervasive disorder (e.g., Dysthymic Disorder), one of the following three exclusion criteria appears in the criteria set for the less pervasive disorder, indicating that only the more pervasive disorder is diagnosed: "Criteria have never been met for . . .," "Criteria are not met for . . .," "does not occur exclusively during the course of. . . ."
- When there are particularly difficult differential diagnostic boundaries, the phrase "not better accounted for by . . ." is included to indicate that clinical judgment is necessary to determine which diagnosis is most appropriate. For example, Panic Disorder With Agoraphobia includes the criterion "not better accounted for by Social Phobia" and Social Phobia includes the criterion "not better accounted for by Panic Disorder With Agoraphobia" in recognition of the fact that this is a particularly difficult boundary to draw. In some cases, both diagnoses might be appropriate.

Criteria for Substance-Induced Disorders

It is often difficult to determine whether presenting symptomatology is substance induced, that is, the direct physiological consequence of Substance Intoxication or Withdrawal, medication use, or toxin exposure. In an effort to provide some assistance in making this determination, the two criteria listed below have been added to each of the Substance-Induced Disorders. These criteria are intended to provide general guidelines, but at the same time allow for clinical judgment in determining whether or not the presenting symptoms are best accounted for by the direct physiological effects of the substance. For further discussion of this issue, see p. 192.

    B. There is evidence from the history, physical examination, or laboratory findings of either (1) or (2):

        (1) the symptoms developed during, or within a month of, Substance Intoxication or Withdrawal

        (2) medication use is etiologically related to the disturbance

    C. The disturbance is not better accounted for by a disorder that is not substance induced. Evidence that the symptoms are better accounted for by a disorder that is not substance induced might include the following: the symptoms precede the onset of the substance use (or medication use); the symptoms persist for a substantial period of time (e.g., about a month) after the cessation of acute withdrawal or severe intoxication, or are substantially in excess of what would be expected given the type, duration, or amount of the substance used; or there is other evidence that suggests the existence of an independent non-substance-induced disorder (e.g., a history of recurrent non-substance-related episodes).

Criteria for a Mental Disorder Due to a General Medical Condition

The criterion listed below is necessary to establish the etiological requirement for each of the Mental Disorders Due to a General Medical Condition (e.g., Mood Disorder Due to Hypothyroidism). For further discussion of this issue, see p. 165.

    There is evidence from the history, physical examination, or laboratory findings that the disturbance is the direct physiological consequence of a general medical condition.

Criteria for Clinical Significance

The definition of *mental disorder* in the introduction to DSM-IV requires that there be clinically significant impairment or distress. To highlight the importance of considering this issue, the criteria sets for most disorders include a clinical significance criterion (usually worded ". . . causes clinically significant distress or impairment in social, occupational, or other important areas of functioning"). This criterion helps establish the threshold for the diagnosis of a disorder in those situations in which the symptomatic presentation by itself (particularly in its milder forms) is not inherently pathological and may be encountered in individuals for whom a diagnosis of "mental disorder" would be inappropriate. Assessing whether this criterion is met, especially in terms of role function, is an inherently difficult clinical judgment. Reliance on information from family members and other third parties (in addition to the individual) regarding the individual's performance is often necessary.

Types of Information in the DSM-IV Text

The text of DSM-IV systematically describes each disorder under the following headings: "Diagnostic Features"; "Subtypes and/or Specifiers"; "Recording Procedures"; "Associated Features and Disorders"; "Specific Culture, Age, and Gender Features"; "Prevalence"; "Course"; "Familial Pattern"; and "Differential Diagnosis." When no information is available for a section, that section is not included. In some instances, when many of the specific disorders in a group of disorders share common features, this information is included in the general introduction to the group.

Diagnostic Features.   This section clarifies the diagnostic criteria and often provides illustrative examples.

Subtypes and/or Specifiers.   This section provides definitions and brief discussions concerning applicable subtypes and/or specifiers.

Recording Procedures.   This section provides guidelines for reporting the name of the disorder and for selecting and recording the appropriate ICD-9-CM diagnostic code. It also includes instructions for applying any appropriate subtypes and/or specifiers.

Associated Features and Disorders.   This section is usually subdivided into three parts:

- *Associated descriptive features and mental disorders.* This section includes clinical features that are frequently associated with the disorder but that are not considered essential to making the diagnosis. In some cases, these features were considered for inclusion as possible diagnostic criteria but were insufficiently sensitive or specific to be included in the final criteria set. Also noted in this section are other mental disorders associated with the disorder being discussed. It is specified (when known) if these disorders precede, co-occur with, or are consequences of the disorder in question (e.g., Alcohol-Induced Persisting Dementia is a consequence of chronic Alcohol Dependence). If available, information on predisposing factors and complications is also included in this section.
- *Associated laboratory findings.* This section provides information on three types of laboratory findings that may be associated with the disorder: 1) those associated laboratory findings that are considered to be "diagnostic" of the disorder—for example, polysomnographic findings in certain sleep disorders; 2) those associated laboratory findings that are not considered to be diagnostic of the disorder but that have been noted to be abnormal in groups of individuals with the disorder relative to control subjects—for example, ventricle size on computed tomography as a validator of the construct of Schizophrenia; and 3) those laboratory findings that are associated with the complications of a disorder—for example, electrolyte imbalances in individuals with Anorexia Nervosa.
- *Associated physical examination findings and general medical conditions.* This section includes information about symptoms elicited by history, or findings noted during physical examination, that may be of diagnostic significance but that are not essential to the diagnosis—for example, dental erosion in Bulimia Nervosa. Also included are those disorders that are coded outside the "Mental and

Behavioural Disorders" chapter of ICD that are associated with the disorder being discussed. As is done for associated mental disorders, the type of association (i.e., precedes, co-occurs with, is a consequence of) is specified if known—for example, that cirrhosis is a consequence of Alcohol Dependence.

Specific Culture, Age, and Gender Features. This section provides guidance for the clinician concerning variations in the presentation of the disorder that may be attributable to the individual's cultural setting, developmental stage (e.g., infancy, childhood, adolescence, adulthood, late life), or gender. This section also includes information on differential prevalence rates related to culture, age, and gender (e.g., sex ratio).

Prevalence. This section provides available data on point and lifetime prevalence, incidence, and lifetime risk. These data are provided for different settings (e.g., community, primary care, outpatient mental health clinics, and inpatient psychiatric settings) when this information is known.

Course. This section describes the typical lifetime patterns of presentation and evolution of the disorder. It contains information on typical *age at onset* and *mode of onset* (e.g., abrupt or insidious) of the disorder; *episodic* versus *continuous course; single episode* versus *recurrent; duration,* characterizing the typical length of the illness and its episodes; and *progression,* describing the general trend of the disorder over time (e.g., stable, worsening, improving).

Familial Pattern. This section describes data on the frequency of the disorder among first-degree biological relatives of those with the disorder compared with the frequency in the general population. It also indicates other disorders that tend to occur more frequently in family members of those with the disorder.

Differential Diagnosis. This section discusses how to differentiate this disorder from other disorders that have some similar presenting characteristics.

DSM-IV Organizational Plan

The DSM-IV disorders are grouped into 16 major diagnostic classes (e.g., Substance-Related Disorders, Mood Disorders, Anxiety Disorders) and one additional section, "Other Conditions That May Be a Focus of Clinical Attention."

The first section is devoted to "Disorders Usually First Diagnosed in Infancy, Childhood, or Adolescence." This division of the Classification according to age at presentation is for convenience only and is not absolute. Although disorders in this section are usually first evident in childhood and adolescence, some individuals diagnosed with disorders located in this section (e.g., Attention-Deficit/Hyperactivity Disorder) may not present for clinical attention until adulthood. In addition, it is not uncommon for the age at onset for many disorders placed in other sections to be during childhood or adolescence (e.g., Major Depressive Disorder, Schizophrenia, Generalized Anxiety Disorder). Clinicians who work primarily with children and adolescents should therefore be familiar with the entire manual, and those who work primarily with adults should also be familiar with this section.

The next three sections—"Delirium, Dementia, and Amnestic and Other Cognitive Disorders"; "Mental Disorders Due to a General Medical Condition"; and "Substance-Related Disorders"—were grouped together in DSM-III-R under the single heading of "Organic Mental Syndromes and Disorders." The term "organic mental disorder" is no longer used in DSM-IV because it incorrectly implies that the other mental disorders in the manual do not have a biological basis. As in DSM-III-R, these sections are placed before the remaining disorders in the manual because of their priority in differential diagnosis (e.g., substance-related causes of depressed mood must be ruled out before making a diagnosis of Major Depressive Disorder). To facilitate differential diagnosis, complete lists of Mental Disorders Due to a General Medical Condition and Substance-Related Disorders appear in these sections, whereas the text and criteria for these disorders are placed in the diagnostic sections with disorders with which they share phenomenology. For example, the text and criteria for Substance-Induced Mood Disorder and Mood Disorder Due to a General Medical Condition are included in the Mood Disorders section.

The organizing principle for all the remaining sections (except for Adjustment Disorders) is to group disorders based on their shared phenomenological features in order to facilitate differential diagnosis. The "Adjustment Disorders" section is organized differently in that these disorders are grouped based on their common etiology (e.g., maladaptive reaction to a stressor). Therefore, the Adjustment Disorders include a variety of heterogeneous clinical presentations (e.g., Adjustment Disorder With Depressed Mood, Adjustment Disorder With Anxiety, Adjustment Disorder With Disturbance of Conduct).

Finally, DSM-IV includes a section for "Other Conditions That May Be a Focus of Clinical Attention."

DSM-IV includes 10 appendixes:

Appendix A: Decision Trees for Differential Diagnosis.   This appendix contains six decision trees (for Mental Disorders Due to a General Medical Condition, Substance-Induced Disorders, Psychotic Disorders, Mood Disorders, Anxiety Disorders, and Somatoform Disorders). Their purpose is to aid the clinician in differential diagnosis and in understanding the hierarchical structure of the DSM-IV Classification.

Appendix B: Criteria Sets and Axes Provided for Further Study.   This appendix contains a number of proposals that were suggested for possible inclusion in DSM-IV. Brief texts and research criteria sets are provided for the following: postconcussional disorder, mild neurocognitive disorder, caffeine withdrawal, postpsychotic depressive disorder of Schizophrenia, simple deteriorative disorder, premenstrual dysphoric disorder, minor depressive disorder, recurrent brief depressive disorder, mixed anxiety-depressive disorder, factitious disorder by proxy, dissociative trance disorder, binge-eating disorder, depressive personality disorder, passive-aggressive personality disorder, Neuroleptic-Induced Parkinsonism, Neuroleptic Malignant Syndrome, Neuroleptic-Induced Acute Dystonia, Neuroleptic-Induced Acute Akathisia, Neuroleptic-Induced Tardive Dyskinesia, and Medication-Induced Postural Tremor. In addition, alternative dimensional descriptors for Schizophrenia and an alternative Criterion B for Dysthymic Disorder are included. Finally, three proposed axes (Defensive Functioning Scale, Global Assessment of Relational Functioning [GARF] Scale, and Social and Occupational Functioning Assessment Scale [SOFAS]) are provided.

Appendix C: Glossary of Technical Terms.   This appendix contains glossary definitions of selected terms to assist users of the manual in the application of the criteria sets.

Appendix D: Annotated Listing of Changes in DSM-IV.   This appendix indicates the major changes from DSM-III-R that have been included in the DSM-IV terms and categories.

Appendix E: Alphabetical Listing of DSM-IV Diagnoses and Codes.   This appendix lists the DSM-IV disorders and conditions (with their ICD-9-CM codes) in alphabetical order. It has been included to facilitate the selection of diagnostic codes.

Appendix F: Numerical Listing of DSM-IV Diagnoses and Codes.   This appendix lists the DSM-IV disorders and conditions (with their ICD-9-CM codes) in numerical order by code. It has been included to facilitate recording of diagnostic terms.

Appendix G: ICD-9-CM Codes for Selected General Medical Conditions and Medication-Induced Disorders.   This appendix contains a list of ICD-9-CM codes for selected general medical conditions and has been provided to facilitate coding on Axis III. This appendix also provides ICD-9-CM E-codes for selected medications, prescribed at therapeutic dose levels, that cause Substance-Induced Disorders. The E-codes may optionally be coded on Axis I immediately following the related disorder (e.g., 292.39 Oral Contraceptive–Induced Mood Disorder, With Depressive Features; E932.2 oral contraceptives).

Appendix H: DSM-IV Classification With ICD-10 Codes.   As of the publication of this manual (in early 1994), the official coding system in use in the United States is the *International Classification of Diseases,* Ninth Revision, Clinical Modification (ICD-9-CM). At some point within the next several years, the U.S. Department of Health and Human Services will require for reporting purposes in the United States the use of codes from the *International Statistical Classification of Diseases and Related Health Problems,* Tenth Revision (ICD-10). To facilitate this transition process, this appendix contains the complete DSM-IV Classification with ICD-10 diagnostic codes.

Appendix I: Outline for Cultural Formulation and Glossary of Culture-Bound Syndromes.   This appendix is divided into two sections. The first provides an outline for cultural formulation designed to assist the clinician in systematically evaluating and reporting the impact of the individual's cultural context. The second is a glossary of culture-bound syndromes.

Appendix J: DSM-IV Contributors.   This appendix lists the names of the advisers and field-trial participants and other individuals and organizations that contributed to the development of DSM-IV.

DSM-IV Classification

NOS = Not Otherwise Specified.

An *x* appearing in a diagnostic code indicates that a specific code number is required.

An ellipsis (. . .) is used in the names of certain disorders to indicate that the name of a specific mental disorder or general medical condition should be inserted when recording the name (e.g., 293.0 Delirium Due to Hypothyroidism).

Numbers in parentheses are page numbers.

If criteria are currently met, one of the following severity specifiers may be noted after the diagnosis:

  Mild
  Moderate
  Severe

If criteria are no longer met, one of the following specifiers may be noted:

  In Partial Remission
  In Full Remission
  Prior History

Disorders Usually First Diagnosed in Infancy, Childhood, or Adolescence (37)

MENTAL RETARDATION (39)
Note: These are coded on Axis II.
317   Mild Mental Retardation (41)
318.0   Moderate Mental Retardation (41)
318.1   Severe Mental Retardation (41)
318.2   Profound Mental Retardation (41)
319   Mental Retardation, Severity
        Unspecified (42)

LEARNING DISORDERS (46)
315.00 Reading Disorder (48)
315.1   Mathematics Disorder (50)
315.2   Disorder of Written Expression (51)
315.9   Learning Disorder NOS (53)

MOTOR SKILLS DISORDER
315.4   Developmental Coordination
        Disorder (53)

COMMUNICATION DISORDERS (55)
315.31 Expressive Language
        Disorder (55)
315.31 Mixed Receptive-Expressive
        Language Disorder (58)
315.39 Phonological Disorder (61)
307.0   Stuttering (63)
307.9   Communication Disorder
        NOS (65)

PERVASIVE DEVELOPMENTAL DISORDERS (65)
299.00 Autistic Disorder (66)
299.80 Rett's Disorder (71)

299.10   Childhood Disintegrative
             Disorder (73)
299.80   Asperger's Disorder (75)
299.80   Pervasive Developmental
             Disorder NOS (77)

**ATTENTION-DEFICIT AND
DISRUPTIVE BEHAVIOR
DISORDERS** (78)
314.xx   Attention-Deficit/Hyperactivity
             Disorder (78)
    .01   Combined Type
    .00   Predominantly Inattentive Type
    .01   Predominantly
                 Hyperactive-Impulsive Type
314.9   Attention-Deficit/Hyperactivity
             Disorder NOS (85)
312.8   Conduct Disorder (85)
             Specify type: Childhood-Onset Type/
             Adolescent-Onset Type
313.81   Oppositional Defiant
             Disorder (91)
312.9   Disruptive Behavior Disorder
             NOS (94)

**FEEDING AND EATING DISORDERS
OF INFANCY OR EARLY
CHILDHOOD** (94)
307.52   Pica (95)
307.53   Rumination Disorder (96)
307.59   Feeding Disorder of Infancy or
             Early Childhood (98)

TIC DISORDERS (100)
307.23   Tourette's Disorder (101)
307.22   Chronic Motor or Vocal Tic
             Disorder (103)
307.21   Transient Tic Disorder (104)
             Specify if: Single Episode/Recurrent
307.20   Tic Disorder NOS (105)

ELIMINATION DISORDERS (106)
——.–   Encopresis (106)
787.6   With Constipation and
                 Overflow Incontinence
307.7   Without Constipation and
                 Overflow Incontinence
307.6   Enuresis (Not Due to a General
             Medical Condition) (108)
             Specify type: Nocturnal Only/Diurnal
             Only/Nocturnal and Diurnal

**OTHER DISORDERS OF INFANCY,
CHILDHOOD, OR ADOLESCENCE**
309.21   Separation Anxiety Disorder (110)
             Specify if: Early Onset
313.23   Selective Mutism (114)
313.89   Reactive Attachment Disorder
             of Infancy or Early
             Childhood (116)
             Specify type: Inhibited Type/
             Disinhibited Type
307.3   Stereotypic Movement
             Disorder (118)
             Specify if: With Self-Injurious Behavior

313.9   Disorder of Infancy, Childhood,
             or Adolescence NOS (121)

**Delirium, Dementia, and
Amnestic and Other Cognitive
Disorders** (123)

DELIRIUM (124)
293.0   Delirium Due to . . . *[Indicate
             the General Medical
             Condition]* (127)
——.–   Substance Intoxication Delirium
             *(refer to Substance-Related
             Disorders for substance-specific
             codes)* (129)
——.–   Substance Withdrawal Delirium
             *(refer to Substance-Related
             Disorders for substance-specific
             codes)* (129)
——.–   Delirium Due to Multiple
             Etiologies *(code each of the
             specific etiologies)* (132)
780.09   Delirium NOS (133)

DEMENTIA (133)
290.xx   Dementia of the Alzheimer's
             Type, With Early Onset *(also
             code 331.0 Alzheimer's disease
             on Axis III)* (139)
    .10   Uncomplicated
    .11   With Delirium
    .12   With Delusions
    .13   With Depressed Mood
             Specify if: With Behavioral Disturbance

290.xx   Dementia of the Alzheimer's
          Type, With Late Onset *(also
          code 331.0 Alzheimer's disease
          on Axis III)* (139)
   .0   Uncomplicated
   .3   With Delirium
   .20   With Delusions
   .21   With Depressed Mood
             Specify if: With Behavioral Disturbance
290.xx   Vascular Dementia (143)
   .40   Uncomplicated
   .41   With Delirium
   .42   With Delusions
   .43   With Depressed Mood
             Specify if: With Behavioral Disturbance
294.9   Dementia Due to HIV Disease
          *(also code 043.1 HIV infection
          affecting central nervous system
          on Axis III)* (148)
294.1   Dementia Due to Head Trauma
          *(also code 854.00 head injury
          on Axis III)* (148)
294.1   Dementia Due to Parkinson's
          Disease *(also code 332.0
          Parkinson's disease on
          Axis III)* (148)
294.1   Dementia Due to Huntington's
          Disease *(also code 333.4
          Huntington's disease on
          Axis III)* (149)
290.10   Dementia Due to Pick's Disease
          *(also code 331.1 Pick's disease
          on Axis III)* (149)
290.10   Dementia Due to
          Creutzfeldt-Jakob Disease *(also
          code 046.1 Creutzfeldt-Jakob
          disease on Axis III)* (150)
294.1   Dementia Due to . . . *[Indicate
          the General Medical Condition
          not listed above]* *(also code the
          general medical condition on
          Axis III)* (151)

——.—   Substance-Induced Persisting
          Dementia *(refer to Substance-
          Related Disorders for substance-
          specific codes)* (152)
——.—   Dementia Due to Multiple
          Etiologies *(code each of the
          specific etiologies)* (154)
294.8   Dementia NOS (155)

AMNESTIC DISORDERS (156)
294.0   Amnestic Disorder Due to . . .
          *[Indicate the General Medical
          Condition]* (158)
          Specify if: Transient/Chronic
——.—   Substance-Induced Persisting
          Amnestic Disorder *(refer to
          Substance-Related Disorders for
          substance-specific codes)* (161)
294.8   Amnestic Disorder NOS (163)

OTHER COGNITIVE DISORDERS (163)
294.9   Cognitive Disorder NOS (163)

Mental Disorders Due to a General Medical Condition Not Elsewhere Classified (165)

293.89   Catatonic Disorder Due to . . .
          *[Indicate the General Medical
          Condition]* (169)
310.1   Personality Change Due to . . .
          *[Indicate the General Medical
          Condition]* (171)
          Specify type: Labile Type/Disinhibited
          Type/Aggressive Type/Apathetic Type/
          Paranoid Type/Other Type/Combined
          Type/Unspecified Type
293.9   Mental Disorder NOS Due to . . .
          *[Indicate the General Medical
          Condition]* (174)

Substance-Related Disorders (175)

[a] *The following specifiers may be applied to Substance Dependence:*

With Physiological Dependence/Without Physiological Dependence

Early Full Remission/Early Partial Remission
Sustained Full Remission/Sustained Partial Remission
On Agonist Therapy/In a Controlled Environment

The following specifiers apply to Substance-Induced Disorders as noted:

[I]With Onset During Intoxication/[W]With Onset During Withdrawal

ALCOHOL-RELATED DISORDERS (194)

Alcohol Use Disorders
303.90   Alcohol Dependence[a] (195)
305.00   Alcohol Abuse (196)

Alcohol-Induced Disorders
303.00   Alcohol Intoxication (196)
291.8   Alcohol Withdrawal (197)
          Specify if: With Perceptual Disturbances
291.0   Alcohol Intoxication Delirium (129)
291.0   Alcohol Withdrawal Delirium (129)
291.2   Alcohol-Induced Persisting Dementia (152)
291.1   Alcohol-Induced Persisting Amnestic Disorder (161)
291.x   Alcohol-Induced Psychotic Disorder (310)
   .5   With Delusions[I,W]
   .3   With Hallucinations[I,W]
291.8   Alcohol-Induced Mood Disorder[I,W] (370)
291.8   Alcohol-Induced Anxiety Disorder[I,W] (439)
291.8   Alcohol-Induced Sexual Dysfunction[I] (519)
291.8   Alcohol-Induced Sleep Disorder[I,W] (601)

291.9   Alcohol-Related Disorder NOS (204)

AMPHETAMINE (OR AMPHETAMINE-LIKE)–RELATED DISORDERS (204)

Amphetamine Use Disorders
304.40   Amphetamine Dependence[a] (206)
305.70   Amphetamine Abuse (206)

Amphetamine-Induced Disorders
292.89   Amphetamine Intoxication (207)
          Specify if: With Perceptual Disturbances
292.0   Amphetamine Withdrawal (208)
292.81   Amphetamine Intoxication Delirium (129)
292.xx   Amphetamine-Induced Psychotic Disorder (310)
   .11   With Delusions[I]
   .12   With Hallucinations[I]
292.84   Amphetamine-Induced Mood Disorder[I,W] (370)
292.89   Amphetamine-Induced Anxiety Disorder[I] (439)
292.89   Amphetamine-Induced Sexual Dysfunction[I] (519)
292.89   Amphetamine-Induced Sleep Disorder[I,W] (601)

292.9   Amphetamine-Related Disorder NOS (211)

CAFFEINE-RELATED DISORDERS (212)

Caffeine-Induced Disorders
305.90   Caffeine Intoxication (212)
292.89   Caffeine-Induced Anxiety Disorder[I] (439)
292.89   Caffeine-Induced Sleep Disorder[I] (601)

292.9   Caffeine-Related Disorder NOS (215)

CANNABIS-RELATED DISORDERS (215)

Cannabis Use Disorders
304.30   Cannabis Dependence[a] (216)
305.20   Cannabis Abuse (217)

Cannabis-Induced Disorders
292.89   Cannabis Intoxication (217)
          Specify if: With Perceptual Disturbances
292.81   Cannabis Intoxication Delirium (129)

292.xx   Cannabis-Induced Psychotic
         Disorder (310)
   .11   With Delusions[I]
   .12   With Hallucinations[I]
292.89   Cannabis-Induced Anxiety
         Disorder[I] (439)

292.9   Cannabis-Related Disorder
         NOS (221)

COCAINE-RELATED DISORDERS (221)

Cocaine Use Disorders
304.20   Cocaine Dependence[a] (222)
305.60   Cocaine Abuse (223)

Cocaine-Induced Disorders
292.89   Cocaine Intoxication (223)
         Specify if: With Perceptual Disturbances
292.0   Cocaine Withdrawal (225)
292.81   Cocaine Intoxication
         Delirium (129)
292.xx   Cocaine-Induced Psychotic
         Disorder (310)
   .11   With Delusions[I]
   .12   With Hallucinations[I]
292.84   Cocaine-Induced Mood
         Disorder[I,W] (370)
292.89   Cocaine-Induced Anxiety
         Disorder[I,W] (439)
292.89   Cocaine-Induced Sexual
         Dysfunction[I] (519)
292.89   Cocaine-Induced Sleep
         Disorder[I,W] (601)

292.9   Cocaine-Related Disorder
         NOS (229)

HALLUCINOGEN-RELATED DISORDERS (229)

Hallucinogen Use Disorders
304.50   Hallucinogen Dependence[a] (230)
305.30   Hallucinogen Abuse (231)

Hallucinogen-Induced Disorders
292.89   Hallucinogen Intoxication (232)
292.89   Hallucinogen Persisting
         Perception Disorder
         (Flashbacks) (233)

292.81   Hallucinogen Intoxication
         Delirium (129)
292.xx   Hallucinogen-Induced Psychotic
         Disorder (310)
   .11   With Delusions[I]
   .12   With Hallucinations[I]
292.84   Hallucinogen-Induced Mood
         Disorder[I] (370)
292.89   Hallucinogen-Induced Anxiety
         Disorder[I] (439)

292.9   Hallucinogen-Related Disorder
         NOS (236)

INHALANT-RELATED DISORDERS (236)

Inhalant Use Disorders
304.60   Inhalant Dependence[a] (238)
305.90   Inhalant Abuse (238)

Inhalant-Induced Disorders
292.89   Inhalant Intoxication (239)
292.81   Inhalant Intoxication
         Delirium (129)
292.82   Inhalant-Induced Persisting
         Dementia (152)
292.xx   Inhalant-Induced Psychotic
         Disorder (310)
   .11   With Delusions[I]
   .12   With Hallucinations[I]
292.84   Inhalant-Induced Mood
         Disorder[I] (370)
292.89   Inhalant-Induced Anxiety
         Disorder[I] (439)

292.9   Inhalant-Related Disorder
         NOS (242)

NICOTINE-RELATED DISORDERS (242)

Nicotine Use Disorder
305.10   Nicotine Dependence[a] (243)

Nicotine-Induced Disorder
292.0   Nicotine Withdrawal (244)

292.9   Nicotine-Related Disorder
         NOS (247)

OPIOID-RELATED DISORDERS (247)

Opioid Use Disorders
304.00   Opioid Dependence[a] (248)
305.50   Opioid Abuse (249)

Opioid-Induced Disorders

292.89   Opioid Intoxication (249)
         Specify if: With Perceptual Disturbances
292.0   Opioid Withdrawal (250)
292.81   Opioid Intoxication Delirium (129)
292.xx   Opioid-Induced Psychotic
         Disorder (310)
    .11   With Delusions[I]
    .12   With Hallucinations[I]
292.84   Opioid-Induced Mood
         Disorder[I] (370)
292.89   Opioid-Induced Sexual
         Dysfunction[I] (519)
292.89   Opioid-Induced Sleep
         Disorder[I,W] (601)

292.9   Opioid-Related Disorder NOS (255)

**PHENCYCLIDINE (OR
PHENCYCLIDINE-LIKE)–
RELATED DISORDERS** (255)

Phencyclidine Use Disorders

304.90   Phencyclidine Dependence[a] (256)
305.90   Phencyclidine Abuse (257)

Phencyclidine-Induced Disorders

292.89   Phencyclidine Intoxication (257)
         Specify if: With Perceptual Disturbances
292.81   Phencyclidine Intoxication
         Delirium (129)
292.xx   Phencyclidine-Induced Psychotic
         Disorder (310)
    .11   With Delusions[I]
    .12   With Hallucinations[I]
292.84   Phencyclidine-Induced Mood
         Disorder[I] (370)
292.89   Phencyclidine-Induced Anxiety
         Disorder[I] (439)

292.9   Phencyclidine-Related Disorder
         NOS (261)

**SEDATIVE-, HYPNOTIC-, OR
ANXIOLYTIC-RELATED
DISORDERS** (261)

**Sedative, Hypnotic, or
Anxiolytic Use Disorders**

304.10   Sedative, Hypnotic, or Anxiolytic
         Dependence[a] (262)

305.40   Sedative, Hypnotic, or Anxiolytic
         Abuse (263)

**Sedative-, Hypnotic-, or
Anxiolytic-Induced Disorders**

292.89   Sedative, Hypnotic, or Anxiolytic
         Intoxication (263)
292.0   Sedative, Hypnotic, or Anxiolytic
         Withdrawal (264)
         Specify if: With Perceptual Disturbances
292.81   Sedative, Hypnotic, or Anxiolytic
         Intoxication Delirium (129)
292.81   Sedative, Hypnotic, or Anxiolytic
         Withdrawal Delirium (129)
292.82   Sedative-, Hypnotic-, or
         Anxiolytic-Induced Persisting
         Dementia (152)
292.83   Sedative-, Hypnotic-, or
         Anxiolytic-Induced Persisting
         Amnestic Disorder (161)
292.xx   Sedative-, Hypnotic-, or
         Anxiolytic-Induced Psychotic
         Disorder (310)
    .11   With Delusions[I,W]
    .12   With Hallucinations[I,W]
292.84   Sedative-, Hypnotic-, or
         Anxiolytic-Induced Mood
         Disorder[I,W] (370)
292.89   Sedative-, Hypnotic-, or
         Anxiolytic-Induced Anxiety
         Disorder[W] (439)
292.89   Sedative-, Hypnotic-, or
         Anxiolytic-Induced Sexual
         Dysfunction[I] (519)
292.89   Sedative-, Hypnotic-, or
         Anxiolytic-Induced Sleep
         Disorder[I,W] (601)

292.9   Sedative-, Hypnotic-, or
         Anxiolytic-Related
         Disorder NOS (269)

**POLYSUBSTANCE-RELATED
DISORDER**

304.80   Polysubstance Dependence[a] (270)

OTHER (OR UNKNOWN) SUBSTANCE–RELATED DISORDERS (270)

Other (or Unknown) Substance Use Disorders

304.90 Other (or Unknown) Substance Dependence[a] (176)
305.90 Other (or Unknown) Substance Abuse (182)

Other (or Unknown) Substance–Induced Disorders

292.89 Other (or Unknown) Substance Intoxication (183)
        Specify if: With Perceptual Disturbances
292.0   Other (or Unknown) Substance Withdrawal (184)
        Specify if: With Perceptual Disturbances
292.81 Other (or Unknown) Substance–Induced Delirium (129)
292.82 Other (or Unknown) Substance–Induced Persisting Dementia (152)
292.83 Other (or Unknown) Substance–Induced Persisting Amnestic Disorder (161)
292.xx Other (or Unknown) Substance–Induced Psychotic Disorder (310)
   .11   With Delusions[I,W]
   .12   With Hallucinations[I,W]
292.84 Other (or Unknown) Substance–Induced Mood Disorder[I,W] (370)
292.89 Other (or Unknown) Substance–Induced Anxiety Disorder[I,W] (439)
292.89 Other (or Unknown) Substance–Induced Sexual Dysfunction[I] (519)
292.89 Other (or Unknown) Substance–Induced Sleep Disorder[I,W] (601)

292.9   Other (or Unknown) Substance–Related Disorder NOS (272)

Schizophrenia and Other Psychotic Disorders (273)

295.xx Schizophrenia (274)

The following Classification of Longitudinal Course applies to all subtypes of Schizophrenia:

Episodic With Interepisode Residual Symptoms (*specify if:* With Prominent Negative Symptoms)/Episodic With No Interepisode Residual Symptoms
Continuous (*specify if:* With Prominent Negative Symptoms)
Single Episode In Partial Remission (*specify if:* With Prominent Negative Symptoms)/Single Episode In Full Remission
Other or Unspecified Pattern

   .30   Paranoid Type (287)
   .10   Disorganized Type (287)
   .20   Catatonic Type (288)
   .90   Undifferentiated Type (289)
   .60   Residual Type (289)

295.40 Schizophreniform Disorder (290)
        Specify if: Without Good Prognostic Features/With Good Prognostic Features
295.70 Schizoaffective Disorder (292)
        Specify type: Bipolar Type/Depressive Type
297.1   Delusional Disorder (296)
        Specify type: Erotomanic Type/Grandiose Type/Jealous Type/Persecutory Type/Somatic Type/Mixed Type/Unspecified Type
298.8   Brief Psychotic Disorder (302)
        Specify if: With Marked Stressor(s)/Without Marked Stressor(s)/With Postpartum Onset
297.3   Shared Psychotic Disorder (305)
293.xx Psychotic Disorder Due to . . . *[Indicate the General Medical Condition]* (306)
   .81   With Delusions
   .82   With Hallucinations
——.–   Substance-Induced Psychotic Disorder *(refer to Substance-Related Disorders for substance-specific codes)* (310)
        Specify if: With Onset During Intoxication/With Onset During Withdrawal
298.9   Psychotic Disorder NOS (315)

Mood Disorders (317)

Code current state of Major Depressive Disorder or Bipolar I Disorder in fifth digit:

    1 = Mild
    2 = Moderate
    3 = Severe Without Psychotic Features
    4 = Severe With Psychotic Features
        Specify: Mood-Congruent Psychotic
        Features/Mood-Incongruent Psychotic
        Features
    5 = In Partial Remission
    6 = In Full Remission
    0 = Unspecified

The following specifiers apply (for current or most recent episode) to Mood Disorders as noted:

[a]Severity/Psychotic/Remission Specifiers/[b]Chronic/[c]With Catatonic Features/[d]With Melancholic Features/[e]With Atypical Features/[f]With Postpartum Onset

The following specifiers apply to Mood Disorders as noted:

[g]With or Without Full Interepisode Recovery/[h]With Seasonal Pattern/[i]With Rapid Cycling

DEPRESSIVE DISORDERS

296.xx Major Depressive Disorder, (339)
    .2x   Single Episode[a,b,c,d,e,f]
    .3x   Recurrent[a,b,c,d,e,f,g,h]
300.4   Dysthymic Disorder (345)
        Specify if: Early Onset/Late Onset
        Specify: With Atypical Features
311   Depressive Disorder NOS (350)

BIPOLAR DISORDERS

296.xx Bipolar I Disorder, (350)
    .0x   Single Manic Episode[a,c,f]
            Specify if: Mixed
    .40   Most Recent Episode
            Hypomanic[g,h,i]
    .4x   Most Recent Episode
            Manic[a,c,f,g,h,i]
    .6x   Most Recent Episode
            Mixed[a,c,f,g,h,i]
    .5x   Most Recent Episode
            Depressed[a,b,c,d,e,f,g,h,i]
    .7   Most Recent Episode
            Unspecified[g,h,i]
296.89 Bipolar II Disorder[a,b,c,d,e,f,g,h,i] (359)
        Specify (current or most recent episode): Hypomanic/Depressed

301.13 Cyclothymic Disorder (363)
296.80 Bipolar Disorder NOS (366)

293.83 Mood Disorder Due to . . .
        [Indicate the General Medical Condition] (366)
        Specify type: With Depressive Features/With Major Depressive–Like Episode/With Manic Features/With Mixed Features
——.—   Substance-Induced Mood Disorder *(refer to Substance-Related Disorders for substance-specific codes)* (370)
        Specify type: With Depressive Features/With Manic Features/With Mixed Features
        Specify if: With Onset During Intoxication/With Onset During Withdrawal

296.90 Mood Disorder NOS (375)

Anxiety Disorders (393)

300.01 Panic Disorder Without Agoraphobia (397)
300.21 Panic Disorder With Agoraphobia (397)
300.22 Agoraphobia Without History of Panic Disorder (403)
300.29 Specific Phobia (405)
        Specify type: Animal Type/Natural Environment Type/Blood-Injection-Injury Type/Situational Type/Other Type
300.23 Social Phobia (411)
        Specify if: Generalized
300.3   Obsessive-Compulsive Disorder (417)
        Specify if: With Poor Insight
309.81 Posttraumatic Stress Disorder (424)
        Specify if: Acute/Chronic
        Specify if: With Delayed Onset
308.3   Acute Stress Disorder (429)
300.02 Generalized Anxiety Disorder (432)
293.89 Anxiety Disorder Due to . . .
        [Indicate the General Medical Condition] (436)
        Specify if: With Generalized Anxiety/With Panic Attacks/With Obsessive-Compulsive Symptoms

——.— Substance-Induced Anxiety
Disorder *(refer to Substance-
Related Disorders for substance-
specific codes)* (439)
Specify if: With Generalized
Anxiety/With Panic Attacks/With
Obsessive-Compulsive Symptoms/
With Phobic Symptoms
Specify if: With Onset During
Intoxication/With Onset During
Withdrawal
300.00 Anxiety Disorder NOS (444)

Somatoform Disorders (445)

300.81 Somatization Disorder (446)
300.81 Undifferentiated Somatoform
Disorder (450)
300.11 Conversion Disorder (452)
Specify type: With Motor Symptom or
Deficit/With Sensory Symptom or
Deficit/With Seizures or
Convulsions/With Mixed
Presentation
307.xx Pain Disorder (458)
.80 Associated With
Psychological Factors
.89 Associated With Both
Psychological Factors and a
General Medical Condition
Specify if: Acute/Chronic
300.7 Hypochondriasis (462)
Specify if: With Poor Insight
300.7 Body Dysmorphic Disorder (466)
300.81 Somatoform Disorder NOS (468)

Factitious Disorders (471)

300.xx Factitious Disorder (471)
.16 With Predominantly
Psychological Signs and
Symptoms
.19 With Predominantly Physical
Signs and Symptoms
.19 With Combined Psychological
and Physical Signs and
Symptoms
300.19 Factitious Disorder NOS (475)

Dissociative Disorders (477)

300.12 Dissociative Amnesia (478)
300.13 Dissociative Fugue (481)
300.14 Dissociative Identity Disorder (484)
300.6 Depersonalization Disorder (488)
300.15 Dissociative Disorder NOS (490)

Sexual and Gender Identity Disorders (493)

SEXUAL DYSFUNCTIONS (493)
*The following specifiers apply to all
primary Sexual Dysfunctions:*
Lifelong Type/Acquired Type
Generalized Type/Situational Type
Due to Psychological Factors/Due to
Combined Factors

Sexual Desire Disorders
302.71 Hypoactive Sexual Desire
Disorder (496)
302.79 Sexual Aversion Disorder (499)

Sexual Arousal Disorders
302.72 Female Sexual Arousal
Disorder (500)
302.72 Male Erectile Disorder (502)

Orgasmic Disorders
302.73 Female Orgasmic Disorder (505)
302.74 Male Orgasmic Disorder (507)
302.75 Premature Ejaculation (509)

Sexual Pain Disorders
302.76 Dyspareunia (Not Due to a
General Medical Condition) (511)
306.51 Vaginismus (Not Due to a
General Medical Condition) (513)

**Sexual Dysfunction Due to a General
Medical Condition** (515)
625.8 Female Hypoactive Sexual
Desire Disorder Due to . . .
*[Indicate the General Medical
Condition]* (515)
608.89 Male Hypoactive Sexual
Desire Disorder Due to . . .
*[Indicate the General Medical
Condition]* (515)

607.84   Male Erectile Disorder Due to . . . *[Indicate the General Medical Condition]* (515)

625.0   Female Dyspareunia Due to . . . *[Indicate the General Medical Condition]* (515)

608.89   Male Dyspareunia Due to . . . *[Indicate the General Medical Condition]* (515)

625.8   Other Female Sexual Dysfunction Due to . . . *[Indicate the General Medical Condition]* (515)

608.89   Other Male Sexual Dysfunction Due to . . . *[Indicate the General Medical Condition]* (515)

——.–   Substance-Induced Sexual Dysfunction *(refer to Substance-Related Disorders for substance-specific codes)* (519)
    Specify if: With Impaired Desire/ With Impaired Arousal/With Impaired Orgasm/With Sexual Pain
    Specify if: With Onset During Intoxication

302.70   Sexual Dysfunction NOS (522)

PARAPHILIAS (522)

302.4   Exhibitionism (525)
302.81   Fetishism (526)
302.89   Frotteurism (527)
302.2   Pedophilia (527)
    Specify if: Sexually Attracted to Males/Sexually Attracted to Females/ Sexually Attracted to Both
    Specify if: Limited to Incest
    Specify type: Exclusive Type/ Nonexclusive Type
302.83   Sexual Masochism (529)
302.84   Sexual Sadism (530)
302.3   Transvestic Fetishism (530)
    Specify if: With Gender Dysphoria
302.82   Voyeurism (532)
302.9   Paraphilia NOS (532)

GENDER IDENTITY DISORDERS (532)

302.xx   Gender Identity Disorder (532)
    .6   in Children
    .85   in Adolescents or Adults
    Specify if: Sexually Attracted to Males/ Sexually Attracted to Females/Sexually Attracted to Both/Sexually Attracted to Neither
302.6   Gender Identity Disorder NOS (538)

302.9   Sexual Disorder NOS (538)

Eating Disorders (539)

307.1   Anorexia Nervosa (539)
    Specify type: Restricting Type; Binge-Eating/Purging Type
307.51   Bulimia Nervosa (545)
    Specify type: Purging Type/ Nonpurging Type
307.50   Eating Disorder NOS (550)

Sleep Disorders (551)

PRIMARY SLEEP DISORDERS (553)

Dyssomnias (553)
307.42   Primary Insomnia (553)
307.44   Primary Hypersomnia (557)
    Specify if: Recurrent
347   Narcolepsy (562)
780.59   Breathing-Related Sleep Disorder (567)
307.45   Circadian Rhythm Sleep Disorder (573)
    Specify type: Delayed Sleep Phase Type/Jet Lag Type/Shift Work Type/ Unspecified Type
307.47   Dyssomnia NOS (579)

Parasomnias (579)
307.47   Nightmare Disorder (580)
307.46   Sleep Terror Disorder (583)
307.46   Sleepwalking Disorder (587)
307.47   Parasomnia NOS (592)

SLEEP DISORDERS RELATED TO ANOTHER MENTAL DISORDER (592)

307.42   Insomnia Related to . . .
         [Indicate the Axis I or Axis II Disorder] (592)
307.44   Hypersomnia Related to . . .
         [Indicate the Axis I or Axis II Disorder] (592)

OTHER SLEEP DISORDERS

780.xx   Sleep Disorder Due to . . .
         [Indicate the General Medical Condition] (597)
    .52   Insomnia Type
    .54   Hypersomnia Type
    .59   Parasomnia Type
    .59   Mixed Type
——.–   Substance-Induced Sleep Disorder
         (refer to Substance-Related Disorders for substance-specific codes) (601)
         Specify type: Insomnia Type/ Hypersomnia Type/Parasomnia Type/ Mixed Type
         Specify if: With Onset During Intoxication/With Onset During Withdrawal

Impulse-Control Disorders Not Elsewhere Classified (609)

312.34   Intermittent Explosive Disorder (609)
312.32   Kleptomania (612)
312.33   Pyromania (614)
312.31   Pathological Gambling (615)
312.39   Trichotillomania (618)
312.30   Impulse-Control Disorder NOS (621)

Adjustment Disorders (623)

309.xx   Adjustment Disorder (623)
    .0   With Depressed Mood
    .24   With Anxiety
    .28   With Mixed Anxiety and Depressed Mood
    .3   With Disturbance of Conduct
    .4   With Mixed Disturbance of Emotions and Conduct
    .9   Unspecified
         Specify if: Acute/Chronic

Personality Disorders (629)

Note: *These are coded on Axis II.*
301.0   Paranoid Personality Disorder (634)
301.20   Schizoid Personality Disorder (638)
301.22   Schizotypal Personality Disorder (641)
301.7   Antisocial Personality Disorder (645)
301.83   Borderline Personality Disorder (650)
301.50   Histrionic Personality Disorder (655)
301.81   Narcissistic Personality Disorder (658)
301.82   Avoidant Personality Disorder (662)
301.6   Dependent Personality Disorder (665)
301.4   Obsessive-Compulsive Personality Disorder (669)
301.9   Personality Disorder NOS (673)

Other Conditions That May Be a Focus of Clinical Attention (675)

PSYCHOLOGICAL FACTORS AFFECTING MEDICAL CONDITION (675)

316   *. . . [Specified Psychological Factor]* Affecting *. . . [Indicate the General Medical Condition]* (675)
         Choose name based on nature of factors:
         Mental Disorder Affecting Medical Condition
         Psychological Symptoms Affecting Medical Condition
         Personality Traits or Coping Style Affecting Medical Condition
         Maladaptive Health Behaviors Affecting Medical Condition
         Stress-Related Physiological Response Affecting Medical Condition
         Other or Unspecified Psychological Factors Affecting Medical Condition

**MEDICATION-INDUCED
MOVEMENT DISORDERS** (678)
332.1   Neuroleptic-Induced
        Parkinsonism (679)
333.92 Neuroleptic Malignant
        Syndrome (679)
333.7   Neuroleptic-Induced Acute
        Dystonia (679)
333.99 Neuroleptic-Induced Acute
        Akathisia (679)
333.82 Neuroleptic-Induced Tardive
        Dyskinesia (679)
333.1   Medication-Induced Postural
        Tremor (680)
333.90 Medication-Induced Movement
        Disorder NOS (680)

**OTHER MEDICATION-INDUCED
DISORDER**
995.2   Adverse Effects of Medication
        NOS (680)

RELATIONAL PROBLEMS (680)
V61.9   Relational Problem Related to
        a Mental Disorder or General
        Medical Condition (681)
V61.20 Parent-Child Relational
        Problem (681)
V61.1   Partner Relational Problem (681)
V61.8   Sibling Relational Problem (681)
V62.81 Relational Problem NOS (681)

**PROBLEMS RELATED TO ABUSE
OR NEGLECT** (682)
V61.21 Physical Abuse of Child (682)
        *(code 995.5 if focus of attention
        is on victim)*
V61.21 Sexual Abuse of Child (682)
        *(code 995.5 if focus of attention
        is on victim)*
V61.21 Neglect of Child (682)
        *(code 995.5 if focus of attention
        is on victim)*
V61.1   Physical Abuse of Adult (682)
        *(code 995.81 if focus of attention
        is on victim)*
V61.1   Sexual Abuse of Adult (682)
        *(code 995.81 if focus of attention
        is on victim)*

**ADDITIONAL CONDITIONS THAT
MAY BE A FOCUS OF CLINICAL
ATTENTION** (683)
V15.81 Noncompliance With
        Treatment (683)
V65.2   Malingering (683)
V71.01 Adult Antisocial Behavior (683)
V71.02 Child or Adolescent Antisocial
        Behavior (684)
V62.89 Borderline Intellectual
        Functioning (684)
        Note: *This is coded on Axis II.*
780.9   Age-Related Cognitive Decline (684)
V62.82 Bereavement (684)
V62.3   Academic Problem (685)
V62.2   Occupational Problem (685)
313.82 Identity Problem (685)
V62.89 Religious or Spiritual Problem (685)
V62.4   Acculturation Problem (685)
V62.89 Phase of Life Problem (685)

Additional Codes

300.9   Unspecified Mental Disorder
        (nonpsychotic) (687)
V71.09 No Diagnosis or Condition on
        Axis I (687)
799.9   Diagnosis or Condition Deferred
        on Axis I (687)
V71.09 No Diagnosis on Axis II (687)
799.9   Diagnosis Deferred on Axis II (687)

Multiaxial System

Axis I   Clinical Disorders
          Other Conditions That May Be a
          Focus of Clinical Attention
Axis II   Personality Disorders
          Mental Retardation
Axis III General Medical Conditions
Axis IV   Psychosocial and Environmental
          Problems
Axis V   Global Assessment of Functioning

Multiaxial Assessment

A multiaxial system involves an assessment on several axes, each of which refers to a different domain of information that may help the clinician plan treatment and predict outcome. There are five axes included in the DSM-IV multiaxial classification:

Axis I	Clinical Disorders
	Other Conditions That May Be a Focus of Clinical Attention
Axis II	Personality Disorders
	Mental Retardation
Axis III	General Medical Conditions
Axis IV	Psychosocial and Environmental Problems
Axis V	Global Assessment of Functioning

The use of the multiaxial system facilitates comprehensive and systematic evaluation with attention to the various mental disorders and general medical conditions, psychosocial and environmental problems, and level of functioning that might be overlooked if the focus were on assessing a single presenting problem. A multiaxial system provides a convenient format for organizing and communicating clinical information, for capturing the complexity of clinical situations, and for describing the heterogeneity of individuals presenting with the same diagnosis. In addition, the multiaxial system promotes the application of the biopsychosocial model in clinical, educational, and research settings.

The rest of this section provides a description of each of the DSM-IV axes. In some settings or situations, clinicians may prefer not to use the multiaxial system. For this reason, guidelines for reporting the results of a DSM-IV assessment without applying the formal multiaxial system are provided at the end of this section.

Axis I: Clinical Disorders
Other Conditions That May Be a Focus of Clinical Attention

Axis I is for reporting all the various disorders or conditions in the Classification except for the Personality Disorders and Mental Retardation (which are reported on Axis II). The major groups of disorders to be reported on Axis I are listed in the box below. Also reported on Axis I are Other Conditions That May Be a Focus of Clinical Attention.

When an individual has more than one Axis I disorder, all of these should be reported (for examples, see p. 33). If more than one Axis I disorder is present, the principal diagnosis or the reason for visit (see p. 3) should be indicated by listing it first. When an individual has both an Axis I and an Axis II disorder, the principal diagnosis or the reason for visit will be assumed to be on Axis I unless the Axis II diagnosis is followed by the qualifying phrase "(Principal Diagnosis)" or "(Reason for Visit)." If no Axis I disorder is present, this should be coded as V71.09. If an Axis I diagnosis is deferred, pending the gathering of additional information, this should be coded as 799.9.

■   Axis I   ■
Clinical Disorders
Other Conditions That May Be a Focus of Clinical Attention

Disorders Usually First Diagnosed in Infancy, Childhood, or Adolescence
    (excluding Mental Retardation, which is diagnosed on Axis II)
Delirium, Dementia, and Amnestic and Other Cognitive Disorders
Mental Disorders Due to a General Medical Condition
Substance-Related Disorders
Schizophrenia and Other Psychotic Disorders
Mood Disorders
Anxiety Disorders
Somatoform Disorders
Factitious Disorders
Dissociative Disorders
Sexual and Gender Identity Disorders
Eating Disorders
Sleep Disorders
Impulse-Control Disorders Not Elsewhere Classified
Adjustment Disorders
Other Conditions That May Be a Focus of Clinical Attention

Axis II: Personality Disorders
Mental Retardation

Axis II is for reporting Personality Disorders and Mental Retardation. It may also be used for noting prominent maladaptive personality features and defense mechanisms. The listing of Personality Disorders and Mental Retardation on a separate axis ensures that consideration will be given to the possible presence of Personality Disorders and Mental Retardation that might otherwise be overlooked when attention is directed to the usually more florid Axis I disorders. The coding of Personality Disorders on Axis II should not be taken to imply that their pathogenesis or range of appropriate treatment is fundamentally different from that for the disorders coded on Axis I. The disorders to be reported on Axis II are listed in the box below.

In the common situation in which an individual has more than one Axis II diagnosis, all should be reported (for examples, see p. 33). When an individual has both an Axis I and an Axis II diagnosis and the Axis II diagnosis is the principal diagnosis or the reason for visit, this should be indicated by adding the qualifying phrase "(Principal Diagnosis)" or "(Reason for Visit)" after the Axis II diagnosis. If no Axis II disorder is present, this should be coded as V71.09. If an Axis II diagnosis is deferred, pending the gathering of additional information, this should be coded as 799.9.

Axis II may also be used to indicate prominent maladaptive personality features that do not meet the threshold for a Personality Disorder (in such instances, no code number should be used—see Example 3 on p. 33). The habitual use of maladaptive defense mechanisms may also be indicated on Axis II (see Appendix B, p. 751, for definitions and Example 1 on p. 33).

■ **Axis II** ■
Personality Disorders
Mental Retardation

Paranoid Personality Disorder	Dependent Personality Disorder
Schizoid Personality Disorder	Obsessive-Compulsive Personality
Schizotypal Personality Disorder	Disorder
Antisocial Personality Disorder	Personality Disorder Not Otherwise
Borderline Personality Disorder	Specified
Histrionic Personality Disorder	
Narcissistic Personality Disorder	Mental Retardation
Avoidant Personality Disorder	

Axis III: General Medical Conditions

Axis III is for reporting current general medical conditions that are potentially relevant to the understanding or management of the individual's mental disorder. These conditions are classified outside the "Mental Disorders" chapter of ICD-9-CM (and outside Chapter V of ICD-10). A listing of the broad categories of general medical conditions is given in the box below. (For a more detailed listing including the specific ICD-9-CM codes, refer to Appendix G.)

As discussed in the "Introduction," the multiaxial distinction among Axis I, II, and III disorders does not imply that there are fundamental differences in their conceptualization, that mental disorders are unrelated to physical or biological factors or processes, or that general medical conditions are unrelated to behavioral or psychosocial factors or processes. The purpose of distinguishing general medical conditions is to encourage thoroughness in evaluation and to enhance communication among health care providers.

General medical conditions can be related to mental disorders in a variety of ways. In some cases it is clear that the general medical condition is directly etiological to the development or worsening of mental symptoms and that the mechanism for this effect is physiological. When a mental disorder is judged to be a direct physiological consequence of the general medical condition, a Mental Disorder Due to a General Medical Condition should be diagnosed on Axis I and the general medical condition should be recorded on both Axis I and Axis III. For example, when hypothyroidism is a direct cause of depressive symptoms, the designation on Axis I is 293.83 Mood Disorder Due to Hypothyroidism, With Depressive Features, and the hypothyroidism is listed again and coded on Axis III as 244.9 (see Example 3, p. 33). For a further discussion, see p. 165.

In those instances in which the etiological relationship between the general medical condition and the mental symptoms is insufficiently clear to warrant an Axis I diagnosis of Mental Disorder Due to a General Medical Condition, the appropriate mental disorder (e.g., Major Depressive Disorder) should be listed and coded on Axis I; the general medical condition should only be coded on Axis III.

There are other situations in which general medical conditions are recorded on Axis III because of their importance to the overall understanding or treatment of the individual with the mental disorder. An Axis I disorder may be a psychological reaction to an Axis III general medical condition (e.g., the development of 309.0 Adjustment Disorder With Depressed Mood as a reaction to the diagnosis of carcinoma of the breast). Some general medical conditions may not be directly related to the mental disorder but nonetheless have important prognostic or treatment implications (e.g., when the diagnosis on Axis I is 296.2 Major Depressive Disorder and on Axis III is 427.9 arrhythmia, the choice of pharmacotherapy is influenced by the general medical condition; or when a person with diabetes mellitus is admitted to the hospital for an exacerbation of Schizophrenia and insulin management must be monitored).

When an individual has more than one clinically relevant Axis III diagnosis, all should be reported. For examples, see p. 33. If no Axis III disorder is present, this should be indicated by the notation "Axis III: None." If an Axis III diagnosis is deferred, pending the gathering of additional information, this should be indicated by the notation "Axis III: Deferred."

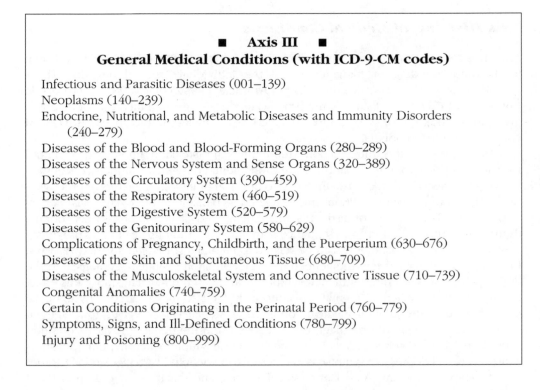

■   **Axis III**   ■
General Medical Conditions (with ICD-9-CM codes)

Infectious and Parasitic Diseases (001–139)
Neoplasms (140–239)
Endocrine, Nutritional, and Metabolic Diseases and Immunity Disorders
    (240–279)
Diseases of the Blood and Blood-Forming Organs (280–289)
Diseases of the Nervous System and Sense Organs (320–389)
Diseases of the Circulatory System (390–459)
Diseases of the Respiratory System (460–519)
Diseases of the Digestive System (520–579)
Diseases of the Genitourinary System (580–629)
Complications of Pregnancy, Childbirth, and the Puerperium (630–676)
Diseases of the Skin and Subcutaneous Tissue (680–709)
Diseases of the Musculoskeletal System and Connective Tissue (710–739)
Congenital Anomalies (740–759)
Certain Conditions Originating in the Perinatal Period (760–779)
Symptoms, Signs, and Ill-Defined Conditions (780–799)
Injury and Poisoning (800–999)

Axis IV: Psychosocial and Environmental Problems

Axis IV is for reporting psychosocial and environmental problems that may affect the diagnosis, treatment, and prognosis of mental disorders (Axes I and II). A psychosocial or environmental problem may be a negative life event, an environmental difficulty or deficiency, a familial or other interpersonal stress, an inadequacy of social support or personal resources, or other problem relating to the context in which a person's difficulties have developed. So-called positive stressors, such as job promotion, should be listed only if they constitute or lead to a problem, as when a person has difficulty adapting to the new situation. In addition to playing a role in the initiation or exacerbation of a mental disorder, psychosocial problems may also develop as a consequence of a person's psychopathology or may constitute problems that should be considered in the overall management plan.

When an individual has multiple psychosocial or environmental problems, the clinician may note as many as are judged to be relevant. In general, the clinician should note only those psychosocial and environmental problems that have been present during the year preceding the current evaluation. However, the clinician may choose to note psychosocial and environmental problems occurring prior to the previous year if these clearly contribute to the mental disorder or have become a focus of treatment—for example, previous combat experiences leading to Posttraumatic Stress Disorder.

In practice, most psychosocial and environmental problems will be indicated on Axis IV. However, when a psychosocial or environmental problem is the primary focus of clinical attention, it should also be recorded on Axis I, with a code derived from the section "Other Conditions That May Be a Focus of Clinical Attention" (see p. 675).

For convenience, the problems are grouped together in the following categories:

- **Problems with primary support group**—e.g., death of a family member; health problems in family; disruption of family by separation, divorce, or estrangement; removal from the home; remarriage of parent; sexual or physical abuse; parental overprotection; neglect of child; inadequate discipline; discord with siblings; birth of a sibling
- **Problems related to the social environment**—e.g., death or loss of friend; inadequate social support; living alone; difficulty with acculturation; discrimination; adjustment to life-cycle transition (such as retirement)
- **Educational problems**—e.g., illiteracy; academic problems; discord with teachers or classmates; inadequate school environment
- **Occupational problems**—e.g., unemployment; threat of job loss; stressful work schedule; difficult work conditions; job dissatisfaction; job change; discord with boss or co-workers
- **Housing problems**—e.g., homelessness; inadequate housing; unsafe neighborhood; discord with neighbors or landlord
- **Economic problems**—e.g., extreme poverty; inadequate finances; insufficient welfare support
- **Problems with access to health care services**—e.g., inadequate health care services; transportation to health care facilities unavailable; inadequate health insurance
- **Problems related to interaction with the legal system/crime**—e.g., arrest; incarceration; litigation; victim of crime

- **Other psychosocial and environmental problems**—e.g., exposure to disasters, war, other hostilities; discord with nonfamily caregivers such as counselor, social worker, or physician; unavailability of social service agencies

When using the Multiaxial Evaluation Report Form (see p. 34), the clinician should identify the relevant categories of psychosocial and environmental problems and indicate the specific factors involved. If a recording form with a checklist of problem categories is not used, the clinician may simply list the specific problems on Axis IV. (See examples on p. 33.)

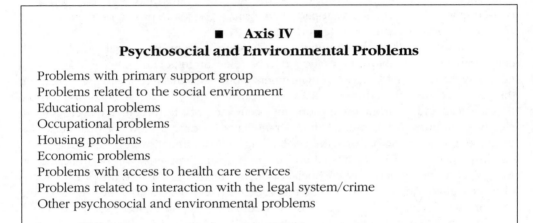

■ **Axis IV** ■
Psychosocial and Environmental Problems

Problems with primary support group
Problems related to the social environment
Educational problems
Occupational problems
Housing problems
Economic problems
Problems with access to health care services
Problems related to interaction with the legal system/crime
Other psychosocial and environmental problems

Axis V: Global Assessment of Functioning

Axis V is for reporting the clinician's judgment of the individual's overall level of functioning. This information is useful in planning treatment and measuring its impact, and in predicting outcome.

The reporting of overall functioning on Axis V is done using the Global Assessment of Functioning (GAF) Scale. The GAF Scale may be particularly useful in tracking the clinical progress of individuals in global terms, using a single measure. The GAF Scale is to be rated with respect only to psychological, social, and occupational functioning. The instructions specify, "Do not include impairment in functioning due to physical (or environmental) limitations." In most instances, ratings on the GAF Scale should be for the current period (i.e., the level of functioning at the time of the evaluation) because ratings of current functioning will generally reflect the need for treatment or care. In some settings, it may be useful to note the GAF Scale rating both at time of admission and at time of discharge. The GAF Scale may also be rated for other time periods (e.g., the highest level of functioning for at least a few months during the past year). The GAF Scale is reported on Axis V as follows: "GAF = ," followed by the GAF rating from 1 to 100, followed by the time period reflected in the rating in parentheses—for example, "(current)," "(highest level in past year)," "(at discharge)." See examples on p. 33.

In some settings, it may be useful to assess social and occupational disability and to track progress in rehabilitation independent of the severity of the psychological symptoms. For this purpose, a proposed Social and Occupational Functioning Assessment Scale (SOFAS) (see p. 760) is included in Appendix B. Two additional proposed scales—Global Assessment of Relational Functioning (GARF) Scale (see p. 758) and Defensive Functioning Scale (see p. 751)—that may be useful in some settings are also included in Appendix B.

Global Assessment of Functioning (GAF) Scale

Consider psychological, social, and occupational functioning on a hypothetical continuum of mental health–illness. Do not include impairment in functioning due to physical (or environmental) limitations.

Code   (**Note:** Use intermediate codes when appropriate, e.g., 45, 68, 72.)

100 | **Superior functioning in a wide range of activities, life's problems never seem to get out of hand, is sought out by others because of his or her many positive qualities. No symptoms.**
91 |

90 | **Absent or minimal symptoms** (e.g., mild anxiety before an exam), **good functioning in all areas, interested and involved in a wide range of activities, socially effective, generally satisfied with life, no more than everyday problems or concerns** (e.g., an occasional argument with family members).
81 |

80 | **If symptoms are present, they are transient and expectable reactions to psychosocial stressors** (e.g., difficulty concentrating after family argument); **no more than slight impairment in social, occupational, or school functioning** (e.g., temporarily falling behind in schoolwork).
71 |

70 | **Some mild symptoms** (e.g., depressed mood and mild insomnia) **OR some difficulty in social, occupational, or school functioning** (e.g., occasional truancy, or theft within the household), **but generally functioning pretty well, has some meaningful interpersonal relationships.**
61 |

60 | **Moderate symptoms** (e.g., flat affect and circumstantial speech, occasional panic attacks) **OR moderate difficulty in social, occupational, or school functioning** (e.g., few friends, conflicts with peers or co-workers).
51 |

50 | **Serious symptoms** (e.g., suicidal ideation, severe obsessional rituals, frequent shoplifting) **OR any serious impairment in social, occupational, or school functioning** (e.g., no friends, unable to keep a job).
41 |

40 | **Some impairment in reality testing or communication** (e.g., speech is at times illogical, obscure, or irrelevant) **OR major impairment in several areas, such as work or school, family relations, judgment, thinking, or mood** (e.g., depressed man avoids friends, neglects family, and is unable to work; child frequently beats up younger children, is defiant at home, and is failing at school).
31 |

30 | **Behavior is considerably influenced by delusions or hallucinations OR serious impairment in communication or judgment** (e.g., sometimes incoherent, acts grossly inappropriately, suicidal preoccupation) **OR inability to function in almost all areas** (e.g., stays in bed all day; no job, home, or friends).
21 |

20 | **Some danger of hurting self or others** (e.g., suicide attempts without clear expectation of death; frequently violent; manic excitement) **OR occasionally fails to maintain minimal personal hygiene** (e.g., smears feces) **OR gross impairment in communication** (e.g., largely incoherent or mute).
11 |

10 | **Persistent danger of severely hurting self or others** (e.g., recurrent violence) **OR persistent inability to maintain minimal personal hygiene OR serious suicidal act with clear expectation of death.**
1 |

0 | Inadequate information.

The rating of overall psychological functioning on a scale of 0–100 was operationalized by Luborsky in the Health-Sickness Rating Scale (Luborsky L: "Clinicians' Judgments of Mental Health." *Archives of General Psychiatry* 7:407–417, 1962). Spitzer and colleagues developed a revision of the Health-Sickness Rating Scale called the Global Assessment Scale (GAS) (Endicott J, Spitzer RL, Fleiss JL, Cohen J: "The Global Assessment Scale: A Procedure for Measuring Overall Severity of Psychiatric Disturbance." *Archives of General Psychiatry* 33:766–771, 1976). A modified version of the GAS was included in DSM-III-R as the Global Assessment of Functioning (GAF) Scale.

Examples of How to Record
Results of a DSM-IV Multiaxial Evaluation

Example 1:

Axis I	296.23	Major Depressive Disorder, Single Episode, Severe Without Psychotic Features
	305.00	Alcohol Abuse
Axis II	301.6	Dependent Personality Disorder
		Frequent use of denial
Axis III		None
Axis IV		Threat of job loss
Axis V	GAF = 35 (current)	

Example 2:

Axis I	300.4	Dysthymic Disorder
	315.00	Reading Disorder
Axis II	V71.09	No diagnosis
Axis III	382.9	Otitis media, recurrent
Axis IV		Victim of child neglect
Axis V	GAF = 53 (current)	

Example 3:

Axis I	293.83	Mood Disorder Due to Hypothyroidism, With Depressive Features
Axis II	V71.09	No diagnosis, histrionic personality features
Axis III	244.9	Hypothyroidism
	365.23	Chronic angle-closure glaucoma
Axis IV		None
Axis V	GAF = 45 (on admission)	
	GAF = 65 (at discharge)	

Example 4:

Axis I	V61.1	Partner Relational Problem
Axis II	V71.09	No diagnosis
Axis III		None
Axis IV		Unemployment
Axis V	GAF = 83 (highest level past year)	

Multiaxial Evaluation Report Form

The following form is offered as one possibility for reporting multiaxial evaluations. In some settings, this form may be used exactly as is; in other settings, the form may be adapted to satisfy special needs.

AXIS I: Clinical Disorders
Other Conditions That May Be a Focus of Clinical Attention

Diagnostic code   DSM-IV name

__ __ __.__ __   _____

__ __ __.__ __   _____

__ __ __.__ __   _____

AXIS II: Personality Disorders
Mental Retardation

Diagnostic code   DSM-IV name

__ __ __.__ __   _____

__ __ __.__ __   _____

AXIS III: General Medical Conditions

ICD-9-CM code   ICD-9-CM name

__ __ __.__ __   _____

__ __ __.__ __   _____

__ __ __.__ __   _____

AXIS IV: Psychosocial and Environmental Problems

Check:
- ☐ **Problems with primary support group** *Specify:* _____
- ☐ **Problems related to the social environment** *Specify:* _____
- ☐ **Educational problems** *Specify:* _____
- ☐ **Occupational problems** *Specify:* _____
- ☐ **Housing problems** *Specify:* _____
- ☐ **Economic problems** *Specify:* _____
- ☐ **Problems with access to health care services** *Specify:* _____
- ☐ **Problems related to interaction with the legal system/crime** *Specify:* _____
- ☐ **Other psychosocial and environmental problems** *Specify:* _____

AXIS V: Global Assessment of Functioning Scale   Score: __ __ __

Time frame: _____

Nonaxial Format

Clinicians who do not wish to use the multiaxial format may simply list the appropriate diagnoses. Those choosing this option should follow the general rule of recording as many coexisting mental disorders, general medical conditions, and other factors as are relevant to the care and treatment of the individual. The Principal Diagnosis or the Reason for Visit should be listed first.

The examples below illustrate the reporting of diagnoses in a format that does not use the multiaxial system.

Example 1:

296.23	Major Depressive Disorder, Single Episode, Severe Without Psychotic Features
305.00	Alcohol Abuse
301.6	Dependent Personality Disorder
	Frequent use of denial

Example 2:

300.4	Dysthymic Disorder
315.00	Reading Disorder
382.9	Otitis media, recurrent

Example 3:

293.83	Mood Disorder Due to Hypothyroidism, With Depressive Features
244.9	Hypothyroidism
365.23	Chronic angle-closure glaucoma
	Histrionic personality features

Example 4:

V61.1	Partner Relational Problem

Disorders Usually First Diagnosed in Infancy, Childhood, or Adolescence

The provision of a separate section for disorders that are usually first diagnosed in infancy, childhood, or adolescence is for convenience only and is not meant to suggest that there is any clear distinction between "childhood" and "adult" disorders. Although most individuals with these disorders present for clinical attention during childhood or adolescence, the disorders sometimes are not diagnosed until adulthood. Moreover, many disorders included in other sections of the manual often have an onset during childhood or adolescence. In evaluating an infant, child, or adolescent, the clinician should consider the diagnoses included in this section but also should refer to the disorders described elsewhere in this manual. Adults may also be diagnosed with disorders included in this section for Disorders Usually First Diagnosed in Infancy, Childhood, or Adolescence if their clinical presentation meets relevant diagnostic criteria (e.g., Stuttering, Pica). Moreover, if an adult had symptoms as a child that met full criteria for a disorder, but now presents with an attenuated or residual form, the In Partial Remission specifier may be indicated (e.g., Attention-Deficit/Hyperactivity Disorder, Combined Type, In Partial Remission). For most (but not all) DSM-IV disorders, a single criteria set is provided that applies to children, adolescents, and adults (e.g., if a child or adolescent has symptoms that meet the criteria for Major Depressive Disorder, this diagnosis should be given, regardless of the individual's age). The variations in the presentation of a disorder that are attributable to an individual's developmental stage are described in a section in the text titled "Specific Culture, Age, and Gender Features." Specific issues related to the diagnosis of Personality Disorders in children or adolescents are discussed on p. 631.

The following disorders are included in this section:

Mental Retardation.   This disorder is characterized by significantly subaverage intellectual functioning (an IQ of approximately 70 or below) with onset before age 18 years and concurrent deficits or impairments in adaptive functioning. Separate codes are provided for **Mild, Moderate, Severe,** and **Profound Mental Retardation** and for **Mental Retardation, Severity Unspecified.**

Learning Disorders.   These disorders are characterized by academic functioning that is substantially below that expected given the person's chronological age, measured intelligence, and age-appropriate education. The specific disorders included in this section are **Reading Disorder, Mathematics Disorder, Disorder of Written Expression,** and **Learning Disorder Not Otherwise Specified.**

Motor Skills Disorder.   This includes **Developmental Coordination Disorder,** which is characterized by motor coordination that is substantially below that expected given the person's chronological age and measured intelligence.

Communication Disorders.   These disorders are characterized by difficulties in speech or language and include **Expressive Language Disorder, Mixed Receptive-Expressive Language Disorder, Phonological Disorder, Stuttering,** and **Communication Disorder Not Otherwise Specified.**

Pervasive Developmental Disorders.   These disorders are characterized by severe deficits and pervasive impairment in multiple areas of development. These include impairment in reciprocal social interaction, impairment in communication, and the presence of stereotyped behavior, interests, and activities. The specific disorders included in this section are **Autistic Disorder, Rett's Disorder, Childhood Disintegrative Disorder, Asperger's Disorder,** and **Pervasive Developmental Disorder Not Otherwise Specified.**

Attention-Deficit and Disruptive Behavior Disorders.   This section includes **Attention-Deficit/Hyperactivity Disorder,** which is characterized by prominent symptoms of inattention and/or hyperactivity-impulsivity. Subtypes are provided for specifying the predominant symptom presentation: **Predominantly Inattentive Type, Predominantly Hyperactive-Impulsive Type,** and **Combined Type.** Also included in this section are the Disruptive Behavior Disorders: **Conduct Disorder** is characterized by a pattern of behavior that violates the basic rights of others or major age-appropriate societal norms or rules; **Oppositional Defiant Disorder** is characterized by a pattern of negativistic, hostile, and defiant behavior. This section also includes two Not Otherwise Specified categories: **Attention-Deficit/Hyperactivity Disorder Not Otherwise Specified** and **Disruptive Behavior Disorder Not Otherwise Specified.**

Feeding and Eating Disorders of Infancy or Early Childhood.   These disorders are characterized by persistent disturbances in feeding and eating. The specific disorders included are **Pica, Rumination Disorder,** and **Feeding Disorder of Infancy or Early Childhood.** Note that Anorexia Nervosa and Bulimia Nervosa are included in the "Eating Disorders" section presented later in the manual (see p. 539).

Tic Disorders.   These disorders are characterized by vocal and/or motor tics. The specific disorders included are **Tourette's Disorder, Chronic Motor or Vocal Tic Disorder, Transient Tic Disorder,** and **Tic Disorder Not Otherwise Specified.**

Elimination Disorders.   This grouping includes **Encopresis,** the repeated passage of feces into inappropriate places, and **Enuresis,** the repeated voiding of urine into inappropriate places.

Other Disorders of Infancy, Childhood, or Adolescence.   This grouping is for disorders that are not covered in the sections listed above. **Separation Anxiety Disorder** is characterized by developmentally inappropriate and excessive anxiety concerning separation from home or from those to whom the child is attached. **Selective Mutism** is characterized by a consistent failure to speak in specific social situations despite speaking in other situations. **Reactive Attachment Disorder of Infancy or Early Childhood** is characterized by markedly disturbed and developmentally inappropriate social relatedness that occurs in most contexts and is associated with grossly pathogenic care. **Stereotypic Movement Disorder** is characterized by repetitive, seemingly driven, and nonfunctional motor behavior that markedly interferes with normal activities and at times may result in bodily injury. **Disorder of Infancy, Childhood, or Adolescence Not Otherwise Specified** is a residual category for coding disorders with onset in infancy, childhood, or adolescence that do not meet criteria for any specific disorder in the Classification.

Children or adolescents may present with problems requiring clinical attention that are not defined as mental disorders (e.g., Relational Problems, Problems Related to Abuse or Neglect, Bereavement, Borderline Intellectual Functioning, Academic Problem, Child or Adolescent Antisocial Behavior, Identity Problem). These are listed at the end of the manual in the section "Other Conditions That May Be a Focus of Clinical Attention" (see p. 675).

DSM-III-R included two anxiety disorders specific to children and adolescents, Overanxious Disorder of Childhood and Avoidant Disorder of Childhood, that have been subsumed under Generalized Anxiety Disorder and Social Phobia, respectively, because of similarities in essential features.

Mental Retardation

Diagnostic Features

The essential feature of Mental Retardation is significantly subaverage general intellectual functioning (Criterion A) that is accompanied by significant limitations in adaptive functioning in at least two of the following skill areas: communication, self-care, home living, social/interpersonal skills, use of community resources, self-direction, functional academic skills, work, leisure, health, and safety (Criterion B). The onset must occur before age 18 years (Criterion C). Mental Retardation has many different etiologies and may be seen as a final common pathway of various pathological processes that affect the functioning of the central nervous system.

General intellectual functioning is defined by the intelligence quotient (IQ or IQ-equivalent) obtained by assessment with one or more of the standardized, individually administered intelligence tests (e.g., Wechsler Intelligence Scales for Children—Revised, Stanford-Binet, Kaufman Assessment Battery for Children). Significantly subaverage intellectual functioning is defined as an IQ of about 70 or below (approximately 2 standard deviations below the mean). It should be noted that there is a measurement error of approximately 5 points in assessing IQ, although this may vary from instrument to instrument (e.g., a Wechsler IQ of 70 is considered to represent a range of 65–75). Thus, it is possible to diagnose Mental Retardation in individuals with

IQs between 70 and 75 who exhibit significant deficits in adaptive behavior. Conversely, Mental Retardation would not be diagnosed in an individual with an IQ lower than 70 if there are no significant deficits or impairments in adaptive functioning. The choice of testing instruments and interpretation of results should take into account factors that may limit test performance (e.g., the individual's sociocultural background, native language, and associated communicative, motor, and sensory handicaps). When there is significant scatter in the subtest scores, the profile of strengths and weaknesses, rather than the mathematically derived full-scale IQ, will more accurately reflect the person's learning abilities. When there is a marked discrepancy across verbal and performance scores, averaging to obtain a full-scale IQ score can be misleading.

Impairments in adaptive functioning, rather than a low IQ, are usually the presenting symptoms in individuals with Mental Retardation. *Adaptive functioning* refers to how effectively individuals cope with common life demands and how well they meet the standards of personal independence expected of someone in their particular age group, sociocultural background, and community setting. Adaptive functioning may be influenced by various factors, including education, motivation, personality characteristics, social and vocational opportunities, and the mental disorders and general medical conditions that may coexist with Mental Retardation. Problems in adaptation are more likely to improve with remedial efforts than is the cognitive IQ, which tends to remain a more stable attribute.

It is useful to gather evidence for deficits in adaptive functioning from one or more reliable independent sources (e.g., teacher evaluation and educational, developmental, and medical history). Several scales have also been designed to measure adaptive functioning or behavior (e.g., the Vineland Adaptive Behavior Scales and the American Association on Mental Retardation Adaptive Behavior Scale). These scales generally provide a clinical cutoff score that is a composite of performance in a number of adaptive skill domains. It should be noted that scores for certain individual domains are not included in some of these instruments and that individual domain scores may vary considerably in reliability. As in the assessment of intellectual functioning, consideration should be given to the suitability of the instrument to the person's sociocultural background, education, associated handicaps, motivation, and cooperation. For instance, the presence of significant handicaps invalidates many adaptive scale norms. In addition, behaviors that would normally be considered maladaptive (e.g., dependency, passivity) may be evidence of good adaptation in the context of a particular individual's life (e.g., in some institutional settings).

Degrees of Severity of Mental Retardation

Four degrees of severity can be specified, reflecting the level of intellectual impairment: Mild, Moderate, Severe, and Profound.

317	**Mild Mental Retardation:**	IQ level 50–55 to approximately 70
318.0	**Moderate Retardation:**	IQ level 35–40 to 50–55
318.1	**Severe Mental Retardation:**	IQ level 20–25 to 35–40
318.2	**Profound Mental Retardation:**	IQ level below 20 or 25

319 Mental Retardation, Severity Unspecified, can be used when there is a strong presumption of Mental Retardation but the person's intelligence is untestable by standard tests (e.g., with individuals too impaired or uncooperative, or with infants).

317   Mild Mental Retardation

Mild Mental Retardation is roughly equivalent to what used to be referred to as the educational category of "educable." This group constitutes the largest segment (about 85%) of those with the disorder. As a group, people with this level of Mental Retardation typically develop social and communication skills during the preschool years (ages 0–5 years), have minimal impairment in sensorimotor areas, and often are not distinguishable from children without Mental Retardation until a later age. By their late teens, they can acquire academic skills up to approximately the sixth-grade level. During their adult years, they usually achieve social and vocational skills adequate for minimum self-support, but may need supervision, guidance, and assistance, especially when under unusual social or economic stress. With appropriate supports, individuals with Mild Mental Retardation can usually live successfully in the community, either independently or in supervised settings.

318.0   Moderate Mental Retardation

Moderate Mental Retardation is roughly equivalent to what used to be referred to as the educational category of "trainable." This outdated term should not be used because it wrongly implies that people with Moderate Mental Retardation cannot benefit from educational programs. This group constitutes about 10% of the entire population of people with Mental Retardation. Most of the individuals with this level of Mental Retardation acquire communication skills during early childhood years. They profit from vocational training and, with moderate supervision, can attend to their personal care. They can also benefit from training in social and occupational skills but are unlikely to progress beyond the second-grade level in academic subjects. They may learn to travel independently in familiar places. During adolescence, their difficulties in recognizing social conventions may interfere with peer relationships. In their adult years, the majority are able to perform unskilled or semiskilled work under supervision in sheltered workshops or in the general work force. They adapt well to life in the community, usually in supervised settings.

318.1   Severe Mental Retardation

The group with Severe Mental Retardation constitutes 3%–4% of individuals with Mental Retardation. During the early childhood years, they acquire little or no communicative speech. During the school-age period, they may learn to talk and can be trained in elementary self-care skills. They profit to only a limited extent from instruction in pre-academic subjects, such as familiarity with the alphabet and simple counting, but can master skills such as learning sight reading of some "survival" words. In their adult years, they may be able to perform simple tasks in closely supervised settings. Most adapt well to life in the community, in group homes or with their families, unless they have an associated handicap that requires specialized nursing or other care.

318.2   Profound Mental Retardation

The group with Profound Mental Retardation constitutes approximately 1%–2% of people with Mental Retardation. Most individuals with this diagnosis have an identified neurological condition that accounts for their Mental Retardation. During the early childhood years, they display considerable impairments in sensorimotor functioning. Optimal development may occur in a highly structured environment with constant aid and supervision and an individualized relationship with a caregiver. Motor development and self-care and communication skills may improve if appropriate training is provided. Some can perform simple tasks in closely supervised and sheltered settings.

319   Mental Retardation, Severity Unspecified

The diagnosis of Mental Retardation, Severity Unspecified, should be used when there is a strong presumption of Mental Retardation but the person cannot be successfully tested by standard intelligence tests. This may be the case when children, adolescents, or adults are too impaired or uncooperative to be tested or, with infants, when there is a clinical judgment of significantly subaverage intellectual functioning, but the available tests (e.g., the Bayley Scales of Infant Development, Cattell Infant Intelligence Scales, and others) do not yield IQ values. In general, the younger the age, the more difficult it is to assess for the presence of Mental Retardation except in those with profound impairment.

Recording Procedures

The specific diagnostic code for Mental Retardation is selected based on the level of severity as indicated above and is coded on Axis II. If Mental Retardation is associated with another mental disorder (e.g., Autistic Disorder), the additional mental disorder is coded on Axis I. If Mental Retardation is associated with a general medical condition (e.g., Down's syndrome), the general medical condition is coded on Axis III.

Associated Features and Disorders

Associated descriptive features and mental disorders.   No specific personality and behavioral features are uniquely associated with Mental Retardation. Some individuals with Mental Retardation are passive, placid, and dependent, whereas others can be aggressive and impulsive. Lack of communication skills may predispose to disruptive and aggressive behaviors that substitute for communicative language. Some general medical conditions associated with Mental Retardation are characterized by certain behavioral symptoms (e.g., the intractable self-injurious behavior associated with Lesch-Nyhan syndrome). Individuals with Mental Retardation may be vulnerable to exploitation by others (e.g., being physically and sexually abused) or being denied rights and opportunities.

Individuals with Mental Retardation have a prevalence of comorbid mental disorders that is estimated to be three to four times greater than in the general population. In some cases, this may result from a shared etiology that is common to Mental Retardation and the associated mental disorder (e.g., head trauma may result in Mental Retardation and in Personality Change Due to Head Trauma). All types of mental disorders may be seen, and there is no evidence that the nature of a given mental disorder is different in individuals who have Mental Retardation. The diagnosis of comorbid mental disorders is, however, often complicated by the fact that the clinical presentation may be modified by the severity of the Mental Retardation and associated handicaps. Deficits in communication skills may result in an inability to provide an adequate history (e.g., the diagnosis of Major Depressive Disorder in a nonverbal adult with Mental Retardation is often based primarily on manifestations such as depressed mood, irritability, anorexia, or insomnia that are observed by others). More often than is the case in individuals without Mental Retardation, it may be difficult to choose a specific diagnosis and in such cases the appropriate Not Otherwise Specified category can be used (e.g., Depressive Disorder Not Otherwise Specified). The most common associated mental disorders are Attention-Deficit/Hyperactivity Disorder, Mood Disorders, Pervasive Developmental Disorders, Stereotypic Movement Disorder, and Mental Disorders Due to a General Medical Condition (e.g., Dementia Due to Head Trauma). Individuals who have Mental Retardation due to Down's syndrome may be at higher risk for developing Dementia of the Alzheimer's Type. Pathological changes in the brain associated with this disorder usually develop by the time these individuals are in their early 40s, although the clinical symptoms of dementia are not evident until later.

Predisposing factors.   Etiological factors may be primarily biological or primarily psychosocial, or some combination of both. In approximately 30%–40% of individuals seen in clinical settings, no clear etiology for the Mental Retardation can be determined despite extensive evaluation efforts. The major predisposing factors include:

Heredity (approximately 5%): These factors include inborn errors of metabolism inherited mostly through autosomal recessive mechanisms (e.g., Tay-Sachs disease), other single-gene abnormalities with Mendelian inheritance and variable expression (e.g., tuberous sclerosis), and chromosomal aberrations (e.g., translocation Down's syndrome, fragile X syndrome).

Early alterations of embryonic development (approximately 30%): These factors include chromosomal changes (e.g., Down's syndrome due to trisomy 21) or prenatal damage due to toxins (e.g., maternal alcohol consumption, infections).

Pregnancy and perinatal problems (approximately 10%): These factors include fetal malnutrition, prematurity, hypoxia, viral and other infections, and trauma.

General medical conditions acquired in infancy or childhood (approximately 5%): These factors include infections, traumas, and poisoning (e.g., due to lead).

Environmental influences and other mental disorders (approximately 15%–20%): These factors include deprivation of nurturance and of social, linguistic, and other stimulation, and severe mental disorders (e.g., Autistic Disorder).

Associated laboratory findings.   Other than the results of psychological and adaptive behavior tests that are necessary for the diagnosis of Mental Retardation, there are no laboratory findings that are uniquely associated with Mental Retardation. Diagnostic laboratory findings may be associated with a specific accompanying general medical condition (e.g., chromosomal findings in various genetic conditions, high blood phenylalanine in phenylketonuria, or abnormalities on central nervous system imaging).

Associated physical examination findings and general medical conditions.
There are no specific physical features associated with Mental Retardation. When Mental Retardation is part of a specific syndrome, the clinical features of that syndrome will be present (e.g., the physical features of Down's syndrome). The more severe the Mental Retardation (especially if it is severe or profound), the greater the likelihood of neurological (e.g., seizures), neuromuscular, visual, auditory, cardiovascular, and other conditions.

Specific Culture, Age, and Gender Features

Care should be taken to ensure that intellectual testing procedures reflect adequate attention to the individual's ethnic or cultural background. This is usually accomplished by using tests in which the individual's relevant characteristics are represented in the standardization sample of the test or by employing an examiner who is familiar with aspects of the individual's ethnic or cultural background. Individualized testing is always required to make the diagnosis of Mental Retardation. The prevalence of Mental Retardation due to known biological factors is similar among children of upper and lower socioeconomic classes, except that certain etiological factors are linked to lower socioeconomic status (e.g., lead poisoning and premature births). In cases in which no specific biological causation can be identified, lower socioeconomic classes are over-represented and the Mental Retardation is usually milder, although all degrees of severity are represented. Developmental considerations should be taken into account in evaluating impairment in adaptive skills because certain of the skill areas are less relevant at different ages (e.g., use of community resources or employment in school-age children). Mental Retardation is more common among males, with a male-to-female ratio of approximately 1.5:1.

Prevalence

The prevalence rate of Mental Retardation has been estimated at approximately 1%. However, different studies have reported different rates depending on definitions used, methods of ascertainment, and population studied.

Course

The diagnosis of Mental Retardation requires that the onset of the disorder be before age 18 years. The age and mode of onset depend on the etiology and severity of the Mental Retardation. More severe retardation, especially when associated with a syndrome with a characteristic phenotype, tends to be recognized early (e.g., Down's syndrome is usually diagnosed at birth). In contrast, Mild Retardation of unknown origin is generally noticed later. In more severe retardation resulting from an acquired cause, the intellectual impairment will develop more abruptly (e.g., retardation following an encephalitis). The course of Mental Retardation is influenced by the course of underlying general medical conditions and by environmental factors (e.g., educational and other opportunities, environmental stimulation, and appropriateness of management). If an underlying general medical condition is static, the course is more likely to be variable and to depend on environmental factors. Mental Retardation is not necessarily a lifelong disorder. Individuals who had Mild Mental Retardation earlier in their lives manifested by failure in academic learning tasks may, with appropriate training and opportunities, develop good adaptive skills in other domains and may no longer have the level of impairment required for a diagnosis of Mental Retardation.

Familial Pattern

Because of its heterogeneous etiology, no familial pattern is applicable to Mental Retardation as a general category. The heritability of Mental Retardation is discussed under "Predisposing Factors" (see p. 43).

Differential Diagnosis

The diagnostic criteria for Mental Retardation do not include an exclusion criterion; therefore, the diagnosis should be made whenever the diagnostic criteria are met, regardless of and in addition to the presence of another disorder. In **Learning Disorders** or **Communication Disorders** (unassociated with Mental Retardation), the development in a specific area (e.g., reading, expressive language) is impaired but there is no generalized impairment in intellectual development and adaptive functioning. A Learning Disorder or Communication Disorder can be diagnosed in an individual with Mental Retardation if the specific deficit is out of proportion to the severity of the Mental Retardation. In **Pervasive Developmental Disorders,** there is qualitative impairment in the development of reciprocal social interaction and in the development of verbal and nonverbal social communication skills. Mental Retardation often accompanies Pervasive Developmental Disorders (75%–80% of individuals with a Pervasive Developmental Disorder also have Mental Retardation).

Some cases of Mental Retardation have their onset after a period of normal functioning and may qualify for the additional diagnosis of **dementia.** A diagnosis of dementia requires that the memory impairment and other cognitive deficits represent a significant decline from a previously higher level of functioning. Because it may be difficult to determine the previous level of functioning in very young children, the diagnosis of dementia may not be appropriate until the child is between ages 4 and 6 years. In general, for individuals under age 18 years, the diagnosis of dementia is made only when the condition is not characterized satisfactorily by the diagnosis of Mental Retardation alone.

Borderline Intellectual Functioning (see p. 684) describes an IQ range that is higher than that for Mental Retardation (generally 71–84). As discussed earlier, an IQ score may involve a measurement error of approximately 5 points, depending on the testing instrument. Thus, it is possible to diagnose Mental Retardation in individuals with IQ scores between 71 and 75 if they have significant deficits in adaptive behavior that meet the criteria for Mental Retardation. Differentiating Mild Mental Retardation from Borderline Intellectual Functioning requires careful consideration of all available information.

Relationship to Other Classifications of Mental Retardation

The classification system of the American Association on Mental Retardation (AAMR) includes the same three criteria (i.e., significantly subaverage intellectual functioning, limitations in adaptive skills, and onset prior to age 18 years). In the AAMR classification, the criterion of significantly subaverage intellectual functioning refers to a standard score of approximately 70–75 or below (which takes into account the potential measurement error of plus or minus 5 points in IQ testing). Furthermore, DSM-IV specifies levels of severity, whereas the AAMR 1992 classification system specifies "Patterns and Intensity of Supports Needed" (i.e., "Intermittent, Limited, Extensive, and Pervasive"), which are not directly comparable with the degrees of severity in DSM-IV. The definition of developmental disabilities in Public Law 95-602 (1978) is not limited to Mental Retardation and is based on functional criteria. This law defines *developmental disability* as a disability attributable to a mental or physical impairment, manifested before age 22 years, likely to continue indefinitely, resulting in substantial limitation in three or more specified areas of functioning, and requiring specific and lifelong or extended care.

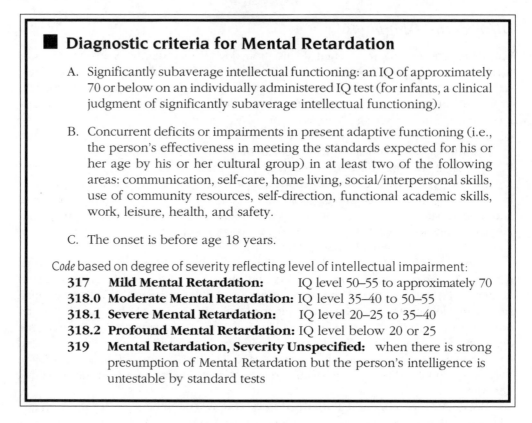

■ **Diagnostic criteria for Mental Retardation**

A. Significantly subaverage intellectual functioning: an IQ of approximately 70 or below on an individually administered IQ test (for infants, a clinical judgment of significantly subaverage intellectual functioning).

B. Concurrent deficits or impairments in present adaptive functioning (i.e., the person's effectiveness in meeting the standards expected for his or her age by his or her cultural group) in at least two of the following areas: communication, self-care, home living, social/interpersonal skills, use of community resources, self-direction, functional academic skills, work, leisure, health, and safety.

C. The onset is before age 18 years.

Code based on degree of severity reflecting level of intellectual impairment:

317   **Mild Mental Retardation:**   IQ level 50–55 to approximately 70
318.0 **Moderate Mental Retardation:** IQ level 35–40 to 50–55
318.1 **Severe Mental Retardation:**   IQ level 20–25 to 35–40
318.2 **Profound Mental Retardation:** IQ level below 20 or 25
319   **Mental Retardation, Severity Unspecified:**   when there is strong presumption of Mental Retardation but the person's intelligence is untestable by standard tests

Learning Disorders
(*formerly* Academic Skills Disorders)

The section on Learning Disorders includes Reading Disorder, Mathematics Disorder, Disorder of Written Expression, and Learning Disorder Not Otherwise Specified.

Diagnostic Features

Learning Disorders are diagnosed when the individual's achievement on individually administered, standardized tests in reading, mathematics, or written expression is substantially below that expected for age, schooling, and level of intelligence. The learning problems significantly interfere with academic achievement or activities of daily living that require reading, mathematical, or writing skills. A variety of statistical approaches can be used to establish that a discrepancy is significant. *Substantially below* is usually defined as a discrepancy of more than 2 standard deviations between achievement and IQ. A smaller discrepancy between achievement and IQ (i.e., between 1 and 2 standard deviations) is sometimes used, especially in cases where an individual's performance on an IQ test may have been compromised by an associated disorder in cognitive processing, a comorbid mental disorder or general medical condition, or the individual's ethnic or cultural background. If a sensory deficit is present, the learning difficulties must be in excess of those usually associated with the deficit. Learning Disorders may persist into adulthood.

Associated Features and Disorders

Demoralization, low self-esteem, and deficits in social skills may be associated with Learning Disorders. The school drop-out rate for children or adolescents with Learning Disorders is reported at nearly 40% (or approximately 1.5 times the average). Adults with Learning Disorders may have significant difficulties in employment or social adjustment. Many individuals (10%–25%) with Conduct Disorder, Oppositional Defiant Disorder, Attention-Deficit/Hyperactivity Disorder, Major Depressive Disorder, or Dysthymic Disorder also have Learning Disorders. There is evidence that developmental delays in language may occur in association with Learning Disorders (particularly Reading Disorder), although these delays may not be sufficiently severe to warrant the separate diagnosis of a Communication Disorder. Learning Disorders may also be associated with a higher rate of Developmental Coordination Disorder.

There may be underlying abnormalities in cognitive processing (e.g., deficits in visual perception, linguistic processes, attention, or memory, or a combination of these) that often precede or are associated with Learning Disorders. Standardized tests to measure these processes are generally less reliable and valid than other psychoeducational tests. Although genetic predisposition, perinatal injury, and various neurological or other general medical conditions may be associated with the development of Learning Disorders, the presence of such conditions does not invariably predict an eventual Learning Disorder, and there are many individuals with Learning Disorders who have no such history. Learning Disorders are, however, frequently found in association with a variety of general medical conditions (e.g., lead poisoning, fetal alcohol syndrome, or fragile X syndrome).

Specific Culture Features

Care should be taken to ensure that intelligence testing procedures reflect adequate attention to the individual's ethnic or cultural background. This is usually accomplished by using tests in which the individual's relevant characteristics are represented in the standardization sample of the test or by employing an examiner who is familiar with aspects of the individual's ethnic or cultural background. Individualized testing is always required to make the diagnosis of a Learning Disorder.

Prevalence

Estimates of the prevalence of Learning Disorders range from 2% to 10% depending on the nature of ascertainment and the definitions applied. Approximately 5% of students in public schools in the United States are identified as having a Learning Disorder.

Differential Diagnosis

Learning Disorders must be differentiated from **normal variations in academic attainment** and from scholastic difficulties due to **lack of opportunity, poor teaching,** or **cultural factors.** Inadequate schooling can result in poor performance on standardized achievement tests. Children from ethnic or cultural backgrounds different from the prevailing school culture or in which English is not the primary language and children who have attended class in schools where teaching has been inadequate may score poorly on achievement tests. Children from these same backgrounds may also be at greater risk for absenteeism due to more frequent illnesses or impoverished or chaotic living environments.

Impaired vision or hearing may affect learning ability and should be investigated through audiometric or visual screening tests. A Learning Disorder may be diagnosed in the presence of such sensory deficits only if the learning difficulties are in excess of those usually associated with these deficits. Accompanying neurological or other general medical conditions should be coded on Axis III.

In **Mental Retardation,** learning difficulties are commensurate with general impairment in intellectual functioning. However, in some cases of Mild Mental Retardation, the level of achievement in reading, mathematics, or written expression is significantly below expected levels given the person's schooling and severity of Mental Retardation. In such cases, the additional diagnosis of the appropriate Learning Disorder should be made.

An additional Learning Disorder diagnosis should be made in the context of a **Pervasive Developmental Disorder** only when academic impairment is significantly below expected levels given the individual's intellectual functioning and schooling. In individuals with **Communication Disorders,** intellectual functioning may have to be assessed using standardized measures of nonverbal intellectual capacity. In cases in which academic achievement is significantly below this measured capacity, the appropriate Learning Disorder should be diagnosed.

Mathematics Disorder and **Disorder of Written Expression** most commonly occur in combination with **Reading Disorder.** When criteria are met for more than one Learning Disorder, all should be diagnosed.

315.00 Reading Disorder

Diagnostic Features

The essential feature of Reading Disorder is reading achievement (i.e., reading accuracy, speed, or comprehension as measured by individually administered standardized tests) that falls substantially below that expected given the individual's chronological age, measured intelligence, and age-appropriate education (Criterion A). The disturbance in reading significantly interferes with academic achievement or with activities of daily living that require reading skills (Criterion B). If a sensory deficit is present, the reading difficulties are in excess of those usually associated with it (Criterion C). If a neurological or other general medical condition or sensory deficit is present, it should be coded on Axis III. In individuals with Reading Disorder (which has also been called "dyslexia"), oral reading is characterized by distortions, substitutions, or omissions; both oral and silent reading are characterized by slowness and errors in comprehension.

Associated Features and Disorders

See the "Associated Features and Disorders" section for Learning Disorders (p. 47). Mathematics Disorder and Disorder of Written Expression are commonly associated with

Reading Disorder, and it is relatively rare for either of these disorders to be found in the absence of Reading Disorder.

Specific Gender Features

From 60% to 80% of individuals diagnosed with Reading Disorder are males. Referral procedures may often be biased toward identifying males, because they more frequently display disruptive behaviors in association with Learning Disorders. The disorder has been found to occur at more equal rates in males and females when careful diagnostic ascertainment and stringent criteria are used rather than traditional school-based referral and diagnostic procedures.

Prevalence

The prevalence of Reading Disorder is difficult to establish because many studies focus on the prevalence of Learning Disorders without careful separation into specific disorders of Reading, Mathematics, or Written Expression. Reading Disorder, alone or in combination with Mathematics Disorder or Disorder of Written Expression, accounts for approximately four of every five cases of Learning Disorder. The prevalence of Reading Disorder in the United States is estimated at 4% of school-age children. Lower incidence and prevalence figures for Reading Disorder may be found in other countries in which stricter criteria are used.

Course

Although symptoms of reading difficulty (e.g., inability to distinguish among common letters or to associate common phonemes with letter symbols) may occur as early as kindergarten, Reading Disorder is seldom diagnosed before the end of kindergarten or the beginning of first grade because formal reading instruction usually does not begin until this point in most school settings. Particularly when Reading Disorder is associated with high IQ, the child may function at or near grade level in the early grades, and the Reading Disorder may not be fully apparent until the fourth grade or later. With early identification and intervention, the prognosis is good in a significant percentage of cases. Reading Disorder may persist into adult life.

Familial Pattern

Reading Disorder aggregates familially and is more prevalent among first-degree biological relatives of individuals with Learning Disorders.

Differential Diagnosis

See the "Differential Diagnosis" section for Learning Disorders (p. 47).

■ **Diagnostic criteria for 315.00 Reading Disorder**

A. Reading achievement, as measured by individually administered standardized tests of reading accuracy or comprehension, is substantially below that expected given the person's chronological age, measured intelligence, and age-appropriate education.

B. The disturbance in Criterion A significantly interferes with academic achievement or activities of daily living that require reading skills.

C. If a sensory deficit is present, the reading difficulties are in excess of those usually associated with it.

Coding note: If a general medical (e.g., neurological) condition or sensory deficit is present, code the condition on Axis III.

315.1   Mathematics Disorder

Diagnostic Features

The essential feature of Mathematics Disorder is mathematical ability (as measured by individually administered standardized tests of mathematical calculation or reasoning) that falls substantially below that expected for the individual's chronological age, measured intelligence, and age-appropriate education (Criterion A). The disturbance in mathematics significantly interferes with academic achievement or with activities of daily living that require mathematical skills (Criterion B). If a sensory deficit is present, the difficulties in mathematical ability are in excess of those usually associated with it (Criterion C). If a neurological or other general medical condition or sensory deficit is present, it should be coded on Axis III. A number of different skills may be impaired in Mathematics Disorder, including "linguistic" skills (e.g., understanding or naming mathematical terms, operations, or concepts, and decoding written problems into mathematical symbols), "perceptual" skills (e.g., recognizing or reading numerical symbols or arithmetic signs, and clustering objects into groups), "attention" skills (e.g., copying numbers or figures correctly, remembering to add in "carried" numbers, and observing operational signs), and "mathematical" skills (e.g., following sequences of mathematical steps, counting objects, and learning multiplication tables).

Associated Features and Disorders

See the "Associated Features and Disorders" section for Learning Disorders (p. 47). Mathematics Disorder is commonly found in combination with Reading Disorder or Disorder of Written Expression.

Prevalence

The prevalence of Mathematics Disorder is difficult to establish because many studies focus on the prevalence of Learning Disorders without careful separation into specific disorders of Reading, Mathematics, or Written Expression. The prevalence of Mathematics Disorder alone (i.e., when not found in association with other Learning Disorders) has been estimated at approximately one in every five cases of Learning Disorder. It is estimated that 1% of school-age children have Mathematics Disorder.

Course

Although symptoms of difficulty in mathematics (e.g., confusion in number concepts or inability to count accurately) may appear as early as kindergarten or first grade, Mathematics Disorder is seldom diagnosed before the end of first grade because sufficient formal mathematics instruction has usually not occurred until this point in most school settings. It usually becomes apparent during second or third grade. Particularly when Mathematics Disorder is associated with high IQ, the child may be able to function at or near grade level in the early grades, and Mathematics Disorder may not be apparent until the fifth grade or later.

Differential Diagnosis

See the "Differential Diagnosis" section for Learning Disorders (p. 47).

■ Diagnostic criteria for 315.1 Mathematics Disorder

A. Mathematical ability, as measured by individually administered standardized tests, is substantially below that expected given the person's chronological age, measured intelligence, and age-appropriate education.

B. The disturbance in Criterion A significantly interferes with academic achievement or activities of daily living that require mathematical ability.

C. If a sensory deficit is present, the difficulties in mathematical ability are in excess of those usually associated with it.

Coding note: If a general medical (e.g., neurological) condition or sensory deficit is present, code the condition on Axis III.

315.2 Disorder of Written Expression

Diagnostic Features

The essential feature of Disorder of Written Expression is writing skills (as measured by an individually administered standardized test or functional assessment of writing skills) that fall substantially below those expected given the individual's chronological age, measured intelligence, and age-appropriate education (Criterion A). The disturbance in written expression significantly interferes with academic achievement or with activities of daily living that require writing skills (Criterion B). If a sensory deficit is present, the difficulties in writing skills are in excess of those usually associated with it (Criterion C). If a neurological or other general medical condition or sensory deficit is present, it should be coded on Axis III. There is generally a combination of difficulties in the individual's ability to compose written texts evidenced by grammatical or punctuation errors within sentences, poor paragraph organization, multiple spelling errors, and excessively poor handwriting. This diagnosis is generally not given if there are only spelling errors or poor handwriting in the absence of other impairment in written expression. Compared with other Learning Disorders, relatively less is known about Disorders of Written Expression and their remediation, particularly when they occur in the absence of Reading Disorder. Except for spelling, standardized tests in this area are less well developed than tests of reading or mathematical ability, and the evaluation of impairment in written skills may require a comparison between extensive samples of the individual's written schoolwork and expected performance for age and IQ. This is especially the case for young children in the early elementary grades. Tasks in which the child is asked to copy, write to dictation, and write spontaneously may all be necessary to establish the presence and extent of this disorder.

Associated Features and Disorders

See the "Associated Features and Disorders" section for Learning Disorders (p. 47). Disorder of Written Expression is commonly found in combination with Reading Disorder or Mathematics Disorder. There is some evidence that language and perceptual-motor deficits may accompany this disorder.

Prevalence

The prevalence of Disorder of Written Expression is difficult to establish because many studies focus on the prevalence of Learning Disorders in general without careful separation into specific disorders of reading, mathematics, or written expression. Disorder of Written Expression is rare when not associated with other Learning Disorders.

Course

Although difficulty in writing (e.g., particularly poor handwriting or copying ability or inability to remember letter sequences in common words) may appear as early as the first grade, Disorder of Written Expression is seldom diagnosed before the end of first grade because sufficient formal writing instruction has usually not occurred until this point in most school settings. The disorder is usually apparent by second grade. Disorder of Written Expression may occasionally be seen in older children or adults, and little is known about its long-term prognosis.

Differential Diagnosis

See the "Differential Diagnosis" section for Learning Disorders (p. 47). A disorder in spelling or handwriting alone, in the absence of other difficulties of written expression, generally does not qualify for a diagnosis of Disorder of Written Expression. If poor handwriting is due to impairment in motor coordination, a diagnosis of **Developmental Coordination Disorder** should be considered.

■ **Diagnostic criteria for 315.2 Disorder of Written Expression**

A. Writing skills, as measured by individually administered standardized tests (or functional assessments of writing skills), are substantially below those expected given the person's chronological age, measured intelligence, and age-appropriate education.

B. The disturbance in Criterion A significantly interferes with academic achievement or activities of daily living that require the composition of written texts (e.g., writing grammatically correct sentences and organized paragraphs).

C. If a sensory deficit is present, the difficulties in writing skills are in excess of those usually associated with it.

Coding note: If a general medical (e.g., neurological) condition or sensory deficit is present, code the condition on Axis III.

315.9 Learning Disorder Not Otherwise Specified

This category is for disorders in learning that do not meet criteria for any specific Learning Disorder. This category might include problems in all three areas (reading, mathematics, written expression) that together significantly interfere with academic achievement even though performance on tests measuring each individual skill is not substantially below that expected given the person's chronological age, measured intelligence, and age-appropriate education.

Motor Skills Disorder

315.4 Developmental Coordination Disorder

Diagnostic Features

The essential feature of Developmental Coordination Disorder is a marked impairment in the development of motor coordination (Criterion A). The diagnosis is made only if this impairment significantly interferes with academic achievement or activities of daily living (Criterion B). The diagnosis is made if the coordination difficulties are not due to a general medical condition (e.g., cerebral palsy, hemiplegia, or muscular dystrophy) and the criteria are not met for Pervasive Developmental Disorder (Criterion C). If Mental Retardation is present, the motor difficulties are in excess of those usually associated with it (Criterion D). The manifestations of this disorder vary with age and development. For example, younger children may display clumsiness and delays in achieving developmental motor milestones (e.g., walking, crawling, sitting, tying shoelaces, buttoning shirts, zipping pants). Older children may display difficulties with the motor aspects of assembling puzzles, building models, playing ball, and printing or handwriting.

Associated Features and Disorders

Problems commonly associated with Developmental Coordination Disorder include delays in other nonmotor milestones. Associated disorders may include Phonological Disorder, Expressive Language Disorder, and Mixed Receptive-Expressive Language Disorder.

Prevalence

Prevalence of Developmental Coordination Disorder has been estimated to be as high as 6% for children in the age range of 5–11 years.

Course

Recognition of Developmental Coordination Disorder usually occurs when the child first attempts such tasks as running, holding a knife and fork, buttoning clothes, or playing ball games. The course is variable. In some cases, lack of coordination continues through adolescence and adulthood.

Differential Diagnosis

Developmental Coordination Disorder must be distinguished from motor impairments that are due to a general medical condition. Problems in coordination may be associated with **specific neurological disorders** (e.g., cerebral palsy, progressive lesions of the cerebellum), but in these cases there is definite neural damage and abnormal findings on neurological examination. If **Mental Retardation** is present, Developmental Coordination Disorder can be diagnosed only if the motor difficulties are in excess of those usually associated with the Mental Retardation. A diagnosis of Developmental Coordination Disorder is not given if the criteria are met for a **Pervasive Developmental Disorder.** Individuals with **Attention-Deficit/Hyperactivity Disorder** may fall, bump into things, or knock things over, but this is usually due to distractibility and impulsiveness, rather than to a motor impairment. If criteria for both disorders are met, both diagnoses can be given.

■ **Diagnostic criteria for 315.4 Developmental Coordination Disorder**

A. Performance in daily activities that require motor coordination is substantially below that expected given the person's chronological age and measured intelligence. This may be manifested by marked delays in achieving motor milestones (e.g., walking, crawling, sitting), dropping things, "clumsiness," poor performance in sports, or poor handwriting.

(continued)

☐ **Diagnostic criteria for 315.4 Developmental Coordination Disorder** (*continued*)

B. The disturbance in Criterion A significantly interferes with academic achievement or activities of daily living.

C. The disturbance is not due to a general medical condition (e.g., cerebral palsy, hemiplegia, or muscular dystrophy) and does not meet criteria for a Pervasive Developmental Disorder.

D. If Mental Retardation is present, the motor difficulties are in excess of those usually associated with it.

Coding note: If a general medical (e.g., neurological) condition or sensory deficit is present, code the condition on Axis III.

Communication Disorders

The following Communication Disorders are included in this section: Expressive Language Disorder, Mixed Receptive-Expressive Language Disorder, Phonological Disorder, Stuttering, and Communication Disorder Not Otherwise Specified. They are included in this classification to familiarize clinicians with the ways in which Communication Disorders present and to facilitate their differential diagnosis.

315.31   Expressive Language Disorder

Diagnostic Features

The essential feature of Expressive Language Disorder is an impairment in expressive language development as demonstrated by scores on standardized individually administered measures of expressive language development substantially below those obtained from standardized measures of both nonverbal intellectual capacity and receptive language development (Criterion A). The difficulties may occur in communication involving both verbal language and sign language. The language difficulties interfere with academic or occupational achievement or with social communication (Criterion B). The symptoms do not meet criteria for Mixed Receptive-Expressive Language Disorder or a Pervasive Developmental Disorder (Criterion C). If Mental Retardation, a speech-motor or sensory deficit, or environmental deprivation is present, the language difficulties are in excess of those usually associated with these problems (Criterion D). If a speech-motor or sensory deficit or neurological condition is present, it should be coded on Axis III.

The linguistic features of the disorder vary depending on its severity and the age of the child. These features include a limited amount of speech, limited range of vocabulary, difficulty acquiring new words, word-finding or vocabulary errors, shortened sentences, simplified grammatical structures, limited varieties of grammatical structures (e.g., verb forms), limited varieties of sentence types (e.g., imperatives, questions), omissions of critical parts of sentences, use of unusual word order, and slow rate of language development. Nonlinguistic functioning (as measured by performance intelligence tests) and language comprehension skills are usually within normal limits. Expressive Language Disorder may be either acquired or developmental. In the acquired type, an impairment in expressive language occurs after a period of normal development as a result of a neurological or other general medical condition (e.g., encephalitis, head trauma, irradiation). In the developmental type, there is an impairment in expressive language that is not associated with a neurological insult of known origin. Children with this type often begin speaking late and progress more slowly than usual through the various stages of expressive language development.

Associated Features and Disorders

The most common associated feature of Expressive Language Disorder in younger children is Phonological Disorder. There may also be a disturbance in fluency and language formulation involving an abnormally rapid rate and erratic rhythm of speech and disturbances in language structure ("cluttering"). When Expressive Language Disorder is acquired, additional speech difficulties are also common and may include motor articulation problems, phonological errors, slow speech, syllable repetitions, and monotonous intonation and stress patterns. Among school-age children, school and learning problems (e.g., writing to dictation, copying sentences, and spelling) that sometimes meet criteria for Learning Disorders are often associated with Expressive Language Disorder. There may also be some mild impairment in receptive language skills, but when this is significant, a diagnosis of Mixed Receptive-Expressive Language Disorder should be made. A history of delay in reaching some motor milestones, Developmental Coordination Disorder, and Enuresis are not uncommon. Social withdrawal and some mental disorders such as Attention-Deficit/Hyperactivity Disorder are also commonly associated. Expressive Language Disorder may be accompanied by EEG abnormalities, abnormal findings on neuroimaging, dysarthric or apraxic behaviors, or other neurological signs.

Specific Culture and Gender Features

Assessments of the development of communication abilities must take into account the individual's cultural and language context, particularly for individuals growing up in bilingual environments. The standardized measures of language development and of nonverbal intellectual capacity must be relevant for the cultural and linguistic group. The developmental type of Expressive Language Disorder is more common in males than in females.

Prevalence

Estimates suggest that 3%–5% of children may be affected by the developmental type of Expressive Language Disorder. The acquired type is less common.

Course

The developmental type of Expressive Language Disorder is usually recognized by age 3 years, although milder forms of the disorder may not become apparent until early adolescence, when language ordinarily becomes more complex. The acquired type of Expressive Language Disorder due to brain lesions, head trauma, or stroke may occur at any age, and the onset is sudden. The outcome of the developmental type of Expressive Language Disorder is variable. Approximately one-half of the children with this disorder appear to outgrow it, whereas one-half appear to have more long-lasting difficulties. Most children ultimately acquire more or less normal language abilities by late adolescence, although subtle deficits may persist. In the acquired type of Expressive Language Disorder, the course and prognosis are related to the severity and location of brain pathology, as well as to the age of the child and the extent of language development at the time the disorder is acquired. Clinical improvement in language abilities is sometimes rapid and complete, whereas in other instances there may be incomplete recovery or progressive deficit.

Familial Pattern

It appears that the developmental type of Expressive Language Disorder is more likely to occur in individuals who have a family history of Communication or Learning Disorders. There is no evidence of familial aggregation in the acquired type.

Differential Diagnosis

Expressive Language Disorder is distinguished from **Mixed Receptive-Expressive Language Disorder** by the presence in the latter of significant impairment in receptive language. Expressive Language Disorder is not diagnosed if the criteria are met for Autistic Disorder or another Pervasive Developmental Disorder. **Autistic Disorder** also involves expressive language impairment but may be distinguished from Expressive and Mixed Receptive-Expressive Language Disorders by the characteristics of the communication impairment (e.g., stereotyped use of language) and by the presence of a qualitative impairment in social interaction and restricted, repetitive, and stereotyped patterns of behavior. Expressive and receptive language development may be impaired due to **Mental Retardation,** a **hearing impairment** or **other sensory deficit,** a **speech-motor deficit,** or **severe environmental deprivation.** The presence of these problems may be established by intelligence testing, audiometric testing, neurological testing, and history. If the language difficulties are in excess of those usually associated with these problems, a concurrent diagnosis of Expressive Language or Mixed Receptive-Expressive Language Disorder may be made. Children with expressive language delays due to environmental deprivation may show rapid gains once the environmental problems are ameliorated. In **Disorder of Written Expression,** there is a disturbance in writing skills. If deficits in oral expression are also present, an additional diagnosis of Expressive Language Disorder may be appropriate. **Selective Mutism** involves limited expressive output that may mimic Expressive or Mixed Receptive-Expressive Language Disorder; careful history and observation are necessary to determine the presence of normal language in some settings. **Acquired aphasia** associated with a general medical condition in childhood is often transient. A diagnosis of Expressive Language Disorder is appropriate only if the language disturbance persists beyond the acute recovery period for the etiological general medical condition (e.g., head trauma, viral infection).

■ **Diagnostic criteria for 315.31 Expressive Language Disorder**

A. The scores obtained from standardized individually administered measures of expressive language development are substantially below those obtained from standardized measures of both nonverbal intellectual capacity and receptive language development. The disturbance may be manifest clinically by symptoms that include having a markedly limited vocabulary, making errors in tense, or having difficulty recalling words or producing sentences with developmentally appropriate length or complexity.

B. The difficulties with expressive language interfere with academic or occupational achievement or with social communication.

C. Criteria are not met for Mixed Receptive-Expressive Language Disorder or a Pervasive Developmental Disorder.

D. If Mental Retardation, a speech-motor or sensory deficit, or environmental deprivation is present, the language difficulties are in excess of those usually associated with these problems.

Coding note: If a speech-motor or sensory deficit or a neurological condition is present, code the condition on Axis III.

315.31   Mixed Receptive-Expressive Language Disorder

Diagnostic Features

The essential feature of Mixed Receptive-Expressive Language Disorder is an impairment in both receptive and expressive language development as demonstrated by scores on standardized individually administered measures of both receptive and expressive language development that are substantially below those obtained from standardized measures of nonverbal intellectual capacity (Criterion A). The difficulties may occur in communication involving both verbal language and sign language. The language difficulties interfere with academic or occupational achievement or with social communication (Criterion B), and the symptoms do not meet criteria for a Pervasive Developmental Disorder (Criterion C). If Mental Retardation, a speech-motor or sensory deficit, or environmental deprivation is present, the language difficulties are in excess of those usually associated with these problems (Criterion D). If a speech-motor or sensory deficit or neurological condition is present, it should be coded on Axis III.

An individual with this disorder has the difficulties associated with Expressive Language Disorder (e.g., a markedly limited vocabulary, errors in tense, difficulty recalling words or producing sentences with developmentally appropriate length or complexity, and general difficulty expressing ideas) and also has impairment in receptive language development (e.g., difficulty understanding words, sentences, or specific types of words). In mild cases, there may be difficulties only in understanding particular types of words (e.g., spatial terms) or statements (e.g., complex "if-then" sentences). In more severe cases, there may be multiple disabilities, including an inability to understand basic vocabulary or simple sentences, and deficits in various areas of auditory processing (e.g., discrimination of sounds, association of sounds and symbols, storage, recall, and sequencing). Because the development of expressive language in childhood relies on the acquisition of receptive skills, a pure receptive language disorder (analogous to a Wernicke's aphasia in adults) is virtually never seen.

Mixed Receptive-Expressive Language Disorder may be either acquired or developmental. In the acquired type, an impairment in receptive and expressive language occurs after a period of normal development as a result of a neurological or other general medical condition (e.g., encephalitis, head trauma, irradiation). In the developmental type, there is an impairment in receptive and expressive language that is not associated with a neurological insult of known origin. This type is characterized by a slow rate of language development in which speech may begin late and advance slowly through the stages of language development.

Associated Features and Disorders

The linguistic features of the production impairment in Mixed Receptive-Expressive Language Disorder are similar to those that accompany Expressive Language Disorder. The comprehension deficit is the primary feature that differentiates this disorder from Expressive Language Disorder and this can vary depending on the severity of the disorder and the age of the child. Impairments in language comprehension can be less obvious than those in language production because they are not as readily apparent to the observer and may appear only on formal assessment. The child may intermittently appear not to hear or to be confused or not paying attention when spoken to. The child may follow commands incorrectly, or not at all, and give tangential or inappropriate responses to questions. The child may be exceptionally quiet or, conversely, very talkative. Conversational skills (e.g., taking turns, maintaining a topic) are often quite poor or inappropriate. Deficits in various areas of sensory information processing are common, especially in temporal auditory processing (e.g., processing rate, association of sounds and symbols, sequence of sounds and memory, attention to and discrimination of sounds). Difficulty in producing motor sequences smoothly and quickly is also characteristic. Phonological Disorder, Learning Disorders, and deficits in speech perception are often present and accompanied by memory impairments. Other associated disorders are Attention-Deficit/Hyperactivity Disorder, Developmental Coordination Disorder, and Enuresis. Mixed Receptive-Expressive Language Disorder may be accompanied by EEG abnormalities, abnormal findings on neuroimaging, and other neurological signs. A form of acquired Mixed Receptive-Expressive Language Disorder that has its onset at about ages 3–9 years and is accompanied by seizures is referred to as Landau-Kleffner syndrome.

Specific Culture and Gender Features

Assessments of the development of communication abilities must take into account the individual's cultural and language context, particularly for individuals growing up in bilingual environments. The standardized measures of language development and of nonverbal intellectual capacity must be relevant for the cultural and linguistic group. The developmental type is more prevalent in males than in females.

Prevalence

It is estimated that the developmental type of Mixed Receptive-Expressive Language Disorder may occur in up to 3% of school-age children but is probably less common than Expressive Language Disorder. Landau-Kleffner syndrome and other forms of the acquired type of the disorder are rarer.

Course

The developmental type of Mixed Receptive-Expressive Language Disorder is usually detectable before age 4 years. Severe forms of the disorder may be apparent by age 2 years. Milder forms may not be recognized until the child reaches elementary school, where deficits in comprehension become more apparent. The acquired type of Mixed Receptive-Expressive Language Disorder due to brain lesions, head trauma, or stroke may occur at any age. The acquired type due to Landau-Kleffner syndrome (acquired epileptic aphasia) usually occurs between ages 3 and 9 years. Many children with Mixed Receptive-Expressive Language Disorder eventually acquire normal language abilities, but the prognosis is worse than for those with Expressive Language Disorder. In the acquired type of Mixed Receptive-Expressive Language Disorder, the course and prognosis are related to the severity and location of brain pathology, as well as to the age of the child and the extent of language development at the time the disorder is acquired. Clinical improvement in language abilities is sometimes complete, whereas in other instances there may be incomplete recovery or progressive deficit. Children with more severe forms are likely to develop Learning Disorders.

Familial Pattern

The developmental type of Mixed Receptive-Expressive Language Disorder is more common among first-degree biological relatives of those with the disorder than in the general population. There is no evidence of familial aggregation in the acquired type of the disorder.

Differential Diagnosis

See the "Differential Diagnosis" section for Expressive Language Disorder (p. 57).

■ **Diagnostic criteria for 315.31 Mixed Receptive-Expressive Language Disorder**

A. The scores obtained from a battery of standardized individually administered measures of both receptive and expressive language development are substantially below those obtained from standardized measures of nonverbal intellectual capacity. Symptoms include those for Expressive Language Disorder as well as difficulty understanding words, sentences, or specific types of words, such as spatial terms.

(continued)

☐ **Diagnostic criteria for 315.31 Mixed Receptive-Expressive Language Disorder** (*continued*)

    B. The difficulties with receptive and expressive language significantly interfere with academic or occupational achievement or with social communication.

    C. Criteria are not met for a Pervasive Developmental Disorder.

    D. If Mental Retardation, a speech-motor or sensory deficit, or environmental deprivation is present, the language difficulties are in excess of those usually associated with these problems.

    Coding note: If a speech-motor or sensory deficit or a neurological condition is present, code the condition on Axis III.

315.39   Phonological Disorder
(*formerly* Developmental Articulation Disorder)

Diagnostic Features

The essential feature of Phonological Disorder is a failure to use developmentally expected speech sounds that are appropriate for the individual's age and dialect (Criterion A). This may involve errors in sound production, use, representation, or organization such as, but not limited to, substitutions of one sound for another (use of /t/ for target /k/ sound) or omissions of sounds (e.g., final consonants). The difficulties in speech sound production interfere with academic or occupational achievement or with social communication (Criterion B). If Mental Retardation, a speech-motor or sensory deficit, or environmental deprivation is present, the speech difficulties are in excess of those usually associated with these problems (Criterion C). If a speech-motor or sensory deficit or neurological condition is present, it should be coded on Axis III.

    Phonological Disorder includes phonological production (i.e., articulation) errors that involve the failure to form speech sounds correctly and cognitively based forms of phonological problems that involve a deficit in linguistic categorization of speech sounds (e.g., a difficulty in sorting out which sounds in the language make a difference in meaning). Severity ranges from little or no effect on speech intelligibility to completely unintelligible speech. Sound omissions are typically viewed as more severe than are sound substitutions, which in turn are more severe than sound distortions. The most frequently misarticulated sounds are those acquired later in the developmental sequence (*l, r, s, z, th, ch*), but in younger or more severely affected individuals, consonants and vowels that develop earlier may also be affected. Lisping (i.e., misarticulation of sibilants) is particularly common. Phonological Disorder may also involve errors of selection and ordering of sounds within syllables and words (e.g., *aks* for *ask*).

Associated Features and Disorders

Although there may be an association with clear causal factors such as hearing impairment, structural deficits of the oral peripheral speech mechanism (e.g., cleft palate), neurological conditions (e.g., cerebral palsy), cognitive limitations (e.g., Mental Retardation), or psychosocial problems, at least 2.5% of preschool children present with Phonological Disorders of unknown or suspect origin, which are often referred to as *functional* or *developmental.* There may be a delayed onset of speech.

Specific Culture and Gender Features

Assessments of the development of communication abilities must take into account the individual's cultural and language context, particularly for individuals growing up in bilingual environments. Phonological Disorder is more prevalent in males.

Prevalence

Approximately 2%–3% of 6- and 7-year-olds present with moderate to severe Phonological Disorder, although the prevalence of milder forms of this disorder is higher. The prevalence falls to 0.5% by age 17 years.

Course

In severe Phonological Disorder, the child's speech may be relatively unintelligible even to family members. Less severe forms of the disorder may not be recognized until the child enters a preschool or school environment and has difficulty being understood by those outside the immediate family. The course of the disorder is variable depending on associated causes and severity. In mild presentations with unknown causes, spontaneous recovery often occurs.

Familial Pattern

A familial pattern has been demonstrated for some forms of Phonological Disorder.

Differential Diagnosis

Speech difficulties may be associated with **Mental Retardation,** a **hearing impairment** or **other sensory deficit,** a **speech-motor deficit,** or **severe environmental deprivation.** The presence of these problems may be established by intelligence testing, audiometric testing, neurological testing, and history. If the speech difficulties are in excess of those usually associated with these problems, a concurrent diagnosis of Phonological Disorder may be made. Problems limited to **speech rhythm** or **voice** are not included as part of Phonological Disorder and instead are diagnosed as **Stuttering** or **Communication Disorder Not Otherwise Specified.** Children with speech difficulties due to environmental deprivation may show rapid gains once the environmental problems are ameliorated.

■ Diagnostic criteria for 315.39 Phonological Disorder

A. Failure to use developmentally expected speech sounds that are appropriate for age and dialect (e.g., errors in sound production, use, representation, or organization such as, but not limited to, substitutions of one sound for another [use of /t/ for target /k/ sound] or omissions of sounds such as final consonants).

B. The difficulties in speech sound production interfere with academic or occupational achievement or with social communication.

C. If Mental Retardation, a speech-motor or sensory deficit, or environmental deprivation is present, the speech difficulties are in excess of those usually associated with these problems.

Coding note: If a speech-motor or sensory deficit or a neurological condition is present, code the condition on Axis III.

307.0   Stuttering

Diagnostic Features

The essential feature of Stuttering is a disturbance in the normal fluency and time patterning of speech that is inappropriate for the individual's age (Criterion A). This disturbance is characterized by frequent repetitions or prolongations of sounds or syllables (Criteria A1 and A2). Various other types of speech dysfluencies may also be involved, including interjections (Criterion A3), broken words (e.g., pauses within a word) (Criterion A4), audible or silent blocking (filled or unfilled pauses in speech) (Criterion A5), circumlocutions (i.e., word substitutions to avoid problematic words) (Criterion A6), words produced with an excess of physical tension (Criterion A7), and monosyllabic whole word repetitions (e.g., "I-I-I-I see him") (Criterion A8). The disturbance in fluency interferes with academic or occupational achievement or with social communication (Criterion B). If a speech-motor or sensory deficit is present, the speech difficulties are in excess of those usually associated with these problems (Criterion C). If a speech-motor or sensory deficit or neurological disorder is present, this condition should also be coded on Axis III. The extent of the disturbance varies from situation to situation and often is more severe when there is special pressure to communicate (e.g., giving a report at school, interviewing for a job). Stuttering is often absent during oral reading, singing, or talking to inanimate objects or to pets.

Associated Features and Disorders

At the onset of Stuttering, the speaker may not be aware of the problem, although awareness and even fearful anticipation of the problem may develop later. The speaker may attempt to avoid stuttering by linguistic mechanisms (e.g., altering the rate of speech, avoiding certain speech situations such as telephoning or public speaking, or avoiding certain words or sounds). Stuttering may be accompanied by motor movements (e.g., eye blinks, tics, tremors of the lips or face, jerking of the head, breathing movements, or fist clenching). Stress or anxiety have been shown to exacerbate Stuttering. Impairment of social functioning may result from associated anxiety, frustration, or low self-esteem. In adults, Stuttering may limit occupational choice or advancement. Phonological Disorder and Expressive Language Disorder occur at a higher frequency in individuals with Stuttering than in the general population.

Prevalence

The prevalence of Stuttering in prepubertal children is 1% and drops to 0.8% in adolescence. The male-to-female ratio is approximately 3:1.

Course

Retrospective studies of individuals with Stuttering report onset typically between ages 2 and 7 years (with peak onset at around age 5 years). Onset occurs before age 10 years in 98% of cases. The onset is usually insidious, covering many months during which episodic, unnoticed speech dysfluencies become a chronic problem. Typically, the disturbance starts gradually, with repetition of initial consonants, words that are usually the first words of a phrase, or long words. The child is generally not aware of Stuttering. As the disorder progresses, there is a waxing and waning course. The dysfluencies become more frequent, and the Stuttering occurs on the most meaningful words or phrases in the utterance. As the child becomes aware of the speech difficulty, mechanisms for avoiding the dysfluencies and emotional responses may occur. Some research suggests that up to 80% of individuals with Stuttering recover, with up to 60% recovering spontaneously. Recovery typically occurs before age 16 years.

Familial Pattern

Family and twin studies provide strong evidence of a genetic factor in the etiology of Stuttering. The presence of a Phonological Disorder or the developmental type of Expressive Language Disorder, or a family history of these, increases the likelihood of Stuttering. The risk of Stuttering among first-degree biological relatives is more than three times the risk in the general population. For men with a history of Stuttering, about 10% of their daughters and 20% of their sons will stutter.

Differential Diagnosis

Speech difficulties may be associated with a **hearing impairment** or **other sensory deficit** or a **speech-motor deficit.** In instances where the speech difficulties are in excess of those usually associated with these problems, a concurrent diagnosis of Stuttering may be made. Stuttering must be distinguished from **normal dysfluencies that occur frequently in young children,** which include whole-word or phrase repetitions (e.g., "I want, I want ice cream"), incomplete phrases, interjections, unfilled pauses, and parenthetical remarks.

> ## ■ Diagnostic criteria for 307.0 Stuttering
>
> A. Disturbance in the normal fluency and time patterning of speech (inappropriate for the individual's age), characterized by frequent occurrences of one or more of the following:
>
>   (1) sound and syllable repetitions
>   (2) sound prolongations
>   (3) interjections
>   (4) broken words (e.g., pauses within a word)
>   (5) audible or silent blocking (filled or unfilled pauses in speech)
>   (6) circumlocutions (word substitutions to avoid problematic words)
>   (7) words produced with an excess of physical tension
>   (8) monosyllabic whole-word repetitions (e.g., "I-I-I-I see him")
>
> B. The disturbance in fluency interferes with academic or occupational achievement or with social communication.
>
> C. If a speech-motor or sensory deficit is present, the speech difficulties are in excess of those usually associated with these problems.
>
> **Coding note:** If a speech-motor or sensory deficit or a neurological condition is present, code the condition on Axis III.

307.9 Communication Disorder Not Otherwise Specified

This category is for disorders in communication that do not meet criteria for any specific Communication Disorder; for example, a voice disorder (i.e., an abnormality of vocal pitch, loudness, quality, tone, or resonance).

Pervasive Developmental Disorders

Pervasive Developmental Disorders are characterized by severe and pervasive impairment in several areas of development: reciprocal social interaction skills, communication skills, or the presence of stereotyped behavior, interests, and activities. The qualitative impairments that define these conditions are distinctly deviant relative to the individual's developmental level or mental age. This section contains Autistic Disorder, Rett's Disorder, Childhood Disintegrative Disorder, Asperger's Disorder, and Pervasive Developmental Disorder Not Otherwise Specified. These disorders are usually evident in the first years of life and are often associated with some degree of Mental Retardation, which, if present, should be coded on Axis II. The Pervasive Developmental Disorders are sometimes observed with a diverse group of other general medical conditions (e.g., chromosomal abnormalities, congenital infections, structural abnormalities of the central nervous system). If such conditions are present, they should be noted on Axis III. Although terms like "psychosis" and "childhood schizophrenia" were once used to refer to individuals with these conditions, there is considerable evidence to suggest that the Pervasive Developmental Disorders are distinct from Schizophrenia (however, an individual with Pervasive Developmental Disorder may occasionally later develop Schizophrenia).

299.00   Autistic Disorder

Diagnostic Features

The essential features of Autistic Disorder are the presence of markedly abnormal or impaired development in social interaction and communication and a markedly restricted repertoire of activity and interests. Manifestations of the disorder vary greatly depending on the developmental level and chronological age of the individual. Autistic Disorder is sometimes referred to as *early infantile autism, childhood autism,* or *Kanner's autism.*

The impairment in reciprocal social interaction is gross and sustained. There may be marked impairment in the use of multiple nonverbal behaviors (e.g., eye-to-eye gaze, facial expression, body postures and gestures) to regulate social interaction and communication (Criterion A1a). There may be failure to develop peer relationships appropriate to developmental level (Criterion A1b) that may take different forms at different ages. Younger individuals may have little or no interest in establishing friendships. Older individuals may have an interest in friendship but lack understanding of the conventions of social interaction. There may be a lack of spontaneous seeking to share enjoyment, interests, or achievements with other people (e.g., not showing, bringing, or pointing out objects they find interesting) (Criterion A1c). Lack of social or emotional reciprocity may be present (e.g., not actively participating in simple social play or games, preferring solitary activities, or involving others in activities only as tools or "mechanical" aids) (Criterion A1d). Often an individual's awareness of others is markedly impaired. Individuals with this disorder may be oblivious to other children (including siblings), may have no concept of the needs of others, or may not notice another person's distress.

The impairment in communication is also marked and sustained and affects both verbal and nonverbal skills. There may be delay in, or total lack of, the development of spoken language (Criterion A2a). In individuals who do speak, there may be marked impairment in the ability to initiate or sustain a conversation with others (Criterion A2b), or a stereotyped and repetitive use of language or idiosyncratic language (Criterion A2c). There may also be a lack of varied, spontaneous make-believe play or social imitative play appropriate to developmental level (Criterion A2d). When speech does develop, the pitch, intonation, rate, rhythm, or stress may be abnormal (e.g., tone of voice may be monotonous or contain questionlike rises at ends of statements). Grammatical structures are often immature and include stereotyped and repetitive use of language (e.g., repetition of words or phrases regardless of meaning; repeating jingles or commercials) or metaphorical language (i.e., language that can only be understood clearly by those familiar with the individual's communication style). A disturbance in the comprehension of language may be evidenced by an inability to understand simple questions, directions, or jokes. Imaginative play is often absent or markedly impaired.

These individuals also tend not to engage in the simple imitation games or routines of infancy or early childhood or do so only out of context or in a mechanical way.

Individuals with Autistic Disorder have restricted, repetitive, and stereotyped patterns of behavior, interests, and activities. There may be an encompassing preoccupation with one or more stereotyped and restricted patterns of interest that is abnormal either in intensity or focus (Criterion A3a); an apparently inflexible adherence to specific, nonfunctional routines or rituals (Criterion A3b); stereotyped and repetitive motor mannerisms (Criterion A3c); or a persistent preoccupation with parts of objects (Criterion A3d). Individuals with Autistic Disorder display a markedly restricted range of interests and are often preoccupied with one narrow interest (e.g., with amassing facts about meteorology or baseball statistics). They may line up an exact number of play things in the same manner over and over again or repetitively mimic the actions of a television actor. They may insist on sameness and show resistance to or distress over trivial changes (e.g., a younger child may have a catastrophic reaction to a minor change in the environment such as a new set of curtains or a change in place at the dinner table). There is often an interest in nonfunctional routines or rituals or an unreasonable insistence on following routines (e.g., taking exactly the same route to school every day). Stereotyped body movements include the hands (clapping, finger flicking) or whole body (rocking, dipping, and swaying). Abnormalities of posture (e.g., walking on tiptoe, odd hand movements and body postures) may be present. These individuals show a persistent preoccupation with parts of objects (buttons, parts of the body). There may also be a fascination with movement (e.g., the spinning wheels of toys, the opening and closing of doors, an electric fan or other rapidly revolving object). The person may be highly attached to some inanimate object (e.g., a piece of string or a rubber band).

The disturbance must be manifest by delays or abnormal functioning in at least one of the following areas prior to age 3 years: social interaction, language as used in social communication, or symbolic or imaginative play (Criterion B). There is typically no period of unequivocally normal development, although 1 or 2 years of relatively normal development has been reported in some instances. In a minority of cases, parents report regression in language development, generally manifest as the cessation of speech after a child has acquired from 5 to 10 words. By definition, if there is a period of normal development, it cannot extend past age 3 years. The disturbance must not be better accounted for by Rett's Disorder or Childhood Disintegrative Disorder (Criterion C).

Associated Features and Disorders

Associated descriptive features and mental disorders.   In most cases, there is an associated diagnosis of Mental Retardation, commonly in the moderate range (IQ 35–50). Approximately 75% of children with Autistic Disorder function at a retarded level. There may be abnormalities in the development of cognitive skills. The profile of cognitive skills is usually uneven, regardless of the general level of intelligence (e.g., a 4½-year-old girl with Autistic Disorder may be able to read, i.e., hyperlexia). In many higher-functioning children with Autistic Disorder, the level of receptive language (i.e., language comprehension) is below that of expressive language (e.g., vocabulary). Individuals with Autistic Disorder may have a range of behavioral symptoms, including hyperactivity, short attention span, impulsivity, aggressiveness, self-injurious behaviors, and, particularly in young children, temper tantrums. There may be odd responses to sensory stimuli (e.g., a high threshold for pain, oversensitivity to sounds or being touched, exaggerated reactions to light or odors, fascination with certain stimuli). There may be abnormalities in eating (e.g., limiting diet to a few foods, Pica) or sleeping (e.g., recurrent awakening at night with rocking). Abnormalities of mood or affect (e.g., giggling or weeping for no apparent reason, an apparent absence of emotional reaction) may be present. There may be a lack of fear in response to real dangers, and excessive fearfulness in response to harmless objects. A variety of self-injurious behaviors may be present (e.g., head banging or finger, hand, or wrist biting). In adolescence or early adult life, individuals with Autistic Disorder who have the intellectual capacity for insight may become depressed in response to the realization of their serious impairment.

Associated laboratory findings.   When Autistic Disorder is associated with a general medical condition, laboratory findings consistent with the general medical condition will be observed. There have been reports of group differences in measures of serotonergic activity, but these are not diagnostic for Autistic Disorder. Imaging studies may be abnormal in some cases, but no specific pattern has been clearly identified. EEG abnormalities are common even in the absence of seizure disorders.

Associated physical examination findings and general medical conditions. Various nonspecific neurological symptoms or signs may be noted (e.g., primitive reflexes, delayed development of hand dominance) in Autistic Disorder. The condition is sometimes observed in association with a neurological or other general medical condition (e.g., encephalitis, phenylketonuria, tuberous sclerosis, fragile X syndrome, anoxia during birth, maternal rubella). Seizures may develop (particularly in adolescence) in as many as 25% of cases. When other general medical conditions are present, they should be noted on Axis III.

Specific Age and Gender Features

The nature of the impairment in social interaction may change over time in Autistic Disorder and may vary depending on the developmental level of the individual. In infants, there may be a failure to cuddle; an indifference or aversion to affection or physical contact; a lack of eye contact, facial responsiveness, or socially directed smiles; and a failure to respond to their parents' voices. As a result, parents may be concerned initially that the child is deaf. Young children with this disorder may treat adults as interchangeable or may cling mechanically to a specific person. Over the course of development, the child may become more willing to be passively engaged in social interaction and may even become more interested in social interaction. However, even in such instances, the child tends to treat other people in unusual ways (e.g., expecting other people to answer ritualized questions in specific ways, having little sense of other people's boundaries, and being inappropriately intrusive in social interaction). In older individuals, tasks involving long-term memory (e.g., train timetables, historical dates, chemical formulas, or recall of the exact words of songs heard years before) may be excellent, but the information tends to be repeated over and over again, regardless of the appropriateness of the information to the social context. Rates of the disorder are four to five times higher in males than in females. Females with the disorder are more likely, however, to exhibit more severe Mental Retardation.

Prevalence

Epidemiological studies suggest rates of Autistic Disorder of 2–5 cases per 10,000 individuals.

Course

By definition, the onset of Autistic Disorder is prior to age 3 years. In some instances, parents will report that they have been worried about the child since birth or shortly afterward because of the child's lack of interest in social interaction. Manifestations of the disorder in infancy are more subtle and difficult to define than those seen after age 2 years. In a minority of cases, the child may be reported to have developed normally for the first year (or even 2 years) of life. Autistic Disorder follows a continuous course. In school-age children and adolescents, developmental gains in some areas are common (e.g., increased interest in social functioning as the child reaches school age). Some individuals deteriorate behaviorally during adolescence, whereas others improve. Language skills (e.g., presence of communicative speech) and overall intellectual level are the strongest factors related to ultimate prognosis. Available follow-up studies suggest that only a small percentage of individuals with the disorder go on as adults to live and work independently. In about one-third of cases, some degree of partial independence is possible. The highest functioning adults with Autistic Disorder typically continue to exhibit problems in social interaction and communication along with markedly restricted interests and activities.

Familial Pattern

There is an increased risk of Autistic Disorder among siblings of individuals with the disorder.

Differential Diagnosis

Periods of developmental regression may be observed in normal development, but these are neither as severe or as prolonged as in Autistic Disorder. Autistic Disorder must be differentiated from **other Pervasive Developmental Disorders. Rett's Disorder** differs from Autistic Disorder in its characteristic sex ratio and pattern of deficits. Rett's Disorder has been diagnosed only in females, whereas Autistic Disorder occurs much more frequently in males. In Rett's Disorder, there is a characteristic pattern of head growth deceleration, loss of previously acquired purposeful hand skills, and the appearance of poorly coordinated gait or trunk movements. Particularly during the preschool years, individuals with Rett's Disorder may exhibit difficulties in social interaction similar to those observed in Autistic Disorder, but these tend to be transient. Autistic Disorder differs from **Childhood Disintegrative Disorder,** which has a distinctive pattern of developmental regression following at least 2 years of normal development. In Autistic Disorder, developmental abnormalities are usually noted within the first year of life. When information on early development is unavailable or when it is not possible to document the required period of normal development, the diagnosis of Autistic Disorder should be made. **Asperger's Disorder** can be distinguished from Autistic Disorder by the lack of delay in language development. Asperger's Disorder is not diagnosed if criteria are met for Autistic Disorder.

Schizophrenia with childhood onset usually develops after years of normal, or near normal, development. An additional diagnosis of Schizophrenia can be made if an individual with Autistic Disorder develops the characteristic features of Schizophrenia (see p. 274) with active-phase symptoms of prominent delusions or hallucinations that last for at least 1 month. In **Selective Mutism,** the child usually exhibits appropriate communication skills in certain contexts and does not have the severe impairment in social interaction and the restricted patterns of behavior associated with Autistic Disorder. In **Expressive Language Disorder** and **Mixed Receptive-Expressive Language Disorder,** there is a language impairment, but it is not associated with the presence of a qualitative impairment in social interaction and restricted, repetitive, and stereotyped patterns of behavior. It is sometimes difficult to determine whether an additional diagnosis of Autistic Disorder is warranted in an individual with **Mental Retardation,** especially if the Mental Retardation is Severe or Profound. An additional diagnosis of Autistic Disorder is reserved for those situations in which there are qualitative deficits in social and communicative skills and the specific behaviors characteristic of Autistic Disorder are present. Motor stereotypies are characteristic of Autistic Disorder; an additional diagnosis of **Stereotypic Movement Disorder** is not given when these are better accounted for as part of the presentation of Autistic Disorder.

■ Diagnostic criteria for 299.00 Autistic Disorder

A. A total of six (or more) items from (1), (2), and (3), with at least two from (1), and one each from (2) and (3):

   (1) qualitative impairment in social interaction, as manifested by at least two of the following:

       (a) marked impairment in the use of multiple nonverbal behaviors such as eye-to-eye gaze, facial expression, body postures, and gestures to regulate social interaction

       (b) failure to develop peer relationships appropriate to developmental level

       (c) a lack of spontaneous seeking to share enjoyment, interests, or achievements with other people (e.g., by a lack of showing, bringing, or pointing out objects of interest)

       (d) lack of social or emotional reciprocity

   (2) qualitative impairments in communication as manifested by at least one of the following:

       (a) delay in, or total lack of, the development of spoken language (not accompanied by an attempt to compensate through alternative modes of communication such as gesture or mime)

       (b) in individuals with adequate speech, marked impairment in the ability to initiate or sustain a conversation with others

       (c) stereotyped and repetitive use of language or idiosyncratic language

       (d) lack of varied, spontaneous make-believe play or social imitative play appropriate to developmental level

(continued)

☐ **Diagnostic criteria for 299.00 Autistic Disorder** (*continued*)

(3) restricted repetitive and stereotyped patterns of behavior, interests, and activities, as manifested by at least one of the following:

(a) encompassing preoccupation with one or more stereotyped and restricted patterns of interest that is abnormal either in intensity or focus

(b) apparently inflexible adherence to specific, nonfunctional routines or rituals

(c) stereotyped and repetitive motor mannerisms (e.g., hand or finger flapping or twisting, or complex whole-body movements)

(d) persistent preoccupation with parts of objects

B. Delays or abnormal functioning in at least one of the following areas, with onset prior to age 3 years: (1) social interaction, (2) language as used in social communication, or (3) symbolic or imaginative play.

C. The disturbance is not better accounted for by Rett's Disorder or Childhood Disintegrative Disorder.

299.80   Rett's Disorder

Diagnostic Features

The essential feature of Rett's Disorder is the development of multiple specific deficits following a period of normal functioning after birth. Individuals have an apparently normal prenatal and perinatal period (Criterion A1) with normal psychomotor development through the first 5 months of life (Criterion A2). Head circumference at birth is also within normal limits (Criterion A3). Between ages 5 and 48 months, head growth decelerates (Criterion B1). There is a loss of previously acquired purposeful hand skills between ages 5 and 30 months, with the subsequent development of characteristic stereotyped hand movements resembling hand-wringing or hand washing (Criterion B2). Interest in the social environment diminishes in the first few years after the onset of the disorder (Criterion B3), although social interaction may often develop later in the course. Problems develop in the coordination of gait or trunk movements (Criterion B4). There is also severe impairment in expressive and receptive language development, with severe psychomotor retardation (Criterion B5).

Associated Features and Disorders

Rett's Disorder is typically associated with Severe or Profound Mental Retardation, which, if present, should be coded on Axis II. There are no specific laboratory findings associated with the disorder. There may be an increased frequency of EEG abnormalities and seizure disorder in individuals with Rett's Disorder. Nonspecific abnormalities on brain imaging have been reported.

Prevalence

Data are limited to mostly case series, and it appears that Rett's Disorder is much less common than Autistic Disorder. This disorder has been reported only in females.

Course

The pattern of developmental regression is highly distinctive. Rett's Disorder has its onset prior to age 4 years, usually in the first or second year of life. The duration of the disorder is lifelong, and the loss of skills is generally persistent and progressive. In most instances, recovery is quite limited, although some very modest developmental gains may be made and interest in social interaction may be observed as individuals enter later childhood or adolescence. The communicative and behavioral difficulties usually remain relatively constant throughout life.

Differential Diagnosis

Periods of developmental regression may be observed in normal development, but these are neither as severe or as prolonged as in Rett's Disorder. For the differential between Rett's Disorder and **Autistic Disorder,** see p. 69. Rett's Disorder differs from **Childhood Disintegrative Disorder** and **Asperger's Disorder** in its characteristic sex ratio, onset, and pattern of deficits. Rett's Disorder has been diagnosed only in females, whereas Childhood Disintegrative Disorder and Asperger's Disorder appear to be more common in males. The onset of symptoms in Rett's Disorder can begin as early as age 5 months, whereas in Childhood Disintegrative Disorder the period of normal development is typically more prolonged (i.e., at least until age 2 years). In Rett's Disorder, there is a characteristic pattern of head growth deceleration, loss of previously acquired purposeful hand skills, and the appearance of poorly coordinated gait or trunk movements. In contrast to Asperger's Disorder, Rett's Disorder is characterized by a severe impairment in expressive and receptive language development.

■ **Diagnostic criteria for 299.80 Rett's Disorder**

A. All of the following:

    (1) apparently normal prenatal and perinatal development

    (2) apparently normal psychomotor development through the first 5 months after birth

    (3) normal head circumference at birth

B. Onset of all of the following after the period of normal development:

    (1) deceleration of head growth between ages 5 and 48 months

(continued)

☐ **Diagnostic criteria for 299.80 Rett's Disorder** (*continued*)

(2)   loss of previously acquired purposeful hand skills between ages 5 and 30 months with the subsequent development of stereotyped hand movements (e.g., hand-wringing or hand washing)
(3)   loss of social engagement early in the course (although often social interaction develops later)
(4)   appearance of poorly coordinated gait or trunk movements
(5)   severely impaired expressive and receptive language development with severe psychomotor retardation

---

299.10   Childhood Disintegrative Disorder

Diagnostic Features

The essential feature of Childhood Disintegrative Disorder is a marked regression in multiple areas of functioning following a period of at least 2 years of apparently normal development (Criterion A). Apparently normal development is reflected in age-appropriate verbal and nonverbal communication, social relationships, play, and adaptive behavior. After the first 2 years of life (but before age 10 years), the child has a clinically significant loss of previously acquired skills in at least two of the following areas: expressive or receptive language, social skills or adaptive behavior, bowel or bladder control, play, or motor skills (Criterion B). Individuals with this disorder exhibit the social and communicative deficits and behavioral features generally observed in Autistic Disorder (see p. 66). There is qualitative impairment in social interaction (Criterion C1) and in communication (Criterion C2), and restricted, repetitive, and stereotyped patterns of behavior, interests, and activities (Criterion C3). The disturbance is not better accounted for by another specific Pervasive Developmental Disorder or by Schizophrenia (Criterion D). This condition has also been termed *Heller's syndrome, dementia infantilis,* or *disintegrative psychosis.*

Associated Features and Disorders

Childhood Disintegrative Disorder is usually associated with Severe Mental Retardation, which, if present, should be coded on Axis II. Various nonspecific neurological symptoms or signs may be noted. There seems to be an increased frequency of EEG abnormalities and seizure disorder. Although it appears likely that the condition is the result of some insult to the developing central nervous system, no precise mechanism has been identified. The condition is occasionally observed in association with a general medical condition (e.g., metachromatic leukodystrophy, Schilder's disease) that might account for the developmental regression. In most instances, however, extensive investigation does not reveal such a condition. If a neurological or other general medical condition is associated with the disorder, it should be recorded on Axis III. The laboratory findings will reflect any associated general medical conditions.

Prevalence

Epidemiological data are limited, but Childhood Disintegrative Disorder appears to be very rare and much less common than Autistic Disorder. Although initial studies suggested an equal sex ratio, the most recent data suggest that the condition is more common among males.

Course

By definition, Childhood Disintegrative Disorder can only be diagnosed if the symptoms are preceded by at least 2 years of normal development and the onset is prior to age 10 years. When the period of normal development has been quite prolonged (5 or more years), it is particularly important to conduct a thorough physical and neurological examination to assess for the presence of a general medical condition. In most cases, the onset is between ages 3 and 4 years and may be insidious or abrupt. Premonitory signs can include increased activity levels, irritability, and anxiety followed by a loss of speech and other skills. Usually the loss of skills reaches a plateau, after which some limited improvement may occur, although improvement is rarely marked. In other instances, especially when the disorder is associated with a progressive neurological condition, the loss of skills is progressive. This disorder follows a continuous course, and in the majority of cases, the duration is lifelong. The social, communicative, and behavioral difficulties remain relatively constant throughout life.

Differential Diagnosis

Periods of regression may be observed in normal development, but these are neither as severe or as prolonged as in Childhood Disintegrative Disorder. Childhood Disintegrative Disorder must be differentiated from **other Pervasive Developmental Disorders.** For the differential diagnosis with **Autistic Disorder,** see p. 69. For the differential diagnosis with **Rett's Disorder,** see p. 72. In contrast to **Asperger's Disorder,** Childhood Disintegrative Disorder is characterized by a clinically significant loss in previously acquired skills and a greater likelihood of Mental Retardation. In Asperger's Disorder, there is no delay in language development and no marked loss of developmental skills.

Childhood Disintegrative Disorder must be differentiated from a **dementia** with onset during infancy or childhood. Dementia occurs as a consequence of the direct physiological effects of a general medical condition (e.g., head trauma), whereas Childhood Disintegrative Disorder typically occurs in the absence of an associated general medical condition.

■ Diagnostic criteria for 299.10 Childhood Disintegrative Disorder

A. Apparently normal development for at least the first 2 years after birth as manifested by the presence of age-appropriate verbal and nonverbal communication, social relationships, play, and adaptive behavior.

(continued)

☐ **Diagnostic criteria for 299.10 Childhood Disintegrative Disorder** (*continued*)

B. Clinically significant loss of previously acquired skills (before age 10 years) in at least two of the following areas:
(1) expressive or receptive language
(2) social skills or adaptive behavior
(3) bowel or bladder control
(4) play
(5) motor skills

C. Abnormalities of functioning in at least two of the following areas:
(1) qualitative impairment in social interaction (e.g., impairment in nonverbal behaviors, failure to develop peer relationships, lack of social or emotional reciprocity)
(2) qualitative impairments in communication (e.g., delay or lack of spoken language, inability to initiate or sustain a conversation, stereotyped and repetitive use of language, lack of varied make-believe play)
(3) restricted, repetitive, and stereotyped patterns of behavior, interests, and activities, including motor stereotypies and mannerisms

D. The disturbance is not better accounted for by another specific Pervasive Developmental Disorder or by Schizophrenia.

299.80 Asperger's Disorder

Diagnostic Features

The essential features of Asperger's Disorder are severe and sustained impairment in social interaction (Criterion A) and the development of restricted, repetitive patterns of behavior, interests, and activities (Criterion B) (see p. 66 in Autistic Disorder for a discussion of Criteria A and B). The disturbance must cause clinically significant impairment in social, occupational, or other important areas of functioning (Criterion C). In contrast to Autistic Disorder, there are no clinically significant delays in language (e.g., single words are used by age 2 years, communicative phrases are used by age 3 years) (Criterion D). In addition, there are no clinically significant delays in cognitive development or in the development of age-appropriate self-help skills, adaptive behavior (other than in social interaction), and curiosity about the environment in childhood (Criterion E). The diagnosis is not given if the criteria are met for any other specific Pervasive Developmental Disorder or for Schizophrenia (Criterion F).

Associated Features and Disorders

Asperger's Disorder is sometimes observed in association with general medical conditions that should be coded on Axis III. Various nonspecific neurological symptoms or signs may be noted. Motor milestones may be delayed, and motor clumsiness is often observed.

Prevalence

Information on the prevalence of Asperger's Disorder is limited, but it appears to be more common in males.

Course

Asperger's Disorder appears to have a somewhat later onset than Autistic Disorder, or at least to be recognized somewhat later. Motor delays or motor clumsiness may be noted in the preschool period. Difficulties in social interaction may become more apparent in the context of school. It is during this time that particular idiosyncratic or circumscribed interests (e.g., a fascination with train schedules) may appear or be recognized as such. As adults, individuals with the condition may have problems with empathy and modulation of social interaction. This disorder apparently follows a continuous course and, in the vast majority of cases, the duration is lifelong.

Familial Pattern

Although the available data are limited, there appears to be an increased frequency of Asperger's Disorder among family members of individuals who have the disorder.

Differential Diagnosis

Asperger's Disorder is not diagnosed if criteria are met for another **Pervasive Developmental Disorder** or for **Schizophrenia.** For the differential diagnosis with **Autistic Disorder,** see p. 69. For the differential diagnosis with **Rett's Disorder,** see p. 72. For the differential diagnosis with **Childhood Disintegrative Disorder,** see p. 74. Asperger's Disorder must also be distinguished from **Obsessive-Compulsive Disorder** and **Schizoid Personality Disorder.** Asperger's Disorder and Obsessive-Compulsive Disorder share repetitive and stereotyped patterns of behavior. In contrast to Obsessive-Compulsive Disorder, Asperger's Disorder is characterized by a qualitative impairment in social interaction and a more restricted pattern of interests and activities. In contrast to Schizoid Personality Disorder, Asperger's Disorder is characterized by stereotyped behaviors and interests and by more severely impaired social interaction.

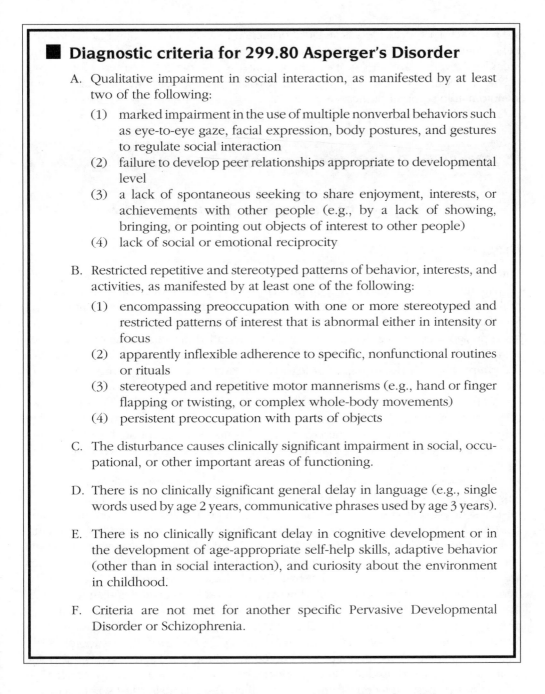

■ **Diagnostic criteria for 299.80 Asperger's Disorder**

A. Qualitative impairment in social interaction, as manifested by at least two of the following:

    (1) marked impairment in the use of multiple nonverbal behaviors such as eye-to-eye gaze, facial expression, body postures, and gestures to regulate social interaction

    (2) failure to develop peer relationships appropriate to developmental level

    (3) a lack of spontaneous seeking to share enjoyment, interests, or achievements with other people (e.g., by a lack of showing, bringing, or pointing out objects of interest to other people)

    (4) lack of social or emotional reciprocity

B. Restricted repetitive and stereotyped patterns of behavior, interests, and activities, as manifested by at least one of the following:

    (1) encompassing preoccupation with one or more stereotyped and restricted patterns of interest that is abnormal either in intensity or focus

    (2) apparently inflexible adherence to specific, nonfunctional routines or rituals

    (3) stereotyped and repetitive motor mannerisms (e.g., hand or finger flapping or twisting, or complex whole-body movements)

    (4) persistent preoccupation with parts of objects

C. The disturbance causes clinically significant impairment in social, occupational, or other important areas of functioning.

D. There is no clinically significant general delay in language (e.g., single words used by age 2 years, communicative phrases used by age 3 years).

E. There is no clinically significant delay in cognitive development or in the development of age-appropriate self-help skills, adaptive behavior (other than in social interaction), and curiosity about the environment in childhood.

F. Criteria are not met for another specific Pervasive Developmental Disorder or Schizophrenia.

299.80   Pervasive Developmental Disorder
Not Otherwise Specified (Including Atypical Autism)

This category should be used when there is a severe and pervasive impairment in the development of reciprocal social interaction or verbal and nonverbal communication skills, or when stereotyped behavior, interests, and activities are present, but the criteria are not met for a specific Pervasive Developmental Disorder, Schizophrenia, Schizotypal Personality Disorder, or Avoidant Personality Disorder. For example, this category includes "atypical autism"—presentations that do not meet the criteria for Autistic Disorder because of late age at onset, atypical symptomatology, or subthreshold symptomatology, or all of these.

Attention-Deficit and Disruptive Behavior Disorders

Attention-Deficit/Hyperactivity Disorder

Diagnostic Features

The essential feature of Attention-Deficit/Hyperactivity Disorder is a persistent pattern of inattention and/or hyperactivity-impulsivity that is more frequent and severe than is typically observed in individuals at a comparable level of development (Criterion A). Some hyperactive-impulsive or inattentive symptoms that cause impairment must have been present before age 7 years, although many individuals are diagnosed after the symptoms have been present for a number of years (Criterion B). Some impairment from the symptoms must be present in at least two settings (e.g., at home and at school or work) (Criterion C). There must be clear evidence of interference with developmentally appropriate social, academic, or occupational functioning (Criterion D). The disturbance does not occur exclusively during the course of a Pervasive Developmental Disorder, Schizophrenia, or other Psychotic Disorder and is not better accounted for by another mental disorder (e.g., a Mood Disorder, Anxiety Disorder, Dissociative Disorder, or Personality Disorder) (Criterion E).

Inattention may be manifest in academic, occupational, or social situations. Individuals with this disorder may fail to give close attention to details or may make careless mistakes in schoolwork or other tasks (Criterion A1a). Work is often messy and performed carelessly and without considered thought. Individuals often have difficulty sustaining attention in tasks or play activities and find it hard to persist with tasks until completion (Criterion A1b). They often appear as if their mind is elsewhere or as if they are not listening or did not hear what has just been said (Criterion A1c). There may be frequent shifts from one uncompleted activity to another. Individuals diagnosed with this disorder may begin a task, move on to another, then turn to yet something else, prior to completing any one task. They often do not follow through on requests or instructions and fail to complete schoolwork, chores, or other duties (Criterion A1d). Failure to complete tasks should be considered in making this diagnosis only if it is due to inattention as opposed to other possible reasons (e.g., a failure to understand instructions). These individuals often have difficulties organizing tasks and activities (Criterion A1e). Tasks that require sustained mental effort are experienced as unpleasant and markedly aversive. As a result, these individuals typically avoid or have a strong dislike for activities that demand sustained self-application and mental effort or that require organizational demands or close concentration (e.g., homework or paperwork) (Criterion A1f). This avoidance must be due to the person's difficulties with attention and not due to a primary oppositional attitude, although secondary oppositionalism may also occur. Work habits are often disorganized and the materials necessary for doing the task are often scattered, lost, or carelessly handled and damaged (Criterion A1g). Individuals with this disorder are easily distracted by irrelevant stimuli and frequently interrupt ongoing tasks to attend to trivial noises or events that are usually and easily ignored by others (e.g., a car honking, a background conversation) (Criterion A1h). They are often forgetful in daily activities (e.g., missing appointments, forgetting to bring lunch) (Criterion A1i). In social situations, inattention may be expressed as frequent shifts in conversation, not listening to others, not keeping one's mind on conversations, and not following details or rules of games or activities.

Hyperactivity may be manifested by fidgetiness or squirming in one's seat (Criterion A2a), by not remaining seated when expected to do so (Criterion A2b), by excessive running or climbing in situations where it is inappropriate (Criterion A2c), by having difficulty playing or engaging quietly in leisure activities (Criterion A2d), by appearing to be often "on the go" or as if "driven by a motor" (Criterion A2e), or by talking excessively (Criterion A2f). Hyperactivity may vary with the individual's age and developmental level, and the diagnosis should be made cautiously in young children. Toddlers and preschoolers with this disorder differ from normally active young children by being constantly on the go and into everything; they dart back and forth, are "out of the door before their coat is on," jump or climb on furniture, run through the house, and have difficulty participating in sedentary group activities in preschool classes (e.g., listening to a story). School-age children display similar behaviors but usually with less frequency or intensity than toddlers and preschoolers. They have difficulty remaining seated, get up frequently, and squirm in, or hang on to the edge of, their seat. They fidget with objects, tap their hands, and shake their feet or legs excessively. They often get up from the table during meals, while watching television, or while doing homework; they talk excessively; and they make excessive noise during quiet activities. In adolescents and adults, symptoms of hyperactivity take the form of feelings of restlessness and difficulty engaging in quiet sedentary activities.

Impulsivity manifests itself as impatience, difficulty in delaying responses, blurting out answers before questions have been completed (Criterion A2g), difficulty awaiting one's turn (Criterion A2h), and frequently interrupting or intruding on others to the point of causing difficulties in social, academic, or occupational settings (Criterion A2i). Others may complain that they cannot get a word in edgewise. Individuals with this disorder typically make comments out of turn, fail to listen to directions, initiate conversations at inappropriate times, interrupt others excessively, intrude on others, grab objects from others, touch things they are not supposed to touch, and clown around. Impulsivity may lead to accidents (e.g., knocking over objects, banging into people, grabbing a hot pan) and to engagement in potentially dangerous activities without consideration of possible consequences (e.g., riding a skateboard over extremely rough terrain).

Behavioral manifestations usually appear in multiple contexts, including home, school, work, and social situations. To make the diagnosis, some impairment must be present in at least two settings (Criterion C). It is very unusual for an individual to display the same level of dysfunction in all settings or within the same setting at all times. Symptoms typically worsen in situations that require sustained attention or mental effort or that lack intrinsic appeal or novelty (e.g., listening to classroom teachers, doing class assignments, listening to or reading lengthy materials, or working on monotonous, repetitive tasks). Signs of the disorder may be minimal or absent when the person is under very strict control, is in a novel setting, is engaged in especially interesting activities, is in a one-to-one situation (e.g., the clinician's office), or while the person experiences frequent rewards for appropriate behavior. The symptoms are more likely to occur in group situations (e.g., in playgroups, classrooms, or work environments). The clinician should therefore inquire about the individual's behavior in a variety of situations within each setting.

Subtypes

Although most individuals have symptoms of both inattention and hyperactivity-impulsivity, there are some individuals in whom one or the other pattern is predominant. The appropriate subtype (for a current diagnosis) should be indicated based on the predominant symptom pattern for the past 6 months.

> **314.01   Attention-Deficit/Hyperactivity Disorder, Combined Type.** This subtype should be used if six (or more) symptoms of inattention and six (or more) symptoms of hyperactivity-impulsivity have persisted for at least 6 months. Most children and adolescents with the disorder have the Combined Type. It is not known whether the same is true of adults with the disorder.
>
> **314.00   Attention Deficit/Hyperactivity Disorder, Predominantly Inattentive Type.** This subtype should be used if six (or more) symptoms of inattention (but fewer than six symptoms of hyperactivity-impulsivity) have persisted for at least 6 months.
>
> **314.01   Attention-Deficit/Hyperactivity Disorder, Predominantly Hyperactive-Impulsive Type.** This subtype should be used if six (or more) symptoms of hyperactivity-impulsivity (but fewer than six symptoms of inattention) have persisted for at least 6 months. Inattention may often still be a significant clinical feature in such cases.

Recording Procedures

Individuals who at an earlier stage of the disorder had the Predominantly Inattentive Type or the Predominantly Hyperactive-Impulsive Type may go on to develop the Combined Type and vice versa. The appropriate subtype (for a current diagnosis) should be indicated based on the predominant symptom pattern for the past 6 months. If clinically significant symptoms remain but criteria are no longer met for any of the subtypes, the appropriate diagnosis is Attention-Deficit/Hyperactivity Disorder, In Partial Remission. When an individual's symptoms do not currently meet full criteria for the disorder and it is unclear whether criteria for the disorder have previously been met, Attention-Deficit/Hyperactivity Disorder Not Otherwise Specified should be diagnosed.

Associated Features and Disorders

Associated descriptive features and mental disorders.   Associated features vary depending on age and developmental stage and may include low frustration tolerance, temper outbursts, bossiness, stubbornness, excessive and frequent insistence that requests be met, mood lability, demoralization, dysphoria, rejection by peers, and poor self-esteem. Academic achievement is often impaired and devalued, typically leading to conflict with the family and school authorities. Inadequate self-application to tasks that require sustained effort is often interpreted by others as indicating laziness, a poor sense of responsibility, and oppositional behavior. Family relationships are often characterized by resentment and antagonism, especially because variability in the individual's symptomatic status often leads parents to believe that all the troublesome behavior is willful. Individuals with Attention-Deficit/Hyperactivity Disorder may obtain less schooling than their peers and have poorer vocational achievement. Intellectual development, as assessed by individual IQ tests, appears to be somewhat lower in children with this disorder. In its severe form, the disorder is very impairing, affecting social, familial, and scholastic adjustment. A substantial proportion of children referred to clinics with Attention-Deficit/Hyperactivity Disorder also have Oppositional Defiant Disorder or Conduct Disorder. There may be a higher prevalence of Mood Disorders, Anxiety Disorders, Learning Disorders, and Communication Disorders in children with Attention-Deficit/Hyperactivity Disorder. This disorder is not infrequent among individuals with Tourette's Disorder; when the two disorders coexist, the onset of Attention-Deficit/Hyperactivity Disorder often precedes the onset of the Tourette's Disorder. There may be a history of child abuse or neglect, multiple foster placements, neurotoxin exposure (e.g., lead poisoning), infections (e.g., encephalitis), drug exposure in utero, low birth weight, and Mental Retardation.

Associated laboratory findings.   There are no laboratory tests that have been established as diagnostic in the clinical assessment of Attention-Deficit/Hyperactivity Disorder. Tests that require effortful mental processing have been noted to be abnormal in groups of individuals with Attention-Deficit/Hyperactivity Disorder compared with control subjects, but it is not yet entirely clear what fundamental cognitive deficit is responsible for this.

Associated physical examination findings and general medical conditions. There are no specific physical features associated with Attention-Deficit/Hyperactivity Disorder, although minor physical anomalies (e.g., hypertelorism, highly arched palate, low-set ears) may occur at a higher rate than in the general population. There may also be a higher rate of physical injury.

Specific Culture, Age, and Gender Features

Attention-Deficit/Hyperactivity Disorder is known to occur in various cultures, with variations in reported prevalence among Western countries probably arising more from different diagnostic practices than from differences in clinical presentation.

It is especially difficult to establish this diagnosis in children younger than age 4 or 5 years, because their characteristic behavior is much more variable than that of older children and may include features that are similar to symptoms of Attention-Deficit/Hyperactivity Disorder. Furthermore, symptoms of inattention in toddlers or preschool children are often not readily observed because young children typically experience few demands for sustained attention. However, even the attention of toddlers can be held in a variety of situations (e.g., the average 2- or 3-year-old child can typically sit with an adult looking through picture books). In contrast, young children with Attention-Deficit/Hyperactivity Disorder move excessively and typically are difficult to contain. Inquiring about a wide variety of behaviors in a young child may be helpful in ensuring that a full clinical picture has been obtained. As children mature, symptoms usually become less conspicuous. By late childhood and early adolescence, signs of excessive gross motor activity (e.g., excessive running and climbing, not remaining seated) are less common, and hyperactivity symptoms may be confined to fidgetiness or an inner feeling of jitteriness or restlessness. In school-age children, symptoms of inattention affect classroom work and academic performance. Impulsive symptoms may also lead to the breaking of familial, interpersonal, and educational rules, especially in adolescence. In adulthood, restlessness may lead to difficulty in participating in sedentary activities and to avoiding pastimes or occupations that provide limited opportunity for spontaneous movement (e.g., desk jobs).

The disorder is much more frequent in males than in females, with male-to-female ratios ranging from 4:1 to 9:1, depending on the setting (i.e., general population or clinics).

Prevalence

The prevalence of Attention-Deficit/Hyperactivity Disorder is estimated at 3%–5% in school-age children. Data on prevalence in adolescence and adulthood are limited.

Course

Most parents first observe excessive motor activity when the children are toddlers, frequently coinciding with the development of independent locomotion. However, because many overactive toddlers will not go on to develop Attention-Deficit/Hyperactivity Disorder, caution should be exercised in making this diagnosis in early years. Usually, the disorder is first diagnosed during elementary school years, when school adjustment is compromised. In the majority of cases seen in clinical settings, the disorder is relatively stable through early adolescence. In most individuals, symptoms attenuate during late adolescence and adulthood, although a minority experience the full complement of symptoms of Attention-Deficit/Hyperactivity Disorder into mid-adulthood. Other adults may retain only some of the symptoms, in which case the diagnosis of Attention-Deficit/Hyperactivity Disorder, In Partial Remission, should be used. This diagnosis applies to individuals who no longer have the full disorder but still retain some symptoms that cause functional impairment.

Familial Pattern

Attention-Deficit/Hyperactivity Disorder has been found to be more common in the first-degree biological relatives of children with Attention-Deficit/Hyperactivity Disorder. Studies also suggest that there is a higher prevalence of Mood and Anxiety Disorders, Learning Disorders, Substance-Related Disorders, and Antisocial Personality Disorder in family members of individuals with Attention-Deficit/Hyperactivity Disorder.

Differential Diagnosis

In early childhood, it may be difficult to distinguish symptoms of Attention-Deficit/Hyperactivity Disorder from **age-appropriate behaviors in active children** (e.g., running around or being noisy).

Symptoms of inattention are common among children with low IQ who are placed in academic settings that are inappropriate to their intellectual ability. These behaviors must be distinguished from similar signs in children with Attention-Deficit/Hyperactivity Disorder. In children with **Mental Retardation,** an additional diagnosis of Attention-

Deficit/Hyperactivity Disorder should be made only if the symptoms of inattention or hyperactivity are excessive for the child's mental age. Inattention in the classroom may also occur when children with high intelligence are placed in academically **understimulating environments.** Attention-Deficit/Hyperactivity Disorder must also be distinguished from difficulty in goal-directed behavior in children from inadequate, disorganized, or chaotic environments. Reports from multiple informants (e.g., babysitters, grandparents, or parents of playmates) are helpful in providing a confluence of observations concerning the child's inattention, hyperactivity, and capacity for developmentally appropriate self-regulation in various settings.

Individuals with **oppositional behavior** may resist work or school tasks that require self-application because of an unwillingness to conform to others' demands. These symptoms must be differentiated from the avoidance of school tasks seen in individuals with Attention-Deficit/Hyperactivity Disorder. Complicating the differential diagnosis is the fact that some individuals with Attention-Deficit/Hyperactivity Disorder develop secondary oppositional attitudes toward such tasks and devalue their importance, often as a rationalization for their failure.

Attention-Deficit/Hyperactivity Disorder is not diagnosed if the symptoms are better accounted for by **another mental disorder** (e.g., Mood Disorder, Anxiety Disorder, Dissociative Disorder, Personality Disorder, Personality Change Due to a General Medical Condition, or a Substance-Related Disorder). In all these disorders, the symptoms of inattention typically have an onset after age 7 years, and the childhood history of school adjustment generally is not characterized by disruptive behavior or teacher complaints concerning inattentive, hyperactive, or impulsive behavior. When a Mood Disorder or Anxiety Disorder co-occurs with Attention-Deficit/Hyperactivity Disorder, each should be diagnosed. Attention-Deficit/Hyperactivity Disorder is not diagnosed if the symptoms of inattention and hyperactivity occur exclusively during the course of a **Pervasive Developmental Disorder** or a **Psychotic Disorder.** Symptoms of inattention, hyperactivity, or impulsivity related to the use of medication (e.g., bronchodilators, isoniazid, akathisia from neuroleptics) in children before age 7 years are not diagnosed as Attention-Deficit/Hyperactivity Disorder but instead are diagnosed as **Other Substance-Related Disorder Not Otherwise Specified.**

■ Diagnostic criteria for Attention-Deficit/Hyperactivity Disorder

A. Either (1) or (2):

    (1)   six (or more) of the following symptoms of **inattention** have persisted for at least 6 months to a degree that is maladaptive and inconsistent with developmental level:

    Inattention
    (a) often fails to give close attention to details or makes careless mistakes in schoolwork, work, or other activities
    (b) often has difficulty sustaining attention in tasks or play activities

(continued)

☐ **Diagnostic criteria for Attention-Deficit/Hyperactivity Disorder** (*continued*)

      (c)   often does not seem to listen when spoken to directly

      (d)   often does not follow through on instructions and fails to finish schoolwork, chores, or duties in the workplace (not due to oppositional behavior or failure to understand instructions)

      (e)   often has difficulty organizing tasks and activities

      (f)   often avoids, dislikes, or is reluctant to engage in tasks that require sustained mental effort (such as schoolwork or homework)

      (g)   often loses things necessary for tasks or activities (e.g., toys, school assignments, pencils, books, or tools)

      (h)   is often easily distracted by extraneous stimuli

      (i)   is often forgetful in daily activities

  (2) six (or more) of the following symptoms of **hyperactivity-impulsivity** have persisted for at least 6 months to a degree that is maladaptive and inconsistent with developmental level:

Hyperactivity

      (a)   often fidgets with hands or feet or squirms in seat

      (b)   often leaves seat in classroom or in other situations in which remaining seated is expected

      (c)   often runs about or climbs excessively in situations in which it is inappropriate (in adolescents or adults, may be limited to subjective feelings of restlessness)

      (d)   often has difficulty playing or engaging in leisure activities quietly

      (e)   is often "on the go" or often acts as if "driven by a motor"

      (f)   often talks excessively

Impulsivity

      (g)   often blurts out answers before questions have been completed

      (h)   often has difficulty awaiting turn

      (i)   often interrupts or intrudes on others (e.g., butts into conversations or games)

B. Some hyperactive-impulsive or inattentive symptoms that caused impairment were present before age 7 years.

C. Some impairment from the symptoms is present in two or more settings (e.g., at school [or work] and at home).

D. There must be clear evidence of clinically significant impairment in social, academic, or occupational functioning.

(continued)

☐ **Diagnostic criteria for Attention-Deficit/Hyperactivity Disorder** (*continued*)

  E. The symptoms do not occur exclusively during the course of a Pervasive Developmental Disorder, Schizophrenia, or other Psychotic Disorder and are not better accounted for by another mental disorder (e.g., Mood Disorder, Anxiety Disorder, Dissociative Disorder, or a Personality Disorder).

Code based on type:
  314.01 Attention-Deficit/Hyperactivity Disorder, Combined Type: if both Criteria A1 and A2 are met for the past 6 months
  314.00 Attention-Deficit/Hyperactivity Disorder, Predominantly Inattentive Type: if Criterion A1 is met but Criterion A2 is not met for the past 6 months
  314.01 Attention-Deficit/Hyperactivity Disorder, Predominantly Hyperactive-Impulsive Type: if Criterion A2 is met but Criterion A1 is not met for the past 6 months

Coding note: For individuals (especially adolescents and adults) who currently have symptoms that no longer meet full criteria, "In Partial Remission" should be specified.

314.9 Attention-Deficit/Hyperactivity Disorder Not Otherwise Specified

This category is for disorders with prominent symptoms of inattention or hyperactivity-impulsivity that do not meet criteria for Attention-Deficit/Hyperactivity Disorder.

312.8 Conduct Disorder

Diagnostic Features

The essential feature of Conduct Disorder is a repetitive and persistent pattern of behavior in which the basic rights of others or major age-appropriate societal norms or rules are violated (Criterion A). These behaviors fall into four main groupings: aggressive conduct that causes or threatens physical harm to other people or animals (Criteria A1–A7), nonaggressive conduct that causes property loss or damage (Criteria A8–A9), deceitfulness or theft (Criteria A10–A12), and serious violations of rules (Criteria A13–A15). Three (or more) characteristic behaviors must have been present during the past 12 months, with at least one behavior present in the past 6 months. The disturbance in behavior causes clinically significant impairment in social, academic, or occupational functioning (Criterion B). Conduct Disorder may be diagnosed in individuals who are older than age 18 years, but only if the criteria for Antisocial Personality Disorder are not met (Criterion C). The behavior pattern is usually present in a variety of settings such as home, school, or the community. Because individuals with Conduct Disorder are likely to minimize their conduct problems, the clinician often must rely on additional informants. However, the informant's knowledge of the child's conduct problems may be limited by inadequate supervision or by the child's not having revealed them.

Children or adolescents with this disorder often initiate aggressive behavior and react aggressively to others. They may display bullying, threatening, or intimidating behavior (Criterion A1); initiate frequent physical fights (Criterion A2); use a weapon that can cause serious physical harm (e.g., a bat, brick, broken bottle, knife, or gun) (Criterion A3); be physically cruel to people (Criterion A4) or animals (Criterion A5); steal while confronting a victim (e.g., mugging, purse snatching, extortion, or armed robbery) (Criterion A6); or force someone into sexual activity (Criterion A7). Physical violence may take the form of rape, assault, or in rare cases, homicide.

Deliberate destruction of others' property is a characteristic feature of this disorder and may include deliberate fire setting with the intention of causing serious damage (Criterion A8) or deliberately destroying other people's property in other ways (e.g., smashing car windows, school vandalism) (Criterion A9).

Deceitfulness or theft is common and may include breaking into someone else's house, building, or car (Criterion A10); frequently lying or breaking promises to obtain goods or favors or to avoid debts or obligations (e.g., "conning" other people) (Criterion A11); or stealing items of nontrivial value without confronting the victim (e.g., shoplifting, forgery) (Criterion A12).

Characteristically, there are also serious violations of rules (e.g., school, parental) by individuals with this disorder. Children with this disorder often have a pattern, beginning before age 13 years, of staying out late at night despite parental prohibitions (Criterion A13). There may be a pattern of running away from home overnight (Criterion A14). To be considered a symptom of Conduct Disorder, the running away must have occurred at least twice (or only once if the individual did not return for a lengthy period). Runaway episodes that occur as a direct consequence of physical or sexual abuse do not typically qualify for this criterion. Children with this disorder may often be truant from school, beginning prior to age 13 years (Criterion A15). In older individuals, this behavior is manifested by often being absent from work without good reason.

Subtypes

Two subtypes of Conduct Disorder are provided based on the age at onset of the disorder (i.e., Childhood-Onset Type and Adolescent-Onset Type). The subtypes differ in regard to the characteristic nature of the presenting conduct problems, developmental course and prognosis, and gender ratio. Both subtypes can occur in a mild, moderate, or severe form. In assessing the age at onset, information should preferably be obtained from the youth and from caregiver(s). Because many of the behaviors may be concealed, caregivers may underreport symptoms and overestimate the age at onset.

> **Childhood-Onset Type.** This subtype is defined by the onset of at least one criterion characteristic of Conduct Disorder prior to age 10 years. Individuals with Childhood-Onset Type are usually male, frequently display physical aggression toward others, have disturbed peer relationships, may have had Oppositional Defiant Disorder during early childhood, and usually have symptoms that meet full criteria for Conduct Disorder prior to puberty. These individuals are more likely to have persistent Conduct Disorder and to develop adult Antisocial Personality Disorder than are those with Adolescent-Onset Type.

Adolescent-Onset Type.   This subtype is defined by the absence of any criteria characteristic of Conduct Disorder prior to age 10 years. Compared with those with the Childhood-Onset Type, these individuals are less likely to display aggressive behaviors and tend to have more normative peer relationships (although they often display conduct problems in the company of others). These individuals are less likely to have persistent Conduct Disorder or to develop adult Antisocial Personality Disorder. The ratio of males to females with Conduct Disorder is lower for the Adolescent-Onset Type than for the Childhood-Onset Type.

Severity Specifiers

Mild.   Few if any conduct problems in excess of those required to make the diagnosis are present, and conduct problems cause relatively minor harm to others (e.g., lying, truancy, staying out after dark without permission).
Moderate.   The number of conduct problems and the effect on others are intermediate between "mild" and "severe" (e.g., stealing without confronting a victim, vandalism).
Severe.   Many conduct problems in excess of those required to make the diagnosis are present, or conduct problems cause considerable harm to others (e.g., forced sex, physical cruelty, use of a weapon, stealing while confronting a victim, breaking and entering).

Associated Features and Disorders

Associated descriptive features and mental disorders.   Individuals with Conduct Disorder may have little empathy and little concern for the feelings, wishes, and well-being of others. Especially in ambiguous situations, aggressive individuals with this disorder frequently misperceive the intentions of others as more hostile and threatening than is the case and respond with aggression that they then feel is reasonable and justified. They may be callous and lack appropriate feelings of guilt or remorse. It can be difficult to evaluate whether displayed remorse is genuine because these individuals learn that expressing guilt may reduce or prevent punishment. Individuals with this disorder may readily inform on their companions and try to blame others for their own misdeeds. Self-esteem is usually low, although the person may project an image of "toughness." Poor frustration tolerance, irritability, temper outbursts, and recklessness are frequent associated features. Accident rates appear to be higher in individuals with Conduct Disorder than in those without it.

Conduct Disorder is often associated with an early onset of sexual behavior, drinking, smoking, use of illegal substances, and reckless and risk-taking acts. Illegal drug use may increase the risk that Conduct Disorder will persist. Conduct Disorder behaviors may lead to school suspension or expulsion, problems in work adjustment, legal difficulties, sexually transmitted diseases, unplanned pregnancy, and physical injury from accidents or fights. These problems may preclude attendance in ordinary schools or living in a parental or foster home. Suicidal ideation, suicide attempts, and completed suicide occur at a higher than expected rate. Conduct Disorder may be associated with lower than average intelligence. Academic achievement, particularly in reading and other verbal skills, is often below the level expected on the basis of age and intelligence and may justify the additional diagnosis of a Learning or Communication Disorder. Attention-

Deficit/Hyperactivity Disorder is common in children with Conduct Disorder. Conduct Disorder may also be associated with one or more of the following mental disorders: Learning Disorders, Anxiety Disorders, Mood Disorders, and Substance-Related Disorders. The following factors may predispose the individual to the development of Conduct Disorder: parental rejection and neglect, difficult infant temperament, inconsistent child-rearing practices with harsh discipline, physical or sexual abuse, lack of supervision, early institutional living, frequent changes of caregivers, large family size, association with a delinquent peer group, and certain kinds of familial psychopathology.

Associated laboratory findings.   In some studies, lower heart rate and lower skin conductance have been noted in individuals with Conduct Disorder compared with those without the disorder. However, levels of physiological arousal are not diagnostic of the disorder.

Specific Culture, Age, and Gender Features

Concerns have been raised that the Conduct Disorder diagnosis may at times be misapplied to individuals in settings where patterns of undesirable behavior are sometimes viewed as protective (e.g., threatening, impoverished, high-crime). Consistent with the DSM-IV definition of mental disorder, the Conduct Disorder diagnosis should be applied only when the behavior in question is symptomatic of an underlying dysfunction within the individual and not simply a reaction to the immediate social context. Moreover, immigrant youth from war-ravaged countries who have a history of aggressive behaviors that may have been necessary for their survival in that context would not necessarily warrant a diagnosis of Conduct Disorder. It may be helpful for the clinician to consider the social and economic context in which the undesirable behaviors have occurred.

Symptoms of the disorder vary with age as the individual develops increased physical strength, cognitive abilities, and sexual maturity. Less severe behaviors (e.g., lying, shoplifting, physical fighting) tend to emerge first, whereas others (e.g., burglary) tend to emerge later. Typically, the most severe conduct problems (e.g., rape, theft while confronting a victim) tend to emerge last. However, there are wide differences among individuals, with some engaging in the more damaging behaviors at an early age.

Conduct Disorder, especially the Childhood-Onset Type, is much more common in males. Gender differences are also found in specific types of conduct problems. Males with a diagnosis of Conduct Disorder frequently exhibit fighting, stealing, vandalism, and school discipline problems. Females with a diagnosis of Conduct Disorder are more likely to exhibit lying, truancy, running away, substance use, and prostitution. Whereas confrontational aggression is more often displayed by males, females tend to use more nonconfrontational behaviors.

Prevalence

The prevalence of Conduct Disorder appears to have increased over the last decades and may be higher in urban than in rural settings. Rates vary widely depending on the nature of the population sampled and methods of ascertainment: for males under age 18 years, rates range from 6% to 16%; for females, rates range from 2% to 9%. Conduct Disorder is one of the most frequently diagnosed conditions in outpatient and inpatient mental health facilities for children.

Course

The onset of Conduct Disorder may occur as early as age 5–6 years but is usually in late childhood or early adolescence. Onset is rare after age 16 years. The course of Conduct Disorder is variable. In a majority of individuals, the disorder remits by adulthood. However, a substantial proportion continue to show behaviors in adulthood that meet criteria for Antisocial Personality Disorder. Many individuals with Conduct Disorder, particularly those with Adolescent-Onset Type and those with few and milder symptoms, achieve adequate social and occupational adjustment as adults. Early onset predicts a worse prognosis and an increased risk in adult life for Antisocial Personality Disorder and Substance-Related Disorders. Individuals with Conduct Disorder are at risk for later Mood or Anxiety Disorders, Somatoform Disorders, and Substance-Related Disorders.

Familial Pattern

Estimates from twin and adoption studies show that Conduct Disorder has both genetic and environmental components. The risk for Conduct Disorder is increased in children with a biological or adoptive parent with Antisocial Personality Disorder or a sibling with Conduct Disorder. The disorder also appears to be more common in children of biological parents with Alcohol Dependence, Mood Disorders, or Schizophrenia or biological parents who have a history of Attention-Deficit/Hyperactivity Disorder or Conduct Disorder.

Differential Diagnosis

Although **Oppositional Defiant Disorder** includes some of the features observed in Conduct Disorder (e.g., disobedience and opposition to authority figures), it does not include the persistent pattern of the more serious forms of behavior in which either the basic rights of others or age-appropriate societal norms or rules are violated. When the individual's pattern of behavior meets the criteria for both Conduct Disorder and Oppositional Defiant Disorder, the diagnosis of Conduct Disorder takes precedence and Oppositional Defiant Disorder is not diagnosed.

Although children with **Attention-Deficit/Hyperactivity Disorder** often exhibit hyperactive and impulsive behavior that may be disruptive, this behavior does not by itself violate age-appropriate societal norms and therefore does not usually meet criteria for Conduct Disorder. When criteria are met for both Attention-Deficit/Hyperactivity Disorder and Conduct Disorder, both diagnoses should be given.

Irritability and conduct problems often occur in children or adolescents having a **Manic Episode.** These can usually be distinguished from the pattern of conduct problems seen in Conduct Disorder based on the episodic course and accompanying symptoms characteristic of a Manic Episode. If criteria for both are met, diagnoses of both Conduct Disorder and Bipolar I Disorder can be given.

The diagnosis of **Adjustment Disorder** (With Disturbance of Conduct or With Mixed Disturbance of Emotions and Conduct) should be considered if clinically significant conduct problems that do not meet the criteria for another specific disorder develop in clear association with the onset of a psychosocial stressor. Isolated conduct problems that do not meet criteria for Conduct Disorder or Adjustment Disorder may be coded as **Child or Adolescent Antisocial Behavior** (see "Other Conditions That May Be a Focus of Clinical Attention," p. 684). Conduct Disorder is diagnosed only if the conduct problems represent a repetitive and persistent pattern that is associated with impairment in social, academic, or occupational functioning.

For individuals over age 18 years, a diagnosis of Conduct Disorder can be given only if the criteria are not also met for **Antisocial Personality Disorder.** The diagnosis of Antisocial Personality Disorder cannot be given to individuals under age 18 years.

■ Diagnostic criteria for 312.8 Conduct Disorder

A. A repetitive and persistent pattern of behavior in which the basic rights of others or major age-appropriate societal norms or rules are violated, as manifested by the presence of three (or more) of the following criteria in the past 12 months, with at least one criterion present in the past 6 months:

Aggression to people and animals

(1) often bullies, threatens, or intimidates others
(2) often initiates physical fights
(3) has used a weapon that can cause serious physical harm to others (e.g., a bat, brick, broken bottle, knife, gun)
(4) has been physically cruel to people
(5) has been physically cruel to animals
(6) has stolen while confronting a victim (e.g., mugging, purse snatching, extortion, armed robbery)
(7) has forced someone into sexual activity

Destruction of property

(8) has deliberately engaged in fire setting with the intention of causing serious damage
(9) has deliberately destroyed others' property (other than by fire setting)

Deceitfulness or theft

(10) has broken into someone else's house, building, or car
(11) often lies to obtain goods or favors or to avoid obligations (i.e., "cons" others)
(12) has stolen items of nontrivial value without confronting a victim (e.g., shoplifting, but without breaking and entering; forgery)

Serious violations of rules

(13) often stays out at night despite parental prohibitions, beginning before age 13 years
(14) has run away from home overnight at least twice while living in parental or parental surrogate home (or once without returning for a lengthy period)
(15) is often truant from school, beginning before age 13 years

(continued)

☐ **Diagnostic criteria for 312.8 Conduct Disorder** (*continued*)

B. The disturbance in behavior causes clinically significant impairment in social, academic, or occupational functioning.

C. If the individual is age 18 years or older, criteria are not met for Antisocial Personality Disorder.

Specify type based on age at onset:
Childhood-Onset Type: onset of at least one criterion characteristic of Conduct Disorder prior to age 10 years
Adolescent-Onset Type: absence of any criteria characteristic of Conduct Disorder prior to age 10 years

Specify severity:
Mild: few if any conduct problems in excess of those required to make the diagnosis **and** conduct problems cause only minor harm to others
Moderate: number of conduct problems and effect on others intermediate between "mild" and "severe"
Severe: many conduct problems in excess of those required to make the diagnosis **or** conduct problems cause considerable harm to others

313.81   Oppositional Defiant Disorder

Diagnostic Features

The essential feature of Oppositional Defiant Disorder is a recurrent pattern of negativistic, defiant, disobedient, and hostile behavior toward authority figures that persists for at least 6 months (Criterion A) and is characterized by the frequent occurrence of at least four of the following behaviors: losing temper (Criterion A1), arguing with adults (Criterion A2), actively defying or refusing to comply with the requests or rules of adults (Criterion A3), deliberately doing things that will annoy other people (Criterion A4), blaming others for his or her own mistakes or misbehavior (Criterion A5), being touchy or easily annoyed by others (Criterion A6), being angry and resentful (Criterion A7), or being spiteful or vindictive (Criterion A8). To qualify for Oppositional Defiant Disorder, the behaviors must occur more frequently than is typically observed in individuals of comparable age and developmental level and must lead to significant impairment in social, academic, or occupational functioning (Criterion B). The diagnosis is not made if the disturbance in behavior occurs exclusively during the course of a Psychotic or Mood Disorder (Criterion C) or if criteria are met for Conduct Disorder or Antisocial Personality Disorder (in an individual over age 18 years).

Negativistic and defiant behaviors are expressed by persistent stubbornness, resistance to directions, and unwillingness to compromise, give in, or negotiate with adults or peers. Defiance may also include deliberate or persistent testing of limits, usually by ignoring orders, arguing, and failing to accept blame for misdeeds. Hostility can be directed at adults or peers and is shown by deliberately annoying others or by verbal aggression (usually without the more serious physical aggression seen in Conduct Disorder). Manifestations of the disorder are almost invariably present in the home setting, but may not be evident at school or in the community. Symptoms of the disorder are typically more evident in interactions with adults or peers whom the individual knows well, and thus may not be apparent during clinical examination. Usually individuals with this disorder do not regard themselves as oppositional or defiant, but justify their behavior as a response to unreasonable demands or circumstances.

Associated Features and Disorders

Associated features and disorders vary as a function of the individual's age and the severity of the Oppositional Defiant Disorder. In males, the disorder has been shown to be more prevalent among those who, in the preschool years, have problematic temperaments (e.g., high reactivity, difficulty being soothed) or high motor activity. During the school years, there may be low self-esteem, mood lability, low frustration tolerance, swearing, and the precocious use of alcohol, tobacco, or illicit drugs. There are often conflicts with parents, teachers, and peers. There may be a vicious cycle in which the parent and child bring out the worst in each other. Oppositional Defiant Disorder is more prevalent in families in which child care is disrupted by a succession of different caregivers or in families in which harsh, inconsistent, or neglectful child-rearing practices are common. Attention-Deficit/Hyperactivity Disorder is common in children with Oppositional Defiant Disorder. Learning Disorders and Communication Disorders also tend to be associated with Oppositional Defiant Disorder.

Specific Age and Gender Features

Because transient oppositional behavior is very common in preschool children and in adolescents, caution should be exercised in making the diagnosis of Oppositional Defiant Disorder especially during these developmental periods. The number of oppositional symptoms tends to increase with age. The disorder is more prevalent in males than in females before puberty, but the rates are probably equal after puberty. Symptoms are generally similar in each gender, except that males may have more confrontational behavior and more persistent symptoms.

Prevalence

Rates of Oppositional Defiant Disorder from 2% to 16% have been reported, depending on the nature of the population sample and methods of ascertainment.

Course

Oppositional Defiant Disorder usually becomes evident before age 8 years and usually not later than early adolescence. The oppositional symptoms often emerge in the home setting but over time may appear in other settings as well. Onset is typically gradual, usually occurring over the course of months or years. In a significant proportion of cases, Oppositional Defiant Disorder is a developmental antecedent to Conduct Disorder.

Familial Pattern

Oppositional Defiant Disorder appears to be more common in families in which at least one parent has a history of a Mood Disorder, Oppositional Defiant Disorder, Conduct Disorder, Attention-Deficit/Hyperactivity Disorder, Antisocial Personality Disorder, or a Substance-Related Disorder. In addition, some studies suggest that mothers with a Depressive Disorder are more likely to have children with oppositional behavior, but it is unclear to what extent maternal depression results from or causes oppositional behavior in children. Oppositional Defiant Disorder is more common in families in which there is serious marital discord.

Differential Diagnosis

The disruptive behaviors of individuals with Oppositional Defiant Disorder are of a less severe nature than those of individuals with Conduct Disorder and typically do not include aggression toward people or animals, destruction of property, or a pattern of theft or deceit. Because all of the features of Oppositional Defiant Disorder are usually present in **Conduct Disorder,** Oppositional Defiant Disorder is not diagnosed if the criteria are met for Conduct Disorder. Oppositional behavior is a common associated feature of **Mood Disorders** and **Psychotic Disorders** presenting in children and adolescents and should not be diagnosed separately if the symptoms occur exclusively during the course of a Mood or Psychotic Disorder. Oppositional behaviors must also be distinguished from the disruptive behavior resulting from inattention and impulsivity in **Attention-Deficit/Hyperactivity Disorder.** When the two disorders co-occur, both diagnoses should be made. In individuals with **Mental Retardation,** a diagnosis of Oppositional Defiant Disorder is given only if the oppositional behavior is markedly greater than is commonly observed among individuals of comparable age, gender, and severity of Mental Retardation. Oppositional Defiant Disorder must also be distinguished from a failure to follow directions that is the result of **impaired language comprehension** (e.g., hearing loss, Mixed Receptive-Expressive Language Disorder). Oppositional behavior is a **typical feature of certain developmental stages** (e.g., early childhood and adolescence). A diagnosis of Oppositional Defiant Disorder should be considered only if the behaviors occur more frequently and have more serious consequences than is typically observed in other individuals of comparable developmental stage and lead to significant impairment in social, academic, or occupational functioning. New onset of oppositional behaviors in adolescence may be due to the process of normal individuation.

■ **Diagnostic criteria for 313.81 Oppositional Defiant Disorder**

  A. A pattern of negativistic, hostile, and defiant behavior lasting at least 6 months, during which four (or more) of the following are present:

    (1) often loses temper
    (2) often argues with adults

(continued)

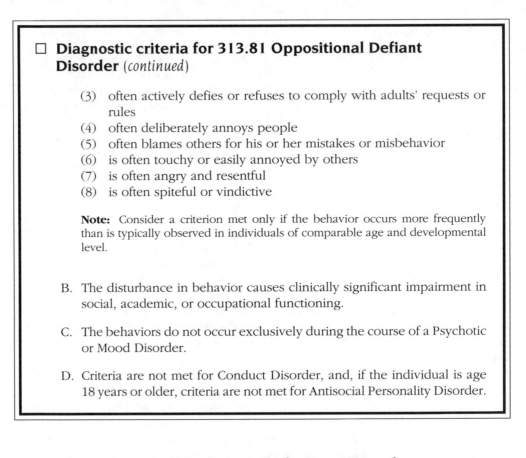

□ **Diagnostic criteria for 313.81 Oppositional Defiant Disorder** (*continued*)

    (3) often actively defies or refuses to comply with adults' requests or rules

    (4) often deliberately annoys people

    (5) often blames others for his or her mistakes or misbehavior

    (6) is often touchy or easily annoyed by others

    (7) is often angry and resentful

    (8) is often spiteful or vindictive

Note: Consider a criterion met only if the behavior occurs more frequently than is typically observed in individuals of comparable age and developmental level.

B. The disturbance in behavior causes clinically significant impairment in social, academic, or occupational functioning.

C. The behaviors do not occur exclusively during the course of a Psychotic or Mood Disorder.

D. Criteria are not met for Conduct Disorder, and, if the individual is age 18 years or older, criteria are not met for Antisocial Personality Disorder.

312.9 Disruptive Behavior Disorder Not Otherwise Specified

This category is for disorders characterized by conduct or oppositional defiant behaviors that do not meet the criteria for Conduct Disorder or Oppositional Defiant Disorder. For example, include clinical presentations that do not meet full criteria either for Oppositional Defiant Disorder or Conduct Disorder, but in which there is clinically significant impairment.

Feeding and Eating Disorders of Infancy or Early Childhood

The Feeding and Eating Disorders of Infancy or Early Childhood are characterized by persistent feeding and eating disturbances. The specific disorders included are Pica, Rumination Disorder, and Feeding Disorder of Infancy or Early Childhood. Note that Anorexia Nervosa and Bulimia Nervosa are included in the "Eating Disorders" section (see p. 539).

307.52 Pica

Diagnostic Features

The essential feature of Pica is the persistent eating of nonnutritive substances for a period of at least 1 month (Criterion A). The typical substance ingested tends to vary with age. Infants and younger children typically eat paint, plaster, string, hair, or cloth. Older children may eat animal droppings, sand, insects, leaves, or pebbles. Adolescents and adults may consume clay or soil. There is no aversion to food. This behavior must be developmentally inappropriate (Criterion B) and not part of a culturally sanctioned practice (Criterion C). The eating of nonnutritive substances is an associated feature of other mental disorders (e.g., Pervasive Developmental Disorder, Mental Retardation). If the eating behavior occurs exclusively during the course of another mental disorder, a separate diagnosis of Pica should be made only if the eating behavior is sufficiently severe to warrant independent clinical attention (Criterion D).

Associated Features and Disorders

Pica is frequently associated with Mental Retardation. Although vitamin or mineral deficiencies have been reported in some instances, usually no specific biological abnormalities are found. In some cases, Pica comes to clinical attention only when the individual presents with any of the various general medical complications that may result (e.g., lead poisoning as a result of ingesting paint or paint-soaked plaster, mechanical bowel problems, intestinal obstruction as a result of hair ball tumors, intestinal perforation, or infections such as toxoplasmosis and toxocariasis as a result of ingesting feces or dirt). Poverty, neglect, lack of parental supervision, and developmental delay increase the risk for the condition.

Specific Culture, Age, and Gender Features

In some cultures, the eating of dirt or other seemingly nonnutritive substances is believed to be of value. Pica is more commonly seen in young children and occasionally in pregnant females.

Prevalence

Epidemiological data on Pica are limited. The condition is not often diagnosed but may not be uncommon in preschool children. Among individuals with Mental Retardation, the prevalence of the disorder appears to increase with the severity of the retardation.

Course

Pica may have its onset in infancy. In most instances, the disorder probably lasts for several months and then remits. It may occasionally continue into adolescence or, less frequently, into adulthood. In individuals with Mental Retardation, the behavior may diminish during adulthood.

Differential Diagnosis

Before approximately ages 18–24 months, mouthing and sometimes eating of nonnutritive substances are relatively common and do not imply the presence of Pica. Pica is diagnosed only when the behavior is judged to be persistent (i.e., present for at least 1 month) and inappropriate given the individual's developmental level. Eating of nonnutritive substances may occur during the course of other mental disorders (e.g., in a **Pervasive Developmental Disorder,** in **Schizophrenia** as a result of delusional beliefs, and in **Kleine-Levin syndrome**). In such instances, an additional diagnosis of Pica should be given only if the eating behavior is sufficiently severe to warrant independent clinical attention. Pica can be distinguished from **other eating disorders** (e.g., Rumination Disorder, Feeding Disorder of Infancy or Early Childhood, Anorexia Nervosa, and Bulimia Nervosa) by the consumption of nonnutritive substances.

■ Diagnostic criteria for 307.52 Pica

A. Persistent eating of nonnutritive substances for a period of at least 1 month.

B. The eating of nonnutritive substances is inappropriate to the developmental level.

C. The eating behavior is not part of a culturally sanctioned practice.

D. If the eating behavior occurs exclusively during the course of another mental disorder (e.g., Mental Retardation, Pervasive Developmental Disorder, Schizophrenia), it is sufficiently severe to warrant independent clinical attention.

307.53   Rumination Disorder

Diagnostic Features

The essential feature of Rumination Disorder is the repeated regurgitation and rechewing of food that develops in an infant or child after a period of normal functioning and lasts for at least 1 month (Criterion A). Partially digested food is brought up into the mouth without apparent nausea, retching, disgust, or associated gastrointestinal disorder. The food is then either ejected from the mouth or, more frequently, chewed and reswallowed. The symptoms are not due to an associated gastrointestinal or other general medical condition (e.g., Sandifer's syndrome, esophageal reflux) (Criterion B) and do not occur exclusively during the course of Anorexia Nervosa or Bulimia Nervosa. If the symptoms occur exclusively during the course of Mental Retardation or a Pervasive Developmental Disorder, they must be sufficiently severe to warrant independent clinical attention

(Criterion C). The disorder is most commonly observed in infants but may be seen in older individuals, particularly those who also have Mental Retardation. Infants with the disorder display a characteristic position of straining and arching the back with the head held back, make sucking movements with their tongues, and give the impression of gaining satisfaction from the activity.

Associated Features and Disorders

Infants with Rumination Disorder are generally irritable and hungry between episodes of regurgitation. Although the infant is apparently hungry and ingests large amounts of food, malnutrition may occur because regurgitation immediately follows the feedings. Weight loss, failure to make expected weight gains, and even death can result (with mortality rates as high as 25% reported). Malnutrition appears to be less likely in older children and adults in whom the disorder may be either continuous or episodic. Psychosocial problems such as lack of stimulation, neglect, stressful life situations, and problems in the parent-child relationship may be predisposing factors. Understimulation of the infant may result if the caregiver becomes discouraged and alienated because of the unsuccessful feeding experiences or the noxious odor of the regurgitated material. In some instances, Feeding Disorder of Infancy or Early Childhood may also develop. In older children and adults, Mental Retardation is a predisposing factor.

Prevalence

Rumination Disorder appears to be uncommon. It may occur more often in males than in females.

Course

The onset of Rumination Disorder may occur in the context of developmental delays. The age at onset is between ages 3 and 12 months, except in individuals with Mental Retardation in whom the disorder may occur at a somewhat later developmental stage. In infants, the disorder frequently remits spontaneously. In some severe cases, however, the course is continuous.

Differential Diagnosis

In infants, **congenital anomalies** (e.g., pyloric stenosis or gastroesophageal reflux) or **other general medical conditions** (e.g., infections of the gastrointestinal system) can cause regurgitation of food and should be ruled out by appropriate physical examinations and laboratory tests. Rumination can be distinguished from **normal vomiting of early infancy** by the apparently voluntary nature of the rumination (e.g., observation of characteristic preparatory movements followed by regurgitation and sucking or chewing movements that appear to be pleasurable). Rumination Disorder is not diagnosed if the symptoms occur exclusively during the course of **Anorexia Nervosa** or **Bulimia Nervosa.**

■ **Diagnostic criteria for 307.53 Rumination Disorder**

A. Repeated regurgitation and rechewing of food for a period of at least 1 month following a period of normal functioning.

B. The behavior is not due to an associated gastrointestinal or other general medical condition (e.g., esophageal reflux).

C. The behavior does not occur exclusively during the course of Anorexia Nervosa or Bulimia Nervosa. If the symptoms occur exclusively during the course of Mental Retardation or a Pervasive Developmental Disorder, they are sufficiently severe to warrant independent clinical attention.

307.59   Feeding Disorder of Infancy or Early Childhood

Diagnostic Features

The essential feature of Feeding Disorder of Infancy or Early Childhood is the persistent failure to eat adequately, as reflected in significant failure to gain weight or significant weight loss over at least 1 month (Criterion A). There is no gastrointestinal or other general medical condition (e.g., esophageal reflux) severe enough to account for the feeding disturbance (Criterion B). The feeding disturbance is also not better accounted for by another Mental Disorder (e.g., Rumination Disorder) or by lack of available food (Criterion C). The onset of the disorder must be before age 6 years (Criterion D).

Associated Features and Disorders

Associated descriptive features and mental disorders.   Infants with feeding disorders are often especially irritable and difficult to console during feeding. They may appear apathetic and withdrawn and may also exhibit developmental delays. In some instances, parent-child interaction problems may contribute to or exacerbate the infant's feeding problem (e.g., presenting food inappropriately or responding to the infant's food refusal as if it were an act of aggression or rejection). Inadequate caloric intake may exacerbate the associated features (e.g., irritability, developmental lags) and further contribute to feeding difficulties. Factors in the infant that may be associated with the condition include neuroregulatory difficulties (e.g., sleep-wake difficulties, frequent regurgitation, unpredictable periods of alertness) and preexisting developmental impairments that make the infant less responsive. Other factors that may be associated with the condition include parental psychopathology and child abuse or neglect.

Associated laboratory findings.   There may be nonspecific findings associated with the malnutrition that is sometimes seen with Feeding Disorder of Infancy or Early Childhood (e.g., anemia and low serum albumin and total protein).

Associated physical examination findings and general medical conditions.
There may be malnutrition that, in severe cases, can be life threatening in Feeding
Disorder of Infancy or Early Childhood.

Specific Age and Gender Features

A later onset (e.g., age 2 or 3 years rather than infancy) is associated with lesser degrees
of developmental delay and malnutrition, although growth retardation may be observed.
Feeding Disorder of Infancy or Early Childhood is equally common in males and females.

Prevalence

Of all pediatric hospital admissions, 1%–5% are for failure to gain adequate weight, and
up to one-half of these may reflect feeding disturbances without any apparent predisposing general medical condition.

Course

Feeding Disorder of Infancy or Early Childhood commonly has its onset in the first year
of life, but may have an onset in children ages 2–3 years. The majority of children have
improved growth after variable lengths of time.

Differential Diagnosis

Minor problems in feeding are common in infancy. The diagnosis of Feeding Disorder
of Infancy or Early Childhood should be made only if the eating problem results in
significant failure to gain weight or loss of weight.

This disorder is not diagnosed if the feeding disturbances are fully explained by a
gastrointestinal, endocrinological, or neurological condition. Children with an
underlying general medical condition may be more difficult to feed, and the diagnosis
of Feeding Disorder of Infancy or Early Childhood should not be made in such cases
unless the degree of disturbance is of greater severity than would be expected on the
basis of the general medical condition alone. The diagnosis is suggested if there is
improvement in feeding and weight gain in response to changing caregivers.

■ Diagnostic criteria for 307.59 Feeding Disorder of Infancy or Early Childhood

A. Feeding disturbance as manifested by persistent failure to eat adequately
    with significant failure to gain weight or significant loss of weight over
    at least 1 month.

B. The disturbance is not due to an associated gastrointestinal or other
    general medical condition (e.g., esophageal reflux).

(continued)

☐ **Diagnostic criteria for 307.59 Feeding Disorder of Infancy or Early Childhood** (*continued*)

C. The disturbance is not better accounted for by another mental disorder (e.g., Rumination Disorder) or by lack of available food.

D. The onset is before age 6 years.

Tic Disorders

Four disorders are included in this section: Tourette's Disorder, Chronic Motor or Vocal Tic Disorder, Transient Tic Disorder, and Tic Disorder Not Otherwise Specified. A *tic* is a sudden, rapid, recurrent, nonrhythmic, stereotyped motor movement or vocalization. It is experienced as irresistible but can be suppressed for varying lengths of time. All forms of tic may be exacerbated by stress and attenuated during absorbing activities (e.g., reading or sewing). Tics are usually markedly diminished during sleep. Both motor and vocal tics may be classified as either simple or complex, although the boundary is not well defined. Common *simple motor tics* include eye blinking, neck jerking, shoulder shrugging, facial grimacing, and coughing. Common *simple vocal tics* include throat clearing, grunting, sniffing, snorting, and barking. Common *complex motor tics* include facial gestures, grooming behaviors, jumping, touching, stamping, and smelling an object. Common *complex vocal tics* include repeating words or phrases out of context, coprolalia (use of socially unacceptable words, frequently obscene), palilalia (repeating one's own sounds or words), and echolalia (repeating the last-heard sound, word, or phrase). Other complex tics include echokinesis (imitation of someone else's movements).

Differential Diagnosis

Tic Disorders must be distinguished from other types of **abnormal movements that may accompany general medical conditions** (e.g., Huntington's disease, stroke, Lesch-Nyhan syndrome, Wilson's disease, Sydenham's chorea, multiple sclerosis, postviral encephalitis, head injury) or may be due to the **direct effects of a substance** (e.g., a neuroleptic medication). **Choreiform movements** are dancing, random, irregular, nonrepetitive movements. **Dystonic movements** are slower, twisting movements interspersed with prolonged states of muscular tension. **Athetoid movements** are slow, irregular, writhing movements, most frequently in the fingers and toes, but often involving the face and neck. **Myoclonic movements** are brief, shocklike muscle contractions that may affect parts of muscles or muscle groups but not synergistically. **Hemiballismic movements** are intermittent, coarse, large-amplitude, unilateral movements of the limbs. **Spasms** are stereotypic, slower, and more prolonged than tics and involve groups of muscles. **Hemifacial spasm** consists of irregular, repetitive, unilateral jerks of facial muscles. **Synkinesis** involves an involuntary movement accompanying a voluntary one (e.g., movement of the corner of the mouth when the person intends to close the eye). This differentiation is further facilitated by considering the presence of features of the underlying general medical condition (e.g., characteristic family history in Huntington's disease) or a history of medication use.

When the tics are a direct physiological consequence of medication use, a **Medication-Induced Movement Disorder Not Otherwise Specified** would be diagnosed instead of a Tic Disorder. In some cases, certain medications (e.g., methylphenidate) may exacerbate a preexisting Tic Disorder, in which case no additional diagnosis of a medication-induced disorder is necessary.

Tics must also be distinguished from stereotyped movements seen in **Stereotypic Movement Disorder** and **Pervasive Developmental Disorders.** Differentiating simple tics (e.g., eye blinking) from the complex movements characteristic of stereotyped movements is relatively straightforward. The distinction between complex motor tics and stereotyped movements is less clear-cut. In general, stereotyped movements appear to be more driven and intentional, whereas tics have a more involuntary quality and are not rhythmic. Tics must be distinguished from **compulsions** (as in Obsessive-Compulsive Disorder). Compulsions are typically quite complex and are performed in response to an obsession or according to rules that must be applied rigidly. In contrast to a compulsion, tics are typically less complex and are not aimed at neutralizing the anxiety resulting from an obsession. Some individuals manifest symptoms of both Obsessive-Compulsive Disorder and a Tic Disorder (especially Tourette's Disorder), so that both diagnoses may be warranted. Certain vocal or motor tics (e.g., barking, echolalia, palilalia) must be distinguished from disorganized or catatonic behavior in **Schizophrenia.**

The Tic Disorders can be distinguished from one another based on duration and variety of tics and age at onset. **Transient Tic Disorder** includes motor and/or vocal tics lasting for at least 4 weeks but for no longer than 12 consecutive months. **Tourette's Disorder** and **Chronic Motor or Vocal Tic Disorder** each have a duration of more than 12 months but are distinguished by the requirement for Tourette's Disorder that there be multiple motor tics and at least one vocal tic. **Tic Disorder Not Otherwise Specified** would be appropriate for clinically significant presentations lasting less than 4 weeks, for presentations with an age at onset above age 18 years, and for the unusual case of an individual with only one motor tic and only one vocal tic.

307.23 Tourette's Disorder

Diagnostic Features

The essential features of Tourette's Disorder are multiple motor tics and one or more vocal tics (Criterion A). These may appear simultaneously or at different periods during the illness. The tics occur many times a day, recurrently throughout a period of more than 1 year (Criterion B). During this period, there is never a tic-free period of more than 3 consecutive months. The disturbance causes marked distress or significant impairment in social, occupational, or other important areas of functioning (Criterion C). The onset of the disorder is before age 18 years (Criterion D). The tics are not due to the direct physiological effects of a substance (e.g., stimulants) or a general medical condition (e.g., Huntington's disease or postviral encephalitis) (Criterion E).

The anatomical location, number, frequency, complexity, and severity of the tics change over time. The tics typically involve the head and, frequently, other parts of the body, such as the torso and upper and lower limbs. The vocal tics include various words or sounds such as clicks, grunts, yelps, barks, sniffs, snorts, and coughs. Coprolalia, a complex vocal tic involving the uttering of obscenities, is present in a few individuals (less than 10%) with this disorder. Complex motor tics involving touching, squatting, deep knee bends, retracing steps, and twirling when walking may be present. In approximately one-half the individuals with this disorder, the first symptoms to appear are bouts of a single tic, most frequently eye blinking, less frequently tics involving another part of the face or the body. Initial symptoms can also include tongue protrusion, squatting, sniffing, hopping, skipping, throat clearing, stuttering, uttering sounds or words, and coprolalia. The other cases begin with multiple symptoms.

Associated Features and Disorders

The most common associated symptoms of Tourette's Disorder are obsessions and compulsions. Hyperactivity, distractibility, and impulsivity are also relatively common. Social discomfort, shame, self-consciousness, and depressed mood frequently occur. Social, academic, and occupational functioning may be impaired because of rejection by others or anxiety about having tics in social situations. In severe cases of Tourette's Disorder, the tics may directly interfere with daily activities (e.g., reading or writing). Rare complications of Tourette's Disorder include physical injury, such as blindness due to retinal detachment (from head banging or striking oneself), orthopedic problems (from knee bending, neck jerking, or head turning), and skin problems (from picking). The severity of the tics may be exacerbated by administration of central nervous system stimulants, which may be a dose-related phenomenon. Obsessive-Compulsive Disorder, Attention-Deficit/Hyperactivity Disorder, and Learning Disorders may be associated with Tourette's Disorder.

Specific Culture and Gender Features

Tourette's Disorder has been widely reported in diverse racial and ethnic groups. The disorder is approximately 1.5–3 times more common in males than in females.

Prevalence

Tourette's Disorder occurs in approximately 4–5 individuals per 10,000.

Course

The age at onset of Tourette's Disorder may be as early as age 2 years, is usually during childhood or early adolescence, and is by definition before age 18 years. The median age at onset for motor tics is 7 years. The duration of the disorder is usually lifelong, though periods of remission lasting from weeks to years may occur. In most cases, the severity, frequency, and variability of the symptoms diminish during adolescence and adulthood. In other cases, the symptoms disappear entirely, usually by early adulthood.

Familial Pattern

The vulnerability to Tourette's Disorder and related disorders is transmitted in an autosomal dominant pattern. "Vulnerability" implies that the child receives the genetic or constitutional basis for developing a Tic Disorder; the precise type or severity of disorder may be different from one generation to another. Not everyone who inherits the genetic vulnerability will express symptoms of a Tic Disorder. Penetrance in female gene carriers is about 70%; penetrance in male gene carriers is about 99%. The range of forms in which the vulnerability may be expressed includes full-blown Tourette's Disorder, Chronic Motor or Vocal Tic Disorder, some forms of Obsessive-Compulsive Disorder, and, perhaps, Attention-Deficit/Hyperactivity Disorder. In about 10% of those with Tourette's Disorder, there is no evidence of a familial pattern. Individuals with these "nongenetic" forms of Tourette's Disorder or another tic disorder often have another mental disorder (e.g., Pervasive Developmental Disorder) or a general medical condition (e.g., a seizure disorder).

Differential Diagnosis

Refer to the "Differential Diagnosis" section for Tic Disorders (p. 100).

■ Diagnostic criteria for 307.23 Tourette's Disorder

A. Both multiple motor and one or more vocal tics have been present at some time during the illness, although not necessarily concurrently. (A *tic* is a sudden, rapid, recurrent, nonrhythmic, stereotyped motor movement or vocalization.)

B. The tics occur many times a day (usually in bouts) nearly every day or intermittently throughout a period of more than 1 year, and during this period there was never a tic-free period of more than 3 consecutive months.

C. The disturbance causes marked distress or significant impairment in social, occupational, or other important areas of functioning.

D. The onset is before age 18 years.

E. The disturbance is not due to the direct physiological effects of a substance (e.g., stimulants) or a general medical condition (e.g., Huntington's disease or postviral encephalitis).

307.22   Chronic Motor or Vocal Tic Disorder

Diagnostic Features

The essential feature of Chronic Motor or Vocal Tic Disorder is the presence of either motor tics *or* vocal tics, but *not both* (Criterion A). This differs from Tourette's Disorder in which there must be both multiple motor and one or more vocal tics. The other essential features (Criteria B, C, D, and E) are the same as for Tourette's Disorder. A diagnosis of Chronic Motor or Vocal Tic Disorder cannot be made if the criteria for Tourette's Disorder have ever been met (Criterion F). The other characteristics of Chronic Motor or Vocal Tic Disorder are generally the same as for Tourette's Disorder (see p. 101), except that the severity of the symptoms and the functional impairment are usually much less. It appears that Chronic Motor or Vocal Tic Disorder and Tourette's Disorder may be genetically related because they often occur in the same families.

Differential Diagnosis

Refer to the "Differential Diagnosis" section for Tic Disorders (p. 100).

■ **Diagnostic criteria for 307.22 Chronic Motor or Vocal Tic Disorder**

A. Single or multiple motor or vocal tics (i.e., sudden, rapid, recurrent, nonrhythmic, stereotyped motor movements or vocalizations), but not both, have been present at some time during the illness.

B. The tics occur many times a day nearly every day or intermittently throughout a period of more than 1 year, and during this period there was never a tic-free period of more than 3 consecutive months.

C. The disturbance causes marked distress or significant impairment in social, occupational, or other important areas of functioning.

D. The onset is before age 18 years.

E. The disturbance is not due to the direct physiological effects of a substance (e.g., stimulants) or a general medical condition (e.g., Huntington's disease or postviral encephalitis).

F. Criteria have never been met for Tourette's Disorder.

307.21   Transient Tic Disorder

Diagnostic Features

The essential feature of Transient Tic Disorder is the presence of single or multiple motor tics and/or vocal tics (Criterion A). The tics occur many times a day, nearly every day for at least 4 weeks, but for no longer than 12 consecutive months (Criterion B). The other essential features (Criteria C, D, and E) are the same as for Tourette's Disorder. Transient Tic Disorder is not diagnosed if the criteria for Tourette's Disorder or Chronic Motor or Vocal Tic Disorder (both of which require a duration of at least 1 year) have ever been met (Criterion F). The other characteristics of the disorder are generally the same as for Tourette's Disorder (see p. 101), except that the severity of the symptoms and the functional impairment are usually much less.

Specifiers

The course of Transient Tic Disorder may be indicated by specifying **Single Episode** or **Recurrent**.

Differential Diagnosis

Refer to the "Differential Diagnosis" section for Tic Disorders (p. 100).

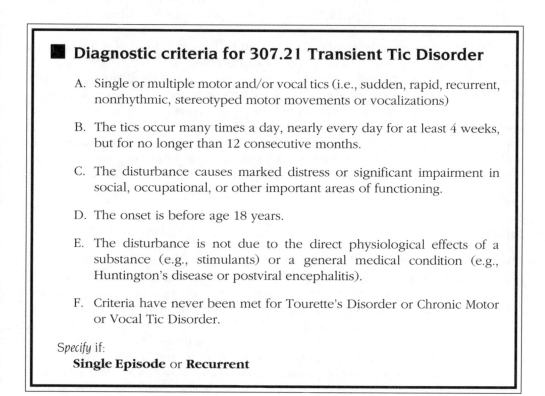

■ **Diagnostic criteria for 307.21 Transient Tic Disorder**

  A. Single or multiple motor and/or vocal tics (i.e., sudden, rapid, recurrent, nonrhythmic, stereotyped motor movements or vocalizations)

  B. The tics occur many times a day, nearly every day for at least 4 weeks, but for no longer than 12 consecutive months.

  C. The disturbance causes marked distress or significant impairment in social, occupational, or other important areas of functioning.

  D. The onset is before age 18 years.

  E. The disturbance is not due to the direct physiological effects of a substance (e.g., stimulants) or a general medical condition (e.g., Huntington's disease or postviral encephalitis).

  F. Criteria have never been met for Tourette's Disorder or Chronic Motor or Vocal Tic Disorder.

Specify if:
  Single Episode or **Recurrent**

307.20 Tic Disorder
Not Otherwise Specified

This category is for disorders characterized by tics that do not meet criteria for a specific Tic Disorder. Examples include tics lasting less than 4 weeks or tics with an onset after age 18 years.

Elimination Disorders

Encopresis

Diagnostic Features

The essential feature of Encopresis is repeated passage of feces into inappropriate places (e.g., clothing or floor) (Criterion A). Most often this is involuntary but occasionally may be intentional. The event must occur at least once a month for at least 3 months (Criterion B), and the chronological age of the child must be at least 4 years (or for children with developmental delays, a mental age of at least 4 years) (Criterion C). The fecal incontinence must not be due exclusively to the direct physiological effects of a substance (e.g., laxatives) or a general medical condition except through a mechanism involving constipation (Criterion D).

When the passage of feces is involuntary rather than intentional, it is often related to constipation, impaction, and retention with subsequent overflow. The constipation may develop for psychological reasons (e.g., anxiety about defecating in a particular place or a more general pattern of anxious or oppositional behavior) leading to avoidance of defecation. Physiological predispositions to constipation include dehydration associated with a febrile illness, hypothyroidism, or a medication side effect. Once constipation has developed, it may be complicated by an anal fissure, painful defecation, and further fecal retention. The consistency of the stool may vary. In some individuals it may be of normal or near-normal consistency. It may be liquid in other individuals who have overflow incontinence secondary to fecal retention.

Subtypes

Encopresis is coded according to the subtype that characterizes the presentation:

787.6 With Constipation and Overflow Incontinence. There is evidence of constipation on physical examination or by history. Feces are characteristically (but not invariably) poorly formed and leakage is continuous, occurring both during the day and during sleep. Only small amounts of feces are passed during toiletting, and the incontinence resolves after treatment of the constipation.

307.7 Without Constipation and Overflow Incontinence. There is no evidence of constipation on physical examination or by history. Feces are likely to be of normal form and consistency, and soiling is intermittent. Feces may be deposited in a prominent location. This is usually associated with the presence of Oppositional Defiant Disorder or Conduct Disorder or may be the consequence of anal masturbation.

Associated Features and Disorders

The child with Encopresis often feels ashamed and may wish to avoid situations (e.g., camp or school) that might lead to embarrassment. The amount of impairment is a function of the effect on the child's self-esteem, the degree of social ostracism by peers, and the anger, punishment, and rejection on the part of caregivers. Smearing feces may be deliberate or accidental resulting from the child's attempt to clean or hide feces that were passed involuntarily. When the incontinence is clearly deliberate, features of Oppositional Defiant Disorder or Conduct Disorder may also be present. Many children with Encopresis also have Enuresis.

Prevalence

It is estimated that approximately 1% of 5-year-olds have Encopresis, and the disorder is more common in males than in females.

Course

Encopresis is not diagnosed until a child has reached a chronological age of at least 4 years (or for children with developmental delays, a mental age of at least 4 years). Inadequate, inconsistent toilet training and psychosocial stress (e.g., entering school or the birth of a sibling) may be predisposing factors. Two types of course have been described: a "primary" type in which the individual has never established fecal continence, and a "secondary" type in which the disturbance develops after a period of established fecal continence. Encopresis can persist with intermittent exacerbations for years but rarely becomes chronic.

Differential Diagnosis

A diagnosis of Encopresis in the presence of a general medical condition is appropriate only if the mechanism involves constipation. Fecal incontinence related to other general medical conditions (e.g., chronic diarrhea) would not warrant a DSM-IV diagnosis of Encopresis.

■ Diagnostic criteria for Encopresis

A. Repeated passage of feces into inappropriate places (e.g., clothing or floor) whether involuntary or intentional.

B. At least one such event a month for at least 3 months.

C. Chronological age is at least 4 years (or equivalent developmental level).

D. The behavior is not due exclusively to the direct physiological effects of a substance (e.g., laxatives) or a general medical condition except through a mechanism involving constipation.

Code as follows:
787.6 With Constipation and Overflow Incontinence
307.7 Without Constipation and Overflow Incontinence

307.6 Enuresis (Not Due to a General Medical Condition)

Diagnostic Features

The essential feature of Enuresis is repeated voiding of urine during the day or at night into bed or clothes (Criterion A). Most often this is involuntary but occasionally may be intentional. To qualify for a diagnosis of Enuresis, the voiding of urine must occur at least twice per week for at least 3 months or else must cause clinically significant distress or impairment in social, academic (occupational), or other important areas of functioning (Criterion B). The individual must have reached an age at which continence is expected (i.e., the chronological age of the child must be at least 5 years, or, for children with developmental delays, a mental age of at least 5 years) (Criterion C). The urinary incontinence is not due exclusively to the direct physiological effects of a substance (e.g., diuretics) or a general medical condition (e.g., diabetes, spina bifida, a seizure disorder) (Criterion D).

Subtypes

The situation in which the Enuresis occurs may be noted by one of the following subtypes:

Nocturnal Only. This is the most common subtype and is defined as passage of urine only during nighttime sleep. The enuretic event typically occurs during the first one-third of the night. Occasionally the voiding takes place during the rapid eye movement (REM) stage of sleep, and the child may recall a dream that involved the act of urinating.

Diurnal Only. This subtype is defined as the passage of urine during waking hours. Diurnal Enuresis is more common in females than in males and is uncommon after age 9 years. The enuretic event most commonly occurs in the early afternoon on school days. Diurnal enuresis is sometimes due to a reluctance to use the toilet because of social anxiety or a preoccupation with school or play activity.

Nocturnal and Diurnal. This subtype is defined as a combination of the two subtypes above.

Associated Features and Disorders

The amount of impairment associated with Enuresis is a function of the limitation on the child's social activities (e.g., ineligibility for sleep-away camp) or its effect on the child's self-esteem, the degree of social ostracism by peers, and the anger, punishment, and rejection on the part of caregivers. Although most children with Enuresis do not have a coexisting mental disorder, the prevalence of coexisting mental and other developmental disorders is higher than in the general population. Encopresis, Sleep-walking Disorder, and Sleep Terror Disorder may be present. Urinary tract infections are more common in children with Enuresis, especially the Diurnal Type, than in those who are continent. The Enuresis commonly persists after appropriate treatment of an associated infection. A number of predisposing factors have been suggested, including delayed or lax toilet training, psychosocial stress, a dysfunction in the ability to concentrate urine, and a lower bladder volume threshold for involuntary voiding.

Prevalence

The prevalence of Enuresis at age 5 years is 7% for males and 3% for females; at age 10 years the prevalence is 3% for males and 2% for females. At age 18 years, the prevalence is 1% for males and less among females.

Course

Two types of course of Enuresis have been described: a "primary" type in which the individual has never established urinary continence, and a "secondary" type in which the disturbance develops after a period of established urinary continence. By definition, primary Enuresis begins at age 5 years. The most common time for the onset of secondary Enuresis is between the ages of 5 and 8 years, but it may occur at any time. After age 5 years, the rate of spontaneous remission is between 5% and 10% per year. Most children with the disorder become continent by adolescence, but in approximately 1% of cases the disorder continues into adulthood.

Familial Pattern

Approximately 75% of all children with Enuresis have a first-degree biological relative who has had the disorder. The concordance for the disorder is greater in monozygotic than in dizygotic twins.

Differential Diagnosis

The diagnosis of Enuresis is not made in the presence of a **neurogenic bladder** or the presence of a **general medical condition that causes polyuria or urgency** (e.g., untreated diabetes mellitus or diabetes insipidus) or during an **acute urinary tract infection.** However, a diagnosis of Enuresis is compatible with such conditions if urinary incontinence was regularly present prior to the development of the general medical condition or if it persists after the institution of appropriate treatment.

■ **Diagnostic criteria for 307.6 Enuresis**

A. Repeated voiding of urine into bed or clothes (whether involuntary or intentional).

B. The behavior is clinically significant as manifested by either a frequency of twice a week for at least 3 consecutive months or the presence of clinically significant distress or impairment in social, academic (occupational), or other important areas of functioning.

C. Chronological age is at least 5 years (or equivalent developmental level).

(continued)

☐ **Diagnostic criteria for 307.6 Enuresis** (*continued*)

    D. The behavior is not due exclusively to the direct physiological effect of a substance (e.g., a diuretic) or a general medical condition (e.g., diabetes, spina bifida, a seizure disorder).

Specify type:
    Nocturnal Only
    Diurnal Only
    Nocturnal and Diurnal

Other Disorders of Infancy, Childhood, or Adolescence

309.21 Separation Anxiety Disorder

Diagnostic Features

The essential feature of Separation Anxiety Disorder is excessive anxiety concerning separation from the home or from those to whom the person is attached (Criterion A). This anxiety is beyond that which is expected for the individual's developmental level. The disturbance must last for a period of at least 4 weeks (Criterion B), begin before age 18 years (Criterion C), and cause clinically significant distress or impairment in social, academic (occupational), or other important areas of functioning (Criterion D). The diagnosis is not made if the anxiety occurs exclusively during the course of a Pervasive Developmental Disorder, Schizophrenia, or other Psychotic Disorder or, in adolescents or adults, if it is better accounted for by Panic Disorder With Agoraphobia (Criterion E).

Individuals with this disorder may experience recurrent excessive distress on separation from home or major attachment figures (Criterion A1). When separated from attachment figures, they often need to know their whereabouts and need to stay in touch with them (e.g., by telephone calls). Some individuals become extremely homesick and uncomfortable to the point of misery when away from home. They may yearn to return home and be preoccupied with reunion fantasies. When separated from major attachment figures, these individuals are often preoccupied with fears that accidents or illness will befall the attachment figures or themselves (Criterion A2). Children with this disorder often express fear of being lost and never being reunited with their parents (Criterion A3). They are often uncomfortable when traveling independently away from the house or from other familiar areas and may avoid going places by themselves. They may be reluctant or refuse to attend school or camp, to visit or sleep at friends' homes, or to go on errands (Criterion A4). These children may be unable to stay in a room by themselves and may display "clinging" behavior, staying close to and "shadowing" the parent around the house (Criterion A5).

Children with this disorder often have difficulty at bedtime and may insist that someone stay with them until they fall asleep (Criterion A6). During the night, they may make their way to their parents' bed (or that of another significant person, such as a sibling); if entry to the parental bedroom is barred, they may sleep outside the parents' door. There may be nightmares whose content expresses the individual's fears (e.g., destruction of the family through fire, murder, or other catastrophe) (Criterion A7). Physical complaints, such as stomachaches, headaches, nausea, and vomiting are common when separation occurs or is anticipated (Criterion A8). Cardiovascular symptoms such as palpitations, dizziness, and feeling faint are rare in younger children but may occur in older individuals.

Specifier

Early Onset.   This specifier may be used to indicate onset of the disorder before age 6 years.

Associated Features and Mental Disorders

Children with Separation Anxiety Disorder tend to come from families that are close-knit. When separated from home or major attachment figures, they may recurrently exhibit social withdrawal, apathy, sadness, or difficulty concentrating on work or play. Depending on their age, individuals may have fears of animals, monsters, the dark, muggers, burglars, kidnappers, car accidents, plane travel, and other situations that are perceived as presenting danger to the integrity of the family or themselves. Concerns about death and dying are common. School refusal may lead to academic difficulties and social avoidance. Children may complain that no one loves them or cares about them and that they wish they were dead. When extremely upset at the prospect of separation, they may show anger or occasionally hit out at someone who is forcing separation. When alone, especially in the evening, young children may report unusual perceptual experiences (e.g., seeing people peering into their room, scary creatures reaching for them, feeling eyes staring at them). Children with this disorder are often described as demanding, intrusive, and in need of constant attention. The child's excessive demands often become a source of parental frustration, leading to resentment and conflict in the family. Sometimes, children with the disorder are described as unusually conscientious, compliant, and eager to please. The children may have somatic complaints that result in physical examinations and medical procedures. Depressed mood is frequently present and may become more persistent over time, justifying an additional diagnosis of Dysthymic Disorder or Major Depressive Disorder. The disorder may precede the development of Panic Disorder With Agoraphobia.

Specific Culture, Age, and Gender Features

There are cultural variations in the degree to which it is considered desirable to tolerate separation. It is important to differentiate Separation Anxiety Disorder from the high value some cultures place on strong interdependence among family members.

The manifestations of the disorder may vary with age. Younger children may not express specific fears of definite threats to parents, home, or themselves. As children get older, worries or fears are often of specific dangers (e.g., kidnapping, mugging). Anxiety and anticipation of separation become manifest in mid-childhood. Although adolescents with this disorder, especially males, may deny anxiety about separation, it may be reflected in their limited independent activity and reluctance to leave home. In older individuals, the disorder may limit the person's ability to handle changes in circumstances (e.g., moving, getting married). Adults with the disorder are typically overconcerned about their offspring and spouses and experience marked discomfort when separated from them. In clinical samples, the disorder is apparently equally common in males and females. In epidemiological samples, the disorder is more frequent in females.

Prevalence

Separation Anxiety Disorder is not uncommon; prevalence estimates average about 4% in children and young adolescents.

Course

Separation Anxiety Disorder may develop after some life stress (e.g., the death of a relative or pet, an illness of the child or a relative, a change of schools, a move to a new neighborhood, or immigration). Onset may be as early as preschool age and may occur at any time before age 18 years, but onset as late as adolescence is uncommon. Typically there are periods of exacerbation and remission. Both the anxiety about possible separation and the avoidance of situations involving separation (e.g., going away to college) may persist for many years.

Familial Pattern

Separation Anxiety Disorder is apparently more common in first-degree biological relatives than in the general population and may be more frequent in children of mothers with Panic Disorder.

Differential Diagnosis

Separation anxiety can be an associated feature of **Pervasive Developmental Disorders, Schizophrenia,** or **other Psychotic Disorders.** If the symptoms of Separation Anxiety Disorder occur exclusively during the course of one of these disorders, a separate diagnosis of Separation Anxiety Disorder is not given. Separation Anxiety Disorder is distinguished from **Generalized Anxiety Disorder** in that the anxiety predominantly concerns separation from home and attachment figures. In children or adolescents with Separation Anxiety Disorder, threats of separation may lead to extreme anxiety and even a Panic Attack. In contrast to Panic Disorder, the anxiety concerns separation from attachment figures or from home rather than being incapacitated by an unexpected Panic Attack. In adults, Separation Anxiety Disorder is rare and should not be given as an additional diagnosis if the separation fears are better accounted for by Agoraphobia in **Panic Disorder With Agoraphobia** or **Agoraphobia Without History of Panic Disorder.** Truancy is common in **Conduct Disorder,** but anxiety about separation is not responsible for school absences and the child usually stays away from, rather than returns to, the home. Some cases of school refusal, especially in adolescence, are due to Social Phobia or Mood Disorders rather than separation anxiety. Unlike the hallucinations in **Psychotic Disorders,** the unusual perceptual experiences in Separation Anxiety Disorder are usually based on a misperception of an actual stimulus, occur only in certain situations (e.g., nighttime), and are reversed by the presence of an attachment figure. Clinical judgment must be used in distinguishing **developmentally appropriate levels of separation anxiety** from the clinically significant concerns about separation seen in Separation Anxiety Disorder.

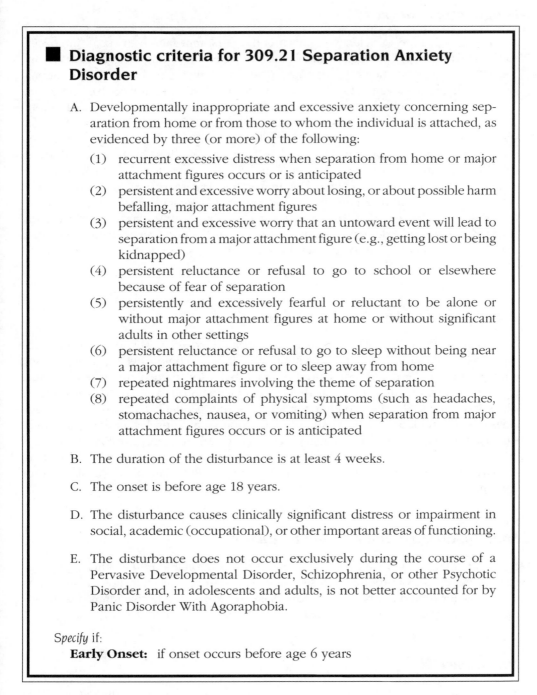

■ **Diagnostic criteria for 309.21 Separation Anxiety Disorder**

A. Developmentally inappropriate and excessive anxiety concerning separation from home or from those to whom the individual is attached, as evidenced by three (or more) of the following:

   (1) recurrent excessive distress when separation from home or major attachment figures occurs or is anticipated
   (2) persistent and excessive worry about losing, or about possible harm befalling, major attachment figures
   (3) persistent and excessive worry that an untoward event will lead to separation from a major attachment figure (e.g., getting lost or being kidnapped)
   (4) persistent reluctance or refusal to go to school or elsewhere because of fear of separation
   (5) persistently and excessively fearful or reluctant to be alone or without major attachment figures at home or without significant adults in other settings
   (6) persistent reluctance or refusal to go to sleep without being near a major attachment figure or to sleep away from home
   (7) repeated nightmares involving the theme of separation
   (8) repeated complaints of physical symptoms (such as headaches, stomachaches, nausea, or vomiting) when separation from major attachment figures occurs or is anticipated

B. The duration of the disturbance is at least 4 weeks.

C. The onset is before age 18 years.

D. The disturbance causes clinically significant distress or impairment in social, academic (occupational), or other important areas of functioning.

E. The disturbance does not occur exclusively during the course of a Pervasive Developmental Disorder, Schizophrenia, or other Psychotic Disorder and, in adolescents and adults, is not better accounted for by Panic Disorder With Agoraphobia.

Specify if:
   Early Onset: if onset occurs before age 6 years

313.23   Selective Mutism
(*formerly* Elective Mutism)

Diagnostic Features

The essential feature of Selective Mutism is the persistent failure to speak in specific social situations (e.g., school, with playmates) where speaking is expected, despite speaking in other situations (Criterion A). The disturbance interferes with educational or occupational achievement or with social communication (Criterion B). The disturbance must last for at least 1 month and is not limited to the first month of school (during which many children may be shy and reluctant to speak) (Criterion C). Selective Mutism should not be diagnosed if the individual's failure to speak is due solely to a lack of knowledge of, or comfort with, the spoken language required in the social situation (Criterion D). It is also not diagnosed if the disturbance is better accounted for by embarrassment related to having a Communication Disorder (e.g., Stuttering) or if it occurs exclusively during a Pervasive Developmental Disorder, Schizophrenia, or other Psychotic Disorder (Criterion E). Instead of communicating by standard verbalization, children with this disorder may communicate by gestures, nodding or shaking the head, or pulling or pushing, or, in some cases, by monosyllabic, short, or monotone utterances, or in an altered voice.

Associated Features and Disorders

Associated features of Selective Mutism may include excessive shyness, fear of social embarrassment, social isolation and withdrawal, clinging, compulsive traits, negativism, temper tantrums, or controlling or oppositional behavior, particularly at home. There may be severe impairment in social and school functioning. Teasing or scapegoating by peers is common. Although children with this disorder generally have normal language skills, there may occasionally be an associated Communication Disorder (e.g., Phonological Disorder, Expressive Language Disorder, or Mixed Receptive-Expressive Language Disorder) or a general medical condition that causes abnormalities of articulation. Anxiety Disorders (especially Social Phobia), Mental Retardation, hospitalization, or extreme psychosocial stressors may be associated with the disorder.

Specific Culture and Gender Features

Immigrant children who are unfamiliar with or uncomfortable in the official language of their new host country may refuse to speak to strangers in their new environment. This behavior should not be diagnosed as Selective Mutism. Selective Mutism is slightly more common in females than in males.

Prevalence

Selective Mutism is apparently rare and is found in fewer than 1% of individuals seen in mental health settings.

Course

Onset of Selective Mutism is usually before age 5 years, but the disturbance may not come to clinical attention until entry into school. Although the disturbance usually lasts for only a few months, it may sometimes persist longer and may even continue for several years.

Differential Diagnosis

Selective Mutism should be distinguished from speech disturbances that are better accounted for by a **Communication Disorder,** such as **Phonological Disorder, Expressive Language Disorder, Mixed Receptive-Expressive Language Disorder,** or **Stuttering.** Unlike Selective Mutism, the speech disturbance in these conditions is not restricted to a specific social situation. Children in families who have immigrated to a country where a different language is spoken may refuse to speak the new language because of **lack of knowledge of the language.** If comprehension of the new language is adequate, but refusal to speak persists, a diagnosis of Selective Mutism may be warranted. Individuals with a **Pervasive Developmental Disorder, Schizophrenia** or **other Psychotic Disorder,** or **severe Mental Retardation** may have problems in social communication and be unable to speak appropriately in social situations. In contrast, Selective Mutism should only be diagnosed in a child who has an established capacity to speak in some social situations (e.g., typically at home). The social anxiety and social avoidance in **Social Phobia** may be associated with Selective Mutism. In such cases, both diagnoses may be given.

■ Diagnostic criteria for 313.23 Selective Mutism

A. Consistent failure to speak in specific social situations (in which there is an expectation for speaking, e.g., at school) despite speaking in other situations.

B. The disturbance interferes with educational or occupational achievement or with social communication.

C. The duration of the disturbance is at least 1 month (not limited to the first month of school).

D. The failure to speak is not due to a lack of knowledge of, or comfort with, the spoken language required in the social situation.

E. The disturbance is not better accounted for by a Communication Disorder (e.g., Stuttering) and does not occur exclusively during the course of a Pervasive Developmental Disorder, Schizophrenia, or other Psychotic Disorder.

313.89   Reactive Attachment Disorder of Infancy or Early Childhood

Diagnostic Features

The essential feature of Reactive Attachment Disorder is markedly disturbed and developmentally inappropriate social relatedness in most contexts that begins before age 5 years and is associated with grossly pathological care (Criterion A). There are two types of presentations. In the Inhibited Type, the child persistently fails to initiate and to respond to most social interactions in a developmentally appropriate way. The child shows a pattern of excessively inhibited, hypervigilant, or highly ambivalent responses (e.g., frozen watchfulness, resistance to comfort, or a mixture of approach and avoidance) (Criterion A1). In the Disinhibited Type, there is a pattern of diffuse attachments. The child exhibits indiscriminate sociability or a lack of selectivity in the choice of attachment figures (Criterion A2). The disturbance is not accounted for solely by developmental delay (e.g., as in Mental Retardation) and does not meet criteria for Pervasive Developmental Disorder (Criterion B). By definition, the condition is associated with grossly pathological care that may take the form of persistent disregard of the child's basic emotional needs for comfort, stimulation, and affection (Criterion C1); persistent disregard of the child's basic physical needs (Criterion C2); or repeated changes of primary caregiver that prevent formation of stable attachments (e.g., frequent changes in foster care) (Criterion C3). The pathological care is presumed to be responsible for the disturbed social relatedness (Criterion D).

Subtypes

The predominant type of disturbance in social relatedness may be indicated by specifying one of the following subtypes for Reactive Attachment Disorder:

Inhibited Type.   In this subtype, the predominant disturbance in social relatedness is the persistent failure to initiate and to respond to most social interactions in a developmentally appropriate way.

Disinhibited Type.   This subtype is used if the predominant disturbance in social relatedness is indiscriminate sociability or a lack of selectivity in the choice of attachment figures.

Associated Features and Disorders

Associated descriptive features and mental disorders.   Certain situations (e.g., prolonged hospitalization of the child, extreme poverty, or parental inexperience) may predispose to the development of pathological care. However, grossly pathological care does not always result in the development of Reactive Attachment Disorder; some children may form stable attachments and social relationships even in the face of marked neglect or abuse. Reactive Attachment Disorder may be associated with developmental delays, Feeding Disorder of Infancy or Early Childhood, Pica, or Rumination Disorder.

Associated laboratory findings.   Laboratory findings consistent with malnutrition may be present.

Associated physical examination findings and general medical conditions.
Physical examination may document associated general medical conditions that might
contribute to, or result from, difficulties in caring for the child (e.g., growth delay,
evidence of physical abuse).

Prevalence

Epidemiological data are limited, but Reactive Attachment Disorder appears to be very
uncommon.

Course

The onset of Reactive Attachment Disorder is usually in the first several years of life and,
by definition, begins before age 5 years. The course appears to vary depending on
individual factors in child and caregivers, the severity and duration of associated
psychosocial deprivation, and the nature of intervention. Considerable improvement or
remission may occur if an appropriately supportive environment is provided. Otherwise,
the disorder follows a continuous course.

Differential Diagnosis

In **Mental Retardation,** appropriate attachments to caregivers usually develop consistent with the child's general developmental level. However, some infants and young
children with Severe Mental Retardation may present particular problems for caregivers
and exhibit symptoms characteristic of Reactive Attachment Disorder. Reactive Attachment Disorder should be diagnosed only if it is clear that the characteristic problems in
formation of selective attachments are not a function of the retardation.

Reactive Attachment Disorder must be differentiated from **Autistic Disorder** and
other Pervasive Developmental Disorders. In the Pervasive Developmental Disorders, selective attachments either fail to develop or are highly deviant, but this usually
occurs in the face of a reasonably supportive psychosocial environment. Autistic Disorder
and other Pervasive Developmental Disorders are also characterized by the presence of
a qualitative impairment in communication and restricted, repetitive, and stereotyped
patterns of behavior. Reactive Attachment Disorder is not diagnosed if the criteria are
met for a Pervasive Developmental Disorder. The Disinhibited Type must be distinguished from the impulsive or hyperactive behavior characteristic of **Attention-Deficit/
Hyperactivity Disorder.** In contrast to Attention-Deficit/Hyperactivity Disorder, the
disinhibited behavior in Reactive Attachment Disorder is characteristically associated
with attempting to form a social attachment after a very brief acquaintance.

Grossly pathogenic care is a defining feature of Reactive Attachment Disorder. An
additional notation of Child Abuse, Child Neglect, or a Parent-Child Relational Problem
may be warranted. When grossly pathogenic care does not result in marked disturbances
in social relatedness, Child Neglect or Parent-Child Relational Problem may be noted
rather than Reactive Attachment Disorder.

■ **Diagnostic criteria for 313.89 Reactive Attachment Disorder of Infancy or Early Childhood**

A. Markedly disturbed and developmentally inappropriate social related-ness in most contexts, beginning before age 5 years, as evidenced by either (1) or (2):

    (1) persistent failure to initiate or respond in a developmentally appropriate fashion to most social interactions, as manifest by excessively inhibited, hypervigilant, or highly ambivalent and contradictory responses (e.g., the child may respond to caregivers with a mixture of approach, avoidance, and resistance to comfort-ing, or may exhibit frozen watchfulness)

    (2) diffuse attachments as manifest by indiscriminate sociability with marked inability to exhibit appropriate selective attachments (e.g., excessive familiarity with relative strangers or lack of selectivity in choice of attachment figures)

B. The disturbance in Criterion A is not accounted for solely by develop-mental delay (as in Mental Retardation) and does not meet criteria for a Pervasive Developmental Disorder.

C. Pathogenic care as evidenced by at least one of the following:

    (1) persistent disregard of the child's basic emotional needs for com-fort, stimulation, and affection

    (2) persistent disregard of the child's basic physical needs

    (3) repeated changes of primary caregiver that prevent formation of stable attachments (e.g., frequent changes in foster care)

D. There is a presumption that the care in Criterion C is responsible for the disturbed behavior in Criterion A (e.g., the disturbances in Criterion A began following the pathogenic care in Criterion C).

Specify type:
    Inhibited Type: if Criterion A1 predominates in the clinical presentation
    Disinhibited Type: if Criterion A2 predominates in the clinical presentation

307.3   Stereotypic Movement Disorder
(*formerly* Stereotypy/Habit Disorder)

Diagnostic Features

The essential feature of Stereotypic Movement Disorder is motor behavior that is repetitive, often seemingly driven, and nonfunctional (Criterion A). This motor behavior markedly interferes with normal activities or results in self-inflicted bodily injury that is significant enough to require medical treatment (or would result in such injury if protective measures were not used) (Criterion B). If Mental Retardation is present, the stereotypic or self-injurious behavior is sufficiently severe to become a focus of treatment (Criterion C). The behavior is not better accounted for by a compulsion (as in Obsessive-Compulsive Disorder), a tic (as in the Tic Disorders), a stereotypy that is part of a Pervasive Developmental Disorder, or hair pulling (as in Trichotillomania) (Criterion D). The behavior is also not due to the direct physiological effects of a substance or a general medical condition (Criterion E). The motor behaviors must persist for at least 4 weeks (Criterion F).

The stereotypic movements may include hand waving, rocking, playing with hands, fiddling with fingers, twirling objects, head banging, self-biting, picking at skin or bodily orifices, or hitting various parts of one's own body. Sometimes the individual uses an object in performing these behaviors. The behaviors may cause permanent and disabling tissue damage and may sometimes be life-threatening. For instance, severe head banging or hitting may lead to cuts, bleeding, infection, retinal detachment, and blindness.

Specifiers

The clinician may specify **With Self-Injurious Behavior** if the behavior results in bodily damage that requires specific treatment (or that would result in bodily damage if protective measures were not used).

Associated Features and Disorders

Associated descriptive features and mental disorders.   The individual may develop methods of self-restraint (e.g., holding hands inside shirts, trousers, or in pockets) to attempt to control the self-injurious behaviors. When the self-restraint is interfered with, the behaviors return. If the behaviors are extreme or repulsive to others, there may be psychosocial complications due to the individual's exclusion from social and community activities. Stereotypic Movement Disorder occurs most commonly in association with Mental Retardation. The more severe the retardation, the higher the risk for self-injurious behaviors. This disorder may also occur in association with severe sensory deficits (blindness and deafness) and may be more common in institutional environments in which the individual receives insufficient stimulation. Self-injurious behaviors occur in certain general medical conditions associated with Mental Retardation (e.g., fragile X syndrome, de Lange syndrome, and especially Lesch-Nyhan syndrome, which is characterized by severe self-biting).

Associated laboratory findings.   If there is self-injury, the laboratory findings will reflect its nature and severity (e.g., anemia may be present if there is a chronic blood loss from self-inflicted rectal bleeding).

Associated physical examination findings and general medical conditions. Signs of chronic tissue damage may be present (e.g., bruises, bite marks, cuts, scratches, skin infections, rectal fissures, foreign bodies in bodily orifices, visual impairment due to eye gouging or traumatic cataract, and fractures or deformed bones). In less severe cases, there may be a chronic skin irritation or calluses from biting, pinching, scratching, or saliva smearing.

Specific Age and Gender Features

Self-injurious behaviors occur in individuals of all ages. There are indications that head banging is more prevalent in males (with about a 3:1 ratio), and self-biting may be more prevalent in females.

Prevalence

There is limited information on the prevalence of Stereotypic Movement Disorder. The estimates of prevalence of self-injurious behaviors in individuals with Mental Retardation vary from 2% and 3% in children and adolescents living in the community to approximately 25% in adults with severe or profound Mental Retardation living in institutions.

Course

There is no typical age at onset or pattern of onset for Stereotypic Movement Disorder. The onset may follow a stressful environmental event. In nonverbal individuals with Severe Mental Retardation, stereotypic movements may be triggered by a painful general medical condition (e.g., a middle ear infection leading to head banging). The stereotypic movements often peak in adolescence and then may gradually decline. However, especially in individuals with Severe or Profound Mental Retardation, the movements may persist for years. The focus of these behaviors often changes (e.g., a person may engage in hand biting that may then subside and head hitting may emerge).

Differential Diagnosis

Stereotypic movements may be associated with **Mental Retardation,** especially for individuals in nonstimulating environments. Stereotypic Movement Disorder should be diagnosed only in individuals in whom the stereotypic or self-injurious behavior is of sufficient severity to become a focus of treatment. Repetitive stereotyped movements are a characteristic feature of **Pervasive Developmental Disorders.** Stereotypic Movement Disorder is not diagnosed if the stereotypies are better accounted for by a Pervasive Developmental Disorder. Compulsions in **Obsessive-Compulsive Disorder** are generally more complex and ritualistic and are performed in response to an obsession or according to rules that must be applied rigidly. Differentiating the complex movements characteristic of Stereotypic Movement Disorder from **simple tics** (e.g., eye blinking) is relatively straightforward, but the differential diagnosis with **complex motor tics** is less clear-cut. In general, stereotyped movements appear to be more driven and intentional, whereas tics have a more involuntary quality and are not rhythmic. In **Trichotillomania,** by definition, the repetitive behavior is limited to hair pulling. The self-induced injuries in Stereotypic Movement Disorder should be distinguished from **Factitious Disorder With Predominantly Physical Signs and Symptoms,** in which the motivation of the self-injury is to assume the sick role. **Self-mutilation associated with certain Psychotic Disorders and Personality Disorders** is premeditated, complex, and sporadic and has a meaning for the individual within the context of the underlying, severe mental disorder (e.g., is the result of delusional thinking). **Involuntary movements associated with neurological conditions** (such as Huntington's disease) usually follow a typical pattern, and the signs and symptoms of the neurological condition are present.

Developmentally appropriate self-stimulatory behaviors in young children (e.g., thumb sucking, rocking, and head banging) are usually self-limited and rarely result in tissue damage requiring treatment. **Self-stimulatory behaviors in individuals with sensory deficits** (e.g., blindness) usually do not result in dysfunction or in self-injury.

■ Diagnostic criteria for 307.3 Stereotypic Movement Disorder

A. Repetitive, seemingly driven, and nonfunctional motor behavior (e.g., hand shaking or waving, body rocking, head banging, mouthing of objects, self-biting, picking at skin or bodily orifices, hitting own body).

B. The behavior markedly interferes with normal activities or results in self-inflicted bodily injury that requires medical treatment (or would result in an injury if preventive measures were not used).

C. If Mental Retardation is present, the stereotypic or self-injurious behavior is of sufficient severity to become a focus of treatment.

D. The behavior is not better accounted for by a compulsion (as in Obsessive-Compulsive Disorder), a tic (as in Tic Disorder), a stereotypy that is part of a Pervasive Developmental Disorder, or hair pulling (as in Trichotillomania).

E. The behavior is not due to the direct physiological effects of a substance or a general medical condition.

F. The behavior persists for 4 weeks or longer.

Specify if:
  With Self-Injurious Behavior: if the behavior results in bodily damage that requires specific treatment (or that would result in bodily damage if protective measures were not used)

313.9   Disorder of Infancy, Childhood, or Adolescence Not Otherwise Specified

This category is a residual category for disorders with onset in infancy, childhood, or adolescence that do not meet criteria for any specific disorder in the Classification.

Delirium, Dementia, and Amnestic and Other Cognitive Disorders

This section includes Delirium, Dementia, Amnestic Disorders, and Cognitive Disorder Not Otherwise Specified. The predominant disturbance is a clinically significant deficit in cognition or memory that represents a significant change from a previous level of functioning. For each disorder in this section, the etiology is either a general medical condition (although the specific general medical condition may not be identifiable) or a substance (i.e., a drug of abuse, medication, or toxin), or a combination of these factors.

In DSM-III-R, these disorders were placed in a section titled "Organic Mental Syndromes and Disorders." The term *organic mental disorder* is no longer used in DSM-IV because it incorrectly implies that "nonorganic" mental disorders do not have a biological basis. In DSM-IV, disorders formerly called "organic mental disorders" have been grouped into three sections: 1) Delirium, Dementia, and Amnestic and Other Cognitive Disorders; 2) Mental Disorders Due to a General Medical Condition; and 3) Substance-Related Disorders.

A **delirium** is characterized by a disturbance of consciousness and a change in cognition that develop over a short period of time. The disorders included in the "Delirium" section are listed according to presumed etiology: Delirium Due to a General Medical Condition, Substance-Induced Delirium (i.e., due to a drug of abuse, a medication, or toxin exposure), Delirium Due to Multiple Etiologies, or Delirium Not Otherwise Specified (if the etiology is indeterminate).

A **dementia** is characterized by multiple cognitive deficits that include impairment in memory. The dementias are also listed according to presumed etiology: Dementia of the Alzheimer's Type, Vascular Dementia, Dementia Due to Other General Medical Conditions (e.g., human immunodeficiency virus [HIV] disease, head trauma, Parkinson's disease, Huntington's disease), Substance-Induced Persisting Dementia (i.e., due to a drug of abuse, a medication, or toxin exposure), Dementia Due to Multiple Etiologies, or Dementia Not Otherwise Specified (if the etiology is indeterminate).

An **amnestic disorder** is characterized by memory impairment in the absence of other significant cognitive impairments. The disorders in the "Amnestic Disorders" section also are listed according to presumed etiology: Amnestic Disorder Due to a

General Medical Condition, Substance-Induced Persisting Amnestic Disorder, or Amnestic Disorder Not Otherwise Specified.

Cognitive Disorder Not Otherwise Specified is for presentations that are characterized by cognitive dysfunction presumed to be due to either a general medical condition or substance use that do not meet criteria for any of the disorders listed elsewhere in this section.

Introductory text is provided that discusses the general features for each group of disorders, regardless of etiology. This is followed by text and criteria for each disorder with specific etiology.

Delirium

The disorders in the "Delirium" section share a common symptom presentation of a disturbance in consciousness and cognition, but are differentiated based on etiology: **Delirium Due to a General Medical Condition, Substance-Induced Delirium** (including medication side effects), and **Delirium Due to Multiple Etiologies.** In addition, **Delirium Not Otherwise Specified** is included in this section for presentations in which the clinician is unable to determine a specific etiology for the delirium.

Diagnostic Features

The essential feature of a delirium is a disturbance of consciousness that is accompanied by a change in cognition that cannot be better accounted for by a preexisting or evolving dementia. The disturbance develops over a short period of time, usually hours to days, and tends to fluctuate during the course of the day. There is evidence from the history, physical examination, or laboratory tests that the delirium is a direct physiological consequence of a general medical condition, Substance Intoxication or Withdrawal, use of a medication, or toxin exposure, or a combination of these factors.

The disturbance in consciousness is manifested by a reduced clarity of awareness of the environment. The ability to focus, sustain, or shift attention is impaired (Criterion A). Questions must be repeated because the individual's attention wanders, or the individual may perseverate with an answer to a previous question rather than appropriately shift attention. The person is easily distracted by irrelevant stimuli. Because of these problems, it may be difficult (or impossible) to engage the person in conversation.

There is an accompanying change in cognition (which may include memory impairment, disorientation, or language disturbance) or development of a perceptual disturbance (Criterion B). Memory impairment is most commonly evident in recent memory and can be tested by asking the person to remember several unrelated objects or a brief sentence, and then to repeat them after a few minutes of distraction. Disorientation is usually manifested by the individual being disoriented to time (e.g., thinking it is morning in the middle of the night) or being disoriented to place (e.g., thinking he or she is home rather than in a hospital). In mild delirium, disorientation to time may be the first symptom to appear. Disorientation to self is less common. Language disturbance may be evident as dysnomia (i.e., the impaired ability to name objects) or dysgraphia (i.e., the impaired ability to write). In some cases, speech is rambling and irrelevant, in others pressured and incoherent, with unpredictable switching from subject to subject. It may be difficult for the clinician to assess for changes in cognitive function because the individual may be inattentive and incoherent. Under these circumstances, it is helpful to review carefully the individual's history and to obtain information from other informants, particularly family members.

Perceptual disturbances may include misinterpretations, illusions, or hallucinations. For example, the banging of a door may be mistaken for a gunshot (misinterpretation); the folds of the bedclothes may appear to be animate objects (illusion); or the person may "see" a group of people hovering over the bed when no one is actually there (hallucination). Although sensory misperceptions are most commonly visual, they may occur in other sensory modalities as well. Misperceptions range from simple and uniform to highly complex. The individual may have a delusional conviction of the reality of the hallucinations and exhibit emotional and behavioral responses in keeping with their content.

The disturbance develops over a short period of time and tends to fluctuate during the course of the day (Criterion C). For example, during morning hospital rounds, the person may be coherent and cooperative, but at night might insist on pulling out intravenous lines and going home to parents who died years ago.

Associated Features and Disorders

Delirium is often associated with a disturbance in the sleep-wake cycle. This disturbance can include daytime sleepiness or nighttime agitation and difficulty falling asleep. In some cases, complete reversal of the night-day sleep-wake cycle can occur. Delirium is frequently accompanied by disturbed psychomotor behavior. Many individuals with delirium are restless or hyperactive. Manifestations of increased psychomotor activity may include groping or picking at the bedclothes, attempting to get out of bed when it is unsafe or untimely, and sudden movements. On the other hand, the individual may show decreased psychomotor activity, with sluggishness and lethargy that approach stupor. Psychomotor activity can shift from one extreme to the other over the course of a day. Impaired judgment may interfere with proper medical treatment.

The individual may exhibit emotional disturbances such as anxiety, fear, depression, irritability, anger, euphoria, and apathy. There may be rapid and unpredictable shifts from one emotional state to another, although some individuals with delirium have a constant emotional tone. Fear often accompanies threatening hallucinations or transient delusions. If fear is marked, the person may attack those who are falsely perceived as threatening. Injuries may be sustained from falling out of bed or trying to escape while attached to intravenous lines, respiratory tubes, urinary catheters, or other medical equipment. The disturbed emotional state may also be evident in calling out, screaming, cursing, muttering, moaning, or other sounds. These behaviors are especially prevalent at night and under conditions in which stimulation and environmental cues are lacking.

In addition to laboratory findings that are characteristic of associated or etiological general medical conditions (or intoxication or withdrawal states), the EEG is typically abnormal, showing either generalized slowing or fast activity.

Specific Culture, Age, and Gender Features

Cultural and educational background should be taken into consideration in the evaluation of an individual's mental capacity. Individuals from certain backgrounds may not be familiar with the information used in certain tests of general knowledge (e.g., names of presidents, geographical knowledge), memory (e.g., date of birth in cultures that do not routinely celebrate birthdays), and orientation (e.g., sense of placement and location may be conceptualized differently in some cultures).

Children may be more susceptible to delirium than adults, especially when it is related to febrile illnesses and certain medications (e.g., anticholinergics). In children, delirium may be mistaken for uncooperative behavior, and eliciting the distinctive cognitive signs may be difficult. If familiar figures cannot soothe the child, this may be suggestive of delirium. The sex ratio for delirium reflects that of the elderly population in general (in which the ratio of women to men increases with increasing age), the group at highest risk for developing delirium.

Prevalence

In individuals over age 65 years who are hospitalized for a general medical condition, approximately 10% are reported to exhibit delirium on admission and another 10%–15% may develop delirium while in the hospital.

Course

The symptoms of delirium usually develop over hours to days. They may begin abruptly (e.g., after a head injury). More typically, single symptoms progress to full-blown delirium within a 3-day period. The delirium may resolve in a few hours, or symptoms may persist for weeks, particularly in individuals with coexisting dementia. If the underlying etiological factor is promptly corrected or is self-limited, recovery is more likely to be complete.

Differential Diagnosis

The most common differential diagnostic issue is whether the person has a **dementia** rather than a delirium, has a delirium alone, or has a delirium superimposed on a preexisting dementia. Memory impairment is common to both a delirium and a dementia, but the person with a dementia alone is alert and does not have the disturbance in consciousness that is characteristic of a delirium. When symptoms of a delirium are present, information from family members, other caretakers, or medical records may be helpful in determining whether the symptoms of a dementia were preexisting. Coding of a delirium superimposed on the different types of dementias is discussed under "Recording Procedures" for each type of delirium.

The presumed etiology determines the specific delirium diagnosis (text and criteria for each delirium diagnosis are provided separately later in this section). If it is judged that the delirium is a consequence of the direct physiological effects of a general medical condition, then Delirium Due to a General Medical Condition is diagnosed. If the delirium results from the direct physiological effects of a drug of abuse, then Substance Intoxication Delirium or Substance Withdrawal Delirium is diagnosed, depending on whether the delirium occurred in association with Substance Intoxication or Substance Withdrawal. If the delirium results from medication use or toxin exposure, then Substance-Induced Delirium is diagnosed. It is not uncommon for the delirium to be due to both a general medical condition and substance (including medication) use. This may be seen, for example, in an elderly individual with a serious general medical condition that is being treated with multiple medications. When there is more than one etiology (e.g., both a substance and a general medical condition), **Delirium Due to Multiple Etiologies** is diagnosed. If it is not possible to establish a specific etiology (i.e., substance induced or due to a general medical condition), Delirium Not Otherwise Specified is diagnosed.

The diagnosis of Substance Intoxication Delirium or Substance Withdrawal Delirium is made instead of **Substance Intoxication** or **Substance Withdrawal** only if the symptoms of the delirium are in excess of those usually associated with the intoxication or withdrawal syndrome and are sufficiently severe to warrant independent clinical attention. Even in individuals with obvious signs of intoxication or withdrawal, other possible causes of the delirium (i.e., **Delirium Due to a General Medical Condition**) must not be overlooked. For example, a head injury that occurs as a result of falls or fighting during intoxication may be responsible for the delirium.

Delirium that is characterized by vivid hallucinations, delusions, language disturbances, and agitation must be distinguished from **Brief Psychotic Disorder, Schizophrenia, Schizophreniform Disorder,** and **other Psychotic Disorders,** as well as from **Mood Disorders With Psychotic Features.** In delirium, the psychotic symptoms fluctuate, are fragmented and unsystematized, occur in the context of a reduced ability to appropriately maintain and shift attention, and are usually associated with EEG abnormalities. There is often memory impairment and disorientation in delirium, but generally not in these other disorders. Finally, in delirium, the person generally shows evidence of an underlying general medical condition, Substance Intoxication or Withdrawal, or medication use.

Delirium must be distinguished from **Malingering** and from **Factitious Disorder.** This distinction is made based on the often atypical presentation in Malingering and Factitious Disorder and the absence of a general medical condition or substance that is etiologically related to the apparent cognitive disturbance.

Individuals may present with some but not all symptoms of delirium. Subsyndromal presentations need to be carefully assessed because they may be harbingers of a full-blown delirium or may signal an as yet undiagnosed underlying general medical condition. Such presentations should be coded as **Cognitive Disorder Not Otherwise Specified.**

293.0   Delirium Due to a General Medical Condition

Diagnostic and Associated Features

The descriptive features of Delirium Due to a General Medical Condition (Criteria A–C) are discussed on pp. 124–125. In addition, to diagnose Delirium Due to a General Medical Condition, there must be evidence from the history, physical examination, or laboratory findings that the cognitive disturbance is the direct physiological consequence of a general medical condition (Criterion D).

In determining whether the delirium is due to a general medical condition, the clinician must first establish the presence of a general medical condition. Further, the clinician must establish that the delirium is etiologically related to the general medical condition. A careful and comprehensive assessment of multiple factors is necessary to make this judgment. Although there are no infallible guidelines, several considerations provide some guidance in this area. One consideration is the presence of a temporal association between the onset, exacerbation, or remission of the general medical condition and that of the delirium. Evidence from the literature that suggests that there can be a direct association between the general medical condition in question and the development of a delirium can provide a useful context in the assessment of a particular situation. In addition, the clinician must also judge that the disturbance is not better accounted for by a Substance-Induced Delirium or a primary mental disorder (e.g., a Manic Episode). This determination is explained in greater detail in the "Mental Disorders Due to a General Medical Condition" section (p. 165).

Delirium can be associated with many different general medical conditions, each of which has characteristic physical examination and laboratory findings. In systemic illnesses, focal neurological signs are not usually found. Various forms of tremor may be present. Asterixis, a flapping movement of the hyperextended hands, was originally described in hepatic encephalopathy but may also be found in association with other causes of delirium. Signs of autonomic hyperactivity (e.g., tachycardia, sweating, flushed face, dilated pupils, and elevated blood pressure) commonly occur. In addition to laboratory findings that are characteristic of etiological general medical conditions (or intoxication or withdrawal states), the EEG is generally abnormal, showing either generalized slowing or fast activity.

Recording Procedures

In recording the diagnosis of Delirium Due to a General Medical Condition, the clinician should note both the delirium and the identified general medical condition judged to be causing the disturbance on Axis I (e.g., 293.0 Delirium Due to Hypoglycemia). The ICD-9-CM code for the general medical condition should also be noted on Axis III (e.g., 251.2 hypoglycemia.) (See Appendix G for a list of selected ICD-9-CM diagnostic codes for general medical conditions.) In an individual with an established history of Dementia of the Alzheimer's Type or Vascular Dementia, a superimposed delirium should be noted by coding the appropriate subtype of the dementia (e.g., 290.3 Dementia of the Alzheimer's Type, With Late Onset, With Delirium). For other dementias, both dementia and delirium should be coded on Axis I (e.g., 294.1 Dementia Due to Parkinson's Disease and 293.0 Delirium Due to Hepatic Encephalopathy). In situations in which it is unclear whether the cognitive deficits are due to delirium or to dementia, it may be useful to make a provisional diagnosis of delirium and observe the person carefully while continuing efforts to identify the nature of the disturbance.

Associated General Medical Conditions

Etiological general medical conditions for delirium include systemic infections, metabolic disorders (e.g., hypoxia, hypercarbia, hypoglycemia), fluid or electrolyte imbalances, hepatic or renal disease, thiamine deficiency, postoperative states, hypertensive encephalopathy, postictal states, and sequelae of head trauma. Certain focal lesions of the right parietal lobe and inferomedial surface of the occipital lobe also may lead to a delirium.

Differential Diagnosis

See p. 126 for a general discussion of the differential diagnosis of delirium.

■ **Diagnostic criteria for 293.0 Delirium Due to . . .**
[*Indicate the General Medical Condition*]

A. Disturbance of consciousness (i.e., reduced clarity of awareness of the environment) with reduced ability to focus, sustain, or shift attention.

B. A change in cognition (such as memory deficit, disorientation, language disturbance) or the development of a perceptual disturbance that is not better accounted for by a preexisting, established, or evolving dementia.

C. The disturbance develops over a short period of time (usually hours to days) and tends to fluctuate during the course of the day.

D. There is evidence from the history, physical examination, or laboratory findings that the disturbance is caused by the direct physiological consequences of a general medical condition.

Coding note: If delirium is superimposed on a preexisting Dementia of the Alzheimer's Type or Vascular Dementia, indicate the delirium by coding the appropriate subtype of the dementia, e.g., 290.3 Dementia of the Alzheimer's Type, With Late Onset, With Delirium.

Coding note: Include the name of the general medical condition on Axis I, e.g., 293.0 Delirium Due to Hepatic Encephalopathy; also code the general medical condition on Axis III (see Appendix G for codes).

Substance-Induced Delirium

Diagnostic and Associated Features

The descriptive features of Substance-Induced Delirium (Criteria A–C) are discussed on pp. 124–125. In addition, to diagnose Substance-Induced Delirium, there must be evidence from the history, physical examination, or laboratory findings of Substance Intoxication or Withdrawal, medication side effects, or toxin exposure judged to be etiologically related to the delirium (Criterion D). A delirium that occurs during Substance Intoxication is diagnosed as Substance Intoxication Delirium; a delirium that occurs during Substance Withdrawal is diagnosed as Substance Withdrawal Delirium; and a delirium that is associated with medication side effects or toxin exposure is diagnosed as Substance-Induced Delirium (see criteria set for Substance Intoxication Delirium, p. 131).

Delirium that occurs during Substance Intoxication may arise within minutes to hours after taking relatively high doses of certain drugs such as cannabis, cocaine, and hallucinogens. With other drugs such as alcohol, barbiturates, or meperidine, delirium sometimes develops only after intoxication is sustained for some days. Usually the delirium resolves as the intoxication ends or within a few hours to days thereafter (although the duration may be longer after intoxication with phencyclidine).

Delirium that is associated with Substance Withdrawal develops as tissue and fluid concentrations of the substance decrease after reduction or termination of sustained, usually high-dose use of certain substances. The duration of the delirium tends to vary with the half-life of the substance involved: longer-acting substances usually are associated with more protracted withdrawal. Substance Withdrawal Delirium may continue for only a few hours or may persist for as long as 2–4 weeks.

This diagnosis should be made instead of a diagnosis of Substance Intoxication or Substance Withdrawal only when the cognitive symptoms are in excess of those usually associated with the intoxication or withdrawal syndrome and when the symptoms are sufficiently severe to warrant independent clinical attention. For a more detailed discussion of the features associated with Substance-Related Disorders, see p. 175.

Recording Procedures

A diagnosis of Substance-Induced Delirium begins with the name of the specific substance (rather than the class of substances) that is presumed to be causing the delirium (e.g., "Diazepam" rather than "Sedative, Hypnotic, or Anxiolytic"). The diagnostic code is selected from the listing of classes of substances provided in the criteria set. For substances that do not fit into any of the classes (e.g., digitalis), the code for "Other Substance" should be used. In addition, for medications prescribed at therapeutic doses, the specific medication can be indicated by listing the appropriate E-code (see Appendix G). For substances that produce intoxication or withdrawal, the name of the substance is followed by the context in which the symptoms developed (e.g., 292.81 Dextro-amphetamine Intoxication Delirium; 291.0 Alcohol Withdrawal Delirium). For medication side effects and toxin exposure, the term "-Induced" is used (e.g., 292.81 Digitalis-Induced Delirium). When more than one substance is judged to play a significant role in the development of the delirium, each should be listed separately. If a substance is judged to be the etiological factor but the specific substance or class of substances is unknown, the diagnosis is 292.81 Unknown Substance–Induced Delirium.

Specific Substances

Substance Intoxication Delirium can occur with the following classes of substances: alcohol; amphetamines and related substances; cannabis; cocaine; hallucinogens; inhalants; opioids; phencyclidine and related substances; sedatives, hypnotics, and anxiolytics; and other or unknown substances. **Substance Withdrawal Delirium** can occur with the following classes of substances: alcohol (often called "delirium tremens"); sedatives, hypnotics, and anxiolytics; and other or unknown substances.

Medications reported to cause delirium include anesthetics, analgesics, antiasthmatic agents, anticonvulsants, antihistamines, antihypertensive and cardiovascular medications, antimicrobials, antiparkinsonian drugs, corticosteroids, gastrointestinal medications, muscle relaxants, and psychotropic medications with anticholinergic side effects. Toxins reported to cause delirium include anticholinesterase, organophosphate insecticides, carbon monoxide, carbon dioxide, and volatile substances such as fuel or paint.

Differential Diagnosis

See p. 126 for a general discussion of the differential diagnosis of delirium and p. 190 for a discussion of the differential diagnosis of Substance Intoxication and Withdrawal.

■ Diagnostic criteria for Substance Intoxication Delirium

A. Disturbance of consciousness (i.e., reduced clarity of awareness of the environment) with reduced ability to focus, sustain, or shift attention.

B. A change in cognition (such as memory deficit, disorientation, language disturbance) or the development of a perceptual disturbance that is not better accounted for by a preexisting, established, or evolving dementia.

C. The disturbance develops over a short period of time (usually hours to days) and tends to fluctuate during the course of the day.

D. There is evidence from the history, physical examination, or laboratory findings of either (1) or (2):

   (1) the symptoms in Criteria A and B developed during Substance Intoxication

   (2) medication use is etiologically related to the disturbance*

Note: This diagnosis should be made instead of a diagnosis of Substance Intoxication only when the cognitive symptoms are in excess of those usually associated with the intoxication syndrome and when the symptoms are sufficiently severe to warrant independent clinical attention.

*Note: The diagnosis should be recorded as Substance-Induced Delirium if related to medication use. Refer to Appendix G for E-codes indicating specific medications.

Code [Specific Substance] Intoxication Delirium:
   (291.0 Alcohol; 292.81 Amphetamine [or Amphetamine-Like Substance]; 292.81 Cannabis; 292.81 Cocaine; 292.81 Hallucinogen; 292.81 Inhalant; 292.81 Opioid; 292.81 Phencyclidine [or Phencyclidine-Like Substance]; 292.81 Sedative, Hypnotic, or Anxiolytic; 292.81 Other [or Unknown] Substance [e.g., cimetidine, digitalis, benztropine])

■ Diagnostic criteria for Substance Withdrawal Delirium

A. Disturbance of consciousness (i.e., reduced clarity of awareness of the environment) with reduced ability to focus, sustain, or shift attention.

B. A change in cognition (such as memory deficit, disorientation, language disturbance) or the development of a perceptual disturbance that is not better accounted for by a preexisting, established, or evolving dementia.

C. The disturbance develops over a short period of time (usually hours to days) and tends to fluctuate during the course of the day.

(continued)

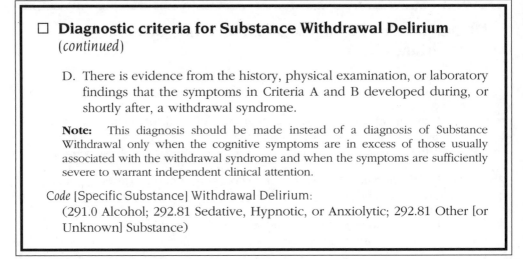

☐ **Diagnostic criteria for Substance Withdrawal Delirium**
(*continued*)

D. There is evidence from the history, physical examination, or laboratory findings that the symptoms in Criteria A and B developed during, or shortly after, a withdrawal syndrome.

Note: This diagnosis should be made instead of a diagnosis of Substance Withdrawal only when the cognitive symptoms are in excess of those usually associated with the withdrawal syndrome and when the symptoms are sufficiently severe to warrant independent clinical attention.

Code [Specific Substance] Withdrawal Delirium:
(291.0 Alcohol; 292.81 Sedative, Hypnotic, or Anxiolytic; 292.81 Other [or Unknown] Substance)

Delirium Due to Multiple Etiologies

The Delirium Due to Multiple Etiologies category is included to alert clinicians to the common situation in which the delirium has more than one etiology. There may be more than one general medical condition etiologically related to the delirium (e.g., Delirium Due to Hepatic Encephalopathy, Delirium Due to Head Trauma), or the delirium may be due to the combined effects of a general medical condition (e.g., viral encephalitis) and substance use (e.g., Alcohol Withdrawal).

Recording Procedures

Delirium Due to Multiple Etiologies does not have its own separate code and should not be recorded as a diagnosis. For example, to code a delirium due to both hepatic encephalopathy and withdrawal from alcohol, the clinician would list both 293.0 Delirium Due to Hepatic Encephalopathy and 291.0 Alcohol Withdrawal Delirium on Axis I and 572.2 hepatic encephalopathy on Axis III.

■ **Diagnostic criteria for Delirium Due to Multiple Etiologies**

A. Disturbance of consciousness (i.e., reduced clarity of awareness of the environment) with reduced ability to focus, sustain, or shift attention.

B. A change in cognition (such as memory deficit, disorientation, language disturbance) or the development of a perceptual disturbance that is not better accounted for by a preexisting, established, or evolving dementia.

(continued)

☐ **Diagnostic criteria for Delirium Due to Multiple Etiologies** (*continued*)

C. The disturbance develops over a short period of time (usually hours to days) and tends to fluctuate during the course of the day.

D. There is evidence from the history, physical examination, or laboratory findings that the delirium has more than one etiology (e.g., more than one etiological general medical condition, a general medical condition plus Substance Intoxication or medication side effect).

Coding note: Use multiple codes reflecting specific delirium and specific etiologies, e.g., 293.0 Delirium Due to Viral Encephalitis; 291.0 Alcohol Withdrawal Delirium.

780.09   Delirium Not Otherwise Specified

This category should be used to diagnose a delirium that does not meet criteria for any of the specific types of delirium described in this section.

Examples include

1. A clinical presentation of delirium that is suspected to be due to a general medical condition or substance use but for which there is insufficient evidence to establish a specific etiology
2. Delirium due to causes not listed in this section (e.g., sensory deprivation)

Dementia

The disorders in the "Dementia" section are characterized by the development of multiple cognitive deficits (including memory impairment) that are due to the direct physiological effects of a general medical condition, to the persisting effects of a substance, or to multiple etiologies (e.g., the combined effects of cerebrovascular disease and Alzheimer's disease). The disorders in this section share a common symptom presentation but are differentiated based on etiology. The diagnostic features listed in the next section pertain to **Dementia of the Alzheimer's Type, Vascular Dementia, Dementia Due to HIV Disease, Dementia Due to Head Trauma, Dementia Due to Parkinson's Disease, Dementia Due to Huntington's Disease, Dementia Due to Pick's Disease, Dementia Due to Creutzfeldt-Jakob Disease, Dementia Due to Other General Medical Conditions, Substance-Induced Persisting Dementia,** and **Dementia Due to Multiple Etiologies.** In addition, **Dementia Not Otherwise Specified** is included in this section for presentations in which the clinician is unable to determine a specific etiology for the multiple cognitive deficits.

Diagnostic Features

The essential feature of a dementia is the development of multiple cognitive deficits that include memory impairment and at least one of the following cognitive disturbances: aphasia, apraxia, agnosia, or a disturbance in executive functioning. The cognitive deficits must be sufficiently severe to cause impairment in occupational or social functioning and must represent a decline from a previously higher level of functioning. A diagnosis of a dementia should not be made if the cognitive deficits occur exclusively during the course of a delirium. However, a dementia and a delirium may both be diagnosed if the dementia is present at times when the delirium is not present. Dementia may be etiologically related to a general medical condition, to the persisting effects of substance use (including toxin exposure), or to a combination of these factors.

Memory impairment is required to make the diagnosis of a dementia and is a prominent early symptom (Criterion A1). Individuals with dementia become impaired in their ability to learn new material, or they forget previously learned material. Most individuals with dementia have both forms of memory impairment, although it is sometimes difficult to demonstrate the loss of previously learned material early in the course of the disorder. They may lose valuables like wallets and keys, forget food cooking on the stove, and become lost in unfamiliar neighborhoods. In advanced stages of dementia, memory impairment is so severe that the person forgets his or her occupation, schooling, birthday, family members, and sometimes even name.

Memory may be formally tested by asking the person to register, retain, recall, and recognize information. The ability to learn new information may be assessed by asking the individual to learn a list of words. The individual is requested to repeat the words (registration), to recall the information after a delay of several minutes (retention, recall), and to recognize the words from a multiple list (recognition). Individuals with difficulty learning new information are not helped by clues or prompts (e.g., multiple-choice questions) because they did not learn the material initially. In contrast, individuals with primarily retrieval deficits can be helped by clues and prompts because their impairment is in the ability to access their memories. Remote memory may be tested by asking the individual to recall personal information or past material that the individual found of interest (e.g., politics, sports, entertainment). It is also useful to determine (from the individual and informants) the impact of the memory disturbances on the individual's functioning (e.g., ability to work, shop, cook, pay bills, return home without getting lost).

Deterioration of language function (aphasia) may be manifested by difficulty producing the names of individuals and objects (Criterion A2a). The speech of individuals with aphasia may become vague or empty, with long circumlocutory phrases and excessive use of terms of indefinite reference such as "thing" and "it." Comprehension of spoken and written language and repetition of language may also be compromised. In the advanced stages of dementia, individuals may be mute or have a deteriorated speech pattern characterized by echolalia (i.e., echoing what is heard) or palilalia (i.e., repeating sounds or words over and over). Language is tested by asking the individual to name objects in the room (e.g., tie, dress, desk, lamp) or body parts (e.g., nose, chin, shoulder), follow commands ("Point at the door and then at the table"), or repeat phrases ("no ifs, ands, or buts").

Individuals with dementia may exhibit apraxia (i.e., impaired ability to execute motor activities despite intact motor abilities, sensory function, and comprehension of the required task) (Criterion A2b). They will be impaired in their ability to pantomime the use of objects (e.g., combing hair) or to execute known motor acts (e.g., waving goodbye). Apraxia may contribute to deficits in cooking, dressing, and drawing. Motor skill disturbances may be tested by asking the individual to execute motor functions (e.g., to show how to brush teeth, to copy intersecting pentagons, to assemble blocks, or to arrange sticks in specific designs).

Individuals with dementia may exhibit agnosia (i.e., failure to recognize or identify objects despite intact sensory function) (Criterion A2c). For example, the individual may have normal visual acuity but lose the ability to recognize objects such as chairs or pencils. Eventually they may be unable to recognize family members or even their own reflection in the mirror. Similarly, they may have normal tactile sensation, but be unable to identify objects placed in their hands by touch alone (e.g., a coin or keys).

Disturbances in executive functioning are a common manifestation of dementia (Criterion A2d) and may be related especially to disorders of the frontal lobe or associated subcortical pathways. Executive functioning involves the ability to think abstractly and to plan, initiate, sequence, monitor, and stop complex behavior. Impairment in abstract thinking may be manifested by the individual having difficulty coping with novel tasks and avoiding situations that require the processing of new and complex information. The ability to abstract can be formally assessed by asking the person to find similarities or differences between related words. Executive dysfunction is also evident in a reduced ability to shift mental sets, to generate novel verbal or nonverbal information, and to execute serial motor activities. Tests for executive function include asking the individual to count to 10, recite the alphabet, subtract serial 7s, state as many animals as possible in 1 minute, or draw a continuous line consisting of alternating m's and n's. It is also useful to determine (from the individual and informants) the impact of the disturbances in executive functioning on the individual's daily life (e.g., ability to work, plan activities, budget).

The items in both Criterion A1 (memory impairment) and Criterion A2 (aphasia, apraxia, agnosia, or disturbance in executive functioning) must be severe enough to cause significant impairment in social or occupational functioning (e.g., going to school, working, shopping, dressing, bathing, handling finances, and other activities of daily living) and must represent a decline from a previous level of functioning (Criterion B). The nature and degree of impairment are variable and often depend on the particular social setting of the individual. The same level of cognitive impairment may significantly impair an individual's ability to perform a complex job, but not a job that is less demanding. Standardized published rating scales that measure physical maintenance (e.g., personal hygiene), intellectual functioning, and the ability to use implements or tools (e.g., telephone, washing machine) can be used to measure the severity of impairment.

Dementia is not diagnosed if these symptoms occur exclusively during the course of a delirium. However, a delirium may be superimposed on a preexisting dementia, in which case both diagnoses should be given.

Associated Features and Disorders

Associated descriptive features and mental disorders. Individuals with dementia may become spatially disoriented and have difficulty with spatial tasks. Visuospatial functioning can be assessed by asking the individual to copy drawings, such as a circle, overlapping pentagons, and a cube. Poor judgment and poor insight are common in dementia. Individuals may exhibit little or no awareness of memory loss or other cognitive abnormalities. They may make unrealistic assessments of their abilities and make plans that are not congruent with their deficits and prognosis (e.g., planning to start a new business). They may underestimate the risks involved in activities (e.g., driving). Occasionally, they may harm others by becoming violent. Suicidal behavior may occur, particularly in early stages when the individual is more capable of carrying out a plan of action. Dementia is sometimes accompanied by motor disturbances of gait leading to falls. Some individuals with dementia show disinhibited behavior, including making inappropriate jokes, neglecting personal hygiene, exhibiting undue familiarity with strangers, or disregarding conventional rules of social conduct. Slurred speech may occur in dementia that is associated with subcortical pathology such as Parkinson's disease, Huntington's disease, and some cases of Vascular Dementia. The multiple cognitive impairments of dementia are often associated with anxiety, mood, and sleep disturbances. Delusions are common, especially those involving themes of persecution (e.g., that misplaced possessions have been stolen). Hallucinations can occur in all sensory modalities, but visual hallucinations are most common. Delirium is frequently superimposed on dementia because the underlying brain disease may increase susceptibility to confusional states that may be produced by medications or other concurrent general medical conditions. Individuals with dementia may be especially vulnerable to physical stressors (e.g., illness or minor surgery) and psychosocial stressors (e.g., going to the hospital, bereavement), which may exacerbate their intellectual deficits and other associated problems.

Associated laboratory findings.   A discussion of associated laboratory findings that are specific to types of dementia is included in the text for each dementia. Invariably there are abnormalities in cognitive and memory functioning, which can be assessed using mental status examinations and neuropsychological testing. Neuroimaging may aid in the differential diagnosis of dementia. Computed tomography (CT) or magnetic resonance imaging (MRI) may reveal cerebral atrophy, focal brain lesions (cortical strokes, tumors, subdural hematomas), hydrocephalus, or periventricular ischemic brain injury. Functional imaging such as positron-emission tomography (PET) or single photon emission computed tomography (SPECT) are not routinely used in the evaluation of dementia, but may provide useful differential diagnostic information (e.g., parietal lobe changes in Alzheimer's disease or frontal lobe alterations in frontal lobe degenerations) in individuals without evidence of structural changes on CT or MRI scans.

Associated physical examination findings and general medical conditions.
The associated physical examination findings of dementia depend on the nature, location, and stage of progression of the underlying pathology. The most common cause of dementia is Alzheimer's disease, followed by vascular disease, and then by multiple etiologies. Other causes of dementia include Pick's disease, normal-pressure hydrocephalus, Parkinson's disease, Huntington's disease, traumatic brain injury, brain tumors, anoxia, infectious disorders (e.g., human immunodeficiency virus [HIV], syphilis), prion diseases (e.g., Creutzfeldt-Jakob disease), endocrine conditions (e.g., hypothyroidism, hypercalcemia, hypoglycemia), vitamin deficiencies (e.g., deficiencies of thiamine, niacin, vitamin B_{12}), immune disorders (e.g., polymyalgia rheumatica, systemic lupus erythematosus), hepatic conditions, metabolic conditions (e.g., Kufs' disease, adreno-leukodystrophy, metachromatic leukodystrophy, and other storage diseases of adulthood and childhood), and other neurological conditions (e.g., multiple sclerosis).

Specific Culture and Age Features

Cultural and educational background should be taken into consideration in the evaluation of an individual's mental capacity. Individuals from certain backgrounds may not be familiar with the information used in certain tests of general knowledge (e.g., names of presidents, geographical knowledge), memory (e.g., date of birth in cultures that do not routinely celebrate birthdays), and orientation (e.g., sense of place and location may be conceptualized differently in some cultures). The prevalence of different causes of dementia (e.g., infections, nutritional deficiencies, traumatic brain injury, endocrine conditions, cerebrovascular diseases, seizure disorders, brain tumors, substance abuse) varies substantially across cultural groups.

The age at onset of dementia depends on the etiology, but is usually late in life, with highest prevalence above age 85 years. A significant deterioration in memory and in multiple cognitive skills, which is necessary for the diagnosis of dementia, may be difficult to document in very young children. Thus, the diagnosis of dementia may not be practical until the child is older (usually between ages 4 and 6 years). In individuals under age 18 years with Mental Retardation, an additional diagnosis of a dementia should be made only if the condition is not characterized satisfactorily by the diagnosis of Mental Retardation alone. Dementia is uncommon in children and adolescents, but can occur as a result of general medical conditions (e.g., head injury, brain tumors, HIV infection, strokes, adrenoleukodystrophies). Dementia in children may present as a deterioration in functioning (as in adults) or as a significant delay or deviation in normal development. Deteriorating school performance may be an early sign.

Prevalence

Reported prevalence of dementia varies among epidemiological studies, depending on the ages of the subjects sampled; methods of determining the presence, severity, and type of cognitive impairment; and the regions or countries studied. Community studies estimated a 1-year prospective prevalence of almost 3.0% with severe cognitive impairment in the adult population. The study assessed individuals with a brief instrument that assessed current cognitive status (the Mini-Mental State Exam), which does not identify specific diagnoses. It is estimated that 2%–4% of the population over age 65 years have Dementia of the Alzheimer's Type, with other types being much less common. The prevalence of dementia, especially Dementia of the Alzheimer's Type and Vascular Dementia, increases with age, particularly after age 75 years, with a prevalence of 20% or more over age 85 years.

Course

Historically, the term *dementia* implied a progressive or irreversible course. The DSM-IV definition of *dementia*, however, is based on the pattern of cognitive deficits and carries no connotation concerning prognosis. Dementia may be progressive, static, or remitting. The reversibility of a dementia is a function of the underlying pathology and of the availability and timely application of effective treatment. The mode of onset and subsequent course of dementia also depend on the underlying etiology. The level of disability depends not only on the severity of the individual's cognitive impairments but also on the available social supports. In advanced dementia, the individual may become totally oblivious to his or her surroundings and require constant care. Individuals with severe dementia are susceptible to accidents and infectious diseases, which often prove fatal.

Differential Diagnosis

Memory impairment occurs in both **delirium** and dementia. Delirium is also characterized by a reduced ability to maintain and shift attention appropriately. The clinical course can help to differentiate between delirium and dementia. Typically, symptoms in delirium fluctuate and symptoms in dementia are relatively stable. Multiple cognitive impairments that persist in an unchanged form for more than a few months suggest dementia rather than delirium. Delirium may be superimposed on a dementia, in which case both disorders are diagnosed. In situations in which it is unclear whether the cognitive deficits are due to a delirium or a dementia, it may be useful to make a provisional diagnosis of delirium and observe the person carefully while continuing efforts to identify the nature of the disturbance.

An **amnestic disorder** is characterized by severe memory impairment without other significant impairments of cognitive functioning (i.e., aphasia, apraxia, agnosia, or disturbances in executive functioning).

The presumed etiology determines the specific dementia diagnosis. If the clinician has determined that the dementia is due to **multiple etiologies,** multiple codes based on the specific dementias and their etiologies should be used (see Dementia Due to Multiple Etiologies, p. 154). In **Vascular Dementia,** focal neurological signs (e.g., exaggeration of deep tendon reflexes, extensor plantar response) and laboratory evidence of vascular disease judged to be related to the dementia are present. The clinical course of Vascular Dementia is variable and typically progresses in stepwise fashion. The presence of **Dementia Due to Other General Medical Conditions** (e.g., Pick's disease, HIV) requires evidence from the history, physical examination, and appropriate laboratory tests that a general medical condition is etiologically related to the dementia. The onset of the deterioration (gradual or sudden) and its course (acute, subacute, or chronic) may be useful in suggesting the etiology. For example, the severity of the impairment in cognitive functioning often remains static after head injury, encephalitis, or stroke.

Multiple cognitive deficits that occur only in the context of substance use are diagnosed as **Substance Intoxication** or **Substance Withdrawal.** If the dementia results from the persisting effects of a substance (i.e., a drug of abuse, a medication, or toxin exposure), then **Substance-Induced Persisting Dementia** is diagnosed. Other causes of dementia (e.g., Dementia Due to a General Medical Condition) should always be considered, even in a person with Substance Dependence. For example, head injury is not infrequent during substance use and may underlie the dementia. **Dementia of the Alzheimer's Type** is currently a diagnosis of exclusion, and other causes for the cognitive deficits (see above) must first be ruled out. In addition, the course is characterized by gradual onset and continuing cognitive decline. In those cases in which there is insufficient evidence to determine whether the dementia is due to a general medical condition or is substance induced, **Dementia Not Otherwise Specified** should be coded. Individuals may present with some but not all of the symptoms of dementia. Such presentations should be coded as **Cognitive Disorder Not Otherwise Specified.**

Mental Retardation is characterized by significantly subaverage current general intellectual functioning, with concurrent impairments in adaptive functioning and with an onset before age 18 years. Mental Retardation is not necessarily associated with memory impairment. In contrast, the age at onset of dementia is usually late in life. If the onset of the dementia is before age 18 years, both dementia and Mental Retardation may be diagnosed if the criteria for both disorders are met. Documenting a significant deterioration in memory and in other cognitive skills, which is necessary for the diagnosis of dementia, may be difficult in persons under age 4 years. In individuals under age 18 years, the diagnosis of dementia should be made only if the condition is not characterized satisfactorily by the diagnosis of Mental Retardation alone.

Schizophrenia can also be associated with multiple cognitive impairments and a decline in functioning, but Schizophrenia is unlike dementia in its generally earlier age at onset, its characteristic symptom pattern, and the absence of a specific etiological general medical condition or substance. Typically, the cognitive impairment associated with Schizophrenia is less severe than that seen in Dementia.

Major Depressive Disorder may be associated with complaints of memory impairment, difficulty thinking and concentrating, and an overall reduction in intellectual abilities. Individuals sometimes perform poorly on mental status examinations and neuropsychological testing. Particularly in elderly persons, it is often difficult to determine whether cognitive symptoms are better accounted for by a dementia or by a Major Depressive Episode. This differential diagnosis may be informed by a thorough medical evaluation and an evaluation of the onset of the disturbance, the temporal sequencing of depressive and cognitive symptoms, the course of illness, family history, and treatment response. The premorbid state of the individual may help to differentiate "pseudodementia" (i.e., cognitive impairments due to the Major Depressive Episode) from dementia. In dementia, there is usually a premorbid history of declining cognitive function, whereas the individual with a Major Depressive Episode is much more likely to have a relatively normal premorbid state and abrupt cognitive decline associated with the depression. If the clinician determines that both a dementia and Major Depressive Disorder are present with independent etiologies, both should be diagnosed.

Dementia must be distinguished from **Malingering** and **Factitious Disorder.** The patterns of cognitive deficits presented in Malingering and Factitious Disorder are usually not consistent over time and are not characteristic of those typically seen in dementia. For example, individuals with Factitious Disorder or Malingering manifesting as dementia may perform calculations while keeping score during a card game, but then claim to be unable to perform similar calculations during a mental status examination.

Dementia must be distinguished from the normal decline in cognitive functioning that occurs with **aging** (as in Age-Related Cognitive Decline). The diagnosis of dementia is warranted only if there is demonstrable evidence of greater memory and other cognitive impairment than would be expected due to normal aging processes and the symptoms cause impairment in social or occupational functioning.

Dementia of the Alzheimer's Type

Diagnostic Features

The cognitive deficits (Criterion A) and the required impairment (Criterion B) are discussed on pp. 133–135. The onset of Dementia of the Alzheimer's Type is gradual and involves continuing cognitive decline (Criterion C). Because of the difficulty of obtaining direct pathological evidence of the presence of Alzheimer's disease, the diagnosis can be made only when other etiologies for the dementia have been ruled out. Specifically, the cognitive deficits are not due to other central nervous system conditions that cause progressive deficits in memory or cognition (e.g., cerebrovascular disease, Parkinson's disease, Huntington's disease), systemic conditions that are known to cause dementia (e.g., hypothyroidism, vitamin B_{12} deficiency, HIV infection), or the persisting effects of a substance (e.g., alcohol) (Criterion D). If there is an additional etiology (e.g., head trauma worsening a Dementia of the Alzheimer's Type), both types of dementia should be coded (see Dementia Due to Multiple Etiologies, p. 154). Dementia of the Alzheimer's Type should not be diagnosed if the symptoms occur exclusively during delirium (Criterion E). However, delirium may be superimposed on a preexisting Dementia of the Alzheimer's Type, in which case the With Delirium subtype should be indicated. Finally, the cognitive deficits are not better accounted for by another Axis I disorder (e.g., Major Depressive Disorder or Schizophrenia) (Criterion F).

Subtypes and Specifiers

The age at onset of Dementia of the Alzheimer's Type can be indicated by the use of one of the following subtypes:

With Early Onset. This subtype is used if the onset of the dementia is age 65 years or under.

With Late Onset. This subtype is used if the onset of the dementia is after age 65 years.

The following subtypes (each of which has its own separate code) must be used to indicate the predominant feature of the current clinical presentation:

With Delirium. This subtype is used if delirium is superimposed on the dementia.

With Delusions. This subtype is used if delusions are the predominant feature.

With Depressed Mood. This subtype is used if depressed mood (including presentations that meet symptom criteria for a Major Depressive Episode) is the predominant feature. A separate diagnosis of Mood Disorder Due to a General Medical Condition is not given.

Uncomplicated. This subtype is used if none of the above predominates in the current clinical presentation.

The specifier **With Behavioral Disturbance** (which cannot be coded) can also be used to indicate clinically significant behavioral disturbances (e.g., wandering).

Recording Procedures

By ICD-9-CM convention, only Dementia of the Alzheimer's Type and Vascular Dementia have codable subtypes. The diagnostic codes are selected as follows:

- For Dementia of the Alzheimer's Type, With Early Onset, the code depends on the subtype for predominant features: 290.11 for With Delirium, 290.12 for With Delusions, 290.13 for With Depressed Mood, 290.10 for Uncomplicated.
- For Dementia of the Alzheimer's Type, With Late Onset, the code also depends on the subtype for predominant features: 290.3 for With Delirium, 290.20 for With Delusions, 290.21 for With Depressed Mood, and 290.0 for Uncomplicated.

The specifier With Behavioral Disturbance is uncoded and can be applied to each of the above subtypes (e.g., 290.21 Dementia of the Alzheimer's Type, With Late Onset, With Depressed Mood, With Behavioral Disturbance). In addition, 331.0 Alzheimer's disease should be coded on Axis III.

Associated Features and Disorders

Associated descriptive features and mental disorders.   See p. 135 for a general discussion of features and disorders associated with dementia. The prevalence of Dementia of the Alzheimer's Type is increased in individuals with Down's syndrome and in individuals with a history of head trauma. Pathological changes that are characteristic of Alzheimer's disease are present in the brains of individuals with Down's syndrome by the time they are in their early 40s, although the clinical symptoms of dementia are not usually evident until later.

Associated laboratory findings.   In the majority of cases, brain atrophy is present in Dementia of the Alzheimer's Type, with wider cortical sulci and larger cerebral ventricles than would be expected given the normal aging process. This may be demonstrated by computed tomography (CT) or magnetic resonance imaging (MRI). Microscopic examination usually reveals histopathological changes, including senile plaques, neurofibrillary tangles, granulovascular degeneration, neuronal loss, astrocytic gliosis, and amyloid angiopathy. Lewy bodies are sometimes seen in the cortical neurons.

Associated physical examination findings and general medical conditions.   In the first years of illness, few motor and sensory signs are associated with Dementia of the Alzheimer's Type. Later in the course, myoclonus and gait disorder may appear. Seizures occur in approximately 10% of individuals with the disorder.

Specific Culture, Age, and Gender Features

See p. 137 for a general discussion of culture and age features associated with dementia. Late onset (after age 65 years) of Dementia of the Alzheimer's Type is much more common than early onset. Few cases develop before age 50 years. The disorder is slightly more common in females than in males.

Prevalence

Between 2% and 4% of the population over age 65 years is estimated to have Dementia of the Alzheimer's Type. The prevalence increases with increasing age, particularly after age 75 years.

Course

See p. 137 for a general discussion of the course of dementia. The course of Dementia of the Alzheimer's Type tends to be slowly progressive, with a loss of 3–4 points per year on a standard assessment instrument such as the Mini-Mental State Exam. Various patterns of deficits are seen. A common pattern is an insidious onset, with early deficits in recent memory followed by the development of aphasia, apraxia, and agnosia after several years. Some individuals may show personality changes or increased irritability in the early stages. In the later stages of the disease, individuals may develop gait and motor disturbances and eventually become mute and bedridden. The average duration of the illness from onset of symptoms to death is 8–10 years.

Familial Pattern

Compared with the general population, first-degree biological relatives of individuals with Dementia of the Alzheimer's Type, With Early Onset, are more likely to develop the disorder. Late-onset cases may also have a genetic component. Dementia of the Alzheimer's Type in some families has been shown to be inherited as a dominant trait with linkage to several chromosomes, including chromosomes 21, 14, and 19. However, the proportion of cases that are related to specific inherited abnormalities is not known.

Differential Diagnosis

See p. 138 for a general discussion of the differential diagnosis of dementia.

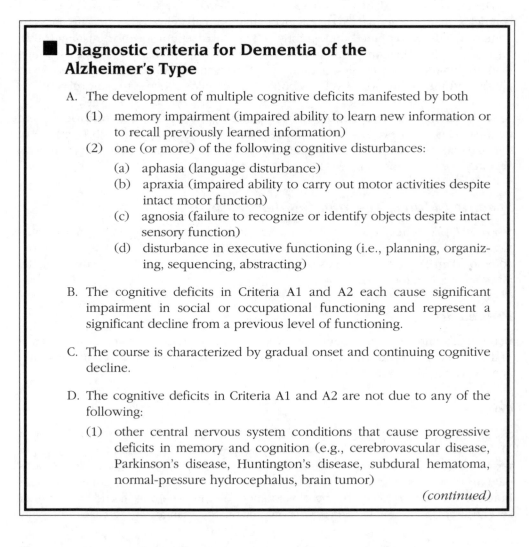

■ **Diagnostic criteria for Dementia of the Alzheimer's Type**

A. The development of multiple cognitive deficits manifested by both

   (1) memory impairment (impaired ability to learn new information or to recall previously learned information)

   (2) one (or more) of the following cognitive disturbances:

      (a) aphasia (language disturbance)

      (b) apraxia (impaired ability to carry out motor activities despite intact motor function)

      (c) agnosia (failure to recognize or identify objects despite intact sensory function)

      (d) disturbance in executive functioning (i.e., planning, organizing, sequencing, abstracting)

B. The cognitive deficits in Criteria A1 and A2 each cause significant impairment in social or occupational functioning and represent a significant decline from a previous level of functioning.

C. The course is characterized by gradual onset and continuing cognitive decline.

D. The cognitive deficits in Criteria A1 and A2 are not due to any of the following:

   (1) other central nervous system conditions that cause progressive deficits in memory and cognition (e.g., cerebrovascular disease, Parkinson's disease, Huntington's disease, subdural hematoma, normal-pressure hydrocephalus, brain tumor)

(continued)

☐ **Diagnostic criteria for Dementia of the Alzheimer's Type**
(continued)

    (2)   systemic conditions that are known to cause dementia (e.g., hypothyroidism, vitamin B_{12} or folic acid deficiency, niacin deficiency, hypercalcemia, neurosyphilis, HIV infection)

    (3)   substance-induced conditions

E. The deficits do not occur exclusively during the course of a delirium.

F. The disturbance is not better accounted for by another Axis I disorder (e.g., Major Depressive Disorder, Schizophrenia).

Code based on type of onset and predominant features:

  With Early Onset: if onset is at age 65 years or below

    290.11 With Delirium: if delirium is superimposed on the dementia

    290.12 With Delusions: if delusions are the predominant feature

    290.13 With Depressed Mood: if depressed mood (including presentations that meet full symptom criteria for a Major Depressive Episode) is the predominant feature. A separate diagnosis of Mood Disorder Due to a General Medical Condition is not given.

    290.10 Uncomplicated: if none of the above predominates in the current clinical presentation

  With Late Onset: if onset is after age 65 years

    290.3   With Delirium: if delirium is superimposed on the dementia

    290.20 With Delusions: if delusions are the predominant feature

    290.21 With Depressed Mood: if depressed mood (including presentations that meet full symptom criteria for a Major Depressive Episode) is the predominant feature. A separate diagnosis of Mood Disorder Due to a General Medical Condition is not given.

    290.0   Uncomplicated: if none of the above predominates in the current clinical presentation

Specify if:

  With Behavioral Disturbance

  Coding note: Also code 331.0 Alzheimer's disease on Axis III.

290.4x Vascular Dementia
(*formerly* Multi-Infarct Dementia)

Diagnostic Features

The cognitive deficits (Criterion A) and the required impairment (Criterion B) in Vascular Dementia are discussed on pp. 133–135. There must be evidence of cerebrovascular disease (i.e., focal neurological signs and symptoms or laboratory evidence) that is judged to be etiologically related to the dementia (Criterion C). The focal neurological signs and symptoms include extensor plantar response, pseudobulbar palsy, gait abnormalities, exaggeration of deep tendon reflexes, or weakness of an extremity. Computed tomography (CT) of the head and magnetic resonance imaging (MRI) usually demonstrate multiple vascular lesions of the cerebral cortex and subcortical structures. Vascular Dementia is not diagnosed if the symptoms occur exclusively during delirium (Criterion D). However, delirium may be superimposed on a preexisting Vascular Dementia, in which case the subtype With Delirium should be indicated.

Subtypes

The following subtypes (each of which has its own separate code) must be used to indicate the predominant feature of the current clinical presentation:

With Delirium. This subtype is used if delirium is superimposed on the dementia.

With Delusions. This subtype is used if delusions are the predominant feature.

With Depressed Mood. This subtype is used if depressed mood (including presentations that meet symptom criteria for a Major Depressive Episode) is the predominant feature. A separate diagnosis of Mood Disorder Due to a General Medical Condition is not given.

Uncomplicated. This subtype is used if none of the above predominates in the current clinical presentation.

The specifier **With Behavioral Disturbance** (which cannot be coded) can also be used to indicate clinically significant behavioral disturbances (e.g., wandering).

Recording Procedures

By ICD-9-CM convention, only Vascular Dementia and Dementia of the Alzheimer's Type have codable subtypes. The diagnostic codes for Vascular Dementia depend on the subtype for predominant features: 290.41 for With Delirium, 290.42 for With Delusions, 290.43 for With Depressed Mood, 290.40 for Uncomplicated. The specifier With Behavioral Disturbance is uncoded and can be applied to each of the above subtypes (e.g., 290.43 Vascular Dementia, With Depressed Mood, With Behavioral Disturbance). In addition, the cerebrovascular condition (e.g., 436 stroke) should be coded on Axis III.

Associated Features and Disorders

Associated descriptive features and mental disorders.   See p. 135 for a general discussion of features and disorders associated with dementia.

Associated laboratory findings.   The extent of central nervous system lesions detected by CT and MRI in Vascular Dementia typically exceeds the extent of changes detected in the brains of healthy elderly persons (e.g., periventricular and white matter hyperintensities noted on MRI scans). Lesions often appear in both white matter and gray matter structures, including subcortical regions and nuclei. Evidence of old infarctions (e.g., focal atrophy) may be detected, as well as findings of more recent disease. EEG findings may reflect focal lesions in the brain. In addition, there may be laboratory evidence of associated cardiac and systemic vascular conditions (e.g., ECG abnormalities, laboratory evidence of renal failure).

Associated physical examination findings and general medical conditions. Common neurological signs (e.g., abnormal reflexes, weakness of an extremity, gait disturbance) are discussed in the "Diagnostic Features" section. There is often evidence of longstanding arterial hypertension (e.g., funduscopic abnormalities, enlarged heart), valvular heart disease (e.g., abnormal heart sounds), or extracranial vascular disease that may be sources of cerebral emboli. A single stroke may cause a relatively circumscribed change in mental state (e.g., an aphasia following damage to the left hemisphere, or an amnestic disorder from infarction in the distribution of the posterior cerebral arteries), but generally does not cause Vascular Dementia, which typically results from the occurrence of multiple strokes, usually at different times.

Specific Culture, Age, and Gender Features

See p. 137 for a general discussion of culture and age features of dementia.

The onset of Vascular Dementia is typically earlier than that of Dementia of the Alzheimer's Type. The disorder is apparently more common in males than in females.

Prevalence

Vascular Dementia is reportedly much less common than Dementia of the Alzheimer's Type.

Course

See p. 137 for a general discussion of the course of dementia.

The onset of Vascular Dementia is typically abrupt, followed by a stepwise and fluctuating course that is characterized by rapid changes in functioning rather than slow progression. The course, however, may be highly variable, and an insidious onset with gradual decline is also encountered. Usually the pattern of deficits is "patchy," depending on which regions of the brain have been destroyed. Certain cognitive functions may be affected early, whereas others remain relatively unimpaired. Early treatment of hypertension and vascular disease may prevent further progression.

Differential Diagnosis

See p. 138 for a general discussion of the differential diagnosis of dementia.

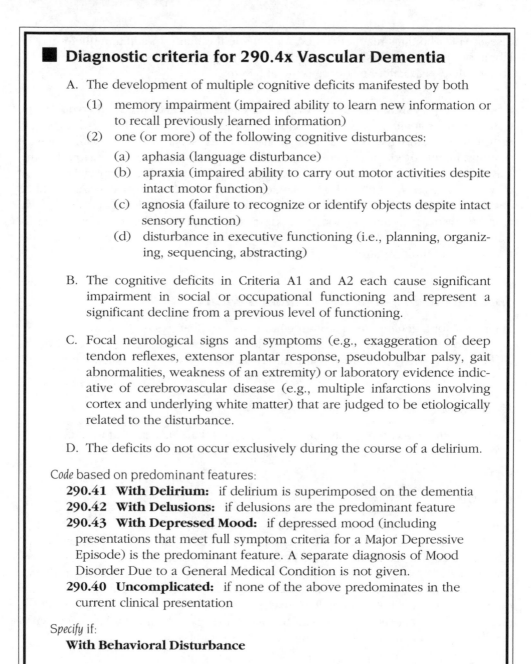

■ **Diagnostic criteria for 290.4x Vascular Dementia**

A. The development of multiple cognitive deficits manifested by both

   (1) memory impairment (impaired ability to learn new information or to recall previously learned information)

   (2) one (or more) of the following cognitive disturbances:

      (a) aphasia (language disturbance)

      (b) apraxia (impaired ability to carry out motor activities despite intact motor function)

      (c) agnosia (failure to recognize or identify objects despite intact sensory function)

      (d) disturbance in executive functioning (i.e., planning, organizing, sequencing, abstracting)

B. The cognitive deficits in Criteria A1 and A2 each cause significant impairment in social or occupational functioning and represent a significant decline from a previous level of functioning.

C. Focal neurological signs and symptoms (e.g., exaggeration of deep tendon reflexes, extensor plantar response, pseudobulbar palsy, gait abnormalities, weakness of an extremity) or laboratory evidence indicative of cerebrovascular disease (e.g., multiple infarctions involving cortex and underlying white matter) that are judged to be etiologically related to the disturbance.

D. The deficits do not occur exclusively during the course of a delirium.

Code based on predominant features:

   290.41 With Delirium: if delirium is superimposed on the dementia

   290.42 With Delusions: if delusions are the predominant feature

   290.43 With Depressed Mood: if depressed mood (including presentations that meet full symptom criteria for a Major Depressive Episode) is the predominant feature. A separate diagnosis of Mood Disorder Due to a General Medical Condition is not given.

   290.40 Uncomplicated: if none of the above predominates in the current clinical presentation

Specify if:

With Behavioral Disturbance

Coding note: Also code cerebrovascular condition on Axis III.

Dementia Due to Other General Medical Conditions

Diagnostic Features

The cognitive deficits (Criterion A) and the required impairment (Criterion B) of Dementia Due to Other General Medical Conditions are discussed on pp. 133–135. There must be evidence from the history, physical examination, or laboratory findings that a general medical condition is etiologically related to the dementia (e.g., infection with human immunodeficiency virus (HIV), traumatic brain injury, Parkinson's disease, Huntington's disease, Pick's disease, Creutzfeldt-Jakob disease, normal-pressure hydrocephalus, hypothyroidism, brain tumor, or vitamin B_{12} deficiency) (Criterion C). Dementia Due to a General Medical Condition is not diagnosed if the symptoms occur exclusively during delirium (Criterion D). However, delirium may be superimposed on a preexisting Dementia Due to a General Medical Condition, in which case both diagnoses should be given.

In determining whether the dementia is due to a general medical condition, the clinician must first establish the presence of a general medical condition. Further, the clinician must establish that the dementia is etiologically related to the general medical condition through a physiological mechanism. A careful and comprehensive assessment of multiple factors is necessary to make this judgment. Although there are no infallible guidelines for determining whether the relationship between the dementia and the general medical condition is etiological, several considerations provide some guidance in this area. One consideration is the presence of a temporal association between the onset or exacerbation of the general medical condition and that of the cognitive deficits. Evidence from the literature that suggests that there can be a direct association between the general medical condition in question and the development of a dementia can provide a useful context in the assessment of a particular situation. In addition, the clinician must also judge that the disturbance is not better accounted for by Dementia of the Alzheimer's Type, Vascular Dementia, a Substance-Induced Persisting Dementia, or another mental disorder (e.g., Major Depressive Disorder). These determinations are explained in greater detail in the "Mental Disorders Due to a General Medical Condition" section (p. 165).

See p. 135 for a general discussion of the features and disorders associated with dementia.

Recording Procedures

Specific codes are available for some of the Dementias Due to a General Medical Condition (see criteria set). The diagnostic codes and terms are selected depending on the specific etiological condition (e.g., 294.1 Dementia Due to Parkinson's disease). The etiological condition (e.g., 332.0 Parkinson's Disease) should also be recorded on Axis III. An "other" category (coded 294.1) is included for etiological conditions not specifically listed and is recorded by noting both the dementia and the specific etiological condition (e.g., 294.1 Dementia Due to Hypothyroidism) on Axis I. The ICD-9-CM code for the etiological condition should also be noted on Axis III (e.g., 244.9 hypothyroidism). (See Appendix G for a list of selected ICD-9-CM diagnostic codes for general medical conditions.)

In an individual with an established history of a dementia, a superimposed Delirium Due to a General Medical Condition should be noted by coding both the dementia and the delirium on Axis I (e.g., 294.1 Dementia Due to Parkinson's Disease and 293.0 Delirium Due to Hepatic Encephalopathy). This is in contrast to Dementia of the Alzheimer's Type and Vascular Dementia, in which the With Delirium subtype is specified.

294.9   Dementia Due to HIV Disease

The essential feature of Dementia Due to HIV Disease is the presence of a dementia that is judged to be the direct pathophysiological consequence of human immunodeficiency virus (HIV) disease. Neuropathological findings most commonly involve diffuse, multifocal destruction of the white matter and subcortical structures. The spinal fluid may show normal or slightly elevated protein and a mild lymphocytosis, and HIV can usually be isolated directly from cerebrospinal fluid. Dementia that is associated with direct HIV infection of the central nervous system is typically characterized by forgetfulness, slowness, poor concentration, and difficulties with problem solving. Behavioral manifestations most commonly include apathy and social withdrawal, and occasionally these may be accompanied by delirium, delusions, or hallucinations. Tremor, impaired rapid repetitive movements, imbalance, ataxia, hypertonia, generalized hyperreflexia, positive frontal release signs, and impaired pursuit and saccadic eye movements may be present on physical examination. Children may also develop Dementia Due to HIV Disease, typically manifested by developmental delay, hypertonia, microcephaly, and basal ganglia calcification. Dementia in association with HIV infection may also result from accompanying central nervous system tumors (e.g., primary central nervous system lymphoma) and from opportunistic infections (e.g., toxoplasmosis, cytomegalovirus infection, cryptococcosis, tuberculosis, and syphilis), in which case the appropriate type of dementia should be diagnosed (e.g., 294.1 Dementia Due to Toxoplasmosis). Unusual systemic infections (e.g., Pneumocystis carinii pneumonia) or neoplasms (e.g., Kaposi's sarcoma) may also be present.

294.1   Dementia Due to Head Trauma

The essential feature of Dementia Due to Head Trauma is the presence of a dementia that is judged to be the direct pathophysiological consequence of head trauma. The degree and type of cognitive impairments or behavioral disturbances depend on the location and extent of the brain injury. Posttraumatic amnesia is frequently present, along with persisting memory impairment. A variety of other behavioral symptoms may be evident, with or without the presence of motor or sensory deficits. These symptoms include aphasia, attentional problems, irritability, anxiety, depression or affective lability, apathy, increased aggression, or other changes in personality. Alcohol or other Substance Intoxication is often present in individuals with acute head injuries, and concurrent Substance Abuse or Dependence may be present. Head injury occurs most often in young males and has been associated with risk-taking behaviors. When it occurs in the context of a single injury, Dementia Due to Head Trauma is usually nonprogressive, but repeated head injury (e.g., from boxing) may lead to a progressive dementia (so called dementia pugilistica). A single head trauma that is followed by a progressive decline in cognitive function should raise the possibility of another superimposed process such as hydrocephalus or a Major Depressive Episode.

294.1   Dementia Due to Parkinson's Disease

The essential feature of Dementia Due to Parkinson's Disease is the presence of a dementia that is judged to be the direct pathophysiological consequence of Parkinson's disease. Parkinson's disease is a slowly progressive neurological condition, characterized by tremor, rigidity, bradykinesia, and postural instability. Dementia has been reported to occur in approximately 20%–60% of individuals with Parkinson's disease and is more likely to be present in older individuals or those with more severe or advanced disease. The dementia associated with Parkinson's disease is characterized by cognitive and motoric slowing, executive dysfunction, and impairment in memory retrieval. Declining cognitive performance in individuals with Parkinson's disease is frequently exacerbated by depression. Findings on physical examination include the characteristic abnormal motor signs of resting tremor, evidence of slowness and poverty of movement (such as micrographia), or muscular rigidity and loss of associated movements. At autopsy, neuronal loss and Lewy bodies are evident in the substantia nigra. There are a number of syndromes that may manifest with dementia, parkinsonian movement disorders, and additional neurological features (e.g., progressive supranuclear palsy, olivoponto-cerebellar degeneration, and Vascular Dementia). Some individuals with Parkinson's disease and dementia are found at autopsy to have coexisting neuropathology indicative of Alzheimer's disease or of diffuse Lewy body disease.

294.1   Dementia Due to Huntington's Disease

The essential feature of Dementia Due to Huntington's Disease is the presence of a dementia that is judged to be the direct pathophysiological consequence of Huntington's disease. Huntington's disease is an inherited progressive degenerative disease of cognition, emotion, and movement. The disease affects men and women equally and is transmitted by a single autosomal dominant gene on the short arm of chromosome 4. The disease is usually diagnosed in the late 30s to early 40s but may begin as early as age 4 years in the juvenile form or as late as age 85 years in the late-onset form. The onset of Huntington's disease is often heralded by insidious changes in behavior and personality, including depression, irritability, and anxiety. Some individuals present with abnormalities of movement that resemble increased fidgeting and that later progress to characteristic generalized choreoathetosis. Difficulties with memory retrieval, executive functioning, and judgment are common early in the course, with more severe memory deficits occurring as the disease progresses. Disorganized speech and psychotic features are sometimes present. Late in the disease, characteristic "boxcar ventricles" may be seen on structural brain imaging due to the atrophy of the striatum. Positron-emission tomography (PET) may show striatal hypometabolism early in the disease. Offspring of individuals with Huntington's disease have a 50% chance of developing the disease. A genetic test is available to determine with relative certainty whether a given at-risk individual is likely to develop the disease; however, such testing may be best adminis-tered by centers with experience in counseling and follow-up of individuals at risk for Huntington's disease.

290.10   Dementia Due to Pick's Disease

The essential feature of Dementia Due to Pick's Disease is the presence of a dementia that is judged to be the direct pathophysiological consequence of Pick's disease. Pick's disease is a degenerative disease of the brain that particularly affects the frontal and temporal lobes. As in other frontal lobe dementias, Pick's disease is characterized clinically by changes in personality early in the course, deterioration of social skills, emotional blunting, behavioral disinhibition, and prominent language abnormalities. Difficulties with memory, apraxia, and other features of dementia usually follow later in the course. Prominent primitive reflexes (snout, suck, grasp) may be present. As the dementia progresses, it may be accompanied by either apathy or extreme agitation. Individuals may develop such severe problems in language, attention, or behavior that it may be difficult to assess their degree of cognitive impairment. Structural brain imaging typically reveals prominent frontal and/or temporal atrophy, and functional brain imaging may localize frontotemporal hypometabolism, even in the absence of clear structural atrophy. The disorder most commonly manifests itself in individuals between ages 50 and 60 years, although it can occur among older individuals. Pick's disease is one of the pathologically distinct etiologies among the heterogeneous group of dementing processes that are associated with frontotemporal brain atrophy. The specific diagnosis of a frontal lobe dementia such as Pick's disease is usually established at autopsy with the pathological finding of characteristic intraneuronal argentophilic Pick inclusion bodies. Clinically, Pick's disease often cannot be distinguished with certainty from atypical cases of Alzheimer's disease or from other dementias that affect the frontal lobes.

290.10   Dementia Due to Creutzfeldt-Jakob Disease

The essential feature of Dementia Due to Creutzfeldt-Jakob Disease is the presence of a dementia that is judged to be the direct pathophysiological consequence of Creutzfeldt-Jakob disease. Jacob-Creutzfeldt disease is one of the subacute spongiform encephalopathies, a group of central nervous system diseases caused by transmissible agents known as "slow viruses" or prions. Typically, individuals with Creutzfeldt-Jakob disease manifest the clinical triad of dementia, involuntary movements (particularly myoclonus), and periodic EEG activity. However, up to 25% of individuals with the disorder may have atypical presentations, and the disease can be confirmed only by biopsy or at autopsy with the demonstration of spongiform neuropathological changes. Creutzfeldt-Jakob disease may develop at any age in adults, but most typically when they are between ages 40 and 60 years. From 5% to 15% of cases may have a familial component. Prodromal symptoms of Creutzfeldt-Jakob disease may include fatigue, anxiety, or problems with appetite, sleeping, or concentration and may be followed after several weeks by incoordination, altered vision, or abnormal gait or other movements that may be myoclonic, choreoathetoid, or ballistic, along with a rapidly progressive dementia. The disease typically progresses very rapidly over several months, although more rarely it can progress over years and appear similar in its course to other dementias. There are no distinctive findings on cerebrospinal fluid analysis, and nonspecific atrophy may be apparent on neuroimaging. In most individuals, the EEG typically reveals periodic sharp, often triphasic and synchronous discharges at a rate of 0.5–2 Hz at some point during the course of the disorder. The transmissible agent thought to be responsible for Creutzfeldt-Jakob disease is resistant to boiling, formalin, alcohol, and ultraviolet radiation, but it can be inactivated by pressured autoclaving or by bleach. Transmission by corneal transplantation and human growth factor injection has been documented, and anecdotal cases of transmission to health care workers have been reported. Therefore, when neurosurgery, brain biopsy, or brain autopsy is undertaken, universal precautions should be taken with both tissue and equipment that comes in contact with tissue.

294.1 Dementia Due to Other General Medical Conditions

In addition to the specific categories described above, a number of other general medical conditions can cause dementia. These conditions include structural lesions (primary or secondary brain tumors, subdural hematoma, slowly progressive or normal-pressure hydrocephalus), endocrine conditions (hypothyroidism, hypercalcemia, hypoglycemia), nutritional conditions (deficiencies of thiamine, niacin, and vitamin B_{12}), other infectious conditions (neurosyphilis, cryptococcosis), derangements of renal and hepatic function, and other neurological conditions such as multiple sclerosis. Unusual causes of central nervous system injury, such as electrical shock or intracranial radiation, are generally evident from the history. Rare disorders such as the childhood and adult storage diseases have a distinctive family history or clinical presentation. Associated physical examination and laboratory findings and other clinical features depend on the nature and severity of the general medical condition.

Differential Diagnosis

See p. 138 for a general discussion of the differential diagnosis of dementia.

■ **Diagnostic criteria for Dementia Due to Other General Medical Conditions**

A. The development of multiple cognitive deficits manifested by both

  (1) memory impairment (impaired ability to learn new information or to recall previously learned information)

  (2) one (or more) of the following cognitive disturbances:

   (a) aphasia (language disturbance)

   (b) apraxia (impaired ability to carry out motor activities despite intact motor function)

   (c) agnosia (failure to recognize or identify objects despite intact sensory function)

   (d) disturbance in executive functioning (i.e., planning, organizing, sequencing, abstracting)

B. The cognitive deficits in Criteria A1 and A2 each cause significant impairment in social or occupational functioning and represent a significant decline from a previous level of functioning.

(continued)

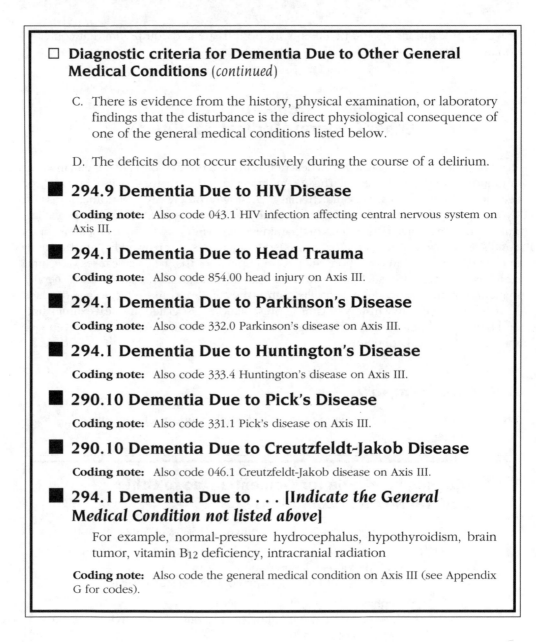

☐ **Diagnostic criteria for Dementia Due to Other General Medical Conditions** (*continued*)

C. There is evidence from the history, physical examination, or laboratory findings that the disturbance is the direct physiological consequence of one of the general medical conditions listed below.

D. The deficits do not occur exclusively during the course of a delirium.

■ **294.9 Dementia Due to HIV Disease**

Coding note: Also code 043.1 HIV infection affecting central nervous system on Axis III.

■ **294.1 Dementia Due to Head Trauma**

Coding note: Also code 854.00 head injury on Axis III.

■ **294.1 Dementia Due to Parkinson's Disease**

Coding note: Also code 332.0 Parkinson's disease on Axis III.

■ **294.1 Dementia Due to Huntington's Disease**

Coding note: Also code 333.4 Huntington's disease on Axis III.

■ **290.10 Dementia Due to Pick's Disease**

Coding note: Also code 331.1 Pick's disease on Axis III.

■ **290.10 Dementia Due to Creutzfeldt-Jakob Disease**

Coding note: Also code 046.1 Creutzfeldt-Jakob disease on Axis III.

■ **294.1 Dementia Due to . . . [*Indicate the General Medical Condition not listed above*]**

For example, normal-pressure hydrocephalus, hypothyroidism, brain tumor, vitamin B_{12} deficiency, intracranial radiation

Coding note: Also code the general medical condition on Axis III (see Appendix G for codes).

Substance-Induced Persisting Dementia

Diagnostic and Associated Features

The cognitive deficits (Criterion A) and the required impairment (Criterion B) are discussed on pp. 133–135. Substance-Induced Persisting Dementia is not diagnosed if the symptoms persist beyond the usual duration of Substance Intoxication or Withdrawal or if they occur exclusively during the course of a delirium (Criterion C). However, delirium may be superimposed on a preexisting Substance-Induced Persisting Dementia, in which case both diagnoses should be given. There must be evidence from the history, physical examination, or laboratory findings that the deficits are etiologically related to the persisting effects of substance use (e.g., a drug of abuse, a medication, toxin exposure) (Criterion D). This disorder is termed "persisting" because the dementia persists long after the individual has experienced the effects of Substance Intoxication or Substance Withdrawal.

Features that are associated with Substance-Induced Persisting Dementia are those associated with dementias generally (see p. 135). Even if currently abstinent from substance use, most individuals with this disorder have previously had a pattern of prolonged and heavy substance use that met criteria for Substance Dependence. Because these disorders persist long after use of the substance has stopped, blood or urine screens may be negative for the etiological substance. The age at onset of Substance-Induced Persisting Dementia is rarely before age 20 years. This disorder usually has an insidious onset and slow progression, typically during a period when the person qualifies for a Substance Dependence diagnosis. The deficits are usually permanent and may worsen even if the substance use stops, although some cases do show improvement.

For a more detailed discussion of the features associated with Substance-Related Disorders, see p. 175.

Recording Procedures

The name of the diagnosis begins with the specific substance (e.g., alcohol) that is presumed to have caused the dementia. The diagnostic code is selected from the listing of classes of substances provided in the criteria set. For substances that do not fit into any of the classes, the code for "Other Substance" should be used. In addition, for medications prescribed at therapeutic doses, the specific medication can be indicated by listing the appropriate E-code (see Appendix G). When more than one substance is judged to play a significant role in the development of the persisting dementia, each should be listed separately (e.g., 291.2 Alcohol-Induced Persisting Dementia; 292.82 Inhalant-Induced Persisting Dementia). If a substance is judged to be the etiological factor, but the specific substance or class of substances is unknown, the diagnosis is 292.82 Unknown Substance–Induced Persisting Dementia.

Specific Substances

Substance-Induced Persisting Dementia can occur in association with the following classes of substances: alcohol; inhalants; sedatives, hypnotics, and anxiolytics; or other or unknown substances. Medications reported to cause dementia include anticonvulsants and intrathecal methotrexate. Toxins reported to evoke symptoms of dementia include lead, mercury, carbon monoxide, organophosphate insecticides, and industrial solvents.

Differential Diagnosis

See p. 138 for a general discussion of the differential diagnosis of dementia.

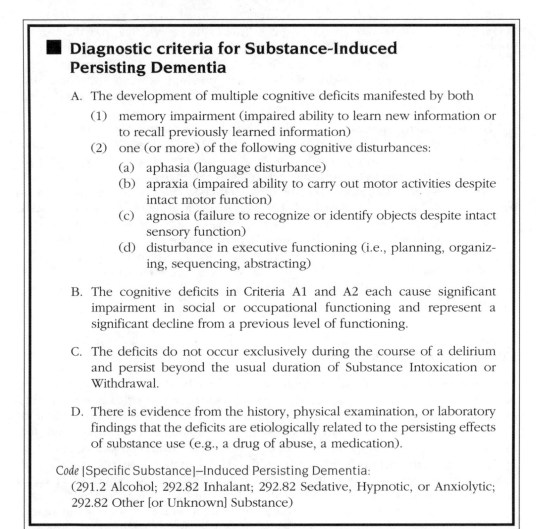

■ **Diagnostic criteria for Substance-Induced Persisting Dementia**

A. The development of multiple cognitive deficits manifested by both

  (1) memory impairment (impaired ability to learn new information or to recall previously learned information)

  (2) one (or more) of the following cognitive disturbances:

  (a) aphasia (language disturbance)

  (b) apraxia (impaired ability to carry out motor activities despite intact motor function)

  (c) agnosia (failure to recognize or identify objects despite intact sensory function)

  (d) disturbance in executive functioning (i.e., planning, organizing, sequencing, abstracting)

B. The cognitive deficits in Criteria A1 and A2 each cause significant impairment in social or occupational functioning and represent a significant decline from a previous level of functioning.

C. The deficits do not occur exclusively during the course of a delirium and persist beyond the usual duration of Substance Intoxication or Withdrawal.

D. There is evidence from the history, physical examination, or laboratory findings that the deficits are etiologically related to the persisting effects of substance use (e.g., a drug of abuse, a medication).

Code [Specific Substance]–Induced Persisting Dementia:
  (291.2 Alcohol; 292.82 Inhalant; 292.82 Sedative, Hypnotic, or Anxiolytic; 292.82 Other [or Unknown] Substance)

Dementia Due to Multiple Etiologies

The Dementia Due to Multiple Etiologies category is included to alert clinicians to the common situation in which the dementia has more than one etiology. More than one general medical condition may be etiologically related to the dementia (e.g., Dementia of the Alzheimer's Type and Dementia Due to Head Trauma), or the dementia may be due to the combined effects of a general medical condition (e.g., Parkinson's disease) and the long-term use of a substance (e.g., Alcohol-Induced Persisting Dementia).

Recording Procedures

Dementia Due to Multiple Etiologies does not have its own separate code and should not be recorded as a diagnosis. For example, both Dementia of the Alzheimer's Type and Vascular Dementia should be diagnosed for an individual with Dementia of the

Alzheimer's Type, With Late Onset, Uncomplicated, who, over the course of several strokes, develops a significant further decline in cognitive functioning. In this example, the clinician would list both 290.0 Dementia of the Alzheimer's Type, With Late Onset, Uncomplicated, and 290.40, Vascular Dementia, Uncomplicated, on Axis I, and 331.0 Alzheimer's Disease and 436 Stroke on Axis III.

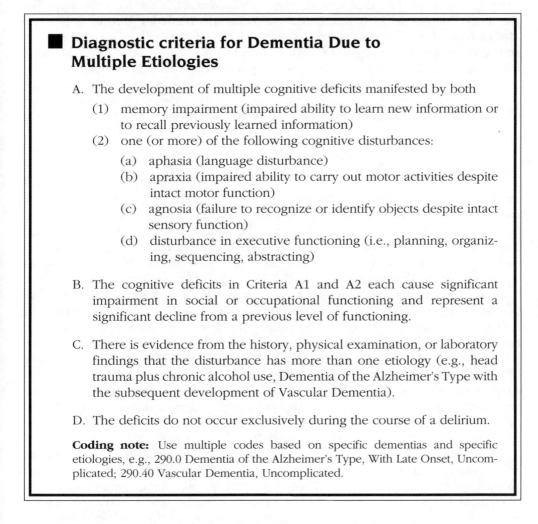

■ **Diagnostic criteria for Dementia Due to Multiple Etiologies**

A. The development of multiple cognitive deficits manifested by both

   (1) memory impairment (impaired ability to learn new information or to recall previously learned information)
   (2) one (or more) of the following cognitive disturbances:

      (a) aphasia (language disturbance)
      (b) apraxia (impaired ability to carry out motor activities despite intact motor function)
      (c) agnosia (failure to recognize or identify objects despite intact sensory function)
      (d) disturbance in executive functioning (i.e., planning, organizing, sequencing, abstracting)

B. The cognitive deficits in Criteria A1 and A2 each cause significant impairment in social or occupational functioning and represent a significant decline from a previous level of functioning.

C. There is evidence from the history, physical examination, or laboratory findings that the disturbance has more than one etiology (e.g., head trauma plus chronic alcohol use, Dementia of the Alzheimer's Type with the subsequent development of Vascular Dementia).

D. The deficits do not occur exclusively during the course of a delirium.

Coding note: Use multiple codes based on specific dementias and specific etiologies, e.g., 290.0 Dementia of the Alzheimer's Type, With Late Onset, Uncomplicated; 290.40 Vascular Dementia, Uncomplicated.

294.8 Dementia Not Otherwise Specified

This category should be used to diagnose a dementia that does not meet criteria for any of the specific types described in this section.

An example is a clinical presentation of dementia for which there is insufficient evidence to establish a specific etiology.

Amnestic Disorders

The disorders in the "Amnestic Disorders" section are characterized by a disturbance in memory that is either due to the direct physiological effects of a general medical condition or due to the persisting effects of a substance (i.e., a drug of abuse, a medication, or toxin exposure). The disorders in this section share the common symptom presentation of memory impairment, but are differentiated based on etiology. The diagnostic features listed below pertain to **Amnestic Disorder Due to a General Medical Condition** (e.g., physical trauma and vitamin deficiency) and **Substance-Induced Persisting Amnestic Disorder** (including medication side effects). In addition, **Amnestic Disorder Not Otherwise Specified** is included in this section for presentations in which the clinician is unable to determine a specific etiology for the memory disturbance. Text and criteria for Dissociative Disorders involving memory loss are not included here and instead are contained in the Dissociative Disorders section (see p. 477).

Diagnostic Features

Individuals with an amnestic disorder are impaired in their ability to learn new information or are unable to recall previously learned information or past events (Criterion A). The memory disturbance must be sufficiently severe to cause marked impairment in social or occupational functioning and must represent a significant decline from a previous level of functioning (Criterion B). The memory disturbance must not occur exclusively during the course of a delirium or a dementia (Criterion C). The ability to learn and recall new information is always affected in an amnestic disorder, whereas problems remembering previously learned information occur more variably, depending on the location and severity of brain damage. The memory deficit is most apparent on tasks that require spontaneous recall and may also be evident when the examiner provides stimuli for the person to recall at a later time. Depending on the specific area of the brain affected, deficits may be predominantly related to verbal or visual stimuli. In some forms of an amnestic disorder, the individual may remember things from the very remote past better than more recent events (e.g., a person may remember in vivid detail a hospital stay that took place a decade before the examination, but may have no idea that he or she is currently in the hospital).

The diagnosis is not made if the memory impairment occurs exclusively during the course of a delirium (i.e., occurs only in the context of reduced ability to maintain and shift attention). The ability to immediately repeat a sequential string of information (e.g., digit span) is typically not impaired in an amnestic disorder. When such impairment is evident, it suggests the presence of an attentional disturbance that may be indicative of a delirium. The diagnosis is also not made in the presence of other cognitive deficits (e.g., aphasia, apraxia, agnosia, disturbance in executive functioning) that are characteristic of a dementia. Individuals with an amnestic disorder may experience major impairment in their social and vocational functioning as a result of their memory deficits, which, at its extreme, may necessitate supervised living situations to ensure appropriate feeding and care.

Associated Features and Disorders

An amnestic disorder is often preceded by an evolving clinical picture that includes confusion and disorientation, occasionally with attentional problems that suggest a delirium (e.g., Amnestic Disorder Due to Thiamine Deficiency). Confabulation, often evidenced by the recitation of imaginary events to fill gaps in memory, may be noted during the early stages of an amnestic disorder but tends to disappear with time. It may therefore be important to obtain corroborating information from family members or other informants. Profound amnesia may result in disorientation to place and time, but rarely to self. Disorientation to self may be encountered in individuals with a dementia but is unusual in an amnestic disorder. Most individuals with a severe Amnestic Disorder lack insight into their memory deficits and may explicitly deny the presence of severe memory impairment despite evidence to the contrary. This lack of insight may lead to accusations against others or, in rare instances, to agitation. Some individuals may acknowledge that they have a problem but appear unconcerned. Apathy, lack of initiative, emotional blandness, or other changes suggestive of altered personality function may be encountered. Individuals may be superficially friendly or agreeable, but they may have a shallow or diminished range of affective expression. Individuals with transient global amnesia often appear bewildered or befuddled. Subtle deficits in other cognitive functions may be noted, but, by definition, they are not severe enough to cause clinically significant impairment. Quantitative neuropsychological testing often demonstrates specific memory deficits in the absence of other cognitive disturbances. Performance on standardized tests that assess recall of well-known historical events or public figures may be variable among individuals with an Amnestic Disorder, depending on the nature and extent of the deficit.

Specific Culture Features

Cultural and educational background should be taken into consideration in the evaluation of memory. Individuals from certain backgrounds may not be familiar with the information used in certain tests of memory (e.g., date of birth in cultures that do not routinely celebrate birthdays).

Course

Age at onset and subsequent course of amnestic disorders may be quite variable, depending on the primary pathological process causing the amnestic disorder. Traumatic brain injury, stroke or other cerebrovascular events, or specific types of neurotoxic exposure (e.g., carbon monoxide poisoning) may lead to an acute onset of an amnestic disorder. Other conditions such as prolonged substance abuse, chronic neurotoxic exposure, or sustained nutritional deficiency may lead to an insidious onset. Transient amnesia due to a cerebrovascular etiology may be recurrent, with episodes lasting from several hours to several days. Amnestic Disorders Due to Head Trauma may last for variable amounts of time, with a characteristic pattern of greatest deficit immediately after injury and improvement during the ensuing 2 years (further improvement beyond 24 months has been noted, but less commonly). Disorders due to destruction of middle-temporal lobe structures (e.g., from infarction, surgical ablation, or malnutrition occurring in the context of Alcohol Dependence) may cause persisting impairments.

Differential Diagnosis

Memory impairment is also a feature of **delirium** and **dementia.** In delirium, memory dysfunction occurs in association with impaired consciousness, with reduced ability to focus, sustain, or shift attention. In dementia, memory impairment must be accompanied by multiple cognitive deficits (i.e., aphasia, apraxia, agnosia, or a disturbance in executive functioning) that lead to clinically significant impairment.

An amnestic disorder must be distinguished from **Dissociative Amnesia** and amnesia occurring in the context of **other Dissociative Disorders** (e.g., **Dissociative Identity Disorder**). By definition, an amnestic disorder is due to the direct physiological effects of a general medical condition or substance use. Furthermore, amnesia in Dissociative Disorders typically does not involve deficits in learning and recalling new information; rather, individuals present with a circumscribed inability to recall previous memories, usually of a traumatic or stressful nature.

For memory disturbances (e.g., blackouts) that occur only during intoxication with or withdrawal from a drug of abuse, the appropriate **Substance Intoxication** or **Substance Withdrawal** should be diagnosed and a separate amnestic disorder diagnosis is not made. For memory disturbances that are associated with the use of medication, Adverse Effects of Medication Not Otherwise Specified (p. 680) may be noted, with the medication indicated by the use of an E-code (see Appendix G).

The presumed etiology of the amnestic disorder determines the diagnosis (text and criteria for each amnestic disorder diagnosis are provided separately later in this section). If it is judged that the memory disturbance is a consequence of the direct physiological effects of a general medical condition (including head trauma), then **Amnestic Disorder Due to a General Medical Condition** is diagnosed. If the memory disturbance results from the persisting effects of a substance (i.e., a drug of abuse, a medication, or toxin exposure), then **Substance-Induced Persisting Amnestic Disorder** is diagnosed. When both a substance (e.g., alcohol) and a general medical condition (e.g., head trauma) have had an etiological role in the development of the memory disturbance, both diagnoses are given. If it is not possible to establish a specific etiology (i.e., dissociative, substance induced, or due to a general medical condition), **Amnestic Disorder Not Otherwise Specified** is diagnosed.

Amnestic disorder must be distinguished from **Malingering** and from **Factitious Disorder.** This difficult distinction can be assisted by systematic memory testing (which often yields inconsistent results in Factitious Disorder or Malingering) and by the absence of a general medical condition or substance use that is etiologically related to the memory impairment.

Amnestic disorder should be distinguished from the less efficient memory characteristic of **Age-Related Cognitive Decline,** which is within the expected age-adjusted normative range for the individual.

294.0 Amnestic Disorder
Due to a General Medical Condition

Diagnostic and Associated Features

The descriptive features of Amnestic Disorder Due to a General Medical Condition (Criteria A–C) are discussed on p. 156. In addition, the diagnosis requires that there must be evidence from the history, physical examination, or laboratory findings that the memory disturbance is the direct physiological consequence of a general medical condition (including physical trauma) (Criterion D).

In determining whether the amnestic disturbance is due to a general medical condition, the clinician must first establish the presence of a general medical condition. Further, the clinician must establish that the amnestic disturbance is etiologically related to the general medical condition through a physiological mechanism. A careful and comprehensive assessment of multiple factors is necessary to make this judgment. Although there are no infallible guidelines for determining whether the relationship between the amnestic disturbance and the general medical condition is etiological, several considerations provide some guidance in this area. One consideration is the presence of a temporal association between the onset, exacerbation, or remission of the general medical condition and that of the amnestic disturbance. A second consideration is the presence of features that are atypical of memory impairment in the context of a dissociative or other mental disorder (e.g., atypical age at onset or course). Evidence from the literature that suggests that there can be a direct association between the general medical condition in question and the development of memory impairment can provide a useful context in the assessment of a particular situation. In addition, the clinician must also judge that the disturbance is not better accounted for by a Dissociative Disorder, Substance-Induced Persisting Amnestic Disorder, or another primary mental disorder (e.g., Major Depressive Disorder). These determinations are explained in greater detail in the "Mental Disorders Due to a General Medical Condition" section (p. 165).

Individuals with Amnestic Disorder Due to a General Medical Condition often show other features of the primary systemic or cerebral disease that caused the memory impairment. However, disordered mental status may be the sole presenting feature. There are no specific or diagnostic features detectable with procedures such as magnetic resonance imaging (MRI) or computed tomography (CT). However, damage to mediotemporal lobe structures is common and may be reflected by enlargement of third ventricle or temporal horns or by structural atrophy detected on MRI.

Specifiers

The following specifiers may be noted to indicate the duration of the disturbance.

> **Transient.**   This specifier is used to indicate durations usually from several hours to a few days and for no more than 1 month. When the diagnosis is made within the first month without waiting for recovery, the term "provisional" may be added. "Transient global amnesia" is a specific form of transient amnestic disorder, characterized by a dense, transitory inability to learn new information and a variable impaired ability to recall events that occurred just before, or in the midst of, the etiological cerebrovascular problem.
>
> **Chronic.**   This specifier is used for disturbances that last for more than 1 month.

Recording Procedures

In recording the diagnosis of Amnestic Disorder Due to a General Medical Condition, the clinician should note the identified general medical condition judged to be causing the disturbance on Axis I (e.g., 294.0 Amnestic Disorder Due to Stroke). The ICD-9-CM code for the general medical condition should also be noted on Axis III (e.g., 436 stroke).

(See Appendix G for a list of selected ICD-9-CM diagnostic codes for general medical conditions.)

Associated General Medical Conditions

An amnestic disorder often occurs as the result of pathological processes (e.g., closed head trauma, penetrating missile wounds, surgical intervention, hypoxia, infarction of the distribution of the posterior cerebral artery, and herpes simplex encephalitis) that cause damage to specific diencephalic and mediotemporal lobe structures (e.g., mammillary bodies, hippocampus, fornix). Pathology is most often bilateral, but deficits may arise from unilateral lesions. Transient Amnestic Disorder, when encountered as "transient global amnesia," is typically associated with cerebrovascular disease and pathology in the vertebrobasilar system. Transient Amnestic Disorder may also arise from episodic general medical conditions (e.g., metabolic conditions or seizures).

Differential Diagnosis

See p. 158 for a discussion of the differential diagnosis of amnestic disorders.

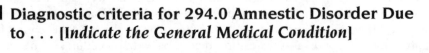
Diagnostic criteria for 294.0 Amnestic Disorder Due to . . . [Indicate the General Medical Condition]

A. The development of memory impairment as manifested by impairment in the ability to learn new information or the inability to recall previously learned information.

B. The memory disturbance causes significant impairment in social or occupational functioning and represents a significant decline from a previous level of functioning.

C. The memory disturbance does not occur exclusively during the course of a delirium or a dementia.

D. There is evidence from the history, physical examination, or laboratory findings that the disturbance is the direct physiological consequence of a general medical condition (including physical trauma).

Specify if:
Transient: if memory impairment lasts for 1 month or less
Chronic: if memory impairment lasts for more than 1 month

Coding note: Include the name of the general medical condition on Axis I, e.g., 294.0 Amnestic Disorder Due to Head Trauma; also code the general medical condition on Axis III (see Appendix G for codes).

Substance-Induced Persisting Amnestic Disorder

Diagnostic and Associated Features

The descriptive features of Substance-Induced Persisting Amnestic Disorder (Criteria A and B) are discussed on p. 156. The memory disturbance does not occur exclusively during the course of a delirium or a dementia and persists beyond the usual duration of Substance Intoxication or Withdrawal (Criterion C). In addition, to diagnose Substance-Induced Persisting Amnestic Disorder, there must be evidence from the history, physical examination, or laboratory findings that the memory disturbance is etiologically related to the persisting effects of substance use (e.g., a drug of abuse, a medication, toxin exposure) (Criterion D). This disorder is termed "persisting" because the memory disturbance persists long after the individual is no longer experiencing the effects of Substance Intoxication or Substance Withdrawal.

Features that are associated with Substance-Induced Persisting Amnestic Disorder are those associated with amnestic disorders generally (see p. 156). Even if currently abstinent from substance use, most individuals with this disorder have previously had a pattern of prolonged and heavy substance use that met criteria for Substance Dependence. Because these disorders persist long after use of the substance has stopped, blood or urine screens may be negative for the etiological substance. The age at onset is rarely before age 20 years. The resulting impairment may remain stable or worsen, even if substance use stops.

For a more detailed discussion of the features associated with Substance-Related Disorders, see p. 175.

Recording Procedures

The name of the diagnosis begins with the specific substance (e.g., alcohol, secobarbital) that is presumed to be causing the memory disturbance. The diagnostic code is selected from the listing of classes of substances provided in the criteria set. For substances that do not fit into any of the classes, the code for "Other Substance" should be used. In addition, for medications prescribed at therapeutic doses, the specific medication can be indicated by listing the appropriate E-code (see Appendix G). When more than one substance is judged to play a significant role in the development of the memory disturbance, each should be listed separately (e.g., 291.1 Alcohol-Induced Persisting Amnestic Disorder; 292.83 Secobarbital-Induced Persisting Amnestic Disorder). If a substance is judged to be the etiological factor but the specific substance or class of substances is unknown, the diagnosis is 292.83 Unknown Substance–Induced Persisting Amnestic Disorder.

Specific Substances

Substance-Induced Persisting Amnestic Disorder can occur in association with the following classes of substances: alcohol; sedatives, hypnotics, and anxiolytics; and other or unknown substances.

Alcohol-Induced Persisting Amnestic Disorder is apparently due to the vitamin deficiency that is associated with prolonged, heavy ingestion of alcohol. Neurological disturbances such as peripheral neuropathy, cerebellar ataxia, and myopathy are among the associated features. Alcohol-Induced Persisting Amnestic Disorder due to thiamine deficiency (Korsakoff's syndrome) often follows an acute episode of Wernicke's encephalopathy, a neurological condition manifested by confusion, ataxia, eye-movement abnormalities (gaze palsies, nystagmus), and other neurological signs. Gradually, these manifestations subside, but a major impairment of memory remains. If Wernicke's encephalopathy is treated early with large doses of thiamine, Alcohol-Induced Persisting Amnestic Disorder may not develop. Although age is not a specific etiological factor in the condition, individuals who develop Alcohol-Induced Persisting Amnestic Disorder generally have histories of many years of heavy alcohol use and are most often over age 40 years. Although the mode of onset is typically abrupt, some individuals may develop deficits insidiously over many years, due to repeated toxic and nutritional insults, prior to the emergence of a final, more dramatically impairing episode apparently related to thiamine deficiency. Once established, Alcohol-Induced Persisting Amnestic Disorder usually persists indefinitely, although there may be slight improvement over time and in a minority of the cases the condition can remit. Impairment is usually quite severe, and lifelong custodial care may be necessary. Sedative-, Hypnotic-, or Anxiolytic-Induced Persisting Amnestic Disorder can follow prolonged and heavy use of drugs from this class. The course is variable, and, unlike Alcohol-Induced Persisting Amnestic Disorder, full recovery can occur. Medications reported to cause amnestic disorders include anticonvulsants and intrathecal methotrexate. Toxins reported to evoke symptoms of amnesia include lead, mercury, carbon monoxide, organophosphate insecticides, and industrial solvents.

Differential Diagnosis

See p. 158 for a general discussion of the differential diagnosis of amnestic disorders.

■ **Diagnostic criteria for Substance-Induced Persisting Amnestic Disorder**

  A. The development of memory impairment as manifested by impairment in the ability to learn new information or the inability to recall previously learned information.

  B. The memory disturbance causes significant impairment in social or occupational functioning and represents a significant decline from a previous level of functioning.

  C. The memory disturbance does not occur exclusively during the course of a delirium or a dementia and persists beyond the usual duration of Substance Intoxication or Withdrawal.

  D. There is evidence from the history, physical examination, or laboratory findings that the memory disturbance is etiologically related to the persisting effects of substance use (e.g., a drug of abuse, a medication).

Code [Specific Substance]–Induced Persisting Amnestic Disorder:
   (291.1 Alcohol; 292.83 Sedative, Hypnotic, or Anxiolytic; 292.83 Other [or Unknown] Substance)

294.8   Amnestic Disorder Not Otherwise Specified

This category should be used to diagnose an amnestic disorder that does not meet criteria for any of the specific types described in this section.

An example is a clinical presentation of amnesia for which there is insufficient evidence to establish a specific etiology (i.e., dissociative, substance induced, or due to a general medical condition).

Other Cognitive Disorders

294.9   Cognitive Disorder Not Otherwise Specified

This category is for disorders that are characterized by cognitive dysfunction presumed to be due to the direct physiological effect of a general medical condition that do not meet criteria for any of the specific deliriums, dementias, or amnestic disorders listed in this section and that are not better classified as Delirium Not Otherwise Specified, Dementia Not Otherwise Specified, or Amnestic Disorder Not Otherwise Specified. For cognitive dysfunction due to a specific or unknown substance, the specific Substance-Related Disorder Not Otherwise Specified category should be used.

Examples include

1. Mild neurocognitive disorder: impairment in cognitive functioning as evidenced by neuropsychological testing or quantified clinical assessment, accompanied by objective evidence of a systemic general medical condition or central nervous system dysfunction (see p. 706 for suggested research criteria)
2. Postconcussional disorder: following a head trauma, impairment in memory or attention with associated symptoms (see p. 704 for suggested research criteria)

Mental Disorders Due to a General Medical Condition

A Mental Disorder Due to a General Medical Condition is characterized by the presence of mental symptoms that are judged to be the direct physiological consequence of a general medical condition. The term *general medical condition* refers to conditions that are coded on Axis III and that are listed outside the "Mental Disorders" chapter of ICD. (See Appendix G for a condensed list of these conditions.) As discussed in the "Introduction" to this manual, maintaining the distinction between mental disorders and general medical conditions does not imply that there are fundamental differences in their conceptualization, that mental disorders are unrelated to physical or biological factors or processes, or that general medical conditions are unrelated to behavioral or psychosocial factors or processes. The purpose of distinguishing general medical conditions from mental disorders is to encourage thoroughness in evaluation and to provide a shorthand term to enhance communication among health care providers. However, in clinical practice, it is expected that more specific terminology will be used to identify the specific condition involved.

In DSM-III-R, the Mental Disorders Due to a General Medical Condition and the Substance-Induced Disorders were called "organic" disorders and were listed together in a single section. This differentiation of "organic" mental disorders as a separate class implied that "nonorganic" or "functional" mental disorders were somehow unrelated to physical or biological factors or processes. DSM-IV eliminates the term *organic* and distinguishes those mental disorders that are due to a general medical condition from those that are substance induced and those that have no specified etiology. The term *primary mental disorder* is used as a shorthand to indicate those mental disorders that are not due to a general medical condition and that are not substance induced.

Text and criteria for three of these disorders (i.e., **Catatonic Disorder Due to a General Medical Condition, Personality Change Due to a General Medical Condition,** and **Mental Disorder Not Otherwise Specified Due to a General Medical Condition**) are included in this section. The text and criteria for the conditions listed below are placed in other sections of the manual with disorders with which they share phenomenology. The manual has been organized in this fashion to alert clinicians to consider these disorders in making a differential diagnosis.

293.0   Delirium Due to a General Medical Condition   Text and criteria are included in the "Delirium, Dementia, and Amnestic and Other Cognitive Disorders" section, p. 127.

——.— Dementia Due to a General Medical Condition   Text and criteria are included in the "Delirium, Dementia, and Amnestic and Other Cognitive Disorders" section, p. 139.

294.0   Amnestic Disorder Due to a General Medical Condition   Text and criteria are included in the "Delirium, Dementia, and Amnestic and Other Cognitive Disorders" section, p. 158.

293.8x   Psychotic Disorder Due to a General Medical Condition   Text and criteria are included in the "Schizophrenia and Other Psychotic Disorders" section, p. 306.

293.83   Mood Disorder Due to a General Medical Condition   Text and criteria are included in the "Mood Disorders" section, p. 366.

293.89   Anxiety Disorder Due to a General Medical Condition   Text and criteria are included in the "Anxiety Disorders" section, p. 436.

——.— Sexual Dysfunction Due to a General Medical Condition   Text and criteria are included in the "Sexual and Gender Identity Disorders" section, p. 515.

780.5x   Sleep Disorder Due to a General Medical Condition   Text and criteria are included in the "Sleep Disorders" section, p. 597.

Diagnostic Features

Three criteria appear in the criteria sets for each of the Mental Disorders Due to a General Medical Condition:

> **B. There is evidence from the history, physical examination, or laboratory findings that the disturbance is the direct physiological consequence of a general medical condition.**

Application of this criterion requires two separate judgments: that a general medical condition is present (ascertained by history, physical examination, or laboratory assessment) and that the disturbance (e.g., psychotic, mood, anxiety symptoms) is etiologically related to the general medical condition through a physiological mechanism. Although there are no infallible guidelines for determining whether the relationship between the disturbance and the general medical condition is etiological, several considerations provide guidance in this area. One consideration is the presence of a temporal association between the onset, exacerbation, or remission of the general medical condition and that of the mental disorder (e.g., symptoms of anxiety in an individual with a parathyroid adenoma that resolve after surgical excision restores a normal serum calcium level). Although evidence of a close temporal relationship is often useful in making a judgment about etiology, there are many exceptions. For example, Psychotic Disorder Due to Epilepsy can emerge many years after the onset of seizures. Alternatively, symptoms and signs of a mental disorder can be among the first manifestations of a systemic or cerebral disease, appearing months or more before the detection of the underlying pathological process (e.g., depressed mood preceding choreiform movements in Huntington's disease). Mental Disorders Due to a General Medical Condition can also persist after the general medical condition has resolved (e.g., depressed mood persisting after thyroid hormone replacement). Moreover, a Mental Disorder Due to a General Medical Condition can be amenable to symptomatic treatment even while the general medical condition remains active (e.g., depression in epilepsy). Treatment targeted to the general medical condition that alleviates the symptoms of both the general medical condition and the mental disturbance may provide stronger evidence of an etiological relationship.

A second important consideration is the presence of features that are atypical of the primary mental disorder. The most common example is an atypical age at onset or course (e.g., first appearance of schizophrenic-like symptoms in a 75-year-old individual). There may be unusual associated features (e.g., visual or tactile hallucinations accompanying major depressive–like episodes) or diagnostic features that are disproportionately more severe than would be expected given the overall presentation (e.g., a 50-pound weight loss in an individual with otherwise mild depressive symptoms might suggest the presence of a underlying general medical condition). The clinician should be alerted especially by the presence of significant cognitive deficits that are out of proportion to those typically encountered with the primary mental disorder.

Evidence from the literature of a well-established or frequently encountered association between the general medical condition and the phenomenology of a specific mental disorder may be useful in the evaluation of a particular situation. Such studies may provide evidence of a plausible etiological association between the mental symptoms and the general medical condition (e.g., lesion location or a known pathophysiological mechanism likely to affect brain function) and of an elevated prevalence rate of the mental symptoms (i.e., above the base rate in an appropriate control population) in individuals with the general medical condition. Although such evidence suggests a possible causal link between a mental disorder and a particular general medical condition, it is not sufficient for making a determination in an individual case because research studies generally reflect group means, whereas the clinician seeks to make a decision regarding an individual. The text for each of the specific Mental Disorders Due to a General Medical Condition contains a list of some of the general medical conditions noted in the literature to be associated with that specific mental disorder.

C. The disturbance is not better accounted for by another mental disorder.

In making the diagnosis of a Mental Disorder Due to a General Medical Condition, it is necessary to rule out primary mental disorders and mental disorders that are substance induced. Ruling out primary mental disorders is often difficult because individuals with primary mental disorders commonly have co-occurring general medical conditions that are *not* causing the mental symptoms through direct physiological mechanisms. There may be a number of other relationships between a mental disorder and a general medical condition: the general medical condition may exacerbate the symptoms or complicate treatment of the mental disorder; the two may be related through nonphysiological mechanisms; or the co-occurrence may be coincidental. For example, when depressive symptoms are precipitated by the general medical condition acting as a psychosocial stressor, rather than resulting from the direct physiological effects of the general medical condition, the diagnosis would be Major Depressive Disorder or Adjustment Disorder With Depressed Mood. In an individual with depressive symptoms that co-occur with a general medical condition, a history of many Major Depressive Episodes or a family history of depression would suggest a diagnosis of Major Depressive Disorder, rather than a Mood Disorder Due to a General Medical Condition. Finally, the clinician should also consider whether the mental symptoms are caused by a drug of abuse, a medication, or toxin exposure (see p. 192 for guidelines). This is especially important because many individuals with general medical conditions receive medications that may have the potential to cause a Substance-Induced Mental Disorder.

D. The disturbance does not occur exclusively during the course of a delirium.

If symptoms (e.g., psychotic, mood, anxiety) occur only during periods of delirium, they are considered to be associated features of the delirium and do not warrant a separate diagnosis. These conditions (e.g., Mood Disorder Due to a General Medical Condition) can be diagnosed separately only if they occur at times other than during the delirium.

Recording Procedures

In recording a Mental Disorder Due to a General Medical Condition, the clinician should note both the type of mental disturbance and the etiological general medical condition on Axis I (e.g., 293.83 Mood Disorder Due to Hypothyroidism, With Depressive Features). The ICD-9-CM code for the general medical condition (e.g., 244.9 hypothyroidism) should also be noted on Axis III. In situations in which the clinician has determined that the mental symptoms are not a direct physiological consequence of the general medical condition, the primary mental disorder should be coded on Axis I and the general medical condition should be coded on Axis III. (See Appendix G for a list of selected ICD-9-CM diagnostic codes for general medical conditions.)

Differential Diagnosis

A Mental Disorder Due to a General Medical Condition is distinguished from a **primary mental disorder** by applying the criteria discussed earlier in this section under "Diagnostic Features." When symptoms of a mental disorder and a general medical condition co-occur, it is especially important to determine whether the etiological relationship, if any, is directly physiological (in which case the diagnosis is Mental Disorder Due to a General Medical Condition) or through another mechanism (in which case the diagnosis is a primary mental disorder). In some cases, the development of a general medical condition or the presence of associated disability may precipitate or exacerbate a mental disorder, with no known physiological link (e.g., the disability associated with osteoarthritis may play a role in the development of depressive symptoms or a Major Depressive Episode, but there is no known physiological mechanism underlying the etiological relationship between the arthritis and the depressive symptoms). In this situation, the primary mental disorder (i.e., Adjustment Disorder or Major Depressive Disorder) should be diagnosed on Axis I and the general medical condition (i.e., osteoarthritis) should be listed on Axis III.

A Mental Disorder Due to a General Medical Condition must also be distinguished from a **Substance-Induced Disorder.** If there is evidence of recent or prolonged use of a substance (including medications with psychoactive effects), withdrawal from a substance, or exposure to a toxin, a Substance-Induced Disorder should be considered. It may be useful to obtain a urine or blood drug screen or other appropriate laboratory evaluation. Symptoms that occur during or shortly after (i.e., within 4 weeks of) significant substance intoxication or withdrawal or medication use may be especially indicative of a Substance-Induced Disorder, depending on the type or the amount of the substance used or the duration of use.

Delirium, dementia, psychotic, mood, anxiety, or sleep symptoms or a sexual dysfunction may be caused by the **combined effects of a general medical condition and substance use** (including medications). In such situations, both diagnoses (e.g., Mood Disorder Due to a General Medical Condition and Substance-Induced Mood Disorder) should be listed. If it is not possible to ascertain whether the mental symptoms are due to a general medical condition or are substance induced, the Not Otherwise Specified category may be used (see discussion below).

When, as often happens, the presentation of a Mental Disorder Due to a General Medical Condition contains a mix of different symptoms (e.g., mood and anxiety), it is generally desirable to assign a single diagnosis based on which symptoms predominate in the clinical presentation. In some situations, it is not possible to determine whether the mental symptoms are primary, due to a general medical condition, or substance induced. The Not Otherwise Specified category should be used in such situations.

293.89   Catatonic Disorder
Due to a General Medical Condition

Diagnostic Features

The essential feature of Catatonic Disorder Due to a General Medical Condition is the presence of catatonia that is judged to be due to the direct physiological effects of a general medical condition. Catatonia is manifested by any of the following: motoric immobility, excessive motor activity, extreme negativism or mutism, peculiarities of voluntary movement, echolalia, or echopraxia (Criterion A). There must be evidence from the history, physical examination, or laboratory findings that the catatonia is the direct physiological consequence of a general medical condition (Criterion B). The diagnosis is not given if the catatonia is better accounted for by another mental disorder (e.g., Manic Episode) (Criterion C) or if it occurs exclusively during the course of a delirium (Criterion D).

Motoric immobility may be manifested by catalepsy (waxy flexibility) or stupor. The excessive motor activity is apparently purposeless and is not influenced by external stimuli. There may be extreme negativism that is manifested by resistance to all instructions or the maintenance of a rigid posture against attempts to be moved. Peculiarities of voluntary movement are manifested by the voluntary assumption of inappropriate or bizarre postures or by prominent grimacing. Echolalia is the pathological, parrotlike, and apparently senseless repetition of a word or phrase just spoken by another person. Echopraxia is the repetitive imitation of the movements of another person.

Recording Procedures

In recording Catatonic Disorder Due to a General Medical Condition, the clinician should note both the specific phenomenology of the disturbance and the identified general medical condition judged to be causing the disturbance on Axis I (e.g., 293.89 Catatonic Disorder Due to Malignant Neoplasm of Brain). The ICD-9-CM code for the general medical condition (e.g., 191.9 malignant neoplasm of brain) should also be noted on Axis III. (See Appendix G for a list of selected ICD-9-CM diagnostic codes for general medical conditions.)

Associated General Medical Conditions

A variety of general medical conditions may cause catatonia, especially neurological conditions (e.g., neoplasms, head trauma, cerebrovascular disease, encephalitis) and metabolic conditions (e.g., hypercalcemia, hepatic encephalopathy, homocystinuria, diabetic ketoacidosis). The associated physical examination findings, laboratory findings, and patterns of prevalence and onset reflect those of the etiological general medical condition.

Differential Diagnosis

A separate diagnosis of Catatonic Disorder Due to a General Medical Condition is not given if the catatonia occurs exclusively during the course of a **delirium.** If the individual is currently taking neuroleptic medication, **Medication-Induced Movement Disorders** should be considered (e.g., abnormal positioning may be due to Neuroleptic-Induced Acute Dystonia). Catatonic symptoms may also be present in Schizophrenia and Mood Disorders. **Schizophrenia, Catatonic Type,** is distinguished by the absence of evidence of a general medical condition that is etiologically related to the catatonia, and by the presence of other symptoms characteristic of Schizophrenia (e.g., delusions, hallucinations, disorganized speech, negative symptoms). A **Mood Disorder With Catatonic Features** is likewise differentiated by the absence of evidence of a general medical condition that is etiologically related to the catatonia, and by the presence of symptoms that meet the criteria for a Major Depressive or Manic Episode.

■ **Diagnostic criteria for 293.89 Catatonic Disorder Due to . . . [Indicate the General Medical Condition]**

   A. The presence of catatonia as manifested by motoric immobility, excessive motor activity (that is apparently purposeless and not influenced by external stimuli), extreme negativism or mutism, peculiarities of voluntary movement, or echolalia or echopraxia.

   B. There is evidence from the history, physical examination, or laboratory findings that the disturbance is the direct physiological consequence of a general medical condition.

(continued)

☐ **Diagnostic criteria for 293.89 Catatonic Disorder Due to . . . [**Indicate the General Medical Condition**]** (continued)

    C. The disturbance is not better accounted for by another mental disorder (e.g., a Manic Episode).

    D. The disturbance does not occur exclusively during the course of a delirium.

    Coding note: Include the name of the general medical condition on Axis I, e.g., 293.89 Catatonic Disorder Due to Hepatic Encephalopathy; also code the general medical condition on Axis III (see Appendix G for codes).

310.1   Personality Change
Due to a General Medical Condition

Diagnostic Features

The essential feature of a Personality Change Due to a General Medical Condition is a persistent personality disturbance that is judged to be due to the direct physiological effects of a general medical condition. The personality disturbance represents a change from the individual's previous characteristic personality pattern. In children, this condition may be manifested as a marked deviation from normal development rather than as a change in a stable personality pattern (Criterion A). There must be evidence from the history, physical examination, or laboratory findings that the personality change is the direct physiological consequence of a general medical condition (Criterion B). The diagnosis is not given if the disturbance is better accounted for by another mental disorder (Criterion C). The diagnosis is not given if the disturbance occurs exclusively during the course of a delirium or if symptoms meet the criteria for a dementia (Criterion D). The disturbance must also cause clinically significant distress or impairment in social, occupational, or other important areas of functioning (Criterion E).

Common manifestations of the personality change include affective instability, poor impulse control, outbursts of aggression or rage grossly out of proportion to any precipitating psychosocial stressor, marked apathy, suspiciousness, or paranoid ideation. The phenomenology of the change is indicated using the subtypes listed below. An individual with the disorder is often characterized by others as "not himself [or herself]." Although it shares the term "personality" with the Axis II Personality Disorders, this diagnosis is coded on Axis I and is distinct by virtue of its specific etiology, different phenomenology, and more variable onset and course.

The clinical presentation in a given individual may depend on the nature and localization of the pathological process. For example, injury to the frontal lobes may yield such symptoms as lack of judgment or foresight, facetiousness, disinhibition, and euphoria. Right hemisphere strokes have often been shown to evoke personality changes in association with unilateral spatial neglect, anosognosia (inability of the individual to recognize a bodily or functional deficit such as the existence of hemiparesis), motor impersistence, and other neurological deficits.

Subtypes

The particular personality change can be specified by indicating the symptom presentation that predominates in the clinical presentation:

Labile Type.   This subtype is used if the predominant feature is affective lability.
Disinhibited Type.   This subtype is used if the predominant feature is poor impulse control (e.g., as evidenced by sexual indiscretions).
Aggressive Type.   This subtype is used if the predominant feature is aggressive behavior.
Apathetic Type.   This subtype is used if the predominant feature is marked apathy and indifference.
Paranoid Type.   This subtype is used if the predominant feature is suspiciousness or paranoid ideation.
Other Type.   This subtype would be used, for example, for a personality change associated with a seizure disorder.
Combined Type.   This subtype is used if more than one feature predominates in the clinical picture.
Unspecified Type.

Recording Procedures

In recording Personality Change Due to a General Medical Condition, the clinician should note both the specific phenomenology of the disturbance, including appropriate subtype, and the general medical condition judged to be causing the disturbance on Axis I (e.g., 310.1 Personality Change Due to Systemic Lupus Erythematosus, Paranoid Type). The ICD-9-CM code for the general medical condition (e.g., 710.0 systemic lupus erythematosus) should also be noted on Axis III. (See Appendix G for a list of selected ICD-9-CM diagnostic codes for general medical conditions.)

Associated General Medical Conditions

A variety of neurological and other general medical conditions may cause personality changes, including central nervous system neoplasms, head trauma, cerebrovascular disease, Huntington's disease, epilepsy, infectious conditions with central nervous system involvement (e.g., human immunodeficiency virus), endocrine conditions (e.g., hypothyroidism, hypo- and hyperadrenocorticism), and autoimmune conditions with central nervous system involvement (e.g., systemic lupus erythematosus). The associated physical examination findings, laboratory findings, and patterns of prevalence and onset reflect those of the neurological or other general medical condition involved.

Differential Diagnosis

Chronic general medical conditions associated with pain and disability can also be associated with changes in personality. The diagnosis of Personality Change Due to a General Medical Condition is given only if a direct pathophysiological mechanism can be established. Personality change is a frequent associated feature of a **dementia** (e.g., Dementia of the Alzheimer's Type). A separate diagnosis of Personality Change Due to a General Medical Condition is not given if criteria are also met for a dementia or if the change occurs exclusively during the course of a **delirium.** Furthermore, the diagnosis of Personality Change Due to a General Medical Condition is not given if the disturbance is better accounted for by **another Mental Disorder Due to a General Medical Condition** (e.g., Mood Disorder Due to Brain Tumor, With Depressive Features).

Personality changes may also occur in the context of **Substance Dependence,** especially if the dependence is long-standing. The clinician should inquire carefully about the nature and extent of substance use. If the clinician wishes to indicate an etiological relationship between the personality change and substance use, the Not Otherwise Specified category for the specific substance (e.g., Cocaine-Related Disorder Not Otherwise Specified) can be used.

Marked personality changes may also be an **associated feature of other mental disorders** (e.g., Schizophrenia, Delusional Disorder, Mood Disorders, Impulse-Control Disorders Not Elsewhere Classified, Panic Disorder). However, in these disorders, no specific physiological factor is judged to be etiologically related to the personality change. Personality Change Due to a General Medical Condition can be distinguished from a **Personality Disorder** by the requirement for a clinically significant change from baseline personality functioning and the presence of a specific etiological general medical condition.

■ **Diagnostic criteria for 310.1 Personality Change Due to . . . [Indicate the General Medical Condition]**

A. A persistent personality disturbance that represents a change from the individual's previous characteristic personality pattern. (In children, the disturbance involves a marked deviation from normal development or a significant change in the child's usual behavior patterns lasting at least 1 year).

B. There is evidence from the history, physical examination, or laboratory findings that the disturbance is the direct physiological consequence of a general medical condition.

C. The disturbance is not better accounted for by another mental disorder (including other Mental Disorders Due to a General Medical Condition).

D. The disturbance does not occur exclusively during the course of a delirium and does not meet criteria for a dementia.

E. The disturbance causes clinically significant distress or impairment in social, occupational, or other important areas of functioning.

Specify type:
   Labile Type: if the predominant feature is affective lability
   Disinhibited Type: if the predominant feature is poor impulse control as evidenced by sexual indiscretions, etc.
   Aggressive Type: if the predominant feature is aggressive behavior

(continued)

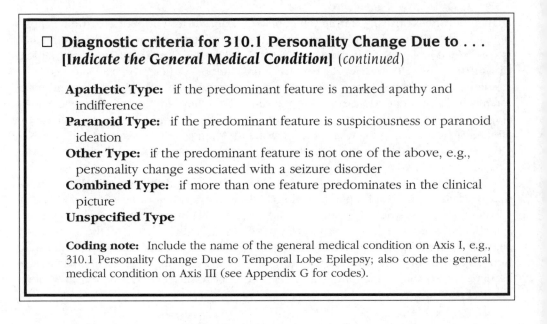

☐ **Diagnostic criteria for 310.1 Personality Change Due to . . . [*Indicate the General Medical Condition*]** (*continued*)

Apathetic Type: if the predominant feature is marked apathy and indifference

Paranoid Type: if the predominant feature is suspiciousness or paranoid ideation

Other Type: if the predominant feature is not one of the above, e.g., personality change associated with a seizure disorder

Combined Type: if more than one feature predominates in the clinical picture

Unspecified Type

Coding note: Include the name of the general medical condition on Axis I, e.g., 310.1 Personality Change Due to Temporal Lobe Epilepsy; also code the general medical condition on Axis III (see Appendix G for codes).

293.9   Mental Disorder Not Otherwise Specified Due to a General Medical Condition

This residual category should be used for situations in which it has been established that the disturbance is caused by the direct physiological effects of a general medical condition, but the criteria are not met for a specific Mental Disorder Due to a General Medical Condition (e.g., dissociative symptoms due to complex partial seizures).

Coding note: Include the name of the general medical condition on Axis I, e.g., 293.9 Mental Disorder Not Otherwise Specified Due to HIV Disease; also code the general medical condition on Axis III (see Appendix G for codes).

Substance-Related Disorders

The Substance-Related Disorders include disorders related to the taking of a drug of abuse (including alcohol), to the side effects of a medication, and to toxin exposure. In this manual, the term *substance* can refer to a drug of abuse, a medication, or a toxin. The substances discussed in this section are grouped into 11 classes: alcohol; amphetamine or similarly acting sympathomimetics; caffeine; cannabis; cocaine; hallucinogens; inhalants; nicotine; opioids; phencyclidine (PCP) or similarly acting arylcyclohexylamines; and sedatives, hypnotics, or anxiolytics. Although these 11 classes appear in alphabetical order, the following classes share similar features: alcohol shares features with the sedatives, hypnotics, and anxiolytics; and cocaine shares features with amphetamines or similarly acting sympathomimetics. Also included in this section are Polysubstance Dependence and Other or Unknown Substance–Related Disorders (which include most disorders related to medications or toxins).

Many prescribed and over-the-counter medications can also cause Substance-Related Disorders. Symptoms are often related to the dosage of the medication and usually disappear when the dosage is lowered or the medication is stopped. However, there may sometimes be an idiosyncratic reaction to a single dose. Medications that may cause Substance-Related Disorders include, but are not limited to, anesthetics and analgesics, anticholinergic agents, anticonvulsants, antihistamines, antihypertensive and cardiovascular medications, antimicrobial medications, antiparkinsonian medications, chemotherapeutic agents, corticosteroids, gastrointestinal medications, muscle relaxants, nonsteroidal anti-inflammatory medications, other over-the-counter medications, antidepressant medications, and disulfiram.

Exposure to a wide range of other chemical substances can also lead to the development of a Substance-Related Disorder. Toxic substances that may cause Substance-Related Disorders include, but are not limited to, heavy metals (e.g., lead or aluminum), rat poisons containing strychnine, pesticides containing acetylcholinesterase inhibitors, nerve gases, ethylene glycol (antifreeze), carbon monoxide, and carbon dioxide. The volatile substances (e.g., fuel, paint) are classified as "inhalants" (see p. 236) if they are used for the purpose of becoming intoxicated; they are considered "toxins" if exposure is accidental or part of intentional poisoning. Impairments in cognition or mood are the most common symptoms associated with toxic substances, although anxiety, hallucinations, delusions, or seizures can also result. Symptoms usually disappear when the individual is no longer exposed to the substance, but resolution of symptoms can take weeks or months and may require treatment.

The Substance-Related Disorders are divided into two groups: the Substance Use Disorders (Substance Dependence and Substance Abuse) and the Substance-Induced Disorders (Substance Intoxication, Substance Withdrawal, Substance-Induced Delirium, Substance-Induced Persisting Dementia, Substance-Induced Persisting Amnestic Disorder, Substance-Induced Psychotic Disorder, Substance-Induced Mood Disorder, Substance-Induced Anxiety Disorder, Substance-Induced Sexual Dysfunction, and Substance-Induced Sleep Disorder). The section begins with the text and criteria sets for Substance Dependence, Abuse, Intoxication, and Withdrawal that are applicable across classes of substances. This is followed by general comments concerning associated features; culture, age, and gender features; course; impairment and complications; familial pattern; differential diagnosis; and recording procedures that apply to all substance classes. The remainder of the section is organized by class of substance and describes the specific aspects of Dependence, Abuse, Intoxication, and Withdrawal for each of the 11 classes of substances. To facilitate differential diagnosis, the text and criteria for the remaining Substance-Induced Disorders are included in the sections of the manual with disorders with which they share phenomenology (e.g., Substance-Induced Mood Disorder is included in the "Mood Disorders" section). The diagnoses associated with each specific group of substances are shown in Table 1.

Substance Use Disorders

Substance Dependence

Features

The essential feature of Substance Dependence is a cluster of cognitive, behavioral, and physiological symptoms indicating that the individual continues use of the substance despite significant substance-related problems. There is a pattern of repeated self-administration that usually results in tolerance, withdrawal, and compulsive drug-taking behavior. A diagnosis of Substance Dependence can be applied to every class of substances except caffeine. The symptoms of Dependence are similar across the various categories of substances, but for certain classes some symptoms are less salient, and in a few instances not all symptoms apply (e.g., withdrawal symptoms are not specified for Hallucinogen Dependence). Although not specifically listed as a criterion item, "craving" (a strong subjective drive to use the substance) is likely to be experienced by most (if not all) individuals with Substance Dependence. Dependence is defined as a cluster of three or more of the symptoms listed below occurring at any time in the same 12-month period.

Tolerance (Criterion 1) is the need for greatly increased amounts of the substance to achieve intoxication (or the desired effect) or a markedly diminished effect with continued use of the same amount of the substance. The degree to which tolerance develops varies greatly across substances. Individuals with heavy use of opioids and stimulants can develop substantial (e.g., tenfold) levels of tolerance, often to a dosage that would be lethal to a nonuser. Alcohol tolerance can also be pronounced, but is usually much less extreme than for amphetamine. Many individuals who smoke

Table 1. Diagnoses associated with class of substances

	Dependence	Abuse	Intoxication	Withdrawal	Intoxication Delirium	Withdrawal Delirium	Dementia	Amnestic Disorder	Psychotic Disorders	Mood Disorders	Anxiety Disorders	Sexual Dysfunctions	Sleep Disorders
Alcohol	X	X	X	X	I	W	P	P	I/W	I/W	I/W	I	I/W
Amphetamines	X	X	X	X	I				I	I/W	I	I	I/W
Caffeine	X		X								I		I
Cannabis	X	X	X		I				I		I		
Cocaine	X	X	X	X	I				I	I/W	I/W	I	I/W
Hallucinogens	X	X	X		I				I*	I	I		
Inhalants	X	X	X		I		P		I	I	I		
Nicotine	X			X									
Opioids	X	X	X	X	I				I	I		I	I/W
Phencyclidine	X	X	X		I				I	I	I		
Sedatives, hypnotics, or anxiolytics	X	X	X	X	I	W	P	P	I/W	I/W	W	I	I/W
Polysubstance	X												
Other	X	X	X	X	I	W	P	P	I/W	I/W	I/W	I	I/W

*Also Hallucinogen Persisting Perception Disorder (Flashbacks).

Note: X, I, W, I/W, or P indicates that the category is recognized in DSM-IV. In addition, *I* indicates that the specifier With Onset During Intoxication may be noted for the category (except for Intoxication Delirium); *W* indicates that the specifier With Onset During Withdrawal may be noted for the category (except for Withdrawal Delirium); and *I/W* indicates that either With Onset During Intoxication or With Onset During Withdrawal may be noted for the category. *P* indicates that the disorder is Persisting.

cigarettes consume more than 20 cigarettes a day, an amount that would have produced symptoms of toxicity when they first started smoking. Individuals with heavy use of cannabis are generally not aware of having developed tolerance (although it has been demonstrated in animal studies and in some individuals). It is uncertain whether any tolerance develops to phencyclidine (PCP). Tolerance may be difficult to determine by history alone when the substance used is illegal and perhaps mixed with various diluents or with other substances. In such situations, laboratory tests may be helpful (e.g., high blood levels of the substance coupled with little evidence of intoxication suggest that tolerance is likely). Tolerance must also be distinguished from individual variability in the initial sensitivity to the effects of particular substances. For example, some first-time drinkers show very little evidence of intoxication with three or four drinks, whereas others of similar weight and drinking histories have slurred speech and incoordination.

Withdrawal (Criterion 2a) is a maladaptive behavioral change, with physiological and cognitive concomitants, that occurs when blood or tissue concentrations of a substance decline in an individual who had maintained prolonged heavy use of the substance. After developing unpleasant withdrawal symptoms, the person is likely to take the substance to relieve or to avoid those symptoms (Criterion 2b), typically using the substance throughout the day beginning soon after awakening. Withdrawal symptoms vary greatly across the classes of substances, and separate criteria sets for Withdrawal are provided for most of the classes. Marked and generally easily measured physiological signs of withdrawal are common with alcohol, opioids, and sedatives, hypnotics, and anxiolytics. Withdrawal signs and symptoms are often present, but may be less apparent, with stimulants such as amphetamines and cocaine, as well as with nicotine. No significant withdrawal is seen even after repeated use of hallucinogens. Withdrawal from phencyclidine and related substances has not yet been described in humans (although it has been demonstrated in animals).

Neither tolerance nor withdrawal is necessary or sufficient for a diagnosis of Substance Dependence. Some individuals (e.g., those with Cannabis Dependence) show a pattern of compulsive use without any signs of tolerance or withdrawal. Conversely, some postsurgical patients without Opioid Dependence may develop a tolerance to prescribed opioids and experience withdrawal symptoms without showing any signs of compulsive use. The specifiers With Physiological Dependence and Without Physiological Dependence are provided to indicate the presence or absence of tolerance or withdrawal.

The following items describe the pattern of compulsive substance use that is characteristic of Dependence. The individual may take the substance in larger amounts or over a longer period than was originally intended (e.g., continuing to drink until severely intoxicated despite having set a limit of only one drink) (Criterion 3). The individual may express a persistent desire to cut down or regulate substance use. Often, there have been many unsuccessful efforts to decrease or discontinue use (Criterion 4). The individual may spend a great deal of time obtaining the substance, using the substance, or recovering from its effects (Criterion 5). In some instances of Substance Dependence, virtually all of the person's daily activities revolve around the substance. Important social, occupational, or recreational activities may be given up or reduced because of substance use (Criterion 6). The individual may withdraw from family activities and hobbies in order to use the substance in private or to spend more time with substance-using friends. Despite recognizing the contributing role of the substance to a psychological or physical problem (e.g., severe depressive symptoms or damage to organ systems), the person continues to use the substance (Criterion 7). The key issue in evaluating this criterion is not the existence of the problem, but rather the individual's failure to abstain from using the substance despite having evidence of the difficulty it is causing.

Specifiers

Tolerance and withdrawal may be associated with a higher risk for immediate general medical problems and a higher relapse rate. Specifiers are provided to note their presence or absence:

With Physiological Dependence. This specifier should be used when Substance Dependence is accompanied by evidence of tolerance (Criterion 1) or withdrawal (Criterion 2).

Without Physiological Dependence. This specifier should be used when there is no evidence of tolerance (Criterion 1) or withdrawal (Criterion 2). In these individuals, Substance Dependence is characterized by a pattern of compulsive use (at least three items from Criteria 3–7).

Course Specifiers

Six course specifiers are available for Substance Dependence. The four Remission specifiers can be applied only after none of the criteria for Substance Dependence or Substance Abuse have been present for at least 1 month. The definition of these four types of Remission is based on the interval of time that has elapsed since the cessation of Dependence (Early versus Sustained Remission) and whether there is continued presence of one or more of the items included in the criteria sets for Dependence or Abuse (Partial versus Full Remission). Because the first 12 months following Dependence is a time of particularly high risk for relapse, this period is designated Early Remission. After 12 months of Early Remission have passed without relapse to Dependence, the person enters into Sustained Remission. For both Early Remission and Sustained Remission, a further designation of Full is given if no criteria for Dependence or Abuse have been met during the period of remission; a designation of Partial is given if at least one of the criteria for Dependence or Abuse has been met, intermittently or continuously, during the period of remission. The differentiation of Sustained Full Remission from recovered (no current Substance Use Disorder) requires consideration of the length of time since the last period of disturbance, the total duration of the disturbance, and the need for continued evaluation. If, after a period of remission or recovery, the individual again becomes dependent, the application of the Early Remission specifier requires that there again be at least 1 month in which no criteria for Dependence or Abuse are met. Two additional specifiers have been provided: On Agonist Therapy and In a Controlled Environment. For an individual to qualify for Early Remission after cessation of agonist therapy or release from a controlled environment, there must be a 1-month period in which none of the criteria for Dependence or Abuse are met.

The following Remission specifiers can be applied only after no criteria for Dependence or Abuse have been met for at least 1 month. Note that these specifiers do not apply if the individual is on agonist therapy or in a controlled environment (see below).

Early Full Remission. This specifier is used if, for at least 1 month, but for less than 12 months, no criteria for Dependence or Abuse have been met.

⊢— Dependence —⊶— 1 —⊶—0–11 months ————————⊣
month

Early Partial Remission. This specifier is used if, for at least 1 month, but less than 12 months, one or more criteria for Dependence or Abuse have been met (but the full criteria for Dependence have not been met).

⊢— Dependence —⊶— 1 —⊶—0–11 months ————————⊣
month

Sustained Full Remission. This specifier is used if none of the criteria for Dependence or Abuse have been met at any time during a period of 12 months or longer.

⊢— Dependence —⊶— 1 —⊶— 11+ months ——————————————⊣
month

Sustained Partial Remission. This specifier is used if full criteria for Dependence have not been met for a period of 12 months or longer; however, one or more criteria for Dependence or Abuse have been met.

⊢— Dependence —⊶— 1 —⊶— 11+ months ——————————————⊣
month

The following specifiers apply if the individual is on agonist therapy or in a controlled environment:

On Agonist Therapy. This specifier is used if the individual is on a prescribed agonist medication, and no criteria for Dependence or Abuse have been met for that class of medication for at least the past month (except tolerance to, or withdrawal from, the agonist). This category also applies to those being treated for Dependence using a partial agonist or an agonist/antagonist.

In a Controlled Environment. This specifier is used if the individual is in an environment where access to alcohol and controlled substances is restricted, and no criteria for Dependence or Abuse have been met for at least the past month. Examples of these environments are closely supervised and substance-free jails, therapeutic communities, or locked hospital units.

■ Criteria for Substance Dependence

A maladaptive pattern of substance use, leading to clinically significant impairment or distress, as manifested by three (or more) of the following, occurring at any time in the same 12-month period:

(1) tolerance, as defined by either of the following:
   (a) a need for markedly increased amounts of the substance to achieve intoxication or desired effect
   (b) markedly diminished effect with continued use of the same amount of the substance

(2) withdrawal, as manifested by either of the following:
   (a) the characteristic withdrawal syndrome for the substance (refer to Criteria A and B of the criteria sets for Withdrawal from the specific substances)
   (b) the same (or a closely related) substance is taken to relieve or avoid withdrawal symptoms

(3) the substance is often taken in larger amounts or over a longer period than was intended

(4) there is a persistent desire or unsuccessful efforts to cut down or control substance use

(5) a great deal of time is spent in activities necessary to obtain the substance (e.g., visiting multiple doctors or driving long distances), use the substance (e.g., chain-smoking), or recover from its effects

(6) important social, occupational, or recreational activities are given up or reduced because of substance use

(7) the substance use is continued despite knowledge of having a persistent or recurrent physical or psychological problem that is likely to have been caused or exacerbated by the substance (e.g., current cocaine use despite recognition of cocaine-induced depression, or continued drinking despite recognition that an ulcer was made worse by alcohol consumption)

Specify if:
   With Physiological Dependence: evidence of tolerance or withdrawal (i.e., either Item 1 or 2 is present)
   Without Physiological Dependence: no evidence of tolerance or withdrawal (i.e., neither Item 1 nor 2 is present)

Course specifiers (see text for definitions):

   Early Full Remission
   Early Partial Remission
   Sustained Full Remission
   Sustained Partial Remission
   On Agonist Therapy
   In a Controlled Environment

Substance Abuse

Features

The essential feature of Substance Abuse is a maladaptive pattern of substance use manifested by recurrent and significant adverse consequences related to the repeated use of substances. There may be repeated failure to fulfill major role obligations, repeated use in situations in which it is physically hazardous, multiple legal problems, and recurrent social and interpersonal problems (Criterion A). These problems must occur recurrently during the same 12-month period. Unlike the criteria for Substance Dependence, the criteria for Substance Abuse do not include tolerance, withdrawal, or a pattern of compulsive use and instead include only the harmful consequences of repeated use. A diagnosis of Substance Abuse is preempted by the diagnosis of Substance Dependence if the individual's pattern of substance use has ever met the criteria for Dependence for that class of substances (Criterion B). Although a diagnosis of Substance Abuse is more likely in individuals who have only recently started taking the substance, some individuals continue to have substance-related adverse social consequences over a long period of time without developing evidence of Substance Dependence. The category of Substance Abuse does not apply to caffeine and nicotine.

The individual may repeatedly demonstrate intoxication or other substance-related symptoms when expected to fulfill major role obligations at work, school, or home (Criterion A1). There may be repeated absences or poor work performance related to recurrent hangovers. A student might have substance-related absences, suspensions, or expulsions from school. While intoxicated, the individual may neglect children or household duties. The person may repeatedly be intoxicated in situations that are physically hazardous (e.g., while driving a car, operating machinery, or engaging in risky recreational behavior such as swimming or rock climbing) (Criterion A2). There may be recurrent substance-related legal problems (e.g., arrests for disorderly conduct, assault and battery, driving under the influence) (Criterion A3). The person may continue to use the substance despite a history of undesirable persistent or recurrent social or interpersonal consequences (e.g., marital difficulties or divorce, verbal or physical fights) (Criterion A4).

■ Criteria for Substance Abuse

A. A maladaptive pattern of substance use leading to clinically significant impairment or distress, as manifested by one (or more) of the following, occurring within a 12-month period:

   (1) recurrent substance use resulting in a failure to fulfill major role obligations at work, school, or home (e.g., repeated absences or poor work performance related to substance use; substance-related absences, suspensions, or expulsions from school; neglect of children or household)

(continued)

☐ **Criteria for Substance Abuse** (*continued*)

    (2)   recurrent substance use in situations in which it is physically hazardous (e.g., driving an automobile or operating a machine when impaired by substance use)

    (3)   recurrent substance-related legal problems (e.g., arrests for substance-related disorderly conduct)

    (4)   continued substance use despite having persistent or recurrent social or interpersonal problems caused or exacerbated by the effects of the substance (e.g., arguments with spouse about consequences of intoxication, physical fights)

B. The symptoms have never met the criteria for Substance Dependence for this class of substance.

Substance-Induced Disorders

Substance Intoxication

Diagnostic Features

The essential feature of Substance Intoxication is the development of a reversible substance-specific syndrome due to the recent ingestion of (or exposure to) a substance (Criterion A). The clinically significant maladaptive behavioral or psychological changes associated with intoxication (e.g., belligerence, mood lability, cognitive impairment, impaired judgment, impaired social or occupational functioning) are due to the direct physiological effects of the substance on the central nervous system and develop during or shortly after use of the substance (Criterion B). The symptoms are not due to a general medical condition and are not better accounted for by another mental disorder (Criterion C). Substance Intoxication is often associated with Substance Abuse or Dependence. This category does not apply to nicotine. Evidence for recent intake of the substance can be obtained from the history, physical examination (e.g., smell of alcohol on the breath), or toxicological analysis of body fluids (e.g., urine or blood).

The most common changes involve disturbances of perception, wakefulness, attention, thinking, judgment, psychomotor behavior, and interpersonal behavior. The specific clinical picture in Substance Intoxication varies dramatically among individuals and also depends on which substance is involved, the dose, the duration or chronicity of dosing, the person's tolerance for the substance, the period of time since the last dose, the expectations of the person as to the substance's effects, and the environment or setting in which the substance is taken. Short-term or "acute" intoxications may have different signs and symptoms from sustained or "chronic" intoxications. For example, moderate cocaine doses may initially produce gregariousness, but social withdrawal may develop if such doses are frequently repeated over days or weeks. Different substances (sometimes even different substance classes) may produce identical symptoms. For example, Amphetamine and Cocaine Intoxication can both present with grandiosity and hyperactivity, accompanied by tachycardia, pupillary dilation, elevated blood pressure, and perspiration or chills.

When used in the physiological sense, the term *intoxication* is broader than Substance Intoxication as defined here. Many substances may produce physiological or psychological changes that are not necessarily maladaptive. For example, an individual with tachycardia from excessive caffeine use has a physiological intoxication, but if this is the only symptom in the absence of maladaptive behavior, the diagnosis of Caffeine Intoxication would not apply. The maladaptive nature of a substance-induced change in behavior depends on the social and environmental context. The maladaptive behavior generally places the individual at significant risk for adverse effects (e.g., accidents, general medical complications, disruption in social and family relationships, vocational or financial difficulties, legal problems). Signs and symptoms of intoxication may sometimes persist for hours or days beyond the time when the substance is detectable in body fluids. This may be due to continuing low concentrations of the substance in certain areas of the brain or to a "hit and run" effect in which the substance alters a physiological process, the recovery of which takes longer than the time for elimination of the substance. These longer-term effects of intoxication must be distinguished from withdrawal (i.e., symptoms initiated by a decline in blood or tissue concentrations of a substance).

■ Criteria for Substance Intoxication

A. The development of a reversible substance-specific syndrome due to recent ingestion of (or exposure to) a substance. **Note:** Different substances may produce similar or identical syndromes.

B. Clinically significant maladaptive behavioral or psychological changes that are due to the effect of the substance on the central nervous system (e.g., belligerence, mood lability, cognitive impairment, impaired judgment, impaired social or occupational functioning) and develop during or shortly after use of the substance.

C. The symptoms are not due to a general medical condition and are not better accounted for by another mental disorder.

Substance Withdrawal

Diagnostic Features

The essential feature of Substance Withdrawal is the development of a substance-specific maladaptive behavioral change, with physiological and cognitive concomitants, that is due to the cessation of, or reduction in, heavy and prolonged substance use (Criterion A). The substance-specific syndrome causes clinically significant distress or impairment in social, occupational, or other important areas of functioning (Criterion B). The symptoms are not due to a general medical condition and are not better accounted for by another mental disorder (Criterion C). Withdrawal is usually, but not always, associated with Substance Dependence (see p. 178). Most (perhaps all) individuals with Withdrawal have a craving to readminister the substance to reduce the symptoms. The diagnosis of Withdrawal is recognized for the following groups of substances: alcohol; amphetamines and other related substances; cocaine; nicotine; opioids; and sedatives, hypnotics, or anxiolytics. The signs and symptoms of Withdrawal vary according to the substance used, with most symptoms being the opposite of those observed in Intoxication with the same substance. The dose and duration of use and other factors such as the presence or absence of additional illnesses also affect withdrawal symptoms. Withdrawal develops when doses are reduced or stopped, whereas signs and symptoms of Intoxication improve (gradually in some cases) after dosing stops.

■ Criteria for Substance Withdrawal

A. The development of a substance-specific syndrome due to the cessation of (or reduction in) substance use that has been heavy and prolonged.

B. The substance-specific syndrome causes clinically significant distress or impairment in social, occupational, or other important areas of functioning.

C. The symptoms are not due to a general medical condition and are not better accounted for by another mental disorder.

Associated Features of Substance Dependence, Abuse, Intoxication, and Withdrawal

Assessment issues.   The diagnosis of Substance Dependence requires obtaining a detailed history from the individual and, whenever possible, from additional sources of information (e.g., medical records; a spouse, relative, or close friend). In addition, physical examination findings and laboratory test results can be helpful.

Route of administration.   The route of administration of a substance is an important factor in determining its effects (including the time course of developing Intoxication, the probability that its use will produce physiological changes associated with Withdrawal, the likelihood that use will lead to Dependence or Abuse, and whether consumption patterns will be characterized by periodic binges or daily use). Routes of administration that produce more rapid and efficient absorption into the bloodstream (e.g., intravenous, smoking, or "snorting") tend to result in a more intense intoxication and an increased likelihood of an escalating pattern of substance use leading to Dependence. Routes of administration that quickly deliver a large amount of the substance to the brain are also associated with higher levels of substance consumption and an increased likelihood of toxic effects. For example, a person who uses intravenous amphetamine is more likely to consume large amounts of the substance and thereby risk an overdose than the person who only takes amphetamine orally or intranasally.

Speed of onset within a class of substance.   Rapidly acting substances are more likely than slower-acting substances to produce immediate intoxication and lead to Dependence or Abuse. For example, because diazepam and alprazolam both have a more rapid onset than oxazepam, they may consequently be more likely to lead to Substance Dependence or Abuse.

Duration of effects.   The duration of effects associated with a particular substance is also important in determining the time course of Intoxication and whether use of the substance will lead to Dependence or Abuse. Relatively short-acting substances (e.g., certain anxiolytics) tend to have a higher potential for the development of Dependence or Abuse than substances with similar effects that have a longer duration of action (e.g., phenobarbital). The half-life of the substance parallels aspects of Withdrawal: the longer the duration of action, the longer the time between cessation and the onset of withdrawal symptoms and the longer the Withdrawal is likely to last.

Use of multiple substances.   Substance Dependence, Abuse, Intoxication, and Withdrawal often involve several substances used simultaneously or sequentially. For example, individuals with Cocaine Dependence frequently also use alcohol, anxiolytics, or opioids, often to counteract lingering cocaine-induced anxiety symptoms. Similarly, individuals with Opioid Dependence or Cannabis Dependence usually have several other Substance-Related Disorders, most often involving alcohol, anxiolytics, amphetamine, or cocaine. When criteria for more than one Substance-Related Disorder are met, multiple diagnoses should be given. The situations in which a diagnosis of Polysubstance Dependence should be given are described on p. 270.

Associated laboratory findings.   Laboratory analyses of blood and urine samples can help determine recent use of a substance. Blood levels offer additional information on the amount of substance still present in the body. It should be noted that a positive blood or urine test does not by itself indicate that the individual has a pattern of substance use that meets criteria for a Substance-Related Disorder and that a negative blood or urine test does not by itself rule out a diagnosis of a Substance-Related Disorder.

In the case of Intoxication, blood and urine tests can help to determine the relevant substance(s) involved. Specific confirmation of the suspected substance may require toxicological analysis, because various substances have similar Intoxication syndromes; individuals often take a number of different substances; and because substitution and contamination of street drugs are frequent, those who obtain substances illicitly often do not know the specific contents of what they have taken. Toxicological tests may also be helpful in differential diagnosis to determine the role of Substance Intoxication or Withdrawal in the etiology (or exacerbation) of symptoms of a variety of mental disorders (e.g., Mood Disorders, Psychotic Disorders). Furthermore, serial blood levels help to differentiate Intoxication from Withdrawal.

The blood level of a substance may be a useful clue in determining whether the person has a high tolerance to a given group of substances (e.g., a person presenting with a blood alcohol level of over 150 mg/dl without signs of Alcohol Intoxication has a significant tolerance to alcohol and is likely to be a chronic user of either alcohol or a sedative, hypnotic, or anxiolytic). Another method for assessing tolerance is to determine the individual's response to an agonist or antagonist medication. For example, a person who does not exhibit any signs of intoxication from a dose of pentobarbital of 200 mg or higher has a significant tolerance to sedatives, hypnotics, or anxiolytics and may need treatment to prevent the development of Withdrawal. Similarly, in cases in which opioid tolerance or Dependence cannot be clearly confirmed by history, the use of an antagonist (e.g., naloxone) to demonstrate whether withdrawal symptoms are induced may be informative.

Laboratory tests can be useful in identifying Withdrawal in individuals with Substance Dependence. Evidence for cessation or reduction of dosing may be obtained by history or by toxicological analysis of body fluids (e.g., urine or blood). Although most substances and their metabolites clear the urine within 48 hours of ingestion, certain metabolites may be present for a longer period in those who use the substance chronically. If the person presents with Withdrawal from an unknown substance, urine tests may help identify the substance from which the person is withdrawing and make it possible to initiate appropriate treatment. Urine tests may also be helpful in differentiating Withdrawal from other mental disorders, because withdrawal symptoms can mimic the symptoms of mental disorders unrelated to use of a substance.

Associated physical examination findings and general medical conditions. As presented in the sections specific to the 11 classes of substance, intoxication and withdrawal states are likely to include physical signs and symptoms that are often the first clue to a substance-related state. In general, intoxication with amphetamines or cocaine is accompanied by increases in blood pressure, respiratory rate, pulse, and body temperature. Intoxication with sedative, hypnotic, or anxiolytic substances or with opioid medication often involves the opposite pattern. Substance Dependence and Abuse are often associated with general medical conditions often related to the toxic effects of the substances on particular organ systems (e.g., cirrhosis in Alcohol Dependence) or the routes of administration (e.g., human immunodeficiency virus [HIV] infection from shared needles).

Associated mental disorders.   Substance use is often a component of the presentation of symptoms of mental disorders. When the symptoms are judged to be a direct physiological consequence of a substance, a Substance-Induced Disorder is diagnosed (see p. 192). Substance-Related Disorders are also commonly comorbid with, and complicate the course and treatment of, many mental disorders (e.g., Conduct Disorder in adolescents; Antisocial and Borderline Personality Disorders, Schizophrenia, Mood Disorders).

Recording Procedures for Dependence, Abuse, Intoxication, and Withdrawal

For drugs of abuse.   The clinician should use the code that applies to the class of substances, but record the name of the specific substance rather than the name of the class. For example, the clinician should record 292.0 Secobarbital Withdrawal (rather than Sedative, Hypnotic, or Anxiolytic Withdrawal) or 305.70 Methamphetamine Abuse (rather than Amphetamine Abuse). For substances that do not fit into any of the classes (e.g., amyl nitrite), the appropriate code for "Other Substance Dependence," "Other

Substance Abuse," "Other Substance Intoxication," or "Other Substance Withdrawal" should be used and the specific substance indicated (e.g., 305.90 Amyl Nitrite Abuse). If the substance taken by the individual is unknown, the code for the class "Other (or Unknown)" should be used (e.g., 292.89 Unknown Substance Intoxication). For a particular substance, if criteria are met for more than one Substance-Related Disorder, all should be diagnosed (e.g., 292.0 Heroin Withdrawal; 304.00 Heroin Dependence). If there are symptoms or problems associated with a particular substance but criteria are not met for any of the substance-specific disorders, the Not Otherwise Specified category can be used (e.g., 292.9 Cannabis-Related Disorder Not Otherwise Specified). If multiple substances are used, all relevant Substance-Related Disorders should be diagnosed (e.g., 292.89 Mescaline Intoxication; 304.20 Cocaine Dependence). The situations in which a diagnosis of 304.80 Polysubstance Dependence should be given are described on p. 270.

For medications and toxins.   For medications not covered above (as well as for toxins), the code for "Other Substance" should be used. The specific medication can coded by also listing the appropriate E-code on Axis I (see Appendix G) (e.g., 292.89 Benztropine Intoxication; E941.1 Benztropine). E-codes should also be used for classes of substances listed above when they are taken as prescribed medications (e.g., opioids).

Specific Culture, Age, and Gender Features

There are wide cultural variations in attitudes toward substance consumption, patterns of substance use, accessibility of substances, physiological reactions to substances, and prevalence of Substance-Related Disorders. Some groups forbid use of alcohol, whereas in others the use of various substances for mood-altering effects is widely accepted. The evaluation of any individual's pattern of substance use must take these factors into account. Patterns of medication use and toxin exposure also vary widely within and between countries.

Individuals between ages 18 and 24 years have relatively high prevalence rates for the use of virtually every substance, including alcohol. For drugs of abuse, Intoxication is usually the initial Substance-Related Disorder and usually begins in the teens. Withdrawal can occur at any age as long as the relevant drug has been taken in high-enough doses over a long-enough period of time. Dependence can also occur at any age, but typically has its initial onset for most drugs of abuse in the 20s, 30s, and 40s. When a Substance-Related Disorder other than Intoxication begins in early adolescence, it is often associated with Conduct Disorder and failure to complete school. For drugs of abuse, Substance-Related Disorders are usually diagnosed more commonly in males than in females, but the sex ratios vary with class of substance.

Course

The course of Dependence, Abuse, Intoxication, and Withdrawal varies with the class of substance, route of administration, and other factors. The "Course" sections for the various classes of substances indicate the specific features characteristic of each. However, some generalizations across substances can be made.

Intoxication usually develops within minutes to hours after a sufficiently large single dose and continues or intensifies with frequently repeated doses. Intoxication usually begins to abate as blood or tissue concentrations of the substance decline, but signs and symptoms may resolve slowly, in some situations lasting for hours or days after the substance is no longer detectable in bodily fluids. The onset of Intoxication may be delayed with slowly absorbed substances or with those that must be metabolized to active compounds. Long-acting substances may produce prolonged intoxications.

Withdrawal develops with the decline of the substance in the central nervous system. Early symptoms of Withdrawal usually develop a few hours after dosing stops for substances with short elimination half-lives (e.g., alcohol, lorazepam, or heroin), although withdrawal seizures may develop several weeks after termination of high doses of long-half-life anxiolytic substances. The more intense signs of Withdrawal usually end within a few days to a few weeks after the cessation of substance use, although some subtle physiological signs may be detectable for many weeks or even months as part of a protracted withdrawal syndrome.

A diagnosis of Substance Abuse is more likely in individuals who have begun using substances only recently. For many individuals, Substance Abuse with a particular class of substances evolves into Substance Dependence for the same class of substance. This is particularly true for those substances that have a high potential for the development of tolerance, withdrawal, and patterns of compulsive use. Some individuals have episodes of Substance Abuse that occur over an extended period of time without ever developing Substance Dependence. This is more true for those substances that have a lower potential for the development of tolerance, withdrawal, and patterns of compulsive use. Once criteria for Substance Dependence are met, a subsequent diagnosis of Substance Abuse cannot be given for any substance in the same class. For a person with Substance Dependence in full remission, any relapses that meet criteria for Substance Abuse would be considered Dependence in partial remission (see course specifiers, p. 179).

The course of Substance Dependence is variable. Although relatively brief and self-limited episodes may occur (particularly during periods of psychosocial stress), the course is usually chronic, lasting years, with periods of exacerbation and partial or full remission. There may be periods of heavy intake and severe problems, periods of total abstinence, and times of nonproblematic use of the substance, sometimes lasting for months. Substance Dependence is sometimes associated with spontaneous, long-term remissions. For example, follow-ups reveal that 20% (or more) of individuals with Alcohol Dependence become permanently abstinent, usually following a severe life stress (e.g., the threat or imposition of social or legal sanctions, discovery of a life-threatening medical complication). During the first 12 months after the onset of remission, the individual is particularly vulnerable to having a relapse. Many individuals underestimate their vulnerability to developing a pattern of Dependence. When in a period of remission, they incorrectly assure themselves that they will have no problem regulating substance use and may experiment with gradually less restrictive rules governing the use of the substance, only to experience a return to Dependence. The presence of co-occurring mental disorders (e.g., Antisocial Personality Disorder, Major Depressive Disorder) often increases the risk of complications and a poor outcome.

Impairment and Complications

Although many individuals with substance-related problems have good functioning (e.g., in personal relationships, job performance, earning abilities), these disorders often cause marked impairment and severe complications. Individuals with Substance-Related

Disorders frequently experience a deterioration in their general health. Malnutrition and other general medical conditions may result from improper diet and inadequate personal hygiene. Intoxication or Withdrawal may be complicated by trauma related to impaired motor coordination or faulty judgment. The materials used to "cut" certain substances can produce toxic or allergic reactions. Using substances intranasally ("snorting") may cause erosion of the nasal septum. Stimulant use can result in sudden death from cardiac arrhythmias, myocardial infarction, a cerebrovascular accident, or respiratory arrest. The use of contaminated needles during intravenous administration of substances can cause human immunodeficiency virus (HIV) infection, hepatitis, tetanus, vasculitis, septicemia, subacute bacterial endocarditis, embolic phenomena, and malaria.

Substance use can be associated with violent or aggressive behavior, which may be manifested by fights or criminal activity, and can result in injury to the person using the substance or to others. Automobile, home, and industrial accidents are a major complication of Substance Intoxication and result in an appreciable rate of morbidity and mortality. Approximately one-half of all highway fatalities involve either a driver or a pedestrian who is intoxicated. In addition, perhaps 10% of individuals with Substance Dependence commit suicide, often in the context of a Substance-Induced Mood Disorder. Finally, because most, if not all, of the substances described in this section cross the placenta, they may have potential adverse effects on the developing fetus (e.g., fetal alcohol syndrome). When taken repeatedly in high doses by the mother, a number of substances (e.g., cocaine, opioids, alcohol, and sedatives, hypnotics, and anxiolytics) are capable of causing physiological dependence in the fetus and a withdrawal syndrome in the newborn.

Familial Pattern

Information about familial associations has been best studied for the Alcohol-Related Disorders (see the detailed discussion on p. 203). There is some evidence for genetically determined differences among individuals in the doses required to produce Alcohol Intoxication. Although Substance Abuse and Dependence appear to aggregate in families, some of this effect may be explained by the concurrent familial distribution of Antisocial Personality Disorder, which may predispose individuals to the development of Substance Abuse or Dependence.

Differential Diagnosis

Substance-Related Disorders are distinguished from **nonpathological substance use** (e.g., **"social" drinking**) and from the **use of medications for appropriate medical purposes** by the presence of tolerance, withdrawal, compulsive use, or substance-related problems (e.g., medical complications, disruption in social and family relationships, vocational or financial difficulties, legal problems). Repeated episodes of **Substance Intoxication** are almost invariably prominent features of **Substance Abuse** or **Dependence.** However, one or more episodes of Intoxication alone are not sufficient for a diagnosis of either Substance Dependence or Abuse.

It may sometimes be difficult to distinguish between **Substance Intoxication** and **Substance Withdrawal.** If a symptom arises during the time of dosing and then gradually abates after dosing stops, it is likely to be part of Intoxication. If the symptom arises after stopping the substance, or reducing its use, it is likely to be part of Withdrawal.

Individuals with Substance-Related Disorders often take more than one substance and may be intoxicated with one substance (e.g., heroin) while withdrawing from another (e.g., diazepam). This differential is further complicated by the fact that the signs and symptoms of Withdrawal from some substances (e.g., sedatives) may partially mimic Intoxication with others (e.g., amphetamines). Substance Intoxication is differentiated from **Substance Intoxication Delirium** (p. 129), **Substance-Induced Psychotic Disorder, With Onset During Intoxication** (p. 310), **Substance-Induced Mood Disorder, With Onset During Intoxication** (p. 370), **Substance-Induced Anxiety Disorder, With Onset During Intoxication** (p. 439), **Substance-Induced Sexual Dysfunction, With Onset During Intoxication** (p. 519), and **Substance-Induced Sleep Disorder, With Onset During Intoxication** (p. 601), by the fact that the symptoms in these latter disorders are in excess of those usually associated with Substance Intoxication and are severe enough to warrant independent clinical attention. Substance Withdrawal is distinguished from **Substance Withdrawal Delirium** (p. 129), **Substance-Induced Psychotic Disorder, With Onset During Withdrawal** (p. 310), **Substance-Induced Mood Disorder, With Onset During Withdrawal** (p. 370), **Substance-Induced Anxiety Disorder, With Onset During Withdrawal** (p. 439), and **Substance-Induced Sleep Disorder, With Onset During Withdrawal** (p. 601), by the fact that the symptoms in these latter disorders are in excess of those usually associated with Substance Withdrawal and are severe enough to warrant independent clinical attention.

The additional Substance-Induced Disorders described above present with symptoms that resemble **non-substance-induced** (i.e., **primary**) **mental disorders.** See p. 193 for a discussion of this important but often difficult differential diagnosis. An additional diagnosis of a Substance-Induced Disorder is usually not made when **symptoms of preexisting mental disorders are exacerbated by Substance Intoxication or Substance Withdrawal** (although a diagnosis of Substance Intoxication or Withdrawal might be appropriate). For example, Intoxication with some substances may exacerbate the mood swings in Bipolar Disorder, the auditory hallucinations and paranoid delusions in Schizophrenia, the intrusive thoughts and terrifying dreams in Posttraumatic Stress Disorder, and the anxiety symptoms in Panic Disorder, Generalized Anxiety Disorder, Social Phobia, and Agoraphobia. Intoxication or Withdrawal may also increase the risk of suicide, violence, and impulsive behavior in individuals with a preexisting Antisocial or Borderline Personality Disorder.

Many neurological (e.g., head injuries) or metabolic conditions produce symptoms that resemble, and are sometimes misattributed to, Intoxication or Withdrawal (e.g., fluctuating levels of consciousness, slurred speech, incoordination). The symptoms of infectious diseases may also resemble Withdrawal from some substances (e.g., viral gastroenteritis can be similar to Opioid Withdrawal). If the symptoms are judged to be a direct physiological consequence of a general medical condition, the appropriate **Mental Disorder Due to a General Medical Condition** should be diagnosed. If the symptoms are judged to be a direct physiological consequence of both substance use and a general medical condition, both a Substance-Related Disorder and a Mental Disorder Due to a General Medical Condition may be diagnosed. If the clinician is unable to determine whether the presenting symptoms are substance induced, due to a general medical condition, or primary, the appropriate **Not Otherwise Specified Category** should be diagnosed (e.g., psychotic symptoms with indeterminate etiology would be diagnosed as Psychotic Disorder Not Otherwise Specified).

Substance-Induced Mental Disorders Included Elsewhere in the Manual

Substance-Induced Disorders cause a variety of symptoms that are characteristic of other mental disorders (see Table 1, p. 177). To facilitate differential diagnosis, the text and criteria for these other Substance-Induced Disorders are included in the sections of the manual with disorders with which they share phenomenology:

Substance-Induced Delirium (see p. 129) is included in the "Delirium, Dementia, and Amnestic and Other Cognitive Disorders" section.

Substance-Induced Persisting Dementia (see p. 152) is included in the "Delirium, Dementia, and Amnestic and Other Cognitive Disorders" section.

Substance-Induced Persisting Amnestic Disorder (see p. 161) is included in the "Delirium, Dementia, and Amnestic and Other Cognitive Disorders" section.

Substance-Induced Psychotic Disorder (see p. 310) is included in the "Schizophrenia and Other Psychotic Disorders" section. (In DSM-III-R these disorders were classified as "organic hallucinosis" and "organic delusional disorder.")

Substance-Induced Mood Disorder (see p. 370) is included in the "Mood Disorders" section.

Substance-Induced Anxiety Disorder (see p. 439) is included in the "Anxiety Disorders" section.

Substance-Induced Sexual Dysfunction (see p. 519) is included in the "Sexual and Gender Identity Disorders" section.

Substance-Induced Sleep Disorder (see p. 601) is included in the "Sleep Disorders" section.

In addition, **Hallucinogen Persisting Perception Disorder (Flashbacks)** (p. 233) is included under "Hallucinogen-Related Disorders" in this section.

In DSM-III-R, the Substance-Induced Disorders and the Mental Disorders Due to a General Medical Condition were called "organic" disorders and were listed together in a single section. This differentiation of "organic" mental disorders as a separate class implied that "nonorganic" or "functional" mental disorders were somehow unrelated to physical or biological factors or processes. DSM-IV eliminates the term *organic* and distinguishes those mental disorders that are substance induced from those that are due to a general medical condition and those that have no specified etiology. The term *primary mental disorder* is used as a shorthand to indicate those mental disorders that are not substance induced and that are not due to a general medical condition.

The context in which a Substance-Induced Disorder develops can have important management implications. Substance-Induced Disorders can develop in the context of Substance Intoxication or Substance Withdrawal, or they can persist long after the substance has been eliminated from the body (Substance-Induced Persisting Disorders). Substance-induced presentations that develop in the context of Substance Intoxication can be indicated by using the specifier With Onset During Intoxication. Substance-induced presentations that develop in the context of Substance Withdrawal can be indicated by the specifier With Onset During Withdrawal. It should be noted that a diagnosis of a Substance-Induced Disorder, With Onset During Intoxication or Withdrawal, should be made instead of a diagnosis of Substance Intoxication or Substance Withdrawal only when the symptoms are in excess of those usually associated with the intoxication or withdrawal syndrome that is characteristic of the particular substance and when they are sufficiently severe to warrant independent clinical attention. Three

Substance-Induced Persisting Disorders are included: Substance-Induced Persisting Dementia (see p. 152) and Substance-Induced Persisting Amnestic Disorder (see p. 161) in the "Delirium, Dementia, and Amnestic and Other Cognitive Disorders" section and Hallucinogen Persisting Perception Disorder under "Hallucinogen-Related Disorders" in this section (see p. 233). The essential feature of a Substance-Induced Persisting Disorder is prolonged or permanent persistence of substance-related symptoms that continue long after the usual course of Intoxication or Withdrawal has ended.

For drugs of abuse, a diagnosis of a Substance-Induced Mental Disorder requires that there be evidence from the history, physical examination, or laboratory findings of Substance Intoxication or Substance Withdrawal. In evaluating whether the symptoms of a mental disorder are the direct physiological effect of substance use, it is important to note the temporal relationship between the onset and offset of substance use and the onset and offset of the symptoms. If the symptoms precede the onset of substance use or persist during extended periods of abstinence from the substance, it is likely that the symptoms are not substance induced. As a rule of thumb, symptoms that persist for more than 4 weeks after the cessation of acute Intoxication or Withdrawal should be considered to be manifestations of an independent non-substance-induced mental disorder or of a Substance-Induced Persisting Disorder. Clinical judgment is necessary in making this distinction, particularly because different substances have different characteristic durations of intoxication and withdrawal and varying relationships with symptoms of mental disorders. Because the withdrawal state for some substances can be relatively protracted, it is useful to carefully observe the course of symptoms for an extended period of time (e.g., 4 weeks or more) after the cessation of acute Intoxication or Withdrawal, making all possible efforts to maintain the individual's abstinence. This can be accomplished in various ways, including inpatient hospitalization or residential treatment, requiring frequent follow-up visits, recruiting friends and family members to help keep the person substance free, regularly evaluating urine or blood for the presence of substances, and, if alcohol is involved, routinely evaluating changes in state markers of heavy drinking such as gamma-glutamyltransferase (GGT).

Another consideration in differentiating a primary mental disorder from a Substance-Induced Disorder is the presence of features that are atypical of the primary disorder (e.g., atypical age at onset or course). For example, the onset of a Manic Episode after age 45 years may suggest a substance-induced etiology. In contrast, factors that suggest that the symptoms are better accounted for by a primary mental disorder include a history of prior episodes of the disturbance that were not substance induced. Finally, the presence or absence of the substance-specific physiological and behavioral features of Intoxication or Withdrawal should be considered. For example, the presence of paranoid delusions would not be surprising in the context of Phencyclidine Intoxication, but would be unusual with Sedative Intoxication, increasing the likelihood that a primary Psychotic Disorder accounts for the symptoms. Furthermore, the dosage of the substance used should be taken into account. For example, the presence of paranoid delusions would be unusual after a single puff of marijuana, but might be compatible with high doses of hashish.

Substance-Induced Disorders can also occur as a side effect of a medication or from exposure to a toxin. Substance-Induced Disorders due to a prescribed treatment for a mental disorder or general medical condition must have their onset while the person is receiving the medication (or during withdrawal if the medication is associated with a withdrawal syndrome). Once the treatment is discontinued, the symptoms will usually remit within days to several weeks (depending on the half-life of the substance, the presence of a withdrawal syndrome, and individual variability). If symptoms persist, a primary mental disorder (not related to a medication) should be considered. Because individuals with general medical conditions often take medications for those conditions, the clinician must consider the possibility that the symptoms are caused by the physiological consequences of the general medical condition rather than the medication, in which case Mental Disorder Due to a General Medical Condition is diagnosed. The history may provide a basis for making this judgment, but a change in the treatment for the general medical condition (e.g., medication substitution or discontinuation) may be needed to determine empirically for that person whether or not the medication is the causative agent.

Recording Procedures for Substance-Induced Mental Disorders Included Elsewhere in the Manual

The name of the diagnosis begins with the specific substance (e.g., cocaine, diazepam, dexamethasone) that is presumed to be causing the symptoms. The diagnostic code is selected from the listing of classes of substances provided in the criteria sets for the particular Substance-Induced Disorder. For substances that do not fit into any of the classes (e.g., dexamethasone), the code for "Other Substance" should be used. In addition, for medications prescribed at therapeutic doses, the specific medication can be indicated by listing the appropriate E-code on Axis I (see Appendix G). The name of the disorder (e.g., Cocaine-Induced Psychotic Disorder; Diazepam-Induced Anxiety Disorder) is followed by the specification of the predominant symptom presentation and the context in which the symptoms developed (e.g., 292.11 Cocaine-Induced Psychotic Disorder, With Delusions, With Onset During Intoxication; 292.89 Diazepam-Induced Anxiety Disorder, With Onset During Withdrawal). When more than one substance is judged to play a significant role in the development of symptoms, each should be listed separately. If a substance is judged to be the etiological factor, but the specific substance or class of substances is unknown, the class "Unknown Substance" should be used.

Alcohol-Related Disorders

In most cultures, alcohol is the most frequently used brain depressant and a cause of considerable morbidity and mortality. At some time in their lives, as many as 90% of adults in the United States have had some experience with alcohol, and a substantial number (60% of males and 30% of females) have had one or more alcohol-related adverse life events (e.g., driving after consuming too much alcohol, missing school or work due to a hangover). Fortunately, most individuals learn from these experiences to moderate their drinking and do not develop Alcohol Dependence or Abuse.

This section contains discussions specific to the Alcohol-Related Disorders. Texts and criteria sets have already been provided earlier for the generic aspects of Substance Dependence (p. 176) and Substance Abuse (p. 182) that apply across all substances. Texts specific to Alcohol Dependence and Abuse are provided below; however, there are no additional specific criteria sets for Alcohol Dependence or Alcohol Abuse. Specific texts and criteria sets for Alcohol Intoxication and Alcohol Withdrawal are also provided below. The Alcohol-Induced Disorders (other than Alcohol Intoxication and Withdrawal) are described in the sections of the manual with disorders with which they share phenomenology (e.g., Alcohol-Induced Mood Disorder is included in the "Mood Disorders" section). Listed below are the Alcohol Use Disorders and the Alcohol-Induced Disorders.

Alcohol Use Disorders

303.90   **Alcohol Dependence** (see p. 195)
305.00   **Alcohol Abuse** (see p. 196)

Alcohol-Induced Disorders

303.00   **Alcohol Intoxication** (see p. 196)
291.8   **Alcohol Withdrawal** (see p. 197) *Specify if:* With Perceptual Disturbances
291.0   **Alcohol Intoxication Delirium** (see p. 129)
291.0   **Alcohol Withdrawal Delirium** (see p. 129)
291.2   **Alcohol-Induced Persisting Dementia** (see p. 152)
291.1   **Alcohol-Induced Persisting Amnestic Disorder** (see p. 161)
291.5   **Alcohol-Induced Psychotic Disorder, With Delusions** (see p. 310)
             Specify if: With Onset During Intoxication/With Onset During Withdrawal
291.3   **Alcohol-Induced Psychotic Disorder, With Hallucinations** (see p. 310)
             Specify if: With Onset During Intoxication/With Onset During Withdrawal
291.8   **Alcohol-Induced Mood Disorder** (see p. 370)
             Specify if: With Onset During Intoxication/With Onset During Withdrawal
291.8   **Alcohol-Induced Anxiety Disorder** (see p. 439)
             Specify if: With Onset During Intoxication/With Onset During Withdrawal
291.8   **Alcohol-Induced Sexual Dysfunction** (see p. 519)
             Specify if: With Onset During Intoxication
291.8   **Alcohol-Induced Sleep Disorder** (see p. 601)
             Specify if: With Onset During Intoxication/With Onset During Withdrawal

291.9   **Alcohol-Related Disorder Not Otherwise Specified** (see p. 204)

Alcohol Use Disorders
303.90 Alcohol Dependence

Also refer to the text and criteria for Substance Dependence (see p. 176). Physiological dependence on alcohol is indicated by evidence of tolerance or symptoms of Withdrawal. Alcohol Withdrawal (see p. 197) is characterized by the development of withdrawal symptoms 12 hours or so after the reduction of intake following prolonged, heavy, alcohol ingestion. Because Withdrawal from alcohol can be unpleasant and intense, individuals with Alcohol Dependence may continue to consume alcohol, despite adverse consequences, often to avoid or to relieve the symptoms of withdrawal. A substantial minority of individuals who have Alcohol Dependence never experience clinically relevant levels of Alcohol Withdrawal, and only about 5% of individuals with Alcohol Dependence ever experience severe complications of withdrawal (e.g., delirium, grand mal seizures). Once a pattern of compulsive use develops, individuals with Dependence may devote substantial periods of time to obtaining and consuming alcoholic beverages. These individuals often continue to use alcohol despite evidence of adverse psychological or physical consequences (e.g., depression, blackouts, liver disease, or other sequelae).

Specifiers

The following specifiers may be applied to a diagnosis of Alcohol Dependence (see p. 179 for more details):

> **With Physiological Dependence**
> **Without Physiological Dependence**
>
> **Early Full Remission**
> **Early Partial Remission**
> **Sustained Full Remission**
> **Sustained Partial Remission**
> **On Agonist Therapy**
> **In a Controlled Environment**

305.00   Alcohol Abuse

Also refer to the text and criteria for Substance Abuse (see p. 182). School and job performance may suffer either from the aftereffects of drinking or from actual intoxication on the job or at school; child care or household responsibilities may be neglected; and alcohol-related absences may occur from school or job. The person may use alcohol in physically hazardous circumstances (e.g., driving an automobile or operating machinery while drunk). Legal difficulties may arise because of alcohol use (e.g., arrests for intoxicated behavior or for driving under the influence). Finally, individuals with Alcohol Abuse may continue to consume alcohol despite the knowledge that continued consumption poses significant social or interpersonal problems for them (e.g., violent arguments with spouse while intoxicated, child abuse). When these problems are accompanied by evidence of tolerance, withdrawal, or compulsive behavior related to alcohol use, a diagnosis of Alcohol Dependence, rather than Alcohol Abuse, should be considered.

Alcohol-Induced Disorders

303.00   Alcohol Intoxication

Refer to the text and criteria for Substance Intoxication (see p. 183). The essential feature of Alcohol Intoxication is the presence of clinically significant maladaptive behavioral or psychological changes (e.g., inappropriate sexual or aggressive behavior, mood lability, impaired judgment, impaired social or occupational functioning) that develop during, or shortly after, the ingestion of alcohol (Criteria A and B). These changes are accompanied by evidence of slurred speech, incoordination, unsteady gait, nystagmus, impairment in attention or memory, or stupor or coma (Criterion C). The symptoms must not be due to a general medical condition and are not better accounted for by another mental disorder (Criterion D). The resulting picture is similar to what is observed during Benzodiazepine or Barbiturate Intoxication. The levels of incoordination can interfere with driving abilities and with performing usual activities to the point of causing accidents. Evidence of alcohol use can be obtained by smelling alcohol on the individual's breath, eliciting a history from the individual or another observer, and, when needed, having the individual undertake breath, blood, or urine toxicology analyses.

■ **Diagnostic criteria for 303.00 Alcohol Intoxication**

A. Recent ingestion of alcohol.

B. Clinically significant maladaptive behavioral or psychological changes (e.g., inappropriate sexual or aggressive behavior, mood lability, impaired judgment, impaired social or occupational functioning) that developed during, or shortly after, alcohol ingestion.

C. One (or more) of the following signs, developing during, or shortly after, alcohol use:
   (1) slurred speech
   (2) incoordination
   (3) unsteady gait
   (4) nystagmus
   (5) impairment in attention or memory
   (6) stupor or coma

D. The symptoms are not due to a general medical condition and are not better accounted for by another mental disorder.

291.8   Alcohol Withdrawal

Also refer to the text and criteria for Substance Withdrawal (see p. 184). The essential feature of Alcohol Withdrawal is the presence of a characteristic withdrawal syndrome that develops after the cessation of (or reduction in) heavy and prolonged alcohol use (Criteria A and B). The withdrawal syndrome includes two or more of the following symptoms: autonomic hyperactivity (e.g., sweating or pulse rate greater than 100); increased hand tremor; insomnia; nausea or vomiting; transient visual, tactile, or auditory hallucinations or illusions; psychomotor agitation; anxiety; and grand mal seizures. When hallucinations or illusions are observed, the clinician can specify With Perceptual Disturbances (see below). The symptoms cause clinically significant distress or impairment in social, occupational, or other important areas of functioning (Criterion C). The symptoms must not be due to a general medical condition and are not better accounted for by another mental disorder (e.g., Sedative, Hypnotic, or Anxiolytic Withdrawal or Generalized Anxiety Disorder) (Criterion D).

Symptoms are usually relieved by administering alcohol or any other brain depressant. The withdrawal symptoms typically begin when blood concentrations of alcohol decline sharply (i.e., within 4–12 hours) after alcohol use has been stopped or reduced. However, withdrawal symptoms can develop after longer periods of time (i.e., for up to a few days). Because of the short half-life of alcohol, symptoms of Alcohol Withdrawal usually peak in intensity during the second day of abstinence and are likely to improve markedly by the fourth or fifth day. Following acute Withdrawal, however, symptoms of anxiety, insomnia, and autonomic dysfunction may persist for up to 3–6 months at lower levels of intensity.

Fewer than 5% of individuals who develop Alcohol Withdrawal develop dramatic symptoms (e.g., severe autonomic hyperactivity, tremors, and Alcohol Withdrawal Delirium). Grand mal seizures occur in fewer than 3% of individuals. Alcohol Withdrawal Delirium (p. 129) includes disturbances in consciousness and cognition and visual, tactile, or auditory hallucinations ("delirium tremens," or "DTs"). When Alcohol Withdrawal Delirium develops, it is likely that a clinically relevant general medical condition may be present (e.g., liver failure, pneumonia, gastrointestinal bleeding, sequelae of head trauma, hypoglycemia, an electrolyte imbalance, or postoperative status).

Specifier

The following specifier may be applied to a diagnosis of Alcohol Withdrawal:

With Perceptual Disturbances. This specifier may be noted when hallucinations with intact reality testing or auditory, visual, or tactile illusions occur in the absence of a delirium. *Intact reality testing* means that the person knows that the hallucinations are induced by the substance and do not represent external reality. When hallucinations occur in the absence of intact reality testing, a diagnosis of Substance-Induced Psychotic Disorder, With Hallucinations, should be considered.

■ Diagnostic criteria for 291.8 Alcohol Withdrawal

A. Cessation of (or reduction in) alcohol use that has been heavy and prolonged.

B. Two (or more) of the following, developing within several hours to a few days after Criterion A:

    (1) autonomic hyperactivity (e.g., sweating or pulse rate greater than 100)

    (2) increased hand tremor

    (3) insomnia

    (4) nausea or vomiting

    (5) transient visual, tactile, or auditory hallucinations or illusions

    (6) psychomotor agitation

    (7) anxiety

    (8) grand mal seizures

(continued)

☐ **Diagnostic criteria for 291.8 Alcohol Withdrawal** (*continued*)

    C. The symptoms in Criterion B cause clinically significant distress or impairment in social, occupational, or other important areas of functioning.

    D. The symptoms are not due to a general medical condition and are not better accounted for by another mental disorder.

Specify if:
With Perceptual Disturbances

Other Alcohol-Induced Disorders

The following Alcohol-Induced Disorders are described in the sections of the manual with disorders with which they share phenomenology: **Alcohol Intoxication Delirium** (p. 129), **Alcohol Withdrawal Delirium** (p. 129), **Alcohol-Induced Persisting Dementia** (p. 152), **Alcohol-Induced Persisting Amnestic Disorder** (p. 161), **Alcohol-Induced Psychotic Disorder** (p. 310), **Alcohol-Induced Mood Disorder** (p. 370), **Alcohol-Induced Anxiety Disorder** (p. 439), **Alcohol-Induced Sexual Dysfunction** (p. 519), and **Alcohol-Induced Sleep Disorder** (p. 601). These disorders are diagnosed instead of Alcohol Intoxication or Alcohol Withdrawal only when the symptoms are in excess of those usually associated with the Alcohol Intoxication or Withdrawal syndrome and when the symptoms are sufficiently severe to warrant independent clinical attention.

Additional Information on Alcohol-Related Disorders

Associated Features and Disorders

Associated descriptive features and mental disorders.   Alcohol Dependence and Abuse are often associated with Dependence on, or Abuse of, other substances (e.g., cannabis; cocaine; heroin; amphetamines; the sedatives, hypnotics, and anxiolytics; and nicotine). Alcohol may be used to alleviate the unwanted effects of these other substances or to substitute for them when they are not available. Symptoms of depression, anxiety, and insomnia frequently accompany Alcohol Dependence and sometimes precede it. Alcohol Intoxication is sometimes associated with an amnesia for the events that occurred during the course of the intoxication ("blackouts"). This phenomenon may be related to the presence of a high blood alcohol level and, perhaps, to the rapidity with which this level is reached.

    Alcohol-Related Disorders are associated with a significant increase in the risk of accidents, violence, and suicide. It is estimated that approximately one-half of all highway fatalities involve either a driver or a pedestrian who has been drinking. Severe Alcohol Intoxication, especially in individuals with Antisocial Personality Disorder, is associated with the commission of criminal acts. For example, more than one-half of all murderers and their victims are believed to have been intoxicated with alcohol at the time of the murder. Severe Alcohol Intoxication also contributes to disinhibition and feelings of sadness and irritability, which contribute to suicide attempts and completed suicides. Alcohol-Related Disorders contribute to absenteeism from work, job-related accidents, and low employee productivity. Alcohol Abuse and Dependence, along with Abuse and Dependence of other substances, are prevalent among homeless individuals in the United States. Mood Disorders, Anxiety Disorders, and Schizophrenia may also be associated with Alcohol Dependence. Although antisocial behavior and Antisocial Personality Disorder are associated with Alcohol-Related Disorders, they are even more common with disorders related to illegal substances (e.g., cocaine, heroin, or amphetamine) whose cost commonly leads to criminal activity.

Associated laboratory findings.   One sensitive laboratory indicator of heavy drinking is an elevation (> 30 units) of gamma-glutamyltransferase (GGT). This finding may be the only laboratory abnormality. At least 70% of individuals with a high GGT level are persistent heavy drinkers. Mean corpuscular volume (MCV) may be elevated to high-normal values in individuals who drink heavily due to deficiencies of some B vitamins, as well as to the direct toxic effects of alcohol on erythropoiesis. Although the MCV can be used to help identify those who drink heavily, it is a poor method of monitoring abstinence because of the long half-life of red blood cells. Liver function tests (e.g., serum glutamic oxaloacetic transaminase [SGOT] and alkaline phosphatase) can reveal liver injury that is a consequence of heavy drinking. Elevations of lipid levels in the blood (e.g., triglycerides and lipoprotein cholesterol) can be observed, resulting from decreases in gluconeogenesis associated with heavy drinking. High fat content in the blood also contributes to the development of fatty liver. High-normal levels of uric acid can occur with heavy drinking, but are relatively nonspecific. The most direct test available to measure alcohol consumption cross-sectionally is blood alcohol concentration, which can also be used to judge tolerance to alcohol. An individual with a concentration of 100 mg of ethanol per deciliter of blood who does not show signs of intoxication can be presumed to have acquired at least some degree of tolerance to alcohol. At 200 mg/dl, most nontolerant individuals demonstrate severe intoxication.

Associated physical examination findings and general medical conditions.
Repeated intake of high doses of alcohol can affect nearly every organ system, especially the gastrointestinal tract, cardiovascular system, and the central and peripheral nervous systems. Gastrointestinal effects include gastritis, stomach or duodenal ulcers, and, in about 15% of those who use alcohol heavily, liver cirrhosis and pancreatitis. There is also an increased rate of cancer of the esophagus, stomach, and other parts of the gastrointestinal tract. One of the most common associated general medical conditions is low-grade hypertension. Cardiomyopathy and other myopathies are less common, but occur at an increased rate among those who drink very heavily. These factors, along with marked increases in levels of triglycerides and low-density lipoprotein cholesterol, contribute to an elevated risk of heart disease. Peripheral neuropathy may be evidenced by muscular weakness, paresthesias, and decreased peripheral sensation. More persistent central nervous system effects include cognitive deficits, severe memory impairment, and degenerative changes in the cerebellum. These effects are related to vitamin deficiencies (particularly of the B vitamins, including thiamine). The most devastating central nervous system effect is the relatively rare Alcohol-Induced Persisting Amnestic

Disorder (p. 161) (Wernicke-Korsakoff syndrome), in which the ability to encode new memory is severely impaired.

Many of the symptoms and physical findings associated with the Alcohol-Related Disorders are a consequence of the disease states noted above. Examples are the dyspepsia, nausea, and bloating that accompany gastritis and the hepatomegaly, esophageal varices, and hemorrhoids that accompany alcohol-induced changes in the liver. Other physical signs include tremor, unsteady gait, insomnia, and erectile dysfunction. Individuals with chronic Alcohol Dependence may exhibit decreased testicular size and feminizing effects associated with reduced testosterone levels. Repeated heavy drinking during pregnancy is associated with spontaneous abortion and fetal alcohol syndrome. Individuals with preexisting histories of epilepsy or severe head trauma are more likely to develop alcohol-related seizures. Alcohol Withdrawal may be associated with nausea, vomiting, gastritis, hematemesis, dry mouth, puffy blotchy complexion, and mild peripheral edema. Alcohol Intoxication may result in falls and accidents that may cause fractures, subdural hematomas, and other forms of brain trauma. Severe, repeated Alcohol Intoxication may also suppress immune mechanisms and predispose individuals to infections and increase the risk for cancers. Finally, unanticipated Alcohol Withdrawal in hospitalized patients for whom a diagnosis of Alcohol Dependence has been overlooked can add to the risks and costs of hospitalization and to time spent in the hospital.

Specific Culture, Age, and Gender Features

The cultural traditions surrounding the use of alcohol in family, religious, and social settings, especially during childhood, can affect both alcohol use patterns and the likelihood that alcohol problems will develop. Marked differences characterize the quantity, frequency, and patterning of alcohol consumption in the countries of the world. In most Asian cultures, the overall prevalence of Alcohol-Related Disorders may be relatively low, and the male-to-female ratio high. These findings appear to relate to the absence, in perhaps 50% of Japanese, Chinese, and Korean individuals, of the form of aldehyde dehydrogenase that eliminates low levels of the first breakdown product of alcohol, acetaldehyde. When such individuals consume alcohol, they experience a flushed face and palpitations and are less likely to consume large amounts. In the United States, whites and African-Americans have nearly identical rates of Alcohol Abuse and Dependence. Latino males have somewhat higher rates, although prevalence is lower among Latino females than among females from other ethnic groups. Low educational level, unemployment, and lower socioeconomic status are associated with Alcohol-Related Disorders, although it is often difficult to separate cause from effect. Years of schooling may not be as important in determining risk as completing the immediate educational goal (i.e., those who drop out of high school or college have particularly high rates of Alcohol-Related Disorders).

Among adolescents, Conduct Disorder and repeated antisocial behavior often co-occur with Alcohol Abuse or Dependence and with other Substance-Related Disorders. Age-related physical changes in elderly persons result in increased brain susceptibility to the depressant effects of alcohol, decreased rates of liver metabolism of a variety of substances, including alcohol, and decreased percentages of body water. These changes can cause older people to develop more severe intoxication and subsequent problems at lower levels of consumption. Alcohol-related problems in older people are also especially likely to be associated with other medical complications.

Alcohol Abuse and Dependence are more common in males than in females, with a male-to-female ratio as high as 5:1. However, this ratio varies substantially depending on the age group. Females tend to start drinking heavily later in life than do males and may develop Alcohol-Related Disorders later. Once Alcohol Abuse or Dependence develops in females, it may progress more rapidly, so that by middle age females may have the same range of health problems and social, interpersonal, and occupational consequences as do males. Females tend to develop higher blood alcohol concentrations than males at a given dose of alcohol per kilogram because of their lower percentage of body water, higher percentage of body fat, and the fact that they tend to metabolize alcohol more slowly (in part because of lower levels of alcohol dehydrogenase in the mucosal lining of the stomach). Because of these higher alcohol levels, they may be at greater risk than males for some of the health-related consequences of heavy alcohol intake (in particular, liver damage).

Prevalence

Alcohol Dependence and Abuse are among the most prevalent mental disorders in the general population. A community study conducted in the United States from 1980 to 1985 using DSM-III criteria found that about 8% of the adult population had Alcohol Dependence and about 5% had Alcohol Abuse at some time in their lives. Approximately 6% had Alcohol Dependence or Abuse during the preceding year. From data collected prospectively, about 7.5% had symptoms that met criteria for an Alcohol-Related Disorder during a 1-year period. A United States national probability sample of noninstitutionalized adults (ages 15–54 years) conducted in 1990–1991 using DSM-III-R criteria reported that around 14% had Alcohol Dependence at some time in their lives, with approximately 7% having had Dependence in the past year.

Course

The first episode of Alcohol Intoxication is likely to occur in the mid-teens, with the age at onset of Alcohol Dependence peaking in the 20s to mid-30s. The large majority of those who develop Alcohol-Related Disorders do so by their late 30s. The first evidence of Withdrawal is not likely to appear until after many other aspects of Dependence have developed. Alcohol Abuse and Dependence have a variable course that is frequently characterized by periods of remission and relapse. A decision to stop drinking, often in response to a crisis, is likely to be followed by weeks or more of abstinence, which is often followed by limited periods of controlled or nonproblematic drinking. However, once alcohol intake resumes, it is highly likely that consumption will rapidly escalate and that severe problems will once again develop. Clinicians often have the erroneous impression that Alcohol Dependence and Abuse are intractable disorders based on the fact that those who present for treatment typically have a history of many years of severe alcohol-related problems. However, these most severe cases represent only a small proportion of individuals with Alcohol Dependence or Abuse, and the typical person with an Alcohol Use Disorder has a much more promising prognosis. Follow-up studies of more highly functioning individuals show a higher than 65% 1-year abstinence rate following treatment. Some individuals (perhaps 20% or more) with Alcohol Dependence achieve long-term sobriety even without active treatment.

During even mild Alcohol Intoxication, different symptoms are likely to be observed at different time points. Early in the drinking period, when blood alcohol levels are rising, symptoms often include talkativeness, a sensation of well-being, and a bright, expansive mood. Later, especially when blood alcohol levels are falling, the individual is likely to become progressively more depressed, withdrawn, and cognitively impaired. At very high blood alcohol levels (e.g., 200–300 mg/dl), a nontolerant individual is likely to fall asleep and enter a first stage of anesthesia. Higher blood alcohol levels (e.g., in excess of 300–400 mg/dl) can cause inhibition of respiration and pulse and even death in nontolerant individuals. The duration of Intoxication depends on how much alcohol was consumed over what period of time. In general, the body is able to metabolize approximately one drink per hour, so that the blood alcohol level generally decreases at a rate of 15–20 mg/dl per hour. Signs and symptoms of intoxication are likely to be more intense when the blood alcohol level is rising than when it is falling.

Familial Pattern

Alcohol Dependence often has a familial pattern, and at least some of the transmission can be traced to genetic factors. The risk for Alcohol Dependence is three to four times higher in close relatives of people with Alcohol Dependence. Higher risk is associated with a greater number of affected relatives, closer genetic relationships, and the severity of the alcohol-related problems in the affected relative. Most studies have found a significantly higher risk for Alcohol Dependence in the monozygotic twin than in the dizygotic twin of a person with Alcohol Dependence. Adoption studies have revealed a three- to fourfold increase in risk for Alcohol Dependence in the children of individuals with Alcohol Dependence when these children were adopted away at birth and raised by adoptive parents who did not have this disorder. However, genetic factors explain only a part of the risk for Alcohol Dependence, with a significant part of the risk coming from environmental or interpersonal factors that may include cultural attitudes toward drinking and drunkenness, the availability of alcohol (including price), expectations of the effects of alcohol on mood and behavior, acquired personal experiences with alcohol, and stress.

Differential Diagnosis

For a general discussion of the differential diagnosis of Substance-Related Disorders, see p. 190. Alcohol-Induced Disorders may be characterized by symptoms (e.g., depressed mood) that resemble **primary mental disorders** (e.g., Major Depressive Disorder versus Alcohol-Induced Mood Disorder, With Depressive Features, With Onset During Intoxication). See p. 193 for a discussion of this differential diagnosis.

The incoordination and impaired judgment that are associated with Alcohol Intoxication can resemble the symptoms of **certain general medical conditions** (e.g., diabetic acidosis, cerebellar ataxias, and other neurological conditions such as multiple sclerosis). Similarly, the symptoms of Alcohol Withdrawal can also be mimicked by **certain general medical conditions** (e.g., hypoglycemia and diabetic ketoacidosis). **Essential tremor,** a disorder that frequently runs in families, may suggest the tremulousness associated with Alcohol Withdrawal.

Alcohol Intoxication (except for the smell of alcohol on the breath) closely resembles **Sedative, Hypnotic, or Anxiolytic Intoxication.** The presence of alcohol on the breath does not by itself exclude intoxications with other substances because multiple substances are not uncommonly used concurrently. Although intoxication at some time during their lives is likely to be a part of the history of most individuals who drink alcohol, when this phenomenon occurs regularly or causes impairment it is important to consider the possibility of a diagnosis of Alcohol Dependence or Alcohol Abuse. **Sedative, Hypnotic, or Anxiolytic Withdrawal** produces a syndrome very similar to that of Alcohol Withdrawal.

Alcohol Intoxication and Alcohol Withdrawal are distinguished from the **other Alcohol-Induced Disorders** (e.g., Alcohol-Induced Anxiety Disorder, With Onset During Withdrawal) because the symptoms in these latter disorders are in excess of those usually associated with Alcohol Intoxication or Alcohol Withdrawal and are severe enough to warrant independent clinical attention. **Alcohol idiosyncratic intoxication,** defined as marked behavioral change, usually aggressiveness, following the ingestion of a relatively small of amount of alcohol, was included in DSM-III-R. Because of limited support in the literature for the validity of this condition, it is no longer included as a separate diagnosis in DSM-IV. Such presentations would most likely be diagnosed as Alcohol Intoxication or Alcohol-Related Disorder Not Otherwise Specified.

291.9   Alcohol-Related Disorder
Not Otherwise Specified

The Alcohol-Related Disorder Not Otherwise Specified category is for disorders associated with the use of alcohol that are not classifiable as Alcohol Dependence, Alcohol Abuse, Alcohol Intoxication, Alcohol Withdrawal, Alcohol Intoxication Delirium, Alcohol Withdrawal Delirium, Alcohol-Induced Persisting Dementia, Alcohol-Induced Persisting Amnestic Disorder, Alcohol-Induced Psychotic Disorder, Alcohol-Induced Mood Disorder, Alcohol-Induced Anxiety Disorder, Alcohol-Induced Sexual Dysfunction, or Alcohol-Induced Sleep Disorder.

Amphetamine
(or Amphetamine-Like)–Related Disorders

The class of amphetamine and amphetamine-like substances includes all substances with a substituted-phenylethylamine structure, such as amphetamine, dextroamphetamine, and methamphetamine ("speed"). Also included are those substances that are structurally different but also have amphetamine-like action, such as methylphenidate and other agents used as appetite suppressants ("diet pills"). These substances are usually taken orally or intravenously, although methamphetamine is also taken by the nasal route ("snorting"). A very pure form of methamphetamine is called "ice" because of the appearance of its crystals when observed under magnification. Due to its high purity and relatively low vaporization point, ice can be smoked to produce an immediate and powerful stimulant effect (as is done with "crack" cocaine). In addition to the synthetic amphetamine-like compounds, there are naturally occurring, plant-derived stimulants such as khat that can produce Abuse or Dependence. Unlike cocaine, which is almost always purchased on the illegal market, amphetamines and other stimulants may be obtained by prescription for the treatment of obesity, Attention-Deficit/Hyperactivity Disorder, and Narcolepsy. Prescribed stimulants have sometimes been diverted into the illegal market, often in the context of weight-control programs. Most of the effects of amphetamines and amphetamine-like drugs are similar to those of cocaine. However, unlike cocaine, these substances do not have local anesthetic (i.e., membrane ion channel) activity; therefore, their risk for inducing certain general medical conditions (e.g., cardiac arrhythmias and seizures) may be lower. The psychoactive effects of most amphetamine-like substances last longer than those of cocaine, and the peripheral sympathomimetic effects may be more potent.

This section contains discussions that are specific to the Amphetamine-Related Disorders. Texts and criteria sets have already been provided for the generic aspects of Substance Dependence (p. 176) and Substance Abuse (p. 182) that apply across all substances. Texts specific to Amphetamine Dependence and Abuse are provided below; however, there are no additional specific criteria sets for Amphetamine Dependence or Amphetamine Abuse. Specific texts and criteria sets for Amphetamine Intoxication and Amphetamine Withdrawal are also provided below. The Amphetamine-Induced Disorders (other than Amphetamine Intoxication and Withdrawal) are described in the sections of the manual with disorders with which they share phenomenology (e.g., Amphetamine-Induced Mood Disorder is included in the "Mood Disorders" section). Listed below are the Amphetamine Use Disorders and the Amphetamine-Induced Disorders.

Amphetamine Use Disorders

304.40   **Amphetamine Dependence** (see p. 206)
305.70   **Amphetamine Abuse** (see p. 206)

Amphetamine-Induced Disorders

292.89   **Amphetamine Intoxication** (see p. 207)
            Specify if: With Perceptual Disturbances
292.0   **Amphetamine Withdrawal** (see p. 208)
292.81   **Amphetamine Intoxication Delirium** (see p. 129)
292.11   **Amphetamine-Induced Psychotic Disorder, With Delusions** (see p. 310)
            Specify if: With Onset During Intoxication
292.12   **Amphetamine-Induced Psychotic Disorder, With Hallucinations**
            (see p. 310) *Specify if:* With Onset During Intoxication
292.84   **Amphetamine-Induced Mood Disorder** (see p. 370)
            Specify if: With Onset During Intoxication/With Onset During Withdrawal
292.89   **Amphetamine-Induced Anxiety Disorder** (see p. 439)
            Specify if: With Onset During Intoxication
292.89   **Amphetamine-Induced Sexual Dysfunction** (see p. 519)
            Specify if: With Onset During Intoxication
292.89   **Amphetamine-Induced Sleep Disorder** (see p. 601)
            Specify if: With Onset During Intoxication/With Onset During Withdrawal

292.9   **Amphetamine-Related Disorder Not Otherwise Specified** (see p. 211)

Amphetamine Use Disorders
304.40   Amphetamine Dependence

Also refer to the text and criteria for Substance Dependence (see p. 176). The patterns of use and course of Amphetamine Dependence are similar to those of Cocaine Dependence because both substances are potent central nervous system stimulants with similar psychoactive and sympathomimetic effects. However, amphetamines are longer acting than cocaine and thus are usually self-administered less frequently. As with Cocaine Dependence, usage may be chronic or episodic, with binges ("speed runs") punctuated by brief drug-free periods. Aggressive or violent behavior is associated with Amphetamine Dependence, especially when high doses are smoked (e.g., "ice") or administered intravenously. As with cocaine, intense but temporary anxiety, as well as paranoid ideation and psychotic episodes that resemble Schizophrenia, Paranoid Type, are often seen, especially in association with high-dose use. Tolerance to amphetamines develops and often leads to substantial escalation of the dose. Conversely, some individuals with Amphetamine Dependence develop reverse tolerance (sensitization). In these cases, small doses may produce marked stimulant and other adverse mental and neurological effects.

Specifiers

The following specifiers may be applied to a diagnosis of Amphetamine Dependence (see p. 179 for more details):

> **With Physiological Dependence**
> **Without Physiological Dependence**
>
> **Early Full Remission**
> **Early Partial Remission**
> **Sustained Full Remission**
> **Sustained Partial Remission**
> **On Agonist Therapy**
> **In a Controlled Environment**

305.70   Amphetamine Abuse

Also refer to the text and criteria for Substance Abuse (see p. 182). Legal difficulties typically arise as a result of behavior while intoxicated with amphetamines (especially aggressive behavior), as a consequence of obtaining the drug on the illegal market, or as a result of drug possession or use. Occasionally, individuals with Amphetamine Abuse will engage in illegal acts (e.g., manufacturing amphetamines, theft) to obtain the drug; however, this behavior is more common among those with Dependence. Individuals may continue to use the substance despite the knowledge that continued use results in arguments with family members while the individual is intoxicated or presents a negative example to children or other close family members. When these problems are accompanied by evidence of tolerance, withdrawal, or compulsive behavior, a diagnosis of Amphetamine Dependence rather than Abuse should be considered.

Amphetamine-Induced Disorders

292.89   Amphetamine Intoxication

Also refer to the text and criteria for Substance Intoxication (see p. 183). The essential feature of Amphetamine Intoxication is the presence of clinically significant maladaptive behavioral or psychological changes that develop during, or shortly after, use of amphetamine or a related substance (Criteria A and B). Amphetamine Intoxication generally begins with a "high" feeling, followed by the development of symptoms such as euphoria with enhanced vigor, gregariousness, hyperactivity, restlessness, hypervigilance, interpersonal sensitivity, talkativeness, anxiety, tension, alertness, grandiosity, stereotypical and repetitive behavior, anger, fighting, and impaired judgment. In the case of chronic intoxication, there may be affective blunting with fatigue or sadness and social withdrawal. These behavioral and psychological changes are accompanied by two or more of the following signs and symptoms: tachycardia or bradycardia; pupillary dilation; elevated or lowered blood pressure; perspiration or chills; nausea or vomiting; evidence of weight loss; psychomotor agitation or retardation; muscular weakness, respiratory depression, chest pain, or cardiac arrhythmias; and confusion, seizures, dyskinesias, dystonias, or coma (Criterion C). Amphetamine Intoxication, either acute or chronic, is often associated with impaired social or occupational functioning. The symptoms must not be due to a general medical condition and are not better accounted for by another mental disorder (Criterion D). The magnitude and manifestations of the behavioral and physiological changes depend on the dose used and individual characteristics of the person using the substance (e.g., tolerance, rate of absorption, chronicity of use). The changes associated with intoxication begin no longer than 1 hour after substance use and sometimes within seconds, depending on the specific drug and method of delivery.

Specifier

The following specifier may be applied to a diagnosis of Amphetamine Intoxication:

> **With Perceptual Disturbances.**   This specifier may be noted when hallucinations with intact reality testing or auditory, visual, or tactile illusions occur in the absence of a delirium. *Intact reality testing* means that the person knows that the hallucinations are induced by the substance and do not represent external reality. When hallucinations occur in the absence of intact reality testing, a diagnosis of Substance-Induced Psychotic Disorder, With Hallucinations, should be considered.

■ **Diagnostic criteria for 292.89 Amphetamine Intoxication**

> A. Recent use of amphetamine or a related substance (e.g., methylphenidate).

> *(continued)*

☐ **Diagnostic criteria for 292.89 Amphetamine Intoxication** (*continued*)

B. Clinically significant maladaptive behavioral or psychological changes (e.g., euphoria or affective blunting; changes in sociability; hypervigilance; interpersonal sensitivity; anxiety, tension, or anger; stereotyped behaviors; impaired judgment; or impaired social or occupational functioning) that developed during, or shortly after, use of amphetamine or a related substance.

C. Two (or more) of the following, developing during, or shortly after, use of amphetamine or a related substance:

(1) tachycardia or bradycardia
(2) pupillary dilation
(3) elevated or lowered blood pressure
(4) perspiration or chills
(5) nausea or vomiting
(6) evidence of weight loss
(7) psychomotor agitation or retardation
(8) muscular weakness, respiratory depression, chest pain, or cardiac arrhythmias
(9) confusion, seizures, dyskinesias, dystonias, or coma

D. The symptoms are not due to a general medical condition and are not better accounted for by another mental disorder.

Specify if:
With Perceptual Disturbances

292.0   Amphetamine Withdrawal

Also refer to the text and criteria for Substance Withdrawal (see p. 184). The essential feature of Amphetamine Withdrawal is the presence of a characteristic withdrawal syndrome that develops within a few hours to several days after cessation of (or reduction in) heavy and prolonged amphetamine use (Criteria A and B). The withdrawal syndrome is characterized by the development of dysphoric mood and two or more of the following physiological changes: fatigue, vivid and unpleasant dreams, insomnia or hypersomnia, increased appetite, and psychomotor retardation or agitation. Anhedonia and drug craving can also be present but are not part of the diagnostic criteria. The symptoms cause clinically significant distress or impairment in social, occupational, or other important areas of functioning (Criterion C). The symptoms must not be due to a general medical condition and are not better accounted for by another mental disorder.

Marked withdrawal symptoms ("crashing") often follow an episode of intense, high-dose use (a "speed run"). These periods are characterized by intense and unpleasant feelings of lassitude and depression, generally requiring several days of rest and recuperation. Weight loss commonly occurs during heavy stimulant use, whereas a marked increase in appetite with rapid weight gain is often observed during withdrawal. Depressive symptoms may last several days and may be accompanied by suicidal ideation.

■ Diagnostic criteria for 292.0 Amphetamine Withdrawal

A. Cessation of (or reduction in) amphetamine (or a related substance) use that has been heavy and prolonged.

B. Dysphoric mood and two (or more) of the following physiological changes, developing within a few hours to several days after Criterion A:

    (1) fatigue
    (2) vivid, unpleasant dreams
    (3) insomnia or hypersomnia
    (4) increased appetite
    (5) psychomotor retardation or agitation

C. The symptoms in Criterion B cause clinically significant distress or impairment in social, occupational, or other important areas of functioning.

D. The symptoms are not due to a general medical condition and are not better accounted for by another mental disorder.

Other Amphetamine-Induced Disorders

The following Amphetamine-Induced Disorders are described in the sections of the manual with disorders with which they share phenomenology: **Amphetamine Intoxication Delirium** (p. 129), **Amphetamine-Induced Psychotic Disorder** (p. 310), **Amphetamine-Induced Mood Disorder** (p. 370), **Amphetamine-Induced Anxiety Disorder** (p. 439), **Amphetamine-Induced Sexual Dysfunction** (p. 519), and **Amphetamine-Induced Sleep Disorder** (p. 601). These disorders are diagnosed instead of Amphetamine Intoxication or Amphetamine Withdrawal only when the symptoms are in excess of those usually associated with Amphetamine Intoxication or Withdrawal and when the symptoms are sufficiently severe to warrant independent clinical attention.

Additional Information on Amphetamine-Related Disorders

Associated Features and Disorders

Acute Amphetamine Intoxication is sometimes associated with confusion, rambling speech, headache, transient ideas of reference, and tinnitus. During intense Amphetamine Intoxication, paranoid ideation, auditory hallucinations in a clear sensorium, and tactile hallucinations may be experienced. Frequently, the person using the substance recognizes these symptoms as resulting from the stimulants. Extreme anger with threats or acting out of aggressive behavior may occur. Mood changes such as depression with suicidal ideation, irritability, anhedonia, emotional lability, or disturbances in attention and concentration are common, especially during withdrawal. Weight loss, anemia, and other signs of malnutrition and impaired personal hygiene are often seen with sustained Amphetamine Dependence.

Amphetamine-Related Disorders and other stimulant-related disorders are often associated with Dependence on or Abuse of other substances, especially those with sedative properties (such as alcohol or benzodiazepines), which are usually taken to reduce the unpleasant, "jittery" feelings that result from stimulant drug effects. The intravenous use of amphetamines is sometimes associated with Opioid Dependence.

The laboratory and physical examination findings and the mental disorders and general medical conditions that are associated with the Amphetamine-Related Disorders are generally similar to those that are associated with the Cocaine-Related Disorders (see p. 226). Urine tests for substances in this class usually remain positive for only 1–3 days, even after a "binge." Adverse pulmonary effects are seen less often than with cocaine because substances in this class are inhaled much less frequently. Fewer maternal and neonatal complications have been attributed to this class of substances than to cocaine. This difference may reflect the greater prevalence of cocaine use rather than lower toxicity from amphetamines. Seizures, human immunodeficiency virus (HIV) infection, malnutrition, gunshot or knife wounds, nosebleeds, and cardiovascular problems are often seen as presenting complaints in individuals with Amphetamine-Related Disorders. A history of childhood Conduct Disorder, Antisocial Personality Disorder, and Attention-Deficit/Hyperactivity Disorder may be associated with the later development of Amphetamine-Related Disorders.

Specific Culture, Age, and Gender Features

Amphetamine Dependence and Abuse are seen throughout all levels of society and are more common among persons between ages 18 and 30 years. Intravenous use is more common among persons from lower socioeconomic groups and has a male-to-female ratio of 3 or 4:1. The male-to-female ratio is more evenly divided among those with nonintravenous use.

Prevalence

A community survey conducted in the United States in 1991 reported that 7% of the population had nonmedical use of amphetamines or amphetamine-like substances one or more times in their lifetime; 1.3% had used them in the last year; and 0.3% had used them in the last month. Because the survey assessed patterns of use rather than diagnoses, it is not known how many of those in the survey who used amphetamines had symptoms that met criteria for Dependence or Abuse. A community study conducted in the United States from 1980 to 1985 that used the more narrowly defined DSM-III criteria found that about 2% of the adult population had Amphetamine Dependence or Abuse at some time in their lives.

Course

Some individuals who abuse or become dependent on amphetamines or amphetamine-like substances begin use in an attempt to control their weight. Others become introduced to these substances through the illegal market. Dependence can occur rapidly when the substance is used intravenously or smoked. Oral administration usually results in a slower progression from use to Dependence. Amphetamine Dependence is associated with two patterns of administration: episodic use or daily (or almost daily) use. In the episodic pattern, substance use is separated by days of nonuse (e.g., intense use over a weekend or on one or more weekdays). These periods of intensive high-dose use (often called "speed runs" or "binges") are often associated with intravenous use. Runs tend to terminate only when drug supplies are depleted. Chronic daily use may involve high or low doses and may occur throughout the day or be restricted to only a few hours. In chronic daily use, there are generally no wide fluctuations in dose on successive days, but there is often an increase in dose over time. Chronic use of high doses often becomes unpleasant because of sensitization and the emergence of dysphoric and other negative drug effects. The few long-term data available indicate that there is a tendency for persons who have been dependent on amphetamines to decrease or stop use after 8–10 years. This appears to result from the development of adverse mental and physical effects that emerge in association with long-term dependence. Little or no data are available on the long-term course of Abuse.

Differential Diagnosis

For a general discussion of the differential diagnosis of Substance-Related Disorders, see p. 190. Amphetamine-Induced Disorders may be characterized by symptoms (e.g., delusions) that resemble **primary mental disorders** (e.g., Schizophreniform Disorder versus Amphetamine-Induced Psychotic Disorder, With Delusions, With Onset During Intoxication). See p. 193 for a discussion of this differential diagnosis.

Cocaine Intoxication, Hallucinogen Intoxication, and **Phencyclidine Intoxication** may cause a similar clinical picture and can sometimes be distinguished from Amphetamine Intoxication only by the presence of amphetamine metabolites in a urine specimen or amphetamine in plasma. Amphetamine Dependence and Abuse should be distinguished from **Cocaine, Phencyclidine,** and **Hallucinogen Dependence** and **Abuse.** Amphetamine Intoxication and Amphetamine Withdrawal are distinguished from the **other Amphetamine-Induced Disorders** (e.g., Amphetamine-Induced Anxiety Disorder, With Onset During Intoxication) because the symptoms in these latter disorders are in excess of those usually associated with Amphetamine Intoxication or Amphetamine Withdrawal and are severe enough to warrant independent clinical attention.

292.9 Amphetamine-Related Disorder Not Otherwise Specified

The Amphetamine-Related Disorder Not Otherwise Specified category is for disorders associated with the use of amphetamine (or a related substance) that are not classifiable as Amphetamine Dependence, Amphetamine Abuse, Amphetamine Intoxication, Amphetamine Withdrawal, Amphetamine Intoxication Delirium, Amphetamine-Induced

Psychotic Disorder, Amphetamine-Induced Mood Disorder, Amphetamine-Induced Anxiety Disorder, Amphetamine-Induced Sexual Dysfunction, or Amphetamine-Induced Sleep Disorder.

Caffeine-Related Disorders

Caffeine can be consumed from a number of different sources, including coffee (brewed = 100 mg/6 oz, instant = 65 mg/6 oz), tea (40 mg/6 oz), caffeinated soda (45 mg/12 oz), over-the-counter analgesics and cold remedies (25–50 mg/tablet), stimulants (100–200 mg/tablet), and weight-loss aids (75–200 mg/tablet). Chocolate and cocoa have much lower levels of caffeine (e.g., 5 mg/chocolate bar). The consumption of caffeine is ubiquitous in much of the United States, with the average caffeine intake being approximately 200 mg/day. Some individuals who drink large amounts of coffee display some aspects of dependence on caffeine and exhibit tolerance and perhaps withdrawal. However, the data are insufficient at this time to determine whether these symptoms are associated with clinically significant impairment that meets the criteria for Substance Dependence or Substance Abuse. In contrast, there is evidence that Caffeine Intoxication can be clinically significant, and specific text and criteria are provided below. Recent evidence also suggests the possible clinical relevance of caffeine withdrawal; a set of research criteria is included on p. 709. The Caffeine-Induced Disorders (other than Caffeine Intoxication) are described in the sections of the manual with disorders with which they share phenomenology (e.g., Caffeine-Induced Anxiety Disorder is included in the "Anxiety Disorders" section). Listed below are the Caffeine-Induced Disorders.

Caffeine-Induced Disorders

305.90   **Caffeine Intoxication** (see p. 212)
292.89   **Caffeine-Induced Anxiety Disorder** (see p. 439)
           Specify if: With Onset During Intoxication
292.89   **Caffeine-Induced Sleep Disorder** (see p. 601)
           Specify if: With Onset During Intoxication

292.9   **Caffeine-Related Disorder Not Otherwise Specified** (see p. 215)

Caffeine-Induced Disorders
305.90   Caffeine Intoxication

Also refer to the text and criteria for Substance Intoxication (see p. 183). The essential feature of Caffeine Intoxication is recent consumption of caffeine and five or more symptoms that develop during, or shortly after, caffeine use (Criteria A and B). Symptoms that can appear following the ingestion of as little as 100 mg of caffeine per day include restlessness, nervousness, excitement, insomnia, flushed face, diuresis, and gastrointestinal complaints. Symptoms that generally appear at levels of more than 1 g/day include muscle twitching, rambling flow of thoughts and speech, tachycardia or cardiac arrhythmia, periods of inexhaustibility, and psychomotor agitation. Caffeine Intoxication may not occur despite high caffeine intake because of the development of tolerance. The symptoms must cause clinically significant distress or impairment in social, occupational, or other important areas of functioning (Criterion C). The symptoms must not be due to a general medical condition and are not better accounted for by another mental disorder (e.g., an Anxiety Disorder) (Criterion D).

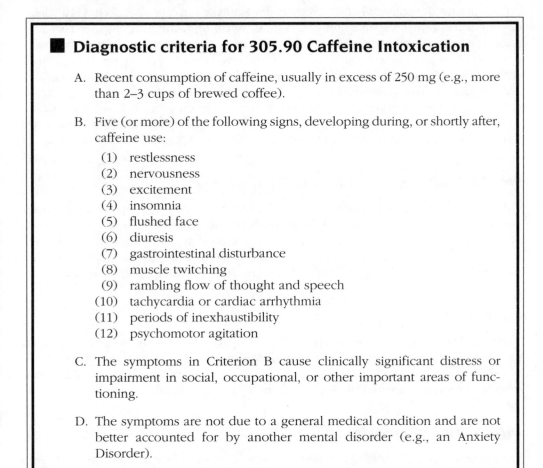

■ **Diagnostic criteria for 305.90 Caffeine Intoxication**

A. Recent consumption of caffeine, usually in excess of 250 mg (e.g., more than 2–3 cups of brewed coffee).

B. Five (or more) of the following signs, developing during, or shortly after, caffeine use:

   (1) restlessness
   (2) nervousness
   (3) excitement
   (4) insomnia
   (5) flushed face
   (6) diuresis
   (7) gastrointestinal disturbance
   (8) muscle twitching
   (9) rambling flow of thought and speech
   (10) tachycardia or cardiac arrhythmia
   (11) periods of inexhaustibility
   (12) psychomotor agitation

C. The symptoms in Criterion B cause clinically significant distress or impairment in social, occupational, or other important areas of functioning.

D. The symptoms are not due to a general medical condition and are not better accounted for by another mental disorder (e.g., an Anxiety Disorder).

Other Caffeine-Induced Disorders

The following Caffeine-Induced Disorders are described in other sections of the manual with disorders with which they share phenomenology: **Caffeine-Induced Anxiety Disorder** (p. 439) and **Caffeine-Induced Sleep Disorder** (p. 601). These disorders are diagnosed instead of Caffeine Intoxication only when the symptoms are in excess of those usually associated with Caffeine Intoxication and when the symptoms are sufficiently severe to warrant independent clinical attention.

Additional Information on Caffeine-Related Disorders

Associated Features and Disorders

Mild sensory disturbances (e.g., ringing in the ears and flashes of light) have been reported at higher doses. Although large doses of caffeine can increase heart rate, smaller doses can slow the pulse. Whether excess caffeine intake can cause headaches is unclear. On physical examination, agitation, restlessness, sweating, tachycardia, flushed face, and increased bowel motility may be seen. Typical patterns of caffeine intake have not been consistently associated with other medical problems. However, heavy use is associated with the development or exacerbation of anxiety and somatic symptoms such as cardiac arrhythmias and gastrointestinal pain or diarrhea. With acute doses exceeding 10 g of caffeine, grand mal seizures and respiratory failure may result in death. Excessive caffeine use is associated with Mood, Eating, Psychotic, Sleep, and Substance-Related Disorders, whereas individuals with Anxiety Disorders are likely to avoid this substance.

Specific Culture, Age, and Gender Features

Caffeine use and the sources from which caffeine is consumed vary widely across cultures. The average caffeine intake in most of the developing world is less than 50 mg/day, compared to as much as 400 mg/day or more in Sweden, the United Kingdom, and other European nations. Caffeine consumption increases during the 20s and often decreases after age 65 years. Intake is greater in males than in females.

Course

The half-life of caffeine is 2–6 hours, so that most symptoms of intoxication are likely to last 6–16 hours after caffeine ingestion. Because tolerance to the behavioral effects of caffeine occurs, Caffeine Intoxication is usually seen in infrequent users or in those who have recently increased their caffeine intake by a substantial amount.

Differential Diagnosis

For a general discussion of the differential diagnosis of Substance-Related Disorders, see p. 190. Caffeine-Induced Disorders may be characterized by symptoms (e.g., Panic Attacks) that resemble **primary mental disorders** (e.g., Panic Disorder versus Caffeine-Induced Anxiety Disorder, With Panic Attacks, With Onset During Intoxication). See p. 193 for a discussion of this differential diagnosis.

To meet criteria for Caffeine Intoxication, the symptoms must not be due to a **general medical condition** or **another mental disorder,** such as an **Anxiety Disorder,** that could better explain them. **Manic Episodes, Panic Disorder, Generalized Anxiety Disorder, Amphetamine Intoxication, Sedative, Hypnotic, or Anxiolytic Withdrawal** or **Nicotine Withdrawal, Sleep Disorders,** and **medication-induced side effects** (e.g., akathisia) can cause a clinical picture that is similar to that of Caffeine Intoxication. The temporal relationship of the symptoms to increased caffeine use or to abstinence from caffeine helps to establish the diagnosis. Caffeine Intoxication is differentiated from **Caffeine-Induced Anxiety Disorder, With Onset During Intoxication** (p. 439), and from **Caffeine-Induced Sleep Disorder, With Onset During Intoxication** (p. 601), by the fact that the symptoms in these latter disorders are in excess of those usually associated with Caffeine Intoxication and are severe enough to warrant independent clinical attention.

292.9   Caffeine-Related Disorder Not Otherwise Specified

The Caffeine-Related Disorder Not Otherwise Specified category is for disorders associated with the use of caffeine that are not classifiable as Caffeine Intoxication, Caffeine-Induced Anxiety Disorder, or Caffeine-Induced Sleep Disorder. An example is caffeine withdrawal (see p. 708 for suggested research criteria).

Cannabis-Related Disorders

This section includes problems that are associated with cannabinoids and chemically similar synthetic compounds. Cannabinoids are substances that are derived from the cannabis plant. When the upper leaves, tops, and stems of the plant are cut, dried, and rolled into cigarettes, the product is usually called marijuana. Hashish is the dried, resinous exudate that seeps from the tops and undersides of cannabis leaves; hashish oil is a concentrated distillate of hashish. Cannabinoids are usually smoked, but may be taken orally and are sometimes mixed with tea or food. The cannabinoid that has been identified as primarily responsible for the psychoactive effects of cannabis is delta-9-tetrahydrocannabinol (also known as THC, or delta-9-THC). This substance itself is rarely available for use in a pure form. The THC content of the marijuana that is generally available varies greatly. The THC content of illicit marijuana has increased significantly since the late 1960s from an average of approximately 1%–5% to as much as 10%–15%. Synthetic delta-9-THC has been used for certain general medical conditions (e.g., for nausea and vomiting caused by chemotherapy, for anorexia and weight loss in individuals with acquired immunodeficiency syndrome [AIDS]).

This section contains discussions specific to the Cannabis-Related Disorders. Texts and criteria sets have already been provided to define the generic aspects of Substance Dependence (p. 176) and Substance Abuse (p. 182) that apply across all substances. Texts specific to Cannabis Dependence and Abuse are provided below; however, there are no additional specific criteria sets for Cannabis Dependence or Cannabis Abuse. A specific text and criteria set for Cannabis Intoxication is also provided below. Symptoms of possible cannabis withdrawal (e.g., irritable or anxious mood accompanied by physiological changes such as tremor, perspiration, nausea, and sleep disturbances) have been described in association with the use of very high doses, but their clinical significance is uncertain. For these reasons, the diagnosis of cannabis withdrawal is not included in this manual. The Cannabis-Induced Disorders (other than Cannabis Intoxication) are described in the sections of the manual with disorders with which they share phenomenology (e.g., Cannabis-Induced Mood Disorder is included in the "Mood Disorders" section). Listed below are the Cannabis Use Disorders and the Cannabis-Induced Disorders.

Cannabis Use Disorders

304.30   **Cannabis Dependence** (see p. 216)
305.20   **Cannabis Abuse** (see p. 217)

Cannabis-Induced Disorders

292.89   **Cannabis Intoxication** (see p. 217)
            Specify if: With Perceptual Disturbances
292.81   **Cannabis Intoxication Delirium** (see p. 129)
292.11   **Cannabis-Induced Psychotic Disorder, With Delusions** (see p. 310)
            Specify if: With Onset During Intoxication
292.12   **Cannabis-Induced Psychotic Disorder, With Hallucinations** (see p. 310)
            Specify if: With Onset During Intoxication
292.89   **Cannabis-Induced Anxiety Disorder** (see p. 439)
            Specify if: With Onset During Intoxication

292.9   **Cannabis-Related Disorder Not Otherwise Specified** (see p. 221)

Cannabis Use Disorders
304.30   Cannabis Dependence

Also refer to the text and criteria for Substance Dependence (see p. 176). Individuals with Cannabis Dependence have compulsive use and do not generally develop physiological dependence, although tolerance to most of the effects of cannabis has been reported in individuals who use cannabis chronically. There have also been some reports of withdrawal symptoms, but they have not yet been reliably shown to be clinically significant. Individuals with Cannabis Dependence may use very potent cannabis throughout the day over a period of months or years, and they may spend several hours a day acquiring and using the substance. This often interferes with family, school, work, or recreational activities. Individuals with Cannabis Dependence may also persist in their use despite knowledge of physical problems (e.g., chronic cough related to smoking) or psychological problems (e.g., excessive sedation resulting from repeated use of high doses).

Specifiers

The following specifiers may be applied to a diagnosis of Cannabis Dependence (see p. 179 for more details):

With Physiological Dependence
Without Physiological Dependence

Early Full Remission
Early Partial Remission
Sustained Full Remission
Sustained Partial Remission
In a Controlled Environment

305.20 Cannabis Abuse

Also refer to the text and criteria for Substance Abuse (see p. 182). Periodic cannabis use and intoxication can interfere with performance at work or school and may be physically hazardous in situations such as driving a car. Legal problems may occur as a consequence of arrests for cannabis possession. There may be arguments with spouses or parents over the possession of cannabis in the home or its use in the presence of children. When there are significant levels of tolerance, or when psychological or physical problems are associated with cannabis in the context of compulsive use, a diagnosis of Cannabis Dependence, rather than Cannabis Abuse, should be considered.

Cannabis-Induced Disorders
292.89 Cannabis Intoxication

Also refer to the text and criteria for Substance Intoxication (see p. 183). The essential feature of Cannabis Intoxication is the presence of clinically significant maladaptive behavioral or psychological changes that develop during, or shortly after, cannabis use (Criteria A and B). Intoxication typically begins with a "high" feeling followed by symptoms that include euphoria with inappropriate laughter and grandiosity, sedation, lethargy, impairment in short-term memory, difficulty carrying out complex mental processes, impaired judgment, distorted sensory perceptions, impaired motor performance, and the sensation that time is passing slowly. Occasionally, anxiety (which can be severe), dysphoria, or social withdrawal occurs. These psychoactive effects are accompanied by two or more of the following signs, developing within 2 hours of cannabis use: conjunctival injection, increased appetite, dry mouth, and tachycardia (Criterion C). The symptoms must not be due to a general medical condition and are not better accounted for by another mental disorder (Criterion D).

Intoxication develops within minutes if the cannabis is smoked, but may take a few hours to develop if ingested orally. The effects usually last 3–4 hours, the duration being somewhat longer when the substance is ingested orally. The magnitude of the behavioral and physiological changes depends on the dose, the method of administration, and the individual characteristics of the person using the substance, such as rate of absorption, tolerance, and sensitivity to the effects of the substance. Because most cannabinoids, including delta-9-THC, are fat soluble, the effects of cannabis or hashish may occasionally persist or reoccur for 12–24 hours due to a slow release of psychoactive substances from fatty tissue or to enterohepatic circulation.

Specifier

The following specifier may be applied to a diagnosis of Cannabis Intoxication:

With Perceptual Disturbances. This specifier may be noted when hallucinations with intact reality testing or auditory, visual, or tactile illusions occur in the absence of a delirium. *Intact reality testing* means that the person knows that the hallucinations are induced by the substance and do not represent external reality. When hallucinations occur in the absence of intact reality testing, a diagnosis of Substance-Induced Psychotic Disorder, With Hallucinations, should be considered.

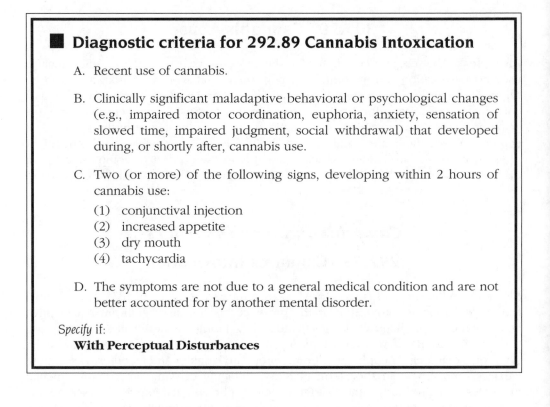

■ **Diagnostic criteria for 292.89 Cannabis Intoxication**

A. Recent use of cannabis.

B. Clinically significant maladaptive behavioral or psychological changes (e.g., impaired motor coordination, euphoria, anxiety, sensation of slowed time, impaired judgment, social withdrawal) that developed during, or shortly after, cannabis use.

C. Two (or more) of the following signs, developing within 2 hours of cannabis use:
   (1) conjunctival injection
   (2) increased appetite
   (3) dry mouth
   (4) tachycardia

D. The symptoms are not due to a general medical condition and are not better accounted for by another mental disorder.

Specify if:
With Perceptual Disturbances

Other Cannabis-Induced Disorders

The following Cannabis-Induced Disorders are described in other sections of the manual with disorders with which they share phenomenology: **Cannabis Intoxication Delirium** (p. 129), **Cannabis-Induced Psychotic Disorder** (p. 310), and **Cannabis-Induced Anxiety Disorder** (p. 439). These disorders are diagnosed instead of Cannabis Intoxication only when the symptoms are in excess of those usually associated with Cannabis Intoxication and when the symptoms are sufficiently severe to warrant independent clinical attention.

Additional Information on Cannabis-Related Disorders

Associated Features and Disorders

Associated descriptive features and mental disorders. Cannabis is often used with other substances, especially nicotine, alcohol, and cocaine. Cannabis (especially marijuana) may be mixed and smoked with opioids, phencyclidine (PCP), or other hallucinogenic drugs. Individuals who regularly use cannabis often report both physical and mental lethargy and anhedonia. Mild forms of depression, anxiety, or irritability are seen in about one-third of individuals who regularly use cannabis (daily or almost daily).

When taken in high doses, cannabinoids have psychoactive effects that can be similar to those of hallucinogens (e.g., lysergic acid diethylamide [LSD]), and individuals who use cannabinoids can experience adverse mental effects that resemble hallucinogen-induced "bad trips." These range from mild to moderate levels of anxiety (e.g., concern that the police will discover the substance use) to severe anxiety reactions resembling Panic Attacks. There may also be paranoid ideation ranging from suspiciousness to frank delusions and hallucinations. Episodes of depersonalization and derealization have also been reported. Fatal traffic accidents have been found to occur more often in individuals who test positive for cannabinoids than in the general population. However, the significance of these findings is unclear because alcohol and other substances are often also present.

Associated laboratory findings.   Urine tests generally identify cannabinoid metabolites. Because these substances are fat soluble, persist in bodily fluids for extended periods of time, and are excreted slowly, routine urine tests for cannabinoids in individuals who use cannabis casually can be positive for 7–10 days; urine of individuals with heavy use of cannabis may test positive for 2–4 weeks. A positive urine test is only consistent with past use; it does not establish Intoxication, Dependence, or Abuse. Biological alterations include temporary (and probably dose-related) suppression of immunological function and suppressed secretion of testosterone and luteinizing hormone (LH), although the clinical significance of these alterations is unclear. Acute cannabinoid use also causes diffuse slowing of background activity on EEG and rapid eye movement (REM) suppression.

Associated physical examination findings and general medical conditions.
Cannabis smoke is highly irritating to the nasopharynx and bronchial lining and thus increases the risk for chronic cough and other signs and symptoms of nasopharyngeal pathology. Chronic cannabis use is sometimes associated with weight gain, probably resulting from overeating and reduced physical activity. Sinusitis, pharyngitis, bronchitis with persistent cough, emphysema, and pulmonary dysplasia may occur with chronic, heavy use. Marijuana smoke contains even larger amounts of known carcinogens than tobacco, and heavy use may increase the risk of developing malignant disease.

Specific Culture, Age, and Gender Features

Cannabis is probably the world's most commonly used illicit substance. It has been taken since ancient times for its psychoactive effects and as a remedy for a wide range of medical conditions. Cannabis is among the first drugs of experimentation (often in the teens) for all cultural groups in the United States. As with most other illicit drugs, Cannabis Use Disorders appear more often in males, and prevalence is most common in persons between ages 18 and 30 years.

Prevalence

Cannabinoids, especially cannabis, are also the most widely used illicit psychoactive substances in the United States, even though lifetime prevalence figures have slowly decreased from the figures obtained by surveys in the 1980s. A community survey conducted in the United States in 1991 reported that about one-third of the population had used marijuana one or more times in their lifetime; 10% had used it in the last year; and 5% had used it in the last month. Because the survey assessed patterns of use rather than diagnoses, it is not known how many of those who used marijuana had symptoms that met criteria for Dependence or Abuse. A community study conducted in the United States from 1980 to 1985 that used the more narrowly defined DSM-III criteria found that about 4% of the adult population had Cannabis Dependence or Abuse at some time in their lives.

Course

Cannabis Dependence and Abuse usually develop over an extended period of time. Those who become dependent typically establish a pattern of chronic use that gradually increases in both frequency and amount. With chronic heavy use, there is sometimes a diminution or loss of the pleasurable effects of the substance. Although there may also be a corresponding increase in dysphoric effects, these are not seen as frequently as in chronic use of other substances such as alcohol, cocaine, or amphetamines. A history of Conduct Disorder in childhood or adolescence and Antisocial Personality Disorder are risk factors for the development of many Substance-Related Disorders, including Cannabis-Related Disorders. Few data are available on the long-term course of Cannabis Dependence or Abuse.

Differential Diagnosis

For a general discussion of the differential diagnosis of Substance-Related Disorders, see p. 190. Cannabis-Induced Disorders may be characterized by symptoms (e.g., anxiety) that resemble **primary mental disorders** (e.g., Generalized Anxiety Disorder versus Cannabis-Induced Anxiety Disorder, With Generalized Anxiety, With Onset During Intoxication). See p. 193 for a discussion of this differential diagnosis. Chronic intake of cannabis can produce symptoms that resemble **Dysthymic Disorder.** Acute adverse reactions to cannabis should be differentiated from the symptoms of **Panic Disorder, Major Depressive Disorder, Delusional Disorder, Bipolar Disorder,** or **Schizophrenia, Paranoid Type.** Physical examination will usually show an increased pulse and injected conjunctivas. Urine toxicological testing can be helpful in making a diagnosis.

In contrast to Cannabis Intoxication, **Alcohol Intoxication** and **Sedative, Hypnotic, or Anxiolytic Intoxication** frequently decrease appetite, increase aggressive behavior, and produce nystagmus or ataxia. **Hallucinogens** in low doses may cause a clinical picture that resembles Cannabis Intoxication. Phencyclidine (PCP), like cannabis, can be smoked and also has hallucinogenic effects, but **Phencyclidine Intoxication** is much more likely to cause ataxia and aggressive behavior. Cannabis Intoxication is distinguished from the **other Cannabis-Induced Disorders** (e.g., Cannabis-Induced Anxiety Disorder, With Onset During Intoxication) because the symptoms in these latter disorders are in excess of those usually associated with Cannabis Intoxication and are severe enough to warrant independent clinical attention.

The distinction between **recreational use of cannabis** and Cannabis Dependence or Abuse can be difficult to make because social, behavioral, or psychological problems may be difficult to attribute to the substance, especially in the context of use of other substances. Denial of heavy use is common, and people appear to seek treatment for

Cannabis Dependence or Abuse less often than for other types of Substance-Related Disorders.

292.9   Cannabis-Related Disorder Not Otherwise Specified

The Cannabis-Related Disorder Not Otherwise Specified category is for disorders associated with the use of cannabis that are not classifiable as Cannabis Dependence, Cannabis Abuse, Cannabis Intoxication, Cannabis Intoxication Delirium, Cannabis-Induced Psychotic Disorder, or Cannabis-Induced Anxiety Disorder.

Cocaine-Related Disorders

Cocaine, a naturally occurring substance produced by the coca plant, is consumed in several preparations (e.g., coca leaves, coca paste, cocaine hydrochloride, and cocaine alkaloid) that differ in potency due to varying levels of purity and speed of onset. Cocaine is the active ingredient in each preparation. Chewing coca leaves is a practice generally limited to native populations in Central and South America, where cocaine is grown. The use of coca paste, a crude extract of the coca plant, occurs almost exclusively in cocaine-producing countries in Central and South America, where its nickname is "basulca." Solvents used in the preparation of coca paste often contaminate the paste and may cause toxic effects in the central nervous system and other organ systems when the paste is smoked. Cocaine hydrochloride powder is usually "snorted" through the nostrils ("snorting") or dissolved in water and injected intravenously. It is sometimes mixed with heroin, yielding a drug combination known as a "speedball."

A commonly used form of cocaine in the United States is "crack," a cocaine alkaloid that is extracted from its powdered hydrochloride salt by mixing it with sodium bicarbonate and allowing it to dry into small "rocks." Crack differs from other forms of cocaine primarily because it is easily vaporized and inhaled and thus its effects have an extremely rapid onset. The clinical syndrome and adverse effects that are associated with crack use are identical to those produced by comparable doses of other cocaine preparations. Before the advent of crack, cocaine was separated from its hydrochloride base by heating it with ether, ammonia, or some other volatile solvent. The resulting "free base" cocaine was then smoked. This process was dangerous because of the risk that the solvents could ignite and harm the user.

This section contains discussions specific to the Cocaine-Related Disorders. Texts and criteria sets have already been provided to define the generic aspects of Substance Dependence (p. 176) and Substance Abuse (p. 182) that apply across all substances. Texts specific to Cocaine Dependence and Abuse are provided below; however, there are no additional specific criteria sets for Cocaine Dependence or Cocaine Abuse. Specific texts and criteria sets for Cocaine Intoxication and Cocaine Withdrawal are also provided below. The Cocaine-Induced Disorders (other than Cocaine Intoxication and Withdrawal) are described in the sections of the manual with disorders with which they share phenomenology (e.g., Cocaine-Induced Mood Disorder is included in the "Mood Disorders" section). Listed below are the Cocaine Use Disorders and the Cocaine-Induced Disorders.

Cocaine Use Disorders

304.20 **Cocaine Dependence** (see p. 222)
305.60 **Cocaine Abuse** (see p. 223)

Cocaine-Induced Disorders

292.89 **Cocaine Intoxication** (see p. 223) *Specify if:* With Perceptual Disturbances
292.0 **Cocaine Withdrawal** (see p. 225)
292.81 **Cocaine Intoxication Delirium** (see p. 129)
292.11 **Cocaine-Induced Psychotic Disorder, With Delusions** (see p. 310)
　　　　Specify if: With Onset During Intoxication
292.12 **Cocaine-Induced Psychotic Disorder, With Hallucinations** (see p. 310)
　　　　Specify if: With Onset During Intoxication
292.84 **Cocaine-Induced Mood Disorder** (see p. 370)
　　　　Specify if: With Onset During Intoxication/With Onset During Withdrawal
292.89 **Cocaine-Induced Anxiety Disorder** (see p. 439)
　　　　Specify if: With Onset During Intoxication/With Onset During Withdrawal
292.89 **Cocaine-Induced Sexual Dysfunction** (see p. 519)
　　　　Specify if: With Onset During Intoxication
292.89 **Cocaine-Induced Sleep Disorder** (see p. 601)
　　　　Specify if: With Onset During Intoxication/With Onset During Withdrawal

292.9 **Cocaine-Related Disorder Not Otherwise Specified** (see p. 229)

Cocaine Use Disorders

304.20 Cocaine Dependence

Also refer to the text and criteria for Substance Dependence (see p. 176). Cocaine has extremely potent euphoric effects, and individuals exposed to it can develop Dependence after using cocaine for very short periods of time. An early sign of Cocaine Dependence is when the individual finds it increasingly difficult to resist using cocaine whenever it is available. Because of its short half-life, there is a need for frequent dosing to maintain a "high." Persons with Cocaine Dependence can spend extremely large amounts of money on the drug within a very short period of time. As a result, the person using the substance may become involved in theft, prostitution, or drug dealing or may request salary advances to obtain funds to purchase the drug. Individuals with Cocaine Dependence often find it necessary to discontinue use for several days to rest or to obtain additional funds. Important responsibilities such as work or child care may be grossly neglected to obtain or use cocaine. Mental or physical complications of chronic use such as paranoid ideation, aggressive behavior, anxiety, depression, and weight loss are common. Regardless of the route of administration, tolerance occurs with repeated use. Withdrawal symptoms, particularly dysphoric mood, can be seen, but are usually transitory and associated with high-dose use.

Specifiers

The following specifiers may be applied to a diagnosis of Cocaine Dependence (see p. 179 for more details):

With Physiological Dependence
Without Physiological Dependence
Early Full Remission
Early Partial Remission
Sustained Full Remission
Sustained Partial Remission
On Agonist Therapy
In a Controlled Environment

305.60   Cocaine Abuse

Also refer to the text and criteria for Substance Abuse (see p. 182). The intensity and frequency of cocaine administration is less in Cocaine Abuse as compared with Dependence. Episodes of problematic use, neglect of responsibilities, and interpersonal conflict often occur around paydays or special occasions, resulting in a pattern of brief periods (hours to a few days) of high-dose use followed by much longer periods (weeks to months) of occasional, nonproblematic use or abstinence. Legal difficulties may result from possession or use of the drug. When the problems associated with use are accompanied by evidence of tolerance, withdrawal, or compulsive behavior related to obtaining and administering cocaine, a diagnosis of Cocaine Dependence rather than Cocaine Abuse should be considered.

Cocaine-Induced Disorders

292.89   Cocaine Intoxication

Also refer to the text and criteria for Substance Intoxication (see p. 183). The essential feature of Cocaine Intoxication is the presence of clinically significant maladaptive behavioral or psychological changes that develop during, or shortly after, use of cocaine (Criteria A and B). Cocaine Intoxication usually begins with a "high" feeling and includes one or more of the following: euphoria with enhanced vigor, gregariousness, hyper-activity, restlessness, hypervigilance, interpersonal sensitivity, talkativeness, anxiety, tension, alertness, grandiosity, stereotyped and repetitive behavior, anger, and impaired judgment, and in the case of chronic intoxication, affective blunting with fatigue or sadness and social withdrawal. These behavioral and psychological changes are accompanied by two or more of the following signs and symptoms that develop during or shortly after cocaine use: tachycardia or bradycardia; pupillary dilation; elevated or lowered blood pressure; perspiration or chills; nausea or vomiting; evidence of weight loss; psychomotor agitation or retardation; muscular weakness, respiratory depression, chest pain, or cardiac arrhythmias; and confusion, seizures, dyskinesias, dystonias, or coma (Criterion C). Intoxication, either acute or chronic, is often associated with impaired social or occupational functioning. Severe intoxication can lead to coma. To make a diagnosis of Cocaine Intoxication, the symptoms must not be due to a general medical condition and are not better accounted for by another mental disorder (Criterion D).

The magnitude and direction of the behavioral and physiological changes depend on many variables, including the dose used and the individual characteristics of the person using the substance (e.g., tolerance, rate of absorption, chronicity of use, context in which it is taken). Stimulant effects such as euphoria, increased pulse and blood pressure, and psychomotor activity are most commonly seen. Depressant effects such as sadness, bradycardia, decreased blood pressure, and decreased psychomotor activity are less common and generally emerge only with chronic high-dose use.

Specifier

The following specifier may be applied to a diagnosis of Cocaine Intoxication:

> **With Perceptual Disturbances.** This specifier may be noted when hallucinations with intact reality testing or auditory, visual, or tactile illusions occur in the absence of a delirium. *Intact reality testing* means that the person knows that the hallucinations are induced by the substance and do not represent external reality. When hallucinations occur in the absence of intact reality testing, a diagnosis of Substance-Induced Psychotic Disorder, With Hallucinations, should be considered.

■ Diagnostic criteria for 292.89 Cocaine Intoxication

A. Recent use of cocaine.

B. Clinically significant maladaptive behavioral or psychological changes (e.g., euphoria or affective blunting; changes in sociability; hypervigilance; interpersonal sensitivity; anxiety, tension, or anger; stereotyped behaviors; impaired judgment; or impaired social or occupational functioning) that developed during, or shortly after, use of cocaine.

C. Two (or more) of the following, developing during, or shortly after, cocaine use:

   (1) tachycardia or bradycardia
   (2) pupillary dilation
   (3) elevated or lowered blood pressure
   (4) perspiration or chills
   (5) nausea or vomiting
   (6) evidence of weight loss
   (7) psychomotor agitation or retardation
   (8) muscular weakness, respiratory depression, chest pain, or cardiac arrhythmias
   (9) confusion, seizures, dyskinesias, dystonias, or coma

(continued)

☐ **Diagnostic criteria for 292.89 Cocaine Intoxication**
(continued)

    D. The symptoms are not due to a general medical condition and are not better accounted for by another mental disorder.

Specify if:
With Perceptual Disturbances

292.0 Cocaine Withdrawal

Also refer to the text and criteria for Substance Withdrawal (see p. 184). The essential feature of Cocaine Withdrawal is the presence of a characteristic withdrawal syndrome that develops within a few hours to several days after the cessation of (or reduction in) cocaine use that has been heavy and prolonged (Criteria A and B). The withdrawal syndrome is characterized by the development of dysphoric mood accompanied by two or more of the following physiological changes: fatigue, vivid and unpleasant dreams, insomnia or hypersomnia, increased appetite, and psychomotor retardation or agitation. Anhedonia and drug craving can often be present but are not part of the diagnostic criteria. These symptoms cause clinically significant distress or impairment in social, occupational, or other important areas of functioning (Criterion C). The symptoms must not be due to a general medical condition and are not better accounted for by another mental disorder (Criterion D).

Acute withdrawal symptoms ("a crash") are often seen after periods of repetitive high-dose use ("runs" or "binges"). These periods are characterized by intense and unpleasant feelings of lassitude and depression, generally requiring several days of rest and recuperation. Depressive symptoms with suicidal ideation or behavior can occur and are generally the most serious problems seen during "crashing" or other forms of Cocaine Withdrawal. A substantial number of individuals with Cocaine Dependence have few or no clinically evident withdrawal symptoms on cessation of use.

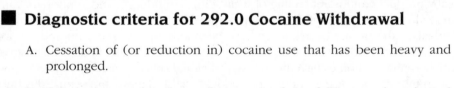

■ **Diagnostic criteria for 292.0 Cocaine Withdrawal**

    A. Cessation of (or reduction in) cocaine use that has been heavy and prolonged.

    B. Dysphoric mood and two (or more) of the following physiological changes, developing within a few hours to several days after Criterion A:

        (1) fatigue
        (2) vivid, unpleasant dreams
        (3) insomnia or hypersomnia

(continued)

☐ **Diagnostic criteria for 292.0 Cocaine Withdrawal** (*continued*)

      (4)   increased appetite
      (5)   psychomotor retardation or agitation

  C. The symptoms in Criterion B cause clinically significant distress or impairment in social, occupational, or other important areas of functioning.

  D. The symptoms are not due to a general medical condition and are not better accounted for by another mental disorder.

Other Cocaine-Induced Disorders

The following Cocaine-Induced Disorders are described in other sections of the manual with disorders with which they share phenomenology: **Cocaine Intoxication Delirium** (p. 129), **Cocaine-Induced Psychotic Disorder** (p. 310), **Cocaine-Induced Mood Disorder** (p. 370), **Cocaine-Induced Anxiety Disorder** (p. 439), **Cocaine-Induced Sexual Dysfunction** (p. 519), and **Cocaine-Induced Sleep Disorder** (p. 601). These disorders are diagnosed instead of Cocaine Intoxication or Cocaine Withdrawal only when the symptoms are in excess of those usually associated with the Cocaine Intoxication or Withdrawal syndrome and when the symptoms are sufficiently severe to warrant independent clinical attention.

Additional Information on Cocaine-Related Disorders

Associated Features and Disorders

Associated descriptive features and mental disorders.   Cocaine is a short-acting drug that produces rapid and powerful effects on the central nervous system, especially when taken intravenously or smoked as "crack." When injected or smoked, cocaine typically produces an instant feeling of well-being, confidence, and euphoria. Dramatic behavioral changes can rapidly develop, especially in association with dependence. Individuals with Cocaine Dependence have been known to spend thousands of dollars for the substance within very short periods of time, resulting in financial catastrophes in which savings or homes have been lost. Individuals may engage in criminal activities to obtain money for cocaine. Erratic behavior, social isolation, and sexual dysfunction are often seen in the context of long-term Cocaine Dependence. Aggressive behavior can result from the effects of cocaine; violence is also associated with the cocaine "trade." Promiscuous sexual behavior either as a result of increased desire or using sex for the purpose of obtaining cocaine (or for money to purchase cocaine) has become a factor in the spread of sexually transmitted diseases, including human immunodeficiency virus (HIV).

    Acute Intoxication with high doses of cocaine may be associated with rambling speech, headache, transient ideas of reference, and tinnitus. There may also be paranoid ideation, auditory hallucinations in a clear sensorium, and tactile hallucinations ("coke bugs"), which the user usually recognizes as effects of cocaine. Extreme anger with threats or acting out of aggressive behavior may occur. Mood changes such as depression, suicidal ideation, irritability, anhedonia, emotional lability, or disturbances in attention and concentration are common, especially during Cocaine Withdrawal.

Individuals with Cocaine Dependence often have temporary depressive symptoms that meet symptomatic and duration criteria for Major Depressive Disorder (see Substance-Induced Mood Disorder, p. 370). Histories consistent with repeated Panic Attacks, social phobic–like behavior, and generalized anxiety–like syndromes are not uncommon (see Substance-Induced Anxiety Disorder, p. 439). Eating Disorders may also be associated with this substance. One of the most extreme instances of cocaine toxicity is Cocaine-Induced Psychotic Disorder (see p. 310), a disorder with delusions and hallucinations that resembles Schizophrenia, Paranoid Type. Mental disturbances that occur in association with cocaine use usually resolve within hours to days after cessation of use, although they can persist for weeks.

Individuals with Cocaine Dependence often develop conditioned responses to cocaine-related stimuli (e.g., craving on seeing any white powder–like substance). These responses probably contribute to relapse, are difficult to extinguish, and typically persist long after detoxification is completed. Cocaine Use Disorders are often associated with other Substance Dependence or Abuse, especially involving alcohol, marijuana, and benzodiazepines, which are often taken to reduce the anxiety and other unpleasant stimulant side effects of cocaine. Cocaine Dependence may be associated with Posttraumatic Stress Disorder, Antisocial Personality Disorder, Attention-Deficit/Hyperactivity Disorder, and Pathological Gambling.

Associated laboratory findings.   Most laboratories test for benzoylecgonine, a metabolite of cocaine that typically remains in the urine for 1–3 days after a single dose and may be present for 7–12 days in those using repeated high doses. Mildly elevated liver function tests can be seen in individuals who inject cocaine or use alcohol excessively in association with cocaine. Hepatitis, sexually transmitted diseases including HIV, and tuberculosis may be associated with cocaine use. Pneumonitis or pneumothorax are occasionally observed on chest X ray. Discontinuation of chronic cocaine use is often associated with EEG changes, alterations in secretion patterns of prolactin, and down-regulation of dopamine receptors.

Associated physical examination findings and general medical conditions.   A wide range of general medical conditions may occur that are specific to the route of administration of cocaine. Persons who use cocaine intranasally ("snort") often develop sinusitis, irritation and bleeding of the nasal mucosa, and a perforated nasal septum. Those who smoke cocaine are at increased risk for respiratory problems (e.g., coughing, bronchitis, and pneumonitis due to irritation and inflammation of the tissues lining the respiratory tract). Persons who inject cocaine have puncture marks and "tracks," most commonly on their forearms, as seen in those with Opioid Dependence. HIV infection is associated with Cocaine Dependence due to the frequent intravenous injections and the increase in promiscuous sexual behavior. Other sexually transmitted diseases, hepatitis, and tuberculosis and other lung infections are also seen. Cocaine Dependence (with any route of administration) is commonly associated with signs of weight loss and malnutrition because of its appetite-suppressing effects. Chest pain may also be a common symptom. Pneumothorax can result from performing Valsalva-like maneuvers that are done to better absorb cocaine that has been inhaled. Myocardial infarction, sudden death from respiratory or cardiac arrest, and stroke have been associated with cocaine use among young and otherwise healthy persons. These incidents are probably caused by the ability of cocaine to increase blood pressure, cause vasoconstriction, or alter the electrical activity of the heart. Seizures have been observed in association with cocaine use, as have palpitations and arrhythmias. Traumatic injuries due to disputes resulting in violent behavior are common, especially among persons who sell cocaine. Among pregnant females, cocaine use is associated with irregularities in placental blood flow, abruptio placentae, premature labor and delivery, and an increased prevalence of infants with very low birth weights.

Specific Culture, Age, and Gender Features

Cocaine use and its attendant disorders affect all race, socioeconomic, age, and gender groups in the United States. Cocaine-Related Disorders are most commonly found in persons between ages 18 and 30 years. Although the current cocaine epidemic started in the 1970s among more affluent individuals, it has shifted to include lower socio-economic groups living in large metropolitan areas. Rural areas that previously had been spared the problems associated with illicit drug use have also been affected. Unlike most other Substance-Related Disorders, with which males are more commonly affected than females, Cocaine Use Disorders are almost equally distributed between males and females.

Prevalence

A community survey conducted in the United States in 1991 reported that 12% of the population had used cocaine one or more times in their lifetime; 3% had used it in the last year; and less than 1% had used it in the last month. Because the survey assessed patterns of use rather than diagnoses, it is not known how many of those who used cocaine had symptoms that met criteria for Dependence or Abuse. A community study conducted in the United States from 1980 to 1985 that used the more narrowly defined DSM-III criteria that only recognized Cocaine Abuse found that about 0.2% of the adult population had Cocaine Abuse at some time in their lives. Among those who had ever had Cocaine Abuse, 17% reported use in the last month and 46% reported having had a problem with cocaine in the last year. These figures predate the increased use of cocaine experienced since the mid-1980s.

Course

As with amphetamines, Cocaine Dependence is associated with either of two patterns of self-administration: episodic or daily (or almost daily) use. In the episodic pattern, the cocaine use tends to be separated by 2 or more days of nonuse (e.g., intense use over a weekend or on one or more weekdays). "Binges" are a form of episodic use that typically involve continuous high-dose use over a period of hours or days and are often associated with Dependence. Binges usually terminate only when cocaine supplies are depleted. Chronic daily use may involve high or low doses and may occur throughout the day or be restricted to only a few hours. In chronic daily use, there are generally no wide fluctuations in dose on successive days, but there is often an increase in dose over time.

Cocaine smoking and intravenous use tend to be particularly associated with a rapid progression from use to abuse or dependence, often occurring over weeks to months. Intranasal use is associated with a more gradual progression, usually occurring over months to years. Dependence is commonly associated with a progressive tolerance to the desirable effects of cocaine leading to increasing doses. With continuing use, there is a diminution of pleasurable effects due to tolerance and an increase in dysphoric effects. Few data are available on the long-term course of Cocaine Use Disorders.

Differential Diagnosis

For a general discussion of the differential diagnosis of Substance-Related Disorders, see p. 190. Cocaine-Induced Disorders may be characterized by symptoms (e.g., depressed mood) that resemble **primary mental disorders** (e.g., Major Depressive Disorder versus Cocaine-Induced Mood Disorder, With Depressive Features, With Onset During Withdrawal). See p. 193 for a discussion of this differential diagnosis. The marked mental disturbances that can result from the effects of cocaine should be distinguished from the symptoms of **Schizophrenia, Paranoid Type, Bipolar** and **other Mood Disorders, Generalized Anxiety Disorder,** and **Panic Disorder.**

Amphetamine Intoxication and **Phencyclidine Intoxication** may cause a similar clinical picture and can often only be distinguished from Cocaine Intoxication by the presence of cocaine metabolites in a urine specimen or cocaine in plasma. Cocaine Intoxication and Cocaine Withdrawal are distinguished from the other **Cocaine-Induced Disorders** (e.g., Cocaine-Induced Anxiety Disorder, With Onset During Intoxication) because the symptoms in these latter disorders are in excess of those usually associated with Cocaine Intoxication or Cocaine Withdrawal and are severe enough to warrant independent clinical attention.

292.9   Cocaine-Related Disorder Not Otherwise Specified

The Cocaine-Related Disorder Not Otherwise Specified category is for disorders associated with the use of cocaine that are not classifiable as Cocaine Dependence, Cocaine Abuse, Cocaine Intoxication, Cocaine Withdrawal, Cocaine Intoxication Delirium, Cocaine-Induced Psychotic Disorder, Cocaine-Induced Mood Disorder, Cocaine-Induced Anxiety Disorder, Cocaine-Induced Sexual Dysfunction, or Cocaine-Induced Sleep Disorder.

Hallucinogen-Related Disorders

This diverse group of substances includes ergot and related compounds (lysergic acid diethylamide [LSD], morning glory seeds), phenylalkylamines (mescaline, "STP" [2,5-dimethoxy-4-methylamphetamine], and MDMA [3,4-methylenedioxymethamphetamine; also called "Ecstasy"]), indole alkaloids (psilocybin, DMT [dimethyltryptamine]), and miscellaneous other compounds. Excluded from this group are phencyclidine (PCP)

(p. 255) and cannabis and its active compound, delta-9-tetrahydrocannabinol (THC) (p. 215). Although these substances can have hallucinogenic effects, they are discussed separately because of significant differences in their other psychological and behavioral effects. Hallucinogens are usually taken orally, although DMT is smoked, and use by injection does occur.

This section contains discussions specific to the Hallucinogen-Related Disorders. Texts and criteria sets have already been provided to define the generic aspects of Substance Dependence (p. 176) and Substance Abuse (p. 182) that apply across all substances. Texts specific to Hallucinogen Dependence and Abuse are provided below; however, there are no additional specific criteria sets for Hallucinogen Dependence or Hallucinogen Abuse. A specific text and criteria set for Hallucinogen Intoxication is also provided below. Tolerance develops with repeated use, but a withdrawal from these substances has not been well documented. For this reason, the diagnosis of hallucinogen withdrawal is not included in this manual. The Hallucinogen-Induced Disorders (other than Hallucinogen Intoxication) are described in the sections of the manual with disorders with which they share phenomenology (e.g., Hallucinogen-Induced Mood Disorder is included in the "Mood Disorders" section). Listed below are the Hallucinogen Use Disorders and the Hallucinogen-Induced Disorders.

Hallucinogen Use Disorders

304.50   **Hallucinogen Dependence** (see p. 230)
305.30   **Hallucinogen Abuse** (see p. 231)

Hallucinogen-Induced Disorders

292.89   **Hallucinogen Intoxication** (see p. 232)
292.89   **Hallucinogen Persisting Perception Disorder (Flashbacks)** (see p. 233)
292.81   **Hallucinogen Intoxication Delirium** (see p. 129)
292.11   **Hallucinogen-Induced Psychotic Disorder, With Delusions** (see p. 310)
   Specify if: With Onset During Intoxication
292.12   **Hallucinogen-Induced Psychotic Disorder, With Hallucinations**
   (see p. 310) *Specify if:* With Onset During Intoxication
292.84   **Hallucinogen-Induced Mood Disorder** (see p. 370)
   Specify if: With Onset During Intoxication
292.89   **Hallucinogen-Induced Anxiety Disorder** (see p. 439)
   Specify if: With Onset During Intoxication

292.9   **Hallucinogen-Related Disorder Not Otherwise Specified** (see p. 236)

Hallucinogen Use Disorders
304.50   Hallucinogen Dependence

Also refer to the text and criteria for Substance Dependence (see p. 176). Some of the generic Dependence criteria do not apply to hallucinogens and others require further explanation. Tolerance has been reported to develop rapidly to the euphoric and psychedelic effects of hallucinogens but not to the autonomic effects such as pupillary dilation, hyperreflexia, increased blood pressure, increased body temperature, piloerection, and tachycardia. Cross-tolerance exists between LSD and other hallucinogens (e.g., psilocybin and mescaline). Hallucinogen use, even among individuals with presentations that meet full criteria for Dependence, is often limited to only a few times a week. This relatively low frequency of use (as compared with use of other substances) may be related to the desire to suppress the development of tolerance to the psychological effects of the hallucinogens. Withdrawal has not been demonstrated, but clear reports of "craving" after stopping hallucinogens are known. Due to the long half-life and extended duration of action of most hallucinogens, individuals with Hallucinogen Dependence often spend hours to days using and recovering from their effects. In contrast, some hallucinogenic "designer drugs" (e.g., DMT) are quite short acting. Hallucinogens may continue to be used despite the knowledge of adverse effects (e.g., memory impairment while intoxicated; "bad trips," which are usually panic reactions; or flashbacks). Some individuals who use MDMA (a designer drug with hallucinogenic effects) describe a "hangover" the day after use that is characterized by insomnia, fatigue, drowsiness, sore jaw muscles from teeth clenching, loss of balance, and headaches. Because adulterants or substitutes are often sold as "acid" or other hallucinogens, some of the reported adverse effects may be due to substances such as strychnine, phencyclidine, or amphetamine. Some individuals can manifest dangerous behavioral reactions (e.g., jumping out of a window under the belief that one can "fly") due to lack of insight and judgment while intoxicated. These adverse effects appear to be more common among those who have preexisting mental disorders.

Specifiers

The following specifiers may be applied to a diagnosis of Hallucinogen Dependence (see p. 179 for more details):

> **Early Full Remission**
> **Early Partial Remission**
> **Sustained Full Remission**
> **Sustained Partial Remission**
> **In a Controlled Environment**

305.30 Hallucinogen Abuse

Also refer to the text and criteria for Substance Abuse (see p. 182). Persons who abuse hallucinogens use them much less often than do those with Dependence. However, they may repeatedly fail to fulfill major role obligations at school, work, or home due to behavioral impairment caused by Hallucinogen Intoxication. The individual may use hallucinogens in situations in which it is physically hazardous (e.g., while driving a motorcycle or a car), and legal difficulties may arise due to behaviors that result from intoxication or possession of hallucinogens. There may be recurrent social or interpersonal problems due to the individual's behavior while intoxicated, isolated lifestyle, or arguments with significant others.

Hallucinogen-Induced Disorders

292.89   Hallucinogen Intoxication

Also refer to the text and criteria for Substance Intoxication (see p. 183). The essential feature of Hallucinogen Intoxication is the presence of clinically significant maladaptive behavioral or psychological changes (e.g., marked anxiety or depression, ideas of reference, fear of losing one's mind, paranoid ideation, impaired judgment, or impaired social or occupational functioning) that develop during, or shortly after (within minutes to a few hours), hallucinogen use (Criteria A and B). Perceptual changes develop during or shortly after hallucinogen use and occur in a state of full wakefulness and alertness (Criterion C). These changes include subjective intensification of perceptions, depersonalization, derealization, illusions, hallucinations, and synesthesias. In addition, the diagnosis requires that two of the following physiological signs are also present: pupillary dilation, tachycardia, sweating, palpitations, blurring of vision, tremors, and incoordination (Criterion D). The symptoms must not be due to a general medical condition and are not better accounted for by another mental disorder (Criterion E).

Hallucinogen Intoxication usually begins with some stimulant effects such as restlessness and autonomic activation. Nausea may occur. A sequence of experiences then follows, with higher doses producing more intense symptoms. Feelings of euphoria may alternate rapidly with depression or anxiety. Initial visual illusions or enhanced sensory experience may give way to hallucinations. At low doses, the perceptual changes frequently do not include hallucinations. Synesthesias (a blending of senses) may result, for example, in sounds being "seen." The hallucinations are usually visual, often of geometric forms or figures, sometimes of persons and objects. More rarely, auditory or tactile hallucinations are experienced. In most cases, reality testing is preserved (i.e., the individual knows that the effects are substance induced).

> ■ **Diagnostic criteria for 292.89 Hallucinogen Intoxication**
>
> A. Recent use of a hallucinogen.
>
> B. Clinically significant maladaptive behavioral or psychological changes (e.g., marked anxiety or depression, ideas of reference, fear of losing one's mind, paranoid ideation, impaired judgment, or impaired social or occupational functioning) that developed during, or shortly after, hallucinogen use.
>
> C. Perceptual changes occurring in a state of full wakefulness and alertness (e.g., subjective intensification of perceptions, depersonalization, derealization, illusions, hallucinations, synesthesias) that developed during, or shortly after, hallucinogen use.
>
> *(continued)*

☐ **Diagnostic criteria for 292.89 Hallucinogen Intoxication**
(*continued*)

D. Two (or more) of the following signs, developing during, or shortly after, hallucinogen use:

(1) pupillary dilation
(2) tachycardia
(3) sweating
(4) palpitations
(5) blurring of vision
(6) tremors
(7) incoordination

E. The symptoms are not due to a general medical condition and are not better accounted for by another mental disorder.

292.89 Hallucinogen Persisting Perception Disorder (Flashbacks)

The essential feature of Hallucinogen Persisting Perception Disorder (Flashbacks) is the transient recurrence of disturbances in perception that are reminiscent of those experienced during one or more earlier Hallucinogen Intoxications. The person must have had no recent Hallucinogen Intoxication and must show no current drug toxicity (Criterion A). This reexperiencing of perceptual symptoms causes clinically significant distress or impairment in social, occupational, or other important areas of functioning (Criterion B). The symptoms are not due to a general medical condition (e.g., anatomical lesions and infections of the brain or visual epilepsies) and are not better accounted for by another mental disorder (e.g., delirium, dementia, or Schizophrenia) or by hypnopompic hallucinations (Criterion C). The perceptual disturbances may include geometric forms, peripheral-field images, flashes of color, intensified colors, trailing images (images left suspended in the path of a moving object as seen in stroboscopic photography), perceptions of entire objects, afterimages (a same-colored or complementary-colored "shadow" of an object remaining after removal of the object), halos around objects, macropsia, and micropsia. The abnormal perceptions that are associated with Hallucinogen Persisting Perception Disorder occur episodically and may be self-induced (e.g., by thinking about them) or triggered by entry into a dark environment, various drugs, anxiety or fatigue, or other stressors. The episodes may abate after several months, but many persons report persisting episodes for 5 years or longer. Reality testing remains intact (i.e., the person recognizes that the perception is a drug effect and does not represent external reality). In contrast, if the person has a delusional interpretation concerning the etiology of the perceptual disturbance, the appropriate diagnosis would be Psychotic Disorder Not Otherwise Specified.

■ **Diagnostic criteria for 292.89 Hallucinogen Persisting Perception Disorder (Flashbacks)**

A. The reexperiencing, following cessation of use of a hallucinogen, of one or more of the perceptual symptoms that were experienced while intoxicated with the hallucinogen (e.g., geometric hallucinations, false perceptions of movement in the peripheral visual fields, flashes of color, intensified colors, trails of images of moving objects, positive after-images, halos around objects, macropsia, and micropsia).

B. The symptoms in Criterion A cause clinically significant distress or impairment in social, occupational, or other important areas of functioning.

C. The symptoms are not due to a general medical condition (e.g., anatomical lesions and infections of the brain, visual epilepsies) and are not better accounted for by another mental disorder (e.g., delirium, dementia, Schizophrenia) or hypnopompic hallucinations.

Other Hallucinogen-Induced Disorders

The following Hallucinogen-Induced Disorders are described in other sections of the manual with disorders with which they share phenomenology: **Hallucinogen Intoxication Delirium** (p. 129), **Hallucinogen-Induced Psychotic Disorder** (p. 310), **Hallucinogen-Induced Mood Disorder** (p. 370), and **Hallucinogen-Induced Anxiety Disorder** (p. 439). These disorders are diagnosed instead of Hallucinogen Intoxication only when the symptoms are in excess of those usually associated with the Hallucinogen Intoxication syndrome and when the symptoms are sufficiently severe to warrant independent clinical attention.

Additional Information on Hallucinogen-Related Disorders

Associated Features and Disorders

When intoxicated with a hallucinogen, individuals may be voluble and discursive and show rapid alternation of moods. Fearfulness and anxiety may become intense, with dread of insanity or death. Many hallucinogenic substances have stimulant effects (e.g., tachycardia, mild hypertension, hyperthermia, and pupillary dilation) and may cause some of the features of Amphetamine Intoxication. The perceptual disturbances and impaired judgment associated with Hallucinogen Intoxication may result in injuries or fatalities from automobile accidents, physical fights, or attempts to "fly" from high places. Environmental factors and the personality and expectations of the individual using the hallucinogen may contribute to the nature and severity of Hallucinogen Intoxication.

Hallucinogen Persisting Perception Disorder may produce considerable anxiety and concern and may be more common in suggestible persons. Hallucinogen Dependence and Abuse may co-occur with chronic psychotic conditions. It remains controversial whether the chronic hallucinogen use produces a Psychotic Disorder de novo, triggers psychotic symptoms only in vulnerable persons, or is simply an early and continuing sign of an evolving psychotic process. Hallucinogen Abuse and Dependence also frequently occur in persons with preexisting adolescent Conduct Disorder or adult Antisocial Personality Disorder. LSD intoxication may be confirmed by urine toxicology.

Specific Culture, Age, and Gender Features

Hallucinogens may be used as part of established religious practices. Within the United States, there are regional differences in their use. Hallucinogen Intoxication usually first occurs in adolescence, and younger users may tend to experience more disruptive emotions. Hallucinogen use and Intoxication appear to be three times more common among males than among females.

Prevalence

A community survey conducted in the United States in 1991 reported that 8% of the population had used hallucinogens or phencyclidine (PCP) at least one or more times in their lifetime. The cohort with the highest lifetime use was persons ages 26–34 years, among whom 26% had ever tried hallucinogens. However, recent use was most common among those ages 18–25 years, with 2% of this group having used hallucinogens within the last month. A community study conducted in the United States from 1980 to 1985 that used the more narrowly defined DSM-III criteria found that about 0.3% of the adult population had Hallucinogen Abuse at some time in their lives.

Course

Hallucinogen Intoxication may be a brief and isolated event or may occur repeatedly. The intoxication may be prolonged if doses are frequently repeated during an episode. Frequent dosing, however, tends to reduce the intoxicating effects because of the development of tolerance. Depending on the drug and its route of administration, peak effects occur within a few minutes to a few hours, and intoxication ends within a few hours to a few days after dosing ends. The high prevalence of "ever having used" hallucinogens among those ages 26–34 years and the lower prevalence of recent use in that group suggest that many individuals may stop using hallucinogens as they get older. Some individuals who use hallucinogen report "flashbacks" that are not associated with any impairment or distress. On the other hand, flashbacks can cause impairment or distress in some individuals (Hallucinogen Persisting Perception Disorder; see above).

Differential Diagnosis

For a general discussion of the differential diagnosis of Substance-Related Disorders, see p. 190. Hallucinogen-Induced Disorders may be characterized by symptoms (e.g., delusions) that resemble **primary mental disorders** (e.g., Schizophreniform Disorder versus Hallucinogen-Induced Psychotic Disorder, With Delusions, With Onset During Intoxication). See p. 193 for a discussion of this differential diagnosis.

Hallucinogen Intoxication should be differentiated from **Amphetamine** or **Phencyclidine Intoxication.** Toxicological tests are useful in making this distinction. **Intoxication with anticholinergics** can also produce hallucinations, but they are often associated with physical findings of fever, dry mouth and skin, flushed face, and visual disturbances. Hallucinogen Intoxication is distinguished from the **other Hallucinogen-Induced Disorders** (e.g., Hallucinogen-Induced Anxiety Disorder, With Onset During Intoxication) because the symptoms in these latter disorders are in excess of those usually associated with Hallucinogen Intoxication and are severe enough to warrant independent clinical attention.

Hallucinogen Intoxication is distinguished from **Hallucinogen Persisting Perception Disorder (Flashbacks)** by the fact that the latter continues episodically for weeks (or longer) after the most recent intoxication. In Hallucinogen Persisting Perception Disorder, the individual does not believe that the perception represents external reality, whereas a person with a **Psychotic Disorder** often believes that the perception is real. Hallucinogen Persisting Perception Disorder may be distinguished from **migraine, epilepsy,** or a **neurological condition** by neuro-ophthalmological history, physical examination, and appropriate laboratory evaluation.

292.9 Hallucinogen-Related Disorder Not Otherwise Specified

The Hallucinogen-Related Disorder Not Otherwise Specified category is for disorders associated with the use of hallucinogens that are not classifiable as Hallucinogen Dependence, Hallucinogen Abuse, Hallucinogen Intoxication, Hallucinogen Persisting Perception Disorder, Hallucinogen Intoxication Delirium, Hallucinogen-Induced Psychotic Disorder, Hallucinogen-Induced Mood Disorder, or Hallucinogen-Induced Anxiety Disorder.

Inhalant-Related Disorders

This section includes disorders induced by inhaling the aliphatic and aromatic hydrocarbons found in substances such as gasoline, glue, paint thinners, and spray paints. Less commonly used are halogenated hydrocarbons (found in cleaners, typewriter correction fluid, spray-can propellants) and other volatile compounds containing esters, ketones, and glycols. Most compounds that are inhaled are a mixture of several substances that can produce psychoactive effects, and it is often difficult to ascertain the exact substance responsible for the disorder. Unless there is clear evidence that a single, unmixed substance has been used, the general term *inhalant* should be used in recording the diagnosis. These volatile substances are available in a wide variety of commercial products and may be used interchangeably, depending on availability and personal preference. Although there may be subtle differences in the psychoactive and physical effects of the different compounds, not enough is known about their differential effects to distinguish among them. All are capable of producing Dependence, Abuse, and Intoxication.

Several methods are used to inhale intoxicating vapors. Most commonly, a rag soaked with the substance is applied to the mouth and nose, and the vapors are breathed in. The substance may also be placed in a paper or plastic bag and the gases in the bag inhaled. Substances may also be inhaled directly from containers or from aerosols sprayed in the mouth or nose. There are reports of individuals heating these compounds to accelerate vaporization. The inhalants reach the lungs, bloodstream, and target sites very rapidly.

This section contains discussions specific to the Inhalant-Related Disorders. Texts and criteria sets have already been provided for generic aspects of Substance Dependence (p. 176) and Substance Abuse (p. 182) that apply across all substances. Texts specific to Inhalant Dependence and Abuse are provided below; however, there are no additional specific criteria sets for Inhalant Dependence or Inhalant Abuse. A specific text and criteria set for Inhalant Intoxication is also provided below. Tolerance has been reported among individuals with heavy use, but a withdrawal syndrome from these substances has not been well documented. For this reason, the diagnosis of inhalant withdrawal is not included in this manual. The Inhalant-Induced Disorders (other than Inhalant Intoxication) are described in the sections of the manual with disorders with which they share phenomenology (e.g., Inhalant-Induced Mood Disorder is included in the "Mood Disorders" section). Listed below are the Inhalant Use Disorders and the Inhalant-Induced Disorders. Reflecting their different modes of action and profiles of associated problems, disorders resulting from the use of anesthetic gases (e.g., nitrous oxide, ether) and short-acting vasodilators (e.g., amyl or butyl nitrite) are excluded from the category of Inhalant-Related Disorders and should be classified under Other Substance–Related Disorders.

Inhalant Use Disorders

304.60   **Inhalant Dependence** (see p. 238)
305.90   **Inhalant Abuse** (see p. 238)

Inhalant-Induced Disorders

292.89   **Inhalant Intoxication** (see p. 239)
292.81   **Inhalant Intoxication Delirium** (see p. 129)
292.82   **Inhalant-Induced Persisting Dementia** (see p. 152)
292.11   **Inhalant-Induced Psychotic Disorder, With Delusions** (see p. 310)
             Specify if: With Onset During Intoxication
292.12   **Inhalant-Induced Psychotic Disorder, With Hallucinations** (see p. 310)
             Specify if: With Onset During Intoxication
292.84   **Inhalant-Induced Mood Disorder** (see p. 370)
             Specify if: With Onset During Intoxication
292.89   **Inhalant-Induced Anxiety Disorder** (see p. 439)
             Specify if: With Onset During Intoxication

292.9   **Inhalant-Related Disorder Not Otherwise Specified** (see p. 242)

Inhalant Use Disorders

304.60   Inhalant Dependence

Also refer to the text and criteria for Substance Dependence (see p. 176). Some of the generic Dependence criteria do not apply to inhalants, whereas others require further explanation. Tolerance to the effects of inhalants has been reported among individuals with heavy use, although its prevalence and clinical significance are unknown. A possible withdrawal syndrome beginning 24–48 hours after cessation of use and lasting from 2 to 5 days has been described, with symptoms including sleep disturbances, tremor, irritability, diaphoresis, nausea, and fleeting illusions. However, this syndrome has not been well documented and appears not to be clinically significant. Thus, Inhalant Dependence includes neither a characteristic withdrawal syndrome nor evidence of inhalant use to relieve or avoid withdrawal symptoms. However, inhalants may be taken over longer periods of time or in larger amounts than was originally intended, and individuals who use them may find it difficult to cut down or regulate inhalant use. Because inhalants are inexpensive, legal, and easily available, spending a great deal of time attempting to procure inhalants would be rare. However, substantial amounts of time may be spent on using and recuperating from the effects of inhalant use. Recurrent inhalant use may result in the individual giving up or reducing important social, occupational, or recreational activities, and substance use may continue despite the individual's knowledge of physical problems (e.g., liver disease or central and peripheral nervous system damage) or psychological problems (e.g., severe depression) caused by the use.

Specifiers

The following specifiers may be applied to a diagnosis of Inhalant Dependence (see p. 179 for more details):

> **Early Full Remission**
> **Early Partial Remission**
> **Sustained Full Remission**
> **Sustained Partial Remission**
> **In a Controlled Environment**

305.90   Inhalant Abuse

Also refer to the text and criteria for Substance Abuse (see p. 182). Individuals who abuse inhalants may use them in hazardous circumstances (e.g., driving an automobile or operating machinery when judgment and coordination are impaired by Inhalant Intoxication). Repeated intake of inhalants may be associated with family conflict and school problems (e.g., truancy, poor grades, dropping out of school).

Inhalant-Induced Disorders

292.89 Inhalant Intoxication

Also refer to the text and criteria for Substance Intoxication (see p. 183). The essential feature of Inhalant Intoxication is the presence of clinically significant maladaptive behavioral or psychological changes (e.g., belligerence, assaultiveness, apathy, impaired judgment, impaired social or occupational functioning) that develop during, or shortly after, the intentional use of, or short-term, high-dose exposure to, volatile inhalants (Criteria A and B). The maladaptive changes are accompanied by signs that include dizziness or visual disturbances (blurred vision or diplopia), nystagmus, incoordination, slurred speech, an unsteady gait, tremor, and euphoria. Higher doses of inhalants may lead to the development of lethargy and psychomotor retardation, generalized muscle weakness, depressed reflexes, stupor, or coma (Criterion C). The disturbance must not be due to a general medical condition and is not better accounted for by another mental disorder (Criterion D).

■ Diagnostic criteria for 292.89 Inhalant Intoxication

A. Recent intentional use or short-term, high-dose exposure to volatile inhalants (excluding anesthetic gases and short-acting vasodilators).

B. Clinically significant maladaptive behavioral or psychological changes (e.g., belligerence, assaultiveness, apathy, impaired judgment, impaired social or occupational functioning) that developed during, or shortly after, use of or exposure to volatile inhalants.

C. Two (or more) of the following signs, developing during, or shortly after, inhalant use or exposure:

   (1) dizziness
   (2) nystagmus
   (3) incoordination
   (4) slurred speech
   (5) unsteady gait
   (6) lethargy
   (7) depressed reflexes
   (8) psychomotor retardation
   (9) tremor
   (10) generalized muscle weakness
   (11) blurred vision or diplopia
   (12) stupor or coma
   (13) euphoria

D. The symptoms are not due to a general medical condition and are not better accounted for by another mental disorder.

Other Inhalant-Induced Disorders

The following Inhalant-Induced Disorders are described in other sections of the manual with disorders with which they share phenomenology: **Inhalant Intoxication Delirium** (p. 129), **Inhalant-Induced Persisting Dementia** (p. 152), **Inhalant-Induced Psychotic Disorder** (p. 310), **Inhalant-Induced Mood Disorder** (p. 370), and **Inhalant-Induced Anxiety Disorder** (p. 439). These disorders are diagnosed instead of Inhalant Intoxication only when the symptoms are in excess of those usually associated with Inhalant Intoxication and when the symptoms are sufficiently severe to warrant independent clinical attention.

Additional Information on Inhalant-Related Disorders

Associated Features and Disorders

Associated descriptive features and mental disorders.   Individuals with Inhalant Intoxication may present with auditory, visual, or tactile hallucinations or other perceptual disturbances (macropsia, micropsia, illusionary misperceptions, alterations in time perception). Delusions (such as believing one can fly) may develop during periods of Inhalant Intoxication, especially those characterized by marked confusion; in some cases, these delusions may be acted on with resultant injury. Anxiety may also be present. Repeated but episodic intake of inhalants may first be associated with school problems (e.g., truancy, poor grades, dropping out of school) as well as family conflict. Use by older adolescents and young adults is often associated with social and work problems (e.g., delinquency, unemployment). Most commonly, inhalants are used by adolescents in a group setting. Solitary use tends to be more typical of those with long-term, heavy use. The use of inhalants as the predominant substance among those seeking help for Substance Dependence appears to be rare, but inhalants may be a secondary drug used by individuals with Dependence on other substances. In some individuals, there may be a progression to a stage at which inhalants become the preferred substance.

Associated laboratory findings.   Direct assay for inhalants is rarely used clinically and is generally not part of routine screening for drugs of abuse. Damage to muscles, kidneys, liver, and other organs can result in laboratory tests being indicative of these pathological conditions.

Associated physical examination findings and general medical conditions.
The odor of paint or solvents may be present on the breath or clothes of individuals who use inhalants, or there may be a residue of the substance on clothing or skin. A "glue sniffer's rash" may be evident around the nose and mouth, and conjunctival irritation may be noted. There may be evidence of trauma due to disinhibited behavior or burns due to the flammable nature of these compounds. Nonspecific respiratory findings include evidence of upper- or lower-airway irritation, including coughing, sinus discharge, dyspnea, rales, or rhonchi; rarely, cyanosis may result from pneumonitis or asphyxia. There may also be headache, generalized weakness, abdominal pain, nausea, and vomiting. Inhalants can cause both central and peripheral nervous system damage,

which may be permanent. Examination of the individual who chronically uses inhalants may reveal a number of neurological deficits, including generalized weakness and peripheral neuropathies. Cerebral atrophy, cerebellar degeneration, and white matter lesions resulting in cranial nerve or pyramidal tract signs have been reported among individuals with heavy use. Recurrent use may lead to the development of hepatitis (which may progress to cirrhosis) or metabolic acidosis consistent with distal renal tubular acidosis. Chronic renal failure, hepatorenal syndrome, and proximal renal tubular acidosis have also been reported, as has bone marrow suppression. Some inhalants (e.g., methylene chloride) may be metabolized to carbon monoxide. Death may occur from respiratory or cardiovascular depression; in particular, "sudden sniffing death" may result from acute arrhythmia, hypoxia, or electrolyte abnormalities.

Specific Culture, Age, and Gender Features

Because of their low cost and easy availability, inhalants are often the first drugs of experimentation for young people, and there may be a higher incidence among those living in economically depressed areas. Inhalant use may begin by ages 9–12 years, appears to peak in adolescence, and is less common after age 35 years. Males account for 70%–80% of inhalant-related emergency-room visits.

Prevalence

Inhalant Dependence and Abuse appear to occur in only a small proportion of individuals who use inhalants.

Course

It can be difficult to match inhalant dose to effect because the different methods of administration and the varying concentrations of inhalants in the products used cause highly variable concentrations in the body. The time course of Inhalant Intoxication is related to the pharmacological characteristics of the specific substance used, but it is typically brief, lasting from a few minutes to an hour. Onset is rapid, peaking within a few minutes after inhaling. Younger children diagnosed as having Inhalant Dependence may use inhalants several times a week, often on weekends and after school. Severe dependence in adults may involve varying periods of intoxication throughout each day and occasional periods of heavier use that may last several days. This pattern may persist for years, with recurrent need for treatment. Individuals who use inhalants may have a preferred level or degree of intoxication, and the method of administration (typically sniffing from a container or breathing through a rag soaked in the substance) may allow the individual to maintain that level for several hours. Cases have also been reported of the development of Dependence in industrial workers who have long-term occupational exposure and access to inhalants. A worker may begin to use the compound for its psychoactive effects and subsequently develop a pattern of Dependence. Use leading to Dependence may also occur in people who do not have access to other substances (e.g., prisoners, isolated military personnel, and adolescents or young adults in isolated rural areas).

Differential Diagnosis

For a general discussion of the differential diagnosis of Substance-Related Disorders, see p. 190. Inhalant-Induced Disorders may be characterized by symptoms (e.g., depressed mood) that resemble **primary mental disorders** (e.g., Major Depressive Disorder versus Inhalant-Induced Mood Disorder, With Depressive Features, With Onset During Intoxication). See p. 193 for a discussion of this differential diagnosis.

The symptoms of mild to moderate Inhalant Intoxication can be similar to those of **Alcohol Intoxication** and **Sedative, Hypnotic, or Anxiolytic Intoxication.** Breath odor or residues on body or clothing may be important differentiating clues, but should not be relied on exclusively. Individuals who chronically use inhalants are likely to use other substances frequently and heavily, further complicating the diagnostic picture. Concomitant use of alcohol may also make the differentiation difficult. History of the drug used and characteristic findings (including odor of solvent or paint residue) may differentiate Inhalant Intoxication from other substance intoxications; additionally, symptoms may subside faster with Inhalant Intoxication than with other substance intoxications. Rapid onset and resolution may also differentiate Inhalant Intoxication from other mental disorders and neurological conditions. Inhalant Intoxication is distinguished from the **other Inhalant-Induced Disorders** (e.g., Inhalant-Induced Mood Disorder, With Onset During Intoxication) because the symptoms in these latter disorders are in excess of those usually associated with Inhalant Intoxication and are severe enough to warrant independent clinical attention.

Industrial workers may occasionally be **accidentally exposed to volatile chemicals** and suffer physiological intoxication. The category "Other Substance–Related Disorders" should be used for such toxin exposures.

292.9   Inhalant-Related Disorder Not Otherwise Specified

The Inhalant-Related Disorder Not Otherwise Specified category is for disorders associated with the use of inhalants that are not classifiable as Inhalant Dependence, Inhalant Abuse, Inhalant Intoxication, Inhalant Intoxication Delirium, Inhalant-Induced Persisting Dementia, Inhalant-Induced Psychotic Disorder, Inhalant-Induced Mood Disorder, or Inhalant-Induced Anxiety Disorder.

Nicotine-Related Disorders

Nicotine Dependence and Withdrawal can develop with use of all forms of tobacco (cigarettes, chewing tobacco, snuff, pipes, and cigars) and with prescription medications (nicotine gum and patch). The relative ability of these products to produce Dependence or to induce Withdrawal is associated with the rapidity characteristic of the route of administration (smoked over oral over transdermal) and the nicotine content of the product.

This section contains discussions specific to the Nicotine-Related Disorders. Texts and criteria sets have already been provided to define the generic aspects of Substance Dependence (p. 176) that apply across all substances. Text specific to Nicotine Dependence is provided below. Nicotine intoxication and nicotine abuse are not included in DSM-IV; nicotine intoxication rarely occurs and has not been well studied, and nicotine abuse is not likely to be observed in the absence of Dependence. A specific text and criteria set for Nicotine Withdrawal is also provided below. Listed below are the Nicotine-Related Disorders.

Nicotine Use Disorder

305.10   Nicotine Dependence (see p. 243)

Nicotine-Induced Disorder

292.0   Nicotine Withdrawal (see p. 244)

292.9   Nicotine-Related Disorder Not Otherwise Specified (see p. 247)

Nicotine Use Disorder
305.10   Nicotine Dependence

Also refer to the text and criteria for Substance Dependence (see p. 176). Some of the generic Dependence criteria do not appear to apply to nicotine, whereas others require further explanation. Tolerance to nicotine is manifested by the absence of nausea, dizziness, and other characteristic symptoms despite using substantial amounts of nicotine or a diminished effect observed with continued use of the same amount of nicotine-containing products. Cessation of nicotine use produces a well-defined withdrawal syndrome that is described below. Many individuals who use nicotine take nicotine to relieve or to avoid withdrawal symptoms when they wake up in the morning or after being in a situation where use is restricted (e.g., at work or on an airplane). Individuals who smoke and other individuals who use nicotine are likely to find that they use up their supply of cigarettes or other nicotine-containing products faster than originally intended. Although over 80% of individuals who smoke express a desire to stop smoking and 35% try to stop each year, less than 5% are successful in unaided attempts to quit. Spending a great deal of time in using the substance is best exemplified by chain-smoking. Because nicotine sources are readily and legally available, spending a great deal of time attempting to procure nicotine would be rare. Giving up important social, occupational, or recreational activities can occur when an individual forgoes an activity because it occurs in smoking-restricted areas. Continued use despite knowledge of medical problems related to smoking is a particularly important health problem (e.g., an individual who continues to smoke despite having a tobacco-induced general medical condition such as bronchitis or chronic obstructive lung disease).

Specifiers

The following specifiers may be applied to a diagnosis of Nicotine Dependence (see p. 179 for more details):

        With Physiological Dependence
        Without Physiological Dependence

Early Full Remission
Early Partial Remission
Sustained Full Remission
Sustained Partial Remission
On Agonist Therapy

Nicotine-Induced Disorder

292.0   Nicotine Withdrawal

Also refer to the text and criteria for Substance Withdrawal (see p. 184). The essential feature of Nicotine Withdrawal is the presence of a characteristic withdrawal syndrome that develops after the abrupt cessation of, or reduction in, the use of nicotine-containing products following a prolonged period (at least several weeks) of daily use (Criteria A and B). The withdrawal syndrome includes four or more of the following: dysphoric or depressed mood; insomnia; irritability, frustration, or anger; anxiety; difficulty concentrating; restlessness or impatience; decreased heart rate; and increased appetite or weight gain. The withdrawal symptoms cause clinically significant distress or impairment in social, occupational, or other important areas of functioning (Criterion C). The symptoms must not be due to a general medical condition and are not better accounted for by another mental disorder (Criterion D).

These symptoms are in large part due to nicotine deprivation and are typically more intense among individuals who smoke cigarettes than among individuals who use other nicotine-containing products. The more rapid onset of nicotine effects with cigarette smoking leads to a more intensive habit pattern that is more difficult to give up because of the frequency and rapidity of reinforcement and the greater physical dependence on nicotine. In individuals who smoke cigarettes, heart rate decreases by 5 to 12 beats per minute in the first few days after stopping smoking, and weight increases an average of 2–3 kg over the first year after stopping smoking. Mild symptoms of withdrawal may occur after switching to low-tar/nicotine cigarettes and after stopping the use of smokeless (chewing) tobacco, nicotine gum, or nicotine patches.

 **Diagnostic criteria for 292.0 Nicotine Withdrawal**

A. Daily use of nicotine for at least several weeks.

B. Abrupt cessation of nicotine use, or reduction in the amount of nicotine used, followed within 24 hours by four (or more) of the following signs:

   (1)   dysphoric or depressed mood
   (2)   insomnia
   (3)   irritability, frustration, or anger
   (4)   anxiety
   (5)   difficulty concentrating

(continued)

☐ **Diagnostic criteria for 292.0 Nicotine Withdrawal** (*continued*)

    (6)   restlessness

    (7)   decreased heart rate

    (8)   increased appetite or weight gain

C. The symptoms in Criterion B cause clinically significant distress or impairment in social, occupational, or other important areas of functioning.

D. The symptoms are not due to a general medical condition and are not better accounted for by another mental disorder.

Additional Information on Nicotine-Related Disorders

Associated Features and Disorders

Associated descriptive features and mental disorders.   Craving is an important element in Nicotine Withdrawal and may account for the difficulty that individuals have in giving up nicotine-containing products. Other symptoms associated with Nicotine Withdrawal include a desire for sweets and impaired performance on tasks requiring vigilance. Several features associated with Nicotine Dependence appear to predict a greater level of difficulty in stopping nicotine use: smoking soon after waking, smoking when ill, difficulty refraining from smoking, reporting the first cigarette of the day to be the one most difficult to give up, and smoking more in the morning than in the afternoon. The number of cigarettes smoked per day, the nicotine yield of the cigarette, and the number of pack-years also are related to the likelihood of an individual stopping smoking. Nicotine Dependence is more common among individuals with other mental disorders. Depending on the population studied, from 55% to 90% of individuals with other mental disorders smoke, compared to 30% in the general population. Mood, Anxiety, and other Substance-Related Disorders may be more common in individuals who smoke than in those who are ex-smokers and those who have never smoked.

Associated laboratory findings.   Withdrawal symptoms are associated with a slowing on EEG, decreases in catecholamine and cortisol levels, rapid eye movement (REM) changes, impairment on neuropsychological testing, and decreased metabolic rate. Smoking increases the metabolism of many medications prescribed for the treatment of mental disorders and of other substances. Thus, cessation of smoking can increase the blood levels of these medications and other substances, sometimes to a clinically significant degree. This effect does not appear to be due to nicotine but rather to other compounds in tobacco. Nicotine and its metabolite cotinine can be measured in blood, saliva, or urine. Persons who smoke also often have diminished pulmonary function tests and increased mean corpuscular volume (MCV).

Associated physical examination findings and general medical conditions.
Nicotine Withdrawal may be associated with a dry or productive cough, decreased heart rate, increased appetite or weight gain, and a dampened orthostatic response. The most common signs of Nicotine Dependence are tobacco odor, cough, evidence of chronic obstructive pulmonary disease, and excessive skin wrinkling. Tobacco stains on the fingers can occur but are rare. Tobacco use can markedly increase the risk of lung, oral, and other cancers; cardiovascular and cerebrovascular conditions; chronic obstructive and other lung diseases; ulcers; maternal and fetal complications; and other conditions. Although most of these problems appear to be caused by the carcinogens and carbon monoxide in tobacco smoke rather than by nicotine itself, nicotine may increase the risk for cardiovascular events. Those who have never smoked but are chronically exposed to tobacco smoke appear to be at increased risk for conditions such as lung cancer and heart disease.

Specific Culture, Age, and Gender Features

The prevalence of smoking is decreasing in most industrialized nations, but is increasing in the developing areas. In the United States, the prevalence of smoking is slightly higher in males than in females; however, the prevalence of smoking is decreasing more rapidly in males than in females. In other countries, smoking is often much more prevalent among males.

Prevalence

In the United States, approximately 45% of the general population have never smoked. The remainder fall into one or more of the following categories: 25% are ex-smokers, 30% currently smoke cigarettes, 4% use pipes or cigars, and 3% use smokeless tobacco. In the United States, the prevalence of smoking has been decreasing approximately 0.7%–1.0% per year. The lifetime prevalence of Nicotine Dependence in the general population is estimated to be 20%. In the United States, between 50% and 80% of individuals who currently smoke have Nicotine Dependence. Lifetime prevalence of Nicotine Withdrawal among persons who smoke appears to be about 50%. Prospectively, it is estimated that about 50% of those who quit smoking on their own and about 75% of those in treatment programs experience Nicotine Withdrawal when they stop smoking.

Course

Smoking usually begins in the early teens. How quickly dependence develops is unclear. Among those who continue to smoke through age 20 years, 95% become regular, daily smokers. Of those who successfully quit, less than 25% quit on their first attempt. Most individuals who smoke have 3–4 failures before they stop smoking for good. In the United States, about 45% of those who have ever smoked eventually stop smoking. Withdrawal symptoms can begin within a few hours of cessation, typically peak in 1–4 days, and last for 3–4 weeks. Depressive symptoms postcessation may be associated with a relapse to smoking. Whether other Nicotine Withdrawal symptoms play a major role in relapse to smoking is debatable. Increased hunger and weight gain often persist for at least 6 months. Six months postcessation, 50% of individuals who have quit smoking report having had a desire for a cigarette in the last 24 hours.

Familial Pattern

The risk for smoking increases threefold if a first-degree biological relative smokes. Twin and adoption studies indicate that genetic factors contribute to the onset and continuation of smoking, with the degree of heritability equivalent to that observed with Alcohol Dependence.

Differential Diagnosis

For a general discussion of the differential diagnosis of Substance-Related Disorders, see p. 190.

The symptoms of Nicotine Withdrawal overlap with those of **other substance withdrawal syndromes; Caffeine Intoxication; Anxiety, Mood,** and **Sleep Disorders; and medication-induced akathisia.** Admission to smoke-free inpatient units can induce withdrawal symptoms that might mimic, intensify, or disguise other diagnoses. Reduction of symptoms associated with the resumption of smoking or nicotine-replacement therapy confirms the diagnosis.

Because regular nicotine use does not appear to impair mental functioning, Nicotine Dependence is not readily confused with other Substance-Related Disorders and mental disorders.

292.9   Nicotine-Related Disorder
Not Otherwise Specified

The Nicotine-Related Disorder Not Otherwise Specified category is for disorders associated with the use of nicotine that are not classifiable as Nicotine Dependence or Nicotine Withdrawal.

Opioid-Related Disorders

The opioids include natural opioids (e.g., morphine), semisynthetics (e.g., heroin), and synthetics with morphine-like action (e.g., codeine, hydromorphone, methadone, oxycodone, meperidine, fentanyl). Medications such as pentazocine and buprenorphine that have both opiate agonist and antagonist effects are also included in this class because their agonist properties produce similar physiological and behavioral effects. Opioids are prescribed as analgesics, anesthetics, antidiarrheal agents, or cough suppressants. Heroin is one of the most commonly abused drugs of this class and is usually taken by injection, although it can be smoked or "snorted" when very pure heroin is available. Fentanyl is injected, whereas cough suppressants and antidiarrheal agents are taken orally. The other opioids are taken both by injection and orally.

This section contains discussions specific to the Opioid-Related Disorders. Texts and criteria sets have already been provided for the generic aspects of Substance Dependence (p. 176) and Substance Abuse (p. 182) that apply across all substances. Texts specific to Opioid Dependence and Abuse are provided below; however, there are no additional specific criteria sets for Opioid Dependence or Opioid Abuse. Specific text and criteria sets for Opioid Intoxication and Opioid Withdrawal are also provided below. The Opioid-Induced Disorders (other than Opioid Intoxication and Withdrawal) are described in the sections of the manual with disorders with which they share phenomenology (e.g., Opioid-Induced Mood Disorder is included in the "Mood Disorders" section). Listed below are the Opioid Use Disorders and the Opioid-Induced Disorders.

Opioid Use Disorders

304.00   **Opioid Dependence** (see p. 248)
305.50   **Opioid Abuse** (see p. 249)

Opioid-Induced Disorders

292.89   **Opioid Intoxication** (see p. 249) *Specify if:* With Perceptual Disturbances
292.0   **Opioid Withdrawal** (see p. 250)
292.81   **Opioid Intoxication Delirium** (see p. 129)
292.11   **Opioid-Induced Psychotic Disorder, With Delusions** (see p. 310)
        Specify if: With Onset During Intoxication
292.12   **Opioid-Induced Psychotic Disorder, With Hallucinations** (see p. 310)
        Specify if: With Onset During Intoxication
292.84   **Opioid-Induced Mood Disorder** (see p. 370)
        Specify if: With Onset During Intoxication
292.89   **Opioid-Induced Sexual Dysfunction** (see p. 519)
        Specify if: With Onset During Intoxication
292.89   **Opioid-Induced Sleep Disorder** (see p. 601)
        Specify if: With Onset During Intoxication/With Onset During Withdrawal

292.9   **Opioid-Related Disorder Not Otherwise Specified** (see p. 255)

Opioid Use Disorders
304.00 Opioid Dependence

Also refer to the text and criteria for Substance Dependence (see p. 176). Most individuals with Opioid Dependence have significant levels of tolerance and will experience withdrawal on abrupt discontinuation of opioid substances. Opioid Dependence includes signs and symptoms that reflect compulsive, prolonged self-administration of opioid substances that are used for no legitimate medical purpose or, if a general medical condition is present that requires opioid treatment, that are used in doses that are greatly in excess of the amount needed for pain relief. Persons with Opioid Dependence tend to develop such regular patterns of compulsive drug use that daily activities are typically planned around obtaining and administering opioids. Opioids are usually purchased on the illegal market, but may also be obtained from physicians by faking or exaggerating general medical problems or by receiving simultaneous prescriptions from several physicians. Health care professionals with Opioid Dependence will often obtain opioids by writing prescriptions for themselves or by diverting opioids that have been prescribed for patients or from pharmacy supplies.

Specifiers

The following specifiers may be applied to a diagnosis of Opioid Dependence (see p. 179 for more details):

With Physiological Dependence
Without Physiological Dependence
Early Full Remission
Early Partial Remission
Sustained Full Remission
Sustained Partial Remission
On Agonist Therapy
In a Controlled Environment

305.50   Opioid Abuse

Also refer to the text and criteria for Substance Abuse (see p. 182). Legal difficulties may arise as a result of behavior while intoxicated with opioids or because an individual has resorted to illegal sources of supply. Persons who abuse opioids typically use these substances much less often than do those with dependence and do not develop significant tolerance or withdrawal. When problems related to opioid use are accompanied by evidence of tolerance, withdrawal, or compulsive behavior related to the use of opioids, a diagnosis of Opioid Dependence, rather than Opioid Abuse, should be considered.

Opioid-Induced Disorders

292.89   Opioid Intoxication

Also refer to the text and criteria for Substance Intoxication (see p. 183). The essential feature of Opioid Intoxication is the presence of clinically significant maladaptive behavioral or psychological changes (e.g., initial euphoria followed by apathy, dysphoria, psychomotor agitation or retardation, impaired judgment, or impaired social or occupational functioning) that develop during, or shortly after, opioid use (Criteria A and B). Intoxication is accompanied by pupillary constriction (unless there has been a severe overdose with consequent anoxia and pupillary dilation) and one or more of the following signs: drowsiness (described as being "on the nod") or even coma, slurred speech, and impairment in attention or memory (Criterion C). Individuals with Opioid Intoxication may demonstrate inattention to the environment, even to the point of ignoring potentially harmful events. The symptoms must not be due to a general medical condition and are not better accounted for by another mental disorder (Criterion D).

The magnitude of the behavioral and physiological changes that result from opioid use depends on the dose as well as characteristics of the individual using the substance (e.g., tolerance, rate of absorption, chronicity of use). Symptoms of Opioid Intoxication usually last for several hours, a time frame that is consistent with the half-life of most opioid drugs. Severe intoxication following an opioid overdose can lead to coma, respiratory depression, pupillary dilation, unconsciousness, and even death.

Specifier

The following specifier may be applied to a diagnosis of Opioid Intoxication:

With Perceptual Disturbances. This specifier may be noted when hallucinations with intact reality testing or auditory, visual, or tactile illusions occur in the absence of a delirium. *Intact reality testing* means that the person knows that the hallucinations are induced by the substance and do not represent external reality. When hallucinations occur in the absence of intact reality testing, a diagnosis of Substance-Induced Psychotic Disorder, With Hallucinations, should be considered.

■ Diagnostic criteria for 292.89 Opioid Intoxication

A. Recent use of an opioid.

B. Clinically significant maladaptive behavioral or psychological changes (e.g., initial euphoria followed by apathy, dysphoria, psychomotor agitation or retardation, impaired judgment, or impaired social or occupational functioning) that developed during, or shortly after, opioid use.

C. Pupillary constriction (or pupillary dilation due to anoxia from severe overdose) and one (or more) of the following signs, developing during, or shortly after, opioid use:

(1)   drowsiness or coma
(2)   slurred speech
(3)   impairment in attention or memory

D. The symptoms are not due to a general medical condition and are not better accounted for by another mental disorder.

Specify if:
With Perceptual Disturbances

292.0   Opioid Withdrawal

Also refer to the text and criteria for Substance Withdrawal (see p. 184). The essential feature of Opioid Withdrawal is the presence of a characteristic withdrawal syndrome that develops after the cessation of (or reduction in) opioid use that has been heavy and prolonged (Criterion A1). The withdrawal syndrome can be also precipitated by administration of an opioid antagonist (e.g., naloxone or naltrexone) after a period of opioid use (Criterion A2). Opioid Withdrawal is characterized by a pattern of signs and symptoms that are opposite to the acute agonist effects. The first of these are subjective and consist of complaints of anxiety, restlessness, and an "achy feeling" that is often located in the back and legs, accompanied by a wish to obtain opioids ("craving") and drug-seeking behavior, along with irritability and increased sensitivity to pain. Three or more of the following must be present to make a diagnosis of Opioid Withdrawal: dysphoric mood; nausea or vomiting; muscle aches; lacrimation or rhinorrhea; pupillary dilation, piloerection, or increased sweating; diarrhea; yawning; fever; and insomnia (Criterion B). Piloerection and fever are associated with severe withdrawal and are not often seen in routine clinical practice because individuals with Opioid Dependence usually obtain substances before withdrawal becomes that far advanced. These symptoms of Opioid Withdrawal must cause clinically significant distress or impairment in social, occupational, or other important areas of functioning (Criterion C). The symptoms must not be due to a general medical condition and are not better accounted for by another mental disorder (Criterion D).

In most individuals who are dependent on short-acting drugs such as heroin, withdrawal symptoms occur within 6–24 hours after the last dose. Symptoms may take 2–4 days to emerge in the case of longer-acting drugs such as methadone or LAAM (L-alphacetylmethadol). Acute withdrawal symptoms for a short-acting opioid such as heroin usually peak within 1–3 days and gradually subside over a period of 5–7 days. Less acute withdrawal symptoms can last for weeks to months. These more chronic symptoms include anxiety, dysphoria, anhedonia, insomnia, and drug craving.

■ Diagnostic criteria for 292.0 Opioid Withdrawal

A. Either of the following:

   (1) cessation of (or reduction in) opioid use that has been heavy and prolonged (several weeks or longer)

   (2) administration of an opioid antagonist after a period of opioid use

B. Three (or more) of the following, developing within minutes to several days after Criterion A:

   (1) dysphoric mood
   (2) nausea or vomiting
   (3) muscle aches
   (4) lacrimation or rhinorrhea
   (5) pupillary dilation, piloerection, or sweating
   (6) diarrhea
   (7) yawning
   (8) fever
   (9) insomnia

C. The symptoms in Criterion B cause clinically significant distress or impairment in social, occupational, or other important areas of functioning.

D. The symptoms are not due to a general medical condition and are not better accounted for by another mental disorder.

Other Opioid-Induced Disorders

The following Opioid-Induced Disorders are described in other sections of the manual with disorders with which they share phenomenology: **Opioid Intoxication Delirium** (p. 129), **Opioid-Induced Psychotic Disorder** (p. 310), **Opioid-Induced Mood Disorder** (p. 370), **Opioid-Induced Sexual Dysfunction** (p. 519), and **Opioid-Induced Sleep Disorder** (p. 601). These disorders are diagnosed instead of Opioid Intoxication or Opioid Withdrawal only when the symptoms are in excess of those usually associated with the Opioid Intoxication or Withdrawal syndrome and when the symptoms are sufficiently severe to warrant independent clinical attention.

Additional Information on Opioid-Related Disorders

Associated Features and Disorders

Associated descriptive features and mental disorders.   Opioid Dependence is commonly associated with a history of drug-related crimes (e.g., possession or distribution of drugs, forgery, burglary, robbery, larceny, or receiving stolen goods). Among health care professionals and individuals who have ready access to controlled substances, there is often a different pattern of illegal activities involving problems with state licensing boards, professional staffs of hospitals, or other administrative agencies. Divorce, unemployment, or irregular employment are often associated with Opioid Dependence at all socioeconomic levels.

For many individuals, the effect of taking an opioid for the first time is dysphoric rather than euphoric, and nausea and vomiting may result. Individuals with Opioid Dependence are especially at risk for the development of brief depressive symptoms and for episodes of mild to moderate depression that meet symptomatic and duration criteria for Major Depressive Disorder. These symptoms may represent an Opioid-Induced Mood Disorder (see p. 370) or exacerbations of a preexisting primary depressive disorder. Periods of depression are especially common during chronic intoxication or in association with psychosocial stressors that are related to the Opioid Dependence. Insomnia is common, especially during withdrawal. Antisocial Personality Disorder is much more common in individuals with Opioid Dependence than in the general population. Posttraumatic Stress Disorder is also seen with increased frequency. A history of Conduct Disorder in childhood or adolescence has been identified as a significant risk factor for Substance-Related Disorders, especially Opioid Dependence.

Associated laboratory findings.   Routine urine toxicology tests are often positive for opioid drugs in individuals with Opioid Dependence. Urine tests remain positive for most opioids for 12–36 hours after administration. Longer-acting opioids (e.g., methadone and LAAM) can be identified in urine for several days. Fentanyl is not detected by standard urine tests but can be identified by more specialized procedures. Laboratory evidence of the presence of other substances (e.g., cocaine, marijuana, alcohol, amphetamines, benzodiazepines) is common. Hepatitis screening tests are often positive, either for hepatitis antigen (signifying active infection) or hepatitis antibody (signifying past infection). Mildly elevated liver function tests are common, either as a result of resolving hepatitis or from toxic injury to the liver due to contaminants that have been mixed with the injected opioid. Subtle changes in cortisol secretion patterns and body temperature regulation have been observed for up to 6 months following opioid detoxification.

Associated physical examination findings and general medical conditions. Acute and chronic opioid use are associated with a lack of secretions, causing dry mouth and nose, slowing of gastrointestinal activity, and constipation. Visual acuity may be impaired as a result of pupillary constriction. In individuals who use opioids intravenously, sclerosed veins ("tracks") and puncture marks on the lower portions of the upper extremities are common. Veins sometimes become so badly sclerosed that peripheral edema develops and individuals switch to veins in the legs, neck, or groin. When these veins become unusable or otherwise unavailable, individuals often inject directly into their subcutaneous tissue ("skin-popping"), resulting in cellulitis, abscesses, and circular-appearing scars from healed skin lesions. Tetanus is a relatively rare but extremely serious consequence of injecting opioids. Infections may also occur in other organs and include bacterial endocarditis, hepatitis, and human immunodeficiency virus (HIV) infection. Tuberculosis is a particularly serious problem among individuals who use drugs intravenously, especially those dependent on heroin. Infection with the tubercle bacillus is usually asymptomatic and evident only by the presence of a positive tuberculin skin test. However, many cases of active tuberculosis have been found, especially among those who are infected with HIV. These individuals often have a newly acquired infection, but also are likely to experience reactivation of a prior infection due to impaired immune function. Persons who sniff heroin or other opioids ("snorting") often develop irritation of the nasal mucosa, sometimes accompanied by perforation of the nasal septum. Difficulties in sexual functioning are common. Males often experience erectile dysfunction during intoxication or chronic use. Females commonly have disturbances of reproductive function and irregular menses.

The incidence of HIV infection is high among individuals who use intravenous drugs, a large proportion of whom are individuals with Opioid Dependence. HIV infection rates have been reported to be as high as 60% among persons dependent on heroin in some areas of the United States.

In addition to infections such as cellulitis, hepatitis, HIV, tuberculosis, and endocarditis, Opioid Dependence is associated with a very high death rate—at the level of approximately 10 per 1,000 per year among untreated persons. Death most often results from overdose, accidents, injuries, or other general medical complications. Accidents and injuries due to violence that is associated with buying or selling drugs are common. In some areas, violence accounts for more opioid-related deaths than overdose or HIV infection. Physiological dependence on opioids may occur in about half of the infants born to females with Opioid Dependence; this can produce a severe withdrawal syndrome requiring medical treatment. Although low birth weight is also seen in children of mothers with Opioid Dependence, it is usually not marked and is generally not associated with serious adverse consequences.

Specific Culture, Age, and Gender Features

Since the 1920s, in the United States, members of minority groups living in economically deprived areas have been overrepresented among persons with Opioid Dependence.

However, in the late 1800s and early 1900s, Opioid Dependence was seen more often among white middle-class individuals, suggesting that differences in use reflect the availability of opioid drugs and other social factors. Medical personnel who have ready access to opioids may have an increased risk for Opioid Abuse and Dependence.

Increasing age appears to be associated with a decrease in prevalence. This tendency for Dependence to remit generally begins after age 40 years and has been called "maturing out." However, many persons have remained opioid dependent for 50 years or longer. Males are more commonly affected, with the male-to-female ratio typically being 3 or 4:1.

Prevalence

A community survey conducted in the United States in 1991 reported that 6% of the population sampled ever used analgesics for nonmedical purposes; 2.5% had used them within the past year; and 0.7% has used them in the last month. The survey also showed that 1.3% had used heroin in their lifetime, and 0.2% had used it in the last year (use in the last month was not reported). Because the survey assessed patterns of use rather than diagnoses, it is not known how many of those who used analgesics or heroin had symptoms that met criteria for Dependence or Abuse. A community study conducted in the United States from 1980 to 1985 that used the more narrowly defined DSM-III criteria found that 0.7% of the adult population had Opioid Dependence or Abuse at some time in their lives. Among those with Dependence or Abuse, 18% reported use in the last month and 42% reported having had a problem with opioids in the last year.

Course

Opioid Dependence can begin at any age, but problems associated with opioid use are most commonly first observed in the late teens or early 20s. Once Dependence develops, it is usually continuous over a period of many years, even though brief periods of abstinence are frequent. Relapse following abstinence is common, even after many years of incarceration. One exception to the typical chronic course of Opioid Dependence was observed in service personnel who became dependent on opioids in Vietnam. On their return to the United States, less than 10% of those who had been dependent on opioids relapsed, although they experienced increased rates of Alcohol or Amphetamine Dependence. Few data are available on the course of Opioid Abuse.

Familial Pattern

The family members of individuals with Opioid Dependence are likely to have higher levels of psychopathology, especially an increased incidence of other Substance-Related Disorders and Antisocial Personality Disorder.

Differential Diagnosis

For a general discussion of the differential diagnosis of Substance-Related Disorders, see p. 190. Opioid-Induced Disorders may be characterized by symptoms (e.g., depressed mood) that resemble **primary mental disorders** (e.g., Dysthymia versus Opioid-Induced Mood Disorder, With Depressive Features, With Onset During Intoxication).

See p. 193 for a discussion of this differential diagnosis. Opioids are less likely to produce symptoms of mental disturbance than are most other drugs of abuse and, in some instances, will even reduce such symptoms. In these cases, mental symptoms or disorders may emerge after opioid use is discontinued.

Alcohol Intoxication and **Sedative, Hypnotic, or Anxiolytic Intoxication** can cause a clinical picture that resembles Opioid Intoxication. A diagnosis of Alcohol or Sedative, Hypnotic, or Anxiolytic Intoxication can usually be made based on the absence of pupillary constriction or the lack of a response to a naloxone challenge. In some cases, intoxication may be due both to opioids and to alcohol or other sedatives. In these cases, the naloxone challenge will not reverse all of the sedative effects. The anxiety and restlessness associated with Opioid Withdrawal resemble symptoms seen in **Sedative, Hypnotic, or Anxiolytic Withdrawal.** However, Opioid Withdrawal is also accompanied by rhinorrhea, lacrimation, and pupillary dilation, which are not seen in sedative-type withdrawal. Dilated pupils are also seen in **Hallucinogen Intoxication, Amphetamine Intoxication,** and **Cocaine Intoxication.** However, others signs or symptoms of Opioid Withdrawal such as nausea, vomiting, diarrhea, abdominal cramps, rhinorrhea, or lacrimation are not present. Opioid Intoxication and Opioid Withdrawal are distinguished from the **other Opioid-Induced Disorders** (e.g., Opioid-Induced Mood Disorder, With Onset During Intoxication) because the symptoms in these latter disorders are in excess of those usually associated with Opioid Intoxication or Opioid Withdrawal and are severe enough to warrant independent clinical attention.

292.9   Opioid-Related Disorder Not Otherwise Specified

The Opioid-Related Disorder Not Otherwise Specified category is for disorders associated with the use of opioids that are not classifiable as Opioid Dependence, Opioid Abuse, Opioid Intoxication, Opioid Withdrawal, Opioid Intoxication Delirium, Opioid-Induced Psychotic Disorder, Opioid-Induced Mood Disorder, Opioid-Induced Sexual Dysfunction, or Opioid-Induced Sleep Disorder.

Phencyclidine (or Phencyclidine-Like)–Related Disorders

The phencyclidines (or phencyclidine-like) substances include phencyclidine (PCP, Sernylan) and similarly acting compounds such as ketamine (Ketalar, Ketaject) and the thiophene analogue of phencyclidine (TCP; 1-[1-2-thienyl-cyclohexyl]piperidine). These substances were first developed as dissociative anesthetics in the 1950s and became street drugs in the 1960s. They can be taken orally or intravenously or can be smoked. Phencyclidine (sold illicitly under a variety of names such as PCP, Hog, Tranq, Angel Dust, and PeaCe Pill) is the most commonly abused substance in this class.

This section contains discussions specific to the Phencyclidine-Related Disorders. Texts and criteria sets have already been provided for the generic aspects of Substance Dependence (p. 176) and Substance Abuse (p. 182) that apply across all substances. Texts specific to Phencyclidine Dependence and Abuse are provided below; however, there are no additional specific criteria sets for Phencyclidine Dependence or Phencyclidine Abuse. A specific text and criteria set for Phencyclidine Intoxication is also provided below. Although symptoms of phencyclidine withdrawal may occur, their clinical significance is uncertain, and a diagnosis of phencyclidine withdrawal is not included in this manual. The Phencyclidine-Induced Disorders (other than Phencyclidine Intoxication) are described in the sections of the manual with disorders with which they share phenomenology (e.g., Phencyclidine-Induced Psychotic Disorder is included in the "Schizophrenia and Other Psychotic Disorders" section). Listed below are the Phencyclidine Use Disorders and the Phencyclidine-Induced Disorders.

Phencyclidine Use Disorders

304.90   Phencyclidine Dependence (see p. 256)
305.90   Phencyclidine Abuse (see p. 257)

Phencyclidine-Induced Disorders

292.89   Phencyclidine Intoxication (see p. 257)
         Specify if: With Perceptual Disturbances
292.81   Phencyclidine Intoxication Delirium (see p. 129)
292.11   Phencyclidine-Induced Psychotic Disorder, With Delusions (see p. 310)
         Specify if: With Onset During Intoxication
292.12   Phencyclidine-Induced Psychotic Disorder, With Hallucinations
         (see p. 310) *Specify if:* With Onset During Intoxication
292.84   Phencyclidine-Induced Mood Disorder (see p. 370)
         Specify if: With Onset During Intoxication
292.89   Phencyclidine-Induced Anxiety Disorder (see p. 439)
         Specify if: With Onset During Intoxication

292.9   Phencyclidine-Related Disorder Not Otherwise Specified (see p. 261)

Phencyclidine Use Disorders
304.90   Phencyclidine Dependence

Also refer to the text and criteria for Substance Dependence (see p. 176). Some of the generic criteria for Substance Dependence do not apply to phencyclidine. Although "craving" has been reported by individuals with heavy use, neither tolerance nor withdrawal symptoms have been clearly demonstrated in humans (although both have been shown to occur in animal studies). Phencyclidine is usually not difficult to obtain, and individuals with Phencyclidine Dependence often smoke it at least 2–3 times per day, thus spending a significant proportion of their time using the substance and experiencing its effects. Phencyclidine use may continue despite the presence of psychological problems (e.g., disinhibition, anxiety, rage, aggression, panic, flashbacks) or medical problems (e.g., hyperthermia, hypertension, seizures) that the individual knows are caused by the substance. Individuals with Phencyclidine Dependence can manifest dangerous behavioral reactions due to lack of insight and judgment while intoxicated. Aggressive behavior involving fighting has been identified as an especially problematic adverse effect of phencyclidine. As with hallucinogens, adverse reactions to phencyclidine may be more common among individuals with preexisting mental disorders.

Specifiers

The following specifiers may be applied to a diagnosis of Phencyclidine Dependence (see p. 179 for more details):

Early Full Remission
Early Partial Remission
Sustained Full Remission
Sustained Partial Remission
In a Controlled Environment

305.90   Phencyclidine Abuse

Also refer to the text and criteria for Substance Abuse (see p. 182). Although individuals who abuse phencyclidine use the substance much less often than those with Dependence, they may repeatedly fail to fulfill major role obligations at school, work, or home because of Phencyclidine Intoxication. Individuals may use phencyclidine in situations where it is physically hazardous (such as while operating heavy machinery or driving a motorcycle or car). Legal difficulties may arise due to possession of phencyclidine or to behaviors resulting from Intoxication (e.g., fighting). There may be recurrent social or interpersonal problems due to the individual's behavior while intoxicated or to the chaotic lifestyle, multiple legal problems, or arguments with significant others.

Phencyclidine-Induced Disorders
292.89   Phencyclidine Intoxication

Also refer to the text and criteria for Substance Intoxication (see p. 183). The essential feature of Phencyclidine Intoxication is the presence of clinically significant maladaptive behavioral changes (e.g., belligerence, assaultiveness, impulsiveness, unpredictability, psychomotor agitation, impaired judgment, or impaired social or occupational functioning) that develop during, or shortly after, use of phencyclidine (or a related substance) (Criteria A and B). These changes are accompanied by two or more of the following signs that develop within an hour of using the substance (or less when it is smoked, "snorted," or used intravenously): vertical or horizontal nystagmus, hypertension or tachycardia, numbness or diminished responsiveness to pain, ataxia, dysarthria, muscle rigidity, seizures or coma, and hyperacusis (Criterion C). The symptoms must not be due to a general medical condition and are not better accounted for by another mental disorder (Criterion D).

Specific signs and symptoms are dose related. Lower doses of phencyclidine produce vertigo, ataxia, nystagmus, mild hypertension, abnormal involuntary movements, slurred speech, nausea, weakness, slowed reaction times, euphoria or affective dulling, loquacity, and lack of concern. Disorganized thinking, changed body image and sensory perception, depersonalization, and feelings of unreality occur at intermediate doses.

Higher doses produce amnesia and coma, with analgesia sufficient for surgery, and seizures with respiratory depression occur at the highest doses. Effects begin almost immediately after an intravenous or transpulmonary dose, reaching a peak within minutes. Peak effects occur about 2 hours after oral doses. In milder intoxications, the effects resolve after 8–20 hours, whereas signs and symptoms of severe intoxications may persist for several days. Phencyclidine-Induced Psychotic Disorder (p. 310) may persist for weeks.

Specifier

The following specifier may be applied to a diagnosis of Phencyclidine Intoxication:

> **With Perceptual Disturbances.** This specifier may be noted when hallucinations with intact reality testing or auditory, visual, or tactile illusions occur in the absence of a delirium. *Intact reality testing* means that the person knows that the hallucinations are induced by the substance and do not represent external reality. When hallucinations occur in the absence of intact reality testing, a diagnosis of Substance-Induced Psychotic Disorder, With Hallucinations, should be considered.

■ Diagnostic criteria for 292.89 Phencyclidine Intoxication

A. Recent use of phencyclidine (or a related substance).

B. Clinically significant maladaptive behavioral changes (e.g., belligerence, assaultiveness, impulsiveness, unpredictability, psychomotor agitation, impaired judgment, or impaired social or occupational functioning) that developed during, or shortly after, phencyclidine use.

C. Within an hour (less when smoked, "snorted," or used intravenously), two (or more) of the following signs:

(1) vertical or horizontal nystagmus
(2) hypertension or tachycardia
(3) numbness or diminished responsiveness to pain
(4) ataxia
(5) dysarthria
(6) muscle rigidity
(7) seizures or coma
(8) hyperacusis

D. The symptoms are not due to a general medical condition and are not better accounted for by another mental disorder.

Specify if:
With Perceptual Disturbances

Other Phencyclidine-Induced Disorders

The following Phencyclidine-Induced Disorders are described in other sections of the manual with disorders with which they share phenomenology: **Phencyclidine Intoxication Delirium** (p. 129), **Phencyclidine-Induced Psychotic Disorder** (p. 310), **Phencyclidine-Induced Mood Disorder** (p. 370), and **Phencyclidine-Induced Anxiety Disorder** (p. 439). These disorders are diagnosed instead of Phencyclidine Intoxication only when the symptoms are in excess of those usually associated with the Phencyclidine Intoxication syndrome and when the symptoms are sufficiently severe to warrant independent clinical attention.

Additional Information on Phencyclidine-Related Disorders

Associated Features and Disorders

Associated descriptive features and mental disorders.   Although individuals with Phencyclidine Intoxication may remain alert and oriented, they may show delirium, coma, psychotic symptoms, or catatonic mutism with posturing. Repeated intoxications may lead to job, family, social, or legal problems. Violence, agitation, and bizarre behavior (e.g., confused wandering) may occur. Individuals with Phencyclidine Dependence or Abuse may report repeated intoxication-induced hospitalizations, emergency-room visits, and arrests for confused or bizarre behavior or for fighting. Conduct Disorder in adolescents and Antisocial Personality Disorder in adults may be associated with phencyclidine use. Dependence on other substances (especially cocaine, alcohol, and amphetamines) is common among those who have Phencyclidine Dependence.

Associated laboratory findings.   Phencyclidine (or a related substance) is present in the urine of individuals who are acutely intoxicated with one of these substances. The substance may be detectable in urine for several weeks after the end of prolonged or very high dose use. Phencyclidine may be detected more readily in acidic urine. Creatine phosphokinase (CPK) and serum glutamic-oxaloacetic transaminase (SGOT) are often elevated.

Associated physical examination findings and general medical conditions. Phencyclidine Intoxication produces extensive cardiovascular and neurological (e.g., seizures, dystonias, dyskinesias, catalepsy, and hypothermia or hyperthermia) toxicity. In those with Phencyclidine Dependence or Abuse, there may be physical evidence of injuries from accidents, fights, and falls. Needle tracks, hepatitis, human immunodeficiency virus (HIV) disease, and bacterial endocarditis may be found among the relatively few individuals who take phencyclidine intravenously. Drowning, even in small volumes of water, has been reported. Respiratory problems arise with apnea, bronchospasm, bronchorrhea, aspiration during coma, and hypersalivation. Rhabdomyolysis with renal impairment is seen in about 2% of individuals who seek emergency care. Cardiac arrest is a rare outcome.

Specific Culture, Age, and Gender Features

The prevalence of phencyclidine-related problems appears to be higher among males (about twofold), among those between ages 20 and 40 years, and among ethnic minorities (about twofold). Males compose about three-quarters of those with phencyclidine-related emergency-room visits.

Prevalence

Medical examiners nationally report that phencyclidine is involved in about 3% of deaths associated with substance use. It is mentioned as a problem in about 3% of substance-related emergency-room visits. The percentage of high-school seniors who report ever having used phencyclidine fell from about 13% in 1980 to about 3% in 1990.

Differential Diagnosis

For a general discussion of the differential diagnosis of Substance-Related Disorders, see p. 190. Phencyclidine-Induced Disorders may be characterized by symptoms (e.g., depressed mood) that resemble **primary mental disorders** (e.g., Major Depressive Disorder versus Phencyclidine-Induced Mood Disorder, With Depressive Features, With Onset During Intoxication). See p. 193 for a discussion of this differential diagnosis. Recurring episodes of psychotic or mood symptoms due to Phencyclidine Intoxication may mimic **Schizophrenia** or **Mood Disorders.** History or laboratory evidence of phencyclidine use establishes a role for the substance, but does not rule out the co-occurrence of other primary mental disorders. Rapid onset of symptoms also suggests Phencyclidine Intoxication rather than Schizophrenia, but phencyclidine use may induce acute psychotic episodes in individuals with preexisting Schizophrenia. Rapid resolution of symptoms and the absence of a history of Schizophrenia may aid in this differentiation. Drug-related violence or impaired judgment may co-occur with, or may mimic aspects of, **Conduct Disorder** or **Antisocial Personality Disorder.** Absence of behavioral problems before the onset of substance use, or during abstinence, may help to clarify this differentiation.

Phencyclidine and related substances may produce perceptual disturbances (e.g., scintillating lights, perception of sounds, illusions, or formed visual images) that the person usually recognizes as resulting from the drug use. If reality testing remains intact and the person neither believes that the perceptions are real nor acts on them, the specifier With Perceptual Disturbances is noted for Phencyclidine Intoxication. If reality testing is impaired, the diagnosis of **Phencyclidine-Induced Psychotic Disorder** should be considered.

Differentiating Phencyclidine Intoxication from **other Substance Intoxications** (with which it often coexists) depends on a history of having taken the substance, the presence of characteristic findings (e.g., nystagmus and mild hypertension), and positive urine toxicological tests. Individuals who use phencyclidine often use other drugs as well, and comorbid Abuse or Dependence on other drugs must be considered. Phencyclidine Intoxication is distinguished from the **other Phencyclidine-Induced Disorders** (e.g., Phencyclidine-Induced Mood Disorder, With Onset During Intoxication) because the symptoms in these latter disorders are in excess of those usually associated with Phencyclidine Intoxication and are severe enough to warrant independent clinical attention.

292.9 Phencyclidine-Related Disorder Not Otherwise Specified

The Phencyclidine-Related Disorder Not Otherwise Specified category is for disorders associated with the use of phencyclidine that are not classifiable as Phencyclidine Dependence, Phencyclidine Abuse, Phencyclidine Intoxication, Phencyclidine Intoxication Delirium, Phencyclidine-Induced Psychotic Disorder, Phencyclidine-Induced Mood Disorder, or Phencyclidine-Induced Anxiety Disorder.

Sedative-, Hypnotic-, or Anxiolytic-Related Disorders

The sedative, hypnotic, and anxiolytic (antianxiety) substances include the benzodiazepines, the carbamates (e.g., glutethimide, meprobamate), the barbiturates (e.g., secobarbital), and the barbiturate-like hypnotics (e.g., glutethimide, methaqualone). This class of substances includes all prescription sleeping medications and almost all prescription antianxiety medications. The nonbenzodiazepine antianxiety agents (e.g., buspirone, gepirone) are not included in this class. Some medications in this class have other important clinical uses (e.g., as anticonvulsants). Like alcohol, these agents are brain depressants and can produce similar Substance-Induced and Substance Use Disorders. At high doses, sedatives, hypnotics, and anxiolytics can be lethal, particularly when mixed with alcohol. Sedatives, hypnotics, and anxiolytics are available both by prescription and from illegal sources. Occasionally, individuals who obtain these substances by prescription will abuse them; conversely, some of those who purchase substances from this class "on the street" do not develop Dependence or Abuse. Medications with rapid onset and/or short to intermediate lengths of action may be especially vulnerable to being abused.

This section contains discussions specific to the Sedative-, Hypnotic-, or Anxiolytic-Related Disorders. Texts and criteria sets have already been provided to define the generic aspects of Substance Dependence (p. 176) and Substance Abuse (p. 182) that apply across all substances. Texts specific to Sedative, Hypnotic, or Anxiolytic Dependence and Abuse are provided below; however, there are no additional specific criteria sets for Sedative, Hypnotic, or Anxiolytic Dependence or Sedative, Hypnotic, or Anxiolytic Abuse. Specific texts and criteria sets for Sedative, Hypnotic, or Anxiolytic Intoxication and Sedative, Hypnotic, or Anxiolytic Withdrawal are also provided below. The Sedative-, Hypnotic-, or Anxiolytic-Induced Disorders (other than Sedative, Hypnotic, or Anxiolytic Intoxication and Withdrawal) are described in the sections of the manual with disorders with which they share phenomenology (e.g., Sedative-, Hypnotic-, or Anxiolytic-Induced Anxiety Disorder is included in the "Anxiety Disorders" section). Listed below are the Sedative, Hypnotic, or Anxiolytic Use Disorders and the Sedative-, Hypnotic-, or Anxiolytic-Induced Disorders.

Sedative, Hypnotic, or Anxiolytic Use Disorders

304.10 Sedative, Hypnotic, or Anxiolytic Dependence (see p. 262)
305.40 Sedative, Hypnotic, or Anxiolytic Abuse (see p. 263)

Sedative-, Hypnotic-, or Anxiolytic-Induced Disorders

292.89   **Sedative, Hypnotic, or Anxiolytic Intoxication** (see p. 263)
292.0   **Sedative, Hypnotic, or Anxiolytic Withdrawal** (see p. 264)
    Specify if: With Perceptual Disturbances
292.81   **Sedative, Hypnotic, or Anxiolytic Intoxication Delirium** (see p. 129)
292.81   **Sedative, Hypnotic, or Anxiolytic Withdrawal Delirium** (see p. 129)
292.82   **Sedative-, Hypnotic-, or Anxiolytic-Induced Persisting Dementia**
    (see p. 152)
292.83   **Sedative-, Hypnotic-, or Anxiolytic-Induced Persisting Amnestic
    Disorder** (see p. 161)
292.11   **Sedative-, Hypnotic-, or Anxiolytic-Induced Psychotic Disorder,
    With Delusions** (see p. 310)
    Specify if: With Onset During Intoxication/With Onset During Withdrawal
292.12   **Sedative-, Hypnotic-, or Anxiolytic-Induced Psychotic Disorder,
    With Hallucinations** (see p. 310)
    Specify if: With Onset During Intoxication/With Onset During Withdrawal
292.84   **Sedative-, Hypnotic-, or Anxiolytic-Induced Mood Disorder** (see p. 370)
    Specify if: With Onset During Intoxication/With Onset During Withdrawal
292.89   **Sedative-, Hypnotic-, or Anxiolytic-Induced Anxiety Disorder**
    (see p. 439) *Specify if:* With Onset During Withdrawal
292.89   **Sedative-, Hypnotic-, or Anxiolytic-Induced Sexual Dysfunction**
    (see p. 519) *Specify if:* With Onset During Intoxication
292.89   **Sedative-, Hypnotic-, or Anxiolytic-Induced Sleep Disorder** (see p. 601)
    Specify if: With Onset During Intoxication/With Onset During Withdrawal

292.9   **Sedative-, Hypnotic-, or Anxiolytic-Related Disorder
    Not Otherwise Specified** (see p. 269)

Sedative, Hypnotic, or Anxiolytic Use Disorders

304.10   Sedative, Hypnotic, or Anxiolytic Dependence

Also refer to the text and criteria for Substance Dependence (see p. 176). Very significant levels of physiological dependence, marked by both tolerance and withdrawal, can develop to the sedatives, hypnotics, and anxiolytics. The timing and severity of the withdrawal syndrome will differ depending on the specific substance and its pharmacokinetics and pharmacodynamics. For example, withdrawal from shorter-acting substances that are rapidly absorbed and that have no active metabolites (e.g., triazolam) can begin within hours after the substance is stopped; withdrawal from substances with long-acting metabolites (e.g., diazepam) may not begin for 1–2 days or longer. The withdrawal syndrome produced by substances in this class may be characterized by the development of a delirium that can be life threatening. There may be evidence of tolerance and withdrawal in the absence of a diagnosis of Substance Dependence in an individual who has abruptly discontinued benzodiazepines that were taken for long periods of time at prescribed and therapeutic doses. A diagnosis of Substance Dependence should be considered only when, in addition to having physiological dependence, the individual using the substance shows evidence of a range of problems (e.g., an individual who has developed drug-seeking behavior to the extent that important activities are given up or reduced to obtain the substance).

Specifiers

The following specifiers may be applied to a diagnosis of Sedative, Hypnotic, or Anxiolytic Dependence (see p. 179 for more details):

With Physiological Dependence
Without Physiological Dependence

Early Full Remission
Early Partial Remission
Sustained Full Remission
Sustained Partial Remission
On Agonist Therapy
In a Controlled Environment

305.40   Sedative, Hypnotic, or Anxiolytic Abuse

Also refer to the text and criteria for Substance Abuse (see p. 182). Abuse of substances from this class may occur on its own or in conjunction with use of other substances. For example, individuals may use intoxicating doses of sedatives or benzodiazepines to "come down" from cocaine or amphetamines or use high doses of benzodiazepines in combination with methadone to "boost" its effects. Abuse of substances from this class may result in use in hazardous situations, such as getting "high" and then driving. The individual may miss work or school or neglect home duties as a result of intoxication or get into arguments with spouses or parents about episodes of substance use. When these problems are accompanied by evidence of tolerance, withdrawal, or compulsive behavior related to the use of sedatives, hypnotics, or anxiolytics, a diagnosis of Sedative, Hypnotic, or Anxiolytic Dependence should be considered.

Sedative-, Hypnotic-, or Anxiolytic-Induced Disorders

292.89   Sedative, Hypnotic, or Anxiolytic Intoxication

Also refer to the text and criteria for Substance Intoxication (see p. 183). The essential feature of Sedative, Hypnotic, or Anxiolytic Intoxication is the presence of clinically significant maladaptive behavioral or psychological changes (e.g., inappropriate sexual or aggressive behavior, mood lability, impaired judgment, impaired social or occupational functioning) that develop during, or shortly after, use of a sedative, hypnotic, or anxiolytic substance (Criteria A and B). As with other brain depressants, these behaviors may be accompanied by slurred speech, an unsteady gait, nystagmus, memory or attentional problems, levels of incoordination that can interfere with driving abilities and with performing usual activities to the point of causing accidents, and stupor or coma (Criterion C). Memory impairment is a prominent feature of Sedative, Hypnotic, or Anxiolytic Intoxication and is most often characterized by an anterograde amnesia that resembles "alcoholic blackouts," which can be quite disturbing to the individual. The symptoms must not be due to a general medical condition and are not better accounted for by another mental disorder (Criterion D). Intoxication may occur in individuals who are receiving these substances by prescription, are borrowing the medication from friends or relatives, or are deliberately taking the substance to achieve intoxication.

■ **Diagnostic criteria for 292.89 Sedative, Hypnotic, or Anxiolytic Intoxication**

A. Recent use of a sedative, hypnotic, or anxiolytic.

B. Clinically significant maladaptive behavioral or psychological changes (e.g., inappropriate sexual or aggressive behavior, mood lability, impaired judgment, impaired social or occupational functioning) that developed during, or shortly after, sedative, hypnotic, or anxiolytic use.

C. One (or more) of the following signs, developing during, or shortly after, sedative, hypnotic, or anxiolytic use:

   (1) slurred speech
   (2) incoordination
   (3) unsteady gait
   (4) nystagmus
   (5) impairment in attention or memory
   (6) stupor or coma

D. The symptoms are not due to a general medical condition and are not better accounted for by another mental disorder.

292.0 Sedative, Hypnotic, or Anxiolytic Withdrawal

Also refer to the text and criteria for Substance Withdrawal (see p. 184). The essential feature of Sedative, Hypnotic, or Anxiolytic Withdrawal is the presence of a characteristic syndrome that develops after a marked decrease in or cessation of intake after several weeks or more of regular use (Criteria A and B). This withdrawal syndrome is characterized by two or more symptoms (similar to Alcohol Withdrawal) that include autonomic hyperactivity (e.g., increases in heart rate, respiratory rate, blood pressure, or body temperature, along with sweating); a tremor of the hands; insomnia, anxiety, and nausea sometimes accompanied by vomiting; and psychomotor agitation. A grand mal seizure may occur in perhaps as many as 20%–30% of individuals undergoing untreated withdrawal from these substances. In severe Withdrawal, visual, tactile, or auditory hallucinations or illusions can occur. If the person's reality testing is intact (i.e., he or she knows the substance is causing the hallucinations) and the illusions occur in a clear sensorium, the specifier With Perceptual Disturbances can be noted (see below). The symptoms cause clinically significant distress or impairment in social, occupational, or other important areas of functioning (Criterion C). The symptoms must not be due to a general medical condition and are not better accounted for by another mental disorder (e.g., Alcohol Withdrawal or Generalized Anxiety Disorder) (Criterion D). Relief of withdrawal symptoms with administration of any sedative-hypnotic agent would support a diagnosis of Sedative, Hypnotic, or Anxiolytic Withdrawal.

The withdrawal syndrome is characterized by signs and symptoms that are generally the opposite of the acute effects that are likely to be observed in a first-time user of these agents. The time course of the withdrawal syndrome is generally predicted by the half-life of the substance. Medications whose actions typically last about 10 hours or less (e.g., lorazepam, oxazepam, and temazepam) produce withdrawal symptoms within 6–8 hours of decreasing blood levels that peak in intensity on the second day and improve markedly by the fourth or fifth day. For substances with longer half-lives (e.g., diazepam), symptoms may not develop for more than a week, peak in intensity during the second week, and decrease markedly during the third or fourth week. There may be additional longer-term symptoms at a much lower level of intensity that persist for several months. As with alcohol, these lingering withdrawal symptoms (e.g., anxiety, moodiness, and trouble sleeping) can be mistaken for non-substance-induced Anxiety or Depressive Disorders (e.g., Generalized Anxiety Disorder).

The longer the substance has been taken and the higher the dosages used, the more likely it is that there will be severe Withdrawal. However, Withdrawal has been reported with as little as 15 mg of diazepam (or its equivalent in other benzodiazepines) when taken daily for several months. Dosages of approximately 40 mg of diazepam (or its equivalent) daily are more likely to produce clinically relevant withdrawal symptoms, and even higher doses (e.g., 100 mg of diazepam) are more likely to be followed by withdrawal seizures or delirium. Sedative, Hypnotic, or Anxiolytic Withdrawal Delirium (see p. 129) is characterized by disturbances in consciousness and cognition, with visual, tactile, or auditory hallucinations. When present, Sedative, Hypnotic, or Anxiolytic Withdrawal Delirium should be diagnosed instead of Withdrawal.

Specifier

The following specifier may be applied to a diagnosis of Sedative, Hypnotic, or Anxiolytic Withdrawal:

> **With Perceptual Disturbances.** This specifier may be noted when hallucinations with intact reality testing or auditory, visual, or tactile illusions occur in the absence of a delirium. *Intact reality testing* means that the person knows that the hallucinations are induced by the substance and do not represent external reality. When hallucinations occur in the absence of intact reality testing, a diagnosis of Substance-Induced Psychotic Disorder, With Hallucinations, should be considered.

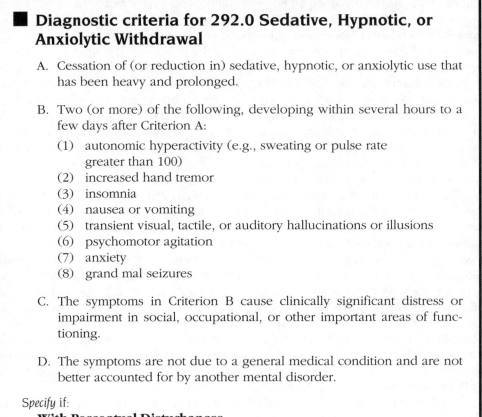

■ **Diagnostic criteria for 292.0 Sedative, Hypnotic, or Anxiolytic Withdrawal**

A. Cessation of (or reduction in) sedative, hypnotic, or anxiolytic use that has been heavy and prolonged.

B. Two (or more) of the following, developing within several hours to a few days after Criterion A:
    (1) autonomic hyperactivity (e.g., sweating or pulse rate greater than 100)
    (2) increased hand tremor
    (3) insomnia
    (4) nausea or vomiting
    (5) transient visual, tactile, or auditory hallucinations or illusions
    (6) psychomotor agitation
    (7) anxiety
    (8) grand mal seizures

C. The symptoms in Criterion B cause clinically significant distress or impairment in social, occupational, or other important areas of functioning.

D. The symptoms are not due to a general medical condition and are not better accounted for by another mental disorder.

Specify if:
With Perceptual Disturbances

Other Sedative-, Hypnotic-, or Anxiolytic-Induced Disorders

The following Sedative-, Hypnotic-, or Anxiolytic-Induced Disorders are described in other sections of the manual with disorders with which they share phenomenology: **Sedative, Hypnotic, or Anxiolytic Intoxication Delirium** (p. 129), **Sedative, Hypnotic, or Anxiolytic Withdrawal Delirium** (p. 129), **Sedative-, Hypnotic-, or Anxiolytic-Induced Persisting Dementia** (p. 152), **Sedative-, Hypnotic-, or Anxiolytic-Induced Persisting Amnestic Disorder** (p. 161), **Sedative-, Hypnotic-, or Anxiolytic-Induced Psychotic Disorder** (p. 310), **Sedative-, Hypnotic-, or Anxiolytic-Induced Mood Disorder** (p. 370), **Sedative-, Hypnotic-, or Anxiolytic-Induced Anxiety Disorder** (p. 439), **Sedative-, Hypnotic-, or Anxiolytic-Induced Sexual Dysfunction** (p. 519), and **Sedative-, Hypnotic-, or Anxiolytic-Induced Sleep Disorder** (p. 601). These disorders are diagnosed instead of Sedative, Hypnotic, or Anxiolytic Intoxication or Sedative, Hypnotic, or Anxiolytic Withdrawal only when the symptoms are in excess of those usually associated with the Sedative, Hypnotic, or Anxiolytic Intoxication or Withdrawal syndrome and when the symptoms are sufficiently severe to warrant independent clinical attention.

Additional Information on
Sedative-, Hypnotic-, or Anxiolytic-Related Disorders

Associated Features and Disorders

Associated descriptive features and mental disorders.   Sedative, Hypnotic, or Anxiolytic Dependence and Abuse may often be associated with Dependence on, or Abuse of, other substances (e.g., alcohol, cannabis, cocaine, heroin, amphetamines). Sedatives are often used to alleviate the unwanted effects of these other substances. Acute Intoxication can result in accidental injury through falls and automobile accidents. For elderly individuals, even short-term use of these sedating medications at prescribed doses can be associated with an increased risk for cognitive problems and falls. Some data indicate that the disinhibiting effects of these agents can, like alcohol, actually contribute to overly aggressive behavior, with subsequent interpersonal and legal problems. Intense or repeated Sedative, Hypnotic, or Anxiolytic Intoxication may be associated with severe depressions that, although temporary, can be intense enough to lead to suicide attempts and completed suicides. Accidental or deliberate overdoses, similar to those observed for Alcohol Abuse or Dependence or repeated Alcohol Intoxication, can occur. In contrast to their wide margin of safety when used alone, benzodiazepines taken in combination with alcohol appear to be particularly dangerous, and accidental overdoses have been reported. Accidental overdoses have also been reported in individuals who deliberately abuse barbiturates and other nonbenzodiazepine sedatives (e.g., methaqualone). With repeated use in search of euphoria, tolerance develops to the sedative effects, and a progressively higher dose is used. However, tolerance to brain stem depressant effects develops much more slowly, and as the person takes more substance to achieve euphoria, there may be a sudden onset of respiratory depression and hypotension, which may result in death. Antisocial behavior and Antisocial Personality Disorder are associated with Sedative, Hypnotic, or Anxiolytic Dependence and Abuse, especially when the substances are obtained illegally.

Associated laboratory findings.   Almost all of these substances can be identified through laboratory evaluations of urine or blood (which can quantify the amounts of these agents in the body). Urine tests are likely to remain positive for up to a week or so after the use of long-acting substances (e.g., flurazepam).

Associated physical examination findings and general medical conditions.
Physical examination is likely to reveal evidence of a mild decrease in most aspects of autonomic nervous system functioning, including a slower pulse, a slightly decreased respiratory rate, and a slight drop in blood pressure (most likely to occur with postural changes). Overdoses of sedatives, hypnotics, and anxiolytics may be associated with a deterioration in vital signs that may signal an impending medical emergency (e.g., respiratory arrest from barbiturates). There may be consequences of trauma (e.g., internal bleeding or a subdural hematoma) from accidents that occur while intoxicated. Intravenous use of these substances can result in medical complications related to the use of contaminated needles (e.g., hepatitis and human immunodeficiency virus [HIV] infection).

Specific Culture, Age, and Gender Features

There are marked variations in prescription patterns (and availability) of this class of substances in different countries, which may lead to variations in prevalence of Sedative-, Hypnotic-, or Anxiolytic-Related Disorders. Deliberate Intoxication to achieve a "high" is most likely to be observed in teenagers and individuals in their 20s. Withdrawal, Dependence, and Abuse are also seen in individuals in their 40s and older who escalate the dose of prescribed medications. Both acute and chronic toxic effects of these substances, especially effects on cognition, memory, and motor coordination, are likely to increase with age as a consequence of pharmacodynamic and pharmacokinetic age-related changes. Individuals with dementia are more likely to develop Intoxication and impaired physiological functioning at lower doses. Women may be at higher risk for prescription drug abuse of substances of this class.

Prevalence

In the United States, up to 90% of individuals hospitalized for medical care or surgery receive orders for sedative, hypnotic, or anxiolytic medications during their hospital stay, and more than 15% of American adults use these medications (usually by prescription) during any 1 year. Most of these individuals take the medication as directed, without evidence of misuse. Among the medications in this class, the benzodiazepines are the most widely used, with perhaps 10% of adults having taken a benzodiazepine for at least 1 month during the prior year. A community survey conducted in the United States in 1991 reported that about 4% of the population sampled had ever used sedatives for nonmedical purposes; approximately 1% had such use in the last year; and 0.4% in the last month. For antianxiety agents, around 6% of the population had ever used them for nonmedical purposes; almost 2% had such use in the last year; and 0.5% in the last month. Because the survey assessed patterns of use rather than diagnoses, it is not known how many of those who used substances from this class had symptoms that met criteria for Dependence or Abuse. A community study conducted in the United States from 1980 to 1985 that used the more narrowly defined DSM-III criteria found that 1.1% of the population surveyed had met criteria for Sedative, Hypnotic, or Anxiolytic Abuse or Dependence at some time in their lives.

Course

The more usual course involves young people in their teens or 20s who may escalate their "recreational" use of sedatives, hypnotics, and anxiolytics to the point at which they develop problems that might qualify for a diagnosis of Dependence or Abuse. This pattern may be especially likely among individuals who have other Substance Use Disorders (e.g., related to alcohol, opioids, cocaine, amphetamine). An initial pattern of intermittent use at parties can lead to daily use and high levels of tolerance. Once this occurs, an increasing level of interpersonal, work, and legal difficulties, as well as increasingly severe episodes of memory impairment and physiological withdrawal, can be expected to ensue.

   The second and less frequently observed clinical course begins with an individual who originally obtained the medication by prescription from a physician, usually for the treatment of anxiety, insomnia, or somatic complaints. Although the great majority of those who are prescribed a medication from this class do not develop problems, a small proportion do. In these individuals, as either tolerance or a need for higher doses of the medication develops, there is a gradual increase in the dose and frequency of self-administration. The person is likely to continue to justify use on the basis of the original symptoms of anxiety or insomnia, but substance-seeking behavior becomes more prominent and the person may seek out multiple physicians to obtain sufficient supplies of the medication. Tolerance can reach high levels, and Withdrawal (including seizures and Withdrawal Delirium) may occur. Other individuals at heightened risk might include those with Alcohol Dependence who may receive repeated prescriptions in response to their complaints of alcohol-related anxiety or insomnia.

Differential Diagnosis

For a general discussion of the differential diagnosis of Substance-Related Disorders, see p. 190. Sedative-, Hypnotic-, or Anxiolytic-Induced Disorders may present with symptoms (e.g., anxiety) that resemble **primary mental disorders** (e.g., Generalized Anxiety Disorder versus Sedative-, Hypnotic-, or Anxiolytic-Induced Anxiety Disorder, With Onset During Withdrawal). See p. 193 for a discussion of this differential diagnosis.

Sedative, Hypnotic, or Anxiolytic Intoxication closely resembles **Alcohol Intoxication,** except for the smell of alcohol on the breath. In older persons, the clinical picture of intoxication can resemble a **progressive dementia.** In addition, the slurred speech, incoordination, and other associated features characteristic of Sedative, Hypnotic, or Anxiolytic Intoxication could be the result of a **general medical condition** (e.g., multiple sclerosis) or of a **prior head trauma** (e.g., a subdural hematoma).

Alcohol Withdrawal produces a syndrome very similar to that of Sedative, Hypnotic, or Anxiolytic Withdrawal. The anxiety, insomnia, and autonomic nervous system hyperactivity that is a consequence of **intoxication with other drugs** (e.g., stimulants such as amphetamines or cocaine), that are **consequences of physiological conditions** (e.g., hyperthyroidism), or that are related to **primary Anxiety Disorders** (e.g., Panic Disorder or Generalized Anxiety Disorder) can resemble some aspects of Sedative, Hypnotic, or Anxiolytic Withdrawal.

Sedative, Hypnotic, or Anxiolytic Intoxication and Withdrawal are distinguished from the **other Sedative-, Hypnotic-, or Anxiolytic-Induced Disorders** (e.g., Sedative-, Hypnotic-, or Anxiolytic-Induced Anxiety Disorder, With Onset During Withdrawal) because the symptoms in these latter disorders are in excess of those usually associated with Sedative, Hypnotic, or Anxiolytic Intoxication or Withdrawal and are severe enough to warrant independent clinical attention.

It should be noted that there are individuals who continue to take benzodiazepine medication according to a physician's direction for a legitimate medical indication over extended periods of time. Even if physiologically dependent on the medication, many of these individuals do not develop symptoms that meet the criteria for Dependence because they are not preoccupied with obtaining the substance and its use does not interfere with their performance of usual social or occupational roles.

292.9   Sedative-, Hypnotic-, or Anxiolytic-Related Disorder Not Otherwise Specified

The Sedative-, Hypnotic-, or Anxiolytic-Related Disorder Not Otherwise Specified category is for disorders associated with the use of sedatives, hypnotics, or anxiolytics that are not classifiable as Sedative, Hypnotic, or Anxiolytic Dependence; Sedative, Hypnotic, or Anxiolytic Abuse; Sedative, Hypnotic, or Anxiolytic Intoxication; Sedative, Hypnotic, or Anxiolytic Withdrawal; Sedative, Hypnotic, or Anxiolytic Intoxication Delirium; Sedative, Hypnotic, or Anxiolytic Withdrawal Delirium; Sedative-, Hypnotic-, or Anxiolytic-Induced Persisting Dementia; Sedative-, Hypnotic-, or Anxiolytic-Induced Persisting Amnestic Disorder; Sedative-, Hypnotic-, or Anxiolytic-Induced Psychotic Disorder; Sedative-, Hypnotic-, or Anxiolytic-Induced Mood Disorder; Sedative-, Hypnotic-, or Anxiolytic-Induced Anxiety Disorder; Sedative-, Hypnotic-, or Anxiolytic-Induced Sexual Dysfunction; or Sedative-, Hypnotic-, or Anxiolytic-Induced Sleep Disorder.

Polysubstance-Related Disorder

304.80   Polysubstance Dependence

This diagnosis is reserved for behavior during the same 12-month period in which the person was repeatedly using at least three groups of substances (not including caffeine and nicotine), but no single substance predominated. Further, during this period, the Dependence criteria were met for substances as a group but not for any specific substance.

Other (or Unknown) Substance–Related Disorders

The Other (or Unknown) Substance–Related Disorders category is for classifying Substance-Related Disorders associated with substances not listed above. Examples of these substances, which are described in more detail below, include anabolic steroids, nitrite inhalants ("poppers"), nitrous oxide, over-the-counter and prescription medications not otherwise covered by the 11 categories (e.g., cortisol, antihistamines, benztropine), and other substances that have psychoactive effects. In addition, this category may be used when the specific substance is unknown (e.g., an intoxication after taking a bottle of unlabeled pills).

Anabolic steroids sometimes produce an initial sense of enhanced well-being (or even euphoria), which is replaced after repeated use by lack of energy, irritability, and other forms of dysphoria. Continued use of these substances may lead to more severe symptoms (e.g., depressive symptomatology) and general medical conditions (liver disease).

Nitrite inhalants ("poppers"—forms of amyl, butyl, and isobutyl nitrite) produce an intoxication that is characterized by a feeling of fullness in the head, mild euphoria, a change in the perception of time, relaxation of smooth muscles, and a possible increase in sexual feelings. In addition to possible compulsive use, these substances carry dangers of potential impairment of immune functioning, irritation of the respiratory system, a decrease in the oxygen-carrying capacity of the blood, and a toxic reaction that can include vomiting, severe headache, hypotension, and dizziness.

Nitrous oxide ("laughing gas") causes rapid onset of an intoxication that is characterized by light-headedness and a floating sensation that clears in a matter of minutes after administration is stopped. There are reports of temporary but clinically relevant confusion and reversible paranoid states when nitrous oxide is used regularly.

Other substances that are capable of producing mild intoxications include **catnip,** which can produce states similar to those observed with marijuana and which in high doses is reported to result in LSD-type perceptions; **betel nut,** which is chewed in many cultures to produce a mild euphoria and floating sensation; and **kava** (a substance derived from the South Pacific pepper plant), which produces sedation, incoordination, weight loss, mild forms of hepatitis, and lung abnormalities. In addition, individuals can develop dependence and impairment through repeated self-administration of **over-the-counter** and **prescription drugs,** including **cortisol, antiparkinsonian agents** that have anticholinergic properties, and **antihistamines.** A discussion of how to code medication-related disorders is found on p. 188.

Texts and criteria sets have already been provided to define the generic aspects of Substance Dependence (p. 176), Substance Abuse (p. 182), Substance Intoxication (p. 183), and Substance Withdrawal (p. 184) that are applicable across classes of substances. The Other (or Unknown) Substance–Induced Disorders are described in the sections of the manual with disorders with which they share phenomenology (e.g., Other (or Unknown) Substance–Induced Mood Disorder is included in the "Mood Disorders" section). Listed below are the Other (or Unknown) Substance Use Disorders and the Other (or Unknown) Substance–Induced Disorders.

Other (or Unknown) Substance Use Disorders

304.90   Other (or Unknown) Substance Dependence (see p. 176)
305.90   Other (or Unknown) Substance Abuse (see p. 182)

Other (or Unknown) Substance–Induced Disorders

292.89   Other (or Unknown) Substance Intoxication (see p. 183)
            Specify if: With Perceptual Disturbances
292.0   Other (or Unknown) Substance Withdrawal (see p. 184)
            Specify if: With Perceptual Disturbances
292.81   Other (or Unknown) Substance-Induced Delirium (see p. 129)
292.82   Other (or Unknown) Substance–Induced Persisting Dementia
            (see p. 152)
**292.83   Other (or Unknown) Substance–Induced Persisting Amnestic
            Disorder** (see p. 161)
**292.11   Other (or Unknown) Substance–Induced Psychotic Disorder,
            With Delusions** (see p. 310) *Specify if:* With Onset During Intoxication/
            With Onset During Withdrawal
**292.12   Other (or Unknown) Substance–Induced Psychotic Disorder,
            With Hallucinations** (see p. 310)
            Specify if: With Onset During Intoxication/With Onset During Withdrawal
292.84   Other (or Unknown) Substance–Induced Mood Disorder (see p. 370)
            Specify if: With Onset During Intoxication/With Onset During Withdrawal

292.89   Other (or Unknown) Substance–Induced Anxiety Disorder (see p. 439)
Specify if: With Onset During Intoxication/With Onset During Withdrawal

292.89   Other (or Unknown) Substance–Induced Sexual Dysfunction
(see p. 519) *Specify if:* With Onset During Intoxication

292.89   Other (or Unknown) Substance–Induced Sleep Disorder (see p. 601)
Specify if: With Onset During Intoxication/With Onset During Withdrawal

**292.9   Other (or Unknown) Substance–Related Disorder
Not Otherwise Specified**

Schizophrenia and Other Psychotic Disorders

The disorders included in this section are all characterized by having psychotic symptoms as the defining feature. Other disorders that may present with psychotic symptoms (but not as defining features) are included elsewhere in the manual (e.g., Dementia of the Alzheimer's Type and Substance-Induced Delirium in the "Delirium, Dementia, and Amnestic and Other Cognitive Disorders" section; Major Depressive Disorder, With Psychotic Features, in the "Mood Disorders" section).

The term *psychotic* has historically received a number of different definitions, none of which has achieved universal acceptance. The narrowest definition of *psychotic* is restricted to delusions or prominent hallucinations, with the hallucinations occurring in the absence of insight into their pathological nature. A slightly less restrictive definition would also include prominent hallucinations that the individual realizes are hallucinatory experiences. Broader still is a definition that also includes other positive symptoms of Schizophrenia (i.e., disorganized speech, grossly disorganized or catatonic behavior). Unlike these definitions based on symptoms, the definition used in earlier classifications (e.g., DSM-II and ICD-9) was probably far too inclusive and focused on the severity of functional impairment, so that a mental disorder was termed "psychotic" if it resulted in "impairment that grossly interferes with the capacity to meet ordinary demands of life." Finally, the term has been defined conceptually as a loss of ego boundaries or a gross impairment in reality testing. The different disorders in this section emphasize different aspects of the various definitions of *psychotic*. In Schizophrenia, Schizophreniform Disorder, Schizoaffective Disorder, and Brief Psychotic Disorder, the term *psychotic* refers to delusions, any prominent hallucinations, disorganized speech, or disorganized or catatonic behavior. In Psychotic Disorder Due to a General Medical Condition and in Substance-Induced Psychotic Disorder, *psychotic* refers to delusions or only those hallucinations that are not accompanied by insight. Finally, in Delusional Disorder and Shared Psychotic Disorder, *psychotic* is equivalent to delusional.

The following disorders are included in this section:

Schizophrenia is a disturbance that lasts for at least 6 months and includes at least 1 month of active-phase symptoms (i.e., two [or more] of the following: delusions, hallucinations, disorganized speech, grossly disorganized or catatonic behavior, negative symptoms). Definitions for the Schizophrenia subtypes (Paranoid, Disorganized, Catatonic, Undifferentiated, and Residual) are also included in this section.

Schizophreniform Disorder is characterized by a symptomatic presentation that is equivalent to Schizophrenia except for its duration (i.e., the disturbance lasts from 1 to 6 months) and the absence of a requirement that there be a decline in functioning.

Schizoaffective Disorder is a disturbance in which a mood episode and the active-phase symptoms of Schizophrenia occur together and were preceded or are followed by at least 2 weeks of delusions or hallucinations without prominent mood symptoms.

Delusional Disorder is characterized by at least 1 month of nonbizarre delusions without other active-phase symptoms of Schizophrenia.

Brief Psychotic Disorder is a psychotic disturbance that lasts more than 1 day and remits by 1 month.

Shared Psychotic Disorder is a disturbance that develops in an individual who is influenced by someone else who has an established delusion with similar content.

In **Psychotic Disorder Due to a General Medical Condition,** the psychotic symptoms are judged to be a direct physiological consequence of a general medical condition.

In **Substance-Induced Psychotic Disorder,** the psychotic symptoms are judged to be a direct physiological consequence of a drug of abuse, a medication, or toxin exposure.

Psychotic Disorder Not Otherwise Specified is included for classifying psychotic presentations that do not meet the criteria for any of the specific Psychotic Disorders defined in this section or psychotic symptomatology about which there is inadequate or contradictory information.

Schizophrenia

The essential features of Schizophrenia are a mixture of characteristic signs and symptoms (both positive and negative) that have been present for a significant portion of time during a 1-month period (or for a shorter time if successfully treated), with some signs of the disorder persisting for at least 6 months (Criteria A and C). These signs and symptoms are associated with marked social or occupational dysfunction (Criterion B). The disturbance is not better accounted for by Schizoaffective Disorder or a Mood Disorder With Psychotic Features and is not due to the direct physiological effects of a substance or a general medical condition (Criteria D and E). In individuals with a previous diagnosis of Autistic Disorder (or another Pervasive Developmental Disorder), the additional diagnosis of Schizophrenia is warranted only if prominent delusions or hallucinations are present for at least a month (Criterion F). The characteristic symptoms of Schizophrenia involve a range of cognitive and emotional dysfunctions that include perception, inferential thinking, language and communication, behavioral monitoring, affect, fluency and productivity of thought and speech, hedonic capacity, volition and drive, and attention. No single symptom is pathognomonic of Schizophrenia; the diagnosis involves the recognition of a constellation of signs and symptoms associated with impaired occupational or social functioning.

Characteristic symptoms (Criterion A) may be conceptualized as falling into two broad categories—positive and negative. The positive symptoms appear to reflect an excess or distortion of normal functions, whereas the negative symptoms appear to reflect a diminution or loss of normal functions. The positive symptoms (Criteria A1–A4) include distortions or exaggerations of inferential thinking (delusions), perception (hallucinations), language and communication (disorganized speech), and behavioral monitoring (grossly disorganized or catatonic behavior). These positive symptoms may comprise two distinct dimensions, which may in turn be related to different underlying neural mechanisms and clinical correlations: the "psychotic dimension" includes delusions and hallucinations, whereas the "disorganization dimension" includes disorganized speech and behavior. Negative symptoms (Criterion A5) include restrictions in the range and intensity of emotional expression (affective flattening), in the fluency and productivity of thought and speech (alogia), and in the initiation of goal-directed behavior (avolition).

Delusions (Criterion A1) are erroneous beliefs that usually involve a misinterpretation of perceptions or experiences. Their content may include a variety of themes (e.g., persecutory, referential, somatic, religious, or grandiose). Persecutory delusions are most common; the person believes he or she is being tormented, followed, tricked, spied on, or subjected to ridicule. Referential delusions are also common; the person believes that certain gestures, comments, passages from books, newspapers, song lyrics, or other environmental cues are specifically directed at him or her. The distinction between a delusion and a strongly held idea is sometimes difficult to make and depends on the degree of conviction with which the belief is held despite clear contradictory evidence.

Although bizarre delusions are considered to be especially characteristic of Schizophrenia, "bizarreness" may be difficult to judge, especially across different cultures. Delusions are deemed bizarre if they are clearly implausible and not understandable and do not derive from ordinary life experiences. An example of a bizarre delusion is a person's belief that a stranger has removed his or her internal organs and has replaced them with someone else's organs without leaving any wounds or scars. An example of a nonbizarre delusion is a person's false belief that he or she is under surveillance by the police. Delusions that express a loss of control over mind or body (i.e., those included among Schneider's list of "first-rank symptoms") are generally considered to be bizarre; these include a person's belief that his or her thoughts have been taken away by some outside force ("thought withdrawal"), that alien thoughts have been put into his or her mind ("thought insertion"), or that his or her body or actions are being acted on or manipulated by some outside force ("delusions of control"). If the delusions are judged to be bizarre, only this single symptom is needed to satisfy Criterion A for Schizophrenia.

Hallucinations (Criterion A2) may occur in any sensory modality (e.g., auditory, visual, olfactory, gustatory, and tactile), but auditory hallucinations are by far the most common and characteristic of Schizophrenia. Auditory hallucinations are usually experienced as voices, whether familiar or unfamiliar, that are perceived as distinct from the person's own thoughts. The content may be quite variable, although pejorative or threatening voices are especially common. Certain types of auditory hallucinations (i.e., two or more voices conversing with one another or voices maintaining a running commentary on the person's thoughts or behavior) have been considered to be particularly characteristic of Schizophrenia and were included among Schneider's list of first-rank symptoms. If these types of hallucinations are present, then only this single symptom is needed to satisfy Criterion A. The hallucinations must occur in the context of a clear sensorium; those that occur while falling asleep (hypnagogic) or waking up (hypnopompic) are considered to be within the range of normal experience. Isolated experiences of hearing one's name called or experiences that lack the quality of an external percept (e.g., a humming in one's head) are also not considered to be hallucinations characteristic of Schizophrenia. Hallucinations may also be a normal part of religious experience in certain cultural contexts.

Disorganized thinking ("formal thought disorder," "loosening of associations") has been argued by some (Bleuler, in particular) to be the single most important feature of Schizophrenia. Because of the difficulty inherent in developing an objective definition of "thought disorder," and because in a clinical setting inferences about thought are based primarily on the individual's speech, the concept of disorganized speech (Criterion A3) has been emphasized in the definition for Schizophrenia used in this manual. The speech of individuals with Schizophrenia may be disorganized in a variety of ways. The person may "slip off the track" from one topic to another ("derailment" or "loose associations"); answers to questions may be obliquely related or completely unrelated ("tangentiality"); and, rarely, speech may be so severely disorganized that it is nearly incomprehensible and resembles receptive aphasia in its linguistic disorganization ("incoherence" or "word salad"). Because mildly disorganized speech is common and nonspecific, the symptom must be severe enough to substantially impair effective communication. Less severe disorganized thinking or speech may occur during the prodromal and residual periods of Schizophrenia (see Criterion C).

Grossly disorganized behavior (Criterion A4) may manifest itself in a variety of ways, ranging from childlike silliness to unpredictable agitation. Problems may be noted in any form of goal-directed behavior, leading to difficulties in performing activities of daily living such as organizing meals or maintaining hygiene. The person may appear markedly disheveled, may dress in an unusual manner (e.g., wearing multiple overcoats, scarves, and gloves on a hot day), or may display clearly inappropriate sexual behavior (e.g., public masturbation) or unpredictable and untriggered agitation (e.g., shouting or swearing). Care should be taken not to apply this criterion too broadly. Grossly disorganized behavior must be distinguished from behavior that is merely aimless or generally unpurposeful and from organized behavior that is motivated by delusional beliefs. Similarly, a few instances of restless, angry, or agitated behavior should not be considered to be evidence of Schizophrenia, especially if the motivation is understandable.

Catatonic motor behaviors (Criterion A4) include a marked decrease in reactivity to the environment, sometimes reaching an extreme degree of complete unawareness (catatonic stupor), maintaining a rigid posture and resisting efforts to be moved (catatonic rigidity), active resistance to instructions or attempts to be moved (catatonic negativism), the assumption of inappropriate or bizarre postures (catatonic posturing), or purposeless and unstimulated excessive motor activity (catatonic excitement). Although catatonia has historically been associated with Schizophrenia, the clinician should keep in mind that catatonic symptoms are nonspecific and may occur in other mental disorders (see Mood Disorders With Catatonic Features, p. 382), in general medical conditions (see Catatonic Disorder Due to a General Medical Condition, p. 169), and Medication-Induced Movement Disorders (see Neuroleptic-Induced Parkinsonism, p. 736).

The negative symptoms of Schizophrenia (Criterion A5) account for a substantial degree of the morbidity associated with the disorder. Three negative symptoms—affective flattening, alogia, and avolition—are included in the definition of Schizophrenia; other negative symptoms (e.g., anhedonia) are noted in the "Associated Features and Disorders" section below. Affective flattening is especially common and is characterized by the person's face appearing immobile and unresponsive, with poor eye contact and reduced body language. Although a person with affective flattening may smile and warm up occasionally, his or her range of emotional expressiveness is clearly diminished most of the time. It may be useful to observe the person interacting with peers to determine whether affective flattening is sufficiently persistent to meet the criterion. Alogia (poverty of speech) is manifested by brief, laconic, empty replies. The individual with alogia appears to have a diminution of thoughts that is reflected in decreased fluency and productivity of speech. This must be differentiated from an unwillingness to speak, a clinical judgment that may require observation over time and in a variety of situations. Avolition is characterized by an inability to initiate and persist in goal-directed activities. The person may sit for long periods of time and show little interest in participating in work or social activities.

Although quite ubiquitous in Schizophrenia, negative symptoms are difficult to evaluate because they occur on a continuum with normality, are nonspecific, and may be due to a variety of other factors (e.g., as a consequence of positive symptoms, medication side effects, a Mood Disorder, environmental understimulation, or demoralization). Social isolation or impoverished speech may not be best conceived of as negative symptoms if they occur as a consequence of a positive symptom (e.g., a paranoid delusion or a prominent hallucination). For example, the behavior of an individual who has the delusional belief that he will be in danger if he leaves his room or talks to anyone may mimic alogia and avolition. Neuroleptic medications often produce extrapyramidal side effects that closely resemble affective flattening or avolition. The distinction between true negative symptoms and medication side effects depends on clinical judgment concerning the severity of negative symptoms, the nature and type of neuroleptic medication, the effects of dosage adjustment, and the effects of anticholinergic medications. The difficult distinction between negative symptoms and depressive symptoms may be informed by the other accompanying symptoms that are present and the fact that individuals with symptoms of depression typically experience an intense painful affect, whereas those with Schizophrenia have a diminution or emptiness of affect. Finally, chronic environmental understimulation or demoralization may result in learned apathy and avolition. In establishing the presence of negative symptoms, perhaps the best test is their persistence for a considerable period of time despite efforts directed at resolving each of the potential causes described above. It has been suggested that enduring negative symptoms be referred to as "deficit" symptoms.

Criterion A for Schizophrenia requires that at least two of the five items be present concurrently for much of at least 1 month. However, if delusions are bizarre or hallucinations involve "voices commenting" or "voices conversing," then the presence of only one item is required. The presence of this relatively severe constellation of signs and symptoms is referred to as the "active phase." In those situations in which the active-phase symptoms remit within a month in response to treatment, Criterion A can still be considered to have been met if the clinician judges that the symptoms would have persisted for a month in the absence of effective treatment. In children, evaluation of the characteristic symptoms should include due consideration of the presence of other disorders or developmental difficulties. For example, the disorganized speech in a child with a Communication Disorder should not count toward a diagnosis of Schizophrenia unless the degree of disorganization is significantly greater than would be expected on the basis of the Communication Disorder alone.

Schizophrenia involves dysfunction in one or more major areas of functioning (e.g., interpersonal relations, work or education, or self-care) (Criterion B). Typically, functioning is clearly below that which had been achieved before the onset of symptoms. If the disturbance begins in childhood or adolescence, however, there may be a failure to achieve what would have been expected for the individual rather than a deterioration in functioning. Comparing the individual with unaffected siblings may be helpful in making this determination. Educational progress is frequently disrupted, and the individual may be unable to finish school. Many individuals are unable to hold a job for sustained periods of time and are employed at a lower level than their parents ("downward drift"). The majority (60%–70%) of individuals with Schizophrenia do not marry, and most have relatively limited social contacts. The dysfunction persists for a substantial period during the course of the disorder and does not appear to be a direct result of any single feature. For example, if a woman quits her job because of the circumscribed delusion that her boss is trying to kill her, this alone is not sufficient evidence for this criterion unless there is a more pervasive pattern of difficulties (usually in multiple domains of functioning).

Some signs of the disturbance must persist for a continuous period of at least 6 months (Criterion C). During that time period, there must be at least 1 month of symptoms (or less than 1 month if symptoms are successfully treated) that meet Criterion A of Schizophrenia (the active phase). Prodromal symptoms are often present prior to the active phase, and residual symptoms may follow it. Some prodromal and residual symptoms are relatively mild or subthreshold forms of the positive symptoms specified in Criterion A. Individuals may express a variety of unusual or odd beliefs that are not of delusional proportions (e.g., ideas of reference or magical thinking); they may have unusual perceptual experiences (e.g., sensing the presence of an unseen person or force in the absence of formed hallucinations); their speech may be generally understandable but digressive, vague, or overly abstract or concrete; and their behavior may be peculiar but not grossly disorganized (e.g., mumbling to themselves, collecting odd and apparently worthless objects). In addition to these positive-like symptoms, negative symptoms are particularly common in the prodromal and residual phases and can often be quite severe. Individuals who had been socially active may become withdrawn; they lose interest in previously pleasurable activities; they may become less talkative and inquisitive; and they may spend the bulk of their time in bed. Such negative symptoms are often the first sign to the family that something is wrong; family members may ultimately report that they experienced the individual as "gradually slipping away."

Subtypes and Course Specifiers

The diagnosis of a particular subtype is based on the clinical picture that occasioned the most recent evaluation or admission to clinical care and may therefore change over time. Separate text and criteria are provided for each of the following subtypes:

295.30 Paranoid Type (see p. 287)
295.10 Disorganized Type (see p. 287)
295.20 Catatonic Type (see p. 288)
295.90 Undifferentiated Type (see p. 289)
295.60 Residual Type (see p. 289)

The following specifiers may be used to indicate the characteristic course of symptoms of Schizophrenia over time. These specifiers can be applied only after at least 1 year has elapsed since the initial onset of active-phase symptoms. During this initial 1-year period, no course specifiers can be given.

Episodic With Interepisode Residual Symptoms. This specifier applies when the course is characterized by episodes in which Criterion A for Schizophrenia is met and there are clinically significant residual symptoms between the episodes. **With Prominent Negative Symptoms** can be added if prominent negative symptoms are present during these residual periods.

Episodic With No Interepisode Residual Symptoms. This specifier applies when the course is characterized by episodes in which Criterion A for Schizophrenia is met and there are no clinically significant residual symptoms between the episodes.
Continuous. This specifier applies when characteristic symptoms of Criterion A are met throughout all (or most) of the course. **With Prominent Negative Symptoms** can be added if prominent negative symptoms are also present.
Single Episode In Partial Remission. This specifier applies when there has been a single episode in which Criterion A for Schizophrenia is met and some clinically significant residual symptoms remain. **With Prominent Negative Symptoms** can be added if these residual symptoms include prominent negative symptoms.
Single Episode In Full Remission. This specifier applies when there has been a single episode in which Criterion A for Schizophrenia has been met and no clinically significant residual symptoms remain.
Other or Unspecified Pattern. This specifier is used if another or an unspecified course pattern has been present.

Recording Procedures

The diagnostic code for Schizophrenia is selected based on the appropriate subtype: 295.30 for Paranoid Type, 295.10 for Disorganized Type, 295.20 for Catatonic Type, 295.90 for Undifferentiated Type, and 295.60 for Residual Type. There are no fifth-digit codes available for the course specifiers. In recording the name of the disorder, the course specifiers are noted after the appropriate subtype (e.g., 295.30 Schizophrenia, Paranoid Type, Episodic With Interepisode Residual Symptoms, With Prominent Negative Symptoms).

Associated Features and Disorders

Associated descriptive features and mental disorders. The individual with Schizophrenia may display inappropriate affect (e.g., smiling, laughing, or a silly facial expression in the absence of an appropriate stimulus), which is one of the defining features of the Disorganized Type. Anhedonia is common and is manifested by a loss of interest or pleasure. Dysphoric mood may take the form of depression, anxiety, or anger. There may be disturbances in sleep pattern (e.g., sleeping during the day and nighttime activity or restlessness). The individual may show a lack of interest in eating or may refuse food as a consequence of delusional beliefs. Often there are abnormalities of psychomotor activity (e.g., pacing, rocking, or apathetic immobility). Difficulty concentrating is frequently evident and may reflect problems with focusing attention or distractibility due to preoccupation with internal stimuli. Although basic intellectual functions are classically considered to be intact in Schizophrenia, some indications of cognitive dysfunction are often present. The individual may be confused or disoriented or may have memory impairment during a period of exacerbation of active symptoms or in the presence of very severe negative symptoms. Lack of insight is common and may be one of the best predictors of poor outcome, perhaps because it predisposes the individual to noncompliance with treatment. Depersonalization, derealization, and somatic concerns may occur and sometimes reach delusional proportions. Motor abnormalities (e.g., grimacing, posturing, odd mannerisms, ritualistic or stereotyped behavior) are sometimes present. The life expectancy of individuals with Schizophrenia is shorter than that of the general population for a variety of reasons. Suicide is an important factor, because approximately 10% of individuals with Schizophrenia commit suicide. Risk factors for suicide include being male, age under 30 years, depressive symptoms, unemployment, and recent hospital discharge. There is conflicting evidence with regard to whether the frequency of violent acts is greater than in the general population. Comorbidity with Substance-Related Disorders (including Nicotine Dependence) is common. Schizotypal, Schizoid, or Paranoid Personality Disorder may sometimes precede the onset of Schizophrenia. Whether these Personality Disorders are simply prodromal to Schizophrenia or whether they constitute a separate earlier disorder is not clear.

Associated laboratory findings.   No laboratory findings have been identified that are diagnostic of Schizophrenia. However, a variety of laboratory findings have been noted to be abnormal in groups of individuals with Schizophrenia relative to control subjects. Structural abnormalities in the brain have consistently been demonstrated in individuals with Schizophrenia as a group; the most common structural abnormalities include enlargement of the ventricular system and prominent sulci in the cortex. A variety of other abnormalities have also been noted using structural imaging techniques (e.g., decreased temporal and hippocampal size, increased size of the basal ganglia, decreased cerebral size). Functional imaging techniques have indicated that some individuals may have abnormal cerebral blood flow or glucose utilization in specific brain regions (e.g., prefrontal cortex). Neuropsychological assessments may show a broad range of dysfunctions (e.g., difficulty in changing response set, focusing attention, formulating abstract concepts). Neurophysiological findings include a slowing in reaction times, abnormalities in eye tracking, or impairments in sensory gating. Abnormal laboratory findings may also be noted as either a complication of Schizophrenia or of its treatment. Some individuals with Schizophrenia drink excessive amounts of fluid ("water intoxication") and develop abnormalities in urine specific gravity or electrolyte imbalances. Elevated creatine phosphokinase (CPK) may result from Neuroleptic Malignant Syndrome (see p. 739).

Associated physical examination findings and general medical conditions. Individuals with Schizophrenia are sometimes physically awkward and may display neurological "soft signs," such as left/right confusion, poor coordination, or mirroring. Some minor physical anomalies (e.g., highly arched palate, narrow- or wide-set eyes or subtle malformations of the ears) may be more common among individuals with Schizophrenia. Perhaps the most common associated physical findings are motor abnormalities. Most of these are likely to be related to side effects from treatment with antipsychotic medications. Motor abnormalities that are secondary to neuroleptic treatment include Neuroleptic-Induced Tardive Dyskinesia (see p. 747), Neuroleptic-Induced Parkinsonism (see p. 736), Neuroleptic-Induced Acute Akathisia (see p. 744), Neuroleptic-Induced Acute Dystonia (see p. 742), and Neuroleptic Malignant Syndrome (see p. 739). Spontaneous motor abnormalities resembling those that may be induced by neuroleptics (e.g., sniffing, tongue clucking, grunting) had been described in the preneuroleptic era and are also still observed, although they may be difficult to distinguish from neuroleptic effects. Other physical findings may be related to frequently associated disorders. For example, because Nicotine Dependence is so common in

Schizophrenia, these individuals are more likely to develop cigarette-related pathology (e.g., emphysema and other pulmonary and cardiac problems).

Specific Culture, Age, and Gender Features

Clinicians assessing the symptoms of Schizophrenia in socioeconomic or cultural situations that are different from their own must take cultural differences into account. Ideas that may appear to be delusional in one culture (e.g., sorcery and witchcraft) may be commonly held in another. In some cultures, visual or auditory hallucinations with a religious content may be a normal part of religious experience (e.g., seeing the Virgin Mary or hearing God's voice). In addition, the assessment of disorganized speech may be made difficult by linguistic variation in narrative styles across cultures that affects the logical form of verbal presentation. The assessment of affect requires sensitivity to differences in styles of emotional expression, eye contact, and body language, which vary across cultures. If the assessment is conducted in a language that is different from the individual's primary language, care must be taken to ensure that alogia is not related to linguistic barriers. Because the cultural meaning of self-initiated, goal-directed activity can be expected to vary across diverse settings, disturbances of volition must also be carefully assessed. There is some evidence that clinicians may have a tendency to overdiagnose Schizophrenia (instead of Bipolar Disorder) in some ethnic groups. Cultural differences have been noted in the presentation, course, and outcome of Schizophrenia. Catatonic behavior has been reported as relatively uncommon among individuals with Schizophrenia in the United States but is more common in non-Western countries. Individuals with Schizophrenia in developing nations tend to have a more acute course and a better outcome than do individuals in industrialized nations.

The onset of Schizophrenia typically occurs between the late teens and the mid-30s, with onset prior to adolescence rare (although cases with age at onset of 5 or 6 years have been reported). The essential features of the condition are the same in children, but it may be particularly difficult to make the diagnosis in this age group. In children, delusions and hallucinations may be less elaborated than those observed in adults, and visual hallucinations may be more common. Disorganized speech is observed in a number of disorders with childhood onset (e.g., Communication Disorders, Pervasive Developmental Disorders), as is disorganized behavior (e.g., Attention-Deficit/Hyperactivity Disorder, Stereotypic Movement Disorder). These symptoms should not be attributed to Schizophrenia without due consideration of these more common disorders of childhood. Schizophrenia can also begin later in life (e.g., after age 45 years). Late-onset cases tend to be similar to earlier-onset Schizophrenia, except for a higher ratio of women, a better occupational history, and a greater frequency of having been married. The clinical presentation is more likely to include paranoid delusions and hallucinations, and less likely to include disorganized and negative symptoms. The course is usually chronic, although individuals are often quite responsive to antipsychotic medications in lower doses. Among those with the oldest age at onset (i.e., over age 60 years), sensory deficits (e.g., hearing loss) apparently occur more commonly than in the general adult population. Their specific role in pathogenesis remains unknown.

There are gender differences in the presentation and course of Schizophrenia. Women are more likely to have a later onset, more prominent mood symptoms, and a better prognosis. Although it has long been held that males and females are affected in roughly equal numbers, estimates of sex ratio are confounded by issues of ascertainment and definition. Hospital-based studies suggest a higher rate of Schizophrenia in males, whereas community-based surveys have mostly suggested an equal sex ratio. Broader definitions of Schizophrenia with respect to the boundary with Mood Disorders will yield a higher female-to-male ratio than the relatively narrow construct of Schizophrenia used in this manual.

Prevalence

There is variability in the reported prevalence of Schizophrenia because different studies have used different methods of ascertainment (e.g., rural versus urban, community versus clinic or hospital) and different definitions of Schizophrenia (narrow versus broad, criterion-based versus clinical). Estimates of prevalence have ranged from 0.2% to 2.0% across many large studies. Prevalence rates are similar throughout the world, but pockets of high prevalence have been reported in some specific areas. Taking all these sources of information into account, the lifetime prevalence of Schizophrenia is usually estimated to be between 0.5% and 1%. Because Schizophrenia tends to be chronic, incidence rates are considerably lower than prevalence rates and are estimated to be approximately 1 per 10,000 per year.

Course

The median age at onset for the first psychotic episode of Schizophrenia is in the early to mid-20s for men and in the late 20s for women. The onset may be abrupt or insidious, but the majority of individuals display some type of prodromal phase manifested by the slow and gradual development of a variety of signs and symptoms (e.g., social withdrawal, loss of interest in school or work, deterioration in hygiene and grooming, unusual behavior, outbursts of anger). Family members may find this behavior difficult to interpret and assume that the person is "going through a phase." Eventually, however, the appearance of some active-phase symptom marks the disturbance as Schizophrenia. The age at onset may have both pathophysiological and prognostic significance. Individuals with an early age at onset are more often male and have a poorer premorbid adjustment, lower educational achievement, more evidence of structural brain abnormalities, more prominent negative signs and symptoms, more evidence of cognitive impairment as assessed with neuropsychological testing, and a worse outcome. Conversely, individuals with a later onset are more often female, have less evidence of structural brain abnormalities or cognitive impairment, and display a better outcome.

Most studies of course and outcome in Schizophrenia suggest that the course may be variable, with some individuals displaying exacerbations and remissions, whereas others remain chronically ill. Because of variability in definition and ascertainment, an accurate summary of the long-term outcome of Schizophrenia is not possible. Complete remission (i.e., a return to full premorbid functioning) is probably not common in this disorder. Of those who remain ill, some appear to have a relatively stable course, whereas others show a progressive worsening associated with severe disability. Early in the illness, negative symptoms may be prominent, appearing primarily as prodromal features. Subsequently, positive symptoms appear. Because these positive symptoms are particularly responsive to treatment, they typically diminish, but in many individuals, negative symptoms persist between episodes of positive symptoms. There is some suggestion that negative symptoms may become steadily more prominent in some individuals during the course of the illness. Numerous studies have indicated a group of factors that are associated with a better prognosis. These include good premorbid adjustment, acute onset, later age at onset, being female, precipitating events, associated mood disturbance, brief duration of active-phase symptoms, good interepisode functioning, minimal residual symptoms, absence of structural brain abnormalities, normal neurological functioning, a family history of Mood Disorder, and no family history of Schizophrenia.

Familial Pattern

The first-degree biological relatives of individuals with Schizophrenia have a risk for Schizophrenia that is about 10 times greater than that of the general population. Concordance rates for Schizophrenia are higher in monozygotic twins than in dizygotic twins. Adoption studies have shown that biological relatives of individuals with Schizophrenia have a substantially increased risk for Schizophrenia, whereas adoptive relatives have no increased risk. Although much evidence suggests the importance of genetic factors in the etiology of Schizophrenia, the existence of a substantial discordance rate in monozygotic twins also indicates the importance of environmental factors.

Differential Diagnosis

A wide variety of general medical conditions can present with psychotic symptoms. **Psychotic Disorder Due to a General Medical Condition, delirium,** or **dementia** is diagnosed when there is evidence from the history, physical examination, or laboratory tests that indicates that the delusions or hallucinations are the direct physiological consequence of a general medical condition (e.g., Cushing's syndrome, brain tumor) (see p. 306). **Substance-Induced Psychotic Disorder, Substance-Induced Delirium,** and **Substance-Induced Persisting Dementia** are distinguished from Schizophrenia by the fact that a substance (e.g., a drug of abuse, a medication, or exposure to a toxin) is judged to be etiologically related to the delusions or hallucinations (see p. 310). Many different types of **Substance-Related Disorders** may produce symptoms similar to those of Schizophrenia (e.g., sustained amphetamine or cocaine use may produce delusions or hallucinations; phencyclidine use may produce a mixture of positive and negative symptoms). Based on a variety of features that characterize the course of Schizophrenia and Substance-Related Disorders, the clinician must determine whether the psychotic symptoms have been initiated and maintained by the substance use. Ideally, the clinician should attempt to observe the individual during a sustained period (e.g., 4 weeks) of abstinence. However, because such prolonged periods of abstinence are often difficult to achieve, the clinician may need to consider other evidence, such as whether the psychotic symptoms appear to be exacerbated by the substance and to diminish when it has been discontinued, the relative severity of psychotic symptoms in relation to the amount and duration of substance use, and knowledge of the characteristic symptoms produced by a particular substance (e.g., amphetamines typically produce delusions and stereotypies, but not affective blunting or prominent negative symptoms). Distinguishing Schizophrenia from **Mood Disorder With Psychotic Features** and **Schizoaffective Disorder** is made difficult by the fact that mood disturbance is common during the prodromal, active, and residual phases of Schizophrenia. If psychotic symptoms occur exclusively during periods of mood disturbance, the diagnosis is Mood Disorder With Psychotic Features. In Schizoaffective Disorder, there must be a mood episode that is concurrent with the active-phase symptoms of Schizophrenia, mood symptoms must be present for a substantial portion of the total duration of the disturbance, and delusions or hallucinations must be present for at least 2 weeks in the absence of prominent mood symptoms. In contrast, mood symptoms in Schizophrenia either have a duration that is brief in relation to the total duration of the disturbance, occur only during the prodromal or residual phases, or do not meet full criteria for a mood episode. When mood symptoms that meet full criteria for a mood episode are superimposed on Schizophrenia and are of particular clinical significance, an additional diagnosis of **Depressive Disorder Not Otherwise Specified** or **Bipolar Disorder Not Otherwise Specified** may be given. Schizophrenia, Catatonic Type, may be difficult to distinguish from a **Mood Disorder With Catatonic Features.**

By definition, Schizophrenia differs from **Schizophreniform Disorder** on the basis of duration. Schizophrenia involves the presence of symptoms (including prodromal or residual symptoms) for at least 6 months, whereas the total duration of symptoms in Schizophreniform Disorder must be at least 1 month but less than 6 months. Schizophreniform Disorder also does not require a decline in functioning. **Brief Psychotic Disorder** is defined by the presence of delusions, hallucinations, disorganized speech, or grossly disorganized or catatonic behavior lasting for at least 1 day but for less than 1 month.

The differential diagnosis between Schizophrenia and **Delusional Disorder** rests on the nature of the delusions (nonbizarre in Delusional Disorder) and the absence of other characteristic symptoms of Schizophrenia (e.g., hallucinations, disorganized speech or behavior, or prominent negative symptoms). Delusional Disorder is particularly difficult to differentiate from the Paranoid Type of Schizophrenia, because this subtype does not include prominent disorganized speech, disorganized behavior, or flat or inappropriate affect and is often associated with less decline in functioning than is characteristic of the other subtypes of Schizophrenia. When poor psychosocial functioning is present in Delusional Disorder, it arises directly from the delusional beliefs themselves.

A diagnosis of **Psychotic Disorder Not Otherwise Specified** may be made if insufficient information is available to choose between Schizophrenia and other Psychotic Disorders (e.g., Schizoaffective Disorder) or to determine whether the presenting symptoms are substance induced or are the result of a general medical condition. Such uncertainty is particularly likely to occur early in the course of the disorder.

Although Schizophrenia and **Pervasive Developmental Disorders** (e.g., Autistic Disorder) share disturbances in language, affect, and interpersonal relatedness, they can be distinguished in a number of ways. Pervasive Developmental Disorders are characteristically recognized during infancy or early childhood (usually before age 3 years), whereas such early onset is rare in Schizophrenia. Moreover, in Pervasive Developmental Disorders, there is an absence of prominent delusions and hallucinations; more pronounced abnormalities in affect; and speech that is absent or minimal and characterized by stereotypies and abnormalities in prosody. Schizophrenia may occasionally develop in individuals with a Pervasive Developmental Disorder; a diagnosis of Schizophrenia is warranted in individuals with a preexisting diagnosis of Autistic Disorder or another Pervasive Developmental Disorder only if prominent hallucinations or delusions have been present for at least a month. Childhood-onset Schizophrenia must be distinguished from **childhood presentations combining disorganized speech** (from a **Communication Disorder**) and disorganized behavior (from **Attention-Deficit/Hyperactivity Disorder**).

Schizophrenia shares features (e.g., paranoid ideation, magical thinking, social avoidance, and vague and digressive speech) with and may be preceded by **Schizotypal, Schizoid,** or **Paranoid Personality Disorder.** An additional diagnosis of Schizophrenia is appropriate when the symptoms are severe enough to satisfy Criterion A of Schizophrenia. The preexisting Personality Disorder may be noted on Axis II followed by "Premorbid" in parentheses [e.g., Schizotypal Personality Disorder (Premorbid)].

■ Diagnostic criteria for Schizophrenia

A. *Characteristic symptoms:* Two (or more) of the following, each present for a significant portion of time during a 1-month period (or less if successfully treated):

  (1)   delusions
  (2)   hallucinations
  (3)   disorganized speech (e.g., frequent derailment or incoherence)
  (4)   grossly disorganized or catatonic behavior
  (5)   negative symptoms, i.e., affective flattening, alogia, or avolition

  Note: Only one Criterion A symptom is required if delusions are bizarre or hallucinations consist of a voice keeping up a running commentary on the person's behavior or thoughts, or two or more voices conversing with each other.

B. *Social/occupational dysfunction:* For a significant portion of the time since the onset of the disturbance, one or more major areas of functioning such as work, interpersonal relations, or self-care are markedly below the level achieved prior to the onset (or when the onset is in childhood or adolescence, failure to achieve expected level of interpersonal, academic, or occupational achievement).

C. *Duration:* Continuous signs of the disturbance persist for at least 6 months. This 6-month period must include at least 1 month of symptoms (or less if successfully treated) that meet Criterion A (i.e., active-phase symptoms) and may include periods of prodromal or residual symptoms. During these prodromal or residual periods, the signs of the disturbance may be manifested by only negative symptoms or two or more symptoms listed in Criterion A present in an attenuated form (e.g., odd beliefs, unusual perceptual experiences).

D. *Schizoaffective and Mood Disorder exclusion:* Schizoaffective Disorder and Mood Disorder With Psychotic Features have been ruled out because either (1) no Major Depressive, Manic, or Mixed Episodes have occurred concurrently with the active-phase symptoms; or (2) if mood episodes have occurred during active-phase symptoms, their total

(continued)

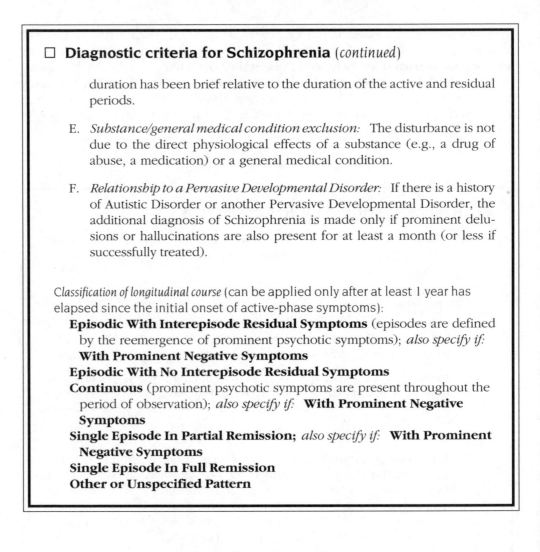

□ **Diagnostic criteria for Schizophrenia** (*continued*)

duration has been brief relative to the duration of the active and residual periods.

E. *Substance/general medical condition exclusion:* The disturbance is not due to the direct physiological effects of a substance (e.g., a drug of abuse, a medication) or a general medical condition.

F. *Relationship to a Pervasive Developmental Disorder:* If there is a history of Autistic Disorder or another Pervasive Developmental Disorder, the additional diagnosis of Schizophrenia is made only if prominent delusions or hallucinations are also present for at least a month (or less if successfully treated).

Classification of longitudinal course (can be applied only after at least 1 year has elapsed since the initial onset of active-phase symptoms):

Episodic With Interepisode Residual Symptoms (episodes are defined by the reemergence of prominent psychotic symptoms); *also specify if:*
With Prominent Negative Symptoms
Episodic With No Interepisode Residual Symptoms
Continuous (prominent psychotic symptoms are present throughout the period of observation); *also specify if:* **With Prominent Negative Symptoms**
Single Episode In Partial Remission; *also specify if:* **With Prominent Negative Symptoms**
Single Episode In Full Remission
Other or Unspecified Pattern

Schizophrenia Subtypes

The subtypes of Schizophrenia are defined by the predominant symptomatology at the time of evaluation. Although the prognostic and treatment implications of the subtypes are variable, the Paranoid and Disorganized Types tend to be the least and most severe, respectively. The diagnosis of a particular subtype is based on the clinical picture that occasioned the most recent evaluation or admission to clinical care and may therefore change over time. Not infrequently, the presentation may include symptoms that are characteristic of more than one subtype. The choice among subtypes depends on the following algorithm: Catatonic Type is assigned whenever prominent catatonic symptoms are present (regardless of the presence of other symptoms); Disorganized Type is assigned whenever disorganized speech and behavior and flat or inappropriate affect are prominent (unless Catatonic Type is also present); Paranoid Type is assigned whenever there is a preoccupation with delusions or frequent hallucinations are prominent (unless the Catatonic or Disorganized Type is present). Undifferentiated Type is a residual category describing presentations that include prominent active-phase symptoms not meeting criteria for the Catatonic, Disorganized, or Paranoid Type; and Residual Type is for presentations in which there is continuing evidence of the disturbance, but the criteria for the active-phase symptoms are no longer met.

A dimensional alternative to the traditional Schizophrenia subtypes is described in Appendix B (see p. 710). The suggested dimensions are the psychotic dimension, the disorganized dimension, and the negative dimension.

295.30   Paranoid Type

The essential feature of the Paranoid Type of Schizophrenia is the presence of prominent delusions or auditory hallucinations in the context of a relative preservation of cognitive functioning and affect. Symptoms characteristic of the Disorganized and Catatonic Types (e.g., disorganized speech, flat or inappropriate affect, catatonic or disorganized behavior) are not prominent. Delusions are typically persecutory or grandiose, or both, but delusions with other themes (e.g., jealousy, religiosity, or somatization) may also occur. The delusions may be multiple, but are usually organized around a coherent theme. Hallucinations are also typically related to the content of the delusional theme. Associated features include anxiety, anger, aloofness, and argumentativeness. The individual may have a superior and patronizing manner and either a stilted, formal quality or extreme intensity in interpersonal interactions. The persecutory themes may predispose the individual to suicidal behavior, and the combination of persecutory and grandiose delusions with anger may predispose the individual to violence. Onset tends to be later in life than the other types of Schizophrenia, and the distinguishing characteristics may be more stable over time. These individuals usually show little or no impairment on neuropsychological or other cognitive testing. Some evidence suggests that the prognosis for the Paranoid Type may be considerably better than for the other types of Schizophrenia, particularly with regard to occupational functioning and capacity for independent living.

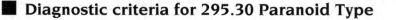 **Diagnostic criteria for 295.30 Paranoid Type**

A type of Schizophrenia in which the following criteria are met:

A.   Preoccupation with one or more delusions or frequent auditory hallucinations.

B.   None of the following is prominent: disorganized speech, disorganized or catatonic behavior, or flat or inappropriate affect.

295.10   Disorganized Type

The essential features of the Disorganized Type of Schizophrenia are disorganized speech, disorganized behavior, and flat or inappropriate affect. The disorganized speech may be accompanied by silliness and laughter that are not closely related to the content of the speech. The behavioral disorganization (i.e., lack of goal orientation) may lead to severe disruption in the ability to perform activities of daily living (e.g., showering, dressing, or preparing meals). Criteria for the Catatonic Type of Schizophrenia are not met, and delusions or hallucinations, if present, are fragmentary and not organized into a coherent theme. Associated features include grimacing, mannerisms, and other oddities of behavior. Impaired performance may be noted on a variety of neuropsychological and cognitive tests. This subtype is also usually associated with poor premorbid personality, early and insidious onset, and a continuous course without significant remissions. Historically, and in other classification systems, this type is termed *hebephrenic*.

■ Diagnostic criteria for 295.10 Disorganized Type

A type of Schizophrenia in which the following criteria are met:

A. All of the following are prominent:
    (1) disorganized speech
    (2) disorganized behavior
    (3) flat or inappropriate affect

B. The criteria are not met for Catatonic Type.

295.20   Catatonic Type

The essential feature of the Catatonic Type of Schizophrenia is a marked psychomotor disturbance that may involve motoric immobility, excessive motor activity, extreme negativism, mutism, peculiarities of voluntary movement, echolalia, or echopraxia. Motoric immobility may be manifested by catalepsy (waxy flexibility) or stupor. The excessive motor activity is apparently purposeless and is not influenced by external stimuli. There may be extreme negativism that is manifested by the maintenance of a rigid posture against attempts to be moved or resistance to all instructions. Peculiarities of voluntary movement are manifested by the voluntary assumption of inappropriate or bizarre postures or by prominent grimacing. Echolalia is the pathological, parrotlike, and apparently senseless repetition of a word or phrase just spoken by another person. Echopraxia is the repetitive imitation of the movements of another person. Additional features include stereotypies, mannerisms, and automatic obedience or mimicry. During severe catatonic stupor or excitement, the person may need careful supervision to avoid self-harm or harming others. There are potential risks from malnutrition, exhaustion, hyperpyrexia, or self-inflicted injury. To diagnose this subtype, the individual's presentation must first meet the full criteria for Schizophrenia and not be better accounted for by another etiology: substance induced (e.g., Neuroleptic-Induced Parkinsonism, see p. 736), a general medical condition (see p. 169), or a Manic or Major Depressive Episode (see p. 382).

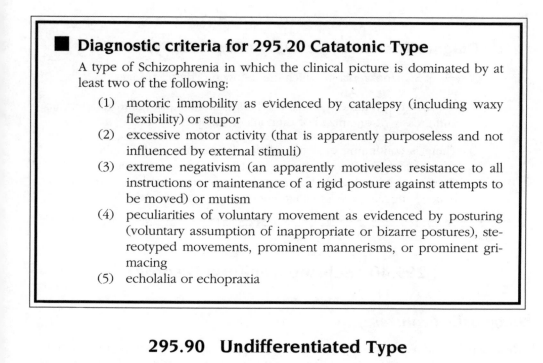

■ **Diagnostic criteria for 295.20 Catatonic Type**

A type of Schizophrenia in which the clinical picture is dominated by at least two of the following:

   (1) motoric immobility as evidenced by catalepsy (including waxy flexibility) or stupor
   (2) excessive motor activity (that is apparently purposeless and not influenced by external stimuli)
   (3) extreme negativism (an apparently motiveless resistance to all instructions or maintenance of a rigid posture against attempts to be moved) or mutism
   (4) peculiarities of voluntary movement as evidenced by posturing (voluntary assumption of inappropriate or bizarre postures), stereotyped movements, prominent mannerisms, or prominent grimacing
   (5) echolalia or echopraxia

295.90   Undifferentiated Type

The essential feature of the Undifferentiated Type of Schizophrenia is the presence of symptoms that meet Criterion A of Schizophrenia but that do not meet criteria for the Paranoid, Disorganized, or Catatonic Type.

■ **Diagnostic criteria for 295.90 Undifferentiated Type**

A type of Schizophrenia in which symptoms that meet Criterion A are present, but the criteria are not met for the Paranoid, Disorganized, or Catatonic Type.

295.60   Residual Type

The Residual Type of Schizophrenia should be used when there has been at least one episode of Schizophrenia, but the current clinical picture is without prominent positive psychotic symptoms (e.g., delusions, hallucinations, disorganized speech or behavior). There is continuing evidence of the disturbance as indicated by the presence of negative symptoms (e.g., flat affect, poverty of speech, or avolition) or two or more attenuated positive symptoms (e.g., eccentric behavior, mildly disorganized speech, or odd beliefs). If delusions or hallucinations are present, they are not prominent and are not accompanied by strong affect. The course of the Residual Type may be time limited and represent a transition between a full-blown episode and complete remission. However, it may also be continuously present for many years, with or without acute exacerbations.

■ Diagnostic criteria for 295.60 Residual Type

A type of Schizophrenia in which the following criteria are met:

A. Absence of prominent delusions, hallucinations, disorganized speech, and grossly disorganized or catatonic behavior.

B. There is continuing evidence of the disturbance, as indicated by the presence of negative symptoms or two or more symptoms listed in Criterion A for Schizophrenia, present in an attenuated form (e.g., odd beliefs, unusual perceptual experiences).

295.40   Schizophreniform Disorder

Diagnostic Features

The essential features of Schizophreniform Disorder are identical to those of Schizophrenia (Criterion A) except for two differences: the total duration of the illness (including prodromal, active, and residual phases) is at least 1 month but less than 6 months (Criterion B) and impaired social or occupational functioning during some part of the illness is not required (although it may occur). The duration requirement for Schizophreniform Disorder is intermediate between that for Brief Psychotic Disorder (in which symptoms last for at least 1 day but for less than 1 month) and Schizophrenia (in which the symptoms persist for at least 6 months). The diagnosis of Schizophreniform Disorder is made under two conditions. In the first, the diagnosis is applied without qualification to an episode of illness of between 1 and 6 months' duration from which the individual has already recovered. In the second instance, the diagnosis is applied when a person who, although symptomatic, has been so for less than the 6 months required for a diagnosis of Schizophrenia. In this case, the diagnosis of Schizophreniform Disorder should be qualified as "Provisional" because there is no certainty that the individual will actually recover from the disturbance within the 6-month period. If the disturbance persists beyond 6 months, the diagnosis would be changed to Schizophrenia.

Specifiers

The following specifiers for Schizophreniform Disorder may be used to indicate the presence or absence of features that may be associated with a better prognosis:

With Good Prognostic Features. This specifier is used if at least two of the following features are present: onset of prominent psychotic symptoms within 4 weeks of the first noticeable change in usual behavior or functioning, confusion or perplexity at the height of the psychotic episode, good premorbid social and occupational functioning, and absence of blunted or flat affect.
Without Good Prognostic Features. This specifier is used if two or more of the above features have not been present.

Associated Features and Disorders

Also see the discussion in the "Associated Features and Disorders" section for Schizophrenia, p. 279. Unlike Schizophrenia, impairment in social or occupational functioning is not required for a diagnosis of Schizophreniform Disorder. However, most individuals do experience dysfunction in various areas of daily functioning (e.g., work or school, interpersonal relationships, and self-care).

Specific Culture, Age, and Gender Features

For additional discussion of culture, age, and gender factors relevant to the diagnosis of Schizophreniform Disorder, see the "Specific Culture, Age, and Gender Features" section for Schizophrenia (p. 281). There are suggestions that in developing countries, recovery from Psychotic Disorders may be more rapid, which would result in higher rates of Schizophreniform Disorder than of Schizophrenia.

Prevalence

Community studies have reported a lifetime prevalence of Schizophreniform Disorder of around 0.2%, with a 1-year prevalence of 0.1%.

Course

There is little available information on the course of Schizophreniform Disorder. Approximately one-third of individuals with an initial diagnosis of Schizophreniform Disorder (Provisional) recover within the 6-month period and receive Schizophreniform Disorder as their final diagnosis. The remaining two-thirds will progress to the diagnosis of Schizophrenia or Schizoaffective Disorder.

Differential Diagnosis

Because the diagnostic criteria for Schizophrenia and Schizophreniform Disorder differ primarily in terms of duration of illness, the discussion of the differential diagnosis of Schizophrenia (p. 283) also applies to Schizophreniform Disorder. Schizophreniform Disorder differs from **Brief Psychotic Disorder,** which has a duration of less than 1 month.

■ **Diagnostic criteria for 295.40 Schizophreniform Disorder**

   A. Criteria A, D, and E of Schizophrenia are met.

   B. An episode of the disorder (including prodromal, active, and residual phases) lasts at least 1 month but less than 6 months. (When the diagnosis must be made without waiting for recovery, it should be qualified as "Provisional.")

(continued)

☐ **Criteria for 295.40 Schizophreniform Disorder** (*continued*)

Specify if:
Without Good Prognostic Features
With Good Prognostic Features: as evidenced by two (or more) of the
following:
   (1)   onset of prominent psychotic symptoms within 4 weeks of the first
         noticeable change in usual behavior or functioning
   (2)   confusion or perplexity at the height of the psychotic episode
   (3)   good premorbid social and occupational functioning
   (4)   absence of blunted or flat affect

295.70   Schizoaffective Disorder

Diagnostic Features

The essential feature of Schizoaffective Disorder is an uninterrupted period of illness during which, at some time, there is a Major Depressive, Manic, or Mixed Episode concurrent with symptoms that meet Criterion A for Schizophrenia (Criterion A). In addition, during the same period of illness, there have been delusions or hallucinations for at least 2 weeks in the absence of prominent mood symptoms (Criterion B). Finally, the mood symptoms are present for a substantial portion of the total duration of the illness (Criterion C). The symptoms must not be due to the direct physiological effects of a substance (e.g., cocaine) or a general medical condition (e.g., hyperthyroidism or temporal lobe epilepsy) (Criterion D). To meet criteria for Schizoaffective Disorder, the essential features must occur within a single uninterrupted period of illness. The phrase "period of illness" as used here refers to a time period during which the individual continues to display active or residual symptoms of psychotic illness. For some individuals, this period of illness may last for years or even decades. A period of illness is considered to have ended when the individual has completely recovered for a significant interval of time and no longer demonstrates any significant symptoms of the disorder.

The phase of the illness with concurrent mood and psychotic symptoms is characterized by the full criteria being met for both the active phase of Schizophrenia (i.e., Criterion A) (see p. 274) and for a Major Depressive Episode (p. 320), a Manic Episode (p. 328), or a Mixed Episode (p. 333). The duration of the Major Depressive Episode must be at least 2 weeks; the duration of the Manic or Mixed Episode must be at least 1 week. Because the psychotic symptoms must have a total duration of at least 1 month to meet Criterion A for Schizophrenia, the minimum duration of a schizoaffective episode is also 1 month. An essential feature of a Major Depressive Episode is the presence of either depressed mood or markedly diminished interest or pleasure. Because loss of interest or pleasure is so common in nonaffective Psychotic Disorders, to meet Criterion A for Schizoaffective Disorder the Major Depressive Episode must include pervasive depressed mood (i.e., the presence of markedly diminished interest or pleasure is not sufficient). The phase of the illness with psychotic symptoms alone is characterized by delusions or hallucinations that last at least 2 weeks. Although some mood symptoms may be present during this phase, they are not prominent. This determination can be difficult and may require longitudinal observation and multiple sources of information.

The symptoms of Schizoaffective Disorder may occur in a variety of temporal patterns. The following is a typical pattern: An individual may have pronounced auditory hallucinations and persecutory delusions for 2 months before the onset of a prominent Major Depressive Episode. The psychotic symptoms and the full Major Depressive Episode are then present for 3 months. Then, the person recovers completely from the Major Depressive Episode, but the psychotic symptoms persist for another month before they too disappear. During this period of illness, the individual's symptoms concurrently met criteria for a Major Depressive Episode and Criterion A for Schizophrenia, and, during this same period of illness, auditory hallucinations and delusions were present both before and after the depressive phase. The total period of illness lasted for about 6 months, with psychotic symptoms alone present during the initial 2 months, both depressive and psychotic symptoms present during the next 3 months, and psychotic symptoms alone present during the last month. In this instance, the duration of the depressive episode was not brief relative to the total duration of the psychotic disturbance, and thus the presentation qualifies for a diagnosis of Schizoaffective Disorder.

Criterion C for Schizoaffective Disorder specifies that mood symptoms that meet criteria for a mood episode must be present for a substantial portion of the entire period of illness. If the mood symptoms are present for only a relatively brief period of time, the diagnosis is Schizophrenia, not Schizoaffective Disorder. In evaluating this criterion, the clinician should determine the proportion of time during the continuous period of psychotic illness (i.e., both active and residual symptoms) in which there were significant mood symptoms accompanying the psychotic symptoms. The operationalization of what is meant by "a substantial portion of time" requires clinical judgment. For example, an individual with a 4-year history of active and residual symptoms of Schizophrenia develops a superimposed Major Depressive Episode that lasts for 5 weeks during which the psychotic symptoms persist. This presentation would not meet the criterion for "a substantial portion of the total duration" because the symptoms that meet criteria for a mood episode occurred for only 5 weeks out of a total of 4 years of disturbance. The diagnosis in this example remains Schizophrenia with the additional diagnosis of Depressive Disorder Not Otherwise Specified to indicate the superimposed Major Depressive Episode.

Subtypes

Two subtypes of Schizoaffective Disorder may be noted based on the mood component of the disorder:

Bipolar Type.   This subtype applies if a Manic Episode or Mixed Episode is part of the presentation. Major Depressive Episodes may also occur.
Depressive Type.   This subtype applies if only Major Depressive Episodes are part of the presentation.

Associated Features and Disorders

There may be poor occupational functioning, a restricted range of social contact, difficulties with self-care, and increased risk of suicide associated with Schizoaffective Disorder. Residual and negative symptoms are usually less severe and less chronic than those seen in Schizophrenia. Individuals with Schizoaffective Disorder may be at increased risk for later developing episodes of pure Mood Disorder (e.g., Major Depressive or Bipolar Disorder) or of Schizophrenia or Schizophreniform Disorder. There may be associated Alcohol and other Substance-Related Disorders. Limited clinical evidence suggests that Schizoaffective Disorder may be preceded by Schizoid, Schizotypal, Borderline, or Paranoid Personality Disorder.

Specific Culture, Age, and Gender Features

For additional discussion of culture, age, and gender factors relevant to evaluating psychotic symptoms, see the text for Schizophrenia (p. 281), and for a discussion of such factors relevant to diagnosing Mood Disorders, see p. 341 and p. 352. Schizoaffective Disorder, Bipolar Type, may be more common in young adults, whereas Schizoaffective Disorder, Depressive Type, may be more common in older adults. Compared with Schizophrenia, Schizoaffective Disorder probably occurs more often in women.

Prevalence

Detailed information is lacking, but Schizoaffective Disorder appears to be less common than Schizophrenia.

Course

The typical age at onset of Schizoaffective Disorder is probably in early adulthood, although onset can occur anywhere from adolescence to late in life. The prognosis for Schizoaffective Disorder is somewhat better than the prognosis for Schizophrenia, but considerably worse than the prognosis for Mood Disorders. Substantial occupational and social dysfunction are not uncommon. The outcome for Schizoaffective Disorder, Bipolar Type, may be better than that for Schizoaffective Disorder, Depressive Type.

Familial Pattern

There is substantial evidence that there is an increased risk for Schizophrenia in first-degree biological relatives of individuals with Schizoaffective Disorder. Most studies also show that relatives of individuals with Schizoaffective Disorder are at increased risk for Mood Disorders.

Differential Diagnosis

General medical conditions and substance use can present with a combination of psychotic and mood symptoms. **Psychotic Disorder Due to a General Medical Condition,** a **delirium,** or a **dementia** is diagnosed when there is evidence from the history, physical examination, or laboratory tests indicating that the symptoms are the direct physiological consequence of a specific general medical condition (see p. 306). **Substance-Induced Psychotic Disorder** and **Substance-Induced Delirium** are distinguished from Schizoaffective Disorder by the fact that a substance (e.g., a drug of abuse, a medication, or exposure to a toxin) is judged to be etiologically related to the symptoms (see p. 310).

Distinguishing Schizoaffective Disorder from Schizophrenia and from Mood Disorder

295.70 Schizoaffective Disorder   295

With Psychotic Features is often difficult. In Schizoaffective Disorder, there must be a mood episode that is concurrent with the active-phase symptoms of Schizophrenia, mood symptoms must be present for a substantial portion of the total duration of the disturbance, and delusions or hallucinations must be present for at least 2 weeks in the absence of prominent mood symptoms. In contrast, mood symptoms in Schizophrenia either have a duration that is brief relative to the total duration of the disturbance, occur only during the prodromal or residual phases, or do not meet full criteria for a mood episode. If psychotic symptoms occur exclusively during periods of mood disturbance, the diagnosis is Mood Disorder With Psychotic Features. In Schizoaffective Disorder, symptoms should not be counted toward a mood episode if they are clearly the result of symptoms of Schizophrenia (e.g., difficulty sleeping because of disturbing auditory hallucinations, weight loss because food is considered poisoned, difficulty concentrating because of psychotic disorganization). Loss of interest or pleasure is common in nonaffective Psychotic Disorders; therefore, to meet Criterion A for Schizoaffective Disorder, the Major Depressive Episode must include pervasive depressed mood.

Because the relative proportion of mood to psychotic symptoms may change over the course of the disturbance, the appropriate diagnosis for an individual episode of illness may change from Schizoaffective Disorder to Schizophrenia (e.g., a diagnosis of Schizoaffective Disorder for a severe and prominent Major Depressive Episode lasting 3 months during the first 6 months of a chronic psychotic illness would be changed to Schizophrenia if active psychotic or prominent residual symptoms persist over several years without a recurrence of another mood episode). The diagnosis may also change for different episodes of illness separated by a period of recovery. For example, an individual may have an episode of psychotic symptoms that meet Criterion A for Schizophrenia during a Major Depressive Episode, recover fully from this episode, and then later develop 6 weeks of delusions and hallucinations without prominent mood symptoms. The diagnosis in this instance would not be Schizoaffective Disorder because the period of delusions and hallucinations was not continuous with the initial period of disturbance. Instead, the appropriate diagnoses for the first episode would be Mood Disorder With Psychotic Features, In Full Remission, and Schizophreniform Disorder (Provisional) for the current episode.

Mood disturbances, especially depression, commonly develop during the course of **Delusional Disorder.** However, such presentations do not meet criteria for Schizoaffective Disorder because the psychotic symptoms in Delusional Disorder are restricted to nonbizarre delusions and therefore do not meet Criterion A for Schizoaffective Disorder.

If there is insufficient information concerning the relationship between psychotic and mood symptoms, **Psychotic Disorder Not Otherwise Specified** may be the most appropriate diagnosis.

◨ Diagnostic criteria for 295.70 Schizoaffective Disorder

A. An uninterrupted period of illness during which, at some time, there is either a Major Depressive Episode, a Manic Episode, or a Mixed Episode concurrent with symptoms that meet Criterion A for Schizophrenia.

Note: The Major Depressive Episode must include Criterion A1: depressed mood.

(continued)

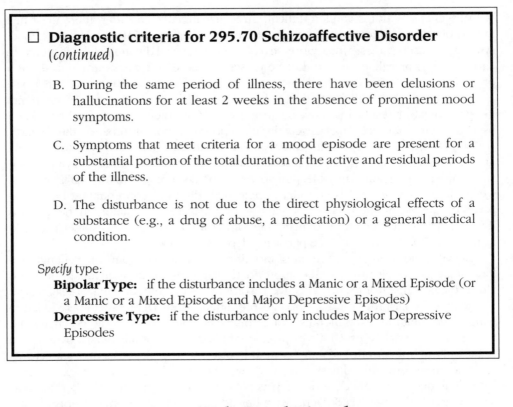

☐ **Diagnostic criteria for 295.70 Schizoaffective Disorder**
(continued)

B. During the same period of illness, there have been delusions or hallucinations for at least 2 weeks in the absence of prominent mood symptoms.

C. Symptoms that meet criteria for a mood episode are present for a substantial portion of the total duration of the active and residual periods of the illness.

D. The disturbance is not due to the direct physiological effects of a substance (e.g., a drug of abuse, a medication) or a general medical condition.

Specify type:
Bipolar Type: if the disturbance includes a Manic or a Mixed Episode (or a Manic or a Mixed Episode and Major Depressive Episodes)
Depressive Type: if the disturbance only includes Major Depressive Episodes

297.1   Delusional Disorder

Diagnostic Features

The essential feature of Delusional Disorder is the presence of one or more nonbizarre delusions that persist for at least 1 month (Criterion A). A diagnosis of Delusional Disorder is not given if the individual has ever had a symptom presentation that met Criterion A for Schizophrenia (Criterion B). Auditory or visual hallucinations, if present, are not prominent. Tactile or olfactory hallucinations may be present (and prominent) if they are related to the delusional theme (e.g., the sensation of being infested with insects associated with delusions of infestation, or the perception that one emits a foul odor from a body orifice associated with delusions of reference). Apart from the direct impact of the delusions, psychosocial functioning is not markedly impaired, and behavior is neither obviously odd nor bizarre (Criterion C). If mood episodes occur concurrently with the delusions, the total duration of these mood episodes is relatively brief compared to the total duration of the delusional periods (Criterion D). The delusions are not due to the direct physiological effects of a substance (e.g., cocaine) or a general medical condition (e.g., Alzheimer's disease, systemic lupus erythematosus) (Criterion E).

Although the determination of whether delusions are bizarre is considered to be especially important in distinguishing between Delusional Disorder and Schizophrenia, "bizarreness" may be difficult to judge, especially across different cultures. Delusions are deemed bizarre if they are clearly implausible, not understandable, and not derived from ordinary life experiences (e.g., an individual's belief that a stranger has removed his or her internal organs and replaced them with someone else's organs without leaving any wounds or scars). In contrast, nonbizarre delusions involve situations that can conceivably occur in real life (e.g., being followed, poisoned, infected, loved at a distance, or deceived by one's spouse or lover).

Psychosocial functioning is variable. Some individuals may appear to be relatively unimpaired in their interpersonal and occupational roles. In others, the impairment may be substantial and include low or absent occupational functioning and social isolation. When poor psychosocial functioning is present in Delusional Disorder, it arises directly from the delusional beliefs themselves. For example, an individual who is convinced that he will be murdered by "Mafia hit men" may quit his job and refuse to leave his house except late at night and only when dressed in clothes quite different from his normal attire. All of this behavior is an understandable attempt to prevent being identified and killed by his presumed assassins. In contrast, poor functioning in Schizophrenia may be due to both positive and negative symptoms (particularly avolition). Similarly, a common characteristic of individuals with Delusional Disorder is the apparent normality of their behavior and appearance when their delusional ideas are not being discussed or acted on. In general, social and marital functioning are more likely to be impaired than intellectual and occupational functioning.

Subtypes

The type of Delusional Disorder may be specified based on the predominant delusional theme:

Erotomanic Type. This subtype applies when the central theme of the delusion is that another person is in love with the individual. The delusion often concerns idealized romantic love and spiritual union rather than sexual attraction. The person about whom this conviction is held is usually of higher status (e.g., a famous person or a superior at work), but can be a complete stranger. Efforts to contact the object of the delusion (through telephone calls, letters, gifts, visits, and even surveillance and stalking) are common, although occasionally the person keeps the delusion secret. Most individuals with this subtype in clinical samples are female; most individuals with this subtype in forensic samples are male. Some individuals with this subtype, particularly males, come into conflict with the law in their efforts to pursue the object of their delusion or in a misguided effort to "rescue" him or her from some imagined danger.

Grandiose Type. This subtype applies when the central theme of the delusion is the conviction of having some great (but unrecognized) talent or insight or having made some important discovery. Less commonly, the individual may have the delusion of having a special relationship with a prominent person (e.g., an adviser to the President) or being a prominent person (in which case the actual person may be regarded as an impostor). Grandiose delusions may have a religious content (e.g., the person believes that he or she has a special message from a deity).

Jealous Type. This subtype applies when the central theme of the person's delusion is that his or her spouse or lover is unfaithful. This belief is arrived at without due cause and is based on incorrect inferences supported by small bits of "evidence" (e.g., disarrayed clothing or spots on the sheets), which are collected and used to justify the delusion. The individual with the delusion usually confronts the spouse or lover and attempts to intervene in the imagined infidelity (e.g., restricting the spouse's autonomy, secretly following the spouse, investigating the imagined lover, attacking the spouse).

Persecutory Type. This subtype applies when the central theme of the delusion involves the person's belief that he or she is being conspired against, cheated, spied on, followed, poisoned or drugged, maliciously maligned, harassed, or obstructed in the pursuit of long-term goals. Small slights may be exaggerated and become the focus of a delusional system. The focus of the delusion is often on some injustice that must be remedied by legal action ("querulous paranoia"), and the affected person may engage in repeated attempts to obtain satisfaction by appeal to the courts and other government agencies. Individuals with persecutory delusions are often resentful and angry and may resort to violence against those they believe are hurting them.

Somatic Type. This subtype applies when the central theme of the delusion involves bodily functions or sensations. Somatic delusions can occur in several forms. Most common are the person's conviction that he or she emits a foul odor from the skin, mouth, rectum, or vagina; that there is an infestation of insects on or in the skin; that there is an internal parasite; that certain parts of the body are definitely (contrary to all evidence) misshapen or ugly; or that parts of the body (e.g., the large intestine) are not functioning.

Mixed Type. This subtype applies when no one delusional theme predominates.

Unspecified Type. This subtype applies when the dominant delusional belief cannot be clearly determined or is not described in the specific types (e.g., referential delusions without a prominent persecutory or grandiose component).

Associated Features and Disorders

Social, marital, or work problems can result from the delusional beliefs of Delusional Disorder. Ideas of reference (e.g., that random events are of special significance) are common in individuals with this disorder. Their interpretation of these events is usually consistent with the content of their delusional beliefs. Many individuals with Delusional Disorder develop irritable or dysphoric mood, which can usually be understood as a reaction to their delusional beliefs. Especially with the Persecutory and Jealous Types, marked anger and violent behavior can occur. The individual may engage in litigious behavior, sometimes leading to hundreds of letters of protest to government and judicial officials and many court appearances. Legal difficulties can occur in Delusional Disorder, Jealous Type and Erotomanic Type. Individuals with Delusional Disorder, Somatic Type, may be subject to unnecessary medical tests and procedures. Hearing deficiency, severe psychosocial stressors (e.g., immigration), and low socioeconomic status may predispose an individual to the development of Delusional Disorder. Major Depressive Episodes probably occur in individuals with Delusional Disorder more frequently than in the general population. Typically, the depression is relatively mild and begins after the onset of prominent delusional beliefs. Delusional Disorder may be associated with Obsessive-Compulsive Disorder, Body Dysmorphic Disorder, and Paranoid, Schizoid, or Avoidant Personality Disorders.

Specific Culture and Gender Features

An individual's cultural and religious background must be taken into account in evaluating the possible presence of Delusional Disorder. Some cultures have widely held and culturally sanctioned beliefs that might be considered delusional in other cultures. The content of delusions also varies in different cultures and subcultures. Delusional Disorder, Jealous Type, is probably more common in men than in women, but there appears to be no major gender difference in the overall frequency of Delusional Disorder.

Prevalence

Delusional Disorder is relatively uncommon in clinical settings, with most studies suggesting that the disorder accounts for 1%–2% of admissions to inpatient mental health facilities. Precise information about the population prevalence of this disorder is lacking, but the best estimate is around 0.03%. Because of its usually late age at onset, the lifetime morbidity risk may be between 0.05% and 0.1%.

Course

The age at onset of Delusional Disorder is generally middle or late adult life, but can be at a younger age. The Persecutory Type is the most common subtype. The course is quite variable. Especially in the Persecutory Type, the disorder may be chronic, although a waxing and waning of the preoccupation with the delusional beliefs often occurs. In other cases, full periods of remission may be followed by subsequent relapses. In yet other cases, the disorder remits within a few months, often without subsequent relapse. Some evidence suggests that the Jealous Type may have a better prognosis than the Persecutory Type.

Familial Pattern

Some studies have found that Delusional Disorder is more common among relatives of individuals with Schizophrenia than would be expected by chance, whereas other studies have found no familial relationship between Delusional Disorder and Schizophrenia. There is limited evidence that Avoidant and Paranoid Personality Disorders may be especially common among first-degree biological relatives of individuals with Delusional Disorder.

Differential Diagnosis

The diagnosis of Delusional Disorder is made only when the delusion is not due to the direct physiological effects of a substance or a general medical condition. A **delirium,** a **dementia,** and **Psychotic Disorder Due to a General Medical Condition** may present with symptoms that suggest Delusional Disorder. For example, simple persecutory delusions (e.g., "someone comes into my room at night and steals my clothes") in the early phase of Dementia of the Alzheimer's Type would be diagnosed as Dementia of the Alzheimer's Type, With Delusions. A **Substance-Induced Psychotic Disorder,** especially due to stimulants such as amphetamines or cocaine, cross-sectionally may be identical in symptomatology to Delusional Disorder, but can usually be distinguished by the chronological relationship of substance use to the onset and remission of the delusional beliefs.

Delusional Disorder can be distinguished from **Schizophrenia** and **Schizophreni-**

form Disorder by the absence of the other characteristic symptoms of the active phase of Schizophrenia (e.g., prominent auditory or visual hallucinations, bizarre delusions, disorganized speech, grossly disorganized or catatonic behavior, negative symptoms). Compared with Schizophrenia, Delusional Disorder usually produces less impairment in occupational and social functioning.

It can be difficult to differentiate **Mood Disorders With Psychotic Features** from Delusional Disorder, because the psychotic features associated with Mood Disorders usually involve nonbizarre delusions without prominent hallucinations, and Delusional Disorder frequently has associated mood symptoms. The distinction depends on the temporal relationship between the mood disturbance and the delusions and on the severity of the mood symptoms. If delusions occur exclusively during mood episodes, the diagnosis is Mood Disorder With Psychotic Features. Although depressive symptoms are common in Delusional Disorder, they are usually mild, remit while the delusional symptoms persist, and do not warrant a separate Mood Disorder diagnosis. Occasionally, mood symptoms that meet full criteria for a mood episode are superimposed on the delusional disturbance. Delusional Disorder can be diagnosed only if the total duration of all mood episodes remains brief relative to the total duration of the delusional disturbance. If symptoms that meet criteria for a mood episode are present for a substantial portion of the delusional disturbance (i.e., the delusional equivalent of Schizoaffective Disorder), then a diagnosis of **Psychotic Disorder Not Otherwise Specified** accompanied by either **Depressive Disorder Not Otherwise Specified** or **Bipolar Disorder Not Otherwise Specified** is appropriate.

Individuals with **Shared Psychotic Disorder** can present with symptoms that are similar to those seen in Delusional Disorder, but the disturbance has a characteristic etiology and course. In Shared Psychotic Disorder, the delusions arise in the context of a close relationship with another person, are identical in form to the delusions of that other person, and diminish or disappear when the individual with Shared Psychotic Disorder is separated from the individual with the primary Psychotic Disorder. **Brief Psychotic Disorder** is differentiated from Delusional Disorder by the fact that the delusional symptoms last less than 1 month. A diagnosis of **Psychotic Disorder Not Otherwise Specified** may be made if insufficient information is available to choose between Delusional Disorder and other Psychotic Disorders or to determine whether the presenting symptoms are substance induced or the result of a general medical condition.

It may be difficult to differentiate **Hypochondriasis** (especially With Poor Insight) from Delusional Disorder. In Hypochondriasis, the fears of having a serious disease or the concern that one has such a serious disease are held with less than delusional intensity (i.e., the individual can entertain the possibility that the feared disease is not present). **Body Dysmorphic Disorder** involves a preoccupation with some imagined defect in appearance. Many individuals with this disorder hold their beliefs with less than delusional intensity and recognize that their view of their appearance is distorted. However, a significant proportion of individuals whose symptoms meet criteria for Body Dysmorphic Disorder hold their beliefs with delusional intensity. When criteria for both disorders are met, both Body Dysmorphic Disorder and Delusional Disorder, Somatic Type, may be diagnosed. The boundary between **Obsessive-Compulsive Disorder** (especially With Poor Insight) and Delusional Disorder can sometimes be difficult to establish. The ability of individuals with Obsessive-Compulsive Disorder to recognize that the obsessions or compulsions are excessive or unreasonable occurs on a continuum. In some individuals, reality testing may be lost, and the obsession may reach delusional proportions (e.g., the belief that one has caused the death of another person by having willed it). If the obsessions develop into sustained delusional beliefs that represent a major part of the clinical picture, an additional diagnosis of Delusional Disorder may be appropriate.

In contrast to Delusional Disorder, there are no clear-cut or persisting delusional beliefs in **Paranoid Personality Disorder.** Whenever a person with a Delusional Disorder has a preexisting Personality Disorder, the Personality Disorder should be listed on Axis II, followed by "Premorbid" in parentheses.

■ Diagnostic criteria for 297.1 Delusional Disorder

A. Nonbizarre delusions (i.e., involving situations that occur in real life, such as being followed, poisoned, infected, loved at a distance, or deceived by spouse or lover, or having a disease) of at least 1 month's duration.

B. Criterion A for Schizophrenia has never been met. **Note:** Tactile and olfactory hallucinations may be present in Delusional Disorder if they are related to the delusional theme.

C. Apart from the impact of the delusion(s) or its ramifications, functioning is not markedly impaired and behavior is not obviously odd or bizarre.

D. If mood episodes have occurred concurrently with delusions, their total duration has been brief relative to the duration of the delusional periods.

E. The disturbance is not due to the direct physiological effects of a substance (e.g., a drug of abuse, a medication) or a general medical condition.

Specify type (the following types are assigned based on the predominant delusional theme):
   Erotomanic Type: delusions that another person, usually of higher status, is in love with the individual
   Grandiose Type: delusions of inflated worth, power, knowledge, identity, or special relationship to a deity or famous person
   Jealous Type: delusions that the individual's sexual partner is unfaithful
   Persecutory Type: delusions that the person (or someone to whom the person is close) is being malevolently treated in some way
   Somatic Type: delusions that the person has some physical defect or general medical condition
   Mixed Type: delusions characteristic of more than one of the above types but no one theme predominates
   Unspecified Type

298.8   Brief Psychotic Disorder

Diagnostic Features

The essential feature of Brief Psychotic Disorder is a disturbance that involves the sudden onset of at least one of the following positive psychotic symptoms: delusions, hallucinations, disorganized speech (e.g., frequent derailment or incoherence), or grossly disorganized or catatonic behavior (Criterion A). An episode of the disturbance lasts at least 1 day but less than 1 month, and the individual eventually has a full return to the premorbid level of functioning (Criterion B). The disturbance is not better accounted for by a Mood Disorder With Psychotic Features, by Schizoaffective Disorder, or by Schizophrenia and is not due to the direct physiological effects of a substance (e.g., a hallucinogen) or a general medical condition (e.g., subdural hematoma) (Criterion C).

Specifiers

The following specifiers for Brief Psychotic Disorder may be noted based on the presence or absence of precipitating stressors:

> **With Marked Stressor(s).** This specifier may be noted if the psychotic symptoms develop shortly after and apparently in response to one or more events that, singly or together, would be markedly stressful to almost anyone in similar circumstances in that person's culture. This type of Brief Psychotic Disorder was called "brief reactive psychosis" in DSM-III-R. The precipitating event(s) may be any major stress, such as the loss of a loved one or the psychological trauma of combat. Determining whether a specific stressor was a precipitant or a consequence of the illness may sometimes be clinically difficult. In such instances, the decision will depend on related factors such as the temporal relationship between the stressor and the onset of the symptoms, ancillary information from a spouse or friend about level of functioning prior to the stressor, and history of similar responses to stressful events in the past.
>
> **Without Marked Stressor(s).** This specifier may be noted if the psychotic symptoms are not apparently in response to events that would be markedly stressful to almost anyone in similar circumstances in the person's culture.
>
> **With Postpartum Onset.** This specifier may be noted if the onset of the psychotic symptoms is within 4 weeks postpartum.

Associated Features and Disorders

Individuals with Brief Psychotic Disorder typically experience emotional turmoil or overwhelming confusion. They may have rapid shifts from one intense affect to another. Although brief, the level of impairment may be severe, and supervision may be required to ensure that nutritional and hygienic needs are met and that the individual is protected from the consequences of poor judgment, cognitive impairment, or acting on the basis of delusions. There appears to be an increased risk of mortality (with a particularly high risk for suicide), especially among younger individuals. Preexisting Personality Disorders (e.g., Paranoid, Histrionic, Narcissistic, Schizotypal, or Borderline Personality Disorder) may predispose the individual to the development of the disorder.

Specific Culture Features

It is important to distinguish symptoms of Brief Psychotic Disorder from culturally sanctioned response patterns. For example, in some religious ceremonies, an individual may report hearing voices, but these do not generally persist and are not perceived as abnormal by most members of the person's community.

Prevalence

Limited available evidence suggests that Brief Psychotic Disorder is uncommon.

Course

Brief Psychotic Disorder may appear in adolescence or early adulthood, with the average age at onset being in the late 20s or early 30s. By definition, a diagnosis of Brief Psychotic Disorder requires a full remission of all symptoms and a return to the premorbid level of functioning within 1 month of the onset of the disturbance. In some individuals, the duration of psychotic symptoms may be quite brief (e.g., a few days).

Familial Pattern

Some evidence suggests that Brief Psychotic Disorder may be related to Mood Disorders, whereas other evidence suggests that it may be distinct from both Schizophrenia and Mood Disorders.

Differential Diagnosis

A wide variety of general medical conditions can present with psychotic symptoms of short duration. **Psychotic Disorder Due to a General Medical Condition** or a **delirium** is diagnosed when there is evidence from the history, physical examination, or laboratory tests that indicates that the delusions or hallucinations are the direct physiological consequence of a specific general medical condition (e.g., Cushing's syndrome, brain tumor) (see p. 306). **Substance-Induced Psychotic Disorder, Substance-Induced Delirium,** and **Substance Intoxication** are distinguished from Brief Psychotic Disorder by the fact that a substance (e.g., a drug of abuse, a medication, or exposure to a toxin) is judged to be etiologically related to the psychotic symptoms (see p. 310). Laboratory tests, such as a urine drug screen or a blood alcohol level, may be helpful in making this determination, as may a careful history of substance use with attention to temporal relationships between substance intake and onset of the symptoms and the nature of the substance being used.

The diagnosis of Brief Psychotic Disorder cannot be made if the psychotic symptoms are better accounted for by a **mood episode** (i.e., the psychotic symptoms occur exclusively during a full Major Depressive, Manic, or Mixed Episode). If the psychotic symptoms persist for 1 month or longer, the diagnosis is either **Schizophreniform Disorder, Delusional Disorder, Mood Disorder With Psychotic Features,** or **Psychotic Disorder Not Otherwise Specified,** depending on the other symptoms in the presentation. The differential diagnosis between Brief Psychotic Disorder and Schizophreniform Disorder is difficult when the psychotic symptoms have remitted before 1 month in response to successful treatment with medication. Because recurrent episodes of Brief Psychotic Disorder are rare, careful attention should be given to the possibility that a recurrent disorder (e.g., Bipolar Disorder, recurrent acute exacerbations of Schizophrenia) may be responsible for any recurring psychotic episodes.

An episode of **Factitious Disorder, With Predominantly Psychological Signs and Symptoms,** may have the appearance of Brief Psychotic Disorder, but in such cases there is evidence that the symptoms are intentionally produced. When **Malingering** involves apparently psychotic symptoms, there is usually evidence that the illness was feigned for an understandable goal.

In certain individuals with **Personality Disorders,** psychosocial stressors may precipitate brief periods of psychotic symptoms. These are usually transient and do not warrant a separate diagnosis. If psychotic symptoms persist for at least 1 day, an additional diagnosis of Brief Psychotic Disorder may be appropriate.

■ **Diagnostic criteria for 298.8 Brief Psychotic Disorder**

A. Presence of one (or more) of the following symptoms:
   (1) delusions
   (2) hallucinations
   (3) disorganized speech (e.g., frequent derailment or incoherence)
   (4) grossly disorganized or catatonic behavior

   Note: Do not include a symptom if it is a culturally sanctioned response pattern.

B. Duration of an episode of the disturbance is at least 1 day but less than 1 month, with eventual full return to premorbid level of functioning.

C. The disturbance is not better accounted for by a Mood Disorder With Psychotic Features, Schizoaffective Disorder, or Schizophrenia and is not due to the direct physiological effects of a substance (e.g., a drug of abuse, a medication) or a general medical condition.

Specify if:
   With Marked Stressor(s) (brief reactive psychosis): if symptoms occur shortly after and apparently in response to events that, singly or together, would be markedly stressful to almost anyone in similar circumstances in the person's culture
   Without Marked Stressor(s): if psychotic symptoms do *not* occur shortly after, or are not apparently in response to events that, singly or together, would be markedly stressful to almost anyone in similar circumstances in the person's culture
   With Postpartum Onset: if onset within 4 weeks postpartum

297.3 Shared Psychotic Disorder (Folie à Deux)

Diagnostic Features

The essential feature of Shared Psychotic Disorder (Folie à Deux) is a delusion that develops in an individual who is involved in a close relationship with another person (sometimes termed the "inducer" or "the primary case") who already has a Psychotic Disorder with prominent delusions (Criterion A). The individual comes to share the delusional beliefs of the primary case in whole or in part (Criterion B). The delusion is not better accounted for by another Psychotic Disorder (e.g., Schizophrenia) or a Mood Disorder With Psychotic Features and is not due to the direct physiological effects of a substance (e.g., amphetamine) or a general medical condition (e.g., brain tumor) (Criterion C). Schizophrenia is probably the most common diagnosis of the primary case, although other diagnoses may include Delusional Disorder or Mood Disorder With Psychotic Features. The content of the shared delusional beliefs may be dependent on the diagnosis of the primary case and can include relatively bizarre delusions (e.g., that radiation is being transmitted into an apartment from a hostile foreign power, causing indigestion and diarrhea), mood-congruent delusions (e.g., that the primary case will soon receive a film contract for $2 million, allowing the family to purchase a much larger home with a swimming pool), or the nonbizarre delusions that are characteristic of Delusional Disorder (e.g., the FBI is tapping the family telephone and trailing family members when they go out). Usually the primary case in Shared Psychotic Disorder is dominant in the relationship and gradually imposes the delusional system on the more passive and initially healthy second person. Individuals who come to share delusional beliefs are often related by blood or marriage and have lived together for a long time, sometimes in relative social isolation. If the relationship with the primary case is interrupted, the delusional beliefs of the other individual usually diminish or disappear. Although most commonly seen in relationships of only two people, Shared Psychotic Disorder can occur among a larger number of individuals, especially in family situations in which the parent is the primary case and the children, sometimes to varying degrees, adopt the parent's delusional beliefs. Individuals with this disorder rarely seek treatment and usually are brought to clinical attention when the primary case receives treatment.

Associated Features and Disorders

Aside from the delusional beliefs, behavior is usually not otherwise odd or unusual in Shared Psychotic Disorder. Impairment is often less severe in the individual with Shared Psychotic Disorder than in the primary case.

Prevalence

Little systematic information about the prevalence of Shared Psychotic Disorder is available. This disorder is rare in clinical settings, although it has been argued that some cases go unrecognized. Limited evidence suggests that Shared Psychotic Disorder is somewhat more common in women than in men.

Course

Little is known about the age at onset of Shared Psychotic Disorder, but it appears to be quite variable. Without intervention, the course is usually chronic, because this disorder most commonly occurs in relationships that are long-standing and resistant to change. With separation from the primary case, the individual's delusional beliefs disappear, sometimes quickly and sometimes quite slowly.

Differential Diagnosis

The diagnosis of Shared Psychotic Disorder is made only when the delusion is not due to the direct physiological effects of a substance or a general medical condition. Differential diagnosis is rarely a problem because the history of close association with the primary case and the similarity of delusions between the two individuals is unique to Shared Psychotic Disorder. In **Schizophrenia, Delusional Disorder, Schizoaffective Disorder,** and **Mood Disorder With Psychotic Features,** there is either no close relationship with a dominant person who has a Psychotic Disorder and shares similar delusional beliefs or, if there is such a person, the psychotic symptoms usually precede the onset of any shared delusions. In rare cases, an individual may present with what appears to be Shared Psychotic Disorder, but the delusions do not disappear when the individual is separated from the primary case. In such a situation, it is probably appropriate to consider another Psychotic Disorder diagnosis.

■ **Diagnostic criteria for 297.3 Shared Psychotic Disorder**

A. A delusion develops in an individual in the context of a close relationship with another person(s), who has an already-established delusion.

B. The delusion is similar in content to that of the person who already has the established delusion.

C. The disturbance is not better accounted for by another Psychotic Disorder (e.g., Schizophrenia) or a Mood Disorder With Psychotic Features and is not due to the direct physiological effects of a substance (e.g., a drug of abuse, a medication) or a general medical condition.

Psychotic Disorder Due to a General Medical Condition

Diagnostic Features

The essential features of Psychotic Disorder Due to a General Medical Condition are prominent hallucinations or delusions that are judged to be due to the direct physiological effects of a general medical condition (Criterion A). There must be evidence from the history, physical examination, or laboratory findings that the delusions or hallucinations are the direct physiological consequence of a general medical condition (Criterion B). The psychotic disturbance is not better accounted for by another mental disorder (e.g., the symptoms are not a psychologically mediated response to a severe general medical condition, in which case a diagnosis of Brief Psychotic Disorder, With Marked Stressor, would be appropriate) (Criterion C). The diagnosis is not made if the disturbance occurs only during the course of a delirium (Criterion D). A separate diagnosis of Psychotic Disorder Due to a General Medical Condition is not given if delusions occur only during the course of Dementia of the Alzheimer's Type or Vascular Dementia; a diagnosis of Dementia of the Alzheimer's Type or Vascular Dementia with the subtype With Delusions is given instead.

Hallucinations can occur in any sensory modality (i.e., visual, olfactory, gustatory, tactile, or auditory), but certain etiological factors are likely to evoke specific hallucinatory phenomena. Olfactory hallucinations, especially those involving the smell of burning rubber or other unpleasant smells, are highly suggestive of temporal lobe epilepsy. Hallucinations may vary from simple and unformed to highly complex and organized, depending on etiological factors, environmental surroundings, nature and focus of the insult rendered to the central nervous system, and the reactive response to impairment. Psychotic Disorder Due to a General Medical Condition is generally not diagnosed if the individual maintains reality testing for the hallucination and appreciates that the perceptual experiences result from the general medical condition. Delusions may express a variety of themes, including somatic, grandiose, religious, and, most commonly, persecutory. Religious delusions have been specifically associated in some cases with temporal lobe epilepsy. Individuals with right parietal brain lesions can develop a contralateral neglect syndrome in which they may disown parts of their body to a delusional extent. On the whole, however, associations between delusions and particular general medical conditions appear to be less specific than is the case for hallucinations.

In determining whether the psychotic disturbance is due to a general medical condition, the clinician must first establish the presence of a general medical condition. Further, the clinician must establish that the psychotic disturbance is etiologically related to the general medical condition through a physiological mechanism. A careful and comprehensive assessment of multiple factors is necessary to make this judgment. Although there are no infallible guidelines for determining whether the relationship between the psychotic disturbance and the general medical condition is etiological, several considerations provide some guidance in this area. One consideration is the presence of a temporal association between the onset, exacerbation, or remission of the general medical condition and that of the psychotic disturbance. A second consideration is the presence of features that are atypical for a primary Psychotic Disorder (e.g., atypical age at onset or presence of visual or olfactory hallucinations). Evidence from the literature that suggests that there can be a direct association between the general medical condition in question and the development of psychotic symptoms can provide a useful context in the assessment of a particular situation. In addition, the clinician must also judge that the disturbance is not better accounted for by a primary Psychotic Disorder, a Substance-Induced Psychotic Disorder, or another primary mental disorder (e.g., Adjustment Disorder). This determination is explained in greater detail in the "Mental Disorders Due to a General Medical Condition" section (p. 165).

Subtypes

One of the following subtypes may be used to indicate the predominant symptom presentation. If both delusions and hallucinations are present, code whichever is predominant:

> **293.81   With Delusions.** This subtype is used if delusions are the predominant symptom.
> **293.82   With Hallucinations.** This subtype is used if hallucinations are the predominant symptom.

Recording Procedures

In recording the diagnosis of Psychotic Disorder Due to a General Medical Condition, the clinician should first note the presence of the Psychotic Disorder, then the identified general medical condition judged to be causing the disturbance, and finally the appropriate specifier indicating the predominant symptom presentation on Axis I (e.g., Psychotic Disorder Due to Thyrotoxicosis, With Hallucinations). The diagnostic code on Axis I is selected based on the subtype: 293.81 for Psychotic Disorder Due to a General Medical Condition, With Delusions, and 293.82 for Psychotic Disorder Due to a General Medical Condition, With Hallucinations. The ICD-9-CM code for the general medical condition should also be noted on Axis III (e.g., 242.9 thyrotoxicosis). (See Appendix G for a list of ICD-9-CM diagnostic codes for selected general medical conditions.)

Associated General Medical Conditions

A variety of general medical conditions may cause psychotic symptoms, including neurological conditions (e.g., neoplasms, cerebrovascular disease, Huntington's disease, epilepsy, auditory nerve injury, deafness, migraine, central nervous system infections), endocrine conditions (e.g., hyper- and hypothyroidism, hyper- and hypoparathyroidism, hypoadrenocorticism), metabolic conditions (e.g., hypoxia, hypercarbia, hypoglycemia), fluid or electrolyte imbalances, hepatic or renal diseases, and autoimmune disorders with central nervous system involvement (e.g., systemic lupus erythematosus). Those neurological conditions that involve subcortical structures or the temporal lobe are more commonly associated with delusions. The associated physical examination findings, laboratory findings, and patterns of prevalence or onset reflect the etiological general medical condition.

Differential Diagnosis

Hallucinations and delusions commonly occur in the context of a **delirium;** however, a separate diagnosis of Psychotic Disorder Due to a General Medical Condition is not given if the disturbance occurs exclusively during the course of a delirium. When delusions develop during the course of **Dementia of the Alzheimer's Type** or **Vascular Dementia,** a diagnosis of Dementia of the Alzheimer's Type or Vascular Dementia with the subtype With Delusions is given; a separate diagnosis of Psychotic Disorder Due to a General Medical Condition is not given. If the presentation includes a mix of different types of symptoms (e.g., psychotic and anxiety), the diagnosis is usually Psychotic Disorder Due to a General Medical Condition because in such situations psychotic symptoms typically predominate in the clinical picture.

If there is evidence of recent or prolonged substance use (including medications with psychoactive effects), withdrawal from a substance, or exposure to a toxin (e.g., LSD Intoxication, Alcohol Withdrawal), a **Substance-Induced Psychotic Disorder** should be considered. It may be useful to obtain a urine or blood drug screen or other appropriate laboratory evaluation. Symptoms that occur during or shortly after (i.e., within 4 weeks of) Substance Intoxication or Withdrawal or after medication use may be especially indicative of a Substance-Induced Psychotic Disorder, depending on the character, duration, or amount of the substance used. If the clinician has ascertained that the disturbance is due to both a general medical condition and substance use, both diagnoses (i.e., Psychotic Disorder Due to a General Medical Condition and Substance-Induced Psychotic Disorder) can be given.

Psychotic Disorder Due to a General Medical Condition must be distinguished from a **primary Psychotic Disorder** (e.g., Schizophrenia, Delusional Disorder, Schizoaffective Disorder) or a **primary Mood Disorder With Psychotic Features.** In primary Psychotic Disorders and in primary Mood Disorders With Psychotic Features, no specific and direct causative physiological mechanisms associated with a general medical condition can be demonstrated. Late age at onset (e.g., the first appearance of delusions in an individual over age 35 years) and the absence of a personal or family history of Schizophrenia or Delusional Disorder suggest the need for a thorough assessment to rule out the diagnosis of Psychotic Disorder Due to a General Medical Condition. Auditory hallucinations that involve voices speaking complex sentences are more characteristic of Schizophrenia than of Psychotic Disorder Due to a General Medical Condition. Other types of hallucinations (e.g., visual, olfactory) commonly signal a Psychotic Disorder Due to a General Medical Condition or a Substance-Induced Psychotic Disorder.

Psychotic Disorder Not Otherwise Specified is diagnosed when the clinician cannot determine if the psychotic disturbance is primary, substance induced, or due to a general medical condition. **Hypnagogic** and **hypnopompic hallucinations** may occur in individuals without a mental disorder, but they occur only on falling asleep or on awakening.

■ **Diagnostic criteria for 293.xx Psychotic Disorder Due to . . . [Indicate the General Medical Condition]**

A. Prominent hallucinations or delusions.

B. There is evidence from the history, physical examination, or laboratory findings that the disturbance is the direct physiological consequence of a general medical condition.

C. The disturbance is not better accounted for by another mental disorder.

D. The disturbance does not occur exclusively during the course of a delirium.

(continued)

☐ **Diagnostic criteria for 293.xx Psychotic Disorder Due to . . . [Indicate the General Medical Condition]** (continued)

Code based on predominant symptom:
- **.81 With Delusions:** if delusions are the predominant symptom
- **.82 With Hallucinations:** if hallucinations are the predominant symptom

Coding note: Include the name of the general medical condition on Axis I, e.g., 293.81 Psychotic Disorder Due to Malignant Lung Neoplasm, With Delusions; also code the general medical condition on Axis III (see Appendix G for codes).

Coding note: If delusions are part of a preexisting dementia, indicate the delusions by coding the appropriate subtype of the dementia if one is available, e.g., 290.20 Dementia of the Alzheimer's Type, With Late Onset, With Delusions.

Substance-Induced Psychotic Disorder

Diagnostic Features

The essential features of Substance-Induced Psychotic Disorder are prominent hallucinations or delusions (Criterion A) that are judged to be due to the direct physiological effects of a substance (i.e., a drug of abuse, a medication, or toxin exposure) (Criterion B). Hallucinations that the individual realizes are substance induced are not included here and instead would be diagnosed as Substance Intoxication or Substance Withdrawal with the accompanying specifier With Perceptual Disturbances. The disturbance must not be better accounted for by a Psychotic Disorder that is not substance induced (Criterion C). The diagnosis is not made if the psychotic symptoms occur only during the course of a delirium (Criterion D). This diagnosis should be made instead of a diagnosis of Substance Intoxication or Substance Withdrawal only when the psychotic symptoms are in excess of those usually associated with the intoxication or withdrawal syndrome and when the symptoms are sufficiently severe to warrant independent clinical attention. For a more detailed discussion of Substance-Related Disorders, see p. 175.

A Substance-Induced Psychotic Disorder is distinguished from a primary Psychotic Disorder by considering the onset, course, and other factors. For drugs of abuse, there must be evidence from the history, physical examination, or laboratory findings of intoxication or withdrawal. Substance-Induced Psychotic Disorders arise only in association with intoxication or withdrawal states, whereas primary Psychotic Disorders may precede the onset of substance use or may occur during times of sustained abstinence. Once initiated, the psychotic symptoms may continue as long as the substance use continues. Because the withdrawal state for some substances can be relatively protracted, the onset of psychotic symptoms can occur up to 4 weeks after the cessation of substance use. Another consideration is the presence of features that are atypical of a primary Psychotic Disorder (e.g., atypical age at onset or course). For example, the appearance of delusions de novo in a person over age 35 years without a known history of a primary Psychotic Disorder should alert the clinician to the possibility of a Substance-Induced Psychotic Disorder. Even a prior history of a primary Psychotic Disorder does not rule out the possibility of a Substance-Induced Psychotic Disorder. It has been suggested that 9 out of 10 nonauditory hallucinations are the product of a Substance-Induced Psychotic Disorder or a Psychotic Disorder Due to a General Medical Condition. In contrast, factors that suggest that the psychotic symptoms are better accounted for by a primary Psychotic Disorder include persistence of psychotic symptoms for a substantial period of time (i.e., about a month) after the end of Substance Intoxication or acute Substance Withdrawal; the development of symptoms that are substantially in excess of what would be expected given the type or amount of the substance used or the duration of use; or a history of prior recurrent primary Psychotic Disorders. Other causes of psychotic symptoms must be considered even in a person with Intoxication or Withdrawal, because substance use problems are not uncommon among persons with (presumably) non-substance-induced Psychotic Disorders.

Subtypes and Specifiers

One of the following subtypes may be used to indicate the predominant symptom presentation. If both delusions and hallucinations are present, code whichever is predominant:

> **With Delusions.** This subtype is used if delusions are the predominant symptom.
> **With Hallucinations.** This subtype is used if hallucinations are the predominant symptom.

The context of the development of the psychotic symptoms may be indicated by using one of the specifiers listed below:

> **With Onset During Intoxication.** This specifier should be used if criteria for intoxication with the substance are met and the symptoms develop during the intoxication syndrome.
> **With Onset During Withdrawal.** This specifier should be used if criteria for withdrawal from the substance are met and the symptoms develop during, or shortly after, a withdrawal syndrome.

Recording Procedures

The name of the Substance-Induced Psychotic Disorder begins with the specific substance (e.g., cocaine, methylphenidate, dexamethasone) that is presumed to be causing the psychotic symptoms. The diagnostic code is selected from the listing of classes of substances provided in the criteria set. For substances that do not fit into any of the classes (e.g., dexamethasone), the code for "Other Substance" should be used. In addition, for medications prescribed at therapeutic doses, the specific medication can be indicated by listing the appropriate E-code on Axis I (see Appendix G). The code for each of the specific Substance-Induced Psychotic Disorders depends on whether the presentation is predominated by delusions or hallucinations: 292.11 for With Delusions and 292.12 for With Hallucinations, except for alcohol, for which the code is 291.5 for With Delusions and 291.3 for With Hallucinations. The name of the disorder (e.g., Cocaine-Induced Psychotic Disorder; Methylphenidate-Induced Psychotic Disorder) is followed by the subtype indicating the predominant symptom presentation and the specifier indicating the context in which the symptoms developed (e.g., 292.11 Cocaine-

Induced Psychotic Disorder, With Delusions, With Onset During Intoxication; 292.12 Phencyclidine-Induced Psychotic Disorder, With Hallucinations, With Onset During Intoxication). When more than one substance is judged to play a significant role in the development of the psychotic symptoms, each should be listed separately. If a substance is judged to be the etiological factor, but the specific substance or class of substance is unknown, the category 292.11 Unknown Substance–Induced Psychotic Disorder, With Delusions, or 292.12 Unknown Substance–Induced Psychotic Disorder, With Hallucinations, may be used.

Specific Substances

Psychotic Disorders can occur in association with **intoxication** with the following classes of substances: alcohol; amphetamine and related substances; cannabis; cocaine; hallucinogens; inhalants; opioids (meperidine); phencyclidine and related substances; sedatives, hypnotics, and anxiolytics; and other or unknown substances. Psychotic Disorders can occur in association with **withdrawal** from the following classes of substances: alcohol; sedatives, hypnotics, and anxiolytics; and other or unknown substances. The initiation of the disorder may vary considerably with the substance. For example, smoking a high dose of cocaine may produce psychosis within minutes, whereas days or weeks of high-dose alcohol or sedative use may be required to produce psychosis. Hallucinations may occur in any modality. In Alcohol-Induced Psychotic Disorder, With Hallucinations, With Onset During Withdrawal, vivid, persistent, and usually unpleasant hallucinations develop shortly (within 48 hours) after cessation of or reduction in alcohol ingestion. This disorder occurs only after prolonged, heavy ingestion of alcohol in people who apparently have Alcohol Dependence. The auditory hallucinations are usually voices, but there may also be visual or tactile hallucinations.

The Psychotic Disorders induced by intoxication with amphetamine and cocaine share similar clinical features. Persecutory delusions may rapidly develop shortly after use of amphetamine or a similarly acting sympathomimetic. Distortion of body image and misperception of people's faces may occur. The hallucination of bugs or vermin crawling in or under the skin (formication) can lead to scratching and extensive skin excoriations. Cannabis-Induced Psychotic Disorder may develop shortly after cannabis use and usually involves persecutory delusions. The disorder is apparently rare. Marked anxiety, emotional lability, depersonalization, and subsequent amnesia for the episode can occur. The disorder usually remits within a day, but in some cases may persist for a few days. Hallucinations associated with Cannabis Intoxication are rare except when very high blood levels are reached.

Substance-Induced Psychotic Disorders may at times not resolve promptly when the offending agent is removed. Agents such as amphetamines, phencyclidine, and cocaine have been reported to evoke temporary psychotic states that can sometimes persist for weeks or longer despite removal of the agent and treatment with neuroleptics. These may be initially difficult to distinguish from non-substance-induced Psychotic Disorders.

Some of the medications reported to evoke psychotic symptoms include anesthetics and analgesics, anticholinergic agents, anticonvulsants, antihistamines, antihypertensive and cardiovascular medications, antimicrobial medications, antiparkinsonian medications, chemotherapeutic agents (e.g., cyclosporine and procarbazine), corticosteroids, gastrointestinal medications, muscle relaxants, nonsteroidal anti-inflammatory medications, other over-the-counter medications (e.g., phenylephrine, pseudoephedrine), antidepressant medication, and disulfiram. Toxins reported to induce psychotic symptoms include anticholinesterase, organophosphate insecticides, nerve gases, carbon monoxide, carbon dioxide, and volatile substances such as fuel or paint.

Differential Diagnosis

A diagnosis of Substance-Induced Psychotic Disorder should be made instead of a diagnosis of **Substance Intoxication** or **Substance Withdrawal** only when the psychotic symptoms are judged to be in excess of those usually associated with the intoxication or withdrawal syndrome and when the symptoms are sufficiently severe to warrant independent clinical attention. Individuals intoxicated with stimulants, cannabis, the opioid meperidine, or phencyclidine, or those withdrawing from alcohol or sedatives, may experience altered perceptions (scintillating lights, sounds, visual illusions) that they recognize as drug effects. If reality testing for these experiences remains intact (i.e., the person recognizes that the perception is substance induced and neither believes in nor acts on it), the diagnosis is not Substance-Induced Psychotic Disorder. Instead, **Substance Intoxication** or **Withdrawal, With Perceptual Disturbances,** is diagnosed (e.g., Cocaine Intoxication, With Perceptual Disturbances). "Flashback" hallucinations that can occur long after the use of hallucinogens has stopped are diagnosed as **Hallucinogen Persisting Perception Disorder** (see p. 233). Moreover, if substance-induced psychotic symptoms occur exclusively during the course of a **delirium,** as in some severe forms of Alcohol Withdrawal, the psychotic symptoms are considered to be an associated feature of the delirium and are not diagnosed separately.

A Substance-Induced Psychotic Disorder is distinguished from a **primary Psychotic Disorder** by the fact that a substance is judged to be etiologically related to the symptoms (see p. 310).

A Substance-Induced Psychotic Disorder due to a prescribed treatment for a mental or general medical condition must have its onset while the person is receiving the medication (or during withdrawal, if there is a withdrawal syndrome associated with the medication). Once the treatment is discontinued, the psychotic symptoms will usually remit within days to several weeks (depending on the half-life of the substance and the presence of a withdrawal syndrome). If symptoms persist beyond 4 weeks, other causes for the psychotic symptoms should be considered. Because individuals with general medical conditions often take medications for those conditions, the clinician must consider the possibility that the psychotic symptoms are caused by the physiological consequences of the general medical condition rather than the medication, in which case **Psychotic Disorder Due to a General Medical Condition** is diagnosed. The history often provides the primary basis for such a judgment. At times, a change in the treatment for the general medical condition (e.g., medication substitution or discontinuation) may be needed to determine empirically for that person whether the medication is the causative agent. If the clinician has ascertained that the disturbance is due to both a general medical condition and substance use, both diagnoses (i.e., Psychotic Disorder Due to a General Medical Condition and Substance-Induced Psychotic Disorder) may be given. When there is insufficient evidence to determine whether the psychotic symptoms are due to a substance (including a medication) or to a general medical condition or are primary (i.e., not due to either a substance or a general medical condition), **Psychotic Disorder Not Otherwise Specified** would be indicated.

■ **Diagnostic criteria for Substance-Induced Psychotic Disorder**

A. Prominent hallucinations or delusions. **Note:** Do not include hallucinations if the person has insight that they are substance induced.

B. There is evidence from the history, physical examination, or laboratory findings of either (1) or (2):

  (1) the symptoms in Criterion A developed during, or within a month of, Substance Intoxication or Withdrawal

  (2) medication use is etiologically related to the disturbance

C. The disturbance is not better accounted for by a Psychotic Disorder that is not substance induced. Evidence that the symptoms are better accounted for by a Psychotic Disorder that is not substance induced might include the following: the symptoms precede the onset of the substance use (or medication use); the symptoms persist for a substantial period of time (e.g., about a month) after the cessation of acute withdrawal or severe intoxication, or are substantially in excess of what would be expected given the type or amount of the substance used or the duration of use; or there is other evidence that suggests the existence of an independent non-substance-induced Psychotic Disorder (e.g., a history of recurrent non-substance-related episodes).

D. The disturbance does not occur exclusively during the course of a delirium.

Note: This diagnosis should be made instead of a diagnosis of Substance Intoxication or Substance Withdrawal only when the symptoms are in excess of those usually associated with the intoxication or withdrawal syndrome and when the symptoms are sufficiently severe to warrant independent clinical attention.

Code [Specific Substance]–Induced Psychotic Disorder:

  (291.5 Alcohol, With Delusions; 291.3 Alcohol, With Hallucinations; 292.11 Amphetamine [or Amphetamine-Like Substance], With Delusions; 292.12 Amphetamine [or Amphetamine-Like Substance], With Hallucinations; 292.11 Cannabis, With Delusions; 292.12 Cannabis, With Hallucinations; 292.11 Cocaine, With Delusions; 292.12 Cocaine, With Hallucinations; 292.11 Hallucinogen, With Delusions; 292.12 Hallucinogen, With Hallucinations; 292.11 Inhalant, With Delusions; 292.12 Inhalant, With Hallucinations; 292.11 Opioid, With Delusions; 292.12 Opioid, With Hallucinations; 292.11 Phencyclidine [or Phencyclidine-Like Substance], With Delusions; 292.12 Phencyclidine [or Phencyclidine-Like Substance], With Hallucinations; 292.11 Sedative, Hypnotic, or Anxiolytic, With Delusions; 292.12 Sedative, Hypnotic, or Anxiolytic, With Hallucinations; 292.11 Other [or Unknown] Substance, With Delusions; 292.12 Other [or Unknown] Substance, With Hallucinations)

(continued)

☐ **Diagnostic criteria for Substance-Induced Psychotic Disorder** (*continued*)

Specify if (see table on p. 177 for applicability by substance):
With Onset During Intoxication: if criteria are met for Intoxication with the substance and the symptoms develop during the intoxication syndrome
With Onset During Withdrawal: if criteria are met for Withdrawal from the substance and the symptoms develop during, or shortly after, a withdrawal syndrome

298.9 Psychotic Disorder Not Otherwise Specified

This category includes psychotic symptomatology (i.e., delusions, hallucinations, disorganized speech, grossly disorganized or catatonic behavior) about which there is inadequate information to make a specific diagnosis or about which there is contradictory information, or disorders with psychotic symptoms that do not meet the criteria for any specific Psychotic Disorder.

Examples include

1. Postpartum psychosis that does not meet criteria for Mood Disorder With Psychotic Features, Brief Psychotic Disorder, Psychotic Disorder Due to a General Medical Condition, or Substance-Induced Psychotic Disorder
2. Psychotic symptoms that have lasted for less than 1 month but that have not yet remitted, so that the criteria for Brief Psychotic Disorder are not met
3. Persistent auditory hallucinations in the absence of any other features
4. Persistent nonbizarre delusions with periods of overlapping mood episodes that have been present for a substantial portion of the delusional disturbance
5. Situations in which the clinician has concluded that a Psychotic Disorder is present, but is unable to determine whether it is primary, due to a general medical condition, or substance induced

Mood Disorders

The Mood Disorders section includes disorders that have a disturbance in mood as the predominant feature. The section is divided into three parts. The first part describes mood episodes (Major Depressive Episode, Manic Episode, Mixed Episode, and Hypomanic Episode) that have been included separately at the beginning of this section for convenience in diagnosing the various Mood Disorders. These episodes do not have their own diagnostic codes and cannot be diagnosed as separate entities; however, they serve as the building blocks for the disorder diagnoses. The second part describes the Mood Disorders (e.g., Major Depressive Disorder, Dysthymic Disorder, Bipolar I Disorder). The criteria sets for most of the Mood Disorders require the presence or absence of the mood episodes described in the first part of the section. The third part includes the specifiers that describe either the most recent mood episode or the course of recurrent episodes.

The Mood Disorders are divided into the Depressive Disorders ("unipolar depression"), the Bipolar Disorders, and two disorders based on etiology—Mood Disorder Due to a General Medical Condition and Substance-Induced Mood Disorder. The Depressive Disorders (i.e., Major Depressive Disorder, Dysthymic Disorder, and Depressive Disorder Not Otherwise Specified) are distinguished from the Bipolar Disorders by the fact that there is no history of ever having had a Manic, Mixed, or Hypomanic Episode. The Bipolar Disorders (i.e., Bipolar I Disorder, Bipolar II Disorder, Cyclothymic Disorder, and Bipolar Disorder Not Otherwise Specified) involve the presence (or history) of Manic Episodes, Mixed Episodes, or Hypomanic Episodes, usually accompanied by the presence (or history) of Major Depressive Episodes.

Major Depressive Disorder is characterized by one or more Major Depressive Episodes (i.e., at least 2 weeks of depressed mood or loss of interest accompanied by at least four additional symptoms of depression).

Dysthymic Disorder is characterized by at least 2 years of depressed mood for more days than not, accompanied by additional depressive symptoms that do not meet criteria for a Major Depressive Episode.

Depressive Disorder Not Otherwise Specified is included for coding disorders with depressive features that do not meet criteria for Major Depressive Disorder, Dysthymic Disorder, Adjustment Disorder With Depressed Mood, or Adjustment Disorder With Mixed Anxiety and Depressed Mood (or depressive symptoms about which there is inadequate or contradictory information).

Bipolar I Disorder is characterized by one or more Manic or Mixed Episodes, usually accompanied by Major Depressive Episodes.

Bipolar II Disorder is characterized by one or more Major Depressive Episodes accompanied by at least one Hypomanic Episode.

Cyclothymic Disorder is characterized by at least 2 years of numerous periods of hypomanic symptoms that do not meet criteria for a Manic Episode and numerous periods of depressive symptoms that do not meet criteria for a Major Depressive Episode.

Bipolar Disorder Not Otherwise Specified is included for coding disorders with bipolar features that do not meet criteria for any of the specific Bipolar Disorders defined in this section (or bipolar symptoms about which there is inadequate or contradictory information).

Mood Disorder Due to a General Medical Condition is characterized by a prominent and persistent disturbance in mood that is judged to be a direct physiological consequence of a general medical condition.

Substance-Induced Mood Disorder is characterized by a prominent and persistent disturbance in mood that is judged to be a direct physiological consequence of a drug of abuse, a medication, another somatic treatment for depression, or toxin exposure.

Mood Disorder Not Otherwise Specified is included for coding disorders with mood symptoms that do not meet the criteria for any specific Mood Disorder and in which it is difficult to choose between Depressive Disorder Not Otherwise Specified and Bipolar Disorder Not Otherwise Specified (e.g., acute agitation).

The specifiers described in the third part of the section are provided to increase diagnostic specificity, create more homogeneous subgroups, assist in treatment selection, and improve the prediction of prognosis. Some of the specifiers describe the current (or most recent) mood episode (i.e., **Severity/Psychotic/Remission, Chronic, With Catatonic Features, With Melancholic Features, With Atypical Features, With Postpartum Onset**). Table 1 (p. 376) indicates which episode specifiers apply to each codable Mood Disorder. Other specifiers describe the course of recurrent mood episodes (i.e., **Longitudinal Course Specifiers, With Seasonal Pattern, With Rapid Cycling**). Table 2 (p. 388) indicates which course specifiers apply to each codable Mood Disorder. The specifiers that indicate severity, remission, and psychotic features can be coded in the fifth digit of the diagnostic code for most of the Mood Disorders. The other specifiers cannot be coded.

The Mood Disorders section is organized as follows:

- **Mood Episodes**

  Major Depressive Episode (p. 320)
  Manic Episode (p. 328)
  Mixed Episode (p. 333)
  Hypomanic Episode (p. 335)

- **Depressive Disorders**

  296.xx   Major Depressive Disorder (p. 339)
  300.4   Dysthymic Disorder (p. 345)
  311   Depressive Disorder Not Otherwise Specified (p. 350)

- **Bipolar Disorders**

  296.xx   Bipolar I Disorder (p. 350)
  296.89   Bipolar II Disorder (p. 359)
  301.13   Cyclothymic Disorder (p. 363)
  296.80   Bipolar Disorder Not Otherwise Specified (p. 366)

- **Other Mood Disorders**

  293.83 Mood Disorder Due to . . . *[Indicate the General Medical Condition]*
         (p. 366)
  29x.xx Substance-Induced Mood Disorder (p. 370)
  296.90 Mood Disorder Not Otherwise Specified (p. 375)

- **Specifiers describing the most recent mood episode**

  Mild, Moderate, Severe Without Psychotic Features, Severe With Psychotic
      Features, In Partial Remission, In Full Remission (for Major Depressive
      Episode, p. 376; for Manic Episode, p. 378; for Mixed Episode, p. 380)
  Chronic (p. 382)
  With Catatonic Features (p. 382)
  With Melancholic Features (p. 383)
  With Atypical Features (p. 384)
  With Postpartum Onset (p. 386)

- **Specifiers describing course of recurrent episodes**

  Longitudinal Course Specifiers (With or Without Full Interepisode Recovery)
      (p. 387)
  With Seasonal Pattern (p. 389)
  With Rapid Cycling (p. 390)

Recording Procedures for Major Depressive Disorder and Bipolar I and Bipolar II Disorders

Selecting diagnostic codes.   The diagnostic codes are selected as follows:

For Major Depressive Disorder:
1. The first three digits are 296.
2. The fourth digit is either 2 (if there is only a single Major Depressive Episode) or 3 (if there are recurrent Major Depressive Episodes).
3. The fifth digit indicates the following: 1 for Mild severity, 2 for Moderate severity, 3 for Severe Without Psychotic Features, 4 for Severe With Psychotic Features, 5 for In Partial Remission, 6 for In Full Remission, and 0 if Unspecified.

For Bipolar I Disorder:
1. The first three digits are also 296.
2. The fourth digit is 0 if there is a single Manic Episode. For recurrent episodes, the fourth digit is 4 if the current or most recent episode is a Hypomanic Episode or a Manic Episode, 6 if it is a Mixed Episode, 5 if it is a Major Depressive Episode, and 7 if the current or most recent episode is Unspecified.
3. The fifth digit (except for Bipolar I Disorder, Most Recent Episode Hypomanic, and Bipolar I Disorder, Most Recent Episode Unspecified) indicates the following: 1 for Mild severity, 2 for Moderate severity, 3 for Severe Without Psychotic Features, 4 for Severe With Psychotic Features, 5 for In Partial Remission, 6 for In Full Remission, and 0 if Unspecified. For Bipolar I Disorder, Most Recent Episode Hypomanic, the fifth digit is always "0." For Bipolar Disorder, Most Recent Episode Unspecified, there is no fifth digit.

For Bipolar II Disorder, the diagnostic code is 296.89.

Recording the name of the diagnosis.   In recording the name of a diagnosis, terms should be listed in the following order:

1. Name of disorder (e.g., Major Depressive Disorder, Bipolar Disorder)
2. Specifiers coded in the fourth digit (e.g., Recurrent, Most Recent Episode Manic)
3. Specifiers coded in the fifth digit (e.g., Mild, Severe With Psychotic Features, In Partial Remission)
4. As many specifiers (without codes) as apply to the most recent episode (e.g., With Melancholic Features, With Postpartum Onset)
5. As many specifiers (without codes) as apply to the course of recurrent episodes (e.g., With Seasonal Pattern, With Rapid Cycling)

The following examples illustrate how to record a Mood Disorder diagnosis with specifiers:

*   296.32 Major Depressive Disorder, Recurrent, Moderate, With Atypical Features, With Seasonal Pattern, With Full Interepisode Recovery
*   296.54 Bipolar I Disorder, Most Recent Episode Depressed, Severe With Psychotic Features, With Melancholic Features, With Rapid Cycling

Mood Episodes

Major Depressive Episode

Episode Features

The essential feature of a Major Depressive Episode is a period of at least 2 weeks during which there is either depressed mood or the loss of interest or pleasure in nearly all activities. In children and adolescents, the mood may be irritable rather than sad. The individual must also experience at least four additional symptoms drawn from a list that includes changes in appetite or weight, sleep, and psychomotor activity; decreased energy; feelings of worthlessness or guilt; difficulty thinking, concentrating, or making decisions; or recurrent thoughts of death or suicidal ideation, plans, or attempts. To count toward a Major Depressive Episode, a symptom must either be newly present or must have clearly worsened compared with the person's preepisode status. The symptoms must persist for most of the day, nearly every day, for at least 2 consecutive weeks. The episode must be accompanied by clinically significant distress or impairment in social, occupational, or other important areas of functioning. For some individuals with milder episodes, functioning may appear to be normal, but requires markedly increased effort.

The mood in a Major Depressive Episode is often described by the person as depressed, sad, hopeless, discouraged, or "down in the dumps" (Criterion A1). In some cases, sadness may be denied at first, but may subsequently be elicited by interview (e.g., by pointing out that the individual looks as if he or she is about to cry). In some individuals who complain of feeling "blah," having no feelings, or feeling anxious, the presence of a depressed mood can be inferred from the person's facial expression and demeanor. Some individuals emphasize somatic complaints (e.g., bodily aches and pains) rather than reporting feelings of sadness. Many individuals report or exhibit increased irritability (e.g., persistent anger, a tendency to respond to events with angry outbursts or blaming others, or an exaggerated sense of frustration over minor matters). In children and adolescents, an irritable or cranky mood may develop rather than a sad or dejected mood. This presentation should be differentiated from a "spoiled child" pattern of irritability when frustrated.

Loss of interest or pleasure is nearly always present, at least to some degree. Individuals may report feeling less interested in hobbies, "not caring anymore," or not feeling any enjoyment in activities that were previously considered pleasurable (Criterion A2). Family members often notice social withdrawal or neglect of pleasurable avocations (e.g., a formerly avid golfer no longer plays, a child who used to enjoy soccer finds excuses not to practice). In some individuals, there is a significant reduction from previous levels of sexual interest or desire.

Appetite is usually reduced, and many individuals feel that they have to force themselves to eat. Other individuals, particularly those encountered in ambulatory settings, may have increased appetite and may crave specific foods (e.g., sweets or other carbohydrates). When appetite changes are severe (in either direction), there may be a significant loss or gain in weight, or, in children, a failure to make expected weight gains may be noted (Criterion A3).

The most common sleep disturbance associated with a Major Depressive Episode is insomnia (Criterion A4). Individuals typically have middle insomnia (i.e., waking up during the night and having difficulty returning to sleep) or terminal insomnia (i.e., waking too early and being unable to return to sleep). Initial insomnia (i.e., difficulty falling asleep) may also occur. Less frequently, individuals present with oversleeping (hypersomnia) in the form of prolonged sleep episodes at night or increased daytime sleep. Sometimes the reason that the individual seeks treatment is for the disturbed sleep.

Psychomotor changes include agitation (e.g., the inability to sit still, pacing, hand-wringing; or pulling or rubbing of the skin, clothing, or other objects) or retardation (e.g., slowed speech, thinking, and body movements; increased pauses before answering; speech that is decreased in volume, inflection, amount, or variety of content, or muteness) (Criterion A5). The psychomotor agitation or retardation must be severe enough to be observable by others and not represent merely subjective feelings.

Decreased energy, tiredness, and fatigue are common (Criterion A6). A person may report sustained fatigue without physical exertion. Even the smallest tasks seem to require substantial effort. The efficiency with which tasks are accomplished may be reduced. For example, an individual may complain that washing and dressing in the morning are exhausting and take twice as long as usual.

The sense of worthlessness or guilt associated with a Major Depressive Episode may include unrealistic negative evaluations of one's worth or guilty preoccupations or ruminations over minor past failings (Criterion A7). Such individuals often misinterpret neutral or trivial day-to-day events as evidence of personal defects and have an exaggerated sense of responsibility for untoward events. For example, a realtor may become preoccupied with self-blame for failing to make sales even when the market has collapsed generally and other realtors are equally unable to make sales. The sense of worthlessness or guilt may be of delusional proportions (e.g., an individual who is convinced that he or she is personally responsible for world poverty). Blaming oneself for being sick and for failing to meet occupational or interpersonal responsibilities as a result of the depression is very common and, unless delusional, is not considered sufficient to meet this criterion.

Many individuals report impaired ability to think, concentrate, or make decisions (Criterion A8). They may appear easily distracted or complain of memory difficulties. Those in intellectually demanding academic or occupational pursuits are often unable to function adequately even when they have mild concentration problems (e.g., a computer programmer who can no longer perform complicated but previously manageable tasks). In children, a precipitous drop in grades may reflect poor concentration. In elderly individuals with a Major Depressive Episode, memory difficulties may be the chief complaint and may be mistaken for early signs of a dementia ("pseudodementia"). When the Major Depressive Episode is successfully treated, the memory problems often fully abate. However, in some individuals, particularly elderly persons, a Major Depressive Episode may sometimes be the initial presentation of an irreversible dementia.

Frequently there may be thoughts of death, suicidal ideation, or suicide attempts (Criterion A9). These thoughts range from a belief that others would be better off if the person were dead, to transient but recurrent thoughts of committing suicide, to actual specific plans of how to commit suicide. The frequency, intensity, and lethality of these thoughts can be quite variable. Less severely suicidal individuals may report transient (1- to 2-minute), recurrent (once or twice a week) thoughts. More severely suicidal individuals may have acquired materials (e.g., a rope or a gun) to be used in the suicide attempt and may have established a location and time when they will be isolated from others so that they can accomplish the suicide. Although these behaviors are associated statistically with suicide attempts and may be helpful in identifying a high-risk group, many studies have shown that it is not possible to predict accurately whether or when a particular individual with depression will attempt suicide. Motivations for suicide may include a desire to give up in the face of perceived insurmountable obstacles or an intense wish to end an excruciatingly painful emotional state that is perceived by the person to be without end.

A diagnosis of a Major Depressive Episode is not made if the symptoms meet criteria for a Mixed Episode (Criterion B). A Mixed Episode is characterized by the symptoms of both a Manic Episode and a Major Depressive Episode occurring nearly every day for at least a 1-week period.

The degree of impairment associated with a Major Depressive Episode varies, but even in mild cases, there must be either clinically significant distress or some interference in social, occupational, or other important areas of functioning (Criterion C). If impairment is severe, the person may lose the ability to function socially or occupationally. In extreme cases, the person may be unable to perform minimal self-care (e.g., feeding or clothing self) or to maintain minimal personal hygiene.

A careful interview is essential to elicit symptoms of a Major Depressive Episode. Reporting may be compromised by difficulties in concentrating, impaired memory, or a tendency to deny, discount, or explain away symptoms. Information from additional informants can be especially helpful in clarifying the course of current or prior Major Depressive Episodes and in assessing whether there have been any Manic or Hypomanic Episodes. Because Major Depressive Episodes can begin gradually, a review of clinical information that focuses on the worst part of the current episode may be most likely to detect the presence of symptoms. The evaluation of the symptoms of a Major Depressive Episode is especially difficult when they occur in an individual who also has a general medical condition (e.g., cancer, stroke, myocardial infarction, diabetes). Some of the criterion items of a Major Depressive Episode are identical to the characteristic signs and symptoms of general medical conditions (e.g., weight loss with untreated diabetes, fatigue with cancer). Such symptoms should count toward a Major Depressive Episode except when they are clearly and fully accounted for by a general medical condition. For example, weight loss in a person with ulcerative colitis who has many bowel movements and little food intake should not be counted toward a Major Depressive Episode. On the other hand, when sadness, guilt, insomnia, or weight loss are present in a person with a recent myocardial infarction, each symptom would count toward a Major Depressive Episode because these are not clearly and fully accounted for by the physiological effects of a myocardial infarction. Similarly, when symptoms are clearly due to mood-incongruent delusions or hallucinations (e.g., a 30-pound weight loss related to not eating because of a delusion that one's food is being poisoned), these symptoms do not count toward a Major Depressive Episode.

By definition, a Major Depressive Episode is not due to the direct physiological effects of a drug of abuse (e.g., in the context of Alcohol Intoxication or Cocaine Withdrawal), to the side effects of medications or treatments (e.g., steroids), or to toxin exposure. Similarly, the episode is not due to the direct physiological effects of a general medical condition (e.g., hypothyroidism) (Criterion D). Moreover, if the symptoms begin within 2 months of the loss of a loved one and do not persist beyond these 2 months, they are generally considered to result from Bereavement (see p. 684), unless they are associated with marked functional impairment or include morbid preoccupation with worthlessness, suicidal ideation, psychotic symptoms, or psychomotor retardation (Criterion E).

Associated Features and Disorders

Associated descriptive features and mental disorders.   Individuals with a Major Depressive Episode frequently present with tearfulness, irritability, brooding, obsessive rumination, anxiety, phobias, excessive worry over physical health, and complaints of pain (e.g., headaches or joint, abdominal, or other pains). During a Major Depressive Episode, some individuals have Panic Attacks that occur in a pattern that meets criteria for Panic Disorder. In children, separation anxiety may occur. Some individuals note difficulty in intimate relationships, less satisfying social interactions, or difficulties in sexual functioning (e.g., anorgasmia in women or erectile dysfunction in men). There may be marital problems (e.g., divorce), occupational problems (e.g., loss of job), academic problems (e.g., truancy, school failure), Alcohol or Other Substance Abuse, or increased utilization of medical services. The most serious consequence of a Major Depressive Episode is attempted or completed suicide. Suicide risk is especially high for individuals with psychotic features, a history of previous suicide attempts, a family history of completed suicides, or concurrent substance use. There may also be an increased rate of premature death from general medical conditions. Major Depressive Episodes often follow psychosocial stressors (e.g., the death of a loved one, marital separation, divorce). Childbirth may precipitate a Major Depressive Episode, in which case the specifier With Postpartum Onset is noted (see p. 386).

Associated laboratory findings.   No laboratory findings that are diagnostic of a Major Depressive Episode have been identified. However, a variety of laboratory findings have been noted to be abnormal in groups of individuals with Major Depressive Episodes compared with control subjects. It appears that the same laboratory abnormalities are associated with a Major Depressive Episode regardless of whether the episode is part of a Major Depressive, Bipolar I, or Bipolar II Disorder. Most laboratory abnormalities are state dependent (i.e., affected by the presence or absence of depressive symptoms), but some findings may precede the onset of the episode or persist after its remission. Laboratory tests are more likely to be abnormal in episodes with melancholic or psychotic features and in more severely depressed individuals.

Sleep EEG abnormalities may be evident in 40%–60% of outpatients and in up to 90% of inpatients with a Major Depressive Episode. The most frequently associated polysomnographic findings include 1) sleep continuity disturbances, such as prolonged sleep latency, increased intermittent wakefulness, and early morning awakening; 2) reduced non–rapid eye movement (NREM) stages 3 and 4 sleep (slow-wave sleep), with a shift in slow-wave activity away from the first NREM period; 3) decreased rapid eye movement (REM) latency (i.e., shortened duration of the first NREM period); 4) increased phasic REM activity (i.e., the number of actual eye movements during REM); and 5) increased duration of REM sleep early in the night. Some evidence suggests that these sleep abnormalities may sometimes persist after clinical remission or may precede the onset of the initial Major Depressive Episode.

Neurotransmitters implicated in the pathophysiology of a Major Depressive Episode include norepinephrine, serotonin, acetylcholine, dopamine, and gamma-aminobutyric acid. Evidence that implicates these neurotransmitters includes measures of their levels in blood, cerebrospinal fluid, or urine and platelet receptor functioning. Other laboratory tests that have demonstrated abnormalities include the dexamethasone suppression test, other neuroendocrine challenges, functional and structural brain imaging, evoked potentials, and waking EEG.

Specific Culture, Age, and Gender Features

Culture can influence the experience and communication of symptoms of depression. Underdiagnosis or misdiagnosis can be reduced by being alert to ethnic and cultural specificity in the presenting complaints of a Major Depressive Episode. For example, in some cultures, depression may be experienced largely in somatic terms, rather than with sadness or guilt. Complaints of "nerves" and headaches (in Latino and Mediterranean cultures), of weakness, tiredness, or "imbalance" (in Chinese and Asian cultures), of problems of the "heart" (in Middle Eastern cultures), or of being "heartbroken" (among Hopi) may express the depressive experience. Such presentations combine features of the Depressive, Anxiety, and Somatoform Disorders. Cultures also may differ in judgments about the seriousness of experiencing or expressing dysphoria (e.g., irritability may provoke greater concern than sadness or withdrawal). Culturally distinctive experiences (e.g., fear of being hexed or bewitched, feelings of "heat in the head" or crawling sensations of worms or ants, or vivid feelings of being visited by those who have died) must be distinguished from actual hallucinations or delusions that may be part of a Major Depressive Episode, With Psychotic Features. It is also imperative that the clinician not routinely dismiss a symptom merely because it is viewed as the "norm" for a culture.

The core symptoms of a Major Depressive Episode are the same for children and adolescents, although there are data that suggest that the prominence of characteristic symptoms may change with age. Certain symptoms such as somatic complaints, irritability, and social withdrawal are particularly common in children, whereas psychomotor retardation, hypersomnia, and delusions are less common in prepuberty than in adolescence and adulthood. In prepubertal children, Major Depressive Episodes occur more frequently in conjunction with other mental disorders (especially Disruptive Behavior Disorders, Attention-Deficit Disorders, and Anxiety Disorders) than in isolation. In adolescents, Major Depressive Episodes are frequently associated with Disruptive Behavior Disorders, Attention-Deficit Disorders, Anxiety Disorders, Substance-Related Disorders, and Eating Disorders. In elderly adults, cognitive symptoms (e.g., disorientation, memory loss, and distractibility) may be particularly prominent.

A significant proportion of women report a worsening of the symptoms of a Major Depressive Episode several days before the onset of menses. Studies indicate that depressive episodes occur twice as frequently in women as in men. See the corresponding sections of the texts for Major Depressive Disorder (p. 341), Bipolar I Disorder (p. 352), and Bipolar II Disorder (p. 360) for specific information on gender.

Course

Symptoms of a Major Depressive Episode usually develop over days to weeks. A prodromal period that may include anxiety symptoms and mild depressive symptoms may last for weeks to months before the onset of a full Major Depressive Episode. The duration of a Major Depressive Episode is also variable. An untreated episode typically lasts 6 months or longer, regardless of age at onset. In a majority of cases, there is complete remission of symptoms, and functioning returns to the premorbid level. In a significant proportion of cases (perhaps 20%–30%), some depressive symptoms insufficient to meet full criteria for a Major Depressive Episode may persist for months to years and may be associated with some disability or distress (in which case the specifier In Partial Remission may be noted; p. 377). Partial remission following a Major Depressive Episode appears to be predictive of a similar pattern after subsequent episodes. In some individuals (5%–10%), the full criteria for a Major Depressive Episode continue to be met for 2 or more years (in which case the specifier Chronic may be noted; see p. 382).

Differential Diagnosis

A Major Depressive Episode must be distinguished from a **Mood Disorder Due to a General Medical Condition.** The appropriate diagnosis would be Mood Disorder Due to a General Medical Condition if the mood disturbance is judged to be the direct physiological consequence of a specific general medical condition (e.g., multiple sclerosis, stroke, hypothyroidism) (see p. 366). This determination is based on the history, laboratory findings, or physical examination. If both a Major Depressive Episode and a general medical condition are present but it is judged that the depressive symptoms are not the direct physiological consequence of the general medical condition, then the primary Mood Disorder is recorded on Axis I (e.g., Major Depressive Disorder) and the general medical condition is recorded on Axis III (e.g., myocardial infarction). This would be the case, for example, if the Major Depressive Episode is considered to be the psychological consequence of having the general medical condition or if there is no etiological relationship between the Major Depressive Episode and the general medical condition.

A **Substance-Induced Mood Disorder** is distinguished from a Major Depressive Episode by the fact that a substance (e.g., a drug of abuse, a medication, or a toxin) is judged to be etiologically related to the mood disturbance (see p. 370). For example, depressed mood that occurs only in the context of withdrawal from cocaine would be diagnosed as Cocaine-Induced Mood Disorder, With Depressive Features, With Onset During Withdrawal.

In elderly persons, it is often difficult to determine whether cognitive symptoms (e.g., disorientation, apathy, difficulty concentrating, memory loss) are better accounted for by a **dementia** or by a Major Depressive Episode. A thorough medical evaluation and an evaluation of the onset of the disturbance, temporal sequencing of depressive and cognitive symptoms, course of illness, and treatment response are helpful in making this determination. The premorbid state of the individual may help to differentiate a Major Depressive Episode from a dementia. In a dementia, there is usually a premorbid history of declining cognitive function, whereas the individual with a Major Depressive Episode is much more likely to have a relatively normal premorbid state and abrupt cognitive decline associated with the depression.

Major Depressive Episodes with prominent irritable mood may be difficult to distinguish from **Manic Episodes with irritable mood** or from **Mixed Episodes.** This distinction requires a careful clinical evaluation of the presence of manic symptoms. If criteria are met for both a Manic Episode and a Major Depressive Episode (except for the 2-week duration) nearly every day for at least a 1-week period, this would constitute a Mixed Episode.

Distractibility and low frustration tolerance can occur in both **Attention-Deficit/ Hyperactivity Disorder** and a Major Depressive Episode; if the criteria are met for both, Attention-Deficit/Hyperactivity Disorder may be diagnosed in addition to the Mood Disorder. However, the clinician must be cautious not to overdiagnose a Major Depressive Episode in children with Attention-Deficit/Hyperactivity Disorder whose disturbance in mood is characterized by irritability rather than by sadness or loss of interest.

A Major Depressive Episode that occurs in response to a psychosocial stressor is distinguished from **Adjustment Disorder With Depressed Mood** by the fact that the full criteria for a Major Depressive Episode are not met in Adjustment Disorder. After the loss of a loved one, even if depressive symptoms are of sufficient duration and number to meet criteria for a Major Depressive Episode, they should be attributed to **Bereavement** rather than to a Major Depressive Episode, unless they persist for more than 2 months or include marked functional impairment, morbid preoccupation with worthlessness, suicidal ideation, psychotic symptoms, or psychomotor retardation.

Finally, **periods of sadness** are inherent aspects of the human experience. These periods should not be diagnosed as a Major Depressive Episode unless criteria are met for severity (i.e., five out of nine symptoms), duration (i.e., most of the day, nearly every day for at least 2 weeks), and clinically significant distress or impairment. The diagnosis **Depressive Disorder Not Otherwise Specified** may be appropriate for presentations of depressed mood with clinically significant impairment that do not meet criteria for duration or severity.

■ Criteria for Major Depressive Episode

A. Five (or more) of the following symptoms have been present during the same 2-week period and represent a change from previous functioning; at least one of the symptoms is either (1) depressed mood or (2) loss of interest or pleasure.

Note: Do not include symptoms that are clearly due to a general medical condition, or mood-incongruent delusions or hallucinations.

   (1) depressed mood most of the day, nearly every day, as indicated by either subjective report (e.g., feels sad or empty) or observation made by others (e.g., appears tearful). **Note:** In children and adolescents, can be irritable mood.
   (2) markedly diminished interest or pleasure in all, or almost all, activities most of the day, nearly every day (as indicated by either subjective account or observation made by others)
   (3) significant weight loss when not dieting or weight gain (e.g., a change of more than 5% of body weight in a month), or decrease or increase in appetite nearly every day. **Note:** In children, consider failure to make expected weight gains.
   (4) insomnia or hypersomnia nearly every day
   (5) psychomotor agitation or retardation nearly every day (observable by others, not merely subjective feelings of restlessness or being slowed down)
   (6) fatigue or loss of energy nearly every day
   (7) feelings of worthlessness or excessive or inappropriate guilt (which may be delusional) nearly every day (not merely self-reproach or guilt about being sick)
   (8) diminished ability to think or concentrate, or indecisiveness, nearly every day (either by subjective account or as observed by others)
   (9) recurrent thoughts of death (not just fear of dying), recurrent suicidal ideation without a specific plan, or a suicide attempt or a specific plan for committing suicide

B. The symptoms do not meet criteria for a Mixed Episode (see p. 335).

C. The symptoms cause clinically significant distress or impairment in social, occupational, or other important areas of functioning.

D. The symptoms are not due to the direct physiological effects of a substance (e.g., a drug of abuse, a medication) or a general medical condition (e.g., hypothyroidism).

E. The symptoms are not better accounted for by Bereavement, i.e., after the loss of a loved one, the symptoms persist for longer than 2 months or are characterized by marked functional impairment, morbid preoccupation with worthlessness, suicidal ideation, psychotic symptoms, or psychomotor retardation.

Manic Episode

Episode Features

A Manic Episode is defined by a distinct period during which there is an abnormally and persistently elevated, expansive, or irritable mood. This period of abnormal mood must last at least 1 week (or less if hospitalization is required) (Criterion A). The mood disturbance must be accompanied by at least three additional symptoms from a list that includes inflated self-esteem or grandiosity, decreased need for sleep, pressure of speech, flight of ideas, distractibility, increased involvement in goal-directed activities or psycho-motor agitation, and excessive involvement in pleasurable activities with a high potential for painful consequences. If the mood is irritable (rather than elevated or expansive), at least four of the above symptoms must be present (Criterion B). The symptoms do not meet criteria for a Mixed Episode, which is characterized by the symptoms of both a Manic Episode and a Major Depressive Episode occurring nearly every day for at least a 1-week period (Criterion C). The disturbance must be sufficiently severe to cause marked impairment in social or occupational functioning or to require hospitalization, or it is characterized by the presence of psychotic features (Criterion D). The episode must not be due to the direct physiological effects of a drug of abuse, a medication, other somatic treatments for depression (e.g., electroconvulsive therapy or light therapy) or toxin exposure. The episode must also not be due to the direct physiological effects of a general medical condition (e.g., multiple sclerosis, brain tumor) (Criterion E).

The elevated mood of a Manic Episode may be described as euphoric, unusually good, cheerful, or high. Although the person's mood may initially have an infectious quality for the uninvolved observer, it is recognized as excessive by those who know the person well. The expansive quality of the mood is characterized by unceasing and indiscriminate enthusiasm for interpersonal, sexual, or occupational interactions. For example, the person may spontaneously start extensive conversations with strangers in public places, or a salesperson may telephone strangers at home in the early morning hours to initiate sales. Although elevated mood is considered the prototypical symptom, the predominant mood disturbance may be irritability, particularly when the person's wishes are thwarted. Lability of mood (e.g., the alternation between euphoria and irritability) is frequently seen.

Inflated self-esteem is typically present, ranging from uncritical self-confidence to marked grandiosity, and may reach delusional proportions (Criterion B1). Individuals may give advice on matters about which they have no special knowledge (e.g., how to run the United Nations). Despite lack of any particular experience or talent, the individual may embark on writing a novel or composing a symphony or seek publicity for some impractical invention. Grandiose delusions are common (e.g., having a special relation-ship to God or to some public figure from the political, religious, or entertainment world).

Almost invariably, there is a decreased need for sleep (Criterion B2). The person usually awakens several hours earlier than usual, feeling full of energy. When the sleep disturbance is severe, the person may go for days without sleep and yet not feel tired.

Manic speech is typically pressured, loud, rapid, and difficult to interrupt (Criterion B3). Individuals may talk nonstop, sometimes for hours on end, and without regard for others' wishes to communicate. Speech is sometimes characterized by joking, punning, and amusing irrelevancies. The individual may become theatrical, with dramatic mannerisms and singing. Sounds rather than meaningful conceptual relationships may govern word choice (i.e., clanging). If the person's mood is more irritable than expansive, speech may be marked by complaints, hostile comments, or angry tirades.

The individual's thoughts may race, often at a rate faster than can be articulated (Criterion B4). Some individuals with Manic Episodes report that this experience resembles watching two or three television programs simultaneously. Frequently there is flight of ideas evidenced by a nearly continuous flow of accelerated speech, with abrupt changes from one topic to another. For example, while talking about a potential business deal to sell computers, a salesperson may shift to discussing in minute detail the history of the computer chip, the industrial revolution, or applied mathematics. When flight of ideas is severe, speech may become disorganized and incoherent.

Distractibility (Criterion B5) is evidenced by an inability to screen out irrelevant external stimuli (e.g., the interviewer's tie, background noises or conversations, or furnishings in the room). There may be a reduced ability to differentiate between thoughts that are germane to the topic and thoughts that are only slightly relevant or clearly irrelevant.

The increase in goal-directed activity often involves excessive planning of, and excessive participation in, multiple activities (e.g., sexual, occupational, political, religious) (Criterion B6). Increased sexual drive, fantasies, and behavior are often present. The person may simultaneously take on multiple new business ventures without regard for the apparent risks or the need to complete each venture satisfactorily. Almost invariably, there is increased sociability (e.g., renewing old acquaintances or calling friends or even strangers at all hours of the day or night), without regard to the intrusive, domineering, and demanding nature of these interactions. Individuals often display psychomotor agitation or restlessness by pacing or by holding multiple conversations simultaneously (e.g., by telephone and in person at the same time). Some individuals write a torrent of letters on many different topics to friends, public figures, or the media.

Expansiveness, unwarranted optimism, grandiosity, and poor judgment often lead to an imprudent involvement in pleasurable activities such as buying sprees, reckless driving, foolish business investments, and sexual behavior unusual for the person, even though these activities are likely to have painful consequences (Criterion B7). The individual may purchase many unneeded items (e.g., 20 pairs of shoes, expensive antiques) without the money to pay for them. Unusual sexual behavior may include infidelity or indiscriminate sexual encounters with strangers.

The impairment resulting from the disturbance must be severe enough to cause marked impairment in functioning or to require hospitalization to protect the individual from the negative consequences of actions that result from poor judgment (e.g., financial losses, illegal activities, loss of employment, assaultive behavior). By definition, the presence of psychotic features during a Manic Episode constitutes marked impairment in functioning (Criterion D).

Symptoms like those seen in a Manic Episode may be due to the direct effects of antidepressant medication, electroconvulsive therapy, light therapy, or medication prescribed for other general medical conditions (e.g., corticosteroids). Such presentations are not considered Manic Episodes and do not count toward the diagnosis of Bipolar I Disorder. For example, if a person with recurrent Major Depressive Disorder develops manic symptoms following a course of antidepressant medication, the episode is diagnosed as a Substance-Induced Mood Disorder, With Manic Features, and there is no switch from a diagnosis of Major Depressive Disorder to Bipolar I Disorder. Some evidence suggests that there may be a bipolar "diathesis" in individuals who develop manic-like episodes following somatic treatment for depression. Such individuals may have an increased likelihood of future Manic, Mixed, or Hypomanic Episodes that are not related to substances or somatic treatments for depression. This may be an especially important consideration in children and adolescents.

Associated Features and Disorders

Associated descriptive features and mental disorders.   Individuals with a Manic Episode frequently do not recognize that they are ill and resist efforts to be treated. They may travel impulsively to other cities, losing contact with relatives and caretakers. They may change their dress, makeup, or personal appearance to a more sexually suggestive or dramatically flamboyant style that is out of character for them. They may engage in activities that have a disorganized or bizarre quality (e.g., distributing candy, money, or advice to passing strangers). Gambling and antisocial behaviors may accompany the Manic Episode. Ethical concerns may be disregarded even by those who are typically very conscientious (e.g., a stockbroker inappropriately buys and sells stock without the clients' knowledge or permission; a scientist incorporates the findings of others). The person may be hostile and physically threatening to others. Some individuals, especially those with psychotic features, may become physically assaultive or suicidal. Adverse consequences of a Manic Episode (e.g., involuntary hospitalization, difficulties with the law, or serious financial difficulties) often result from poor judgment and hyperactivity. When no longer in the Manic Episode, most individuals are regretful for behaviors engaged in during the Manic Episode. Some individuals describe having a much sharper sense of smell, hearing, or vision (e.g., colors appear very bright). When catatonic symptoms (e.g., stupor, mutism, negativism, and posturing) are present, the specifier With Catatonic Features may be indicated (see p. 382).

Mood may shift rapidly to anger or depression. Depressive symptoms may last moments, hours, or, more rarely, days. Not uncommonly, the depressive symptoms and manic symptoms occur simultaneously. If the criteria for both a Major Depressive Episode and a Manic Episode are prominent every day for at least 1 week, the episode is considered to be a Mixed Episode (see p. 333). As the Manic Episode develops, there is often a substantial increase in the use of alcohol or stimulants, which may exacerbate or prolong the episode.

Associated laboratory findings.   No laboratory findings that are diagnostic of a Manic Episode have been identified. However, a variety of laboratory findings have been noted to be abnormal in groups of individuals with Manic Episodes compared with control subjects. Laboratory findings in Manic Episodes include polysomnographic abnormalities, increased cortisol secretion, and absence of dexamethasone nonsuppression. There may be abnormalities involving the norepinephrine, serotonin, acetylcholine, dopamine, or gamma-aminobutyric acid neurotransmitter systems, as demonstrated by studies of neurotransmitter metabolites, receptor functioning, pharmacological provocation, and neuroendocrine function.

Specific Culture, Age, and Gender Features

Cultural considerations that were suggested for Major Depressive Episodes are also relevant to Manic Episodes (see p. 324). Manic Episodes in adolescents are more likely to include psychotic features and may be associated with school truancy, antisocial behavior, school failure, or substance use. A significant minority of adolescents appear to have a history of long-standing behavior problems that precede the onset of a frank Manic Episode. It is unclear whether these problems represent a prolonged prodrome to Bipolar Disorder or an independent disorder. See the corresponding sections of the texts for Bipolar I Disorder (p. 352) and Bipolar II Disorder (p. 360) for specific information on gender.

Course

The mean age at onset for a first Manic Episode is the early 20s, but some cases start in adolescence and others start after age 50 years. Manic Episodes typically begin suddenly, with a rapid escalation of symptoms over a few days. Frequently, Manic Episodes occur following psychosocial stressors. The episodes usually last from a few weeks to several months and are briefer and end more abruptly than Major Depressive Episodes. In many instances (50%–60%), a Major Depressive Episode immediately precedes or immediately follows a Manic Episode, with no intervening period of euthymia. If the Manic Episode occurs in the postpartum period, there may be an increased risk for recurrence in subsequent postpartum periods and the specifier With Postpartum Onset is applicable (see p. 386).

Differential Diagnosis

A Manic Episode must be distinguished from a **Mood Disorder Due to a General Medical Condition.** The appropriate diagnosis would be Mood Disorder Due to a General Medical Condition if the mood disturbance is judged to be the direct physiological consequence of a specific general medical condition (e.g., multiple sclerosis, brain tumor, Cushing's syndrome) (see p. 366). This determination is based on the history, laboratory findings, or physical examination. If it is judged that the manic symptoms are not the direct physiological consequence of the general medical condition, then the primary Mood Disorder is recorded on Axis I (e.g., Bipolar I Disorder) and the general medical condition is recorded on Axis III (e.g., myocardial infarction). A late onset of a first Manic Episode (e.g., after age 50 years) should alert the clinician to the possibility of an etiological general medical condition or substance.

A **Substance-Induced Mood Disorder** is distinguished from a Manic Episode by the fact that a substance (e.g., a drug of abuse, a medication, or exposure to a toxin) is judged to be etiologically related to the mood disturbance (see p. 370). Symptoms like those seen in a Manic Episode may be precipitated by a drug of abuse (e.g., manic symptoms that occur only in the context of intoxication with cocaine would be diagnosed as Cocaine-Induced Mood Disorder, With Manic Features, With Onset During Intoxication). Symptoms like those seen in a Manic Episode may also be precipitated by antidepressant treatment such as medication, electroconvulsive therapy, or light therapy. Such episodes are also diagnosed as Substance-Induced Mood Disorders (e.g., Amitriptyline-Induced Mood Disorder, With Manic Features; Electroconvulsive Therapy–Induced Mood Disorder, With Manic Features).

Manic Episodes should be distinguished from **Hypomanic Episodes.** Although Manic Episodes and Hypomanic Episodes have an identical list of characteristic symptoms, the disturbance in Hypomanic Episodes is not sufficiently severe to cause marked impairment in social or occupational functioning or to require hospitalization. Some Hypomanic Episodes may evolve into full Manic Episodes.

Major Depressive Episodes with prominent irritable mood may be difficult to distinguish from Manic Episodes with irritable mood or from **Mixed Episodes.** This determination requires a careful clinical evaluation of the presence of manic symptoms. If criteria are met for both a Manic Episode and a Major Depressive Episode nearly every day for at least a 1-week period, this would constitute a Mixed Episode.

Attention-Deficit/Hyperactivity Disorder and a Manic Episode are both characterized by excessive activity, impulsive behavior, poor judgment, and denial of problems. Attention-Deficit/Hyperactivity Disorder is distinguished from a Manic Episode by its characteristic early onset (i.e., before age 7 years), chronic rather than episodic course, lack of relatively clear onsets and offsets, and the absence of abnormally expansive or elevated mood or psychotic features.

■ Criteria for Manic Episode

A. A distinct period of abnormally and persistently elevated, expansive, or irritable mood, lasting at least 1 week (or any duration if hospitalization is necessary).

B. During the period of mood disturbance, three (or more) of the following symptoms have persisted (four if the mood is only irritable) and have been present to a significant degree:

    (1) inflated self-esteem or grandiosity

    (2) decreased need for sleep (e.g., feels rested after only 3 hours of sleep)

    (3) more talkative than usual or pressure to keep talking

    (4) flight of ideas or subjective experience that thoughts are racing

    (5) distractibility (i.e., attention too easily drawn to unimportant or irrelevant external stimuli)

    (6) increase in goal-directed activity (either socially, at work or school, or sexually) or psychomotor agitation

    (7) excessive involvement in pleasurable activities that have a high potential for painful consequences (e.g., engaging in unrestrained buying sprees, sexual indiscretions, or foolish business investments)

C. The symptoms do not meet criteria for a Mixed Episode (see p. 335).

D. The mood disturbance is sufficiently severe to cause marked impairment in occupational functioning or in usual social activities or relationships with others, or to necessitate hospitalization to prevent harm to self or others, or there are psychotic features.

E. The symptoms are not due to the direct physiological effects of a substance (e.g., a drug of abuse, a medication, or other treatment) or a general medical condition (e.g., hyperthyroidism).

Note: Manic-like episodes that are clearly caused by somatic antidepressant treatment (e.g., medication, electroconvulsive therapy, light therapy) should not count toward a diagnosis of Bipolar I Disorder.

Mixed Episode

Episode Features

A Mixed Episode is characterized by a period of time (lasting at least 1 week) in which the criteria are met both for a Manic Episode and for a Major Depressive Episode nearly every day (Criterion A). The individual experiences rapidly alternating moods (sadness, irritability, euphoria) accompanied by symptoms of a Manic Episode (see p. 328) and a Major Depressive Episode (see p. 320). The symptom presentation frequently includes agitation, insomnia, appetite dysregulation, psychotic features, and suicidal thinking. The disturbance must be sufficiently severe to cause marked impairment in social or occupational functioning or to require hospitalization, or it is characterized by the presence of psychotic features (Criterion B). The disturbance is not due to the direct physiological effects of a substance (e.g., a drug of abuse, a medication, or other treatment) or a general medical condition (e.g., hyperthyroidism) (Criterion C). Symptoms like those seen in a Mixed Episode may be due to the direct effects of antidepressant medication, electroconvulsive therapy, light therapy, or medication prescribed for other general medical conditions (e.g., corticosteroids). Such presentations are not considered Mixed Episodes and do not count toward a diagnosis of Bipolar I Disorder. For example, if a person with recurrent Major Depressive Disorder develops a mixed symptom picture during a course of antidepressant medication, the diagnosis of the episode is Substance-Induced Mood Disorder, With Mixed Features, and there is no switch from a diagnosis of Major Depressive Disorder to Bipolar I Disorder. Some evidence suggests that there may be a bipolar "diathesis" in individuals who develop mixed-like episodes following somatic treatment for depression. Such individuals may have an increased likelihood of future Manic, Mixed, or Hypomanic Episodes that are not related to substances or somatic treatments for depression. This may be an especially important consideration in children and adolescents.

Associated Features and Disorders

Associated descriptive features and mental disorders.   Associated features of a Mixed Episode are similar to those for Manic Episodes and Major Depressive Episodes. Individuals may be disorganized in their thinking or behavior. Because individuals in Mixed Episodes experience more dysphoria than do those in Manic Episodes, they may be more likely to seek help.

Associated laboratory findings.   Laboratory findings for Mixed Episode are not well studied, although evidence to date suggests physiological and endocrine findings that are similar to those found in severe Major Depressive Episodes.

Specific Culture, Age, and Gender Features

Cultural considerations suggested for Major Depressive Episodes are relevant to Mixed Episodes as well (see p. 324). Mixed episodes appear to be more common in younger individuals and in individuals over age 60 years with Bipolar Disorder and may be more common in males than in females.

Course

Mixed Episodes can evolve from a Manic Episode or from a Major Depressive Episode or may arise de novo. For example, the diagnosis would be changed from Bipolar I Disorder, Most Recent Episode Manic, to Bipolar I Disorder, Most Recent Episode Mixed, for an individual with 3 weeks of manic symptoms followed by 1 week of both manic symptoms and depressive symptoms. Mixed episodes may last weeks to several months and may remit to a period with few or no symptoms or evolve into a Major Depressive Episode. It is far less common for a Mixed Episode to evolve into a Manic Episode.

Differential Diagnosis

A Mixed Episode must be distinguished from a **Mood Disorder Due to a General Medical Condition.** The diagnosis is Mood Disorder Due to a General Medical Condition if the mood disturbance is judged to be the direct physiological consequence of a specific general medical condition (e.g., multiple sclerosis, brain tumor, Cushing's syndrome) (see p. 366). This determination is based on the history, laboratory findings, or physical examination. If it is judged that the mixed manic and depressive symptoms are not the direct physiological consequence of the general medical condition, then the primary Mood Disorder is recorded on Axis I (e.g., Bipolar I Disorder) and the general medical condition is recorded on Axis III (e.g., myocardial infarction).

A **Substance-Induced Mood Disorder** is distinguished from a Mixed Episode by the fact that a substance (e.g., a drug of abuse, a medication, or exposure to a toxin) is judged to be etiologically related to the mood disturbance (see p. 370). Symptoms like those seen in a Mixed Episode may be precipitated by use of a drug of abuse (e.g., mixed manic and depressive symptoms that occur only in the context of intoxication with cocaine would be diagnosed as Cocaine-Induced Mood Disorder, With Mixed Features, With Onset During Intoxication). Symptoms like those seen in a Mixed Episode may also be precipitated by antidepressant treatment such as medication, electroconvulsive therapy, or light therapy. Such episodes are also diagnosed as Substance-Induced Mood Disorders (e.g., Amitriptyline-Induced Mood Disorder, With Mixed Features; Electroconvulsive Therapy–Induced Mood Disorder, With Mixed Features).

Major Depressive Episodes with prominent irritable mood and **Manic Episodes with prominent irritable mood** may be difficult to distinguish from Mixed Episodes. This determination requires a careful clinical evaluation of the simultaneous presence of symptoms that are characteristic of both a full Manic Episode and a full Major Depressive Episode (except for duration).

Attention-Deficit/Hyperactivity Disorder and a Mixed Episode are both characterized by excessive activity, impulsive behavior, poor judgment, and denial of problems. Attention-Deficit/Hyperactivity Disorder is distinguished from a Mixed Episode by its characteristic early onset (i.e., before age 7 years), chronic rather than episodic course, lack of relatively clear onsets and offsets, and the absence of abnormally expansive or elevated mood or psychotic features. Children with Attention-Deficit/Hyperactivity Disorder also sometimes show depressive symptoms such as low self-esteem and frustration tolerance. If criteria are met for both, Attention-Deficit/Hyperactivity Disorder may be diagnosed in addition to the Mood Disorder.

■ **Criteria for Mixed Episode**

A. The criteria are met both for a Manic Episode (see p. 332) and for a Major Depressive Episode (see p. 327) (except for duration) nearly every day during at least a 1-week period.

B. The mood disturbance is sufficiently severe to cause marked impairment in occupational functioning or in usual social activities or relationships with others, or to necessitate hospitalization to prevent harm to self or others, or there are psychotic features.

C. The symptoms are not due to the direct physiological effects of a substance (e.g., a drug of abuse, a medication, or other treatment) or a general medical condition (e.g., hyperthyroidism).

Note: Mixed-like episodes that are clearly caused by somatic antidepressant treatment (e.g., medication, electroconvulsive therapy, light therapy) should not count toward a diagnosis of Bipolar I Disorder.

Hypomanic Episode

Episode Features

A Hypomanic Episode is defined as a distinct period during which there is an abnormally and persistently elevated, expansive, or irritable mood that lasts at least 4 days (Criterion A). This period of abnormal mood must be accompanied by at least three additional symptoms from a list that includes inflated self-esteem or grandiosity (nondelusional), decreased need for sleep, pressure of speech, flight of ideas, distractibility, increased involvement in goal-directed activities or psychomotor agitation, and excessive involvement in pleasurable activities that have a high potential for painful consequences (Criterion B). If the mood is irritable rather than elevated or expansive, at least four of the above symptoms must be present. This list of additional symptoms is identical to those that define a Manic Episode (see p. 328) except that delusions or hallucinations cannot be present. The mood during a Hypomanic Episode must be clearly different from the individual's usual nondepressed mood, and there must be a clear change in functioning that is not characteristic of the individual's usual functioning (Criterion C). Because the changes in mood and functioning must be observable by others (Criterion D), the evaluation of this criterion will often require interviewing other informants (e.g., family members). History from other informants is particularly important in the evaluation of adolescents. In contrast to a Manic Episode, a Hypomanic Episode is not severe enough to cause marked impairment in social or occupational functioning or to require hospitalization, and there are no psychotic features (Criterion E). The change in functioning for some individuals may take the form of a marked increase in efficiency, accomplishments, or creativity. However, for others, hypomania can cause some social or occupational impairment.

The mood disturbance and other symptoms must not be due to the direct physiological effects of a drug of abuse, a medication, other treatment for depression (electroconvulsive therapy or light therapy), or toxin exposure. The episode must also not be due to the direct physiological effects of a general medical condition (e.g., multiple sclerosis, brain tumor) (Criterion F). Symptoms like those seen in a Hypomanic Episode may be due to the direct effects of antidepressant medication, electroconvulsive therapy, light therapy, or medication prescribed for other general medical conditions (e.g., corticosteroids). Such presentations are not considered Hypomanic Episodes and do not count toward the diagnosis of Bipolar II Disorder. For example, if a person with recurrent Major Depressive Disorder develops symptoms of a hypomanic-like episode during a course of antidepressant medication, the episode is diagnosed as a Substance-Induced Mood Disorder, With Manic Features, and there is no switch from a diagnosis of Major Depressive Disorder to Bipolar II Disorder. Some evidence suggests that there may be a bipolar "diathesis" in individuals who develop manic- or hypomanic-like episodes following somatic treatment for depression. Such individuals may have an increased likelihood of future Manic or Hypomanic Episodes that are not related to substances or somatic treatments for depression.

The elevated mood in a Hypomanic Episode is described as euphoric, unusually good, cheerful, or high. Although the person's mood may have an infectious quality for the uninvolved observer, it is recognized as a distinct change from the usual self by those who know the person well. The expansive quality of the mood disturbance is characterized by enthusiasm for social, interpersonal, or occupational interactions. Although elevated mood is considered prototypical, the mood disturbance may be irritable or may alternate between euphoria and irritability. Characteristically, inflated self-esteem, usually at the level of uncritical self-confidence rather than marked grandiosity, is present (Criterion B1). There is very often a decreased need for sleep (Criterion B2); the person awakens before the usual time with increased energy. The speech of a person with a Hypomanic Episode is often somewhat louder and more rapid than usual, but is not typically difficult to interrupt. It may be full of jokes, puns, plays on words, and irrelevancies (Criterion B3). Flight of ideas is uncommon and, if present, lasts for very brief periods (Criterion B4).

Distractibility is often present, as evidenced by rapid changes in speech or activity as a result of responding to various irrelevant external stimuli (Criterion B5). The increase in goal-directed activity may involve planning of, and participation in, multiple activities (Criterion B6). These activities are often creative and productive (e.g., writing a letter to the editor, clearing up paperwork). Sociability is usually increased, and there may be an increase in sexual activity. There may be impulsive activity such as buying sprees, reckless driving, or foolish business investments (Criterion B7). However, such activities are usually organized, are not bizarre, and do not result in the level of impairment that is characteristic of a Manic Episode.

Specific Culture and Age Features

Cultural considerations that were suggested for Major Depressive Episodes are relevant to Hypomanic Episodes as well (see p. 324). In younger (e.g., adolescent) persons, Hypomanic Episodes may be associated with school truancy, antisocial behavior, school failure, or substance use.

Course

A Hypomanic Episode typically begins suddenly, with a rapid escalation of symptoms within a day or two. Episodes may last for several weeks to months and are usually more abrupt in onset and briefer than Major Depressive Episodes. In many cases, the Hypomanic Episode may be preceded or followed by a Major Depressive Episode. Studies suggest that 5%–15% of individuals with hypomania will ultimately develop a Manic Episode.

Differential Diagnosis

A Hypomanic Episode must be distinguished from a **Mood Disorder Due to a General Medical Condition.** The diagnosis is Mood Disorder Due to a General Medical Condition if the mood disturbance is judged to be the direct physiological consequence of a specific general medical condition (e.g., multiple sclerosis, brain tumor, Cushing's syndrome) (see p. 366). This determination is based on the history, laboratory findings, or physical examination. If it is judged that the hypomanic symptoms are not the direct physiological consequence of the general medical condition, then the primary Mood Disorder is recorded on Axis I (e.g., Bipolar II Disorder) and the general medical condition is recorded on Axis III (e.g., myocardial infarction).

A **Substance-Induced Mood Disorder** is distinguished from a Hypomanic Episode by the fact that a substance (e.g., a drug of abuse, a medication, or exposure to a toxin) is judged to be etiologically related to the mood disturbance (see p. 370). Symptoms like those seen in a Hypomanic Episode may be precipitated by a drug of abuse (e.g., hypomanic symptoms that occur only in the context of intoxication with cocaine would be diagnosed as Cocaine-Induced Mood Disorder, With Manic Features, With Onset During Intoxication). Symptoms like those seen in a Hypomanic Episode may also be precipitated by antidepressant treatment such as medication, electroconvulsive therapy, or light therapy. Such episodes are also diagnosed as Substance-Induced Mood Disorders (e.g., Amitriptyline-Induced Mood Disorder, With Manic Features; Electroconvulsive Therapy–Induced Mood Disorder, With Manic Features).

Manic Episodes should be distinguished from Hypomanic Episodes. Although Manic Episodes and Hypomanic Episodes have identical lists of characteristic symptoms, the mood disturbance in Hypomanic Episodes is not sufficiently severe to cause marked impairment in social or occupational functioning or to require hospitalization. Some Hypomanic Episodes may evolve into full Manic Episodes.

Attention-Deficit/Hyperactivity Disorder and a Hypomanic Episode are both characterized by excessive activity, impulsive behavior, poor judgment, and denial of problems. Attention-Deficit/Hyperactivity Disorder is distinguished from a Hypomanic Episode by its characteristic early onset (i.e., before age 7 years), chronic rather than episodic course, lack of relatively clear onsets and offsets, and the absence of abnormally expansive or elevated mood.

A Hypomanic Episode must be distinguished from **euthymia**, particularly in individuals who have been chronically depressed and are unaccustomed to the experience of a nondepressed mood state.

■ Criteria for Hypomanic Episode

A. A distinct period of persistently elevated, expansive, or irritable mood, lasting throughout at least 4 days, that is clearly different from the usual nondepressed mood.

B. During the period of mood disturbance, three (or more) of the following symptoms have persisted (four if the mood is only irritable) and have been present to a significant degree:

(1) inflated self-esteem or grandiosity

(2) decreased need for sleep (e.g., feels rested after only 3 hours of sleep)

(3) more talkative than usual or pressure to keep talking

(4) flight of ideas or subjective experience that thoughts are racing

(5) distractibility (i.e., attention too easily drawn to unimportant or irrelevant external stimuli)

(6) increase in goal-directed activity (either socially, at work or school, or sexually) or psychomotor agitation

(7) excessive involvement in pleasurable activities that have a high potential for painful consequences (e.g., the person engages in unrestrained buying sprees, sexual indiscretions, or foolish business investments)

C. The episode is associated with an unequivocal change in functioning that is uncharacteristic of the person when not symptomatic.

D. The disturbance in mood and the change in functioning are observable by others.

E. The episode is not severe enough to cause marked impairment in social or occupational functioning, or to necessitate hospitalization, and there are no psychotic features.

F. The symptoms are not due to the direct physiological effects of a substance (e.g., a drug of abuse, a medication, or other treatment) or a general medical condition (e.g., hyperthyroidism).

Note: Hypomanic-like episodes that are clearly caused by somatic antidepressant treatment (e.g., medication, electroconvulsive therapy, light therapy) should not count toward a diagnosis of Bipolar II Disorder.

Depressive Disorders

Major Depressive Disorder

Diagnostic Features

The essential feature of Major Depressive Disorder is a clinical course that is character-ized by one or more Major Depressive Episodes (see p. 320) without a history of Manic, Mixed, or Hypomanic Episodes (Criteria A and C). Episodes of Substance-Induced Mood Disorder (due to the direct physiological effects of a drug of abuse, a medication, or toxin exposure) or of Mood Disorder Due to a General Medical Condition do not count toward a diagnosis of Major Depressive Disorder. In addition, the episodes must not be better accounted for by Schizoaffective Disorder and are not superimposed on Schizo-phrenia, Schizophreniform Disorder, Delusional Disorder, or Psychotic Disorder Not Otherwise Specified (Criterion B).

The fourth digit in the diagnostic code for Major Depressive Disorder indicates whether it is a Single Episode (used only for first episodes) or Recurrent. It is sometimes difficult to distinguish between a single episode with waxing and waning symptoms and two separate episodes. For purposes of this manual, an episode is considered to have ended when the full criteria for the Major Depressive Episode have not been met for at least 2 consecutive months. During this 2-month period, there is either complete resolution of symptoms or the presence of depressive symptoms that no longer meet the full criteria for a Major Depressive Episode (In Partial Remission).

The fifth digit in the diagnostic code for Major Depressive Disorder indicates the current state of the disturbance. If the criteria for a Major Depressive Episode are met, the severity of the episode is noted as Mild, Moderate, Severe Without Psychotic Features, or Severe With Psychotic Features. If the criteria for a Major Depressive Episode are not currently met, the fifth digit is used to indicate whether the disorder is In Partial Remission or In Full Remission (see p. 377).

If Manic, Mixed, or Hypomanic Episodes develop in the course of Major Depressive Disorder, the diagnosis is changed to a Bipolar Disorder. However, if manic or hypomanic symptoms occur as a direct effect of antidepressant treatment, use of other medications, substance use, or toxin exposure, the diagnosis of Major Depressive Disorder remains appropriate and an additional diagnosis of Substance-Induced Mood Disorder, With Manic Features (or With Mixed Features), should be noted. Similarly, if manic or hypomanic symptoms occur as a direct effect of a general medical condition, the diagnosis of Major Depressive Disorder remains appropriate and an additional diagnosis of Mood Disorder Due to a General Medical Condition, With Manic Features (or With Mixed Features), should be noted.

Specifiers

The following specifiers may be used to describe the current Major Depressive Episode (or, if criteria are not currently met for a Major Depressive Episode, the most recent Major Depressive Episode):

Mild, Moderate, Severe Without Psychotic Features, Severe With Psychotic Features, In Partial Remission, In Full Remission (see p. 376)

Chronic (see p. 382)
With Catatonic Features (see p. 382)
With Melancholic Features (see p. 383)
With Atypical Features (see p. 384)
With Postpartum Onset (see p. 386)

The following specifiers may be used to indicate the pattern of the episodes and the presence of interepisode symptomatology for Major Depressive Disorder, Recurrent:

Longitudinal Course Specifiers (With or Without Full Interepisode Recovery) (see p. 387)
With Seasonal Pattern (see p. 389)

Recording Procedures

The diagnostic codes for Major Depressive Disorder are selected as follows:

1. The first three digits are 296.
2. The fourth digit is either 2 (if there is only a single Major Depressive Episode) or 3 (if there are recurrent Major Depressive Episodes).
3. The fifth digit indicates the following: 1 for Mild severity, 2 for Moderate severity, 3 for Severe Without Psychotic Features, 4 for Severe With Psychotic Features, 5 for In Partial Remission, 6 for In Full Remission, and 0 if Unspecified. Other specifiers for Major Depressive Disorder cannot be coded.

In recording the name of a diagnosis, terms should be listed in the following order: Major Depressive Disorder, specifiers coded in the fourth digit (e.g., Recurrent), specifiers coded in the fifth digit (e.g., Mild, Severe With Psychotic Features, In Partial Remission), as many specifiers (without codes) as apply to the most recent episode (e.g., With Melancholic Features, With Postpartum Onset), and as many specifiers (without codes) as apply to the course of episodes (e.g., With Full Interepisode Recovery); for example, 296.32 Major Depressive Disorder, Recurrent, Moderate, With Atypical Features, With Seasonal Pattern, With Full Interepisode Recovery.

Associated Features and Disorders

Associated descriptive features and mental disorders.   Major Depressive Disorder is associated with high mortality. Up to 15% of individuals with severe Major Depressive Disorder die by suicide. Epidemiological evidence also suggests that there is a fourfold increase in death rates in individuals with Major Depressive Disorder who are over age 55 years. Individuals with Major Depressive Disorder admitted to nursing homes may have a markedly increased likelihood of death in the first year. Among individuals seen in general medical settings, those with Major Depressive Disorder have more pain and physical illness and decreased physical, social, and role functioning.

Major Depressive Disorder may be preceded by Dysthymic Disorder (10% in epidemiological samples and 15%–25% in clinical samples). It is also estimated that each year approximately 10% of individuals with Dysthymic Disorder alone will go on to have a first Major Depressive Episode. Other mental disorders frequently co-occur with Major Depressive Disorder (e.g., Substance-Related Disorders, Panic Disorder, Obsessive-Compulsive Disorder, Anorexia Nervosa, Bulimia Nervosa, Borderline Personality Disorder).

Associated laboratory findings.   The laboratory abnormalities that are associated with Major Depressive Disorder are those associated with Major Depressive Episode (see p. 323). None of these findings are diagnostic of Major Depressive Disorder, but they have been noted to be abnormal in groups of individuals with Major Depressive Disorder compared with control subjects. Most laboratory abnormalities are state dependent (i.e., are present only when depressive symptoms are present). However, evidence suggests that some sleep EEG abnormalities persist into clinical remission or may precede the onset of the Major Depressive Episode.

Associated physical examination findings and general medical conditions. Major Depressive Disorder may be associated with chronic general medical conditions. Up to 20%–25% of individuals with certain general medical conditions (e.g., diabetes, myocardial infarction, carcinomas, stroke) will develop Major Depressive Disorder during the course of their general medical condition. The management of the general medical condition is more complex and the prognosis is less favorable if Major Depressive Disorder is present.

Specific Culture, Age, and Gender Features

Specific culture-related features are discussed in the text for Major Depressive Episode (see p. 324). Major Depressive Disorder (Single or Recurrent) is twice as common in adolescent and adult females as in adolescent and adult males. In prepubertal children, boys and girls are equally affected. Rates in men and women are highest in the 25- to 44-year-old age group, whereas rates are lower for both men and women over age 65 years.

Prevalence

Studies of Major Depressive Disorder have reported a wide range of values for the proportion of the adult population with the disorder. The lifetime risk for Major Depressive Disorder in community samples has varied from 10% to 25% for women and from 5% to 12% for men. The point prevalence of Major Depressive Disorder in adults in community samples has varied from 5% to 9% for women and from 2% to 3% for men. The prevalence rates for Major Depressive Disorder appear to be unrelated to ethnicity, education, income, or marital status.

Course

Major Depressive Disorder may begin at any age, with an average age at onset in the mid-20s. Epidemiological data suggest that the age at onset is decreasing for those born more recently. The course of Major Depressive Disorder, Recurrent, is variable. Some people have isolated episodes that are separated by many years without any depressive symptoms, whereas others have clusters of episodes, and still others have increasingly frequent episodes as they grow older. Some evidence suggests that the periods of remission generally last longer early in the course of the disorder. The number of prior episodes predicts the likelihood of developing a subsequent Major Depressive Episode. Approximately 50%–60% of individuals with Major Depressive Disorder, Single Episode, can be expected to have a second episode. Individuals who have had two episodes have a 70% chance of having a third, and individuals who have had three episodes have a 90% chance of having a fourth. About 5%–10% of individuals with Major Depressive Disorder, Single Episode, subsequently develop a Manic Episode (i.e., develop Bipolar I Disorder).

Major Depressive Episodes may end completely (in about two-thirds of cases), or only partially or not at all (in about one-third of cases). For individuals who have only partial remission, there is a greater likelihood of developing additional episodes and of continuing the pattern of partial interepisode recovery. The longitudinal course specifiers With Full Interepisode Recovery and Without Full Interepisode Recovery (see p. 387) may therefore have prognostic value. A number of individuals have preexisting Dysthymic Disorder prior to the onset of Major Depressive Disorder, Single Episode. Some evidence suggests that these individuals are more likely to have additional Major Depressive Episodes, have poorer interepisode recovery, and may require additional acute-phase treatment and a longer period of continuing treatment to attain and maintain a more thorough and longer-lasting euthymic state.

Follow-up naturalistic studies suggested that 1 year after the diagnosis of a Major Depressive Episode, 40% of individuals still have symptoms that are sufficiently severe to meet criteria for a full Major Depressive Episode, roughly 20% continue to have some symptoms that no longer meet full criteria for a Major Depressive Episode (i.e., Major Depressive Disorder, In Partial Remission), and 40% have no Mood Disorder. The severity of the initial Major Depressive Episode appears to predict persistence. Chronic general medical conditions are also a risk factor for more persistent episodes.

Episodes of Major Depressive Disorder often follow a severe psychosocial stressor, such as the death of a loved one or divorce. Studies suggest that psychosocial events (stressors) may play a more significant role in the precipitation of the first or second episodes of Major Depressive Disorder and may play less of a role in the onset of subsequent episodes. Chronic general medical conditions and Substance Dependence (particularly Alcohol or Cocaine Dependence) may contribute to the onset or exacerbation of Major Depressive Disorder.

It is difficult to predict whether the first episode of a Major Depressive Disorder in a young person will ultimately evolve into a Bipolar Disorder. Some data suggest that the acute onset of severe depression, especially with psychotic features and psychomotor retardation, in a young person without prepubertal psychopathology is more likely to predict a bipolar course. A family history of Bipolar Disorder may also be suggestive of subsequent development of Bipolar Disorder.

Familial Pattern

Major Depressive Disorder is 1.5–3 times more common among first-degree biological relatives of persons with this disorder than among the general population. There is evidence for an increased risk of Alcohol Dependence in adult first-degree biological relatives, and there may be an increased incidence of Attention-Deficit/Hyperactivity Disorder in the children of adults with this disorder.

Differential Diagnosis

See the "Differential Diagnosis" section for Major Depressive Episode (p. 325). A history of a **Manic, Mixed,** or **Hypomanic Episode** precludes the diagnosis of Major

Depressive Disorder. The presence of Hypomanic Episodes (without any history of Manic Episodes) indicates a diagnosis of Bipolar II Disorder. The presence of Manic or Mixed Episodes (with or without Hypomanic Episodes) indicates a diagnosis of Bipolar I Disorder.

Major Depressive Episodes in Major Depressive Disorder must be distinguished from a **Mood Disorder Due to a General Medical Condition.** The diagnosis is Mood Disorder Due to a General Medical Condition if the mood disturbance is judged to be the direct physiological consequence of a specific general medical condition (e.g., multiple sclerosis, stroke, hypothyroidism) (see p. 366). This determination is based on the history, laboratory findings, or physical examination. If it is judged that the depressive symptoms are not the direct physiological consequence of the general medical condition, then the primary Mood Disorder is recorded on Axis I (e.g., Major Depressive Disorder) and the general medical condition is recorded on Axis III (e.g., myocardial infarction). This would be the case, for example, if the Major Depressive Episode is considered to be the psychological consequence of having the general medical condition or if there is no etiological relationship between the Major Depressive Episode and the general medical condition.

A **Substance-Induced Mood Disorder** is distinguished from Major Depressive Episodes in Major Depressive Disorder by the fact that a substance (e.g., a drug of abuse, a medication, or exposure to a toxin) is judged to be etiologically related to the mood disturbance (see p. 370). For example, depressed mood that occurs only in the context of withdrawal from cocaine would be diagnosed as Cocaine-Induced Mood Disorder, With Depressive Features, With Onset During Withdrawal.

Dysthymic Disorder and Major Depressive Disorder are differentiated based on severity, chronicity, and persistence. In Major Depressive Disorder, the depressed mood must be present for most of the day, nearly every day, for a period of at least 2 weeks, whereas Dysthymic Disorder must be present for more days than not over a period of at least 2 years. The differential diagnosis between Dysthymic Disorder and Major Depressive Disorder is made particularly difficult by the fact that the two disorders share similar symptoms and that the differences between them in onset, duration, persistence, and severity are not easy to evaluate retrospectively. Usually Major Depressive Disorder consists of one or more discrete Major Depressive Episodes that can be distinguished from the person's usual functioning, whereas Dysthymic Disorder is characterized by chronic, less severe depressive symptoms that have been present for many years. If the initial onset of chronic depressive symptoms is of sufficient severity and number to meet criteria for a Major Depressive Episode, the diagnosis would be Major Depressive Disorder, Chronic (if the criteria are still met), or Major Depressive Disorder, In Partial Remission (if the criteria are no longer met). The diagnosis of Dysthymic Disorder is made following Major Depressive Disorder only if the Dysthymic Disorder was estab- lished prior to the first Major Depressive Episode (i.e., no Major Depressive Episodes during the first 2 years of dysthymic symptoms), or if there has been a full remission of the Major Depressive Episode (i.e., lasting at least 2 months) before the onset of the Dysthymic Disorder.

Schizoaffective Disorder differs from Major Depressive Disorder, With Psychotic Features, by the requirement that in Schizoaffective Disorder there must be at least 2 weeks of delusions or hallucinations occurring in the absence of prominent mood symptoms. Depressive symptoms may be present during **Schizophrenia, Delusional Disorder,** and **Psychotic Disorder Not Otherwise Specified.** Most commonly, such depressive symptoms can be considered associated features of these disorders and do not merit a separate diagnosis. However, when the depressive symptoms meet full criteria for a Major Depressive Episode (or are of particular clinical significance), a diagnosis of Depressive Disorder Not Otherwise Specified may be made in addition to the diagnosis of Schizophrenia, Delusional Disorder, or Psychotic Disorder Not Otherwise Specified. Schizophrenia, Catatonic Type, may be difficult to distinguish from Major Depressive Disorder, With Catatonic Features. Prior history or family history may be helpful in making this distinction.

In elderly individuals, it is often difficult to determine whether cognitive symptoms (e.g., disorientation, apathy, difficulty concentrating, memory loss) are better accounted for by a **dementia** or by a Major Depressive Episode in Major Depressive Disorder. This differential diagnosis may be informed by a thorough general medical evaluation and consideration of the onset of the disturbance, temporal sequencing of depressive and cognitive symptoms, course of illness, and treatment response. The premorbid state of the individual may help to differentiate a Major Depressive Disorder from dementia. In dementia, there is usually a premorbid history of declining cognitive function, whereas the individual with Major Depressive Disorder is much more likely to have a relatively normal premorbid state and abrupt cognitive decline associated with the depression.

■ Diagnostic criteria for 296.2x Major Depressive Disorder, Single Episode

A. Presence of a single Major Depressive Episode (see p. 327).

B. The Major Depressive Episode is not better accounted for by Schizoaffective Disorder and is not superimposed on Schizophrenia, Schizophreniform Disorder, Delusional Disorder, or Psychotic Disorder Not Otherwise Specified.

C. There has never been a Manic Episode (see p. 332), a Mixed Episode (see p. 335), or a Hypomanic Episode (see p. 338). **Note:** This exclusion does not apply if all of the manic-like, mixed-like, or hypomanic-like episodes are substance or treatment induced or are due to the direct physiological effects of a general medical condition.

Specify (for current or most recent episode):
Severity/Psychotic/Remission Specifiers (see p. 376)
Chronic (see p. 382)
With Catatonic Features (see p. 382)
With Melancholic Features (see p. 383)
With Atypical Features (see p. 384)
With Postpartum Onset (see p. 386)

■ **Diagnostic criteria for 296.3x Major Depressive Disorder, Recurrent**

A. Presence of two or more Major Depressive Episodes (see p. 327).

   Note: To be considered separate episodes, there must be an interval of at least 2 consecutive months in which criteria are not met for a Major Depressive Episode.

B. The Major Depressive Episodes are not better accounted for by Schizoaffective Disorder and are not superimposed on Schizophrenia, Schizophreniform Disorder, Delusional Disorder, or Psychotic Disorder Not Otherwise Specified.

C. There has never been a Manic Episode (see p. 332), a Mixed Episode (see p. 335), or a Hypomanic Episode (see p. 338).   **Note:** This exclusion does not apply if all of the manic-like, mixed-like, or hypomanic-like episodes are substance or treatment induced or are due to the direct physiological effects of a general medical condition.

Specify (for current or most recent episode):
   Severity/Psychotic/Remission Specifiers (see p. 376)
   Chronic (see p. 382)
   With Catatonic Features (see p. 382)
   With Melancholic Features (see p. 383)
   With Atypical Features (see p. 384)
   With Postpartum Onset (see p. 386)

Specify:
   Longitudinal Course Specifiers (With and Without Interepisode Recovery) (see p. 387)
   With Seasonal Pattern (see p. 389)

300.4   Dysthymic Disorder

Diagnostic Features

The essential feature of Dysthymic Disorder is a chronically depressed mood that occurs for most of the day more days than not for at least 2 years (Criterion A). Individuals with Dysthymic Disorder describe their mood as sad or "down in the dumps." In children, the mood may be irritable rather than depressed, and the required minimum duration is only 1 year. During periods of depressed mood, at least two of the following additional symptoms are present: poor appetite or overeating, insomnia or hypersomnia, low energy or fatigue, low self-esteem, poor concentration or difficulty making decisions, and feelings of hopelessness (Criterion B). Individuals may note the prominent presence of low interest and self-criticism, often seeing themselves as uninteresting or incapable. Because these symptoms have become so much a part of the individual's day-to-day experience (e.g., "I've always been this way," "That's just how I am"), they are often not reported unless directly asked about by the interviewer.

During the 2-year period (1 year for children or adolescents), any symptom-free intervals last no longer than 2 months (Criterion C). The diagnosis of Dysthymic Disorder can be made only if the initial 2-year period of dysthymic symptoms is free of Major Depressive Episodes (Criterion D). If the chronic depressive symptoms include a Major Depressive Episode during the initial 2 years, then the diagnosis is Major Depressive Disorder, Chronic (if full criteria for a Major Depressive Episode are met), or Major Depressive Disorder, In Partial Remission (if full criteria for a Major Depressive Episode are not currently met). After the initial 2 years of the Dysthymic Disorder, Major Depressive Episodes may be superimposed on the Dysthymic Disorder. In such cases ("double depression"), both Major Depressive Disorder and Dysthymic Disorder are diagnosed. Once the person returns to a dysthymic baseline (i.e., criteria for a Major Depressive Episode are no longer met but dysthymic symptoms persist), only Dysthymic Disorder is diagnosed.

The diagnosis of Dysthymic Disorder is not made if the individual has ever had a Manic Episode (p. 328), a Mixed Episode (p. 333), or a Hypomanic Episode (p. 335) or if criteria have ever been met for Cyclothymic Disorder (Criterion E). A separate diagnosis of Dysthymic Disorder is not made if the depressive symptoms occur exclusively during the course of a chronic Psychotic Disorder, such as Schizophrenia or Delusional Disorder (Criterion F), in which case they are regarded as associated features of these disorders. Dysthymic Disorder is also not diagnosed if the disturbance is due to the direct physiological effects of a substance (e.g., alcohol, antihypertensive medications) or a general medical condition (e.g., hypothyroidism, Alzheimer's disease) (Criterion G). The symptoms must cause clinically significant distress or impairment in social, occupational (or academic), or other important areas of functioning (Criterion H).

Specifiers

Age at onset and the characteristic pattern of symptoms in Dysthymic Disorder may be indicated by using the following specifiers:

Early Onset. This specifier should be used if the onset of the dysthymic symptoms occurs before age 21 years. Such individuals are more likely to develop subsequent Major Depressive Episodes.

Late Onset. This specifier should be used if the onset of the dysthymic symptoms occurs at age 21 or older.

With Atypical Features. This specifier should be used if the pattern of symptoms during the most recent 2 years of the disorder meets the criteria for With Atypical Features (see p. 384).

Associated Features and Disorders

Associated descriptive features and mental disorders.   The associated features of Dysthymic Disorder are similar to those for a Major Depressive Episode (p. 323). Several studies suggest that the most commonly encountered symptoms in Dysthymic Disorder may be feelings of inadequacy; generalized loss of interest or pleasure; social withdrawal; feelings of guilt or brooding about the past; subjective feelings of irritability or excessive anger; and decreased activity, effectiveness, or productivity. (Appendix B provides an alternative for Criterion B for use in research studies that includes these items.) In individuals with Dysthymic Disorder, vegetative symptoms (e.g., sleep, appetite, weight change, and psychomotor symptoms) appear to be less common than for persons in a Major Depressive Episode. When Dysthymic Disorder without prior Major Depressive Disorder is present, it is a risk factor for developing Major Depressive Disorder (10% of individuals with Dysthymic Disorder will develop Major Depressive Disorder over the next year). Dysthymic Disorder may be associated with Borderline, Histrionic, Narcissistic, Avoidant, and Dependent Personality Disorders. However, the assessment of features of a Personality Disorder is difficult in such individuals because chronic mood symptoms may contribute to interpersonal problems or be associated with distorted self-perception. Other chronic Axis I disorders (e.g., Substance Dependence) or chronic psychosocial stressors may be associated with Dysthymic Disorder in adults. In children, Dysthymic Disorder may be associated with Attention-Deficit/Hyperactivity Disorder, Conduct Disorder, Anxiety Disorders, Learning Disorders, and Mental Retardation.

Associated laboratory findings. About 25%–50% of adults with Dysthymic Disorder have some of the same polysomnographic features that are found in some individuals with Major Depressive Disorder (e.g., reduced rapid eye movement (REM) latency, increased REM density, reduced slow-wave sleep, impaired sleep continuity). Those individuals with polysomnographic abnormalities more often have a positive family history for Major Depressive Disorder (and may respond better to antidepressant medications) than those with Dysthymic Disorder without such findings. Whether polysomnographic abnormalities are also found in those with "pure" Dysthymic Disorder (i.e., those with no prior history of Major Depressive Episodes) is not clear. Dexamethasone nonsuppression in Dysthymic Disorder is not common, unless criteria are also met for a Major Depressive Episode.

Specific Age and Gender Features

In children, Dysthymic Disorder seems to occur equally in both sexes and often results in impaired school performance and social interaction. Children and adolescents with Dysthymic Disorder are usually irritable and cranky as well as depressed. They have low self-esteem and poor social skills and are pessimistic. In adulthood, women are two to three times more likely to develop Dysthymic Disorder than are men.

Prevalence

The lifetime prevalence of Dysthymic Disorder (with or without superimposed Major Depressive Disorder) is approximately 6%. The point prevalence of Dysthymic Disorder is approximately 3%.

Course

Dysthymic Disorder often has an early and insidious onset (i.e., in childhood, adolescence, or early adult life) as well as a chronic course. In clinical settings, individuals with Dysthymic Disorder usually have superimposed Major Depressive Disorder, which is often the reason for seeking treatment. If Dysthymic Disorder precedes the onset of Major Depressive Disorder, there is less likelihood that there will be spontaneous full interepisode recovery between Major Depressive Episodes and a greater likelihood of having more frequent subsequent episodes.

Familial Pattern

Dysthymic Disorder is more common among first-degree biological relatives of people with Major Depressive Disorder than among the general population.

Differential Diagnosis

See the "Differential Diagnosis" section for Major Depressive Disorder (p. 342). The differential diagnosis between Dysthymic Disorder and **Major Depressive Disorder** is made particularly difficult by the facts that the two disorders share similar symptoms and that the differences between them in onset, duration, persistence, and severity are not easy to evaluate retrospectively. Usually Major Depressive Disorder consists of one or more discrete Major Depressive Episodes that can be distinguished from the person's usual functioning, whereas Dysthymic Disorder is characterized by chronic, less severe depressive symptoms that have been present for many years. When Dysthymic Disorder is of many years' duration, the mood disturbance may not be easily distinguished from the person's "usual" functioning. If the initial onset of chronic depressive symptoms is of sufficient severity and number to meet full criteria for a Major Depressive Episode, the diagnosis would be Major Depressive Disorder, Chronic (if the full criteria are still met), or Major Depressive Disorder, In Partial Remission (if the full criteria are no longer met). The diagnosis of Dysthymic Disorder can be made following Major Depressive Disorder only if the Dysthymic Disorder was established prior to the first Major Depressive Episode (i.e., no Major Depressive Episodes during the first 2 years of dysthymic symptoms), or if there has been a full remission of the Major Depressive Disorder (i.e., lasting at least 2 months) before the onset of the Dysthymic Disorder.

Depressive symptoms may be a common associated feature of **chronic Psychotic Disorders** (e.g., Schizoaffective Disorder, Schizophrenia, Delusional Disorder). A separate diagnosis of Dysthymic Disorder is not made if the symptoms occur only during the course of the Psychotic Disorder (including residual phases).

Dysthymic Disorder must be distinguished from a **Mood Disorder Due to a General Medical Condition.** The diagnosis is Mood Disorder Due to a General Medical Condition, With Depressive Features, if the mood disturbance is judged to be the direct physiological consequence of a specific, usually chronic, general medical condition (e.g., multiple sclerosis) (see p. 366). This determination is based on the history, laboratory findings, or physical examination. If it is judged that the depressive symptoms are not the direct physiological consequence of the general medical condition, then the primary Mood Disorder is recorded on Axis I (e.g., Dysthymic Disorder) and the general medical condition is recorded on Axis III (e.g., diabetes mellitus). This would be the case, for example, if the depressive symptoms are considered to be the psychological consequence of having a chronic general medical condition or if there is no etiological relationship between the depressive symptoms and the general medical condition. A **Substance-Induced Mood Disorder** is distinguished from a Dysthymic Disorder by the fact that a substance (e.g., a drug of abuse, a medication, or exposure to a toxin) is judged to be etiologically related to the mood disturbance (see p. 370).

Often there is evidence of a **coexisting personality disturbance.** When an individual's presentation meets the criteria for both Dysthymic Disorder and a Personality Disorder, both diagnoses are given.

■ **Diagnostic criteria for 300.4 Dysthymic Disorder**

A. Depressed mood for most of the day, for more days than not, as indicated either by subjective account or observation by others, for at least 2 years. **Note:** In children and adolescents, mood can be irritable and duration must be at least 1 year.

B. Presence, while depressed, of two (or more) of the following:
   (1) poor appetite or overeating
   (2) insomnia or hypersomnia
   (3) low energy or fatigue
   (4) low self-esteem
   (5) poor concentration or difficulty making decisions
   (6) feelings of hopelessness

C. During the 2-year period (1 year for children or adolescents) of the disturbance, the person has never been without the symptoms in Criteria A and B for more than 2 months at a time.

D. No Major Depressive Episode (see p. 327) has been present during the first 2 years of the disturbance (1 year for children and adolescents); i.e., the disturbance is not better accounted for by chronic Major Depressive Disorder, or Major Depressive Disorder, In Partial Remission.

   Note: There may have been a previous Major Depressive Episode provided there was a full remission (no significant signs or symptoms for 2 months) before development of the Dysthymic Disorder. In addition, after the initial 2 years (1 year in children or adolescents) of Dysthymic Disorder, there may be superimposed episodes of Major Depressive Disorder, in which case both diagnoses may be given when the criteria are met for a Major Depressive Episode.

E. There has never been a Manic Episode (see p. 332), a Mixed Episode (see p. 335), or a Hypomanic Episode (see p. 338), and criteria have never been met for Cyclothymic Disorder.

F. The disturbance does not occur exclusively during the course of a chronic Psychotic Disorder, such as Schizophrenia or Delusional Disorder.

G. The symptoms are not due to the direct physiological effects of a substance (e.g., a drug of abuse, a medication) or a general medical condition (e.g., hypothyroidism).

H. The symptoms cause clinically significant distress or impairment in social, occupational, or other important areas of functioning.

Specify if:
   Early Onset: if onset is before age 21 years
   Late Onset: if onset is age 21 years or older

Specify (for most recent 2 years of Dysthymic Disorder):
   With Atypical Features (see p. 384)

311   Depressive Disorder Not Otherwise Specified

The Depressive Disorder Not Otherwise Specified category includes disorders with depressive features that do not meet the criteria for Major Depressive Disorder, Dysthymic Disorder, Adjustment Disorder With Depressed Mood (see p. 623), or Adjustment Disorder With Mixed Anxiety and Depressed Mood (see p. 624). Sometimes depressive symptoms can present as part of an Anxiety Disorder Not Otherwise Specified (see p. 444). Examples of Depressive Disorder Not Otherwise Specified include

1. Premenstrual dysphoric disorder: in most menstrual cycles during the past year, symptoms (e.g., markedly depressed mood, marked anxiety, marked affective lability, decreased interest in activities) regularly occurred during the last week of the luteal phase (and remitted within a few days of the onset of menses). These symptoms must be severe enough to markedly interfere with work, school, or usual activities and be entirely absent for at least 1 week postmenses (see p. 715 for suggested research criteria).
2. Minor depressive disorder: episodes of at least 2 weeks of depressive symptoms but with fewer than the five items required for Major Depressive Disorder (see p. 719 for suggested research criteria).
3. Recurrent brief depressive disorder: depressive episodes lasting from 2 days up to 2 weeks, occurring at least once a month for 12 months (not associated with the menstrual cycle) (see p. 721 for suggested research criteria).
4. Postpsychotic depressive disorder of Schizophrenia: a Major Depressive Episode that occurs during the residual phase of Schizophrenia (see p. 711 for suggested research criteria).
5. A Major Depressive Episode superimposed on Delusional Disorder, Psychotic Disorder Not Otherwise Specified, or the active phase of Schizophrenia.
6. Situations in which the clinician has concluded that a depressive disorder is present but is unable to determine whether it is primary, due to a general medical condition, or substance induced.

Bipolar Disorders

This section includes Bipolar I Disorder, Bipolar II Disorder, Cyclothymia, and Bipolar Disorder Not Otherwise Specified. There are six separate criteria sets for Bipolar I Disorder: Single Manic Episode, Most Recent Episode Hypomanic, Most Recent Episode Manic, Most Recent Episode Mixed, Most Recent Episode Depressed, and Most Recent Episode Unspecified. Bipolar I Disorder, Single Manic Episode, is used to describe individuals who are having a first episode of mania. The remaining criteria sets are used to specify the nature of the current (or most recent) episode in individuals who have had recurrent mood episodes.

Bipolar I Disorder

Diagnostic Features

The essential feature of Bipolar I Disorder is a clinical course that is characterized by the occurrence of one or more Manic Episodes (see p. 328) or Mixed Episodes (see

p. 333). Often individuals have also had one or more Major Depressive Episodes (see p. 320). Episodes of Substance-Induced Mood Disorder (due to the direct effects of a medication, other somatic treatments for depression, a drug of abuse, or toxin exposure) or of Mood Disorder Due to a General Medical Condition do not count toward a diagnosis of Bipolar I Disorder. In addition, the episodes are not better accounted for by Schizoaffective Disorder and are not superimposed on Schizophrenia, Schizophreniform Disorder, Delusional Disorder, or Psychotic Disorder Not Otherwise Specified. Bipolar I Disorder is subclassified in the fourth digit of the code according to whether the individual is experiencing a first episode (i.e., Single Manic Episode) or whether the disorder is recurrent. Recurrence is indicated by either a shift in the polarity of the episode or an interval between episodes of at least 2 months without manic symptoms. A shift in polarity is defined as a clinical course in which a Major Depressive Episode evolves into a Manic Episode or a Mixed Episode or in which a Manic Episode or a Mixed Episode evolves into a Major Depressive Episode. In contrast, a Hypomanic Episode that evolves into a Manic Episode or a Mixed Episode, or a Manic Episode that evolves into a Mixed Episode (or vice versa), is considered to be only a single episode. For recurrent Bipolar I Disorders, the nature of the current (or most recent) episode can be specified (Most Recent Episode Hypomanic, Most Recent Episode Manic, Most Recent Episode Mixed, Most Recent Episode Depressed, Most Recent Episode Unspecified).

Specifiers

The following specifiers for Bipolar I Disorder can be used to describe the current Manic, Mixed, or Major Depressive Episode (or, if criteria are not currently met for a Manic, Mixed, or Major Depressive Episode, the most recent Manic, Mixed, or Major Depressive Episode):

> **Mild, Moderate, Severe Without Psychotic Features, Severe With Psychotic Features, In Partial Remission, In Full Remission** (see p. 376)
> **With Catatonic Features** (see p. 382)
> **With Postpartum Onset** (see p. 386)

The following specifiers apply only to the current (or most recent) Major Depressive Episode only if it is the most recent type of mood episode:

> **Chronic** (see p. 382)
> **With Melancholic Features** (see p. 383)
> **With Atypical Features** (see p. 384)

The following specifiers can be used to indicate the pattern of episodes:

> **Longitudinal Course Specifiers (With or Without Full Interepisode Recovery)** (see p. 387)
> **With Seasonal Pattern** (applies only to the pattern of Major Depressive Episodes) (see p. 389)
> **With Rapid Cycling** (see p. 390)

Recording Procedures

The diagnostic codes for Bipolar I Disorder are selected as follows:

1. The first three digits are 296.

2. The fourth digit is 0 if there is a single Manic Episode. For recurrent episodes, the fourth digit is 4 if the current or most recent episode is a Hypomanic Episode or a Manic Episode, 6 if it is a Mixed Episode, 5 if it is a Major Depressive Episode, and 7 if the current or most recent episode is Unspecified.
3. The fifth digit (except for Bipolar I Disorder, Most Recent Episode Hypomanic, and Bipolar I Disorder, Most Recent Episode Unspecified) indicates the following: 1 for Mild severity, 2 for Moderate severity, 3 for Severe Without Psychotic Features, 4 for Severe With Psychotic Features, 5 for In Partial Remission, 6 for In Full Remission, and 0 if Unspecified. Other specifiers for Bipolar I Disorder cannot be coded. For Bipolar I Disorder, Most Recent Episode Hypomanic, the fifth digit is always 0. For Bipolar Disorder, Most Recent Episode Unspecified, there is no fifth digit.

In recording the name of a diagnosis, terms should be listed in the following order: Bipolar I Disorder, specifiers coded in the fourth digit (e.g., Most Recent Episode Manic), specifiers coded in the fifth digit (e.g., Mild, Severe With Psychotic Features, In Partial Remission), as many specifiers (without codes) as apply to the most recent episode (e.g., With Melancholic Features, With Postpartum Onset), and as many specifiers (without codes) as apply to the course of episodes (e.g., With Rapid Cycling); for example, 296.54 Bipolar I Disorder, Most Recent Episode Depressed, Severe With Psychotic Features, With Melancholic Features, With Rapid Cycling.

Note that if the single episode of Bipolar I Disorder is a Mixed Episode, the diagnosis would be indicated as 296.0x Bipolar I Disorder, Single Manic Episode, Mixed.

Associated Features and Disorders

Associated descriptive features and mental disorders.   Completed suicide occurs in 10%–15% of individuals with Bipolar I Disorder. Child abuse, spouse abuse, or other violent behavior may occur during severe Manic Episodes or during those with psychotic features. Other associated problems include school truancy, school failure, occupational failure, divorce, or episodic antisocial behavior. Other associated mental disorders include Anorexia Nervosa, Bulimia Nervosa, Attention-Deficit/Hyperactivity Disorder, Panic Disorder, Social Phobia, Substance-Related Disorders.

Associated laboratory findings.   There appear to be no laboratory features that distinguish Major Depressive Episodes found in Major Depressive Disorder from those in Bipolar I Disorder.

Associated physical examination findings and general medical conditions. An age at onset for a first Manic Episode after age 40 years should alert the clinician to the possibility that the symptoms may be due to a general medical condition or substance use. There is some evidence that untreated thyroid disease worsens the prognosis of Bipolar I Disorder.

Specific Culture, Age, and Gender Features

There are no reports of differential incidence of Bipolar I Disorder based on race or ethnicity. There is some evidence that clinicians may have a tendency to overdiagnose

Schizophrenia (instead of Bipolar Disorder) in some ethnic groups and in younger individuals.

Approximately 10%–15% of adolescents with recurrent Major Depressive Episodes will go on to develop Bipolar I Disorder. Mixed Episodes appear to be more likely in adolescents and young adults than in older adults.

Recent epidemiological studies in the United States indicate that Bipolar I Disorder is approximately equally common in men and women (unlike Major Depressive Disorder, which is more common in women). Gender appears to be related to the order of appearance of Manic and Major Depressive Episodes. The first episode in males is more likely to be a Manic Episode. The first episode in females is more likely to be a Major Depressive Episode. Women with Bipolar I Disorder have an increased risk of developing subsequent episodes (often psychotic) in the immediate postpartum period. Some women have their first episode during the postpartum period. The specifier With Postpartum Onset may be used to indicate that the onset of the episode is within 4 weeks of delivery (see p. 386). The premenstrual period may be associated with worsening of an ongoing Major Depressive, Manic, Mixed, or Hypomanic Episode.

Prevalence

The lifetime prevalence of Bipolar I Disorder in community samples has varied from 0.4% to 1.6%.

Course

Bipolar I Disorder is a recurrent disorder—more than 90% of individuals who have a single Manic Episode go on to have future episodes. Roughly 60%–70% of Manic Episodes occur immediately before or after a Major Depressive Episode. Manic Episodes often precede or follow the Major Depressive Episodes in a characteristic pattern for a particular person. The number of lifetime episodes (both Manic and Major Depressive) tends to be higher for Bipolar I Disorder compared with Major Depressive Disorder, Recurrent. Studies of the course of Bipolar I Disorder prior to lithium maintenance treatment suggest that, on average, four episodes occur in 10 years. The interval between episodes tends to decrease as the individual ages. There is some evidence that changes in sleep-wake schedule such as occur during time zone changes or sleep deprivation may precipitate or exacerbate a Manic, Mixed, or Hypomanic Episode. Approximately 5%–15% of individuals with Bipolar I Disorder have multiple (four or more) mood episodes (Major Depressive, Manic, Mixed, or Hypomanic) that occur within a given year. If this pattern is present, it is noted by the specifier With Rapid Cycling (see p. 390). A rapid-cycling pattern is associated with a poorer prognosis.

Although the majority of individuals with Bipolar I Disorder return to a fully functional level between episodes, some (20%–30%) continue to display mood lability and interpersonal or occupational difficulties. Psychotic symptoms may develop after days or weeks in what was previously a nonpsychotic Manic or Mixed Episode. When an individual has Manic Episodes with psychotic features, subsequent Manic Episodes are more likely to have psychotic features. Incomplete interepisode recovery is more common when the current episode is accompanied by mood-incongruent psychotic features.

Familial Pattern

First-degree biological relatives of individuals with Bipolar I Disorder have elevated rates of Bipolar I Disorder (4%–24%), Bipolar II Disorder (1%–5%), and Major Depressive Disorder (4%–24%). Twin and adoption studies provide strong evidence of a genetic influence for Bipolar I Disorder.

Differential Diagnosis

Major Depressive, Manic, Mixed, and Hypomanic Episodes in Bipolar I Disorder must be distinguished from episodes of a **Mood Disorder Due to a General Medical Condition.** The diagnosis is Mood Disorder Due to a General Medical Condition for episodes that are judged to be the direct physiological consequence of a specific general medical condition (e.g., multiple sclerosis, stroke, hypothyroidism) (see p. 366). This determination is based on the history, laboratory findings, or physical examination.

A **Substance-Induced Mood Disorder** is distinguished from Major Depressive, Manic, or Mixed Episodes that occur in Bipolar I Disorder by the fact that a substance (e.g., a drug of abuse, a medication, or exposure to a toxin) is judged to be etiologically related to the mood disturbance (see p. 370). Symptoms like those seen in a Manic, Mixed, or Hypomanic Episode may be part of an intoxication with or withdrawal from a drug of abuse and should be diagnosed as a Substance-Induced Mood Disorder (e.g., euphoric mood that occurs only in the context of intoxication with cocaine would be diagnosed as Cocaine-Induced Mood Disorder, With Manic Features, With Onset During Intoxication). Symptoms like those seen in a Manic or Mixed Episode may also be precipitated by antidepressant treatment such as medication, electroconvulsive therapy, or light therapy. Such episodes may be diagnosed as a Substance-Induced Mood Disorder (e.g., Amitriptyline-Induced Mood Disorder, With Manic Features; Electroconvulsive Therapy–Induced Mood Disorder, With Manic Features) and would not count toward a diagnosis of Bipolar I Disorder. However, when the substance use or medication is judged not to fully account for the episode (e.g., the episode continues for a considerable period autonomously after the substance is discontinued), the episode would count toward a diagnosis of Bipolar I Disorder.

Bipolar I Disorder is distinguished from **Major Depressive Disorder** and **Dysthymic Disorder** by the lifetime history of at least one Manic or Mixed Episode. Bipolar I Disorder is distinguished from **Bipolar II Disorder** by the presence of one or more Manic or Mixed Episodes. When an individual previously diagnosed with Bipolar II Disorder develops a Manic or Mixed Episode, the diagnosis is changed to Bipolar I Disorder.

In **Cyclothymic Disorder,** there are numerous periods of hypomanic symptoms that do not meet criteria for a Manic Episode and periods of depressive symptoms that do not meet symptom or duration criteria for a Major Depressive Episode. Bipolar I Disorder is distinguished from Cyclothymic Disorder by the presence of one or more Manic or Mixed Episodes. If a Manic or Mixed Episode occurs after the first 2 years of Cyclothymic Disorder, then Cyclothymic Disorder and Bipolar I Disorder may both be diagnosed.

The differential diagnosis between **Psychotic Disorders** (e.g., Schizoaffective Disorder, Schizophrenia, and Delusional Disorder) and Bipolar I Disorder may be difficult (especially in adolescents) because these disorders may share a number of presenting symptoms (e.g., grandiose and persecutory delusions, irritability, agitation, and catatonic symptoms), particularly cross-sectionally and early in their course. In contrast to Bipolar I Disorder, Schizophrenia, Schizoaffective Disorder, and Delusional Disorder are all characterized by periods of psychotic symptoms that occur in the absence of prominent mood symptoms. Other helpful considerations include the accompanying symptoms, previous course, and family history. Manic and depressive symptoms may be present during Schizophrenia, Delusional Disorder, and Psychotic Disorder Not Otherwise Specified, but rarely with sufficient number, duration, and pervasiveness to meet criteria for a Manic Episode or a Major Depressive Episode. However, when full criteria are met (or the symptoms are of particular clinical significance), a diagnosis of **Bipolar Disorder Not Otherwise Specified** may be made in addition to the diagnosis of Schizophrenia, Delusional Disorder, or Psychotic Disorder Not Otherwise Specified.

If there is a very rapid alternation (over days) between manic symptoms and depressive symptoms (e.g., several days of purely manic symptoms followed by several days of purely depressive symptoms) that do not meet minimal duration criteria for a Manic Episode or Major Depressive Episode, the diagnosis is **Bipolar Disorder Not Otherwise Specified.**

■ Diagnostic criteria for 296.0x Bipolar I Disorder, Single Manic Episode

A. Presence of only one Manic Episode (see p. 332) and no past Major Depressive Episodes.

Note: Recurrence is defined as either a change in polarity from depression or an interval of at least 2 months without manic symptoms.

B. The Manic Episode is not better accounted for by Schizoaffective Disorder and is not superimposed on Schizophrenia, Schizophreniform Disorder, Delusional Disorder, or Psychotic Disorder Not Otherwise Specified.

Specify if:
   Mixed: if symptoms meet criteria for a Mixed Episode (see p. 335)

Specify (for current or most recent episode):
   Severity/Psychotic/Remission Specifiers (see p. 378)
   With Catatonic Features (see p. 382)
   With Postpartum Onset (see p. 386)

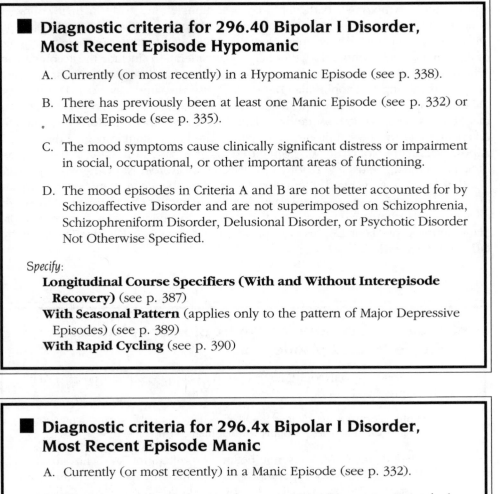

■ **Diagnostic criteria for 296.40 Bipolar I Disorder, Most Recent Episode Hypomanic**

A. Currently (or most recently) in a Hypomanic Episode (see p. 338).

B. There has previously been at least one Manic Episode (see p. 332) or Mixed Episode (see p. 335).

C. The mood symptoms cause clinically significant distress or impairment in social, occupational, or other important areas of functioning.

D. The mood episodes in Criteria A and B are not better accounted for by Schizoaffective Disorder and are not superimposed on Schizophrenia, Schizophreniform Disorder, Delusional Disorder, or Psychotic Disorder Not Otherwise Specified.

Specify:
Longitudinal Course Specifiers (With and Without Interepisode Recovery) (see p. 387)
With Seasonal Pattern (applies only to the pattern of Major Depressive Episodes) (see p. 389)
With Rapid Cycling (see p. 390)

■ **Diagnostic criteria for 296.4x Bipolar I Disorder, Most Recent Episode Manic**

A. Currently (or most recently) in a Manic Episode (see p. 332).

B. There has previously been at least one Major Depressive Episode (see p. 327), Manic Episode (see p. 332), or Mixed Episode (see p. 335).

C. The mood episodes in Criteria A and B are not better accounted for by Schizoaffective Disorder and are not superimposed on Schizophrenia, Schizophreniform Disorder, Delusional Disorder, or Psychotic Disorder Not Otherwise Specified.

Specify (for current or most recent episode):
Severity/Psychotic/Remission Specifiers (see p. 378)
With Catatonic Features (see p. 382)
With Postpartum Onset (see p. 386)

Specify:
Longitudinal Course Specifiers (With and Without Interepisode Recovery) (see p. 387)
With Seasonal Pattern (applies only to the pattern of Major Depressive Episodes) (see p. 389)
With Rapid Cycling (see p. 390)

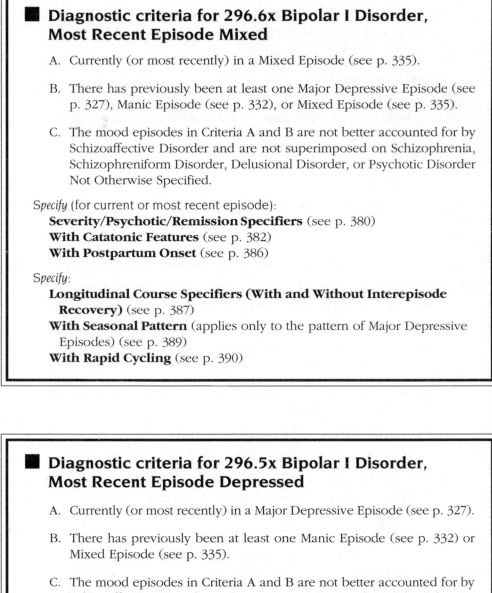

■ **Diagnostic criteria for 296.6x Bipolar I Disorder, Most Recent Episode Mixed**

A. Currently (or most recently) in a Mixed Episode (see p. 335).

B. There has previously been at least one Major Depressive Episode (see p. 327), Manic Episode (see p. 332), or Mixed Episode (see p. 335).

C. The mood episodes in Criteria A and B are not better accounted for by Schizoaffective Disorder and are not superimposed on Schizophrenia, Schizophreniform Disorder, Delusional Disorder, or Psychotic Disorder Not Otherwise Specified.

Specify (for current or most recent episode):
  Severity/Psychotic/Remission Specifiers (see p. 380)
  With Catatonic Features (see p. 382)
  With Postpartum Onset (see p. 386)

Specify:
  Longitudinal Course Specifiers (With and Without Interepisode Recovery) (see p. 387)
  With Seasonal Pattern (applies only to the pattern of Major Depressive Episodes) (see p. 389)
  With Rapid Cycling (see p. 390)

■ **Diagnostic criteria for 296.5x Bipolar I Disorder, Most Recent Episode Depressed**

A. Currently (or most recently) in a Major Depressive Episode (see p. 327).

B. There has previously been at least one Manic Episode (see p. 332) or Mixed Episode (see p. 335).

C. The mood episodes in Criteria A and B are not better accounted for by Schizoaffective Disorder and are not superimposed on Schizophrenia, Schizophreniform Disorder, Delusional Disorder, or Psychotic Disorder Not Otherwise Specified.

Specify (for current or most recent episode):
  Severity/Psychotic/Remission Specifiers (see p. 376)
  Chronic (see p. 382)
  With Catatonic Features (see p. 382)
  With Melancholic Features (see p. 383)

(continued)

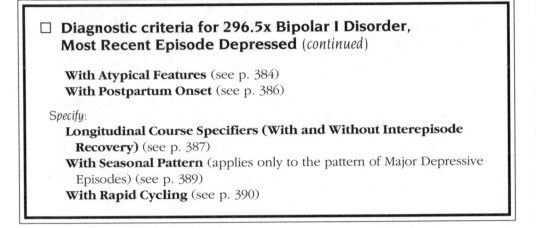

☐ **Diagnostic criteria for 296.5x Bipolar I Disorder, Most Recent Episode Depressed** (*continued*)

With Atypical Features (see p. 384)
With Postpartum Onset (see p. 386)

Specify:
Longitudinal Course Specifiers (With and Without Interepisode Recovery) (see p. 387)
With Seasonal Pattern (applies only to the pattern of Major Depressive Episodes) (see p. 389)
With Rapid Cycling (see p. 390)

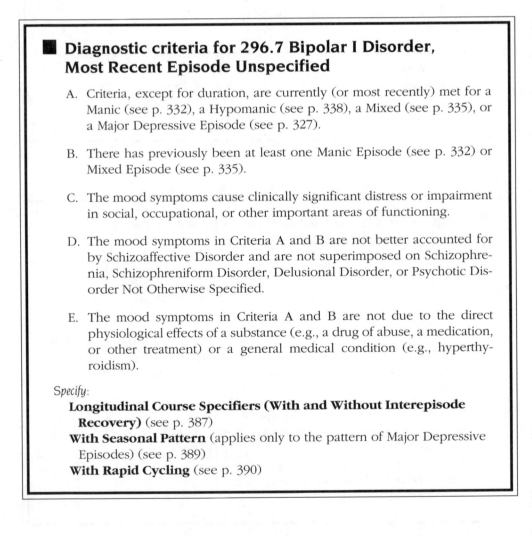

■ **Diagnostic criteria for 296.7 Bipolar I Disorder, Most Recent Episode Unspecified**

A. Criteria, except for duration, are currently (or most recently) met for a Manic (see p. 332), a Hypomanic (see p. 338), a Mixed (see p. 335), or a Major Depressive Episode (see p. 327).

B. There has previously been at least one Manic Episode (see p. 332) or Mixed Episode (see p. 335).

C. The mood symptoms cause clinically significant distress or impairment in social, occupational, or other important areas of functioning.

D. The mood symptoms in Criteria A and B are not better accounted for by Schizoaffective Disorder and are not superimposed on Schizophrenia, Schizophreniform Disorder, Delusional Disorder, or Psychotic Disorder Not Otherwise Specified.

E. The mood symptoms in Criteria A and B are not due to the direct physiological effects of a substance (e.g., a drug of abuse, a medication, or other treatment) or a general medical condition (e.g., hyperthyroidism).

Specify:
Longitudinal Course Specifiers (With and Without Interepisode Recovery) (see p. 387)
With Seasonal Pattern (applies only to the pattern of Major Depressive Episodes) (see p. 389)
With Rapid Cycling (see p. 390)

296.89   Bipolar II Disorder
(Recurrent Major Depressive Episodes With Hypomanic Episodes)

Diagnostic Features

The essential feature of Bipolar II Disorder is a clinical course that is characterized by the occurrence of one or more Major Depressive Episodes (Criterion A) accompanied by at least one Hypomanic Episode (Criterion B). Hypomanic Episodes should not be confused with the several days of euthymia that may follow remission of a Major Depressive Episode. The presence of a Manic or Mixed Episode precludes the diagnosis of Bipolar II Disorder (Criterion C). Episodes of Substance-Induced Mood Disorder (due to the direct physiological effects of a medication, other somatic treatments for depression, drugs of abuse, or toxin exposure) or of Mood Disorder Due to a General Medical Condition do not count toward a diagnosis of Bipolar II Disorder. In addition, the episodes must not be better accounted for by Schizoaffective Disorder and are not superimposed on Schizophrenia, Schizophreniform Disorder, Delusional Disorder, or Psychotic Disorder Not Otherwise Specified (Criterion D). The symptoms must cause clinically significant distress or impairment in social, occupational, or other important areas of functioning (Criterion E). In some cases, the Hypomanic Episodes themselves do not cause impairment. Instead, the impairment may result from the Major Depressive Episodes or from a chronic pattern of unpredictable mood episodes and fluctuating unreliable interpersonal or occupational functioning.

Individuals with Bipolar II Disorder may not view the Hypomanic Episodes as pathological, although others may be troubled by the individuals' erratic behavior. Often individuals, particularly when in the midst of a Major Depressive Episode, do not recall periods of hypomania without reminders from close friends or relatives. Information from other informants is often critical in establishing the diagnosis of Bipolar II Disorder.

Specifiers

The following specifiers for Bipolar II Disorder should be used to indicate the current or most recent episode:

Hypomanic. This specifier is used if the current (or most recent) episode is a Hypomanic Episode.

Depressed. This specifier is used if the current (or most recent) episode is a Major Depressive Episode.

The following specifiers may be used to describe the current Major Depressive Episode in Bipolar II Disorder (or the most recent Major Depressive Episode if currently in remission only if it is the most recent type of mood episode):

Mild, Moderate, Severe Without Psychotic Features, Severe With Psychotic Features, In Partial Remission, In Full Remission (see p. 376)
Chronic (see p. 382)
With Catatonic Features (see p. 382)
With Melancholic Features (see p. 383)
With Atypical Features (see p. 384)
With Postpartum Onset (see p. 386)

The following specifiers may be used to indicate the pattern or frequency of episodes:

> **Longitudinal Course Specifiers (With and Without Interepisode Recovery)** (see p. 387)
>
> **With Seasonal Pattern** (applies only to the pattern of Major Depressive Episodes) (see p. 389)
>
> **With Rapid Cycling** (see p. 390)

Recording Procedures

The diagnostic code for Bipolar II Disorder is 296.89; none of the specifiers are codable. In recording the name of the diagnosis, terms should be listed in the following order: Bipolar II Disorder, specifiers indicating current or most recent episode (e.g., Hypomanic, Depressed), as many specifiers as apply to the current or most recent Major Depressive Episode (e.g., Moderate, With Melancholic Features, With Postpartum Onset), and as many specifiers as apply to the course of episodes (e.g., With Seasonal Pattern); for example, 296.89 Bipolar II Disorder, Depressed, Severe With Psychotic Features, With Melancholic Features, With Seasonal Pattern.

Associated Features and Disorders

Associated descriptive features and mental disorders.   Completed suicide (usually during Major Depressive Episodes) is a significant risk, occurring in 10%–15% of persons with Bipolar II Disorder. School truancy, school failure, occupational failure, or divorce may be associated with Bipolar II Disorder. Associated mental disorders include Substance Abuse or Dependence, Anorexia Nervosa, Bulimia Nervosa, Attention-Deficit/Hyperactivity Disorder, Panic Disorder, Social Phobia, and Borderline Personality Disorder.

Associated laboratory findings.   There appear to be no laboratory features that distinguish Major Depressive Episodes found in Major Depressive Disorder from those in Bipolar II Disorder.

Specific Gender Features

Bipolar II Disorder may be more common in women than in men. Women with Bipolar II Disorder may be at increased risk of developing subsequent episodes in the immediate postpartum period.

Prevalence

Community studies suggest a lifetime prevalence of Bipolar II Disorder of approximately 0.5%.

Course

Roughly 60%–70% of the Hypomanic Episodes in Bipolar II Disorder occur immediately before or after a Major Depressive Episode. Hypomanic Episodes often precede or follow the Major Depressive Episodes in a characteristic pattern for a particular person. The number of lifetime episodes (both Hypomanic Episodes and Major Depressive Episodes) tends to be higher for Bipolar II Disorder compared with Major Depressive Disorder, Recurrent. The interval between episodes tends to decrease as the individual ages. Approximately 5%–15% of individuals with Bipolar II Disorder have multiple (four or more) mood episodes (Hypomanic or Major Depressive) that occur within a given year. If this pattern is present, it is noted by the specifier With Rapid Cycling (see p. 390). A rapid-cycling pattern is associated with a poorer prognosis.

Although the majority of individuals with Bipolar II Disorder return to a fully functional level between episodes, approximately 15% continue to display mood lability and interpersonal or occupational difficulties. Psychotic symptoms do not occur in Hypomanic Episodes, and they appear to be less frequent in the Major Depressive Episodes in Bipolar II Disorder than is the case for Bipolar I Disorder. Some evidence is consistent with the notion that marked changes in sleep-wake schedule such as occur during time zone changes or sleep deprivation may precipitate or exacerbate Hypomanic or Major Depressive Episodes. If a Manic or Mixed Episode develops in the course of Bipolar II Disorder, the diagnosis is changed to Bipolar I Disorder. Over 5 years, about 5%–15% of individuals with Bipolar II Disorder will develop a Manic Episode.

Familial Pattern

Some studies have indicated that first-degree biological relatives of individuals with Bipolar II Disorder have elevated rates of Bipolar II Disorder, Bipolar I Disorder, and Major Depressive Disorder compared with the general population.

Differential Diagnosis

Hypomanic and Major Depressive Episodes in Bipolar II Disorder must be distinguished from episodes of a **Mood Disorder Due to a General Medical Condition.** The diagnosis is Mood Disorder Due to a General Medical Condition for episodes that are judged to be the direct physiological consequence of a specific general medical condition (e.g., multiple sclerosis, stroke, hypothyroidism) (see p. 366). This determination is based on the history, laboratory findings, or physical examination.

A **Substance-Induced Mood Disorder** is distinguished from Hypomanic or Major Depressive Episodes that occur in Bipolar II Disorder by the fact that a substance (e.g., a drug of abuse, a medication, or exposure to a toxin) is judged to be etiologically related to the mood disturbance (see p. 370). Symptoms like those seen in a Hypomanic Episode may be part of an intoxication with or withdrawal from a drug of abuse and should be diagnosed as a Substance-Induced Mood Disorder (e.g., a major depressive–like episode occurring only in the context of withdrawal from cocaine would be diagnosed as Cocaine-Induced Mood Disorder, With Depressive Features, With Onset During Withdrawal). Symptoms like those seen in a Hypomanic Episode may also be precipitated by antidepressant treatment such as medication, electroconvulsive therapy, or light therapy. Such episodes may be diagnosed as a Substance-Induced Mood Disorder (e.g., Amitriptyline-Induced Mood Disorder, With Manic Features; Electroconvulsive Therapy–Induced Mood Disorder, With Manic Features) and would not count toward a diagnosis of Bipolar II Disorder. However, when the substance use or medication is judged not to fully account for the episode (e.g., the episode continues for a considerable period autonomously after the substance is discontinued), the episode would count toward a diagnosis of Bipolar II Disorder.

Bipolar II Disorder is distinguished from **Major Depressive Disorder** and **Dysthymic Disorder** by the lifetime history of at least one Hypomanic Episode. Bipolar II Disorder is distinguished from **Bipolar I Disorder** by the presence of one or more Manic or Mixed Episodes in the latter. When an individual previously diagnosed with Bipolar II Disorder develops a Manic or Mixed Episode, the diagnosis is changed to Bipolar I disorder.

In **Cyclothymic Disorder,** there are numerous periods of hypomanic symptoms and numerous periods of depressive symptoms that do not meet symptom or duration criteria for a Major Depressive Episode. Bipolar II Disorder is distinguished from Cyclothymic Disorder by the presence of one or more Major Depressive Episodes. If a Major Depressive Episode occurs after the first 2 years of Cyclothymic Disorder, the additional diagnosis of Bipolar II Disorder is given.

Bipolar II Disorder must be distinguished from **Psychotic Disorders** (e.g., Schizoaffective Disorder, Schizophrenia, and Delusional Disorder). Schizophrenia, Schizoaffective Disorder, and Delusional Disorder are all characterized by periods of psychotic symptoms that occur in the absence of prominent mood symptoms. Other helpful considerations include the accompanying symptoms, previous course, and family history.

■ Diagnostic criteria for 296.89 Bipolar II Disorder

A. Presence (or history) of one or more Major Depressive Episodes (see p. 327).

B. Presence (or history) of at least one Hypomanic Episode (see p. 338).

C. There has never been a Manic Episode (see p. 332) or a Mixed Episode (see p. 335).

D. The mood symptoms in Criteria A and B are not better accounted for by Schizoaffective Disorder and are not superimposed on Schizophrenia, Schizophreniform Disorder, Delusional Disorder, or Psychotic Disorder Not Otherwise Specified.

E. The symptoms cause clinically significant distress or impairment in social, occupational, or other important areas of functioning.

Specify current or most recent episode:
Hypomanic: if currently (or most recently) in a Hypomanic Episode (see p. 338)
Depressed: if currently (or most recently) in a Major Depressive Episode (see p. 327)

(continued)

☐ **Diagnostic criteria for 296.89 Bipolar II Disorder** (*continued*)

Specify (for current or most recent Major Depressive Episode only if it is the most recent type of mood episode):
    Severity/Psychotic/Remission Specifiers (see p. 376) **Note:** Fifth-digit codes specified on p. 377 cannot be used here because the code for Bipolar II Disorder already uses the fifth digit.
    Chronic (see p. 382)
    With Catatonic Features (see p. 382)
    With Melancholic Features (see p. 383)
    With Atypical Features (see p. 384)
    With Postpartum Onset (see p. 386)

Specify:
    Longitudinal Course Specifiers (With and Without Interepisode Recovery) (see p. 387)
    With Seasonal Pattern (applies only to the pattern of Major Depressive Episodes) (see p. 389)
    With Rapid Cycling (see p. 390)

301.13   Cyclothymic Disorder

Diagnostic Features

The essential feature of Cyclothymic Disorder is a chronic, fluctuating mood disturbance involving numerous periods of hypomanic symptoms (see p. 335) and numerous periods of depressive symptoms (see p. 320) (Criterion A). The hypomanic symptoms are of insufficient number, severity, pervasiveness, or duration to meet full criteria for a Manic Episode, and the depressive symptoms are of insufficient number, severity, pervasiveness, or duration to meet full criteria for a Major Depressive Episode. During the 2-year period (1 year for children or adolescents), any symptom-free intervals last no longer than 2 months (Criterion B). The diagnosis of Cyclothymic Disorder is made only if the initial 2-year period of cyclothymic symptoms is free of Major Depressive, Manic, and Mixed Episodes (Criterion C). After the initial 2 years of the Cyclothymic Disorder, Manic or Mixed Episodes may be superimposed on the Cyclothymic Disorder, in which case both Cyclothymic Disorder and Bipolar I Disorder are diagnosed. Similarly, after the initial 2 years of Cyclothymic Disorder, Major Depressive Episodes may be superimposed on the Cyclothymic Disorder, in which case both Cyclothymic Disorder and Bipolar II Disorder are diagnosed. The diagnosis is not made if the pattern of mood swings is better accounted for by Schizoaffective Disorder or is superimposed on a Psychotic Disorder, such as Schizophrenia, Schizophreniform Disorder, Delusional Disorder, or Psychotic Disorder Not Otherwise Specified (Criterion D), in which case the mood symptoms are considered to be associated features of the Psychotic Disorder. The mood disturbance must also not be due to the direct physiological effects of a substance (e.g., a drug of abuse, a medication) or a general medical condition (e.g., hyperthyroidism) (Criterion E). Although some people may function particularly well during some of the periods of hypomania, overall there must be clinically significant distress or impairment in social, occupational, or other important areas of functioning as a result of the mood disturbance (Criterion F). The impairment may develop as a result of prolonged periods of cyclical, often unpredictable mood changes (e.g., the person may be regarded as temperamental, moody, unpredictable, inconsistent, or unreliable).

Associated Features and Disorders

Associated descriptive features and mental disorders.   Substance-Related Disorders and Sleep Disorders (i.e., difficulties in initiating and maintaining sleep) may be present.

Specific Age and Gender Features

Cyclothymic Disorder often begins early in life and is sometimes considered to reflect a temperamental predisposition to other Mood Disorders (especially Bipolar Disorders). In community samples, Cyclothymic Disorder is apparently equally common in men and in women. In clinical settings, women with Cyclothymic Disorder may be more likely to present for treatment than men.

Prevalence

Studies have reported a lifetime prevalence of Cyclothymic Disorder of from 0.4% to 1%. Prevalence in mood disorders clinics may range from 3% to 5%.

Course

Cyclothymic Disorder usually begins in adolescence or early adult life. Onset of Cyclothymic Disorder late in adult life may suggest a Mood Disorder Due to a General Medical Condition such as multiple sclerosis. Cyclothymic Disorder usually has an insidious onset and a chronic course. There is a 15%–50% risk that the person will subsequently develop Bipolar I or II Disorder.

Familial Pattern

Major Depressive Disorder and Bipolar I or II Disorder appear to be more common among first-degree biological relatives of persons with Cyclothymic Disorder than among the general population. There may also be an increased familial risk of Substance-Related Disorders.

Differential Diagnosis

Cyclothymic Disorder must be distinguished from a **Mood Disorder Due to a General Medical Condition.** The diagnosis is Mood Disorder Due to a General Medical Condition, With Mixed Features, when the mood disturbance is judged to be the direct physiological consequence of a specific, usually chronic general medical condition (e.g., hyperthyroidism) (see p. 366). This determination is based on the history, laboratory findings, or physical examination. If it is judged that the depressive symptoms are not the direct physiological consequence of the general medical condition, then the primary Mood Disorder is recorded on Axis I (e.g., Cyclothymic Disorder) and the general medical condition is recorded on Axis III. This would be the case, for example, if the mood symptoms are considered to be the psychological consequence of having a chronic general medical condition or if there is no etiological relationship between the mood symptoms and the general medical condition.

A **Substance-Induced Mood Disorder** is distinguished from Cyclothymic Disorder by the fact that a substance (especially stimulants) is judged to be etiologically related to the mood disturbance (see p. 370). The frequent mood swings that are suggestive of Cyclothymic Disorder usually dissipate following cessation of drug use.

Bipolar I Disorder, With Rapid Cycling, and **Bipolar II Disorder, With Rapid Cycling,** both may resemble Cyclothymic Disorder by virtue of the frequent marked shifts in mood. By definition, the mood states in Cyclothymic Disorder do not meet the full criteria for a Major Depressive, Manic, or Mixed Episode, whereas the specifier With Rapid Cycling requires that full mood episodes be present. If a Major Depressive, Manic, or Mixed Episode occurs during the course of an established Cyclothymic Disorder, the diagnosis of either Bipolar I Disorder (for a Manic or Mixed Episode) or Bipolar II Disorder (for a Major Depressive Episode) is given along with the diagnosis of Cyclothymic Disorder.

Borderline Personality Disorder is associated with marked shifts in mood that may suggest Cyclothymic Disorder. If the criteria are met for each disorder, both Borderline Personality Disorder and Cyclothymic Disorder may be diagnosed.

■ **Diagnostic criteria for 301.13 Cyclothymic Disorder**

A. For at least 2 years, the presence of numerous periods with hypomanic symptoms (see p. 338) and numerous periods with depressive symptoms that do not meet criteria for a Major Depressive Episode. **Note:** In children and adolescents, the duration must be at least 1 year.

B. During the above 2-year period (1 year in children and adolescents), the person has not been without the symptoms in Criterion A for more than 2 months at a time.

C. No Major Depressive Episode (p. 327), Manic Episode (p. 332), or Mixed Episode (see p. 335) has been present during the first 2 years of the disturbance.

   Note: After the initial 2 years (1 year in children and adolescents) of Cyclothymic Disorder, there may be superimposed Manic or Mixed Episodes (in which case both Bipolar I Disorder and Cyclothymic Disorder may be diagnosed) or Major Depressive Episodes (in which case both Bipolar II Disorder and Cyclothymic Disorder may be diagnosed).

(continued)

☐ **Diagnostic criteria for 301.13 Cyclothymic Disorder**
(*continued*)

  D. The symptoms in Criterion A are not better accounted for by Schizoaffective Disorder and are not superimposed on Schizophrenia, Schizophreniform Disorder, Delusional Disorder, or Psychotic Disorder Not Otherwise Specified.

  E. The symptoms are not due to the direct physiological effects of a substance (e.g., a drug of abuse, a medication) or a general medical condition (e.g., hyperthyroidism).

  F. The symptoms cause clinically significant distress or impairment in social, occupational, or other important areas of functioning.

296.80   Bipolar Disorder Not Otherwise Specified

The Bipolar Disorder Not Otherwise Specified category includes disorders with bipolar features that do not meet criteria for any specific Bipolar Disorder. Examples include

  1. Very rapid alternation (over days) between manic symptoms and depressive symptoms that do not meet minimal duration criteria for a Manic Episode or a Major Depressive Episode
  2. Recurrent Hypomanic Episodes without intercurrent depressive symptoms
  3. A Manic or Mixed Episode superimposed on Delusional Disorder, residual Schizophrenia, or Psychotic Disorder Not Otherwise Specified
  4. Situations in which the clinician has concluded that a Bipolar Disorder is present but is unable to determine whether it is primary, due to a general medical condition, or substance induced

Other Mood Disorders

293.83   Mood Disorder
Due to a General Medical Condition

Diagnostic Features

The essential feature of Mood Disorder Due to a General Medical Condition is a prominent and persistent disturbance in mood that is judged to be due to the direct physiological effects of a general medical condition. The mood disturbance may involve depressed mood; markedly diminished interest or pleasure; or elevated, expansive, or irritable mood (Criterion A). Although the clinical presentation of the mood disturbance may resemble that of a Major Depressive, Manic, Mixed, or Hypomanic Episode, the full criteria for one of these episodes need not be met; the predominant symptom type may be indicated by using one of the following subtypes: With Depressive Features, With Major Depressive–Like Episode, With Manic Features, or With Mixed Features. There must be evidence from the history, physical examination, or laboratory findings that the disturbance is the direct physiological consequence of a general medical condition (Criterion B). The mood disturbance is not better accounted for by another mental disorder (e.g., Adjustment Disorder With Depressed Mood that occurs in response to the psychosocial stress of having the general medical condition) (Criterion C). The diagnosis is also not made if the mood disturbance occurs only during the course of a delirium (Criterion D). The mood disturbance must cause clinically significant distress or impairment in social, occupational, or other important areas of functioning (Criterion E). In some cases, the individual may still be able to function, but only with markedly increased effort.

In determining whether the mood disturbance is due to a general medical condition, the clinician must first establish the presence of a general medical condition. Further, the clinician must establish that the mood disturbance is etiologically related to the general medical condition through a physiological mechanism. A careful and comprehensive assessment of multiple factors is necessary to make this judgment. Although there are no infallible guidelines for determining whether the relationship between the mood disturbance and the general medical condition is etiological, several considerations provide some guidance in this area. One consideration is the presence of a temporal association between the onset, exacerbation, or remission of the general medical condition and that of the mood disturbance. A second consideration is the presence of features that are atypical of primary Mood Disorders (e.g., atypical age at onset or course or absence of family history). Evidence from the literature that suggests that there can be a direct association between the general medical condition in question and the development of mood symptoms can provide a useful context in the assessment of a particular situation. In addition, the clinician must also judge that the disturbance is not better accounted for by a primary Mood Disorder, a Substance-Induced Mood Disorder, or other primary mental disorders (e.g., Adjustment Disorder). This determination is explained in greater detail in the "Mental Disorders Due to a General Medical Condition" section (p. 165).

In contrast to Major Depressive Disorder, Mood Disorder Due to a General Medical Condition, With Depressive Features, appears to be nearly equally distributed by gender. Mood Disorder Due to a General Medical Condition increases the risk of attempted and completed suicide. Rates of suicide are variable depending on the particular general medical condition, with chronic, incurable, and painful conditions (e.g., malignancy, spinal cord injury, peptic ulcer disease, Huntington's disease, acquired immunodeficiency syndrome [AIDS], end-stage renal disease, head injury) carrying the greatest risk for suicide.

Subtypes

One of the following subtypes may be used to indicate which of the following symptom presentations predominates:

   With Depressive Features.   This subtype is used if the predominant mood is depressed, but the full criteria for a Major Depressive Episode are not met.
   With Major Depressive–Like Episode.   This subtype is used if the full criteria (except Criterion D) for a Major Depressive Episode (see p. 327) are met.

With Manic Features. This subtype is used if the predominant mood is elevated, euphoric, or irritable.

With Mixed Features. This subtype is used if the symptoms of both mania and depression are present but neither predominates.

Recording Procedures

In recording the diagnosis of Mood Disorder Due to a General Medical Condition, the clinician should note both the specific phenomenology of the disturbance, including the appropriate subtype, and the identified general medical condition judged to be causing the disturbance on Axis I (e.g., 293.83 Mood Disorder Due to Thyrotoxicosis, With Manic Features). The ICD-9-CM code for the general medical condition should also be noted on Axis III (e.g., 242.9 thyrotoxicosis). (See Appendix G for a list of selected ICD-9-CM diagnostic codes for general medical conditions.)

A separate diagnosis of Mood Disorder Due to a General Medical Condition is not given if the depressive symptoms develop exclusively during the course of Dementia of the Alzheimer's Type or Vascular Dementia. In this case, the depressive symptoms are indicated by specifying the subtype With Depressed Mood (e.g., 290.21 Dementia of the Alzheimer's Type, With Late Onset, With Depressed Mood).

Associated General Medical Conditions

A variety of general medical conditions may cause mood symptoms. These conditions include degenerative neurological conditions (e.g., Parkinson's disease, Huntington's disease), cerebrovascular disease (e.g., stroke), metabolic conditions (e.g., vitamin B_{12} deficiency), endocrine conditions (e.g., hyper- and hypothyroidism, hyper- and hypoparathyroidism, hyper- and hypoadrenocorticism), autoimmune conditions (e.g., systemic lupus erythematosus), viral or other infections (e.g., hepatitis, mononucleosis, human immunodeficiency virus [HIV]), and certain cancers (e.g., carcinoma of the pancreas). The associated physical examination findings, laboratory findings, and patterns of prevalence or onset reflect the etiological general medical condition.

Prevalence

Prevalence estimates for Mood Disorder Due to a General Medical Condition are confined to those presentations with depressive features. It has been observed that 25%–40% of individuals with certain neurological conditions (including Parkinson's disease, Huntington's disease, multiple sclerosis, stroke, and Alzheimer's disease) will develop a marked depressive disturbance at some point during the course of the illness. For general medical conditions without direct central nervous system involvement, rates are far more variable, ranging from more than 60% in Cushing's syndrome to less than 8% in end-stage renal disease.

Differential Diagnosis

A separate diagnosis of Mood Disorder Due to a General Medical Condition is not given if the mood disturbance occurs exclusively during the course of a **delirium.** When the clinician wishes to indicate the presence of clinically significant mood symptoms that occur in the context of a **Dementia Due to a General Medical Condition,** a separate diagnosis of Mood Disorder Due to a General Medical Condition can be indicated. An exception to this is when depressive symptoms occur exclusively during the course of **Dementia of the Alzheimer's Type** or **Vascular Dementia.** In these cases, only a diagnosis of Dementia of the Alzheimer's Type or of Vascular Dementia with the subtype With Depressed Mood is given; a separate diagnosis of Mood Disorder Due to a General Medical Condition is not made. If the presentation includes a mix of different types of symptoms (e.g., mood and anxiety), the specific mental disorder due to a general medical condition depends on which symptoms predominate in the clinical picture.

If there is evidence of recent or prolonged substance use (including medications with psychoactive effects), withdrawal from a substance, or exposure to a toxin, a **Substance-Induced Mood Disorder** should be considered. It may be useful to obtain a urine or blood drug screen or other appropriate laboratory evaluation. Symptoms that occur during or shortly after (i.e., within 4 weeks of) Substance Intoxication or Withdrawal or after medication use may be especially indicative of a Substance-Induced Disorder, depending on the character, duration, or amount of the substance used. If the clinician has ascertained that the disturbance is due to both a general medical condition and substance use, both diagnoses (i.e., Mood Disorder Due to a General Medical Condition and Substance-Induced Mood Disorder) are given.

Mood Disorder Due to a General Medical Condition must be distinguished from **Major Depressive Disorder, Bipolar I Disorder, Bipolar II Disorder,** and **Adjustment Disorder With Depressed Mood** (e.g., a maladaptive response to the stress of having a general medical condition). In Major Depressive, Bipolar, and Adjustment Disorders, no specific and direct causative physiological mechanisms associated with a general medical condition can be demonstrated. It is often difficult to determine whether certain symptoms (e.g., weight loss, insomnia, fatigue) represent a mood disturbance or are a direct manifestation of a general medical condition (e.g., cancer, stroke, myocardial infarction, diabetes). Such symptoms count toward a diagnosis of a Major Depressive Episode except in cases where they are clearly and fully accounted for by a general medical condition. If the clinician cannot determine whether the mood disturbance is primary, substance induced, or due to a general medical condition, **Mood Disorder Not Otherwise Specified** may be diagnosed.

■ **Diagnostic criteria for 293.83 Mood Disorder Due to . . . [*Indicate the General Medical Condition*]**

A. A prominent and persistent disturbance in mood predominates in the clinical picture and is characterized by either (or both) of the following:

   (1) depressed mood or markedly diminished interest or pleasure in all, or almost all, activities

   (2) elevated, expansive, or irritable mood

B. There is evidence from the history, physical examination, or laboratory findings that the disturbance is the direct physiological consequence of a general medical condition.

(continued)

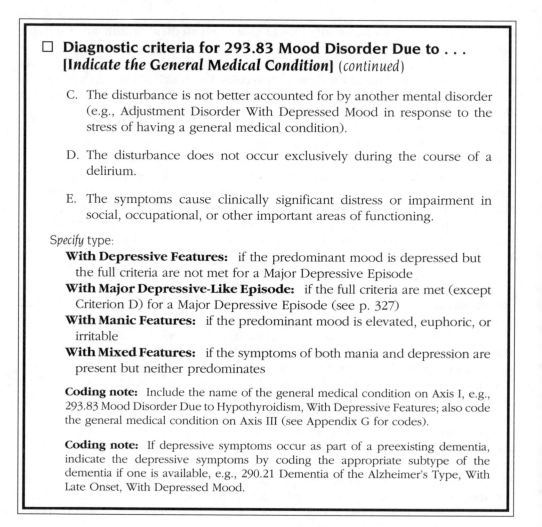

☐ **Diagnostic criteria for 293.83 Mood Disorder Due to . . . [Indicate the General Medical Condition]** (continued)

  C. The disturbance is not better accounted for by another mental disorder (e.g., Adjustment Disorder With Depressed Mood in response to the stress of having a general medical condition).

  D. The disturbance does not occur exclusively during the course of a delirium.

  E. The symptoms cause clinically significant distress or impairment in social, occupational, or other important areas of functioning.

Specify type:
 With Depressive Features: if the predominant mood is depressed but the full criteria are not met for a Major Depressive Episode
 With Major Depressive-Like Episode: if the full criteria are met (except Criterion D) for a Major Depressive Episode (see p. 327)
 With Manic Features: if the predominant mood is elevated, euphoric, or irritable
 With Mixed Features: if the symptoms of both mania and depression are present but neither predominates

 Coding note: Include the name of the general medical condition on Axis I, e.g., 293.83 Mood Disorder Due to Hypothyroidism, With Depressive Features; also code the general medical condition on Axis III (see Appendix G for codes).

 Coding note: If depressive symptoms occur as part of a preexisting dementia, indicate the depressive symptoms by coding the appropriate subtype of the dementia if one is available, e.g., 290.21 Dementia of the Alzheimer's Type, With Late Onset, With Depressed Mood.

Substance-Induced Mood Disorder

Diagnostic Features

The essential feature of Substance-Induced Mood Disorder is a prominent and persistent disturbance in mood (Criterion A) that is judged to be due to the direct physiological effects of a substance (i.e., a drug of abuse, a medication, other somatic treatment for depression, or toxin exposure) (Criterion B). Depending on the nature of the substance and the context in which the symptoms occur (i.e., during intoxication or withdrawal), the disturbance may involve depressed mood or markedly diminished interest or pleasure or elevated, expansive, or irritable mood. Although the clinical presentation of the mood disturbance may resemble that of a Major Depressive, Manic, Mixed, or Hypomanic Episode, the full criteria for one of these episodes need not be met. The predominant symptom type may be indicated by using one of the following subtypes: With Depressive Features, With Manic Features, With Mixed Features. The disturbance must not be better accounted for by a Mood Disorder that is not substance induced

(Criterion C). The diagnosis is not made if the mood disturbance occurs only during the course of a delirium (Criterion D). The symptoms must cause clinically significant distress or impairment in social, occupational, or other important areas of functioning (Criterion E). In some cases, the individual may still be able to function, but only with markedly increased effort. This diagnosis should be made instead of a diagnosis of Substance Intoxication or Substance Withdrawal only when the mood symptoms are in excess of those usually associated with the intoxication or withdrawal syndrome and when the mood symptoms are sufficiently severe to warrant independent clinical attention.

A Substance-Induced Mood Disorder is distinguished from a primary Mood Disorder by considering the onset, course, and other factors. For drugs of abuse, there must be evidence from the history, physical examination, or laboratory findings of intoxication or withdrawal. Substance-Induced Mood Disorders arise only in association with intoxication or withdrawal states, whereas primary Mood Disorders may precede the onset of substance use or may occur during times of sustained abstinence. Because the withdrawal state for some substances can be relatively protracted, the onset of the mood symptoms can occur up to 4 weeks after the cessation of substance use. Another consideration is the presence of features that are atypical of primary Mood Disorders (e.g., atypical age at onset or course). For example, the onset of a Manic Episode after age 45 years may suggest a substance-induced etiology. In contrast, factors that suggest that the mood symptoms are better accounted for by a primary Mood Disorder include persistence of mood symptoms for a substantial period of time (i.e., about a month) after the end of Substance Intoxication or acute Substance Withdrawal; the development of mood symptoms that are substantially in excess of what would be expected given the type or amount of the substance used or the duration of use; or a history of prior recurrent primary episodes of Mood Disorder.

Some medications (e.g., stimulants, steroids, l-dopa, antidepressants) or other somatic treatments for depression (e.g., electroconvulsive therapy or light therapy) can induce manic-like mood disturbances. Clinical judgment is essential to determine whether the treatment is truly causal or whether a primary Mood Disorder happened to have its onset while the person was receiving the treatment. For example, manic symptoms that develop in a person while he or she is taking lithium would not be diagnosed as Substance-Induced Mood Disorder because lithium is not likely to induce manic-like episodes. On the other hand, a depressive episode that developed within the first several weeks of beginning alpha-methyldopa (an antihypertensive agent) in a person with no history of Mood Disorder would qualify for the diagnosis of alpha-Methyldopa–Induced Mood Disorder, With Depressive Features. In some cases, a previously established condition (e.g., Major Depressive Disorder, Recurrent) can recur while the person is coincidentally taking a medication that has the capacity to cause depressive symptoms (e.g., l-dopa, birth-control pills). In such cases, the clinician must make a judgment as to whether the medication is causative in this particular situation. For a more detailed discussion of Substance-Related Disorders, see p. 175.

Subtypes and Specifiers

One of the following subtypes may be used to indicate which of the following symptom presentations predominates:

> **With Depressive Features.** This subtype is used if the predominant mood is depressed.

With Manic Features. This subtype is used if the predominant mood is elevated, euphoric, or irritable.

With Mixed Features. This subtype is used if the symptoms of both mania and depression are present but neither predominates.

The context of the development of the mood symptoms may be indicated by using one of the following specifiers:

With Onset During Intoxication. This specifier should be used if criteria for intoxication with the substance are met and the symptoms develop during the intoxication syndrome.

With Onset During Withdrawal. This specifier should be used if criteria for withdrawal from the substance are met and the symptoms develop during, or shortly after, a withdrawal syndrome.

Recording Procedures

The name of the Substance-Induced Mood Disorder begins with the specific substance or somatic treatment (e.g., cocaine, amitriptyline, electroconvulsive therapy) that is presumed to be causing the mood symptoms. The diagnostic code is selected from the listing of classes of substances provided in the criteria set. For substances that do not fit into any of the classes (e.g., amitriptyline) and for other somatic treatments (e.g., electroconvulsive therapy), the code for "Other Substance" should be used. In addition, for medications prescribed at therapeutic doses, the specific medication can be indicated by listing the appropriate E-code (see Appendix G). The name of the disorder (e.g., Cocaine-Induced Mood Disorder) is followed by the subtype indicating the predominant symptom presentation and the specifier indicating the context in which the symptoms developed (e.g., 292.84 Cocaine-Induced Mood Disorder, With Depressive Features, With Onset During Withdrawal). When more than one substance is judged to play a significant role in the development of mood symptoms, each should be listed separately (e.g., 292.84 Cocaine-Induced Mood Disorder, With Manic Features, With Onset During Withdrawal; 292.84 Light Therapy–Induced Mood Disorder, With Manic Features). If a substance is judged to be the etiological factor but the specific substance or class of substances is unknown, the category 292.84 Unknown Substance–Induced Mood Disorder may be used.

Specific Substances

Mood Disorders can occur in association with **intoxication** with the following classes of substances: alcohol; amphetamine and related substances; cocaine; hallucinogens; inhalants; opioids; phencyclidine and related substances; sedatives, hypnotics, and anxiolytics; and other or unknown substances. Mood Disorders can occur in association with **withdrawal** from the following classes of substances: alcohol; amphetamine and related substances; cocaine; sedatives, hypnotics, and anxiolytics; and other or unknown substances.

Some of the medications reported to evoke mood symptoms include anesthetics, analgesics, anticholinergics, anticonvulsants, antihypertensives, antiparkinsonian medications, antiulcer medications, cardiac medications, oral contraceptives, psychotropic medications (e.g., antidepressants, benzodiazepines, antipsychotics, disulfiram), muscle relaxants, steroids, and sulfonamides. Some medications have an especially high likelihood of producing depressive features (e.g., high doses of reserpine, cortico-steroids, anabolic steroids). Note that this is not an exhaustive list of possible medications and that many medications may occasionally produce an idiosyncratic depressive reaction. Heavy metals and toxins (e.g., volatile substances such as gasoline and paint, organophosphate insecticides, nerve gases, carbon monoxide, carbon dioxide) may also cause mood symptoms.

Differential Diagnosis

Mood symptoms occur commonly in **Substance Intoxication** and **Substance Withdrawal,** and the diagnosis of the substance-specific intoxication or substance-specific withdrawal will usually suffice to categorize the symptom presentation. A diagnosis of Substance-Induced Mood Disorder should be made instead of a diagnosis of Substance Intoxication or Substance Withdrawal only when the mood symptoms are judged to be in excess of those usually associated with the intoxication or withdrawal syndrome and when the mood symptoms are sufficiently severe to warrant independent clinical attention. For example, dysphoric mood is a characteristic feature of Cocaine Withdrawal. Cocaine-Induced Mood Disorder should be diagnosed instead of Cocaine Withdrawal only if the mood disturbance is substantially more intense than what is usually encountered with Cocaine Withdrawal and is sufficiently severe to be a separate focus of attention and treatment.

If substance-induced mood symptoms occur exclusively during the course of a **delirium,** the mood symptoms are considered to be an associated feature of the delirium and are not diagnosed separately. In **substance-induced presentations that contain a mix of different types of symptoms** (e.g., mood, psychotic, and anxiety symptoms), the specific type of Substance-Induced Disorder to be diagnosed depends on which type of symptoms predominates in the clinical presentation.

A Substance-Induced Mood Disorder is distinguished from a **primary Mood Disorder** by the fact that a substance is judged to be etiologically related to the symptoms (p. 371).

A Substance-Induced Mood Disorder due to a prescribed treatment for a mental disorder or general medical condition must have its onset while the person is receiving the medication (e.g., antihypertensive medication) (or during withdrawal, if there is a withdrawal syndrome associated with the medication). Once the treatment is discontinued, the mood symptoms will usually remit within days to several weeks (depending on the half-life of the substance and the presence of a withdrawal syndrome). If symptoms persist beyond 4 weeks, other causes for the mood symptoms should be considered.

Because individuals with general medical conditions often take medications for those conditions, the clinician must consider the possibility that the mood symptoms are caused by the physiological consequences of the general medical condition rather than the medication, in which case **Mood Disorder Due to a General Medical Condition** is diagnosed. The history often provides the primary basis for such a judgment. At times, a change in the treatment for the general medical condition (e.g., medication substitution or discontinuation) may be needed to determine empirically for that person whether the medication is the causative agent. If the clinician has ascertained that the disturbance is due to both a general medical condition and substance use, both diagnoses (i.e., Mood

Disorder Due to a General Medical Condition and Substance-Induced Mood Disorder) may be given. When there is insufficient evidence to determine whether the mood symptoms are due to a substance (including a medication) or to a general medical condition or are primary (i.e., not due to either a substance or a general medical condition), **Depressive Disorder Not Otherwise Specified** or **Bipolar Disorder Not Otherwise Specified** would be indicated.

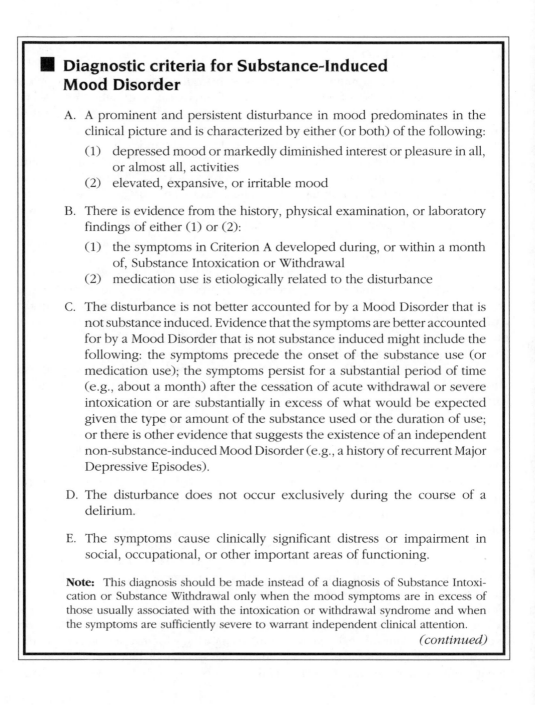

■ **Diagnostic criteria for Substance-Induced Mood Disorder**

A. A prominent and persistent disturbance in mood predominates in the clinical picture and is characterized by either (or both) of the following:
   (1) depressed mood or markedly diminished interest or pleasure in all, or almost all, activities
   (2) elevated, expansive, or irritable mood

B. There is evidence from the history, physical examination, or laboratory findings of either (1) or (2):
   (1) the symptoms in Criterion A developed during, or within a month of, Substance Intoxication or Withdrawal
   (2) medication use is etiologically related to the disturbance

C. The disturbance is not better accounted for by a Mood Disorder that is not substance induced. Evidence that the symptoms are better accounted for by a Mood Disorder that is not substance induced might include the following: the symptoms precede the onset of the substance use (or medication use); the symptoms persist for a substantial period of time (e.g., about a month) after the cessation of acute withdrawal or severe intoxication or are substantially in excess of what would be expected given the type or amount of the substance used or the duration of use; or there is other evidence that suggests the existence of an independent non-substance-induced Mood Disorder (e.g., a history of recurrent Major Depressive Episodes).

D. The disturbance does not occur exclusively during the course of a delirium.

E. The symptoms cause clinically significant distress or impairment in social, occupational, or other important areas of functioning.

Note: This diagnosis should be made instead of a diagnosis of Substance Intoxication or Substance Withdrawal only when the mood symptoms are in excess of those usually associated with the intoxication or withdrawal syndrome and when the symptoms are sufficiently severe to warrant independent clinical attention.

(continued)

☐ **Diagnostic criteria for Substance-Induced Mood Disorder**
(*continued*)

Code [Specific Substance]–Induced Mood Disorder:
(291.8 Alcohol; 292.84 Amphetamine [or Amphetamine-Like Substance];
292.84 Cocaine; 292.84 Hallucinogen; 292.84 Inhalant; 292.84 Opioid;
292.84 Phencyclidine [or Phencyclidine-Like Substance]; 292.84 Sedative,
Hypnotic, or Anxiolytic; 292.84 Other [or Unknown] Substance)

Specify type:
With Depressive Features: if the predominant mood is depressed
With Manic Features: if the predominant mood is elevated, euphoric, or
irritable
With Mixed Features: if symptoms of both mania and depression are
present and neither predominates

Specify if (see table on p. 177 for applicability by substance):
With Onset During Intoxication: if the criteria are met for Intoxication
with the substance and the symptoms develop during the intoxication
syndrome
With Onset During Withdrawal: if criteria are met for Withdrawal from
the substance and the symptoms develop during, or shortly after, a
withdrawal syndrome

296.90   Mood Disorder Not Otherwise Specified

This category includes disorders with mood symptoms that do not meet the criteria for
any specific Mood Disorder and in which it is difficult to choose between Depressive
Disorder Not Otherwise Specified and Bipolar Disorder Not Otherwise Specified (e.g.,
acute agitation).

Specifiers Describing Most Recent Episode

A number of specifiers for Mood Disorders are provided to increase diagnostic specificity
and create more homogeneous subgroups, assist in treatment selection, and improve
the prediction of prognosis. The following specifiers pertain to the current (or most
recent) mood episode: Severity/Psychotic/Remission, Chronic, With Catatonic Features,
With Melancholic Features, With Atypical Features, and With Postpartum Onset. The
specifiers that indicate severity, remission, and psychotic features can be coded in the
fifth digit of the diagnostic code for most of the Mood Disorders. The other specifiers
cannot be coded. Table 1 indicates which episode specifiers apply to each Mood
Disorder (see p. 376).

Table 1.   Episode specifiers that apply to Mood Disorders

	Severity/ Psychotic/ Remission	Chronic	With Catatonic Features	With Melancholic Features	With Atypical Features	With Postpartum Onset
Major Depressive Disorder, Single Episode	X	X	X	X	X	X
Major Depressive Disorder, Recurrent	X	X	X	X	X	X
Dysthymic Disorder					X	
Bipolar I Disorder, Single Manic Episode	X		X			X
Bipolar I Disorder, Most Recent Episode Hypomanic						
Bipolar I Disorder, Most Recent Episode Manic	X		X			X
Bipolar I Disorder, Most Recent Episode Mixed	X		X			X
Bipolar I Disorder, Most Recent Episode Depressed	X	X	X	X	X	X
Bipolar I Disorder, Most Recent Episode Unspecified						
Bipolar II Disorder, Hypomanic						
Bipolar II Disorder, Depressed	X	X	X	X	X	X
Cyclothymic Disorder						

Severity/Psychotic/Remission Specifiers for Major Depressive Episode

These specifiers apply to the most recent Major Depressive Episode in Major Depressive Disorder and to a Major Depressive Episode in Bipolar I or II Disorder only if it is the most recent type of mood episode. If criteria are currently met for the Major Depressive Episode, it can be classified as Mild, Moderate, Severe Without Psychotic Features, or Severe With Psychotic Features. If the criteria are no longer met, the specifier indicates whether the episode is in partial or full remission. For Major Depressive Disorder and most of the Bipolar I Disorders, the specifier is reflected in the fifth-digit coding for the disorder.

1—Mild, 2—Moderate, 3—Severe Without Psychotic Features.   Severity is judged to be mild, moderate, or severe based on the number of criteria symptoms, the severity of the symptoms, and the degree of functional disability and distress. *Mild* episodes are characterized by the presence of only five or six depressive symptoms and either mild disability or the capacity to function normally but with substantial and unusual effort. Episodes that are *Severe Without Psychotic Features* are characterized by the presence of most of the criteria symptoms and clear-cut, observable disability (e.g., inability to work or care for children). *Moderate* episodes have a severity that is intermediate between mild and severe.

4—Severe With Psychotic Features.   This specifier indicates the presence of either delusions or hallucinations (typically auditory). Most commonly, the content of the delusions or hallucinations is consistent with the depressive themes. Such *mood-congruent psychotic features* include delusions of guilt (e.g., of being responsible for illness in a loved one), delusions of deserved punishment (e.g., of being punished because of a moral transgression or some personal inadequacy), nihilistic delusions (e.g., of world or personal destruction), somatic delusions (e.g., of cancer or one's body "rotting away"), or delusions of poverty (e.g., of being bankrupt). Hallucinations, when present, are usually transient and not elaborate and may involve voices that berate the person for shortcomings or sins.

Less commonly, the content of the hallucinations or delusions has no apparent relationship to depressive themes. Such *mood-incongruent psychotic features* include persecutory delusions (without depressive themes that the individual deserves to be persecuted), delusions of thought insertion (i.e., one's thoughts are not one's own), delusions of thought broadcasting (i.e., others can hear one's thoughts) and delusions of control (i.e., one's actions are under outside control). These features are associated with a poorer prognosis. The clinician can indicate the nature of the psychotic features by specifying With Mood-Congruent Features or With Mood-Incongruent Features.

5—In Partial Remission, 6—In Full Remission.   Full Remission requires a period of at least 2 months in which there are no significant symptoms of depression. There are two ways for the episode to be In Partial Remission: 1) some symptoms of a Major Depressive Episode are still present, but full criteria are no longer met; or 2) there are no longer any significant symptoms of a Major Depressive Episode, but the period of remission has been less than 2 months. If the Major Depressive Episode has been superimposed on Dysthymic Disorder, the diagnosis of Major Depressive Disorder, In Partial Remission, is not given once the full criteria for a Major Depressive Episode are no longer met; instead, the diagnosis is Dysthymic Disorder and Major Depressive Disorder, Prior History.

■ **Criteria for Severity/Psychotic/Remission Specifiers for current (or most recent) Major Depressive Episode**

Note: Code in fifth digit. Can be applied to the most recent Major Depressive Episode in Major Depressive Disorder and to a Major Depressive Episode in Bipolar I or II Disorder only if it is the most recent type of mood episode.

.x1—Mild: Few, if any, symptoms in excess of those required to make the diagnosis and symptoms result in only minor impairment in occupational functioning or in usual social activities or relationships with others.
.x2—Moderate: Symptoms or functional impairment between "mild" and "severe."

(continued)

☐ **Criteria for Severity/Psychotic/Remission Specifiers for current (or most recent) Major Depressive Episode** (*continued*)

.x3—Severe Without Psychotic Features: Several symptoms in excess of those required to make the diagnosis, **and** symptoms markedly interfere with occupational functioning or with usual social activities or relationships with others.

.x4—Severe With Psychotic Features: Delusions or hallucinations. If possible, specify whether the psychotic features are mood-congruent or mood-incongruent:

Mood-Congruent Psychotic Features: Delusions or hallucinations whose content is entirely consistent with the typical depressive themes of personal inadequacy, guilt, disease, death, nihilism, or deserved punishment.

Mood-Incongruent Psychotic Features: Delusions or hallucinations whose content does not involve typical depressive themes of personal inadequacy, guilt, disease, death, nihilism, or deserved punishment. Included are such symptoms as persecutory delusions (not directly related to depressive themes), thought insertion, thought broadcasting, and delusions of control.

.x5—In Partial Remission: Symptoms of a Major Depressive Episode are present but full criteria are not met, or there is a period without any significant symptoms of a Major Depressive Episode lasting less than 2 months following the end of the Major Depressive Episode. (If the Major Depressive Episode was superimposed on Dysthymic Disorder, the diagnosis of Dysthymic Disorder alone is given once the full criteria for a Major Depressive Episode are no longer met.)

.x6—In Full Remission: During the past 2 months, no significant signs or symptoms of the disturbance were present.

.x0—Unspecified.

Severity/Psychotic/Remission Specifiers for Manic Episode

These specifiers apply to a Manic Episode in Bipolar I Disorder only if it is the most recent type of mood episode. If criteria are currently met for the Manic Episode, it can be classified as Mild, Moderate, Severe Without Psychotic Features, or Severe With Psychotic Features. If the criteria are no longer met, the specifier indicates whether the episode is in partial or full remission. These specifiers are reflected in the fifth-digit coding for the disorder.

1—Mild, 2—Moderate, 3—Severe Without Psychotic Features.   Severity is judged to be mild, moderate, or severe based on the number of criteria symptoms, the severity of the symptoms, the degree of functional disability, and the need for supervision. *Mild* episodes are characterized by the presence of only three or four manic symptoms. *Moderate* episodes are characterized by an extreme increase in activity or impairment in judgment. Episodes that are *Severe Without Psychotic Features* are characterized by the need for almost continual supervision to protect the individual from harm to self or others.

4—Severe With Psychotic Features. This specifier indicates the presence of either delusions or hallucinations (typically auditory). Most commonly, the content of the delusions or hallucinations is consistent with the manic themes, that is, they are *mood-congruent psychotic features*. For example, God's voice may be heard explaining that the person has a special mission. Persecutory delusions may be based on the idea that the person is being persecuted because of some special relationship or attribute.

Less commonly, the content of the hallucinations or delusions has no apparent relationship to manic themes, that is, they are *mood-incongruent psychotic features*. These may include persecutory delusions (not directly related to grandiose themes), delusions of thought insertion (i.e., one's thoughts are not one's own), delusions of thought broadcasting (i.e., others can hear one's thoughts), and delusions of control (i.e., one's actions are under outside control). The presence of these features may be associated with a poorer prognosis. The clinician can indicate the nature of the psychotic features by specifying With Mood-Congruent Features or With Mood-Incongruent Features.

5—In Partial Remission, 6—In Full Remission. Full Remission requires a period of at least 2 months in which there are no significant symptoms of mania. There are two ways for the episode to be In Partial Remission: 1) symptoms of a Manic Episode are still present, but full criteria are no longer met; or 2) there are no longer any significant symptoms of a Manic Episode, but the period of remission has been less than 2 months.

■ **Criteria for Severity/Psychotic/Remission Specifiers for current (or most recent) Manic Episode**

Note: Code in fifth digit. Can be applied to a Manic Episode in Bipolar I Disorder only if it is the most recent type of mood episode.

.x1—Mild: Minimum symptom criteria are met for a Manic Episode.

.x2—Moderate: Extreme increase in activity or impairment in judgment.

.x3—Severe Without Psychotic Features: Almost continual supervision required to prevent physical harm to self or others.

.x4—Severe With Psychotic Features: Delusions or hallucinations. If possible, specify whether the psychotic features are mood-congruent or mood-incongruent:

> **Mood-Congruent Psychotic Features:** Delusions or hallucinations whose content is entirely consistent with the typical manic themes of inflated worth, power, knowledge, identity, or special relationship to a deity or famous person.

(continued)

☐ **Criteria for Severity/Psychotic/Remission Specifiers for current (or most recent) Manic Episode** (*continued*)

Mood-Incongruent Psychotic Features: Delusions or hallucinations whose content does not involve typical manic themes of inflated worth, power, knowledge, identity, or special relationship to a deity or famous person. Included are such symptoms as persecutory delusions (not directly related to grandiose ideas or themes), thought insertion, and delusions of being controlled.

.x5—In Partial Remission: Symptoms of a Manic Episode are present but full criteria are not met, or there is a period without any significant symptoms of a Manic Episode lasting less than 2 months following the end of the Manic Episode.

.x6—In Full Remission: During the past 2 months no significant signs or symptoms of the disturbance were present.

.x0—Unspecified.

Severity/Psychotic/Remission Specifiers for Mixed Episode

These specifiers apply to a Mixed Episode in Bipolar I Disorder only if it is the most recent type of mood episode. If criteria are currently met for the Mixed Episode, it can be classified as Mild, Moderate, Severe Without Psychotic Features, or Severe With Psychotic Features. If the criteria are no longer met, the specifier indicates whether the episode is in partial or full remission. These specifiers are reflected in the fifth-digit coding for the disorder.

1—Mild, 2—Moderate, 3—Severe Without Psychotic Features.   Severity is judged to be mild, moderate, or severe based on the number of criteria symptoms, the severity of the symptoms, the degree of functional disability, and the need for supervision. *Mild* episodes are characterized by the presence of only three or four manic symptoms and five or six depressive symptoms. *Moderate* episodes are characterized by an extreme increase in activity or impairment in judgment. Episodes that are *Severe Without Psychotic Features* are characterized by the need for almost continual supervision to protect the individual from harm to self or others.

4—Severe With Psychotic Features.   This specifier indicates the presence of either delusions or hallucinations (typically auditory). Most commonly, the content of the delusions or hallucinations is consistent with either the manic or depressive themes, that is, they are *mood-congruent psychotic features*. For example, God's voice may be heard explaining that the person has a special mission. Persecutory delusions may be based on the idea that the person is being persecuted because of being especially deserving of punishment or having some special relationship or attribute.

Less commonly, the content of the hallucinations or delusions has no apparent relationship to either manic or depressive themes, that is, they are *mood-incongruent psychotic features*. These may include delusions of thought insertion (i.e., one's thoughts are not one's own), delusions of thought broadcasting (i.e., others can hear one's thoughts), and delusions of control (i.e., one's actions are under outside control). These features are associated with a poorer prognosis. The clinician can indicate the nature of the psychotic features by specifying With Mood-Congruent Features or With Mood-Incongruent Features.

5—In Partial Remission, 6—In Full Remission.   Full Remission requires a period of at least 2 months in which there are no significant symptoms of mania or depression. There are two ways for the episode to be In Partial Remission: 1) symptoms of a Mixed Episode are still present, but full criteria are no longer met; or 2) there are no longer any significant symptoms of a Mixed Episode, but the period of remission has been less than 2 months.

■ **Criteria for Severity/Psychotic/Remission Specifiers for current (or most recent) Mixed Episode**

Note: Code in fifth digit. Can be applied to a Mixed Episode in Bipolar I Disorder only if it is the most recent type of mood episode.

.x1—Mild: No more than minimum symptom criteria are met for both a Manic Episode and a Major Depressive Episode.

.x2—Moderate: Symptoms or functional impairment between "mild" and "severe."

.x3—Severe Without Psychotic Features: Almost continual supervision required to prevent physical harm to self or others.

.x4—Severe With Psychotic Features: Delusions or hallucinations. If possible, specify whether the psychotic features are mood-congruent or mood-incongruent:

> **Mood-Congruent Psychotic Features:** Delusions or hallucinations whose content is entirely consistent with the typical manic or depressive themes.

> **Mood-Incongruent Psychotic Features:** Delusions or hallucinations whose content does not involve typical manic or depressive themes. Included are such symptoms as persecutory delusions (not directly related to grandiose or depressive themes), thought insertion, and delusions of being controlled.

.x5—In Partial Remission: Symptoms of a Mixed Episode are present but full criteria are not met, or there is a period without any significant symptoms of a Mixed Episode lasting less than 2 months following the end of the Mixed Episode.

.x6—In Full Remission: During the past 2 months, no significant signs or symptoms of the disturbance were present.

.x0—Unspecified.

Chronic Specifier for a Major Depressive Episode

This specifier indicates the chronic nature of a Major Depressive Episode. This specifier applies to the current or most recent Major Depressive Episode in Major Depressive Disorder and to a Major Depressive Episode in Bipolar I or Bipolar II Disorder only if it is the most recent type of mood episode.

■ Criteria for Chronic Specifier

Specify if:
  Chronic (can be applied to the current or most recent Major Depressive Episode in Major Depressive Disorder and to a Major Depressive Episode in Bipolar I or II Disorder only if it is the most recent type of mood episode)

  Full criteria for a Major Depressive Episode have been met continuously for at least the past 2 years.

Catatonic Features Specifier

The specifier With Catatonic Features can be applied to the current (or most recent) Major Depressive, Manic, or Mixed Episode in Major Depressive Disorder, Bipolar I Disorder, or Bipolar II Disorder. The specifier With Catatonic Features is appropriate when the clinical picture is characterized by marked psychomotor disturbance that may involve motoric immobility, excessive motor activity, extreme negativism, mutism, peculiarities of voluntary movement, echolalia, or echopraxia. Motoric immobility may be manifested by catalepsy (waxy flexibility) or stupor. The excessive motor activity is apparently purposeless and is not influenced by external stimuli. There may be extreme negativism that is manifested by the maintenance of a rigid posture against attempts to be moved or resistance to all instructions. Peculiarities of voluntary movement are manifested by the assumption of inappropriate or bizarre postures or by prominent grimacing. Echolalia (the pathological, parrotlike, and apparently senseless repetition of a word or phrase just spoken by another person) and echopraxia (the repetitive imitation of the movements of another person) are often present. Additional features may include stereotypies, mannerisms, and automatic obedience or mimicry. During severe catatonic stupor or excitement, the person may need careful supervision to avoid self-harm or harm to others. Potential consequences include malnutrition, exhaustion, hyperpyrexia, or self-inflicted injury. The differential diagnosis of a Mood Episode With Catatonic Features includes **Catatonic Disorder Due to a General Medical Condition** (p. 169), **Schizophrenia, Catatonic Type** (p. 288), or a **side effect of a medication** (e.g., a Medication-Induced Movement Disorder, p. 678).

■ **Criteria for Catatonic Features Specifier**

Specify if:

With Catatonic Features (can be applied to the current or most recent Major Depressive Episode, Manic Episode, or Mixed Episode in Major Depressive Disorder, Bipolar I Disorder, or Bipolar II Disorder)

The clinical picture is dominated by at least two of the following:

(1) motoric immobility as evidenced by catalepsy (including waxy flexibility) or stupor

(2) excessive motor activity (that is apparently purposeless and not influenced by external stimuli)

(3) extreme negativism (an apparently motiveless resistance to all instructions or maintenance of a rigid posture against attempts to be moved) or mutism

(4) peculiarities of voluntary movement as evidenced by posturing (voluntary assumption of inappropriate or bizarre postures), stereotyped movements, prominent mannerisms, or prominent grimacing

(5) echolalia or echopraxia

Melancholic Features Specifier

The specifier With Melancholic Features can be applied to the current (or most recent) Major Depressive Episode that occurs in the course of Major Depressive Disorder and to a Major Depressive Episode in Bipolar I or II Disorder only if it is the most recent type of mood episode. The essential feature of a Major Depressive Episode, With Melancholic Features is loss of interest or pleasure in all, or almost all, activities or a lack of reactivity to usually pleasurable stimuli. The individual's depressed mood does not improve, even temporarily, when something good happens (Criterion A). In addition, at least three of the following symptoms are present: a distinct quality of the depressed mood, depression that is regularly worse in the morning, early morning awakening, psychomotor retardation or agitation, significant anorexia or weight loss, or excessive or inappropriate guilt (Criterion B).

The specifier With Melancholic Features is applied if these features are present at the nadir of the episode. There is a near-complete absence of the capacity for pleasure, not merely a diminution. A guideline for evaluating the lack of reactivity of mood is that, even for very desired events, the depressed mood does not brighten at all or brightens only partially (e.g., up to 20%–40% of normal for only minutes at a time). The distinct quality of mood that is characteristic of the With Melancholic Features specifier is experienced by individuals as qualitatively different from the sadness experienced during bereavement or a nonmelancholic depressive episode. This may be elicited by asking the person to compare the quality of the current depressed mood with the mood experienced after the death of a loved one. A depressed mood that is described as merely more severe, longer-lasting, or present without a reason is not considered distinct in quality. Psychomotor changes are nearly always present and are observable by others.

Individuals with melancholic features are less likely to have a premorbid Personality Disorder, to have a clear precipitant to the episode, and to respond to a trial of placebo medication. They are more likely to have responded to antidepressant medications or electroconvulsive therapy in the past and are also more likely to respond in the current episode. Melancholic features are encountered equally in both genders, but are more likely in older individuals. These features exhibit only a modest tendency to repeat across episodes in the same individual. They are more frequent in inpatients, as opposed to outpatients, and are less likely to occur in milder than in more severe Major Depressive Episodes and are more likely to occur in those with psychotic features. Melancholic features are more frequently associated with laboratory findings of dexamethasone nonsuppression, hyperadrenocorticism, reduced rapid eye movement (REM) latency, abnormal tyramine challenge test, and an abnormal asymmetry on dichotic listening tasks.

■ Criteria for Melancholic Features Specifier

Specify if:

With Melancholic Features (can be applied to the current or most recent Major Depressive Episode in Major Depressive Disorder and to a Major Depressive Episode in Bipolar I or Bipolar II Disorder only if it is the most recent type of mood episode)

A. Either of the following, occurring during the most severe period of the current episode:

  (1) loss of pleasure in all, or almost all, activities
  (2) lack of reactivity to usually pleasurable stimuli (does not feel much better, even temporarily, when something good happens)

B. Three (or more) of the following:

  (1) distinct quality of depressed mood (i.e., the depressed mood is experienced as distinctly different from the kind of feeling experienced after the death of a loved one)
  (2) depression regularly worse in the morning
  (3) early morning awakening (at least 2 hours before usual time of awakening)
  (4) marked psychomotor retardation or agitation
  (5) significant anorexia or weight loss
  (6) excessive or inappropriate guilt

Atypical Features Specifier

The specifier With Atypical Features can be applied to the current (or most recent) Major Depressive Episode in Major Depressive Disorder and to a Major Depressive Episode in Bipolar I or Bipolar II Disorder only if it is the most recent type of mood episode, or to Dysthymic Disorder. The essential features are mood reactivity (Criterion A) and the presence of at least two of the following features (Criterion B): increased appetite or weight gain, hypersomnia, leaden paralysis, and a long-standing pattern of extreme sensitivity to perceived interpersonal rejection. These features predominate during the most recent 2-week period (or the most recent 2-year period for Dysthymic Disorder). The specifier With Atypical Features is not given if the criteria for With Melancholic Features or With Catatonic Features have been met during the same Major Depressive Episode.

Mood reactivity is the capacity to be cheered up when presented with positive events (e.g., a visit from children, compliments from others). Mood may become euthymic (not sad) even for extended periods of time if the external circumstances remain favorable. Increased appetite may be manifested by an obvious increase in food intake or by weight gain. Hypersomnia may include either an extended period of nighttime sleep or daytime napping that totals at least 10 hours of sleep per day (or at least 2 hours more than when not depressed). Leaden paralysis is defined as feeling heavy, leaden, or weighted down, usually in the arms or legs; this is generally present for at least an hour a day but often lasts for many hours at a time. Unlike the other atypical features, pathological sensitivity to perceived interpersonal rejection is a trait that has an early onset and persists throughout most of adult life. Rejection sensitivity occurs both when the person is and is not depressed, though it may be exacerbated during depressive periods. The problems that result from rejection sensitivity must be significant enough to result in functional impairment. There may be stormy relationships with frequent disruptions and an inability to sustain a longer-lasting relationship. The individual's reaction to rebuff or criticism may be manifested by leaving work early, using substances excessively, or displaying other clinically significant maladaptive behavioral responses. There may also be avoidance of relationships due to the fear of interpersonal rejection. Being occasionally touchy or overemotional does not qualify as a manifestation of interpersonal rejection sensitivity. Personality Disorders (e.g., Avoidant Personality Disorder) and Anxiety Disorders (e.g., Separation Anxiety Disorder, Specific Phobia, or Social Phobia) may be more common in those with atypical features. The laboratory findings associated with a Major Depressive Episode With Melancholic Features are generally not present in association with an episode with atypical features.

Atypical features are two to three times more common in women. Individuals with atypical features report an earlier age at onset of their depressive episodes (e.g., while in high school) and frequently have a more chronic, less episodic course, with only partial interepisode recovery. Younger individuals may be more likely to have episodes with atypical features, whereas older individuals may more often have episodes with melancholic features. Episodes with atypical features are more common in Bipolar I Disorder, Bipolar II Disorder, and in Major Depressive Disorder, Recurrent, occurring in a seasonal pattern.

■ **Criteria for Atypical Features Specifier**

Specify if:

   With Atypical Features (can be applied when these features predominate
      during the most recent 2 weeks of a Major Depressive Episode in Major
      Depressive Disorder or in Bipolar I or Bipolar II Disorder when the Major
      Depressive Episode is the most recent type of mood episode, or when these
      features predominate during the most recent 2 years of Dysthymic Disorder)
                                                                    (continued)

☐ **Criteria for Atypical Features Specifier** (*continued*)

A. Mood reactivity (i.e., mood brightens in response to actual or potential positive events)

B. Two (or more) of the following features:
   (1) significant weight gain or increase in appetite
   (2) hypersomnia
   (3) leaden paralysis (i.e., heavy, leaden feelings in arms or legs)
   (4) long-standing pattern of interpersonal rejection sensitivity (not limited to episodes of mood disturbance) that results in significant social or occupational impairment

C. Criteria are not met for With Melancholic Features or With Catatonic Features during the same episode.

Postpartum Onset Specifier

The specifier With Postpartum Onset can be applied to the current (or most recent) Major Depressive, Manic, or Mixed Episode of Major Depressive Disorder, Bipolar I Disorder, or Bipolar II Disorder or to Brief Psychotic Disorder (p. 302) if onset is within 4 weeks after delivery of a child. In general, the symptomatology of the postpartum Major Depressive, Manic, or Mixed Episode does not differ from the symptomatology in nonpostpartum mood episodes and may include psychotic features. A fluctuating course and mood lability may be more common in postpartum episodes. When delusions are present, they often concern the newborn infant (e.g., the newborn is possessed by the devil, has special powers, or is destined for a terrible fate). In both the psychotic and nonpsychotic presentations, there may be suicidal ideation, obsessional thoughts regarding violence to the child, lack of concentration, and psychomotor agitation. Women with postpartum Major Depressive Episodes often have severe anxiety, Panic Attacks, spontaneous crying long after the usual duration of "baby blues" (i.e., 3–7 days postpartum), disinterest in their new infant, and insomnia (more likely to manifest as difficulty falling asleep than as early morning awakening).

Many women feel especially guilty about having depressive feelings at a time when they believe they should be happy. They may be reluctant to discuss their symptoms or their negative feelings toward the child. Less-than-optimal development of the mother-infant relationship may result from the clinical condition itself or from separations from the infant. Infanticide is most often associated with postpartum psychotic episodes that are characterized by command hallucinations to kill the infant or delusions that the infant is possessed, but it can also occur in severe postpartum mood episodes without such specific delusions or hallucinations. Postpartum mood (Major Depressive, Manic, or Mixed) episodes with psychotic features appear to occur in from 1 in 500 to 1 in 1000 deliveries and may be more common in primiparous women. The risk of postpartum episodes with psychotic features is particularly increased for women with prior postpartum mood episodes but is also elevated for those with a prior history of a Mood Disorder (especially Bipolar I Disorder). Once a woman has had a postpartum episode with psychotic features, the risk of recurrence with each subsequent delivery is between 30% and 50%. There is also some evidence of increased risk of postpartum psychotic mood episodes among women without a history of Mood Disorders with a family history of Bipolar Disorders. Postpartum episodes must be differentiated from delirium occurring in the postpartum period, which is distinguished by a decreased level of awareness or attention.

■ **Criteria for Postpartum Onset Specifier**

Specify if:

With Postpartum Onset (can be applied to the current or most recent Major Depressive, Manic, or Mixed Episode in Major Depressive Disorder, Bipolar I Disorder, or Bipolar II Disorder; or to Brief Psychotic Disorder)

Onset of episode within 4 weeks postpartum

Specifiers Describing Course of Recurrent Episodes

A number of specifiers for Mood Disorders are provided to increase diagnostic specificity and create more homogeneous subgroups, assist in treatment selection, and improve the prediction of prognosis. Specifiers that describe the course of recurrent episodes include Longitudinal Course Specifiers (With or Without Full Interepisode Recovery), Seasonal Pattern, and Rapid Cycling. These specifiers cannot be coded. Table 2 indicates which course specifiers apply to each Mood Disorder (see p. 388).

Longitudinal Course Specifiers
(With and Without Full Interepisode Recovery)

The specifiers With Full Interepisode Recovery and Without Full Interepisode Recovery are provided to help characterize the course of illness in individuals with Recurrent Major Depressive Disorder, Bipolar I Disorder, or Bipolar II Disorder. These specifiers should be applied to the period of time between the two most recent episodes. The characterization of course is further enhanced by noting the presence of antecedent Dysthymic Disorder.

The four graphs below depict prototypical courses. *A* shows the course of Major Depressive Disorder, Recurrent, in which there is no antecedent Dysthymic Disorder and there is a period of full remission between the episodes. This course pattern predicts the best future prognosis. *B* shows the course of Major Depressive Disorder, Recurrent, in which there is no antecedent Dysthymic Disorder but in which prominent symptoms persist between the two most recent episodes—that is, no more than partial remission is attained. *C* shows the rare pattern (present in fewer than 3% of individuals with Major Depressive Disorder) of Major Depressive Disorder, Recurrent, with antecedent Dysthy-

Table 2. Course specifiers that apply to Mood Disorders

	With/Without Interepisode Recovery	Seasonal Pattern	Rapid Cycling
Major Depressive Disorder, Single Episode			
Major Depressive Disorder, Recurrent	X	X	
Dysthymic Disorder			
Bipolar I Disorder, Single Manic Episode			
Bipolar I Disorder, Most Recent Episode Hypomanic	X	X	X
Bipolar I Disorder, Most Recent Episode Manic	X	X	X
Bipolar I Disorder, Most Recent Episode Mixed	X	X	X
Bipolar I Disorder, Most Recent Episode Depressed	X	X	X
Bipolar I Disorder, Most Recent Episode Unspecified	X	X	X
Bipolar II Disorder, Hypomanic	X	X	X
Bipolar II Disorder, Depressed	X	X	X
Cyclothymic Disorder			

mic Disorder but with full interepisode recovery between the two most recent episodes. *D* shows the course of Major Depressive Disorder, Recurrent, in which there is antecedent Dysthymic Disorder and in which there is no period of full remission between the two most recent episodes. This pattern, commonly referred to as "double depression" (see p. 346), is seen in about 20%–25% of individuals with Major Depressive Disorder.

In general, individuals with a history of Without Full Interepisode Recovery between episodes have a persistence of that pattern between subsequent episodes. They also appear more likely to have more Major Depressive Episodes than those with full interepisode recovery. Dysthymic Disorder prior to the first episode of Major Depressive Disorder is most likely to be associated with lack of full interepisode recovery subsequently. These specifiers may also be applied to the period of time between the most recent mood episodes in Bipolar I Disorder or Bipolar II Disorder to indicate presence or absence of mood symptomatology.

A. Recurrent, with full interepisode recovery, with no Dysthymic Disorder

B. Recurrent, without full interepisode recovery, with no Dysthymic Disorder

C. Recurrent, with full interepisode recovery, super-imposed on Dysthymic Disorder (also code 300.4)

D. Recurrent, without full interepisode recovery, super-imposed on Dysthymic Disorder (also code 300.4)

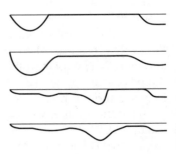

■ **Criteria for Longitudinal Course Specifiers**

Specify if (can be applied to Recurrent Major Depressive Disorder or Bipolar I or II Disorder):
   With Full Interepisode Recovery: if full remission is attained between the two most recent Mood Episodes
   Without Full Interepisode Recovery: if full remission is not attained between the two most recent Mood Episodes

Seasonal Pattern Specifier

The specifier With Seasonal Pattern can be applied to the pattern of Major Depressive Episodes in Bipolar I Disorder, Bipolar II Disorder, or Major Depressive Disorder, Recurrent. The essential feature is the onset and remission of Major Depressive Episodes at characteristic times of the year. In most cases, the episodes begin in fall or winter and remit in spring. Less commonly, there may be recurrent summer depressive episodes. This pattern of onset and remission of episodes must have occurred during the last 2 years, without any nonseasonal episodes occurring during this period. In addition, the seasonal depressive episodes must substantially outnumber any nonseasonal depressive episodes over the individual's lifetime. This specifier does not apply to those situations in which the pattern is better explained by seasonally linked psychosocial stressors (e.g., seasonal unemployment or school schedule). Major Depressive Episodes that occur in a seasonal pattern are often characterized by prominent anergy, hypersomnia, over-eating, weight gain, and a craving for carbohydrates. It is unclear whether a seasonal pattern is more likely in Major Depressive Disorder, Recurrent, or in Bipolar Disorders. However, within the Bipolar Disorders group, a seasonal pattern appears to be more likely in Bipolar II Disorder than in Bipolar I Disorder. In some individuals, the onset of Manic or Hypomanic Episodes may also be linked to a particular season. Bright visible-spectrum light used in treatment may be associated with switches into Manic or Hypomanic Episodes.

The prevalence of winter-type seasonal pattern appears to vary with latitude, age, and sex. Prevalence increases with higher latitudes. Age is also a strong predictor of seasonality, with younger persons at higher risk for winter depressive episodes. Women comprise 60%–90% of persons with seasonal pattern, but it is unclear whether female gender is a specific risk factor over and above the risk associated with recurrent Major Depressive Disorder. Although this specifier applies to seasonal occurrence of full Major Depressive Episodes, some research suggests that a seasonal pattern may also describe the presentation in some individuals with recurrent winter depressive episodes that do not meet criteria for a Major Depressive Episode.

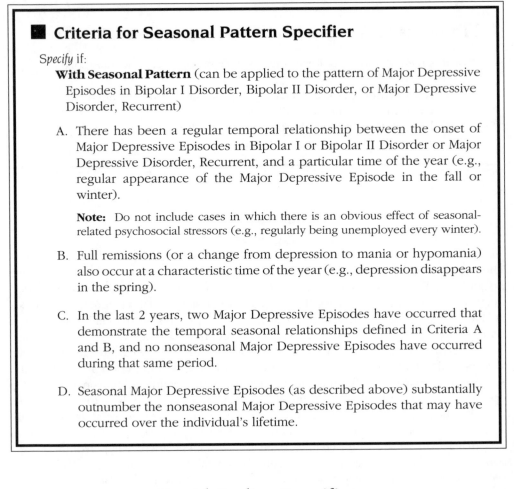

■ Criteria for Seasonal Pattern Specifier

Specify if:

With Seasonal Pattern (can be applied to the pattern of Major Depressive Episodes in Bipolar I Disorder, Bipolar II Disorder, or Major Depressive Disorder, Recurrent)

A. There has been a regular temporal relationship between the onset of Major Depressive Episodes in Bipolar I or Bipolar II Disorder or Major Depressive Disorder, Recurrent, and a particular time of the year (e.g., regular appearance of the Major Depressive Episode in the fall or winter).

   Note: Do not include cases in which there is an obvious effect of seasonal-related psychosocial stressors (e.g., regularly being unemployed every winter).

B. Full remissions (or a change from depression to mania or hypomania) also occur at a characteristic time of the year (e.g., depression disappears in the spring).

C. In the last 2 years, two Major Depressive Episodes have occurred that demonstrate the temporal seasonal relationships defined in Criteria A and B, and no nonseasonal Major Depressive Episodes have occurred during that same period.

D. Seasonal Major Depressive Episodes (as described above) substantially outnumber the nonseasonal Major Depressive Episodes that may have occurred over the individual's lifetime.

Rapid-Cycling Specifier

The specifier With Rapid Cycling can be applied to Bipolar I Disorder or Bipolar II Disorder. The essential feature of a rapid-cycling Bipolar Disorder is the occurrence of four or more mood episodes during the previous 12 months. These episodes can occur in any combination and order. The episodes must meet both the duration and symptom criteria for a Major Depressive, Manic, Mixed, or Hypomanic Episode and must be demarcated by either a period of full remission or by a switch to an episode of the opposite polarity. Manic, Hypomanic, and Mixed Episodes are counted as being on the same pole (e.g., a Manic Episode immediately followed by a Mixed Episode counts as only one episode in considering the specifier With Rapid Cycling). Except for the fact that they occur more frequently, the episodes that occur in a rapid-cycling pattern are no different from those that occur in a non-rapid-cycling pattern. Mood episodes that count toward defining a rapid-cycling pattern exclude those episodes directly caused by a substance (e.g., cocaine, corticosteroids) or a general medical condition.

Rapid cycling occurs in approximately 5%–15% of persons with Bipolar Disorder seen in mood disorders clinics. Whereas in Bipolar Disorder in general the sex ratio is equal, women comprise 70%–90% of individuals with a rapid-cycling pattern. The mood episodes are not linked to any phase of the menstrual cycle and occur in both pre- and postmenopausal women. Rapid cycling may be associated with hypothyroidism, certain neurological conditions (e.g., multiple sclerosis), Mental Retardation, head injury, or antidepressant treatment. Rapid cycling can occur at any time during the course of Bipolar Disorder and may appear and disappear, particularly if it is associated with antidepressant use. The development of rapid cycling is associated with a poorer longer-term prognosis.

■ Criteria for Rapid-Cycling Specifier

Specify if:

With Rapid Cycling (can be applied to Bipolar I Disorder or Bipolar II Disorder)

At least four episodes of a mood disturbance in the previous 12 months that meet criteria for a Major Depressive, Manic, Mixed, or Hypomanic Episode.

Note: Episodes are demarcated either by partial or full remission for at least 2 months or a switch to an episode of opposite polarity (e.g., Major Depressive Episode to Manic Episode).

Anxiety Disorders

The following disorders are contained in this section: Panic Disorder Without Agoraphobia, Panic Disorder With Agoraphobia, Agoraphobia Without History of Panic Disorder, Specific Phobia, Social Phobia, Obsessive-Compulsive Disorder, Posttraumatic Stress Disorder, Acute Stress Disorder, Generalized Anxiety Disorder, Anxiety Disorder Due to a General Medical Condition, Substance-Induced Anxiety Disorder, and Anxiety Disorder Not Otherwise Specified. Because Panic Attacks and Agoraphobia occur in the context of several of these disorders, criteria sets for a Panic Attack and for Agoraphobia are listed separately at the beginning of this section.

A **Panic Attack** is a discrete period in which there is the sudden onset of intense apprehension, fearfulness, or terror, often associated with feelings of impending doom. During these attacks, symptoms such as shortness of breath, palpitations, chest pain or discomfort, choking or smothering sensations, and fear of "going crazy" or losing control are present.

Agoraphobia is anxiety about, or avoidance of, places or situations from which escape might be difficult (or embarrassing) or in which help may not be available in the event of having a Panic Attack or panic-like symptoms.

Panic Disorder Without Agoraphobia is characterized by recurrent unexpected Panic Attacks about which there is persistent concern. **Panic Disorder With Agoraphobia** is characterized by both recurrent unexpected Panic Attacks and Agoraphobia.

Agoraphobia Without History of Panic Disorder is characterized by the presence of Agoraphobia and panic-like symptoms without a history of unexpected Panic Attacks.

Specific Phobia is characterized by clinically significant anxiety provoked by exposure to a specific feared object or situation, often leading to avoidance behavior.

Social Phobia is characterized by clinically significant anxiety provoked by exposure to certain types of social or performance situations, often leading to avoidance behavior.

Obsessive-Compulsive Disorder is characterized by obsessions (which cause marked anxiety or distress) and/or by compulsions (which serve to neutralize anxiety).

Posttraumatic Stress Disorder is characterized by the reexperiencing of an extremely traumatic event accompanied by symptoms of increased arousal and by avoidance of stimuli associated with the trauma.

Acute Stress Disorder is characterized by symptoms similar to those of Posttraumatic Stress Disorder that occur immediately in the aftermath of an extremely traumatic event.

Generalized Anxiety Disorder is characterized by at least 6 months of persistent and excessive anxiety and worry.

Anxiety Disorder Due to a General Medical Condition is characterized by prominent symptoms of anxiety that are judged to be a direct physiological consequence of a general medical condition.

Substance-Induced Anxiety Disorder is characterized by prominent symptoms of anxiety that are judged to be a direct physiological consequence of a drug of abuse, a medication, or toxin exposure.

Anxiety Disorder Not Otherwise Specified is included for coding disorders with prominent anxiety or phobic avoidance that do not meet criteria for any of the specific Anxiety Disorders defined in this section (or anxiety symptoms about which there is inadequate or contradictory information).

Because Separation Anxiety Disorder (characterized by anxiety related to separation from parental figures) usually develops in childhood, it is included in the "Disorders Usually First Diagnosed in Infancy, Childhood, or Adolescence" section (see p. 110). Phobic avoidance that is limited to genital sexual contact with a sexual partner is classified as Sexual Aversion Disorder and is included in the "Sexual and Gender Identity Disorders" section (see p. 499).

Panic Attack

Features

Because Panic Attacks occur in the context of several different Anxiety Disorders, the text and criteria set for a Panic Attack are provided separately in this section. The essential feature of a Panic Attack is a discrete period of intense fear or discomfort that is accompanied by at least 4 of 13 somatic or cognitive symptoms. The attack has a sudden onset and builds to a peak rapidly (usually in 10 minutes or less) and is often accompanied by a sense of imminent danger or impending doom and an urge to escape. The 13 somatic or cognitive symptoms are palpitations, sweating, trembling or shaking, sensations of shortness of breath or smothering, feeling of choking, chest pain or discomfort, nausea or abdominal distress, dizziness or lightheadedness, derealization or depersonalization, fear of losing control or "going crazy," fear of dying, paresthesias, and chills or hot flushes. Attacks that meet all other criteria but that have fewer than 4 somatic or cognitive symptoms are referred to as limited-symptom attacks.

Individuals seeking care for unexpected Panic Attacks will usually describe the fear as intense and report that they thought they were about to die, lose control, have a heart attack or stroke, or "go crazy." They also usually report an urgent desire to flee from wherever the attack is occurring. With recurrent attacks, some of the intense fearfulness may wane. Shortness of breath is a common symptom in Panic Attacks associated with Panic Disorder With and Without Agoraphobia. Blushing is common in situationally bound Panic Attacks related to social or performance anxiety. The anxiety that is characteristic of a Panic Attack can be differentiated from generalized anxiety by its intermittent, almost paroxysmal nature and its typically greater severity.

Panic Attacks can occur in a variety of Anxiety Disorders (e.g., Panic Disorder, Social Phobia, Specific Phobia, Posttraumatic Stress Disorder, Acute Stress Disorder). In determining the differential diagnostic significance of a Panic Attack, it is important to consider the context in which the Panic Attack occurs. There are three characteristic types of Panic Attacks with different relationships between the onset of the attack and the presence or absence of situational triggers: **unexpected (uncued) Panic Attacks,** in which the onset of the Panic Attack is not associated with a situational trigger (i.e., occurring spontaneously "out of the blue"); **situationally bound (cued) Panic Attacks,** in which the Panic Attack almost invariably occurs immediately on exposure to, or in anticipation of, the situational cue or trigger (e.g., seeing a snake or dog always triggers an immediate Panic Attack); and **situationally predisposed Panic Attacks,** which are more likely to occur on exposure to the situational cue or trigger, but are not invariably associated with the cue and do not necessarily occur immediately after the exposure (e.g., attacks are more likely to occur while driving, but there are times when the individual drives and does not have a Panic Attack or times when the Panic Attack occurs after driving for a half hour).

The occurrence of unexpected Panic Attacks is required for a diagnosis of Panic Disorder (with or without Agoraphobia). Situationally bound Panic Attacks are most characteristic of Social and Specific Phobias. Situationally predisposed Panic Attacks are especially frequent in Panic Disorder but may at times occur in Specific Phobia or Social Phobia. The differential diagnosis of Panic Attacks is complicated by the fact that an exclusive relationship does not always exist between the diagnosis and the type of Panic Attack. For instance, although Panic Disorder definitionally requires that at least some of the Panic Attacks be unexpected, individuals with Panic Disorder frequently report having situationally bound attacks, particularly later in the course of the disorder. The diagnostic issues for boundary cases are discussed in the "Differential Diagnosis" sections of the texts for the disorders in which Panic Attacks may appear.

■ Criteria for Panic Attack

Note: A Panic Attack is not a codable disorder. Code the specific diagnosis in which the Panic Attack occurs (e.g., 300.21 Panic Disorder With Agoraphobia [p. 402]).

A discrete period of intense fear or discomfort, in which four (or more) of the following symptoms developed abruptly and reached a peak within 10 minutes:

   (1) palpitations, pounding heart, or accelerated heart rate
   (2) sweating
   (3) trembling or shaking
   (4) sensations of shortness of breath or smothering
   (5) feeling of choking
   (6) chest pain or discomfort
   (7) nausea or abdominal distress
   (8) feeling dizzy, unsteady, lightheaded, or faint
   (9) derealization (feelings of unreality) or depersonalization (being detached from oneself)
  (10) fear of losing control or going crazy
  (11) fear of dying
  (12) paresthesias (numbness or tingling sensations)
  (13) chills or hot flushes

Agoraphobia

Features

Because Agoraphobia occurs in the context of Panic Disorder With Agoraphobia and Agoraphobia Without History of Panic Disorder, the text and criteria set for Agoraphobia are provided separately in this section. The essential feature of Agoraphobia is anxiety about being in places or situations from which escape might be difficult (or embarrassing) or in which help may not be available in the event of having a Panic Attack (see p. 394) or panic-like symptoms (e.g., fear of having a sudden attack of dizziness or a sudden attack of diarrhea) (Criterion A). The anxiety typically leads to a pervasive avoidance of a variety of situations that may include being alone outside the home or being home alone; being in a crowd of people; traveling in a automobile, bus, or airplane; or being on a bridge or in an elevator. Some individuals are able to expose themselves to the feared situations but endure these experiences with considerable dread. Often an individual is better able to confront a feared situation when accompanied by a companion (Criterion B). Individuals' avoidance of situations may impair their ability to travel to work or to carry out homemaking responsibilities (e.g., grocery shopping, taking children to the doctor). The anxiety or phobic avoidance is not better accounted for by another mental disorder (Criterion C). The differential diagnosis to distinguish Agoraphobia from Social and Specific Phobia and from severe Separation Anxiety Disorder can be difficult because all of these conditions are characterized by avoidance of specific situations. The diagnostic issues for boundary cases are discussed in the "Differential Diagnosis" sections of the texts for the disorders in which avoidant behavior is an essential or associated feature.

■ Criteria for Agoraphobia

Note: Agoraphobia is not a codable disorder. Code the specific disorder in which the Agoraphobia occurs (e.g., 300.21 Panic Disorder With Agoraphobia [p. 402] or 300.22 Agoraphobia Without History of Panic Disorder [p. 404]).

A. Anxiety about being in places or situations from which escape might be difficult (or embarrassing) or in which help may not be available in the event of having an unexpected or situationally predisposed Panic Attack or panic-like symptoms. Agoraphobic fears typically involve characteristic clusters of situations that include being outside the home alone; being in a crowd or standing in a line; being on a bridge; and traveling in a bus, train, or automobile.

Note: Consider the diagnosis of Specific Phobia if the avoidance is limited to one or only a few specific situations, or Social Phobia if the avoidance is limited to social situations.

B. The situations are avoided (e.g., travel is restricted) or else are endured with marked distress or with anxiety about having a Panic Attack or panic-like symptoms, or require the presence of a companion.

(continued)

□ **Criteria for Agoraphobia** (*continued*)

    C. The anxiety or phobic avoidance is not better accounted for by another mental disorder, such as Social Phobia (e.g., avoidance limited to social situations because of fear of embarrassment), Specific Phobia (e.g., avoidance limited to a single situation like elevators), Obsessive-Compulsive Disorder (e.g., avoidance of dirt in someone with an obsession about contamination), Posttraumatic Stress Disorder (e.g., avoidance of stimuli associated with a severe stressor), or Separation Anxiety Disorder (e.g., avoidance of leaving home or relatives).

Panic Disorder

Diagnostic Features

The essential feature of Panic Disorder is the presence of recurrent, unexpected Panic Attacks (see p. 394) followed by at least 1 month of persistent concern about having another Panic Attack, worry about the possible implications or consequences of the Panic Attacks, or a significant behavioral change related to the attacks (Criterion A). The Panic Attacks are not due to the direct physiological effects of a substance (e.g., Caffeine Intoxication) or a general medical condition (e.g., hyperthyroidism) (Criterion C). Finally, the Panic Attacks are not better accounted for by another mental disorder (e.g., Specific or Social Phobia, Obsessive-Compulsive Disorder, Posttraumatic Stress Disorder, or Separation Anxiety Disorder) (Criterion D). Depending on whether criteria are also met for Agoraphobia (see p. 396), 300.21 Panic Disorder With Agoraphobia or 300.01 Panic Disorder Without Agoraphobia is diagnosed (Criterion B).

An unexpected (spontaneous, uncued) Panic Attack is defined as one that is not associated with a situational trigger (i.e., it occurs "out of the blue"). At least two unexpected Panic Attacks are required for the diagnosis, but most individuals have considerably more. Individuals with Panic Disorder frequently also have situationally predisposed Panic Attacks (i.e., those more likely to occur on, but not invariably associated with, exposure to a situational trigger). Situationally bound attacks (i.e., those that occur almost invariably and immediately on exposure to a situational trigger) can occur but are less common.

The frequency and severity of the Panic Attacks vary widely. For example, some individuals have moderately frequent attacks (e.g., once a week) that occur regularly for months at a time. Others report short bursts of more frequent attacks (e.g., daily for a week) separated by weeks or months without any attacks or with less frequent attacks (e.g., two each month) over many years. Limited-symptom attacks (i.e., attacks that are identical to "full" Panic Attacks except that the sudden fear or anxiety is accompanied by fewer than 4 of the 13 additional symptoms) are very common in individuals with Panic Disorder. Although the distinction between full Panic Attacks and limited-symptom attacks is somewhat arbitrary, full Panic Attacks are associated with greater morbidity. Most individuals who have limited-symptom attacks have had full Panic Attacks at some time during the course of the disorder.

Individuals with Panic Disorder display characteristic concerns or attributions about the implications or consequences of the Panic Attacks. Some fear that the attacks indicate the presence of an undiagnosed, life-threatening illness (e.g., cardiac disease, seizure disorder). Despite repeated medical testing and reassurance, they may remain frightened and unconvinced that they do not have a life-threatening illness. Others fear that the Panic Attacks are an indication that they are "going crazy" or losing control or are emotionally weak. Some individuals with recurrent Panic Attacks significantly change their behavior (e.g., quit a job) in response to the attacks, but deny either fear of having another attack or concerns about the consequences of their Panic Attacks. Concerns about the next attack, or its implications, are often associated with development of avoidant behavior that may meet criteria for Agoraphobia (see p. 396), in which case Panic Disorder With Agoraphobia is diagnosed.

Associated Features and Disorders

Associated descriptive features and mental disorders.   In addition to worry about Panic Attacks and their implications, many individuals with Panic Disorder also report constant or intermittent feelings of anxiety that are not focused on any specific situation or event. Others become excessively apprehensive about the outcome of routine activities and experiences, particularly those related to health or separation from loved ones. For example, individuals with Panic Disorder often anticipate a catastrophic outcome from a mild physical symptom or medication side effect (e.g., thinking that a headache indicates a brain tumor or a hypertensive crisis). Such individuals are also much less tolerant of medication side effects and generally need continued reassurance in order to take medication. In individuals whose Panic Disorder has not been treated or was misdiagnosed, the belief that they have an undetected life-threatening illness may lead to both chronic debilitating anxiety and excessive visits to health care facilities. This pattern can be both emotionally and financially disruptive.

In some cases, loss or disruption of important interpersonal relationships (e.g., leaving home to live on one's own, divorce) is associated with the onset or exacerbation of Panic Disorder. Demoralization is a common consequence, with many individuals becoming discouraged, ashamed, and unhappy about the difficulties of carrying out their normal routines. They often attribute this problem to a lack of "strength" or "character." This demoralization can become generalized to areas beyond specific panic-related problems. These individuals may frequently be absent from work or school for doctor and emergency-room visits, which can lead to unemployment or dropping out of school.

Major Depressive Disorder occurs frequently (50%–65%) in individuals with Panic Disorder. In approximately one-third of individuals with both disorders, the depression precedes the onset of Panic Disorder. In the remaining two-thirds, depression occurs coincident with or following the onset of Panic Disorder. A subset of individuals, some of whom may develop a Substance-Related Disorder as a consequence, treat their anxiety with alcohol or medications. Comorbidity with other Anxiety Disorders is also common, especially in clinical settings and in individuals with more severe Agoraphobia (Social Phobia has been reported in 15%–30% of individuals with Panic Disorder; Obsessive-Compulsive Disorder in 8%–10%; Specific Phobia in 10%–20%; and Generalized Anxiety Disorder in 25%). Separation Anxiety Disorder in childhood has been associated with this disorder.

Associated laboratory findings.   No laboratory findings have been identified that are diagnostic of Panic Disorder. However, a variety of laboratory findings have been noted to be abnormal in groups of individuals with Panic Disorder relative to control subjects. Some individuals with Panic Disorder show signs of compensated respiratory alkalosis (i.e., decreased carbon dioxide and decreased bicarbonate levels with an almost normal pH). Panic Attacks in response to sodium lactate infusion or carbon dioxide inhalation are more common in Panic Disorder than in other Anxiety Disorders.

Associated physical examination findings and general medical conditions. Transient tachycardia and moderate elevation of systolic blood pressure may occur during some Panic Attacks. Although studies have suggested that both mitral valve prolapse and thyroid disease are more common among individuals with Panic Disorder than in the general population, others have found no differences in prevalence.

Specific Culture and Gender Features

In some cultures, Panic Attacks may involve intense fear of witchcraft or magic. Panic Disorder as described here has been found in epidemiological studies throughout the world. Moreover, a number of conditions included in the "Glossary of Culture-Bound Syndromes" (see Appendix I) may be related to Panic Disorder. Some cultural or ethnic groups restrict the participation of women in public life, and this must be distinguished from Agoraphobia. Panic Disorder Without Agoraphobia is diagnosed twice as often and Panic Disorder With Agoraphobia three times as often in women as in men.

Prevalence

Epidemiological studies throughout the world consistently indicate the lifetime prevalence of Panic Disorder (With or Without Agoraphobia) to be between 1.5% and 3.5%. One-year prevalence rates are between 1% and 2%. Approximately one-third to one-half of individuals diagnosed with Panic Disorder in community samples also have Agoraphobia, although a much higher rate of Agoraphobia is encountered in clinical samples.

Course

Age at onset for Panic Disorder varies considerably, but is most typically between late adolescence and the mid-30s. There may be a bimodal distribution, with one peak in late adolescence and a second smaller peak in the mid-30s. A small number of cases begin in childhood, and onset after age 45 years is unusual but can occur. Retrospective descriptions by individuals seen in clinical settings suggest that the usual course is chronic but waxing and waning. Some individuals may have episodic outbreaks with years of remission in between, and others may have continuous severe symptomatology. Although Agoraphobia may develop at any point, its onset is usually within the first year of occurrence of recurrent Panic Attacks. The course of Agoraphobia and its relationship to the course of Panic Attacks are variable. In some cases, a decrease or remission of Panic Attacks may be followed closely by a corresponding decrease in agoraphobic avoidance and anxiety. In others, Agoraphobia may become chronic regardless of the presence or absence of Panic Attacks. Some individuals report that they can reduce the frequency of Panic Attacks by avoiding certain situations. Naturalistic follow-up studies of individuals treated in tertiary care settings (which may select for a poor-prognosis group) suggest that, at 6–10 years posttreatment, about 30% of individuals are well, 40%–50% are improved but symptomatic, and the remaining 20%–30% have symptoms that are the same or slightly worse.

Familial Pattern

First-degree biological relatives of individuals with Panic Disorder have a four to seven times greater chance of developing Panic Disorder. However, in clinical settings, as many as one-half to three-quarters of individuals with Panic Disorder do not have an affected first-degree biological relative. Twin studies indicate a genetic contribution to the development of Panic Disorder.

Differential Diagnosis

Panic Disorder is not diagnosed if the Panic Attacks are judged to be a direct physiological consequence of a general medical condition, in which case an **Anxiety Disorder Due to a General Medical Condition** is diagnosed (see p. 436). Examples of general medical conditions that can cause Panic Attacks include hyperthyroidism, hyperparathyroidism, pheochromocytoma, vestibular dysfunctions, seizure disorders, and cardiac conditions (e.g., arrhythmias, supraventricular tachycardia). Appropriate laboratory tests (e.g., serum calcium levels for hyperparathyroidism) or physical examinations (e.g., for cardiac conditions) may be helpful in determining the etiological role of a general medical condition. Panic Disorder is not diagnosed if the Panic Attacks are judged to be a direct physiological consequence of a substance (i.e., a drug of abuse, a medication), in which case a **Substance-Induced Anxiety Disorder** is diagnosed (see p. 439). Intoxication with central nervous system stimulants (e.g., cocaine, amphetamines, caffeine) or cannabis and withdrawal from central nervous system depressants (e.g., alcohol, barbiturates) can precipitate a Panic Attack. However, if Panic Attacks continue to occur outside of the context of substance use (e.g., long after the effects of intoxication or withdrawal have ended), a diagnosis of Panic Disorder should be considered. Features such as onset after age 45 years or the presence of atypical symptoms during a Panic Attack (e.g., vertigo, loss of consciousness, loss of bladder or bowel control, headaches, slurred speech, or amnesia) suggest the possibility that a general medical condition or a substance may be causing the Panic Attack symptoms.

Panic Disorder must be distinguished from other mental disorders (e.g., **other Anxiety Disorders** and **Psychotic Disorders**) that have Panic Attacks as an associated feature. By definition, Panic Disorder is characterized by recurrent, unexpected (spontaneous, uncued, "out of the blue") Panic Attacks. As discussed earlier (see p. 394), there are three types of Panic Attacks—unexpected, situationally bound, and situationally predisposed. The presence of recurrent unexpected Panic Attacks either initially or later in the course is required for the diagnosis of Panic Disorder. In contrast, Panic Attacks that occur in the context of other Anxiety Disorders are situationally bound or situationally predisposed (e.g., in **Social Phobia** cued by social situations; in **Specific Phobia** cued by an object or situation; in **Obsessive-Compulsive Disorder** cued by exposure to the object of an obsession [e.g., exposure to dirt in someone with an obsession about contamination]; in **Posttraumatic Stress Disorder** cued by stimuli recalling the stressor).

The focus of the anxiety also helps to differentiate Panic Disorder With Agoraphobia from other disorders characterized by avoidant behaviors. Agoraphobic avoidance is associated with the fear of having a Panic Attack, whereas avoidance in other disorders is associated with specific situations (e.g., fears of scrutiny, humiliation, and embarrassment in Social Phobia; fears of heights, elevators, or crossing bridges in Specific Phobia; separation concerns in **Separation Anxiety Disorder;** persecution fears in **Delusional Disorder**).

Differentiation of Specific Phobia, Situational Type, from Panic Disorder With Agoraphobia may be particularly difficult because both disorders may include Panic Attacks and avoidance of similar types of situations (e.g., driving, flying, public transportation, enclosed places). Prototypically, Panic Disorder With Agoraphobia is characterized by the initial onset of unexpected Panic Attacks and the subsequent avoidance of multiple situations thought to be likely triggers of the Panic Attacks. Prototypically, Specific Phobia, Situational Type, is characterized by situational avoidance in the absence of recurrent unexpected Panic Attacks. Some presentations fall between these prototypes and require clinical judgment in the selection of the most appropriate diagnosis. Four factors can be helpful in making this judgment: the focus of fear, the type and number of Panic Attacks, the number of situations avoided, and the level of intercurrent anxiety. For example, an individual who had not previously feared or avoided elevators has a Panic Attack in an elevator and begins to dread going to work because of the need to take the elevator to his office on the 24th floor. If this individual subsequently has Panic Attacks only in elevators (even if the focus of fear is on the Panic Attack), then a diagnosis of Specific Phobia may be appropriate. If, however, the individual experiences unexpected Panic Attacks in other situations and begins to avoid or endure with dread other situations because of fear of a Panic Attack, then a diagnosis of Panic Disorder With Agoraphobia would be warranted. Furthermore, the presence of pervasive apprehension about having a Panic Attack even when not anticipating exposure to a phobic situation also supports a diagnosis of Panic Disorder With Agoraphobia. If the individual has additional unexpected Panic Attacks in other situations but no additional avoidance or endurance with dread develops, then the appropriate diagnosis would be Panic Disorder Without Agoraphobia. If the focus of avoidance is not related to having a Panic Attack but concerns some other catastrophe (e.g., injury due to the elevator cable breaking), then an additional diagnosis of Specific Phobia may be considered.

Similarly, distinguishing between Social Phobia and Panic Disorder With Agoraphobia can be difficult, especially when there is avoidance only of social situations. The focus of fear and the type of Panic Attacks can be helpful in making this distinction. For example, an individual who had not previously had a fear of public speaking has a Panic Attack while giving a talk and begins to dread giving presentations. If this individual subsequently has Panic Attacks only in social performance situations (even if the focus of fear is on the possibility of having another Panic Attack), then a diagnosis of Social Phobia may be appropriate. If, however, the individual continues to experience unexpected Panic Attacks in other situations, then a diagnosis of Panic Disorder With Agoraphobia would be warranted. Individuals with Social Phobia fear scrutiny and rarely have a Panic Attack when alone, whereas individuals with Panic Disorder With Agoraphobia may be more anxious in situations where they must be without a trusted companion. In addition, nocturnal Panic Attacks that awaken an individual from sleep are characteristic of Panic Disorder.

When criteria are met for both Panic Disorder and another Anxiety or Mood Disorder, both disorders should be diagnosed. However, if unexpected Panic Attacks occur in the context of another disorder (e.g., Major Depressive Disorder or Generalized Anxiety Disorder) but are not accompanied by a month or more of fear of having additional attacks, associated concerns, or behavior change, the additional diagnosis of Panic Disorder is not made. Because individuals with Panic Disorder may self-medicate their symptoms, comorbid Substance-Related Disorders (most notably related to cannabis, alcohol, and cocaine) are not uncommon.

■ **Diagnostic criteria for 300.01 Panic Disorder Without Agoraphobia**

A. Both (1) and (2):

(1) recurrent unexpected Panic Attacks (see p. 395)
(2) at least one of the attacks has been followed by 1 month (or more) of one (or more) of the following:

(a) persistent concern about having additional attacks
(b) worry about the implications of the attack or its consequences (e.g., losing control, having a heart attack, "going crazy")
(c) a significant change in behavior related to the attacks

B. Absence of Agoraphobia (see p. 396).

C. The Panic Attacks are not due to the direct physiological effects of a substance (e.g., a drug of abuse, a medication) or a general medical condition (e.g., hyperthyroidism).

D. The Panic Attacks are not better accounted for by another mental disorder, such as Social Phobia (e.g., occurring on exposure to feared social situations), Specific Phobia (e.g., on exposure to a specific phobic situation), Obsessive-Compulsive Disorder (e.g., on exposure to dirt in someone with an obsession about contamination), Posttraumatic Stress Disorder (e.g., in response to stimuli associated with a severe stressor), or Separation Anxiety Disorder (e.g., in response to being away from home or close relatives).

■ **Diagnostic criteria for 300.21 Panic Disorder With Agoraphobia**

A. Both (1) and (2):

(1) recurrent unexpected Panic Attacks (see p. 395)
(2) at least one of the attacks has been followed by 1 month (or more) of one (or more) of the following:

(a) persistent concern about having additional attacks
(b) worry about the implications of the attack or its consequences (e.g., losing control, having a heart attack, "going crazy")
(c) a significant change in behavior related to the attacks

B. The presence of Agoraphobia (see p. 396).

C. The Panic Attacks are not due to the direct physiological effects of a substance (e.g., a drug of abuse, a medication) or a general medical condition (e.g., hyperthyroidism).

(continued)

☐ **Diagnostic criteria for 300.21 Panic Disorder With Agoraphobia** (*continued*)

   D. The Panic Attacks are not better accounted for by another mental disorder, such as Social Phobia (e.g., occurring on exposure to feared social situations), Specific Phobia (e.g., on exposure to a specific phobic situation), Obsessive-Compulsive Disorder (e.g., on exposure to dirt in someone with an obsession about contamination), Posttraumatic Stress Disorder (e.g., in response to stimuli associated with a severe stressor), or Separation Anxiety Disorder (e.g., in response to being away from home or close relatives).

300.22 Agoraphobia Without History of Panic Disorder

Diagnostic Features

The essential features of Agoraphobia Without History of Panic Disorder are similar to those of Panic Disorder With Agoraphobia except that the focus of fear is on the occurrence of incapacitating or extremely embarrassing panic-like symptoms or limited-symptom attacks rather than full Panic Attacks. Individuals with this disorder have Agoraphobia (see p. 396) (Criterion A). The "panic-like symptoms" include any of the 13 symptoms listed for Panic Attack (see p. 394) or other symptoms that may be incapacitating or embarrassing (e.g., loss of bladder control). For example, an individual may be afraid to leave home because of a fear of becoming dizzy, fainting, and then being left helpless on the ground. To qualify for this diagnosis, the full criteria for Panic Disorder must never have been met (Criterion B) and the symptoms must not be due to the direct physiological effects of a substance (e.g., a drug of abuse, a medication) or a general medical condition (Criterion C). If an associated general medical condition is present (e.g., a cardiac condition), the fear of being incapacitated or embarrassed by the development of symptoms (e.g., fainting) is clearly in excess of that usually associated with the condition (Criterion D).

Specific Culture and Gender Features

Some cultural or ethnic groups restrict the participation of women in public life, and this must be distinguished from Agoraphobia. This disorder is diagnosed far more often in females than in males.

Prevalence

In clinical settings, almost all individuals (over 95%) who present with Agoraphobia also have a current diagnosis (or history) of Panic Disorder. In contrast, the prevalence of Agoraphobia Without History of Panic Disorder in epidemiological samples has been reported to be higher than that for Panic Disorder With Agoraphobia. However, problems with assessment appear to have inflated the rates reported in epidemiological studies. Recently, individuals who were given a diagnosis of Agoraphobia Without History of Panic Disorder in an epidemiological study were reevaluated by clinicians using standard interview schedules. The majority were found to have Specific Phobias, but not Agoraphobia.

Course

Relatively little is known about the course of Agoraphobia Without History of Panic Disorder. Anecdotal evidence suggests that some cases may persist for years and be associated with considerable impairment.

Differential Diagnosis

Agoraphobia Without History of Panic Disorder is distinguished from **Panic Disorder With Agoraphobia** by the absence of a history of recurrent unexpected Panic Attacks. The avoidance in Agoraphobia Without History of Panic Disorder results from fear of incapacitation or humiliation due to unpredictable, sudden, panic-like symptoms rather than from fear of a full Panic Attack as in Panic Disorder With Agoraphobia. The diagnosis of Panic Disorder With Agoraphobia remains appropriate in cases in which Panic Attacks go into remission but Agoraphobia continues to be experienced.

Other reasons for avoidance must also be distinguished from Agoraphobia Without History of Panic Disorder. In **Social Phobia,** individuals avoid social or performance situations in which they fear that they might act in a way that is humiliating or embarrassing. In **Specific Phobia,** the individual avoids a specific feared object or situation. In **Major Depressive Disorder,** the individual may avoid leaving home due to apathy, loss of energy, and anhedonia. Persecutory fears (as in **Delusional Disorder**) and fears of contamination (as in **Obsessive-Compulsive Disorder**) can also lead to widespread avoidance. In **Separation Anxiety Disorder,** children avoid situations that take them away from home or close relatives.

Individuals with certain general medical conditions may avoid situations due to **realistic concerns** about being incapacitated (e.g., fainting in an individual with transient ischemic attacks) or being embarrassed (e.g., diarrhea in an individual with Crohn's disease). The diagnosis of Agoraphobia Without History of Panic Disorder should be given only if the fear or avoidance is clearly in excess of that usually associated with the general medical condition.

■ **Diagnostic criteria for 300.22 Agoraphobia Without History of Panic Disorder**

A. The presence of Agoraphobia (see p. 396) related to fear of developing panic-like symptoms (e.g., dizziness or diarrhea).

B. Criteria have never been met for Panic Disorder (see p. 402).

(continued)

☐ **Diagnostic criteria for 300.22 Agoraphobia Without History of Panic Disorder** (*continued*)

C. The disturbance is not due to the direct physiological effects of a substance (e.g., a drug of abuse, a medication) or a general medical condition.

D. If an associated general medical condition is present, the fear described in Criterion A is clearly in excess of that usually associated with the condition.

300.29 Specific Phobia
(*formerly* Simple Phobia)

Diagnostic Features

The essential feature of Specific Phobia is marked and persistent fear of clearly discernible, circumscribed objects or situations (Criterion A). Exposure to the phobic stimulus almost invariably provokes an immediate anxiety response (Criterion B). This response may take the form of a situationally bound or situationally predisposed Panic Attack (see p. 394). Although adolescents and adults with this disorder recognize that their fear is excessive or unreasonable (Criterion C), this may not be the case with children. Most often, the phobic stimulus is avoided, although it is sometimes endured with dread (Criterion D). The diagnosis is appropriate only if the avoidance, fear, or anxious anticipation of encountering the phobic stimulus interferes significantly with the person's daily routine, occupational functioning, or social life, or if the person is markedly distressed about having the phobia (Criterion E). In individuals under age 18 years, symptoms must have persisted for at least 6 months before Specific Phobia is diagnosed (Criterion F). The anxiety, Panic Attacks, or phobic avoidance are not better accounted for by another mental disorder (e.g., Obsessive-Compulsive Disorder, Posttraumatic Stress Disorder, Separation Anxiety Disorder, Social Phobia, Panic Disorder With Agoraphobia, or Agoraphobia Without History of Panic Disorder) (Criterion G).

The individual experiences a marked, persistent, and excessive or unreasonable fear when in the presence of, or when anticipating an encounter with, a specific object or situation. The focus of the fear may be anticipated harm from some aspect of the object or situation (e.g., an individual may fear air travel because of a concern about crashing, may fear dogs because of concerns about being bitten, or may fear driving because of concerns about being hit by other vehicles on the road). Specific Phobias may also involve concerns about losing control, panicking, and fainting that might occur on exposure to the feared object. For example, individuals afraid of blood and injury may also worry about the possibility of fainting; people afraid of heights may also worry about dizziness; and people afraid of closed-in situations may also worry about losing control and screaming.

Anxiety is almost invariably felt immediately on confronting the phobic stimulus (e.g., a person with a Specific Phobia of cats will almost invariably have an immediate anxiety response when forced to confront a cat). The level of anxiety or fear usually varies as a function of both the degree of proximity to the phobic stimulus (e.g., fear intensifies as the cat approaches and decreases as the cat withdraws) and the degree to which escape from the phobic stimulus is limited (e.g., fear intensifies as the elevator approaches the midway point between floors and decreases as the doors open at the next floor). However, the intensity of the fear may not always relate predictably to the phobic stimulus (e.g., a person afraid of heights may experience variable amounts of fear when crossing the same bridge on different occasions). Sometimes full-blown Panic Attacks are experienced in response to the phobic stimulus, especially when the person must remain in the situation or believes that escape will be impossible. Because marked anticipatory anxiety occurs if the person is confronted with the necessity of entering into the phobic situation, such situations are usually avoided. Less commonly, the person forces himself or herself to endure the phobic situation, but it is experienced with intense anxiety.

Adults with this disorder recognize that the phobia is excessive or unreasonable. The diagnosis would be Delusional Disorder instead of Specific Phobia for an individual who avoids an elevator because of a conviction that it has been sabotaged and who does not recognize that this fear is excessive and unreasonable. Moreover, the diagnosis should not be given if the fear is reasonable given the context of the stimuli (e.g., fear of being shot in a hunting area or a dangerous neighborhood). Insight into the excessive or unreasonable nature of the fear tends to increase with age and is not required to make the diagnosis in children.

Fears of circumscribed objects or situations are very common, especially in children, but in many cases the degree of impairment is insufficient to warrant a diagnosis. If the phobia does not significantly interfere with the individual's functioning or cause marked distress, the diagnosis is not made. For example, a person who is afraid of snakes to the point of expressing intense fear in the presence of snakes would not receive a diagnosis of Specific Phobia if he or she lives in an area devoid of snakes, is not restricted in activities by the fear of snakes, and is not distressed about having a fear of snakes.

Subtypes

The following subtypes may be specified to indicate the focus of fear or avoidance in Specific Phobia (e.g., Specific Phobia, Animal Type).

> **Animal Type.** This subtype should be specified if the fear is cued by animals or insects. This subtype generally has a childhood onset.
> **Natural Environment Type.** This subtype should be specified if the fear is cued by objects in the natural environment, such as storms, heights, or water. This subtype generally has a childhood onset.
> **Blood-Injection-Injury Type.** This subtype should be specified if the fear is cued by seeing blood or an injury or by receiving an injection or other invasive medical procedure. This subtype is highly familial and is often characterized by a strong vasovagal response.
> **Situational Type.** This subtype should be specified if the fear is cued by a specific situation such as public transportation, tunnels, bridges, elevators, flying, driving, or enclosed places. This subtype has a bimodal age-at-onset distribution, with one peak in childhood and another peak in the mid-20s. This subtype

appears to be similar to Panic Disorder With Agoraphobia in its characteristic sex ratios, familial aggregation pattern, and age at onset.

Other Type. This subtype should be specified if the fear is cued by other stimuli. These stimuli might include the fear or avoidance of situations that might lead to choking, vomiting, or contracting an illness; "space" phobia (i.e., the individual is afraid of falling down if away from walls or other means of physical support); and children's fears of loud sounds or costumed characters.

The frequency of the subtypes in adult clinical settings, from most to least frequent, is Situational; Natural Environment; Blood-Injection-Injury; and Animal. In many cases, more than one subtype of Specific Phobia is present. Having one phobia of a specific subtype tends to increase the likelihood of having another phobia from within the same subtype (e.g., fear of cats *and* snakes). When more than one subtype applies, they should all be noted (e.g., Specific Phobia, Animal and Natural Environment Types).

Associated Features and Disorders

Associated descriptive features and mental disorders. Specific Phobia may result in a restricted lifestyle or interference with certain occupations, depending on the type of phobia. For example, job promotion may be threatened by avoidance of air travel, and social activities may be restricted by fears of crowded or closed-in places. Specific Phobias frequently co-occur with other Anxiety Disorders but are rarely the focus of clinical attention in these situations. The Specific Phobia is usually associated with less distress or less interference with functioning than the comorbid main diagnosis. There is a particularly frequent co-occurrence between Specific Phobias and Panic Disorder With Agoraphobia.

Associated physical examination findings and general medical conditions. A vasovagal fainting response is characteristic of Blood-Injection-Injury Type Specific Phobias; approximately 75% of such individuals report a history of fainting in these situations. The physiological response is characterized by an initial brief acceleration of heart rate followed by a deceleration of heart rate and a drop in blood pressure, which contrasts with the usual acceleration of heart rate in other Specific Phobias. Certain general medical conditions may be exacerbated as a consequence of phobic avoidance. For example, Specific Phobias, Blood-Injection-Injury Type, may have detrimental effects on dental or physical health, because the individual may avoid obtaining necessary medical care. Similarly, fears of choking may have a detrimental effect on health when food is limited to substances that are easy to swallow or when oral medication is avoided.

Specific Culture, Age, and Gender Features

The content of phobias as well as their prevalence varies with culture and ethnicity. For example, fears of magic or spirits are present in many cultures and should be considered a Specific Phobia only if the fear is excessive in the context of that culture and causes significant impairment or distress.

In children, the anxiety may be expressed by crying, tantrums, freezing, or clinging. Children often do not recognize that the fears are excessive or unreasonable and rarely report distress about having the phobias. Fears of animals and other objects in the natural environment are particularly common and are usually transitory in childhood. A diagnosis of Specific Phobia is not warranted unless the fears lead to clinically significant impairment (e.g., unwillingness to go to school for fear of encountering a dog on the street).

The sex ratio varies across different types of Specific Phobias. Approximately 75%–90% of individuals with the Animal and Natural Environment Type are female (except for fear of heights, where the percentage of females is 55%–70%). Similarly, approximately 75%–90% of individuals with the Situational Type are female. Approximately 55%–70% of individuals with the Blood-Injection-Injury Type are female.

Prevalence

Although phobias are common in the general population, they rarely result in sufficient impairment or distress to warrant a diagnosis of Specific Phobia. The reported prevalence may vary depending on the threshold used to determine impairment or distress and the number of types of phobias surveyed. In community samples, a 1-year prevalence rate of about 9% has been reported, with lifetime rates ranging from 10% to 11.3%.

Course

The mean age at onset varies according to the type of Specific Phobia. Age at onset for Specific Phobia, Situational Type, tends to be bimodally distributed, with a peak in childhood and a second peak in the mid-20s. Specific Phobias, Natural Environment Type (e.g., height phobia), tend to begin primarily in childhood, although many new cases of height phobia develop in early adulthood. The ages at onset for Specific Phobias, Animal Type, and for Specific Phobias, Blood-Injection-Injury Type, are also usually in childhood.

Predisposing factors to the onset of Specific Phobias include traumatic events (such as being attacked by an animal or trapped in a closet), unexpected Panic Attacks in the to-be-feared situation, observation of others undergoing trauma or demonstrating fearfulness (such as observing others fall from heights or become afraid in the presence of certain animals), and informational transmission (e.g., repeated parental warnings about the dangers of certain animals or media coverage of airplane crashes). Feared objects or situations tend to involve things that may actually represent a threat or have represented a threat at some point in the course of human evolution. Phobias that result from traumatic events or unexpected Panic Attacks tend to be particularly acute in their development. Phobias of traumatic origin do not have a characteristic age at onset (e.g., fear of choking, which usually follows a choking or near-choking incident, may develop at almost any age). Phobias that persist into adulthood remit only infrequently (around 20% of cases).

Familial Pattern

Preliminary evidence suggests that there may be an aggregation within families by type of phobia (e.g., first-degree biological relatives of persons with Specific Phobias, Animal Type, are likely to have animal phobias, although not necessarily of the same animal, and first-degree biological relatives of persons with Specific Phobias, Situational Type, are likely to have phobias of situations). Fears of blood and injury have particularly strong familial patterns.

Differential Diagnosis

Specific Phobias differ from most other Anxiety Disorders in levels of intercurrent anxiety. Typically, individuals with Specific Phobia, unlike those with **Panic Disorder With Agoraphobia,** do not present with pervasive anxiety, because their fear is limited to specific, circumscribed objects or situations. However, generalized anxious anticipation may emerge under conditions in which encounters with the phobic stimulus become more likely (e.g., when a person who is fearful of snakes moves to a desert area) or when life events force immediate confrontation with the phobic stimulus (e.g., when a person who is fearful of flying is forced by circumstances to fly).

Differentiation of Specific Phobia, Situational Type, from Panic Disorder With Agoraphobia may be particularly difficult because both disorders may include Panic Attacks and avoidance of similar types of situations (e.g., driving, flying, public transportation, and enclosed places). Prototypically, Panic Disorder With Agoraphobia is characterized by the initial onset of unexpected Panic Attacks and the subsequent avoidance of multiple situations thought to be likely triggers of the Panic Attacks. Prototypically, Specific Phobia, Situational Type, is characterized by situational avoidance in the absence of recurrent unexpected Panic Attacks. Some presentations fall between these prototypes and require clinical judgment in the selection of the most appropriate diagnosis. Four factors can be helpful in making this judgment: the focus of fear, the type and number of Panic Attacks, the number of situations avoided, and the level of intercurrent anxiety. For example, an individual who had not previously feared or avoided elevators has a Panic Attack in an elevator and begins to dread going to work because of the need to take the elevator to his office on the 24th floor. If this individual subsequently has Panic Attacks only in elevators (even if the focus of fear is on the Panic Attack), then a diagnosis of Specific Phobia may be appropriate. If, however, the individual experiences unexpected Panic Attacks in other situations and begins to avoid or endure with dread other situations because of fear of a Panic Attack, then a diagnosis of Panic Disorder With Agoraphobia would be warranted. Furthermore, the presence of pervasive apprehension about having a Panic Attack even when not anticipating exposure to a phobic situation also supports a diagnosis of Panic Disorder With Agoraphobia. If the individual has additional unexpected Panic Attacks in other situations but no additional avoidance or endurance with dread develops, then the appropriate diagnosis would be Panic Disorder Without Agoraphobia.

Concurrent diagnoses of Specific Phobia and Panic Disorder With Agoraphobia are sometimes warranted. In these cases, consideration of the focus of the individual's concern about the phobic situation may be helpful. For example, avoidance of being alone because of concern about having unexpected Panic Attacks warrants a diagnosis of Panic Disorder With Agoraphobia (if other criteria are met), whereas the additional phobic avoidance of air travel, if due to worries about bad weather conditions and crashing, may warrant an additional diagnosis of Specific Phobia.

Specific Phobia and **Social Phobia** can be differentiated on the basis of the focus of the fears. For example, avoidance of eating in a restaurant may be based on concerns about negative evaluation from others (i.e., Social Phobia) or concerns about choking (i.e., Specific Phobia). In contrast to the avoidance in Specific Phobia, the avoidance in

Posttraumatic Stress Disorder follows a life-threatening stressor and is accompanied by additional features (e.g., reexperiencing the trauma and restricted affect). In **Obsessive-Compulsive Disorder,** the avoidance is associated with the content of the obsession (e.g., dirt, contamination). In individuals with **Separation Anxiety Disorder,** a diagnosis of Specific Phobia is not given if the avoidance behavior is exclusively limited to fears of separation from persons to whom the individual is attached. Moreover, children with Separation Anxiety Disorder often have associated exaggerated fears of people or events (e.g., of muggers, burglars, kidnappers, car accidents, airplane travel) that might threaten the integrity of the family. A separate diagnosis of Specific Phobia would rarely be warranted.

The differentiation between **Hypochondriasis** and a Specific Phobia, Other Type (i.e., avoidance of situations that may lead to contracting an illness), depends on the presence or absence of disease conviction. Individuals with Hypochondriasis are preoccupied with fears of having a disease, whereas individuals with a Specific Phobia fear contracting a disease (but do not believe it is already present). In individuals with **Anorexia Nervosa** and **Bulimia Nervosa,** a diagnosis of Specific Phobia is not given if the avoidance behavior is exclusively limited to avoidance of food and food-related cues. An individual with **Schizophrenia** or **another Psychotic Disorder** may avoid certain activities in response to delusions, but does not recognize that the fear is excessive or unreasonable.

Fears are very common, particularly in childhood, but they do not warrant a diagnosis of Specific Phobia unless there is significant interference with social, educational, or occupational functioning or marked distress about having the phobia.

■ Diagnostic criteria for 300.29 Specific Phobia

A. Marked and persistent fear that is excessive or unreasonable, cued by the presence or anticipation of a specific object or situation (e.g., flying, heights, animals, receiving an injection, seeing blood).

B. Exposure to the phobic stimulus almost invariably provokes an immediate anxiety response, which may take the form of a situationally bound or situationally predisposed Panic Attack.   **Note:** In children, the anxiety may be expressed by crying, tantrums, freezing, or clinging.

C. The person recognizes that the fear is excessive or unreasonable. **Note:** In children, this feature may be absent.

D. The phobic situation(s) is avoided or else is endured with intense anxiety or distress.

E. The avoidance, anxious anticipation, or distress in the feared situation(s) interferes significantly with the person's normal routine, occupational (or academic) functioning, or social activities or relationships, or there is marked distress about having the phobia.

(continued)

☐ **Diagnostic criteria for 300.29 Specific Phobia** (*continued*)

F. In individuals under age 18 years, the duration is at least 6 months.

G. The anxiety, Panic Attacks, or phobic avoidance associated with the specific object or situation are not better accounted for by another mental disorder, such as Obsessive-Compulsive Disorder (e.g., fear of dirt in someone with an obsession about contamination), Posttraumatic Stress Disorder (e.g., avoidance of stimuli associated with a severe stressor), Separation Anxiety Disorder (e.g., avoidance of school), Social Phobia (e.g., avoidance of social situations because of fear of embarrassment), Panic Disorder With Agoraphobia, or Agoraphobia Without History of Panic Disorder.

Specify type:
Animal Type
Natural Environment Type (e.g., heights, storms, water)
Blood-Injection-Injury Type
Situational Type (e.g., airplanes, elevators, enclosed places)
Other Type (e.g., phobic avoidance of situations that may lead to choking, vomiting, or contracting an illness; in children, avoidance of loud sounds or costumed characters)

300.23 Social Phobia
(Social Anxiety Disorder)

Diagnostic Features

The essential feature of Social Phobia is a marked and persistent fear of social or performance situations in which embarrassment may occur (Criterion A). Exposure to the social or performance situation almost invariably provokes an immediate anxiety response (Criterion B). This response may take the form of a situationally bound or situationally predisposed Panic Attack (see p. 394). Although adolescents and adults with this disorder recognize that their fear is excessive or unreasonable (Criterion C), this may not be the case with children. Most often, the social or performance situation is avoided, although it is sometimes endured with dread (Criterion D). The diagnosis is appropriate only if the avoidance, fear, or anxious anticipation of encountering the social or performance situation interferes significantly with the person's daily routine, occupational functioning, or social life, or if the person is markedly distressed about having the phobia (Criterion E). In individuals younger than age 18 years, symptoms must have persisted for at least 6 months before Social Phobia is diagnosed (Criterion F). The fear or avoidance is not due to the direct physiological effects of a substance or a general medical condition and is not better accounted for by another mental disorder (e.g., Panic Disorder, Separation Anxiety Disorder, Body Dysmorphic Disorder, a Pervasive Developmental Disorder, or Schizoid Personality Disorder) (Criterion G). If another mental disorder or general medical condition is present (e.g., Stuttering, Parkinson's disease, Anorexia Nervosa), the fear or avoidance is not limited to concern about its social impact (Criterion H).

In feared social or performance situations, individuals with Social Phobia experience concerns about embarrassment and are afraid that others will judge them to be anxious, weak, "crazy," or stupid. They may fear public speaking because of concern that others will notice their trembling hands or voice or they may experience extreme anxiety when conversing with others because of fear that they will appear inarticulate. They may avoid eating, drinking, or writing in public because of a fear of being embarrassed by having others see their hands shake. Individuals with Social Phobia almost always experience symptoms of anxiety (e.g., palpitations, tremors, sweating, gastrointestinal discomfort, diarrhea, muscle tension, blushing, confusion) in the feared social situations, and, in severe cases, these symptoms may meet the criteria for a Panic Attack (see p. 395). Blushing may be more typical of Social Phobia.

Adults with Social Phobia recognize that the fear is excessive or unreasonable, although this is not always the case in children. For example, the diagnosis would be Delusional Disorder instead of Social Phobia for an individual who avoids eating in public because of a conviction that he or she will be observed by the police and who does not recognize that this fear is excessive and unreasonable. Moreover, the diagnosis should not be given if the fear is reasonable given the context of the stimuli (e.g., fear of being called on in class when unprepared).

The person with Social Phobia typically will avoid the feared situations. Less commonly, the person forces himself or herself to endure the social or performance situation, but experiences it with intense anxiety. Marked anticipatory anxiety may also occur far in advance of upcoming social or public situations (e.g., worrying every day for several weeks before attending a social event). There may be a vicious cycle of anticipatory anxiety leading to fearful cognition and anxiety symptoms in the feared situations, which leads to actual or perceived poor performance in the feared situations, which leads to embarrassment and increased anticipatory anxiety about the feared situations, and so on.

The fear or avoidance must interfere significantly with the person's normal routine, occupational or academic functioning, or social activities or relationships, or the person must experience marked distress about having the phobia. For example, a person who is afraid of speaking in public would not receive a diagnosis of Social Phobia if this activity is not routinely encountered in job or classroom and the person is not particularly distressed about it. Fears of being embarrassed in social situations are common, but usually the degree of distress or impairment is insufficient to warrant a diagnosis of Social Phobia. Transient social anxiety or avoidance is especially common in childhood and adolescence (e.g., an adolescent girl may avoid eating in front of boys for a short time, then resume usual behavior). In those younger than age 18 years, only symptoms that persist for at least 6 months qualify for the diagnosis of Social Phobia.

Specifier

Generalized. This specifier can be used when the fears are related to most social situations (e.g., initiating or maintaining conversations, participating in small groups, dating, speaking to authority figures, attending parties). Individuals with Social Phobia, Generalized, usually fear both public performance situations and social interactional situations. Because individuals with Social Phobia often do not spontaneously report the full range of their social fears, it is useful for the clinician to review a list of social and performance situations with the individual. Individuals whose clinical manifestations do not meet the definition of Generalized compose a heterogeneous group that includes persons who fear a single performance situation as well as those who fear several, but not most, social situations. Individuals with Social Phobia, Generalized, may be more likely to manifest deficits in social skills and to have severe social and work impairment.

Associated Features and Disorders

Associated descriptive features and mental disorders. Common associated features of Social Phobia include hypersensitivity to criticism, negative evaluation, or rejection; difficulty being assertive; and low self-esteem or feelings of inferiority. Individuals with Social Phobia also often fear indirect evaluation by others, such as taking a test. They may manifest poor social skills (e.g., poor eye contact) or observable signs of anxiety (e.g., cold clammy hands, tremors, shaky voice). Individuals with Social Phobia often underachieve in school due to test anxiety or avoidance of classroom participation. They may underachieve at work because of anxiety during, or avoidance of, speaking in groups, in public, or to authority figures and colleagues. Persons with Social Phobia often have decreased social support networks and are less likely to marry. In more severe cases, individuals may drop out of school, be unemployed and not seek work due to difficulty interviewing for jobs, have no friends or cling to unfulfilling relationships, completely refrain from dating, or remain with their family of origin.

Social Phobia may be associated with Panic Disorder With Agoraphobia, Agoraphobia Without History of Panic Disorder, Obsessive-Compulsive Disorder, Mood Disorders, Substance-Related Disorders, and Somatization Disorder and usually precedes these disorders. In clinical samples, Avoidant Personality Disorder is frequently present in individuals with Social Phobia, Generalized.

Associated laboratory findings. Compared with those with Panic Disorder, individuals with Social Phobia are less likely to develop a Panic Attack in response to sodium lactate infusion or carbon dioxide inhalation. This finding supports the differentiation of Social Phobia from Panic Disorder, although none of these findings are considered to be diagnostic of these disorders.

Specific Culture, Age, and Gender Features

Clinical presentation and resulting impairment may differ across cultures, depending on social demands. In certain cultures (e.g., Japan and Korea), individuals with Social Phobia may develop persistent and excessive fears of giving offense to others in social situations, instead of being embarrassed. These fears may take the form of extreme anxiety that blushing, eye-to-eye contact, or one's body odor will be offensive to others (*taijin kyofusho* in Japan).

In children, crying, tantrums, freezing, clinging or staying close to a familiar person, and inhibited interactions to the point of mutism may be present. Young children may appear excessively timid in unfamiliar social settings, shrink from contact with others, refuse to participate in group play, typically stay on the periphery of social activities, and attempt to remain close to familiar adults. Unlike adults, children with Social Phobia usually do not have the option of avoiding feared situations altogether and may be unable to identify the nature of their anxiety. There may be a decline in classroom performance, school refusal, or avoidance of age-appropriate social activities and dating. To make the diagnosis in children, there must be evidence of capacity for social relationships with familiar people and the social anxiety must occur in peer settings, not just in interactions with adults. Because of the disorder's early onset and chronic course, impairment in children tends to take the form of failure to achieve an expected level of functioning, rather than a decline from an optimal level of functioning. In contrast, when the onset is in adolescence, the disorder may lead to decrements in social and academic performance.

Epidemiological and community-based studies suggest that Social Phobia is more common in women than in men. In most clinical samples, however, the sexes are either equally represented or the majority are male.

Prevalence

Epidemiological and community-based studies have reported a lifetime prevalence of Social Phobia ranging from 3% to 13%. The reported prevalence may vary depending on the threshold used to determine distress or impairment and the number of types of social situations specifically surveyed. In one study, 20% reported excessive fear of public speaking and performance, but only about 2% appeared to experience enough impairment or distress to warrant a diagnosis of Social Phobia. In the general population, most individuals with Social Phobia fear public speaking, whereas somewhat less than half fear speaking to strangers or meeting new people. Other performance fears (e.g., eating, drinking, or writing in public, or using a public restroom) appear to be less common. In clinical settings, the vast majority of persons with Social Phobia fear more than one type of social situation. Social Phobia is rarely the reason for admission to inpatient settings. In outpatient clinics, rates of Social Phobia have ranged between 10% and 20% of individuals with Anxiety Disorders, but rates vary widely by site.

Course

Social Phobia typically has an onset in the mid-teens, sometimes emerging out of a childhood history of social inhibition or shyness. Some individuals report an onset in early childhood. Onset may abruptly follow a stressful or humiliating experience, or it may be insidious. The course of Social Phobia is often continuous. Duration is frequently lifelong, although the disorder may attenuate in severity or remit during adulthood. Severity of impairment may fluctuate with life stressors and demands. For example, Social Phobia may diminish after a person with fear of dating marries and reemerge after death of a spouse. A job promotion to a position requiring public speaking may result in the emergence of Social Phobia in someone who previously never needed to speak in public.

Familial Pattern

Social Phobia appears to occur more frequently among first-degree biological relatives of those with the disorder compared with the general population.

Differential Diagnosis

Individuals with both Panic Attacks and social avoidance sometimes present a potentially difficult diagnostic problem. Prototypically, **Panic Disorder With Agoraphobia** is characterized by the initial onset of unexpected Panic Attacks and the subsequent avoidance of multiple situations thought to be likely triggers of the Panic Attacks. Although social situations may be avoided in Panic Disorder due to the fear of being seen while having a Panic Attack, Panic Disorder is characterized by recurrent unexpected Panic Attacks that are not limited to social situations, and the diagnosis of Social Phobia is not made when the only social fear is of being seen while having a Panic Attack. Prototypically, Social Phobia is characterized by the avoidance of social situations in the absence of recurrent unexpected Panic Attacks. When Panic Attacks do occur, they take the form of situationally bound or situationally predisposed Panic Attacks (e.g., a person with fear of embarrassment when speaking in public experiences Panic Attacks cued only by public speaking or other social situations). Some presentations fall between these prototypes and require clinical judgment in the selection of the most appropriate diagnosis. For example, an individual who had not previously had a fear of public speaking has a Panic Attack while giving a talk and begins to dread giving presentations. If this individual subsequently has Panic Attacks only in social performance situations (even if the focus of fear is on the panic), then a diagnosis of Social Phobia may be appropriate. If, however, the individual continues to experience unexpected Panic Attacks, then a diagnosis of Panic Disorder With Agoraphobia would be warranted. If criteria are met for both Social Phobia and Panic Disorder, both diagnoses may be given. For example, an individual with lifelong fear and avoidance of most social situations (Social Phobia) later develops Panic Attacks in nonsocial situations and a variety of additional avoidance behaviors (Panic Disorder With Agoraphobia).

Avoidance of situations because of a fear of possible humiliation is highly prominent in Social Phobia, but may also at times occur in **Panic Disorder With Agoraphobia** and **Agoraphobia Without History of Panic Disorder.** The situations avoided in Social Phobia are limited to those involving possible scrutiny by other people. Fears in Agoraphobia Without History of Panic Disorder typically involve characteristic clusters of situations that may or may not involve scrutiny by others (e.g., being alone outside the home or being home alone; being on a bridge or in an elevator; traveling in a bus, train, automobile, or airplane). The role of a companion also may be useful in distinguishing Social Phobia from Agoraphobia (With and Without Panic Disorder). Typically, individuals with agoraphobic avoidance prefer to be with a trusted companion when in the feared situation, whereas individuals with Social Phobia may have marked anticipatory anxiety, but characteristically do not have Panic Attacks when alone. A person with Social Phobia who fears crowded stores would feel scrutinized with or without a companion and might be less anxious without the added burden of perceived scrutiny by the companion.

Children with **Separation Anxiety Disorder** may avoid social settings due to concerns about being separated from their caretaker, concerns about being embarrassed by needing to leave prematurely to return home, or concerns about requiring the presence of a parent when it is not developmentally appropriate. A separate diagnosis of Social Phobia is generally not warranted. Children with Separation Anxiety Disorder are usually comfortable in social settings in their own home, whereas those with Social Phobia display signs of discomfort even when feared social situations occur at home.

Although fear of embarrassment or humiliation may be present in **Generalized**

Anxiety Disorder or **Specific Phobia** (e.g., embarrassment about fainting when having blood drawn), this is not the main focus of the individual's fear or anxiety. Children with Generalized Anxiety Disorder have excessive worries about the quality of their performance, but these occur even when they are not evaluated by others, whereas in Social Phobia the potential evaluation by others is the key to the anxiety.

In a **Pervasive Developmental Disorder** and **Schizoid Personality Disorder,** social situations are avoided because of lack of interest in relating to other individuals. In contrast, individuals with Social Phobia have a capacity for and interest in social relationships with familiar people. In particular, for children to qualify for a diagnosis of Social Phobia, they must have at least one age-appropriate social relationship with someone outside the immediate family (e.g., a child who feels uncomfortable in social gatherings with peers and avoids such situations, but who has an active interest in and a relationship with one familiar same-age friend).

Avoidant Personality Disorder shares a number of features with Social Phobia and appears to overlap extensively with Social Phobia, Generalized. For individuals with Social Phobia, Generalized, the additional diagnosis of Avoidant Personality Disorder should be considered.

Social anxiety and avoidance of social situations are **associated features of many other mental disorders** (e.g., Major Depressive Disorder, Dysthymic Disorder, Schizophrenia, Body Dysmorphic Disorder). If the symptoms of social anxiety or avoidance occur only during the course of another mental disorder and are judged to be better accounted for by that disorder, the additional diagnosis of Social Phobia is not made.

Individuals with Social Phobia may be vulnerable to a worsening of social anxiety and avoidance related to a general medical condition or mental disorder with potentially embarrassing symptoms (e.g., tremor in Parkinson's disease, abnormal eating behavior in Anorexia Nervosa, obesity, strabismus, or facial scarring). However, if social anxiety and avoidance are limited to concerns about the general medical condition or mental disorder, by convention the diagnosis of Social Phobia is not made. If the social avoidance is clinically significant, a separate diagnosis of **Anxiety Disorder Not Otherwise Specified** may be given.

Performance anxiety, stage fright, and **shyness** in social situations that involve unfamiliar people are common and should not be diagnosed as Social Phobia unless the anxiety or avoidance leads to clinically significant impairment or marked distress. Children commonly exhibit social anxiety, particularly when interacting with unfamiliar adults. A diagnosis of Social Phobia should not be made in children unless the social anxiety is also evident in peer settings and persists for at least 6 months.

■ Diagnostic criteria for 300.23 Social Phobia

A. A marked and persistent fear of one or more social or performance situations in which the person is exposed to unfamiliar people or to possible scrutiny by others. The individual fears that he or she will act in a way (or show anxiety symptoms) that will be humiliating or embarrassing. **Note:** In children, there must be evidence of the capacity for age-appropriate social relationships with familiar people and the anxiety must occur in peer settings, not just in interactions with adults.

(continued)

☐ **Diagnostic criteria for 300.23 Social Phobia** (*continued*)

B. Exposure to the feared social situation almost invariably provokes anxiety, which may take the form of a situationally bound or situationally predisposed Panic Attack. **Note:** In children, the anxiety may be expressed by crying, tantrums, freezing, or shrinking from social situations with unfamiliar people.

C. The person recognizes that the fear is excessive or unreasonable. **Note:** In children, this feature may be absent.

D. The feared social or performance situations are avoided or else are endured with intense anxiety or distress.

E. The avoidance, anxious anticipation, or distress in the feared social or performance situation(s) interferes significantly with the person's normal routine, occupational (academic) functioning, or social activities or relationships, or there is marked distress about having the phobia.

F. In individuals under age 18 years, the duration is at least 6 months.

G. The fear or avoidance is not due to the direct physiological effects of a substance (e.g., a drug of abuse, a medication) or a general medical condition and is not better accounted for by another mental disorder (e.g., Panic Disorder With or Without Agoraphobia, Separation Anxiety Disorder, Body Dysmorphic Disorder, a Pervasive Developmental Disorder, or Schizoid Personality Disorder).

H. If a general medical condition or another mental disorder is present, the fear in Criterion A is unrelated to it, e.g., the fear is not of Stuttering, trembling in Parkinson's disease, or exhibiting abnormal eating behavior in Anorexia Nervosa or Bulimia Nervosa.

Specify if:
   Generalized: if the fears include most social situations (also consider the additional diagnosis of Avoidant Personality Disorder)

300.3 Obsessive-Compulsive Disorder

Diagnostic Features

The essential features of Obsessive-Compulsive Disorder are recurrent obsessions or compulsions (Criterion A) that are severe enough to be time consuming (i.e., they take more than 1 hour a day) or cause marked distress or significant impairment (Criterion C). At some point during the course of the disorder, the person has recognized that the obsessions or compulsions are excessive or unreasonable (Criterion B). If another Axis I disorder is present, the content of the obsessions or compulsions is not restricted to it

(Criterion D). The disturbance is not due to the direct physiological effects of a substance (e.g., a drug of abuse, a medication) or a general medical condition (Criterion E).

Obsessions are persistent ideas, thoughts, impulses, or images that are experienced as intrusive and inappropriate and that cause marked anxiety or distress. The intrusive and inappropriate quality of the obsessions has been referred to as "ego-dystonic." This refers to the individual's sense that the content of the obsession is alien, not within his or her own control, and not the kind of thought that he or she would expect to have. However, the individual is able to recognize that the obsessions are the product of his or her own mind and are not imposed from without (as in thought insertion).

The most common obsessions are repeated thoughts about contamination (e.g., becoming contaminated by shaking hands), repeated doubts (e.g., wondering whether one has performed some act such as having hurt someone in a traffic accident or having left a door unlocked), a need to have things in a particular order (e.g., intense distress when objects are disordered or asymmetrical), aggressive or horrific impulses (e.g., to hurt one's child or to shout an obscenity in church), and sexual imagery (e.g., a recurrent pornographic image). The thoughts, impulses, or images are not simply excessive worries about real-life problems (e.g., concerns about current ongoing difficulties in life, such as financial, work, or school problems) and are unlikely to be related to a real-life problem.

The individual with obsessions usually attempts to ignore or suppress such thoughts or impulses or to neutralize them with some other thought or action (i.e., a compulsion). For example, an individual plagued by doubts about having turned off the stove attempts to neutralize them by repeatedly checking to ensure that it is off.

Compulsions are repetitive behaviors (e.g., hand washing, ordering, checking) or mental acts (e.g., praying, counting, repeating words silently) the goal of which is to prevent or reduce anxiety or distress, not to provide pleasure or gratification. In most cases, the person feels driven to perform the compulsion to reduce the distress that accompanies an obsession or to prevent some dreaded event or situation. For example, individuals with obsessions about being contaminated may reduce their mental distress by washing their hands until their skin is raw; individuals distressed by obsessions about having left a door unlocked may be driven to check the lock every few minutes; individuals distressed by unwanted blasphemous thoughts may find relief in counting to 10 backward and forward 100 times for each thought. In some cases, individuals perform rigid or stereotyped acts according to idiosyncratically elaborated rules without being able to indicate why they are doing them. By definition, compulsions are either clearly excessive or are not connected in a realistic way with what they are designed to neutralize or prevent. The most common compulsions involve washing and cleaning, counting, checking, requesting or demanding assurances, repeating actions, and ordering.

By definition, adults with Obsessive-Compulsive Disorder have at some point recognized that the obsessions or compulsions are excessive or unreasonable. This requirement does not apply to children because they may lack sufficient cognitive awareness to make this judgment. However, even in adults there is a broad range of insight into the reasonableness of the obsessions or compulsions. Some individuals are uncertain about the reasonableness of their obsessions or compulsions, and any given individual's insight may vary across times and situations. For example, the person may recognize a contamination compulsion as unreasonable when discussing it in a "safe situation" (e.g., in the therapist's office), but not when forced to handle money. At those times when the individual recognizes that the obsessions and compulsions are unreasonable, he or she may desire or attempt to resist them. When attempting to resist a compulsion, the individual may have a sense of mounting anxiety or tension that is often relieved by yielding to the compulsion. In the course of the disorder, after repeated failure to resist the obsessions or compulsions, the individual may give in to them, no longer experience a desire to resist them, and may incorporate the compulsions into his or her daily routines.

The obsessions or compulsions must cause marked distress, be time consuming (take more than 1 hour per day), or significantly interfere with the individual's normal routine, occupational functioning, or usual social activities or relationships with others. Obsessions or compulsions can displace useful and satisfying behavior and can be highly disruptive to overall functioning. Because obsessive intrusions can be distracting, they frequently result in inefficient performance of cognitive tasks that require concentration, such as reading or computation. In addition, many individuals avoid objects or situations that provoke obsessions or compulsions. Such avoidance can become extensive and can severely restrict general functioning.

Specifier

With Poor Insight. This specifier can be applied when, for most of the time during the current episode, the individual does not recognize that the obsessions or compulsions are excessive or unreasonable.

Associated Features and Disorders

Associated descriptive features and mental disorders. Frequently there is avoidance of situations that involve the content of the obsessions, such as dirt or contamination. For example, a person with obsessions about dirt may avoid public restrooms or shaking hands with strangers. Hypochondriacal concerns are common, with repeated visits to physicians to seek reassurance. Guilt, a pathological sense of responsibility, and sleep disturbances may be present. There may be excessive use of alcohol or of sedative, hypnotic, or anxiolytic medications. Performing compulsions may become a major life activity, leading to serious marital, occupational, or social disability. Pervasive avoidance may leave an individual housebound.

Obsessive-Compulsive Disorder may be associated with Major Depressive Disorder, other Anxiety Disorders (Specific Phobia, Social Phobia, Panic Disorder), Eating Disorders, and Obsessive-Compulsive Personality Disorder. There is a high incidence of Obsessive-Compulsive Disorder in individuals with Tourette's Disorder, with estimates ranging from approximately 35% to 50%. The incidence of Tourette's Disorder in Obsessive-Compulsive Disorder is lower, with estimates ranging between 5% and 7%. Between 20% and 30% of individuals with Obsessive-Compulsive Disorder have reported current or past tics.

Associated laboratory findings. No laboratory findings have been identified that are diagnostic of Obsessive-Compulsive Disorder. However, a variety of laboratory findings have been noted to be abnormal in groups of individuals with Obsessive-Compulsive Disorder relative to control subjects. There is some evidence that some serotonin agonists given acutely cause increased symptoms in some individuals with the disorder. Individuals with the disorder may exhibit increased autonomic activity when confronted in the laboratory with circumstances that trigger an obsession. Physiological reactivity decreases after the performance of compulsions.

Associated physical examination findings and general medical conditions. Dermatological problems caused by excessive washing with water or caustic cleaning agents may be observed.

Specific Culture, Age, and Gender Features

Culturally prescribed ritual behavior is not in itself indicative of Obsessive-Compulsive Disorder unless it exceeds cultural norms, occurs at times and places judged inappropriate by others of the same culture, and interferes with social role functioning. Important life transitions and mourning may lead to an intensification of ritual behavior that may appear to be an obsession to a clinician who is not familiar with the cultural context.

Presentations of Obsessive-Compulsive Disorder in children are generally similar to those in adulthood. Washing, checking, and ordering rituals are particularly common in children. Children generally do not request help, and the symptoms may not be ego-dystonic. More often the problem is identified by parents, who bring the child in for treatment. Gradual declines in schoolwork secondary to impaired ability to concentrate have been reported. Like adults, children are more prone to engage in rituals at home than in front of peers, teachers, or strangers.

This disorder is equally common in males and females.

Prevalence

Although Obsessive-Compulsive Disorder was previously thought to be relatively rare in the general population, recent community studies have estimated a lifetime prevalence of 2.5% and 1-year prevalence of 1.5%–2.1%.

Course

Although Obsessive-Compulsive Disorder usually begins in adolescence or early adulthood, it may begin in childhood. Modal age at onset is earlier in males than in females: between ages 6 and 15 years for males and between ages 20 and 29 years for females. For the most part, onset is gradual, but acute onset has been noted in some cases. The majority of individuals have a chronic waxing and waning course, with exacerbation of symptoms that may be related to stress. About 15% show progressive deterioration in occupational and social functioning. About 5% have an episodic course with minimal or no symptoms between episodes.

Familial Pattern

The concordance rate for Obsessive-Compulsive Disorder is higher for monozygotic twins than it is for dizygotic twins. The rate of Obsessive-Compulsive Disorder in first-degree biological relatives of individuals with Obsessive-Compulsive Disorder and in first-degree biological relatives of individuals with Tourette's Disorder is higher than that in the general population.

Differential Diagnosis

Obsessive-Compulsive Disorder must be distinguished from **Anxiety Disorder Due to a General Medical Condition.** The diagnosis is Anxiety Disorder Due to a General Medical Condition when the obsessions or compulsions are judged to be a direct physiological consequence of a specific general medical condition (see p. 436. This determination is based on history, laboratory findings, or physical examination. A **Substance-Induced Anxiety Disorder** is distinguished from Obsessive-Compulsive Disorder by the fact that a substance (i.e., a drug of abuse, a medication, or exposure to a toxin) is judged to be etiologically related to the obsessions or compulsions (see p. 439).

Recurrent or intrusive thoughts, impulses, images, or behaviors may occur in the context of many other mental disorders. Obsessive-Compulsive Disorder is not diagnosed if the content of the thoughts or the activities is exclusively related to another mental disorder (e.g., preoccupation with appearance in **Body Dysmorphic Disorder,** preoccupation with a feared object or situation in **Specific** or **Social Phobia,** hair pulling in **Trichotillomania**). An additional diagnosis of Obsessive-Compulsive Disorder may still be warranted if there are obsessions or compulsions whose content is unrelated to the other mental disorder.

In a **Major Depressive Episode,** persistent brooding about potentially unpleasant circumstances or about possible alternative actions is common and is considered a mood-congruent aspect of depression rather than an obsession. For example, a depressed individual who ruminates that he is worthless would not be considered to have obsessions because such brooding is not ego-dystonic.

Generalized Anxiety Disorder is characterized by excessive worry, but such worries are distinguished from obsessions by the fact that the person experiences them as excessive concerns about real-life circumstances. For example, an excessive concern that one may lose one's job would constitute a worry, not an obsession. In contrast, the content of obsessions does not typically involve real-life problems, and the obsessions are experienced as inappropriate by the individual (e.g., the intrusive distressing idea that "God" is "dog" spelled backward).

If recurrent distressing thoughts are exclusively related to fears of having, or the idea that one has, a serious disease based on misinterpretation of bodily symptoms, then **Hypochondriasis** should be diagnosed instead of Obsessive-Compulsive Disorder. However, if the concern about having an illness is accompanied by rituals such as excessive washing or checking behavior related to concerns about the illness or about spreading it to other people, then an additional diagnosis of Obsessive-Compulsive Disorder may be indicated. If the major concern is about contracting an illness (rather than having an illness) and no rituals are involved, then a **Specific Phobia** of illness may be the more appropriate diagnosis.

The ability of individuals to recognize that the obsessions or compulsions are excessive or unreasonable occurs on a continuum. In some individuals with Obsessive-Compulsive Disorder, reality testing may be lost, and the obsession may reach delusional proportions (e.g., the belief that one has caused the death of another person by having willed it). In such cases, the presence of psychotic features may be indicated by an additional diagnosis of **Delusional Disorder** or **Psychotic Disorder Not Otherwise Specified.** The specifier With Poor Insight may be useful in those situations that are on the boundary between obsession and delusion (e.g., an individual whose extreme preoccupation with contamination, although exaggerated, is less intense than in a

Delusional Disorder and is justified by the fact that germs are indeed ubiquitous).

The ruminative delusional thoughts and bizarre stereotyped behaviors that occur in **Schizophrenia** are distinguished from obsessions and compulsions by the fact that they are not ego-dystonic and not subject to reality testing. However, some individuals manifest symptoms of both Obsessive-Compulsive Disorder and Schizophrenia and warrant both diagnoses.

Tics (in **Tic Disorder**) and stereotyped movements (in **Stereotypic Movement Disorder**) must be distinguished from compulsions. A *tic* is a sudden, rapid, recurrent, nonrhythmic stereotyped motor movement or vocalization (e.g., eye blinking, tongue protrusion, throat clearing). A *stereotyped movement* is a repetitive, seemingly driven nonfunctional motor behavior (e.g., head banging, body rocking, self-biting). In contrast to a compulsion, tics and stereotyped movements are typically less complex and are not aimed at neutralizing an obsession. Some individuals manifest symptoms of both Obsessive-Compulsive Disorder and a Tic Disorder (especially Tourette's Disorder), and both diagnoses may be warranted.

Some activities, such as eating (e.g., **Eating Disorders**), sexual behavior (e.g., **Paraphilias**), gambling (e.g., **Pathological Gambling**), or substance use (e.g., **Alcohol Dependence** or **Abuse**), when engaged in excessively, have been referred to as "compulsive." However, these activities are not considered to be compulsions as defined in this manual because the person usually derives pleasure from the activity and may wish to resist it only because of its deleterious consequences.

Although **Obsessive-Compulsive Personality Disorder** and Obsessive-Compulsive Disorder have similar names, the clinical manifestations of these disorders are quite different. Obsessive-Compulsive Personality Disorder is not characterized by the presence of obsessions or compulsions and instead involves a pervasive pattern of preoccupation with orderliness, perfectionism, and control and must begin by early adulthood. If an individual manifests symptoms of both Obsessive-Compulsive Disorder and Obsessive-Compulsive Personality Disorder, both diagnoses can be given.

Superstitions and **repetitive checking behaviors** are commonly encountered in everyday life. A diagnosis of Obsessive-Compulsive Disorder should be considered only if they are particularly time consuming or result in clinically significant impairment or distress.

■ Diagnostic criteria for 300.3 Obsessive-Compulsive Disorder

A. Either obsessions or compulsions:

Obsessions as defined by (1), (2), (3), and (4):

(1) recurrent and persistent thoughts, impulses, or images that are experienced, at some time during the disturbance, as intrusive and inappropriate and that cause marked anxiety or distress

(2) the thoughts, impulses, or images are not simply excessive worries about real-life problems

(continued)

☐ **Diagnostic criteria for 300.3 Obsessive-Compulsive Disorder** (*continued*)

    (3)   the person attempts to ignore or suppress such thoughts, impulses, or images, or to neutralize them with some other thought or action

    (4)   the person recognizes that the obsessional thoughts, impulses, or images are a product of his or her own mind (not imposed from without as in thought insertion)

Compulsions as defined by (1) and (2):

    (1)   repetitive behaviors (e.g., hand washing, ordering, checking) or mental acts (e.g., praying, counting, repeating words silently) that the person feels driven to perform in response to an obsession, or according to rules that must be applied rigidly

    (2)   the behaviors or mental acts are aimed at preventing or reducing distress or preventing some dreaded event or situation; however, these behaviors or mental acts either are not connected in a realistic way with what they are designed to neutralize or prevent or are clearly excessive

B. At some point during the course of the disorder, the person has recognized that the obsessions or compulsions are excessive or unreasonable. **Note:** This does not apply to children.

C. The obsessions or compulsions cause marked distress, are time consuming (take more than 1 hour a day), or significantly interfere with the person's normal routine, occupational (or academic) functioning, or usual social activities or relationships.

D. If another Axis I disorder is present, the content of the obsessions or compulsions is not restricted to it (e.g., preoccupation with food in the presence of an Eating Disorder; hair pulling in the presence of Trichotillomania; concern with appearance in the presence of Body Dysmorphic Disorder; preoccupation with drugs in the presence of a Substance Use Disorder; preoccupation with having a serious illness in the presence of Hypochondriasis; preoccupation with sexual urges or fantasies in the presence of a Paraphilia; or guilty ruminations in the presence of Major Depressive Disorder).

E. The disturbance is not due to the direct physiological effects of a substance (e.g., a drug of abuse, a medication) or a general medical condition.

Specify if:

    With Poor Insight: if, for most of the time during the current episode, the person does not recognize that the obsessions and compulsions are excessive or unreasonable

309.81   Posttraumatic Stress Disorder

Diagnostic Features

The essential feature of Posttraumatic Stress Disorder is the development of characteristic symptoms following exposure to an extreme traumatic stressor involving direct personal experience of an event that involves actual or threatened death or serious injury, or other threat to one's physical integrity; or witnessing an event that involves death, injury, or a threat to the physical integrity of another person; or learning about unexpected or violent death, serious harm, or threat of death or injury experienced by a family member or other close associate (Criterion A1). The person's response to the event must involve intense fear, helplessness, or horror (or in children, the response must involve disorganized or agitated behavior) (Criterion A2). The characteristic symptoms resulting from the exposure to the extreme trauma include persistent reexperiencing of the traumatic event (Criterion B), persistent avoidance of stimuli associated with the trauma and numbing of general responsiveness (Criterion C), and persistent symptoms of increased arousal (Criterion D). The full symptom picture must be present for more than 1 month (Criterion E), and the disturbance must cause clinically significant distress or impairment in social, occupational, or other important areas of functioning (Criterion F).

Traumatic events that are experienced directly include, but are not limited to, military combat, violent personal assault (sexual assault, physical attack, robbery, mugging), being kidnapped, being taken hostage, terrorist attack, torture, incarceration as a prisoner of war or in a concentration camp, natural or manmade disasters, severe automobile accidents, or being diagnosed with a life-threatening illness. For children, sexually traumatic events may include developmentally inappropriate sexual experiences without threatened or actual violence or injury. Witnessed events include, but are not limited to, observing the serious injury or unnatural death of another person due to violent assault, accident, war, or disaster or unexpectedly witnessing a dead body or body parts. Events experienced by others that are learned about include, but are not limited to, violent personal assault, serious accident, or serious injury experienced by a family member or a close friend; learning about the sudden, unexpected death of a family member or a close friend; or learning that one's child has a life-threatening disease. The disorder may be especially severe or long lasting when the stressor is of human design (e.g., torture, rape). The likelihood of developing this disorder may increase as the intensity of and physical proximity to the stressor increase.

The traumatic event can be reexperienced in various ways. Commonly the person has recurrent and intrusive recollections of the event (Criterion B1) or recurrent distressing dreams during which the event is replayed (Criterion B2). In rare instances, the person experiences dissociative states that last from a few seconds to several hours, or even days, during which components of the event are relived and the person behaves as though experiencing the event at that moment (Criterion B3). Intense psychological distress (Criterion B4) or physiological reactivity (Criterion B5) often occurs when the person is exposed to triggering events that resemble or symbolize an aspect of the traumatic event (e.g., anniversaries of the traumatic event; cold, snowy weather or uniformed guards for survivors of death camps in cold climates; hot, humid weather for combat veterans of the South Pacific; entering any elevator for a woman who was raped in an elevator).

Stimuli associated with the trauma are persistently avoided. The person commonly makes deliberate efforts to avoid thoughts, feelings, or conversations about the traumatic event (Criterion C1) and to avoid activities, situations, or people who arouse recollections of it (Criterion C2). This avoidance of reminders may include amnesia for an important aspect of the traumatic event (Criterion C3). Diminished responsiveness to the external world, referred to as "psychic numbing" or "emotional anesthesia," usually begins soon after the traumatic event. The individual may complain of having markedly diminished interest or participation in previously enjoyed activities (Criterion C4), of feeling detached or estranged from other people (Criterion C5), or of having markedly reduced ability to feel emotions (especially those associated with intimacy, tenderness, and sexuality) (Criterion C6). The individual may have a sense of a foreshortened future (e.g., not expecting to have a career, marriage, children, or a normal life span) (Criterion C7).

The individual has persistent symptoms of anxiety or increased arousal that were not present before the trauma. These symptoms may include difficulty falling or staying asleep that may be due to recurrent nightmares during which the traumatic event is relived (Criterion D1), hypervigilance (Criterion D4), and exaggerated startle response (Criterion D5). Some individuals report irritability or outbursts of anger (Criterion D2) or difficulty concentrating or completing tasks (Criterion D3).

Specifiers

The following specifiers may be used to specify onset and duration of the symptoms of Posttraumatic Stress Disorder:

Acute. This specifier should be used when the duration of symptoms is less than 3 months.

Chronic. This specifier should be used when the symptoms last 3 months or longer.

With Delayed Onset. This specifier indicates that at least 6 months have passed between the traumatic event and the onset of the symptoms.

Associated Features and Disorders

Associated descriptive features and mental disorders. Individuals with Posttraumatic Stress Disorder may describe painful guilt feelings about surviving when others did not survive or about the things they had to do to survive. Phobic avoidance of situations or activities that resemble or symbolize the original trauma may interfere with interpersonal relationships and lead to marital conflict, divorce, or loss of job. The following associated constellation of symptoms may occur and are more commonly seen in association with an interpersonal stressor (e.g., childhood sexual or physical abuse, domestic battering, being taken hostage, incarceration as a prisoner of war or in a concentration camp, torture): impaired affect modulation; self-destructive and impulsive behavior; dissociative symptoms; somatic complaints; feelings of ineffectiveness, shame, despair, or hopelessness; feeling permanently damaged; a loss of previously sustained beliefs; hostility; social withdrawal; feeling constantly threatened; impaired relationships with others; or a change from the individual's previous personality characteristics.

There may be increased risk of Panic Disorder, Agoraphobia, Obsessive-Compulsive Disorder, Social Phobia, Specific Phobia, Major Depressive Disorder, Somatization Disorder, and Substance-Related Disorders. It is not known to what extent these disorders precede or follow the onset of Posttraumatic Stress Disorder.

Associated laboratory findings.   Increased arousal may be measured through studies of autonomic functioning (e.g., heart rate, electromyography, sweat gland activity).

Associated physical examination findings and general medical conditions.
General medical conditions may occur as a consequence of the trauma (e.g., head injury, burns).

Specific Culture and Age Features

Individuals who have recently emigrated from areas of considerable social unrest and civil conflict may have elevated rates of Posttraumatic Stress Disorder. Such individuals may be especially reluctant to divulge experiences of torture and trauma due to their vulnerable political immigrant status. Specific assessments of traumatic experiences and concomitant symptoms are needed for such individuals.

In younger children, distressing dreams of the event may, within several weeks, change into generalized nightmares of monsters, of rescuing others, or of threats to self or others. Young children usually do not have the sense that they are reliving the past; rather, the reliving of the trauma may occur through repetitive play (e.g., a child who was involved in a serious automobile accident repeatedly reenacts car crashes with toy cars). Because it may be difficult for children to report diminished interest in significant activities and constriction of affect, these symptoms should be carefully evaluated with reports from parents, teachers, and other observers. In children, the sense of a foreshortened future may be evidenced by the belief that life will be too short to include becoming an adult. There may also be "omen formation"—that is, belief in an ability to foresee future untoward events. Children may also exhibit various physical symptoms, such as stomachaches and headaches.

Prevalence

Community-based studies reveal a lifetime prevalence for Posttraumatic Stress Disorder ranging from 1% to 14%, with the variability related to methods of ascertainment and the population sampled. Studies of at-risk individuals (e.g., combat veterans, victims of volcanic eruptions or criminal violence) have yielded prevalence rates ranging from 3% to 58%.

Course

Posttraumatic Stress Disorder can occur at any age, including childhood. Symptoms usually begin within the first 3 months after the trauma, although there may be a delay of months, or even years, before symptoms appear. Frequently, the disturbance initially meets criteria for Acute Stress Disorder (see p. 429) in the immediate aftermath of the trauma. The symptoms of the disorder and the relative predominance of reexperiencing, avoidance, and hyperarousal symptoms may vary over time. Duration of the symptoms varies, with complete recovery occurring within 3 months in approximately half of cases, with many others having persisting symptoms for longer than 12 months after the trauma.

The severity, duration, and proximity of an individual's exposure to the traumatic event are the most important factors affecting the likelihood of developing this disorder. There is some evidence that social supports, family history, childhood experiences, personality variables, and preexisting mental disorders may influence the development of Posttraumatic Stress Disorder. This disorder can develop in individuals without any predisposing conditions, particularly if the stressor is especially extreme.

Differential Diagnosis

In Posttraumatic Stress Disorder, the stressor must be of an extreme (i.e., life-threatening) nature. In contrast, in **Adjustment Disorder,** the stressor can be of any severity. The diagnosis of Adjustment Disorder is appropriate both for situations in which the response to an extreme stressor does not meet the criteria for Posttraumatic Stress Disorder (or another specific mental disorder) and for situations in which the symptom pattern of Posttraumatic Stress Disorder occurs in response to a stressor that is not extreme (e.g., spouse leaving, being fired).

Not all psychopathology that occurs in individuals exposed to an extreme stressor should necessarily be attributed to Posttraumatic Stress Disorder. **Symptoms of avoidance, numbing, and increased arousal that are present before exposure to the stressor** do not meet criteria for the diagnosis of Posttraumatic Stress Disorder and require consideration of other diagnoses (e.g., a Mood Disorder or another Anxiety Disorder). Moreover, if the symptom response pattern to the extreme stressor meets criteria for **another mental disorder** (e.g., Brief Psychotic Disorder, Conversion Disorder, Major Depressive Disorder), these diagnoses should be given instead of, or in addition to, Posttraumatic Stress Disorder.

Acute Stress Disorder is distinguished from Posttraumatic Stress Disorder because the symptom pattern in Acute Stress Disorder must occur within 4 weeks of the traumatic event and resolve within that 4-week period. If the symptoms persist for more than 1 month and meet criteria for Posttraumatic Stress Disorder, the diagnosis is changed from Acute Stress Disorder to Posttraumatic Stress Disorder.

In **Obsessive-Compulsive Disorder,** there are recurrent intrusive thoughts, but these are experienced as inappropriate and are not related to an experienced traumatic event. Flashbacks in Posttraumatic Stress Disorder must be distinguished from illusions, hallucinations, and other perceptual disturbances that may occur in **Schizophrenia, other Psychotic Disorders, Mood Disorder With Psychotic Features,** a **delirium, Substance-Induced Disorders,** and **Psychotic Disorders Due to a General Medical Condition.**

Malingering should be ruled out in those situations in which financial remuneration, benefit eligibility, and forensic determinations play a role.

■ Diagnostic criteria for 309.81 Posttraumatic Stress Disorder

A. The person has been exposed to a traumatic event in which both of the following were present:

(1) the person experienced, witnessed, or was confronted with an event or events that involved actual or threatened death or serious injury, or a threat to the physical integrity of self or others

(continued)

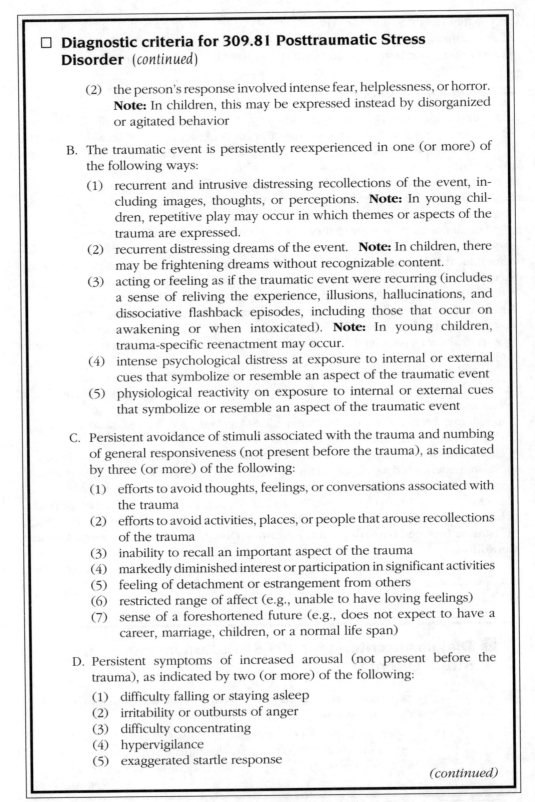

☐ **Diagnostic criteria for 309.81 Posttraumatic Stress Disorder** (*continued*)

   (2)   the person's response involved intense fear, helplessness, or horror. **Note:** In children, this may be expressed instead by disorganized or agitated behavior

B.   The traumatic event is persistently reexperienced in one (or more) of the following ways:

   (1)   recurrent and intrusive distressing recollections of the event, including images, thoughts, or perceptions. **Note:** In young children, repetitive play may occur in which themes or aspects of the trauma are expressed.

   (2)   recurrent distressing dreams of the event. **Note:** In children, there may be frightening dreams without recognizable content.

   (3)   acting or feeling as if the traumatic event were recurring (includes a sense of reliving the experience, illusions, hallucinations, and dissociative flashback episodes, including those that occur on awakening or when intoxicated). **Note:** In young children, trauma-specific reenactment may occur.

   (4)   intense psychological distress at exposure to internal or external cues that symbolize or resemble an aspect of the traumatic event

   (5)   physiological reactivity on exposure to internal or external cues that symbolize or resemble an aspect of the traumatic event

C.   Persistent avoidance of stimuli associated with the trauma and numbing of general responsiveness (not present before the trauma), as indicated by three (or more) of the following:

   (1)   efforts to avoid thoughts, feelings, or conversations associated with the trauma

   (2)   efforts to avoid activities, places, or people that arouse recollections of the trauma

   (3)   inability to recall an important aspect of the trauma

   (4)   markedly diminished interest or participation in significant activities

   (5)   feeling of detachment or estrangement from others

   (6)   restricted range of affect (e.g., unable to have loving feelings)

   (7)   sense of a foreshortened future (e.g., does not expect to have a career, marriage, children, or a normal life span)

D.   Persistent symptoms of increased arousal (not present before the trauma), as indicated by two (or more) of the following:

   (1)   difficulty falling or staying asleep

   (2)   irritability or outbursts of anger

   (3)   difficulty concentrating

   (4)   hypervigilance

   (5)   exaggerated startle response

(continued)

☐ **Diagnostic criteria for 309.81 Posttraumatic Stress Disorder** (*continued*)

  E. Duration of the disturbance (symptoms in Criteria B, C, and D) is more than 1 month.

  F. The disturbance causes clinically significant distress or impairment in social, occupational, or other important areas of functioning.

Specify if:
  Acute: if duration of symptoms is less than 3 months
  Chronic: if duration of symptoms is 3 months or more

Specify if:
  With Delayed Onset: if onset of symptoms is at least 6 months after the stressor

308.3 Acute Stress Disorder

Diagnostic Features

The essential feature of Acute Stress Disorder is the development of characteristic anxiety, dissociative, and other symptoms that occurs within 1 month after exposure to an extreme traumatic stressor (Criterion A). For a discussion of the types of stressors involved, see the description of Posttraumatic Stress Disorder (p. 424). Either while experiencing the traumatic event or after the event, the individual has at least three of the following dissociative symptoms: a subjective sense of numbing, detachment, or absence of emotional responsiveness; a reduction in awareness of his or her surroundings; derealization; depersonalization; or dissociative amnesia (Criterion B). Following the trauma, the traumatic event is persistently reexperienced (Criterion C), and the individual displays marked avoidance of stimuli that may arouse recollections of the trauma (Criterion D) and has marked symptoms of anxiety or increased arousal (Criterion E). The symptoms must cause clinically significant distress, significantly interfere with normal functioning, or impair the individual's ability to pursue necessary tasks (Criterion F). The disturbance lasts for at least 2 days and does not persist beyond 4 weeks after the traumatic event (Criterion G). The symptoms are not due to the direct physiological effects of a substance (i.e., a drug of abuse, a medication) or a general medical condition, are not better accounted for by Brief Psychotic Disorder, and are not merely an exacerbation of a preexisting mental disorder (Criterion H).

As a response to the traumatic event, the individual develops dissociative symptoms. Individuals with Acute Stress Disorder have a decrease in emotional responsiveness, often finding it difficult or impossible to experience pleasure in previously enjoyable activities, and frequently feel guilty about pursuing usual life tasks. They may experience difficulty concentrating, feel detached from their bodies, experience the world as unreal or dreamlike, or have increasing difficulty recalling specific details of the traumatic event (dissociative amnesia). In addition, at least one symptom from each of the symptom clusters required for Posttraumatic Stress Disorder is present. First, the traumatic event is persistently reexperienced (e.g., recurrent recollections, images, thoughts, dreams, illusions, flashback episodes, a sense of reliving the event, or distress on exposure to reminders of the event). Second, reminders of the trauma (e.g., places, people, activities) are avoided. Finally, hyperarousal in response to stimuli reminiscent of the trauma is present (e.g., difficulty sleeping, irritability, poor concentration, hypervigilance, an exaggerated startle response, and motor restlessness).

Associated Features and Disorders

Associated descriptive features and mental disorders.   Symptoms of despair and hopelessness may be experienced in Acute Stress Disorder and may be sufficiently severe and persistent to meet criteria for a Major Depressive Episode, in which case an additional diagnosis of Major Depressive Disorder may be warranted. If the trauma led to another's death or to serious injury, survivors may feel guilt about having remained intact or about not providing enough help to others. Individuals with this disorder often perceive themselves to have greater responsibility for the consequences of the trauma than is warranted. Problems may result from the individual's neglect of basic health and safety needs associated with the aftermath of the trauma. Individuals with this disorder are at increased risk for the development of Posttraumatic Stress Disorder. Impulsive and risk-taking behavior may occur after the trauma.

Associated physical examination findings and general medical conditions. General medical conditions may occur as a consequence of the trauma (e.g., head injury, burns).

Specific Culture Features

Although some events are likely to be universally experienced as traumatic, the severity and pattern of response may be modulated by cultural differences in the implications of loss. There may also be culturally prescribed coping behaviors that are characteristic of particular cultures. For example, dissociative symptoms may be a more prominent part of the acute stress response in cultures in which such behaviors are sanctioned. For further discussion of cultural factors related to traumatic events, see p. 426.

Prevalence

The prevalence of Acute Stress Disorder in a population exposed to a serious traumatic stress depends on the severity and persistence of the trauma and the degree of exposure to it.

Course

Symptoms of Acute Stress Disorder are experienced during or immediately after the trauma, last for at least 2 days, and either resolve within 4 weeks after the conclusion of the traumatic event or the diagnosis is changed. When symptoms persist beyond 1 month, a diagnosis of Posttraumatic Stress Disorder may be appropriate if the full criteria for Posttraumatic Stress Disorder are met. The severity, duration, and proximity of an individual's exposure to the traumatic event are the most important factors in determining the likelihood of development of Acute Stress Disorder. There is some evidence that social supports, family history, childhood experiences, personality variables, and preexisting mental disorders may influence the development of Acute Stress Disorder. This disorder can develop in individuals without any predisposing conditions, particularly if the stressor is especially extreme.

Differential Diagnosis

Some symptomatology following exposure to an extreme stress is ubiquitous and often does not require any diagnosis. Acute Stress Disorder should only be considered if the symptoms last at least 2 days and cause clinically significant distress or impairment in social, occupational, or other important areas of functioning or impair the individual's ability to pursue some necessary task (e.g., obtaining necessary assistance or mobilizing personal resources by telling family members about the traumatic experience).

Acute Stress Disorder must be distinguished from a **Mental Disorder Due to a General Medical Condition** (e.g., head trauma) (see p. 165) and from a **Substance-Induced Disorder** (e.g., related to Alcohol Intoxication) (see p. 192), which may be common consequences of exposure to an extreme stressor. In some individuals, psychotic symptoms may occur following an extreme stressor. In such cases, **Brief Psychotic Disorder** is diagnosed instead of Acute Stress Disorder. If a **Major Depressive Episode** develops after the trauma, a diagnosis of Major Depressive Disorder should be considered in addition to a diagnosis of Acute Stress Disorder. A separate diagnosis of Acute Stress Disorder should not be made if the symptoms are an **exacerbation of a preexisting mental disorder.**

By definition, a diagnosis of Acute Stress Disorder is appropriate only for symptoms that occur within 1 month of the extreme stressor. Because **Posttraumatic Stress Disorder** requires more than 1 month of symptoms, this diagnosis cannot be made during this initial 1-month period. For individuals with the diagnosis of Acute Stress Disorder whose symptoms persist for longer than 1 month, the diagnosis of Posttraumatic Stress Disorder should be considered. For individuals who have an extreme stressor but who develop a symptom pattern that does not meet criteria for Acute Stress Disorder, a diagnosis of **Adjustment Disorder** should be considered.

Malingering must be ruled out in those situations in which financial remuneration, benefit eligibility, or forensic determinations play a role.

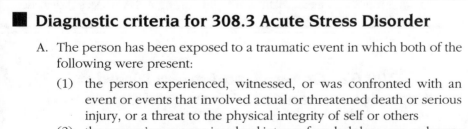

■ Diagnostic criteria for 308.3 Acute Stress Disorder

A. The person has been exposed to a traumatic event in which both of the following were present:

   (1) the person experienced, witnessed, or was confronted with an event or events that involved actual or threatened death or serious injury, or a threat to the physical integrity of self or others

   (2) the person's response involved intense fear, helplessness, or horror

B. Either while experiencing or after experiencing the distressing event, the individual has three (or more) of the following dissociative symptoms:

(continued)

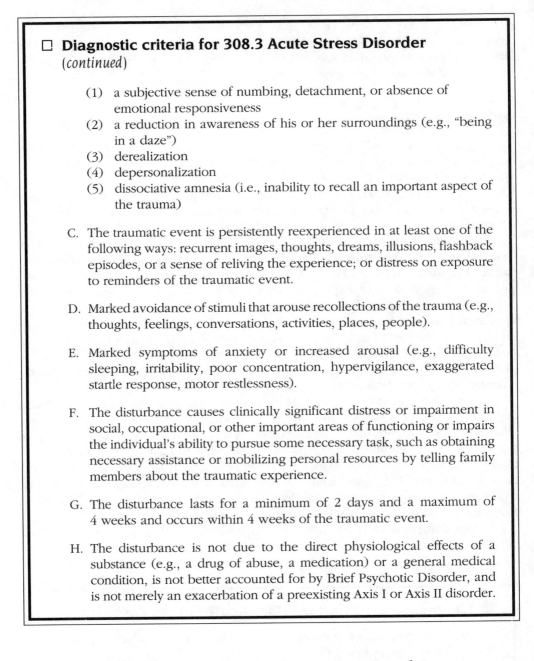

□ **Diagnostic criteria for 308.3 Acute Stress Disorder**
(*continued*)

  (1) a subjective sense of numbing, detachment, or absence of emotional responsiveness
  (2) a reduction in awareness of his or her surroundings (e.g., "being in a daze")
  (3) derealization
  (4) depersonalization
  (5) dissociative amnesia (i.e., inability to recall an important aspect of the trauma)

C. The traumatic event is persistently reexperienced in at least one of the following ways: recurrent images, thoughts, dreams, illusions, flashback episodes, or a sense of reliving the experience; or distress on exposure to reminders of the traumatic event.

D. Marked avoidance of stimuli that arouse recollections of the trauma (e.g., thoughts, feelings, conversations, activities, places, people).

E. Marked symptoms of anxiety or increased arousal (e.g., difficulty sleeping, irritability, poor concentration, hypervigilance, exaggerated startle response, motor restlessness).

F. The disturbance causes clinically significant distress or impairment in social, occupational, or other important areas of functioning or impairs the individual's ability to pursue some necessary task, such as obtaining necessary assistance or mobilizing personal resources by telling family members about the traumatic experience.

G. The disturbance lasts for a minimum of 2 days and a maximum of 4 weeks and occurs within 4 weeks of the traumatic event.

H. The disturbance is not due to the direct physiological effects of a substance (e.g., a drug of abuse, a medication) or a general medical condition, is not better accounted for by Brief Psychotic Disorder, and is not merely an exacerbation of a preexisting Axis I or Axis II disorder.

300.02   Generalized Anxiety Disorder
(Includes Overanxious Disorder of Childhood)

Diagnostic Features

The essential feature of Generalized Anxiety Disorder is excessive anxiety and worry (apprehensive expectation), occurring more days than not for a period of at least 6 months, about a number of events or activities (Criterion A). The individual finds it difficult to control the worry (Criterion B). The anxiety and worry are accompanied by at least three additional symptoms from a list that includes restlessness, being easily fatigued, difficulty concentrating, irritability, muscle tension, and disturbed sleep (only one additional symptom is required in children) (Criterion C). The focus of the anxiety and worry is not confined to features of another Axis I disorder such as having a Panic Attack (as in Panic Disorder), being embarrassed in public (as in Social Phobia), being contaminated (as in Obsessive-Compulsive Disorder), being away from home or close relatives (as in Separation Anxiety Disorder), gaining weight (as in Anorexia Nervosa), having multiple physical complaints (as in Somatization Disorder), or having a serious illness (as in Hypochondriasis), and the anxiety and worry do not occur exclusively during Posttraumatic Stress Disorder (Criterion D). Although individuals with Generalized Anxiety Disorder may not always identify the worries as "excessive," they report subjective distress due to constant worry, have difficulty controlling the worry, or experience related impairment in social, occupational, or other important areas of functioning (Criterion E). The disturbance is not due to the direct physiological effects of a substance (i.e., a drug of abuse, a medication, or toxin exposure) or a general medical condition and does not occur exclusively during a Mood Disorder, a Psychotic Disorder, or a Pervasive Developmental Disorder (Criterion F).

The intensity, duration, or frequency of the anxiety and worry is far out of proportion to the actual likelihood or impact of the feared event. The person finds it difficult to keep worrisome thoughts from interfering with attention to tasks at hand and has difficulty stopping the worry. Adults with Generalized Anxiety Disorder often worry about everyday, routine life circumstances such as possible job responsibilities, finances, the health of family members, misfortune to their children, or minor matters (such as household chores, car repairs, or being late for appointments). Children with Generalized Anxiety Disorder tend to worry excessively about their competence or the quality of their performance. During the course of the disorder, the focus of worry may shift from one concern to another.

Associated Features and Disorders

Associated with muscle tension, there may be trembling, twitching, feeling shaky, and muscle aches or soreness. Many individuals with Generalized Anxiety Disorder also experience somatic symptoms (e.g., cold, clammy hands; dry mouth; sweating; nausea or diarrhea; urinary frequency; trouble swallowing or a "lump in the throat") and an exaggerated startle response. Depressive symptoms are also common.

Generalized Anxiety Disorder very frequently co-occurs with Mood Disorders (e.g., Major Depressive Disorder or Dysthymic Disorder), with other Anxiety Disorders (e.g., Panic Disorder, Social Phobia, Specific Phobia), and with Substance-Related Disorders (e.g., Alcohol or Sedative, Hypnotic, or Anxiolytic Dependence or Abuse). Other conditions that may be associated with stress (e.g., irritable bowel syndrome, headaches) frequently accompany Generalized Anxiety Disorder.

Specific Culture, Age, and Gender Features

There is considerable cultural variation in the expression of anxiety (e.g., in some cultures, anxiety is expressed predominantly through somatic symptoms, in others through cognitive symptoms). It is important to consider the cultural context when evaluating whether worries about certain situations are excessive.

In children and adolescents with Generalized Anxiety Disorder, the anxieties and worries often concern the quality of their performance or competence at school or in sporting events, even when their performance is not being evaluated by others. There may be excessive concerns about punctuality. They may also worry about catastrophic events such as earthquakes or nuclear war. Children with the disorder may be overly conforming, perfectionist, and unsure of themselves and tend to redo tasks because of excessive dissatisfaction with less-than-perfect performance. They are typically over-zealous in seeking approval and require excessive reassurance about their performance and their other worries.

In clinical settings, the disorder is diagnosed somewhat more frequently in women than in men (about 55%–60% of those presenting with the disorder are female). In epidemiological studies, the sex ratio is approximately two-thirds female.

Prevalence

In a community sample, the 1-year prevalence rate for Generalized Anxiety Disorder was approximately 3%, and the lifetime prevalence rate was 5%. In anxiety disorder clinics, approximately 12% of the individuals present with Generalized Anxiety Disorder.

Course

Many individuals with Generalized Anxiety Disorder report that they have felt anxious and nervous all their lives. Although over half of those presenting for treatment report onset in childhood or adolescence, onset occurring after age 20 years is not uncommon. The course is chronic but fluctuating and often worsens during times of stress.

Familial Pattern

Anxiety as a trait has a familial association. Inconsistent findings have been reported regarding familial patterns for Generalized Anxiety Disorder, with most reports failing to find specific familial aggregation.

Differential Diagnosis

Generalized Anxiety Disorder must be distinguished from an **Anxiety Disorder Due to a General Medical Condition.** The diagnosis is Anxiety Disorder Due to a General Medical Condition if the anxiety symptoms are judged to be a direct physiological consequence of a specific general medical condition (e.g., pheochromocytoma, hyperthyroidism) (see p. 436). This determination is based on history, laboratory findings, or physical examination. A **Substance-Induced Anxiety Disorder** is distinguished from Generalized Anxiety Disorder by the fact that a substance (i.e., a drug of abuse, a medication, or exposure to a toxin) is judged to be etiologically related to the anxiety disturbance (see p. 439). For example, severe anxiety that occurs only in the context of heavy coffee consumption would be diagnosed as Caffeine-Induced Anxiety Disorder, With Generalized Anxiety.

When another Axis I disorder is present, an additional diagnosis of Generalized Anxiety Disorder should be made only when the focus of the anxiety and worry is unrelated to the other disorder, that is, the excessive worry is not restricted to having a

Panic Attack (as in **Panic Disorder**), being embarrassed in public (as in **Social Phobia**), being contaminated (as in **Obsessive-Compulsive Disorder**), gaining weight (as in **Anorexia Nervosa**), having a serious illness (as in **Hypochondriasis**), having multiple physical complaints (as in **Somatization Disorder**), or to concerns about the welfare of close relations or being away from them or from home (as in **Separation Anxiety Disorder**). For example, the anxiety present in Social Phobia is focused on upcoming social situations in which the individual must perform or be evaluated by others, whereas individuals with Generalized Anxiety Disorder experience anxiety whether or not they are being evaluated.

Several features distinguish the excessive worry of Generalized Anxiety Disorder from the **obsessional thoughts** of Obsessive-Compulsive Disorder. Obsessional thoughts are not simply excessive worries about everyday or real-life problems, but rather are ego-dystonic intrusions that often take the form of urges, impulses, and images in addition to thoughts. Finally, most obsessions are accompanied by compulsions that reduce the anxiety associated with the obsessions.

Anxiety is invariably present in **Posttraumatic Stress Disorder.** Generalized Anxiety Disorder is not diagnosed if the anxiety occurs exclusively during the course of Posttraumatic Stress Disorder. Anxiety may also be present in **Adjustment Disorder,** but this residual category should be used only when the criteria are not met for any other Anxiety Disorder (including Generalized Anxiety Disorder). Moreover, in Adjustment Disorder the anxiety occurs in response to a life stressor and does not persist for more than 6 months after the termination of the stressor or its consequences. Generalized anxiety is a common associated feature of **Mood Disorders** and **Psychotic Disorders** and should not be diagnosed separately if it occurs exclusively during the course of these conditions.

Several features distinguish Generalized Anxiety Disorder from **nonpathological anxiety.** First, the worries associated with Generalized Anxiety Disorder are difficult to control and typically interfere significantly with functioning, whereas the worries of everyday life are perceived as more controllable and can be put off until later. Second, the worries associated with Generalized Anxiety Disorder are more pervasive, pronounced, distressing, and of longer duration and frequently occur without precipitants. The more life circumstances about which a person worries excessively (finances, children's safety, job performance, car repairs), the more likely the diagnosis. Third, everyday worries are much less likely to be accompanied by physical symptoms (e.g., excessive fatigue, restlessness, feeling keyed up or on edge, irritability), although this is less true of children.

■ Diagnostic criteria for 300.02 Generalized Anxiety Disorder

A. Excessive anxiety and worry (apprehensive expectation), occurring more days than not for at least 6 months, about a number of events or activities (such as work or school performance).

B. The person finds it difficult to control the worry.

(continued)

☐ **Diagnostic criteria for 300.02 Generalized Anxiety Disorder** (*continued*)

C. The anxiety and worry are associated with three (or more) of the following six symptoms (with at least some symptoms present for more days than not for the past 6 months). **Note:** Only one item is required in children.

   (1) restlessness or feeling keyed up or on edge
   (2) being easily fatigued
   (3) difficulty concentrating or mind going blank
   (4) irritability
   (5) muscle tension
   (6) sleep disturbance (difficulty falling or staying asleep, or restless unsatisfying sleep)

D. The focus of the anxiety and worry is not confined to features of an Axis I disorder, e.g., the anxiety or worry is not about having a Panic Attack (as in Panic Disorder), being embarrassed in public (as in Social Phobia), being contaminated (as in Obsessive-Compulsive Disorder), being away from home or close relatives (as in Separation Anxiety Disorder), gaining weight (as in Anorexia Nervosa), having multiple physical complaints (as in Somatization Disorder), or having a serious illness (as in Hypochondriasis), and the anxiety and worry do not occur exclusively during Posttraumatic Stress Disorder.

E. The anxiety, worry, or physical symptoms cause clinically significant distress or impairment in social, occupational, or other important areas of functioning.

F. The disturbance is not due to the direct physiological effects of a substance (e.g., a drug of abuse, a medication) or a general medical condition (e.g., hyperthyroidism) and does not occur exclusively during a Mood Disorder, a Psychotic Disorder, or a Pervasive Developmental Disorder.

293.89 Anxiety Disorder
Due to a General Medical Condition

Diagnostic Features

The essential feature of Anxiety Disorder Due to a General Medical Condition is clinically significant anxiety that is judged to be due to the direct physiological effects of a general medical condition. Symptoms can include prominent, generalized anxiety symptoms, Panic Attacks, or obsessions or compulsions (Criterion A). There must be evidence from the history, physical examination, or laboratory findings that the disturbance is the direct physiological consequence of a general medical condition (Criterion B). The disturbance is not better accounted for by another mental disorder, such as Adjustment Disorder With Anxiety, in which the stressor is the general medical condition (Criterion C). The diagnosis is not made if the anxiety symptoms occur only during the course of a delirium (Criterion D). The anxiety symptoms must cause clinically significant distress or impairment in social, occupational, or other important areas of functioning (Criterion E).

In determining whether the anxiety symptoms are due to a general medical condition, the clinician must first establish the presence of a general medical condition. Further, the clinician must establish that the anxiety symptoms are etiologically related to the general medical condition through a physiological mechanism. A careful and comprehensive assessment of multiple factors is necessary to make this judgment. Although there are no infallible guidelines for determining whether the relationship between the anxiety symptoms and the general medical condition is etiological, several considerations provide some guidance in this area. One consideration is the presence of a temporal association between the onset, exacerbation, or remission of the general medical condition and the anxiety symptoms. A second consideration is the presence of features that are atypical of a primary Anxiety Disorder (e.g., atypical age at onset or course, or absence of family history). Evidence from the literature that suggests that there can be a direct association between the general medical condition in question and the development of anxiety symptoms may provide a useful context in the assessment of a particular situation. In addition, the clinician must also judge that the disturbance is not better accounted for by a primary Anxiety Disorder, a Substance-Induced Anxiety Disorder, or other primary mental disorders (e.g., Adjustment Disorder). These determinations are explained in greater detail in the "Mental Disorders Due to a General Medical Condition" section (p. 165).

Specifiers

The following specifiers can be used to indicate which symptom presentation predominates in Anxiety Disorder Due to a General Medical Condition:

> **With Generalized Anxiety.**   This specifier may be used if excessive anxiety or worry about a number of events or activities predominates in the clinical presentation.
> **With Panic Attacks.**   This specifier may be used if Panic Attacks (see p. 394) predominate in the clinical presentation.
> **With Obsessive-Compulsive Symptoms.**   This specifier may be used if obsessions or compulsions predominate in the clinical presentation.

Recording Procedures

In recording the diagnosis of Anxiety Disorder Due to a General Medical Condition, the clinician should first note the presence of the Anxiety Disorder, then the identified general medical condition judged to be causing the disturbance, and finally the appropriate specifier indicating the predominant symptom presentation on Axis I (e.g., 293.89 Anxiety Disorder Due to Thyrotoxicosis, With Generalized Anxiety). The ICD-9-CM code for the general medical condition should also be noted on Axis III (e.g., 242.9 thyrotoxicosis). See Appendix G for a list of ICD-9-CM diagnostic codes for selected general medical conditions.

Associated General Medical Conditions

A variety of general medical conditions may cause anxiety symptoms, including endocrine conditions (e.g., hyper- and hypothyroidism, pheochromocytoma, hypoglycemia, hyperadrenocorticism), cardiovascular conditions (e.g., congestive heart failure, pulmonary embolism, arrhythmia), respiratory conditions (e.g., chronic obstructive pulmonary disease, pneumonia, hyperventilation), metabolic conditions (e.g., vitamin B_{12} deficiency, porphyria), and neurological conditions (e.g., neoplasms, vestibular dysfunction, encephalitis). The associated physical examination findings, laboratory findings, and patterns of prevalence or onset reflect the etiological general medical condition.

Differential Diagnosis

A separate diagnosis of Anxiety Disorder Due to a General Medical Condition is not given if the anxiety disturbance occurs exclusively during the course of a **delirium.** If the presentation includes a mix of different types of symptoms (e.g., mood and anxiety), the specific Mental Disorder Due to a General Medical Condition depends on which symptoms predominate in the clinical picture.

If there is evidence of recent or prolonged substance use (including medications with psychoactive effects), withdrawal from a substance, or exposure to a toxin, a **Substance-Induced Anxiety Disorder** should be considered. It may be useful to obtain a urine or blood drug screen or other appropriate laboratory evaluation. Symptoms that occur during or shortly after (i.e., within 4 weeks of) Substance Intoxication or Withdrawal or after medication use may be especially indicative of a Substance-Induced Anxiety Disorder, depending on the type, duration, or amount of the substance used. If the clinician has ascertained that the disturbance is due to both a general medical condition and substance use, both diagnoses (i.e., Anxiety Disorder Due to a General Medical Condition and Substance-Induced Anxiety Disorder) can be given.

Anxiety Disorder Due to a General Medical Condition should be distinguished from a **primary Anxiety Disorder** (especially Panic Disorder, Generalized Anxiety Disorder, and Obsessive-Compulsive Disorder) and from **Adjustment Disorder With Anxiety** or **With Mixed Anxiety and Depressed Mood** (e.g., a maladaptive response to the stress of having a general medical condition). In primary mental disorders, no specific and direct causative physiological mechanisms associated with a general medical condition can be demonstrated. Late age at onset and the absence of a personal or family history of Anxiety Disorders suggest the need for a thorough assessment to rule out the diagnosis of Anxiety Disorder Due to a General Medical Condition. In addition, anxiety symptoms may be an **associated feature of another mental disorder** (e.g., Schizophrenia, Anorexia Nervosa).

Anxiety Disorder Not Otherwise Specified is diagnosed if the clinician cannot determine whether the anxiety disturbance is primary, substance induced, or due to a general medical condition.

■ Diagnostic criteria for 293.89 Anxiety Disorder Due to . . . [*Indicate the General Medical Condition*]

A. Prominent anxiety, Panic Attacks, or obsessions or compulsions predominate in the clinical picture.

B. There is evidence from the history, physical examination, or laboratory findings that the disturbance is the direct physiological consequence of a general medical condition.

C. The disturbance is not better accounted for by another mental disorder (e.g., Adjustment Disorder With Anxiety in which the stressor is a serious general medical condition).

D. The disturbance does not occur exclusively during the course of a delirium.

E. The disturbance causes clinically significant distress or impairment in social, occupational, or other important areas of functioning.

Specify if:
With Generalized Anxiety: if excessive anxiety or worry about a number of events or activities predominates in the clinical presentation
With Panic Attacks: if Panic Attacks (see p. 395) predominate in the clinical presentation
With Obsessive-Compulsive Symptoms: if obsessions or compulsions predominate in the clinical presentation

Coding note: Include the name of the general medical condition on Axis I, e.g., 293.89 Anxiety Disorder Due to Pheochromocytoma, With Generalized Anxiety; also code the general medical condition on Axis III (see Appendix G for codes).

Substance-Induced Anxiety Disorder

Diagnostic Features

The essential features of Substance-Induced Anxiety Disorder are prominent anxiety symptoms (Criterion A) that are judged to be due to the direct physiological effects of a substance (i.e., a drug of abuse, a medication, or toxin exposure) (Criterion B). Depending on the nature of the substance and the context in which the symptoms occur (i.e., during intoxication or withdrawal), the disturbance may involve prominent anxiety, Panic Attacks, phobias, or obsessions or compulsions. Although the clinical presentation of the Substance-Induced Anxiety Disorder may resemble that of Panic Disorder, Generalized Anxiety Disorder, Social Phobia, or Obsessive-Compulsive Disorder, the full criteria for one of these disorders need not be met. The disturbance must not be better accounted for by a mental disorder (e.g., another Anxiety Disorder) that is not substance induced (Criterion C). The diagnosis is not made if the anxiety symptoms occur only during the course of a delirium (Criterion D). The symptoms must cause clinically significant distress or impairment in social, occupational, or other important areas of functioning (Criterion E). This diagnosis should be made instead of a diagnosis of Substance Intoxication or Substance Withdrawal only when the anxiety symptoms are in excess of those usually associated with the intoxication or withdrawal syndrome and when the anxiety symptoms are sufficiently severe to warrant independent clinical attention. For a more detailed discussion of Substance-Related Disorders, see p. 175.

A Substance-Induced Anxiety Disorder is distinguished from a primary Anxiety Disorder by considering the onset, course, and other factors. For drugs of abuse, there must be evidence from the history, physical examination, or laboratory findings of intoxication or withdrawal. Substance-Induced Anxiety Disorders arise only in association with intoxication or withdrawal states, whereas primary Anxiety Disorders may precede the onset of substance use or occur during times of sustained abstinence. Because the withdrawal state for some substances (e.g., some benzodiazepines) can be relatively protracted, the onset of the anxiety symptoms can occur up to 4 weeks after cessation of substance use. Another consideration is the presence of features that are atypical of a primary Anxiety Disorder (e.g., atypical age at onset or course). For example, the onset of Panic Disorder after age 45 years (which is rare) or the presence of atypical symptoms during a Panic Attack (e.g., true vertigo; loss of balance, consciousness, or bladder or bowel control; headaches; slurred speech; or amnesia) may suggest a substance-induced etiology. In contrast, factors suggesting that the anxiety symptoms are better accounted for by a primary Anxiety Disorder include persistence of anxiety symptoms for a substantial period of time (i.e., about a month) after the end of Substance Intoxication or acute Withdrawal; the development of symptoms that are substantially in excess of what would be expected given the type or amount of the substance used or the duration of use; or a history of prior recurrent primary Anxiety Disorders.

Specifiers

The following specifiers can be used to indicate which symptom presentation predominates:

> **With Generalized Anxiety.** This specifier may be used if excessive anxiety or worry about a number of events or activities predominates in the clinical presentation.
>
> **With Panic Attacks.** This specifier may be used if Panic Attacks (see p. 394) predominate in the clinical presentation.
>
> **With Obsessive-Compulsive Symptoms.** This specifier may be used if obsessions or compulsions predominate in the clinical presentation.
>
> **With Phobic Symptoms.** This specifier may be used if phobic symptoms predominate in the clinical presentation.

The context of the development of the anxiety symptoms may be indicated by using one of the following specifiers:

> **With Onset During Intoxication.** This specifier should be used if criteria for intoxication with the substance are met and the symptoms develop during the intoxication syndrome.

With Onset During Withdrawal. This specifier should be used if criteria for withdrawal from the substance are met and the symptoms develop during, or shortly after, a withdrawal syndrome.

Recording Procedures

The name of the diagnosis of Substance-Induced Anxiety Disorder begins with the specific substance (e.g., alcohol, methylphenidate, thyroxine) that is presumed to be causing the anxiety symptoms. The diagnostic code is selected from the listing of classes of substances provided in the criteria set. For substances that do not fit into any of the classes (e.g., thyroxine), the code for "Other Substance" should be used. In addition, for medications prescribed at therapeutic doses, the specific medication can be indicated by listing the appropriate E-code on Axis I (see Appendix G). The name of the disorder (e.g., Caffeine-Induced Anxiety Disorder) is followed by the specification of the predominant symptom presentation and the context in which the symptoms developed (e.g., 292.89 Caffeine-Induced Anxiety Disorder, With Panic Attacks, With Onset During Intoxication). When more than one substance is judged to play a significant role in the development of anxiety symptoms, each should be listed separately (e.g., 292.89 Cocaine-Induced Anxiety Disorder, With Generalized Anxiety, With Onset During Intoxication; 291.8 Alcohol-Induced Anxiety Disorder, With Generalized Anxiety, With Onset During Withdrawal). If a substance is judged to be the etiological factor, but the specific substance or class of substances is unknown, the category 292.89 Unknown Substance–Induced Anxiety Disorder should be used.

Specific Substances

Anxiety Disorders can occur in association with **intoxication** with the following classes of substances: alcohol; amphetamine and related substances; caffeine; cannabis; cocaine; hallucinogens; inhalants; phencyclidine and related substances; and other or unknown substances. Anxiety Disorders can occur in association with **withdrawal** from the following classes of substances: alcohol; cocaine; sedatives, hypnotics, and anxiolytics; and other or unknown substances.

Some of the medications reported to evoke anxiety symptoms include anesthetics and analgesics, sympathomimetics or other bronchodilators, anticholinergics, insulin, thyroid preparations, oral contraceptives, antihistamines, antiparkinsonian medications, corticosteroids, antihypertensive and cardiovascular medications, anticonvulsants, lithium carbonate, antipsychotic medications, and antidepressant medications. Heavy metals and toxins (e.g., volatile substances such as gasoline and paint, organophosphate insecticides, nerve gases, carbon monoxide, carbon dioxide) may also cause anxiety symptoms.

Differential Diagnosis

Anxiety symptoms commonly occur in **Substance Intoxication** and **Substance Withdrawal.** The diagnosis of the substance-specific intoxication or substance-specific withdrawal will usually suffice to categorize the symptom presentation. A diagnosis of Substance-Induced Anxiety Disorder should be made instead of a diagnosis of Substance Intoxication or Substance Withdrawal only when the anxiety symptoms are judged to be in excess of those usually associated with the intoxication or withdrawal syndrome and when the anxiety symptoms are sufficiently severe to warrant independent clinical attention. For example, anxiety symptoms are a characteristic feature of Alcohol Withdrawal. Alcohol-Induced Anxiety Disorder should be diagnosed instead of Alcohol Withdrawal only if the anxiety symptoms are more severe than those usually encountered with Alcohol Withdrawal and are sufficiently severe to be a separate focus of attention and treatment. If substance-induced anxiety symptoms occur exclusively during the course of a **delirium,** the anxiety symptoms are considered to be an associated feature of the delirium and are not diagnosed separately. In **substance-induced presentations that contain a mix of different types of symptoms** (e.g., mood, psychotic, and anxiety), the specific type of Substance-Induced Disorder to be diagnosed depends on which type of symptoms predominates in the clinical presentation.

A Substance-Induced Anxiety Disorder is distinguished from a **primary Anxiety Disorder** by the fact that a substance is judged to be etiologically related to the symptoms (see p. 440).

A Substance-Induced Anxiety Disorder due to a prescribed treatment for a mental disorder or general medical condition must have its onset while the person is receiving the medication (or during withdrawal, if a withdrawal syndrome is associated with the medication). Once the treatment is discontinued, the anxiety symptoms will usually remit within days to several weeks (depending on the half-life of the substance and the presence of a withdrawal syndrome). If symptoms persist beyond 4 weeks, other causes for the anxiety symptoms should be considered.

Because individuals with general medical conditions often take medications for those conditions, the clinician must consider the possibility that the anxiety symptoms are caused by the physiological consequences of the general medical condition rather than the medication, in which case **Anxiety Disorder Due to a General Medical Condition** is diagnosed. The history often provides the primary basis for such a judgment. At times, a change in the treatment for the general medical condition (e.g., medication substitution or discontinuation) may be needed to determine empirically for that person whether or not the medication is the causative agent. If the clinician has ascertained that the disturbance is due to both a general medical condition and substance use, both diagnoses (i.e., Anxiety Disorder Due to a General Medical Condition and Substance-Induced Anxiety Disorder) may be given. When there is insufficient evidence to determine whether the anxiety symptoms are due to a substance (including a medication) or to a general medical condition or are primary (i.e., not due to either a substance or a general medical condition), **Anxiety Disorder Not Otherwise Specified** would be indicated.

■ Diagnostic criteria for Substance-Induced Anxiety Disorder

A. Prominent anxiety, Panic Attacks, or obsessions or compulsions pre-dominate in the clinical picture.

B. There is evidence from the history, physical examination, or laboratory findings of either (1) or (2):

   (1) the symptoms in Criterion A developed during, or within 1 month of, Substance Intoxication or Withdrawal

   (2) medication use is etiologically related to the disturbance

C. The disturbance is not better accounted for by an Anxiety Disorder that is not substance induced. Evidence that the symptoms are better accounted for by an Anxiety Disorder that is not substance induced might include the following: the symptoms precede the onset of the substance use (or medication use); the symptoms persist for a substantial period of time (e.g., about a month) after the cessation of acute withdrawal or severe intoxication or are substantially in excess of what would be expected given the type or amount of the substance used or the duration of use; or there is other evidence suggesting the existence of an independent non-substance-induced Anxiety Disorder (e.g., a history of recurrent non-substance-related episodes).

D. The disturbance does not occur exclusively during the course of a delirium.

E. The disturbance causes clinically significant distress or impairment in social, occupational, or other important areas of functioning.

Note: This diagnosis should be made instead of a diagnosis of Substance Intoxi-cation or Substance Withdrawal only when the anxiety symptoms are in excess of those usually associated with the intoxication or withdrawal syndrome and when the anxiety symptoms are sufficiently severe to warrant independent clinical attention.

Code [Specific Substance]–Induced Anxiety Disorder
   (291.8 Alcohol; 292.89 Amphetamine (or Amphetamine-Like Substance); 292.89 Caffeine; 292.89 Cannabis; 292.89 Cocaine; 292.89 Hallucinogen; 292.89 Inhalant; 292.89 Phencyclidine (or Phencyclidine-Like Substance); 292.89 Sedative, Hypnotic, or Anxiolytic; 292.89 Other [or Unknown] Substance)

Specify if:
   With Generalized Anxiety: if excessive anxiety or worry about a number of events or activities predominates in the clinical presentation
   With Panic Attacks: if Panic Attacks (see p. 395) predominate in the clinical presentation

(continued)

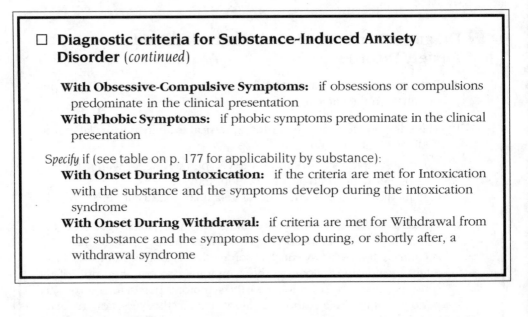

☐ **Diagnostic criteria for Substance-Induced Anxiety Disorder** (*continued*)

With Obsessive-Compulsive Symptoms: if obsessions or compulsions predominate in the clinical presentation
With Phobic Symptoms: if phobic symptoms predominate in the clinical presentation

Specify if (see table on p. 177 for applicability by substance):
With Onset During Intoxication: if the criteria are met for Intoxication with the substance and the symptoms develop during the intoxication syndrome
With Onset During Withdrawal: if criteria are met for Withdrawal from the substance and the symptoms develop during, or shortly after, a withdrawal syndrome

300.00   Anxiety Disorder Not Otherwise Specified

This category includes disorders with prominent anxiety or phobic avoidance that do not meet criteria for any specific Anxiety Disorder, Adjustment Disorder With Anxiety, or Adjustment Disorder With Mixed Anxiety and Depressed Mood. Examples include

1. Mixed anxiety-depressive disorder: clinically significant symptoms of anxiety and depression, but the criteria are not met for either a specific Mood Disorder or a specific Anxiety Disorder (see p. 723 for suggested research criteria)
2. Clinically significant social phobic symptoms that are related to the social impact of having a general medical condition or mental disorder (e.g., Parkinson's disease, dermatological conditions, Stuttering, Anorexia Nervosa, Body Dysmorphic Disorder)
3. Situations in which the clinician has concluded that an Anxiety Disorder is present but is unable to determine whether it is primary, due to a general medical condition, or substance induced

Somatoform Disorders

The common feature of the Somatoform Disorders is the presence of physical symptoms that suggest a general medical condition (hence, the term *somatoform*) and are not fully explained by a general medical condition, by the direct effects of a substance, or by another mental disorder (e.g., Panic Disorder). The symptoms must cause clinically significant distress or impairment in social, occupational, or other areas of functioning. In contrast to Factitious Disorders and Malingering, the physical symptoms are not intentional (i.e., under voluntary control). Somatoform Disorders differ from Psychological Factors Affecting Medical Condition in that there is no diagnosable general medical condition to fully account for the physical symptoms. The grouping of these disorders in a single section is based on clinical utility (i.e., the need to exclude occult general medical conditions or substance-induced etiologies for the bodily symptoms) rather than on assumptions regarding shared etiology or mechanism. These disorders are often encountered in general medical settings.

The following Somatoform Disorders are included in this section:

Somatization Disorder (historically referred to as hysteria or Briquet's syndrome) is a polysymptomatic disorder that begins before age 30 years, extends over a period of years, and is characterized by a combination of pain, gastrointestinal, sexual, and pseudoneurological symptoms.

Undifferentiated Somatoform Disorder is characterized by unexplained physical complaints, lasting at least 6 months, that are below the threshold for a diagnosis of Somatization Disorder.

Conversion Disorder involves unexplained symptoms or deficits affecting voluntary motor or sensory function that suggest a neurological or other general medical condition. Psychological factors are judged to be associated with the symptoms or deficits.

Pain Disorder is characterized by pain as the predominant focus of clinical attention. In addition, psychological factors are judged to have an important role in its onset, severity, exacerbation, or maintenance.

Hypochondriasis is the preoccupation with the fear of having, or the idea that one has, a serious disease based on the person's misinterpretation of bodily symptoms or bodily functions.

Body Dysmorphic Disorder is the preoccupation with an imagined or exaggerated defect in physical appearance.

Somatoform Disorder Not Otherwise Specified is included for coding disorders with somatoform symptoms that do not meet the criteria for any of the specific Somatoform Disorders.

300.81   Somatization Disorder

Diagnostic Features

The essential feature of Somatization Disorder is a pattern of recurring, multiple, clinically significant somatic complaints. A somatic complaint is considered to be clinically significant if it results in medical treatment (e.g., the taking of medication) or causes significant impairment in social, occupational, or other important areas of functioning. The somatic complaints must begin before age 30 years and occur over a period of several years (Criterion A). The multiple somatic complaints cannot be fully explained by any known general medical condition or the direct effects of a substance. If they occur in the presence of a general medical condition, the physical complaints or resulting social or occupational impairment are in excess of what would be expected from the history, physical examination, or laboratory tests (Criterion C). There must be a history of pain related to at least four different sites (e.g., head, abdomen, back, joints, extremities, chest, rectum) or functions (e.g., menstruation, sexual intercourse, urination) (Criterion B1). There also must be a history of at least two gastrointestinal symptoms other than pain (Criterion B2). Most individuals with the disorder describe the presence of nausea and abdominal bloating. Vomiting, diarrhea, and food intolerance are less common. Gastrointestinal complaints often lead to frequent X-ray examinations and can result in abdominal surgery that in retrospect was unnecessary. There must be a history of at least one sexual or reproductive symptom other than pain (Criterion B3). In women, this may consist of irregular menses, menorrhagia, or vomiting throughout pregnancy. In men, there may be symptoms such as erectile or ejaculatory dysfunction. Both women and men may be subject to sexual indifference. Finally, there must also be a history of at least one symptom, other than pain, that suggests a neurological condition (conversion symptoms such as impaired coordination or balance, paralysis or localized weakness, difficulty swallowing or lump in throat, aphonia, urinary retention, hallucinations, loss of touch or pain sensation, double vision, blindness, deafness, or seizures; dissociative symptoms such as amnesia; or loss of consciousness other than fainting) (Criterion B4). The symptoms in each of the groups have been listed in the approximate order of their reported frequency. Finally, the unexplained symptoms in Somatization Disorder are not intentionally feigned or produced (as in Factitious Disorder or Malingering) (Criterion D).

Associated Features and Disorders

Associated descriptive features and mental disorders.   Individuals with Somatization Disorder usually describe their complaints in colorful, exaggerated terms, but specific factual information is often lacking. They are often inconsistent historians, so that a checklist approach to diagnostic interviewing may be less effective than a thorough review of medical treatments and hospitalizations to document a pattern of frequent somatic complaints. They often seek treatment from several physicians concurrently, which may lead to complicated and sometimes hazardous combinations of treatments. Prominent anxiety symptoms and depressed mood are very common and may be the reason for being seen in mental health settings. There may be impulsive and antisocial behavior, suicide threats and attempts, and marital discord. The lives of these individuals, particularly those with associated Personality Disorders, are often as chaotic and complicated as their medical histories. Frequent use of medications may lead to side effects and Substance-Related Disorders. These individuals commonly undergo numerous medical examinations, diagnostic procedures, surgeries, and hospitalizations, which expose the person to an increased risk of morbidity associated with these procedures. Major Depressive Disorder, Panic Disorder, and Substance-Related Disorders are frequently associated with Somatization Disorder. Histrionic, Borderline, and Antisocial Personality Disorders are the most frequently associated Personality Disorders.

Associated laboratory findings.   Laboratory test results are remarkable for the absence of findings to support the subjective complaints.

Associated physical examination findings and general medical conditions. Physical examination is remarkable for the absence of objective findings to fully explain the many subjective complaints of individuals with Somatization Disorder. These individuals may be diagnosed with so-called functional disorders (e.g., irritable bowel syndrome). However, because these syndromes are as yet without established objective signs or specific laboratory findings, their symptoms may count toward a diagnosis of Somatization Disorder.

Specific Culture and Gender Features

The type and frequency of somatic symptoms may differ across cultures. For example, burning hands and feet or the nondelusional experience of worms in the head or ants crawling under the skin represent pseudoneurological symptoms that are more common in Africa and South Asia than in North America. Symptoms related to male reproductive function may be more prevalent in cultures in which there is widespread concern about semen loss (e.g., *dhat* syndrome in India). Accordingly, the symptom reviews should be adjusted to the culture. The symptoms listed in this manual are examples that have been found most diagnostic in the United States. It should be noted that the order of frequency was derived from studies done in the United States.

Somatization Disorder occurs only rarely in men in the United States, but the higher reported frequency in Greek and Puerto Rican men suggests that cultural factors may influence the sex ratio.

Prevalence

Studies have reported widely variable lifetime prevalence rates of Somatization Disorder, ranging from 0.2% to 2% among women and less than 0.2% in men. Differences in rates may depend on whether the interviewer is a physician, on the method of assessment, and on the demographic variables in the samples studied. When nonphysician interviewers are used, Somatization Disorder is much less frequently diagnosed.

Course

Somatization Disorder is a chronic but fluctuating disorder that rarely remits completely. A year seldom passes without the individual seeking some medical attention prompted by unexplained somatic complaints. Diagnostic criteria are typically met before age 25 years, but initial symptoms are often present by adolescence. Menstrual difficulties may be one of the earliest symptoms in women. Sexual symptoms are often associated with marital discord.

Familial Pattern

Somatization Disorder is observed in 10%–20% of female first-degree biological relatives of women with Somatization Disorder. The male relatives of women with this disorder show an increased risk of Antisocial Personality Disorder and Substance-Related Disorders. Adoption studies indicate that both genetic and environmental factors contribute to the risk for Antisocial Personality Disorder, Substance-Related Disorders, and Somatization Disorder. Having a biological or adoptive parent with any of these disorders increases the risk of developing either Antisocial Personality Disorder, a Substance-Related Disorder, or Somatization Disorder.

Differential Diagnosis

The symptom picture encountered in Somatization Disorder is frequently nonspecific and can overlap with a multitude of **general medical conditions.** Three features that suggest a diagnosis of Somatization Disorder rather than a general medical condition include 1) involvement of multiple organ systems, 2) early onset and chronic course without development of physical signs or structural abnormalities, and 3) absence of laboratory abnormalities that are characteristic of the suggested general medical condition. It is still necessary to rule out general medical conditions that are characterized by vague, multiple, and confusing somatic symptoms (e.g., hyperparathyroidism, acute intermittent porphyria, multiple sclerosis, systemic lupus erythematosus). Moreover, Somatization Disorder does not protect individuals from having other independent general medical conditions. Objective findings should be evaluated without undue reliance on subjective complaints. The onset of multiple physical symptoms late in life is almost always due to a general medical condition.

Schizophrenia with multiple somatic delusions needs to be differentiated from the nondelusional somatic complaints of individuals with Somatization Disorder. In rare instances, individuals with Somatization Disorder also have Schizophrenia, in which case both diagnoses should be noted. Furthermore, hallucinations can occur as pseudoneurological symptoms and must be distinguished from the typical hallucinations seen in Schizophrenia (see p. 275).

It can be very difficult to distinguish between **Anxiety Disorders** and Somatization Disorder. In **Panic Disorder,** multiple somatic symptoms are also present, but these occur primarily during Panic Attacks. However, Panic Disorder may coexist with Somatization Disorder; when the somatic symptoms occur at times other than during Panic Attacks, both diagnoses may be made. Individuals with **Generalized Anxiety Disorder** may have a multitude of physical complaints associated with their generalized anxiety, but the focus of the anxiety and worry is not limited to the physical complaints. Individuals with **Mood Disorders,** particularly **Depressive Disorders,** may present with somatic complaints, most commonly headache, gastrointestinal disturbances, or unexplained pain. Individuals with Somatization Disorder have physical complaints recurrently throughout most of their lives, regardless of their current mood state, whereas physical complaints in Depressive Disorders are limited to episodes of depressed mood. Individuals with Somatization Disorder also often present with depressive complaints. If criteria are met for both Somatization Disorder and a Mood Disorder, both may be diagnosed.

By definition, all individuals with Somatization Disorder have a history of pain symptoms, sexual symptoms, and conversion or dissociative symptoms. Therefore, if these symptoms occur exclusively during the course of Somatization Disorder, there should not be an additional diagnosis of **Pain Disorder Associated With Psychological Factors, a Sexual Dysfunction, Conversion Disorder,** or a **Dissociative Disorder. Hypochondriasis** is not be diagnosed if preoccupation with fears of having a serious illness occurs exclusively during the course of Somatization Disorder.

The criteria for Somatization Disorder in this manual are slightly more restrictive than the original criteria for **Briquet's syndrome.** Somatoform presentations that do not meet criteria for Somatization Disorder should be classified as **Undifferentiated Somatoform Disorder** if the duration of the syndrome is 6 months or longer, or **Somatoform Disorder Not Otherwise Specified** for presentations of shorter duration.

In **Factitious Disorder With Predominantly Physical Signs and Symptoms** and **Malingering,** somatic symptoms may be intentionally produced to assume the sick role or for gain, respectively. Symptoms that are intentionally produced should not count toward a diagnosis of Somatization Disorder. However, the presence of some factitious or malingered symptoms, mixed with other nonintentional symptoms, is not uncommon. In such mixed cases, both Somatization Disorder and a Factitious Disorder or Malingering should be diagnosed.

■ Diagnostic criteria for 300.81 Somatization Disorder

A. A history of many physical complaints beginning before age 30 years that occur over a period of several years and result in treatment being sought or significant impairment in social, occupational, or other important areas of functioning.

B. Each of the following criteria must have been met, with individual symptoms occurring at any time during the course of the disturbance:

   (1) *four pain symptoms:* a history of pain related to at least four different sites or functions (e.g., head, abdomen, back, joints, extremities, chest, rectum, during menstruation, during sexual intercourse, or during urination)

   (2) *two gastrointestinal symptoms:* a history of at least two gastrointestinal symptoms other than pain (e.g., nausea, bloating, vomiting other than during pregnancy, diarrhea, or intolerance of several different foods)

   (3) *one sexual symptom:* a history of at least one sexual or reproductive symptom other than pain (e.g., sexual indifference, erectile or ejaculatory dysfunction, irregular menses, excessive menstrual bleeding, vomiting throughout pregnancy)

   (4) *one pseudoneurological symptom:* a history of at least one symptom or deficit suggesting a neurological condition not limited to pain (conversion symptoms such as impaired coordination or balance, paralysis or localized weakness, difficulty swallowing or lump in throat, aphonia, urinary retention, hallucinations, loss of touch or pain sensation, double vision, blindness, deafness, seizures; dissociative symptoms such as amnesia; or loss of consciousness other than fainting)

(continued)

☐ **Diagnostic criteria for 300.81 Somatization Disorder**
(continued)

C. Either (1) or (2):

(1) after appropriate investigation, each of the symptoms in Criterion B cannot be fully explained by a known general medical condition or the direct effects of a substance (e.g., a drug of abuse, a medication)

(2) when there is a related general medical condition, the physical complaints or resulting social or occupational impairment are in excess of what would be expected from the history, physical examination, or laboratory findings

D. The symptoms are not intentionally produced or feigned (as in Factitious Disorder or Malingering).

300.81 Undifferentiated Somatoform Disorder

Diagnostic Features

The essential feature of Undifferentiated Somatoform Disorder is one or more physical complaints (Criterion A) that persist for 6 months or longer (Criterion D). The most frequent complaints are chronic fatigue, loss of appetite, or gastrointestinal or genito-urinary symptoms. These symptoms cannot be fully explained by any known general medical condition or the direct effects of a substance (e.g., the effects of injury, substance use, or medication side effects), or the physical complaints or resultant impairment are grossly in excess of what would be expected from the history, physical examination, or laboratory findings (Criterion B). The symptoms must cause clinically significant distress or impairment in social, occupational, or other important areas of functioning (Criterion C). The diagnosis is not made when the symptoms are better accounted for by another mental disorder (e.g., another Somatoform Disorder, Sexual Dysfunction, Mood Disorder, Anxiety Disorder, Sleep Disorder, or Psychotic Disorder) (Criterion E). The symptoms are not intentionally produced or feigned (as in Factitious Disorder or Malingering) (Criterion F).

This is a residual category for those persistent somatoform presentations that do not meet the full criteria for Somatization Disorder or another Somatoform Disorder. Symptoms that may be seen include the examples listed for Somatization Disorder. There may be a single circumscribed symptom, such as nausea, or, more commonly, multiple physical symptoms. The chronic unexplained physical complaints often lead to medical consultation, typically with a primary care physician.

Specific Culture, Age, and Gender Features

Medically unexplained symptoms and worry about physical illness may constitute culturally shaped "idioms of distress" that are employed to express concerns about a broad range of personal and social problems, without necessarily indicating psychopathology. The highest frequency of unexplained physical complaints occurs in young women of low socioeconomic status, but such symptoms are not limited to any age, gender, or sociocultural group. "Neurasthenia," a syndrome described frequently in many parts of the world and characterized by fatigue and weakness, is classified in DSM-IV as Undifferentiated Somatoform Disorder if symptoms have persisted for longer than 6 months.

Course

The course of individual unexplained physical complaints is unpredictable. The eventual diagnosis of a general medical condition or another mental disorder is frequent.

Differential Diagnosis

Also refer to the "Differential Diagnosis" section for Somatization Disorder (see p. 448). Undifferentiated Somatoform Disorder is differentiated from **Somatization Disorder** by the requirement in Somatization Disorder of a multiplicity of symptoms of several years' duration and an onset before age 30 years. Individuals with Somatization Disorder are typically inconsistent historians, so that at one evaluation they may report many symptoms that fulfill criteria for Somatization Disorder, whereas at another time they may report many fewer symptoms that fail to meet full criteria. If the physical complaints have persisted for less than 6 months, a diagnosis of **Somatoform Disorder Not Otherwise Specified** should be made. Undifferentiated Somatoform Disorder is not diagnosed if the symptoms are better accounted for by another mental disorder. Other mental disorders that frequently include unexplained physical complaints are **Major Depressive Disorder, Anxiety Disorders,** and **Adjustment Disorder.** In contrast to Undifferentiated Somatoform Disorder, the physical symptoms of **Factitious Disorders** and **Malingering** are intentionally produced or feigned. In Factitious Disorder, the motivation is to assume the sick role and to obtain medical evaluation and treatment, whereas in Malingering, more external incentives are apparent, such as financial compensation, avoidance of duty, evasion of criminal prosecution, or obtaining drugs.

■ **Diagnostic criteria for 300.81 Undifferentiated Somatoform Disorder**

A. One or more physical complaints (e.g., fatigue, loss of appetite, gastrointestinal or urinary complaints).

B. Either (1) or (2):

(1) after appropriate investigation, the symptoms cannot be fully explained by a known general medical condition or the direct effects of a substance (e.g., a drug of abuse, a medication)

(continued)

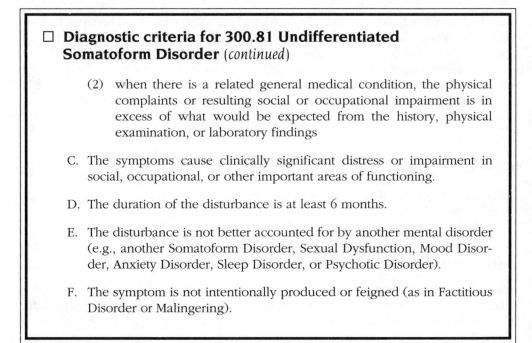

☐ **Diagnostic criteria for 300.81 Undifferentiated Somatoform Disorder** (*continued*)

    (2) when there is a related general medical condition, the physical complaints or resulting social or occupational impairment is in excess of what would be expected from the history, physical examination, or laboratory findings

C. The symptoms cause clinically significant distress or impairment in social, occupational, or other important areas of functioning.

D. The duration of the disturbance is at least 6 months.

E. The disturbance is not better accounted for by another mental disorder (e.g., another Somatoform Disorder, Sexual Dysfunction, Mood Disorder, Anxiety Disorder, Sleep Disorder, or Psychotic Disorder).

F. The symptom is not intentionally produced or feigned (as in Factitious Disorder or Malingering).

300.11   Conversion Disorder

Diagnostic Features

The essential feature of Conversion Disorder is the presence of symptoms or deficits affecting voluntary motor or sensory function that suggest a neurological or other general medical condition (Criterion A). Psychological factors are judged to be associated with the symptom or deficit, a judgment based on the observation that the initiation or exacerbation of the symptom or deficit is preceded by conflicts or other stressors (Criterion B). The symptoms are not intentionally produced or feigned, as in Factitious Disorder or Malingering (Criterion C). Conversion Disorder is not diagnosed if the symptoms or deficits are fully explained by a neurological or other general medical condition, by the direct effects of a substance, or as a culturally sanctioned behavior or experience (Criterion D). The problem must be clinically significant as evidenced by marked distress; impairment in social, occupational, or other important areas of functioning; or the fact that it warrants medical evaluation (Criterion E). Conversion Disorder is not diagnosed if symptoms are limited to pain or sexual dysfunction, occur exclusively during the course of Somatization Disorder, or are better accounted for by another mental disorder (Criterion F).

    Conversion symptoms are related to voluntary motor or sensory functioning and are thus referred to as "pseudoneurological." Motor symptoms or deficits include impaired coordination or balance, paralysis or localized weakness, aphonia, difficulty swallowing or a sensation of a lump in the throat, and urinary retention. Sensory symptoms or deficits include loss of touch or pain sensation, double vision, blindness, deafness, and hallucinations. Symptoms may also include seizures or convulsions. The more medically naive the person, the more implausible are the presenting symptoms. More sophisticated persons tend to have more subtle symptoms and deficits that may closely simulate neurological or other general medical conditions.

A diagnosis of Conversion Disorder should be made only after a thorough medical investigation has been performed to rule out an etiological neurological or general medical condition. Because a general medical etiology for many cases of apparent Conversion Disorder can take years to become evident, the diagnosis should be viewed as tentative and provisional. In early studies, general medical etiologies were later found in from one-quarter to one-half of persons initially diagnosed with conversion symptoms. In more recent studies, misdiagnosis is less evident, perhaps reflecting increased awareness of the disorder, as well as improved knowledge and diagnostic techniques. A history of other unexplained somatic (especially conversion) or dissociative symptoms signifies a greater likelihood that an apparent conversion symptom is not due to a general medical condition, especially if criteria for Somatization Disorder have been met in the past.

Conversion symptoms typically do not conform to known anatomical pathways and physiological mechanisms, but instead follow the individual's conceptualization of a condition. A "paralysis" may involve inability to perform a particular movement or to move an entire body part, rather than a deficit corresponding to patterns of motor innervation. Conversion symptoms are often inconsistent. A "paralyzed" extremity will be moved inadvertently while dressing or when attention is directed elsewhere. If placed above the head and released, a "paralyzed" arm will briefly retain its position, then fall to the side, rather than striking the head. Unacknowledged strength in antagonistic muscles, normal muscle tone, and intact reflexes may be demonstrated. An electro-myogram will be normal. Difficulty swallowing will be equal with liquids and solids. Conversion "anesthesia" of a foot or a hand may follow a so-called stocking-glove distribution with uniform (no proximal to distal gradient) loss of all sensory modalities (i.e., touch, temperature, and pain) sharply demarcated at an anatomical landmark rather than according to dermatomes. A conversion "seizure" will vary from convulsion to convulsion, and paroxysmal activity will not be evident on an EEG.

Even when following such guidelines carefully, caution must be exercised. Knowl-edge of anatomical and physiological mechanisms is incomplete and available methods of objective assessment have limitations. A broad range of neurological conditions may be misdiagnosed as Conversion Disorder. Prominent among them are multiple sclerosis, myasthenia gravis, and idiopathic or substance-induced dystonias. However, the pres-ence of a neurological condition does not preclude a diagnosis of Conversion Disorder. As many as one-third of individuals with conversion symptoms have a current or prior neurological condition. Conversion Disorder may be diagnosed in the presence of a neurological or other general medical condition if the symptoms are not fully explained given the nature and severity of the neurological or other general medical condition.

Traditionally, the term *conversion* derived from the hypothesis that the individual's somatic symptom represents a symbolic resolution of an unconscious psychological conflict, reducing anxiety and serving to keep the conflict out of awareness ("primary gain"). The individual might also derive "secondary gain" from the conversion symp-tom—that is, external benefits are obtained or noxious duties or responsibilities are evaded. Although the DSM-IV criteria set for Conversion Disorder does not necessarily imply that the symptoms involve such constructs, it does require that psychological factors be associated with their onset or exacerbation. Because psychological factors are so ubiquitously present in relation to general medical conditions, it can be difficult to establish whether a specific psychological factor is etiologically related to the symptom or deficit. However, a close temporal relationship between a conflict or stressor and the initiation or exacerbation of a symptom may be helpful in this determination, especially if the person has developed conversion symptoms under similar circumstances in the past.

Although the individual may derive secondary gain from the conversion symptom, unlike in Malingering or Factitious Disorder the symptoms are not intentionally produced to obtain the benefits. The determination that a symptom is not intentionally produced or feigned can also be difficult. Generally, it must be inferred from a careful evaluation of the context in which the symptom develops, especially relative to potential external rewards or the assumption of the sick role. Supplementing the person's self-report with additional sources of information (e.g., from associates or records) may be helpful.

Conversion Disorder is not diagnosed if a symptom is fully explained as a culturally sanctioned behavior or experience. For example, "visions" or "spells" that occur as part of religious rituals in which such behaviors are encouraged and expected would not justify a diagnosis of Conversion Disorder unless the symptom exceeded what is contextually expected and caused undue distress or impairment. In "epidemic hysteria," shared symptoms develop in a circumscribed group of people following "exposure" to a common precipitant. A diagnosis of Conversion Disorder should be made only if the individual experiences clinically significant distress or impairment.

Subtypes

The following subtypes are noted based on the nature of the presenting symptom or deficit:

With Motor Symptom or Deficit. This subtype includes such symptoms as impaired coordination or balance, paralysis or localized weakness, difficulty swallowing or "lump in throat," aphonia, and urinary retention.

With Sensory Symptom or Deficit. This subtype includes such symptoms as loss of touch or pain sensation, double vision, blindness, deafness, and hallucinations.

With Seizures or Convulsions. This subtype includes seizures or convulsions with voluntary motor or sensory components.

With Mixed Presentation. This subtype is used if symptoms of more than one category are evident.

Associated Features and Disorders

Associated descriptive features and mental disorders. Individuals with conversion symptoms may show *la belle indifference* (i.e., a relative lack of concern about the nature or implications of the symptom) or may also present in a dramatic or histrionic fashion. Because these individuals are often suggestible, their symptoms may be modified or resolved based on external cues; however, it must be cautioned that this is not specific to Conversion Disorder and may also occur with general medical conditions. Symptoms may be more common following extreme psychosocial stress (e.g., warfare or the recent death of a significant figure). Dependency and the adoption of a sick role may be fostered in the course of treatment. Other nonconversion somatic complaints are common. Associated mental disorders include Dissociative Disorders, Major Depressive Disorder, and Histrionic, Antisocial, and Dependent Personality Disorders.

Associated laboratory findings.   No specific laboratory abnormalities are associated with Conversion Disorder. In fact, it is the absence of expected findings that suggests and supports the diagnosis of Conversion Disorder. However, laboratory findings consistent with a general medical condition do not exclude the diagnosis of Conversion Disorder, because it only requires that a symptom not be fully explained by such a condition.

Associated physical examination findings and general medical conditions. Symptoms of Conversion Disorder typically do not conform to known anatomical pathways and physiological mechanisms. Thus, expected objective signs (e.g., reflex changes) are rarely present. However, a person may develop symptoms that resemble those observed in others or in themselves (e.g., individuals with epilepsy may simulate "seizures" that resemble those they have observed in others or how their own seizures were described to them). Generally, individual conversion symptoms are self-limited and do not lead to physical changes or disabilities. Rarely, physical changes such as atrophy and contractures may occur as a result of disuse or as sequelae to diagnostic or therapeutic procedures. It is important to note, however, that conversion symptoms can occur in individuals with neurological conditions.

Specific Culture, Age, and Gender Features

Conversion Disorder has been reported to be more common in rural populations, individuals of lower socioeconomic status, and individuals less knowledgeable about medical and psychological concepts. Higher rates of conversion symptoms are reported in developing regions, with the incidence generally declining with increasing development. Falling down with loss or alteration of consciousness is a feature of a variety of culture-specific syndromes. The form of conversion symptoms reflects local cultural ideas about acceptable and credible ways to express distress. Changes resembling conversion symptoms (as well as dissociative symptoms) are common aspects of certain culturally sanctioned religious and healing rituals. The clinician must assess whether such symptoms are fully explained in the particular social context, and whether they result in clinically significant distress, disability, or role impairment.

Conversion symptoms in children under age 10 years are usually limited to gait problems or seizures. Conversion Disorder appears to be more frequent in women than in men, with reported ratios varying from 2:1 to 10:1. Especially in women, symptoms are much more common on the left than on the right side of the body. Women (rarely men) presenting with conversion symptoms may later manifest the full picture of Somatization Disorder. Particularly in men, an association with Antisocial Personality Disorder is evident. In men, Conversion Disorder is often seen in the context of industrial accidents or the military, in which cases it must be carefully differentiated from Malingering.

Prevalence

Reported rates of Conversion Disorder have varied widely, ranging from 11/100,000 to 300/100,000 in general population samples. It has been reported as a focus of treatment in 1%–3% of outpatient referrals to mental health clinics.

Course

The onset of Conversion Disorder is generally from late childhood to early adulthood, rarely before age 10 years or after age 35 years, but onset as late as the ninth decade of life has been reported. When an apparent Conversion Disorder first develops in middle or old age, the probability of an occult neurological or other general medical condition is high. The onset of Conversion Disorder is generally acute, but gradually increasing symptomatology may also occur. Typically, individual conversion symptoms are of short duration. In individuals hospitalized with conversion symptoms, symptoms will remit within 2 weeks in most cases. Recurrence is common, occurring in from one-fifth to one-quarter of individuals within 1 year, with a single recurrence predicting future episodes. Factors that are associated with good prognosis include acute onset, presence of clearly identifiable stress at the time of onset, a short interval between onset and the institution of treatment, and above average intelligence. Symptoms of paralysis, aphonia, and blindness are associated with a good prognosis, whereas tremor and seizures are not.

Familial Pattern

Limited data suggest that conversion symptoms are more frequent in relatives of individuals with Conversion Disorder. Increased risk of Conversion Disorder in monozygotic but not in dizygotic twin pairs has been reported.

Differential Diagnosis

The major diagnostic concern in evaluating potential conversion symptoms is the exclusion of **occult neurological** or **other general medical conditions** and **substance (including medication)–induced etiologies.** Appropriate evaluation of potential general medical conditions (e.g., multiple sclerosis, myasthenia gravis) should include careful review of the current presentation, the overall medical history, neurological and general physical examinations, and appropriate laboratory studies, including investigation for use of alcohol and other substances.

Pain Disorder or a **Sexual Dysfunction** is diagnosed instead of Conversion Disorder if the symptoms are limited to pain or to sexual dysfunction, respectively. An additional diagnosis of Conversion Disorder should not be made if conversion symptoms occur exclusively during the course of **Somatization Disorder.** Conversion Disorder is not diagnosed if symptoms are better accounted for by **another mental disorder** (e.g., catatonic symptoms or somatic delusions in **Schizophrenia** or **other Psychotic Disorders** or **Mood Disorder** or difficulty swallowing during a **Panic Attack**). In **Hypochondriasis,** the individual is preoccupied with the "serious disease" underlying the pseudoneurological symptoms, whereas in Conversion Disorder the focus is on the presenting symptom and there may be *la belle indifférence.* In **Body Dysmorphic Disorder,** the emphasis is on a preoccupation with an imagined or slight defect in appearance, rather than a change in voluntary motor or sensory function. Conversion Disorder shares features with **Dissociative Disorders.** Both disorders involve symptoms that suggest neurological dysfunction and may also have shared antecedents. If both conversion and dissociative symptoms occur in the same individual (which is common), both diagnoses should be made.

It is controversial whether hallucinations ("pseudohallucinations") can be considered as the presenting symptom of Conversion Disorder. As distinguished from **hallucina-**

tions that occur in the context of a Psychotic Disorder (e.g., Schizophrenia or another Psychotic Disorder, a Psychotic Disorder Due to a General Medical Condition, a Substance-Related Disorder, or a Mood Disorder With Psychotic Features), hallucinations in Conversion Disorder generally occur with intact insight in the absence of other psychotic symptoms, often involve more than one sensory modality (e.g., a hallucination involving visual, auditory, and tactile components), and often have a naive, fantastic, or childish content. They are often psychologically meaningful and tend to be described by the individual as an interesting story.

Symptoms of **Factitious Disorders** and **Malingering** are intentionally produced or feigned. In Factitious Disorder, the motivation is to assume the sick role and to obtain medical evaluation and treatment, whereas more obvious goals such as financial compensation, avoidance of duty, evasion of criminal prosecution, or obtaining drugs are apparent in Malingering. Such goals may resemble "secondary gain" in conversion symptoms, with the distinguishing feature of conversion symptoms being the lack of conscious intent in the production of the symptom.

■ **Diagnostic criteria for 300.11 Conversion Disorder**

A. One or more symptoms or deficits affecting voluntary motor or sensory function that suggest a neurological or other general medical condition.

B. Psychological factors are judged to be associated with the symptom or deficit because the initiation or exacerbation of the symptom or deficit is preceded by conflicts or other stressors.

C. The symptom or deficit is not intentionally produced or feigned (as in Factitious Disorder or Malingering).

D. The symptom or deficit cannot, after appropriate investigation, be fully explained by a general medical condition, or by the direct effects of a substance, or as a culturally sanctioned behavior or experience.

E. The symptom or deficit causes clinically significant distress or impairment in social, occupational, or other important areas of functioning or warrants medical evaluation.

F. The symptom or deficit is not limited to pain or sexual dysfunction, does not occur exclusively during the course of Somatization Disorder, and is not better accounted for by another mental disorder.

Specify type of symptom or deficit:
With Motor Symptom or Deficit
With Sensory Symptom or Deficit
With Seizures or Convulsions
With Mixed Presentation

Pain Disorder

Diagnostic Features

The essential feature of Pain Disorder is pain that is the predominant focus of the clinical presentation and is of sufficient severity to warrant clinical attention (Criterion A). The pain causes significant distress or impairment in social, occupational, or other important areas of functioning (Criterion B). Psychological factors are judged to play a significant role in the onset, severity, exacerbation, or maintenance of the pain (Criterion C). The pain is not intentionally produced or feigned as in Factitious Disorder or Malingering (Criterion D). Pain Disorder is not diagnosed if the pain is better accounted for by a Mood, Anxiety, or Psychotic Disorder, or if the pain presentation meets criteria for Dyspareunia (Criterion E). Examples of impairment resulting from the pain include inability to work or attend school, frequent use of the health care system, the pain becoming a major focus of the individual's life, substantial use of medications, and relational problems such as marital discord and disruption of the family's normal lifestyle. The psychological factors involved may consist of another Axis I or Axis II disorder (which would also be diagnosed) or may be of a nature that does not reach the threshold for such a disorder (e.g., reactions to psychosocial stressors).

Subtypes and Specifiers

Pain Disorder is coded according to the subtype that best characterizes the factors involved in the etiology and maintenance of the pain:

> **307.80 Pain Disorder Associated With Psychological Factors.** This subtype is used when psychological factors are judged to have the major role in the onset, severity, exacerbation, or maintenance of the pain. In this subtype, general medical conditions play either no role or a minimal role in the onset or maintenance of the pain. This subtype is not diagnosed if criteria for Somatization Disorder are met.
>
> **307.89 Pain Disorder Associated With Both Psychological Factors and a General Medical Condition.** This subtype is used when both psychological factors and a general medical condition are judged to have important roles in the onset, severity, exacerbation, or maintenance of the pain. The anatomical site of the pain or associated general medical condition is coded on Axis III (see "Recording Procedures").
>
> **Pain Disorder Associated With a General Medical Condition.** This subtype of Pain Disorder *is not considered a mental disorder and is coded on Axis III*. It is listed in this section to facilitate differential diagnosis. The pain results from a general medical condition, and psychological factors are judged to play either no role or a minimal role in the onset or maintenance of the pain. The ICD-9-CM code for this subtype is selected based on the location of the pain or the associated general medical condition if this has been established (see "Recording Procedures").

For Pain Disorder Associated With Psychological Factors and Pain Disorder Associated With Both Psychological Factors and a General Medical Condition, the following specifiers may be noted to indicate the duration of the pain:

Acute. This specifier is used if the duration of the pain is less than 6 months.
Chronic. This specifier is used if the duration of the pain is 6 months or longer.

Recording Procedures

The diagnostic code for Pain Disorder is selected based on the subtype described above. The code is 307.80 for Pain Disorder Associated With Psychological Factors. For Pain Disorder Associated With Both Psychological Factors and a General Medical Condition, 307.89 is coded on Axis I and the associated general medical condition or anatomical site of pain is coded on Axis III (e.g., 307.89 Pain Disorder Associated With Both Psychological Factors and a General Medical Condition on Axis I; 357.2 Diabetic Polyneuropathy on Axis III). For Pain Disorder Associated With a General Medical Condition, the diagnostic code for the pain is selected based on the associated general medical condition if one has been established (see Appendix G) or on the anatomical location of the pain if the underlying general medical condition is not yet clearly established—for example, low back (724.2), sciatic (724.3), pelvic (625.9), headache (784.0), facial (784.0), chest (786.50), joint (719.4), bone (733.90), abdominal (789.0), breast (611.71), renal (788.0), ear (388.70), eye (379.91), throat (784.1), tooth (525.9), and urinary (788.0).

Associated Features and Disorders

Associated descriptive features and mental disorders.   Pain may severely disrupt various aspects of daily life. Unemployment, disability, and family problems are frequently encountered among individuals with chronic forms of Pain Disorder. Iatrogenic Opioid Dependence or Abuse and Benzodiazepine Dependence or Abuse may develop. Individuals whose pain is associated with severe depression and those whose pain is related to a terminal illness, most notably cancer, appear to be at increased risk for suicide. Individuals with recurrent acute or chronic pain are sometimes convinced that there is a health professional somewhere who has the "cure" for the pain. They may spend a considerable amount of time and money seeking an unattainable goal. Pain may lead to inactivity and social isolation, which in turn can lead to additional psychological problems (e.g., depression) and a reduction in physical endurance that results in fatigue and additional pain. Pain Disorder appears to be associated with other mental disorders, especially Mood and Anxiety Disorders. Chronic pain appears to be most frequently associated with Depressive Disorders, whereas acute pain appears to be more commonly associated with Anxiety Disorders. The associated mental disorders may precede the Pain Disorder (and possibly predispose the individual to it), co-occur with it, or result from it. Both the acute and chronic forms of Pain Disorder are frequently associated with insomnia.

Associated laboratory findings.   In Pain Disorder Associated With Both Psychological Factors and a General Medical Condition, appropriate laboratory testing may reveal pathology that is associated with the pain (e.g., finding of a herniated lumbar disc on a magnetic resonance imaging (MRI) scan in an individual with radicular low-back pain). However, general medical conditions may also be present in the absence of objective findings. Conversely, the presence of such findings may be coincidental to the pain.

Associated physical examination findings and general medical conditions.   In Pain Disorder Associated With Both Psychological Factors and a General Medical Condition, the physical examination may reveal pathology that is associated with the pain. Pain Disorder can be associated with many general medical conditions. Among the most common general medical conditions associated with pain are various musculoskeletal conditions (e.g., disc herniation, osteoporosis, osteoarthritis or rheumatoid arthritis, myofascial syndromes), neuropathies (e.g., diabetic neuropathies, post-herpetic neuralgia), and malignancies (e.g., metastatic lesions in bone, tumor infiltration of nerves). Attempts to treat the pain may lead to additional problems, some of which can cause more pain (e.g., use of nonsteroidal anti-inflammatory drugs resulting in gastrointestinal distress, surgery resulting in adhesions).

Specific Culture, Age, and Gender Features

There may be differences in how various ethnic and cultural groups respond to painful stimuli and how they express their reactions to pain. However, because there is so much individual variation, these factors are of limited usefulness in the evaluation and management of individuals with Pain Disorder.

Pain Disorder may occur at any age. Females appear to experience certain chronic pain conditions, most notably headaches and musculoskeletal pain, more often than do males.

Prevalence

Pain Disorder appears to be relatively common. For example, it is estimated that, in any given year, 10%–15% of adults in the United States have some form of work disability due to back pain alone.

Course

Most acute pain resolves in relatively short periods of time. There is a wide range of variability in the onset of chronic pain. In most cases, the symptom has persisted for many years by the time the individual comes to the attention of the mental health profession. Important factors that appear to influence recovery from Pain Disorder are the individual's participation in regularly scheduled activities (e.g., work) despite the pain and resistance to allowing the pain to become the determining factor in his or her lifestyle.

Familial Pattern

Depressive Disorders, Alcohol Dependence, and chronic pain may be more common in the first-degree biological relatives of individuals with chronic Pain Disorder.

Differential Diagnosis

Pain symptoms are included in the diagnostic criteria for **Somatization Disorder.** If the pain associated with psychological factors occurs exclusively during the course of Somatization Disorder, an additional diagnosis of Pain Disorder Associated With

Psychological Factors is not made. Similarly, if the pain presentation meets criteria for **Dyspareunia** (i.e., pain associated with sexual intercourse), an additional diagnosis of Pain Disorder is not given. Pain complaints may be prominent in individuals with **Conversion Disorder,** but by definition, Conversion Disorder is not limited to pain symptoms. Pain symptoms are common associated features of **other mental disorders** (e.g., Depressive Disorders, Anxiety Disorders, Psychotic Disorders). An additional diagnosis of Pain Disorder should be considered only if the pain is an independent focus of clinical attention, leads to clinically significant distress or impairment, and is in excess of that usually associated with the other mental disorder.

Pain symptoms may be intentionally produced or feigned in **Factitious Disorder** or **Malingering.** In Factitious Disorder, the motivation is to assume the sick role and to obtain medical evaluation and treatment, whereas more obvious goals such as financial compensation, avoidance of duties related to military service or incarceration, evasion of criminal prosecution, or obtaining drugs are apparent in Malingering.

Relationship to the Taxonomy Proposed by The International Association for the Study of Pain

The Subcommittee on Taxonomy of The International Association for the Study of Pain proposed a five-axis system for categorizing chronic pain according to I) anatomical region, II) organ system, III) temporal characteristics of pain and pattern of occurrence, IV) patient's statement of intensity and time since onset of pain, and V) etiology. This five-axis system focuses primarily on the physical manifestations of pain. It provides for comments on psychological factors on both the second axis where the involvement of a mental disorder can be coded and the fifth axis where possible etiologies include "psychophysiological" and "psychological."

■ **Diagnostic criteria for Pain Disorder**

    A. Pain in one or more anatomical sites is the predominant focus of the clinical presentation and is of sufficient severity to warrant clinical attention.

    B. The pain causes clinically significant distress or impairment in social, occupational, or other important areas of functioning.

    C. Psychological factors are judged to have an important role in the onset, severity, exacerbation, or maintenance of the pain.

    D. The symptom or deficit is not intentionally produced or feigned (as in Factitious Disorder or Malingering).

    E. The pain is not better accounted for by a Mood, Anxiety, or Psychotic Disorder and does not meet criteria for Dyspareunia.

(continued)

□ **Diagnostic criteria for Pain Disorder** (*continued*)

Code as follows:

307.80 Pain Disorder Associated With Psychological Factors: psychological factors are judged to have the major role in the onset, severity, exacerbation, or maintenance of the pain. (If a general medical condition is present, it does not have a major role in the onset, severity, exacerbation, or maintenance of the pain.) This type of Pain Disorder is not diagnosed if criteria are also met for Somatization Disorder.

Specify if:
Acute: duration of less than 6 months
Chronic: duration of 6 months or longer

307.89 Pain Disorder Associated With Both Psychological Factors and a General Medical Condition: both psychological factors and a general medical condition are judged to have important roles in the onset, severity, exacerbation, or maintenance of the pain. The associated general medical condition or anatomical site of the pain (see below) is coded on Axis III.

Specify if:
Acute: duration of less than 6 months
Chronic: duration of 6 months or longer

Note: The following is not considered to be a mental disorder and is included here to facilitate differential diagnosis.

Pain Disorder Associated With a General Medical Condition: a general medical condition has a major role in the onset, severity, exacerbation, or maintenance of the pain. (If psychological factors are present, they are not judged to have a major role in the onset, severity, exacerbation, or maintenance of the pain.) The diagnostic code for the pain is selected based on the associated general medical condition if one has been established (see Appendix G) or on the anatomical location of the pain if the underlying general medical condition is not yet clearly established—for example, low back (724.2), sciatic (724.3), pelvic (625.9), headache (784.0), facial (784.0), chest (786.50), joint (719.4), bone (733.90), abdominal (789.0), breast (611.71), renal (788.0), ear (388.70), eye (379.91), throat (784.1), tooth (525.9), and urinary (788.0).

300.7 Hypochondriasis

Diagnostic Features

The essential feature of Hypochondriasis is preoccupation with fears of having, or the idea that one has, a serious disease based on a misinterpretation of one or more bodily signs or symptoms (Criterion A). A thorough medical evaluation does not identify a general medical condition that fully accounts for the person's concerns about disease or for the physical signs or symptoms (although a coexisting general medical condition may be present). The unwarranted fear or idea of having a disease persists despite medical reassurance (Criterion B). However, the belief is not of delusional intensity (i.e., the person can acknowledge the possibility that he or she may be exaggerating the extent of the feared disease, or that there may be no disease at all). The belief is also not restricted to a circumscribed concern about appearance, as seen in Body Dysmorphic Disorder (Criterion C). The preoccupation with bodily symptoms causes clinically significant distress or impairment in social, occupational, or other important areas of functioning (Criterion D) and lasts for at least 6 months (Criterion E). The preoccupation is not better accounted for by Generalized Anxiety Disorder, Obsessive-Compulsive Disorder, Panic Disorder, a Major Depressive Episode, Separation Anxiety, or another Somatoform Disorder (Criterion F).

The preoccupation in Hypochondriasis may be with bodily functions (e.g., heartbeat, sweating, or peristalsis); with minor physical abnormalities (e.g., a small sore or an occasional cough); or with vague and ambiguous physical sensations (e.g., "tired heart," "aching veins"). The person attributes these symptoms or signs to the suspected disease and is very concerned with their meaning, authenticity, and etiology. The concerns may involve several body systems, at different times or simultaneously. Alternatively, there may be preoccupation with a specific organ or a single disease (e.g., fear of having cardiac disease). Repeated physical examinations, diagnostic tests, and reassurance from the physician do little to allay the concern about bodily disease or affliction. For example, an individual preoccupied with having cardiac disease will not be reassured by the repeated lack of findings on physical examination, ECG, or even cardiac angiography. Individuals with Hypochondriasis may become alarmed by reading or hearing about disease, knowing someone who becomes sick, or from observations, sensations, or occurrences within their own bodies. Concern about the feared illness often becomes a central feature of the individual's self-image, a topic of social discourse, and a response to life stresses.

Specifier

With Poor Insight. This specifier is used if, for most of the time during the current episode, the individual does not recognize that the concern about having a serious illness is excessive or unreasonable.

Associated Features and Disorders

Associated descriptive features and mental disorders. The medical history is often presented in great detail and at length in Hypochondriasis. "Doctor-shopping" and deterioration in doctor-patient relationships, with frustration and anger on both sides, are common. Individuals with this disorder often believe that they are not getting proper care and may strenuously resist referral to mental health settings. Complications may result from repeated diagnostic procedures that carry their own risks and are costly. However, because these individuals have a history of multiple complaints without a clear physical basis, they may receive cursory evaluations and the presence of a general medical condition may be missed. Social relationships become strained because the individual with Hypochondriasis is preoccupied with his or her condition and often expects special treatment and consideration. Family life may become disturbed as it becomes centered around the individual's physical well-being. There may be no effect on functioning at work if the individual limits the hypochondriacal preoccupation to nonwork time. More often, the preoccupation interferes with performance and causes the person to miss time from work. In more severe cases, the individual with Hypochondriasis may become a complete invalid.

Serious illnesses, particularly in childhood, and past experience with disease in a family member are associated with the occurrence of Hypochondriasis. Psychosocial stressors, in particular the death of someone close to the individual, are thought to precipitate Hypochondriasis in some cases. Individuals with Hypochondriasis often have other mental disorders (particularly Anxiety and Depressive Disorders).

Associated laboratory findings.   Laboratory findings do not confirm the individual's preoccupation.

Associated physical examination findings and general medical conditions. Physical examination findings do not confirm the individual's preoccupation.

Specific Culture and Gender Features

Whether it is unreasonable for the preoccupation with disease to persist despite appropriate medical evaluation and reassurance must be judged relative to the individual's cultural background and explanatory models. The diagnosis of Hypochondriasis should be made cautiously if the individual's ideas about disease have been reinforced by traditional healers who may disagree with the reassurances provided by medical evaluations. The disorder is equally common in males and in females.

Prevalence

The prevalence of Hypochondriasis in the general population is unknown. The prevalence in general medical practice has been reported to be between 4% and 9%.

Course

Hypochondriasis can begin at any age, with the most common age at onset thought to be in early adulthood. The course is usually chronic, with waxing and waning symptoms, but complete recovery sometimes occurs. It appears that acute onset, general medical comorbidity, the absence of a Personality Disorder, and the absence of secondary gain are favorable prognostic indicators. Because of its chronicity, some view this disorder as having prominent "traitlike" characteristics (i.e., a long-standing preoccupation with bodily complaints and focus on bodily symptoms).

Differential Diagnosis

The most important differential diagnostic consideration in Hypochondriasis is an underlying **general medical condition,** such as the early stages of neurological conditions (e.g., multiple sclerosis or myasthenia gravis), endocrine conditions (e.g., thyroid or parathyroid disease), diseases that affect multiple body systems (e.g., systemic lupus erythematosus), and occult malignancies. Although the presence of a general medical condition does not rule out the possibility of coexisting Hypochondriasis, transient preoccupations related to a current general medical condition do not constitute

Hypochondriasis. **Somatic symptoms** (e.g., abdominal pain) are common **in children** and should not be diagnosed as Hypochondriasis unless the child has a prolonged preoccupation with having a serious illness. Bodily preoccupations and fears of debility may be frequent in elderly persons. However, the onset of **health concerns in old age** is more likely to be realistic or to reflect a Mood Disorder rather than Hypochondriasis.

Hypochondriasis is diagnosed only when the individual's health concerns are not better accounted for by **Generalized Anxiety Disorder, Obsessive-Compulsive Disorder, Panic Disorder,** a **Major Depressive Episode, Separation Anxiety Disorder,** or **another Somatoform Disorder.** Individuals with Hypochondriasis may have intrusive thoughts about having a disease and also may have associated compulsive behaviors (e.g., asking for reassurances). A separate diagnosis of Obsessive-Compulsive Disorder is given only when the obsessions or compulsions are not restricted to concerns about illness (e.g., checking locks). In **Body Dysmorphic Disorder,** the concern is limited to the person's physical appearance. In contrast to a **Specific** ("disease") **Phobia** in which the individual is fearful of being exposed to a disease, Hypochondriasis is characterized by a preoccupation that one has the disease.

In Hypochondriasis, the disease conviction does not reach delusional proportions (i.e., the individual can entertain the possibility that the feared disease is not present), as opposed to somatic delusions that can occur in **Psychotic Disorders** (e.g., Schizophrenia, Delusional Disorder, Somatic Type, and Major Depressive Disorder, With Psychotic Features).

■ Diagnostic criteria for 300.7 Hypochondriasis

A. Preoccupation with fears of having, or the idea that one has, a serious disease based on the person's misinterpretation of bodily symptoms.

B. The preoccupation persists despite appropriate medical evaluation and reassurance.

C. The belief in Criterion A is not of delusional intensity (as in Delusional Disorder, Somatic Type) and is not restricted to a circumscribed concern about appearance (as in Body Dysmorphic Disorder).

D. The preoccupation causes clinically significant distress or impairment in social, occupational, or other important areas of functioning.

E. The duration of the disturbance is at least 6 months.

F. The preoccupation is not better accounted for by Generalized Anxiety Disorder, Obsessive-Compulsive Disorder, Panic Disorder, a Major Depressive Episode, Separation Anxiety, or another Somatoform Disorder.

Specify if:

With Poor Insight: if, for most of the time during the current episode, the person does not recognize that the concern about having a serious illness is excessive or unreasonable

300.7   Body Dysmorphic Disorder

Diagnostic Features

The essential feature of Body Dysmorphic Disorder (historically known as dysmorphophobia) is a preoccupation with a defect in appearance (Criterion A). The defect is either imagined, or, if a slight physical anomaly is present, the individual's concern is markedly excessive (Criterion A). The preoccupation must cause significant distress or impairment in social, occupational, or other important areas of functioning (Criterion B). The preoccupation is not better accounted for by another mental disorder (e.g., dissatisfaction with body shape and size in Anorexia Nervosa) (Criterion C).

Complaints commonly involve imagined or slight flaws of the face or head such as hair thinning, acne, wrinkles, scars, vascular markings, paleness or redness of the complexion, swelling, facial asymmetry or disproportion, or excessive facial hair. Other common preoccupations include the shape, size, or some other aspect of the nose, eyes, eyelids, eyebrows, ears, mouth, lips, teeth, jaw, chin, cheeks, or head. However, any other body part may be the focus of concern (e.g., the genitals, breasts, buttocks, abdomen, arms, hands, feet, legs, hips, shoulders, spine, larger body regions, or overall body size). The preoccupation may simultaneously focus on several body parts. Although the complaint is often specific (e.g., a "crooked" lip or a "bumpy" nose), it is sometimes vague (e.g., a "falling" face or "inadequately firm" eyes). Because of embarrassment over their concerns, some individuals with Body Dysmorphic Disorder avoid describing their "defects" in detail and may instead refer only to their general ugliness.

Most individuals with this disorder experience marked distress over their supposed deformity, often describing their preoccupations as "intensely painful," "tormenting," or "devastating." Most find their preoccupations difficult to control, and they may make little or no attempt to resist them. As a result, they often spend hours a day thinking about their "defect," to the point where these thoughts may dominate their lives. Significant impairment in many areas of functioning generally occurs. Feelings of self-consciousness about their "defect" may lead to avoidance of work or public situations.

Associated Features and Disorders

Frequent mirror checking and checking of the "defect" in other available reflecting surfaces (e.g., store windows, car bumpers, watch faces) can consume many hours a day. Some individuals use special lighting or magnifying glasses to scrutinize their "defect." There may be excessive grooming behavior (e.g., excessive hair combing, hair removal, ritualized makeup application, or skin picking). Although the checking and grooming are intended by some individuals to diminish anxiety about the "defect," they often intensify the preoccupation and associated anxiety. Consequently, some individuals avoid mirrors, sometimes covering them or removing them from their environment. Others appear to alternate between periods of excessive mirror checking and avoidance. There may be frequent requests for reassurance about the "defect," but such reassurance leads to only temporary, if any, relief. Individuals with the disorder may also frequently compare their "ugly" body part with that of others. Ideas of reference related to the imagined defect are also common. Individuals with this disorder often think that others may be (or are) taking special notice of their supposed flaw, perhaps talking about it or mocking it. They may try to camouflage the "defect" (e.g., growing a beard to cover imagined facial scars, wearing a hat to hide imagined hair loss, stuffing their shorts to enhance a "small" penis). Some individuals may be excessively preoccupied with fears that the "ugly" body part will malfunction or is extremely fragile and in constant danger of being damaged.

Avoidance of usual activities may lead to extreme social isolation. In some cases, individuals may leave their homes only at night, when they cannot be seen, or become housebound, sometimes for years. Individuals with this disorder may drop out of school, avoid job interviews, work at jobs below their capacity, or not work at all. They may have few friends, avoid dating and other social interactions, have marital difficulties, or get divorced because of their symptoms. The distress and dysfunction associated with this disorder, although variable, can lead to repeated hospitalization and to suicidal ideation, suicide attempts, and completed suicide. Individuals with Body Dysmorphic Disorder often pursue and receive general medical, dental, or surgical treatments to rectify their imagined defects. Such treatment may cause the disorder to worsen, leading to intensified or new preoccupations, which may in turn lead to further unsuccessful procedures, so that individuals may eventually possess "synthetic" noses, ears, breasts, and hips, which they are still dissatisfied with. Body Dysmorphic Disorder may be associated with Major Depressive Disorder, Delusional Disorder, Social Phobia, and Obsessive-Compulsive Disorder.

Specific Culture and Gender Features

Cultural concerns about physical appearance and the importance of proper physical self-presentation may influence or amplify preoccupations about an imagined physical deformity. Preliminary evidence suggests that Body Dysmorphic Disorder is diagnosed with approximately equal frequency in women and in men.

Prevalence

Reliable information is lacking, but Body Dysmorphic Disorder may be more common than was previously thought.

Course

Body Dysmorphic Disorder usually begins during adolescence, but may not be diagnosed for many years, often because individuals with the disorder are reluctant to reveal their symptoms. The onset may be either gradual or abrupt. The disorder often has a fairly continuous course, with few symptom-free intervals, although the intensity of symptoms may wax and wane over time. The part of the body on which concern is focused may remain the same or may change.

Differential Diagnosis

Unlike **normal concerns about appearance,** the preoccupation with appearance in Body Dysmorphic Disorder is excessively time consuming and associated with significant distress or impairment in social, occupational, or other areas of functioning. However, Body Dysmorphic Disorder may be underrecognized in settings in which cosmetic procedures are performed.

The diagnosis of Body Dysmorphic Disorder should not be made if the preoccupation is better accounted for by **another mental disorder.** Body Dysmorphic Disorder should not be diagnosed if the excessive preoccupation is restricted to concerns about "fatness" in **Anorexia Nervosa**, if the individual's preoccupation is limited to discomfort with or a sense of inappropriateness about his or her primary and secondary sex characteristics occurring in **Gender Identity Disorder**, or if the preoccupation is limited to mood-congruent ruminations involving appearance that occur exclusively during a **Major Depressive Episode.** Individuals with **Avoidant Personality Disorder** or **Social Phobia** may worry about being embarrassed by real defects in appearance, but this concern is usually not prominent, persistent, distressing, time consuming, and impairing. Although individuals with Body Dysmorphic Disorder have obsessional preoccupations about their appearance and may have associated compulsive behaviors (e.g., mirror checking), a separate diagnosis of **Obsessive-Compulsive Disorder** is given only when the obsessions or compulsions are not restricted to concerns about appearance.

Individuals with Body Dysmorphic Disorder can receive an additional diagnosis of **Delusional Disorder, Somatic Type,** if their preoccupation with an imagined defect in appearance is held with a delusional intensity.

Koro is a culture-bound syndrome that occurs primarily in Southeast Asia that may be related to Body Dysmorphic Disorder. It is characterized by the preoccupation that the penis is shrinking and will disappear into the abdomen, resulting in death. Koro differs from Body Dysmorphic Disorder by its usually brief duration, different associated features (primarily acute anxiety and fear of death), positive response to reassurance, and occasional occurrence as an epidemic.

■ **Diagnostic criteria for 300.7 Body Dysmorphic Disorder**

A. Preoccupation with an imagined defect in appearance. If a slight physical anomaly is present, the person's concern is markedly excessive.

B. The preoccupation causes clinically significant distress or impairment in social, occupational, or other important areas of functioning.

C. The preoccupation is not better accounted for by another mental disorder (e.g., dissatisfaction with body shape and size in Anorexia Nervosa).

300.81   Somatoform Disorder Not Otherwise Specified

This category includes disorders with somatoform symptoms that do not meet the criteria for any specific Somatoform Disorder. Examples include

1. Pseudocyesis: a false belief of being pregnant that is associated with objective signs of pregnancy, which may include abdominal enlargement (although the

umbilicus does not become everted), reduced menstrual flow, amenorrhea, subjective sensation of fetal movement, nausea, breast engorgement and secretions, and labor pains at the expected date of delivery. Endocrine changes may be present, but the syndrome cannot be explained by a general medical condition that causes endocrine changes (e.g., a hormone-secreting tumor).

2. A disorder involving nonpsychotic hypochondriacal symptoms of less than 6 months' duration.

3. A disorder involving unexplained physical complaints (e.g., fatigue or body weakness) of less than 6 months' duration that are not due to another mental disorder.

Factitious Disorders

Factitious Disorders are characterized by physical or psychological symptoms that are intentionally produced or feigned in order to assume the sick role. The judgment that a particular symptom is intentionally produced is made both by direct evidence and by excluding other causes of the symptom. For example, an individual presenting with hematuria is found to have anticoagulants in his possession. The person denies having taken them, but blood studies are consistent with the ingestion of anticoagulants. A reasonable inference, in the absence of evidence that accidental ingestion occurred, is that the individual may have taken the medication intentionally. It should be noted that the presence of factitious symptoms does not preclude the coexistence of true physical or psychological symptoms.

Factitious Disorders are distinguished from acts of Malingering. In Malingering, the individual also produces the symptoms intentionally, but has a goal that is obviously recognizable when the environmental circumstances are known. For example, the intentional production of symptoms to avoid jury duty, standing trial, or conscription into the military would be classified as Malingering. Similarly, if an individual who is hospitalized for treatment of a mental disorder simulates an exacerbation of illness to avoid transfer to another, less desirable facility, this would be an act of Malingering. In contrast, in Factitious Disorder, the motivation is a psychological need to assume the sick role, as evidenced by an absence of external incentives for the behavior. Malingering may be considered to be adaptive under certain circumstances (e.g., in hostage situations), but by definition a diagnosis of a Factitious Disorder always implies psychopathology.

Factitious Disorder

The essential feature of Factitious Disorder is the intentional production of physical or psychological signs or symptoms (Criterion A). The presentation may include fabrication of subjective complaints (e.g., complaints of acute abdominal pain in the absence of any such pain), self-inflicted conditions (e.g., the production of abscesses by injection of saliva into the skin), exaggeration or exacerbation of preexisting general medical conditions (e.g., feigning of a grand mal seizure by an individual with a previous history of seizure disorder), or any combination or variation of these. The motivation for the behavior is to assume the sick role (Criterion B). External incentives for the behavior (e.g., economic gain, avoiding legal responsibility, or improving physical well-being, as in Malingering) are absent (Criterion C).

Individuals with Factitious Disorder usually present their history with dramatic flair, but are extremely vague and inconsistent when questioned in greater detail. They may engage in pathological lying, in a manner that is intriguing to the listener, about any aspect of their history or symptoms (i.e., pseudologia fantastica). They often have extensive knowledge of medical terminology and hospital routines. Complaints of pain and requests for analgesics are very common. After an extensive workup of their initial chief complaints has proved negative, they often complain of other physical or psychological problems and produce more factitious symptoms. Individuals with this disorder may eagerly undergo multiple invasive procedures and operations. While in the hospital, they usually have few visitors. Eventually, a point may be reached at which the factitious nature of the individual's symptoms is revealed (e.g., the person is recognized by someone who encountered the patient during a previous admission; other hospitals confirm multiple prior hospitalizations for factitious symptomatology). When confronted with evidence that their symptoms are factitious, individuals with this disorder usually deny the allegations or rapidly discharge themselves against medical advice. Frequently, they will be admitted to another hospital soon after. Their repeated hospitalizations often take them to numerous cities, states, and countries.

Subtypes

Factitious Disorder is coded according to the subtype that best characterizes the predominant symptoms.

300.16 With Predominantly Psychological Signs and Symptoms. This subtype describes a clinical presentation in which psychological signs and symptoms predominate. It is characterized by the intentional production or feigning of psychological (often psychotic) symptoms that are suggestive of a mental disorder. The individual's goal is apparently to assume the "patient" role and is not otherwise understandable in light of environmental circumstances (in contrast to the case in Malingering). This subtype may be suggested by a wide-ranging symptomatology that often does not correspond to a typical syndromal pattern, an unusual course and response to treatment, and the worsening of symptoms when the individual is aware of being observed. Individuals with this subtype of Factitious Disorder may claim depression and suicidal ideation following the death of a spouse (the death not being confirmed by other informants), memory loss (recent and remote), hallucinations (auditory and visual), and dissociative symptoms. These individuals may be extremely suggestible and may endorse many of the symptoms brought up during a review of systems. Conversely, they may be extremely negativistic and uncooperative when questioned. The presentation usually represents the individual's concept of mental disorder and may not conform to any recognized diagnostic category.

300.19 With Predominantly Physical Signs and Symptoms. This subtype describes a clinical presentation in which signs and symptoms of an apparent general medical condition predominate. The individual's entire life may consist of trying to get admitted to, or stay in, hospitals (known as "Munchausen syndrome"). Common clinical pictures include severe right-lower-quadrant pain associated with nausea and vomiting, dizziness and blacking out, massive hemoptysis, generalized rashes and abscesses, fevers of undetermined origin, bleeding secondary to ingestion of anticoagulants, and "lupus-like" syndromes. All organ systems are potential targets, and the symptoms presented are limited only by the individual's medical knowledge, sophistication, and imagination.

300.19   With Combined Psychological and Physical Signs and Symptoms. This subtype describes a clinical presentation in which both psychological and physical signs and symptoms are present, but neither predominates.

Associated Features and Disorders

In Factitious Disorder With Predominantly Psychological Signs and Symptoms, the giving of approximate answers may occur (e.g., 8 times 8 equals 65). The individual may surreptitiously use psychoactive substances for the purpose of producing symptoms that suggest a mental disorder (e.g., stimulants to produce restlessness or insomnia, hallucinogens to induce altered perceptual states, analgesics to induce euphoria, and hypnotics to induce lethargy). Combinations of psychoactive substances can produce very unusual presentations.

Individuals with Factitious Disorder With Predominantly Physical Signs and Symptoms may also present with Substance Abuse, particularly of prescribed analgesics and sedatives. Multiple hospitalizations frequently lead to iatrogenically induced general medical conditions (e.g., the formation of scar tissue from unnecessary surgery, or adverse drug reactions). Individuals with the chronic form of this disorder may acquire a "gridiron abdomen" from multiple surgical procedures. Factitious Disorder is usually incompatible with the individual's maintaining steady employment, family ties, and interpersonal relationships. Possible predisposing factors to Factitious Disorder may include the presence of other mental disorders or general medical conditions during childhood or adolescence that led to extensive medical treatment and hospitalization; a grudge against the medical profession; employment in a medically related position; the presence of a severe Personality Disorder; and an important relationship with a physician in the past.

Prevalence

There is limited information on prevalence of Factitious Disorder. Although it is a rarely reported diagnosis, it often may not be recognized. On the other hand, the chronic form of the disorder may be overreported because affected individuals appear to different physicians at different hospitals, often under different names. The disorder is apparently more common in males than in females.

Course

The course of Factitious Disorder may be limited to one or more brief episodes, but is usually chronic. The onset is usually in early adulthood, often after a hospitalization for a general medical condition or other mental disorder. In the chronic form of this disorder, a pattern of successive hospitalizations may become a lifelong pattern.

Differential Diagnosis

A Factitious Disorder must be distinguished from a **true general medical condition** and from a **true mental disorder.** Suspicion that an apparent mental disorder or general medical condition in fact represents Factitious Disorder should be aroused if any combination of the following is noted in a hospitalized individual: an atypical or dramatic presentation that does not conform to an identifiable general medical condition or mental disorder; symptoms or behaviors that are present only when the individual is being observed; pseudologia fantastica; disruptive behavior on the ward (e.g., noncompliance with hospital regulations, arguing excessively with nurses and physicians); extensive knowledge of medical terminology and hospital routines; covert use of substances; evidence of multiple treatment interventions (e.g., repeated surgery, repeated courses of electroconvulsive therapy); extensive history of traveling; few, if any, visitors while hospitalized; and a fluctuating clinical course, with rapid development of "complications" or new "pathology" once the initial workup proves to be negative.

In **Somatoform Disorders,** physical complaints that are not fully attributable to a true general medical condition are also present, but the symptoms are not intentionally produced. **Malingering** differs from Factitious Disorder in that the motivation for the symptom production in Malingering is an external incentive, whereas in Factitious Disorder external incentives are absent. Individuals with Malingering may seek hospitalization by producing symptoms in attempts to obtain compensation, evade the police, or simply "get a bed for the night." However, the goal is usually apparent, and they can "stop" the symptoms when the symptoms are no longer useful to them.

■ Diagnostic criteria for Factitious Disorder

A. Intentional production or feigning of physical or psychological signs or symptoms.

B. The motivation for the behavior is to assume the sick role.

C. External incentives for the behavior (such as economic gain, avoiding legal responsibility, or improving physical well-being, as in Malingering) are absent.

Code based on type:

300.16 With Predominantly Psychological Signs and Symptoms: if psychological signs and symptoms predominate in the clinical presentation

300.19 With Predominantly Physical Signs and Symptoms: if physical signs and symptoms predominate in the clinical presentation

300.19 With Combined Psychological and Physical Signs and Symptoms: if both psychological and physical signs and symptoms are present but neither predominates in the clinical presentation

---

300.19   Factitious Disorder Not Otherwise Specified

This category includes disorders with factitious symptoms that do not meet the criteria for Factitious Disorder. An example is factitious disorder by proxy: the intentional production or feigning of physical or psychological signs or symptoms in another person who is under the individual's care for the purpose of indirectly assuming the sick role (see p. 725 for suggested research criteria).

Dissociative Disorders

The essential feature of the Dissociative Disorders is a disruption in the usually integrated functions of consciousness, memory, identity, or perception of the environment. The disturbance may be sudden or gradual, transient or chronic. The following disorders are included in this section:

Dissociative Amnesia is characterized by an inability to recall important personal information, usually of a traumatic or stressful nature, that is too extensive to be explained by ordinary forgetfulness.

Dissociative Fugue is characterized by sudden, unexpected travel away from home or one's customary place of work, accompanied by an inability to recall one's past and confusion about personal identity or the assumption of a new identity.

Dissociative Identity Disorder (formerly Multiple Personality Disorder) is characterized by the presence of two or more distinct identities or personality states that recurrently take control of the individual's behavior accompanied by an inability to recall important personal information that is too extensive to be explained by ordinary forgetfulness.

Depersonalization Disorder is characterized by a persistent or recurrent feeling of being detached from one's mental processes or body that is accompanied by intact reality testing.

Dissociative Disorder Not Otherwise Specified is included for coding disorders in which the predominant feature is a dissociative symptom, but that do not meet the criteria for any specific Dissociative Disorder.

Dissociative symptoms are also included in the criteria sets for Acute Stress Disorder, Posttraumatic Stress Disorder, and Somatization Disorder. An additional Dissociative Disorder diagnosis is not given if the dissociative symptoms occur exclusively during the course of one of these disorders. In some classifications, conversion reaction is considered to be a dissociative phenomenon; however, in DSM-IV, Conversion Disorder is placed in the "Somatoform Disorders" section to emphasize the importance of considering neurological or other general medical conditions in the differential diagnosis.

A cross-cultural perspective is particularly important in the evaluation of Dissociative Disorders because dissociative states are a common and accepted expression of cultural activities or religious experience in many societies. Dissociation should not be considered inherently pathological and often does not lead to significant distress, impairment, or help-seeking behavior. However, a number of culturally defined syndromes characterized by dissociation do cause distress and impairment and are recognized indigenously as manifestations of pathology (see p. 727 and p. 843).

300.12   Dissociative Amnesia
(*formerly* Psychogenic Amnesia)

Diagnostic Features

The essential feature of Dissociative Amnesia is an inability to recall important personal information, usually of a traumatic or stressful nature, that is too extensive to be explained by normal forgetfulness (Criterion A). This disorder involves a reversible memory impairment in which memories of personal experience cannot be retrieved in a verbal form (or, if temporarily retrieved, cannot be wholly retained in consciousness). The disturbance does not occur exclusively during the course of Dissociative Identity Disorder, Dissociative Fugue, Posttraumatic Stress Disorder, Acute Stress Disorder, or Somatization Disorder and is not due to the direct physiological effects of a substance or a neurological or other general medical condition (Criterion B). The symptoms must cause clinically significant distress or impairment in social, occupational, or other important areas of functioning (Criterion C).

Dissociative Amnesia most commonly presents as a retrospectively reported gap or series of gaps in recall for aspects of the individual's life history. These gaps are usually related to traumatic or extremely stressful events. Some individuals may have amnesia for episodes of self-mutilation, violent outbursts, or suicide attempts. Less commonly, Dissociative Amnesia presents as a florid episode with sudden onset. This acute form is more likely to occur during wartime or in response to a natural disaster.

Several types of memory disturbances have been described in Dissociative Amnesia. In *localized amnesia,* the individual fails to recall events that occurred during a circumscribed period of time, usually the first few hours following a profoundly disturbing event (e.g., the uninjured survivor of a car accident in which a family member has been killed may not be able to recall anything that happened from the time of the accident until 2 days later). In *selective amnesia,* the person can recall some, but not all, of the events during a circumscribed period of time (e.g., a combat veteran can recall only some parts of a series of violent combat experiences). Three other types of amnesia—generalized, continuous, and systematized—are less common. In *generalized amnesia,* failure of recall encompasses the person's entire life. Individuals with this rare disorder usually present to the police, to emergency rooms, or to general hospital consultation-liaison services. *Continuous amnesia* is defined as the inability to recall events subsequent to a specific time up to and including the present. *Systematized amnesia* is loss of memory for certain categories of information, such as all memories relating to one's family or to a particular person. Individuals who exhibit these latter three types of Dissociative Amnesia may ultimately be diagnosed as having a more complex form of Dissociative Disorder (e.g., Dissociative Identity Disorder).

Associated Features and Disorders

Associated descriptive features and mental disorders.   Some individuals with Dissociative Amnesia report depressive symptoms, depersonalization, trance states, analgesia, and spontaneous age regression. They may provide approximate inaccurate answers to questions (e.g., "2 plus 2 equals 5") as in Ganser syndrome. Other problems that sometimes accompany this disorder include sexual dysfunction, impairment in work and interpersonal relationships, self-mutilation, aggressive impulses, and suicidal impulses and acts. Individuals with Dissociative Amnesia may also have symptoms that meet criteria for Conversion Disorder, a Mood Disorder, or a Personality Disorder.

Associated laboratory findings.   Individuals with Dissociative Amnesia often display high hypnotizability as measured by standardized testing.

Specific Age Features

Dissociative Amnesia is especially difficult to assess in preadolescent children, because it may be confused with inattention, anxiety, oppositional behavior, Learning Disorders, psychotic disturbances, and developmentally appropriate childhood amnesia (i.e., the decreased recall of autobiographical events that occurred before age 5). Serial observation or evaluations by several different examiners (e.g., teacher, therapist, case worker) may be needed to make an accurate diagnosis of Dissociative Amnesia in children.

Prevalence

In recent years in the United States, there has been an increase in reported cases of Dissociative Amnesia that involves previously forgotten early childhood traumas. This increase has been subject to very different interpretations. Some believe that the greater awareness of the diagnosis among mental health professionals has resulted in the identification of cases that were previously undiagnosed. In contrast, others believe that the syndrome has been overdiagnosed in individuals who are highly suggestible.

Course

Dissociative Amnesia can present in any age group, from young children to adults. The main manifestation in most individuals is a retrospective gap in memory. The reported duration of the events for which there is amnesia may be minutes to years. Only a single episode of amnesia may be reported, although two or more episodes are also commonly described. Individuals who have had one episode of Dissociative Amnesia may be predisposed to develop amnesia for subsequent traumatic circumstances. Acute amnesia may resolve spontaneously after the individual is removed from the traumatic circumstances with which the amnesia was associated (e.g., a soldier with localized amnesia after several days of intense combat may spontaneously regain memory of these experiences after being removed from the battlefield). Some individuals with chronic amnesia may gradually begin to recall dissociated memories. Other individuals may develop a chronic form of amnesia.

Differential Diagnosis

Dissociative Amnesia must be distinguished from **Amnestic Disorder Due to a General Medical Condition,** in which the amnesia is judged to be the direct physiological consequence of a specific neurological or other general medical condition (e.g., head trauma, epilepsy) (see p. 158). This determination is based on history, laboratory findings, or physical examination. In **Amnestic Disorder Due to a Brain Injury,** the disturbance of recall, though circumscribed, is often retrograde, encompassing a period of time before the head trauma, and there is usually a history of a clear-cut physical trauma, a period of unconsciousness, or clinical evidence of brain injury. In contrast, in Dissociative Amnesia, the disturbance of recall is almost always anterograde (i.e., memory loss is restricted to the period after the trauma). The rare case of Dissociative Amnesia with retrograde amnesia can be distinguished by the diagnostic use of hypnosis; the prompt recovery of the lost memories suggests a dissociative basis for the disturbance. In **seizure disorders,** the memory impairment is sudden in onset, motor abnormalities may be present, and repeated EEGs reveal typical abnormalities. In **delirium** and **dementia,** the memory loss for personal information is embedded in a far more extensive set of cognitive, linguistic, affective, attentional, perceptual, and behavioral disturbances. In contrast, in Dissociative Amnesia, the memory loss is primarily for autobiographical information and cognitive abilities generally are preserved. The amnesia associated with a general medical condition usually cannot be reversed.

Memory loss associated with the use of substances or medications must be distinguished from Dissociative Amnesia. **Substance-Induced Persisting Amnestic Disorder** should be diagnosed if it is judged that there is a persistent loss of memory that is related to the direct physiological effects of a substance (e.g., a drug of abuse or a medication) (see p. 161). Whereas the ability to lay down new memories is preserved in Dissociative Amnesia, in Substance-Induced Persisting Amnestic Disorder, short-term memory is impaired (i.e., events may be recalled immediately after they occur, but not after a few minutes have passed). Memory loss associated with **Substance Intoxication** (e.g., "blackouts") can be distinguished from Dissociative Amnesia by the association of the memory loss with heavy substance use and the fact that the amnesia usually cannot be reversed.

The dissociative symptom of amnesia is a characteristic feature of both Dissociative Fugue and Dissociative Identity Disorder. Therefore, if the dissociative amnesia occurs exclusively during the course of **Dissociative Fugue** or **Dissociative Identity Disorder,** a separate diagnosis of Dissociative Amnesia is not made. Because depersonalization is an associated feature of Dissociative Amnesia, depersonalization that occurs only during Dissociative Amnesia should not be diagnosed separately as **Depersonalization Disorder.**

In **Posttraumatic Stress Disorder** and **Acute Stress Disorder,** there can be amnesia for the traumatic event. Similarly, dissociative symptoms such as amnesia are included in the criteria set for **Somatization Disorder.** Dissociative Amnesia is not diagnosed if it occurs exclusively during the course of these disorders.

There are no tests or set of procedures that invariably distinguish Dissociative Amnesia from **Malingering,** but individuals with Dissociative Amnesia usually score high on standard measures of hypnotizability and dissociative capacity. Malingered amnesia is more common in individuals presenting with acute, florid symptoms in a context in which potential secondary gain is evident—for example, financial or legal problems or the desire to avoid combat, although true amnesia may also be associated with such stressors.

Care must be exercised in evaluating the accuracy of retrieved memories, because the informants are often highly suggestible. There has been considerable controversy concerning amnesia related to reported physical or sexual abuse, particularly when abuse is alleged to have occurred during early childhood. Some clinicians believe that there has been an underreporting of such events, especially because the victims are often children and perpetrators are inclined to deny or distort their actions. However, other clinicians are concerned that there may be overreporting, particularly given the unreliability of childhood memories. There is currently no method for establishing with certainty the accuracy of such retrieved memories in the absence of corroborative evidence.

Dissociative Amnesia must also be differentiated from memory loss related to **Age-Related Cognitive Decline** and **nonpathological forms of amnesia** including everyday memory loss, posthypnotic amnesia, infantile and childhood amnesia, and amnesia for sleep and dreaming. Dissociative Amnesia can be distinguished from normal gaps in memory by the intermittent and involuntary nature of the inability to recall and by the presence of significant distress or impairment.

■ Diagnostic criteria for 300.12 Dissociative Amnesia

A. The predominant disturbance is one or more episodes of inability to recall important personal information, usually of a traumatic or stressful nature, that is too extensive to be explained by ordinary forgetfulness.

B. The disturbance does not occur exclusively during the course of Dissociative Identity Disorder, Dissociative Fugue, Posttraumatic Stress Disorder, Acute Stress Disorder, or Somatization Disorder and is not due to the direct physiological effects of a substance (e.g., a drug of abuse, a medication) or a neurological or other general medical condition (e.g., Amnestic Disorder Due to Head Trauma).

C. The symptoms cause clinically significant distress or impairment in social, occupational, or other important areas of functioning.

300.13 Dissociative Fugue
(*formerly* Psychogenic Fugue)

Diagnostic Features

The essential feature of Dissociative Fugue is sudden, unexpected, travel away from home or one's customary place of daily activities, with inability to recall some or all of one's past (Criterion A). This is accompanied by confusion about personal identity or even the assumption of a new identity (Criterion B). The disturbance does not occur exclusively during the course of Dissociative Identity Disorder and is not due to the direct physiological effects of a substance or a general medical condition (Criterion C). The symptoms must cause clinically significant distress or impairment in social, occupational, or other important areas of functioning (Criterion D).

Travel may range from brief trips over relatively short periods of time (i.e., hours or days) to complex, usually unobtrusive wandering over long time periods (e.g., weeks or months), with some individuals reportedly crossing numerous national borders and traveling thousands of miles. During a fugue, individuals generally appear to be without psychopathology and do not attract attention. At some point, the individual is brought to clinical attention, usually because of amnesia for recent events or a lack of awareness of personal identity. Once the individual returns to the prefugue state, there may be no memory for the events that occurred during the fugue.

Most fugues do not involve the formation of a new identity. If a new identity is assumed during a fugue, it is usually characterized by more gregarious and uninhibited traits than characterized the former identity. The person may assume a new name, take up a new residence, and engage in complex social activities that are well integrated and that do not suggest the presence of a mental disorder.

Associated Features and Disorders

Associated descriptive features and mental disorders.   After return to the pre-fugue state, amnesia for traumatic events in the person's past may be noted (e.g., after termination of a long fugue, a soldier remains amnestic for wartime events that occurred several years previously in which the soldier's closest friend was killed). Depression, dysphoria, grief, shame, guilt, psychological stress, conflict, and suicidal and aggressive impulses may be present. The person may provide approximate inaccurate answers to questions (e.g., "2 plus 2 equals 5") as in Ganser syndrome. The extent and duration of the fugue may determine the degree of other problems, such as loss of employment or severe disruption of personal or family relationships. Individuals with Dissociative Fugue may have a Mood Disorder, Posttraumatic Stress Disorder, or a Substance-Related Disorder.

Specific Culture Features

Individuals with various culturally defined "running" syndromes (e.g., *pibloktoq* among native peoples of the Arctic, *grisi siknis* among the Miskito of Honduras and Nicaragua, Navajo "frenzy" witchcraft, and some forms of *amok* in Western Pacific cultures) may have symptoms that meet diagnostic criteria for Dissociative Fugue. These are conditions characterized by a sudden onset of a high level of activity, a trancelike state, potentially dangerous behavior in the form of running or fleeing, and ensuing exhaustion, sleep, and amnesia for the episode. (See also Dissociative Trance Disorder in Appendix B, p. 727.)

Prevalence

A prevalence rate of 0.2% for Dissociative Fugue has been reported in the general population. The prevalence may increase during times of extremely stressful events such as wartime or natural disaster.

Course

The onset of Dissociative Fugue is usually related to traumatic, stressful, or overwhelming life events. Most cases are described in adults. Single episodes are most commonly reported and may last from hours to months. Recovery is usually rapid, but refractory Dissociative Amnesia may persist in some cases.

Differential Diagnosis

Dissociative Fugue must be distinguished from symptoms that are judged to be the **direct physiological consequence of a specific general medical condition** (e.g., head injury) (see p. 165). This determination is based on history, laboratory findings, or physical examination. Individuals with **complex partial seizures** have been noted to exhibit wandering or semipurposeful behavior during seizures or during postictal states for which there is subsequent amnesia. However, an epileptic fugue can usually be recognized because the individual may have an aura, motor abnormalities, stereotyped behavior, perceptual alterations, a postictal state, and abnormal findings on serial EEGs. Dissociative symptoms that are judged to be the direct physiological consequence of a general medical condition should be diagnosed as **Mental Disorder Not Otherwise Specified Due to a General Medical Condition.** Dissociative Fugue must also be distinguished from symptoms caused by the **direct physiological effects of a substance** (see p. 192).

If the fugue symptoms only occur during the course of **Dissociative Identity Disorder,** Dissociative Fugue should not be diagnosed separately. **Dissociative Amnesia** and **Depersonalization Disorder** should not be diagnosed separately if the amnesia or depersonalization symptoms occur only during the course of a Dissociative Fugue. Wandering and purposeful travel that occur during a **Manic Episode** must be distinguished from Dissociative Fugue. As in Dissociative Fugue, individuals in a Manic Episode may report amnesia for some period of their life, particularly for behavior that occurs during euthymic or depressed states. However, in a Manic Episode, the travel is associated with grandiose ideas and other manic symptoms and such individuals often call attention to themselves by inappropriate behavior. Assumption of an alternate identity does not occur.

Peripatetic behavior may also occur in **Schizophrenia.** Memory for events during wandering episodes in individuals with Schizophrenia may be difficult to ascertain due to the individual's disorganized speech. However, individuals with Dissociative Fugue generally do not demonstrate any of the psychopathology associated with Schizophrenia (e.g., delusions, negative symptoms).

Individuals with Dissociative Fugue usually score high on standard measures of hypnotizability and dissociative capacity. However, there are no tests or set of procedures that invariably distinguish true dissociative symptoms from those that are malingered. **Malingering** of fugue states may occur in individuals who are attempting to flee a situation involving legal, financial, or personal difficulties, as well as in soldiers who are attempting to avoid combat or unpleasant military duties (although true Dissociative Fugue may also be associated with such stressors). Malingering of dissociative symptoms can be maintained even during hypnotic or barbiturate-facilitated interviews. In the forensic context, the examiner should always give careful consideration to the diagnosis of malingering when fugue is claimed. Criminal conduct that is bizarre or with little actual gain may be more consistent with a true dissociative disturbance.

■ Diagnostic criteria for 300.13 Dissociative Fugue

A. The predominant disturbance is sudden, unexpected travel away from home or one's customary place of work, with inability to recall one's past.

B. Confusion about personal identity or assumption of a new identity (partial or complete).

C. The disturbance does not occur exclusively during the course of Dissociative Identity Disorder and is not due to the direct physiological effects of a substance (e.g., a drug of abuse, a medication) or a general medical condition (e.g., temporal lobe epilepsy).

D. The symptoms cause clinically significant distress or impairment in social, occupational, or other important areas of functioning.

300.14   Dissociative Identity Disorder (*formerly* Multiple Personality Disorder)

Diagnostic Features

The essential feature of Dissociative Identity Disorder is the presence of two or more distinct identities or personality states (Criterion A) that recurrently take control of behavior (Criterion B). There is an inability to recall important personal information, the extent of which is too great to be explained by ordinary forgetfulness (Criterion C). The disturbance is not due to the direct physiological effects of a substance or a general medical condition (Criterion D). In children, the symptoms cannot be attributed to imaginary playmates or other fantasy play.

Dissociative Identity Disorder reflects a failure to integrate various aspects of identity, memory, and consciousness. Each personality state may be experienced as if it has a distinct personal history, self-image, and identity, including a separate name. Usually there is a primary identity that carries the individual's given name and is passive, dependent, guilty, and depressed. The alternate identities frequently have different names and characteristics that contrast with the primary identity (e.g., are hostile, controlling, and self-destructive). Particular identities may emerge in specific circumstances and may differ in reported age and gender, vocabulary, general knowledge, or predominant affect. Alternate identities are experienced as taking control in sequence, one at the expense of the other, and may deny knowledge of one another, be critical of one another, or appear to be in open conflict. Occasionally, one or more powerful identities allocate time to the others. Aggressive or hostile identities may at times interrupt activities or place the others in uncomfortable situations.

Individuals with this disorder experience frequent gaps in memory for personal history, both remote and recent. The amnesia is frequently asymmetrical. The more passive identities tend to have more constricted memories, whereas the more hostile, controlling, or "protector" identities have more complete memories. An identity that is not in control may nonetheless gain access to consciousness by producing auditory or visual hallucinations (e.g., a voice giving instructions). Evidence of amnesia may be uncovered by reports from others who have witnessed behavior that is disavowed by the individual or by the individual's own discoveries (e.g., finding items of clothing at home that the individual cannot remember having bought). There may be loss of memory not only for recurrent periods of time, but also an overall loss of biographical memory for some extended period of childhood. Transitions among identities are often triggered by psychosocial stress. The time required to switch from one identity to another is usually a matter of seconds, but, less frequently, may be gradual. The number of identities reported ranges from 2 to more than 100. Half of reported cases include individuals with 10 or fewer identities.

Associated Features and Disorders

Associated descriptive features and mental disorders.   Individuals with Dissociative Identity Disorder frequently report having experienced severe physical and sexual abuse, especially during childhood. Controversy surrounds the accuracy of such reports, because childhood memories may be subject to distortion and individuals with this disorder tend to be highly hypnotizable and especially vulnerable to suggestive influences. On the other hand, those responsible for acts of physical and sexual abuse may be prone to deny or distort their behavior. Individuals with Dissociative Identity Disorder may manifest posttraumatic symptoms (e.g., nightmares, flashbacks, and startle responses) or Posttraumatic Stress Disorder. Self-mutilation and suicidal and aggressive behavior may occur. Some individuals may have a repetitive pattern of relationships involving physical and sexual abuse. Certain identities may experience conversion symptoms (e.g., pseudoseizures) or have unusual abilities to control pain or other physical symptoms. Individuals with this disorder may also have symptoms that meet criteria for Mood, Substance-Related, Sexual, Eating, or Sleep Disorders. Self-mutilative behavior, impulsivity, and sudden and intense changes in relationships may warrant a concurrent diagnosis of Borderline Personality Disorder.

Associated laboratory findings.   Individuals with Dissociative Identity Disorder score toward the upper end of the distribution on measures of hypnotizability and dissociative capacity. There are reports of variation in physiological function across identity states (e.g., differences in visual acuity, pain tolerance, symptoms of asthma, sensitivity to allergens, and response of blood glucose to insulin).

Associated physical examination findings and general medical conditions. There may be scars from self-inflicted injuries or physical abuse. Individuals with this disorder may have migraine and other types of headaches, irritable bowel syndrome, and asthma.

Specific Culture, Age, and Gender Features

It has been suggested that the recent relatively high rates of the disorder reported in the United States might indicate that this is a culture-specific syndrome. In preadolescent children, particular care is needed in making the diagnosis because the manifestations may be less distinctive than in adolescents and adults. Dissociative Identity Disorder is diagnosed three to nine times more frequently in adult females than in adult males; in childhood, the female-to-male ratio may be more even, but data are limited. Females tend to have more identities than do males, averaging 15 or more, whereas males average approximately 8 identities.

Prevalence

The sharp rise in reported cases of Dissociative Identity Disorder in the United States in recent years has been subject to very different interpretations. Some believe that the greater awareness of the diagnosis among mental health professionals has resulted in the identification of cases that were previously undiagnosed. In contrast, others believe that the syndrome has been overdiagnosed in individuals who are highly suggestible.

Course

Dissociative Identity Disorder appears to have a fluctuating clinical course that tends to be chronic and recurrent. The average time period from first symptom presentation to diagnosis is 6–7 years. Episodic and continuous courses have both been described. The disorder may become less manifest as individuals age beyond their late 40s, but may reemerge during episodes of stress or trauma or with Substance Abuse.

Familial Pattern

Several studies suggest that Dissociative Identity Disorder is more common among the first-degree biological relatives of persons with the disorder than in the general population.

Differential Diagnosis

Dissociative Identity Disorder must be distinguished from **symptoms that are caused by the direct physiological effects of a general medical condition** (e.g., seizure disorder) (see p. 165). This determination is based on history, laboratory findings, or physical examination. Dissociative Identity Disorder should be distinguished from **dissociative symptoms due to complex partial seizures,** although the two disorders may co-occur. Seizure episodes are generally brief (30 seconds to 5 minutes) and do not involve the complex and enduring structures of identity and behavior typically found in Dissociative Identity Disorder. Also, a history of physical and sexual abuse is less common in individuals with complex partial seizures. EEG studies, especially sleep deprived and with nasopharyngeal leads, may help clarify the differential diagnosis. Symptoms caused by the **direct physiological effects of a substance** can be distinguished from Dissociative Identity Disorder by the fact that a substance (e.g., a drug of abuse or a medication) is judged to be etiologically related to the disturbance (see p. 192).

The diagnosis of Dissociative Identity Disorder takes precedence over **Dissociative Amnesia, Dissociative Fugue,** and **Depersonalization Disorder.** Individuals with Dissociative Identity Disorder can be distinguished from those with trance and possession trance symptoms that would be diagnosed as **Dissociative Disorder Not Other-**

wise Specified by the fact that those with trance and possession trance symptoms typically describe external spirits or entities that have entered their bodies and taken control.

Controversy exists concerning the differential diagnosis between Dissociative Identity Disorder and a variety of **other mental disorders,** including **Schizophrenia** and **other Psychotic Disorders, Bipolar Disorder, With Rapid Cycling, Anxiety Disorders, Somatization Disorders,** and **Personality Disorders.** Some clinicians believe that Dissociative Identity Disorder has been underdiagnosed (e.g., the presence of more than one dissociated personality state may be mistaken for a delusion or the communication from one identity to another may be mistaken for an auditory hallucination, leading to confusion with the Psychotic Disorders; shifts between identity states may be confused with cyclical mood fluctuations leading to confusion with Bipolar Disorder). In contrast, others are concerned that Dissociative Identity Disorder may be overdiagnosed relative to other mental disorders based on the media interest in the disorder and the suggestible nature of the individuals. Factors that may support a diagnosis of Dissociative Identity Disorder are the presence of clear-cut dissociative symptomatology with sudden shifts in identity states, reversible amnesia, and high scores on measures of dissociation and hypnotizability in individuals who do not have the characteristic presentations of another mental disorder.

Dissociative Identity Disorder must be distinguished from **Malingering** in situations in which there may be financial or forensic gain and from **Factitious Disorder** in which there may be a pattern of help-seeking behavior.

■ Diagnostic criteria for 300.14 Dissociative Identity Disorder

A. The presence of two or more distinct identities or personality states (each with its own relatively enduring pattern of perceiving, relating to, and thinking about the environment and self).

B. At least two of these identities or personality states recurrently take control of the person's behavior.

C. Inability to recall important personal information that is too extensive to be explained by ordinary forgetfulness.

D. The disturbance is not due to the direct physiological effects of a substance (e.g., blackouts or chaotic behavior during Alcohol Intoxication) or a general medical condition (e.g., complex partial seizures). **Note:** In children, the symptoms are not attributable to imaginary playmates or other fantasy play.

300.6   Depersonalization Disorder

Diagnostic Features

The essential features of Depersonalization Disorder are persistent or recurrent episodes of depersonalization characterized by a feeling of detachment or estrangement from one's self (Criterion A). The individual may feel like an automaton or as if he or she is living in a dream or a movie. There may be a sensation of being an outside observer of one's mental processes, one's body, or parts of one's body. Various types of sensory anesthesia, lack of affective response, and a sensation of lacking control of one's actions, including speech, are often present. The individual with Depersonalization Disorder maintains intact reality testing (e.g., awareness that it is only a feeling and that he or she is not really an automaton) (Criterion B). Depersonalization is a common experience, and this diagnosis should be made only if the symptoms are sufficiently severe to cause marked distress or impairment in functioning (Criterion C). Because depersonalization is a common associated feature of many other mental disorders, a separate diagnosis of Depersonalization Disorder is not made if the experience occurs exclusively during the course of another mental disorder (e.g., Schizophrenia, Panic Disorder, Acute Stress Disorder, or another Dissociative Disorder). In addition, the disturbance is not due to the direct physiological effects of a substance or a general medical condition (Criterion D).

Associated Features and Disorders

Associated descriptive features and mental disorders.   Often individuals with Depersonalization Disorder may have difficulty describing their symptoms and may fear that these experiences signify that they are "crazy." Derealization may also be present and is experienced as the sense that the external world is strange or unreal. The individual may perceive an uncanny alteration in the size or shape of objects (macropsia or micropsia), and people may seem unfamiliar or mechanical. Other common associated features include anxiety symptoms, depressive symptoms, obsessive rumination, somatic concerns, and a disturbance in one's sense of time. In some cases, the loss of feeling that is characteristic of depersonalization may mimic Major Depressive Disorder and, in other cases, may coexist with it. Hypochondriasis and Substance-Related Disorders may also coexist with Depersonalization Disorder. Depersonalization and derealization are very frequent symptoms of Panic Attacks. A separate diagnosis of Depersonalization Disorder should not be made when the depersonalization and derealization occur exclusively during such attacks.

Associated laboratory findings.   Individuals with Depersonalization Disorder may display high hypnotizability and high dissociative capacity as measured by standardized testing.

Specific Culture Features

Voluntarily induced experiences of depersonalization or derealization form part of meditative and trance practices that are prevalent in many religions and cultures and should not be confused with Depersonalization Disorder.

Prevalence

The lifetime prevalence of Depersonalization Disorder in community and clinical settings is unknown. At some time in their lives, approximately half of all adults may have experienced a single brief episode of depersonalization, usually precipitated by severe stress. A transient experience of depersonalization develops in nearly one-third of individuals exposed to life-threatening danger and in close to 40% of patients hospitalized for mental disorders.

Course

Individuals with Depersonalization Disorder usually present for treatment in adolescence or adulthood, although the disorder may have an undetected onset in childhood. Because depersonalization is rarely the presenting complaint, individuals with recurrent depersonalization often present with another symptom such as anxiety, panic, or depression. Duration of episodes of depersonalization can vary from very brief (seconds) to persistent (years). Depersonalization subsequent to life-threatening situations (e.g., military combat, traumatic accidents, being a victim of violent crime) usually develops suddenly on exposure to the trauma. The course may be chronic and marked by remissions and exacerbations. Most often the exacerbations occur in association with actual or perceived stressful events.

Differential Diagnosis

Depersonalization Disorder must be distinguished from **symptoms that are due to the physiological consequences of a specific general medical condition** (e.g., epilepsy) (see p. 165). This determination is based on history, laboratory findings, or physical examination. **Depersonalization that is caused by the direct physiological effects of a substance** is distinguished from Depersonalization Disorder by the fact that a substance (e.g., a drug of abuse or a medication) is judged to be etiologically related to the depersonalization (see p. 192). **Acute Intoxication** or **Withdrawal** from alcohol and a variety of other substances can result in depersonalization. On the other hand, substance use may intensify the symptoms of a preexisting Depersonalization Disorder. Thus, accurate diagnosis of Depersonalization Disorder in individuals with a history of alcohol- or substance-induced depersonalization should include a longitudinal history of Substance Abuse and depersonalization symptoms.

Depersonalization Disorder should not be diagnosed separately when the symptoms occur only during a Panic Attack that is part of **Panic Disorder, Social or Specific Phobia,** or **Posttraumatic** or **Acute Stress Disorders.** In contrast to **Schizophrenia,** intact reality testing is maintained in Depersonalization Disorder. The loss of feeling associated with depersonalization (e.g., numbness) may mimic a **depression.** However, the absence of feeling in individuals with Depersonalization Disorder is associated with other manifestations of depersonalization (e.g., a sense of detachment from one's self) and occurs even when the individual is not depressed.

■ **Diagnostic criteria for 300.6 Depersonalization Disorder**

A. Persistent or recurrent experiences of feeling detached from, and as if one is an outside observer of, one's mental processes or body (e.g., feeling like one is in a dream).

B. During the depersonalization experience, reality testing remains intact.

C. The depersonalization causes clinically significant distress or impairment in social, occupational, or other important areas of functioning.

D. The depersonalization experience does not occur exclusively during the course of another mental disorder, such as Schizophrenia, Panic Disorder, Acute Stress Disorder, or another Dissociative Disorder, and is not due to the direct physiological effects of a substance (e.g., a drug of abuse, a medication) or a general medical condition (e.g., temporal lobe epilepsy).

300.15   Dissociative Disorder Not Otherwise Specified

This category is included for disorders in which the predominant feature is a dissociative symptom (i.e., a disruption in the usually integrated functions of consciousness, memory, identity, or perception of the environment) that does not meet the criteria for any specific Dissociative Disorder. Examples include

1. Clinical presentations similar to Dissociative Identity Disorder that fail to meet full criteria for this disorder. Examples include presentations in which a) there are not two or more distinct personality states, or b) amnesia for important personal information does not occur.
2. Derealization unaccompanied by depersonalization in adults.
3. States of dissociation that occur in individuals who have been subjected to periods of prolonged and intense coercive persuasion (e.g., brainwashing, thought reform, or indoctrination while captive).
4. Dissociative trance disorder: single or episodic disturbances in the state of consciousness, identity, or memory that are indigenous to particular locations and cultures. Dissociative trance involves narrowing of awareness of immediate surroundings or stereotyped behaviors or movements that are experienced as being beyond one's control. Possession trance involves replacement of the customary sense of personal identity by a new identity, attributed to the influence of a spirit, power, deity, or other person, and associated with stereotyped "involuntary" movements or amnesia. Examples include *amok* (Indonesia), *bebainan* (Indonesia), *latah* (Malaysia), *pibloktoq* (Arctic), *ataque de nervios* (Latin America), and possession (India). The dissociative or trance disorder is

not a normal part of a broadly accepted collective cultural or religious practice. (See p. 727 for suggested research criteria.)

5. Loss of consciousness, stupor, or coma not attributable to a general medical condition.

6. Ganser syndrome: the giving of approximate answers to questions (e.g., "2 plus 2 equals 5") when not associated with Dissociative Amnesia or Dissociative Fugue.

Sexual and Gender Identity Disorders

This section contains the Sexual Dysfunctions, the Paraphilias, and the Gender Identity Disorders. The **Sexual Dysfunctions** are characterized by disturbance in sexual desire and in the psychophysiological changes that characterize the sexual response cycle and cause marked distress and interpersonal difficulty. The Sexual Dysfunctions include Sexual Desire Disorders (i.e., Hypoactive Sexual Desire Disorder, Sexual Aversion Disorder), Sexual Arousal Disorders (i.e., Female Sexual Arousal Disorder, Male Erectile Disorder), Orgasmic Disorders (i.e., Female Orgasmic Disorder, Male Orgasmic Disorder, Premature Ejaculation), Sexual Pain Disorders (i.e., Dyspareunia, Vaginismus), Sexual Dysfunction Due to a General Medical Condition, Substance-Induced Sexual Dysfunction, and Sexual Dysfunction Not Otherwise Specified.

The **Paraphilias** are characterized by recurrent, intense sexual urges, fantasies, or behaviors that involve unusual objects, activities, or situations and cause clinically significant distress or impairment in social, occupational, or other important areas of functioning. The Paraphilias include Exhibitionism, Fetishism, Frotteurism, Pedophilia, Sexual Masochism, Sexual Sadism, Transvestic Fetishism, Voyeurism, and Paraphilia Not Otherwise Specified.

Gender Identity Disorders are characterized by strong and persistent cross-gender identification accompanied by persistent discomfort with one's assigned sex.

Sexual Disorder Not Otherwise Specified is included for coding disorders of sexual functioning that are not classifiable in any of the specific categories. It is important to note that notions of deviance, standards of sexual performance, and concepts of appropriate gender role can vary from culture to culture.

Sexual Dysfunctions

A Sexual Dysfunction is characterized by a disturbance in the processes that characterize the sexual response cycle or by pain associated with sexual intercourse. The sexual response cycle can be divided into the following phases:

1. *Desire:* This phase consists of fantasies about sexual activity and the desire to have sexual activity.

---

2. *Excitement:* This phase consists of a subjective sense of sexual pleasure and accompanying physiological changes. The major changes in the male consist of penile tumescence and erection. The major changes in the female consist of vasocongestion in the pelvis, vaginal lubrication and expansion, and swelling of the external genitalia.
3. *Orgasm:* This phase consists of a peaking of sexual pleasure, with release of sexual tension and rhythmic contraction of the perineal muscles and reproductive organs. In the male, there is the sensation of ejaculatory inevitability, which is followed by ejaculation of semen. In the female, there are contractions (not always subjectively experienced as such) of the wall of the outer third of the vagina. In both genders, the anal sphincter rhythmically contracts.
4. *Resolution:* This phase consists of a sense of muscular relaxation and general well-being. During this phase, males are physiologically refractory to further erection and orgasm for a variable period of time. In contrast, females may be able to respond to additional stimulation almost immediately.

Disorders of sexual response may occur at one or more of these phases. Whenever more than one Sexual Dysfunction is present, all are recorded. No attempt is made in the criteria sets to specify a minimum frequency or range of settings, activities, or types of sexual encounters in which the dysfunction must occur. This judgment must be made by the clinician, taking into account such factors as the age and experience of the individual, frequency and chronicity of the symptom, subjective distress, and effect on other areas of functioning. The words "persistent or recurrent" in the diagnostic criteria indicate the need for such a clinical judgment. If sexual stimulation is inadequate in either focus, intensity, or duration, the diagnosis of Sexual Dysfunction involving excitement or orgasm is not made.

Subtypes

Subtypes are provided to indicate the onset, context, and etiological factors associated with the Sexual Dysfunctions. If multiple Sexual Dysfunctions are present, the appropriate subtypes for each may be noted. These subtypes do not apply to a diagnosis of Sexual Dysfunction Due to a General Medical Condition or Substance-Induced Sexual Dysfunction.

One of the following subtypes may be used to indicate the nature of the onset of the Sexual Dysfunction:

Lifelong Type. This subtype applies if the sexual dysfunction has been present since the onset of sexual functioning.

Acquired Type. This subtype applies if the sexual dysfunction develops only after a period of normal functioning.

One of the following subtypes may be used to indicate the context in which the Sexual Dysfunction occurs:

Generalized Type. This subtype applies if the sexual dysfunction is not limited to certain types of stimulation, situations, or partners.

Situational Type. This subtype applies if the sexual dysfunction is limited to certain types of stimulation, situations, or partners. Although in most instances the dysfunctions occur during sexual activity with a partner, in some cases it may be appropriate to identify dysfunctions that occur during masturbation.

One of the following subtypes may be used to indicate etiological factors associated with the Sexual Dysfunction:

Due to Psychological Factors. This subtype applies when psychological factors are judged to have the major role in the onset, severity, exacerbation, or maintenance of the Sexual Dysfunction, and general medical conditions and substances play no role in the etiology of the Sexual Dysfunction.

Due to Combined Factors. This subtype applies when 1) psychological factors are judged to have a role in the onset, severity, exacerbation, or maintenance of the Sexual Dysfunction; and 2) a general medical condition or substance use is also judged to be contributory but is not sufficient to account for the Sexual Dysfunction. If a general medical condition or substance use (including medication side effects) is sufficient to account for the Sexual Dysfunction, Sexual Dysfunction Due to a General Medical Condition (p. 515) and/or Substance-Induced Sexual Dysfunction (p. 519) is diagnosed.

Specific Culture, Age, and Gender Features

Clinical judgments about the presence of a Sexual Dysfunction should take into account the individual's ethnic, cultural, religious, and social background, which may influence sexual desire, expectations, and attitudes about performance. For example, in some societies, sexual desires on the part of the female are given less relevance (especially when fertility is the primary concern). Aging may be associated with a lowering of sexual interest and functioning (especially in males), but there are wide individual differences in age effects.

Prevalence

There are very few systematic epidemiological data regarding the prevalence of the various sexual dysfunctions, and these show extremely wide variability, probably reflecting differences in assessment methods, definitions used, and characteristics of sampled populations.

Differential Diagnosis

If the Sexual Dysfunction is judged to be caused exclusively by the physiological effects of a specified general medical condition, the diagnosis is **Sexual Dysfunction Due to a General Medical Condition** (p. 515). This determination is based on history, laboratory findings, or physical examination. If the Sexual Dysfunction is judged to be caused exclusively by the physiological effects of a drug of abuse, a medication, or toxin exposure, the diagnosis is **Substance-Induced Sexual Dysfunction** (see p. 519). The clinician should inquire carefully about the nature and extent of substance use, including medications. Symptoms that occur during or shortly after (i.e., within 4 weeks of) Substance Intoxication or after medication use may be especially indicative of a Substance-Induced Sexual Dysfunction, depending on the type or amount of the substance used or the duration of use.

If the clinician has ascertained that the sexual dysfunction is due to both a general medical condition and substance use, both diagnoses (i.e., Sexual Dysfunction Due to a General Medical Condition and Substance-Induced Sexual Dysfunction) can be given. A primary Sexual Dysfunction diagnosis with the subtype **Due to Combined Factors** is made if a combination of psychological factors and either a general medical condition or a substance is judged to have an etiological role, but no one etiology is sufficient to account for the dysfunction. If the clinician cannot determine the etiological roles of psychological factors, a general medical condition, and substance use, **Sexual Dysfunction Not Otherwise Specified** is diagnosed.

The diagnosis of a Sexual Dysfunction is also not made if the dysfunction is better accounted for by another Axis I disorder (e.g., if diminished sexual desire occurs only in the context of a Major Depressive Episode). However, if the disturbance in sexual functioning antedates the Axis I disorder or is a focus of independent clinical attention, an additional diagnosis of Sexual Dysfunction can also be made. Commonly, if one Sexual Dysfunction is present (e.g., a Sexual Arousal Disorder), additional Sexual Dysfunctions will also be present (e.g., Hypoactive Sexual Desire Disorder). In such cases, all should be diagnosed. A **Personality Disorder** may coexist with a Sexual Dysfunction. In such cases, the Sexual Dysfunction should be recorded on Axis I and the Personality Disorder should be recorded on Axis II. If another clinical condition, such as a **Relational Problem,** is associated with the disturbance in sexual functioning, the Sexual Dysfunction should be diagnosed and the other clinical condition is also noted on Axis I. Occasional problems with sexual desire, arousal, or orgasm that are not persistent or recurrent or are not accompanied by marked distress or interpersonal difficulty are not considered to be Sexual Dysfunctions.

Sexual Desire Disorders

302.71 Hypoactive Sexual Desire Disorder

Diagnostic Features

The essential feature of Hypoactive Sexual Desire Disorder is a deficiency or absence of sexual fantasies and desire for sexual activity (Criterion A). The disturbance must cause marked distress or interpersonal difficulty (Criterion B). The dysfunction is not better accounted for by another Axis I disorder (except another Sexual Dysfunction) and is not due exclusively to the direct physiological effects of a substance (including medications) or a general medical condition (Criterion C). Low sexual desire may be global and encompass all forms of sexual expression or may be situational and limited to one partner or to a specific sexual activity (e.g., intercourse but not masturbation). There is little motivation to seek stimuli and diminished frustration when deprived of the opportunity for sexual expression. The individual usually does not initiate sexual activity or may only engage in it reluctantly when it is initiated by the partner. Although the frequency of sexual experiences is usually low, pressure from the partner or nonsexual needs (e.g., for physical comfort or intimacy) may increase the frequency of sexual encounters. Because of a lack of normative age- or gender-related data on frequency or degree of sexual desire, the diagnosis must rely on clinical judgment based on the individual's characteristics, the interpersonal determinants, the life context, and the cultural setting. The clinician may need to assess both partners when discrepancies in sexual desire prompt the call for professional attention. Apparent "low desire" in one partner may instead reflect an excessive need for sexual expression by the other partner. Alternatively, both partners may have levels of desire within the normal range but at different ends of the continuum.

Subtypes

Subtypes are provided to indicate onset (**Lifelong** versus **Acquired**), context (**Generalized** versus **Situational**) and etiological factors (**Due to Psychological Factors, Due to Combined Factors**) for Hypoactive Sexual Desire Disorder. (See descriptions on p. 494.)

Associated Features and Disorders

Low sexual interest is frequently associated with problems of sexual arousal or with orgasm difficulties. The deficiency in sexual desire may be the primary dysfunction or may be the consequence of emotional distress induced by disturbances in excitement or orgasm. However, some individuals with low sexual desire retain the capacity for adequate sexual excitement and orgasm in response to sexual stimulation. General medical conditions may have a nonspecific deleterious effect on sexual desire due to weakness, pain, problems with body image, or concerns about survival. Depressive disorders are often associated with low sexual desire, and the onset of depression may precede, co-occur with, or be the consequence of the deficient sexual desire. Individuals with Hypoactive Sexual Desire Disorder may have difficulties developing stable sexual relationships and may have marital dissatisfaction and disruption.

Course

The age at onset for individuals with Lifelong forms of Hypoactive Sexual Desire Disorder is puberty. More frequently, the disorder develops in adulthood, after a period of adequate sexual interest, in association with psychological distress, stressful life events, or interpersonal difficulties. The loss of sexual desire may be continuous or episodic, depending on psychosocial or relationship factors. An episodic pattern of loss of sexual desire occurs in some individuals in relation to problems with intimacy and commitment.

Differential Diagnosis

Hypoactive Sexual Desire Disorder must be distinguished from **Sexual Dysfunction Due to a General Medical Condition.** The appropriate diagnosis would be Sexual Dysfunction Due to a General Medical Condition when the dysfunction is judged to be due exclusively to the physiological effects of a specified general medical condition (see p. 515). This determination is based on history, laboratory findings, or physical examination. Certain general medical conditions such as neurological, hormonal, and metabolic abnormalities may specifically impair the physiological substrates of sexual desire. Abnormalities in total and bioavailable testosterone and prolactin may indicate hormonal disorders responsible for loss of sexual desire. If both Hypoactive Sexual Desire Disorder and a general medical condition are present, but it is judged that the sexual dysfunction is not due exclusively to the direct physiological effects of the general medical condition, then Hypoactive Sexual Desire Disorder, Due to Combined Factors, is diagnosed.

In contrast to Hypoactive Sexual Desire Disorder, a **Substance-Induced Sexual Dysfunction** is judged to be due exclusively to the direct physiological effects of a substance (e.g., antihypertensive medication, a drug of abuse) (see p. 519). If both Hypoactive Sexual Desire Disorder and substance use are present, but it is judged that the sexual dysfunction is not due exclusively to the direct physiological effects of the substance use, then Hypoactive Sexual Desire Disorder, Due to Combined Factors, is diagnosed. If the low sexual desire is judged to be due exclusively to the physiological effects of both a general medical condition and substance use, both Sexual Dysfunction Due to a General Medical Condition and Substance-Induced Sexual Dysfunction are diagnosed.

Hypoactive Sexual Desire Disorder may also occur in association with other Sexual Dysfunctions (e.g., Male Erectile Dysfunction). If so, both should be noted. An additional diagnosis of Hypoactive Sexual Desire Disorder is usually not made if the low sexual desire is better accounted for by **another Axis I disorder** (e.g., Major Depressive Disorder, Obsessive-Compulsive Disorder, Posttraumatic Stress Disorder). The additional diagnosis may be appropriate when the low desire predates the Axis I disorder or is a focus of independent clinical attention. **Occasional problems with sexual desire** that are not persistent or recurrent or are not accompanied by marked distress or interpersonal difficulty are not considered to be Hypoactive Sexual Desire Disorder.

■ Diagnostic criteria for 302.71 Hypoactive Sexual Desire Disorder

A. Persistently or recurrently deficient (or absent) sexual fantasies and desire for sexual activity. The judgment of deficiency or absence is made by the clinician, taking into account factors that affect sexual functioning, such as age and the context of the person's life.

B. The disturbance causes marked distress or interpersonal difficulty.

C. The sexual dysfunction is not better accounted for by another Axis I disorder (except another Sexual Dysfunction) and is not due exclusively to the direct physiological effects of a substance (e.g., a drug of abuse, a medication) or a general medical condition.

Specify type:
   Lifelong Type
   Acquired Type

Specify type:
   Generalized Type
   Situational Type

Specify:
   Due to Psychological Factors
   Due to Combined Factors

302.79 Sexual Aversion Disorder

Diagnostic Features

The essential feature of Sexual Aversion Disorder is the aversion to and active avoidance of genital sexual contact with a sexual partner (Criterion A). The disturbance must cause marked distress or interpersonal difficulty (Criterion B). The dysfunction is not better accounted for by another Axis I disorder (except another Sexual Dysfunction) (Criterion C). The individual reports anxiety, fear, or disgust when confronted by a sexual opportunity with a partner. The aversion to genital contact may be focused on a particular aspect of sexual experience (e.g., genital secretions, vaginal penetration). Some individuals experience generalized revulsion to all sexual stimuli, including kissing and touching. The intensity of the individual's reaction when exposed to the aversive stimulus may range from moderate anxiety and lack of pleasure to extreme psychological distress.

Subtypes

Subtypes are provided to indicate onset (**Lifelong** versus **Acquired**), context (**Generalized** versus **Situational**), and etiological factors (**Due to Psychological Factors, Due to Combined Factors**) for Sexual Aversion Disorder. (See descriptions on p. 494.)

Associated Features and Disorders

When confronted with a sexual situation, some individuals with severe Sexual Aversion Disorder may experience Panic Attacks with extreme anxiety, feelings of terror, faintness, nausea, palpitations, dizziness, and breathing difficulties. There may be markedly impaired interpersonal relations (e.g., marital dissatisfaction). Individuals may avoid sexual situations or potential sexual partners by covert strategies (e.g., going to sleep early, traveling, neglecting personal appearance, using substances, and being over-involved in work, social, or family activities).

Differential Diagnosis

Sexual Aversion Disorder may also occur in association with other Sexual Dysfunctions (e.g., Dyspareunia). If so, both should be noted. An additional diagnosis of Sexual Aversion Disorder is usually not made if the sexual aversion is better accounted for by **another Axis I disorder** (e.g., Major Depressive Disorder, Obsessive-Compulsive Disorder, Posttraumatic Stress Disorder). The additional diagnosis may be made when the aversion predates the Axis I disorder or is a focus of independent clinical attention. Although sexual aversion may technically meet the criteria for **Specific Phobia,** this additional diagnosis is not given. **Occasional sexual aversion** that is not persistent or recurrent or is not accompanied by marked distress or interpersonal difficulty is not considered to be a Sexual Aversion Disorder.

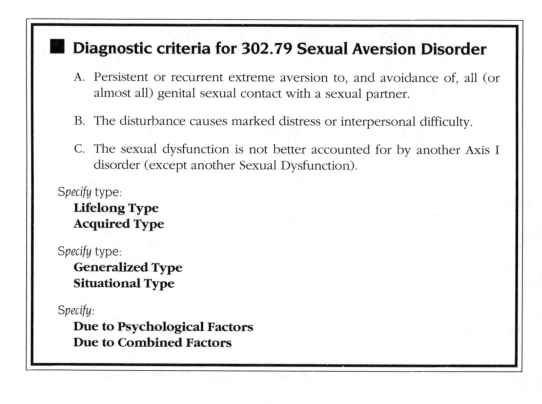

■ **Diagnostic criteria for 302.79 Sexual Aversion Disorder**

A. Persistent or recurrent extreme aversion to, and avoidance of, all (or almost all) genital sexual contact with a sexual partner.

B. The disturbance causes marked distress or interpersonal difficulty.

C. The sexual dysfunction is not better accounted for by another Axis I disorder (except another Sexual Dysfunction).

Specify type:
Lifelong Type
Acquired Type

Specify type:
Generalized Type
Situational Type

Specify:
Due to Psychological Factors
Due to Combined Factors

Sexual Arousal Disorders

302.72   Female Sexual Arousal Disorder

Diagnostic Features

The essential feature of Female Sexual Arousal Disorder is a persistent or recurrent inability to attain, or to maintain until completion of the sexual activity, an adequate lubrication-swelling response of sexual excitement (Criterion A). The arousal response consists of vasocongestion in the pelvis, vaginal lubrication and expansion, and swelling of the external genitalia. The disturbance must cause marked distress or interpersonal difficulty (Criterion B). The dysfunction is not better accounted for by another Axis I disorder (except another Sexual Dysfunction) and is not due exclusively to the direct physiological effects of a substance (including medications) or a general medical condition (Criterion C).

Subtypes

Subtypes are provided to indicate onset (**Lifelong** versus **Acquired**), context (**Generalized** versus **Situational**), and etiological factors (**Due to Psychological Factors, Due to Combined Factors**) for Female Sexual Arousal Disorder. (See descriptions on p. 494.)

Associated Features and Disorders

Limited evidence suggests that Female Sexual Arousal Disorder is often accompanied by Sexual Desire Disorders and Female Orgasmic Disorder. The individual with Female Sexual Arousal Disorder may have little or no subjective sense of sexual arousal. The disorder may result in painful intercourse, sexual avoidance, and the disturbance of marital or sexual relationships.

Differential Diagnosis

Female Sexual Arousal Disorder must be distinguished from a **Sexual Dysfunction Due to a General Medical Condition.** The appropriate diagnosis would be Sexual Dysfunction Due to a General Medical Condition when the dysfunction is judged to be due exclusively to the physiological effects of a specified general medical condition (e.g., menopausal or postmenopausal reductions in estrogen levels, atrophic vaginitis, diabetes mellitus, radiotherapy of the pelvis) (see p. 515). Reduced lubrication has also been reported in association with lactation. This determination is based on history, laboratory findings, or physical examination. If both Female Sexual Arousal Disorder and a general medical condition are present but it is judged that the sexual dysfunction is not due exclusively to the direct physiological consequences of the general medical condition, then Female Sexual Arousal Disorder, Due to Combined Factors, is diagnosed.

In contrast to Female Sexual Arousal Disorder, a **Substance-Induced Sexual Dysfunction** is judged to be due exclusively to the direct physiological effects of a substance (e.g., reduced lubrication caused by antihypertensives or antihistamines) (see p. 519). If both Female Sexual Arousal Disorder and substance use are present but it is judged that the sexual dysfunction is not due exclusively to the direct physiological effects of the substance use, then Female Sexual Arousal Disorder, Due to Combined Factors, is diagnosed.

If the arousal problems are judged to be due exclusively to the physiological effects of both a general medical condition and substance use, both Sexual Dysfunction Due to a General Medical Condition and Substance-Induced Sexual Dysfunction are diagnosed.

Female Sexual Arousal Disorder may also occur in association with other Sexual Dysfunctions (e.g., Female Orgasmic Disorder). If so, both should be noted. An additional diagnosis of Female Sexual Arousal Disorder is usually not made if the sexual arousal problem is better accounted for by **another Axis I disorder** (e.g., Major Depressive Disorder, Obsessive-Compulsive Disorder, Posttraumatic Stress Disorder). The additional diagnosis may be made when the problem with sexual arousal predates the Axis I disorder or is a focus of independent clinical attention. **Occasional problems with sexual arousal** that are not persistent or recurrent or are not accompanied by marked distress or interpersonal difficulty are not considered to be Female Sexual Arousal Disorder. A diagnosis of Female Sexual Arousal Disorder is also not appropriate if the problems in arousal are due to sexual stimulation that is not adequate in focus, intensity, and duration.

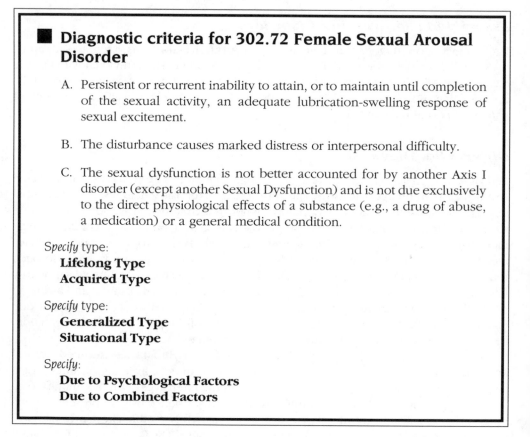

■ **Diagnostic criteria for 302.72 Female Sexual Arousal Disorder**

A. Persistent or recurrent inability to attain, or to maintain until completion of the sexual activity, an adequate lubrication-swelling response of sexual excitement.

B. The disturbance causes marked distress or interpersonal difficulty.

C. The sexual dysfunction is not better accounted for by another Axis I disorder (except another Sexual Dysfunction) and is not due exclusively to the direct physiological effects of a substance (e.g., a drug of abuse, a medication) or a general medical condition.

Specify type:
Lifelong Type
Acquired Type

Specify type:
Generalized Type
Situational Type

Specify:
Due to Psychological Factors
Due to Combined Factors

302.72   Male Erectile Disorder

Diagnostic Features

The essential feature of Male Erectile Disorder is a persistent or recurrent inability to attain, or to maintain until completion of the sexual activity, an adequate erection (Criterion A). The disturbance must cause marked distress or interpersonal difficulty (Criterion B). The dysfunction is not better accounted for by another Axis I disorder (except another Sexual Dysfunction) and is not due exclusively to the direct physiological effects of a substance (including medications) or a general medical condition (Criterion C).

There are different patterns of erectile dysfunction. Some individuals will report the inability to obtain any erection from the outset of a sexual experience. Others will complain of first experiencing an adequate erection and then losing tumescence when attempting penetration. Still others will report that they have an erection that is sufficiently firm for penetration but that they then lose tumescence before or during thrusting. Some males may report being able to experience an erection only during self-masturbation or on awakening. Masturbatory erections may be lost as well, but this is not common.

Subtypes

Subtypes are provided to indicate onset (**Lifelong** versus **Acquired**), context (**Generalized** versus **Situational**), and etiological factors (**Due to Psychological Factors, Due to Combined Factors**) for Male Erectile Disorder. (See descriptions on p. 494.)

Associated Features and Disorders

The erectile difficulties in Male Erectile Disorder are frequently associated with sexual anxiety, fear of failure, concerns about sexual performance, and a decreased subjective sense of sexual excitement and pleasure. Erectile dysfunction can disrupt existing marital or sexual relationships and may be the cause of unconsummated marriages and infertility. This disorder may be associated with Hypoactive Sexual Desire Disorder and Premature Ejaculation. Individuals with Mood Disorders and Substance-Related Disorders often report problems with sexual arousal.

Course

The various forms of Male Erectile Disorder follow different courses, and the age at onset varies substantially. The few individuals who have never been able to experience an erection of sufficient quality to complete sexual activity with a partner typically have a chronic, lifelong disorder. Acquired cases may remit spontaneously 15%–30% of the time. Situational cases may be dependent on a type of partner or the intensity or quality of the relationship and are episodic and frequently recurrent.

Differential Diagnosis

Male Erectile Disorder must be distinguished from **Sexual Dysfunction Due to a General Medical Condition.** The appropriate diagnosis would be Sexual Dysfunction Due to a General Medical Condition when the dysfunction is judged to be due exclusively to the physiological effects of a specified general medical condition (e.g., diabetes mellitus, multiple sclerosis, renal failure, peripheral neuropathy, peripheral vascular disease, spinal cord injury, injury of the autonomic nervous system by surgery or radiation) (see p. 515). This determination is based on history (e.g., impaired erectile functioning during masturbation), laboratory findings, or physical examination. Nocturnal penile tumescence studies can demonstrate whether erections occur during sleep and may be helpful in differentiating primary erectile disorders from Male Erectile Disorder Due to a General Medical Condition. Penile blood pressure, pulse-wave assessments, or duplex ultrasound studies can indicate vasculogenic loss of erectile functioning. Invasive procedures such as intracorporeal pharmacological testing or angiography can assess the presence of arterial flow problems. Cavernosography can evaluate venous competence. If both Male Erectile Disorder and a general medical condition are present but it is judged that the erectile dysfunction is not due exclusively to the direct physiological effects of the general medical condition, then Male Erectile Disorder, Due to Combined Factors, is diagnosed.

   A **Substance-Induced Sexual Dysfunction** is distinguished from Male Erectile Disorder by the fact that the sexual dysfunction is judged to be due exclusively to the direct physiological effects of a substance (e.g., antihypertensive medication, antidepressant medication, neuroleptic medication, a drug of abuse) (see p. 519). If both Male Erectile Disorder and substance use are present but it is judged that the erectile dysfunction is not due exclusively to the direct physiological effects of the substance use, then Male Erectile Disorder, Due to Combined Factors, is diagnosed.

If the arousal problems are judged to be due exclusively to the physiological effects of both a general medical condition and substance use, both Sexual Dysfunction Due to a General Medical Condition and Substance-Induced Sexual Dysfunction are diagnosed.

Male Erectile Disorder may also occur in association with other Sexual Dysfunctions (e.g., Premature Ejaculation). If so, both should be noted. An additional diagnosis of Male Erectile Disorder is usually not made if the erectile dysfunction is better accounted for by **another Axis I disorder** (e.g., Major Depressive Disorder, Obsessive-Compulsive Disorder). The additional diagnosis may be made when the erectile dysfunction predates the Axis I disorder or is a focus of independent clinical attention. **Occasional problems with having erections** that are not persistent or recurrent or are not accompanied by marked distress or interpersonal difficulty are not considered to be Male Erectile Disorder. A diagnosis of Male Erectile Disorder is also not appropriate if the erectile dysfunction is due to sexual stimulation that is not adequate in focus, intensity, and duration. Older males may require more stimulation or take longer to achieve a full erection. These physiological changes should not be considered to be Male Erectile Disorder.

■ Diagnostic criteria for 302.72 Male Erectile Disorder

A. Persistent or recurrent inability to attain, or to maintain until completion of the sexual activity, an adequate erection.

B. The disturbance causes marked distress or interpersonal difficulty.

C. The erectile dysfunction is not better accounted for by another Axis I disorder (other than a Sexual Dysfunction) and is not due exclusively to the direct physiological effects of a substance (e.g., a drug of abuse, a medication) or a general medical condition.

Specify type:
  Lifelong Type
  Acquired Type

Specify type:
  Generalized Type
  Situational Type

Specify:
  Due to Psychological Factors
  Due to Combined Factors

Orgasmic Disorders

302.73 Female Orgasmic Disorder
(*formerly* Inhibited Female Orgasm)

Diagnostic Features

The essential feature of Female Orgasmic Disorder is a persistent or recurrent delay in, or absence of, orgasm following a normal sexual excitement phase (Criterion A). Women exhibit wide variability in the type or intensity of stimulation that triggers orgasm. The diagnosis of Female Orgasmic Disorder should be based on the clinician's judgment that the woman's orgasmic capacity is less than would be reasonable for her age, sexual experience, and the adequacy of sexual stimulation she receives. The disturbance must cause marked distress or interpersonal difficulty (Criterion B). The dysfunction is not better accounted for by another Axis I disorder (except another Sexual Dysfunction) and is not due exclusively to the direct physiological effects of a substance (including medications) or a general medical condition (Criterion C).

Subtypes

Subtypes are provided to indicate onset (**Lifelong** versus **Acquired**), context (**Generalized** versus **Situational**), and etiological factors (**Due to Psychological Factors, Due to Combined Factors**) for Female Orgasmic Disorder. (See descriptions on p. 494.)

Associated Features and Disorders

No association has been found between specific patterns of personality traits or psychopathology and orgasmic dysfunction in females. Female Orgasmic Disorder may affect body image, self-esteem, or relationship satisfaction. According to controlled studies, orgasmic capacity is not correlated with vaginal size or pelvic muscle strength. Although females with spinal cord lesions, removal of the vulva, or vaginal excision and reconstruction have reported reaching orgasm, orgasmic dysfunction is commonly reported in women with these conditions. In general, however, chronic general medical conditions like diabetes or pelvic cancer are more likely to impair the arousal phase of the sexual response, leaving orgasmic capacity relatively intact.

Course

Because orgasmic capacity in females increases with age, Female Orgasmic Disorder may be more prevalent in younger women. Most female orgasmic disorders are lifelong rather than acquired. Once a female learns how to reach orgasm, it is uncommon for her to lose that capacity, unless poor sexual communication, relationship conflict, a traumatic experience (e.g., rape), a Mood Disorder, or a general medical condition intervenes. When orgasmic dysfunction occurs only in certain situations, difficulty with sexual desire and arousal are often present in addition to the orgasmic disorder. Many females increase their orgasmic capacity as they experience a wider variety of stimulation and acquire more knowledge about their own bodies.

Differential Diagnosis

Female Orgasmic Disorder must be distinguished from a **Sexual Dysfunction Due to a General Medical Condition.** The appropriate diagnosis would be Sexual Dysfunction Due to a General Medical Condition when the dysfunction is judged to be due exclusively to the physiological effects of a specified general medical condition (e.g., spinal cord lesion) (see p. 515). This determination is based on history, laboratory findings, or physical examination. If both Female Orgasmic Disorder and a general medical condition are present but it is judged that the sexual dysfunction is not due exclusively to the direct physiological effects of the general medical condition, then Female Orgasmic Disorder, Due to Combined Factors, is diagnosed.

In contrast to Female Orgasmic Disorder, a **Substance-Induced Sexual Dysfunction** is judged to be due exclusively to the direct physiological effects of a substance (e.g., antidepressants, benzodiazepines, neuroleptics, antihypertensives, opioids) (see p. 519). If both Female Orgasmic Disorder and substance use are present but it is judged that the sexual dysfunction is not due exclusively to the direct physiological effects of the substance use, then Female Orgasmic Disorder, Due to Combined Factors, is diagnosed.

If the sexual dysfunction is judged to be due exclusively to the physiological effects of both a general medical condition and substance use, both Sexual Dysfunction Due to a General Medical Condition and Substance-Induced Sexual Dysfunction are diagnosed.

Female Orgasmic Disorder may also occur in association with other Sexual Dysfunctions (e.g., Female Sexual Arousal Disorder). If so, both should be noted. An additional diagnosis of Female Orgasmic Disorder is usually not made if the orgasmic difficulty is better accounted for by **another Axis I disorder** (e.g., Major Depressive Disorder). This additional diagnosis may be made when the orgasmic difficulty predates the Axis I disorder or is a focus of independent clinical attention. **Occasional orgasmic problems** that are not persistent or recurrent or are not accompanied by marked distress or interpersonal difficulty are not considered to be Female Orgasmic Disorder. A diagnosis of Female Orgasmic Disorder is also not appropriate if the problems are due to sexual stimulation that is not adequate in focus, intensity, and duration.

■ **Diagnostic criteria for 302.73 Female Orgasmic Disorder**

A. Persistent or recurrent delay in, or absence of, orgasm following a normal sexual excitement phase. Women exhibit wide variability in the type or intensity of stimulation that triggers orgasm. The diagnosis of Female Orgasmic Disorder should be based on the clinician's judgment that the woman's orgasmic capacity is less than would be reasonable for her age, sexual experience, and the adequacy of sexual stimulation she receives.

B. The disturbance causes marked distress or interpersonal difficulty.

(continued)

☐ **Diagnostic criteria for 302.73 Female Orgasmic Disorder**
(*continued*)

    C. The orgasmic dysfunction is not better accounted for by another Axis I disorder (except another Sexual Dysfunction) and is not due exclusively to the direct physiological effects of a substance (e.g., a drug of abuse, a medication) or a general medical condition.

Specify type:
Lifelong Type
Acquired Type

Specify type:
Generalized Type
Situational Type

Specify:
Due to Psychological Factors
Due to Combined Factors

302.74   Male Orgasmic Disorder
(*formerly* Inhibited Male Orgasm)

Diagnostic Features

The essential feature of Male Orgasmic Disorder is a persistent or recurrent delay in, or absence of, orgasm following a normal sexual excitement phase. In judging whether the orgasm is delayed, the clinician should take into account the person's age and whether the stimulation is adequate in focus, intensity, and duration (Criterion A). The disturbance must cause marked distress or interpersonal difficulty (Criterion B). The orgasmic dysfunction is not better accounted for by another Axis I disorder (except another Sexual Dysfunction) and is not due exclusively to the direct physiological effects of a substance (including medications) or a general medical condition (Criterion C). In the most common form of Male Orgasmic Disorder, a male cannot reach orgasm during intercourse, although he can ejaculate from a partner's manual or oral stimulation. Some males with Male Orgasmic Disorder can reach coital orgasm but only after very prolonged and intense noncoital stimulation. Some can ejaculate only from masturbation. An even smaller subgroup have experienced orgasm only at the moment of waking from an erotic dream.

Subtypes

Subtypes are provided to indicate onset (**Lifelong** versus **Acquired**), context (**Generalized** versus **Situational**), and etiological factors (**Due to Psychological Factors, Due to Combined Factors**) for Male Orgasmic Disorder. (See descriptions on p. 494.)

Associated Features and Disorders

Many coitally inorgasmic males describe feeling aroused at the beginning of a sexual encounter but that thrusting gradually becomes a chore rather than a pleasure. A pattern of paraphiliac sexual arousal may be present. When a man has hidden his lack of coital orgasms from his wife, the couple may present with infertility of unknown cause. The disorder may result in the disturbance of existing marital or sexual relationships. Males can usually reach orgasm even when vascular or neurological conditions interfere with erectile rigidity. Both the sensation of orgasm and striated muscle contractions at orgasm remain intact in males who lose their prostate and seminal vesicles with radical pelvic cancer surgery. Orgasm also can occur in the absence of emission of semen (e.g., when sympathetic ganglia are damaged by surgery or autonomic neuropathy).

Differential Diagnosis

Male Orgasmic Disorder must be distinguished from a **Sexual Dysfunction Due to a General Medical Condition.** The appropriate diagnosis would be Sexual Dysfunction Due to a General Medical Condition when the dysfunction is judged to be due exclusively to the physiological effects of a specified general medical condition (e.g., hyperprolactinemia) (see p. 515). This determination is based on history, laboratory findings, or physical examination. Sensory threshold testing may demonstrate reduced sensation in the skin on the penis that is due to a neurological condition (e.g., spinal cord injuries, sensory neuropathies). If both Male Orgasmic Disorder and a general medical condition are present but it is judged that the sexual dysfunction is not due exclusively to the direct physiological effects of the general medical condition, then Male Orgasmic Disorder, Due to Combined Factors, is diagnosed.

In contrast to Male Orgasmic Disorder, a **Substance-Induced Sexual Dysfunction** is judged to be due exclusively to the direct physiological effects of a substance (e.g., alcohol, opioids, antihypertensives, antidepressants, neuroleptics) (see p. 519). If both Male Orgasmic Disorder and substance use are present but it is judged that the sexual dysfunction is not due exclusively to the direct physiological effects of the substance use, then Male Orgasmic Disorder, Due to Combined Factors, is diagnosed.

If the orgasmic dysfunction is judged to be due exclusively to the physiological effects of both a general medical condition and substance use, both Sexual Dysfunction Due to a General Medical Condition and Substance-Induced Sexual Dysfunction are diagnosed.

Male Orgasmic Disorder may also occur in association with other Sexual Dysfunctions (e.g., Male Erectile Disorder). If so, both should be noted. An additional diagnosis of Male Orgasmic Disorder is usually not made if the orgasmic difficulty is better accounted for by **another Axis I disorder** (e.g., Major Depressive Disorder). An additional diagnosis may be made when the orgasmic difficulty predates the Axis I disorder or is a focus of independent clinical attention. Several types of Sexual Dysfunction (e.g., ejaculation but without pleasurable orgasm, orgasm that occurs without ejaculation of semen or with seepage of semen rather than propulsive ejaculation) would be diagnosed as **Sexual Dysfunction Not Otherwise Specified** rather than as Male Orgasmic Disorder.

Occasional orgasmic problems that are not persistent or recurrent or are not accompanied by marked distress or interpersonal difficulty are not considered to be

Male Orgasmic Disorder. As males age, they may require a longer period of stimulation to achieve orgasm. The clinician must also ascertain that there has been sufficient stimulation to attain orgasm.

■ **Diagnostic criteria for 302.74 Male Orgasmic Disorder**

A. Persistent or recurrent delay in, or absence of, orgasm following a normal sexual excitement phase during sexual activity that the clinician, taking into account the person's age, judges to be adequate in focus, intensity, and duration.

B. The disturbance causes marked distress or interpersonal difficulty.

C. The orgasmic dysfunction is not better accounted for by another Axis I disorder (except another Sexual Dysfunction) and is not due exclusively to the direct physiological effects of a substance (e.g., a drug of abuse, a medication) or a general medical condition.

Specify type:
   Lifelong Type
   Acquired Type

Specify type:
   Generalized Type
   Situational Type

Specify:
   Due to Psychological Factors
   Due to Combined Factors

302.75 Premature Ejaculation

Diagnostic Features

The essential feature of Premature Ejaculation is the persistent or recurrent onset of orgasm and ejaculation with minimal sexual stimulation before, on, or shortly after penetration and before the person wishes it (Criterion A). The clinician must take into account factors that affect duration of the excitement phase, such as age, novelty of the sexual partner or situation, and recent frequency of sexual activity. The majority of males with this disorder can delay orgasm during self-masturbation for a considerably longer time than during coitus. Partners' estimates of the duration of time from the beginning of sexual activity until ejaculation as well as their judgment of whether Premature Ejaculation is a problem can be quite disparate. The disturbance must cause marked distress or interpersonal difficulty (Criterion B). The premature ejaculation is not due exclusively to the direct effects of a substance (e.g., withdrawal from opioids) (Criterion C).

Subtypes

Subtypes are provided to indicate onset (**Lifelong** versus **Acquired**), context (**Generalized** versus **Situational**), and etiological factors (**Due to Psychological Factors, Due to Combined Factors**) for Premature Ejaculation. (See descriptions on p. 494.)

Associated Features and Disorders

Like other Sexual Dysfunctions, Premature Ejaculation may create tension in a relationship. Some unmarried males hesitate to begin dating new partners out of fear of embarrassment from the disorder. This can contribute to social isolation.

Course

A majority of young males learn to delay orgasm with sexual experience and aging, but some continue to ejaculate prematurely and may seek help for the disorder. Some males are able to delay ejaculation in a long-term relationship but experience a recurrence of Premature Ejaculation when they have a new partner. Typically, Premature Ejaculation is seen in young men and is present from their first attempts at intercourse. However, some males lose the ability to delay orgasm after a period of adequate function. When onset occurs after a period of adequate sexual function, the context is often a decreased frequency of sexual activity, intense performance anxiety with a new partner, or loss of ejaculatory control related to difficulty achieving or maintaining erections. Some males who have stopped regular use of alcohol may develop Premature Ejaculation because they relied on their drinking to delay orgasm instead of learning behavioral strategies.

Differential Diagnosis

Premature Ejaculation should be distinguished from **erectile dysfunction related to the development of a general medical condition** (see p. 515). Some individuals with erectile dysfunction may omit their usual strategies for delaying orgasm. Others require prolonged noncoital stimulation to develop a degree of erection sufficient for intromission. In such individuals, sexual arousal may be so high that ejaculation occurs immediately. **Occasional problems with premature ejaculation** that are not persistent or recurrent or are not accompanied by marked distress or interpersonal difficulty do not qualify for the diagnosis of Premature Ejaculation. The clinician should also take into account the individual's age, overall sexual experience, recent sexual activity, and the novelty of the partner. When problems with Premature Ejaculation are due exclusively to substance use (e.g., Opioid Withdrawal), a **Substance-Induced Sexual Dysfunction** can be diagnosed (see p. 519).

■ **Diagnostic criteria for 302.75 Premature Ejaculation**

A. Persistent or recurrent ejaculation with minimal sexual stimulation before, on, or shortly after penetration and before the person wishes it. The clinician must take into account factors that affect duration of the excitement phase, such as age, novelty of the sexual partner or situation, and recent frequency of sexual activity.

B. The disturbance causes marked distress or interpersonal difficulty.

C. The premature ejaculation is not due exclusively to the direct effects of a substance (e.g., withdrawal from opioids).

Specify type:
Lifelong Type
Acquired Type

Specify type:
Generalized Type
Situational Type

Specify:
Due to Psychological Factors
Due to Combined Factors

Sexual Pain Disorders

302.76   Dyspareunia
(Not Due to a General Medical Condition)

Diagnostic Features

The essential feature of Dyspareunia is genital pain that is associated with sexual intercourse (Criterion A). Although it is most commonly experienced during coitus, it may also occur before or after intercourse. The disorder can occur in both males and females. In females, the pain may be described as superficial during intromission or as deep during penile thrusting. The intensity of the symptoms may range from mild discomfort to sharp pain. The disturbance must cause marked distress or interpersonal difficulty (Criterion B). The disturbance is not caused exclusively by Vaginismus or lack of lubrication, is not better accounted for by another Axis I disorder (except for another Sexual Dysfunction), and is not due exclusively to the direct physiological effects of a substance (e.g., a drug of abuse, a medication) or a general medical condition (Criterion C).

Subtypes

Subtypes are provided to indicate onset (**Lifelong** versus **Acquired**), context (**Generalized** versus **Situational**), and etiological factors (**Due to Psychological Factors, Due to Combined Factors**) for Dyspareunia. (See descriptions on p. 494.)

Associated Features and Disorders

Dyspareunia is rarely a chief complaint in mental health settings. Individuals with Dyspareunia typically seek treatment in general medical settings. The physical examination for individuals with this disorder typically does not demonstrate genital abnormalities. The repeated experience of genital pain during coitus may result in the avoidance of sexual experience, disrupting existing sexual relationships or limiting the development of new sexual relationships.

Course

The limited amount of information available suggests that the course of Dyspareunia tends to be chronic.

Differential Diagnosis

Dyspareunia must be distinguished from **Sexual Dysfunction Due to a General Medical Condition** (see p. 515). The appropriate diagnosis would be Sexual Dysfunction Due to a General Medical Condition when the dysfunction is judged to be due exclusively to the physiological effects of a specified general medical condition (e.g., insufficient vaginal lubrication; pelvic pathology such as vaginal or urinary tract infections, vaginal scar tissue, endometriosis, or adhesions; postmenopausal vaginal atrophy; temporary estrogen deprivation during lactation; urinary tract irritation or infection; or gastrointestinal conditions). This determination is based on history, laboratory findings, or physical examination. If both Dyspareunia and a general medical condition are present but it is judged that the sexual dysfunction is not due exclusively to the direct physiological effects of the general medical condition, then a diagnosis of Dyspareunia, Due to Combined Factors, is made.

In contrast to Dyspareunia, a **Substance-Induced Sexual Dysfunction** is judged to be due exclusively to the direct physiological effects of a substance (see p. 519). Painful orgasm has been reported with fluphenazine, thioridazine, and amoxapine. If both Dyspareunia and substance use are present but it is judged that the sexual dysfunction is not due exclusively to the direct physiological effects of the substance use, then Dyspareunia, Due to Combined Factors, is diagnosed.

If the sexual pain is judged to be due exclusively to the physiological effects of both a general medical condition and substance use, both Sexual Dysfunction Due to a General Medical Condition and Substance-Induced Sexual Dysfunction are diagnosed.

Dyspareunia is not diagnosed if it is caused exclusively by Vaginismus or a lack of lubrication. An additional diagnosis of Dyspareunia is usually not made if the sexual dysfunction is better accounted for by **another Axis I disorder** (e.g., Somatization Disorder). The additional diagnosis may be made when the orgasmic difficulty predates the Axis I disorder or is a focus of independent clinical attention. Dyspareunia can also occur in association with other Sexual Dysfunctions (except Vaginismus) and if criteria for both are met, both should be coded. **Occasional pain associated with sexual intercourse** that is not persistent or recurrent or is not accompanied by marked distress or interpersonal difficulty is not considered to be Dyspareunia.

■ **Diagnostic criteria for 302.76 Dyspareunia**

A. Recurrent or persistent genital pain associated with sexual intercourse in either a male or a female.

B. The disturbance causes marked distress or interpersonal difficulty.

C. The disturbance is not caused exclusively by Vaginismus or lack of lubrication, is not better accounted for by another Axis I disorder (except another Sexual Dysfunction), and is not due exclusively to the direct physiological effects of a substance (e.g., a drug of abuse, a medication) or a general medical condition.

Specify type:
   Lifelong Type
   Acquired Type

Specify type:
   Generalized Type
   Situational Type

Specify:
   Due to Psychological Factors
   Due to Combined Factors

306.51   Vaginismus
(Not Due to a General Medical Condition)

Diagnostic Features

The essential feature of Vaginismus is the recurrent or persistent involuntary contraction of the perineal muscles surrounding the outer third of the vagina when vaginal penetration with penis, finger, tampon, or speculum is attempted (Criterion A). The disturbance must cause marked distress or interpersonal difficulty (Criterion B). The disturbance is not better accounted for by another Axis I disorder (except another Sexual Dysfunction) and is not due exclusively to the direct physiological effects of a general medical condition (Criterion C). In some females, even the anticipation of vaginal insertion may result in muscle spasm. The contraction may range from mild, inducing some tightness and discomfort, to severe, preventing penetration.

Subtypes

Subtypes are provided to indicate onset (**Lifelong** versus **Acquired**), context (**Generalized** versus **Situational**), and etiological factors (**Due to Psychological Factors, Due to Combined Factors**) for Vaginismus. (See descriptions on p. 494.)

Associated Features and Disorders

Sexual responses (e.g., desire, pleasure, orgasmic capacity) may not be impaired unless penetration is attempted or anticipated. The physical obstruction due to muscle contraction usually prevents coitus. The condition, therefore, can limit the development of sexual relationships and disrupt existing relationships. Cases of unconsummated marriages and infertility have been found to be associated with this condition. The diagnosis is often made during routine gynecological examinations when response to the pelvic examination results in the readily observed contraction of the vaginal outlet. In some cases, the intensity of the contraction may be so severe or prolonged as to cause pain. However, Vaginismus occurs in some women during sexual activity but not during a gynecological examination. The disorder is more often found in younger than in older females, in females with negative attitudes toward sex, and in females who have a history of being sexually abused or traumatized.

Course

Lifelong Vaginismus usually has an abrupt onset, first manifest during initial attempts at sexual penetration by a partner or during the first gynecological examination. Once the disorder is established, the course is usually chronic unless ameliorated by treatment. Acquired Vaginismus also may occur suddenly in response to a sexual trauma or a general medical condition.

Differential Diagnosis

Vaginismus must be distinguished from a **Sexual Dysfunction Due to a General Medical Condition** (see p. 515). The appropriate diagnosis would be Sexual Dysfunction Due to a General Medical Condition when the dysfunction is judged to be due exclusively to the physiological effects of a specified general medical condition (e.g., endometriosis or vaginal infection). This determination is based on history, laboratory findings, or physical examination. Vaginismus may remain as a residual problem after resolution of the general medical condition. If both Vaginismus and a general medical condition are present but it is judged that the vaginal spasms are not due exclusively to the direct physiological effects of the general medical condition, a diagnosis of Vaginismus, Due to Combined Factors, is made.

Vaginismus may also occur in association with other Sexual Dysfunctions (e.g., Hypoactive Sexual Desire Disorder). If so, both should be noted. Although pain associated with sexual intercourse may occur with Vaginismus, an additional diagnosis of **Dyspareunia** is not given. An additional diagnosis of Vaginismus is usually not made if the vaginal spasms are better accounted for by **another Axis I condition** (e.g., Somatization Disorder). The additional diagnosis may be made when the vaginal spasms predate the Axis I disorder or are a focus of independent clinical attention.

■ **Diagnostic criteria for 306.51 Vaginismus**

A. Recurrent or persistent involuntary spasm of the musculature of the outer third of the vagina that interferes with sexual intercourse.

B. The disturbance causes marked distress or interpersonal difficulty.

C. The disturbance is not better accounted for by another Axis I disorder (e.g., Somatization Disorder) and is not due exclusively to the direct physiological effects of a general medical condition.

Specify type:
   Lifelong Type
   Acquired Type

Specify type:
   Generalized Type
   Situational Type

Specify:
   Due to Psychological Factors
   Due to Combined Factors

Sexual Dysfunction Due to a General Medical Condition

Diagnostic Features

The essential feature of Sexual Dysfunction Due to a General Medical Condition is the presence of clinically significant sexual dysfunction that is judged to be due exclusively to the direct physiological effects of a general medical condition. The sexual dysfunction can involve pain associated with intercourse, hypoactive sexual desire, male erectile dysfunction, or other forms of sexual dysfunction (e.g., Orgasmic Disorders) and must cause marked distress or interpersonal difficulty (Criterion A). There must be evidence from the history, physical examination, or laboratory findings that the dysfunction is fully explained by the direct physiological effects of a general medical condition (Criterion B). The disturbance is not better accounted for by another mental disorder (e.g., Major Depressive Disorder) (Criterion C).

In determining whether the sexual dysfunction is exclusively due to a general medical condition, the clinician must first establish the presence of a general medical condition. Further, the clinician must establish that the sexual dysfunction is etiologically related to the general medical condition through a physiological mechanism. A careful and comprehensive assessment of multiple factors is necessary to make this judgment. Although there are no infallible guidelines for determining whether the relationship between the sexual dysfunction and the general medical condition is etiological, several considerations provide some guidance in this area. One consideration is the presence of a temporal association between the onset, exacerbation, or remission of the general medical condition and that of the sexual dysfunction. A second consideration is the presence of features that are atypical of a primary Sexual Dysfunction (e.g., atypical age at onset or course). Evidence from the literature that suggests that there can be a direct association between the general medical condition in question and the development of the sexual dysfunction can provide a useful context in the assessment of a particular situation. In addition, the clinician must also judge that the disturbance is not better accounted for by a primary Sexual Dysfunction, a Substance-Induced Sexual Dysfunction, or another primary mental disorder (e.g., Major Depressive Disorder). These determinations are explained in greater detail in the "Mental Disorders Due to a General Medical Condition" section (p. 165).

In contrast, a Sexual Dysfunction diagnosis with the subtype "Due to Combined Factors" is made if a combination of psychological factors and either a general medical condition or a substance is judged to have an etiological role, but no one etiology is sufficient to account for the dysfunction.

Subtypes

The diagnostic code and term for a Sexual Dysfunction Due to a General Medical Condition is selected based on the predominant Sexual Dysfunction. The terms listed below should be used instead of the overall rubric "Sexual Dysfunction Due to a General Medical Condition."

625.8 Female Hypoactive Sexual Desire Disorder Due to . . . *[Indicate the General Medical Condition].* This term is used if, in a female, deficient or absent sexual desire is the predominant feature.

608.89 Male Hypoactive Sexual Desire Disorder Due to . . . *[Indicate the General Medical Condition].* This term is used if, in a male, deficient or absent sexual desire is the predominant feature.

607.84 Male Erectile Disorder Due to . . . *[Indicate the General Medical Condition].* This term is used if male erectile dysfunction is the predominant feature.

625.0 Female Dyspareunia Due to . . . *[Indicate the General Medical Condition].* This term is used if, in a female, pain associated with intercourse is the predominant feature.

608.89 Male Dyspareunia Due to . . . *[Indicate the General Medical Condition].* This term is used if, in a male, pain associated with intercourse is the predominant feature.

625.8 Other Female Sexual Dysfunction Due to . . . *[Indicate the General Medical Condition].* This term is used if, in a female, some other feature is predominant (e.g., Orgasmic Disorder) or no feature predominates.

608.89 Other Male Sexual Dysfunction Due to . . . *[Indicate the General Medical Condition].* This term is used if, in a male, some other feature is predominant (e.g., Orgasmic Disorder) or no feature predominates.

Recording Procedures

In recording the diagnosis of Sexual Dysfunction Due to a General Medical Condition, the clinician should note both the specific phenomenology of the dysfunction (from the list above) and the identified general medical condition judged to be causing the dysfunction on Axis I (e.g., 607.84 Male Erectile Disorder Due to Diabetes Mellitus). The ICD-9-CM code for the general medical condition is also noted on Axis III (e.g., 250.0 diabetes mellitus). (See Appendix G for a list of selected ICD-9-CM diagnostic codes for general medical conditions.)

Associated General Medical Conditions

A variety of general medical conditions can cause sexual dysfunction, including neurological conditions (e.g., multiple sclerosis, spinal cord lesions, neuropathy, temporal lobe lesions), endocrine conditions (e.g., diabetes mellitus, hypothyroidism, hyper- and hypoadrenocorticism, hyperprolactinemia, hypogonadal states, pituitary dysfunction), vascular conditions, and genitourinary conditions (e.g., testicular disease, Peyronie's disease, urethral infections, postprostatectomy complications, genital injury or infection, atrophic vaginitis, infections of the vagina and external genitalia, postsurgical complications such as episiotomy scars, shortened vagina, cystitis, endometriosis, uterine prolapse, pelvic infections, neoplasms). Current clinical experience suggests that Sexual Dysfunction Due to a General Medical Condition is usually generalized. The associated physical examination findings, laboratory findings, and patterns of prevalence or onset reflect the etiological general medical condition.

Differential Diagnosis

Sexual Dysfunction Due to a General Medical Condition is diagnosed only if the sexual dysfunction is fully explained by the direct effects of a general medical condition. If psychological factors also play a role in the onset, severity, exacerbation, or maintenance of a sexual dysfunction, the diagnosis is the **primary Sexual Dysfunction** (with the subtype **Due to Combined Factors**). In determining whether the sexual dysfunction is primary or exclusively due to the direct effects of a general medical condition, a comprehensive psychosexual and medical history is the most important component of the evaluation. For males, tests such as nocturnal penile tumescence, vascular studies, and injection of tissue activators may be helpful in the assessment. Careful gynecological examination is important in making these determinations in women, especially in assessing Sexual Pain Disorders in females. Neurological evaluation and endocrine assessment may be helpful in both men and women.

If there is evidence of recent or prolonged substance use (including medications), withdrawal from a substance, or exposure to a toxin, and that the sexual dysfunction is fully explained by the direct effects of the substance, a **Substance-Induced Sexual Dysfunction** should be considered. The clinician should inquire carefully about the nature and extent of substance use, including medications. Symptoms that occur during or shortly after (i.e., within 4 weeks of) Substance Intoxication or after medication use may be especially indicative of a Substance-Induced Sexual Dysfunction, depending on the type or amount of the substance used or the duration of use. If the clinician has ascertained that the sexual dysfunction is due to both a general medical condition and substance use, both diagnoses (i.e., Sexual Dysfunction Due to a General Medical Condition and Substance-Induced Sexual Dysfunction) can be given.

Hypoactive sexual desire, arousal dysfunction, and, to a lesser extent, orgasmic dysfunction can also occur as symptoms of **Major Depressive Disorder.** In Major Depressive Disorder, no specific and direct causative pathophysiological mechanisms associated with a general medical condition can be demonstrated. Sexual Dysfunction Due to a General Medical Condition must be distinguished from the **diminished sexual interest and functioning that may accompany aging.**

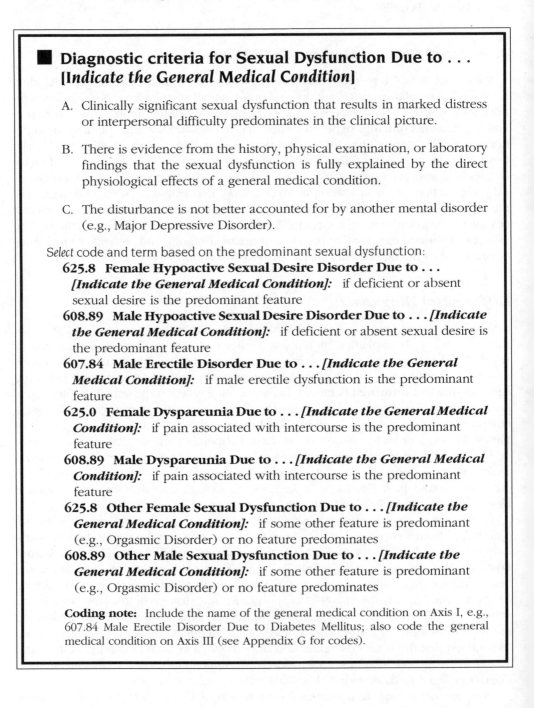

■ **Diagnostic criteria for Sexual Dysfunction Due to . . . [Indicate the General Medical Condition]**

A. Clinically significant sexual dysfunction that results in marked distress or interpersonal difficulty predominates in the clinical picture.

B. There is evidence from the history, physical examination, or laboratory findings that the sexual dysfunction is fully explained by the direct physiological effects of a general medical condition.

C. The disturbance is not better accounted for by another mental disorder (e.g., Major Depressive Disorder).

Select code and term based on the predominant sexual dysfunction:

625.8 Female Hypoactive Sexual Desire Disorder Due to . . . [Indicate the General Medical Condition]: if deficient or absent sexual desire is the predominant feature

608.89 Male Hypoactive Sexual Desire Disorder Due to . . . [Indicate the General Medical Condition]: if deficient or absent sexual desire is the predominant feature

607.84 Male Erectile Disorder Due to . . . [Indicate the General Medical Condition]: if male erectile dysfunction is the predominant feature

625.0 Female Dyspareunia Due to . . . [Indicate the General Medical Condition]: if pain associated with intercourse is the predominant feature

608.89 Male Dyspareunia Due to . . . [Indicate the General Medical Condition]: if pain associated with intercourse is the predominant feature

625.8 Other Female Sexual Dysfunction Due to . . . [Indicate the General Medical Condition]: if some other feature is predominant (e.g., Orgasmic Disorder) or no feature predominates

608.89 Other Male Sexual Dysfunction Due to . . . [Indicate the General Medical Condition]: if some other feature is predominant (e.g., Orgasmic Disorder) or no feature predominates

Coding note: Include the name of the general medical condition on Axis I, e.g., 607.84 Male Erectile Disorder Due to Diabetes Mellitus; also code the general medical condition on Axis III (see Appendix G for codes).

Substance-Induced
Sexual Dysfunction

Diagnostic Features

The essential feature of Substance-Induced Sexual Dysfunction is a clinically significant sexual dysfunction that results in marked distress or interpersonal difficulty (Criterion A). Depending on the substance involved, the dysfunction may involve impaired desire, impaired arousal, impaired orgasm, or sexual pain. The dysfunction is judged to be fully explained by the direct physiological effects of a substance (i.e., a drug of abuse, a medication, or toxin exposure) (Criterion B). The disturbance must not be better accounted for by a Sexual Dysfunction that is not substance induced (Criterion C). This diagnosis should be made instead of a diagnosis of Substance Intoxication only when the sexual symptoms are in excess of those usually associated with the intoxication syndrome and when the symptoms are sufficiently severe to warrant independent clinical attention. For a more detailed discussion of Substance-Related Disorders, see p. 175.

A Substance-Induced Sexual Dysfunction is distinguished from a primary Sexual Dysfunction by considering onset and course. For drugs of abuse, there must be evidence of intoxication from the history, physical examination, or laboratory findings. Substance-Induced Sexual Dysfunctions arise only in association with intoxication, whereas primary Sexual Dysfunctions may precede the onset of substance use or occur during times of sustained abstinence from the substance. Factors suggesting that the dysfunction is better accounted for by a primary Sexual Dysfunction include persistence of the dysfunction for a substantial period of time (i.e., about a month) after the end of Substance Intoxication; the development of a dysfunction that is substantially in excess of what would be expected given the type or amount of the substance used or the duration of use; or a history of prior recurrent primary Sexual Dysfunctions.

Specifiers

The following specifiers for Substance-Induced Sexual Dysfunction are selected based on the predominant sexual dysfunction. Although the clinical presentation of the sexual dysfunction may resemble one of the specific primary Sexual Dysfunctions, the full criteria for one of these disorders need not be met.

>**With Impaired Desire.**   This specifier is used if deficient or absent sexual desire is the predominant feature.
>**With Impaired Arousal.**   This specifier is used if impaired sexual arousal (e.g., erectile dysfunction, impaired lubrication) is the predominant feature.
>**With Impaired Orgasm.**   This specifier is used if impaired orgasm is the predominant feature.
>**With Sexual Pain.**   This specifier is used if pain associated with intercourse is the predominant feature.

Substance-Induced Sexual Dysfunctions usually have their onset during Substance Intoxication, and this may be indicated by noting **With Onset During Intoxication.**

Recording Procedures

The name of the Substance-Induced Sexual Dysfunction begins with the specific substance (e.g., alcohol, fluoxetine) that is presumed to be causing the sexual dysfunction. The diagnostic code is selected from the listing of classes of substances provided in the criteria set. For substances that do not fit into any of the classes (e.g., fluoxetine), the code for "Other Substance" should be used. In addition, for medications prescribed at therapeutic doses, the specific medication can be indicated by listing the appropriate E-code on Axis I (see Appendix G). The name of the disorder is followed by the specification of predominant symptom presentation (e.g., 292.89 Cocaine-Induced Sexual Dysfunction, With Impaired Arousal). When more than one substance is judged to play a significant role in the development of the sexual dysfunction, each should be listed separately (e.g., 291.8 Alcohol-Induced Sexual Dysfunction, With Impaired Arousal; 292.89 Fluoxetine-Induced Sexual Dysfunction, With Impaired Orgasm). If a substance is judged to be the etiological factor, but the specific substance or class of substances is unknown, the category 292.89 Unknown Substance–Induced Sexual Dysfunction may be used.

Specific Substances

Sexual Dysfunctions can occur in association with **intoxication** with the following classes of substances: alcohol; amphetamine and related substances; cocaine; opioids; sedatives, hypnotics, and anxiolytics; and other or unknown substances. Acute intoxication with or chronic abuse of substances of abuse has been reported to decrease sexual interest and cause arousal problems in both sexes. A decrease in sexual interest (both sexes), arousal disorders (both sexes), and orgasmic disorders (more common in men) may also be caused by prescribed medications including antihypertensives, histamine H_2 receptor antagonists, antidepressants, neuroleptics, anxiolytics, anabolic steroids, and antiepileptics. Painful orgasm has been reported with fluphenazine, thioridazine, and amoxapine. Priapism has been reported with use of chlorpromazine, trazodone, and clozapine and following penile injections of papaverine or prostaglandin. Serotonin reuptake blockers may cause decreased sexual desire or arousal disorders. Medications such as antihypertensive agents or anabolic steroids may also promote depressed or irritable mood in addition to the sexual dysfunction, and an additional diagnosis of Substance-Induced Mood Disorder may be warranted. Current clinical experience strongly suggests that Substance-Induced Sexual Dysfunction is usually generalized.

Differential Diagnosis

Sexual dysfunctions commonly occur in **Substance Intoxication.** The diagnosis of the substance-specific Intoxication will usually suffice to categorize the symptom presentation. A diagnosis of Substance-Induced Sexual Dysfunction should be made instead of a diagnosis of Substance Intoxication only when the dysfunction is judged to be in excess of that usually associated with the intoxication syndrome and when the symptoms are sufficiently severe to warrant independent clinical attention. If psychological factors also play a role in the onset, severity, exacerbation, or maintenance of a sexual dysfunction, the diagnosis is the primary Sexual Dysfunction (with the subtype Due to Combined Factors).

A Substance-Induced Sexual Dysfunction is distinguished from a **primary Sexual**

Dysfunction by the fact that the symptoms are judged to be fully explained by the direct effects of a substance (see p. 519).

A Substance-Induced Sexual Dysfunction due to a prescribed treatment for a mental disorder or general medical condition must have its onset while the person is receiving the medication (e.g., antihypertensive medication). Once the treatment is discontinued, the sexual dysfunction will remit within days to several weeks (depending on the half-life of the substance). If the sexual dysfunction persists, other causes for the dysfunction should be considered. Side effects of prescribed medications that affect sexual function may lead individuals to be noncompliant with the medication regimen if they value sexual performance over the benefits of the medication.

Because individuals with general medical conditions often take medications for those conditions, the clinician must consider the possibility that the sexual dysfunction is caused by the physiological consequences of the general medical condition rather than the medication, in which case **Sexual Dysfunction Due to a General Medical Condition** is diagnosed. The history often provides the primary basis for such a judgment. At times, a change in the treatment for the general medical condition (e.g., medication substitution or discontinuation) may be needed to determine empirically for that person whether the medication is the causative agent. If the clinician has ascertained that the dysfunction is due to both a general medical condition and substance use, both diagnoses (i.e., Sexual Dysfunction Due to a General Medical Condition and Substance-Induced Sexual Dysfunction) are given. When there is insufficient evidence to determine whether the Sexual Dysfunction is due to a substance (including a medication) or to a general medical condition or is primary (i.e., not due to either a substance or a general medical condition), **Sexual Dysfunction Not Otherwise Specified** would be indicated.

■ Diagnostic criteria for Substance-Induced Sexual Dysfunction

A. Clinically significant sexual dysfunction that results in marked distress or interpersonal difficulty predominates in the clinical picture.

B. There is evidence from the history, physical examination, or laboratory findings that the sexual dysfunction is fully explained by substance use as manifested by either (1) or (2):

   (1) the symptoms in Criterion A developed during, or within a month of, Substance Intoxication

   (2) medication use is etiologically related to the disturbance

C. The disturbance is not better accounted for by a Sexual Dysfunction that is not substance induced. Evidence that the symptoms are better accounted for by a Sexual Dysfunction that is not substance induced might include the following: the symptoms precede the onset of the substance use or dependence (or medication use); the symptoms persist for a substantial period of time (e.g., about a month) after the cessation of intoxication, or are substantially in excess of what would be expected

(continued)

☐ **Diagnostic criteria for Substance-Induced Sexual Dysfunction** (*continued*)

given the type or amount of the substance used or the duration of use; or there is other evidence that suggests the existence of an independent non-substance-induced Sexual Dysfunction (e.g., a history of recurrent non-substance-related episodes).

Note: This diagnosis should be made instead of a diagnosis of Substance Intoxication only when the sexual dysfunction is in excess of that usually associated with the intoxication syndrome and when the dysfunction is sufficiently severe to warrant independent clinical attention.

Code [Specific Substance]–Induced Sexual Dysfunction:
(291.8 Alcohol; 292.89 Amphetamine [or Amphetamine-Like Substance]; 292.89 Cocaine; 292.89 Opioid; 292.89 Sedative, Hypnotic, or Anxiolytic; 292.89 Other [or Unknown] Substance)

Specify if:
With Impaired Desire
With Impaired Arousal
With Impaired Orgasm
With Sexual Pain

Specify if:
With Onset During Intoxication: if the criteria are met for Intoxication with the substance and the symptoms develop during the intoxication syndrome

302.70   Sexual Dysfunction Not Otherwise Specified

This category includes sexual dysfunctions that do not meet criteria for any specific Sexual Dysfunction. Examples include

1. No (or substantially diminished) subjective erotic feelings despite otherwise-normal arousal and orgasm
2. Situations in which the clinician has concluded that a sexual dysfunction is present but is unable to determine whether it is primary, due to a general medical condition, or substance induced

Paraphilias

Diagnostic Features

The essential features of a Paraphilia are recurrent, intense sexually arousing fantasies, sexual urges, or behaviors generally involving 1) nonhuman objects, 2) the suffering or humiliation of oneself or one's partner, or 3) children or other nonconsenting persons, that occur over a period of at least 6 months (Criterion A). For some individuals, paraphiliac fantasies or stimuli are obligatory for erotic arousal and are always included in sexual activity. In other cases, the paraphiliac preferences occur only episodically (e.g., perhaps during periods of stress), whereas at other times the person is able to function sexually without paraphiliac fantasies or stimuli. The behavior, sexual urges, or fantasies cause clinically significant distress or impairment in social, occupational, or other important areas of functioning (Criterion B).

Paraphiliac imagery may be acted out with a nonconsenting partner in a way that may be injurious to the partner (as in Sexual Sadism or Pedophilia). The individual may be subject to arrest and incarceration. Sexual offenses against children constitute a significant proportion of all reported criminal sex acts, and individuals with Exhibitionism, Pedophilia, and Voyeurism make up the majority of apprehended sex offenders. In some situations, acting out the paraphiliac imagery may lead to self-injury (as in Sexual Masochism). Social and sexual relationships may suffer if others find the unusual sexual behavior shameful or repugnant or if the individual's sexual partner refuses to cooperate in the unusual sexual preferences. In some instances, the unusual behavior (e.g., exhibitionistic acts or the collection of fetish objects) may become the major sexual activity in the individual's life. These individuals are rarely self-referred and usually come to the attention of mental health professionals only when their behavior has brought them into conflict with sexual partners or society.

The Paraphilias described here are conditions that have been specifically identified by previous classifications. They include Exhibitionism (exposure of genitals), Fetishism (use of nonliving objects), Frotteurism (touching and rubbing against a nonconsenting person), Pedophilia (focus on prepubescent children), Sexual Masochism (receiving humiliation or suffering), Sexual Sadism (inflicting humiliation or suffering), Transvestic Fetishism (cross-dressing), and Voyeurism (observing sexual activity). A residual category, Paraphilia Not Otherwise Specified, includes other Paraphilias that are less frequently encountered. Not uncommonly, individuals have more than one Paraphilia.

Recording Procedures

The individual Paraphilias are differentiated based on the characteristic paraphiliac focus. However, if the individual's sexual preferences meet criteria for more than one Paraphilia, all should be diagnosed. The diagnostic code and terms are as follows: 302.4 Exhibitionism, 302.81 Fetishism, 302.89 Frotteurism, 302.2 Pedophilia, 302.83 Sexual Masochism, 302.84 Sexual Sadism, 302.82 Voyeurism, 302.3 Transvestic Fetishism, and 302.9 Paraphilia Not Otherwise Specified.

Associated Features and Disorders

Associated descriptive features and mental disorders.   The preferred stimulus, even within a particular Paraphilia, may be highly specific. Individuals who do not have a consenting partner with whom their fantasies can be acted out may purchase the services of prostitutes or may act out their fantasies with unwilling victims. Individuals with a Paraphilia may select an occupation or develop a hobby or volunteer work that brings them into contact with the desired stimulus (e.g., selling women's shoes or lingerie [Fetishism], working with children [Pedophilia], or driving an ambulance [Sexual

Sadism]). They may selectively view, read, purchase, or collect photographs, films, and textual depictions that focus on their preferred type of paraphiliac stimulus. Many individuals with these disorders assert that the behavior causes them no distress and that their only problem is social dysfunction as a result of the reaction of others to their behavior. Others report extreme guilt, shame, and depression at having to engage in an unusual sexual activity that is socially unacceptable or that they regard as immoral. There is often impairment in the capacity for reciprocal, affectionate sexual activity, and Sexual Dysfunctions may be present. Personality disturbances are also frequent and may be severe enough to warrant a diagnosis of a Personality Disorder. Symptoms of depression may develop in individuals with Paraphilias and may be accompanied by an increase in the frequency and intensity of the paraphiliac behavior.

Associated laboratory findings.   Penile plethysmography has been used in research settings to assess various Paraphilias by measuring an individual's sexual arousal in response to visual and auditory stimuli. The reliability and validity of this procedure in clinical assessment have not been well established, and clinical experience suggests that subjects can simulate response by manipulating mental images.

Associated general medical conditions.   Frequent, unprotected sex may result in infection with, or transmission of, a sexually transmitted disease. Sadistic or masochistic behaviors may lead to injuries ranging in extent from minor to life threatening.

Specific Culture and Gender Features

The diagnosis of Paraphilias across cultures or religions is complicated by the fact that what is considered deviant in one cultural setting may be more acceptable in another setting. Except for Sexual Masochism, where the sex ratio is estimated to be 20 males for each female, the other Paraphilias are almost never diagnosed in females, although some cases have been reported.

Prevalence

Although Paraphilias are rarely diagnosed in general clinical facilities, the large commercial market in paraphiliac pornography and paraphernalia suggests that its prevalence in the community is likely to be higher. The most common presenting problems in clinics that specialize in the treatment of Paraphilias are Pedophilia, Voyeurism, and Exhibitionism. Sexual Masochism and Sexual Sadism are much less commonly seen. Approximately one-half of the individuals with Paraphilias seen clinically are married.

Course

Certain of the fantasies and behaviors associated with Paraphilias may begin in childhood or early adolescence but become better defined and elaborated during adolescence and early adulthood. Elaboration and revision of paraphiliac fantasies may continue over the lifetime of the individual. By definition, the fantasies and urges associated with these disorders are recurrent. Many individuals report that the fantasies are always present but that there are periods of time when the frequency of the fantasies and intensity of the urges vary substantially. The disorders tend to be chronic and lifelong, but both the fantasies and the behaviors often diminish with advancing age in adults. The behaviors may increase in response to psychosocial stressors, in relation to other mental disorders, or with increased opportunity to engage in the Paraphilia.

Differential Diagnosis

A Paraphilia must be distinguished from the **nonpathological use of sexual fantasies, behaviors, or objects as a stimulus for sexual excitement** in individuals without a Paraphilia. Fantasies, behaviors, or objects are paraphiliac only when they lead to clinically significant distress or impairment (e.g., are obligatory, result in sexual dysfunction, require participation of nonconsenting individuals, lead to legal complications, interfere with social relationships).

In **Mental Retardation, Dementia, Personality Change Due to a General Medical Condition, Substance Intoxication,** a **Manic Episode** or **Schizophrenia,** there may be a decrease in judgment, social skills, or impulse control that, in rare instances, leads to unusual sexual behavior. This can be distinguished from a Paraphilia by the fact that the unusual sexual behavior is not the individual's preferred or obligatory pattern, the sexual symptoms occur exclusively during the course of these mental disorders, and the unusual sexual acts tend to be isolated rather than recurrent and usually have a later age at onset.

The individual Paraphilias can be distinguished based on differences in the characteristic paraphiliac focus. However, if the individual's sexual preferences meet criteria for more than one Paraphilia, all can be diagnosed. **Exhibitionism** must be distinguished from **public urination,** which is sometimes offered as an explanation for the behavior. **Fetishism** and **Transvestic Fetishism** both often involve articles of feminine clothing. In Fetishism, the focus of sexual arousal is on the article of clothing itself (e.g., panties), whereas in Transvestic Fetishism the sexual arousal comes from the act of cross-dressing. Cross-dressing, which is present in **Transvestic Fetishism,** may also be present in **Sexual Masochism.** In Sexual Masochism, it is the humiliation of being forced to cross-dress, not the garments themselves, that is sexually exciting.

Cross-dressing may be associated with gender dysphoria. If some gender dysphoria is present but the full criteria for Gender Identity Disorder are not met, the diagnosis is **Transvestic Fetishism, With Gender Dysphoria.** Individuals should receive the additional diagnosis of **Gender Identity Disorder** if their presentation meets the full criteria for Gender Identity Disorder.

302.4 Exhibitionism

The paraphiliac focus in Exhibitionism involves the exposure of one's genitals to a stranger. Sometimes the individual masturbates while exposing himself (or while fantasizing exposing himself). If the person acts on these urges, there is generally no attempt at further sexual activity with the stranger. In some cases, the individual is aware of a desire to surprise or shock the observer. In other cases, the individual has the sexually arousing fantasy that the observer will become sexually aroused. The onset usually occurs before age 18 years, although it can begin at a later age. Few arrests are made in the older age groups, which may suggest that the condition becomes less severe after age 40 years.

■ **Diagnostic criteria for 302.4 Exhibitionism**

A. Over a period of at least 6 months, recurrent, intense sexually arousing fantasies, sexual urges, or behaviors involving the exposure of one's genitals to an unsuspecting stranger.

B. The fantasies, sexual urges, or behaviors cause clinically significant distress or impairment in social, occupational, or other important areas of functioning.

302.81   Fetishism

The paraphiliac focus in Fetishism involves the use of nonliving objects (the "fetish"). Among the more common fetish objects are women's underpants, bras, stockings, shoes, boots, or other wearing apparel. The person with Fetishism frequently masturbates while holding, rubbing, or smelling the fetish object or may ask the sexual partner to wear the object during their sexual encounters. Usually the fetish is required or strongly preferred for sexual excitement, and in its absence there may be erectile dysfunction in males. This Paraphilia is not diagnosed when the fetishes are limited to articles of female clothing used in cross-dressing, as in Transvestic Fetishism, or when the object is genitally stimulating because it has been designed for that purpose (e.g., a vibrator). Usually the Paraphilia begins by adolescence, although the fetish may have been endowed with special significance earlier in childhood. Once established, Fetishism tends to be chronic.

■ **Diagnostic criteria for 302.81 Fetishism**

A. Over a period of at least 6 months, recurrent, intense sexually arousing fantasies, sexual urges, or behaviors involving the use of nonliving objects (e.g., female undergarments).

B. The fantasies, sexual urges, or behaviors cause clinically significant distress or impairment in social, occupational, or other important areas of functioning.

C. The fetish objects are not limited to articles of female clothing used in cross-dressing (as in Transvestic Fetishism) or devices designed for the purpose of tactile genital stimulation (e.g., a vibrator).

302.89 Frotteurism

The paraphiliac focus of Frotteurism involves touching and rubbing against a noncon-senting person. The behavior usually occurs in crowded places from which the individual can more easily escape arrest (e.g., on busy sidewalks or in public transportation vehicles). He rubs his genitals against the victim's thighs and buttocks or fondles her genitalia or breasts with his hands. While doing this he usually fantasizes an exclusive, caring relationship with the victim. However, he recognizes that to avoid possible prosecution, he must escape detection after touching his victim. Usually the paraphilia begins by adolescence. Most acts of frottage occur when the person is ages 15–25 years, after which there is a gradual decline in frequency.

■ **Diagnostic criteria for 302.89 Frotteurism**

    A. Over a period of at least 6 months, recurrent, intense sexually arousing fantasies, sexual urges, or behaviors involving touching and rubbing against a nonconsenting person.

    B. The fantasies, sexual urges, or behaviors cause clinically significant distress or impairment in social, occupational, or other important areas of functioning.

302.2 Pedophilia

The paraphiliac focus of Pedophilia involves sexual activity with a prepubescent child (generally age 13 years or younger). The individual with Pedophilia must be age 16 years or older and at least 5 years older than the child. For individuals in late adolescence with Pedophilia, no precise age difference is specified, and clinical judgment must be used; both the sexual maturity of the child and the age difference must be taken into account. Individuals with Pedophilia generally report an attraction to children of a particular age range. Some individuals prefer males, others females, and some are aroused by both males and females. Those attracted to females usually prefer 8- to 10-year-olds, whereas those attracted to males usually prefer slightly older children. Pedophilia involving female victims is reported more often than Pedophilia involving male victims. Some individuals with Pedophilia are sexually attracted only to children (Exclusive Type), whereas others are sometimes attracted to adults (Nonexclusive Type). Individuals with Pedophilia who act on their urges with children may limit their activity to undressing the child and looking, exposing themselves, masturbating in the presence of the child, or gentle touching and fondling of the child. Others, however, perform fellatio or cunnilingus on the child or penetrate the child's vagina, mouth, or anus with their fingers, foreign objects, or penis and use varying degrees of force to do so. These activities are commonly explained with excuses or rationalizations that they have "educational value" for the child, that the child derives "sexual pleasure" from them, or that the child was "sexually provocative"—themes that are also common in pedophiliac pornography.

Individuals may limit their activities to their own children, stepchildren, or relatives or may victimize children outside their families. Some individuals with Pedophilia threaten the child to prevent disclosure. Others, particularly those who frequently victimize children, develop complicated techniques for obtaining access to children, which may include winning the trust of a child's mother, marrying a woman with an attractive child, trading children with other individuals with Pedophilia, or, in rare instances, taking in foster children from nonindustrialized countries or abducting children from strangers. Except in cases in which the disorder is associated with Sexual Sadism, the person may be attentive to the child's needs in order to gain the child's affection, interest, and loyalty and to prevent the child from reporting the sexual activity. The disorder usually begins in adolescence, although some individuals with Pedophilia report that they did not become aroused by children until middle age. The frequency of pedophiliac behavior often fluctuates with psychosocial stress. The course is usually chronic, especially in those attracted to males. The recidivism rate for individuals with Pedophilia involving a preference for males is roughly twice that for those who prefer females.

■ Diagnostic criteria for 302.2 Pedophilia

A. Over a period of at least 6 months, recurrent, intense sexually arousing fantasies, sexual urges, or behaviors involving sexual activity with a prepubescent child or children (generally age 13 years or younger).

B. The fantasies, sexual urges, or behaviors cause clinically significant distress or impairment in social, occupational, or other important areas of functioning.

C. The person is at least age 16 years and at least 5 years older than the child or children in Criterion A.

   Note: Do not include an individual in late adolescence involved in an ongoing sexual relationship with a 12- or 13-year-old.

Specify if:
   Sexually Attracted to Males
   Sexually Attracted to Females
   Sexually Attracted to Both

Specify if:
   Limited to Incest

Specify type:
   Exclusive Type (attracted only to children)
   Nonexclusive Type

302.83   Sexual Masochism

The paraphiliac focus of Sexual Masochism involves the act (real, not simulated) of being humiliated, beaten, bound, or otherwise made to suffer. Some individuals are bothered by their masochistic fantasies, which may be invoked during sexual intercourse or masturbation but not otherwise acted on. In such cases, the masochistic fantasies usually involve being raped while being held or bound by others so that there is no possibility of escape. Others act on the masochistic sexual urges by themselves (e.g., binding themselves, sticking themselves with pins, shocking themselves electrically, or self-mutilation) or with a partner. Masochistic acts that may be sought with a partner include restraint (physical bondage), blindfolding (sensory bondage), paddling, spanking, whipping, beating, electrical shocks, cutting, "pinning and piercing" (infibulation), and humiliation (e.g., being urinated or defecated on, being forced to crawl and bark like a dog, or being subjected to verbal abuse). Forced cross-dressing may be sought for its humiliating associations. The individual may have a desire to be treated as a helpless infant and clothed in diapers ("infantilism"). One particularly dangerous form of Sexual Masochism, called "hypoxyphilia," involves sexual arousal by oxygen deprivation obtained by means of chest compression, noose, ligature, plastic bag, mask, or chemical (often a volatile nitrite that produces a temporary decrease in brain oxygenation by peripheral vasodilation). Oxygen-depriving activities may be engaged in alone or with a partner. Because of equipment malfunction, errors in the placement of the noose or ligature, or other mistakes, accidental deaths sometimes occur. Data from the United States, England, Australia, and Canada indicate that one to two hypoxyphilia-caused deaths per million population are detected and reported each year. Some males with Sexual Masochism also have Fetishism, Transvestic Fetishism, or Sexual Sadism. Masochistic sexual fantasies are likely to have been present in childhood. The age at which masochistic activities with partners first begins is variable, but is commonly by early adulthood. Sexual Masochism is usually chronic, and the person tends to repeat the same masochistic act. Some individuals with Sexual Masochism may engage in masochistic acts for many years without increasing the potential injuriousness of their acts. Others, however, increase the severity of the masochistic acts over time or during periods of stress, which may eventually result in injury or even death.

■ Diagnostic criteria for 302.83 Sexual Masochism

A. Over a period of at least 6 months, recurrent, intense sexually arousing fantasies, sexual urges, or behaviors involving the act (real, not simulated) of being humiliated, beaten, bound, or otherwise made to suffer.

B. The fantasies, sexual urges, or behaviors cause clinically significant distress or impairment in social, occupational, or other important areas of functioning.

302.84   Sexual Sadism

The paraphiliac focus of Sexual Sadism involves acts (real, not simulated) in which the individual derives sexual excitement from the psychological or physical suffering (including humiliation) of the victim. Some individuals with this Paraphilia are bothered by their sadistic fantasies, which may be invoked during sexual activity but not otherwise acted on; in such cases the sadistic fantasies usually involve having complete control over the victim, who is terrified by anticipation of the impending sadistic act. Others act on the sadistic sexual urges with a consenting partner (who may have Sexual Masochism) who willingly suffers pain or humiliation. Still others with Sexual Sadism act on their sadistic sexual urges with nonconsenting victims. In all of these cases, it is the suffering of the victim that is sexually arousing. Sadistic fantasies or acts may involve activities that indicate the dominance of the person over the victim (e.g., forcing the victim to crawl or keeping the victim in a cage). They may also involve restraint, blindfolding, paddling, spanking, whipping, pinching, beating, burning, electrical shocks, rape, cutting, stabbing, strangulation, torture, mutilation, or killing. Sadistic sexual fantasies are likely to have been present in childhood. The age at onset of sadistic activities is variable, but is commonly by early adulthood. Sexual Sadism is usually chronic. When Sexual Sadism is practiced with nonconsenting partners, the activity is likely to be repeated until the person with Sexual Sadism is apprehended. Some individuals with Sexual Sadism may engage in sadistic acts for many years without a need to increase the potential for inflicting serious physical damage. Usually, however, the severity of the sadistic acts increases over time. When Sexual Sadism is severe, and especially when it is associated with Antisocial Personality Disorder, individuals with Sexual Sadism may seriously injure or kill their victims.

■ Diagnostic criteria for 302.84 Sexual Sadism

A. Over a period of at least 6 months, recurrent, intense sexually arousing fantasies, sexual urges, or behaviors involving acts (real, not simulated) in which the psychological or physical suffering (including humiliation) of the victim is sexually exciting to the person.

B. The fantasies, sexual urges, or behaviors cause clinically significant distress or impairment in social, occupational, or other important areas of functioning.

302.3   Transvestic Fetishism

The paraphiliac focus of Transvestic Fetishism involves cross-dressing. Usually the male with Transvestic Fetishism keeps a collection of female clothes that he intermittently uses to cross-dress. While cross-dressed, he usually masturbates, imagining himself to be both the male subject and the female object of his sexual fantasy. This disorder has been described only in heterosexual males. Transvestic Fetishism is not diagnosed when cross-dressing occurs exclusively during the course of Gender Identity Disorder. Transvestic phenomena range from occasional solitary wearing of female clothes to extensive involvement in a transvestic subculture. Some males wear a single item of women's apparel (e.g., underwear or hosiery) under their masculine attire. Other males with Transvestic Fetishism dress entirely as females and wear makeup. The degree to which the cross-dressed individual successfully appears to be a female varies, depending on mannerisms, body habitus, and cross-dressing skill. When not cross-dressed, the male with Transvestic Fetishism is usually unremarkably masculine. Although his basic preference is heterosexual, he tends to have few sexual partners and may have engaged in occasional homosexual acts. An associated feature may be the presence of Sexual Masochism. The disorder typically begins with cross-dressing in childhood or early adolescence. In many cases, the cross-dressing is not done in public until adulthood. The initial experience may involve partial or total cross-dressing; partial cross-dressing often progresses to complete cross-dressing. A favored article of clothing may become erotic in itself and may be used habitually, first in masturbation and later in intercourse. In some individuals, the motivation for cross-dressing may change over time, temporarily or permanently, with sexual arousal in response to the cross-dressing diminishing or disappearing. In such instances, the cross-dressing becomes an antidote to anxiety or depression or contributes to a sense of peace and calm. In other individuals, gender dysphoria may emerge, especially under situational stress with or without symptoms of depression. For a small number of individuals, the gender dysphoria becomes a fixed part of the clinical picture and is accompanied by the desire to dress and live permanently as a female and to seek hormonal or surgical reassignment. Individuals with Transvestic Fetishism often seek treatment when gender dysphoria emerges. The subtype With Gender Dysphoria is provided to allow the clinician to note the presence of gender dysphoria as part of Transvestic Fetishism.

■ **Diagnostic criteria for 302.3 Transvestic Fetishism**

A. Over a period of at least 6 months, in a heterosexual male, recurrent, intense sexually arousing fantasies, sexual urges, or behaviors involving cross-dressing.

B. The fantasies, sexual urges, or behaviors cause clinically significant distress or impairment in social, occupational, or other important areas of functioning.

Specify if:
   With Gender Dysphoria: if the person has persistent discomfort with gender role or identity

302.82   Voyeurism

The paraphiliac focus of Voyeurism involves the act of observing unsuspecting individuals, usually strangers, who are naked, in the process of disrobing, or engaging in sexual activity. The act of looking ("peeping") is for the purpose of achieving sexual excitement, and generally no sexual activity with the observed person is sought. Orgasm, usually produced by masturbation, may occur during the voyeuristic activity or later in response to the memory of what the person has witnessed. Often these individuals have the fantasy of having a sexual experience with the observed person, but in reality this rarely occurs. In its severe form, peeping constitutes the exclusive form of sexual activity. The onset of voyeuristic behavior is usually before age 15 years. The course tends to be chronic.

■ **Diagnostic criteria for 302.82 Voyeurism**

A. Over a period of at least 6 months, recurrent, intense sexually arousing fantasies, sexual urges, or behaviors involving the act of observing an unsuspecting person who is naked, in the process of disrobing, or engaging in sexual activity.

B. The fantasies, sexual urges, or behaviors cause clinically significant distress or impairment in social, occupational, or other important areas of functioning.

302.9   Paraphilia Not Otherwise Specified

This category is included for coding Paraphilias that do not meet the criteria for any of the specific categories. Examples include, but are not limited to, telephone scatologia (obscene phone calls), necrophilia (corpses), partialism (exclusive focus on part of body), zoophilia (animals), coprophilia (feces), klismaphilia (enemas), and urophilia (urine).

Gender Identity Disorders

Gender Identity Disorder

Diagnostic Features

There are two components of Gender Identity Disorder, both of which must be present to make the diagnosis. There must be evidence of a strong and persistent cross-gender identification, which is the desire to be, or the insistence that one is, of the other sex

(Criterion A). This cross-gender identification must not merely be a desire for any perceived cultural advantages of being the other sex. There must also be evidence of persistent discomfort about one's assigned sex or a sense of inappropriateness in the gender role of that sex (Criterion B). The diagnosis is not made if the individual has a concurrent physical intersex condition (e.g., androgen insensitivity syndrome or congenital adrenal hyperplasia) (Criterion C). To make the diagnosis, there must be evidence of clinically significant distress or impairment in social, occupational, or other important areas of functioning (Criterion D).

In boys, the cross-gender identification is manifested by a marked preoccupation with traditionally feminine activities. They may have a preference for dressing in girls' or women's clothes or may improvise such items from available materials when genuine articles are unavailable. Towels, aprons, and scarves are often used to represent long hair or skirts. There is a strong attraction for the stereotypical games and pastimes of girls. They particularly enjoy playing house, drawing pictures of beautiful girls and princesses, and watching television or videos of their favorite female characters. Stereotypical female-type dolls, such as Barbie, are often their favorite toys, and girls are their preferred playmates. When playing "house," these boys role-play female figures, most commonly "mother roles," and often are quite preoccupied with female fantasy figures. They avoid rough-and-tumble play and competitive sports and have little interest in cars and trucks or other nonaggressive but stereotypical boy's toys. They may express a wish to be a girl and assert that they will grow up to be a woman. They may insist on sitting to urinate and pretend not to have a penis by pushing it in between their legs. More rarely, boys with Gender Identity Disorder may state that they find their penis or testes disgusting, that they want to remove them, or that they have, or wish to have, a vagina.

Girls with Gender Identity Disorder display intense negative reactions to parental expectations or attempts to have them wear dresses or other feminine attire. Some may refuse to attend school or social events where such clothes may be required. They prefer boy's clothing and short hair, are often misidentified by strangers as boys, and may ask to be called by a boy's name. Their fantasy heroes are most often powerful male figures, such as Batman or Superman. These girls prefer boys as playmates, with whom they share interests in contact sports, rough-and-tumble play, and traditional boyhood games. They show little interest in dolls or any form of feminine dress up or role-play activity. A girl with this disorder may occasionally refuse to urinate in a sitting position. She may claim that she has or will grow a penis and may not want to grow breasts or to menstruate. She may assert that she will grow up to be a man. Such girls typically reveal marked cross-gender identification in role-play, dreams, and fantasies.

Adults with Gender Identity Disorder are preoccupied with their wish to live as a member of the other sex. This preoccupation may be manifested as an intense desire to adopt the social role of the other sex or to acquire the physical appearance of the other sex through hormonal or surgical manipulation. Adults with this disorder are uncomfortable being regarded by others as, or functioning in society as, a member of their designated sex. To varying degrees, they adopt the behavior, dress, and mannerisms of the other sex. In private, these individuals may spend much time cross-dressed and working on the appearance of being the other sex. Many attempt to pass in public as the other sex. With cross-dressing and hormonal treatment (and for males, electrolysis), many individuals with this disorder may pass convincingly as the other sex. The sexual activity of these individuals with same-sex partners is generally constrained by the preference that their partners neither see nor touch their genitals. For some males who present later in life, (often following marriage), sexual activity with a woman is accompanied by the fantasy of being lesbian lovers or that his partner is a man and he is a woman.

In adolescents, the clinical features may resemble either those of children or those of adults, depending on the individual's developmental level, and the criteria should be applied accordingly. In a younger adolescent, it may be more difficult to arrive at an accurate diagnosis because of the adolescent's guardedness. This may be increased if the adolescent feels ambivalent about cross-gender identification or feels that it is unacceptable to the family. The adolescent may be referred because the parents or teachers are concerned about social isolation or peer teasing and rejection. In such circumstances, the diagnosis should be reserved for those adolescents who appear quite cross-gender identified in their dress and who engage in behaviors that suggest significant cross-gender identification (e.g., shaving legs in males). Clarifying the diagnosis in children and adolescents may require monitoring over an extended period of time.

Distress or disability in individuals with Gender Identity Disorder is manifested differently across the life cycle. In young children, distress is manifested by the stated unhappiness about their assigned sex. Preoccupation with cross-gender wishes often interferes with ordinary activities. In older children, failure to develop age-appropriate same-sex peer relationships and skills often leads to isolation and distress, and some children may refuse to attend school because of teasing or pressure to dress in attire stereotypical of their assigned sex. In adolescents and adults, preoccupation with cross-gender wishes often interferes with ordinary activities. Relationship difficulties are common and functioning at school or at work may be impaired.

Specifiers

For sexually mature individuals, the following specifiers may be noted based on the individual's sexual orientation: **Sexually Attracted to Males, Sexually Attracted to Females, Sexually Attracted to Both,** and **Sexually Attracted to Neither.** Males with Gender Identity Disorder include substantial proportions with all four specifiers. Virtually all females with Gender Identity Disorder will receive the same specifier—Sexually Attracted to Females—although there are exceptional cases involving females who are Sexually Attracted to Males.

Recording Procedures

The assigned diagnostic code depends on the individual's current age: if the disorder occurs in childhood, the code 302.6 is used; for an adolescent or adult, 302.85 is used.

Associated Features and Disorders

Associated descriptive features and mental disorders. Many individuals with Gender Identity Disorder become socially isolated. Isolation and ostracism contribute to low self-esteem and may lead to school aversion or dropping out of school. Peer ostracism and teasing are especially common sequelae for boys with the disorder. Boys with Gender Identity Disorder often show marked feminine mannerisms and speech patterns.

The disturbance can be so pervasive that the mental lives of some individuals revolve only around those activities that lessen gender distress. They are often preoccupied with appearance, especially early in the transition to living in the opposite sex role. Relationships with one or both parents also may be seriously impaired. Some males with Gender Identity Disorder resort to self-treatment with hormones and may very rarely perform their own castration or penectomy. Especially in urban centers, some males with the disorder may engage in prostitution, which places them at high risk for human immunodeficiency virus (HIV) infection. Suicide attempts and Substance-Related Disorders are commonly associated.

Children with Gender Identity Disorder may manifest coexisting Separation Anxiety Disorder, Generalized Anxiety Disorder, and symptoms of depression. Adolescents are particularly at risk for depression and suicidal ideation and suicide attempts. In adults, anxiety and depressive symptoms may be present. Some adult males have a history of Transvestic Fetishism as well as other Paraphilias. Associated Personality Disorders are more common among males than among females being evaluated at adult gender clinics.

Associated laboratory findings.   There is no diagnostic test specific for Gender Identity Disorder. In the presence of a normal physical examination, karyotyping for sex chromosomes and sex hormone assays are usually not indicated. Psychological testing may reveal cross-gender identification or behavior patterns.

Associated physical examination findings and general medical conditions. Individuals with Gender Identity Disorder have normal genitalia (in contrast to the ambiguous genitalia or hypogonadism found in physical intersex conditions). Adolescent and adult males with Gender Identity Disorder may show breast enlargement resulting from hormone ingestion, hair denuding from temporary or permanent epilation, and other physical changes as a result of procedures such as rhinoplasty or thyroid cartilage shaving (surgical reduction of the Adam's apple). Distorted breasts or breast rashes may be seen in females who wear breast binders. Postsurgical complications in genetic females include prominent chest wall scars, and in genetic males, vaginal strictures, rectovaginal fistulas, urethral stenoses, and misdirected urinary streams. Adult females with Gender Identity Disorder may have a higher than expected likelihood of polycystic ovarian disease.

Specific Age and Gender Features

Females with Gender Identity Disorders generally experience less ostracism because of cross-gender interests and may suffer less from peer rejection, at least until adolescence. In child clinic samples, there are approximately five boys for each girl referred with this disorder. In adult clinic samples, men outnumber women by about two or three times. In children, the referral bias toward males may partly reflect the greater stigma that cross-gender behavior carries for boys than for girls.

Prevalence

There are no recent epidemiological studies to provide data on prevalence of Gender Identity Disorder. Data from smaller countries in Europe with access to total population statistics and referrals suggest that roughly 1 per 30,000 adult males and 1 per 100,000 adult females seek sex-reassignment surgery.

Course

For clinically referred children, onset of cross-gender interests and activities is usually between ages 2 and 4 years, and some parents report that their child has always had cross-gender interests. Only a very small number of children with Gender Identity Disorder will continue to have symptoms that meet criteria for Gender Identity Disorder in later adolescence or adulthood. Typically, children are referred around the time of school entry because of parental concern that what they regarded as a "phase" does not appear to be passing. Most children with Gender Identity Disorder display less overt cross-gender behaviors with time, parental intervention, or response from peers. By late adolescence or adulthood, about three-quarters of boys who had a childhood history of Gender Identity Disorder report a homosexual or bisexual orientation, but without concurrent Gender Identity Disorder. Most of the remainder report a heterosexual orientation, also without concurrent Gender Identity Disorder. The corresponding percentages for sexual orientation in girls are not known. Some adolescents may develop a clearer cross-gender identification and request sex-reassignment surgery or may continue in a chronic course of gender confusion or dysphoria.

In adult males, there are two different courses for the development of Gender Identity Disorder. The first is a continuation of Gender Identity Disorder that had an onset in childhood or early adolescence. These individuals typically present in late adolescence or adulthood. In the other course, the more overt signs of cross-gender identification appear later and more gradually, with a clinical presentation in early to mid-adulthood usually following, but sometimes concurrent with, Transvestic Fetishism. The later-onset group may be more fluctuating in the degree of cross-gender identification, more ambivalent about sex-reassignment surgery, more likely to be sexually attracted to women, and less likely to be satisfied after sex-reassignment surgery. Males with Gender Identity Disorder who are sexually attracted to males tend to present in adolescence or early adulthood with a lifelong history of gender dysphoria. In contrast, those who are sexually attracted to females, to both males and females, or to neither sex tend to present later and typically have a history of Transvestic Fetishism. If Gender Identity Disorder is present in adulthood, it tends to have a chronic course, but spontaneous remission has been reported.

Differential Diagnosis

Gender Identity Disorder can be distinguished from simple **nonconformity to stereotypical sex role behavior** by the extent and pervasiveness of the cross-gender wishes, interests, and activities. This disorder is not meant to describe a child's nonconformity to stereotypic sex-role behavior as, for example, in "tomboyishness" in girls or "sissyish" behavior in boys. Rather, it represents a profound disturbance of the individual's sense of identity with regard to maleness or femaleness. Behavior in children that merely does not fit the cultural stereotype of masculinity or femininity should not be given the diagnosis unless the full syndrome is present, including marked distress or impairment.

Transvestic Fetishism occurs in heterosexual (or bisexual) men for whom the cross-dressing behavior is for the purpose of sexual excitement. Aside from cross-dressing, most individuals with Transvestic Fetishism do not have a history of childhood cross-gender behaviors. Males with a presentation that meets full criteria for Gender Identity Disorder as well as Transvestic Fetishism should be given both diagnoses. If gender dysphoria is present in an individual with Transvestic Fetishism but full criteria for Gender Identity Disorder are not met, the specifier With Gender Dysphoria can be used.

The category **Gender Identity Disorder Not Otherwise Specified** can be used for individuals who have a gender identity problem with a **concurrent congenital intersex condition** (e.g., androgen insensitivity syndrome or congenital adrenal hyperplasia).

In **Schizophrenia,** there may rarely be delusions of belonging to the other sex. Insistence by a person with a Gender Identity Disorder that he or she is of the other sex is not considered a delusion, because what is invariably meant is that the person feels like a member of the other sex rather than truly believes that he or she is a member of the other sex. In very rare cases, however, Schizophrenia and severe Gender Identity Disorder may coexist.

■ **Diagnostic criteria for Gender Identity Disorder**

A. A strong and persistent cross-gender identification (not merely a desire for any perceived cultural advantages of being the other sex).

In children, the disturbance is manifested by four (or more) of the following:

(1) repeatedly stated desire to be, or insistence that he or she is, the other sex

(2) in boys, preference for cross-dressing or simulating female attire; in girls, insistence on wearing only stereotypical masculine clothing

(3) strong and persistent preferences for cross-sex roles in make-believe play or persistent fantasies of being the other sex

(4) intense desire to participate in the stereotypical games and pastimes of the other sex

(5) strong preference for playmates of the other sex

In adolescents and adults, the disturbance is manifested by symptoms such as a stated desire to be the other sex, frequent passing as the other sex, desire to live or be treated as the other sex, or the conviction that he or she has the typical feelings and reactions of the other sex.

B. Persistent discomfort with his or her sex or sense of inappropriateness in the gender role of that sex.

In children, the disturbance is manifested by any of the following: in boys, assertion that his penis or testes are disgusting or will disappear or assertion that it would be better not to have a penis, or aversion toward rough-and-tumble play and rejection of male stereotypical toys, games, and activities; in girls, rejection of urinating in a sitting position, assertion that she has or will grow a penis, or assertion that she does not want to grow breasts or menstruate, or marked aversion toward normative feminine clothing.

(continued)

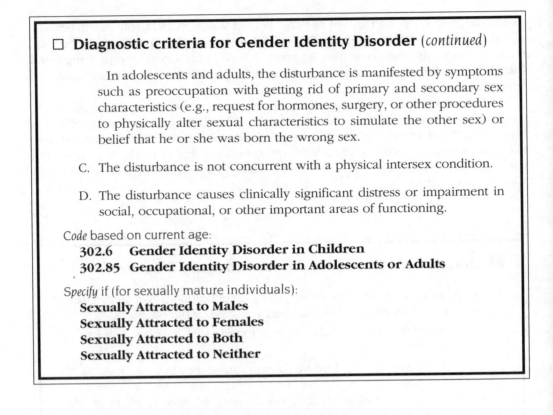

☐ **Diagnostic criteria for Gender Identity Disorder** (*continued*)

In adolescents and adults, the disturbance is manifested by symptoms such as preoccupation with getting rid of primary and secondary sex characteristics (e.g., request for hormones, surgery, or other procedures to physically alter sexual characteristics to simulate the other sex) or belief that he or she was born the wrong sex.

C. The disturbance is not concurrent with a physical intersex condition.

D. The disturbance causes clinically significant distress or impairment in social, occupational, or other important areas of functioning.

Code based on current age:
302.6   Gender Identity Disorder in Children
302.85 Gender Identity Disorder in Adolescents or Adults

Specify if (for sexually mature individuals):
Sexually Attracted to Males
Sexually Attracted to Females
Sexually Attracted to Both
Sexually Attracted to Neither

302.6   Gender Identity Disorder Not Otherwise Specified

This category is included for coding disorders in gender identity that are not classifiable as a specific Gender Identity Disorder. Examples include

1. Intersex conditions (e.g., androgen insensitivity syndrome or congenital adrenal hyperplasia) and accompanying gender dysphoria
2. Transient, stress-related cross-dressing behavior
3. Persistent preoccupation with castration or penectomy without a desire to acquire the sex characteristics of the other sex

302.9   Sexual Disorder Not Otherwise Specified

This category is included for coding a sexual disturbance that does not meet the criteria for any specific Sexual Disorder and is neither a Sexual Dysfunction nor a Paraphilia. Examples include

1. Marked feelings of inadequacy concerning sexual performance or other traits related to self-imposed standards of masculinity or femininity
2. Distress about a pattern of repeated sexual relationships involving a succession of lovers who are experienced by the individual only as things to be used
3. Persistent and marked distress about sexual orientation

Eating Disorders

The Eating Disorders are characterized by severe disturbances in eating behavior. This section includes two specific diagnoses, Anorexia Nervosa and Bulimia Nervosa. **Anorexia Nervosa** is characterized by a refusal to maintain a minimally normal body weight. **Bulimia Nervosa** is characterized by repeated episodes of binge eating followed by inappropriate compensatory behaviors such as self-induced vomiting; misuse of laxatives, diuretics, or other medications; fasting; or excessive exercise. A disturbance in perception of body shape and weight is an essential feature of both Anorexia Nervosa and Bulimia Nervosa. An Eating Disorder Not Otherwise Specified category is also provided for coding disorders that do not meet criteria for a specific Eating Disorder.

Simple obesity is included in the *International Classification of Diseases* (ICD) as a general medical condition, but does not appear in DSM-IV because it has not been established that it is consistently associated with a psychological or behavioral syndrome. However, when there is evidence that psychological factors are of importance in the etiology or course of a particular case of obesity, this can be indicated by noting the presence of Psychological Factors Affecting Medical Condition (p. 675).

Disorders of Feeding and Eating that are usually first diagnosed in infancy or early childhood (i.e., Pica, Rumination Disorder, and Feeding Disorder of Infancy or Early Childhood) are included in the section "Feeding and Eating Disorders of Infancy or Early Childhood" (p. 94).

307.1 Anorexia Nervosa

Diagnostic Features

The essential features of Anorexia Nervosa are that the individual refuses to maintain a minimally normal body weight, is intensely afraid of gaining weight, and exhibits a significant disturbance in the perception of the shape or size of his or her body. In addition, postmenarcheal females with this disorder are amenorrheic. (The term *anorexia* is a misnomer because loss of appetite is rare.)

The individual maintains a body weight that is below a minimally normal level for age and height (Criterion A). When Anorexia Nervosa develops in an individual during childhood or early adolescence, there may be failure to make expected weight gains (i.e., while growing in height) instead of weight loss.

Criterion A provides a guideline for determining when the individual meets the threshold for being underweight. It suggests that the individual weigh less than 85% of that weight that is considered normal for that person's age and height (usually computed using one of several published versions of the Metropolitan Life Insurance tables or pediatric growth charts). An alternative and somewhat stricter guideline (used in the ICD-10 Diagnostic Criteria for Research) requires that the individual have a body mass index (BMI) (calculated as weight in kilograms/height in meters^2) equal to or below 17.5 kg/m^2. These cutoffs are provided only as suggested guidelines for the clinician, since it is unreasonable to specify a single standard for minimally normal weight that applies to all individuals of a given age and height. In determining a minimally normal weight, the clinician should consider not only such guidelines but also the individual's body build and weight history.

Usually weight loss is accomplished primarily through reduction in total food intake. Although individuals may begin by excluding from their diet what they perceive to be highly caloric foods, most eventually end up with a very restricted diet that is sometimes limited to only a few foods. Additional methods of weight loss include purging (i.e., self-induced vomiting or the misuse of laxatives or diuretics) and increased or excessive exercise.

Individuals with this disorder intensely fear gaining weight or becoming fat (Criterion B). This intense fear of becoming fat is usually not alleviated by the weight loss. In fact, concern about weight gain often increases even as actual weight continues to decrease.

The experience and significance of body weight and shape are distorted in these individuals (Criterion C). Some individuals feel globally overweight. Others realize that they are thin, but are still concerned that certain parts of their bodies, particularly the abdomen, buttocks, and thighs, are "too fat." They may employ a wide variety of techniques to estimate their body size or weight, including excessive weighing, obsessive measuring of body parts, and persistently using a mirror to check for perceived areas of "fat." The self-esteem of individuals with Anorexia Nervosa is highly dependent on their body shape and weight. Weight loss is viewed as an impressive achievement and a sign of extraordinary self-discipline, whereas weight gain is perceived as an unacceptable failure of self-control. Though some individuals with this disorder may acknowledge being thin, they typically deny the serious medical implications of their malnourished state.

In postmenarcheal females, amenorrhea (due to abnormally low levels of estrogen secretion that are due in turn to diminished pituitary secretion of follicle-stimulating hormone [FSH] and luteinizing hormone [LH]) is an indicator of physiological dysfunction in Anorexia Nervosa (Criterion D). Amenorrhea is usually a consequence of the weight loss but, in a minority of individuals, may actually precede it. In prepubertal females, menarche may be delayed by the illness.

The individual is often brought to professional attention by family members after marked weight loss (or failure to make expected weight gains) has occurred. If individuals seek help on their own, it is usually because of their subjective distress over the somatic and psychological sequelae of starvation. It is rare for an individual with Anorexia Nervosa to complain of weight loss per se. Individuals with Anorexia Nervosa frequently lack insight into, or have considerable denial of, the problem and may be unreliable historians. It is therefore often necessary to obtain information from parents or other outside sources to evaluate the degree of weight loss and other features of the illness.

Subtypes

The following subtypes can be used to specify the presence or absence of regular binge eating or purging during the current episode of Anorexia Nervosa:

Restricting Type. This subtype describes presentations in which weight loss is accomplished primarily through dieting, fasting, or excessive exercise. During the current episode, these individuals have not regularly engaged in binge eating or purging.

Binge-Eating/Purging Type. This subtype is used when the individual has regularly engaged in binge eating or purging (or both) during the current episode. Most individuals with Anorexia Nervosa who binge eat also purge through self-induced vomiting or the misuse of laxatives, diuretics, or enemas. Some individuals included in this subtype do not binge eat, but do regularly purge after the consumption of small amounts of food. It appears that most individuals with Binge-Eating/Purging Type engage in these behaviors at least weekly, but sufficient information is not available to justify the specification of a minimum frequency.

Associated Features and Disorders

Associated descriptive features and mental disorders. When seriously underweight, many individuals with Anorexia Nervosa manifest depressive symptoms such as depressed mood, social withdrawal, irritability, insomnia, and diminished interest in sex. Such individuals may have symptomatic presentations that meet criteria for Major Depressive Disorder. Because these features are also observed in individuals without Anorexia Nervosa who are undergoing starvation, many of the depressive features may be secondary to the physiological sequelae of semistarvation. Symptoms of mood disturbance must therefore be reassessed after partial or complete weight restoration.

Obsessive-compulsive features, both related and unrelated to food, are often prominent. Most individuals with Anorexia Nervosa are preoccupied with thoughts of food. Some collect recipes or hoard food. Observations of behaviors associated with other forms of starvation suggest that obsessions and compulsions related to food may be caused or exacerbated by undernutrition. When individuals with Anorexia Nervosa exhibit obsessions and compulsions that are not related to food, body shape, or weight, an additional diagnosis of Obsessive-Compulsive Disorder may be warranted.

Other features sometimes associated with Anorexia Nervosa include concerns about eating in public, feelings of ineffectiveness, a strong need to control one's environment, inflexible thinking, limited social spontaneity, and overly restrained initiative and emotional expression.

Compared with individuals with Anorexia Nervosa, Restricting Type, those with the Binge-Eating/Purging Type are more likely to have other impulse-control problems, to abuse alcohol or other drugs, to exhibit more mood lability, and to be sexually active.

Associated laboratory findings. Although some individuals with Anorexia Nervosa exhibit no laboratory abnormalities, the semistarvation characteristic of this disorder can affect most major organ systems and produce a variety of disturbances. The induced vomiting and abuse of laxatives, diuretics, and enemas can also cause a number of disturbances leading to abnormal laboratory findings.

Hematology: Leukopenia and mild anemia are common; thrombocytopenia occurs rarely.

Chemistry: Dehydration may be reflected by an elevated blood urea nitrogen (BUN). Hypercholesterolemia is common. Liver function tests may be elevated. Hypomagnesemia, hypozincemia, hypophosphatemia, and hyperamylasemia are occasionally found. Induced vomiting may lead to metabolic alkalosis (elevated serum bicarbonate), hypochloremia, and hypokalemia, and laxative abuse may cause a metabolic acidosis. Serum thyroxine (T_4) levels are usually in the low-normal range; triiodothyronine (T_3) levels are decreased. Hyperadrenocorticism and abnormal responsiveness to a variety of neuroendocrine challenges are common.

In females, low serum estrogen levels are present, whereas males have low levels of serum testosterone. There is a regression of the hypothalamic-pituitary-gonadal axis in both sexes in that the 24-hour pattern of secretion of luteinizing hormone (LH) resembles that normally seen in prepubertal or pubertal individuals.

Electrocardiography: Sinus bradycardia and, rarely, arrhythmias are observed.

Electroencephalography: Diffuse abnormalities, reflecting a metabolic encephalopathy, may result from significant fluid and electrolyte disturbances.

Brain imaging: An increase in the ventricular-brain ratio secondary to starvation is often seen.

Resting energy expenditure: This is often significantly reduced.

Associated physical examination findings and general medical conditions. Many of the physical signs and symptoms of Anorexia Nervosa are attributable to starvation. In addition to amenorrhea, there may be complaints of constipation, abdominal pain, cold intolerance, lethargy, and excess energy. The most obvious finding on physical examination is emaciation. There may also be significant hypotension, hypothermia, and dryness of skin. Some individuals develop lanugo, a fine downy body hair, on their trunks. Most individuals with Anorexia Nervosa exhibit bradycardia. Some develop peripheral edema, especially during weight restoration or on cessation of laxative and diuretic abuse. Rarely, petechiae, usually on the extremities, may indicate a bleeding diathesis. Some individuals evidence a yellowing of the skin associated with hypercarotenemia. Hypertrophy of the salivary glands, particularly the parotid glands, may be present. Individuals who induce vomiting may have dental enamel erosion and some may have scars or calluses on the dorsum of the hand from contact with the teeth when using the hand to induce vomiting.

The semistarvation of Anorexia Nervosa, and the purging behaviors sometimes associated with it, can result in significant associated general medical conditions. These include the development of normochromic normocytic anemia, impaired renal function (associated with chronic dehydration and hypokalemia), cardiovascular problems (severe hypotension, arrhythmias), dental problems, and osteoporosis (resulting from low calcium intake and absorption, reduced estrogen secretion, and increased cortisol secretion).

Specific Culture, Age, and Gender Features

Anorexia Nervosa appears to be far more prevalent in industrialized societies, in which there is an abundance of food and in which, especially for females, being considered attractive is linked to being thin. The disorder is probably most common in the United States, Canada, Europe, Australia, Japan, New Zealand, and South Africa, but little systematic work has examined prevalence in other cultures. Immigrants from cultures in which the disorder is rare who emigrate to cultures in which the disorder is more prevalent may develop Anorexia Nervosa as thin-body ideals are assimilated. Cultural factors may also influence the manifestations of the disorder. For example, in some cultures, disturbed perception of the body may not be prominent and the expressed motivation for food restriction may have a different content, such as epigastric discomfort or distaste for food.

Anorexia Nervosa rarely begins before puberty, but there are suggestions that the severity of associated mental disturbances may be greater among prepubertal individuals who develop the illness. However, data also suggest that when the illness begins during early adolescence (between ages 13 and 18 years), it may be associated with a better prognosis. More than 90% of cases of Anorexia Nervosa occur in females.

Prevalence

Prevalence studies among females in late adolescence and early adulthood have found rates of 0.5%–1.0% for presentations that meet full criteria for Anorexia Nervosa. Individuals who are subthreshold for the disorder (i.e., with Eating Disorder Not Otherwise Specified) are more commonly encountered. There are limited data concerning the prevalence of this disorder in males. The incidence of Anorexia Nervosa appears to have increased in recent decades.

Course

The mean age at onset for Anorexia Nervosa is 17 years, with some data suggesting bimodal peaks at ages 14 and 18 years. The onset of this disorder rarely occurs in females over age 40 years. The onset of illness is often associated with a stressful life event, such as leaving home for college. The course and outcome of Anorexia Nervosa are highly variable. Some individuals with Anorexia Nervosa recover fully after a single episode, some exhibit a fluctuating pattern of weight gain followed by relapse, and others experience a chronically deteriorating course of the illness over many years. Hospitalization may be required to restore weight and to address fluid and electrolyte imbalances. Of individuals admitted to university hospitals, the long-term mortality from Anorexia Nervosa is over 10%. Death most commonly results from starvation, suicide, or electrolyte imbalance.

Familial Pattern

There is an increased risk of Anorexia Nervosa among first-degree biological relatives of individuals with the disorder. An increased risk of Mood Disorders has also been found among first-degree biological relatives of individuals with Anorexia Nervosa, particularly relatives of individuals with the Binge-Eating/Purging Type. Studies of Anorexia Nervosa in twins have found concordance rates for monozygotic twins to be significantly higher than those for dizygotic twins.

Differential Diagnosis

Other possible causes of significant weight loss should be considered in the differential diagnosis of Anorexia Nervosa, especially when the presenting features are atypical (such as an onset of illness after age 40 years). In **general medical conditions** (e.g., gastrointestinal disease, brain tumors, occult malignancies, and acquired immunodeficiency syndrome [AIDS]), serious weight loss may occur, but individuals with such disorders usually do not have a distorted body image and a desire for further weight loss. The **superior mesenteric artery syndrome** (characterized by postprandial vomiting secondary to intermittent gastric outlet obstruction) should be distinguished from Anorexia Nervosa, although this syndrome may sometimes develop in individuals with Anorexia Nervosa because of their emaciation. In **Major Depressive Disorder,** severe weight loss may occur, but most individuals with Major Depressive Disorder do not have a desire for excessive weight loss or excessive fear of gaining weight. In **Schizophrenia,** individuals may exhibit odd eating behavior and occasionally experience significant weight loss, but they rarely show the fear of gaining weight and the body image disturbance required for a diagnosis of Anorexia Nervosa.

Some of the features of Anorexia Nervosa are part of the criteria sets for **Social Phobia, Obsessive-Compulsive Disorder,** and **Body Dysmorphic Disorder.** Specifically, individuals may be humiliated or embarrassed to be seen eating in public, as in Social Phobia; may exhibit obsessions and compulsions related to food, as in Obsessive-Compulsive Disorder; or may be preoccupied with an imagined defect in bodily appearance, as in Body Dysmorphic Disorder. If the individual with Anorexia Nervosa has social fears that are limited to eating behavior alone, the diagnosis of Social Phobia should not be made, but social fears unrelated to eating behavior (e.g., excessive fear of speaking in public) may warrant an additional diagnosis of Social Phobia. Similarly, an additional diagnosis of Obsessive-Compulsive Disorder should be considered only if the individual exhibits obsessions and compulsions unrelated to food (e.g., an excessive fear of contamination), and an additional diagnosis of Body Dysmorphic Disorder should be considered only if the distortion is unrelated to body shape and size (e.g., preoccupation that one's nose is too big).

In **Bulimia Nervosa,** individuals exhibit recurrent episodes of binge eating, engage in inappropriate behavior to avoid weight gain (e.g., self-induced vomiting), and are overly concerned with body shape and weight. However, unlike individuals with Anorexia Nervosa, Binge-Eating/Purging Type, individuals with Bulimia Nervosa are able to maintain body weight at or above a minimally normal level.

■ Diagnostic criteria for 307.1 Anorexia Nervosa

A. Refusal to maintain body weight at or above a minimally normal weight for age and height (e.g., weight loss leading to maintenance of body weight less than 85% of that expected; or failure to make expected weight gain during period of growth, leading to body weight less than 85% of that expected).

B. Intense fear of gaining weight or becoming fat, even though underweight.

(continued)

☐ **Diagnostic criteria for 307.1 Anorexia Nervosa** (*continued*)

    C. Disturbance in the way in which one's body weight or shape is experienced, undue influence of body weight or shape on self-evaluation, or denial of the seriousness of the current low body weight.

    D. In postmenarcheal females, amenorrhea, i.e., the absence of at least three consecutive menstrual cycles. (A woman is considered to have amenorrhea if her periods occur only following hormone, e.g., estrogen, administration.)

Specify type:

Restricting Type: during the current episode of Anorexia Nervosa, the person has not regularly engaged in binge-eating or purging behavior (i.e., self-induced vomiting or the misuse of laxatives, diuretics, or enemas)

Binge-Eating/Purging Type: during the current episode of Anorexia Nervosa, the person has regularly engaged in binge-eating or purging behavior (i.e., self-induced vomiting or the misuse of laxatives, diuretics, or enemas)

307.51 Bulimia Nervosa

Diagnostic Features

The essential features of Bulimia Nervosa are binge eating and inappropriate compensatory methods to prevent weight gain. In addition, the self-evaluation of individuals with Bulimia Nervosa is excessively influenced by body shape and weight. To qualify for the diagnosis, the binge eating and the inappropriate compensatory behaviors must occur, on average, at least twice a week for 3 months (Criterion C).

A *binge* is defined as eating in a discrete period of time an amount of food that is definitely larger than most individuals would eat under similar circumstances (Criterion A1). The clinician should consider the context in which the eating occurred—what would be regarded as excessive consumption at a typical meal might be considered normal during a celebration or holiday meal. A "discrete period of time" refers to a limited period, usually less than 2 hours. A single episode of binge eating need not be restricted to one setting. For example, an individual may begin a binge in a restaurant and then continue it on returning home. Continual snacking on small amounts of food throughout the day would not be considered a binge.

Although the type of food consumed during binges varies, it typically includes sweet, high-calorie foods such as ice cream or cake. However, binge eating appears to be characterized more by an abnormality in the amount of food consumed than by a craving for a specific nutrient, such as carbohydrate. Although individuals with Bulimia Nervosa consume more calories during an episode of binge eating than persons without Bulimia Nervosa consume during a meal, the fractions of calories derived from protein, fat, and carbohydrate are similar.

Individuals with Bulimia Nervosa are typically ashamed of their eating problems and attempt to conceal their symptoms. Binge eating usually occurs in secrecy, or as inconspicuously as possible. An episode may or may not be planned in advance and is usually (but not always) characterized by rapid consumption. The binge eating often continues until the individual is uncomfortably, or even painfully, full. Binge eating is typically triggered by dysphoric mood states, interpersonal stressors, intense hunger following dietary restraint, or feelings related to body weight, body shape, and food. Binge eating may transiently reduce dysphoria, but disparaging self-criticism and depressed mood often follow.

An episode of binge eating is also accompanied by a sense of lack of control (Criterion A2). An individual may be in a frenzied state while binge eating, especially early in the course of the disorder. Some individuals describe a dissociative quality during, or following, the binge episodes. After Bulimia Nervosa has persisted for some time, individuals may report that their binge-eating episodes are no longer characterized by an acute feeling of loss of control, but rather by behavioral indicators of impaired control, such as difficulty resisting binge eating or difficulty stopping a binge once it has begun. The impairment in control associated with binge eating in Bulimia Nervosa is not absolute; for example, an individual may continue binge eating while the telephone is ringing, but will cease if a roommate or spouse unexpectedly enters the room.

Another essential feature of Bulimia Nervosa is the recurrent use of inappropriate compensatory behaviors to prevent weight gain (Criterion B). Many individuals with Bulimia Nervosa employ several methods in their attempt to compensate for binge eating. The most common compensatory technique is the induction of vomiting after an episode of binge eating. This method of purging is employed by 80%–90% of individuals with Bulimia Nervosa who present for treatment at eating disorders clinics. The immediate effects of vomiting include relief from physical discomfort and reduction of fear of gaining weight. In some cases, vomiting becomes a goal in itself, and the person will binge in order to vomit or will vomit after eating a small amount of food. Individuals with Bulimia Nervosa may use a variety of methods to induce vomiting, including the use of fingers or instruments to stimulate the gag reflex. Individuals generally become adept at inducing vomiting and are eventually able to vomit at will. Rarely, individuals consume syrup of ipecac to induce vomiting. Other purging behaviors include the misuse of laxatives and diuretics. Approximately one-third of those with Bulimia Nervosa misuse laxatives after binge eating. Rarely, individuals with the disorder will misuse enemas following episodes of binge eating, but this is seldom the sole compensatory method employed.

Individuals with Bulimia Nervosa may fast for a day or more or exercise excessively in an attempt to compensate for binge eating. Exercise may be considered to be excessive when it significantly interferes with important activities, when it occurs at inappropriate times or in inappropriate settings, or when the individual continues to exercise despite injury or other medical complications. Rarely, individuals with this disorder may take thyroid hormone in an attempt to avoid weight gain. Individuals with diabetes mellitus and Bulimia Nervosa may omit or reduce insulin doses in order to reduce the metabolism of food consumed during eating binges.

Individuals with Bulimia Nervosa place an excessive emphasis on body shape and weight in their self-evaluation, and these factors are typically the most important ones in determining self-esteem (Criterion D). Individuals with this disorder may closely resemble those with Anorexia Nervosa in their fear of gaining weight, in their desire to lose weight, and in the level of dissatisfaction with their bodies. However, a diagnosis of Bulimia Nervosa should not be given when the disturbance occurs only during episodes of Anorexia Nervosa (Criterion E).

Subtypes

The following subtypes can be used to specify the presence or absence of regular use of purging methods as a means to compensate for the binge eating:

Purging Type. This subtype describes presentations in which the person has regularly engaged in self-induced vomiting or the misuse of laxatives, diuretics, or enemas during the current episode.

Nonpurging Type. This subtype describes presentations in which the person has used other inappropriate compensatory behaviors, such as fasting or excessive exercise, but has not regularly engaged in self-induced vomiting or the misuse of laxatives, diuretics, or enemas during the current episode.

Associated Features and Disorders

Associated descriptive features and mental disorders. Individuals with Bulimia Nervosa typically are within the normal weight range, although some may be slightly underweight or overweight. The disorder occurs but is uncommon among moderately and morbidly obese individuals. There are suggestions that, prior to the onset of the Eating Disorder, individuals with Bulimia Nervosa are more likely to be overweight than their peers. Between binges, individuals with Bulimia Nervosa typically restrict their total caloric consumption and preferentially select low-calorie ("diet") foods while avoiding foods they perceive to be fattening or likely to trigger a binge.

There is an increased frequency of depressive symptoms (e.g., low self-esteem) or Mood Disorders (particularly Dysthymic Disorder and Major Depressive Disorder) in individuals with Bulimia Nervosa. In many or most individuals, the mood disturbance begins at the same time as or following the development of Bulimia Nervosa, and individuals often ascribe their mood disturbances to Bulimia Nervosa. However, in some individuals, the mood disturbance clearly precedes the development of Bulimia Nervosa. There may also be an increased frequency of anxiety symptoms (e.g., fear of social situations) or Anxiety Disorders. These mood and anxiety disturbances frequently remit following effective treatment of Bulimia Nervosa. Substance Abuse or Dependence, particularly involving alcohol and stimulants, occurs in about one-third of individuals with Bulimia Nervosa. Stimulant use often begins in an attempt to control appetite and weight. Probably between one-third and one-half of individuals with Bulimia Nervosa also have personality features that meet criteria for one or more Personality Disorders (most frequently Borderline Personality Disorder).

Preliminary evidence suggests that individuals with Bulimia Nervosa, Purging Type, show more symptoms of depression and greater concern with shape and weight than individuals with Bulimia Nervosa, Nonpurging Type.

Associated laboratory findings. Frequent purging behavior of any kind can produce fluid and electrolyte abnormalities, most frequently hypokalemia, hyponatremia, and hypochloremia. The loss of stomach acid through vomiting may produce a metabolic alkalosis (elevated serum bicarbonate), and the frequent induction of diarrhea through laxative abuse can cause metabolic acidosis. Some individuals with Bulimia Nervosa exhibit mildly elevated levels of serum amylase, probably reflecting an increase in the salivary isoenzyme.

Associated physical examination findings and general medical conditions. Recurrent vomiting eventually leads to a significant and permanent loss of dental enamel, especially from lingual surfaces of the front teeth. These teeth may become chipped and appear ragged and "moth-eaten." There may also be an increased frequency of dental cavities. In some individuals, the salivary glands, particularly the parotid glands, may become notably enlarged. Individuals who induce vomiting by manually stimulating the gag reflex may develop calluses or scars on the dorsal surface of the hand from repeated trauma from the teeth. Serious cardiac and skeletal myopathies have been reported among individuals who regularly use syrup of ipecac to induce vomiting.

Menstrual irregularity or amenorrhea sometimes occurs among females with Bulimia Nervosa; whether such disturbances are related to weight fluctuations, to nutritional deficiencies, or to emotional stress is uncertain. Individuals who chronically abuse laxatives may become dependent on their use to stimulate bowel movements. The fluid and electrolyte disturbances resulting from the purging behavior are sometimes sufficiently severe to constitute medically serious problems. Rare but potentially fatal complications include esophageal tears, gastric rupture, and cardiac arrhythmias. Compared with individuals with Bulimia Nervosa, Nonpurging Type, those with the Purging Type are much more likely to have physical problems such as fluid and electrolyte disturbances.

Specific Culture, Age, and Gender Features

Bulimia Nervosa has been reported to occur with roughly similar frequencies in most industrialized countries, including the United States, Canada, Europe, Australia, Japan, New Zealand, and South Africa. Few studies have examined the prevalence of Bulimia Nervosa in other cultures. In clinical studies of Bulimia Nervosa in the United States, individuals presenting with this disorder are primarily white, but the disorder has also been reported among other ethnic groups.

In clinic and population samples, at least 90% of individuals with Bulimia Nervosa are female. Some data suggest that males with Bulimia Nervosa have a higher prevalence of premorbid obesity than do females with Bulimia Nervosa.

Prevalence

The prevalence of Bulimia Nervosa among adolescent and young adult females is approximately 1%–3%; the rate of occurrence of this disorder in males is approximately one-tenth of that in females.

Course

Bulimia Nervosa usually begins in late adolescence or early adult life. The binge eating frequently begins during or after an episode of dieting. Disturbed eating behavior persists for at least several years in a high percentage of clinic samples. The course may be chronic or intermittent, with periods of remission alternating with recurrences of binge eating. The long-term outcome of Bulimia Nervosa is not known.

Familial Pattern

Several studies have suggested an increased frequency of Bulimia Nervosa, of Mood Disorders, and of Substance Abuse and Dependence in the first-degree biological relatives of individuals with Bulimia Nervosa. A familial tendency toward obesity may exist, but this has not been definitively established.

Differential Diagnosis

Individuals whose binge-eating behavior occurs only during Anorexia Nervosa are given the diagnosis **Anorexia Nervosa, Binge-Eating/Purging Type,** and should *not* be given the additional diagnosis of Bulimia Nervosa. For an individual who binges and purges but whose presentation no longer meets the full criteria for Anorexia Nervosa, Binge-Eating/Purging Type (e.g., when weight is normal or menses have become regular), it is a matter of clinical judgment whether the most appropriate current diagnosis is Anorexia Nervosa, Binge-Eating/Purging Type, In Partial Remission, or Bulimia Nervosa.

In certain neurological or other general medical conditions, such as **Kleine-Levin syndrome,** there is disturbed eating behavior, but the characteristic psychological features of Bulimia Nervosa, such as overconcern with body shape and weight, are not present. Overeating is common in **Major Depressive Disorder, With Atypical Features,** but such individuals do not engage in inappropriate compensatory behavior and do not exhibit the characteristic overconcern with body shape and weight. If criteria for both disorders are met, both diagnoses should be given. Binge-eating behavior is included in the impulsive behavior criterion that is part of the definition of **Borderline Personality Disorder.** If the full criteria for both disorders are met, both diagnoses can be given.

■ **Diagnostic criteria for 307.51 Bulimia Nervosa**

A. Recurrent episodes of binge eating. An episode of binge eating is characterized by both of the following:

   (1) eating, in a discrete period of time (e.g., within any 2-hour period), an amount of food that is definitely larger than most people would eat during a similar period of time and under similar circumstances

   (2) a sense of lack of control over eating during the episode (e.g., a feeling that one cannot stop eating or control what or how much one is eating)

B. Recurrent inappropriate compensatory behavior in order to prevent weight gain, such as self-induced vomiting; misuse of laxatives, diuretics, enemas, or other medications; fasting; or excessive exercise.

C. The binge eating and inappropriate compensatory behaviors both occur, on average, at least twice a week for 3 months.

(continued)

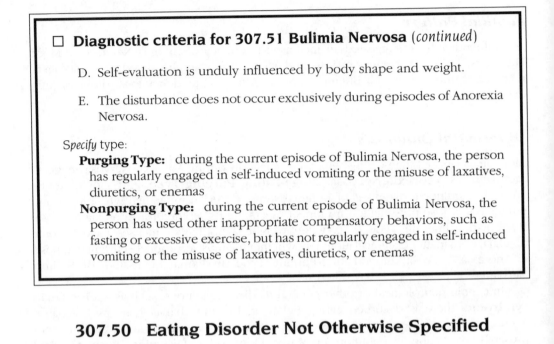

□ **Diagnostic criteria for 307.51 Bulimia Nervosa** (*continued*)

D. Self-evaluation is unduly influenced by body shape and weight.

E. The disturbance does not occur exclusively during episodes of Anorexia Nervosa.

Specify type:
Purging Type: during the current episode of Bulimia Nervosa, the person has regularly engaged in self-induced vomiting or the misuse of laxatives, diuretics, or enemas
Nonpurging Type: during the current episode of Bulimia Nervosa, the person has used other inappropriate compensatory behaviors, such as fasting or excessive exercise, but has not regularly engaged in self-induced vomiting or the misuse of laxatives, diuretics, or enemas

307.50 Eating Disorder Not Otherwise Specified

The Eating Disorder Not Otherwise Specified category is for disorders of eating that do not meet the criteria for any specific Eating Disorder. Examples include

1. For females, all of the criteria for Anorexia Nervosa are met except that the individual has regular menses.
2. All of the criteria for Anorexia Nervosa are met except that, despite significant weight loss, the individual's current weight is in the normal range.
3. All of the criteria for Bulimia Nervosa are met except that the binge eating and inappropriate compensatory mechanisms occur at a frequency of less than twice a week or for a duration of less than 3 months.
4. The regular use of inappropriate compensatory behavior by an individual of normal body weight after eating small amounts of food (e.g., self-induced vomiting after the consumption of two cookies).
5. Repeatedly chewing and spitting out, but not swallowing, large amounts of food.
6. Binge-eating disorder: recurrent episodes of binge eating in the absence of the regular use of inappropriate compensatory behaviors characteristic of Bulimia Nervosa (see p. 729 for suggested research criteria).

Sleep Disorders

The sleep disorders are organized into four major sections according to presumed etiology. **Primary Sleep Disorders** are those in which none of the etiologies listed below (i.e., another mental disorder, a general medical condition, or a substance) is responsible. Primary Sleep Disorders are presumed to arise from endogenous abnormalities in sleep-wake generating or timing mechanisms, often complicated by conditioning factors. Primary Sleep Disorders in turn are subdivided into **Dyssomnias** (characterized by abnormalities in the amount, quality, or timing of sleep) and **Parasomnias** (characterized by abnormal behavioral or physiological events occurring in association with sleep, specific sleep stages, or sleep-wake transitions).

Sleep Disorder Related to Another Mental Disorder involves a prominent complaint of sleep disturbance that results from a diagnosable mental disorder (often a Mood Disorder or Anxiety Disorder) but that is sufficiently severe to warrant independent clinical attention. Presumably, the pathophysiological mechanisms responsible for the mental disorder also affect sleep-wake regulation.

Sleep Disorder Due to a General Medical Condition involves a prominent complaint of sleep disturbance that results from the direct physiological effects of a general medical condition on the sleep-wake system.

Substance-Induced Sleep Disorder involves prominent complaints of sleep disturbance that result from the concurrent use, or recent discontinuation of use, of a substance (including medications).

The systematic assessment in individuals who present with prominent complaints of sleep disturbance includes an evaluation of the specific type of sleep complaint and a consideration of concurrent mental disorders, general medical conditions, and substance (including medication) use that may be responsible for the sleep disturbance.

Five distinct sleep stages can be measured by polysomnography: rapid eye movement (REM) sleep and four stages of non–rapid eye movement (NREM) sleep (stages 1, 2, 3, and 4). Stage 1 NREM sleep is a transition from wakefulness to sleep and occupies about 5% of time spent asleep in healthy adults. Stage 2 NREM sleep, which is characterized by specific EEG waveforms (sleep spindles and K complexes), occupies about 50% of time spent asleep. Stages 3 and 4 NREM sleep (also known collectively as slow-wave sleep) are the deepest levels of sleep and occupy about 10%–20% of sleep time. REM sleep, during which the majority of typical storylike dreams occur, occupies about 20%–25% of total sleep.

These sleep stages have a characteristic temporal organization across the night. NREM stages 3 and 4 tend to occur in the first one-third to one-half of the night and increase in duration in response to sleep deprivation. REM sleep occurs cyclically throughout the night, alternating with NREM sleep about every 80–100 minutes. REM sleep periods increase in duration toward the morning. Human sleep also varies characteristically across the life span. After relative stability with large amounts of slow-wave sleep in childhood and early adolescence, sleep continuity and depth deteriorate across the adult age range. This deterioration is reflected by increased wakefulness and stage 1 sleep and decreased stages 3 and 4 sleep. Because of this, age must be considered in the diagnosis of a Sleep Disorder in any individual.

Polysomnography is the monitoring of multiple electrophysiological parameters during sleep and generally includes measurement of EEG activity, electrooculographic activity, and electromyographic activity. Additional polysomnographic measures may include oral or nasal airflow, respiratory effort, chest and abdominal wall movement, oxyhemoglobin saturation, or exhaled carbon dioxide concentration; these measures are used to monitor respiration during sleep and to detect the presence and severity of sleep apnea. Measurement of peripheral electromyographic activity may be used to detect abnormal movements during sleep. Most polysomnographic studies are conducted during the person's usual sleeping hours—that is, at night. However, daytime poly-somnographic studies also are used to quantify daytime sleepiness. The most common daytime procedure is the Multiple Sleep Latency Test (MSLT), in which the individual is instructed to lie down in a dark room and not resist falling asleep; this protocol is repeated five times during the day. Sleep latency (the amount of time required to fall asleep) is measured on each trial and is used as an index of physiological sleepiness. The converse of the MSLT is also used: In the Repeated Test of Sustained Wakefulness (RTSW), the individual is placed in a quiet, dimly lit room and instructed to remain awake; this protocol is repeated several times during the day. Again, sleep latency is measured, but it is used here as an index of the individual's ability to maintain wakefulness.

Standard terminology for polysomnographic measures is used throughout the text in this section. *Sleep continuity* refers to the overall balance of sleep and wakefulness during a night of sleep. "Better" sleep continuity indicates consolidated sleep with little wakefulness; "worse" sleep continuity indicates disrupted sleep with more wakefulness. Specific sleep continuity measures include *sleep latency*—the amount of time required to fall asleep (expressed in minutes); *intermittent wakefulness*—the amount of awake time after initial sleep onset (expressed in minutes); and *sleep efficiency*—the ratio of actual time spent asleep to time spent in bed (expressed as a percentage, with higher numbers indicating better sleep continuity). *Sleep architecture* refers to the amount and distribution of specific sleep stages. Sleep architecture measures include absolute amounts of REM sleep and each NREM sleep stage (in minutes), relative amount of REM sleep and NREM sleep stages (expressed as a percentage of total sleep time), and latency between sleep onset and the first REM period (REM latency).

The text for each of the Sleep Disorders contains a section describing its relationship to corresponding disorders in the *The International Classification of Sleep Disorders: (ICSD) Diagnostic and Coding Manual,* published in 1990 by the American Sleep Disorders Association.

Primary Sleep Disorders

Dyssomnias

Dyssomnias are primary disorders of initiating or maintaining sleep or of excessive sleepiness and are characterized by a disturbance in the amount, quality, or timing of sleep. This section includes Primary Insomnia, Primary Hypersomnia, Narcolepsy, Breathing-Related Sleep Disorder, Circadian Rhythm Sleep Disorder, and Dyssomnia Not Otherwise Specified.

307.42 Primary Insomnia

Diagnostic Features

The essential feature of Primary Insomnia is a complaint of difficulty initiating or maintaining sleep or of nonrestorative sleep that lasts for at least 1 month (Criterion A) and causes clinically significant distress or impairment in social, occupational, or other important areas of functioning (Criterion B). The disturbance in sleep does not occur exclusively during the course of another sleep disorder (Criterion C) or mental disorder (Criterion D) and is not due to the direct physiological effects of a substance or a general medical condition (Criterion E).

Individuals with Primary Insomnia most often report a combination of difficulty falling asleep and intermittent wakefulness during sleep. Less commonly, these individuals may complain only of nonrestorative sleep, that is, feeling that their sleep was restless, light, or of poor quality. Primary Insomnia is often associated with increased physiological or psychological arousal at nighttime in combination with negative conditioning for sleep. A marked preoccupation with and distress due to the inability to sleep may contribute to the development of a vicious cycle: the more the individual strives to sleep, the more frustrated and distressed the individual becomes and the less he or she is able to sleep. Lying in a bed in which the individual has frequently spent sleepless nights may cause frustration and conditioned arousal. Conversely, the individual may fall asleep more easily when not trying to do so (e.g., while watching television, reading, or riding in a car). Some individuals with increased arousal and negative conditioning report that they sleep better away from their own bedrooms and their usual routines. Chronic insomnia may lead to decreased feelings of well-being during the day (e.g., deterioration of mood and motivation; decreased attention, energy, and concentration; and an increase in fatigue and malaise). Although individuals often have the subjective complaint of daytime fatigue, polysomnographic studies usually do not demonstrate an increase in physiological signs of sleepiness.

Associated Features and Disorders

Associated descriptive features and mental disorders.   Many individuals with Primary Insomnia have a history of "light" or easily disturbed sleep prior to the development of more persistent sleep problems. Other associated factors may include anxious overconcern with general health and increased sensitivity to the daytime effects of mild sleep loss. Symptoms of anxiety or depression that do not meet criteria for a specific mental disorder may be present. Interpersonal, social, and occupational problems may develop as a result of overconcern with sleep, increased daytime irritability, and poor concentration. Problems with inattention and concentration may also lead to accidents. Individuals with Primary Insomnia may have a history of mental disorders, particularly Mood Disorders and Anxiety Disorders. Conversely, the chronic sleep disturbance that characterizes Primary Insomnia constitutes a risk factor for (or perhaps an early symptom of) subsequent Mood Disorders and Anxiety Disorders. Individuals with Primary Insomnia sometimes use medications inappropriately: hypnotics or alcohol to help with nighttime sleep, anxiolytics to combat tension or anxiety, and caffeine or other stimulants to combat excessive fatigue. In some cases, this type of substance use may progress to Substance Abuse or Substance Dependence.

Associated laboratory findings.   Polysomnography may demonstrate poor sleep continuity (e.g., increased sleep latency, increased intermittent wakefulness, and decreased sleep efficiency), increased stage 1 sleep, decreased stages 3 and 4 sleep, increased muscle tension, or increased amounts of EEG alpha activity during sleep. These features must be interpreted within the context of age-appropriate norms. Some individuals may report better sleep in the laboratory than at home, suggesting a conditioned basis for sleep complaints. Other psychophysiological tests may also show high arousal (e.g., increased muscle tension or excessive physiological reactivity to stress). Individuals with Primary Insomnia may also have elevated scores on self-report psychological or personality inventories (e.g., on profiles indicating chronic, mild depression and anxiety; an "internalizing" style of conflict resolution; and a somatic focus).

Associated physical examination findings and general medical conditions. Individuals with Primary Insomnia may appear fatigued or haggard, but show no other characteristic abnormalities on physical examination. There may be an increased incidence of stress-related psychophysiological problems (e.g., tension headache, increased muscle tension, gastric distress).

Specific Age and Gender Features

Survey data consistently demonstrate that complaints of insomnia are more prevalent with increasing age and among women. Young adults more often complain of difficulty falling asleep, whereas midlife and elderly adults are more likely to have difficulty with maintaining sleep and early morning awakening. Paradoxically, despite the greater prevalence of insomnia complaints among elderly women, polysomnographic studies generally indicate better preservation of sleep continuity and slow-wave sleep in elderly females than in elderly males. The reason for this discrepancy between self-report and laboratory data is not known.

Prevalence

The true prevalence rate of Primary Insomnia in the general population is unknown. Population surveys indicate a 1-year prevalence of insomnia complaints of 30%–40% in adults (although the percentage of those whose sleep disturbance would meet criteria for Primary Insomnia has not been studied). In clinics specializing in sleep disorders, approximately 15%–25% of individuals with chronic insomnia are diagnosed with Primary Insomnia.

Course

The factors that precipitate Primary Insomnia may differ from those that perpetuate it. Most cases have a fairly sudden onset at a time of psychological, social, or medical stress. Primary Insomnia often persists long after the original causative factors resolve, due to the development of heightened arousal and negative conditioning. For example, a person with a painful injury who spends a great deal of time in bed and has difficulty sleeping may then develop negative associations for sleep. Negative associations, increased arousal, and conditioned awakenings may then persist beyond the convalescent period, leading to Primary Insomnia. A similar scenario may develop in association with insomnia that occurs in the context of an acute psychological stress or a mental disorder. For instance, insomnia that occurs during an episode of Major Depressive Disorder can become a focus of attention with consequent negative conditioning, and insomnia may persist long after resolution of the depressive episode. In some cases, Primary Insomnia may develop gradually without a clear stressor.

Primary Insomnia typically begins in young adulthood or middle age and is rare in childhood or adolescence. In exceptional cases, the insomnia can be documented back to childhood. The course of Primary Insomnia is variable. It may be limited to a period of several months, particularly if precipitated by a psychosocial or medical stressor that later resolves. The more typical course consists of an initial phase of progressive worsening over weeks to months, followed by a chronic phase of stable sleep difficulty that may last for many years. Some individuals experience an episodic course, with periods of better or worse sleep occurring in response to life events such as vacations or stress.

Familial Pattern

The predisposition toward light and disrupted sleep has a familial association. Formal genetic and/or family studies have not been conducted.

Differential Diagnosis

"Normal" sleep duration varies considerably in the general population. Some individuals who require little sleep ("short sleepers") may be concerned about their sleep duration. **Short sleepers** are distinguished from those with Primary Insomnia by their lack of difficulty falling asleep and by the absence of characteristic symptoms of Primary Insomnia (e.g., intermittent wakefulness, fatigue, concentration problems, or irritability).

Daytime sleepiness, which is a characteristic feature of **Primary Hypersomnia,** can also occur in Primary Insomnia, but is not as severe in Primary Insomnia. When daytime sleepiness is judged to be due to insomnia, an additional diagnosis of Primary Hypersomnia is not given.

Jet Lag and Shift Work Types of **Circadian Rhythm Sleep Disorder** are distinguished from Primary Insomnia by the history of recent transmeridian travel or shift work. Individuals with the Delayed Sleep Phase Type of Circadian Rhythm Sleep Disorder report sleep-onset insomnia only when they try to sleep at socially normal times, but they do not report difficulty falling asleep or staying asleep when they sleep at their preferred times.

Narcolepsy may cause insomnia complaints, particularly in older adults. However, Narcolepsy rarely involves a major complaint of insomnia and is distinguished from Primary Insomnia by symptoms of prominent daytime sleepiness, cataplexy, sleep paralysis, and sleep-related hallucinations.

A **Breathing-Related Sleep Disorder,** particularly central sleep apnea, may involve a complaint of chronic insomnia and daytime impairment. A careful history may reveal periodic pauses in breathing during sleep or crescendo-decrescendo breathing (Cheyne-Stokes respiration). A history of central nervous system injury or disease may further suggest a Breathing-Related Sleep Disorder. Polysomnography can confirm the presence of apneic events. Most individuals with Breathing-Related Sleep Disorder have obstructive apnea that can be distinguished from Primary Insomnia by a history of loud snoring, breathing pauses during sleep, and excessive daytime sleepiness.

Parasomnias are characterized by a complaint of unusual behavior or events during sleep that sometimes may lead to intermittent awakenings. However, it is these behavioral events that dominate the clinical picture in a Parasomnia rather than the insomnia.

Primary Insomnia must be distinguished from **mental disorders that include insomnia as an essential or associated feature** (e.g., Major Depressive Disorder, Generalized Anxiety Disorder, Schizophrenia). The diagnosis of Primary Insomnia is not given if insomnia occurs exclusively during the course of another mental disorder. A thorough investigation for the presence of other mental disorders is essential before considering the diagnosis of Primary Insomnia. A diagnosis of Primary Insomnia can be made in the presence of another current or past mental disorder if the mental disorder is judged to not account for the insomnia or if the insomnia and the mental disorder have an independent course. In contrast, when insomnia occurs as a manifestation of, and exclusively during the course of, another mental disorder (e.g., a Mood, Anxiety, Somatoform, or Psychotic Disorder), the diagnosis of **Insomnia Related to Another Mental Disorder** may be more appropriate. This diagnosis should only be considered when the insomnia is the predominant complaint and is sufficiently severe to warrant independent clinical attention; otherwise, no separate diagnosis is necessary.

Primary Insomnia must be distinguished from **Sleep Disorder Due to a General Medical Condition, Insomnia Type.** The diagnosis should be Sleep Disorder Due to a General Medical Condition when the insomnia is judged to be the direct physiological consequence of a specific general medical condition (e.g., pheochromocytoma, hyperthyroidism) (see p. 597). This determination is based on history, laboratory findings, or physical examination. **Substance-Induced Sleep Disorder, Insomnia Type,** is distinguished from Primary Insomnia by the fact that a substance (i.e., a drug of abuse, a medication, or exposure to a toxin) is judged to be etiologically related to the insomnia (see p. 601). For example, insomnia occurring only in the context of heavy coffee consumption would be diagnosed as Caffeine-Induced Sleep Disorder, Insomnia Type, With Onset During Intoxication.

Relationship to International Classification of Sleep Disorders

Primary Insomnia subsumes a number of insomnia diagnoses in the International Classification of Sleep Disorders (ICSD), including Psychophysiological Insomnia, Sleep

State Misperception, Idiopathic Insomnia, and some cases of Inadequate Sleep Hygiene. Psychophysiological Insomnia most closely resembles Primary Insomnia, particularly in terms of arousal and conditioning factors. Sleep State Misperception is a condition characterized by complaints of insomnia with a marked discrepancy between subjective and objective estimates of sleep. Idiopathic Insomnia includes those cases with onset in childhood and a lifelong course, presumably due to an abnormality in the neurological control of the sleep-wake system. Inadequate Sleep Hygiene refers to insomnia resulting from behavioral practices that increase arousal or disrupt sleep organization (e.g., working late into the night, taking excessive daytime naps, or keeping irregular sleep hours).

■ Diagnostic criteria for 307.42 Primary Insomnia

A. The predominant complaint is difficulty initiating or maintaining sleep, or nonrestorative sleep, for at least 1 month.

B. The sleep disturbance (or associated daytime fatigue) causes clinically significant distress or impairment in social, occupational, or other important areas of functioning.

C. The sleep disturbance does not occur exclusively during the course of Narcolepsy, Breathing-Related Sleep Disorder, Circadian Rhythm Sleep Disorder, or a Parasomnia.

D. The disturbance does not occur exclusively during the course of another mental disorder (e.g., Major Depressive Disorder, Generalized Anxiety Disorder, a delirium).

E. The disturbance is not due to the direct physiological effects of a substance (e.g., a drug of abuse, a medication) or a general medical condition.

307.44 Primary Hypersomnia

Diagnostic Features

The essential feature of Primary Hypersomnia is excessive sleepiness for at least 1 month as evidenced either by prolonged sleep episodes or by daytime sleep episodes occurring almost daily (Criterion A). The excessive sleepiness must be sufficiently severe to cause clinically significant distress or impairment in social, occupational, or other important areas of functioning (Criterion B). The excessive sleepiness does not occur exclusively during the course of another Sleep Disorder (Criterion C) or mental disorder (Criterion D) and is not due to the direct physiological effects of a substance or a general medical condition (Criterion E).

In individuals with Primary Hypersomnia, the duration of the major sleep episode (for most individuals, nocturnal sleep) may range from 8 to 12 hours and is often followed by difficulty awakening in the morning. The actual quality of nocturnal sleep is normal. Excessive sleepiness during normal waking hours takes the form of intentional naps or inadvertent episodes of sleep. Objective measurements demonstrate increased physiological sleepiness. Daytime naps tend to be relatively long (often lasting an hour or more), are experienced as unrefreshing, and often do not lead to improved alertness. Individuals typically feel sleepiness developing over a period of time, rather than experiencing a sudden sleep "attack." Unintentional sleep episodes typically occur in low-stimulation and low-activity situations (e.g., while attending lectures, reading, watching television, or driving long distances).

Hypersomnia can lead to significant distress and dysfunction in work and social relationships. Prolonged nocturnal sleep and difficulty awakening can result in difficulty in meeting morning obligations. Unintentional daytime sleep episodes can be embarrassing and even dangerous, if, for instance, the individual is driving or operating machinery when the episode occurs. The low level of alertness that occurs while an individual fights sleepiness can lead to poor efficiency, poor concentration, and poor memory during daytime activities. Sleepiness, often misattributed to boredom or laziness, can also disrupt social and family relationships.

Specifier

Recurrent. This specifier is used if there are periods of excessive sleepiness that last at least 3 days occurring several times a year for at least 2 years.

Most individuals with Primary Hypersomnia have consistent and persistent symptoms. In contrast, the Recurrent form should be noted if symptoms occur periodically for several days to several weeks, with symptomatic periods recurring several times per year. Between periods of excessive sleepiness, sleep duration and daytime alertness are normal. In the recurrent form of Primary Hypersomnia known as Kleine-Levin syndrome, individuals may spend 18–20 hours asleep or in bed. The recurrent periods of sleepiness are associated with other characteristic clinical features indicating disinhibition. Indiscriminate hypersexuality including inappropriate sexual advances and overt masturbation can be seen in males (and less often in females). Compulsive overeating with acute weight gain may occur. Irritability, depersonalization, depression, confusion, and occasional hallucinations have been described in some individuals, and impulsive behaviors can also occur. Other recurrent forms of hypersomnia can be seen in the absence of these features. For instance, some females report regularly occurring periods of hypersomnia at specific times of their menstrual cycle.

Associated Features and Disorders

Associated descriptive features and mental disorders.   In Primary Hypersomnia, sleep tends to be continuous but nonrestorative. Individuals with this disorder fall asleep quickly and have good sleep efficiency, but may have difficulty waking up in the morning, sometimes appearing confused, combative, or ataxic. This prolonged impairment of alertness at the sleep-wake transition is often referred to as "sleep drunkenness."

Persistent daytime sleepiness can lead to automatic behavior (usually of a very routine, low-complexity type) that the individual carries out with little or no subsequent recall. For example, individuals may find themselves having driven several miles from where they thought they were, unaware of the "automatic" driving they did in the preceding minutes.

Although precise data are not available regarding comorbidity with mental disorders, many individuals with Primary Hypersomnia have symptoms of depression that may meet criteria for Major Depressive Disorder. This may be related to the psychosocial consequences of excessive sleepiness. Individuals with hypersomnia are also at risk for Substance-Related Disorders, particularly related to self-medication with stimulants.

Associated laboratory findings.   In Primary Hypersomnia, nocturnal polysomnography demonstrates a normal to prolonged sleep duration, short sleep latency, normal to increased sleep continuity, and normal distributions of rapid eye movement (REM) and non–rapid eye movement (NREM) sleep. Some individuals with this disorder may have increased amounts of slow-wave sleep. Sleep-onset REM periods (the occurrence of REM sleep within 20 minutes of sleep onset), breathing-related sleep disturbances, and frequent limb movements disrupting sleep are not present. The Multiple Sleep Latency Test (MSLT) documents excessive physiological daytime sleepiness, typically indicated by mean sleep latency values of 5–10 minutes. REM sleep does not occur during the daytime sleep episodes. Nocturnal polysomnography and the MSLT do not reveal findings characteristic of other causes of hypersomnia.

In the Recurrent Kleine-Levin form of Primary Hypersomnia, routine EEG studies performed during the periods of hypersomnia show general slowing of the background rhythm and paroxysmal bursts of theta activity. Nocturnal polysomnography shows an increase in total sleep time and short REM sleep latency. MSLT studies confirm increased physiological sleepiness, with sleep latencies generally less than 10 minutes. Sleep-onset REM periods may be seen during symptomatic periods.

Associated physical examination findings and general medical conditions.
Individuals with Primary Hypersomnia often appear sleepy and may even fall asleep in the clinician's waiting area. A subset of individuals with Primary Hypersomnia have a family history of hypersomnia and also have symptoms of autonomic nervous system dysfunction, including recurrent vascular-type headaches, reactivity of the peripheral vascular system (Raynaud's phenomenon), and fainting. Individuals with the Recurrent Kleine-Levin form may have nonspecific neurological examination findings including depressed deep tendon reflexes, dysarthria, and nystagmus.

Specific Age or Gender Features

Voluntary napping increases with age, but this normal phenomenon is distinct from Primary Hypersomnia. Kleine-Levin syndrome affects males about three times more often than it affects females.

Prevalence

The true prevalence of Primary Hypersomnia in the general population is not known. Approximately 5%–10% of individuals who present to sleep disorders clinics with complaints of daytime sleepiness are diagnosed as having Primary Hypersomnia. The Recurrent form of Primary Hypersomnia known as Kleine-Levin syndrome is rare.

Population surveys find a complaint of daytime sleepiness in 0.5%–5.0% of adults, without regard to specific causes or diagnoses.

Course

Primary Hypersomnia typically begins between ages 15 and 30 years, with a gradual progression over weeks to months. For most individuals, the course is then chronic and stable, unless treatment is initiated. Kleine-Levin syndrome also begins during adolescence and may continue its periodic course for decades, although it often resolves during middle age.

Familial Pattern

The subgroup of individuals with autonomic dysfunction are more likely than other individuals with Primary Hypersomnia to have family members with Primary Hypersomnia. Kleine-Levin syndrome does not demonstrate familial aggregation.

Differential Diagnosis

"Normal" sleep duration varies considerably in the general population. **"Long sleepers"** (i.e., individuals who require a greater than average amount of sleep) do not have excessive daytime sleepiness, sleep drunkenness, or automatic behavior when they obtain their required amount of nocturnal sleep. If social or occupational demands lead to shorter nocturnal sleep, daytime symptoms may appear. In Primary Hypersomnia, by contrast, symptoms of excessive sleepiness occur regardless of nocturnal sleep duration.

An **inadequate amount of nocturnal sleep** can produce symptoms of daytime sleepiness very similar to those of Primary Hypersomnia. An average sleep duration of fewer than 7 hours per night strongly suggests inadequate nocturnal sleep, and an average of more than 9 hours of sleep per 24-hour period suggests Primary Hypersomnia. Individuals with inadequate nocturnal sleep typically "catch up" with longer sleep durations on days when they are free from social or occupational demands or on vacations. Unlike Primary Hypersomnia, insufficient nocturnal sleep is unlikely to persist unabated for decades. A diagnosis of Primary Hypersomnia should not be made if there is a question regarding the adequacy of nocturnal sleep duration. A diagnostic and therapeutic trial of sleep extension for 10–14 days can often clarify the diagnosis.

Daytime sleepiness, which is a characteristic feature of Primary Hypersomnia, can also occur in **Primary Insomnia,** but the sleepiness is less severe in individuals with Primary Insomnia. When daytime sleepiness is judged to be due to insomnia, an additional diagnosis of Primary Hypersomnia is not given.

Primary Hypersomnia and **Narcolepsy** are similar with respect to the degree of daytime sleepiness, age at onset, and stable course over time, but can be distinguished based on distinctive clinical and laboratory features. Individuals with Primary Hypersomnia typically have longer and less disrupted nocturnal sleep, greater difficulty awakening, more persistent daytime sleepiness (as opposed to more discrete "sleep attacks" in Narcolepsy), longer and less refreshing daytime sleep episodes, and little or no dreaming during daytime naps. By contrast, individuals with Narcolepsy have cataplexy and recurrent intrusions of elements of REM sleep into the transition between sleep and wakefulness (e.g., sleep-related hallucinations and sleep paralysis). The MSLT typically demonstrates shorter sleep latencies (i.e., greater physiological sleepiness) as well as the presence of multiple sleep-onset REM periods in individuals with Narcolepsy.

Individuals with Primary Hypersomnia and **Breathing-Related Sleep Disorder** may have similar patterns of excessive sleepiness. Breathing-Related Sleep Disorder is suggested by a history of loud snoring, pauses in breathing during sleep, brain injury, or cardiovascular disease and by the presence of obesity, oropharyngeal anatomical abnormalities, hypertension, or heart failure on physical examination. Polysomnographic studies can confirm the presence of apneic events in Breathing-Related Sleep Disorder (and their absence in Primary Hypersomnia).

Circadian Rhythm Sleep Disorder is often characterized by daytime sleepiness. A history of an abnormal sleep-wake schedule (with shifted or irregular hours) is present in individuals with Circadian Rhythm Sleep Disorder. **Parasomnias** rarely produce the prolonged, undisturbed nocturnal sleep or daytime sleepiness characteristic of Primary Hypersomnia.

Primary Hypersomnia must be distinguished from **mental disorders that include hypersomnia as an essential or associated feature.** In particular, complaints of daytime sleepiness may occur in a **Major Depressive Episode, With Atypical Features,** and in the depressed phase of **Bipolar Disorder.** The diagnosis of Primary Hypersomnia is not given if hypersomnia occurs exclusively during the course of another mental disorder. A thorough investigation for the presence of other mental disorders is essential before considering the diagnosis of Primary Hypersomnia. A diagnosis of Primary Hypersomnia can be made in the presence of another current or past mental disorder if the mental disorder is judged to not account for the hypersomnia or if the hypersomnia and the mental disorder have an independent course (e.g., in an individual with chronic hypersomnia who later develops a Major Depressive Disorder). In contrast, when hypersomnia occurs as a manifestation of, and exclusively during the course of, another mental disorder, the diagnosis of Hypersomnia Related to Another Mental Disorder may be more appropriate. This diagnosis should only be considered when the hypersomnia is the predominant complaint and is sufficiently severe to warrant independent clinical attention; otherwise, no separate diagnosis is necessary.

Primary Hypersomnia must be distinguished from **Sleep Disorder Due to a General Medical Condition, Hypersomnia Type.** The diagnosis is Sleep Disorder Due to a General Medical Condition when the hypersomnia is judged to be a direct physiological consequence of a specific general medical condition (e.g., brain tumor) (see p. 597). This determination is based on history, laboratory findings, or physical examination. **Substance-Induced Sleep Disorder, Hypersomnia Type,** is distinguished from Primary Hypersomnia by the fact that a substance (i.e., a drug of abuse, a medication, or exposure to a toxin) is judged to be etiologically related to the hypersomnia (see p. 601). For example, hypersomnia occurring only in the context of withdrawal from cocaine would be diagnosed as Cocaine-Induced Sleep Disorder, Hypersomnia Type, With Onset During Withdrawal.

Relationship to the International Classification of Sleep Disorders

Primary Hypersomnia is analogous to the diagnosis of Idiopathic Hypersomnia in the International Classification of Sleep Disorders (ICSD). In addition, the ICSD includes a separate category for Recurrent Hypersomnia, which is analogous to the Recurrent form of Primary Hypersomnia.

■ **Diagnostic criteria for 307.44 Primary Hypersomnia**

A. The predominant complaint is excessive sleepiness for at least 1 month (or less if recurrent) as evidenced by either prolonged sleep episodes or daytime sleep episodes that occur almost daily.

B. The excessive sleepiness causes clinically significant distress or impairment in social, occupational, or other important areas of functioning.

C. The excessive sleepiness is not better accounted for by insomnia and does not occur exclusively during the course of another Sleep Disorder (e.g., Narcolepsy, Breathing-Related Sleep Disorder, Circadian Rhythm Sleep Disorder, or a Parasomnia) and cannot be accounted for by an inadequate amount of sleep.

D. The disturbance does not occur exclusively during the course of another mental disorder.

E. The disturbance is not due to the direct physiological effects of a substance (e.g., a drug of abuse, a medication) or a general medical condition.

Specify if:
   Recurrent: if there are periods of excessive sleepiness that last at least 3 days occurring several times a year for at least 2 years

347   Narcolepsy

Diagnostic Features

The essential features of Narcolepsy are repeated irresistible attacks of refreshing sleep, cataplexy, and recurrent intrusions of elements of rapid eye movement (REM) sleep into the transition period between sleep and wakefulness. The individual's sleepiness typically decreases after a sleep attack, only to return several hours later. The sleep attacks must occur daily over a period of at least 3 months to establish the diagnosis (Criterion A), although most individuals describe many years of sleep attacks prior to seeking clinical attention. In addition to sleepiness, individuals with Narcolepsy experience one or both of the following: cataplexy (i.e., episodes of sudden, bilateral, reversible loss of muscle tone that last for seconds to minutes and are usually precipitated by intense emotion) (Criterion B1) or recurrent intrusions of elements of rapid eye movement (REM) sleep into the transition between sleep and wakefulness as manifested by paralysis of voluntary muscles or dreamlike hallucinations (Criterion B2). Many sleep experts allow the diagnosis to be made in the absence of cataplexy or intrusions of REM sleep elements if the individual demonstrates pathological sleepiness and two or more sleep-onset REM periods during a Multiple Sleep Latency Test (MSLT). The symptoms must not be due to the direct physiological effects of a substance (including a medication) or another general medical condition (Criterion C). Although Narcolepsy is classified in the chapter of ICD devoted to neurological conditions, it is included in this section to assist in differential diagnosis in individuals with excessive sleepiness and is coded on Axis I.

Episodes of sleepiness in Narcolepsy are often described as irresistible, resulting in unintended sleep in inappropriate situations (e.g., while driving an automobile, attending meetings, or carrying on a conversation). Low-stimulation, low-activity situations typically exaggerate the degree of sleepiness (e.g., falling asleep while reading, watching television, or attending lectures). Sleep episodes generally last 10–20 minutes but can last up to an hour if uninterrupted. Dreaming is frequently reported. Individuals have varying abilities to "fight off" these sleep attacks. Some individuals take naps intentionally in order to manage their sleepiness. Individuals with Narcolepsy typically have 2–6 episodes of sleep (intentional and unintentional) per day when untreated. Sleep episodes are usually superimposed on a more normal degree of alertness, although some individuals describe constant sleepiness of some degree.

Cataplexy often develops several years after the onset of daytime sleepiness and occurs in approximately 70% of individuals with the disorder. The loss of muscle tone with cataplexy may be subtle, leading to a sagging jaw or drooping eyelids, head, or arms not noticeable to observers. Cataplexy can also be more dramatic, and the individual may drop objects being carried, buckle at the knees, or actually fall to the ground. Respiratory and eye muscles are not affected. The muscle weakness usually lasts only seconds, although periods of up to a half hour have been reported. Episodes are followed by a full return of normal muscle strength. Full consciousness and alertness are preserved during cataplectic episodes. Individuals can clearly describe events and have no confusion before or after the episode. Rarely, prolonged episodes of cataplexy may lead into sleep episodes. Cataplexy is usually triggered by a strong emotional stimulus (e.g., anger, surprise, laughter). Sleep deprivation typically increases the frequency and severity of episodes of cataplexy.

Approximately 20%–40% of individuals with Narcolepsy also experience intense dreamlike imagery just before falling asleep (hypnagogic hallucinations) or just after awakening (hypnopompic hallucinations). Most sleep-related hallucinations are visual and incorporate elements of the actual environment. For instance, individuals may describe objects appearing through cracks in the wall or describe objects moving in a picture on the wall. The hallucinations may also be auditory (e.g., hearing intruders in the home) or kinetic (e.g., sensation of flying). Approximately 30%–50% of individuals with Narcolepsy also experience sleep paralysis just on falling asleep or awakening. In this condition, individuals describe being awake but unable to move or speak. They may also complain of feeling unable to breathe, although the diaphragm is spared and respiration continues. Sleep-related hallucinations and sleep paralysis may occur simultaneously, resulting in an often terrifying experience of seeing or hearing unusual things and being unable to move. Both sleep-related hallucinations and sleep paralysis last for seconds to a few minutes and terminate spontaneously. Both phenomena (vivid mental imagery and skeletal muscle atonia) are thought to result from dissociated elements of REM sleep intruding into wakefulness.

Associated Features and Disorders

Associated descriptive features and mental disorders. Some individuals with Narcolepsy experience generalized daytime sleepiness between the discrete sleep attacks. They may describe being able to sleep at any time in any situation. Automatic behavior, in which the individual engages in activity without full awareness, can occur as a result of profound sleepiness. Individuals may drive, converse, or even work during episodes of automatic behavior. Frequent, intense, and vivid dreams may occur during nocturnal sleep. Individuals with Narcolepsy often experience fragmented nighttime sleep as a result of spontaneous awakenings or periodic limb movements. Rarely, individuals may present with a chief complaint of insomnia, rather than hypersomnia.

Individuals with Narcolepsy may hesitate to engage in social activities because they fear falling asleep or having an episode of cataplexy. They may also strive to prevent attacks of cataplexy by exerting control over their emotions, which may lead to a generalized lack of expressiveness that interferes with social relations. Narcolepsy can severely limit daytime functioning because of repeated, uncontrollable sleep attacks, automatic behavior, and episodes of cataplexy. Individuals with Narcolepsy are at risk for accidental injury to themselves or others because of falling asleep in dangerous situations (e.g., while driving an automobile or operating machinery).

A concurrent mental disorder or history of another mental disorder can be found in approximately 40% of individuals with Narcolepsy. The most common associated disorders are Mood Disorders (primarily Major Depressive Disorder and Dysthymia), followed by Substance-Related Disorders and Generalized Anxiety Disorder. A history of Parasomnias such as Sleepwalking Disorder, bruxism (clenching of the jaw and grinding teeth), and Enuresis appears to be more common in individuals with Narcolepsy.

Associated laboratory findings.   Findings from the daytime Multiple Sleep Latency Test (MSLT) include an average sleep latency of less than 5 minutes and the appearance of REM sleep during two or more naps on a five-nap MSLT. Sleep latencies of less than 10 minutes and sleep-onset REM periods during nocturnal polysomnographic studies are also found frequently. Additional findings on polysomnography may include frequent transient arousals, decreased sleep efficiency, increased stage 1 sleep, increased REM sleep, and an increase in the frequency of eye movements within the REM periods ("REM density"). Periodic limb movements and episodes of sleep apnea are often noted, but the latter occur less frequently than in Breathing-Related Sleep Disorder.

Human leukocyte antigen (HLA) typing of individuals with Narcolepsy shows the presence of HLA-DR2 (also known as DQw6) and DQw1 (also known as DRw15) in 90%–100% of individuals. However, these HLA antigens are also present in 10%–35% of the general population.

Associated physical examination findings and general medical conditions.
Individuals with Narcolepsy frequently appear sleepy during the clinical interview and examination and may actually fall asleep in the waiting area or examination room. During episodes of cataplexy, individuals may slump in the chair and have slurred speech or drooping eyelids.

Prevalence

Epidemiological studies indicate a prevalence of 0.02%–0.16% for Narcolepsy in the adult population, with equal rates in females and males.

Course

Daytime sleepiness is almost always the first symptom of Narcolepsy and usually becomes clinically significant during adolescence. However, on careful review, some degree of sleepiness may have been present even during preschool and early school ages. Onset after age 40 years is unusual. Acute psychosocial stressors or acute alterations in the sleep-wake schedule herald the onset in roughly half of cases. Cataplexy may develop concurrently with sleepiness, but often appears months, years, or even decades after the onset of sleepiness. Sleep-related hallucinations and sleep paralysis are more variable symptoms of the disorder and may not occur in some individuals. Disrupted nocturnal sleep usually develops later in the course of the disorder, often when individuals are in their 40s or 50s.

The excessive sleepiness of Narcolepsy has a stable course over time. The development of other Sleep Disorders (e.g., periodic limb movements or Breathing-Related Sleep Disorder) may worsen the degree of sleepiness, whereas treatment with stimulant medications may improve it. Cataplexy usually has a stable course as well, although some individuals report decreased symptoms or even complete cessation of symptoms after many years. Similarly, the sleep-related hallucinations and sleep paralysis may go into remission while the daytime sleepiness and sleep attacks persist.

Familial Pattern

Data from HLA studies and family studies strongly suggest a role for genetic factors in the development of Narcolepsy. The mode of inheritance has not been determined but is likely multifactorial. Approximately 5%–15% of first-degree biological relatives of probands with Narcolepsy have the disorder. Approximately 25%–50% of the first-degree biological relatives of individuals with Narcolepsy have other disorders characterized by excessive sleepiness (such as Primary Hypersomnia).

Differential Diagnosis

Narcolepsy must be differentiated from normal variations in sleep, sleep deprivation, other primary Sleep Disorders, and Sleep Disorder Related to Another Mental Disorder, Hypersomnia Type. Many individuals feel some sleepiness during the day, particularly in the afternoon hours when an increase in physiological sleepiness occurs. However, such individuals do not have irresistible sleep at other times of the day and can "fight through" their sleepiness with increased mental and physical effort. They generally do not experience cataplexy, sleep-related hallucinations, or sleep paralysis.

Sleep deprivation from any cause produces daytime sleepiness. Narcolepsy should be diagnosed only if the individual has demonstrated a regular sleep-wake schedule with an adequate amount of nocturnal sleep. Sleep deprivation and irregular sleep schedules may rarely lead to sleep-related hallucinations or sleep paralysis, but not to cataplexy.

The degree of daytime sleepiness may be similar in individuals with Narcolepsy and **Primary Hypersomnia.** Compared with individuals with Narcolepsy, individuals with Primary Hypersomnia generally describe prolonged and less disrupted nocturnal sleep. Daytime sleepiness in Primary Hypersomnia consists of more prolonged, unrefreshing sleep periods, which have less urgency than the sleep "attacks" of Narcolepsy and are less often associated with dreaming. Individuals with Primary Hypersomnia do not manifest cataplexy, sleep-related hallucinations, or sleep paralysis. Nocturnal poly-somnography confirms less disrupted sleep and normal REM latency in individuals with Primary Hypersomnia, and the MSLT does not show sleep-onset REM periods.

Individuals with **Breathing-Related Sleep Disorder** often experience excessive sleepiness that is equal in magnitude to that of individuals with Narcolepsy. Furthermore, many individuals with Narcolepsy may develop some degree of sleep apnea. Breathing-Related Sleep Disorder is distinguished from Narcolepsy by a history of loud snoring; breathing pauses that disrupt nocturnal sleep; lengthy, unrefreshing daytime sleep episodes; and the absence of accessory symptoms such as cataplexy. Polysomnography can identify breathing pauses (apneas) in individuals with Breathing-Related Sleep Disorder. Apneas in individuals with Narcolepsy tend to be less frequent and associated with less oxyhemoglobin desaturation. If an individual presents an unambiguous history of Narcolepsy together with confirmatory polysomnographic findings (sleep-onset REM) and also has evidence of Breathing-Related Sleep Disorder during polysomnography, both diagnoses can be made. If an individual has sleep-onset REM and sleep apnea activity during polysomnography, but does not have the full clinical syndrome of Narcolepsy, then only a diagnosis of Breathing-Related Sleep Disorder should be made.

Individuals with **Hypersomnia Related to Another Mental Disorder** may report excessive sleepiness and intense dreams. In particular, Major Depressive Episodes With Atypical Features and Bipolar Disorder, Most Recent Episode Depressed, often involve an intense need for sleep during the daytime. However, individuals with Mood Disorders typically have prolonged nocturnal sleep in contrast to the short, fragmented sleep of Narcolepsy. Daytime naps are not refreshing in individuals with Mood Disorders. Furthermore, these individuals do not have the accessory symptoms that are character-istic of Narcolepsy (e.g., cataplexy), although individuals who have Major Depressive Disorder, With Psychotic Features, may complain of hallucinations near sleep and at other times. Polysomnographic studies of individuals with Mood Disorders may reveal short REM latency, but typically not as short as that seen in Narcolepsy. Nocturnal sleep latency is also longer in individuals with Mood Disorders. Finally, daytime testing with the MSLT shows a much lower degree of physiological sleepiness and infrequent sleep-onset REM periods in individuals with Mood Disorders. Thus, the "sleepiness" in these individuals appears to be more a manifestation of psychomotor retardation and anergy.

The **use of, or withdrawal from, substances** (including medications) may produce some symptoms of Narcolepsy. Cholinergic agonists (including anticholinester-ase pesticides) can disrupt sleep continuity and enhance REM sleep. Similar effects can result from the abrupt discontinuation of anticholinergic agents, including tricyclic antidepressants. Reserpine and methyldopa can enhance REM sleep and produce sleepiness. Withdrawal from stimulants can produce severe somnolence. A diagnosis of **Substance-Induced Sleep Disorder, Hypersomnia Type,** might be warranted if the symptoms are judged to be due to the direct physiological effects of a substance (see p. 601). Conversely, a diagnosis of Narcolepsy should not be made if the individual is taking or has recently discontinued taking such substances.

Narcolepsy must be distinguished from **Sleep Disorder Due to a General Medical Condition, Hypersomnia Type.** The diagnosis is Sleep Disorder Due to a General Medical Condition when the symptoms are judged to be the direct physiological consequence of a specific general medical condition (e.g., closed head injury or hypothalamic tumor) (see p. 597).

Relationship to the International Classification of Sleep Disorders

The International Classification of Sleep Disorders (ICSD) diagnosis of Narcolepsy includes the same essential features as the DSM-IV diagnosis.

■ Diagnostic criteria for 347 Narcolepsy

A. Irresistible attacks of refreshing sleep that occur daily over at least 3 months.

B. The presence of one or both of the following:

(1) cataplexy (i.e., brief episodes of sudden bilateral loss of muscle tone, most often in association with intense emotion)

(2) recurrent intrusions of elements of rapid eye movement (REM) sleep into the transition between sleep and wakefulness, as manifested by either hypnopompic or hypnagogic hallucinations or sleep paralysis at the beginning or end of sleep episodes

C. The disturbance is not due to the direct physiological effects of a substance (e.g., a drug of abuse, a medication) or another general medical condition.

780.59   Breathing-Related Sleep Disorder

Diagnostic Features

The essential feature of Breathing-Related Sleep Disorder is sleep disruption, leading to excessive sleepiness or insomnia, that is judged to be due to abnormalities of ventilation during sleep (e.g., sleep apnea or central alveolar hypoventilation) (Criterion A). This sleep disruption must not be better accounted for by a mental disorder and is not due to the direct physiological effects of a substance (including medication) or a general medical condition that produces sleep symptoms through a mechanism other than abnormal breathing (Criterion B).

Excessive sleepiness is the most common presenting complaint of individuals with Breathing-Related Sleep Disorder. Sleepiness results from frequent arousals during nocturnal sleep as the individual attempts to breathe normally. The sleepiness is most evident in relaxing situations, such as when the individual is reading or watching television. The individual's inability to control the sleepiness can be evident in boring meetings or while attending movies, theater, or concerts. When sleepiness is extreme, the person may fall asleep while actively conversing, eating, walking, or driving. Naps tend to be unrefreshing and may be accompanied by a dull headache on awakening. However, there can be considerable variation in the intensity of the sleepiness. The impact of the sleepiness may be minimized by the individual, who may express pride about being able to sleep anywhere at anytime.

Insomnia, frequent awakenings, or unrefreshing sleep are less frequent than daytime sleepiness as the presenting complaint in individuals with Breathing-Related Sleep Disorder. Some individuals may complain of difficulty breathing while lying supine or sleeping.

Abnormal respiratory events during sleep in Breathing-Related Sleep Disorder include apneas (episodes of breathing cessation), hypopneas (abnormally slow or shallow respiration), and hypoventilation (abnormal blood oxygen and carbon dioxide levels). Three forms of Breathing-Related Sleep Disorder have been described: obstructive sleep apnea syndrome, central sleep apnea syndrome, and central alveolar hypoventilation syndrome.

Obstructive sleep apnea syndrome is the most common form of Breathing-Related Sleep Disorder. It is characterized by repeated episodes of upper-airway obstruction (apneas and hypopneas) during sleep. The central drive for respiration and respiratory movements in the chest and abdomen are preserved. It usually occurs in overweight individuals and leads to a complaint of excessive sleepiness. Obstructive sleep apnea syndrome is characterized by loud snores or brief gasps that alternate with episodes of silence that usually last 20–30 seconds. Snoring is caused by breathing through a partially obstructed airway. Silent periods are caused by obstructive apneas, with the cessation in breathing caused by complete airway obstruction. Typically the loud snoring has been present for many years, often since childhood, but an increase in its severity may lead the individual to seek evaluation. The snoring is commonly loud enough to disturb the sleep of others in close proximity. The cessation of breathing, sometimes lasting as long as 60–90 seconds and associated with cyanosis, may also be of concern to bedpartners. The termination of the apneic event can be associated with loud "resuscitative" snores, gasps, moans or mumbling, or whole-body movements. The bedpartner may have to move to a separate bed or another room as a result of the affected individual's snoring, gasps, and movements. Most affected individuals are unaware of the loud snoring, breathing difficulty, and frequent arousals. However, some persons, particularly elderly persons, are intensely aware of the sleep disturbance and present with a complaint of frequent awakenings and unrefreshing sleep.

Central sleep apnea syndrome is characterized by episodic cessation of ventilation during sleep (apneas and hypopneas) without airway obstruction. Thus, in contrast to obstructive apnea events, central apneas are not associated with continued chest wall and abdominal breathing movements and occur more commonly in elderly persons as a result of cardiac or neurological conditions that affect ventilatory regulation. Individuals most often present with complaints of insomnia due to repeated awakenings, which they may or may not associate with breathing difficulties. Individuals with central sleep apnea may have mild snoring, but it is not a prominent complaint.

The *central alveolar hypoventilation syndrome* is characterized by an impairment in ventilatory control that results in abnormally low arterial oxygen levels further worsened by sleep (hypoventilation without apneas or hypopneas). The lungs in individuals with this disorder have normal mechanical properties. This form most commonly occurs in very overweight individuals and can be associated with a complaint of either excessive sleepiness or insomnia.

Associated Features and Disorders

Associated descriptive features and mental disorders.   The individual with Breathing-Related Sleep Disorder may complain of nocturnal chest discomfort, choking, suffocation, or intense anxiety in association with apneic events or hypoventilation. Body movements associated with breathing difficulties can be violent, and individuals with Breathing-Related Sleep Disorder are often described as restless sleepers. Individuals with this disorder typically feel unrefreshed on awakening and may describe feeling more tired in the morning than when they went to sleep. They may also describe sleep drunkenness (i.e., extreme difficulty awakening, confusion, and inappropriate behavior). Severe dryness of the mouth is common and often leads the person to drink water during the night or on awakening in the morning. Nocturia occurs more often with the progression of symptoms. Dull, generalized morning headaches can last for 1–2 hours after awakening.

The sleepiness can lead to memory disturbance, poor concentration, irritability, and personality changes. Mood Disorders (particularly Major Depressive Disorder and Dysthymic Disorder), Anxiety Disorders (particularly Panic Disorder), and dementia are commonly associated with Breathing-Related Sleep Disorder. Individuals can also have reduced libido and erectile ability. Rarely, erectile dysfunction is the presenting complaint of the obstructive sleep apnea syndrome. Children with Breathing-Related Sleep Disorder may have developmental delay and learning difficulties. Excessive daytime sleepiness can result in injuries (e.g., falling asleep while driving a vehicle) and can also cause severe social and occupational impairment resulting in job loss, marital and family problems, and decreased school performance.

Associated laboratory findings.   Each of the major Breathing-Related Sleep Disorder syndromes produces specific abnormalities. In the obstructive sleep apnea syndrome, nocturnal polysomnography shows apneic episodes longer than 10 seconds in duration (usually 20–40 seconds), with rare episodes lasting up to several minutes. Hypopneas are characterized by a reduction of airflow. Both types of events are associated with a reduction in oxyhemoglobin saturation. The central sleep apnea syndrome may include Cheyne-Stokes respiration (i.e., a pattern of periodic breathing consisting of an apnea, a 10- to 60-second episode of hyperventilation following the apnea, and a gradual decrease in ventilation culminating in another apnea). In the central alveolar hypoventilation syndrome, periods of decreased respiration lasting up to several minutes occur, with sustained arterial oxygen desaturation and increased carbon dioxide levels. Other features of nocturnal polysomnography in individuals with Breathing-Related Sleep Disorder include short sleep duration, frequent awakenings, increased amounts of stage 1 sleep, and decreased amounts of slow-wave sleep and rapid eye movement (REM) sleep. The arousals that occur at the termination of the apneic and hypoventilation events may be quite brief (several seconds).

Apneas, hypopneas, and hypoventilation may produce other disturbances: oxyhemoglobin desaturation, ECG abnormalities, elevated pulmonary and systemic arterial pressure, and transient arousals as the individual terminates an episode of breathing disturbance. Cardiac arrhythmias commonly occur during sleep in individuals with Breathing-Related Sleep Disorder and may include sinus arrhythmias, premature ventricular contractions, atrioventricular block, or sinus arrest. Bradycardia followed by tachycardia is commonly seen in association with apneic episodes. Frequent nocturnal awakenings and oxyhemoglobin desaturation can result in excessive sleepiness that may be detected by the Multiple Sleep Latency Test (MSLT) or other tests of daytime sleepiness. Mean sleep latency on the MSLT is often less than 10 minutes and can be less than 5 minutes (normal is 10–20 minutes).

Arterial blood gas measurements while the person is awake are usually normal, but some individuals with severe obstructive sleep apnea syndrome or central alveolar hypoventilation syndrome can have waking hypoxemia or hypercarbia. Cephalometric X rays, magnetic resonance imaging (MRI), computed tomography (CT), and fiber-optic endoscopy can show obstruction of the upper airway. Cardiac testing may show evidence of impaired right ventricular function. Individuals may also have elevated hemoglobin or hematocrit values due to repeated nocturnal hypoxemia.

Associated physical examination findings and general medical conditions. The majority of individuals with the obstructive sleep apnea syndrome and the central alveolar hypoventilation syndrome are overweight and notice an increase in the severity of symptoms with increasing body weight. Upper-airway narrowing can occur due to excessive bulk of soft tissues. Obstructive sleep apnea syndrome occurring in individuals of normal or below-normal body weight suggests upper-airway obstruction due to definable, localized structural abnormality, such as a maxillomandibular malformation or adenotonsillar enlargement. Individuals may have noisy breathing even while awake. Gastroesophageal reflux with severe "heartburn" pain may occur in the obstructive sleep apnea syndrome in association with the effort to reestablish breathing during sleep. Individuals with central sleep apnea syndrome less frequently are overweight or have demonstrable upper-airway obstructions.

Mild systemic hypertension with elevated diastolic pressure is commonly associated with Breathing-Related Sleep Disorder. Some individuals, particularly those with chronic obstructive pulmonary disease or alveolar hypoventilation, have continuously low oxygen saturation values during sleep and are predisposed to developing pulmonary hypertension and associated right-sided cardiac failure, hepatic congestion, and ankle edema.

Individuals with Breathing-Related Sleep Disorder may have an underlying abnormality in the neurological control of the upper-airway musculature or ventilation during sleep. Disorders affecting neurological control of ventilation usually manifest as the central sleep apnea syndrome. Some individuals with neurological conditions have a specific lesion affecting the control of pharyngeal muscles, which may lead to the obstructive sleep apnea syndrome.

Breathing-Related Sleep Disorder can be associated with systemic general medical or neurological conditions. For instance, obstructive sleep apnea may result from tongue enlargement due to acromegaly, lingual thyroid tissue or cysts, or vocal cord paralysis as seen in Shy-Drager syndrome. Impaired cardiac function due to reduced cardiac output can result in central sleep apnea, as can neurological conditions that affect the brain stem control of respiration, such as syringobulbia or brain stem tumors.

Specific Age and Gender Features

In young children, the signs and symptoms of Breathing-Related Sleep Disorder (almost exclusively the obstructive sleep apnea syndrome) are more subtle than those in adults and the diagnosis is more difficult to establish. In children, polysomnography is especially useful in confirming the diagnosis. Snoring, which is characteristic of adult obstructive sleep apnea syndrome, might not be present. Agitated arousals and unusual sleep postures, such as sleeping on the hands and knees, commonly occur. Nocturnal enuresis is also common and should raise the suspicion of obstructive sleep apnea syndrome if it recurs in a child who was previously dry at night. Children may also manifest excessive daytime sleepiness, although this is not as common or pronounced as in adults. Daytime mouth breathing, difficulty in swallowing, and poor speech articulation are also common features in children. On physical examination, pectus excavatum and rib flaring can be seen. If associated with adenotonsillar enlargement, typical "adenoid facies" can be seen with a dull expression, periorbital edema, and mouth breathing.

The obstructive sleep apnea syndrome is most common in middle-aged, overweight males and prepubertal children with enlarged tonsils. The central alveolar hypoventilation syndrome is more common in obese young-adult males. Aging leads to an increase in the frequency of both obstructive and central apnea events, even among asymptomatic healthy individuals. Because some degree of apnea may be normative with aging, polysomnographic results must be interpreted within this context. On the other hand, significant clinical symptoms of insomnia and hypersomnia should be investigated regardless of the individual's age, and a diagnosis of Breathing-Related Sleep Disorder should be made if a breathing disturbance best explains the symptoms.

In adults, the male-to-female ratio of obstructive sleep apnea syndrome is about 8:1. There is no sex difference among prepubertal children. In adults, central apneic events appear to be more prevalent in males than in females, although this difference is less apparent after menopause.

Prevalence

The prevalence of Breathing-Related Sleep Disorder associated with obstructive sleep apnea is estimated to be approximately 1%–10% in the adult population, but may be higher in elderly individuals. The prevalence of Breathing-Related Sleep Disorder also varies considerably as a function of the threshold for the frequency of apnea events.

Course

The obstructive sleep apnea syndrome can occur at any age, but most individuals present for evaluation when they are between ages 40 and 60 years (with females more likely to develop obstructive sleep apnea after menopause). Central sleep apnea is more commonly seen in elderly individuals with central nervous system or cardiac disease. The central alveolar hypoventilation syndrome and central sleep apnea syndrome can develop at any age.

Breathing-Related Sleep Disorder usually has an insidious onset, gradual progression, and chronic course. Most often, the disorder will have been present for years by the time it is diagnosed. Spontaneous resolution of the obstructive sleep apnea syndrome has been reported with weight loss, but usually the course is progressive and can ultimately lead to premature death due to cardiovascular disease or arrhythmia. The central sleep apnea syndrome also has a chronic unremitting course, although management of underlying medical conditions may improve the breathing disturbance. Adults with the central alveolar hypoventilation syndrome have a slowly progressive course.

Familial Pattern

A familial tendency for obstructive sleep apnea syndrome has been described.

Differential Diagnosis

Breathing-Relating Sleep Disorder must be differentiated from other causes of sleepiness, such as Narcolepsy, Primary Hypersomnia, and Circadian Rhythm Sleep Disorder. Breathing-Related Sleep Disorder can be differentiated from **Narcolepsy** by the absence of cataplexy, sleep-related hallucinations, and sleep paralysis and by the presence of loud snoring, gasping during sleep, or observed apneas or shallow breathing in sleep. Daytime sleep episodes in Narcolepsy are characteristically shorter, more refreshing, and more often associated with dreaming. Breathing-Related Sleep Disorder shows characteristic apneas or hypoventilation during nocturnal polysomnographic studies, and Narcolepsy results in multiple sleep-onset REM periods during the MSLT. Some individuals have concurrent Narcolepsy and Breathing-Related Sleep Disorder. Breathing-Related Sleep Disorder may be distinguished from **Primary Hypersomnia** and **Circadian Rhythm Sleep Disorder** based on the presence of clinical or laboratory findings of obstructive sleep apnea, central sleep apnea, or central alveolar hypoventilation syndromes. Definitive differential diagnosis between Primary Hypersomnia and Breathing-Related Sleep Disorder may require polysomnographic studies.

Hypersomnia related to a Major Depressive Episode can be distinguished from Breathing-Related Sleep Disorder by the presence or absence of other characteristic symptoms (e.g., depressed mood and loss of interest in a Major Depressive Episode and snoring and gasping during sleep in Breathing-Related Sleep Disorder).

Individuals with Breathing-Related Sleep Disorder must also be differentiated from otherwise **asymptomatic adults who snore.** This differentiation can be made based on the presenting complaint of insomnia or hypersomnia, the greater intensity of snoring, and the presence of the characteristic history, signs, and symptoms of Breathing-Related Sleep Disorder. For individuals complaining of insomnia, **Primary Insomnia** can be differentiated from Breathing-Related Sleep Disorder by the absence of complaints (or reports from bedpartners) of difficulty breathing during sleep and the absence of the history, signs, and symptoms characteristic of Breathing-Related Sleep Disorder.

Nocturnal Panic Attacks may include symptoms of gasping or choking during sleep that may be difficult to distinguish clinically from Breathing-Related Sleep Disorder. However, the lower frequency of episodes, intense autonomic arousal, and the lack of excessive sleepiness differentiates nocturnal Panic Attacks from Breathing-Related Sleep Disorder. Polysomnography in individuals with nocturnal Panic Attacks does not reveal the typical pattern of apneas, hypoventilation, or oxygen desaturation characteristic of Breathing-Related Sleep Disorder.

The diagnosis of Breathing-Related Sleep Disorder is appropriate in the presence of a **general medical condition** that causes insomnia or hypersomnia through the mechanism of impaired ventilation during sleep. For example, an individual with tonsillar hypertrophy who has sleep difficulty related to snoring and obstructive sleep apneas should receive a diagnosis of Breathing-Related Sleep Disorder on Axis I and tonsillar hypertrophy on Axis III. In contrast, Sleep Disorder Due to a General Medical Condition is appropriate if a general medical or neurological condition causes sleep-related symptoms through a mechanism other than breathing disturbance. For instance, individuals with arthritis or renal impairment may complain of insomnia or hypersomnia, but this does not result from breathing impairment during sleep.

The **use of, or withdrawal from, substances** (including medications) can produce insomnia or hypersomnia similar to that in Breathing-Related Sleep Disorder. A careful history is usually sufficient to identify the relevant substance, and follow-up shows improvement of the sleep disturbance after discontinuation of the substance. In other cases, the use of a substance (e.g., alcohol, barbiturates, or benzodiazepines) can exacerbate Breathing-Related Sleep Disorder. An individual with symptoms and signs consistent with Breathing-Related Sleep Disorder should receive that diagnosis, even in the presence of concurrent substance use that is exacerbating the condition.

Relationship to the International Classification of Sleep Disorders

Breathing-Related Sleep Disorder is identified as three more specific syndromes in the International Classification of Sleep Disorders (ICSD): Obstructive Sleep Apnea Syndrome, Central Sleep Apnea Syndrome, and Central Alveolar Hypoventilation Syndrome.

■ **Diagnostic criteria for 780.59 Breathing-Related Sleep Disorder**

A. Sleep disruption, leading to excessive sleepiness or insomnia, that is judged to be due to a sleep-related breathing condition (e.g., obstructive or central sleep apnea syndrome or central alveolar hypoventilation syndrome).

B. The disturbance is not better accounted for by another mental disorder and is not due to the direct physiological effects of a substance (e.g., a drug of abuse, a medication) or another general medical condition (other than a breathing-related disorder).

Coding note: Also code sleep-related breathing disorder on Axis III.

307.45   Circadian Rhythm Sleep Disorder
(formerly Sleep-Wake Schedule Disorder)

Diagnostic Features

The essential feature of Circadian Rhythm Sleep Disorder is a persistent or recurrent pattern of sleep disruption that results from a mismatch between the individual's endogenous circadian sleep-wake system on the one hand, and exogenous demands regarding the timing and duration of sleep on the other (Criterion A). In contrast to other primary Sleep Disorders, Circadian Rhythm Sleep Disorder does not result from the mechanisms generating sleep and wakefulness per se. As a result of this circadian mismatch, individuals with this disorder may complain of insomnia at certain times during the day and excessive sleepiness at other times, with resulting impairment in social, occupational, or other important areas of functioning or marked subjective distress (Criterion B). The sleep problems are not better accounted for by other Sleep Disorders or other mental disorders (Criterion C) and are not due to the direct physiological effects of a substance or a general medical condition (Criterion D).

The diagnosis of Circadian Rhythm Sleep Disorder should be reserved for those presentations in which the individual has significant social or occupational impairment or marked distress related to the sleep disturbance. Individuals vary widely in their ability to adapt to circadian changes and requirements. Many, if not most, individuals with circadian-related symptoms of sleep disturbance do not seek treatment and do not have symptoms of sufficient severity to warrant a diagnosis. Those who present for evaluation because of this disorder are most often troubled by the severity or persistence of their symptoms. For example, it is not unusual for shift workers to present for evaluation after falling asleep while on the job or while driving.

The diagnosis of Circadian Rhythm Sleep Disorder rests primarily on the clinical history, including the pattern of work, sleep, naps, and "free time." The history should also examine past attempts at coping with symptoms, such as attempts at advancing the sleep-wake schedule in Delayed Sleep Phase Type. Prospective sleep-wake diaries or sleep charts are often a useful adjunct to diagnosis.

Subtypes

Delayed Sleep Phase Type. This type of Circadian Rhythm Sleep Disorder results from an endogenous sleep-wake cycle that is delayed relative to the demands of society. Measurement of endogenous circadian rhythms (e.g., core body temperature) reflects this delay. Individuals with this subtype ("night owls") are hypothesized to have an abnormally diminished ability to phase-advance sleep-wake hours (i.e., to move sleep and wakefulness to earlier clock times). As a result, these individuals are "locked in" to habitually late sleep hours and cannot move these sleep hours forward to an earlier time. The circadian phase of sleep is stable: individuals will fall asleep and awaken at consistent, albeit delayed, times when left to their own schedule (e.g., on weekends or vacations). Affected individuals complain of difficulty falling asleep at socially acceptable hours, but once sleep is initiated, it is normal. There is concomitant difficulty awakening at socially acceptable hours (e.g., multiple alarm clocks are often unable to arouse the individual). Because many individuals with this disorder will be chronically sleep deprived, sleepiness during the desired wake period may occur.

Jet Lag Type. In this type of Circadian Rhythm Sleep Disorder, the endogenous circadian sleep-wake cycle is normal and the disturbance arises from conflict between the pattern of sleep and wakefulness generated by the circadian system and the pattern of sleep and wakefulness required by a new time zone. Individuals with this type complain of a mismatch between desired and required hours of sleep and wakefulness. The severity of the mismatch is proportional to the number of time zones traveled through, with maximal difficulties often noted after traveling through eight or more time zones in less than 24 hours. Eastward travel (advancing sleep-wake hours) is typically more difficult for most individuals to tolerate than westward travel (delaying sleep-wake hours).

Shift Work Type. In this type of Circadian Rhythm Sleep Disorder, the endogenous circadian sleep-wake cycle is normal and the disturbance arises from conflict between the pattern of sleep and wakefulness generated by the circadian system and the desired pattern of sleep and wakefulness required by shift work.

Rotating-shift schedules are the most disruptive because they force sleep and wakefulness into aberrant circadian positions and prevent any consistent adjustment. Night- and rotating-shift workers typically have a shorter sleep duration and more frequent disturbances in sleep continuity than morning and afternoon workers. Conversely, there may also be sleepiness during the desired wake period, that is, in the middle of the night work shift. The circadian mismatch of the Shift Work Type is further exacerbated by insufficient sleep time, social and family demands, and environmental disturbances (e.g., telephone, traffic noise) during intended sleep times.

Unspecified Type. This type of Circadian Rhythm Sleep Disorder should be indicated if another pattern of circadian sleep disturbance (e.g., advanced sleep phase, non-24-hour sleep-wake pattern, or irregular sleep-wake pattern) is present. An "advanced sleep phase pattern" is the analog of Delayed Sleep Phase Type, but in the opposite direction: individuals complain of an inability to stay awake in the evening and spontaneous awakening in the early morning hours. "Non-24-hour sleep-wake pattern" denotes a free-running cycle: the sleep-wake schedule follows the endogenous circadian rhythm period of approximately 24–25 hours despite the presence of 24-hour time cues in the environment. In contrast to the stable sleep-wake pattern of the Delayed or advanced sleep phase types, these individuals' sleep-wake schedules become progressively delayed relative to the 24-hour clock, resulting in a changing sleep-wake pattern over successive days. "Irregular sleep-wake pattern" indicates the absence of an identifiable pattern of sleep and wakefulness.

Associated Features and Disorders

Associated descriptive features and mental disorders.   In Delayed Sleep Phase Type, individuals frequently go to bed later and wake up later on weekends or during vacations, with a reduction in sleep-onset difficulties and difficulty awakening. They will typically give many examples of school, work, and social difficulties arising from their inability to awaken at socially desired times. If awakened earlier than the time dictated by the circadian timekeeping system, the individual may demonstrate "sleep drunkenness" (i.e., extreme difficulty awakening, confusion, and inappropriate behavior). Performance often also follows a delayed phase, with peak efficiency occurring in late-evening hours.

Jet Lag and Shift Work Types may be more common in individuals who are "morning types." Performance is often impaired during desired waking hours, following the pattern that would be predicted by the underlying endogenous circadian rhythms. Jet lag is often accompanied by nonspecific symptoms (e.g., headache, fatigue, indigestion) that relate to travel conditions, such as sleep deprivation, alcohol and caffeine use, and decreased ambient air pressure in airplane cabins. Dysfunction in occupational, family, and social roles is often observed in individuals who have difficulty coping with shift work. Individuals with any Circadian Rhythm Sleep Disorder may have a history of alcohol, sedative-hypnotic, or stimulant use resulting from attempts to control their inappropriately phased sleep-wake tendencies. The use of these substances may in turn exacerbate the Circadian Rhythm Sleep Disorder.

Delayed Sleep Phase Type has been associated with schizoid, schizotypal, and avoidant personality features, particularly in adolescents. "Non-24-hour sleep-wake pattern" and "irregular sleep-wake pattern" have also been associated with these same features. Jet Lag and Shift Work Types may precipitate or exacerbate a Manic or Major Depressive Episode or an episode of a Psychotic Disorder.

Associated laboratory findings.   Sleep studies yield different results depending on what time they are performed. For individuals with Delayed Sleep Phase Type, studies conducted at the preferred sleep times will be essentially normal for age. However, when studied at socially normal sleep times, these individuals have prolonged sleep latency, spontaneous awakening occurring late relative to social convention, and (in some individuals) moderately short REM sleep latency. Sleep continuity is normal for age. Laboratory procedures designed to measure the phase of the endogenous circadian pacemaker (e.g., core body temperature) reveal the expected phase delay in the timing of acrophase (peak time) and nadir.

When studied during their habitual workweek sleep hours, individuals with Shift Work Type usually have normal or short sleep latency, reduced sleep duration, and more frequent sleep continuity disturbances compared with age-matched individuals with "normal" nocturnal sleep patterns. There is a specific reduction in stage 2 and REM sleep in many cases. Tests of sleep tendency, such as the Multiple Sleep Latency Test (MSLT), show a high degree of sleepiness during desired wake times (e.g., during the night shift). When studied after a period of adjustment to a normal diurnal schedule, these individuals have normal nocturnal sleep and normal levels of daytime sleepiness.

Laboratory studies of 6-hour simulated jet lag demonstrate prolonged sleep latency, impaired sleep efficiency, reductions in REM sleep, and minor reductions in slow-wave sleep. These features recover toward baseline values over 1–2 weeks.

Associated physical examination findings and general medical conditions. No specific physical findings are described for Circadian Rhythm Sleep Disorder. Shift workers may appear haggard or sleepy and may have an excess of cardiovascular and gastrointestinal disturbances, including gastritis and peptic ulcer disease. The roles of caffeine and alcohol consumption and altered eating patterns have not been fully evaluated in these cases. "Non-24-hour sleep-wake pattern" often occurs in blind individuals. Circadian Rhythm Sleep Disorder may exacerbate preexisting general medical conditions.

Specific Age Features

Shift work and jet lag symptoms are often reported to be more severe, or more easily induced, in late-middle-aged and elderly individuals compared with young adults. "Advanced sleep phase pattern" also increases with age. These findings may result from age-related deterioration in nocturnal sleep and shortening of the endogenous circadian period.

Prevalence   The prevalence for any of the types of Circadian Rhythm Sleep Disorder has not been well established. Surveys suggest a prevalence of up to 7% for Delayed Sleep Phase Type in adolescents and of up to 60% for Shift Work Type in night-shift workers.

Course

Without intervention, Delayed Sleep Phase Type typically lasts for years or decades but may "correct" itself given the tendency for endogenous circadian rhythm phase to advance with age. Treatment with progressive phase delay of the sleep-wake schedule can often normalize sleep hours at least temporarily, but there is a persistent vulnerability for falling back to delayed sleep hours.

Shift Work Type typically persists for as long as the individual works that particular schedule. Reversal of symptoms generally occurs within 2 weeks of a return to a normal diurnal sleep-wake schedule.

Experimental and field data concerning jet lag indicate that it takes approximately 1 day per time zone traveled for the circadian system to resynchronize itself to the new local time. Different circadian rhythms (such as core body temperature, hormonal level, alertness, and sleep patterns) may readjust at different rates.

Differential Diagnosis

Circadian Rhythm Sleep Disorder must be distinguished from **normal patterns of sleep** and **normal adjustments following a change in schedule.** The key to such distinctions lies in the persistence of the disturbance and the presence and degree of social or occupational impairment. For instance, many adolescents and young adults maintain delayed sleep-wake schedules, but without distress or interference with school or work routines. Almost anyone who travels across time zones will experience transient sleep disruption. The diagnosis of the Jet Lag Type should be reserved for an individual with frequent travel requirements and associated severe sleep disturbances and work disruption.

Delayed Sleep Phase Type must be differentiated from **volitional patterns of delayed sleep hours.** Some individuals who voluntarily delay sleep onset to participate in social or work activities may complain of difficulty awakening. When permitted to do so, these individuals fall asleep readily at earlier times and, after a period of recovery sleep, have no significant difficulty awakening in the morning. In such cases, the primary problem is sleep deprivation rather than a Circadian Rhythm Sleep Disorder. Other individuals (particularly children and adolescents) may volitionally shift sleep hours to avoid school or family demands. The pattern of difficulty awakening vanishes when desired activities are scheduled in the morning hours. In a similar way, younger children involved in limit-setting battles with parents may present as having Delayed Sleep Phase Type.

Jet Lag and Shift Work Types must be distinguished mainly from other primary Sleep Disorders, such as **Primary Insomnia** and **Primary Hypersomnia.** The history of jet lag or shift work, with undisturbed sleep on other schedules, usually provides sufficient evidence to exclude these other disorders. In some cases, other primary Sleep Disorders, such as Breathing-Related Sleep Disorder or periodic limb movements during sleep, may complicate Shift Work or Jet Lag Types. This possibility should be suspected when reversion to a normal diurnal schedule does not provide relief from sleep-related symptoms. Other types of Circadian Rhythm Sleep Disorder, such as "non-24-hour sleep-wake pattern" and "irregular sleep-wake pattern," are distinguished from the Delayed Sleep Phase Type by the stably delayed sleep-wake hours characteristic of the latter.

Patterns of delayed or advanced sleep that occur exclusively during another mental disorder are not diagnosed separately (e.g., a pattern of early morning awakening in Major Depressive Disorder or a pattern of delayed sleep in Schizophrenia).

Substances (including medications) can cause delayed sleep onset or awakening in the morning. For instance, consumption of caffeine or nicotine in the evening may delay sleep onset, and the use of hypnotic medications in the middle of the night may delay the time of awakening. A diagnosis of **Substance-Induced Sleep Disorder** may be considered if the sleep disturbance is judged to be a direct physiological consequence of regular substance use and warrants independent clinical attention (see p. 601). General medical conditions rarely cause fixed delays or advances of the sleep-wake schedule and typically pose no difficulty in differential diagnosis.

Relationship to the International Classification of Sleep Disorders

The International Classification of Sleep Disorders (ICSD) includes categories for Delayed Sleep Phase Syndrome, Shift Work Sleep Disorder and Time Zone Change (Jet Lag) Syndrome, and specific categories for three other Circadian Rhythm Sleep Disorders (Irregular Sleep-Wake Pattern, Advanced Sleep Phase Syndrome, and Non-24-Hour Sleep-Wake Syndrome).

■ Diagnostic criteria for 307.45 Circadian Rhythm Sleep Disorder

A. A persistent or recurrent pattern of sleep disruption leading to excessive sleepiness or insomnia that is due to a mismatch between the sleep-wake schedule required by a person's environment and his or her circadian sleep-wake pattern.

B. The sleep disturbance causes clinically significant distress or impairment in social, occupational, or other important areas of functioning.

C. The disturbance does not occur exclusively during the course of another Sleep Disorder or other mental disorder.

D. The disturbance is not due to the direct physiological effects of a substance (e.g., a drug of abuse, a medication) or a general medical condition.

Specify type:
  Delayed Sleep Phase Type: a persistent pattern of late sleep onset and late awakening times, with an inability to fall asleep and awaken at a desired earlier time
  Jet Lag Type: sleepiness and alertness that occur at an inappropriate time of day relative to local time, occurring after repeated travel across more than one time zone
  Shift Work Type: insomnia during the major sleep period or excessive sleepiness during the major awake period associated with night shift work or frequently changing shift work
  Unspecified Type

307.47   Dyssomnia Not Otherwise Specified

The Dyssomnia Not Otherwise Specified category is for insomnias, hypersomnias, or circadian rhythm disturbances that do not meet criteria for any specific Dyssomnia. Examples include

1. Complaints of clinically significant insomnia or hypersomnia that are attributable to environmental factors (e.g., noise, light, frequent interruptions).
2. Excessive sleepiness that is attributable to ongoing sleep deprivation.
3. Idiopathic "Restless Legs Syndrome": uncomfortable sensations (e.g., discomfort, crawling sensations, or restlessness) that lead to an intense urge to move the legs. Typically, the sensations begin in the evening before sleep onset and are temporarily relieved by moving the legs or walking, only to begin again when the legs are immobile. The sensations can delay sleep onset or awaken the individual from sleep.
4. Idiopathic periodic limb movements ("nocturnal myoclonus"): repeated low-amplitude brief limb jerks, particularly in the lower extremities. These movements begin near sleep onset and decrease during stage 3 or 4 non–rapid eye movement (NREM) and rapid eye movement (REM) sleep. Movements usually occur rhythmically every 20–60 seconds, leading to repeated, brief arousals. Individuals are typically unaware of the actual movements, but may complain of insomnia, frequent awakenings, or daytime sleepiness if the number of movements is very large.
5. Situations in which the clinician has concluded that a Dyssomnia is present but is unable to determine whether it is primary, due to a general medical condition, or substance induced.

Parasomnias

Parasomnias are disorders characterized by abnormal behavioral or physiological events occurring in association with sleep, specific sleep stages, or sleep-wake transitions. Unlike dyssomnias, parasomnias do not involve abnormalities of the mechanisms generating sleep-wake states, nor of the timing of sleep and wakefulness. Rather, parasomnias represent the activation of physiological systems at inappropriate times during the sleep-wake cycle. In particular, these disorders involve activation of the autonomic nervous system, motor system, or cognitive processes during sleep or sleep-wake transitions. Different parasomnias occur at different times during sleep, and specific parasomnias often occur during specific sleep stages. Individuals with parasomnias usually present with complaints of unusual behavior during sleep, rather than complaints of insomnia or excessive daytime sleepiness. This section includes Nightmare Disorder, Sleep Terror Disorder, Sleepwalking Disorder, and Parasomnia Not Otherwise Specified.

307.47 Nightmare Disorder
(formerly Dream Anxiety Disorder)

Diagnostic Features

The essential feature of Nightmare Disorder is the repeated occurrence of frightening dreams that lead to awakenings from sleep (Criterion A). The individual becomes fully alert on awakening (Criterion B). The frightening dreams or sleep interruptions resulting from the awakenings cause the individual significant distress or result in social or occupational dysfunction (Criterion C). This disorder is not diagnosed if the nightmares occur exclusively during the course of another mental disorder or are due to the direct physiological effects of a substance (e.g., a drug of abuse or a medication) or a general medical condition (Criterion D).

Nightmares typically occur in a lengthy, elaborate dream sequence that is highly anxiety provoking or terrifying. Dream content most often focuses on imminent physical danger to the individual (e.g., pursuit, attack, injury). In other cases, the perceived danger may be more subtle, involving personal failure or embarrassment. Nightmares that occur after traumatic experiences may replicate the original dangerous or threatening situation, but most nightmares do not recount actual events. On awakening, individuals with this disorder can describe the dream sequence and content in detail. Individuals may report multiple nightmares within a given night, often with a recurrent theme. Nightmares arise almost exclusively during rapid eye movement (REM) sleep. Because REM episodes occur periodically throughout nocturnal sleep (approximately every 90–110 minutes), nightmares may also occur at any time during the sleep episode. However, because REM sleep periods typically become longer and dreaming more intense in the second half of the night, nightmares are also more likely to occur later in the night.

Nightmares usually terminate with an awakening that is associated with a rapid return of full alertness and a lingering sense of fear or anxiety. These factors often lead to difficulty returning to sleep. Nightmare Disorder causes significant subjective distress more often than it causes demonstrable social or occupational impairment. However, if nocturnal awakenings are frequent, or if the individual avoids sleeping because of fear of nightmares, the individual may experience excessive sleepiness, poor concentration, depression, anxiety, or irritability that can disrupt daytime functioning.

Associated Features and Disorders

Associated descriptive features and mental disorders.   In individuals with Nightmare Disorder, mild autonomic arousal (e.g., sweating, tachycardia, tachypnea) may be evident on awakening. Depressive and anxiety symptoms that do not meet criteria for a specific diagnosis are common among individuals with Nightmare Disorder. Body movements and vocalization are not characteristic of Nightmare Disorder because of the loss of skeletal muscle tone that normally occurs during REM sleep. When talking, screaming, or striking out do occur, these are most likely to appear as brief phenomena that terminate a nightmare. These behaviors are also more likely to occur in the nightmares that accompany Posttraumatic Stress Disorder, because these nightmares may occur during non–rapid eye movement (NREM) sleep.

Associated laboratory findings.   Polysomnographic studies demonstrate abrupt awakenings from REM sleep that correspond to the individual's report of nightmares.

These awakenings usually occur during the second half of the night. In most cases, the REM sleep episode will have lasted for more than 10 minutes and may include a greater-than-average number of eye movements. Heart rate and respiratory rate may increase or show increased variability before the awakening. Nightmares following traumatic events (e.g., in individuals with Posttraumatic Stress Disorder) may arise during NREM sleep, particularly stage 2, as well as during REM sleep. Other polysomnographic features, including sleep continuity and sleep architecture, are not characteristically abnormal in Nightmare Disorder.

Specific Culture, Age, and Gender Features

The significance attributed to nightmares may vary with cultural background. For instance, some cultures may relate nightmares to spiritual or supernatural phenomena, whereas others may view nightmares as indicators of mental or physical disturbance. Because nightmares frequently occur during childhood, this diagnosis should not be given unless there is persistent significant distress or impairment that warrants independent clinical attention. Nightmare Disorder is most likely to appear in children exposed to severe psychosocial stressors. Although specific dream content may reflect the age of the individual having the nightmares, the essential features of the disorder are the same across age groups. Females report having nightmares more often than do men, at a ratio of approximately 2–4:1. It is not clear to what extent this difference reflects a true discrepancy in the number of nightmares as opposed to a variance in reporting.

Prevalence

Between 10% and 50% of children ages 3–5 years have nightmares of sufficient intensity to disturb their parents. In the adult population, as many as 50% of individuals may report at least an occasional nightmare. However, the actual prevalence of Nightmare Disorder is unknown.

Course

Nightmares often begin between ages 3 and 6 years. When the frequency is high (e.g., several per week), the dreams may become a source of concern and distress to both children and parents. Most children who develop a nightmare problem outgrow it. In a minority, the dreams may persist at high frequency into adulthood, becoming virtually a lifelong disturbance. A tendency toward amelioration of the disorder in later decades has been described.

Differential Diagnosis

Nightmare Disorder should be differentiated from **Sleep Terror Disorder.** Both disorders include awakenings or partial awakenings with fearfulness and autonomic activation, but can be differentiated by several clinical features. Nightmares typically occur later in the night during REM sleep and produce vivid dream imagery, complete awakenings, mild autonomic arousal, and detailed recall of the event. Sleep terrors typically arise in the first third of the night during stage 3 or 4 NREM sleep and produce either no dream recall or single images without the storylike quality that is typical of nightmares. Sleep terrors lead to partial awakenings in which the individual is confused, disoriented, and only partially responsive and has significant autonomic arousal. In contrast to Nightmare Disorder, the individual with Sleep Terror Disorder has amnesia for the event on awakening in the morning.

Breathing-Related Sleep Disorder can lead to awakenings with autonomic arousal, but these are not accompanied by recall of frightening dreams. Nightmares are a frequent complaint of individuals with **Narcolepsy,** but the presence of excessive sleepiness and cataplexy differentiates this condition from Nightmare Disorder. **Panic Attacks** arising during sleep can also produce abrupt awakenings with autonomic arousal and fearfulness, but the individual does not report frightening dreams and can identify these symptoms as consistent with other Panic Attacks. The presence of complex motor activity during frightening dreams should prompt further evaluation for other Sleep Disorders, such as "REM sleep behavior disorder" (see **Parasomnia Not Otherwise Specified**).

Numerous medications that affect the autonomic nervous system can precipitate nightmares. Examples include L-dopa and other dopaminergic agonists; beta-adrenergic antagonists and other antihypertensive medications; amphetamine, cocaine, and other stimulants; and antidepressant medications. Conversely, withdrawal of medications that suppress REM sleep, such as antidepressant medications and alcohol, can lead to a REM sleep "rebound" accompanied by nightmares. If the nightmares are sufficiently severe to warrant independent clinical attention, a diagnosis of **Substance-Induced Sleep Disorder, Parasomnia Type,** may be considered (see p. 601). Nightmare Disorder also should not be diagnosed if the disturbing dreams arise as a direct physiological effect of a general medical condition (e.g., central nervous system infection, vascular lesions of the brain stem, general medical conditions causing delirium). If the nightmares are sufficiently severe to warrant independent clinical attention, **Sleep Disorder Due to a General Medical Condition, Parasomnia Type,** may be considered (see p. 597). Although nightmares may frequently occur during a **delirium,** a separate diagnosis of Nightmare Disorder is not given.

Nightmares occur frequently as part of **other mental disorders** (e.g., Posttraumatic Stress Disorder, Schizophrenia, Mood Disorders, other Anxiety Disorders, Adjustment Disorders, and Personality Disorders). If the nightmares occur exclusively during the course of another mental disorder, the diagnosis of Nightmare Disorder is not given.

Many individuals experience an occasional, isolated nightmare. Nightmare Disorder is not diagnosed unless the frequency and severity of nightmares result in significant distress or impairment.

Relationship to the International Classification of Sleep Disorders

Nightmare Disorder corresponds to the diagnosis of Nightmares in the International Classification of Sleep Disorders (ICSD).

■ Diagnostic criteria for 307.47 Nightmare Disorder

A. Repeated awakenings from the major sleep period or naps with detailed recall of extended and extremely frightening dreams, usually involving threats to survival, security, or self-esteem. The awakenings generally occur during the second half of the sleep period.

B. On awakening from the frightening dreams, the person rapidly becomes oriented and alert (in contrast to the confusion and disorientation seen in Sleep Terror Disorder and some forms of epilepsy). '

C. The dream experience, or the sleep disturbance resulting from the awakening, causes clinically significant distress or impairment in social, occupational, or other important areas of functioning.

D. The nightmares do not occur exclusively during the course of another mental disorder (e.g., a delirium, Posttraumatic Stress Disorder) and are not due to the direct physiological effects of a substance (e.g., a drug of abuse, a medication) or a general medical condition.

307.46 Sleep Terror Disorder

Diagnostic Features

The essential feature of Sleep Terror Disorder is the repeated occurrence of sleep terrors, that is, abrupt awakenings from sleep usually beginning with a panicky scream or cry (Criterion A). Sleep terrors usually begin during the first third of the major sleep episode and last 1–10 minutes. The episodes are accompanied by autonomic arousal and behavioral manifestations of intense fear (Criterion B). During an episode, the individual is difficult to awaken or comfort (Criterion C). If the individual awakens after the sleep terror, no dream is recalled, or only fragmentary, single images are recalled. On awakening the following morning, the individual has amnesia for the event (Criterion D). The sleep terror episodes must cause clinically significant distress or impairment in social, occupational, or other important areas of functioning (Criterion E). Sleep Terror Disorder should not be diagnosed if the recurrent events are due to the direct physiological effects of a substance (e.g., a drug of abuse, a medication) or a general medical condition (Criterion F). Sleep terrors are also called "night terrors" or pavor nocturnus.

During a typical episode, the individual abruptly sits up in bed screaming or crying, with a frightened expression and autonomic signs of intense anxiety (e.g., tachycardia, rapid breathing, flushing of the skin, sweating, dilation of the pupils, increased muscle tone). The individual is usually unresponsive to the efforts of others to awaken or comfort him or her. If awakened, the person is confused and disoriented for several minutes and recounts a vague sense of terror, usually without dream content. Although fragmentary vivid dream images may occur, a storylike dream sequence (as in nightmares) is not reported. Most commonly, the individual does not awaken fully, but returns to sleep, and has amnesia for the episode on awakening the next morning. Some individuals may vaguely recall having an "episode" during the previous night, but do not have detailed recall. Usually only one episode will occur on any one night, although occasionally several episodes may occur at intervals throughout the night.

For the diagnosis to be made, the individual must experience clinically significant distress or impairment. Embarrassment concerning the episodes can impair social relationships. Individuals may avoid situations in which others might become aware of the disturbance, such as going to camp, visiting friends overnight, or sleeping with bedpartners.

Associated Features and Disorders

Associated descriptive features and mental disorders.   The episode is usually accompanied by yelling, screaming, crying, or incoherent vocalizations. The individual may actively resist being held or touched, or even demonstrate more elaborate motor activity (e.g., swinging, punching, rising from the bed, or fleeing). These behaviors appear to represent attempts at self-protection or flight from a threat and may result in physical injury. Episodes that simultaneously include features of sleep terror and sleepwalking can occur. Alcohol or sedative use, sleep deprivation, sleep-wake schedule disruptions, fatigue, and physical or emotional stress increase the likelihood of episodes.

Children with Sleep Terror Disorder do not have a higher incidence of psychopathology or mental disorders than does the general population. Psychopathology is more likely to be associated with Sleep Terror Disorder in adults. Sleep Terror Disorder may occur with an increased frequency in individuals with Axis I disorders, particularly Posttraumatic Stress Disorder and Generalized Anxiety Disorder. Personality Disorders may occur in individuals with Sleep Terror Disorder, especially Dependent, Schizoid, and Borderline Personality Disorders. Elevated scores for depression and anxiety have been noted on personality inventories.

Associated laboratory findings.   Sleep terrors begin during deep NREM sleep that is characterized by slow-frequency EEG activity (delta). This EEG activity is most prevalent during stages 3 and 4 NREM sleep, which are concentrated in the first third of the major sleep episode. Therefore, sleep terrors are also most likely to occur in the first third of the night. However, episodes can occur during slow-wave sleep at any time, even during daytime naps. The onset of sleep terror episodes is typically heralded by very high voltage EEG delta activity, an increase in muscle tone, and a twofold to fourfold increase in heart rate, often to over 120 beats per minute. During the episode, the polysomnogram may be obscured with movement artifact. In the absence of such artifact, the EEG typically shows theta or alpha activity during the episode, indicating partial arousal. Individuals with Sleep Terror Disorder may also have abrupt arousals from deep NREM sleep that do not progress to full episodes of sleep terror. Such episodes can include abrupt tachycardia.

Associated physical examination findings and general medical conditions.
Fever and sleep deprivation can produce an increased frequency of sleep terror episodes.

Specific Culture, Age, and Gender Features

No reports have provided clear evidence of culturally related differences in the manifestations of Sleep Terror Disorder, although it is likely that the significance and cause attributed to sleep terror episodes will differ between cultures. Older children and adults provide a more detailed recollection of fearful images associated with sleep terrors than do younger children, who are more likely to have complete amnesia or to report only a vague sense of fear. Among children, Sleep Terror Disorder is more common in males than in females. Among adults, the sex ratio is even.

Prevalence

There are limited data on Sleep Terror Disorder in the general population. The prevalence of sleep terror episodes (as opposed to Sleep Terror Disorder in which there is recurrence and distress or impairment) has been estimated at 1%–6% among children and at less than 1% of adults.

Course

Sleep Terror Disorder usually begins in children between ages 4 and 12 years and resolves spontaneously during adolescence. In adults, it most commonly begins between ages 20 and 30 years and often follows a chronic course, with the frequency and severity of episodes waxing and waning over time. The frequency of episodes varies both within and among individuals. Episodes usually occur at intervals of days or weeks, but may occur on consecutive nights.

Familial Pattern

Individuals with Sleep Terror Disorder frequently report a positive family history of either sleep terrors or sleepwalking. Some studies indicate a tenfold increase in the prevalence of the disorder among first-degree biological relatives. The exact mode of inheritance is unknown.

Differential Diagnosis

Many individuals suffer from isolated episodes of sleep terrors at some time in their lives. The distinction between individual episodes of sleep terrors and Sleep Terror Disorder rests on repeated occurrence, intensity, clinically significant impairment or distress, and the potential for injury to self or others.

Sleep Terror Disorder must be differentiated from other disorders that produce complete or partial awakenings at night or unusual behavior during sleep. The most important differential diagnoses for Sleep Terror Disorder include Nightmare Disorder, Sleepwalking Disorder, other parasomnias (see Parasomnia Not Otherwise Specified), Breathing-Related Sleep Disorder, and seizures occurring during sleep. In contrast to individuals with Sleep Terror Disorder, individuals with **Nightmare Disorder** typically awaken easily and completely, report vivid storylike dreams accompanying the episodes, and tend to have episodes later in the night. The degree of autonomic arousal and motor activity is not as great as that in Sleep Terror Disorder, and recall is more complete. Sleep terrors usually occur during slow-wave sleep, whereas nightmares occur during REM sleep. Parents of children with Sleep Terror Disorder may misinterpret reports of fearfulness and fragmentary imagery reports as nightmares.

Sleepwalking Disorder may be difficult to differentiate from cases of Sleep Terror

Disorder that involve prominent motor activity. In fact, the two disorders frequently occur together, and family history commonly involves both disorders. The prototypical case of Sleep Terror Disorder involves a predominance of autonomic arousal and fear, with a lesser degree of motor activity that tends to be abrupt and disorganized. The prototypical case of Sleepwalking Disorder involves little autonomic arousal or fear and a greater degree of organized motor activity.

Parasomnias Not Otherwise Specified include several presentations that can resemble Sleep Terror Disorder. The most common example is "REM sleep behavior disorder," which also produces subjective fear, violent motor activity, and the potential for injury. Because this occurs during REM sleep, it involves vivid storylike dreams, more immediate and complete awakening, and motor activity that clearly follows dream content. "Nocturnal paroxysmal dystonia" also includes awakenings from sleep with motor activity, but this activity is longer in duration, more rhythmic and stereotyped, and not associated with subjective reports or signs of fear.

Hypnagogic hallucinations, experienced sporadically by many otherwise-asymptomatic individuals, as well as more regularly by those with **Narcolepsy,** may be associated with anxiety. Their occurrence at sleep onset, vivid images, and subjective sensation of wakefulness differentiate these episodes from sleep terrors.

Rarely, an individual with a **Breathing-Related Sleep Disorder** may have episodes of awakenings associated with fear and panic that resemble those in Sleep Terror Disorder. The association with snoring, obesity, and respiratory symptoms such as witnessed apneas, an inability to breathe, or choking episodes distinguishes Breathing-Related Sleep Disorder. A single episode of sleep terror can also occur during the slow-wave sleep rebound that follows the abrupt treatment of obstructive sleep apnea syndrome (e.g., following nasal continuous positive airway pressure [CPAP] therapy).

Seizures that occur during sleep can produce subjective sensations of fear and stereotyped behaviors, followed by confusion and difficulty awakening. Most nocturnal seizures occur at sleep-wake transitions, but they may occur during slow-wave sleep. Incontinence and tonic-clonic movements suggest a seizure disorder, but frontal and temporal lobe seizures can produce more complex behaviors as well. An EEG often reveals interictal findings in individuals with sleep-related seizures, but EEG monitoring during nocturnal sleep may be needed for definitive differential diagnosis. Sleep disruption related to seizures should be diagnosed as **Sleep Disorder Due to a General Medical Condition, Parasomnia Type** (see p. 597). Sleep Disorders Due to a General Medical Condition other than sleep-related seizures may rarely cause unusual behavioral episodes at night. The new onset of abnormal behavior during sleep in a middle-aged or older adult should prompt consideration of a closed head injury or central nervous system pathology such as tumor or infection.

Sleep terror episodes also may be exacerbated or induced by medications such as central nervous system depressants. If episodes are judged to be a direct physiological effect of taking a medication or substance, the disorder should be classified as a **Substance-Induced Sleep Disorder, Parasomnia Type** (see p. 601).

Panic Disorder may also cause abrupt awakenings from deep NREM sleep accompanied by fearfulness, but these episodes produce rapid and complete awakening without the confusion, amnesia, or motor activity typical of Sleep Terror Disorder. Individuals who have Panic Attacks during sleep report that these symptoms are virtually identical to those of Panic Attacks that occur during the day. The presence of Agoraphobia may also help differentiate the two disorders.

Relationship to the International Classification of Sleep Disorders

Sleep Terror Disorder is virtually identical to Sleep Terrors in the International Classification of Sleep Disorders (ICSD). Confusional Arousals, which can occur as an independent disorder or in conjunction with Sleep Terror Disorder, are also described in the ICSD. Confusional Arousals are characterized by brief awakenings from slow-wave sleep with confusion, but without terror or ambulation.

■ **Diagnostic criteria for 307.46 Sleep Terror Disorder**

A. Recurrent episodes of abrupt awakening from sleep, usually occurring during the first third of the major sleep episode and beginning with a panicky scream.

B. Intense fear and signs of autonomic arousal, such as tachycardia, rapid breathing, and sweating, during each episode.

C. Relative unresponsiveness to efforts of others to comfort the person during the episode.

D. No detailed dream is recalled and there is amnesia for the episode.

E. The episodes cause clinically significant distress or impairment in social, occupational, or other important areas of functioning.

F. The disturbance is not due to the direct physiological effects of a substance (e.g., a drug of abuse, a medication) or a general medical condition.

307.46   Sleepwalking Disorder

Diagnostic Features

The essential feature of Sleepwalking Disorder is repeated episodes of complex motor behavior initiated during sleep, including rising from bed and walking about. Sleepwalking episodes begin during slow-wave sleep and therefore most often occur during the first third of the night (Criterion A). During episodes, the individual has reduced alertness and responsiveness, a blank stare, and relative unresponsiveness to communication with others or efforts to be awakened by others (Criterion B). If awakened during the episode (or on awakening the following morning), the individual has limited recall for the events of the episode (Criterion C). After the episode, there may initially be a brief period of confusion or difficulty orienting, followed by full recovery of cognitive function and appropriate behavior (Criterion D). The sleepwalking must cause clinically significant distress or impairment in social, occupational, or other important areas of functioning (Criterion E). Sleepwalking Disorder should not be diagnosed if the behavior is due to the direct physiological effects of a substance (e.g., a drug of abuse, a medication) or a general medical condition (Criterion F).

Sleepwalking episodes can include a variety of behaviors. In mild episodes (sometimes called "confusional arousals"), the individual may simply sit up in bed, look about, or pick at the blanket or sheet. More typically, the individual actually gets out of bed and may walk into closets, out of the room, up and down stairs, and even out of buildings. Individuals may use the bathroom, eat, and talk during episodes. Running and frantic attempts to escape some apparent threat can also occur. Most behaviors during sleepwalking episodes are routine and of low complexity. However, cases of unlocking doors and even operating machinery have been reported. Particularly in childhood, sleepwalking can also include inappropriate behavior (e.g., urinating in a closet). Most episodes last for several minutes to a half hour.

Sleepwalking episodes can terminate in spontaneous arousals followed by a brief period of confusion, or the individual may return to bed and continue to sleep until the morning. Not uncommonly, the individual may awaken the next morning in another place, or with evidence of having performed some activity during the night, but with complete amnesia for the event. Some episodes may be followed by vague recall of fragmentary dream images, but usually not by typical storylike dreams.

During sleepwalking episodes, individuals may talk or even respond to others' questions. However, their articulation is poor, and true dialogue is rare. Individuals may respond to others' requests to cease their activity and return to bed. However, these behaviors are performed with reduced levels of alertness, and awakening an individual from a sleepwalking episode is typically very difficult. If awakened, the individual remains confused for several minutes and then returns to a normal state of alertness.

For the diagnosis to be made, the individual must experience clinically significant distress or impairment. Individuals may avoid situations that would reveal their behavior to others (e.g., children may avoid visiting friends or going to summer camp; adults may avoid sleeping with bedpartners, going on vacation, or staying away from home). Social isolation or occupational difficulties can result.

Associated Features and Disorders

Associated descriptive features and mental disorders. Internal stimuli (e.g., a distended bladder) or external stimuli (e.g., noises) can increase the likelihood of a sleepwalking episode, as can psychosocial stressors and alcohol or sedative use. Some individuals with sleepwalking also report episodes of eating during the night, most often with complete or partial amnesia. They may find evidence of their eating only the next morning. Individuals can injure themselves during sleepwalking episodes by bumping into objects, walking on stairs, going outside, and even walking out of windows. The risk of injury further increases if sleepwalking episodes also include features of sleep terrors, with an attendant fleeing or striking out. Individuals with Sleepwalking Disorder and Sleep Terror Disorder can also injure others during episodes.

Other parasomnias associated with non–rapid eye movement (NREM) sleep (e.g., Sleep Terror Disorder) can also occur in individuals with Sleepwalking Disorder. Sleepwalking Disorder in children usually is not associated with other mental disorders, but in adults it may be associated with Personality Disorders, Mood Disorders, or Anxiety Disorders.

Associated laboratory findings.   Polysomnography, using routine procedures with the addition of audiovisual monitoring, can document episodes of sleepwalking. Episodes begin within the first few hours of sleep during deep (usually NREM stage 3 or 4) sleep. Some individuals (e.g., older adults) may have episodes during NREM stage 2 sleep. Preceding the episode, the EEG often shows rhythmic ("hypersynchronous"), high-voltage delta activity that persists during the arousal. EEG signs of arousal, such as alpha activity, may also appear at the beginning of the episode. Most commonly, the EEG is obscured by movement artifact during the actual episode. Heart rate and respiratory rate may increase at the beginning of the episode. These findings may occur with a full sleepwalking episode or with a more minor behavioral event (such as a confusional arousal). Other polysomnographic findings may include an increased number of transitions out of stages 3 and 4 sleep and reduced sleep efficiency.

Associated physical examination findings and general medical conditions. Fever or sleep deprivation can increase the frequency of sleepwalking episodes. Obstructive sleep apnea syndrome and other disorders that produce severe disruption of slow-wave sleep can also be associated with sleepwalking episodes. An association between migraine headaches and Sleepwalking Disorder has been noted.

Specific Culture, Age, and Gender Features

No reports have provided clear evidence of culturally related differences in the manifestations of Sleepwalking Disorder, but it is likely that the significance and causes attributed to sleepwalking differ among cultures. Violent activity during sleepwalking episodes is more likely to occur in adults. Sleepwalking Disorder occurs with equal frequency in both sexes.

Prevalence

Between 10% and 30% of children have had at least one episode of sleepwalking, but the prevalence of Sleepwalking Disorder (marked by repeated episodes and impairment or distress) is much lower, probably in the range of 1%–5%. Epidemiological surveys report the prevalence of sleepwalking episodes (not Sleepwalking Disorder) to be 1.0%–7.0% among adults.

Course

Sleepwalking can occur at any time after a child is able to walk, but episodes most commonly occur for the first time between ages 4 and 8 years. The peak prevalence occurs at about age 12 years. Episodes rarely occur for the first time in adults. The onset of Sleepwalking Disorder in adults should prompt a search for specific etiologies such as substance use or a neurological condition. Sleepwalking in childhood usually disappears spontaneously during early adolescence, typically by age 15 years. Less commonly, episodes may have a recurrent course, with return of episodes in early adulthood after cessation of episodes in late childhood. Sleepwalking Disorder is adults most often follows a chronic, waxing and waning course. Sleepwalking episodes may occur as isolated events in individuals of any age, but the most common pattern is repeated episodes occurring over a period of several years.

Familial Pattern

Sleepwalking Disorder aggregates among family members. A family history for sleep-walking or sleep terrors has been reported in up to 80% of individuals who sleepwalk. Approximately 10%–20% of individuals who sleepwalk have a first-degree biological relative who also sleepwalks. The risk for sleepwalking is further increased (to as much as 60% of offspring) when both parents have a history of the disorder. Genetic transmission is suggested, but the exact mode of inheritance is not known.

Differential Diagnosis

Many children have isolated or infrequent episodes of sleepwalking, either with or without precipitating events. The exact boundary between **nonclinically significant sleepwalking episodes** and Sleepwalking Disorder is indistinct. Frequent episodes, injuries, more active or violent behavior, and social impairment resulting from sleep-walking are likely to lead the child's parents to seek help and warrant a diagnosis of Sleepwalking Disorder. Episodes that have persisted from childhood to late adolescence, or that occur de novo in adults, are more likely to warrant a diagnosis of Sleepwalking Disorder.

It can be difficult clinically to distinguish Sleepwalking Disorder from **Sleep Terror Disorder** when there is an attempt to "escape" from the terrifying stimulus. In both cases, the individual shows movement, difficulty awakening, and amnesia for the event. An initial scream, signs of intense fear and panic, and autonomic arousal are more characteristic of Sleep Terror Disorder. Sleepwalking Disorder and Sleep Terror Disorder may occur in the same individual, and in such cases both should be diagnosed.

Breathing-Related Sleep Disorder, especially the obstructive sleep apnea syndrome, can also produce confusional arousals with subsequent amnesia. However, Breathing-Related Sleep Disorder is also characterized by characteristic symptoms of snoring, breathing pauses, and daytime sleepiness. In some individuals, Breathing-Related Sleep Disorder may precipitate episodes of sleepwalking.

"REM sleep behavior disorder" is another Parasomnia (see **Parasomnia Not Otherwise Specified**) that may be difficult to distinguish from Sleepwalking Disorder. REM sleep behavior disorder is characterized by episodes of prominent, complex movements, often involving personal injury. In contrast to Sleepwalking Disorder, REM sleep behavior disorder occurs during rapid eye movement (REM) sleep, often in the later part of the night. Individuals awaken easily and report dream content that matches their behaviors. A variety of other behaviors can occur with partial arousals from sleep. Confusional arousals resemble sleepwalking episodes in all respects except the actual movement out of the bed. "Sleep drunkenness" is a state in which the individual shows a prolonged transition from sleep to wakefulness in the morning. It may be difficult to arouse the individual, who may violently resist efforts to awaken him or her. Again, ambulation or other more complex behaviors distinguish Sleepwalking Disorder. However, both confusional arousals and sleep drunkenness may occur in individuals with Sleepwalking Disorder.

Sleep-related epilepsy can produce episodes of unusual behavior that occur only during sleep. The individual is unresponsive and is amnestic for the episode. Typically, sleep-related epilepsy produces more stereotypical, perseverative, low-complexity movements than those in sleepwalking. In most cases, individuals with sleep-related epilepsy also have similar episodes during wakefulness. The EEG shows features of epilepsy, including paroxysmal activity during the episodes and interictal features at other times. However, the presence of sleep-related seizures does not preclude the presence of sleepwalking episodes. Sleep-related epilepsy should be diagnosed as **Sleep Disorder Due to Epilepsy, Parasomnia Type** (see p. 597).

Sleepwalking can be induced by substances or medications (e.g., antipsychotics, tricyclic antidepressants, chloral hydrate). In such cases, **Substance-Induced Sleep Disorder, Parasomnia Type,** should be diagnosed (see p. 601).

Dissociative Fugue bears superficial similarities to Sleepwalking Disorder. Fugue is rare in children, typically begins when the individual is awake, lasts hours or days, and is not characterized by disturbances of consciousness. Although individuals can feign sleepwalking as part of **Malingering,** it is difficult to counterfeit the appearance or behavior of sleepwalking under direct observation.

Relationship to the International Classification of Sleep Disorders

Sleepwalking Disorder is virtually identical to Sleepwalking as described in the International Classification of Sleep Disorders (ICSD). The ICSD includes two other disorders that may have features similar to sleepwalking: Confusional Arousals and Nocturnal Eating (Drinking) Syndrome.

■ Diagnostic criteria for 307.46 Sleepwalking Disorder

A. Repeated episodes of rising from bed during sleep and walking about, usually occurring during the first third of the major sleep episode.

B. While sleepwalking, the person has a blank, staring face, is relatively unresponsive to the efforts of others to communicate with him or her, and can be awakened only with great difficulty.

C. On awakening (either from the sleepwalking episode or the next morning), the person has amnesia for the episode.

D. Within several minutes after awakening from the sleepwalking episode, there is no impairment of mental activity or behavior (although there may initially be a short period of confusion or disorientation).

E. The sleepwalking causes clinically significant distress or impairment in social, occupational, or other important areas of functioning.

F. The disturbance is not due to the direct physiological effects of a substance (e.g., a drug of abuse, a medication) or a general medical condition.

307.47   Parasomnia Not Otherwise Specified

The Parasomnia Not Otherwise Specified category is for disturbances that are characterized by abnormal behavioral or physiological events during sleep or sleep-wake transitions, but that do not meet criteria for a more specific Parasomnia. Examples include

1. REM sleep behavior disorder: motor activity, often of a violent nature, that arises during rapid eye movement (REM) sleep. Unlike sleepwalking, these episodes tend to occur later in the night and are associated with vivid dream recall.
2. Sleep paralysis: an inability to perform voluntary movement during the transition between wakefulness and sleep. The episodes may occur at sleep onset (hypnagogic) or with awakening (hypnopompic). The episodes are usually associated with extreme anxiety and, in some cases, fear of impending death. Sleep paralysis occurs commonly as an ancillary symptom of Narcolepsy and, in such cases, should not be coded separately.
3. Situations in which the clinician has concluded that a Parasomnia is present but is unable to determine whether it is primary, due to a general medical condition, or substance induced.

Sleep Disorders Related to Another Mental Disorder

307.42   Insomnia Related to Another Mental Disorder
307.44   Hypersomnia Related to Another Mental Disorder

Diagnostic Features

The essential feature of Insomnia Related to Another Mental Disorder and Hypersomnia Related to Another Mental Disorder is the presence of either insomnia or hypersomnia that is judged to be related temporally and causally to another mental disorder. Insomnia or Hypersomnia that is the direct physiological consequence of a substance is not included here. Such presentations would be diagnosed as Substance-Induced Sleep Disorder (see p. 601). Insomnia Related to Another Mental Disorder is characterized by a complaint of difficulty falling asleep, frequent awakenings during the night, or a marked feeling of nonrestorative sleep that has lasted for at least 1 month and is associated with daytime fatigue or impaired daytime functioning (Criterion A). Hypersomnia Related to Another Mental Disorder is characterized by a complaint of either prolonged nighttime sleep or repeated daytime sleep episodes for at least 1 month (Criterion A). In both Insomnia and Hypersomnia Related to Another Mental Disorder, the sleep symptoms cause significant distress or impairment in social, occupational, or other important areas of functioning (Criterion B). The insomnia or hypersomnia is not better accounted for by another Sleep Disorder (e.g., Narcolepsy, Breathing-Related Sleep Disorder, or a Parasomnia) and hypersomnia is not better accounted for by an inadequate amount of sleep (Criterion D). The sleep disturbance must not be due to the direct physiological effects of a substance (e.g., a drug of abuse, a medication) or a general medical condition (Criterion E).

Sleep disturbances are common features of other mental disorders. An additional diagnosis of Insomnia or Hypersomnia Related to Another Mental Disorder is made only when the sleep disturbance is a predominant complaint and is sufficiently severe to warrant independent clinical attention (Criterion C). Individuals with this type of insomnia or hypersomnia usually focus on their sleep disturbance to the exclusion of the symptoms characteristic of the related mental disorder, whose presence may become apparent only after specific and persistent questioning. Not infrequently, they attribute their symptoms of mental disorder to the fact that they have slept poorly.

Many mental disorders may at times involve insomnia or hypersomnia as the predominant problems. Individuals with Major Depressive Disorder often complain of difficulty falling asleep or staying asleep or early morning awakening with inability to return to sleep. Hypersomnia Related to Mood Disorder is more often associated with Bipolar Mood Disorder, Most Recent Episode Depressed, or a Major Depressive Episode With Atypical Features. Individuals with Generalized Anxiety Disorder often report difficulty falling asleep and may awaken with anxious ruminations in the middle of the night. Some individuals with Panic Disorder have nocturnal Panic Attacks that can lead to insomnia. Significant insomnia is often seen during exacerbations of Schizophrenia and other Psychotic Disorders but is rarely the predominant complaint. Other mental disorders that may be related to insomnia include Adjustment Disorders, Somatoform Disorders, and Personality Disorders.

Recording Procedures

The name of the diagnosis begins with the type of sleep disturbance (i.e., insomnia or hypersomnia) followed by the name of the specific Axis I or Axis II disorder that it is related to (e.g., 307.42 Insomnia Related to Major Depressive Disorder) on Axis I. The specific related mental disorder should also be coded on Axis I or Axis II as appropriate.

Associated Features and Disorders

Associated descriptive features and mental disorders.   Because, by definition, the criteria are met for the related mental disorder, the associated features of Insomnia or Hypersomnia Related to Another Mental Disorder include the characteristic and associated features of the related mental disorder.

Individuals with Insomnia Related to Another Mental Disorder may demonstrate the same type of conditioned arousal and negative conditioning that individuals with Primary Insomnia demonstrate. For instance, they will note increased anxiety as bedtime approaches, improved sleep when taken out of the usual sleep environment, and a tendency to spend too much time in bed. They may also have a history of multiple or inappropriate medication treatments for their insomnia complaints. Individuals with Hypersomnia Related to Another Mental Disorder will frequently emphasize symptoms of fatigue, "leaden paralysis," or complete lack of energy. On careful questioning, these individuals may be more distressed by such fatigue-related symptoms than by true sleepiness. They may also have a history of inappropriate use of stimulant medications, including caffeine.

Associated laboratory findings.   Characteristic (but not diagnostic) polysomnographic findings in Major Depressive Episode include 1) sleep continuity disturbance, such as prolonged sleep latency, increased intermittent wakefulness, and early morning awakening; 2) reduced non–rapid eye movement (NREM) stages 3 and 4 sleep (slow-wave sleep), with a shift in slow-wave activity away from the first NREM period; 3) decreased rapid eye movement (REM) latency (i.e., shorter duration of the first NREM period); 4) increased REM density (i.e., the number of actual eye movements during REM); and 5) increased duration of REM sleep early in the night. Sleep abnormalities may be evident in 40%–60% of outpatients and in up to 90% of inpatients with a Major Depressive Episode. Evidence suggests that most of these abnormalities persist after clinical remission and may precede the onset of the initial Major Depressive Episode.

Polysomnographic findings in Manic Episodes are similar to those found in Major Depressive Episodes. In Schizophrenia, REM sleep is diminished early in the course of an acute exacerbation, with a gradual return toward normal values as clinical status improves. REM latency may be reduced. Total sleep time is often severely diminished in Schizophrenia, and slow-wave sleep is typically reduced during exacerbations. Individuals with Panic Disorder may have paroxysmal awakenings on entering stages 3 and 4 NREM sleep; these awakenings are accompanied by tachycardia, increased respiratory rate, and cognitive and emotional symptoms with Panic Attacks. Most other mental disorders produce nonspecific patterns of sleep disturbance (e.g., prolonged sleep latency or frequent awakenings).

Associated physical examination findings and general medical conditions. Individuals with Insomnia or Hypersomnia Related to Another Mental Disorder may appear tired, fatigued, or haggard during routine examination. The general medical conditions associated with these Sleep Disorders are the same as those associated with the underlying mental disorder.

Specific Culture, Age, and Gender Features

In some cultures, sleep complaints may be viewed as relatively less stigmatizing than mental disorders. Therefore, individuals from some cultural backgrounds may be more likely to present with complaints of insomnia or hypersomnia rather than with other symptoms (e.g., depression, anxiety).

Children and adolescents with Major Depressive Disorder generally present with less subjective sleep disturbance and fewer polysomnographic changes than do older adults. In general, hypersomnia is a more common feature of Depressive Disorders in adolescents and young adults and insomnia is more common in older adults.

Sleep Disorders Related to Another Mental Disorder are more prevalent in females than in males. This difference probably relates to the increased prevalence of Mood and Anxiety Disorders in women, rather than to any particular difference in susceptibility to sleep problems.

Prevalence

Sleep problems are extremely common in all types of mental disorders, but there are no accurate estimates of the percentage of individuals who present primarily because of sleep disruption. Insomnia Related to Another Mental Disorder is the most frequent diagnosis (35%–50%) among individuals presenting to sleep disorders centers for evaluation of chronic insomnia. Hypersomnia Related to Another Mental Disorder is a much less frequent diagnosis (fewer than 5%) among individuals evaluated for hypersomnia at sleep disorders centers.

Course

The course of Sleep Disorders Related to Another Mental Disorder generally follows the course of the underlying mental disorder itself. The sleep disturbance may be one of the earliest symptoms to appear in individuals who subsequently develop an associated mental disorder. Symptoms of insomnia or hypersomnia often fluctuate considerably over time. For many individuals with depression, particularly those treated with medications, sleep disturbance may improve rapidly, often more quickly than other symptoms of the underlying mental disorder. On the other hand, other individuals have persistent or intermittent insomnia even after the other symptoms of their Major Depressive Disorder remit. Individuals with Bipolar Disorder often have distinctive sleep-related symptoms depending on the nature of the current episode. During Manic Episodes, individuals experience hyposomnia, although they rarely complain about their inability to sleep. On the other hand, such individuals may have marked distress about hypersomnia during Major Depressive Episodes. Individuals with Psychotic Disorders most often have a notable worsening in sleep early during the course of an acute exacerbation, but then report improvement as psychotic symptoms abate.

Differential Diagnosis

Insomnia or Hypersomnia Related to Another Mental Disorder should not be diagnosed in every individual with a mental disorder who also has sleep-related symptoms. A diagnosis of Insomnia or Hypersomnia Related to Another Mental Disorder should be made only when sleep symptoms are severe and are an independent focus of clinical attention. No independent sleep disorder diagnosis is warranted for most individuals with **Major Depressive Disorder** who report difficulties falling or staying asleep in the middle of the night. However, if the individual primarily complains of sleep disturbance or if the insomnia is out of proportion to other symptoms, then an additional diagnosis of Insomnia Related to Another Mental Disorder may be warranted.

Distinguishing **Primary Insomnia** or **Primary Hypersomnia** from Insomnia or Hypersomnia Related to Another Mental Disorder can be especially difficult in individuals who present with both clinically significant sleep disturbance and other symptoms of a mental disorder. The diagnosis of Insomnia or Hypersomnia Related to Another Mental Disorder is based on three judgments. First, the insomnia or hypersomnia must be judged to be attributable to the mental disorder (e.g., the insomnia or hypersomnia occurs exclusively during the mental disorder). Second, the insomnia or hypersomnia must be the predominant complaint and must be sufficiently severe to warrant independent clinical attention. Third, the symptom presentation should meet the full criteria for another mental disorder. A diagnosis of Primary Insomnia or Primary Hypersomnia is appropriate when (as is often the case) the insomnia or hypersomnia is accompanied by symptoms (e.g., anxiety, depressed mood) that do not meet criteria for a specific mental disorder. A diagnosis of Primary Insomnia is also appropriate for individuals with chronic insomnia who later develop a Mood or Anxiety Disorder. If symptoms of insomnia or hypersomnia persist long after the other symptoms of the related mental disorder have remitted completely, the diagnosis would be changed from Insomnia or Hypersomnia Related to Another Mental Disorder to Primary Insomnia or Primary Hypersomnia.

Insomnia or Hypersomnia Related to Another Mental Disorder is not diagnosed if the presentation is better accounted for by **another Sleep Disorder** (e.g., Narcolepsy, Breathing-Related Sleep Disorder, or a Parasomnia).

Insomnia or Hypersomnia Related to Another Mental Disorder must be distinguished from a **Sleep Disorder Due to a General Medical Condition.** The diagnosis is Sleep Disorder Due to a General Medical Condition when the sleep disturbance is judged to be a direct physiological consequence of a specific general medical condition (e.g., pheochromocytoma, hyperthyroidism). This determination is based on history, laboratory findings, and physical examination (see p. 597 for further discussion). A **Substance-Induced Sleep Disorder** is distinguished from Insomnia or Hypersomnia Related to Another Mental Disorder by the fact that a substance (i.e., a drug of abuse, a medication) is judged to be etiologically related to the sleep disturbance (see p. 601 for further discussion). For example, insomnia that occurs only in the context of heavy coffee consumption would be diagnosed as Caffeine-Induced Sleep Disorder, Insomnia Type.

Sleep Disorders Related to Another Mental Disorder must be differentiated from **normal sleep patterns,** as well as from other Sleep Disorders. Although complaints of occasional insomnia or hypersomnia are common in the general population, they are not usually accompanied by the other signs and symptoms of a mental disorder. Transient sleep disturbances are common reactions to stressful life events and generally do not warrant a diagnosis. A separate diagnosis of Insomnia or Hypersomnia Related to Adjustment Disorder should be considered only when the sleep disturbance is particularly severe and prolonged.

Relationship to the International Classification of Sleep Disorders

The International Classification of Sleep Disorders (ICSD) includes analogous diagnoses for Sleep Disorders Related to Another Mental Disorder and specifically lists Psychoses, Mood Disorders, Anxiety Disorders, Panic Disorder, and Alcoholism.

■ **Diagnostic criteria for 307.42 Insomnia Related to . . .** [*Indicate the* Axis I *or* Axis II *disorder*]

  A. The predominant complaint is difficulty initiating or maintaining sleep, or nonrestorative sleep, for at least 1 month that is associated with daytime fatigue or impaired daytime functioning.

  B. The sleep disturbance (or daytime sequelae) causes clinically significant distress or impairment in social, occupational, or other important areas of functioning.

  C. The insomnia is judged to be related to another Axis I or Axis II disorder (e.g., Major Depressive Disorder, Generalized Anxiety Disorder, Adjustment Disorder With Anxiety), but is sufficiently severe to warrant independent clinical attention.

(continued)

☐ **Diagnostic criteria for 307.42 Insomnia Related to . . .
[Indicate the Axis I or Axis II Disorder]** (continued)

   D. The disturbance is not better accounted for by another Sleep Disorder
   (e.g., Narcolepsy, Breathing-Related Sleep Disorder, a Parasomnia).

   E. The disturbance is not due to the direct physiological effects of a
   substance (e.g., a drug of abuse, a medication) or a general medical
   condition.

◼ **Diagnostic criteria for 307.44 Hypersomnia Related
to . . . [Indicate the Axis I or Axis II disorder]**

   A. The predominant complaint is excessive sleepiness for at least 1 month
   as evidenced by either prolonged sleep episodes or daytime sleep
   episodes that occur almost daily.

   B. The excessive sleepiness causes clinically significant distress or impairment in social, occupational, or other important areas of functioning.

   C. The hypersomnia is judged to be related to another Axis I or Axis II
   disorder (e.g., Major Depressive Disorder, Dysthymic Disorder), but is
   sufficiently severe to warrant independent clinical attention.

   D. The disturbance is not better accounted for by another Sleep Disorder
   (e.g., Narcolepsy, Breathing-Related Sleep Disorder, a Parasomnia) or
   by an inadequate amount of sleep.

   E. The disturbance is not due to the direct physiological effects of a
   substance (e.g., a drug of abuse, a medication) or a general medical
   condition.

Other Sleep Disorders

780.xx   Sleep Disorder
Due to a General Medical Condition

Diagnostic Features

The essential feature of Sleep Disorder Due to a General Medical Condition is a
prominent disturbance in sleep that is severe enough to warrant independent clinical
attention (Criterion A) and is due to a general medical condition. Symptoms may include

insomnia, hypersomnia, a Parasomnia, or some combination of these. There must be evidence from the history, physical examination, or laboratory findings that the sleep disturbance is the direct physiological consequence of a general medical condition (Criterion B). The disturbance is not better accounted for by another mental disorder, such as Adjustment Disorder, in which the stressor is a serious general medical condition (Criterion C). The diagnosis is not made if the sleep disturbance occurs only during the course of a delirium (Criterion D). By convention, sleep disturbances due to a Sleep-Related Breathing Disorder (e.g., sleep apnea) or to Narcolepsy are not included in this category (Criterion E). The sleep symptoms must cause clinically significant distress or impairment in social, occupational, or other important areas of functioning (Criterion F).

In determining whether the sleep disturbance is due to a general medical condition, the clinician must first establish the presence of a general medical condition. Further, the clinician must establish that the sleep disturbance is etiologically related to the general medical condition through a physiological mechanism. A careful and comprehensive assessment of multiple factors is necessary to make this judgment. Although there are no infallible guidelines for determining whether the relationship between the sleep disturbance and the general medical condition is etiological, several considerations provide some guidance in this area. One consideration is the presence of a temporal association between the onset, exacerbation, or remission of the general medical condition and that of the sleep disturbance. A second consideration is the presence of features that are atypical of primary Sleep Disorders (e.g., atypical age at onset or course or absence of family history). Evidence from the literature that suggests that there can be a direct association between the general medical condition in question and the development of a sleep disturbance can provide a useful context in the assessment of a particular situation. In addition, the clinician must also judge that the disturbance is not better accounted for by a primary Sleep Disorder, a Substance-Induced Sleep Disorder, or other primary mental disorders (e.g., Adjustment Disorder). This determination is explained in greater detail in the "Mental Disorders Due to a General Medical Condition" section (p. 165).

Subtypes

The subtypes listed below can be used to indicate which of the following symptom presentations predominates. The clinical presentation of the specific Sleep Disorder Due to a General Medical Condition may resemble that of the analogous primary Sleep Disorder. However, the full criteria for the analogous primary Sleep Disorder do not need to be met to assign a diagnosis of Sleep Disorder Due to a General Medical Condition.

Insomnia Type. This subtype refers to a sleep complaint characterized primarily by difficulty falling asleep, difficulty maintaining sleep, or a feeling of nonrestorative sleep.

Hypersomnia Type. This subtype is used when the predominant complaint is one of excessively long nocturnal sleep or of excessive sleepiness during waking hours.

Parasomnia Type. This subtype refers to a sleep disturbance characterized primarily by abnormal behavioral events that occur in association with sleep or sleep transitions.

Mixed Type. This subtype should be used to designate a sleep problem due to a general medical condition characterized by multiple sleep symptoms but no symptom clearly predominates.

Recording Procedures

In recording the diagnosis of Sleep Disorder Due to a General Medical Condition, the clinician should note both the specific phenomenology of the disturbance, including the appropriate subtype, and the specific general medical condition judged to be causing the disturbance on Axis I (e.g., 780.52 Sleep Disorder Due to Thyrotoxicosis, Insomnia Type). The ICD-9-CM code for the general medical condition should also be noted on Axis III (e.g., 242.9 thyrotoxicosis). (See Appendix G for a list of selected ICD-9-CM diagnostic codes for general medical conditions.)

Associated Features and Disorders

Associated laboratory findings.   Laboratory findings are consistent with the underlying general medical condition. There are no polysomnographic findings that are specific to the entire group of Sleep Disorders Due to a General Medical Condition. Most general medical conditions cause a decrease in total sleep duration, an increase in awakenings, a decrease in slow-wave sleep, and (less consistently) a decrease in rapid eye movement (REM) sleep or phasic REM density. Some medical conditions produce more specific polysomnographic findings. For example, individuals with fibromyalgia syndrome complain of nonrestorative sleep and often have a distinct pattern of alpha EEG activity during non–rapid eye movement (NREM) sleep. Sleep-related seizures result in specific EEG discharges that are consistent with the underlying seizure type.

Associated physical examination findings and general medical conditions. Individuals with a Sleep Disorder Due to a General Medical Condition are expected to have the typical physical findings of the underlying general medical condition. Sleep disturbances may result from a variety of general medical and neurological conditions including (but not limited to) degenerative neurological illnesses (e.g., Parkinson's disease, Huntington's disease), cerebrovascular disease (e.g., insomnia following vascular lesions to the upper brain stem), endocrine conditions (e.g., hypo- or hyperthyroidism, hypo- or hyperadrenocorticism), viral and bacterial infections (e.g., hypersomnia related to viral encephalitis), coughing related to pulmonary disease other than sleep-related breathing conditions (e.g., chronic bronchitis), and pain from musculoskeletal disease (e.g., rheumatoid arthritis, fibromyalgia).

Differential Diagnosis

Sleep Disorder Due to a General Medical Condition must be differentiated from expected disruptions in sleep patterns, primary Sleep Disorders, Sleep Disorders Related to Another Mental Disorder, and Substance-Induced Sleep Disorders. Many individuals experience **sleep disruption during the course of a general medical or neurological condition.** In the majority of cases, such complaints do not merit an additional diagnosis of a Sleep Disorder. Rather, a diagnosis of Sleep Disorder Due to a General Medical Condition should be reserved for cases in which the sleep disturbance is a very prominent clinical feature, atypical symptoms are present, or the individual is sufficiently distressed by the sleep symptom or attendant impairment that specific treatment for this disturbance is required.

Sleep Disorders Due to a General Medical Condition are characterized by symptoms similar to those in **primary Sleep Disorders.** The differential diagnosis rests not on specific symptoms, but rather on the presence or absence of a medical condition judged to be etiologically related to the sleep complaint. In the specific cases of **Narcolepsy** and **Breathing-Related Sleep Disorder**, the underlying etiology of the sleep disturbance is assumed to be a general medical condition. However, in these two specific examples, the general medical condition does not exist independent of sleep symptoms. For this reason, these two disorders are included in the "Primary Sleep Disorders" section.

Differentiating a Sleep Disorder Due to a General Medical Condition from **Substance-Induced Sleep Disorder** can prove very difficult. In many cases, individuals with a significant general medical condition often take medication for that condition; these medications in turn may cause sleep-related symptoms. For example, an individual may have sleep disruption related to asthma. However, that individual may also be treated with theophylline preparations, which in some cases can themselves cause sleep disturbance. Differentiating a Sleep Disorder Due to a General Medical Condition from a Substance-Induced Sleep Disorder often rests on chronology, response to treatment or discontinuation of medications, and longitudinal course. In some cases, concurrent diagnoses of Sleep Disorder Due to a General Medical Condition and Substance-Induced Sleep Disorder may be appropriate. In cases in which a drug of abuse is suspected to be the cause for the Sleep Disorder, a urine or blood drug screen may help to differentiate this problem from a Sleep Disorder Due to a General Medical Condition.

If the clinician cannot determine whether the sleep disturbance is primary, related to another mental disorder, due to a general medical condition, or substance induced, the appropriate diagnosis is Dyssomnia or Parasomnia Not Otherwise Specified.

Relationship to the International Classification of Sleep Disorders

The International Classification of Sleep Disorders (ICSD) contains the general section "Medical/Psychiatric Sleep Disorders." Specific diagnoses are presented for Sleep Disorders that are associated with neurological disorders (with 7 examples listed) and Sleep Disorders that are associated with other medical disorders (with 7 examples listed). Although only 14 medical/neurological disorders are specifically cited in the ICSD, the clinician may diagnose a Sleep Disorder associated with any other medical disorder simply by using the appropriate ICD-9-CM codes.

■ Diagnostic criteria for 780.xx Sleep Disorder Due to . . . [*Indicate the General Medical Condition*]

A. A prominent disturbance in sleep that is sufficiently severe to warrant independent clinical attention.

B. There is evidence from the history, physical examination, or laboratory findings that the sleep disturbance is the direct physiological consequence of a general medical condition.

(continued)

☐ **Diagnostic criteria for 780.xx Sleep Disorder Due to . . .
[Indicate the General Medical Condition]** (continued)

    C. The disturbance is not better accounted for by another mental disorder (e.g., an Adjustment Disorder in which the stressor is a serious medical illness).

    D. The disturbance does not occur exclusively during the course of a delirium.

    E. The disturbance does not meet the criteria for Breathing-Related Sleep Disorder or Narcolepsy.

    F. The sleep disturbance causes clinically significant distress or impairment in social, occupational, or other important areas of functioning.

Specify type:
    .52 Insomnia Type: if the predominant sleep disturbance is insomnia
    .54 Hypersomnia Type: if the predominant sleep disturbance is hypersomnia
    .59 Parasomnia Type: if the predominant sleep disturbance is a Parasomnia
    .59 Mixed Type: if more than one sleep disturbance is present and none predominates

Coding note: Include the name of the general medical condition on Axis I, e.g., 780.52 Sleep Disorder Due to Chronic Obstructive Pulmonary Disease, Insomnia Type; also code the general medical condition on Axis III (see Appendix G for codes).

Substance-Induced Sleep Disorder

Diagnostic Features

The essential feature of Substance-Induced Sleep Disorder is a prominent disturbance in sleep that is sufficiently severe to warrant independent clinical attention (Criterion A) and is judged to be due to the direct physiological effects of a substance (i.e., a drug of abuse, a medication, or toxin exposure) (Criterion B). Depending on the substance involved, one of four types of sleep disturbance may be noted. Insomnia and Hypersomnia Types are most common, and Parasomnia Type is seen less often. A Mixed Type may also be noted when more than one type of sleep disturbance is present and none predominates. The disturbance must not be better accounted for by a mental disorder (e.g., another Sleep Disorder) that is not substance induced (Criterion C). The diagnosis is not made if the sleep disturbance occurs only during the course of a delirium (Criterion D). The symptoms must cause clinically significant distress or impairment in social, occupational, or other important areas of functioning (Criterion E). This diagnosis should be made instead of a diagnosis of Substance Intoxication or Substance Withdrawal only when the symptoms are in excess of those usually associated with the intoxication or withdrawal syndrome and when the symptoms are sufficiently severe to warrant independent clinical attention. For a more detailed discussion of Substance-Related Disorders, see p. 175.

A Substance-Induced Sleep Disorder is distinguished from a primary Sleep Disorder and from Insomnia or Hypersomnia Related to Another Mental Disorder by considering the onset and course. For drugs of abuse, there must be evidence from the history, physical examination, or laboratory findings of intoxication or withdrawal. Substance-Induced Sleep Disorder arises only in association with intoxication or withdrawal states, whereas the primary Sleep Disorders may precede the onset of substance use or occur during times of sustained abstinence. Because the withdrawal state for some substances (e.g., some benzodiazepines) can be relatively protracted, the onset of the sleep disturbance can occur up to 4 weeks after cessation of substance use. Another consideration is the presence of features that are atypical of primary Sleep Disorders (e.g., atypical age at onset or course). In contrast, factors that suggest that the sleep disturbance is better accounted for by a primary Sleep Disorder include persistence of the sleep disturbance for more than about 4 weeks after the end of intoxication or acute withdrawal; the development of symptoms that are substantially in excess of what would be expected given the type or amount of the substance used or the duration of use; or a history of a prior primary Sleep Disorder.

Subtypes and Specifiers

The subtypes listed below can be used to indicate which of the following symptom presentations predominates. The clinical presentation of the specific Substance-Induced Sleep Disorder may resemble that of the analogous primary Sleep Disorder. However, the full criteria for the analogous primary Sleep Disorder do not need to be met to assign a diagnosis of Substance-Induced Sleep Disorder.

> **Insomnia Type.**   This subtype refers to a sleep complaint characterized primarily by difficulty falling asleep, difficulty maintaining sleep, or a feeling of nonrestorative sleep.
>
> **Hypersomnia Type.**   This subtype is used when the predominant complaint is one of excessively long nocturnal sleep or of excessive sleepiness during waking hours.
>
> **Parasomnia Type.**   This subtype refers to a sleep disturbance characterized primarily by abnormal behavioral events that occur in association with sleep or sleep-wake transitions.
>
> **Mixed Type.**   This subtype should be used to designate a substance-induced sleep problem characterized by multiple types of sleep symptoms but no symptom clearly predominates.

The context of the development of the sleep symptoms may be indicated by using one of the following specifiers:

> **With Onset During Intoxication.**   This specifier should be used if criteria are met for intoxication with the substance and symptoms develop during the intoxication syndrome.
>
> **With Onset During Withdrawal.**   This specifier should be used if criteria are met for withdrawal from the substance and the symptoms develop during, or shortly after, a withdrawal syndrome.

Recording Procedures

The name of the Substance-Induced Sleep Disorder begins with the specific substance (e.g., alcohol, methylphenidate, thyroxine) that is presumed to be causing the sleep disturbance. The diagnostic code is selected from the listing of classes of substances provided in the criteria set for Substance-Induced Sleep Disorder. For substances that do not fit into any of the classes (e.g., thyroxine), the code for "Other Substance" should be used. In addition, for medications prescribed at therapeutic doses, the specific medication can be indicated by listing the appropriate E-code (see Appendix G). The name of the disorder (e.g., Caffeine-Induced Sleep Disorder) is followed by the subtype indicating the predominant symptom presentation and the specifier indicating the context in which the symptoms developed (e.g., 292.89 Caffeine-Induced Sleep Disorder, Insomnia Type, With Onset During Intoxication). When more than one substance is judged to play a significant role in the development of the sleep disturbance, each should be listed separately (e.g., 292.89 Cocaine-Induced Sleep Disorder, Insomnia Type, With Onset During Intoxication; 291.8 Alcohol-Induced Sleep Disorder, Insomnia Type, With Onset During Withdrawal). If a substance is judged to be the etiological factor but the specific substance or class of substance is unknown, the category 292.89 Unknown Substance-Induced Sleep Disorder may be used.

Specific Substances

Substance-Induced Sleep Disorder most commonly occurs during **intoxication** with the following classes of substances: alcohol; amphetamine and related substances; caffeine; cocaine; opioids; and sedatives, hypnotics, and anxiolytics. Sleep disturbances are also seen less commonly with use of other types of substances. Substance-Induced Sleep Disorder can also occur in association with **withdrawal** from the following classes of substances: alcohol; amphetamine and related stimulants; cocaine; opioids; and sedatives, hypnotics, and anxiolytics. Each of the Substance-Induced Sleep Disorders produces EEG sleep patterns that are associated with, but cannot be considered diagnostic of, the disorder. The EEG sleep profile for each substance is further related to the stage of use, whether intoxication, chronic use, or withdrawal following discontinuation of the substance.

Alcohol. Alcohol-Induced Sleep Disorder typically occurs as the Insomnia Type. During acute intoxication, alcohol typically produces an immediate sedative effect, with increased sleepiness and reduced wakefulness for 3–4 hours. This is accompanied by an increase in stages 3 and 4 non–rapid eye movement (NREM) sleep and reduced rapid eye movement (REM) sleep during EEG sleep studies. Following these initial effects, the individual has increased wakefulness, restless sleep, and, often, vivid and anxiety-laden dreams for the rest of the sleep period. EEG sleep studies show that, in the second half of sleep after alcohol ingestion, stages 3 and 4 sleep is reduced, wakefulness is increased, and REM sleep is increased. Alcohol can aggravate Breathing-Related Sleep Disorder by increasing the number of obstructive apnea events. With continued habitual use, alcohol continues to show a short-lived sedative effect for several hours, followed by sleep continuity disruption for several hours.

During Alcohol Withdrawal, sleep is grossly disturbed. The individual typically has extremely disrupted sleep continuity, accompanied by an increase in the amount and intensity of REM sleep. This is often accompanied by an increase in vivid dreaming and, in the most extreme example, constitutes part of Alcohol Withdrawal Delirium. After acute withdrawal, individuals who have chronically used alcohol may continue to complain of light, fragmented sleep for weeks to years. EEG sleep studies confirm a persistent deficit in slow-wave sleep and persistent sleep continuity disturbance in these cases.

Amphetamines and related stimulants.   Amphetamine-Induced Sleep Disorder is characterized by insomnia during intoxication and by hypersomnia during withdrawal. During the period of acute intoxication, amphetamine reduces the total amount of sleep, increases sleep latency and sleep continuity disturbances, increases body movements, and decreases REM sleep. Slow-wave sleep tends to be reduced. During withdrawal from chronic amphetamine use, individuals typically experience hypersomnia, with both prolonged nocturnal sleep duration and excessive sleepiness during the daytime. REM and slow-wave sleep may rebound to above baseline values. Multiple Sleep Latency Tests (MSLTs) may show increased daytime sleepiness during the withdrawal phase as well.

Caffeine.   Caffeine-Induced Sleep Disorder typically produces insomnia, although some individuals may present with a complaint of hypersomnia and daytime sleepiness related to withdrawal (see p. 708). Caffeine exerts a dose-dependent effect, with increasing doses causing increased wakefulness and decreased sleep continuity. Polysomnography may show prolonged sleep latency, increased wakefulness, and a decrease in slow-wave sleep. Consistent effects on REM sleep have not been described. Abrupt withdrawal from chronic caffeine use can produce hypersomnia. Some individuals may also experience hypersomnia between daytime doses of caffeine, as the immediate stimulant effect wanes.

Cocaine.   As with other stimulants, cocaine typically produces insomnia during acute intoxication and hypersomnia during withdrawal. During acute intoxication, the total amount of sleep may be drastically reduced, with only short bouts of very disrupted sleep. Conversely, withdrawal after a cocaine binge is often associated with extremely prolonged sleep duration.

Opioids.   During acute short-term use, opioids typically produce an increase in sleepiness and in subjective depth of sleep. REM sleep is typically reduced by acute administration of opioids, with little overall change in wakefulness or total sleep time. With continued administration, most individuals become tolerant to the sedative effects of opioids and may begin to complain of insomnia. This is mirrored by increased wakefulness and decreased sleep time in polysomnographic studies. Withdrawal from opioids is typically accompanied by hypersomnia complaints, although few objective studies have documented this finding.

Sedatives, hypnotics, and anxiolytics.   Drugs within this class (e.g., barbiturates, benzodiazepines, meprobamate, glutethimide, and methyprylon) have similar, but not identical, effects on sleep. Differences in duration of action and half-life may affect sleep complaints and objective measures of sleep. In general, barbiturates and the older nonbarbiturate, nonbenzodiazepine drugs more consistently produce tolerance, dependence, and severe withdrawal, but these phenomena can be noted with benzodiazepines as well.

During acute intoxication, sedative-hypnotic drugs produce the expected increase in sleepiness and decrease in wakefulness. Polysomnographic studies confirm these subjective effects during acute administration, as well as a decrease in REM sleep and an increase in sleep-spindle activity. Chronic use (particularly of barbiturates and the older nonbarbiturate, nonbenzodiazepine drugs) may cause tolerance with the resulting return of insomnia. If the individual then increases the dose, daytime hypersomnia may occur. Sedative-hypnotic drugs can aggravate Breathing-Related Sleep Disorder by increasing the frequency and severity of obstructive sleep apnea events.

The abrupt discontinuation of chronic sedative-hypnotic use can lead to withdrawal insomnia. In addition to decreased sleep duration, withdrawal can produce increased anxiety, tremulousness, and ataxia. Barbiturates and the older nonbarbiturate, non-benzodiazepine drugs are also associated with a high incidence of withdrawal seizures, which are much less frequently observed with benzodiazepines. Typically, sedative-hypnotic drugs with short durations of action are most likely to produce complaints of withdrawal insomnia, whereas those with longer durations of action are more often associated with daytime hypersomnia during active use. However, any sedative-hypnotic drug can potentially cause either daytime sedation or withdrawal insomnia. Withdrawal from sedative-hypnotic agents can be confirmed by polysomnographic studies, which show reduced sleep duration, increased sleep disruption, and REM sleep "rebound."

Other substances.   Other substances may produce sleep disturbances. Common examples include medications that affect the central or autonomic nervous systems (including adrenergic agonists and antagonists, dopamine agonists and antagonists, cholinergic agonists and antagonists, serotonergic agonists and antagonists, antihistamines, and corticosteroids). Clinically, such medications are prescribed for the control of hypertension and cardiac arrhythmias, chronic obstructive pulmonary disease, gastrointestinal motility problems, or inflammatory processes.

Differential Diagnosis

Sleep disturbances are commonly encountered in the context of Substance Intoxication or Substance Withdrawal. A diagnosis of Substance-Induced Sleep Disorder should be made instead of a diagnosis of **Substance Intoxication** or **Substance Withdrawal** only when the sleep disturbance is judged to be in excess of that usually associated with the intoxication or withdrawal syndrome and when the disturbance is sufficiently severe to warrant independent clinical attention. For example, insomnia is a characteristic feature of Sedative, Hypnotic, or Anxiolytic Withdrawal. Sedative-, Hypnotic-, or Anxiolytic-Induced Sleep Disorder should be diagnosed instead of Sedative, Hypnotic, or Anxiolytic Withdrawal only if the insomnia is more severe than that usually encountered with Sedative, Hypnotic, or Anxiolytic Withdrawal and requires special attention and treatment. If the substance-induced sleep disturbance occurs exclusively during the course of a **delirium,** the sleep disturbance is considered to be an associated feature of the delirium and is not diagnosed separately. In **substance-induced presentations that contain a mix of different types of symptoms** (e.g., sleep, mood, and anxiety), the specific type of Substance-Induced Disorder to be diagnosed depends on which type of symptoms predominates in the clinical presentation.

A Substance-Induced Sleep Disorder is distinguished from a **primary Sleep Disorder** and from **Insomnia** or **Hypersomnia Related to Another Mental Disorder** by the fact that a substance is judged to be etiologically related to the symptoms (see p. 602).

A Substance-Induced Sleep Disorder due to a prescribed treatment for a mental disorder or general medical condition must have its onset while the person is receiving the medication (or during withdrawal, if there is a withdrawal syndrome associated with the medication). Once the treatment is discontinued, the sleep disturbance will usually remit within days to several weeks (depending on the half-life of the substance and the presence of a withdrawal syndrome). If symptoms persist beyond 4 weeks, other causes for the sleep disturbance should be considered. Not infrequently, individuals with a primary Sleep Disorder use medications or drugs of abuse to relieve their symptoms. If the clinician judges that the substance is playing a significant role in the exacerbation of the sleep disturbance, an additional diagnosis of a Substance-Induced Sleep Disorder may be warranted.

A Substance-Induced Sleep Disorder and **Sleep Disorder Due to a General Medical Condition** can also be difficult to distinguish. Both may produce similar symptoms of insomnia, hypersomnia, or (more rarely) a Parasomnia. Furthermore, many individuals with general medical conditions that cause a sleep complaint are treated with medications that may also cause disturbances in sleep. The chronology of symptoms is the most important factor in distinguishing between these two causes of sleep disturbance. For instance, a sleep disturbance that clearly preceded the use of any medication for treatment of a general medical condition would suggest a diagnosis of Sleep Disorder Due to a General Medical Condition. Conversely, sleep symptoms that appear only after the institution of a particular medication or substance would suggest a Substance-Induced Sleep Disorder. In a similar way, a sleep disturbance that appears during treatment for a general medical condition but that improves after the medication is discontinued suggests a diagnosis of Substance-Induced Sleep Disorder. If the clinician has ascertained that the disturbance is due to both a general medical condition and substance use, both diagnoses (i.e., Sleep Disorder Due to a General Medical Condition and Substance-Induced Sleep Disorder) are given. When there is insufficient evidence to determine whether the sleep disturbance is due to a substance (including a medication) or to a general medical condition or is primary (i.e., not due to either a substance or a general medical condition), **Parasomnia Not Otherwise Specified** or **Dyssomnia Not Otherwise Specified** would be indicated.

■ Diagnostic criteria for Substance-Induced Sleep Disorder

A. A prominent disturbance in sleep that is sufficiently severe to warrant independent clinical attention.

B. There is evidence from the history, physical examination, or laboratory findings of either (1) or (2):

(1) the symptoms in Criterion A developed during, or within a month of, Substance Intoxication or Withdrawal

(2) medication use is etiologically related to the sleep disturbance

(continued)

☐ **Diagnostic criteria for Substance-Induced Sleep Disorder** (*continued*)

C. The disturbance is not better accounted for by a Sleep Disorder that is not substance induced. Evidence that the symptoms are better accounted for by a Sleep Disorder that is not substance induced might include the following: the symptoms precede the onset of the substance use (or medication use); the symptoms persist for a substantial period of time (e.g., about a month) after the cessation of acute withdrawal or severe intoxication, or are substantially in excess of what would be expected given the type or amount of the substance used or the duration of use; or there is other evidence that suggests the existence of an independent non-substance-induced Sleep Disorder (e.g., a history of recurrent non-substance-related episodes).

D. The disturbance does not occur exclusively during the course of a delirium.

E. The sleep disturbance causes clinically significant distress or impairment in social, occupational, or other important areas of functioning.

Note: This diagnosis should be made instead of a diagnosis of Substance Intoxication or Substance Withdrawal only when the sleep symptoms are in excess of those usually associated with the intoxication or withdrawal syndrome and when the symptoms are sufficiently severe to warrant independent clinical attention.

Code [Specific Substance]–Induced Sleep Disorder:
   (291.8 Alcohol; 292.89 Amphetamine; 292.89 Caffeine; 292.89 Cocaine; 292.89 Opioid; 292.89 Sedative, Hypnotic, or Anxiolytic; 292.89 Other [or Unknown] Substance)

Specify type:
   Insomnia Type: if the predominant sleep disturbance is insomnia
   Hypersomnia Type: if the predominant sleep disturbance is hypersomnia
   Parasomnia Type: if the predominant sleep disturbance is a Parasomnia
   Mixed Type: if more than one sleep disturbance is present and none predominates

Specify if (see table on p. 177 for applicability by substance):
   With Onset During Intoxication: if the criteria are met for Intoxication with the substance and the symptoms develop during the intoxication syndrome
   With Onset During Withdrawal: if criteria are met for Withdrawal from the substance and the symptoms develop during, or shortly after, a withdrawal syndrome

Impulse-Control Disorders Not Elsewhere Classified

This section includes disorders of impulse control that are not classified as part of the presentation of disorders in other sections of the manual (e.g., Substance-Related Disorders, Paraphilias, Antisocial Personality Disorder, Conduct Disorder, Schizophrenia, Mood Disorders may have features that involve problems of impulse control). The essential feature of Impulse-Control Disorders is the failure to resist an impulse, drive, or temptation to perform an act that is harmful to the person or to others. For most of the disorders in this section, the individual feels an increasing sense of tension or arousal before committing the act and then experiences pleasure, gratification, or relief at the time of committing the act. Following the act there may or may not be regret, self-reproach, or guilt. The following disorders are included in this section:

Intermittent Explosive Disorder is characterized by discrete episodes of failure to resist aggressive impulses resulting in serious assaults or destruction of property.

Kleptomania is characterized by the recurrent failure to resist impulses to steal objects not needed for personal use or monetary value.

Pyromania is characterized by a pattern of fire setting for pleasure, gratification, or relief of tension.

Pathological Gambling is characterized by recurrent and persistent maladaptive gambling behavior.

Trichotillomania is characterized by recurrent pulling out of one's hair for pleasure, gratification, or relief of tension that results in noticeable hair loss.

Impulse-Control Disorder Not Otherwise Specified is included for coding disorders of impulse control that do not meet the criteria for any of the specific Impulse-Control Disorders described above or in other sections of the manual.

312.34   Intermittent Explosive Disorder

Diagnostic Features

The essential feature of Intermittent Explosive Disorder is the occurrence of discrete episodes of failure to resist aggressive impulses that result in serious assaultive acts or destruction of property (Criterion A). The degree of aggressiveness expressed during an episode is grossly out of proportion to any provocation or precipitating psychosocial stressor (Criterion B). A diagnosis of Intermittent Explosive Disorder is made only after other mental disorders that might account for episodes of aggressive behavior have been ruled out (e.g., Antisocial Personality Disorder, Borderline Personality Disorder, a Psychotic Disorder, a Manic Episode, Conduct Disorder, or Attention Deficit/ Hyperactivity Disorder) (Criterion C). The aggressive episodes are not due to the direct physiological effects of a substance (e.g., a drug of abuse, a medication) or a general medical condition (e.g., head trauma, Alzheimer's disease) (Criterion C). The individual may describe the aggressive episodes as "spells" or "attacks" in which the explosive behavior is preceded by a sense of tension or arousal and is followed immediately by a sense of relief. Later the individual may feel upset, remorseful, regretful, or embarrassed about the aggressive behavior.

Associated Features and Disorders

Associated descriptive features and mental disorders.   Signs of generalized impulsivity or aggressiveness may be present between explosive episodes. Individuals with narcissistic, obsessive, paranoid, or schizoid traits may be especially prone to having explosive outbursts of anger when under stress. The disorder may result in job loss, school suspension, divorce, difficulties with interpersonal relationships, accidents (e.g., in vehicles), hospitalization (e.g., because of injuries incurred in fights or accidents), or incarcerations.

Associated laboratory findings.   There may be nonspecific EEG findings (e.g., slowing) or evidence of abnormalities on neuropsychological testing (e.g., difficulty with letter reversal). Signs of altered serotonin metabolism have been found in the cerebrospinal fluid of some impulsive and temper-prone individuals, but the specific relationship of these findings to Intermittent Explosive Disorder is unclear.

Associated physical examination findings and general medical conditions. There may be nonspecific or "soft" findings on neurological examinations (e.g., reflex asymmetries or mirror movements). Developmental difficulties indicative of cerebral dysfunction may be present (e.g., delayed speech or poor coordination). A history of neurological conditions (e.g., head injury, episodes of unconsciousness, or febrile seizures in childhood) may be present. However, if the clinician judges that the aggressive behavior is a consequence of the direct physiological effects of a diagnosable general medical condition, the appropriate Mental Disorder Due to a General Medical Condition should be diagnosed instead (e.g., Personality Change Due to Head Trauma, Aggressive Type; Dementia of the Alzheimer's Type, Early Onset, Uncomplicated, With Behavioral Disturbance).

Specific Culture and Gender Features

Amok is characterized by an episode of acute, unrestrained violent behavior for which the person claims amnesia. Although traditionally seen in southeastern Asian countries, cases of amok have been reported in Canada and the United States. Unlike Intermittent Explosive Disorder, amok typically occurs as a single episode rather than as a pattern of aggressive behavior and is often associated with prominent dissociative features. Episodic violent behavior is more common in males than in females.

Prevalence

Reliable information is lacking, but Intermittent Explosive Disorder is apparently rare.

Course

Limited data are available on the age at onset of Intermittent Explosive Disorder, but it appears to be from late adolescence to the third decade of life. Mode of onset may be abrupt and without a prodromal period.

Differential Diagnosis

Aggressive behavior can occur in the context of many other mental disorders. A diagnosis of Intermittent Explosive Disorder should be considered only after all other disorders that are associated with aggressive impulses or behavior have been ruled out. If the aggressive behavior occurs exclusively during the course of a **delirium,** a diagnosis of Intermittent Explosive Disorder is not given. Similarly, when the behavior develops as part of a **dementia,** a diagnosis of Intermittent Explosive Disorder is not made and the appropriate diagnosis is dementia with the specifier With Behavioral Disturbance. Intermittent Explosive Disorder should be distinguished from **Personality Change Due to a General Medical Condition, Aggressive Type,** which is diagnosed when the pattern of aggressive episodes is judged to be due to the direct physiological effects of a diagnosable general medical condition (e.g., an individual who has suffered brain injury from an automobile accident and subsequently manifests a change in personality characterized by aggressive outbursts). A careful history and a thorough neurological evaluation are helpful in making the determination. Note that nonspecific abnormalities on neurological examination (e.g., "soft signs") and nonspecific EEG changes are compatible with a diagnosis of Intermittent Explosive Disorder and only preempt the diagnosis if they are indicative of a diagnosable general medical condition.

Aggressive outbursts may also occur in association with **Substance Intoxication** or **Substance Withdrawal,** particularly associated with alcohol, phencyclidine, cocaine and other stimulants, barbiturates, and inhalants. The clinician should inquire carefully about the nature and extent of substance use, and a blood or urine drug screen may be informative.

Intermittent Explosive Disorder should be distinguished from the aggressive or erratic behavior that can occur in **Oppositional Defiant Disorder, Conduct Disorder, Antisocial Personality Disorder, Borderline Personality Disorder**, a **Manic Episode,** and **Schizophrenia.** If the aggressive behavior is better accounted for as a diagnostic or associated feature of another mental disorder, a separate diagnosis of Intermittent Explosive Disorder is not given. Aggressive behavior may, of course, occur when no mental disorder is present. **Purposeful behavior** is distinguished from Intermittent Explosive Disorder by the presence of motivation and gain in the aggressive act. In forensic settings, individuals may **malinger** Intermittent Explosive Disorder to avoid responsibility for their behavior.

> ### ■ Diagnostic criteria for 312.34 Intermittent Explosive Disorder
>
> A. Several discrete episodes of failure to resist aggressive impulses that result in serious assaultive acts or destruction of property.
>
> B. The degree of aggressiveness expressed during the episodes is grossly out of proportion to any precipitating psychosocial stressors.
>
> C. The aggressive episodes are not better accounted for by another mental disorder (e.g., Antisocial Personality Disorder, Borderline Personality Disorder, a Psychotic Disorder, a Manic Episode, Conduct Disorder, or Attention-Deficit/Hyperactivity Disorder) and are not due to the direct physiological effects of a substance (e.g., a drug of abuse, a medication) or a general medical condition (e.g., head trauma, Alzheimer's disease).

312.32   Kleptomania

Diagnostic Features

The essential feature of Kleptomania is the recurrent failure to resist impulses to steal items even though the items are not needed for personal use or for their monetary value (Criterion A). The individual experiences a rising subjective sense of tension before the theft (Criterion B) and feels pleasure, gratification, or relief when committing the theft (Criterion C). The stealing is not committed to express anger or vengeance, is not done in response to a delusion or hallucination (Criterion D), and is not better accounted for by Conduct Disorder, a Manic Episode, or Antisocial Personality Disorder (Criterion E). The objects are stolen despite the fact that they are typically of little value to the individual, who could have afforded to pay for them and often gives them away or discards them. Occasionally the individual may hoard the stolen objects or surreptitiously return them. Although individuals with this disorder will generally avoid stealing when immediate arrest is probable (e.g., in full view of a police officer), they usually do not preplan the thefts or fully take into account the chances of apprehension. The stealing is done without assistance from, or collaboration with, others.

Associated Features and Disorders

Individuals with Kleptomania experience the impulse to steal as ego-dystonic and are aware that the act is wrong and senseless. The person frequently fears being apprehended and often feels depressed or guilty about the thefts. Mood Disorders (especially Major Depressive Disorder), Anxiety Disorders, Eating Disorders (particularly Bulimia Nervosa), and Personality Disorders may be associated with Kleptomania. The disorder may cause legal, family, career, and personal difficulties.

Prevalence

Kleptomania is a rare condition that appears to occur in fewer than 5% of identified shoplifters. It appears to be much more common in females.

Course

There is little systematic information on the course of Kleptomania, but three typical courses have been described: sporadic with brief episodes and long periods of remission; episodic with protracted periods of stealing and periods of remission; and chronic with some degree of fluctuation. The disorder may continue for years, despite multiple convictions for shoplifting.

Differential Diagnosis

Kleptomania should be distinguished from **ordinary acts of theft or shoplifting.** Ordinary theft (whether planned or impulsive) is deliberate and is motivated by the usefulness of the object or its monetary worth. Some individuals, especially adolescents, may also steal on a dare, as an act of rebellion, or as a rite of passage. The diagnosis is not made unless other characteristic features of Kleptomania are also present. Kleptomania is exceedingly rare, whereas shoplifting is relatively common. In **Malingering,** individuals may simulate the symptoms of Kleptomania to avoid criminal prosecution. **Antisocial Personality Disorder** and **Conduct Disorder** are distinguished from Kleptomania by a general pattern of antisocial behavior. Kleptomania should be distinguished from intentional or inadvertent stealing that may occur during a **Manic Episode,** in response to delusions or hallucinations (e.g., in **Schizophrenia**), or as a result of a **dementia.**

■ Diagnostic criteria for 312.32 Kleptomania

A. Recurrent failure to resist impulses to steal objects that are not needed for personal use or for their monetary value.

B. Increasing sense of tension immediately before committing the theft.

C. Pleasure, gratification, or relief at the time of committing the theft.

D. The stealing is not committed to express anger or vengeance and is not in response to a delusion or a hallucination.

E. The stealing is not better accounted for by Conduct Disorder, a Manic Episode, or Antisocial Personality Disorder.

312.33 Pyromania

Diagnostic Features

The essential feature of Pyromania is the presence of multiple episodes of deliberate and purposeful fire setting (Criterion A). Individuals with this disorder experience tension or affective arousal before setting a fire (Criterion B). There is a fascination with, interest in, curiosity about, or attraction to fire and its situational contexts (e.g., paraphernalia, uses, consequences) (Criterion C). Individuals with this disorder are often regular "watchers" at fires in their neighborhoods, may set off false alarms, and derive pleasure from institutions, equipment, and personnel associated with fire. They may spend time at the local fire department, set fires to be affiliated with the fire department, or even become firefighters. Individuals with this disorder experience pleasure, gratification, or a release of tension when setting the fire, witnessing its effects, or participating in its aftermath (Criterion D). The fire setting is not done for monetary gain, as an expression of sociopolitical ideology, to conceal criminal activity, to express anger or vengeance, to improve one's living circumstances, or in response to a delusion or a hallucination (Criterion E). The fire setting does not result from impaired judgment (e.g., in dementia, Mental Retardation, or Substance Intoxication). The diagnosis is not made if the fire setting is better accounted for by Conduct Disorder, a Manic Episode, or Antisocial Personality Disorder (Criterion F).

Associated Features and Disorders

Individuals with Pyromania may make considerable advance preparation for starting a fire. They may be indifferent to the consequences to life or property caused by the fire, or they may derive satisfaction from the resulting property destruction. The behaviors may lead to property damage, legal consequences, or injury or loss of life to the fire setter or to others.

Specific Age and Gender Features

Although fire setting is a major problem in children and adolescents (over 40% of those arrested for arson offenses in the United States are under age 18 years), Pyromania in childhood appears to be rare. Juvenile fire setting is usually associated with Conduct Disorder, Attention-Deficit/Hyperactivity Disorder, or Adjustment Disorder. Pyromania occurs much more often in males, especially those with poorer social skills and learning difficulties.

Prevalence

Pyromania is apparently rare.

Course

There are insufficient data to establish a typical age at onset of Pyromania. The relationship between fire setting in childhood and Pyromania in adulthood has not been documented. In individuals with Pyromania, fire-setting incidents are episodic and may wax and wane in frequency. Longitudinal course is unknown.

Differential Diagnosis

It is important to rule out other causes of fire setting before giving the diagnosis of Pyromania. Intentional fire setting may occur for **profit, sabotage, or revenge; to conceal a crime; to make a political statement** (e.g., an act of terrorism or protest); or **to attract attention or recognition** (e.g., setting a fire in order to discover it and save the day). Fire setting may also occur as part of **developmental experimentation in childhood** (e.g., playing with matches, lighters, or fire). Some individuals with mental disorders use fire setting to communicate a desire, wish, or need, often directed at gaining a change in the nature or location of services. This form of fire setting has been referred to as "communicative arson" and must be carefully distinguished from Pyromania. A separate diagnosis of Pyromania is not given when fire setting occurs as part of **Conduct Disorder,** a **Manic Episode,** or **Antisocial Personality Disorder,** or if it occurs in response to a delusion or a hallucination (e.g., in **Schizophrenia**). The diagnosis of Pyromania should also not be given when fire setting results from impaired judgment associated with **dementia, Mental Retardation,** or **Substance Intoxication.**

■ Diagnostic criteria for 312.33 Pyromania

A. Deliberate and purposeful fire setting on more than one occasion.

B. Tension or affective arousal before the act.

C. Fascination with, interest in, curiosity about, or attraction to fire and its situational contexts (e.g., paraphernalia, uses, consequences).

D. Pleasure, gratification, or relief when setting fires, or when witnessing or participating in their aftermath.

E. The fire setting is not done for monetary gain, as an expression of sociopolitical ideology, to conceal criminal activity, to express anger or vengeance, to improve one's living circumstances, in response to a delusion or hallucination, or as a result of impaired judgment (e.g., in dementia, Mental Retardation, Substance Intoxication).

F. The fire setting is not better accounted for by Conduct Disorder, a Manic Episode, or Antisocial Personality Disorder.

312.31 Pathological Gambling

Diagnostic Features

The essential feature of Pathological Gambling is persistent and recurrent maladaptive gambling behavior (Criterion A) that disrupts personal, family, or vocational pursuits. The diagnosis is not made if the gambling behavior is better accounted for by a Manic Episode (Criterion B).

The individual may be preoccupied with gambling (e.g., reliving past gambling experiences, planning the next gambling venture, or thinking of ways to get money with which to gamble) (Criterion A1). Most individuals with Pathological Gambling say that they are seeking "action" (an aroused, euphoric state) even more than money. Increasingly larger bets, or greater risks, may be needed to continue to produce the desired level of excitement (Criterion A2). Individuals with Pathological Gambling often continue to gamble despite repeated efforts to control, cut back, or stop the behavior (Criterion A3). There may be restlessness or irritability when attempting to cut down or stop gambling (Criterion A4). The individual may gamble as a way of escaping from problems or to relieve a dysphoric mood (e.g., feelings of helplessness, guilt, anxiety, depression) (Criterion A5). A pattern of "chasing" one's losses may develop, with an urgent need to keep gambling (often with larger bets or the taking of greater risks) to undo a loss or series of losses. The individual may abandon his or her gambling strategy and try to win back losses all at once. Although all gamblers may chase for short periods, it is the long-term chase that is more characteristic of individuals with Pathological Gambling (Criterion A6). The individual may lie to family members, therapists, or others to conceal the extent of involvement with gambling (Criterion A7). When the individual's borrowing resources are strained, the person may resort to antisocial behavior (e.g., forgery, fraud, theft, or embezzlement) to obtain money (Criterion A8). The individual may have jeopardized or lost a significant relationship, job, or educational or career opportunity because of gambling (Criterion A9). The individual may also engage in "bailout" behavior, turning to family or others for help with a desperate financial situation that was caused by gambling (Criterion A10).

Associated Features and Disorders

Distortions in thinking (e.g., denial, superstitions, overconfidence, or a sense of power and control) may be present in individuals with Pathological Gambling. Many individuals with Pathological Gambling believe that money is both the cause of and solution to all their problems. Individuals with Pathological Gambling are frequently highly competitive, energetic, restless, and easily bored. They may be overly concerned with the approval of others and may be generous to the point of extravagance. When not gambling, they may be workaholics or "binge" workers who wait until they are up against deadlines before really working hard. They may be prone to developing general medical conditions that are associated with stress (e.g., hypertension, peptic ulcer disease, migraine). Increased rates of Mood Disorders, Attention-Deficit/Hyperactivity Disorder, Substance Abuse or Dependence, and Antisocial, Narcissistic, and Borderline Personality Disorders have been reported in individuals with Pathological Gambling. Of individuals in treatment for Pathological Gambling, 20% are reported to have attempted suicide.

Specific Culture and Gender Features

There are cultural variations in the prevalence and type of gambling activities (e.g., pai go, cockfights, horse racing, the stock market). Approximately one-third of individuals with Pathological Gambling are females. Females with the disorder are more apt to be depressed and to gamble as an escape. Females are underrepresented in treatment programs for gambling and represent only 2%–4% of the population of Gamblers

Anonymous. This may be a function of the greater stigma attached to female gamblers.

Prevalence

The limited data available suggest that the prevalence of Pathological Gambling may be as high as 1%–3% of the adult population.

Course

Pathological Gambling typically begins in early adolescence in males and later in life in females. Although a few individuals are "hooked" with their very first bet, for most the course is more insidious. There may be years of social gambling followed by an abrupt onset that may be precipitated by greater exposure to gambling or by a stressor. The gambling pattern may be regular or episodic, and the course of the disorder is typically chronic. There is generally a progression in the frequency of gambling, the amount wagered, and the preoccupation with gambling and obtaining money with which to gamble. The urge to gamble and gambling activity generally increase during periods of stress or depression.

Familial Pattern

Pathological Gambling and Alcohol Dependence are both more common among the parents of individuals with Pathological Gambling than among the general population.

Differential Diagnosis

Pathological Gambling must be distinguished from social gambling and professional gambling. **Social gambling** typically occurs with friends or colleagues and lasts for a limited period of time, with predetermined acceptable losses. In **professional gambling,** risks are limited and discipline is central. Some individuals can experience problems associated with their gambling (e.g., short-term chasing behavior and loss of control) that do not meet the full criteria for Pathological Gambling.

Loss of judgment and excessive gambling may occur during a **Manic Episode.** An additional diagnosis of Pathological Gambling should only be given if the gambling behavior is not better accounted for by the Manic Episode (e.g., a history of maladaptive gambling behavior at times other than during a Manic Episode). Alternatively, an individual with Pathological Gambling may exhibit behavior during a gambling binge that resembles a Manic Episode. However, once the individual is away from the gambling, these manic-like features dissipate. Problems with gambling may occur in individuals with **Antisocial Personality Disorder;** if criteria are met for both disorders, both can be diagnosed.

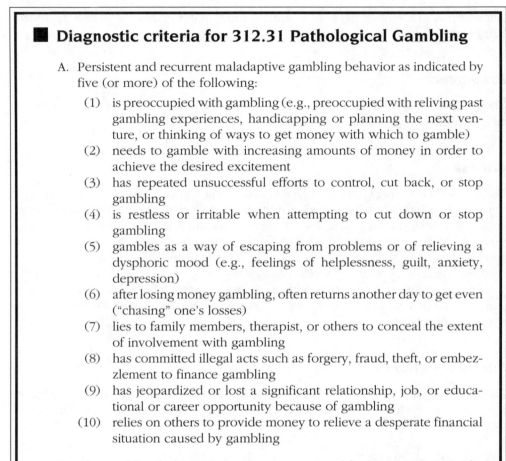

■ **Diagnostic criteria for 312.31 Pathological Gambling**

A. Persistent and recurrent maladaptive gambling behavior as indicated by five (or more) of the following:

(1) is preoccupied with gambling (e.g., preoccupied with reliving past gambling experiences, handicapping or planning the next venture, or thinking of ways to get money with which to gamble)

(2) needs to gamble with increasing amounts of money in order to achieve the desired excitement

(3) has repeated unsuccessful efforts to control, cut back, or stop gambling

(4) is restless or irritable when attempting to cut down or stop gambling

(5) gambles as a way of escaping from problems or of relieving a dysphoric mood (e.g., feelings of helplessness, guilt, anxiety, depression)

(6) after losing money gambling, often returns another day to get even ("chasing" one's losses)

(7) lies to family members, therapist, or others to conceal the extent of involvement with gambling

(8) has committed illegal acts such as forgery, fraud, theft, or embezzlement to finance gambling

(9) has jeopardized or lost a significant relationship, job, or educational or career opportunity because of gambling

(10) relies on others to provide money to relieve a desperate financial situation caused by gambling

B. The gambling behavior is not better accounted for by a Manic Episode.

312.39 Trichotillomania

Diagnostic Features

The essential feature of Trichotillomania is the recurrent pulling out of one's own hair that results in noticeable hair loss (Criterion A). Sites of hair pulling may include any region of the body in which hair may grow (including axillary, pubic, and perirectal regions), with the most common sites being the scalp, eyebrows, and eyelashes. Hair pulling may occur in brief episodes scattered throughout the day or in less frequent but more sustained periods that can continue for hours. Stressful circumstances frequently increase hair-pulling behavior, but increased hair pulling also occurs in states of relaxation and distraction (e.g., when reading a book or watching television). An increasing sense of tension is present immediately before pulling out the hair (Criterion B). For some, tension does not necessarily precede the act but is associated with attempts to resist the urge. There is gratification, pleasure, or a sense of relief when pulling out the hair (Criterion C). Some individuals experience an "itchlike" sensation in the scalp that is eased by the act of pulling hair. The diagnosis is not given if the hair pulling is better accounted for by another mental disorder (e.g., in response to a delusion or a hallucination) or is due to a general medical condition (e.g., inflammation of the skin or other dermatological conditions) (Criterion D). The disturbance must cause significant distress or impairment in social, occupational, or other important areas of functioning (Criterion E).

Associated Features and Disorders

Associated descriptive features and mental disorders.   Examining the hair root, twirling it off, pulling the strand between the teeth, or trichophagia (eating hairs) may occur with Trichotillomania. Hair pulling does not usually occur in the presence of other people (except immediate family members), and social situations may be avoided. Individuals commonly deny their hair-pulling behavior and conceal or camouflage the resulting alopecia. Some individuals have urges to pull hairs from other people and may sometimes try to find opportunities to do so surreptitiously. They may pull hairs from pets, dolls, and other fibrous materials (e.g., sweaters or carpets). Nail biting, scratching, gnawing, and excoriation may be associated with Trichotillomania. Individuals with Trichotillomania may also have Mood Disorders, Anxiety Disorders, or Mental Retardation.

Associated laboratory findings.   Certain histological findings are considered characteristic and may aid diagnosis when Trichotillomania is suspected and the affected individual denies symptoms. Biopsy samples from involved areas may reveal short and broken hairs. Histological examination will reveal normal and damaged follicles in the same area, as well as an increased number of catagen hairs. Some hair follicles may show signs of trauma (wrinkling of the outer root sheath). Involved follicles may be empty or may contain a deeply pigmented keratinous material. The absence of inflammation distinguishes Trichotillomania-induced alopecia from alopecia areata.

Associated physical examination findings and general medical conditions. Pain is not routinely reported to accompany the hair pulling; pruritus and tingling in the involved areas may be present. The patterns of hair loss are highly variable. Areas of complete alopecia are common, as well as areas of noticeably thinned hair density. When the scalp is involved, there may be a predilection for the crown or parietal regions. The surface of the scalp usually shows no evidence of excoriation. There may be a pattern of nearly complete baldness except for a narrow perimeter around the outer margins of the scalp, particularly at the nape of the neck ("tonsure trichotillomania"). Eyebrows and eyelashes may be completely absent. Thinning of pubic hairs may be apparent on inspection. There may be areas of absent hair on the limbs or torso. Trichophagia may result in bezoars (hair balls) that may lead to anemia, abdominal pain, hematemesis, nausea and vomiting, and bowel obstruction and even perforation.

Specific Culture, Age, and Gender Features

Among children with Trichotillomania, males and females are equally represented. Among adults, Trichotillomania appears to be much more common among females than among males. This may reflect the true gender ratio of the condition or it may reflect differential treatment seeking based on cultural or gender-based attitudes regarding appearance (e.g., acceptance of normative hair loss among males).

Prevalence

No systematic data are available on the prevalence of Trichotillomania. Although Trichotillomania was previously thought to be an uncommon condition, it is now believed to occur more frequently. Recent surveys of college samples suggest that 1%–2% of students have a past or current history of Trichotillomania.

Course

Transient periods of hair pulling in early childhood may be considered a benign "habit" with a self-limited course. However, many individuals who present with chronic Trichotillomania in adulthood report onset in early childhood. The age at onset is usually before young adulthood, with peaks at around ages 5–8 years and age 13 years. Some individuals have continuous symptoms for decades. For others, the disorder may come and go for weeks, months, or years at a time. Sites of hair pulling may vary over time.

Differential Diagnosis

Other causes of alopecia should be considered in individuals who deny hair pulling (e.g., alopecia areata, male-pattern baldness, chronic discoid lupus erythematosus, lichen planopilaris, folliculitis decalvans, pseudopelade, and alopecia mucinosa). A separate diagnosis of Trichotillomania is not given if the behavior is better accounted for by **another mental disorder** (e.g., in response to a delusion or a hallucination in Schizophrenia). The repetitive hair pulling in Trichotillomania must be distinguished from a compulsion, as in **Obsessive-Compulsive Disorder.** In Obsessive-Compulsive Disorder, the repetitive behaviors are performed in response to an obsession, or according to rules that must be applied rigidly. An additional diagnosis of **Stereotypic Movement Disorder** is not made if the repetitive behavior is limited to hair pulling. The self-induced alopecia in Trichotillomania must be distinguished from **Factitious Disorder With Predominantly Physical Signs and Symptoms,** in which the motivation for the behavior is assuming the sick role.

Many individuals twist and play with hair, especially during states of heightened anxiety, but this behavior does not usually qualify for a diagnosis of Trichotillomania. Some individuals may present with features of Trichotillomania, but the resulting hair damage may be so slight as to be virtually undetectable. In such situations, the diagnosis should only be considered if the individual experiences significant distress. In children, self-limited periods of hair pulling are common and may be considered a temporary "habit." Therefore, among children, the diagnosis should be reserved for situations in which the behavior has persisted for several months.

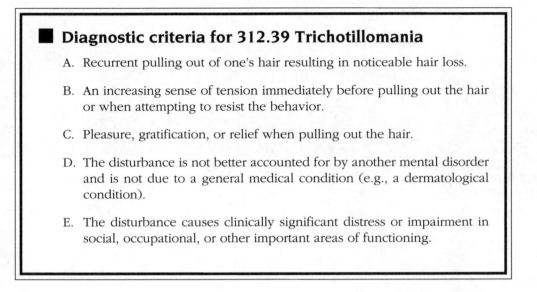

■ **Diagnostic criteria for 312.39 Trichotillomania**

A. Recurrent pulling out of one's hair resulting in noticeable hair loss.

B. An increasing sense of tension immediately before pulling out the hair or when attempting to resist the behavior.

C. Pleasure, gratification, or relief when pulling out the hair.

D. The disturbance is not better accounted for by another mental disorder and is not due to a general medical condition (e.g., a dermatological condition).

E. The disturbance causes clinically significant distress or impairment in social, occupational, or other important areas of functioning.

312.30 Impulse-Control Disorder Not Otherwise Specified

This category is for disorders of impulse control that do not meet the criteria for any specific Impulse-Control Disorder or for another mental disorder having features involving impulse control described elsewhere in the manual (e.g., Substance Dependence, a Paraphilia).

Adjustment Disorders

Diagnostic Features

The essential feature of an Adjustment Disorder is the development of clinically significant emotional or behavioral symptoms in response to an identifiable psychosocial stressor or stressors. The symptoms must develop within 3 months after the onset of the stressor(s) (Criterion A). The clinical significance of the reaction is indicated either by marked distress that is in excess of what would be expected given the nature of the stressor, or by significant impairment in social or occupational (academic) functioning (Criterion B). This category should not be used if the disturbance meets the criteria for another specific Axis I disorder (e.g., a specific Anxiety or Mood Disorder) or is merely an exacerbation of a preexisting Axis I or II disorder (Criterion C). However, an Adjustment Disorder may be diagnosed in the presence of another Axis I or Axis II disorder if the latter does not account for the pattern of symptoms that have occurred in response to the stressor. The diagnosis of an Adjustment Disorder also does not apply when the symptoms represent Bereavement (Criterion D). By definition, an Adjustment Disorder must resolve within 6 months of the termination of the stressor (or its consequences) (Criterion E). However, the symptoms may persist for a prolonged period (i.e., longer than 6 months) if they occur in response to a chronic stressor (e.g., a chronic, disabling general medical condition) or to a stressor that has enduring consequences (e.g., the financial and emotional difficulties resulting from a divorce).

The stressor may be a single event (e.g., termination of a romantic relationship), or there may be multiple stressors (e.g., marked business difficulties and marital problems). Stressors may be recurrent (e.g., associated with seasonal business crises) or continuous (e.g., living in a crime-ridden neighborhood). Stressors may affect a single individual, an entire family, or a larger group or community (e.g., as in a natural disaster). Some stressors may accompany specific developmental events (e.g., going to school, leaving the parental home, getting married, becoming a parent, failing to attain occupational goals, retirement).

Subtypes and Specifiers

Adjustment Disorders are coded according to the subtype that best characterizes the predominant symptoms:

> **309.0 With Depressed Mood.** This subtype should be used when the predominant manifestations are symptoms such as depressed mood, tearfulness, or feelings of hopelessness.

309.24 With Anxiety. This subtype should be used when the predominant manifestations are symptoms such as nervousness, worry, or jitteriness or, in children, fears of separation from major attachment figures.

309.28 With Mixed Anxiety and Depressed Mood. This subtype should be used when the predominant manifestation is a combination of depression and anxiety.

309.3 With Disturbance of Conduct. This subtype should be used when the predominant manifestation is a disturbance in conduct in which there is violation of the rights of others or of major age-appropriate societal norms and rules (e.g., truancy, vandalism, reckless driving, fighting, defaulting on legal responsibilities).

309.4 With Mixed Disturbance of Emotions and Conduct. This subtype should be used when the predominant manifestations are both emotional symptoms (e.g., depression, anxiety) and a disturbance of conduct (see above subtype).

309.9 Unspecified. This subtype should be used for maladaptive reactions (e.g., physical complaints, social withdrawal, or work or academic inhibition) to psychosocial stressors that are not classifiable as one of the specific subtypes of Adjustment Disorder.

The duration of the symptoms of an Adjustment Disorder can be indicated by choosing one of the following specifiers:

Acute. This specifier can be used to indicate persistence of symptoms for less than 6 months.

Chronic. This specifier can be used to indicate persistence of symptoms for 6 months or longer. By definition, symptoms cannot persist for more than 6 months after the termination of the stressor or its consequences. The Chronic specifier therefore applies when the duration of the disturbance is longer than 6 months in response to a chronic stressor or to a stressor that has enduring consequences.

Reporting Procedures

The predominant symptom presentation for an Adjustment Disorder should be indicated by choosing the diagnostic code and term from the list above, followed, if desired, by the Acute or Chronic specifier (e.g., 309.0 Adjustment Disorder With Depressed Mood, Acute). In a multiaxial assessment, the nature of the stressor can be indicated by listing it on Axis IV (e.g., Divorce).

Associated Features and Disorders

The subjective distress or impairment in functioning associated with Adjustment Disorders is frequently manifested as decreased performance at work or school and temporary changes in social relationships. Adjustment Disorders are associated with an increased risk of suicide attempts and suicide. The presence of an Adjustment Disorder may complicate the course of illness in individuals who have a general medical condition (e.g., decreased compliance with the recommended medical regimen or increased length of hospital stay).

Specific Culture, Age, and Gender Features

The context of the individual's cultural setting should be taken into account in making the clinical judgment of whether the individual's response to the stressor is maladaptive or whether the associated distress is in excess of what would be expected. The nature, meaning, and experience of the stressors and the evaluation of the response to the stressors may vary across cultures. Adjustment Disorders may occur in any age group, and males and females are equally affected.

Prevalence

Adjustment Disorders are apparently common, although epidemiological figures vary widely as a function of the population studied and the assessment methods used. The percentage of individuals in outpatient mental health treatment with a principal diagnosis of Adjustment Disorder ranges from approximately 5% to 20%. Individuals from disadvantaged life circumstances experience a high rate of stressors and may be at increased risk for the disorder.

Course

By definition, the disturbance in Adjustment Disorder begins within 3 months of onset of a stressor and lasts no longer than 6 months after the stressor or its consequences have ceased. If the stressor is an acute event (e.g., being fired from a job), the onset of the disturbance is usually immediate (or within a few days) and the duration is relatively brief (e.g., no more than a few months). If the stressor or its consequences persist, the Adjustment Disorder may also persist.

Differential Diagnosis

Adjustment Disorder is a residual category used to describe presentations that are a response to an identifiable stressor and that do not meet the criteria for another specific Axis I disorder. For example, if an individual has symptoms that meet criteria for a Major Depressive Episode in response to a stressor, the diagnosis of Adjustment Disorder is not applicable. Adjustment Disorder can be diagnosed in addition to another Axis I disorder only if the latter does not account for the particular symptoms that occur in reaction to the stressor. For example, an individual may develop Adjustment Disorder With Depressed Mood after losing a job and at the same time have a diagnosis of Obsessive-Compulsive Disorder.

Because **Personality Disorders** are frequently exacerbated by stress, the additional diagnosis of Adjustment Disorder is usually not made. However, if symptoms that are not characteristic of the Personality Disorder appear in response to a stressor (e.g., a person with Paranoid Personality Disorder develops depressed mood in response to job loss), the additional diagnosis of Adjustment Disorder may be appropriate.

The diagnosis of Adjustment Disorder requires the presence of an identifiable stressor, in contrast to the atypical or subthreshold presentations that would be diagnosed as a **Not Otherwise Specified disorder** (e.g., Anxiety Disorder Not Otherwise Specified). If the symptoms of Adjustment Disorder persist for more than 6 months after the stressor or its consequences have ceased, the diagnosis should be changed to another mental disorder, usually in the appropriate Not Otherwise Specified category.

Adjustment Disorder, **Posttraumatic Stress Disorder,** and **Acute Stress Disorder** all require the presence of a psychosocial stressor. Posttraumatic Stress Disorder and Acute Stress Disorder are characterized by the presence of an extreme stressor and a specific constellation of symptoms. In contrast, Adjustment Disorder can be triggered by a stressor of any severity and may involve a wide range of possible symptoms.

In **Psychological Factors Affecting Medical Condition,** specific psychological symptoms, behaviors, or other factors exacerbate a general medical condition, complicate treatment for a general medical condition, or otherwise increase the risks of developing a general medical condition. In Adjustment Disorder, the relationship is the reverse (i.e., the psychological symptoms develop in response to the stress of having or being diagnosed with a general medical condition). Both conditions may be present in some individuals.

Bereavement is generally diagnosed instead of Adjustment Disorder when the reaction is an expectable response to the death of a loved one. The diagnosis of Adjustment Disorder may be appropriate when the reaction is in excess of, or more prolonged than, what would be expected. Adjustment Disorder should also be distinguished from other **nonpathological reactions to stress** that do not lead to marked distress in excess of what is expected and that do not cause significant impairment in social or occupational functioning.

■ **Diagnostic criteria for Adjustment Disorders**

A. The development of emotional or behavioral symptoms in response to an identifiable stressor(s) occurring within 3 months of the onset of the stressor(s).

B. These symptoms or behaviors are clinically significant as evidenced by either of the following:

(1) marked distress that is in excess of what would be expected from exposure to the stressor

(2) significant impairment in social or occupational (academic) functioning

C. The stress-related disturbance does not meet the criteria for another specific Axis I disorder and is not merely an exacerbation of a preexisting Axis I or Axis II disorder.

D. The symptoms do not represent Bereavement.

E. Once the stressor (or its consequences) has terminated, the symptoms do not persist for more than an additional 6 months.

Specify if:
Acute: if the disturbance lasts less than 6 months
Chronic: if the disturbance lasts for 6 months or longer

(continued)

☐ **Diagnostic criteria for Adjustment Disorders** (*continued*)

Adjustment Disorders are coded based on the subtype, which is selected according to the predominant symptoms. The specific stressor(s) can be specified on Axis IV.

309.0	**With Depressed Mood**
309.24	**With Anxiety**
309.28	**With Mixed Anxiety and Depressed Mood**
309.3	**With Disturbance of Conduct**
309.4	**With Mixed Disturbance of Emotions and Conduct**
309.9	**Unspecified**

Personality Disorders

This section begins with a general definition of Personality Disorder that applies to each of the 10 specific Personality Disorders. A Personality Disorder is an enduring pattern of inner experience and behavior that deviates markedly from the expectations of the individual's culture, is pervasive and inflexible, has an onset in adolescence or early adulthood, is stable over time, and leads to distress or impairment. The Personality Disorders included in this section are listed below.

Paranoid Personality Disorder is a pattern of distrust and suspiciousness such that others' motives are interpreted as malevolent.

Schizoid Personality Disorder is a pattern of detachment from social relationships and a restricted range of emotional expression.

Schizotypal Personality Disorder is a pattern of acute discomfort in close relationships, cognitive or perceptual distortions, and eccentricities of behavior.

Antisocial Personality Disorder is a pattern of disregard for, and violation of, the rights of others.

Borderline Personality Disorder is a pattern of instability in interpersonal relationships, self-image, and affects, and marked impulsivity.

Histrionic Personality Disorder is a pattern of excessive emotionality and attention seeking.

Narcissistic Personality Disorder is a pattern of grandiosity, need for admiration, and lack of empathy.

Avoidant Personality Disorder is a pattern of social inhibition, feelings of inadequacy, and hypersensitivity to negative evaluation.

Dependent Personality Disorder is a pattern of submissive and clinging behavior related to an excessive need to be taken care of.

Obsessive-Compulsive Personality Disorder is a pattern of preoccupation with orderliness, perfectionism, and control.

Personality Disorder Not Otherwise Specified is a category provided for two situations: 1) the individual's personality pattern meets the general criteria for a Personality Disorder and traits of several different Personality Disorders are present, but the criteria for any specific Personality Disorder are not met; or 2) the individual's personality pattern meets the general criteria for a Personality Disorder, but the individual is considered to have a Personality Disorder that is not included in the Classification (e.g., passive-aggressive personality disorder).

The Personality Disorders are grouped into three clusters based on descriptive similarities. Cluster A includes the Paranoid, Schizoid, and Schizotypal Personality Disorders. Individuals with these disorders often appear odd or eccentric. Cluster B includes the Antisocial, Borderline, Histrionic, and Narcissistic Personality Disorders. Individuals with these disorders often appear dramatic, emotional, or erratic. Cluster C includes the Avoidant, Dependent, and Obsessive-Compulsive Personality Disorders. Individuals with these disorders often appear anxious or fearful. It should be noted that this clustering system, although useful in some research and educational situations, has serious limitations and has not been consistently validated. Moreover, individuals frequently present with co-occurring Personality Disorders from different clusters.

Diagnostic Features

Personality traits are enduring patterns of perceiving, relating to, and thinking about the environment and oneself that are exhibited in a wide range of social and personal contexts. Only when personality traits are inflexible and maladaptive and cause significant functional impairment or subjective distress do they constitute Personality Disorders. The essential feature of a Personality Disorder is an enduring pattern of inner experience and behavior that deviates markedly from the expectations of the individual's culture and is manifested in at least two of the following areas: cognition, affectivity, interpersonal functioning, or impulse control (Criterion A). This enduring pattern is inflexible and pervasive across a broad range of personal and social situations (Criterion B) and leads to clinically significant distress or impairment in social, occupational, or other important areas of functioning (Criterion C). The pattern is stable and of long duration, and its onset can be traced back at least to adolescence or early adulthood (Criterion D). The pattern is not better accounted for as a manifestation or consequence of another mental disorder (Criterion E) and is not due to the direct physiological effects of a substance (e.g., a drug of abuse, a medication, exposure to a toxin) or a general medical condition (e.g., head trauma) (Criterion F). Specific diagnostic criteria are also provided for each of the Personality Disorders included in this section. The items in the criteria sets for each of the specific Personality Disorders are listed in order of decreasing diagnostic importance as measured by relevant data on diagnostic efficiency (when available).

The diagnosis of Personality Disorders requires an evaluation of the individual's long-term patterns of functioning, and the particular personality features must be evident by early adulthood. The personality traits that define these disorders must also be distinguished from characteristics that emerge in response to specific situational stressors or more transient mental states (e.g., Mood or Anxiety Disorders, Substance Intoxication). The clinician should assess the stability of personality traits over time and across different situations. Although a single interview with the person is sometimes sufficient for making the diagnosis, it is often necessary to conduct more than one interview and to space these over time. Assessment can also be complicated by the fact that the characteristics that define a Personality Disorder may not be considered problematic by the individual (i.e., the traits are often ego-syntonic). To help overcome this difficulty, supplementary information from other informants may be helpful.

Recording Procedures

Personality Disorders are coded on Axis II. When (as is often the case) an individual's pattern of behavior meets criteria for more than one Personality Disorder, the clinician should list all relevant Personality Disorder diagnoses in order of importance. When an

Axis I disorder is not the principal diagnosis or the reason for visit, the clinician is encouraged to indicate which Personality Disorder is the principal diagnosis or the reason for visit by noting "Principal Diagnosis" or "Reason for Visit" in parentheses. In most cases, the principal diagnosis or the reason for visit is also the main focus of attention or treatment. Personality Disorder Not Otherwise Specified is the appropriate diagnosis for a "mixed" presentation in which criteria are not met for any single Personality Disorder but features of several Personality Disorders are present and involve clinically significant impairment.

Specific maladaptive personality traits that do not meet the threshold for a Personality Disorder may also be listed on Axis II. In such instances, no specific code should be used; for example, the clinician might record "Axis II: V71.09 No diagnosis on Axis II, histrionic personality traits." The use of particular defense mechanisms may also be indicated on Axis II. For example, a clinician might record "Axis II: 301.6 Dependent Personality Disorder; Frequent use of denial." Glossary definitions for specific defense mechanisms and the Defensive Functioning Scale appear in Appendix B (p. 751).

When an individual has a chronic Axis I Psychotic Disorder (e.g., Schizophrenia) that was preceded by a preexisting Personality Disorder (e.g., Schizotypal, Schizoid, Paranoid), the Personality Disorder should be recorded on Axis II, followed by "Premorbid" in parentheses. For example: Axis I: 295.30 Schizophrenia, Paranoid Type; Axis II: 301.20 Schizoid Personality Disorder (Premorbid).

Specific Culture, Age, and Gender Features

Judgments about personality functioning must take into account the individual's ethnic, cultural, and social background. Personality Disorders should not be confused with problems associated with acculturation following immigration or with the expression of habits, customs, or religious and political values professed by the individual's culture of origin. Especially when evaluating someone from a different background, it is useful for the clinician to obtain additional information from informants who are familiar with the person's cultural background.

Personality Disorder categories may be applied to children or adolescents in those relatively unusual instances in which the individual's particular maladaptive personality traits appear to be pervasive, persistent, and unlikely to be limited to a particular developmental stage or an episode of an Axis I disorder. It should be recognized that the traits of a Personality Disorder that appear in childhood will often not persist unchanged into adult life. To diagnose a Personality Disorder in an individual under age 18 years, the features must have been present for at least 1 year. The one exception to this is Antisocial Personality Disorder, which cannot be diagnosed in individuals under age 18 years (see p. 645). Although, by definition, a Personality Disorder requires an onset no later than early adulthood, individuals may not come to clinical attention until relatively late in life. A Personality Disorder may be exacerbated following the loss of significant supporting persons (e.g., a spouse) or previously stabilizing social situations (e.g., a job). However, the development of a change in personality in middle adulthood or later life warrants a thorough evaluation to determine the possible presence of a Personality Change Due to a General Medical Condition or an unrecognized Substance-Related Disorder.

Certain Personality Disorders (e.g., Antisocial Personality Disorder) are diagnosed more frequently in men. Others (e.g., Borderline, Histrionic, and Dependent Personality

Disorders) are diagnosed more frequently in women. Although these differences in prevalence probably reflect real gender differences in the presence of such patterns, clinicians must be cautious not to overdiagnose or underdiagnose certain Personality Disorders in females or in males because of social stereotypes about typical gender roles and behaviors.

Course

The features of a Personality Disorder usually become recognizable during adolescence or early adult life. By definition, a Personality Disorder is an enduring pattern of thinking, feeling, and behaving that is relatively stable over time. Some types of Personality Disorder (notably, Antisocial and Borderline Personality Disorders) tend to become less evident or to remit with age, whereas this appears to be less true for some other types (e.g., Obsessive-Compulsive and Schizotypal Personality Disorders).

Differential Diagnosis

Many of the specific criteria for the Personality Disorders describe features (e.g., suspiciousness, dependency, or insensitivity) that are also characteristic of episodes of **Axis I mental disorders.** A Personality Disorder should be diagnosed only when the defining characteristics appeared before early adulthood, are typical of the individual's long-term functioning, and do not occur exclusively during an episode of an Axis I disorder. It may be particularly difficult (and not particularly useful) to distinguish Personality Disorders from those Axis I disorders (e.g., Dysthymic Disorder) that have an early onset and a chronic, relatively stable course. Some Personality Disorders may have a "spectrum" relationship to particular Axis I conditions (e.g., Schizotypal Personality Disorder with Schizophrenia; Avoidant Personality Disorder with Social Phobia) based on phenomenological or biological similarities or familial aggregation.

For the three Personality Disorders that may be related to the **Psychotic Disorders** (i.e., Paranoid, Schizoid, and Schizotypal), there is an exclusion criterion stating that the pattern of behavior must not have occurred exclusively during the course of Schizophrenia, a Mood Disorder With Psychotic Features, or another Psychotic Disorder. When an individual has a chronic Axis I Psychotic Disorder (e.g., Schizophrenia) that was preceded by a preexisting Personality Disorder, the Personality Disorder should also be recorded, on Axis II, followed by "Premorbid" in parentheses.

The clinician must be cautious in diagnosing Personality Disorders during an episode of a **Mood Disorder** or an **Anxiety Disorder** because these conditions may have cross-sectional symptom features that mimic personality traits and may make it more difficult to evaluate retrospectively the individual's long-term patterns of functioning. When personality changes emerge and persist after an individual has been exposed to extreme stress, a diagnosis of **Posttraumatic Stress Disorder** should be considered (see p. 424). When a person has a **Substance-Related Disorder,** it is important not to make a Personality Disorder diagnosis based solely on behaviors that are consequences of Substance Intoxication or Withdrawal or that are associated with activities in the service of sustaining a dependency (e.g., antisocial behavior). When enduring changes in personality arise as a result of the direct physiological effects of a general medical condition (e.g., brain tumor), a diagnosis of **Personality Change Due to a General Medical Condition** (p. 171) should be considered.

Personality Disorders must be distinguished from **personality traits that do not reach the threshold for a Personality Disorder.** Personality traits are diagnosed as a Personality Disorder only when they are inflexible, maladaptive, and persisting and cause significant functional impairment or subjective distress.

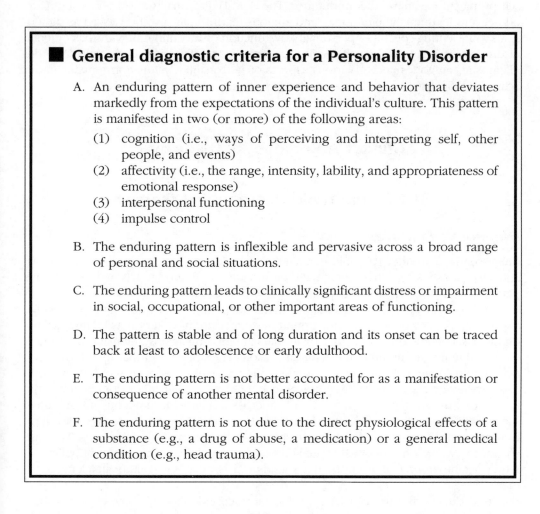

■ General diagnostic criteria for a Personality Disorder

A. An enduring pattern of inner experience and behavior that deviates markedly from the expectations of the individual's culture. This pattern is manifested in two (or more) of the following areas:

    (1) cognition (i.e., ways of perceiving and interpreting self, other people, and events)

    (2) affectivity (i.e., the range, intensity, lability, and appropriateness of emotional response)

    (3) interpersonal functioning

    (4) impulse control

B. The enduring pattern is inflexible and pervasive across a broad range of personal and social situations.

C. The enduring pattern leads to clinically significant distress or impairment in social, occupational, or other important areas of functioning.

D. The pattern is stable and of long duration and its onset can be traced back at least to adolescence or early adulthood.

E. The enduring pattern is not better accounted for as a manifestation or consequence of another mental disorder.

F. The enduring pattern is not due to the direct physiological effects of a substance (e.g., a drug of abuse, a medication) or a general medical condition (e.g., head trauma).

Dimensional Models for Personality Disorders

The diagnostic approach used in this manual represents the categorical perspective that Personality Disorders represent qualitatively distinct clinical syndromes. An alternative to the categorical approach is the dimensional perspective that Personality Disorders represent maladaptive variants of personality traits that merge imperceptibly into normality and into one another. There have been many different attempts to identify the most fundamental dimensions that underlie the entire domain of normal and pathological personality functioning. One model consists of the following five dimensions: neuroticism, introversion versus extroversion, closedness versus openness to experience, antagonism versus agreeableness, and conscientiousness. Another approach is to describe more specific areas of personality dysfunction, including as many as 15–40 dimensions (e.g., affective reactivity, social apprehensiveness, cognitive distortion, impulsivity, insincerity, self-centeredness). Other dimensions that have been studied include novelty seeking, reward dependence, harm avoidance, dominance, affiliation, constraint, persistence, positive emotionality versus negative emotionality, pleasure seeking versus pain avoidance, passive accommodation versus active modification, and self-propagation versus other nurturance. The DSM-IV Personality Disorder clusters (i.e., odd-eccentric, dramatic-emotional, and anxious-fearful) may also be viewed as dimensions representing spectra of personality dysfunction on a continuum with Axis I mental disorders. The relationship of the various dimensional models to the Personality Disorder diagnostic categories and to various aspects of personality dysfunction remains under active investigation.

Cluster A Personality Disorders

301.0   Paranoid Personality Disorder

Diagnostic Features

The essential feature of Paranoid Personality Disorder is a pattern of pervasive distrust and suspiciousness of others such that their motives are interpreted as malevolent. This pattern begins by early adulthood and is present in a variety of contexts.

Individuals with this disorder assume that other people will exploit, harm, or deceive them, even if no evidence exists to support this expectation (Criterion A1). They suspect on the basis of little or no evidence that others are plotting against them and may attack them suddenly, at any time and without reason. They often feel that they have been deeply and irreversibly injured by another person or persons even when there is no objective evidence for this. They are preoccupied with unjustified doubts about the loyalty or trustworthiness of their friends and associates, whose actions are minutely scrutinized for evidence of hostile intentions (Criterion A2). Any perceived deviation from trustworthiness or loyalty serves to support their underlying assumptions. They are so amazed when a friend or associate shows loyalty that they cannot trust or believe it. It they get into trouble, they expect that friends and associates will either attack or ignore them.

Individuals with this disorder are reluctant to confide in or become close to others because they fear that the information they share will be used against them (Criterion A3). They may refuse to answer personal questions, saying that the information is "nobody's business." They read hidden meanings that are demeaning and threatening into benign remarks or events (Criterion A4). For example, an individual with this disorder may misinterpret an honest mistake by a store clerk as a deliberate attempt to shortchange or may view a casual humorous remark by a co-worker as a serious character attack. Compliments are often misinterpreted (e.g., a compliment on a new acquisition is misinterpreted as a criticism for selfishness; a compliment on an accomplishment is misinterpreted as an attempt to coerce more and better performance). They may view an offer of help as a criticism that they are not doing well enough on their own.

Individuals with this disorder persistently bear grudges and are unwilling to forgive the insults, injuries, or slights that they think they have received (Criterion A5). Minor slights arouse major hostility, and the hostile feelings persist for a long time. Because they are constantly vigilant to the harmful intentions of others, they very often feel that their character or reputation has been attacked or that they have been slighted in some other way. They are quick to counterattack and react with anger to perceived insults (Criterion A6). Individuals with this disorder may be pathologically jealous, often suspecting that their spouse or sexual partner is unfaithful without any adequate justification (Criterion A7). They may gather trivial and circumstantial "evidence" to support their jealous beliefs. They want to maintain complete control of intimate relationships to avoid being betrayed and may constantly question and challenge the whereabouts, actions, intentions, and fidelity of their spouse or partner.

Paranoid Personality Disorder should not be diagnosed if the pattern of behavior occurs exclusively during the course of Schizophrenia, a Mood Disorder With Psychotic Features, or another Psychotic Disorder or if it is due to the direct physiological effects of a neurological (e.g., temporal lobe epilepsy) or other general medical condition (Criterion B).

Associated Features and Disorders

Individuals with Paranoid Personality Disorder are generally difficult to get along with and often have problems with close relationships. Their excessive suspiciousness and hostility may be expressed in overt argumentativeness, in recurrent complaining, or by quiet, apparently hostile aloofness. Because they are hypervigilant for potential threats, they may act in a guarded, secretive, or devious manner and appear to be "cold" and lacking in tender feelings. Although they may appear to be objective, rational, and unemotional, they more often display a labile range of affect, with hostile, stubborn, and sarcastic expressions predominating. Their combative and suspicious nature may elicit a hostile response in others, which then serves to confirm their original expectations.

Because individuals with Paranoid Personality Disorder lack trust in others, they have an excessive need to be self-sufficient and a strong sense of autonomy. They also need to have a high degree of control over those around them. They are often rigid, critical of others, and unable to collaborate, although they have great difficulty accepting criticism themselves. They may blame others for their own shortcomings. Because of their quickness to counterattack in response to the threats they perceive around them, they may be litigious and frequently become involved in legal disputes. Individuals with this disorder seek to confirm their preconceived negative notions regarding people or situations they encounter, attributing malevolent motivations to others that are projections of their own fears. They may exhibit thinly hidden, unrealistic grandiose fantasies, are often attuned to issues of power and rank, and tend to develop negative stereotypes of others, particularly those from population groups distinct from their own. Attracted by simplistic formulations of the world, they are often wary of ambiguous situations. They may be perceived as "fanatics" and form tightly knit "cults" or groups with others who share their paranoid belief systems.

Particularly in response to stress, individuals with this disorder may experience very brief psychotic episodes (lasting minutes to hours). In some instances, Paranoid Personality Disorder may appear as the premorbid antecedent of Delusional Disorder or Schizophrenia. Individuals with this disorder may develop Major Depressive Disorder and may be at increased risk for Agoraphobia and Obsessive-Compulsive Disorder. Alcohol and other Substance Abuse or Dependence frequently occur. The most common co-occurring Personality Disorders appear to be Schizotypal, Schizoid, Narcissistic, Avoidant, and Borderline.

Specific Culture, Age, and Gender Features

Some behaviors that are influenced by sociocultural contexts or specific life circumstances may be erroneously labeled paranoid and may even be reinforced by the process of clinical evaluation. Members of minority groups, immigrants, political and economic refugees, or individuals of different ethnic backgrounds may display guarded or defensive behaviors due to unfamiliarity (e.g., language barriers or lack of knowledge of rules and regulations) or in response to the perceived neglect or indifference of the majority society. These behaviors can, in turn, generate anger and frustration in those who deal with these individuals, thus setting up a vicious cycle of mutual mistrust, which should not be confused with Paranoid Personality Disorder. Some ethnic groups also display culturally related behaviors that can be misinterpreted as paranoid.

Paranoid Personality Disorder may be first apparent in childhood and adolescence with solitariness, poor peer relationships, social anxiety, underachievement in school, hypersensitivity, peculiar thoughts and language, and idiosyncratic fantasies. These children may appear to be "odd" or "eccentric" and attract teasing. In clinical samples, this disorder appears to be more commonly diagnosed in males.

Prevalence

The prevalence of Paranoid Personality Disorder has been reported to be 0.5%–2.5% in the general population, 10%–30% among those in inpatient psychiatric settings, and 2%–10% among those in outpatient mental health clinics.

Familial Pattern

There is some evidence for an increased prevalence of Paranoid Personality Disorder in relatives of probands with chronic Schizophrenia and for a more specific familial relationship with Delusional Disorder, Persecutory Type.

Differential Diagnosis

Paranoid Personality Disorder can be distinguished from **Delusional Disorder, Persecutory Type, Schizophrenia, Paranoid Type,** and **Mood Disorder With Psychotic Features** because these disorders are all characterized by a period of persistent psychotic symptoms (e.g., delusions and hallucinations). To give an additional diagnosis of Paranoid Personality Disorder, the Personality Disorder must have been present before the onset of psychotic symptoms and must persist when the psychotic symptoms are in remission. When an individual has a chronic Axis I Psychotic Disorder (e.g., Schizophrenia) that was preceded by Paranoid Personality Disorder, Paranoid Personality Disorder should be recorded on Axis II, followed by "Premorbid" in parentheses.

Paranoid Personality Disorder must be distinguished from **Personality Change Due to a General Medical Condition,** in which the traits emerge due to the direct effects of a general medical condition on the central nervous system. It must also be distinguished from **symptoms that may develop in association with chronic**

substance use (e.g., Cocaine-Related Disorder Not Otherwise Specified). Finally, it must also be distinguished from **paranoid traits associated with the development of physical handicaps** (e.g., a hearing impairment).

Other Personality Disorders may be confused with Paranoid Personality Disorder because they have certain features in common. It is, therefore, important to distinguish among these disorders based on differences in their characteristic features. However, if an individual has personality features that meet criteria for one or more Personality Disorders in addition to Paranoid Personality Disorder, all can be diagnosed. Paranoid Personality Disorder and **Schizotypal Personality Disorder** share the traits of suspiciousness, interpersonal aloofness, and paranoid ideation, but Schizotypal Personality Disorder also includes symptoms such as magical thinking, unusual perceptual experiences, and odd thinking and speech. Individuals with behaviors that meet criteria for **Schizoid Personality Disorder** are often perceived as strange, eccentric, cold, and aloof, but they do not usually have prominent paranoid ideation. The tendency of individuals with Paranoid Personality Disorder to react to minor stimuli with anger is also seen in **Borderline** and **Histrionic Personality Disorders.** However, these disorders are not necessarily associated with pervasive suspiciousness. People with **Avoidant Personality Disorder** may also be reluctant to confide in others, but more because of a fear of being embarrassed or found inadequate than from fear of others' malicious intent. Although antisocial behavior may be present in some individuals with Paranoid Personality Disorder, it is not usually motivated by a desire for personal gain or to exploit others as in **Antisocial Personality Disorder,** but rather is more often due to a desire for revenge. Individuals with **Narcissistic Personality Disorder** may occasionally display suspiciousness, social withdrawal, or alienation, but this derives primarily from fears of having their imperfections or flaws revealed.

Paranoid traits may be adaptive, particularly in threatening environments. Paranoid Personality Disorder should be diagnosed only when these traits are inflexible, maladaptive, and persisting and cause significant functional impairment or subjective distress.

■ **Diagnostic criteria for 301.0 Paranoid Personality Disorder**

A. A pervasive distrust and suspiciousness of others such that their motives are interpreted as malevolent, beginning by early adulthood and present in a variety of contexts, as indicated by four (or more) of the following:

   (1) suspects, without sufficient basis, that others are exploiting, harming, or deceiving him or her

   (2) is preoccupied with unjustified doubts about the loyalty or trustworthiness of friends or associates

   (3) is reluctant to confide in others because of unwarranted fear that the information will be used maliciously against him or her

   (4) reads hidden demeaning or threatening meanings into benign remarks or events

   (5) persistently bears grudges, i.e., is unforgiving of insults, injuries, or slights

(continued)

☐ **Diagnostic criteria for 301.0 Paranoid Personality Disorder** (*continued*)

       (6)   perceives attacks on his or her character or reputation that are not apparent to others and is quick to react angrily or to counterattack

       (7)   has recurrent suspicions, without justification, regarding fidelity of spouse or sexual partner

  B. Does not occur exclusively during the course of Schizophrenia, a Mood Disorder With Psychotic Features, or another Psychotic Disorder and is not due to the direct physiological effects of a general medical condition.

Note: If criteria are met prior to the onset of Schizophrenia, add "Premorbid," e.g., "Paranoid Personality Disorder (Premorbid)."

301.20   Schizoid Personality Disorder

Diagnostic Features

The essential feature of Schizoid Personality Disorder is a pervasive pattern of detachment from social relationships and a restricted range of expression of emotions in interpersonal settings. This pattern begins by early adulthood and is present in a variety of contexts.

    Individuals with Schizoid Personality Disorder appear to lack a desire for intimacy, seem indifferent to opportunities to develop close relationships, and do not seem to derive much satisfaction from being part of a family or other social group (Criterion A1). They prefer spending time by themselves, rather than being with other people. They often appear to be socially isolated or "loners" and almost always choose solitary activities or hobbies that do not include interaction with others (Criterion A2). They prefer mechanical or abstract tasks, such as computer or mathematical games. They may have very little interest in having sexual experiences with another person (Criterion A3) and take pleasure in few, if any, activities (Criterion A4). There is usually a reduced experience of pleasure from sensory, bodily, or interpersonal experiences, such as walking on a beach at sunset or having sex. These individuals have no close friends or confidants, except possibly a first-degree relative (Criterion A5).

    Individuals with Schizoid Personality Disorder often seem indifferent to the approval or criticism of others and do not appear to be bothered by what others may think of them (Criterion A6). They may be oblivious to the normal subtleties of social interaction and often do not respond appropriately to social cues so that they seem socially inept or superficial and self-absorbed. They usually display a "bland" exterior without visible emotional reactivity and rarely reciprocate gestures or facial expressions, such as smiles or nods (Criterion A7). They claim that they rarely experience strong emotions such as anger and joy. They often display a constricted affect and appear cold and aloof. However, in those very unusual circumstances in which these individuals become at least temporarily comfortable in revealing themselves, they may acknowledge having painful feelings, particularly related to social interactions.

Schizoid Personality Disorder should not be diagnosed if the pattern of behavior occurs exclusively during the course of Schizophrenia, a Mood Disorder With Psychotic Features, another Psychotic Disorder, or a Pervasive Developmental Disorder or if it is due to the direct physiological effects of a neurological (e.g., temporal lobe epilepsy) or other general medical condition (Criterion B).

Associated Features and Disorders

Individuals with Schizoid Personality Disorder may have particular difficulty expressing anger, even in response to direct provocation, which contributes to the impression that they lack emotion. Their lives sometimes seem directionless, and they may appear to "drift" in their goals. Such individuals often react passively to adverse circumstances and have difficulty responding appropriately to important life events. Because of their lack of social skills and lack of desire for sexual experiences, individuals with this disorder have few friendships, date infrequently, and often do not marry. Occupational functioning may be impaired, particularly if interpersonal involvement is required, but individuals with this disorder may do well when they work under conditions of social isolation. Particularly in response to stress, individuals with this disorder may experience very brief psychotic episodes (lasting minutes to hours). In some instances, Schizoid Personality Disorder may appear as the premorbid antecedent of Delusional Disorder or Schizophrenia. Individuals with this disorder may sometimes develop Major Depressive Disorder. Schizoid Personality Disorder most often co-occurs with Schizotypal, Paranoid, and Avoidant Personality Disorders.

Specific Culture, Age, and Gender Features

Individuals from a variety of cultural backgrounds sometimes exhibit defensive behaviors and interpersonal styles that may be erroneously labeled as schizoid. For example, those who have moved from rural to metropolitan environments may react with "emotional freezing" that may last for several months and be manifested by solitary activities, constricted affect, and other deficits in communication. Immigrants from other countries are sometimes mistakenly perceived as cold, hostile, or indifferent.

Schizoid Personality Disorder may be first apparent in childhood and adolescence with solitariness, poor peer relationships, and underachievement in school, which mark these children or adolescents as different and make them subject to teasing.

Schizoid Personality Disorder is diagnosed slightly more often in males and may cause more impairment in them.

Prevalence

Schizoid Personality Disorder is uncommon in clinical settings.

Familial Pattern

Schizoid Personality Disorder may have increased prevalence in the relatives of individuals with Schizophrenia or Schizotypal Personality Disorder.

Differential Diagnosis

Schizoid Personality Disorder can be distinguished from **Delusional Disorder, Schizophrenia,** and **Mood Disorder With Psychotic Features** because these disorders are all characterized by a period of persistent psychotic symptoms (e.g., delusions and hallucinations). To give an additional diagnosis of Schizoid Personality Disorder, the Personality Disorder must have been present before the onset of psychotic symptoms and must persist when the psychotic symptoms are in remission. When an individual has a chronic Axis I Psychotic Disorder (e.g., Schizophrenia) that was preceded by Schizoid Personality Disorder, Schizoid Personality Disorder should be recorded on Axis II followed by "Premorbid" in parentheses.

There may be great difficulty differentiating individuals with Schizoid Personality Disorder from those with milder forms of **Autistic Disorder** and from those with **Asperger's Disorder.** Milder forms of Autistic Disorder and Asperger's Disorder are differentiated by more severely impaired social interaction and stereotyped behaviors and interests.

Schizoid Personality Disorder must be distinguished from **Personality Change Due to a General Medical Condition,** in which the traits emerge due to the direct effects of a general medical condition on the central nervous system. It must also be distinguished from **symptoms that may develop in association with chronic substance use** (e.g., Cocaine-Related Disorder Not Otherwise Specified).

Other Personality Disorders may be confused with Schizoid Personality Disorder because they have certain features in common. It is, therefore, important to distinguish among these disorders based on differences in their characteristic features. However, if an individual has personality features that meet criteria for one or more Personality Disorders in addition to Schizoid Personality Disorder, all can be diagnosed. Although characteristics of social isolation and restricted affectivity are common to Schizoid, Schizotypal, and Paranoid Personality Disorders, Schizoid Personality Disorder can be distinguished from **Schizotypal Personality Disorder** by the lack of cognitive and perceptual distortions and from **Paranoid Personality Disorder** by the lack of suspiciousness and paranoid ideation. The social isolation of Schizoid Personality Disorder can be distinguished from that of **Avoidant Personality Disorder,** which is due to fear of being embarrassed or found inadequate and excessive anticipation of rejection. In contrast, people with Schizoid Personality Disorder have a more pervasive detachment and limited desire for social intimacy. Individuals with **Obsessive-Compulsive Personality Disorder** may also show an apparent social detachment stemming from devotion to work and discomfort with emotions, but they do have an underlying capacity for intimacy.

Individuals who are "loners" may display personality traits that might be considered schizoid. Only when these traits are inflexible and maladaptive and cause significant functional impairment or subjective distress do they constitute Schizoid Personality Disorder.

■ **Diagnostic criteria for 301.20 Schizoid Personality Disorder**

A. A pervasive pattern of detachment from social relationships and a restricted range of expression of emotions in interpersonal settings, beginning by early adulthood and present in a variety of contexts, as indicated by four (or more) of the following:

(1) neither desires nor enjoys close relationships, including being part of a family

(2) almost always chooses solitary activities

(3) has little, if any, interest in having sexual experiences with another person

(4) takes pleasure in few, if any, activities

(5) lacks close friends or confidants other than first-degree relatives

(6) appears indifferent to the praise or criticism of others

(7) shows emotional coldness, detachment, or flattened affectivity

B. Does not occur exclusively during the course of Schizophrenia, a Mood Disorder With Psychotic Features, another Psychotic Disorder, or a Pervasive Developmental Disorder and is not due to the direct physiological effects of a general medical condition.

Note: If criteria are met prior to the onset of Schizophrenia, add "Premorbid," e.g., "Schizoid Personality Disorder (Premorbid)."

301.22   Schizotypal Personality Disorder

Diagnostic Features

The essential feature of Schizotypal Personality Disorder is a pervasive pattern of social and interpersonal deficits marked by acute discomfort with, and reduced capacity for, close relationships as well as by cognitive or perceptual distortions and eccentricities of behavior. This pattern begins by early adulthood and is present in a variety of contexts.

Individuals with Schizotypal Personality Disorder often have ideas of reference (i.e., incorrect interpretations of casual incidents and external events as having a particular and unusual meaning specifically for the person) (Criterion A1). These should be distinguished from delusions of reference, in which the beliefs are held with delusional conviction. These individuals may be superstitious or preoccupied with paranormal phenomena that are outside the norms of their subculture (Criterion A2). They may feel that they have special powers to sense events before they happen or to read others' thoughts. They may believe that they have magical control over others, which can be implemented directly (e.g., believing that their spouse taking the dog out for a walk is the direct result of thinking it should be done an hour earlier) or indirectly through compliance with magical rituals (e.g., walking past a specific object three times to avoid a certain harmful outcome). Perceptual alterations may be present (e.g., sensing that another person is present or hearing a voice murmuring his or her name) (Criterion A3). Their speech may include unusual or idiosyncratic phrasing and construction. It is often loose, digressive, or vague, but without actual derailment or incoherence (Criterion A4). Responses can be either overly concrete or overly abstract, and words or concepts are sometimes applied in unusual ways (e.g., the person may state that he or she was not "talkable" at work).

Individuals with this disorder are often suspicious and may have paranoid ideation (e.g., believing their colleagues at work are intent on undermining their reputation with the boss) (Criterion A5). They are usually not able to negotiate the full range of affects and interpersonal cuing required for successful relationships and thus often appear to interact with others in an inappropriate, stiff, or constricted fashion (Criterion A6). These individuals are often considered to be odd or eccentric because of unusual mannerisms, an often unkempt manner of dress that does not quite "fit together," and inattention to the usual social conventions (e.g., the person may avoid eye contact, wear clothes that are ink stained and ill-fitting, and be unable to join in the give-and-take banter of co-workers) (Criterion A7).

Individuals with Schizotypal Personality Disorder experience interpersonal relatedness as problematic and are uncomfortable relating to other people. Although they may express unhappiness about their lack of relationships, their behavior suggests a decreased desire for intimate contacts. As a result, they usually have no or few close friends or confidants other than a first-degree relative (Criterion A8). They are anxious in social situations, particularly those involving unfamiliar people (Criterion A9). They will interact with other people when they have to, but prefer to keep to themselves because they feel that they are different and just do not "fit in." Their social anxiety does not easily abate, even when they spend more time in the setting or become more familiar with the other people, because their anxiety tends to be associated with suspiciousness regarding others' motivations. For example, when attending a dinner party, the individual with Schizotypal Personality Disorder will not become more relaxed as time goes on, but rather may become increasingly tense and suspicious.

Schizotypal Personality Disorder should not be diagnosed if the pattern of behavior occurs exclusively during the course of Schizophrenia, a Mood Disorder With Psychotic Features, another Psychotic Disorder, or a Pervasive Developmental Disorder (Criterion B).

Associated Features and Disorders

Individuals with Schizotypal Personality Disorder often seek treatment for the associated symptoms of anxiety, depression, or other dysphoric affects rather than for the personality disorder features per se. Particularly in response to stress, individuals with this disorder may experience transient psychotic episodes (lasting minutes to hours), although they usually are insufficient in duration to warrant an additional diagnosis such as Brief Psychotic Disorder or Schizophreniform Disorder. In some cases, clinically significant psychotic symptoms may develop that meet criteria for Brief Psychotic Disorder, Schizophreniform Disorder, Delusional Disorder, or Schizophrenia. Over half may have a history of at least one Major Depressive Episode. From 30% to 50% of individuals diagnosed with this disorder have a concurrent diagnosis of Major Depressive Disorder when admitted to a clinical setting. There is considerable co-occurrence with Schizoid, Paranoid, Avoidant, and Borderline Personality Disorders.

Specific Culture, Age, and Gender Features

Cognitive and perceptual distortions must be evaluated in the context of the individual's cultural milieu. Pervasive culturally determined characteristics, particularly those regarding religious beliefs and rituals, can appear to be schizotypal to the uninformed outsider (e.g., voodoo, speaking in tongues, life beyond death, shamanism, mind reading, sixth sense, evil eye, and magical beliefs related to health and illness).

Schizotypal Personality Disorder may be first apparent in childhood and adolescence with solitariness, poor peer relationships, social anxiety, underachievement in school, hypersensitivity, peculiar thoughts and language, and bizarre fantasies. These children may appear "odd" or "eccentric" and attract teasing. Schizotypal Personality Disorder may be slightly more common in males.

Prevalence

Schizotypal Personality Disorder has been reported to occur in approximately 3% of the general population.

Course

Schizotypal Personality Disorder has a relatively stable course, with only a small proportion of individuals going on to develop Schizophrenia or another Psychotic Disorder.

Familial Pattern

Schizotypal Personality Disorder appears to aggregate familially and is more prevalent among the first-degree biological relatives of individuals with Schizophrenia than among the general population. There may also be a modest increase in Schizophrenia and other Psychotic Disorders in the relatives of probands with Schizotypal Personality Disorder.

Differential Diagnosis

Schizotypal Personality Disorder can be distinguished from **Delusional Disorder, Schizophrenia,** and **Mood Disorder With Psychotic Features** because these disorders are all characterized by a period of persistent psychotic symptoms (e.g., delusions and hallucinations). To give an additional diagnosis of Schizotypal Personality Disorder, the Personality Disorder must have been present before the onset of psychotic symptoms and persist when the psychotic symptoms are in remission. When an individual has a chronic Axis I Psychotic Disorder (e.g., Schizophrenia) that was preceded by Schizotypal Personality Disorder, Schizotypal Personality Disorder should be recorded on Axis II followed by "Premorbid" in parentheses.

There may be great difficulty differentiating children with Schizotypal Personality Disorder from the heterogeneous group of solitary, odd children whose behavior is characterized by marked social isolation, eccentricity, or peculiarities of language and whose diagnoses would probably include milder forms of **Autistic Disorder, Asperger's Disorder,** and **Expressive** and **Mixed Receptive-Expressive Language**

Disorders. Communication Disorders may be differentiated by the primacy and severity of the disorder in language accompanied by compensatory efforts by the child to communicate by other means (e.g., gestures) and by the characteristic features of impaired language found in a specialized language assessment. Milder forms of Autistic Disorder and Asperger's Disorder are differentiated by the even greater lack of social awareness and emotional reciprocity and stereotyped behaviors and interests.

Schizotypal Personality Disorder must be distinguished from **Personality Change Due to a General Medical Condition,** in which the traits emerge due to the direct effects of a general medical condition on the central nervous system. It must also be distinguished from **symptoms that may develop in association with chronic substance use** (e.g., Cocaine-Related Disorder Not Otherwise Specified).

Other Personality Disorders may be confused with Schizotypal Personality Disorder because they have certain features in common. It is, therefore, important to distinguish among these disorders based on differences in their characteristic features. However, if an individual has personality features that meet criteria for one or more Personality Disorders in addition to Schizotypal Personality Disorder, all can be diagnosed. Although **Paranoid** and **Schizoid Personality Disorders** may also be characterized by social detachment and restricted affect, Schizotypal Personality Disorder can be distinguished from these two diagnoses by the presence of cognitive or perceptual distortions and marked eccentricity or oddness. Close relationships are limited in both Schizotypal Personality Disorder and **Avoidant Personality Disorder**; however, in Avoidant Personality Disorder an active desire for relationships is constrained by a fear of rejection, whereas in Schizotypal Personality Disorder there is a lack of desire for relationships and persistent detachment. Individuals with **Narcissistic Personality Disorder** may also display suspiciousness, social withdrawal, or alienation, but in Narcissistic Personality Disorder these qualities derive primarily from fears of having imperfections or flaws revealed. Individuals with **Borderline Personality Disorder** may also have transient, psychotic-like symptoms, but these are usually more closely related to affective shifts in response to stress (e.g., intense anger, anxiety, or disappointment) and are usually more dissociative (e.g., derealization or depersonalization). In contrast, individuals with Schizotypal Personality Disorder are more likely to have enduring psychotic-like symptoms that may worsen under stress but are less likely to be invariably associated with pronounced affective symptoms. Although social isolation may occur in Borderline Personality Disorder, this is usually secondary to repeated interpersonal failures due to angry outbursts and frequent mood shifts, rather than a result of a persistent lack of social contacts and desire for intimacy. Furthermore, individuals with Schizotypal Personality Disorder do not usually demonstrate the impulsive or manipulative behaviors of the individual with Borderline Personality Disorder. However, there is a high rate of co-occurrence between the two disorders, so that making such distinctions is not always feasible. **Schizotypal features during adolescence** may be reflective of transient emotional turmoil, rather than an enduring personality disorder.

■ **Diagnostic criteria for 301.22 Schizotypal Personality Disorder**

A. A pervasive pattern of social and interpersonal deficits marked by acute discomfort with, and reduced capacity for, close relationships as well as by cognitive or perceptual distortions and eccentricities of behavior, beginning by early adulthood and present in a variety of contexts, as indicated by five (or more) of the following:

(1) ideas of reference (excluding delusions of reference)
(2) odd beliefs or magical thinking that influences behavior and is inconsistent with subcultural norms (e.g., superstitiousness, belief in clairvoyance, telepathy, or "sixth sense"; in children and adolescents, bizarre fantasies or preoccupations)
(3) unusual perceptual experiences, including bodily illusions
(4) odd thinking and speech (e.g., vague, circumstantial, metaphorical, overelaborate, or stereotyped)
(5) suspiciousness or paranoid ideation
(6) inappropriate or constricted affect
(7) behavior or appearance that is odd, eccentric, or peculiar
(8) lack of close friends or confidants other than first-degree relatives
(9) excessive social anxiety that does not diminish with familiarity and tends to be associated with paranoid fears rather than negative judgments about self

B. Does not occur exclusively during the course of Schizophrenia, a Mood Disorder With Psychotic Features, another Psychotic Disorder, or a Pervasive Developmental Disorder.

Note: If criteria are met prior to the onset of Schizophrenia, add "Premorbid," e.g., "Schizotypal Personality Disorder (Premorbid)."

Cluster B Personality Disorders

301.7 Antisocial Personality Disorder

Diagnostic Features

The essential feature of Antisocial Personality Disorder is a pervasive pattern of disregard for, and violation of, the rights of others that begins in childhood or early adolescence and continues into adulthood.

This pattern has also been referred to as psychopathy, sociopathy, or dyssocial personality disorder. Because deceit and manipulation are central features of Antisocial Personality Disorder, it may be especially helpful to integrate information acquired from systematic clinical assessment with information collected from collateral sources.

For this diagnosis to be given, the individual must be at least age 18 years (Criterion B) and must have had a history of some symptoms of Conduct Disorder before age 15 years (Criterion C). Conduct Disorder involves a repetitive and persistent pattern of behavior in which the basic rights of others or major age-appropriate societal norms or rules are violated. The specific behaviors characteristic of Conduct Disorder fall into one of four categories: aggression to people and animals, destruction of property, deceitfulness or theft, or serious violation of rules. These are described in more detail on p. 85.

The pattern of antisocial behavior continues into adulthood. Individuals with Antisocial Personality Disorder fail to conform to social norms with respect to lawful behavior (Criterion A1). They may repeatedly perform acts that are grounds for arrest (whether they are arrested or not), such as destroying property, harassing others, stealing, or pursuing illegal occupations. Persons with this disorder disregard the wishes, rights, or feelings of others. They are frequently deceitful and manipulative in order to gain personal profit or pleasure (e.g., to obtain money, sex, or power) (Criterion A2). They may repeatedly lie, use an alias, con others, or malinger. A pattern of impulsivity may be manifested by a failure to plan ahead (Criterion A3). Decisions are made on the spur of the moment, without forethought, and without consideration for the consequences to self or others; this may lead to sudden changes of jobs, residences, or relationships. Individuals with Antisocial Personality Disorder tend to be irritable and aggressive and may repeatedly get into physical fights or commit acts of physical assault (including spouse beating or child beating) (Criterion A4). Aggressive acts that are required to defend oneself or someone else are not considered to be evidence for this item. These individuals also display a reckless disregard for the safety of themselves or others (Criterion A5). This may be evidenced in their driving behavior (recurrent speeding, driving while intoxicated, multiple accidents). They may engage in sexual behavior or substance use that has a high risk for harmful consequences. They may neglect or fail to care for a child in a way that puts the child in danger.

Individuals with Antisocial Personality Disorder also tend to be consistently and extremely irresponsible (Criterion A6). Irresponsible work behavior may be indicated by significant periods of unemployment despite available job opportunities, or by abandonment of several jobs without a realistic plan for getting another job. There may also be a pattern of repeated absences from work that are not explained by illness either in themselves or in their family. Financial irresponsibility is indicated by acts such as defaulting on debts, failing to provide child support, or failing to support other dependents on a regular basis. Individuals with Antisocial Personality Disorder show little remorse for the consequences of their acts (Criterion A7). They may be indifferent to, or provide a superficial rationalization for, having hurt, mistreated, or stolen from someone (e.g., "life's unfair," "losers deserve to lose," or "he had it coming anyway"). These individuals may blame the victims for being foolish, helpless, or deserving their fate; they may minimize the harmful consequences of their actions; or they may simply indicate complete indifference. They generally fail to compensate or make amends for their behavior. They may believe that everyone is out to "help number one" and that one should stop at nothing to avoid being pushed around.

The antisocial behavior must not occur exclusively during the course of Schizophrenia or a Manic Episode (Criterion D).

Associated Features and Disorders

Individuals with Antisocial Personality Disorder frequently lack empathy and tend to be callous, cynical, and contemptuous of the feelings, rights, and sufferings of others. They may have an inflated and arrogant self-appraisal (e.g., feel that ordinary work is beneath them or lack a realistic concern about their current problems or their future) and may be excessively opinionated, self-assured, or cocky. They may display a glib, superficial charm and can be quite voluble and verbally facile (e.g., using technical terms or jargon that might impress someone who is unfamiliar with the topic). Lack of empathy, inflated self-appraisal, and superficial charm are features that have been commonly included in traditional conceptions of psychopathy and may be particularly distinguishing of Antisocial Personality Disorder in prison or forensic settings where criminal, delinquent, or aggressive acts are likely to be nonspecific. These individuals may also be irresponsible and exploitative in their sexual relationships. They may have a history of many sexual partners and may never have sustained a monogamous relationship. They may be irresponsible as parents, as evidenced by malnutrition of a child, an illness in the child resulting from a lack of minimal hygiene, a child's dependence on neighbors or nonresident relatives for food or shelter, a failure to arrange for a caretaker for a young child when the individual is away from home, or repeated squandering of money required for household necessities. These individuals may receive dishonorable discharges from the armed services, may fail to be self-supporting, may become impoverished or even homeless, or may spend many years in penal institutions. Individuals with Antisocial Personality Disorder are more likely than people in the general population to die prematurely by violent means (e.g., suicide, accidents, and homicides).

Individuals with this disorder may also experience dysphoria, including complaints of tension, inability to tolerate boredom, and depressed mood. They may have associated Anxiety Disorders, Depressive Disorders, Substance-Related Disorders, Somatization Disorder, Pathological Gambling, and other disorders of impulse control. Individuals with Antisocial Personality Disorder also often have personality features that meet criteria for other Personality Disorders, particularly Borderline, Histrionic, and Narcissistic Personality Disorders. The likelihood of developing Antisocial Personality Disorder in adult life is increased if the individual experienced an early onset of Conduct Disorder (before age 10 years) and accompanying Attention-Deficit/Hyperactivity Disorder. Child abuse or neglect, unstable or erratic parenting, or inconsistent parental discipline may increase the likelihood that Conduct Disorder will evolve into Antisocial Personality Disorder.

Specific Culture, Age, and Gender Features

Antisocial Personality Disorder appears to be associated with low socioeconomic status and urban settings. Concerns have been raised that the diagnosis may at times be misapplied to individuals in settings in which seemingly antisocial behavior may be part of a protective survival strategy. In assessing antisocial traits, it is helpful for the clinician to consider the social and economic context in which the behaviors occur.

By definition, Antisocial Personality cannot be diagnosed before age 18 years. Antisocial Personality Disorder is much more common in males than in females. There has been some concern that Antisocial Personality Disorder may be underdiagnosed in females, particularly because of the emphasis on aggressive items in the definition of Conduct Disorder.

Prevalence

The overall prevalence of Antisocial Personality Disorder in community samples is about 3% in males and about 1% in females. Prevalence estimates within clinical settings have varied from 3% to 30%, depending on the predominant characteristics of the populations being sampled. Even higher prevalence rates are associated with substance abuse treatment settings and prison or forensic settings.

Course

Antisocial Personality Disorder has a chronic course but may become less evident or remit as the individual grows older, particularly by the fourth decade of life. Although this remission tends to be particularly evident with respect to engaging in criminal behavior, there is likely to be a decrease in the full spectrum of antisocial behaviors and substance use.

Familial Pattern

Antisocial Personality Disorder is more common among the first-degree biological relatives of those with the disorder than among the general population. The risk to biological relatives of females with the disorder tends to be higher than the risk to biological relatives of males with the disorder. Biological relatives of persons with this disorder are also at increased risk for Somatization Disorder and Substance-Related Disorders. Within a family that has a member with Antisocial Personality Disorder, males more often have Antisocial Personality Disorder and Substance-Related Disorders, whereas females more often have Somatization Disorder. However, in such families, there is an increase in prevalence of all of these disorders in both males and females compared with the general population. Adoption studies indicate that both genetic and environmental factors contribute to the risk of this group of disorders. Both adopted and biological children of parents with Antisocial Personality Disorder have an increased risk of developing Antisocial Personality Disorder, Somatization Disorder, and Substance-Related Disorders. Adopted-away children resemble their biological parents more than their adoptive parents, but the adoptive family environment influences the risk of developing a Personality Disorder and related psychopathology.

Differential Diagnosis

The diagnosis of Antisocial Personality Disorder is not given to individuals under age 18 years and is given only if there is a history of some symptoms of Conduct Disorder before age 15 years. For individuals over age 18 years, a diagnosis of Conduct Disorder is given only if the criteria for Antisocial Personality Disorder are not met.

When antisocial behavior in an adult is associated with a **Substance-Related Disorder,** the diagnosis of Antisocial Personality Disorder is not made unless the signs of Antisocial Personality Disorder were also present in childhood and have continued into adulthood. When substance use and antisocial behavior both began in childhood and continued into adulthood, both a Substance-Related Disorder and Antisocial Personality Disorder should be diagnosed if the criteria for both are met, even though some antisocial acts may be a consequence of the Substance-Related Disorder (e.g., illegal selling of drugs or thefts to obtain money for drugs). Antisocial behavior that occurs exclusively during the course of **Schizophrenia** or a **Manic Episode** should not be diagnosed as Antisocial Personality Disorder.

Other Personality Disorders may be confused with Antisocial Personality Disorder because they have certain features in common. It is, therefore, important to distinguish among these disorders based on differences in their characteristic features. However, if an individual has personality features that meet criteria for one or more Personality Disorders in addition to Antisocial Personality Disorder, all can be diagnosed. Individuals with Antisocial Personality Disorder and **Narcissistic Personality Disorder** share a tendency to be tough-minded, glib, superficial, exploitative, and unempathic. However, Narcissistic Personality Disorder does not include characteristics of impulsivity, aggression, and deceit. In addition, individuals with Antisocial Personality Disorder may not be as needy of the admiration and envy of others, and persons with Narcissistic Personality Disorder usually lack the history of Conduct Disorder in childhood or criminal behavior in adulthood. Individuals with Antisocial Personality Disorder and **Histrionic Personality Disorder** share a tendency to be impulsive, superficial, excitement seeking, reckless, seductive, and manipulative, but persons with Histrionic Personality Disorder tend to be more exaggerated in their emotions and do not characteristically engage in antisocial behaviors. Individuals with Histrionic and **Borderline Personality Disorders** are manipulative to gain nurturance, whereas those with Antisocial Personality Disorder are manipulative to gain profit, power, or some other material gratification. Individuals with Antisocial Personality Disorder tend to be less emotionally unstable and more aggressive than those with Borderline Personality Disorder. Although antisocial behavior may be present in some individuals with **Paranoid Personality Disorder,** it is not usually motivated by a desire for personal gain or to exploit others as in Antisocial Personality Disorder, but rather is more often due to a desire for revenge.

Antisocial Personality Disorder must be distinguished from criminal behavior undertaken for gain that is not accompanied by the personality features characteristic of this disorder. **Adult Antisocial Behavior** (listed in the "Other Conditions That May Be a Focus of Clinical Attention" section, p. 683) can be used to describe criminal, aggressive, or other antisocial behavior that comes to clinical attention but that does not meet the full criteria for Antisocial Personality Disorder. Only when antisocial personality traits are inflexible, maladaptive, and persistent and cause significant functional impairment or subjective distress do they constitute Antisocial Personality Disorder.

■ **Diagnostic criteria for 301.7 Antisocial Personality Disorder**

A. There is a pervasive pattern of disregard for and violation of the rights of others occurring since age 15 years, as indicated by three (or more) of the following:

   (1) failure to conform to social norms with respect to lawful behaviors as indicated by repeatedly performing acts that are grounds for arrest

(continued)

☐ **Diagnostic criteria for 301.7 Antisocial Personality Disorder** (*continued*)

  (2) deceitfulness, as indicated by repeated lying, use of aliases, or conning others for personal profit or pleasure
  (3) impulsivity or failure to plan ahead
  (4) irritability and aggressiveness, as indicated by repeated physical fights or assaults
  (5) reckless disregard for safety of self or others
  (6) consistent irresponsibility, as indicated by repeated failure to sustain consistent work behavior or honor financial obligations
  (7) lack of remorse, as indicated by being indifferent to or rationalizing having hurt, mistreated, or stolen from another

B. The individual is at least age 18 years.

C. There is evidence of Conduct Disorder (see p. 90) with onset before age 15 years.

D. The occurrence of antisocial behavior is not exclusively during the course of Schizophrenia or a Manic Episode.

301.83   Borderline Personality Disorder

Diagnostic Features

The essential feature of Borderline Personality Disorder is a pervasive pattern of instability of interpersonal relationships, self-image, and affects, and marked impulsivity that begins by early adulthood and is present in a variety of contexts.

Individuals with Borderline Personality Disorder make frantic efforts to avoid real or imagined abandonment (Criterion 1). The perception of impending separation or rejection, or the loss of external structure, can lead to profound changes in self-image, affect, cognition, and behavior. These individuals are very sensitive to environmental circumstances. They experience intense abandonment fears and inappropriate anger even when faced with a realistic time-limited separation or when there are unavoidable changes in plans (e.g., sudden despair in reaction to a clinician's announcing the end of the hour; panic or fury when someone important to them is just a few minutes late or must cancel an appointment). They may believe that this "abandonment" implies they are "bad." These abandonment fears are related to an intolerance of being alone and a need to have other people with them. Their frantic efforts to avoid abandonment may include impulsive actions such as self-mutilating or suicidal behaviors, which are described separately in Criterion 5.

Individuals with Borderline Personality Disorder have a pattern of unstable and intense relationships (Criterion 2). They may idealize potential caregivers or lovers at the first or second meeting, demand to spend a lot of time together, and share the most intimate details early in a relationship. However, they may switch quickly from idealizing other people to devaluing them, feeling that the other person does not care enough, does not give enough, is not "there" enough. These individuals can empathize with and nurture other people, but only with the expectation that the other person will "be there" in return to meet their own needs on demand. These individuals are prone to sudden and dramatic shifts in their view of others, who may alternately be seen as beneficent supports or as cruelly punitive. Such shifts often reflect disillusionment with a caregiver whose nurturing qualities had been idealized or whose rejection or abandonment is expected.

There may be an identity disturbance characterized by markedly and persistently unstable self-image or sense of self (Criterion 3). There are sudden and dramatic shifts in self-image, characterized by shifting goals, values, and vocational aspirations. There may be sudden changes in opinions and plans about career, sexual identity, values, and types of friends. These individuals may suddenly change from the role of a needy supplicant for help to a righteous avenger of past mistreatment. Although they usually have a self-image that is based on being bad or evil, individuals with this disorder may at times have feelings that they do not exist at all. Such experiences usually occur in situations in which the individual feels a lack of a meaningful relationship, nurturing, and support. These individuals may show worse performance in unstructured work or school situations.

Individuals with this disorder display impulsivity in at least two areas that are potentially self-damaging (Criterion 4). They may gamble, spend money irresponsibly, binge eat, abuse substances, engage in unsafe sex, or drive recklessly. Individuals with Borderline Personality Disorder display recurrent suicidal behavior, gestures, or threats, or self-mutilating behavior (Criterion 5). Completed suicide occurs in 8%–10% of such individuals, and self-mutilative acts (e.g., cutting or burning) and suicide threats and attempts are very common. Recurrent suicidality is often the reason that these individuals present for help. These self-destructive acts are usually precipitated by threats of separation or rejection or by expectations that they assume increased responsibility. Self-mutilation may occur during dissociative experiences and often brings relief by reaffirming the ability to feel or by expiating the individual's sense of being evil.

Individuals with Borderline Personality Disorder may display affective instability that is due to a marked reactivity of mood (e.g., intense episodic dysphoria, irritability, or anxiety usually lasting a few hours and only rarely more than a few days) (Criterion 6). The basic dysphoric mood of those with Borderline Personality Disorder is often disrupted by periods of anger, panic, or despair and is rarely relieved by periods of well-being or satisfaction. These episodes may reflect the individual's extreme reactivity to interpersonal stresses. Individuals with Borderline Personality Disorder may be troubled by chronic feelings of emptiness (Criterion 7). Easily bored, they may constantly seek something to do. Individuals with Borderline Personality Disorder frequently express inappropriate, intense anger or have difficulty controlling their anger (Criterion 8). They may display extreme sarcasm, enduring bitterness, or verbal outbursts. The anger is often elicited when a caregiver or lover is seen as neglectful, withholding, uncaring, or abandoning. Such expressions of anger are often followed by shame and guilt and contribute to the feeling they have of being evil. During periods of extreme stress, transient paranoid ideation or dissociative symptoms (e.g., depersonalization) may occur (Criterion 9), but these are generally of insufficient severity or duration to warrant an additional diagnosis. These episodes occur most frequently in response to a real or imagined abandonment. Symptoms tend to be transient, lasting minutes or hours.

The real or perceived return of the caregiver's nurturance may result in a remission of symptoms.

Associated Features and Disorders

Individuals with Borderline Personality Disorder may have a pattern of undermining themselves at the moment a goal is about to be realized (e.g., dropping out of school just before graduation; regressing severely after a discussion of how well therapy is going; destroying a good relationship just when it is clear that the relationship could last). Some individuals develop psychotic-like symptoms (e.g., hallucinations, body-image distortions, ideas of reference, and hypnagogic phenomena) during times of stress. Individuals with this disorder may feel more secure with transitional objects (i.e., a pet or inanimate possession) than in interpersonal relationships. Premature death from suicide may occur in individuals with this disorder, especially in those with co-occurring Mood Disorders or Substance-Related Disorders. Physical handicaps may result from self-inflicted abuse behaviors or failed suicide attempts. Recurrent job losses, interrupted education, and broken marriages are common. Physical and sexual abuse, neglect, hostile conflict, and early parental loss or separation are more common in the childhood histories of those with Borderline Personality Disorder. Common co-occurring Axis I disorders include Mood Disorders, Substance-Related Disorders, Eating Disorders (notably Bulimia), Posttraumatic Stress Disorder, and Attention-Deficit/Hyperactivity Disorder. Borderline Personality Disorder also frequently co-occurs with the other Personality Disorders.

Specific Culture, Age, and Gender Features

The pattern of behavior seen in Borderline Personality Disorder has been identified in many settings around the world. Adolescents and young adults with identity problems (especially when accompanied by substance use) may transiently display behaviors that misleadingly give the impression of Borderline Personality Disorder. Such situations are characterized by emotional instability, "existential" dilemmas, uncertainty, anxiety-provoking choices, conflicts about sexual orientation, and competing social pressures to decide on careers. Borderline Personality Disorder is diagnosed predominantly (about 75%) in females.

Prevalence

The prevalence of Borderline Personality Disorder is estimated to be about 2% of the general population, about 10% among individuals seen in outpatient mental health clinics, and about 20% among psychiatric inpatients. It ranges from 30% to 60% among clinical populations with Personality Disorders.

Course

There is considerable variability in the course of Borderline Personality Disorder. The most common pattern is one of chronic instability in early adulthood, with episodes of serious affective and impulsive dyscontrol and high levels of use of health and mental health resources. The impairment from the disorder and the risk of suicide are greatest in the young-adult years and gradually wane with advancing age. During their 30s and 40s, the majority of individuals with this disorder attain greater stability in their relationships and vocational functioning.

Familial Pattern

Borderline Personality Disorder is about five times more common among first-degree biological relatives of those with the disorder than in the general population. There is also an increased familial risk for Substance-Related Disorders, Antisocial Personality Disorder, and Mood Disorders.

Differential Diagnosis

Borderline Personality Disorder often co-occurs with **Mood Disorders,** and when criteria for both are met, both may be diagnosed. Because the cross-sectional presentation of Borderline Personality Disorder can be mimicked by an episode of Mood Disorder, the clinician should avoid giving an additional diagnosis of Borderline Personality Disorder based only on cross-sectional presentation without having documented that the pattern of behavior has an early onset and a long-standing course.

Other Personality Disorders may be confused with Borderline Personality Disorder because they have certain features in common. It is, therefore, important to distinguish among these disorders based on differences in their characteristic features. However, if an individual has personality features that meet criteria for one or more Personality Disorders in addition to Borderline Personality Disorder, all can be diagnosed. Although **Histrionic Personality Disorder** can also be characterized by attention seeking, manipulative behavior, and rapidly shifting emotions, Borderline Personality Disorder is distinguished by self-destructiveness, angry disruptions in close relationships, and chronic feelings of deep emptiness and loneliness. Paranoid ideas or illusions may be present in both Borderline Personality Disorder and **Schizotypal Personality Disorder,** but these symptoms are more transient, interpersonally reactive, and responsive to external structuring in Borderline Personality Disorder. Although **Paranoid Personality Disorder** and **Narcissistic Personality Disorder** may also be characterized by an angry reaction to minor stimuli, the relative stability of self-image as well as the relative lack of self-destructiveness, impulsivity, and abandonment concerns distinguish these disorders from Borderline Personality Disorder. Although **Antisocial Personality Disorder** and Borderline Personality Disorder are both characterized by manipulative behavior, individuals with Antisocial Personality Disorder are manipulative to gain profit, power, or some other material gratification, whereas the goal in Borderline Personality Disorder is directed more toward gaining the concern of caretakers. Both **Dependent Personality Disorder** and Borderline Personality Disorder are characterized by fear of abandonment; however, the individual with Borderline Personality Disorder reacts to abandonment with feelings of emotional emptiness, rage, and demands, whereas the individual with Dependent Personality Disorder reacts with increasing appeasement and submissiveness and urgently seeks a replacement relationship to provide caregiving and support. Borderline Personality Disorder can further be distinguished from Dependent Personality Disorder by the typical pattern of unstable and intense relationships. Borderline Personality Disorder must be distinguished from **Personality Change Due to a General Medical Condition,** in which the traits emerge due to the direct effects of a general medical condition on the central nervous system. It must also be distinguished from **symptoms that may develop in association with chronic substance use** (e.g., Cocaine-Related Disorder Not Otherwise Specified).

Borderline Personality Disorder should be distinguished from **Identity Problem** (see p. 685), which is reserved for identity concerns related to a developmental phase (e.g., adolescence) and does not qualify as a mental disorder.

■ **Diagnostic criteria for 301.83 Borderline Personality Disorder**

A pervasive pattern of instability of interpersonal relationships, self-image, and affects, and marked impulsivity beginning by early adulthood and present in a variety of contexts, as indicated by five (or more) of the following:

    (1)   frantic efforts to avoid real or imagined abandonment. **Note:** Do not include suicidal or self-mutilating behavior covered in Criterion 5.

    (2)   a pattern of unstable and intense interpersonal relationships characterized by alternating between extremes of idealization and devaluation

    (3)   identity disturbance: markedly and persistently unstable self-image or sense of self

    (4)   impulsivity in at least two areas that are potentially self-damaging (e.g., spending, sex, substance abuse, reckless driving, binge eating). **Note:** Do not include suicidal or self-mutilating behavior covered in Criterion 5.

    (5)   recurrent suicidal behavior, gestures, or threats, or self-mutilating behavior

    (6)   affective instability due to a marked reactivity of mood (e.g., intense episodic dysphoria, irritability, or anxiety usually lasting a few hours and only rarely more than a few days)

    (7)   chronic feelings of emptiness

    (8)   inappropriate, intense anger or difficulty controlling anger (e.g., frequent displays of temper, constant anger, recurrent physical fights)

    (9)   transient, stress-related paranoid ideation or severe dissociative symptoms

301.50 Histrionic Personality Disorder

Diagnostic Features

The essential feature of Histrionic Personality Disorder is pervasive and excessive emotionality and attention-seeking behavior. This pattern begins by early adulthood and is present in a variety of contexts.

Individuals with Histrionic Personality Disorder are uncomfortable or feel unappreciated when they are not the center of attention (Criterion 1). Often lively and dramatic, they tend to draw attention to themselves and may initially charm new acquaintances by their enthusiasm, apparent openness, or flirtatiousness. These qualities wear thin, however, as these individuals continually demand to be the center of attention. They commandeer the role of "the life of the party." If they are not the center of attention, they may do something dramatic (e.g., make up stories, create a scene) to draw the focus of attention to themselves. This need is often apparent in their behavior with a clinician (e.g., flattery, bringing gifts, providing dramatic descriptions of physical and psychological symptoms that are replaced by new symptoms each visit).

The appearance and behavior of individuals with this disorder are often inappropriately sexually provocative or seductive (Criterion 2). This behavior is directed not only toward persons in whom the individual has a sexual or romantic interest, but occurs in a wide variety of social, occupational, and professional relationships beyond what is appropriate for the social context. Emotional expression may be shallow and rapidly shifting (Criterion 3). Individuals with this disorder consistently use physical appearance to draw attention to themselves (Criterion 4). They are overly concerned with impressing others by their appearance and expend an excessive amount of time, energy, and money on clothes and grooming. They may "fish for compliments" regarding appearance and be easily and excessively upset by a critical comment about how they look or by a photograph that they regard as unflattering.

These individuals have a style of speech that is excessively impressionistic and lacking in detail (Criterion 5). Strong opinions are expressed with dramatic flair, but underlying reasons are usually vague and diffuse, without supporting facts and details. For example, an individual with Histrionic Personality Disorder may comment that a certain individual is a wonderful human being, yet be unable to provide any specific examples of good qualities to support this opinion. Individuals with this disorder are characterized by self-dramatization, theatricality, and an exaggerated expression of emotion (Criterion 6). They may embarrass friends and acquaintances by an excessive public display of emotions (e.g., embracing casual acquaintances with excessive ardor, sobbing uncontrollably on minor sentimental occasions, or having temper tantrums). However, their emotions often seem to be turned on and off too quickly to be deeply felt, which may lead others to accuse the individual of faking these feelings.

Individuals with Histrionic Personality Disorder have a high degree of suggestibility (Criterion 7). Their opinions and feelings are easily influenced by others and by current fads. They may be overly trusting, especially of strong authority figures whom they see as magically solving their problems. They have a tendency to play hunches and to adopt convictions quickly. Individuals with this disorder often consider relationships more intimate than they actually are, describing almost every acquaintance as "my dear, dear friend" or referring to physicians met only once or twice under professional circumstances by their first names (Criterion 8). Flights into romantic fantasy are common.

Associated Features and Disorders

Individuals with Histrionic Personality Disorder may have difficulty achieving emotional intimacy in romantic or sexual relationships. Without being aware of it, they often act out a role (e.g., "victim" or "princess") in their relationships to others. They may seek to control their partner through emotional manipulation or seductiveness on one level, whereas displaying a marked dependency on them at another level. Individuals with this disorder often have impaired relationships with same-sex friends because their sexually provocative interpersonal style may seem a threat to their friends' relationships. These individuals may also alienate friends with demands for constant attention. They often become depressed and upset when they are not the center of attention. They may crave novelty, stimulation, and excitement and have a tendency to become bored with their usual routine. These individuals are often intolerant of, or frustrated by, situations that involve delayed gratification, and their actions are often directed at obtaining immediate satisfaction. Although they often initiate a job or project with great enthusiasm, their interest may lag quickly. Longer-term relationships may be neglected to make way for the excitement of new relationships.

The actual risk of suicide is not known, but clinical experience suggests that individuals with this disorder are at increased risk for suicidal gestures and threats to get attention and coerce better caregiving. Histrionic Personality Disorder has been associated with higher rates of Somatization Disorder, Conversion Disorder, and Major Depressive Disorder. Borderline, Narcissistic, Antisocial, and Dependent Personality Disorders often co-occur.

Specific Culture, Age, and Gender Features

Norms for interpersonal behavior, personal appearance, and emotional expressiveness vary widely across cultures, genders, and age groups. Before considering the various traits (e.g., emotionality, seductiveness, dramatic interpersonal style, novelty seeking, sociability, charm, impressionability, and a tendency to somatization) to be evidence of Histrionic Personality Disorder, it is important to evaluate whether they cause clinically significant impairment or distress. In clinical settings, this disorder has been diagnosed more frequently in females; however, the sex ratio is not significantly different than the sex ratio of females within the respective clinical setting. In contrast, some studies using structured assessments report similar prevalence rates among males and females. The behavioral expression of Histrionic Personality Disorder may be influenced by sex role stereotypes. For example, a man with this disorder may dress and behave in a manner often identified as "macho" and may seek to be the center of attention by bragging about athletic skills, whereas a woman, for example, may choose very feminine clothes and talk about how much she impressed her dance instructor.

Prevalence

Limited data from general population studies suggest a prevalence of Histrionic Personality Disorder of about 2%–3%. Rates of about 10%–15% have been reported in inpatient and outpatient mental health settings when structured assessment is used.

Differential Diagnosis

Other Personality Disorders may be confused with Histrionic Personality Disorder because they have certain features in common. It is, therefore, important to distinguish among these disorders based on differences in their characteristic features. However, if an individual has personality features that meet criteria for one or more Personality Disorders in addition to Histrionic Personality Disorder, all can be diagnosed. Although **Borderline Personality Disorder** can also be characterized by attention seeking, manipulative behavior, and rapidly shifting emotions, it is distinguished by self-destructiveness, angry disruptions in close relationships, and chronic feelings of deep emptiness and identity disturbance. Individuals with **Antisocial Personality Disorder** and Histrionic Personality Disorder share a tendency to be impulsive, superficial, excitement seeking, reckless, seductive, and manipulative, but persons with Histrionic Personality Disorder tend to be more exaggerated in their emotions and do not characteristically engage in antisocial behaviors. Individuals with Histrionic Personality Disorder are manipulative to gain nurturance, whereas those with Antisocial Personality Disorder are manipulative to gain profit, power, or some other material gratification. Although individuals with **Narcissistic Personality Disorder** also crave attention from others, they usually want praise for their "superiority," whereas the individual with Histrionic Personality Disorder is willing to be viewed as fragile or dependent if this is instrumental in getting attention. Individuals with Narcissistic Personality Disorder may exaggerate the intimacy of their relationships with other people, but they are more apt to emphasize the "VIP" status or wealth of their friends. In **Dependent Personality Disorder,** the person is excessively dependent on others for praise and guidance, but is without the flamboyant, exaggerated, emotional features of Histrionic Personality Disorder.

Histrionic Personality Disorder must be distinguished from **Personality Change Due to a General Medical Condition,** in which the traits emerge due to the direct effects of a general medical condition on the central nervous system. It must also be distinguished from **symptoms that may develop in association with chronic substance use** (e.g., Cocaine-Related Disorder Not Otherwise Specified).

Many individuals may display histrionic personality traits. Only when these traits are inflexible, maladaptive, and persisting and cause significant functional impairment or subjective distress do they constitute Histrionic Personality Disorder.

■ Diagnostic criteria for 301.50 Histrionic Personality Disorder

A pervasive pattern of excessive emotionality and attention seeking, beginning by early adulthood and present in a variety of contexts, as indicated by five (or more) of the following:

   (1) is uncomfortable in situations in which he or she is not the center of attention

   (2) interaction with others is often characterized by inappropriate sexually seductive or provocative behavior

(continued)

☐ **Diagnostic criteria for 301.50 Histrionic Personality Disorder** (*continued*)

  (3) displays rapidly shifting and shallow expression of emotions
  (4) consistently uses physical appearance to draw attention to self
  (5) has a style of speech that is excessively impressionistic and lacking in detail
  (6) shows self-dramatization, theatricality, and exaggerated expression of emotion
  (7) is suggestible, i.e., easily influenced by others or circumstances
  (8) considers relationships to be more intimate than they actually are

---

301.81   Narcissistic Personality Disorder

Diagnostic Features

The essential feature of Narcissistic Personality Disorder is a pervasive pattern of grandiosity, need for admiration, and lack of empathy that begins by early adulthood and is present in a variety of contexts.

Individuals with this disorder have a grandiose sense of self-importance (Criterion 1). They routinely overestimate their abilities and inflate their accomplishments, often appearing boastful and pretentious. They may blithely assume that others attribute the same value to their efforts and may be surprised when the praise they expect and feel they deserve is not forthcoming. Often implicit in the inflated judgments of their own accomplishments is an underestimation (devaluation) of the contributions of others. They are often preoccupied with fantasies of unlimited success, power, brilliance, beauty, or ideal love (Criterion 2). They may ruminate about "long overdue" admiration and privilege and compare themselves favorably with famous or privileged people.

Individuals with Narcissistic Personality Disorder believe that they are superior, special, or unique and expect others to recognize them as such (Criterion 3). They may feel that they can only be understood by, and should only associate with, other people who are special or of high status and may attribute "unique," "perfect," or "gifted" qualities to those with whom they associate. Individuals with this disorder believe that their needs are special and beyond the ken of ordinary people. Their own self-esteem is enhanced (i.e., "mirrored") by the idealized value that they assign to those with whom they associate. They are likely to insist on having only the "top" person (doctor, lawyer, hairdresser, instructor) or being affiliated with the "best" institutions, but may devalue the credentials of those who disappoint them.

Individuals with this disorder generally require excessive admiration (Criterion 4). Their self-esteem is almost invariably very fragile. They may be preoccupied with how well they are doing and how favorably they are regarded by others. This often takes the form of a need for constant attention and admiration. They may expect their arrival to be greeted with great fanfare and are astonished if others do not covet their possessions. They may constantly fish for compliments, often with great charm. A sense of entitlement is evident in these individuals' unreasonable expectation of especially favorable treatment (Criterion 5). They expect to be catered to and are puzzled or furious when this does not happen. For example, they may assume that they do not have to wait in line and that their priorities are so important that others should defer to them, and then get irritated when others fail to assist "in their very important work." This sense of entitlement combined with a lack of sensitivity to the wants and needs of others may result in the conscious or unwitting exploitation of others (Criterion 6). They expect to be given whatever they want or feel they need, no matter what it might mean to others. For example, these individuals may expect great dedication from others and may overwork them without regard for the impact on their lives. They tend to form friendships or romantic relationships only if the other person seems likely to advance their purposes or otherwise enhance their self-esteem. They often usurp special privileges and extra resources that they believe they deserve because they are so special.

Individuals with Narcissistic Personality Disorder generally have a lack of empathy and have difficulty recognizing the desires, subjective experiences, and feelings of others (Criterion 7). They may assume that others are totally concerned about their welfare. They tend to discuss their own concerns in inappropriate and lengthy detail, while failing to recognize that others also have feelings and needs. They are often contemptuous and impatient with others who talk about their own problems and concerns. These individuals may be oblivious to the hurt their remarks may inflict (e.g., exuberantly telling a former lover that "I am now in the relationship of a lifetime!"; boasting of health in front of someone who is sick). When recognized, the needs, desires, or feelings of others are likely to be viewed disparagingly as signs of weakness or vulnerability. Those who relate to individuals with Narcissistic Personality Disorder typically find an emotional coldness and lack of reciprocal interest.

These individuals are often envious of others or believe that others are envious of them (Criterion 8). They may begrudge others their successes or possessions, feeling that they better deserve those achievements, admiration, or privileges. They may harshly devalue the contributions of others, particularly when those individuals have received acknowledgment or praise for their accomplishments. Arrogant, haughty behaviors characterize these individuals. They often display snobbish, disdainful, or patronizing attitudes (Criterion 9). For example, an individual with this disorder may complain about a clumsy waiter's "rudeness" or "stupidity" or conclude a medical evaluation with a condescending evaluation of the physician.

Associated Features and Disorders

Vulnerability in self-esteem makes individuals with Narcissistic Personality Disorder very sensitive to "injury" from criticism or defeat. Although they may not show it outwardly, criticism may haunt these individuals and may leave them feeling humiliated, degraded, hollow, and empty. They may react with disdain, rage, or defiant counterattack. Such experiences often lead to social withdrawal or an appearance of humility that may mask and protect the grandiosity. Interpersonal relations are typically impaired due to problems derived from entitlement, the need for admiration, and the relative disregard for the sensitivities of others. Though overweening ambition and confidence may lead to high achievement, performance may be disrupted due to intolerance of criticism or defeat. Sometimes vocational functioning can be very low, reflecting an unwillingness to take a risk in competitive or other situations in which defeat is possible. Sustained feelings of shame or humiliation and the attendant self-criticism may be associated with social withdrawal, depressed mood, and Dysthymic or Major Depressive Disorder. In contrast, sustained periods of grandiosity may be associated with a hypomanic mood. Narcissistic Personality Disorder is also associated with Anorexia Nervosa and Substance-Related Disorders (especially related to cocaine). Histrionic, Borderline, Antisocial, and Paranoid Personality Disorders may be associated with Narcissistic Personality Disorder.

Specific Age and Gender Features

Narcissistic traits may be particularly common in adolescents and do not necessarily indicate that the individual will go on to have Narcissistic Personality Disorder. Individuals with Narcissistic Personality Disorder may have special difficulties adjusting to the onset of physical and occupational limitations that are inherent in the aging process. Of those diagnosed with Narcissistic Personality Disorder, 50%–75% are male.

Prevalence

Estimates of prevalence of Narcissistic Personality Disorder range from 2% to 16% in the clinical population and are less than 1% in the general population.

Differential Diagnosis

Other Personality Disorders may be confused with Narcissistic Personality Disorder because they have certain features in common. It is, therefore, important to distinguish among these disorders based on differences in their characteristic features. However, if an individual has personality features that meet criteria for one or more Personality Disorders in addition to Narcissistic Personality Disorder, all can be diagnosed. The most useful feature in discriminating Narcissistic Personality Disorder from **Histrionic, Antisocial,** and **Borderline Personality Disorders,** whose interactive styles are respectively coquettish, callous, and needy, is the grandiosity characteristic of Narcissistic Personality Disorder. The relative stability of self-image as well as the relative lack of self-destructiveness, impulsivity, and abandonment concerns also help distinguish Narcissistic Personality Disorder from Borderline Personality Disorder. Excessive pride in achievements, a relative lack of emotional display, and disdain for others' sensitivities help distinguish Narcissistic Personality Disorder from Histrionic Personality Disorder. Although individuals with Borderline, Histrionic, and Narcissistic Personality Disorders may require much attention, those with Narcissistic Personality Disorder specifically need that attention to be admiring. Individuals with Antisocial and Narcissistic Personality Disorders will share a tendency to be tough-minded, glib, superficial, exploitative, and unempathic. However, Narcissistic Personality Disorder does not necessarily include characteristics of impulsivity, aggression, and deceit. In addition, individuals with Antisocial Personality Disorder may not be as needy of the admiration and envy of others, and persons with Narcissistic Personality Disorder usually lack the history of Conduct Disorder in childhood or criminal behavior in adulthood. In both Narcissistic Personality Disorder and **Obsessive-Compulsive Personality Disorder,** the individual may profess a commitment to perfectionism and believe that others cannot do things as well. In contrast to the accompanying self-criticism of those with Obsessive-Compulsive Personality Disorder, individuals with Narcissistic Personality Disorder are more likely to believe that they have achieved perfection. Suspiciousness and social withdrawal usually distinguish those with **Schizotypal** or **Paranoid Personality Disorder** from those with Narcissistic Personality Disorder. When these qualities are present in individuals with Narcissistic Personality Disorder, they derive primarily from fears of having imperfections or flaws revealed. Grandiosity may emerge as part of **Manic** or **Hypomanic Episodes,** but the association with mood change or functional impairments helps distinguish these episodes from Narcissistic Personality Disorder.

Narcissistic Personality Disorder must be distinguished from **Personality Change Due to a General Medical Condition,** in which the traits emerge due to the direct effects of a general medical condition on the central nervous system. It must also be distinguished from **symptoms that may develop in association with chronic substance use** (e.g., Cocaine-Related Disorder Not Otherwise Specified).

Many highly successful individuals display personality traits that might be considered narcissistic. Only when these traits are inflexible, maladaptive, and persisting and cause significant functional impairment or subjective distress do they constitute Narcissistic Personality Disorder.

■ Diagnostic criteria for 301.81 Narcissistic Personality Disorder

A pervasive pattern of grandiosity (in fantasy or behavior), need for admiration, and lack of empathy, beginning by early adulthood and present in a variety of contexts, as indicated by five (or more) of the following:

(1) has a grandiose sense of self-importance (e.g., exaggerates achievements and talents, expects to be recognized as superior without commensurate achievements)

(2) is preoccupied with fantasies of unlimited success, power, brilliance, beauty, or ideal love

(3) believes that he or she is "special" and unique and can only be understood by, or should associate with, other special or high-status people (or institutions)

(4) requires excessive admiration

(5) has a sense of entitlement, i.e., unreasonable expectations of especially favorable treatment or automatic compliance with his or her expectations

(6) is interpersonally exploitative, i.e., takes advantage of others to achieve his or her own ends

(7) lacks empathy: is unwilling to recognize or identify with the feelings and needs of others

(8) is often envious of others or believes that others are envious of him or her

(9) shows arrogant, haughty behaviors or attitudes

Cluster C Personality Disorders

301.82   Avoidant Personality Disorder

Diagnostic Features

The essential feature of Avoidant Personality Disorder is a pervasive pattern of social inhibition, feelings of inadequacy, and hypersensitivity to negative evaluation that begins by early adulthood and is present in a variety of contexts.

Individuals with Avoidant Personality Disorder avoid work or school activities that involve significant interpersonal contact because of fears of criticism, disapproval, or rejection (Criterion 1). Offers of job promotions may be declined because the new responsibilities might result in criticism from co-workers. These individuals avoid making new friends unless they are certain they will be liked and accepted without criticism (Criterion 2). Until they pass stringent tests proving the contrary, other people are assumed to be critical and disapproving. Individuals with this disorder will not join in group activities unless there are repeated and generous offers of support and nurturance. Interpersonal intimacy is often difficult for these individuals, although they are able to establish intimate relationships when there is assurance of uncritical acceptance. They may act with restraint, have difficulty talking about themselves, and withhold intimate feelings for fear of being exposed, ridiculed, or shamed (Criterion 3).

Because individuals with this disorder are preoccupied with being criticized or rejected in social situations, they may have a markedly low threshold for detecting such reactions (Criterion 4). If someone is even slightly disapproving or critical, they may feel extremely hurt. They tend to be shy, quiet, inhibited, and "invisible" because of the fear that any attention would be degrading or rejecting. They expect that no matter what they say, others will see it as "wrong," and so they may say nothing at all. They react strongly to subtle cues that are suggestive of mockery or derision. Despite their longing to be active participants in social life, they fear placing their welfare in the hands of others. Individuals with Avoidant Personality Disorder are inhibited in new interpersonal situations because they feel inadequate and have low self-esteem (Criterion 5). Doubts concerning social competence and personal appeal become especially manifest in settings involving interactions with strangers. These individuals believe themselves to be socially inept, personally unappealing, or inferior to others (Criterion 6). They are unusually reluctant to take personal risks or to engage in any new activities because these may prove embarrassing (Criterion 7). They are prone to exaggerate the potential dangers of ordinary situations, and a restricted lifestyle may result from their need for certainty and security. Someone with this disorder may cancel a job interview for fear of being embarrassed by not dressing appropriately. Marginal somatic symptoms or other problems may become the reason for avoiding new activities.

Associated Features and Disorders

Individuals with Avoidant Personality Disorder often vigilantly appraise the movements and expressions of those with whom they come into contact. Their fearful and tense demeanor may elicit ridicule and derision from others, which in turn confirms their self-doubts. They are very anxious about the possibility that they will react to criticism with blushing or crying. They are described by others as being "shy," "timid," "lonely," and "isolated." The major problems associated with this disorder occur in social and occupational functioning. The low self-esteem and hypersensitivity to rejection are associated with restricted interpersonal contacts. These individuals may become relatively isolated and usually do not have a large social support network that can help them weather crises. They desire affection and acceptance and may fantasize about idealized relationships with others. The avoidant behaviors can also adversely affect occupational functioning because these individuals try to avoid the types of social situations that may be important for meeting the basic demands of the job or for advancement.

Other disorders that are commonly diagnosed with Avoidant Personality Disorder include Mood and Anxiety Disorders (especially Social Phobia of the Generalized Type). Avoidant Personality Disorder is often diagnosed with Dependent Personality Disorder, because individuals with Avoidant Personality Disorder become very attached to and dependent on those few other people with whom they are friends. Avoidant Personality Disorder also tends to be diagnosed with Borderline Personality Disorder and with the Cluster A Personality Disorders (i.e., Paranoid, Schizoid, or Schizotypal Personality Disorders).

Specific Culture, Age, and Gender Features

There may be variation in the degree to which different cultural and ethnic groups regard diffidence and avoidance as appropriate. Moreover, avoidant behavior may be the result of problems in acculturation following immigration. This diagnosis should be used with great caution in children and adolescents for whom shy and avoidant behavior may be developmentally appropriate. Avoidant Personality Disorder appears to be equally frequent in males and females.

Prevalence

The prevalence of Avoidant Personality Disorder in the general population is between 0.5% and 1.0%. Avoidant Personality Disorder has been reported to be present in about 10% of outpatients seen in mental health clinics.

Course

The avoidant behavior often starts in infancy or childhood with shyness, isolation, and fear of strangers and new situations. Although shyness in childhood is a common precursor of Avoidant Personality Disorder, in most individuals it tends to gradually dissipate as they get older. In contrast, individuals who go on to develop Avoidant Personality Disorder may become increasingly shy and avoidant during adolescence and early adulthood, when social relationships with new people become especially important. There is some evidence that in adults Avoidant Personality Disorder tends to become less evident or to remit with age.

Differential Diagnosis

There appears to be a great deal of overlap between Avoidant Personality Disorder and **Social Phobia, Generalized Type,** so much so that they may be alternative conceptualizations of the same or similar conditions. Avoidance also characterizes both Avoidant Personality Disorder and **Panic Disorder With Agoraphobia,** and they often co-occur. The avoidance in Panic Disorder With Agoraphobia typically starts after the onset of Panic Attacks and may vary based on their frequency and intensity. In contrast, the avoidance in Avoidant Personality Disorder tends to have an early onset, an absence of clear precipitants, and a stable course.

Other Personality Disorders may be confused with Avoidant Personality Disorder because they have certain features in common. It is, therefore, important to distinguish among these disorders based on differences in their characteristic features. However, if an individual has personality features that meet criteria for one or more Personality Disorders in addition to Avoidant Personality Disorder, all can be diagnosed. Both Avoidant Personality Disorder and **Dependent Personality Disorder** are characterized by feelings of inadequacy, hypersensitivity to criticism, and a need for reassurance. Although the primary focus of concern in Avoidant Personality Disorder is avoidance of humiliation and rejection, in Dependent Personality Disorder the focus is on being taken care of. However, Avoidant Personality Disorder and Dependent Personality Disorder are particularly likely to co-occur. Like Avoidant Personality Disorder, **Schizoid Personality Disorder** and **Schizotypal Personality Disorder** are characterized by social isolation. However, individuals with Avoidant Personality Disorder want to have relationships with others and feel their loneliness deeply, whereas those with Schizoid or Schizotypal Personality Disorder may be content with and even prefer their social isolation. **Paranoid Personality Disorder** and Avoidant Personality Disorder are both characterized by a reluctance to confide in others. However, in Avoidant Personality Disorder, this reluctance is due more to a fear of being embarrassed or being found inadequate than to a fear of others' malicious intent.

Avoidant Personality Disorder must be distinguished from **Personality Change Due to a General Medical Condition,** in which the traits emerge due to the direct effects of a general medical condition on the central nervous system. It must also be distinguished from **symptoms that may develop in association with chronic substance use** (e.g., Cocaine-Related Disorder Not Otherwise Specified).

Many individuals display avoidant personality traits. Only when these traits are inflexible, maladaptive, and persisting and cause significant functional impairment or subjective distress do they constitute Avoidant Personality Disorder.

■ Diagnostic criteria for 301.82 Avoidant Personality Disorder

A pervasive pattern of social inhibition, feelings of inadequacy, and hypersensitivity to negative evaluation, beginning by early adulthood and present in a variety of contexts, as indicated by four (or more) of the following:

  (1) avoids occupational activities that involve significant interpersonal contact, because of fears of criticism, disapproval, or rejection

(continued)

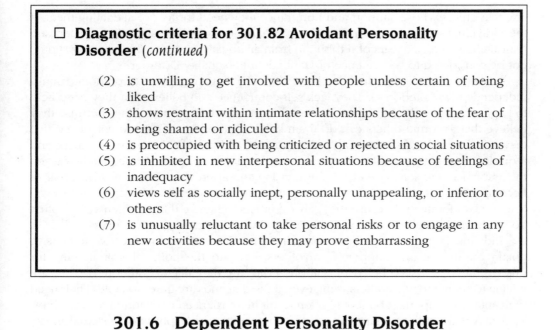

☐ **Diagnostic criteria for 301.82 Avoidant Personality Disorder** (*continued*)

    (2)   is unwilling to get involved with people unless certain of being liked

    (3)   shows restraint within intimate relationships because of the fear of being shamed or ridiculed

    (4)   is preoccupied with being criticized or rejected in social situations

    (5)   is inhibited in new interpersonal situations because of feelings of inadequacy

    (6)   views self as socially inept, personally unappealing, or inferior to others

    (7)   is unusually reluctant to take personal risks or to engage in any new activities because they may prove embarrassing

301.6 Dependent Personality Disorder

Diagnostic Features

The essential feature of Dependent Personality Disorder is a pervasive and excessive need to be taken care of that leads to submissive and clinging behavior and fears of separation. This pattern begins by early adulthood and is present in a variety of contexts. The dependent and submissive behaviors are designed to elicit caregiving and arise from a self-perception of being unable to function adequately without the help of others.

Individuals with Dependent Personality Disorder have great difficulty making everyday decisions (e.g., what color shirt to wear to work or whether to carry an umbrella) without an excessive amount of advice and reassurance from others (Criterion 1). These individuals tend to be passive and to allow other people (often a single other person) to take the initiative and assume responsibility for most major areas of their lives (Criterion 2). Adults with this disorder typically depend on a parent or spouse to decide where they should live, what kind of job they should have, and which neighbors to befriend. Adolescents with this disorder may allow their parent(s) to decide what they should wear, with whom they should associate, how they should spend their free time, and what school or college they should attend. This need for others to assume responsibility goes beyond age-appropriate and situation-appropriate requests for assistance from others (e.g., the specific needs of children, elderly persons, and handicapped persons). Dependent Personality Disorder may occur in an individual who has a serious general medical condition or disability, but in such cases the difficulty in taking responsibility must go beyond what would normally be associated with that condition or disability.

Because they fear losing support or approval, individuals with Dependent Personality Disorder often have difficulty expressing disagreement with other people, especially those on whom they are dependent (Criterion 3). These individuals feel so unable to function alone that they will agree with things that they feel are wrong rather than risk losing the help of those to whom they look for guidance. They do not get appropriately angry at others whose support and nurturance they need for fear of alienating them. If the individual's concerns regarding the consequences of expressing disagreement are realistic (e.g., realistic fears of retribution from an abusive spouse), the behavior should not be considered to be evidence of Dependent Personality Disorder.

Individuals with this disorder have difficulty initiating projects or doing things independently (Criterion 4). They lack self-confidence and believe that they need help to begin and carry through tasks. They will wait for others to start things because they believe that as a rule others can do them better. These individuals are convinced that they are incapable of functioning independently and present themselves as inept and requiring constant assistance. They are, however, likely to function adequately if given the assurance that someone else is supervising and approving. There may be a fear of becoming or appearing to be more competent, because they may believe that this will lead to abandonment. Because they rely on others to handle their problems, they often do not learn the skills of independent living, thus perpetuating dependency.

Individuals with Dependent Personality Disorder may go to excessive lengths to obtain nurturance and support from others, even to the point of volunteering for unpleasant tasks if such behavior will bring the care they need (Criterion 5). They are willing to submit to what others want, even if the demands are unreasonable. Their need to maintain an important bond will often result in imbalanced or distorted relationships. They may make extraordinary self-sacrifices or tolerate verbal, physical, or sexual abuse. (It should be noted that this behavior should be considered evidence of Dependent Personality Disorder only when it can clearly be established that other options are available to the individual). Individuals with this disorder feel uncomfortable or helpless when alone, because of their exaggerated fears of being unable to care for themselves (Criterion 6). They will "tag along" with important others just to avoid being alone, even if they are not interested or involved in what is happening.

When a close relationship ends (e.g., a breakup with a lover; the death of a caregiver), individuals with Dependent Personality Disorder may urgently seek another relationship to provide the care and support they need (Criterion 7). Their belief that they are unable to function in the absence of a close relationship motivates these individuals to become quickly and indiscriminately attached to another person. Individuals with this disorder are often preoccupied with fears of being left to care for themselves (Criterion 8). They see themselves as so totally dependent on the advice and help of an important other person that they worry about being abandoned by that person when there are no grounds to justify such fears. To be considered as evidence of this criterion, the fears must be excessive and unrealistic. For example, an elderly man with cancer who moves into his son's household for care is exhibiting dependent behavior that is appropriate given this person's life circumstances.

Associated Features and Disorders

Individuals with Dependent Personality Disorder are often characterized by pessimism and self-doubt, tend to belittle their abilities and assets, and may constantly refer to themselves as "stupid." They take criticism and disapproval as proof of their worthlessness and lose faith in themselves. They may seek overprotection and dominance from others. Occupational functioning may be impaired if independent initiative is required. They may avoid positions of responsibility and become anxious when faced with decisions. Social relations tend to be limited to those few people on whom the individual is dependent. There may be an increased risk of Mood Disorders, Anxiety Disorders, and Adjustment Disorder. Dependent Personality Disorder often co-occurs with other Personality Disorders, especially Borderline, Avoidant, and Histrionic Personality Disorders. Chronic physical illness or Separation Anxiety Disorder in childhood or adolescence may predispose the individual to the development of this disorder.

Specific Culture, Age, and Gender Features

The degree to which dependent behaviors are considered to be appropriate varies substantially across different age and sociocultural groups. Age and cultural factors need to be considered in evaluating the diagnostic threshold of each criterion. Dependent behavior should be considered characteristic of the disorder only when it is clearly in excess of the individual's cultural norms or reflects unrealistic concerns. An emphasis on passivity, politeness, and deferential treatment is characteristic of some societies and may be misinterpreted as traits of Dependent Personality Disorder. Similarly, societies may differentially foster and discourage dependent behavior in males and females. This diagnosis should be used with great caution, if at all, in children and adolescents, for whom dependent behavior may be developmentally appropriate. In clinical settings, this disorder has been diagnosed more frequently in females; however, the sex ratio of this disorder is not significantly different than the sex ratio of females within the respective clinical setting. Moreover, some studies using structured assessments report similar prevalence rates among males and females.

Prevalence

Dependent Personality Disorder is among the most frequently reported Personality Disorders encountered in mental health clinics.

Differential Diagnosis

Dependent Personality Disorder must be distinguished from dependency arising as a consequence of Axis I disorders (e.g., **Mood Disorders, Panic Disorder,** and **Agoraphobia**) and as a result of **general medical conditions.** Dependent Personality Disorder has an early onset, chronic course, and a pattern of behavior that does not occur exclusively during an Axis I or Axis III disorder.

Other Personality Disorders may be confused with Dependent Personality Disorder because they have certain features in common. It is, therefore, important to distinguish among these disorders based on differences in their characteristic features. However, if an individual has personality features that meet criteria for one or more Personality Disorders in addition to Dependent Personality Disorder, all can be diagnosed. Although many Personality Disorders are characterized by dependent features, Dependent Personality Disorder can be distinguished by its predominantly submissive, reactive, and clinging behavior. Both Dependent Personality Disorder and **Borderline Personality Disorder** are characterized by fear of abandonment; however, the individual with Borderline Personality Disorder reacts to abandonment with feelings of emotional emptiness, rage, and demands, whereas the individual with Dependent Personality Disorder reacts with increasing appeasement and submissiveness and urgently seeks a replacement relationship to provide caregiving and support. Borderline Personality

Disorder can further be distinguished from Dependent Personality Disorder by a typical pattern of unstable and intense relationships. Individuals with **Histrionic Personality Disorder,** like those with Dependent Personality Disorder, have a strong need for reassurance and approval and may appear childlike and clinging. However, unlike Dependent Personality Disorder, which is characterized by self-effacing and docile behavior, Histrionic Personality Disorder is characterized by gregarious flamboyance with active demands for attention. Both Dependent Personality Disorder and **Avoidant Personality Disorder** are characterized by feelings of inadequacy, hypersensitivity to criticism, and a need for reassurance; however, individuals with Avoidant Personality Disorder have such a strong fear of humiliation and rejection that they withdraw until they are certain they will be accepted. In contrast, individuals with Dependent Personality Disorder have a pattern of seeking and maintaining connections to important others, rather than avoiding and withdrawing from relationships.

Dependent Personality Disorder must be distinguished from **Personality Change Due to a General Medical Condition,** in which the traits emerge due to the direct effects of a general medical condition on the central nervous system. It must also be distinguished from **symptoms that may develop in association with chronic substance use** (e.g., Cocaine-Related Disorder Not Otherwise Specified).

Many individuals display dependent personality traits. Only when these traits are inflexible, maladaptive, and persisting and cause significant functional impairment or subjective distress do they constitute Dependent Personality Disorder.

■ Diagnostic criteria for 301.6 Dependent Personality Disorder

A pervasive and excessive need to be taken care of that leads to submissive and clinging behavior and fears of separation, beginning by early adulthood and present in a variety of contexts, as indicated by five (or more) of the following:

(1) has difficulty making everyday decisions without an excessive amount of advice and reassurance from others

(2) needs others to assume responsibility for most major areas of his or her life

(3) has difficulty expressing disagreement with others because of fear of loss of support or approval. **Note:** Do not include realistic fears of retribution.

(4) has difficulty initiating projects or doing things on his or her own (because of a lack of self-confidence in judgment or abilities rather than a lack of motivation or energy)

(5) goes to excessive lengths to obtain nurturance and support from others, to the point of volunteering to do things that are unpleasant

(6) feels uncomfortable or helpless when alone because of exaggerated fears of being unable to care for himself or herself

(continued)

☐ **Diagnostic criteria for 301.6 Dependent Personality Disorder** (*continued*)

    (7) urgently seeks another relationship as a source of care and support when a close relationship ends

    (8) is unrealistically preoccupied with fears of being left to take care of himself or herself

301.4   Obsessive-Compulsive Personality Disorder

Diagnostic Features

The essential feature of Obsessive-Compulsive Personality Disorder is a preoccupation with orderliness, perfectionism, and mental and interpersonal control, at the expense of flexibility, openness, and efficiency. This pattern begins by early adulthood and is present in a variety of contexts.

Individuals with Obsessive-Compulsive Personality Disorder attempt to maintain a sense of control through painstaking attention to rules, trivial details, procedures, lists, schedules, or form to the extent that the major point of the activity is lost (Criterion 1). They are excessively careful and prone to repetition, paying extraordinary attention to detail and repeatedly checking for possible mistakes. They are oblivious to the fact that other people tend to become very annoyed at the delays and inconveniences that result from this behavior. For example, when such individuals misplace a list of things to be done, they will spend an inordinate amount of time looking for the list rather than spending a few moments re-creating it from memory and proceeding to accomplish the tasks. Time is poorly allocated, the most important tasks being left to the last moment. The perfectionism and self-imposed high standards of performance cause significant dysfunction and distress in these individuals. They may become so involved in making every detail of a project absolutely perfect that the project is never finished (Criterion 2). For example, the completion of a written report is delayed by numerous time-consuming rewrites that all come up short of "perfection." Deadlines are missed, and aspects of the individual's life that are not the current focus of activity may fall into disarray.

Individuals with Obsessive-Compulsive Personality Disorder display excessive devotion to work and productivity to the exclusion of leisure activities and friendships (Criterion 3). This behavior is not accounted for by economic necessity. They often feel that they do not have time to take an evening or a weekend day off to go on an outing or to just relax. They may keep postponing a pleasurable activity, such as a vacation, so that it may never occur. When they do take time for leisure activities or vacations, they are very uncomfortable unless they have taken along something to work on so they do not "waste time." There may be a great concentration on household chores (e.g., repeated excessive cleaning so that "one could eat off the floor"). If they spend time with friends, it is likely to be in some kind of formally organized activity (e.g., sports). Hobbies or recreational activities are approached as serious tasks requiring careful organization and hard work to master. The emphasis is on perfect performance. These individuals turn play into a structured task (e.g., correcting an infant for not putting rings on the post in the right order; telling a toddler to ride his or her tricycle in a straight line; turning a baseball game into a harsh "lesson").

Individuals with Obsessive-Compulsive Personality Disorder may be excessively conscientious, scrupulous, and inflexible about matters of morality, ethics, or values (Criterion 4). They may force themselves and others to follow rigid moral principles and very strict standards of performance. They may also be mercilessly self-critical about their own mistakes. Individuals with this disorder are rigidly deferential to authority and rules and insist on quite literal compliance, with no rule bending for extenuating circumstances. For example, the individual will not lend a quarter to a friend who needs one to make a telephone call, because "neither a borrower or lender be" or because it would be "bad" for the person's character. These qualities should not be accounted for by the individual's cultural or religious identification.

Individuals with this disorder may be unable to discard worn-out or worthless objects, even when they have no sentimental value (Criterion 5). Often these individuals will admit to being "pack rats." They regard discarding objects as wasteful because "you never know when you might need something" and will become upset if someone tries to get rid of the things they have saved. Their spouses or roommates may complain about the amount of space taken up by old parts, magazines, broken appliances, and so on.

Individuals with Obsessive-Compulsive Personality Disorder are reluctant to delegate tasks or to work with others (Criterion 6). They stubbornly and unreasonably insist that everything be done their way and that people conform to their way of doing things. They often give very detailed instructions about how things should be done (e.g., there is one and only one way to mow the lawn, wash the dishes, build a doghouse) and are surprised and irritated if others suggest creative alternatives. At other times they may reject offers of help even when behind schedule because they believe no one else can do it right.

Individuals with this disorder may be miserly and stingy and maintain a standard of living far below what they can afford, believing that spending must be tightly controlled to provide for future catastrophes (Criterion 7). Individuals with Obsessive-Compulsive Personality Disorder are characterized by rigidity and stubbornness (Criterion 8). They are so concerned about having things done the one "correct" way that they have trouble going along with anyone else's ideas. These individuals plan ahead in meticulous detail and are unwilling to consider changes. Totally wrapped up in their own perspective, they have difficulty acknowledging the viewpoints of others. Friends and colleagues may become frustrated by this constant rigidity. Even when individuals with Obsessive-Compulsive Personality Disorder recognize that it may be in their interest to compromise, they may stubbornly refuse to do so, arguing that it is "the principle of the thing."

Associated Features and Disorders

When rules and established procedures do not dictate the correct answer, decision making may become a time-consuming, often painful process. Individuals with Obsessive-Compulsive Personality Disorder may have such difficulty deciding which tasks take priority or what is the best way of doing some particular task that they may never get started on anything. They are prone to become upset or angry in situations in which they are not able to maintain control of their physical or interpersonal environment, although the anger is typically not expressed directly. For example, a person may be angry when service in a restaurant is poor, but instead of complaining to the management, the individual ruminates about how much to leave as a tip. On other occasions, anger may be expressed with righteous indignation over a seemingly minor matter. People with this disorder may be especially attentive to their relative status in dominance-submission relationships and may display excessive deference to an authority they respect and excessive resistance to authority that they do not respect.

Individuals with this disorder usually express affection in a highly controlled or stilted fashion and may be very uncomfortable in the presence of others who are emotionally expressive. Their everyday relationships have a formal and serious quality, and they may be stiff in situations in which others would smile and be happy (e.g., greeting a lover at the airport). They carefully hold themselves back until they are sure that whatever they say will be perfect. They may be preoccupied with logic and intellect, and intolerant of affective behavior in others. They often have difficulty expressing tender feelings, rarely paying compliments. Individuals with this disorder may experience occupational difficulties and distress, particularly when confronted with new situations that demand flexibility and compromise.

Although some studies suggest an association with Obsessive-Compulsive Disorder (included in the "Anxiety Disorders" section, p. 417), it appears that the majority of individuals with Obsessive-Compulsive Disorder do not have a pattern of behavior that meets criteria for Obsessive-Compulsive Personality Disorder. Many of the features of Obsessive-Compulsive Personality Disorder overlap with "type A" personality characteristics (e.g., hostility, competitiveness, and time urgency), and these features may be present in people at risk for myocardial infarction. There may be an association between Obsessive-Compulsive Personality Disorder and Mood and Anxiety Disorders.

Specific Culture and Gender Features

In assessing an individual for Obsessive-Compulsive Personality Disorder, the clinician should not include those behaviors that reflect habits, customs, or interpersonal styles that are culturally sanctioned by the individual's reference group. Certain cultures place substantial emphasis on work and productivity; the resulting behaviors in members of those societies need not be considered indications of Obsessive-Compulsive Personality Disorder. In systematic studies, the disorder appears to be diagnosed about twice as often among males.

Prevalence

Studies that have used systematic assessment suggest prevalence estimates of Obsessive-Compulsive Personality Disorder of about 1% in community samples and about 3%–10% in individuals presenting to mental health clinics.

Differential Diagnosis

Despite the similarity in names, **Obsessive-Compulsive Disorder** is usually easily distinguished from Obsessive-Compulsive Personality Disorder by the presence of true obsessions and compulsions. A diagnosis of Obsessive-Compulsive Disorder should be considered especially when hoarding is extreme (e.g., accumulated stacks of worthless objects present a fire hazard and make it difficult for others to walk through the house).

When criteria for both disorders are met, both diagnoses should be recorded.

Other Personality Disorders may be confused with Obsessive-Compulsive Personality Disorder because they have certain features in common. It is, therefore, important to distinguish among these disorders based on differences in their characteristic features. However, if an individual has personality features that meet criteria for one or more Personality Disorders in addition to Obsessive-Compulsive Personality Disorder, all can be diagnosed. Individuals with **Narcissistic Personality Disorder** may also profess a commitment to perfectionism and believe that others cannot do things as well, but these individuals are more likely to believe that they have achieved perfection, whereas those with Obsessive-Compulsive Personality Disorder are usually self-critical. Individuals with Narcissistic or **Antisocial Personality Disorder** lack generosity but will indulge themselves, whereas those with Obsessive-Compulsive Personality Disorder adopt a miserly spending style toward both self and others. Both **Schizoid Personality Disorder** and Obsessive-Compulsive Personality Disorder may be characterized by an apparent formality and social detachment. In Obsessive-Compulsive Personality Disorder, this stems from discomfort with emotions and excessive devotion to work, whereas in Schizoid Personality Disorder there is a fundamental lack of capacity for intimacy.

Obsessive-Compulsive Personality Disorder must be distinguished from **Personality Change Due to a General Medical Condition,** in which the traits emerge due to the direct effects of a general medical condition on the central nervous system. It must also be distinguished from **symptoms that may develop in association with chronic substance use** (e.g., Cocaine-Related Disorder Not Otherwise Specified).

Obsessive-compulsive personality traits in moderation may be especially adaptive, particularly in situations that reward high performance. Only when these traits are inflexible, maladaptive, and persisting and cause significant functional impairment or subjective distress do they constitute Obsessive-Compulsive Personality Disorder.

■ Diagnostic criteria for 301.4 Obsessive-Compulsive Personality Disorder

A pervasive pattern of preoccupation with orderliness, perfectionism, and mental and interpersonal control, at the expense of flexibility, openness, and efficiency, beginning by early adulthood and present in a variety of contexts, as indicated by four (or more) of the following:

(1) is preoccupied with details, rules, lists, order, organization, or schedules to the extent that the major point of the activity is lost

(2) shows perfectionism that interferes with task completion (e.g., is unable to complete a project because his or her own overly strict standards are not met)

(3) is excessively devoted to work and productivity to the exclusion of leisure activities and friendships (not accounted for by obvious economic necessity)

(4) is overconscientious, scrupulous, and inflexible about matters of morality, ethics, or values (not accounted for by cultural or religious identification)

(continued)

☐ **Diagnostic criteria for 301.4 Obsessive-Compulsive Personality Disorder** (*continued*)

    (5)   is unable to discard worn-out or worthless objects even when they have no sentimental value

    (6)   is reluctant to delegate tasks or to work with others unless they submit to exactly his or her way of doing things

    (7)   adopts a miserly spending style toward both self and others; money is viewed as something to be hoarded for future catastrophes

    (8)   shows rigidity and stubbornness

301.9 Personality Disorder Not Otherwise Specified

This category is for disorders of personality functioning that do not meet criteria for any specific Personality Disorder. An example is the presence of features of more than one specific Personality Disorder that do not meet the full criteria for any one Personality Disorder ("mixed personality"), but that together cause clinically significant distress or impairment in one or more important areas of functioning (e.g., social or occupational). This category can also be used when the clinician judges that a specific Personality Disorder that is not included in the Classification is appropriate. Examples include depressive personality disorder and passive-aggressive personality disorder (see p. 732 and p. 733, respectively, for suggested research criteria).

Other Conditions
That May Be a Focus of
Clinical Attention

This section covers other conditions or problems that may be a focus of clinical attention. These are related to the mental disorders described previously in this manual in one of the following ways: 1) the problem is the focus of diagnosis or treatment and the individual has no mental disorder (e.g., a Partner Relational Problem in which neither partner has symptoms that meet criteria for a mental disorder, in which case only the Partner Relational Problem is coded); 2) the individual has a mental disorder but it is unrelated to the problem (e.g., a Partner Relational Problem in which one of the partners has an incidental Specific Phobia, in which case both can be coded); 3) the individual has a mental disorder that is related to the problem, but the problem is sufficiently severe to warrant independent clinical attention (e.g., a Partner Relational Problem sufficiently problematic to be a focus of treatment that is also associated with Major Depressive Disorder in one of the partners, in which case both can be coded). The conditions and problems in this section are coded on Axis I.

Psychological Factors Affecting Medical Condition

316   Psychological Factor Affecting Medical Condition

Diagnostic Features

The essential feature of Psychological Factors Affecting Medical Condition is the presence of one or more specific psychological or behavioral factors that adversely affect a general medical condition. There are several different ways in which these factors can adversely affect the general medical condition. The factors can influence the course of the general medical condition (which can be inferred by a close temporal association between the factors and the development or exacerbation of, or delayed recovery from, the medical condition). The factors may interfere with treatment of the general medical condition.

The factors may constitute an additional health risk for the individual (e.g., continued overeating in an individual with weight-related diabetes). They may precipitate or exacerbate symptoms of a general medical condition by eliciting stress-related physiological responses (e.g., causing chest pain in individuals with coronary artery disease, or bronchospasm in individuals with asthma).

The psychological or behavioral factors that influence general medical conditions include Axis I disorders, Axis II disorders, psychological symptoms or personality traits that do not meet the full criteria for a specific mental disorder, maladaptive health behaviors, or physiological responses to environmental or social stressors.

Psychological or behavioral factors play a potential role in the presentation or treatment of almost every general medical condition. This category should be reserved for those situations in which the psychological factors have a clinically significant effect on the course or outcome of the general medical condition or place the individual at a significantly higher risk for an adverse outcome. There must be reasonable evidence to suggest an association between the psychological factors and the medical condition, although it may often not be possible to demonstrate direct causality or the mechanisms underlying the relationship. Psychological and behavioral factors may affect the course of almost every major category of disease, including cardiovascular conditions, dermatological conditions, endocrinological conditions, gastrointestinal conditions, neoplastic conditions, neurological conditions, pulmonary conditions, renal conditions, and rheumatological conditions.

The Psychological Factors Affecting Medical Condition diagnosis is coded on Axis I, and the accompanying general medical condition is coded on Axis III. (See Appendix G for a list of diagnostic codes for general medical conditions.) To provide greater specificity regarding the type of psychological factor, the name is chosen from the list below. When more than one type of factor is present, the most prominent should be specified.

Mental Disorder Affecting . . . *[Indicate the General Medical Condition]*.   A specific Axis I or Axis II disorder significantly affects the course or treatment of a general medical condition (e.g., Major Depressive Disorder adversely affecting the prognosis of myocardial infarction, renal failure, or hemodialysis; Schizophrenia complicating the treatment of diabetes mellitus). In addition to coding this condition on Axis I, the specific mental disorder is also coded on Axis I or Axis II.

Psychological Symptoms Affecting . . . *[Indicate the General Medical Condition]*. Symptoms that do not meet full criteria for an Axis I disorder significantly affect the course or treatment of a general medical condition (e.g., symptoms of anxiety or depression affecting the course and severity of irritable bowel syndrome or peptic ulcer disease, or complicating recovery from surgery).

Personality Traits or Coping Style Affecting . . . *[Indicate the General Medical Condition]*.   A personality trait or a maladaptive coping style significantly affects the course or treatment of a general medical condition. Personality traits can be subthreshold for an Axis II disorder or represent another pattern that has been demonstrated to be a risk factor for certain illnesses (e.g., "type A," pressured, hostile behavior for coronary artery disease). Problematic personality traits and maladaptive coping styles can impede the working relationship with health care personnel.

Maladaptive Health Behaviors Affecting . . . [Indicate the General Medical Condition].   Maladaptive health behaviors (e.g., sedentary lifestyle, unsafe sexual practices, overeating, excessive alcohol and drug use) significantly affect the course or treatment of a general medical condition. If the maladaptive behaviors are better accounted for by an Axis I disorder (e.g., overeating as part of Bulimia Nervosa, alcohol use as part of Alcohol Dependence), the name "Mental Disorder Affecting Medical Condition" should be used instead.

Stress-Related Physiological Response Affecting . . . [Indicate the General Medical Condition].   Stress-related physiological responses significantly affect the course or treatment of a general medical condition (e.g., precipitate chest pain or arrhythmia in a patient with coronary artery disease).

Other or Unspecified Factors Affecting . . . [Indicate the General Medical Condition].   A factor not included in the subtypes specified above or an unspecified psychological or behavioral factor significantly affects the course or treatment of a general medical condition.

Differential Diagnosis

A temporal association between symptoms of a mental disorder and a general medical condition is also characteristic of a **Mental Disorder Due to a General Medical Condition,** but the presumed causality is in the opposite direction. In a Mental Disorder Due to a General Medical Condition, the general medical condition is judged to be causing the mental disorder through a direct physiological mechanism. In Psychological Factors Affecting Medical Condition, the psychological or behavioral factors are judged to affect the course of the general medical condition.

Substance Use Disorders (e.g., Alcohol Dependence, Nicotine Dependence) adversely affect the prognosis of many general medical conditions. If an individual has a coexisting Substance Use Disorder that adversely affects or causes a general medical condition, Mental Disorder Affecting General Medical Condition can be coded on Axis I in addition to the Substance Use Disorder. For substance use patterns affecting a general medical condition that do not meet the criteria for a Substance Use Disorder, Maladaptive Health Behaviors Affecting Medical Condition can be specified.

Somatoform Disorders are characterized by the presence of both psychological factors and physical symptoms, but there is no general medical condition that can completely account for the physical symptoms. In contrast, in Psychological Factors Affecting Medical Condition, the psychological factors adversely affect a diagnosable general medical condition. Psychological factors affecting pain syndromes are not diagnosed as Psychological Factors Affecting Medical Condition but rather as **Pain Disorder Associated With Psychological Factors** or **Pain Disorder Associated With Both Psychological Factors and a General Medical Condition.**

When noncompliance with treatment for a general medical condition results from psychological factors but becomes the major focus of clinical attention, **Noncompliance With Treatment** (see p. 683) should be coded.

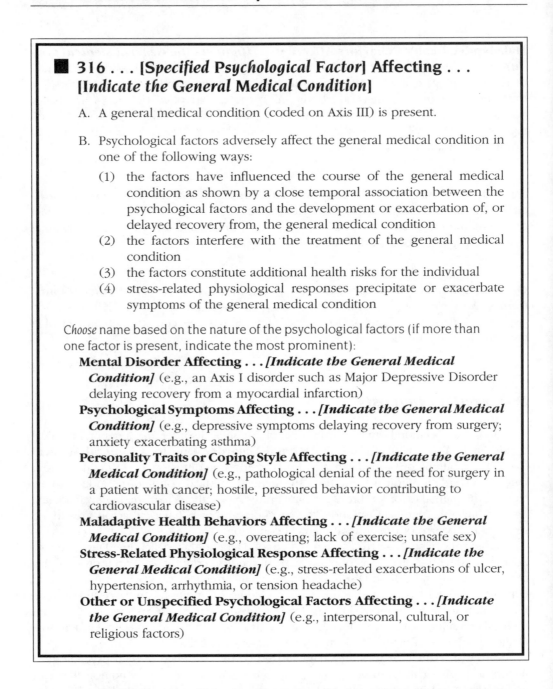

■ **316 . . . [Specified Psychological Factor] Affecting . . . [Indicate the General Medical Condition]**

A. A general medical condition (coded on Axis III) is present.

B. Psychological factors adversely affect the general medical condition in one of the following ways:

    (1) the factors have influenced the course of the general medical condition as shown by a close temporal association between the psychological factors and the development or exacerbation of, or delayed recovery from, the general medical condition

    (2) the factors interfere with the treatment of the general medical condition

    (3) the factors constitute additional health risks for the individual

    (4) stress-related physiological responses precipitate or exacerbate symptoms of the general medical condition

Choose name based on the nature of the psychological factors (if more than one factor is present, indicate the most prominent):

    Mental Disorder Affecting . . . *[Indicate the General Medical Condition]* (e.g., an Axis I disorder such as Major Depressive Disorder delaying recovery from a myocardial infarction)

    Psychological Symptoms Affecting . . . *[Indicate the General Medical Condition]* (e.g., depressive symptoms delaying recovery from surgery; anxiety exacerbating asthma)

    Personality Traits or Coping Style Affecting . . . *[Indicate the General Medical Condition]* (e.g., pathological denial of the need for surgery in a patient with cancer; hostile, pressured behavior contributing to cardiovascular disease)

    Maladaptive Health Behaviors Affecting . . . *[Indicate the General Medical Condition]* (e.g., overeating; lack of exercise; unsafe sex)

    Stress-Related Physiological Response Affecting . . . *[Indicate the General Medical Condition]* (e.g., stress-related exacerbations of ulcer, hypertension, arrhythmia, or tension headache)

    Other or Unspecified Psychological Factors Affecting . . . *[Indicate the General Medical Condition]* (e.g., interpersonal, cultural, or religious factors)

Medication-Induced Movement Disorders

The following Medication-Induced Movement Disorders are included because of their frequent importance in 1) the management by medication of mental disorders or general medical conditions; and 2) the differential diagnosis with Axis I disorders (e.g., Anxiety Disorder versus Neuroleptic-Induced Akathisia; catatonia versus Neuroleptic Malignant Syndrome). Although these disorders are labeled "medication induced," it is often difficult to establish the causal relationship between medication exposure and the development of the movement disorder, especially because some of these movement disorders also occur in the absence of medication exposure. The term *neuroleptic* is used broadly in this manual to refer to medications with dopamine-antagonist properties. These include so-called "typical" antipsychotic agents (e.g., chlorpromazine, haloperidol, fluphenazine), "atypical" antipsychotic agents (e.g., clozapine), certain dopamine receptor blocking drugs used in the treatment of symptoms such as nausea and gastroparesis (e.g., prochlorperazine, promethazine, trimethobenzamide, thiethylperazine, and metoclopramide), and amoxapine, which is marketed as an antidepressant. Medication-Induced Movement Disorders should be coded on Axis I.

332.1   Neuroleptic-Induced Parkinsonism

Parkinsonian tremor, muscular rigidity, or akinesia developing within a few weeks of starting or raising the dose of a neuroleptic medication (or after reducing a medication used to treat extrapyramidal symptoms). (See p. 736 for suggested research criteria.)

333.92   Neuroleptic Malignant Syndrome

Severe muscle rigidity, elevated temperature, and other related findings (e.g., diaphoresis, dysphagia, incontinence, changes in level of consciousness ranging from confusion to coma, mutism, elevated or labile blood pressure, elevated creatine phosphokinase [CPK]) developing in association with the use of neuroleptic medication. (See p. 739 for suggested research criteria.)

333.7   Neuroleptic-Induced Acute Dystonia

Abnormal positioning or spasm of the muscles of the head, neck, limbs, or trunk developing within a few days of starting or raising the dose of a neuroleptic medication (or after reducing a medication used to treat extrapyramidal symptoms). (See p. 742 for suggested research criteria.)

333.99   Neuroleptic-Induced Acute Akathisia

Subjective complaints of restlessness accompanied by observed movements (e.g., fidgety movements of the legs, rocking from foot to foot, pacing, or inability to sit or stand still) developing within a few weeks of starting or raising the dose of a neuroleptic medication (or after reducing a medication used to treat extrapyramidal symptoms). (See p. 744 for suggested research criteria.)

333.82   Neuroleptic-Induced Tardive Dyskinesia

Involuntary choreiform, athetoid, or rhythmic movements (lasting at least a few weeks) of the tongue, jaw, or extremities developing in association with the use of neuroleptic medication for at least a few months (may be for a shorter period of time in elderly persons). (See p. 747 for suggested research criteria.)

333.1   Medication-Induced Postural Tremor

Fine tremor occurring during attempts to maintain a posture that develops in association with the use of medication (e.g., lithium, antidepressants, valproate). (See p. 749 for suggested research criteria.)

333.90   Medication-Induced Movement Disorder Not Otherwise Specified

This category is for Medication-Induced Movement Disorders not classified by any of the specific disorders listed above. Examples include 1) parkinsonism, acute akathisia, acute dystonia, or dyskinetic movement that is associated with a medication other than a neuroleptic; 2) a presentation that resembles neuroleptic malignant syndrome that is associated with a medication other than a neuroleptic; or 3) tardive dystonia.

Other Medication-Induced Disorder

995.2   Adverse Effects of Medication Not Otherwise Specified

This category is available for optional use by clinicians to code side effects of medication (other than movement symptoms) when these adverse effects become a main focus of clinical attention. Examples include severe hypotension, cardiac arrhythmias, and priapism.

Relational Problems

Relational problems include patterns of interaction between or among members of a relational unit that are associated with clinically significant impairment in functioning, or symptoms among one or more members of the relational unit, or impairment in the functioning of the relational unit itself. The following relational problems are included because they are frequently a focus of clinical attention among individuals seen by health professionals. These problems may exacerbate or complicate the management of a mental disorder or general medical condition in one or more members of the relational unit, may be a result of a mental disorder or a general medical condition, may be independent of other conditions that are present, or can occur in the absence of any other condition. When these problems are the principal focus of clinical attention, they should be listed on Axis I. Otherwise, if they are present but not the principal focus of clinical attention, they may be listed on Axis IV. The relevant category is generally applied to all members of a relational unit who are being treated for the problem.

V61.9   Relational Problem Related to a Mental Disorder or General Medical Condition

This category should be used when the focus of clinical attention is a pattern of impaired interaction that is associated with a mental disorder or a general medical condition in a family member.

V61.20   Parent-Child Relational Problem

This category should be used when the focus of clinical attention is a pattern of interaction between parent and child (e.g., impaired communication, overprotection, inadequate discipline) that is associated with clinically significant impairment in individual or family functioning or the development of clinically significant symptoms in parent or child.

V61.1   Partner Relational Problem

This category should be used when the focus of clinical attention is a pattern of interaction between spouses or partners characterized by negative communication (e.g., criticisms), distorted communication (e.g., unrealistic expectations), or noncommunication (e.g., withdrawal) that is associated with clinically significant impairment in individual or family functioning or the development of symptoms in one or both partners.

V61.8   Sibling Relational Problem

This category should be used when the focus of clinical attention is a pattern of interaction among siblings that is associated with clinically significant impairment in individual or family functioning or the development of symptoms in one or more of the siblings.

V62.81   Relational Problem Not Otherwise Specified

This category should be used when the focus of clinical attention is on relational problems that are not classifiable by any of the specific problems listed above (e.g., difficulties with co-workers).

Problems Related to Abuse or Neglect

This section includes categories that should be used when the focus of clinical attention is severe mistreatment of one individual by another through physical abuse, sexual abuse, or child neglect. These problems are included because they are frequently a focus of clinical attention among individuals seen by health professionals. The appropriate V code applies if the focus of attention is on the perpetrator of the abuse or neglect or on the relational unit in which it occurs. If the individual being evaluated or treated is the victim of the abuse or neglect, code 995.5 for a child or 995.81 for an adult.

V61.21   Physical Abuse of Child

This category should be used when the focus of clinical attention is physical abuse of a child.
Coding note: *Specify* **995.5** *if focus of clinical attention is on the victim.*

V61.21   Sexual Abuse of Child

This category should be used when the focus of clinical attention is sexual abuse of a child.
Coding note: *Specify* **995.5** *if focus of clinical attention is on the victim.*

V61.21   Neglect of Child

This category should be used when the focus of clinical attention is child neglect.
Coding note: *Specify* **995.5** *if focus of clinical attention is on the victim.*

V61.1   Physical Abuse of Adult

This category should be used when the focus of clinical attention is physical abuse of an adult (e.g., spouse beating, abuse of elderly parent).
Coding note: *Specify* **995.81** *if focus of clinical attention is on the victim.*

V61.1   Sexual Abuse of Adult

This category should be used when the focus of clinical attention is sexual abuse of an adult (e.g., sexual coercion, rape).
Coding note: *Specify* **995.81** *if focus of clinical attention is on the victim.*

Additional Conditions That May Be a Focus of Clinical Attention

V15.81   Noncompliance With Treatment

This category can be used when the focus of clinical attention is noncompliance with an important aspect of the treatment for a mental disorder or a general medical condition. The reasons for noncompliance may include discomfort resulting from treatment (e.g., medication side effects), expense of treatment, decisions based on personal value judgments or religious or cultural beliefs about the advantages and disadvantages of the proposed treatment, maladaptive personality traits or coping styles (e.g., denial of illness), or the presence of a mental disorder (e.g., Schizophrenia, Avoidant Personality Disorder). This category should be used only when the problem is sufficiently severe to warrant independent clinical attention.

V65.2   Malingering

The essential feature of Malingering is the intentional production of false or grossly exaggerated physical or psychological symptoms, motivated by external incentives such as avoiding military duty, avoiding work, obtaining financial compensation, evading criminal prosecution, or obtaining drugs. Under some circumstances, Malingering may represent adaptive behavior—for example, feigning illness while a captive of the enemy during wartime.

Malingering should be strongly suspected if any combination of the following is noted:

1. Medicolegal context of presentation (e.g., the person is referred by an attorney to the clinician for examination)
2. Marked discrepancy between the person's claimed stress or disability and the objective findings
3. Lack of cooperation during the diagnostic evaluation and in complying with the prescribed treatment regimen
4. The presence of Antisocial Personality Disorder

Malingering differs from Factitious Disorder in that the motivation for the symptom production in Malingering is an external incentive, whereas in Factitious Disorder external incentives are absent. Evidence of an intrapsychic need to maintain the sick role suggests Factitious Disorder. Malingering is differentiated from Conversion Disorder and other Somatoform Disorders by the intentional production of symptoms and by the obvious, external incentives associated with it. In Malingering (in contrast to Conversion Disorder), symptom relief is not often obtained by suggestion or hypnosis.

V71.01   Adult Antisocial Behavior

This category can be used when the focus of clinical attention is adult antisocial behavior that is not due to a mental disorder (e.g., Conduct Disorder, Antisocial Personality

Disorder, or an Impulse-Control Disorder). Examples include the behavior of some professional thieves, racketeers, or dealers in illegal substances.

V71.02   Child or Adolescent Antisocial Behavior

This category can be used when the focus of clinical attention is antisocial behavior in a child or adolescent that is not due to a mental disorder (e.g., Conduct Disorder or an Impulse-Control Disorder). Examples include isolated antisocial acts of children or adolescents (not a pattern of antisocial behavior).

V62.89   Borderline Intellectual Functioning

This category can be used when the focus of clinical attention is associated with borderline intellectual functioning, that is, an IQ in the 71–84 range. Differential diagnosis between Borderline Intellectual Functioning and Mental Retardation (an IQ of 70 or below) is especially difficult when the coexistence of certain mental disorders (e.g., Schizophrenia) is involved.
Coding note: *This is coded on Axis II.*

780.9   Age-Related Cognitive Decline

This category can be used when the focus of clinical attention is an objectively identified decline in cognitive functioning consequent to the aging process that is within normal limits given the person's age. Individuals with this condition may report problems remembering names or appointments or may experience difficulty in solving complex problems. This category should be considered only after it has been determined that the cognitive impairment is not attributable to a specific mental disorder or neurological condition.

V62.82   Bereavement

This category can be used when the focus of clinical attention is a reaction to the death of a loved one. As part of their reaction to the loss, some grieving individuals present with symptoms characteristic of a Major Depressive Episode (e.g., feelings of sadness and associated symptoms such as insomnia, poor appetite, and weight loss). The bereaved individual typically regards the depressed mood as "normal," although the person may seek professional help for relief of associated symptoms such as insomnia or anorexia. The duration and expression of "normal" bereavement vary considerably among different cultural groups. The diagnosis of Major Depressive Disorder is generally not given unless the symptoms are still present 2 months after the loss. However, the presence of certain symptoms that are not characteristic of a "normal" grief reaction may be helpful in differentiating bereavement from a Major Depressive Episode. These include 1) guilt about things other than actions taken or not taken by the survivor at the time of the death; 2) thoughts of death other than the survivor feeling that he or she would be better off dead or should have died with the deceased person; 3) morbid preoccupation with worthlessness; 4) marked psychomotor retardation; 5) prolonged and marked functional impairment; and 6) hallucinatory experiences other than thinking that he or she hears the voice of, or transiently sees the image of, the deceased person.

V62.3   Academic Problem

This category can be used when the focus of clinical attention is an academic problem that is not due to a mental disorder or, if due to a mental disorder, is sufficiently severe to warrant independent clinical attention. An example is a pattern of failing grades or of significant underachievement in a person with adequate intellectual capacity in the absence of a Learning or Communication Disorder or any other mental disorder that would account for the problem.

V62.2   Occupational Problem

This category can be used when the focus of clinical attention is an occupational problem that is not due to a mental disorder or, if it is due to a mental disorder, is sufficiently severe to warrant independent clinical attention. Examples include job dissatisfaction and uncertainty about career choices.

313.82   Identity Problem

This category can be used when the focus of clinical attention is uncertainty about multiple issues relating to identity such as long-term goals, career choice, friendship patterns, sexual orientation and behavior, moral values, and group loyalties.

V62.89   Religious or Spiritual Problem

This category can be used when the focus of clinical attention is a religious or spiritual problem. Examples include distressing experiences that involve loss or questioning of faith, problems associated with conversion to a new faith, or questioning of spiritual values that may not necessarily be related to an organized church or religious institution.

V62.4   Acculturation Problem

This category can be used when the focus of clinical attention is a problem involving adjustment to a different culture (e.g., following migration).

V62.89   Phase of Life Problem

This category can be used when the focus of clinical attention is a problem associated with a particular developmental phase or some other life circumstance that is not due to a mental disorder or, if it is due to a mental disorder, is sufficiently severe to warrant independent clinical attention. Examples include problems associated with entering school, leaving parental control, starting a new career, and changes involved in marriage, divorce, and retirement.

Additional Codes

300.9   Unspecified Mental Disorder (nonpsychotic)

There are several circumstances in which it may be appropriate to assign this code: 1) for a specific mental disorder not included in the DSM-IV Classification, 2) when none of the available Not Otherwise Specified categories is appropriate, or 3) when it is judged that a nonpsychotic mental disorder is present but there is not enough information available to diagnose one of the categories provided in the Classification. In some cases, the diagnosis can be changed to a specific disorder after more information is obtained.

V71.09   No Diagnosis or Condition on Axis I

When no Axis I diagnosis or condition is present, this should be indicated. There may or may not be an Axis II diagnosis.

799.9   Diagnosis or Condition Deferred on Axis I

When there is insufficient information to make any diagnostic judgment about an Axis I diagnosis or condition, this should be noted as Diagnosis or Condition Deferred on Axis I.

V71.09   No Diagnosis on Axis II

When no Axis II diagnosis (e.g., no Personality Disorder) is present, this should be indicated. There may or may not be an Axis I diagnosis or condition.

799.9   Diagnosis Deferred on Axis II

When there is insufficient information to make any diagnostic judgment about an Axis II diagnosis, this should be noted as Diagnosis Deferred on Axis II.

Appendix A

Decision Trees for Differential Diagnosis

The purpose of these decision trees is to aid the clinician in understanding the organization and hierarchical structure of the DSM-IV Classification. Each decision tree starts with a set of clinical features. When one of these features is a prominent part of the presenting clinical picture, the clinician can follow the series of questions to rule in or rule out various disorders. Note that the questions are only approximations of the diagnostic criteria and are not meant to replace them.

The Psychotic Disorders decision tree is the only one that contains disorders that are mutually exclusive (i.e., only one disorder from that section can be diagnosed in a given individual for a particular episode). For the other decision trees, it is important to refer to the individual criteria sets to determine when more than one diagnosis may apply.

Contents

Note: Prepared by Michael B. First, M.D., Allen Frances, M.D., and Harold Alan Pincus, M.D.

Differential Diagnosis of Mental Disorders Due to a General Medical Condition

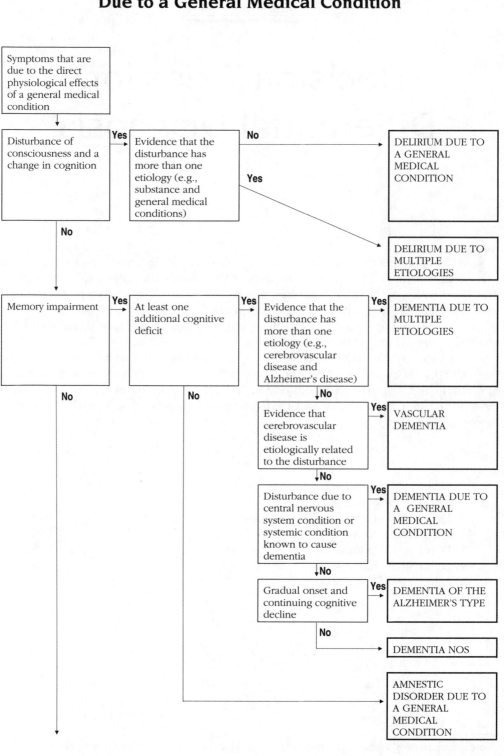

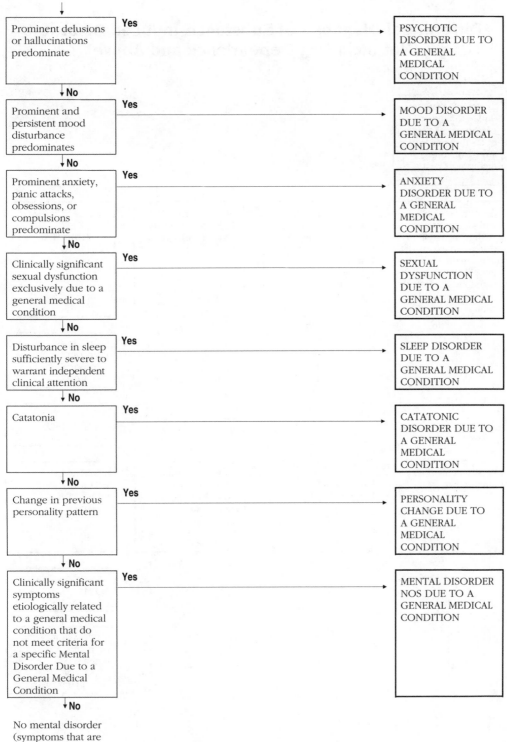

Prominent delusions or hallucinations predominate — Yes → PSYCHOTIC DISORDER DUE TO A GENERAL MEDICAL CONDITION

↓ No

Prominent and persistent mood disturbance predominates — Yes → MOOD DISORDER DUE TO A GENERAL MEDICAL CONDITION

↓ No

Prominent anxiety, panic attacks, obsessions, or compulsions predominate — Yes → ANXIETY DISORDER DUE TO A GENERAL MEDICAL CONDITION

↓ No

Clinically significant sexual dysfunction exclusively due to a general medical condition — Yes → SEXUAL DYSFUNCTION DUE TO A GENERAL MEDICAL CONDITION

↓ No

Disturbance in sleep sufficiently severe to warrant independent clinical attention — Yes → SLEEP DISORDER DUE TO A GENERAL MEDICAL CONDITION

↓ No

Catatonia — Yes → CATATONIC DISORDER DUE TO A GENERAL MEDICAL CONDITION

↓ No

Change in previous personality pattern — Yes → PERSONALITY CHANGE DUE TO A GENERAL MEDICAL CONDITION

↓ No

Clinically significant symptoms etiologically related to a general medical condition that do not meet criteria for a specific Mental Disorder Due to a General Medical Condition — Yes → MENTAL DISORDER NOS DUE TO A GENERAL MEDICAL CONDITION

↓ No

No mental disorder (symptoms that are not clinically significant)

Differential Diagnosis of Substance-Induced Disorders (Not Including Dependence and Abuse)

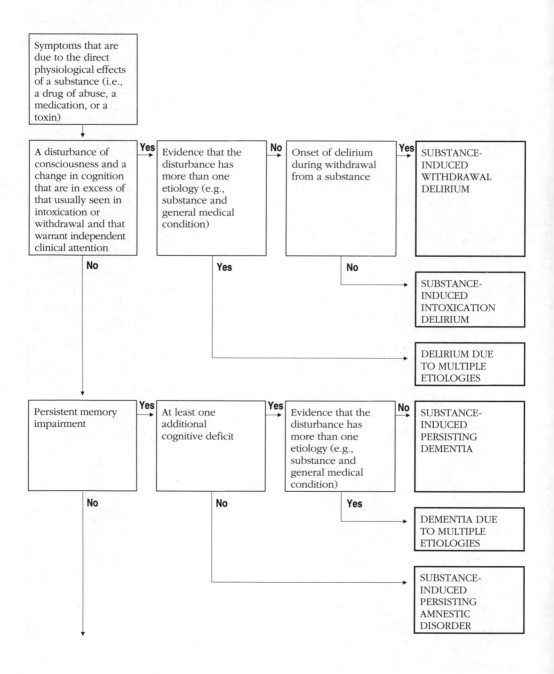

Delusions or hallucinations predominate, are in excess of that usually seen in intoxication or withdrawal, and warrant independent clinical attention

Yes →

SUBSTANCE-INDUCED PSYCHOTIC DISORDER
Specify if onset during intoxication or withdrawal

↓ **No**

A mood disturbance predominates, is in excess of that usually seen in intoxication or withdrawal, and warrants independent clinical attention

Yes →

SUBSTANCE-INDUCED MOOD DISORDER
Specify if onset during intoxication or withdrawal

↓ **No**

Anxiety, panic attacks, or obsessions or compulsions predominate; are in excess of that usually seen in intoxication or withdrawal; and warrant independent clinical attention

Yes →

SUBSTANCE-INDUCED ANXIETY DISORDER
Specify if onset during intoxication or withdrawal

↓ **No**

Clinically significant sexual dysfunction exclusively due to a substance, is in excess of that usually seen in intoxication, and warrants independent clinical attention

Yes →

SUBSTANCE-INDUCED SEXUAL DYSFUNCTION

↓ **No**

Disturbance in sleep that is sufficiently severe to warrant independent clinical attention and is in excess of that usually seen in intoxication or withdrawal

Yes →

SUBSTANCE-INDUCED SLEEP DISORDER
Specify if onset during intoxication or withdrawal

↓ **No**

Development of a reversible syndrome due to recent use of a substance

Yes →

SUBSTANCE INTOXICATION

↓ **No**

Development of a syndrome due to reduction or cessation of use of a substance

Yes →

SUBSTANCE WITHDRAWAL

↓ **No**

Clinically significant symptoms due to a substance that do not meet criteria for one of the Substance-Induced Disorders

Yes →

SUBSTANCE-RELATED DISORDER NOS

↓ **No**

No Substance-Induced Disorder
(substance-induced symptoms that are not clinically significant)

Differential Diagnosis of Psychotic Disorders

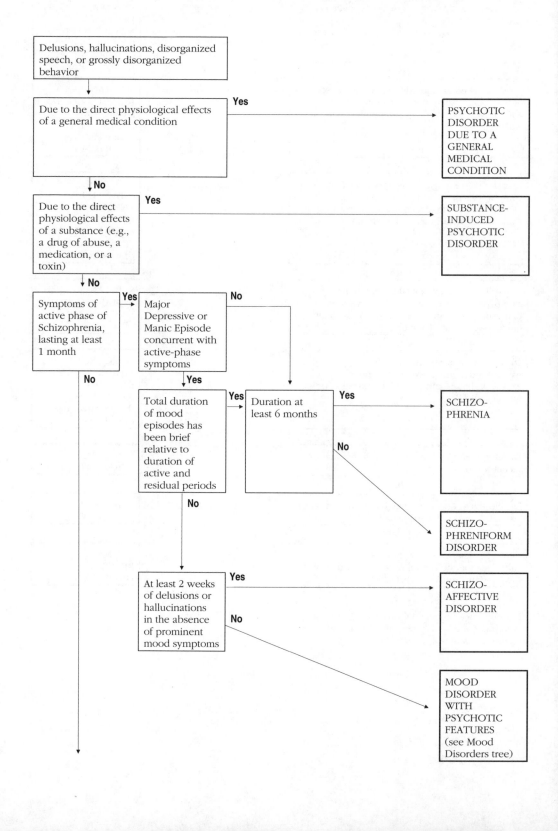

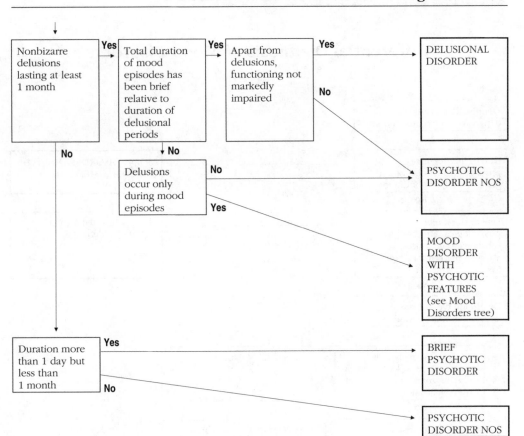

Differential Diagnosis of Mood Disorders

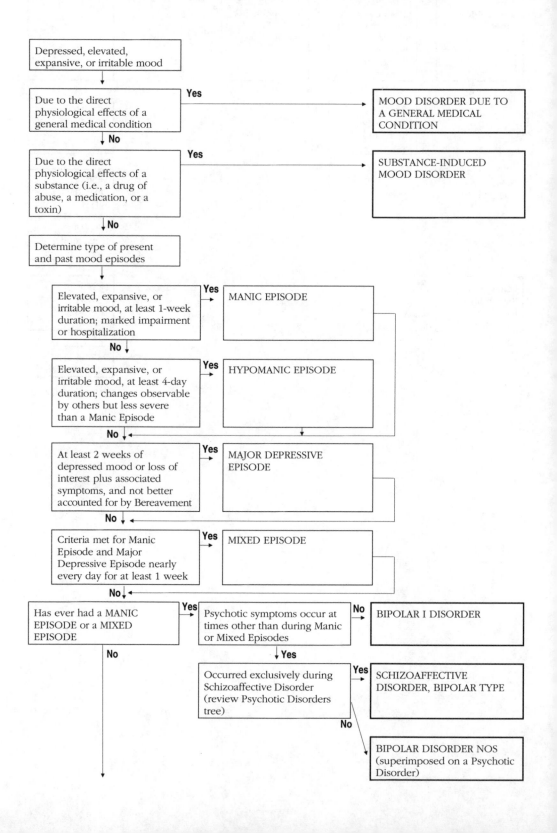

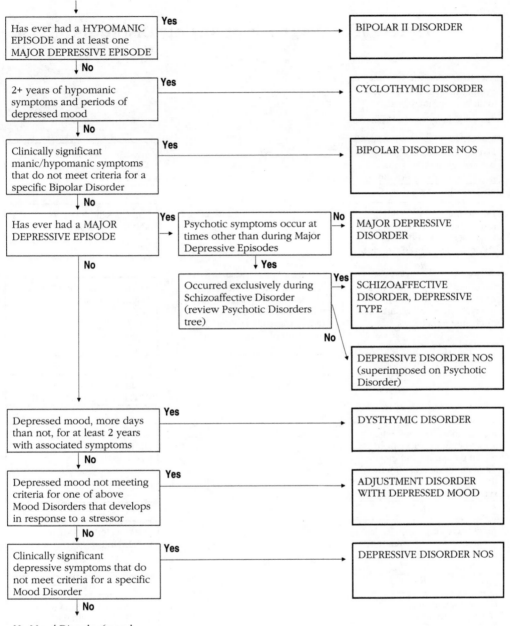

Differential Diagnosis of Anxiety Disorders

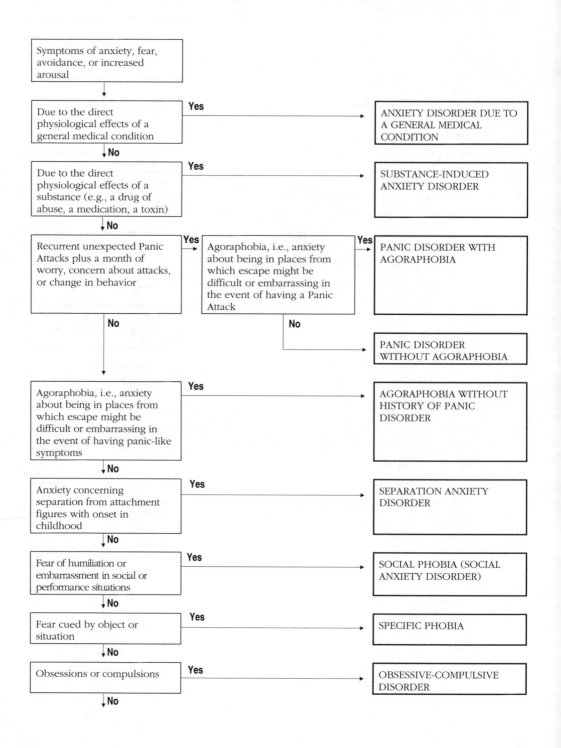

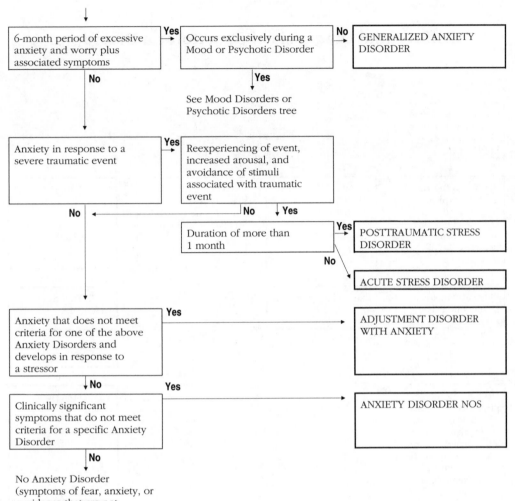

Differential Diagnosis of Somatoform Disorders

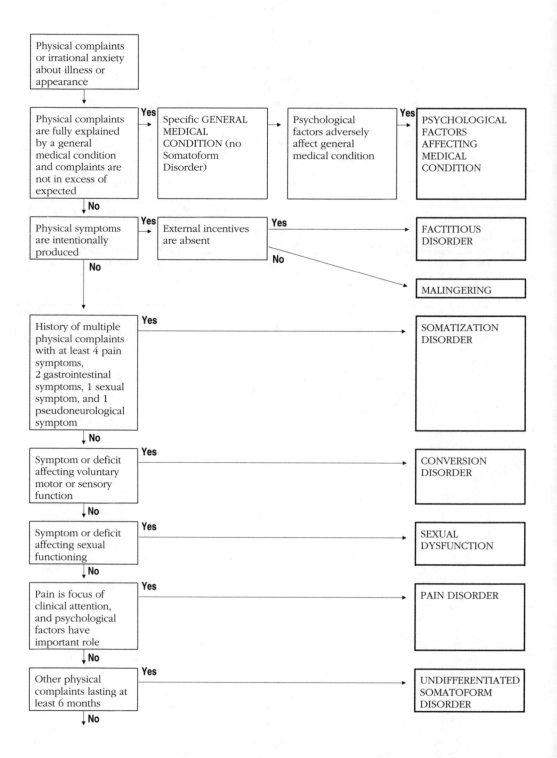

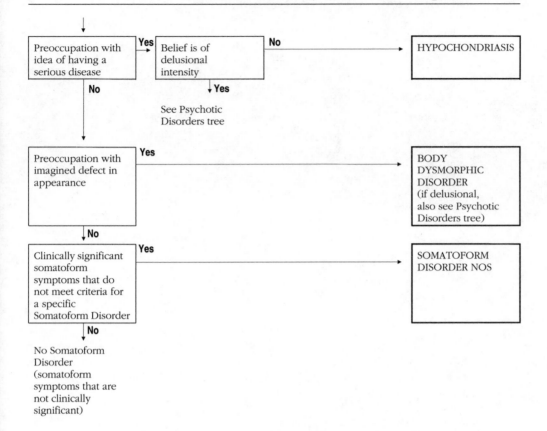

Preoccupation with idea of having a serious disease — **Yes** → Belief is of delusional intensity — **No** → HYPOCHONDRIASIS

Preoccupation with idea of having a serious disease — **No** ↓

Belief is of delusional intensity — **Yes** ↓ See Psychotic Disorders tree

Preoccupation with imagined defect in appearance — **Yes** → BODY DYSMORPHIC DISORDER (if delusional, also see Psychotic Disorders tree)

Preoccupation with imagined defect in appearance — **No** ↓

Clinically significant somatoform symptoms that do not meet criteria for a specific Somatoform Disorder — **Yes** → SOMATOFORM DISORDER NOS

Clinically significant somatoform symptoms that do not meet criteria for a specific Somatoform Disorder — **No** ↓

No Somatoform Disorder (somatoform symptoms that are not clinically significant)

Appendix B

Criteria Sets and Axes Provided for Further Study

This appendix contains a number of proposals for new categories and axes that were suggested for possible inclusion in DSM-IV. The DSM-IV Task Force and Work Groups subjected each of these proposals to a careful empirical review and invited wide commentary from the field. The Task Force determined that there was insufficient information to warrant inclusion of these proposals as official categories or axes in DSM-IV.

The items, thresholds, and durations contained in the research criteria sets are intended to provide a common language for researchers and clinicians who are interested in studying these disorders. It is hoped that such research will help to determine the possible utility of these proposed categories and will result in refinement of the criteria sets. The specific thresholds and durations were set by expert consensus (informed by literature review, data reanalysis, and field-trial results when such information was available) and, as such, should be considered tentative. It would be highly desirable for researchers to study alternative items, thresholds, or durations whenever this is possible.

The following proposals are included in this appendix:

> Postconcussional disorder
> Mild neurocognitive disorder
> Caffeine withdrawal
> Alternative dimensional descriptors for Schizophrenia
> Postpsychotic depressive disorder of Schizophrenia
> Simple deteriorative disorder (simple Schizophrenia)
> Premenstrual dysphoric disorder
> Alternative Criterion B for Dysthymic Disorder
> Minor depressive disorder
> Recurrent brief depressive disorder
> Mixed anxiety-depressive disorder
> Factitious disorder by proxy
> Dissociative trance disorder
> Binge-eating disorder
> Depressive personality disorder

Passive-aggressive personality disorder (negativistic personality disorder)
Medication-Induced Movement Disorders
    Neuroleptic-Induced Parkinsonism
    Neuroleptic Malignant Syndrome
    Neuroleptic-Induced Acute Dystonia
    Neuroleptic-Induced Acute Akathisia
    Neuroleptic-Induced Tardive Dyskinesia
    Medication-Induced Postural Tremor
    Medication-Induced Movement Disorder Not Otherwise Specified

(**Note:** These categories are included in the "Other Conditions That May Be a Focus of Clinical Attention" section. Text and research criteria sets for these conditions are included here.)

Defensive Functioning Scale
Global Assessment of Relational Functioning (GARF) Scale
Social and Occupational Functioning Assessment Scale (SOFAS)

Postconcussional Disorder

Features

The essential feature is an acquired impairment in cognitive functioning, accompanied by specific neurobehavioral symptoms, that occurs as a consequence of closed head injury of sufficient severity to produce a significant cerebral concussion. The manifestations of concussion include loss of consciousness, posttraumatic amnesia, and less commonly, posttraumatic onset of seizures. Specific approaches for defining this criterion need to be refined by further research. Although there is insufficient evidence to establish a definite threshold for the severity of the closed head injury, specific criteria have been suggested, for example, two of the following: 1) a period of unconsciousness lasting more than 5 minutes, 2) a period of posttraumatic amnesia that lasts more than 12 hours after the closed head injury, or 3) a new onset of seizures (or marked worsening of a preexisting seizure disorder) that occurs within the first 6 months after the closed head injury. There must also be documented cognitive deficits in either attention (concentration, shifting focus of attention, performing simultaneous cognitive tasks) or memory (learning or recalling information). Accompanying the cognitive disturbances, there must be three (or more) symptoms that are present for at least 3 months following the closed head injury. These include becoming fatigued easily; disordered sleep; headache; vertigo or dizziness; irritability or aggression on little or no provocation; anxiety, depression, or affective lability; apathy or lack of spontaneity; and other changes in personality (e.g., social or sexual inappropriateness). The cognitive disturbances and the somatic and behavioral symptoms develop after the head trauma has occurred or represent a significant worsening of preexisting symptoms. The cognitive and neurobehavioral sequelae are accompanied by significant impairment in social or occupational functioning and represent a significant decline from a previous level of functioning. In the case of school-age children, there may be significant worsening in academic achievement dating from the trauma. This proposed disorder should not be considered if the individual's symptoms meet the criteria for Dementia Due to Head Trauma or if the symptoms are better accounted for by another mental disorder.

Associated Features

Additional features that may be sequelae of closed head injury include visual or hearing impairments and anosmia (loss of sense of smell). The latter may be related to a lack of interest in food. Specific orthopedic and neurological complications may be present, depending on the cause, nature, and extent of the trauma. Substance-Related Disorders are frequently associated with closed head injury. Closed head injury occurs more often in young males and has been associated with risk-taking behaviors.

Differential Diagnosis

In DSM-IV, individuals whose presentation meets these research criteria would be diagnosed as having **Cognitive Disorder Not Otherwise Specified.**

If the head trauma results in a **dementia** (e.g., memory impairment and at least one other cognitive impairment), postconcussional disorder should not be considered. **Mild neurocognitive disorder,** like postconcussional disorder, is included in this appendix (see p. 706). Postconcussional disorder can be differentiated from mild neurocognitive disorder by the specific pattern of cognitive, somatic, and behavioral symptoms and the presence of a specific etiology (i.e., closed head injury). Individuals with **Somatization Disorder** and **Undifferentiated Somatoform Disorder** may manifest similar behavioral or somatic symptoms; however, these disorders do not have a specific etiology (i.e., closed head injury) or measurable impairment in cognitive functioning. Postconcussional disorder must be distinguished from **Factitious Disorder** (the need to assume the sick role) and **Malingering** (in which the desire for compensation may lead to the production or prolongation of symptoms due to closed head injury).

■ Research criteria for postconcussional disorder

A. A history of head trauma that has caused significant cerebral concussion.

Note: The manifestations of concussion include loss of consciousness, post-traumatic amnesia, and, less commonly, posttraumatic onset of seizures. The specific method of defining this criterion needs to be established by further research.

B. Evidence from neuropsychological testing or quantified cognitive assessment of difficulty in attention (concentrating, shifting focus of attention, performing simultaneous cognitive tasks) or memory (learning or recalling information).

C. Three (or more) of the following occur shortly after the trauma and last at least 3 months:
    (1) becoming fatigued easily
    (2) disordered sleep
    (3) headache

(continued)

☐ **Research criteria for postconcussional disorder** (*continued*)

        (4) vertigo or dizziness
        (5) irritability or aggression on little or no provocation
        (6) anxiety, depression, or affective lability
        (7) changes in personality (e.g., social or sexual inappropriateness)
        (8) apathy or lack of spontaneity

  D. The symptoms in Criteria B and C have their onset following head trauma or else represent a substantial worsening of preexisting symptoms.

  E. The disturbance causes significant impairment in social or occupational functioning and represents a significant decline from a previous level of functioning. In school-age children, the impairment may be manifested by a significant worsening in school or academic performance dating from the trauma.

  F. The symptoms do not meet criteria for Dementia Due to Head Trauma and are not better accounted for by another mental disorder (e.g., Amnestic Disorder Due to Head Trauma, Personality Change Due to Head Trauma).

Mild Neurocognitive Disorder

Features

The essential feature is the development of impairment in neurocognitive functioning that is due to a general medical condition. By definition, the level of cognitive impairment and the impact on everyday functioning is mild (e.g., the individual is able to partially compensate for cognitive impairment with additional effort). Individuals with this condition have a new onset of deficits in at least two areas of cognitive functioning. These may include disturbances in memory (learning or recalling new information), executive functioning (e.g., planning, reasoning), attention or speed of information processing (e.g., concentration, rapidity of assimilating or analyzing information), perceptual motor abilities (e.g., integrating visual, tactile, or auditory information with motor activities), or language (e.g., word-finding difficulties, reduced fluency). The report of cognitive impairment must be corroborated by the results of neuropsychological testing or bedside standardized cognitive assessment techniques. Furthermore, the cognitive deficits cause marked distress or interfere with the individual's social, occupational, or other important areas of functioning and represent a decline from a previous level of functioning. The cognitive disturbance does not meet criteria for a delirium, a dementia, or an amnestic disorder and is not better accounted for by another mental disorder (e.g., a Substance-Related Disorder, Major Depressive Disorder).

Associated Features

The associated features depend on the underlying general medical condition. In the case of certain chronic disorders (e.g., hypoxemia, electrolyte imbalances), the cognitive profile is usually one of a generalized reduction in all cognitive functions. Some neurological and other general medical conditions produce patterns of cognitive impairment that suggest more "subcortical" brain involvement (i.e., disproportionate impairment in the ability to concentrate and learn new facts and in the speed and efficiency of processing information). These include the early phases of Huntington's disease, HIV-associated neurocognitive disorder, and Parkinson's disease. Other conditions (e.g., systemic lupus erythematosus) are more frequently associated with a multifocal or patchy pattern of cognitive loss. The EEG may show mild slowing of background activity or disturbance in evoked potentials. Mild cognitive impairment, even in cases of early Alzheimer's disease, is frequently present without specific changes on neuroanatomical studies using magnetic resonance imaging (MRI) or computed tomography (CT). Abnormalities are more likely to be present in functional brain imaging studies (single photon emission computer tomography [SPECT], positron-emission tomography [PET], functional MRI). The course depends on the underlying etiology. In some instances, the cognitive impairment slowly worsens so that ultimately a diagnosis of dementia becomes appropriate (e.g., early phases of Alzheimer's disease, Huntington's disease, and other slowly progressive neurodegenerative conditions). In other instances, the disturbance may improve slowly, as in gradual recovery from hypothyroidism. In some instances, cognitive disturbances due to severe metabolic derangements or infectious diseases may resolve partially but be characterized by a residual impairment that is permanent.

Differential Diagnosis

In DSM-IV, individuals whose presentation meets these research criteria would be diagnosed as having **Cognitive Disorder Not Otherwise Specified.**

Although there is no clear boundary between mild neurocognitive disorder and **dementia,** mild neurocognitive disorder has less cognitive impairment and less impact on daily activities, and memory impairment is not a requirement. Mild neurocognitive disorder may be confused with a slowly evolving **delirium,** especially early in its course. Mild neurocognitive disorder can be distinguished from an **amnestic disorder** by the requirement that there be cognitive impairment in at least two areas. Mild neurocognitive disorder should not be considered if an individual's symptoms meet criteria for a **Substance-Related Disorder** (including medication side effects). In such cases, the appropriate Substance-Related Disorder Not Otherwise Specified should be diagnosed.

Postconcussional disorder, another category listed in this appendix (see p. 704), is distinguished from mild neurocognitive disorder by the presence of a specific pattern of symptoms and a specific etiology (i.e., closed head injury).

Mild neurocognitive disturbances are a common associated feature of a number of **mental disorders** (e.g., Major Depressive Disorder). Mild neurocognitive disorder should only be considered if the cognitive impairment is better accounted for by the direct effects of a general medical condition than by a mental disorder. Individuals with **Age-Related Cognitive Decline** may have similar levels of cognitive impairment, but the decline is considered to be part of the normative aging process rather than attributable to a general medical condition. Individuals may report **subjective complaints of**

impairment in cognitive functioning that cannot be corroborated by neuropsychological testing or are judged not to be associated with a general medical condition. This proposed disorder should not be considered for such presentations.

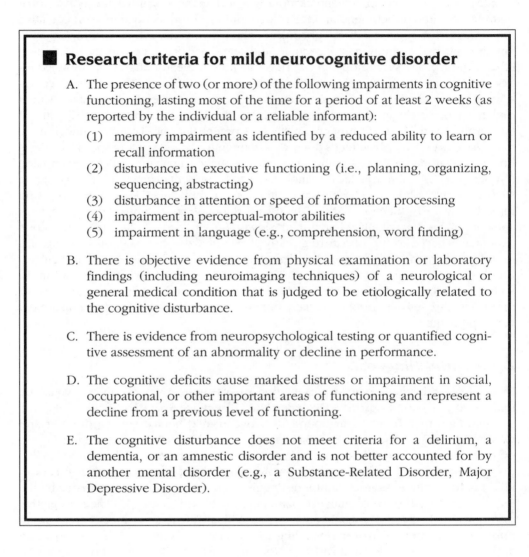

■ **Research criteria for mild neurocognitive disorder**

A. The presence of two (or more) of the following impairments in cognitive functioning, lasting most of the time for a period of at least 2 weeks (as reported by the individual or a reliable informant):

(1) memory impairment as identified by a reduced ability to learn or recall information

(2) disturbance in executive functioning (i.e., planning, organizing, sequencing, abstracting)

(3) disturbance in attention or speed of information processing

(4) impairment in perceptual-motor abilities

(5) impairment in language (e.g., comprehension, word finding)

B. There is objective evidence from physical examination or laboratory findings (including neuroimaging techniques) of a neurological or general medical condition that is judged to be etiologically related to the cognitive disturbance.

C. There is evidence from neuropsychological testing or quantified cognitive assessment of an abnormality or decline in performance.

D. The cognitive deficits cause marked distress or impairment in social, occupational, or other important areas of functioning and represent a decline from a previous level of functioning.

E. The cognitive disturbance does not meet criteria for a delirium, a dementia, or an amnestic disorder and is not better accounted for by another mental disorder (e.g., a Substance-Related Disorder, Major Depressive Disorder).

Caffeine Withdrawal

Features

The essential feature is a characteristic withdrawal syndrome due to the abrupt cessation of, or reduction in, the use of caffeine-containing products after prolonged daily use. The syndrome includes headache and one (or more) of the following symptoms: marked fatigue or drowsiness, marked anxiety or depression, or nausea or vomiting. These symptoms appear to be more prevalent in individuals with heavy use (500 mg/day) but may occur in individuals with light use (100 mg/day). The symptoms must cause clinically significant distress or impairment in social, occupational, or other important areas of functioning. The symptoms must not be due to the direct physiological effects of a general medical condition and must not be better accounted for by another mental disorder.

Associated Features

Associated symptoms include a strong desire for caffeine and worsened cognitive performance (especially on vigilance tasks). Symptoms can begin within 12 hours of cessation of caffeine use, peak around 24–48 hours, and last up to 1 week. Some individuals may seek medical treatment for these symptoms without realizing they are due to caffeine withdrawal.

Differential Diagnosis

In DSM-IV, individuals whose presentation meets these research criteria would be diagnosed as having **Caffeine-Related Disorder Not Otherwise Specified.**

For a general discussion of the differential diagnosis of Substance-Related Disorders, see p. 190. The symptoms must not be due to the direct physiological effects of a **general medical condition** (e.g., migraine, viral illness) and must not be better accounted for by **another mental disorder.** Headaches, fatigue, nausea, or vomiting due to a general medical condition or due to the **initiation or cessation of a medication** can cause a clinical picture similar to caffeine withdrawal. Drowsiness, fatigue, and mood changes from caffeine withdrawal can mimic **Amphetamine** or **Cocaine Withdrawal**. The temporal relationship of symptoms to caffeine cessation and the time-limited course of the symptoms usually establish the diagnosis. If the diagnosis is unclear, a diagnostic trial of caffeine can be of help.

■ Research criteria for caffeine withdrawal

A. Prolonged daily use of caffeine.

B. Abrupt cessation of caffeine use, or reduction in the amount of caffeine used, closely followed by headache and one (or more) of the following symptoms:

    (1) marked fatigue or drowsiness

    (2) marked anxiety or depression

    (3) nausea or vomiting

C. The symptoms in Criterion B cause clinically significant distress or impairment in social, occupational, or other important areas of functioning.

D. The symptoms are not due to the direct physiological effects of a general medical condition (e.g., migraine, viral illness) and are not better accounted for by another mental disorder.

Alternative Dimensional Descriptors for Schizophrenia

Because of limitations in the classical subtyping of Schizophrenia (see p. 286), a three-factor dimensional model (psychotic, disorganized, and negative) has been suggested to describe current and lifetime symptomatology. The psychotic factor includes delusions and hallucinations. The disorganized factor includes disorganized speech, disorganized behavior, and inappropriate affect. The negative factor includes the various negative symptoms. Studies suggest that the severity of symptoms within each of these three factors tends to vary together, both cross-sectionally and over time, whereas this is less true for symptoms across factors. For example, as delusions become more severe, hallucinations tend to become more severe as well. In contrast, the severity of negative or disorganized symptoms is less related to the severity of hallucinations or delusions. One model for understanding the clinical heterogeneity of Schizophrenia suggests that each of these three dimensions may have different underlying pathophysiological processes and treatment responses. Various combinations of severity on the three dimensions are encountered in clinical practice, and it is relatively uncommon for one dimension to be present in the complete absence of both of the others. The following is a system for applying these dimensions in research and clinical studies.

■ Alternative dimensional descriptors for Schizophrenia

Specify: absent, mild, moderate, severe for each dimension. The prominence of these dimensions may be specified for either (or both) the current episode (i.e., previous 6 months) or the lifetime course of the disorder.

psychotic (hallucinations/delusions) dimension: describes the degree to which hallucinations or delusions have been present

disorganized dimension: describes the degree to which disorganized speech, disorganized behavior, or inappropriate affect have been present

negative (deficit) dimension: describes the degree to which negative symptoms (i.e., affective flattening, alogia, avolition) have been present. **Note:** Do not include symptoms that appear to be secondary to depression, medication side effects, or hallucinations or delusions.

Two examples that include the DSM-IV subtype, course specifiers, and the proposed dimensional approach are

Example 1
295.30 Schizophrenia, Paranoid Type, Continuous
Current:
    With severe psychotic dimension
    With absent disorganized dimension
    With moderate negative dimension

Lifetime:
> With mild psychotic dimension
> With absent disorganized dimension
> With mild negative dimension

Example 2
295.60 Schizophrenia, Residual Type, Episodic With Residual Symptoms
Current:
> With mild psychotic dimension
> With mild disorganized dimension
> With mild negative dimension

Lifetime:
> With moderate psychotic dimension
> With mild disorganized dimension
> With mild negative dimension

Postpsychotic Depressive Disorder of Schizophrenia

Features

The essential feature is a Major Depressive Episode (see p. 320) that is superimposed on, and occurs only during, the residual phase of Schizophrenia. The residual phase of Schizophrenia follows the active phase (i.e., symptoms meeting Criterion A) of Schizophrenia. It is characterized by the persistence of negative symptoms or of active-phase symptoms that are in an attenuated form (e.g., odd beliefs, unusual perceptual experiences). The superimposed Major Depressive Episode must include depressed mood (i.e., loss of interest or pleasure cannot serve as an alternate for sad or depressed mood). Most typically, the Major Depressive Episode follows immediately after remission of the active-phase symptoms of the psychotic episode. Sometimes it may follow after a short or extended interval during which there are no psychotic symptoms. Mood symptoms due to the direct physiological effects of a drug of abuse, a medication, or a general medical condition are not counted toward postpsychotic depressive disorder of Schizophrenia.

Associated Features

As compared with individuals with Schizophrenia without postpsychotic depressive episodes, these individuals are more likely to be living alone and to have fewer social supports. Other risk factors may include a larger number of previous hospitalizations, history of psychotic relapses while being treated with antipsychotic medications, insidious onset of psychotic episodes, prior episodes of depression, and prior suicide attempts. There may be recent losses, undesirable life events, and other stressors. Up to 25% of individuals with Schizophrenia may have this condition sometime in the course of their illness. Males and females seem equally vulnerable. These individuals appear more likely to relapse into a psychotic episode or to be rehospitalized than those without depression. Individuals with Schizophrenia who also have first-degree biological relatives with histories of Major Depressive Disorder may be at higher risk for postpsychotic depressions. This condition is associated with suicidal ideation, suicide attempts, and completed suicides.

Differential Diagnosis

In DSM-IV, individuals whose presentation meets these research criteria would be diagnosed as having **Depressive Disorder Not Otherwise Specified.**

Mood Disorder Due to a General Medical Condition is distinguished from this disturbance by the fact that the depressive symptoms are due to the direct physiological effects of a general medical condition (e.g., hypothyroidism). **Substance-Induced Mood Disorder** is distinguished from this disturbance by the fact that the depressive symptoms are due to the direct physiological effects of a drug of abuse (e.g., alcohol, cocaine) or the side effects of a medication. Individuals with Schizophrenia are often on maintenance neuroleptic medications, which can cause dysphoria or Medication-Induced Movement Disorders as side effects. These side effects can be confused with depressive symptoms. **Neuroleptic-Induced Parkinsonism** with akinesia (see p. 736) is characterized by a reduced ability to initiate or sustain behaviors, which can lead to a lack of spontaneity or anhedonia. **Neuroleptic-Induced Akathisia** (see p. 744) may be mistaken for anxiety or agitation, and depressed mood or suicidal ideation may be associated. Adjusting the medication type or dose may assist in reducing these side effects and clarifying the cause of such symptoms.

The differential diagnosis between postpsychotic depressive symptoms and the **negative symptoms of Schizophrenia** (i.e., avolition, alogia, affective flattening) may be particularly difficult. Negative symptoms must be distinguished from the other symptoms of depression (e.g., sadness, guilt, shame, hopelessness, helplessness, and low self-esteem). In **Schizoaffective Disorder** and **Mood Disorder With Psychotic Features,** there must be a period of overlap between the full psychotic episode and the mood episode. In contrast, this proposed disorder requires that the symptoms of a Major Depressive Episode occur only during the residual phase of Schizophrenia.

Demoralization may occur during the course of Schizophrenia but should not be considered postpsychotic depression unless the full criteria for a Major Depressive Episode are met. **Adjustment Disorder With Depressed Mood** is distinguished from postpsychotic depressive symptoms in Schizophrenia because the depressive symptoms in Adjustment Disorder do not meet the criteria for a Major Depressive Episode.

■ Research criteria for postpsychotic depressive disorder of Schizophrenia

A. Criteria are met for a Major Depressive Episode.

   Note: The Major Depressive Episode must include Criterion A1: depressed mood. Do not include symptoms that are better accounted for as medication side effects or negative symptoms of Schizophrenia.

B. The Major Depressive Episode is superimposed on and occurs only during the residual phase of Schizophrenia.

C. The Major Depressive Episode is not due to the direct physiological effects of a substance or a general medical condition.

Simple Deteriorative Disorder (Simple Schizophrenia)

Features

The essential feature is the development of prominent negative symptoms, which represent a clear change from a preestablished baseline. These symptoms are severe enough to result in a marked decline in occupational or academic functioning. If positive psychotic symptoms (e.g., hallucinations, delusions, disorganized speech, disorganized behavior, catatonic behavior) have ever been present, they have not been prominent. This pattern should be considered only after all other possible causes for the deterioration have been ruled out, that is, the presentation is not better accounted for by Schizotypal or Schizoid Personality Disorder; a Psychotic, Mood, or Anxiety Disorder; a dementia; or Mental Retardation; nor are the symptoms due to the direct physiological effects of a substance or a general medical condition. There is an insidious and progressive development of negative symptoms over a period of at least 1 year beginning in adolescence or later. Emotional responses become blunted, shallow, flat, and empty. Speech becomes impoverished of words and meanings. There is a definite change in "personality," with a marked loss of interpersonal rapport. Close relationships lose warmth and mutuality, social interaction generally becomes awkward, and isolation and withdrawal result. Initiative gives way to apathy, and ambition to avolition. Loss of interest extends to the daily details of self-care. The person may appear forgetful and absentminded. Academic or job skills are lost, resulting in a pattern of brief, simple jobs and frequent unemployment.

Associated Features

Any of the features of Schizoid or Schizotypal Personality Disorder may be present. Most common are peculiarities of grooming and behavior, lapses in hygiene, overinvestment in odd ideas, or unusual perceptual experiences such as illusions. This proposed disorder may occur in adolescents and adults of both sexes. Good estimates of prevalence and incidence are not available, but it is clear that the disorder is rare. The course, at least for the first few years, is progressively downhill, with prominent deterioration of functioning. This deterioration in functioning resembles the characteristic course of Schizophrenia and distinguishes this condition from Schizoid and Schizotypal Personality Disorders. Symptoms meeting Criterion A for Schizophrenia may emerge, at which time the diagnosis is changed to Schizophrenia. In these instances, this pattern proves to have been a prolonged prodrome to Schizophrenia. In other cases this pattern recedes in severity, as can happen with Schizophrenia. For the majority of individuals, the course is continuous, with deterioration occurring within the first few years after prodromal symptoms and then plateauing to a marginal and reduced, but stable, functional capacity.

Differential Diagnosis

In DSM-IV, individuals whose presentation meets these research criteria would be diagnosed as having **Unspecified Mental Disorder.**

This pattern should be considered only after all other possible causes of deterioration in functioning have been ruled out. This pattern is distinguished from the disorders included in the "Schizophrenia and Other Psychotic Disorders" section by the absence of prominent positive psychotic symptoms. These disorders include **Schizophrenia, Schizoaffective Disorder, Schizophreniform Disorder, Brief Psychotic Disorder, Delusional Disorder, Shared Psychotic Disorder,** and **Psychotic Disorder Not Otherwise Specified,** all of which require at least one positive symptom for some period of time. This proposed disorder is distinguished from **Schizoid** and **Schizotypal Personality Disorders** as well as other Personality Disorders by the requirement of a clear change in personality and marked deterioration in functioning. In contrast, the Personality Disorders represent lifelong patterns without progressive deterioration. **Mood Disorders** may mimic the apathy and anhedonia of simple deteriorative disorder, but in a Mood Disorder depressive affect (sadness, hopelessness, helplessness, painful guilt) is experienced, and the course tends to be episodic. Furthermore, in simple deteriorative disorder, there is a sense of emptiness rather than a painful or prominently depressive mood, and the course is continuous and progressive. The distinction can be more difficult with **Dysthymic Disorder,** in which the course may also be continuous and in which vegetative symptoms and painfully depressive mood may not be prominent. This proposed disorder may mimic **chronic Substance Dependence** and should only be considered if the personality change and deterioration precede extensive substance use. **Personality Change Due to a General Medical Condition** is distinguished by the presence of an etiological general medical condition. The cognitive impairment of simple deteriorative disorder may be mistaken for **Mental Retardation** or **dementia.** Mental Retardation is distinguished by its typical onset in infancy or childhood. Dementia is distinguished by the presence of an etiological general medical condition or substance use.

Perhaps the most difficult differential diagnosis is with **no mental disorder.** Simple deteriorative disorder often leads a person to become a marginal member of society. It does not follow, however, that marginal members of society necessarily have this proposed disorder. The defining features of simple deteriorative disorder involve negative symptoms, which tend to be more on a continuum with normality than are positive symptoms and which may be mimicked by a variety of factors (see the relevant discussion in the "Schizophrenia" section, p. 276). Therefore, special caution must be taken not to apply this proposed disorder too broadly.

■ **Research criteria for simple deteriorative disorder (simple Schizophrenia)**

A. Progressive development over a period of at least a year of all of the following:

    (1)   marked decline in occupational or academic functioning

    (2)   gradual appearance and deepening of negative symptoms such as affective flattening, alogia, and avolition

    (3)   poor interpersonal rapport, social isolation, or social withdrawal

B. Criterion A for Schizophrenia has never been met.

(continued)

☐ **Research criteria for simple deteriorative disorder (simple Schizophrenia)** (*continued*)

C. The symptoms are not better accounted for by Schizotypal or Schizoid Personality Disorder, a Psychotic Disorder, a Mood Disorder, an Anxiety Disorder, a dementia, or Mental Retardation and are not due to the direct physiological effects of a substance or a general medical condition.

Premenstrual Dysphoric Disorder

Features

The essential features are symptoms such as markedly depressed mood, marked anxiety, marked affective lability, and decreased interest in activities. These symptoms have regularly occurred during the last week of the luteal phase in most menstrual cycles during the past year. The symptoms begin to remit within a few days of the onset of menses (the follicular phase) and are always absent in the week following menses.

Five (or more) of the following symptoms must have been present most of the time during the last week of the luteal phase, with at least one of the symptoms being one of the first four: 1) feeling sad, hopeless, or self-deprecating; 2) feeling tense, anxious or "on edge"; 3) marked lability of mood interspersed with frequent tearfulness; 4) persistent irritability, anger, and increased interpersonal conflicts; 5) decreased interest in usual activities, which may be associated with withdrawal from social relationships; 6) difficulty concentrating; 7) feeling fatigued, lethargic, or lacking in energy; 8) marked changes in appetite, which may be associated with binge eating or craving certain foods; 9) hypersomnia or insomnia; 10) a subjective feeling of being overwhelmed or out of control; and 11) physical symptoms such as breast tenderness or swelling, headaches, or sensations of "bloating" or weight gain, with tightness of fit of clothing, shoes, or rings. There may also be joint or muscle pain. The symptoms may be accompanied by suicidal thoughts.

This pattern of symptoms must have occurred most months for the previous 12 months. The symptoms disappear completely shortly after the onset of menstruation. The most typical pattern seems to be that of dysfunction during the week prior to menses that ends mid-menses. Atypically, some females also have symptoms for a few days around ovulation; a few females with short cycles might, therefore, be symptom free for only 1 week per cycle.

Typically, the symptoms are of comparable severity (but not duration) to those of a Major Depressive Episode and must cause an obvious and marked impairment in the ability to function socially or occupationally in the week prior to menses. Impairment in social functioning may be manifested by marital discord and problems with friends and family. It is very important not to confuse long-standing marital or job problems with the dysfunction that occurs only premenstrually. There is a great contrast between the woman's depressed feelings and difficulty in functioning during these days and her mood and capabilities the rest of the month. These symptoms may be superimposed on another disorder but are not merely an exacerbation of the symptoms of another disorder, such as Major Depressive, Panic, or Dysthymic Disorder, or a Personality Disorder. The presence of the cyclical pattern of symptoms must be confirmed by at least 2 consecutive months of prospective daily symptom ratings. Daily symptom ratings must be done by the woman and can also be done by someone with whom she lives. It is important that these diaries be kept on a daily basis rather than composed retrospectively from memory.

Associated Features

Females who have had recurrent Major Depressive Disorder or Bipolar I or II Disorder or a family history of such disorders may be at greater risk to have a disturbance that meets the research criteria for premenstrual dysphoric disorder. Females who have had severe postpartum Major Depressive, Manic, or psychotic episodes may also be at greater risk for severe premenstrual dysphoric mood changes. Frequently there is a history of prior Mood and Anxiety Disorders. Delusions and hallucinations have been described in the late luteal phase of the menstrual cycle but are very rare.

Although females with the combination of dysmenorrhea (painful menses) and premenstrual dysphoric disorder are somewhat more likely to seek treatment than females with only one of these conditions, most females with either of the conditions do not have the other condition. A wide range of general medical conditions may worsen in the premenstrual or luteal phase (e.g., migraine, asthma, allergies, and seizure disorders). There are no specific laboratory tests that are diagnostic of the disturbance. However, in several small preliminary studies, certain laboratory findings (e.g., serotonin or melatonin secretion patterns, sleep EEG findings) have been noted to be abnormal in groups of females with this proposed disorder relative to control subjects.

It is estimated that at least 75% of women report minor or isolated premenstrual changes. Limited studies suggest an occurrence of "premenstrual syndrome" (variably defined) of 20%–50%, and that 3%–5% of women experience symptoms that may meet the criteria for this proposed disorder. There has been very little systematic study on the course and stability of this condition. Premenstrual symptoms can begin at any age after menarche, with the onset most commonly occurring during the teens to late 20s. Those who seek treatment are usually in their 30s. Symptoms usually remit with menopause. Although symptoms do not necessarily occur every cycle, they are present for the majority of the cycles. Some months the symptoms may be worse than others. Women commonly report that their symptoms worsen with age until relieved by the onset of menopause.

Differential Diagnosis

In DSM-IV, individuals whose presentation meets these research criteria would be diagnosed as having **Depressive Disorder Not Otherwise Specified.**

The transient mood changes that many females experience around the time of their period should not be considered a mental disorder. Premenstrual dysphoric disorder should be considered only when the symptoms markedly interfere with work or school or with usual social activities and relationships with others (e.g., avoidance of social activities, decreased productivity and efficiency at work or school). Premenstrual dysphoric disorder can be distinguished from the far more common **"premenstrual syndrome"** by using prospective daily ratings and the strict criteria listed below. It differs from the "premenstrual syndrome" in its characteristic pattern of symptoms, their severity, and the resulting impairment.

Premenstrual dysphoric disorder must be distinguished from the **premenstrual exacerbation of a current mental disorder** (e.g., Mood Disorders, Anxiety Disorders,

Somatoform Disorders, Bulimia Nervosa, Substance Use Disorders, and Personality Disorders). In such situations (which are far more common than premenstrual dysphoric disorder), there is a premenstrual worsening of the symptoms but the symptoms persist throughout the menstrual cycle. Although this condition should not be considered in females who are experiencing only a premenstrual exacerbation of another mental disorder, it can be considered in addition to the diagnosis of another current mental disorder if the woman experiences symptoms and changes in level of functioning that are characteristic of premenstrual dysphoric disorder and are markedly different from the symptoms experienced as part of the ongoing disorder.

Some individuals with **general medical conditions** may present with dysphoria and fatigue that are exacerbated during the premenstrual period. Examples include seizure disorders, thyroid and other endocrine disorders, cancer, systemic lupus erythematosus, anemias, endometriosis, and various infections. These general medical conditions can be distinguished from premenstrual dysphoric disorder by history, laboratory testing, or physical examination.

■ **Research criteria for premenstrual dysphoric disorder**

A. In most menstrual cycles during the past year, five (or more) of the following symptoms were present for most of the time during the last week of the luteal phase, began to remit within a few days after the onset of the follicular phase, and were absent in the week postmenses, with at least one of the symptoms being either (1), (2), (3), or (4):

    (1) markedly depressed mood, feelings of hopelessness, or self-deprecating thoughts

    (2) marked anxiety, tension, feelings of being "keyed up," or "on edge"

    (3) marked affective lability (e.g., feeling suddenly sad or tearful or increased sensitivity to rejection)

    (4) persistent and marked anger or irritability or increased interpersonal conflicts

    (5) decreased interest in usual activities (e.g., work, school, friends, hobbies)

    (6) subjective sense of difficulty in concentrating

    (7) lethargy, easy fatigability, or marked lack of energy

    (8) marked change in appetite, overeating, or specific food cravings

    (9) hypersomnia or insomnia

    (10) a subjective sense of being overwhelmed or out of control

    (11) other physical symptoms, such as breast tenderness or swelling, headaches, joint or muscle pain, a sensation of "bloating," weight gain

Note: In menstruating females, the luteal phase corresponds to the period between ovulation and the onset of menses, and the follicular phase begins with menses. In nonmenstruating females (e.g., those who have had a hysterectomy), the timing of luteal and follicular phases may require measurement of circulating reproductive hormones.

(continued)

☐ **Research criteria for premenstrual dysphoric disorder**
(*continued*)

B. The disturbance markedly interferes with work or school or with usual social activities and relationships with others (e.g., avoidance of social activities, decreased productivity and efficiency at work or school).

C. The disturbance is not merely an exacerbation of the symptoms of another disorder, such as Major Depressive Disorder, Panic Disorder, Dysthymic Disorder, or a Personality Disorder (although it may be superimposed on any of these disorders).

D. Criteria A, B, and C must be confirmed by prospective daily ratings during at least two consecutive symptomatic cycles. (The diagnosis may be made provisionally prior to this confirmation.)

Alternative Criterion B for Dysthymic Disorder

There has been some controversy concerning which symptoms best define Dysthymic Disorder. The results of the DSM-IV Mood Disorders field trial suggest that the following alternative version of Criterion B may be more characteristic of Dysthymic Disorder than the version of Criterion B that was in DSM-III-R and is in DSM-IV. However, it was decided that additional confirmatory evidence needs to be collected before these items are incorporated in the official definition of Dysthymic Disorder.

■ **Alternative Research Criterion B for Dysthymic Disorder**

B. Presence, while depressed, of three (or more) of the following:

(1) low self-esteem or self-confidence, or feelings of inadequacy
(2) feelings of pessimism, despair, or hopelessness
(3) generalized loss of interest or pleasure
(4) social withdrawal
(5) chronic fatigue or tiredness
(6) feelings of guilt, brooding about the past
(7) subjective feelings of irritability or excessive anger
(8) decreased activity, effectiveness, or productivity
(9) difficulty in thinking, reflected by poor concentration, poor memory, or indecisiveness

Minor Depressive Disorder

Features

The essential feature is one or more periods of depressive symptoms that are identical to Major Depressive Episodes in duration, but which involve fewer symptoms and less impairment. An episode involves either a sad or "depressed" mood or loss of interest or pleasure in nearly all activities. In total, at least two but less than five additional symptoms must be present. See the text for a Major Depressive Episode (p. 320) for a more detailed description of the characteristic symptoms. At the onset of the episode, the symptoms are either newly present or must be clearly worsened compared with the person's preepisode status. During the episode, these symptoms cause clinically significant distress or impairment in social, occupational, or other important areas of functioning. In some individuals, there may be near-normal functioning, but this is accomplished with significantly increased effort.

A number of disorders exclude consideration of this proposed disorder. There has never been a Major Depressive, Manic, Mixed, or Hypomanic Episode, and criteria are not met for Dysthymic or Cyclothymic Disorder. The mood disturbance does not occur exclusively during Schizophrenia, Schizophreniform Disorder, Schizoaffective Disorder, Delusional Disorder, or Psychotic Disorder Not Otherwise Specified.

Associated Features

The prevalence of this proposed disorder as defined here is unclear, but it may be relatively common, especially in primary care and outpatient mental health settings. A number of general medical conditions (e.g., stroke, cancer, and diabetes) appear to be associated. Family studies suggest an increase in this symptom pattern among relatives of probands with Major Depressive Disorder.

Differential Diagnosis

In DSM-IV, individuals whose presentation meets these research criteria would be diagnosed as having **Adjustment Disorder With Depressed Mood** if the depressive symptoms occur in response to a psychosocial stressor; otherwise, the appropriate diagnosis is **Depressive Disorder Not Otherwise Specified.**

An episode of minor depressive disorder is distinguished from a **Major Depressive Episode** by the required number of symptoms (two to four symptoms for minor depressive disorder and at least five symptoms for a Major Depressive Episode). This proposed disorder is considered to be a residual category and is not to be used if there is a history of a **Major Depressive Episode, Manic Episode, Mixed Episode,** or **Hypomanic Episode,** or if the presentation meets criteria for **Dysthymic** or **Cyclo-thymic Disorder.** Symptoms meeting research criteria for minor depressive disorder can be difficult to distinguish from **periods of sadness** that are an inherent part of everyday life. This proposed disorder requires that the depressive symptoms be present for most of the day nearly every day for at least 2 weeks. In addition, the depressive symptoms must cause clinically significant distress or impairment. Depressive symptoms occurring in response to the loss of a loved one are considered **Bereavement** (unless they meet the criteria for a Major Depressive Episode; see p. 320). **Substance-Induced**

Mood Disorder is distinguished from this disturbance in that the depressive symptoms are due to the direct physiological effects of a drug of abuse (e.g., alcohol or cocaine) or the side effects of a medication (e.g., steroids) (see p. 370). **Mood Disorder Due to a General Medical Condition** is distinguished from this disturbance in that the depressive symptoms are due to the direct physiological effects of a general medical condition (e.g., hypothyroidism) (see p. 366). Because depressive symptoms are common associated features of psychotic disorders, they do not receive a separate diagnosis if they occur exclusively during **Schizophrenia, Schizophreniform Disorder, Schizoaffective Disorder, Delusional Disorder,** or **Psychotic Disorder Not Otherwise Specified.** The relationship between this proposed disorder and several other proposed categories included in this appendix (i.e., recurrent brief depressive disorder, depressive personality disorder, and mixed anxiety-depressive disorder) and with other Personality Disorders is not known, but substantial overlap may exist among them.

■ Research criteria for minor depressive disorder

A. A mood disturbance, defined as follows:

(1) at least two (but less than five) of the following symptoms have been present during the same 2-week period and represent a change from previous functioning; at least one of the symptoms is either (a) or (b):

(a) depressed mood most of the day, nearly every day, as indicated by either subjective report (e.g., feels sad or empty) or observation made by others (e.g., appears tearful).
Note: In children and adolescents, can be irritable mood.

(b) markedly diminished interest or pleasure in all, or almost all, activities most of the day, nearly every day (as indicated by either subjective account or observation made by others)

(c) significant weight loss when not dieting or weight gain (e.g., a change of more than 5% of body weight in a month), or decrease or increase in appetite nearly every day. **Note:** In children, consider failure to make expected weight gains.

(d) insomnia or hypersomnia nearly every day

(e) psychomotor agitation or retardation nearly every day (observable by others, not merely subjective feelings of restlessness or being slowed down)

(f) fatigue or loss of energy nearly every day

(g) feelings of worthlessness or excessive or inappropriate guilt (which may be delusional) nearly every day (not merely self-reproach or guilt about being sick)

(h) diminished ability to think or concentrate, or indecisiveness, nearly every day (either by subjective account or as observed by others)

(continued)

☐ **Research criteria for minor depressive disorder** (*continued*)

(i)   recurrent thoughts of death (not just fear of dying), recurrent suicidal ideation without a specific plan, or a suicide attempt or a specific plan for committing suicide

(2)   the symptoms cause clinically significant distress or impairment in social, occupational, or other important areas of functioning

(3)   the symptoms are not due to the direct physiological effects of a substance (e.g., a drug of abuse, a medication) or a general medical condition (e.g., hypothyroidism)

(4)   the symptoms are not better accounted for by Bereavement (i.e., a normal reaction to the death of a loved one)

B.   There has never been a Major Depressive Episode (see p. 327), and criteria are not met for Dysthymic Disorder.

C.   There has never been a Manic Episode (see p. 332), a Mixed Episode (see p. 335), or a Hypomanic Episode (see p. 338), and criteria are not met for Cyclothymic Disorder.   **Note:** This exclusion does not apply if all of the manic-, mixed-, or hypomanic-like episodes are substance or treatment induced.

D.   The mood disturbance does not occur exclusively during Schizophrenia, Schizophreniform Disorder, Schizoaffective Disorder, Delusional Disorder, or Psychotic Disorder Not Otherwise Specified.

Recurrent Brief Depressive Disorder

Features

The essential feature is the recurrence of brief episodes of depressive symptoms that are identical to Major Depressive Episodes in the number and severity of symptoms but that do not meet the 2-week duration requirement. See the text for a Major Depressive Episode (p. 320) for a more detailed description of the characteristic symptoms. The episodes last at least 2 days but less than 2 weeks and most typically have a duration of between 2 and 4 days. Episodes must recur at least once a month for a period of 12 consecutive months, and they must not be associated exclusively with the menstrual cycle. The brief depressive episodes must cause clinically significant distress or impairment in social, occupational, or other important areas of functioning. In some individuals, there may be near-normal functioning, but this is accomplished with significantly increased effort.

A number of disorders exclude consideration of this proposed disorder. There has never been a Major Depressive, Manic, Mixed, or Hypomanic Episode, and criteria are not met for Dysthymic or Cyclothymic Disorder. The mood disturbance does not occur exclusively during Schizophrenia, Schizophreniform Disorder, Schizoaffective Disorder, Delusional Disorder, or Psychotic Disorder Not Otherwise Specified.

Associated Features

The pattern of lifetime or current comorbidity appears to be similar to that of Major Depressive Disorder. Associated disorders may include Substance-Related Disorders and Anxiety Disorders. The episodes may follow a seasonal pattern. The 1-year prevalence of this proposed disorder has been reported to be about 7% (although this was often in association with other established mental disorders). Males and females appear equally likely to experience recurrent brief depressive episodes, and the most typical age at onset appears to be in adolescence. Suicide attempts are the most serious complication. The rate of depressive disorders is increased in the first-degree biological relatives of individuals who have recurrent brief depressive episodes.

Differential Diagnosis

In DSM-IV, individuals whose presentation meets these research criteria would be diagnosed as having **Depressive Disorder Not Otherwise Specified.**

An episode of recurrent brief depressive disorder is distinguished from a **Major Depressive Episode** by the duration of the episode (2–13 days for a brief depressive episode and 2 weeks or longer for a Major Depressive Episode). Recurrent brief depressive disorder is considered to be a residual category and is not to be used if there is a history of a **Major Depressive Episode, Manic Episode, Mixed Episode,** or **Hypomanic Episode,** or if criteria are met for **Cyclothymic Disorder** or **Dysthymic Disorder. Substance-Induced Mood Disorder** is distinguished from this disturbance in that the depressive symptoms are due to the direct physiological effects of a drug of abuse (e.g., alcohol or cocaine) or the side effects of a medication (e.g., steroids) (see p. 370). **Mood Disorder Due to a General Medical Condition** is distinguished from this disturbance in that the depressive symptoms are due to the direct physiological effects of a general medical condition (e.g., hypothyroidism) (see p. 366). Because depressive symptoms are common associated features of psychotic disorders, they do not receive a separate diagnosis if they occur exclusively during **Schizophrenia, Schizophreniform Disorder, Schizoaffective Disorder, Delusional Disorder,** or **Psychotic Disorder Not Otherwise Specified.** Recurrent brief depressive disorder shares some clinical features with **Borderline Personality Disorder** (i.e., both disorders manifest brief and episodic depressive symptoms such as suicidal ideation or sadness). In cases where a Personality Disorder and this proposed disorder are both present, both may be noted (with recurrent brief depressive disorder noted as Depressive Disorder Not Otherwise Specified). The relationship between this proposed disorder and several other proposed categories included in this appendix (i.e., minor depressive disorder, depressive personality disorder, and mixed anxiety-depressive disorder) and with other Personality Disorders is not known, but substantial overlap may exist among them.

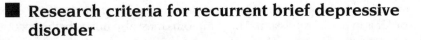 **Research criteria for recurrent brief depressive disorder**

A. Criteria, except for duration, are met for a Major Depressive Episode (see p. 327).

B. The depressive periods in Criterion A last at least 2 days but less than 2 weeks.

C. The depressive periods occur at least once a month for 12 consecutive months and are not associated with the menstrual cycle.

D. The periods of depressed mood cause clinically significant distress or impairment in social, occupational, or other important areas of functioning.

E. The symptoms are not due to the direct physiological effects of a substance (e.g., a drug of abuse, a medication) or a general medical condition (e.g., hypothyroidism).

F. There has never been a Major Depressive Episode (see p. 327), and criteria are not met for Dysthymic Disorder.

G. There has never been a Manic Episode (see p. 332), a Mixed Episode (see p. 335), or a Hypomanic Episode (see p. 338), and criteria are not met for Cyclothymic Disorder. **Note:** This exclusion does not apply if all of the manic-, mixed-, or hypomanic-like episodes are substance or treatment induced.

H. The mood disturbance does not occur exclusively during Schizophrenia, Schizophreniform Disorder, Schizoaffective Disorder, Delusional Disorder, or Psychotic Disorder Not Otherwise Specified.

Mixed Anxiety-Depressive Disorder

Features

The essential feature is a persistent or recurrent dysphoric mood lasting at least 1 month. The dysphoric mood is accompanied by additional symptoms that also must persist for at least 1 month and include at least four of the following: concentration or memory difficulties, sleep disturbance, fatigue or low energy, irritability, worry, being easily moved to tears, hypervigilance, anticipating the worst, hopelessness or pessimism about the future, and low self-esteem or feelings of worthlessness. The symptoms must cause clinically significant distress or impairment in social, occupational, or other important areas of functioning. This proposed disorder should not be considered if the symptoms are due to the direct physiological effects of a substance or a general medical condition or if the criteria for Major Depressive Disorder, Dysthymic Disorder, Panic Disorder, or

Generalized Anxiety Disorder have ever been met. The diagnosis is also not made if the criteria for any other Anxiety or Mood Disorder are currently met, even if the Anxiety or Mood Disorder is in partial remission. The symptoms must also not be better accounted for by any other mental disorder. Much of the initial information about this condition has been collected in primary care settings, in which the disorder appears to be common; it may also be quite common in outpatient mental health settings.

Differential Diagnosis

In DSM-IV, individuals whose presentation meets these research criteria would be diagnosed as having **Anxiety Disorder Not Otherwise Specified.**

Substance-Induced Anxiety Disorder is distinguished from this disturbance in that the symptoms of dysphoria are due to the direct physiological effects of a drug of abuse (e.g., alcohol or cocaine) or the side effects of a medication (e.g., steroids) (see p. 439). **Anxiety Disorder Due to a General Medical Condition** is distinguished from this disturbance in that the symptoms of dysphoria are due to the direct physiological effects of a general medical condition (e.g., pheochromocytoma, hyperthyroidism) (see p. 436). The symptoms described in this presentation are a frequent **associated feature of many mental disorders** and therefore should not be diagnosed separately if better accounted for by any other mental disorder. This condition should also not be considered in individuals with a current or past history of **Major Depressive Disorder, Dysthymic Disorder, Panic Disorder,** or **Generalized Anxiety Disorder** or with any other current Mood or Anxiety Disorder (including those in partial remission). This presentation is also distinguished from **no mental disorder** by the facts that the symptoms are persistent or recurrent and that they cause clinically significant distress or impairment in social, occupational, or other important areas of functioning.

The relationship between this proposed disorder and several other proposed categories included in this appendix (i.e., minor depressive disorder, recurrent brief depressive disorder, and depressive personality disorder) and with other Personality Disorders is not known, but substantial overlap may exist among them.

■ **Research criteria for mixed anxiety-depressive disorder**

A. Persistent or recurrent dysphoric mood lasting at least 1 month.

B. The dysphoric mood is accompanied by at least 1 month of four (or more) of the following symptoms:

(1) difficulty concentrating or mind going blank
(2) sleep disturbance (difficulty falling or staying asleep, or restless unsatisfying sleep)
(3) fatigue or low energy
(4) irritability
(5) worry

(continued)

☐ **Research criteria for mixed anxiety-depressive disorder**
(*continued*)

        (6) being easily moved to tears
        (7) hypervigilance
        (8) anticipating the worst
        (9) hopelessness (pervasive pessimism about the future)
      (10) low self-esteem or feelings of worthlessness

C. The symptoms cause clinically significant distress or impairment in social, occupational, or other important areas of functioning.

D. The symptoms are not due to the direct physiological effects of a substance (e.g., a drug of abuse, a medication) or a general medical condition.

E. All of the following:
    (1) criteria have never been met for Major Depressive Disorder, Dysthymic Disorder, Panic Disorder, or Generalized Anxiety Disorder
    (2) criteria are not currently met for any other Anxiety or Mood Disorder (including an Anxiety or Mood Disorder, In Partial Remission)
    (3) the symptoms are not better accounted for by any other mental disorder

Factitious Disorder by Proxy

Features

The essential feature is the deliberate production or feigning of physical or psychological signs or symptoms in another person who is under the individual's care. Typically the victim is a young child and the perpetrator is the child's mother. The motivation for the perpetrator's behavior is presumed to be a psychological need to assume the sick role by proxy. External incentives for the behavior, such as economic gain, are absent. The behavior is not better accounted for by another mental disorder. The perpetrator induces or simulates the illness or disease process in the victim and then presents the victim for medical care while disclaiming any knowledge about the actual etiology of the problem. The majority of induced and simulated conditions involve the gastrointestinal, the genitourinary, and the central nervous systems; the simulation of mental disorders in the victim is much less frequently reported. The type and severity of signs and symptoms are limited only by the medical sophistication and opportunities of the perpetrator. Cases are often characterized by an atypical clinical course in the victim and inconsistent laboratory test results that are at variance with the seeming health of the victim.

    The victim is usually a preschool child, although newborns, adolescents, and adults may be used as victims. With older children, consideration should be given to the possibility of collaboration with the perpetrator in the production of signs and symptoms. The perpetrator receives a diagnosis of factitious disorder by proxy. For the victim, Physical Abuse of Child (995.5) or Physical Abuse of Adult (995.81) may be noted if appropriate. In the event of voluntary collaboration, an additional diagnosis of Factitious Disorder may be appropriate for the collaborator.

Associated Features

Life stressors, especially marital conflict, may trigger the behavior. Perpetrators may exhibit pathological lying (or pseudologia fantastica) in describing everyday experiences and when presenting the victim for medical care. They commonly have considerable experience in health-related areas and seem to thrive in a medical environment. Despite their medical knowledge, they often seem insufficiently concerned with the apparent severity of the victim's condition. Victims may suffer a significant morbidity and mortality rate as a consequence of the induced conditions and are at increased risk of developing Factitious Disorder themselves as they mature. The perpetrator is usually the mother, and the father usually appears uninvolved. Sometimes, however, the father or husband may collaborate with the mother or may act alone. The perpetrator may also be a spouse or another caregiver (e.g., a baby-sitter). Perpetrators may have a history of having been abused. Somatoform Disorders and Personality Disorders may be present.

This proposed disorder often coexists with Factitious Disorder, which is usually quiescent as long as the perpetrator can induce or simulate a factitious illness in the victim. When confronted with the consequences of their behavior, perpetrators may become depressed and suicidal. Some become angry with the health care providers, deny the accusations, attempt to remove the victim from the hospital against medical advice, and seek care from other providers even at a considerable distance. Perpetrators may face criminal charges ranging from abuse to murder. Typically the perpetrator focuses on only one victim at a time, although other siblings or individuals may have been or might become victims.

Differential Diagnosis

In DSM-IV, an individual (i.e., the perpetrator) whose presentation meets these research criteria would be diagnosed as having **Factitious Disorder Not Otherwise Specified.**

Factitious disorder by proxy must be distinguished from a **general medical condition** or a **mental disorder** in the individual being brought for treatment. Factitious disorder by proxy must also be distinguished from **physical or sexual abuse** that is not related to the goal of indirectly assuming the sick role. **Malingering** differs from factitious disorder by proxy in that the motivation for the symptom production in Malingering is an external incentive, whereas in Factitious Disorder external incentives are absent. Individuals with Malingering may seek hospitalization for an individual under their care by producing symptoms in an attempt to obtain compensation.

■ **Research criteria for factitious disorder by proxy**

    A. Intentional production or feigning of physical or psychological signs or symptoms in another person who is under the individual's care.

    B. The motivation for the perpetrator's behavior is to assume the sick role by proxy.

    C. External incentives for the behavior (such as economic gain) are absent.

    D. The behavior is not better accounted for by another mental disorder.

Dissociative Trance Disorder

Features

The essential feature is an involuntary state of trance that is not accepted by the person's culture as a normal part of a collective cultural or religious practice and that causes clinically significant distress or functional impairment. This proposed disorder should not be considered in individuals who enter trance or possession states voluntarily and without distress in the context of cultural and religious practices that are broadly accepted by the person's cultural group. Such voluntary and nonpathological states are common and constitute the overwhelming majority of trance and possession trance states encountered cross-culturally. However, some individuals undergoing culturally normative trance or possession trance states may develop symptoms that cause distress or impairment and thus could be considered for this proposed disorder. Specific local instances of dissociative trance disorder show considerable variation cross-culturally with regard to the precise nature of the behaviors performed during the altered state, the presence or absence of dissociative sensory alterations (e.g., blindness), the identity assumed during these states, and the degree of amnesia experienced following the altered state (for examples, see Appendix I's Glossary of Culture-Bound Syndromes, p. 844).

In trance, the loss of customary identity is not associated with the appearance of alternate identities, and the actions performed during a trance state are generally not complex (e.g., convulsive movements, falling, running). In possession trance, there is the appearance of one (or several) distinct alternate identities with characteristic behaviors, memories, and attitudes, and the activities performed by the person tend to be more complex (e.g., coherent conversations, characteristic gestures, facial expressions, and specific verbalizations that are culturally established as belonging to a particular possessing agent). Full or partial amnesia is more regularly reported after an episode of possession trance than after an episode of trance (although reports of amnesia after trance are not uncommon). Many individuals with this proposed disorder exhibit features of only one type of trance, but some present with mixed symptomatology or fluctuate between types of trance over time according to local cultural parameters.

Associated Features

Variants of these conditions have been described in nearly every traditional society on every continent. The prevalence appears to decrease with increasing industrialization but remains elevated among traditional ethnic minorities in industrialized societies. There are considerable local variations in age and mode of onset. The course is typically episodic, with variable duration of acute episodes from minutes to hours. It has been reported that during a trance state, individuals may have an increased pain threshold, may consume inedible materials (e.g., glass), and may experience increased muscular strength. The symptoms of a pathological trance may be heightened or reduced in response to environmental cues and the ministrations of others. Presumed possessing agents are usually spiritual in nature (e.g., spirits of the dead, supernatural entities, gods, demons) and are often experienced as making demands or expressing animosity. Individuals with pathological possession trance typically experience a limited number of agents (one to five) in a sequential, not simultaneous, fashion. Complications include suicide attempts, self-mutilation, and accidents. Sudden deaths have been reported as a possible outcome, perhaps due to cardiac arrhythmias.

Differential Diagnosis

In DSM-IV, individuals whose presentation meets these research criteria would be diagnosed as having **Dissociative Disorder Not Otherwise Specified.**

This diagnosis should not be made if the trance state is judged to be due to the direct physiological effects of a general medical condition (in which case the diagnosis would be **Mental Disorder Not Otherwise Specified Due to a General Medical Condition,** see p. 174) or a substance (in which case the diagnosis would be **Substance-Related Disorder Not Otherwise Specified**).

The symptoms of the trance state (e.g., hearing or seeing spiritual beings and being controlled or influenced by others) may be confused with the hallucinations and delusions of **Schizophrenia, Mood Disorder With Psychotic Features,** or **Brief Psychotic Disorder.** The trance state may be distinguished by its cultural congruency, its briefer duration, and the absence of the characteristic symptoms of these other disorders.

Individuals with **Dissociative Identity Disorder** can be distinguished from those with trance and possession symptoms by the fact that those with trance and possession symptoms typically describe external spirits or entities that have entered their bodies and taken over.

This proposed disorder should not be considered in individuals who enter trance or possession states voluntarily and without distress or impairment in the context of cultural and religious practices.

■ Research criteria for dissociative trance disorder

A. Either (1) or (2):

    (1) trance, i.e., temporary marked alteration in the state of consciousness or loss of customary sense of personal identity without replacement by an alternate identity, associated with at least one of the following:

(continued)

☐ **Research criteria for dissociative trance disorder** (*continued*)

  (a) narrowing of awareness of immediate surroundings, or unusually narrow and selective focusing on environmental stimuli

  (b) stereotyped behaviors or movements that are experienced as being beyond one's control

 (2) possession trance, a single or episodic alteration in the state of consciousness characterized by the replacement of customary sense of personal identity by a new identity. This is attributed to the influence of a spirit, power, deity, or other person, as evidenced by one (or more) of the following:

  (a) stereotyped and culturally determined behaviors or movements that are experienced as being controlled by the possessing agent

  (b) full or partial amnesia for the event

B. The trance or possession trance state is not accepted as a normal part of a collective cultural or religious practice.

C. The trance or possession trance state causes clinically significant distress or impairment in social, occupational, or other important areas of functioning.

D. The trance or possession trance state does not occur exclusively during the course of a Psychotic Disorder (including Mood Disorder With Psychotic Features and Brief Psychotic Disorder) or Dissociative Identity Disorder and is not due to the direct physiological effects of a substance or a general medical condition.

Binge-Eating Disorder

Diagnostic Features

The essential features are recurrent episodes of binge eating associated with subjective and behavioral indicators of impaired control over, and significant distress about, the binge eating and the absence of the regular use of inappropriate compensatory behaviors (such as self-induced vomiting, misuse of laxatives and other medications, fasting, and excessive exercise) that are characteristic of Bulimia Nervosa. The characteristics of a binge episode are discussed in the text for Bulimia Nervosa (p. 545). Indicators of impaired control include eating very rapidly, eating until feeling uncomfortably full, eating large amounts of food when not hungry, eating alone because of embarrassment over how much one is eating, and feeling disgust, guilt, or depression after overeating. The marked distress required for the diagnosis includes unpleasant feelings during and after the binge episodes, as well as concerns about the long-term effect of the recurrent binge episodes on body weight and shape.

Binge episodes must occur, on average, at least 2 days a week for a period of at least 6 months. The duration of a binge-eating episode can vary greatly, and many individuals have difficulty separating binge eating into discrete episodes. However, they usually have little difficulty recalling whether or not binge eating occurred on a given day. Thus, it is suggested that the number of days on which binge eating occurs be counted, rather than the number of episodes of binge eating, as is done in making the diagnosis of Bulimia Nervosa. Future research should address this issue.

The symptoms do not occur exclusively during Anorexia Nervosa or Bulimia Nervosa. In addition, although some inappropriate compensatory behavior (e.g., purging, fasting, or excessive exercise) may occur occasionally, it is not regularly employed to counteract the effects of the binge eating. Research studies conducted to date have varied in how they have defined "regular use of inappropriate compensatory behaviors." Some studies have equated "regular" with the twice-a-week frequency criterion of Bulimia Nervosa and have considered individuals who engage in these behaviors less than twice a week (but as often as once a week) to be eligible for the diagnosis of binge-eating disorder. Other studies have excluded individuals who describe any use of inappropriate compensatory behaviors during the episode of illness. Future research should address this issue.

Associated Features and Disorders

Some individuals report that binge eating is triggered by dysphoric moods, such as depression and anxiety. Others are unable to identify specific precipitants but may report a nonspecific feeling of tension that is relieved by the binge eating. Some individuals describe a dissociative quality to the binge episodes (feeling "numb" or "spaced out"). Many individuals eat throughout the day with no planned mealtimes.

Individuals with this eating pattern seen in clinical settings have varying degrees of obesity. Most have a long history of repeated efforts to diet and feel desperate about their difficulty in controlling food intake. Some continue to make attempts to restrict calorie intake, whereas others have given up all efforts to diet because of repeated failures. In weight-control clinics, individuals with this eating pattern are, on average, more obese and have a history of more marked weight fluctuations than individuals without this pattern. In nonpatient community samples, most individuals with this eating pattern are overweight (although some have never been overweight).

Individuals with this eating pattern may report that their eating or weight interferes with their relationships with other people, with their work, and with their ability to feel good about themselves. In comparison with individuals of equal weight without this pattern of eating, they report higher rates of self-loathing, disgust about body size, depression, anxiety, somatic concern, and interpersonal sensitivity. There may be a higher lifetime prevalence of Major Depressive Disorder, Substance-Related Disorders, and Personality Disorders.

In samples drawn from weight-control programs, the overall prevalence varies from approximately 15% to 50% (with a mean of 30%), with females approximately 1.5 times more likely to have this eating pattern than males. In nonpatient community samples, a prevalence rate of 0.7%–4% has been reported. The onset of binge eating typically is in late adolescence or in the early 20s, often coming soon after significant weight loss from dieting. Among individuals presenting for treatment, the course appears to be chronic.

Differential Diagnosis

In DSM-IV, individuals whose presentation meets these research criteria would be diagnosed as having **Eating Disorder Not Otherwise Specified.**

In contrast to **Bulimia Nervosa,** in which inappropriate compensatory mechanisms are employed to counteract the effects of the binges, in binge-eating disorder no such behavior is regularly employed to compensate for the binge eating. Overeating is frequently seen during episodes of **Major Depressive Disorder,** but usually does not involve binge eating. This appendix diagnosis should be considered only when the individual reports that, during episodes of overeating, both the subjective sense of impaired control and three of the associated symptoms listed in Criterion B are present. Many individuals are distressed by episodes of overeating that are not binge-eating episodes.

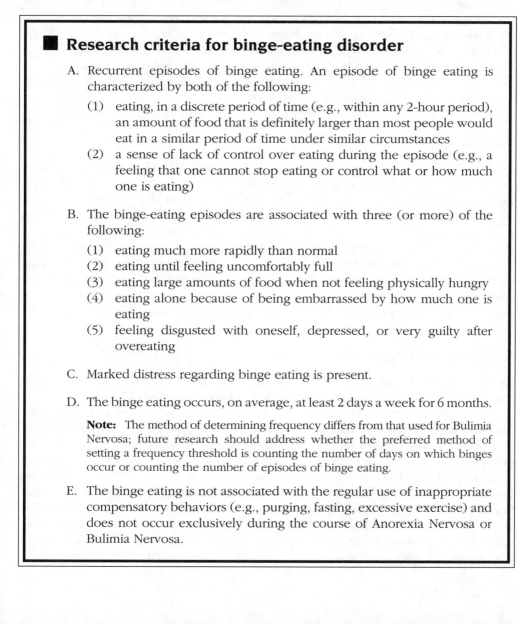

■ Research criteria for binge-eating disorder

A. Recurrent episodes of binge eating. An episode of binge eating is characterized by both of the following:

(1) eating, in a discrete period of time (e.g., within any 2-hour period), an amount of food that is definitely larger than most people would eat in a similar period of time under similar circumstances

(2) a sense of lack of control over eating during the episode (e.g., a feeling that one cannot stop eating or control what or how much one is eating)

B. The binge-eating episodes are associated with three (or more) of the following:

(1) eating much more rapidly than normal

(2) eating until feeling uncomfortably full

(3) eating large amounts of food when not feeling physically hungry

(4) eating alone because of being embarrassed by how much one is eating

(5) feeling disgusted with oneself, depressed, or very guilty after overeating

C. Marked distress regarding binge eating is present.

D. The binge eating occurs, on average, at least 2 days a week for 6 months.

Note: The method of determining frequency differs from that used for Bulimia Nervosa; future research should address whether the preferred method of setting a frequency threshold is counting the number of days on which binges occur or counting the number of episodes of binge eating.

E. The binge eating is not associated with the regular use of inappropriate compensatory behaviors (e.g., purging, fasting, excessive exercise) and does not occur exclusively during the course of Anorexia Nervosa or Bulimia Nervosa.

Depressive Personality Disorder

Features

The essential feature is a pervasive pattern of depressive cognitions and behaviors that begins by early adulthood and that occurs in a variety of contexts. This pattern does not occur exclusively during Major Depressive Episodes and is not better accounted for by Dysthymic Disorder. The depressive cognitions and behaviors include a persistent and pervasive feeling of dejection, gloominess, cheerlessness, joylessness, and unhappiness. These individuals are overly serious, incapable of enjoyment or relaxation, and lack a sense of humor. They may feel that they do not deserve to have fun or to be happy. They also tend to brood and worry, dwelling persistently on their negative and unhappy thoughts. Such individuals view the future as negatively as they view the present; they doubt that things will ever improve, anticipate the worst, and while priding themselves on being realistic, are considered by others to be pessimistic. They may be harsh in self-judgment and prone to feeling excessively guilty for shortcomings and failings. Self-esteem is low and particularly focused on feelings of inadequacy. Individuals with this proposed disorder tend to judge others as harshly as they judge themselves. They often focus on others' failings rather than their positive attributes, and they may be negativistic, critical, and judgmental toward others.

Associated Features

These individuals may be quiet, introverted, passive, and unassertive, preferring to follow others rather than taking the lead. This pattern may occur with approximately equal frequency in females and males. Individuals with this presentation may be predisposed to developing Dysthymic Disorder and possibly Major Depressive Disorder. These conditions may exist on a spectrum, with depressive personality disorder being the early-onset, persistent, traitlike variant of the Depressive Disorders. Preliminary evidence suggests that depressive personality disorder may have an increased prevalence in family members of probands with Major Depressive Disorder. Conversely, Major Depressive Disorder may occur with increased frequency in family members of probands with depressive personality disorder who do not themselves have Major Depressive Disorder.

Differential Diagnosis

In DSM-IV, individuals whose presentation meets these research criteria would be diagnosed as having **Personality Disorder Not Otherwise Specified.**

It remains controversial whether the distinction between depressive personality disorder and **Dysthymic Disorder** is useful. The research criteria given for this proposed disorder differ from the diagnostic criteria for Dysthymic Disorder by their emphasis on cognitive, interpersonal, and intrapsychic personality traits. This proposed disorder should not be considered if the symptoms are better accounted for by Dysthymic Disorder or if they occur exclusively during **Major Depressive Episodes.** This proposed disorder differs from so-called normal depressive traits (e.g., unhappiness, pessimism, self-criticism, and proneness to guilt) in that the pattern is pervasive and causes marked distress or impairment in social or occupational functioning. The relationship between this proposed disorder and several other proposed categories included in this appendix (i.e., minor depressive disorder, recurrent brief depressive disorder, and mixed anxiety-depressive disorder) and with other Personality Disorders is not known, but substantial overlap may exist among them.

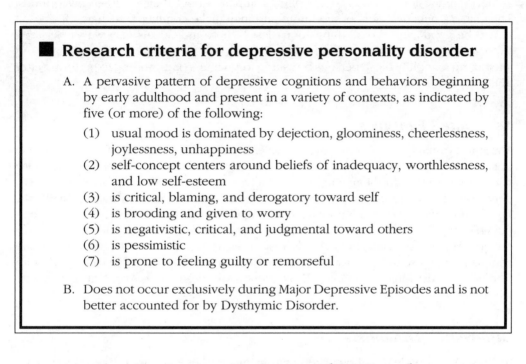

■ **Research criteria for depressive personality disorder**

A. A pervasive pattern of depressive cognitions and behaviors beginning by early adulthood and present in a variety of contexts, as indicated by five (or more) of the following:

   (1) usual mood is dominated by dejection, gloominess, cheerlessness, joylessness, unhappiness

   (2) self-concept centers around beliefs of inadequacy, worthlessness, and low self-esteem

   (3) is critical, blaming, and derogatory toward self

   (4) is brooding and given to worry

   (5) is negativistic, critical, and judgmental toward others

   (6) is pessimistic

   (7) is prone to feeling guilty or remorseful

B. Does not occur exclusively during Major Depressive Episodes and is not better accounted for by Dysthymic Disorder.

Passive-Aggressive Personality Disorder (Negativistic Personality Disorder)

Features

The essential feature is a pervasive pattern of negativistic attitudes and passive resistance to demands for adequate performance in social and occupational situations that begins by early adulthood and that occurs in a variety of contexts. This pattern does not occur exclusively during Major Depressive Episodes and is not better accounted for by Dysthymic Disorder. These individuals habitually resent, oppose, and resist demands to function at a level expected by others. This opposition occurs most frequently in work situations but can also be evident in social functioning. The resistance is expressed by procrastination, forgetfulness, stubbornness, and intentional inefficiency, especially in response to tasks assigned by authority figures. These individuals obstruct the efforts of others by failing to do their share of the work. For example, when an executive gives a subordinate some material to review for a meeting the next morning, the subordinate may misplace or misfile the material rather than point out that there is insufficient time to do the work. These individuals feel cheated, unappreciated, and misunderstood and chronically complain to others. When difficulties appear, they blame their failures on the behaviors of others. They may be sullen, irritable, impatient, argumentative, cynical, skeptical, and contrary. Authority figures (e.g., a superior at work, a teacher at school, a parent, or a spouse who acts the role of a parent) often become the focus of discontent.

Because of their negativism and tendency to externalize blame, these individuals often criticize and voice hostility toward authority figures with minimal provocation. They are also envious and resentful of peers who succeed or who are viewed positively by authority figures. These individuals often complain about their personal misfortunes. They have a negative view of the future and may make comments such as, "It doesn't pay to be good" and "Good things don't last." These individuals may waver between expressing hostile defiance toward those they view as causing their problems and attempting to mollify these persons by asking forgiveness or promising to perform better in the future.

Associated Features

These individuals are often overtly ambivalent, wavering indecisively from one course of action to its opposite. They may follow an erratic path that causes endless wrangles with others and disappointments for themselves. An intense conflict between dependence on others and the desire for self-assertion is characteristic of these individuals. Their self-confidence is often poor despite a superficial bravado. They foresee the worst possible outcome for most situations, even those that are going well. This defeatist outlook can evoke hostile and negative responses from others who are subjected to the complaints of these individuals. This pattern of behavior often occurs in individuals with Borderline, Histrionic, Paranoid, Dependent, Antisocial, and Avoidant Personality Disorders.

Differential Diagnosis

In DSM-IV, individuals whose presentation meets these research criteria would be diagnosed as having **Personality Disorder Not Otherwise Specified.**

In **Oppositional Defiant Disorder,** there is a similar pattern of negativistic attitudes and problems with authority figures, but Oppositional Defiant Disorder is usually diagnosed in children, whereas this proposed disorder should be considered only in adults. This pattern should not be considered if the symptoms are better accounted for by **Dysthymic Disorder** or if they occur exclusively during **Major Depressive Episodes.** Passive-aggressive behaviors are frequently encountered in everyday life, particularly among those in authoritarian situations (e.g., work, military, prison) that do not tolerate other forms of assertiveness. Only when these passive-aggressive personality traits are inflexible, maladaptive, and cause significant functional impairment or subjective distress do they constitute a disorder.

■ Research criteria for passive-aggressive personality disorder

A. A pervasive pattern of negativistic attitudes and passive resistance to demands for adequate performance, beginning by early adulthood and present in a variety of contexts, as indicated by four (or more) of the following:

(continued)

□ **Research criteria for passive-aggressive personality disorder** (*continued*)

    (1) passively resists fulfilling routine social and occupational tasks
    (2) complains of being misunderstood and unappreciated by others
    (3) is sullen and argumentative
    (4) unreasonably criticizes and scorns authority
    (5) expresses envy and resentment toward those apparently more fortunate
    (6) voices exaggerated and persistent complaints of personal misfortune
    (7) alternates between hostile defiance and contrition

  B. Does not occur exclusively during Major Depressive Episodes and is not better accounted for by Dysthymic Disorder.

Medication-Induced Movement Disorders

A consideration of Medication-Induced Movement Disorders is important in the management by medication of mental disorders or general medical conditions and in the differential diagnosis with Axis I disorders (e.g., Anxiety Disorder versus Neuroleptic-Induced Akathisia; catatonia versus Neuroleptic Malignant Syndrome). These conditions can lead to noncompliance with treatment and psychosocial and occupational impairments. Medication-Induced Movement Disorders should be coded on Axis I. Although these disorders are labeled "medication induced," it is often difficult to establish the causal relationship between medication exposure and the development of the movement disorder, especially because some of these conditions also occur in the absence of medication exposure. Criteria and text are provided for these disorders to facilitate research and to encourage appropriate diagnosis and treatment. The following Medication-Induced Movement Disorders are included in this section: Neuroleptic-Induced Parkinsonism, Neuroleptic Malignant Syndrome, Neuroleptic-Induced Acute Dystonia, Neuroleptic-Induced Acute Akathisia, Neuroleptic-Induced Tardive Dyskinesia, and Medication-Induced Postural Tremor. A category for Medication-Induced Movement Disorder Not Otherwise Specified is also provided for medication-induced movement disorders that do not meet the criteria for any of the specific disorders listed above. These include movement disorders (e.g., parkinsonism, acute akathisia) that are associated with a medication other than a neuroleptic (e.g., a serotonin reuptake inhibitor).

The term *neuroleptic* is used broadly in this manual to refer to medications with dopamine-antagonist properties. These include so-called typical antipsychotic agents (e.g., chlorpromazine, haloperidol, fluphenazine), atypical antipsychotic agents (e.g., clozapine), certain dopamine receptor blocking drugs used in the treatment of physical symptoms such as nausea (e.g., prochlorperazine, promethazine, trimethobenzamide, metoclopramide), and amoxapine, which is marketed as an antidepressant.

332.1 Neuroleptic-Induced Parkinsonism

Diagnostic Features

The essential feature of Neuroleptic-Induced Parkinsonism is the presence of parkinsonian signs or symptoms (i.e., tremor, muscular rigidity, or akinesia) that develop in association with the use of neuroleptic medication. These symptoms usually develop within a few weeks of starting or raising the dose of a neuroleptic medication or after reducing a medication (e.g., an anticholinergic medication) that is being used to treat or prevent acute extrapyramidal symptoms. The symptoms must not be better accounted for by a mental disorder (e.g., catatonia, negative symptoms of Schizophrenia, psychomotor retardation in a Major Depressive Episode) and are not due to a neurological or other general medical condition (e.g., idiopathic Parkinson's disease, Wilson's disease). Rigidity and akinesia are most frequent, whereas tremor is somewhat less common. It has been estimated that at least 50% of outpatients receiving long-term neuroleptic treatment develop some parkinsonian signs or symptoms at some point in their course of treatment. Symptoms may develop rapidly after starting or raising the dose of neuroleptic medication or may develop insidiously over time. The most typical course is the development of symptoms 2–4 weeks after starting a neuroleptic medication. The symptoms then tend to continue unchanged or to diminish gradually over the next few months. Symptoms will usually abate with a reduction of the dose (or discontinuation) of the neuroleptic medication, the addition of antiparkinsonian medication, or a switch to a neuroleptic medication with a lower incidence of these side effects.

Parkinsonian tremor is a steady, rhythmic oscillatory movement (3–6 cycles per second) that is typically slower than other tremors and is apparent at rest. It may occur intermittently and be unilateral or bilateral or depend on where the limb is located (positional tremor). The tremor may affect limbs, head, jaw, mouth, lip ("rabbit syndrome"), or tongue. The tremor can be suppressed, especially when the individual attempts to perform a task with the tremulous limb. Individuals may describe the tremor as "shaking" and report that it occurs especially during times of anxiety, stress, or fatigue.

Parkinsonian muscular rigidity is defined as excessive firmness and tensing of resting muscles. It may affect all skeletal muscles or it may only involve discrete muscular areas. Two kinds of rigidity occur: *continuous ("lead-pipe") rigidity* and *cogwheel rigidity*. In lead-pipe rigidity, the limb or joint resists movement and feels locked in place. The rigidity is continuous (i.e., the limb usually does not show moment-to-moment fluctuations). In cogwheel rigidity, as the muscle is stretched around a joint there is a rhythmic, ratchet-like resistance that interrupts the usual smooth motion of the joint. Cogwheel rigidity can be felt by placing the hand over the joint being moved. Cogwheel rigidity occurs when the muscles are passively moved, is most common in the wrists and elbows, and often waxes and wanes. Individuals with parkinsonian rigidity may complain of generalized muscle tenderness or stiffness, muscle or joint pain, body aching, or lack of coordination during sports.

Akinesia is a state of decreased spontaneous motor activity. There is global slowing as well as slowness in initiating and executing movements. Normal everyday behaviors (e.g., grooming) are reduced. Individuals may complain of feeling listless, lacking spontaneity and drive, or oversleeping. Parkinsonian rigidity and akinesia can be manifested as abnormalities in gait or decreases in length of stride, arm swing, or overall spontaneity of walking. Other signs include bent-over neck, stooped shoulders, a staring facial expression, and small shuffling steps. Drooling may arise due to a general decrease in pharyngeal motor activity, although it may be less common in parkinsonism associated with neuroleptic medication because of the anticholinergic properties of these medications.

Associated Features

Associated behavioral symptoms may include depression and worsening of negative signs of Schizophrenia. Other associated signs and symptoms include small handwriting (micrographia), hypophonia, postural instability, inhibited blinking in response to glabellae tapping, and seborrhea. General medical complications can occur when parkinsonian symptoms are severe and result in decreased motor activity (e.g., contractures, bedsores, and pulmonary emboli). Decreased gag reflex and dysphagia can be life threatening and may present as aspiration pneumonia or unexplained weight loss. There may be urinary incontinence and increased rates of hip fractures in elderly persons. Risk factors for developing Neuroleptic-Induced Parkinsonism include a history of prior episodes of Neuroleptic-Induced Parkinsonism; older age; the presence of a coexisting delirium, dementia, or amnestic disorder; or a coexisting neurological condition. Children may also be at higher risk of developing Neuroleptic-Induced Parkinsonism. Furthermore, the risk of developing Neuroleptic-Induced Parkinsonism is associated with the type of neuroleptic medication, the rapidity of increases in dosage, and the absolute dose; the risk is reduced if individuals are taking anticholinergic medications.

Differential Diagnosis

It is important to distinguish between Neuroleptic-Induced Parkinsonism and other causes of parkinsonian symptoms in individuals being treated with a neuroleptic medication. Neuroleptic-Induced Parkinsonism should be distinguished from **parkinsonian symptoms due to another substance or medication** or **due to a neurological or other general medical condition** (e.g., Parkinson's disease, Wilson's disease). Laboratory findings may help to establish other causes for the parkinsonian symptoms (e.g., positive urine heavy metal screen, basal ganglia calcification indicating hypercalcemia, serum ceruloplasmin indicating Wilson's disease). Tremor due to other causes of parkinsonian symptoms, familial tremor, non-neuroleptic-induced tremor, and tremor associated with Substance Withdrawal should be distinguished from tremor in Neuroleptic-Induced Parkinsonism. Nonparkinsonian tremors tend to be finer (e.g., smaller amplitude) and faster (10 cycles per second) and tend to worsen on intention (e.g., when the individual reaches out to hold a cup). Tremor associated with **Substance Withdrawal** will usually have associated hyperreflexia and increased autonomic signs. Tremor from **cerebellar disease** worsens on intention and may have associated nystagmus, ataxia, or scanning speech. Choreiform movements associated with **Neuroleptic-Induced Tardive Dyskinesia** can resemble parkinsonian tremor; however, the parkinsonian tremor is distinguished by its steady rhythmicity. **Strokes** and **other focal lesions of the central nervous system** can cause focal neurological signs as well as causing immobility from flaccid or spastic paralysis. In contrast, muscle strength is initially normal and muscles fatigue later in Neuroleptic-Induced Parkinsonism. Rigidity from parkinsonism also needs to be differentiated from the "clasp knife" phenomenon found in pyramidal lesions and oppositional behavior.

Some indications that the parkinsonian symptoms are not due to neuroleptics include family history of an inherited neurological condition, rapidly progressive parkinsonism not accounted for by recent psychopharmacological changes, the presence of focal nonextrapyramidal neurological signs (e.g., frontal release signs, cranial nerve abnormalities, or a positive Babinski sign), and parkinsonian signs or symptoms that do not reverse within 3 months of neuroleptic discontinuation (or 1 year when the neuroleptic was given in a long-acting intramuscular form). Individuals with **Neuroleptic Malignant Syndrome** have both severe akinesia and rigidity but have additional physical and laboratory findings (e.g., fever, increased creatine phosphokinase [CPK]).

Distinguishing between symptoms of a **primary mental disorder** and behavioral disturbances from Neuroleptic-Induced Parkinsonism can be difficult. Often the diagnosis has to be based on multiple sources of information (e.g., physical examination findings, medication history, mental symptoms). The diagnosis of Neuroleptic-Induced Parkinsonism may have to be made provisionally and can sometimes only be confirmed by a trial of dosage reduction (or elimination) of the neuroleptic medication or by initiating anticholinergic treatment. Neuroleptic-induced akinesia and **Major Depressive Disorder** have many overlapping symptoms. Major Depressive Disorder is more likely to have vegetative signs (e.g., early morning awakening), hopelessness, and despair, whereas apathy is more typical of akinesia. Catatonia associated with **Schizophrenia, Catatonic Type,** or **Mood Disorders With Catatonic Features** can be particularly difficult to distinguish from severe akinesia. The **negative symptoms of Schizophrenia** may also be difficult to differentiate from akinesia. Rigidity may also be associated with **Psychotic Disorders, delirium, dementia, Anxiety Disorders,** and **Conversion Disorder.** The resistance to passive motion is constant through the full range of motion in parkinsonian rigidity, whereas it is inconsistent in mental disorders or other neurological conditions presenting with rigidity. Furthermore, individuals with parkinsonian rigidity generally have a constellation of signs and symptoms, including a characteristic walk and facial expression, drooling, decreased blinking, and other aspects of bradykinesia.

■ Research criteria for 332.1 Neuroleptic-Induced Parkinsonism

A. One (or more) of the following signs or symptoms has developed in association with the use of neuroleptic medication:

   (1) parkinsonian tremor (i.e., a coarse, rhythmic, resting tremor with a frequency between 3 and 6 cycles per second, affecting the limbs, head, mouth, or tongue)

   (2) parkinsonian muscular rigidity (i.e., cogwheel rigidity or continuous "lead-pipe" rigidity)

   (3) akinesia (i.e., a decrease in spontaneous facial expressions, gestures, speech, or body movements)

B. The symptoms in Criterion A developed within a few weeks of starting or raising the dose of a neuroleptic medication, or of reducing a medication used to treat (or prevent) acute extrapyramidal symptoms (e.g., anticholinergic agents).

(continued)

☐ **Research criteria for 332.1 Neuroleptic-Induced Parkinsonism** (*continued*)

C. The symptoms in Criterion A are not better accounted for by a mental disorder (e.g., catatonic or negative symptoms in Schizophrenia, psychomotor retardation in a Major Depressive Episode). Evidence that the symptoms are better accounted for by a mental disorder might include the following: the symptoms precede the exposure to neuroleptic medication or are not compatible with the pattern of pharmacological intervention (e.g., no improvement after lowering the neuroleptic dose or administering anticholinergic medication).

D. The symptoms in Criterion A are not due to a nonneuroleptic substance or to a neurological or other general medical condition (e.g., Parkinson's disease, Wilson's disease). Evidence that the symptoms are due to a general medical condition might include the following: the symptoms precede exposure to neuroleptic medication, unexplained focal neurological signs are present, or the symptoms progress despite a stable medication regimen.

333.92   Neuroleptic Malignant Syndrome

Diagnostic Features

The essential feature of Neuroleptic Malignant Syndrome is the development of severe muscle rigidity and elevated temperature in an individual using neuroleptic medication. This is accompanied by two (or more) of the following symptoms: diaphoresis, dysphagia, tremor, incontinence, changes in level of consciousness ranging from confusion to coma, mutism, tachycardia, elevated or labile blood pressure, leukocytosis, and laboratory evidence of muscle injury (e.g., elevated creatine phosphokinase [CPK]). These symptoms are not due to another substance (e.g., phencyclidine) or to a neurological or other general medical condition (e.g., viral encephalitis) and are not better accounted for by a mental disorder (e.g., Mood Disorder With Catatonic Features). There may be accompanying agitation or acute dystonic reactions.

Elevated temperature ranges from mild elevations (e.g., 99°–100°F) to markedly hyperthermic states (e.g., 106°F). Fever due to a general medical condition (e.g., infection) needs to be ruled out as a cause of the elevated temperature; however, individuals with Neuroleptic Malignant Syndrome often develop other medical conditions that can worsen an already elevated temperature. CPK is typically elevated, ranging from minor elevations to extremely high levels (exceeding 16,000 IU). It should be noted that mild to moderate elevations of CPK can also be seen with muscle damage due to various causes such as intramuscular injection and use of restraints and has also been reported in individuals with acute Psychotic Disorders. White blood cell counts are often high, usually ranging between 10,000 and 20,000. In severe cases, myoglobinuria may occur and may be a harbinger of renal failure.

The presentation and course of Neuroleptic Malignant Syndrome are quite variable. It may have a malignant, potentially fatal course or a relatively benign, self-limited course. There is currently no way to predict the evolution of the syndrome in any particular individual. Neuroleptic Malignant Syndrome usually develops within 4 weeks after starting a neuroleptic medication, with two-thirds of cases developing within the first week. However, some individuals develop Neuroleptic Malignant Syndrome after taking the same dose of neuroleptic medication for many months. After discontinuation of neuroleptic medication, resolution of the condition occurs within a mean duration of 2 weeks for nondepot neuroleptic medication and 1 month for depot neuroleptic medication, although there are cases that continue far beyond the mean duration of 2 weeks. In most cases, there is eventually a total resolution of symptoms. For a minority of individuals, the outcome is fatal. Fatality rates in the literature are in the 10%–20% range, but these rates may be artificially high as a result of reporting bias. With increasing recognition of this condition, estimates of fatality rates have decreased. There have been rare reports of neurological sequelae.

Associated Features

Most cases have been reported to occur in individuals with Schizophrenia, Manic Episodes, and Mental Disorders Due to a General Medical Condition (e.g., a delirium or a dementia). Prior episodes of Neuroleptic Malignant Syndrome, agitation, dehydration, high doses of neuroleptic medication, rapid increase in dosage, and intramuscular injection of neuroleptic medication appear to be risk factors. There is controversy in the literature about whether treatment with lithium carbonate enhances the likelihood of developing Neuroleptic Malignant Syndrome. Although this disorder can occur in both hot and cold environments, environments that are warm and humid may contribute to the development of this condition. Various general medical conditions may occur and complicate the clinical picture, including pneumonia, renal failure, cardiac or respiratory arrest, seizures, sepsis, pulmonary embolism, and disseminated intravascular coagulation.

Estimates of the prevalence of this condition in individuals exposed to neuroleptic medications range from 0.07% to 1.4%. Neuroleptic Malignant Syndrome has been reported to occur somewhat more frequently in males than in females. The condition may occur at any age but has been reported most frequently in young adults. Variations in reported prevalence may be due to a lack of consistency in the definition of caseness, neuroleptic prescribing practices, study design, and the demographics of the population being studied. Neuroleptic Malignant Syndrome may occur more frequently with high-potency neuroleptic medication. Some individuals who have developed this condition may be less likely to be compliant with taking neuroleptic medication. Although many individuals do not experience a recurrence when neuroleptic medication is reinstituted, some do experience a recurrence, especially when the neuroleptic medication is reinstituted soon after an episode of Neuroleptic Malignant Syndrome.

Differential Diagnosis

Neuroleptic Malignant Syndrome must be distinguished from the symptoms of a **neurological or other general medical condition.** An elevated temperature that is due to a general medical condition (e.g., a viral infection) must be distinguished from the elevated temperature associated with Neuroleptic Malignant Syndrome. Extremely elevated temperatures are more likely due to Neuroleptic Malignant Syndrome, especially in the absence of an identifiable general medical condition. In addition, in Neuroleptic Malignant Syndrome, other characteristic features (e.g., severe muscle rigidity) are also present. General medical conditions with a presentation that may resemble Neuroleptic Malignant Syndrome include central nervous system infection, status epilepticus, sub-cortical brain lesions (e.g., stroke, trauma, neoplasms), and systemic conditions (e.g., intermittent acute porphyria, tetanus). **Heat stroke** may mimic Neuroleptic Malignant Syndrome but can be distinguished by the presence of hot, dry skin (rather than diaphoresis), hypotension (rather than fluctuating or elevated blood pressure), and limb flaccidity (rather than rigidity). **Malignant hyperthermia** presents with high elevated temperature and rigidity and usually occurs in genetically susceptible individuals who have received halogenated inhalational anesthetics and depolarizing muscle relaxants. Malignant hyperthermia usually starts within minutes of receiving anesthesia. Because other general medical conditions can co-occur with or result from Neuroleptic Malignant Syndrome, it is important to determine whether the elevated temperature occurred before or subsequent to the superimposed medical problems. Abrupt discontinuation of antiparkinsonian medication in a person with **Parkinson's disease** or **treatment with dopamine-depleting agents** (e.g., reserpine, tetrabenazine) may precipitate a reaction similar to Neuroleptic Malignant Syndrome.

Neuroleptic Malignant Syndrome must be distinguished from similar syndromes resulting from the use of **other psychotropic medications** (e.g., monoamine oxidase inhibitors, monoamine oxidase inhibitor–tricyclic combinations, monoamine oxidase inhibitor–serotonergic agent combinations, monoamine oxidase inhibitor–meperidine combinations, lithium toxicity, anticholinergic delirium, amphetamines, fenfluramine, cocaine, and phencyclidine), all of which may present with hyperthermia, altered mental status, and autonomic changes. In such cases, a diagnosis of **Medication-Induced Movement Disorder Not Otherwise Specified** can be given.

Individuals with Schizophrenia or a Manic Episode who are not receiving a neuroleptic medication may sometimes present with extreme catatonic states (so-called **lethal catatonia**), which can mimic Neuroleptic Malignant Syndrome and may include elevated temperature, autonomic dysfunction, and abnormal laboratory findings. For individuals already receiving a neuroleptic medication, a history of prior extreme catatonic states when the individual was not receiving a neuroleptic is important in making the differential diagnosis. The problem is further confounded by the fact that neuroleptic medication may worsen the symptoms of lethal catatonia.

■ **Research criteria for 333.92 Neuroleptic Malignant Syndrome**

A. The development of severe muscle rigidity and elevated temperature associated with the use of neuroleptic medication.

B. Two (or more) of the following:
   (1) diaphoresis
   (2) dysphagia

(continued)

☐ **Research criteria for 333.92 Neuroleptic Malignant Syndrome** (*continued*)

      (3) tremor

      (4) incontinence

      (5) changes in level of consciousness ranging from confusion to coma

      (6) mutism

      (7) tachycardia

      (8) elevated or labile blood pressure

      (9) leucocytosis

     (10) laboratory evidence of muscle injury (e.g., elevated CPK)

C. The symptoms in Criteria A and B are not due to another substance (e.g., phencyclidine) or a neurological or other general medical condition (e.g., viral encephalitis).

D. The symptoms in Criteria A and B are not better accounted for by a mental disorder (e.g., Mood Disorder With Catatonic Features).

333.7 Neuroleptic-Induced Acute Dystonia

Diagnostic Features

The essential feature of Neuroleptic-Induced Acute Dystonia is sustained abnormal postures or muscle spasms that develop in association with the use of neuroleptic medication. These include abnormal positioning of the head and neck in relation to the body (e.g., retrocollis, torticollis); spasms of the jaw muscles (trismus, gaping, grimacing); impaired swallowing (dysphagia), speaking, or breathing (potentially life-threatening laryngeal-pharyngeal spasm, dysphonia); thickened or slurred speech due to hypertonic tongue (dysarthria, macroglossia); tongue protrusion or tongue dysfunction; eyes deviated up, down, or sideward (oculogyric crisis); or abnormal positioning of the distal limbs or trunk (opisthotonos). There is great variability in the severity of the symptoms and in the body areas that may be affected. Increased tone in the affected muscles is usually present. The signs or symptoms develop within 7 days of starting or rapidly raising the dose of neuroleptic medication or of reducing a medication being used to treat or prevent acute extrapyramidal symptoms (e.g., anticholinergic agents). The symptoms must not be better accounted for by a mental disorder (e.g., catatonic symptoms in Schizophrenia) and must not be due to a nonneuroleptic substance or to a neurological or other general medical condition.

Associated Features

Fear and anxiety often accompany the onset of Neuroleptic-Induced Acute Dystonia, especially in individuals who are unaware of the possibility of developing dystonia and who mistakenly regard the symptom as part of their mental disorder. Some individuals experience pain or cramps in affected muscles. Noncompliance with medication treatment may result following the development of acute dystonic reactions. Neuroleptic-Induced Acute Dystonia occurs most commonly in young males. Risk factors for developing Neuroleptic-Induced Acute Dystonia include prior dystonic reactions to neuroleptic treatment and the use of high-potency neuroleptic medication.

Differential Diagnosis

It is important to distinguish between Neuroleptic-Induced Acute Dystonia and other causes of dystonia in individuals being treated with a neuroleptic medication. Evidence that the symptoms are due to a **neurological or other general medical condition** includes course (e.g., symptoms preceding exposure to the neuroleptic medication or progression of symptoms in the absence of change in medication) and the presence of focal neurological signs. **Spontaneously occurring focal or segmental dystonias** usually persist for several days or weeks independent of medication. Other neurological conditions (e.g., temporal lobe seizures, viral and bacterial infections, trauma, or space-occupying lesions in the peripheral or central nervous system) and endocrinopathies (e.g., hypoparathyroidism) can also produce symptoms (e.g., tetany) that resemble a Neuroleptic-Induced Acute Dystonia.

Neuroleptic Malignant Syndrome can produce dystonia but differs in that it is also accompanied by fever and generalized rigidity. Neuroleptic-Induced Acute Dystonia should be distinguished from **dystonia due to a nonneuroleptic medication** (e.g., anticonvulsant medications such as phenytoin and carbamazepine). In such cases, a diagnosis of **Medication-Induced Movement Disorder Not Otherwise Specified** can be given.

Catatonia associated with a Mood Disorder or Schizophrenia can be distinguished by the temporal relationship between the symptoms and the neuroleptic exposure (e.g., dystonia preceding exposure to neuroleptic medication) and response to pharmacological intervention (e.g., no improvement after lowering of neuroleptic dose or anticholinergic administration). Furthermore, individuals with Neuroleptic-Induced Acute Dystonia are generally distressed about the dystonic reaction and usually seek intervention. In contrast, individuals with catatonia are typically mute and withdrawn and do not express subjective distress about their condition.

■ **Research criteria for 333.7 Neuroleptic-Induced Acute Dystonia**

A. One (or more) of the following signs or symptoms has developed in association with the use of neuroleptic medication:

(1) abnormal positioning of the head and neck in relation to the body (e.g., retrocollis, torticollis)

(2) spasms of the jaw muscles (trismus, gaping, grimacing)

(3) impaired swallowing (dysphagia), speaking, or breathing (laryngeal-pharyngeal spasm, dysphonia)

(continued)

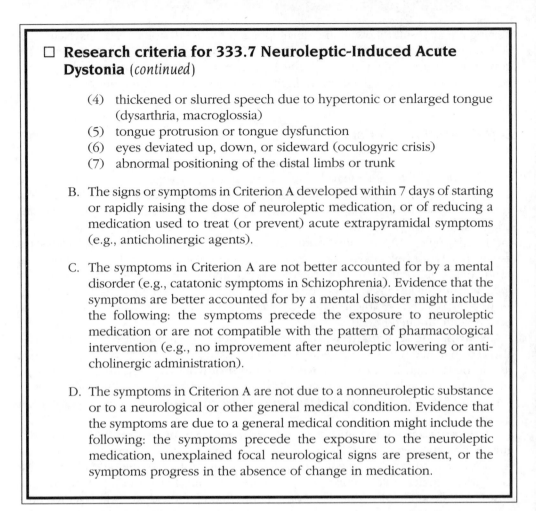

□ **Research criteria for 333.7 Neuroleptic-Induced Acute Dystonia** (*continued*)

   (4) thickened or slurred speech due to hypertonic or enlarged tongue (dysarthria, macroglossia)
   (5) tongue protrusion or tongue dysfunction
   (6) eyes deviated up, down, or sideward (oculogyric crisis)
   (7) abnormal positioning of the distal limbs or trunk

B. The signs or symptoms in Criterion A developed within 7 days of starting or rapidly raising the dose of neuroleptic medication, or of reducing a medication used to treat (or prevent) acute extrapyramidal symptoms (e.g., anticholinergic agents).

C. The symptoms in Criterion A are not better accounted for by a mental disorder (e.g., catatonic symptoms in Schizophrenia). Evidence that the symptoms are better accounted for by a mental disorder might include the following: the symptoms precede the exposure to neuroleptic medication or are not compatible with the pattern of pharmacological intervention (e.g., no improvement after neuroleptic lowering or anticholinergic administration).

D. The symptoms in Criterion A are not due to a nonneuroleptic substance or to a neurological or other general medical condition. Evidence that the symptoms are due to a general medical condition might include the following: the symptoms precede the exposure to the neuroleptic medication, unexplained focal neurological signs are present, or the symptoms progress in the absence of change in medication.

333.99   Neuroleptic-Induced Acute Akathisia

Diagnostic Features

The essential features of Neuroleptic-Induced Acute Akathisia are subjective complaints of restlessness and at least one of the following observed movements: fidgety movements or swinging of the legs while seated, rocking from foot to foot or "walking on the spot" while standing, pacing to relieve the restlessness, or an inability to sit or stand still for at least several minutes. In its most severe form, the individual may be unable to maintain any position for more than a few seconds. The subjective complaints include a sense of inner restlessness, most often in the legs; a compulsion to move one's legs; distress if one is asked not to move one's legs; and dysphoria and anxiety. The symptoms typically occur within 4 weeks of initiating or increasing the dose of a neuroleptic medication and can occasionally follow the reduction of medication used to treat or prevent acute extrapyramidal symptoms (e.g., anticholinergic agents). The symptoms are not better accounted for by a mental disorder (e.g., Schizophrenia, Substance Withdrawal, agitation from a Major Depressive or Manic Episode, hyperactivity in Attention-Deficit/Hyperactivity Disorder) and are not due to a nonneuroleptic substance or to a neurological or other general medical condition (e.g., Parkinson's disease, iron-deficiency anemi).

Associated Features and Disorders

The subjective distress resulting from akathisia is significant and can lead to noncompliance with neuroleptic treatment. Akathisia may be associated with dysphoria, irritability, aggression, or suicide attempts. Worsening of psychotic symptoms or behavioral dyscontrol may lead to an increase in neuroleptic medication dose, which may exacerbate the problem. Akathisia can develop very rapidly after initiating or increasing neuroleptic medication. The development of akathisia appears to be dose dependent and to be more frequently associated with particular neuroleptic medications. Acute akathisia tends to persist for as long as neuroleptic medications are continued, although the intensity may fluctuate over time. The reported prevalence of akathisia among individuals receiving neuroleptic medication has varied widely (20%–75%). Variations in reported prevalence may be due to a lack of consistency in the definition of caseness, neuroleptic prescribing practices, study design, and the demographics of the population being studied.

Differential Diagnosis

Neuroleptic-Induced Acute Akathisia may be clinically indistinguishable from syndromes of restlessness due to certain neurological or other general medical conditions, to nonneuroleptic substances, and to agitation presenting as part of a mental disorder (e.g., a Manic Episode). The akathisia of **Parkinson's disease** and **iron-deficiency anemia** are phenomenologically similar to Neuroleptic-Induced Acute Akathisia. The frequently abrupt appearance of restlessness soon after initiation or increase in neuroleptic medication usually distinguishes Neuroleptic-Induced Acute Akathisia.

Serotonin-specific reuptake inhibitor antidepressant medications may produce akathisia that appears to be identical in phenomenology and treatment response to Neuroleptic-Induced Acute Akathisia. Akathisia due to nonneuroleptic medication can be diagnosed as **Medication-Induced Movement Disorder Not Otherwise Specified.** Other situations that might be included under Medication-Induced Movement Disorders Not Otherwise Specified are acute akathisia with only subjective or only objective complaints, but not both; and akathisia occurring late in the course of treatment (e.g., 6 months after initiation of, or increase in the dose of, a neuroleptic). **Neuroleptic-Induced Tardive Dyskinesia** also often has a component of generalized restlessness that may coexist with akathisia in an individual receiving neuroleptic medication. Neuroleptic-Induced Acute Akathisia is differentiated from Neuroleptic-Induced Tardive Dyskinesia by the nature of the movements and their relationship to the initiation of medication. The time course of symptomatic presentation relative to neuroleptic dose changes may aid in this distinction. An increase in neuroleptic medication will often exacerbate akathisia, whereas it often temporarily relieves the symptoms of Tardive Dyskinesia.

Neuroleptic-Induced Acute Akathisia should be distinguished from symptoms that are better accounted for by a mental disorder. Individuals with **Depressive Episodes, Manic Episodes, Generalized Anxiety Disorder, Schizophrenia and other Psychotic Disorders**, **Attention-Deficit/Hyperactivity Disorder, dementia, delirium,**

Substance Intoxication (e.g., with cocaine), or **Substance Withdrawal** (e.g., from an opioid) may also display agitation that is difficult to distinguish from akathisia. Some of these individuals are able to differentiate akathisia from the anxiety, restlessness, and agitation characteristic of a mental disorder by their experience of akathisia as being different from previously experienced feelings. Other evidence that restlessness or agitation may be better accounted for by a mental disorder includes the onset of agitation prior to exposure to the neuroleptic medication, absence of increasing restlessness with increasing neuroleptic medication doses, and absence of relief with pharmacological interventions (e.g., no improvement after decreasing the neuroleptic dose or treatment with medication intended to treat the akathisia).

■ Research criteria for 333.99 Neuroleptic-Induced Acute Akathisia

A. The development of subjective complaints of restlessness after exposure to a neuroleptic medication.

B. At least one of the following is observed:
    (1) fidgety movements or swinging of the legs
    (2) rocking from foot to foot while standing
    (3) pacing to relieve restlessness
    (4) inability to sit or stand still for at least several minutes

C. The onset of the symptoms in Criteria A and B occurs within 4 weeks of initiating or increasing the dose of the neuroleptic, or of reducing medication used to treat (or prevent) acute extrapyramidal symptoms (e.g., anticholinergic agents).

D. The symptoms in Criterion A are not better accounted for by a mental disorder (e.g., Schizophrenia, Substance Withdrawal, agitation from a Major Depressive or Manic Episode, hyperactivity in Attention-Deficit/Hyperactivity Disorder). Evidence that symptoms may be better accounted for by a mental disorder might include the following: the onset of symptoms preceding the exposure to the neuroleptics, the absence of increasing restlessness with increasing neuroleptic doses, and the absence of relief with pharmacological interventions (e.g., no improvement after decreasing the neuroleptic dose or treatment with medication intended to treat the akathisia).

E. The symptoms in Criterion A are not due to a nonneuroleptic substance or to a neurological or other general medical condition. Evidence that symptoms are due to a general medical condition might include the onset of the symptoms preceding the exposure to neuroleptics or the progression of symptoms in the absence of a change in medication.

333.82   Neuroleptic-Induced Tardive Dyskinesia

Diagnostic Features

The essential features of Neuroleptic-Induced Tardive Dyskinesia are abnormal, involuntary movements of the tongue, jaw, trunk, or extremities that develop in association with the use of neuroleptic medication. The movements are present over a period of at least 4 weeks and may be choreiform (rapid, jerky, nonrepetitive), athetoid (slow, sinuous, continual), or rhythmic (e.g., stereotypies) in nature. The signs or symptoms develop during exposure to a neuroleptic medication or within 4 weeks of withdrawal from an oral (or within 8 weeks of withdrawal from a depot) neuroleptic medication. There must be a history of the use of neuroleptic medication for at least 3 months (or 1 month in individuals age 60 years or older). Although a large number of epidemiological studies have established the etiological relationship between neuroleptic use and Tardive Dyskinesia, any dyskinesia in an individual who is receiving neuroleptic medication is not necessarily Neuroleptic-Induced Tardive Dyskinesia. The movements must not be due to a neurological or other general medical condition (e.g., Huntington's disease, Sydenham's chorea, spontaneous dyskinesia, hyperthyroidism, Wilson's disease), to ill-fitting dentures, or to exposure to other medications that can cause acute reversible dyskinesia (e.g., L-dopa, bromocriptine). The movements should also not be better accounted for by a neuroleptic-induced acute movement disorder (e.g., Neuroleptic-Induced Acute Dystonia, Neuroleptic-Induced Acute Akathisia).

Over three-fourths of the individuals with Tardive Dyskinesia have abnormal orofacial movements, approximately one-half have limb involvement, and up to one-quarter have axial dyskinesia of the trunk. All three regions are affected in approximately 10% of individuals. Involvement of other muscle groups (e.g., pharyngeal, abdominal) may occur but is uncommon, especially in the absence of dyskinesia of the orofacial region, limbs, or trunk. Limb or truncal dyskinesia without orofacial involvement is more common in younger individuals, whereas orofacial dyskinesias are typical in elderly persons.

Associated Features

The symptoms of Tardive Dyskinesia tend to be worsened by stimulants, neuroleptic withdrawal, and anticholinergic medications and may be transiently worsened by emotional arousal, stress, and distraction during voluntary movements in unaffected parts of the body. The abnormal movements of dyskinesia are transiently reduced by relaxation and by voluntary movements in affected parts of the body. They are generally absent during sleep. Dyskinesia may be suppressed, at least temporarily, by increased doses of neuroleptics or sedatives.

The overall prevalence of Neuroleptic-Induced Tardive Dyskinesia in individuals who have received long-term neuroleptic treatment ranges from 20% to 30%. The overall incidence among younger individuals ranges from 3% to 5% per year. Elderly individuals appear to develop Neuroleptic-Induced Tardive Dyskinesia more often, with prevalence figures reported up to 50% and an incidence of 25%–30% after an average of 1 year's cumulative exposure to neuroleptic medication. Prevalence also varies depending on setting, with Tardive Dyskinesia tending to be more common among inpatients (especially chronically institutionalized individuals). Tardive Dyskinesia is diagnosed with approximately equal frequency in young males and females, whereas among elderly individuals it may be seen more often in females than in males. Mood Disorders (especially Major Depressive Disorder), neurological conditions, greater cumulative amount of neuroleptic medication, and early development of extrapyramidal side effects have been suggested as risk factors for Tardive Dyskinesia. Variations in reported prevalence may be due to a lack of consistency in the definition of caseness, neuroleptic prescribing practices, study design, and the demographics of the population being studied.

Onset may occur at any age and is almost always insidious. The signs are typically minimal to mild at onset and escape notice except by a keen observer. In a majority of cases, Tardive Dyskinesia is mild and is primarily a cosmetic problem. In severe cases, however, it may be associated with general medical complications (e.g., ulcers in cheeks and tongue; loss of teeth; macroglossia; difficulty in walking, swallowing, or breathing; muffled speech; weight loss; depression; and suicidal ideation). If the individual with Tardive Dyskinesia remains off neuroleptic medication, the dyskinesia remits within 3 months in one-third of the cases and remits by 12–18 months in more than 50% of cases, although these percentages are lower in elderly persons. When individuals receiving neuroleptic medication are assessed periodically, Tardive Dyskinesia is found to be stable over time in about one-half, to worsen in one-quarter, and to improve in the rest. Younger individuals generally tend to improve more readily; in elderly persons there is a greater likelihood that Tardive Dyskinesia may become more severe or more generalized with continued neuroleptic use. When neuroleptic medications are discontinued, it is estimated that 5%–40% of all cases remit and between 50% and 90% of mild cases remit.

Differential Diagnosis

Dyskinesia that emerges during neuroleptic withdrawal may remit with continued withdrawal from neuroleptic medication. If the dyskinesia persists for at least 4 weeks, a diagnosis of Tardive Dyskinesia may be warranted. Neuroleptic-Induced Tardive Dyskinesia must be distinguished from other causes of orofacial and body dyskinesia. These conditions include **Huntington's disease; Wilson's disease; Sydenham's (rheumatic) chorea; systemic lupus erythematosus; thyrotoxicosis; heavy metal poisoning; ill-fitting dentures; dyskinesia due to other medications such as L-dopa, bromocriptine,** or **amantadine;** and **spontaneous dyskinesias.** Factors that may be helpful in making the distinction are evidence that the symptoms preceded the exposure to the neuroleptic medication or that other focal neurological signs are present. It should be noted that other movement disorders may coexist with Neuroleptic-Induced Tardive Dyskinesia. Because spontaneous dyskinesia can occur in more than 5% of individuals and is also more common in elderly persons, it may be difficult to prove that neuroleptic medications produced Tardive Dyskinesia in a given individual. Neuroleptic-Induced Tardive Dyskinesia must be distinguished from symptoms that are due to a neuroleptic-induced acute movement disorder (e.g., **Neuroleptic-Induced Acute Dystonia** or **Neuroleptic-Induced Acute Akathisia**). Neuroleptic-Induced Acute Dystonia develops within 7 days and Neuroleptic-Induced Acute Akathisia develops within 4 weeks of initiating or increasing the dose of a neuroleptic medication (or reducing the dose of a medication used to treat acute extrapyramidal symptoms). Neuroleptic-Induced Tardive Dyskinesia, on the other hand, develops during exposure to (or withdrawal from) neuroleptic medication in individuals with a history of neuroleptic use for at least 3 months (or 1 month in elderly persons).

■ **Research criteria for 333.82 Neuroleptic-Induced Tardive Dyskinesia**

A. Involuntary movements of the tongue, jaw, trunk, or extremities have developed in association with the use of neuroleptic medication.

B. The involuntary movements are present over a period of at least 4 weeks and occur in any of the following patterns:

    (1) choreiform movements (i.e., rapid, jerky, nonrepetitive)
    (2) athetoid movements (i.e., slow, sinuous, continual)
    (3) rhythmic movements (i.e., stereotypies)

C. The signs or symptoms in Criteria A and B develop during exposure to a neuroleptic medication or within 4 weeks of withdrawal from an oral (or within 8 weeks of withdrawal from a depot) neuroleptic medication.

D. There has been exposure to neuroleptic medication for at least 3 months (1 month if age 60 years or older).

E. The symptoms are not due to a neurological or general medical condition (e.g., Huntington's disease, Sydenham's chorea, spontaneous dyskinesia, hyperthyroidism, Wilson's disease), ill-fitting dentures, or exposure to other medications that cause acute reversible dyskinesia (e.g., L-dopa, bromocriptine). Evidence that the symptoms are due to one of these etiologies might include the following: the symptoms precede the exposure to the neuroleptic medication or unexplained focal neurological signs are present.

F. The symptoms are not better accounted for by a neuroleptic-induced acute movement disorder (e.g., Neuroleptic-Induced Acute Dystonia, Neuroleptic-Induced Acute Akathisia).

333.1   Medication-Induced Postural Tremor

Diagnostic Features

The essential feature of Medication-Induced Postural Tremor is a fine postural tremor that has developed in association with the use of a medication. Medications with which such a tremor may be associated include lithium, beta-adrenergic medications (e.g., isoproterenol), stimulants (e.g., amphetamine), dopaminergic medications, anticonvulsant medications (e.g., valproic acid), neuroleptic medications, antidepressant medications, and methylxanthines (e.g., caffeine, theophylline). The tremor is a regular, rhythmic oscillation of the limbs (most commonly hands and fingers), head, mouth, or tongue with a frequency of between 8 and 12 cycles per second. It is most easily observed when the affected body part is held in a sustained posture (e.g., hands outstretched, mouth held open). When an individual describes a tremor that is consistent with this definition, but the clinician does not directly observe the tremor, it may be helpful to try to re-create the situation in which the tremor occurred (e.g., drinking from a cup and saucer). The symptoms are not due to a preexisting, nonpharmacologically induced tremor and are not better accounted for by Neuroleptic-Induced Parkinsonism.

Associated Features

Most available information concerns lithium-induced tremor. Lithium tremor is a common, usually benign, and well-tolerated side effect of therapeutic doses. However, it may cause social embarrassment, occupational difficulties, and noncompliance in some individuals. As serum lithium levels approach toxic levels, the tremor may become more coarse and be accompanied by muscle twitching, fasciculations, or ataxia. Nontoxic lithium tremor may improve spontaneously over time. A variety of factors may increase the risk of lithium tremor (e.g., increasing age, high serum lithium levels, concurrent antidepressant or neuroleptic medication, excessive caffeine intake, personal or family history of tremor, presence of Alcohol Dependence, and associated anxiety). The frequency of complaints about tremor appears to decrease with duration of lithium treatment. Factors that may exacerbate the tremor include anxiety, stress, fatigue, hypoglycemia, thyrotoxicosis, pheochromocytoma, hypothermia, and Alcohol Withdrawal.

Differential Diagnosis

Medication-Induced Postural Tremor should be distinguished from a **preexisting tremor** that is not caused by the effects of a medication. Factors that help to establish that the tremor was preexisting include its temporal relationship to the initiation of medication, lack of correlation with serum levels of the medication, and persistence after the medication is discontinued. If a preexisting, nonpharmacologically induced tremor is present that worsens with medication, such a tremor would not be considered to meet the criteria for a Medication-Induced Postural Tremor and would be coded as **Medication-Induced Movement Disorder Not Otherwise Specified.** The factors described above that may contribute to the severity of a Medication-Induced Postural Tremor (e.g., anxiety, stress, fatigue, hypoglycemia, thyrotoxicosis, pheochromocytoma, hypothermia, and Alcohol Withdrawal) may also be a cause of tremor independent of the medication.

Medication-Induced Postural Tremor is not diagnosed if the tremor is better accounted for by **Neuroleptic-Induced Parkinsonism.** A Medication-Induced Postural Tremor is usually absent at rest and intensifies when the affected part is brought into action or held in a sustained position. In contrast, the tremor related to Neuroleptic-Induced Parkinsonism is usually lower in frequency, worse at rest, and suppressed during intentional movement and usually occurs in association with other symptoms of Neuroleptic-Induced Parkinsonism (e.g., akinesia, rigidity).

■ **Research criteria for 333.1 Medication-Induced Postural Tremor**

A. A fine postural tremor that has developed in association with the use of a medication (e.g., lithium, antidepressant medication, valproic acid).

B. The tremor (i.e., a regular, rhythmic oscillation of the limbs, head, mouth, or tongue) has a frequency between 8 and 12 cycles per second.

C. The symptoms are not due to a preexisting nonpharmacologically induced tremor. Evidence that the symptoms are due to a preexisting tremor might include the following: the tremor was present prior to the introduction of the medication, the tremor does not correlate with serum levels of the medication, and the tremor persists after discontinuation of the medication.

D. The symptoms are not better accounted for by Neuroleptic-Induced Parkinsonism.

333.90   Medication-Induced Movement Disorder Not Otherwise Specified

This category is for Medication-Induced Movement Disorders that do not meet criteria for any of the specific disorders listed above. Examples include 1) parkinsonism, acute akathisia, acute dystonia, or dyskinetic movement that is associated with a medication other than a neuroleptic; 2) a presentation that resembles Neuroleptic Malignant Syndrome that is associated with a medication other than a neuroleptic; or 3) tardive dystonia.

Proposed Axes for Further Study

Defensive Functioning Scale

Defense mechanisms (or coping styles) are automatic psychological processes that protect the individual against anxiety and from the awareness of internal or external dangers or stressors. Individuals are often unaware of these processes as they operate. Defense mechanisms mediate the individual's reaction to emotional conflicts and to internal and external stressors. The individual defense mechanisms are divided conceptually and empirically into related groups that are referred to as *Defense Levels*.

To use the Defensive Functioning Scale, the clinician should list up to seven of the specific defenses or coping styles (starting with the most prominent) and then indicate the predominant defense level exhibited by the individual. These should reflect the defenses or coping styles employed at the time of evaluation, supplemented by whatever information is available about the individual's defenses or coping patterns during the recent time period that preceded the evaluation. The specific defense mechanisms listed may be drawn from the different Defense Levels.

   The Defensive Functioning Axis is presented first, followed by a recording form. The rest of the section consists of a list of definitions for the specific defense mechanisms and coping styles.

Defense Levels and Individual Defense Mechanisms

High adaptive level.   This level of defensive functioning results in optimal adaptation in the handling of stressors. These defenses usually maximize gratification and allow the conscious awareness of feelings, ideas, and their consequences. They also promote an optimum balance among conflicting motives. Examples of defenses at this level are

- anticipation
- affiliation
- altruism
- humor
- self-assertion
- self-observation
- sublimation
- suppression

Mental inhibitions (compromise formation) level.   Defensive functioning at this level keeps potentially threatening ideas, feelings, memories, wishes, or fears out of awareness. Examples are

- displacement
- dissociation
- intellectualization
- isolation of affect
- reaction formation
- repression
- undoing

Minor image-distorting level.   This level is characterized by distortions in the image of the self, body, or others that may be employed to regulate self-esteem. Examples are

- devaluation
- idealization
- omnipotence

Disavowal level.   This level is characterized by keeping unpleasant or unacceptable stressors, impulses, ideas, affects, or responsibility out of awareness with or without a misattribution of these to external causes. Examples are

- denial
- projection
- rationalization

Major image-distorting level. This level is characterized by gross distortion or misattribution of the image of self or others. Examples are

- autistic fantasy
- projective identification
- splitting of self-image or image of others

Action level. This level is characterized by defensive functioning that deals with internal or external stressors by action or withdrawal. Examples are

- acting out
- apathetic withdrawal
- help-rejecting complaining
- passive aggression

Level of defensive dysregulation. This level is characterized by failure of defensive regulation to contain the individual's reaction to stressors, leading to a pronounced break with objective reality. Examples are

- delusional projection
- psychotic denial
- psychotic distortion

Recording Form: Defensive Functioning Scale

A. Current Defenses or Coping Styles: List in order, beginning with most prominent defenses or coping styles.

1. _____

2. _____

3. _____

4. _____

5. _____

6. _____

7. _____

B. Predominant Current Defense Level: _____

Example

Axis I: 296.32   Major Depressive Disorder, Recurrent, Moderate
            305.40   Sedative, Hypnotic, or Anxiolytic Abuse
Axis II: 301.83   Borderline Personality Disorder
                         Antisocial personality features
Axis III: 881.02   Lacerations of wrist
Axis IV: Recent arrest
                      Expulsion from home by parents
Axis V: GAF = 45 (current)

Recording Form: Defensive Functioning Scale

A. Current Defenses or Coping Styles:

1. splitting
2. projection identification
3. acting out
4. devaluation
5. omnipotence
6. denial
7. projection

B. Predominant Current Defense Level: major image-distorting level

Glossary of Specific Defense Mechanisms and Coping Styles

acting out The individual deals with emotional conflict or internal or external stressors by actions rather than reflections or feelings. This definition is broader than the original concept of the acting out of transference feelings or wishes during psychotherapy and is intended to include behavior arising both within and outside the transference relationship. Defensive acting out is not synonymous with "bad behavior" because it requires evidence that the behavior is related to emotional conflicts.

affiliation The individual deals with emotional conflict or internal or external stressors by turning to others for help or support. This involves sharing problems with others but does not imply trying to make someone else responsible for them.

altruism The individual deals with emotional conflict or internal or external stressors by dedication to meeting the needs of others. Unlike the self-sacrifice sometimes characteristic of reaction formation, the individual receives gratification either vicariously or from the response of others.

anticipation The individual deals with emotional conflict or internal or external stressors by experiencing emotional reactions in advance of, or anticipating conse-quences of, possible future events and considering realistic, alternative responses or solutions.

autistic fantasy The individual deals with emotional conflict or internal or external stressors by excessive daydreaming as a substitute for human relationships, more effective action, or problem solving.

denial The individual deals with emotional conflict or internal or external stressors by refusing to acknowledge some painful aspect of external reality or subjective experience that would be apparent to others. The term *psychotic denial* is used when there is gross impairment in reality testing.

devaluation The individual deals with emotional conflict or internal or external stressors by attributing exaggerated negative qualities to self or others.

displacement The individual deals with emotional conflict or internal or external stressors by transferring a feeling about, or a response to, one object onto another (usually less threatening) substitute object.

dissociation The individual deals with emotional conflict or internal or external stressors with a breakdown in the usually integrated functions of consciousness, memory, perception of self or the environment, or sensory/motor behavior.

help-rejecting complaining The individual deals with emotional conflict or internal or external stressors by complaining or making repetitious requests for help that disguise covert feelings of hostility or reproach toward others, which are then expressed by rejecting the suggestions, advice, or help that others offer. The complaints or requests may involve physical or psychological symptoms or life problems.

humor The individual deals with emotional conflict or external stressors by empha-sizing the amusing or ironic aspects of the conflict or stressor.

idealization The individual deals with emotional conflict or internal or external stressors by attributing exaggerated positive qualities to others.

intellectualization The individual deals with emotional conflict or internal or external stressors by the excessive use of abstract thinking or the making of generalizations to control or minimize disturbing feelings.

isolation of affect The individual deals with emotional conflict or internal or external stressors by the separation of ideas from the feelings originally associated with them. The individual loses touch with the feelings associated with a given idea (e.g., a traumatic event) while remaining aware of the cognitive elements of it (e.g., descriptive details).

omnipotence The individual deals with emotional conflict or internal or external stressors by feeling or acting as if he or she possesses special powers or abilities and is superior to others.

passive aggression The individual deals with emotional conflict or internal or external stressors by indirectly and unassertively expressing aggression toward others. There is a facade of overt compliance masking covert resistance, resentment, or hostility. Passive aggression often occurs in response to demands for independent action or performance or the lack of gratification of dependent wishes but may be adaptive for individuals in subordinate positions who have no other way to express assertiveness more overtly.

projection The individual deals with emotional conflict or internal or external stressors by falsely attributing to another his or her own unacceptable feelings, impulses, or thoughts.

projective identification As in projection, the individual deals with emotional conflict or internal or external stressors by falsely attributing to another his or her own unacceptable feelings, impulses, or thoughts. Unlike simple projection, the individual does not fully disavow what is projected. Instead, the individual remains aware of his or her own affects or impulses but misattributes them as justifiable reactions to the other person. Not infrequently, the individual induces the very feelings in others that were first mistakenly believed to be there, making it difficult to clarify who did what to whom first.

rationalization The individual deals with emotional conflict or internal or external stressors by concealing the true motivations for his or her own thoughts, actions, or feelings through the elaboration of reassuring or self-serving but incorrect explanations.

reaction formation The individual deals with emotional conflict or internal or external stressors by substituting behavior, thoughts, or feelings that are diametrically opposed to his or her own unacceptable thoughts or feelings (this usually occurs in conjunction with their repression).

repression The individual deals with emotional conflict or internal or external stressors by expelling disturbing wishes, thoughts, or experiences from conscious awareness. The feeling component may remain conscious, detached from its associated ideas.

self-assertion The individual deals with emotional conflict or stressors by expressing his or her feelings and thoughts directly in a way that is not coercive or manipulative.

self-observation The individual deals with emotional conflict or stressors by reflecting on his or her own thoughts, feelings, motivation, and behavior, and responding appropriately.

splitting The individual deals with emotional conflict or internal or external stressors by compartmentalizing opposite affect states and failing to integrate the positive and negative qualities of the self or others into cohesive images. Because ambivalent affects cannot be experienced simultaneously, more balanced views and expectations of self or others are excluded from emotional awareness. Self and object images tend to alternate between polar opposites: exclusively loving, powerful, worthy, nurturant, and kind—or exclusively bad, hateful, angry, destructive, rejecting, or worthless.

sublimation The individual deals with emotional conflict or internal or external stressors by channeling potentially maladaptive feelings or impulses into socially acceptable behavior (e.g., contact sports to channel angry impulses).

suppression The individual deals with emotional conflict or internal or external stressors by intentionally avoiding thinking about disturbing problems, wishes, feelings, or experiences.

undoing The individual deals with emotional conflict or internal or external stressors by words or behavior designed to negate or to make amends symbolically for unacceptable thoughts, feelings, or actions.

Global Assessment of Relational Functioning (GARF) Scale

Instructions: The GARF Scale can be used to indicate an overall judgment of the functioning of a family or other ongoing relationship on a hypothetical continuum ranging from competent, optimal relational functioning to a disrupted, dysfunctional relationship. It is analogous to Axis V (Global Assessment of Functioning Scale) provided for individuals in DSM-IV. The GARF Scale permits the clinician to rate the degree to which a family or other ongoing relational unit meets the affective or instrumental needs of its members in the following areas:

A. *Problem solving*—skills in negotiating goals, rules, and routines; adaptability to stress; communication skills; ability to resolve conflict
B. *Organization*—maintenance of interpersonal roles and subsystem boundaries; hierarchical functioning; coalitions and distribution of power, control, and responsibility
C. *Emotional climate*—tone and range of feelings; quality of caring, empathy, involvement, and attachment/commitment; sharing of values; mutual affective responsiveness, respect, and regard; quality of sexual functioning

In most instances, the GARF Scale should be used to rate functioning during the current period (i.e., the level of relational functioning at the time of the evaluation). In some settings, the GARF Scale may also be used to rate functioning for other time periods (i.e., the highest level of relational functioning for at least a few months during the past year).

Note: Use specific, intermediate codes when possible, for example, 45, 68, 72. If detailed information is not adequate to make specific ratings, use midpoints of the five ranges, that is, 90, 70, 50, 30, or 10.

81–100 *Overall:* *Relational unit is functioning satisfactorily from self-report of participants and from perspectives of observers.*

Agreed-on patterns or routines exist that help meet the usual needs of each family/couple member; there is flexibility for change in response to unusual demands or events; and occasional conflicts and stressful transitions are resolved through problem-solving communication and negotiation.

There is a shared understanding and agreement about roles and appropriate tasks, decision making is established for each functional area, and there is recognition of the unique characteristics and merit of each subsystem (e.g., parents/spouses, siblings, and individuals).

There is a situationally appropriate, optimistic atmosphere in the family; a wide range of feelings is freely expressed and managed within the family; and there is a general atmosphere of warmth, caring, and sharing of values among all family members. Sexual relations of adult members are satisfactory.

61–80 *Overall:* *Functioning of relational unit is somewhat unsatisfactory. Over a period of time, many but not all difficulties are resolved without complaints.*

Daily routines are present but there is some pain and difficulty in responding to the unusual. Some conflicts remain unresolved, but do not disrupt family functioning.

Decision making is usually competent, but efforts at control of one another quite often are greater than necessary or are ineffective. Individuals and relationships are clearly demarcated but sometimes a specific subsystem is depreciated or scapegoated.

A range of feeling is expressed, but instances of emotional blocking or tension are evident. Warmth and caring are present but are marred by a family member's irritability and frustrations. Sexual activity of adult members may be reduced or problematic.

41–60 Overall: *Relational unit has occasional times of satisfying and competent functioning together, but clearly dysfunctional, unsatisfying relationships tend to predominate.*

Communication is frequently inhibited by unresolved conflicts that often interfere with daily routines; there is significant difficulty in adapting to family stress and transitional change.

Decision making is only intermittently competent and effective; either excessive rigidity or significant lack of structure is evident at these times. Individual needs are quite often submerged by a partner or coalition.

Pain or ineffective anger or emotional deadness interfere with family enjoyment. Although there is some warmth and support for members, it is usually unequally distributed. Troublesome sexual difficulties between adults are often present.

21–40 Overall: *Relational unit is obviously and seriously dysfunctional; forms and time periods of satisfactory relating are rare.*

Family/couple routines do not meet the needs of members; they are grimly adhered to or blithely ignored. Life cycle changes, such as departures or entries into the relational unit, generate painful conflict and obviously frustrating failures of problem solving.

Decision making is tyrannical or quite ineffective. The unique characteristics of individuals are unappreciated or ignored by either rigid or confusingly fluid coalitions.

There are infrequent periods of enjoyment of life together; frequent distancing or open hostility reflect significant conflicts that remain unresolved and quite painful. Sexual dysfunction among adult members is commonplace.

1–20 Overall: *Relational unit has become too dysfunctional to retain continuity of contact and attachment.*

Family/couple routines are negligible (e.g., no mealtime, sleeping, or waking schedule); family members often do not know where others are or when they will be in or out; there is a little effective communication among family members.

Family/couple members are not organized in such a way that personal or generational responsibilities are recognized. Boundaries of relational unit as a whole and subsystems cannot be identified or agreed on. Family members are physically endangered or injured or sexually attacked.

Despair and cynicism are pervasive; there is little attention to the emotional needs of others; there is almost no sense of attachment, commitment, or concern about one another's welfare.

0 Inadequate information.

Social and Occupational Functioning Assessment Scale (SOFAS)

The SOFAS is a new scale that differs from the Global Assessment of Functioning (GAF) Scale in that it focuses exclusively on the individual's level of social and occupational functioning and is not directly influenced by the overall severity of the individual's psychological symptoms. Also in contrast to the GAF Scale, any impairment in social and occupational functioning that is due to general medical conditions is considered in making the SOFAS rating. The SOFAS is usually used to rate functioning for the current period (i.e., the level of functioning at the time of the evaluation). The SOFAS may also be used to rate functioning for other time periods. For example, for some purposes it may be useful to evaluate functioning for the past year (i.e., the highest level of functioning for at least a few months during the past year).

Social and Occupational Functioning Assessment Scale (SOFAS)

Consider social and occupational functioning on a continuum from excellent functioning to grossly impaired functioning. Include impairments in functioning due to physical limitations, as well as those due to mental impairments. To be counted, impairment must be a direct consequence of mental and physical health problems; the effects of lack of opportunity and other environmental limitations are not to be considered.

Code   (**Note:** Use intermediate codes when appropriate, e.g., 45, 68, 72.)

100   Superior functioning in a wide range of activities.
|
91

90   Good functioning in all areas, occupationally and socially effective.
|
81

80   No more than a slight impairment in social, occupational, or school functioning (e.g., infrequent
| interpersonal conflict, temporarily falling behind in schoolwork).
71

70   Some difficulty in social, occupational, or school functioning, but generally functioning well, has
| some meaningful interpersonal relationships.
61

60   Moderate difficulty in social, occupational, or school functioning (e.g., few friends, conflicts with
| peers or co-workers).
51

50   Serious impairment in social, occupational, or school functioning (e.g., no friends, unable to keep a
| job).
41

40   Major impairment in several areas, such as work or school, family relations (e.g., depressed man
| avoids friends, neglects family, and is unable to work; child frequently beats up younger children,
31   is defiant at home, and is failing at school).

30   Inability to function in almost all areas (e.g., stays in bed all day; no job, home, or friends).
|
21

20   Occasionally fails to maintain minimal personal hygiene; unable to function independently.
|
11

10   Persistent inability to maintain minimal personal hygiene. Unable to function without harming self
| or others or without considerable external support (e.g., nursing care and supervision).
1

0   Inadequate information.

Note: The rating of overall psychological functioning on a scale of 0–100 was operationalized by Luborsky in the Health-Sickness Rating Scale. (Luborsky L: "Clinicians' Judgments of Mental Health." *Archives of General Psychiatry* 7:407–417, 1962). Spitzer and colleagues developed a revision of the Health-Sickness Rating Scale called the Global Assessment Scale (GAS) (Endicott J, Spitzer RL, Fleiss JL, et al.: "The Global Assessment Scale: A Procedure for Measuring Overall Severity of Psychiatric Disturbance." *Archives of General Psychiatry* 33:766–771, 1976). The SOFAS is derived from the GAS and its development is described in Goldman HH, Skodol AE, Lave TR: "Revising Axis V for DSM-IV: A Review of Measures of Social Functioning." *American Journal of Psychiatry* 149:1148–1156, 1992.

Appendix C

Glossary of Technical Terms

affect A pattern of observable behaviors that is the expression of a subjectively experienced feeling state (emotion). Common examples of affect are sadness, elation, and anger. In contrast to *mood,* which refers to a more pervasive and sustained emotional "climate," *affect* refers to more fluctuating changes in emotional "weather." What is considered the normal range of the expression of affect varies considerably, both within and among different cultures. Disturbances in affect include

    blunted Significant reduction in the intensity of emotional expression.

    flat Absence or near absence of any signs of affective expression.

    inappropriate Discordance between affective expression and the content of speech or ideation.

    labile Abnormal variability in affect with repeated, rapid, and abrupt shifts in affective expression.

    restricted or constricted Mild reduction in the range and intensity of emotional expression.

agitation (psychomotor agitation) Excessive motor activity associated with a feeling of inner tension. The activity is usually nonproductive and repetitious and consists of such behavior as pacing, fidgeting, wringing of the hands, pulling of clothes, and inability to sit still.

agonist medication A chemical entity extrinsic to endogenously produced substances that acts on a receptor and is capable of producing the maximal effect that can be produced by stimulating that receptor. A **partial agonist** is capable only of producing less than the maximal effect even when given in a concentration sufficient to bind with all available receptors.

agonist/antagonist medication A chemical entity extrinsic to endogenously produced substances that acts on a family of receptors (such as mu, delta, and kappa opiate

---

Glossary definitions were informed by the following sources: DSM-III; DSM-III-R; *American Psychiatric Glossary,* 6th Edition; *Penguin Dictionary of Psychology;* Campbell's *Psychiatric Dictionary,* 6th Edition; *Stedman's Medical Dictionary,* 19th Edition; *Dorland's Illustrated Medical Dictionary,* 25th Edition; and *Webster's Third New International Dictionary.*

---

receptors) in such a fashion that it is an agonist or partial agonist on one type of receptor and an antagonist on another.

alogia An impoverishment in thinking that is inferred from observing speech and language behavior. There may be brief and concrete replies to questions and restriction in the amount of spontaneous speech *(poverty of speech)*. Sometimes the speech is adequate in amount but conveys little information because it is overconcrete, over-abstract, repetitive, or stereotyped *(poverty of content)*.

amnesia Loss of memory. Types of amnesia include

    anterograde Loss of memory of events that occur after the onset of the etiological condition or agent.
    retrograde Loss of memory of events that occurred before the onset of the etiological condition or agent.

antagonist medication A chemical entity extrinsic to endogenously produced substances that occupies a receptor, produces no physiologic effects, and prevents endogenous and exogenous chemicals from producing an effect on that receptor.

anxiety The apprehensive anticipation of future danger or misfortune accompanied by a feeling of dysphoria or somatic symptoms of tension. The focus of anticipated danger may be internal or external.

aphasia An impairment in the understanding or transmission of ideas by language in any of its forms—reading, writing, or speaking—that is due to injury or disease of the brain centers involved in language.

aphonia An inability to produce speech sounds that require the use of the larynx that is not due to a lesion in the central nervous system.

ataxia Partial or complete loss of coordination of voluntary muscular movement.

attention The ability to focus in a sustained manner on a particular stimulus or activity. A disturbance in attention may be manifested by easy distractibility or difficulty in finishing tasks or in concentrating on work.

avolition An inability to initiate and persist in goal-directed activities. When severe enough to be considered pathological, avolition is pervasive and prevents the person from completing many different types of activities (e.g., work, intellectual pursuits, self-care).

catalepsy Waxy flexibility—rigid maintenance of a body position over an extended period of time.

cataplexy Episodes of sudden bilateral loss of muscle tone resulting in the individual collapsing, often in association with intense emotions such as laughter, anger, fear, or surprise.

catatonic behavior Marked motor abnormalities including *motoric immobility* (i.e., catalepsy or stupor), certain types of *excessive motor activity* (apparently purposeless agitation not influenced by external stimuli), *extreme negativism* (apparent motiveless resistance to instructions or attempts to be moved) or *mutism, posturing* or *stereotyped movements,* and *echolalia* or *echopraxia.*

conversion symptom A loss of, or alteration in, voluntary motor or sensory functioning suggesting a neurological or general medical condition. Psychological factors are judged to be associated with the development of the symptom, and the symptom is not fully explained by a neurological or general medical condition or the direct effects of a substance. The symptom is not intentionally produced or feigned and is not culturally sanctioned.

defense mechanism Automatic psychological process that protects the individual against anxiety and from awareness of internal or external stressors or dangers. Defense mechanisms mediate the individual's reaction to emotional conflicts and to external stressors. Some defense mechanisms (e.g., projection, splitting, and acting out) are almost invariably maladaptive. Others, such as suppression and denial, may be either maladaptive or adaptive, depending on their severity, their inflexibility, and the context in which they occur. Definitions of specific defense mechanisms and how they would be recorded using the Defensive Functioning Scale are presented on p. 751.

delusion A false belief based on incorrect inference about external reality that is firmly sustained despite what almost everyone else believes and despite what constitutes incontrovertible and obvious proof or evidence to the contrary. The belief is not one ordinarily accepted by other members of the person's culture or subculture (e.g., it is not an article of religious faith). When a false belief involves a value judgment, it is regarded as a delusion only when the judgment is so extreme as to defy credibility. Delusional conviction occurs on a continuum and can sometimes be inferred from an individual's behavior. It is often difficult to distinguish between a delusion and an overvalued idea (in which case the individual has an unreasonable belief or idea but does not hold it as firmly as is the case with a delusion).

   Delusions are subdivided according to their content. Some of the more common types are listed below:

   bizarre A delusion that involves a phenomenon that the person's culture would regard as totally implausible.
   delusional jealousy The delusion that one's sexual partner is unfaithful.
   erotomanic A delusion that another person, usually of higher status, is in love with the individual.
   grandiose A delusion of inflated worth, power, knowledge, identity, or special relationship to a deity or famous person.
   mood-congruent *See* mood-congruent psychotic features.
   mood-incongruent *See* mood-incongruent psychotic features.
   of being controlled A delusion in which feelings, impulses, thoughts, or actions are experienced as being under the control of some external force rather than being under one's own control.
   of reference A delusion whose theme is that events, objects, or other persons in one's immediate environment have a particular and unusual significance. These delusions are usually of a negative or pejorative nature, but also may be grandiose in content. This differs from an *idea of reference,* in which the false belief is not as firmly held nor as fully organized into a true belief.
   persecutory A delusion in which the central theme is that one (or someone to

whom one is close) is being attacked, harassed, cheated, persecuted, or conspired against.

somatic A delusion whose main content pertains to the appearance or functioning of one's body.

thought broadcasting The delusion that one's thoughts are being broadcast out loud so that they can be perceived by others.

thought insertion The delusion that certain of one's thoughts are not one's own, but rather are inserted into one's mind.

depersonalization An alteration in the perception or experience of the self so that one feels detached from, and as if one is an outside observer of, one's mental processes or body (e.g., feeling like one is in a dream).

derailment ("loosening of associations") A pattern of speech in which a person's ideas slip off one track onto another that is completely unrelated or only obliquely related. In moving from one sentence or clause to another, the person shifts the topic idiosyncratically from one frame of reference to another and things may be said in juxtaposition that lack a meaningful relationship. This disturbance occurs *between* clauses, in contrast to incoherence, in which the disturbance is *within* clauses. An occasional change of topic without warning or obvious connection does not constitute derailment.

derealization An alteration in the perception or experience of the external world so that it seems strange or unreal (e.g., people may seem unfamiliar or mechanical).

disorientation Confusion about the time of day, date, or season (time), where one is (place), or who one is (person).

dissociation A disruption in the usually integrated functions of consciousness, memory, identity, or perception of the environment. The disturbance may be sudden or gradual, transient or chronic.

distractibility The inability to maintain attention, that is, the shifting from one area or topic to another with minimal provocation, or attention being drawn too frequently to unimportant or irrelevant external stimuli.

dysarthria Imperfect articulation of speech due to disturbances of muscular control.

dyskinesia Distortion of voluntary movements with involuntary muscular activity.

dyssomnia Primary disorders of sleep or wakefulness characterized by insomnia or hypersomnia as the major presenting symptom. Dyssomnias are disorders of the amount, quality, or timing of sleep.

dystonia Disordered tonicity of muscles.

echolalia The pathological, parrotlike, and apparently senseless repetition (echoing) of a word or phrase just spoken by another person.

echopraxia Repetition by imitation of the movements of another. The action is not a willed or voluntary one and has a semiautomatic and uncontrollable quality.

flashback A recurrence of a memory, feeling, or perceptual experience from the past.

flight of ideas A nearly continuous flow of accelerated speech with abrupt changes from topic to topic that are usually based on understandable associations, distracting stimuli, or plays on words. When severe, speech may be disorganized and incoherent.

gender dysphoria A persistent aversion toward some or all of those physical characteristics or social roles that connote one's own biological sex.

gender identity A person's inner conviction of being male or female.

gender role Attitudes, patterns of behavior, and personality attributes defined by the culture in which the person lives as stereotypically "masculine" or "feminine" social roles.

grandiosity An inflated appraisal of one's worth, power, knowledge, importance, or identity. When extreme, grandiosity may be of delusional proportions.

hallucination A sensory perception that has the compelling sense of reality of a true perception but that occurs without external stimulation of the relevant sensory organ. Hallucinations should be distinguished from *illusions,* in which an actual external stimulus is misperceived or misinterpreted. The person may or may not have insight into the fact that he or she is having a hallucination. One person with auditory hallucinations may recognize that he or she is having a false sensory experience, whereas another may be convinced that the source of the sensory experience has an independent physical reality. The term *hallucination* is not ordinarily applied to the false perceptions that occur during dreaming, while falling asleep *(hypnagogic),* or when awakening *(hypno-pompic).* Transient hallucinatory experiences may occur in people without a mental disorder.
Types of hallucinations include

auditory A hallucination involving the perception of sound, most commonly of voices. Some clinicians and investigators would not include those experiences perceived as coming from inside the head and would instead limit the concept of true auditory hallucinations to those sounds whose source is perceived as being external. However, as used in DSM-IV, no distinction is made as to whether the source of the voices is perceived as being inside or outside of the head.
gustatory A hallucination involving the perception of taste (usually unpleasant).
mood-congruent *See* mood-congruent psychotic features.
mood-incongruent *See* mood-incongruent psychotic features.
olfactory A hallucination involving the perception of odor, such as of burning rubber or decaying fish.
somatic A hallucination involving the perception of a physical experience localized within the body (such as a feeling of electricity). A somatic hallucination is to be distinguished from physical sensations arising from an as-yet undiagnosed general medical condition, from hypochondriacal preoccupation with normal physical sensations, and from a tactile hallucination.
tactile A hallucination involving the perception of being touched or of something being under one's skin. The most common tactile hallucinations are the sensation of electric shocks and *formication* (the sensation of something creeping or crawling on or under the skin).
visual A hallucination involving sight, which may consist of formed images, such as of people, or of unformed images, such as flashes of light. Visual hallucinations should be distinguished from illusions, which are misperceptions of real external stimuli.

hyperacusis Painful sensitivity to sounds.

hypersomnia Excessive sleepiness, as evidenced by prolonged nocturnal sleep, difficulty maintaining an alert awake state during the day, or undesired daytime sleep episodes.

ideas of reference The feeling that casual incidents and external events have a particular and unusual meaning that is specific to the person. This is to be distinguished from a *delusion of reference,* in which there is a belief that is held with delusional conviction.

illusion A misperception or misinterpretation of a real external stimulus, such as hearing the rustling of leaves as the sound of voices. *See also* hallucination.

incoherence Speech or thinking that is essentially incomprehensible to others because words or phrases are joined together without a logical or meaningful connection. This disturbance occurs *within* clauses, in contrast to derailment, in which the disturbance is *between* clauses. This has sometimes been referred to as "word salad" to convey the degree of linguistic disorganization. Mildly ungrammatical constructions or idiomatic usages characteristic of particular regional or cultural backgrounds, lack of education, or low intelligence should not be considered incoherence. The term is generally not applied when there is evidence that the disturbance in speech is due to an aphasia.

insomnia A subjective complaint of difficulty falling or staying asleep or poor sleep quality. Types of insomnia include

> **initial insomnia** Difficulty in falling asleep.
> **middle insomnia** Awakening in the middle of the night followed by eventually falling back to sleep, but with difficulty.
> **terminal insomnia** Awakening before one's usual waking time and being unable to return to sleep.

intersex condition A condition in which an individual shows intermingling, in various degrees, of the characteristics of each sex, including physical form, reproductive organs, and sexual behavior.

macropsia The visual perception that objects are larger than they actually are.

magical thinking The erroneous belief that one's thoughts, words, or actions will cause or prevent a specific outcome in some way that defies commonly understood laws of cause and effect. Magical thinking may be a part of normal child development.

micropsia The visual perception that objects are smaller than they actually are.

mood A pervasive and sustained emotion that colors the perception of the world. Common examples of mood include depression, elation, anger, and anxiety. In contrast to *affect,* which refers to more fluctuating changes in emotional "weather," mood refers to a more pervasive and sustained emotional "climate."
> Types of mood include

> **dysphoric** An unpleasant mood, such as sadness, anxiety, or irritability.
> **elevated** An exaggerated feeling of well-being, or euphoria or elation. A person

with elevated mood may describe feeling "high," "ecstatic," "on top of the world," or "up in the clouds."

euthymic Mood in the "normal" range, which implies the absence of depressed or elevated mood.

expansive Lack of restraint in expressing one's feelings, frequently with an overvaluation of one's significance or importance.

irritable Easily annoyed and provoked to anger.

mood-congruent psychotic features Delusions or hallucinations whose content is entirely consistent with the typical themes of a depressed or manic mood. If the mood is depressed, the content of the delusions or hallucinations would involve themes of personal inadequacy, guilt, disease, death, nihilism, or deserved punishment. The content of the delusion may include themes of persecution if these are based on self-derogatory concepts such as deserved punishment. If the mood is manic, the content of the delusions or hallucinations would involve themes of inflated worth, power, knowledge, or identity, or a special relationship to a deity or a famous person. The content of the delusion may include themes of persecution if these are based on concepts such as inflated worth or deserved punishment.

mood-incongruent psychotic features Delusions or hallucinations whose content is not consistent with the typical themes of a depressed or manic mood. In the case of depression, the delusions or hallucinations would not involve themes of personal inadequacy, guilt, disease, death, nihilism, or deserved punishment. In the case of mania, the delusions or hallucinations would not involve themes of inflated worth, power, knowledge, or identity, or a special relationship to a deity or a famous person. Examples of mood-incongruent psychotic features include persecutory delusions (without self-derogatory or grandiose content), thought insertion, thought broadcasting, and delusions of being controlled whose content has no apparent relationship to any of the themes listed above.

nystagmus Involuntary rhythmic movements of the eyes that consist of small-amplitude rapid tremors in one direction and a larger, slower, recurrent sweep in the opposite direction. Nystagmus may be horizontal, vertical, or rotary.

overvalued idea An unreasonable and sustained belief that is maintained with less than delusional intensity (i.e., the person is able to acknowledge the possibility that the belief may not be true). The belief is not one that is ordinarily accepted by other members of the person's culture or subculture.

panic attacks Discrete periods of sudden onset of intense apprehension, fearfulness, or terror, often associated with feelings of impending doom. During these attacks there are symptoms such as shortness of breath or smothering sensations; palpitations, pounding heart, or accelerated heart rate; chest pain or discomfort; choking; and fear of going crazy or losing control. Panic attacks may be **unexpected** (uncued), in which the onset of the attack is not associated with a situational trigger and instead occurs "out of the blue"; **situationally bound,** in which the panic attack almost invariably occurs immediately on exposure to, or in anticipation of, a situational trigger ("cue"); and **situationally predisposed**, in which the panic attack is more likely to occur on exposure to a situational trigger but is not invariably associated with it.

paranoid ideation Ideation, of less than delusional proportions, involving suspiciousness or the belief that one is being harassed, persecuted, or unfairly treated.

parasomnia Abnormal behavior or physiological events occurring during sleep or sleep-wake transitions.

personality Enduring patterns of perceiving, relating to, and thinking about the environment and oneself. *Personality traits* are prominent aspects of personality that are exhibited in a wide range of important social and personal contexts. Only when personality traits are inflexible and maladaptive and cause either significant functional impairment or subjective distress do they constitute a Personality Disorder.

phobia A persistent, irrational fear of a specific object, activity, or situation (the phobic stimulus) that results in a compelling desire to avoid it. This often leads either to avoidance of the phobic stimulus or to enduring it with dread.

pressured speech Speech that is increased in amount, accelerated, and difficult or impossible to interrupt. Usually it is also loud and emphatic. Frequently the person talks without any social stimulation and may continue to talk even though no one is listening.

prodrome An early or premonitory sign or symptom of a disorder.

psychomotor agitation *See* agitation.

psychomotor retardation Visible generalized slowing of movements and speech.

psychotic This term has historically received a number of different definitions, none of which has achieved universal acceptance. The narrowest definition of *psychotic* is restricted to delusions or prominent hallucinations, with the hallucinations occurring in the absence of insight into their pathological nature. A slightly less restrictive definition would also include prominent hallucinations that the individual realizes are hallucinatory experiences. Broader still is a definition that also includes other positive symptoms of Schizophrenia (i.e., disorganized speech, grossly disorganized or catatonic behavior). Unlike these definitions based on symptoms, the definition used in DSM-II and ICD-9 was probably far too inclusive and focused on the severity of functional impairment, so that a mental disorder was termed *psychotic* if it resulted in "impairment that grossly interferes with the capacity to meet ordinary demands of life." Finally, the term has been defined conceptually as a loss of ego boundaries or a gross impairment in reality testing. Based on their characteristic features, the different disorders in DSM-IV emphasize different aspects of the various definitions of *psychotic*.

residual phase The phase of an illness that occurs after remission of the florid symptoms or the full syndrome.

sex A person's biological status as male, female, or uncertain. Depending on the circumstances, this determination may be based on the appearance of the external genitalia or on karyotyping.

sign An objective manifestation of a pathological condition. Signs are observed by the examiner rather than reported by the affected individual.

stereotyped movements Repetitive, seemingly driven, and nonfunctional motor behavior (e.g., hand shaking or waving, body rocking, head banging, mouthing of objects, self-biting, picking at skin or body orifices, hitting one's own body).

stressor, psychosocial Any life event or life change that may be associated temporally (and perhaps causally) with the onset, occurrence, or exacerbation of a mental disorder.

stupor A state of unresponsiveness with immobility and mutism.

symptom A subjective manifestation of a pathological condition. Symptoms are reported by the affected individual rather than observed by the examiner.

syndrome A grouping of signs and symptoms, based on their frequent co-occurrence, that may suggest a common underlying pathogenesis, course, familial pattern, or treatment selection.

synesthesia A condition in which a sensory experience associated with one modality occurs when another modality is stimulated, for example, a sound produces the sensation of a particular color.

tic An involuntary, sudden, rapid, recurrent, nonrhythmic, stereotyped motor movement or vocalization.

transsexualism Severe gender dysphoria, coupled with a persistent desire for the physical characteristics and social roles that connote the opposite biological sex.

Appendix D

Annotated Listing of Changes in DSM-IV

This appendix outlines the major changes from DSM-III-R that have been included in the DSM-IV terms and categories. The disorders listed are in the order in which they appear in the DSM-IV Classification. The annotation includes lists of those diagnoses that have been introduced into DSM-IV and those DSM-III-R diagnoses that have been deleted or subsumed into other DSM-IV categories. Please refer to "Use of the Manual" for an explanation of the conventions, text sections, and organizational plan used in DSM-IV.

Multiaxial system. Pervasive Developmental Disorders, Learning Disorders, Motor Skills Disorder, and Communication Disorders (which were coded on Axis II in DSM-III-R) are all coded on Axis I in DSM-IV. For DSM-IV, only Personality Disorders and Mental Retardation remain coded on Axis II. Axis III continues to be used for coding general medical conditions. (Appendix G, which lists selected general medical conditions with their ICD-9-CM codes, has been introduced into DSM-IV.) In DSM-IV, Axis IV is used for reporting psychosocial and environmental problems; in contrast, DSM-III-R Axis IV provided a rating scale for severity of stressors. Axis V (the Global Assessment of Functioning Scale) is essentially the same as in DSM-III-R, except that the scale extends over 100 points to include the highest level of functioning. Optional scales (for social and occupational functioning apart from symptomatology, for relational functioning, and for defense mechanisms) are included in Appendix B, on p. 751.

Disorders Usually First Diagnosed in Infancy, Childhood, or Adolescence

Mental Retardation. The criteria have been modified to be more compatible with the American Association of Mental Retardation definition.

Learning Disorders. The name has been changed from the DSM-III-R Academic Skills Disorders to reflect common clinical usage. The exclusion criterion (Criterion C) has been modified to allow a diagnosis of Learning Disorder in the presence of a sensory deficit so long as the learning difficulties are in excess of those usually associated with the sensory deficit. In addition, the DSM-III-R exclusion criterion has been modified to allow the diagnosis of a Learning Disorder in the presence of a general medical (neurological) condition. In contrast to DSM-III-R, Learning Disorders are coded on Axis I in DSM-IV.

Communication Disorders.   This section brings together under one heading all of the speech and language disorders that in DSM-III-R were listed in two separate sections—the Specific Developmental Disorders and Speech Disorders Not Elsewhere Classified.

Expressive Language Disorder.   This diagnosis is no longer excluded in the presence of a speech-motor deficit, a sensory deficit, or environmental deprivation so long as the language difficulties are in excess of those usually associated with these problems. In contrast to DSM-III-R, Expressive Language Disorder is coded on Axis I in DSM-IV.

Mixed Receptive-Expressive Language Disorder.   This diagnosis replaces DSM-III-R Developmental Receptive Language Disorder in recognition of the fact that receptive language problems do not occur in isolation without accompanying expressive language problems. This diagnosis is no longer excluded in the presence of a speech-motor deficit, sensory deficit, or environmental deprivation so long as the language difficulties are in excess of those usually associated with these problems. In contrast to DSM-III-R, Mixed Receptive-Expressive Language Disorder is coded on Axis I in DSM-IV.

Phonological Disorder.   The name has been changed from DSM-III-R Developmental Articulation Disorder to conform to current terminology. This diagnosis is no longer excluded in the presence of a speech-motor deficit, sensory deficit, or environmental deprivation so long as the language difficulties are in excess of those usually associated with these problems. In contrast to DSM-III-R, Phonological Disorder is coded on Axis I in DSM-IV.

Stuttering.   The DSM-III-R criteria set consisted of a one-sentence definition. An expanded and more specific criteria set has been added.

Pervasive Developmental Disorders.   In contrast to DSM-III-R, Pervasive Developmental Disorders are coded on Axis I in DSM-IV.

Autistic Disorder.   The DSM-III-R defining features (impaired social interaction, communication, and stereotyped patterns of behavior) are retained in DSM-IV, but the individual items and the overall diagnostic algorithm have been modified to 1) improve clinical utility by reducing the number of items from 16 to 12 and by increasing the clarity of individual items; 2) increase compatibility with the ICD-10 Diagnostic Criteria for Research; and 3) narrow the definition of caseness so that it conforms more closely with clinical judgment, DSM-III, and ICD-10. In addition, an "age at onset" requirement (before age 3 years in DSM-IV), which had been dropped in DSM-III-R, has been reinstated to conform to clinical usage and to increase the homogeneity of this category.

Rett's Disorder, Childhood Disintegrative Disorder, and Asperger's Disorder. These three disorders have been included to improve differential diagnosis and to provide greater specificity in describing those individuals who would have been diagnosed with either Autistic Disorder or Pervasive Developmental Disorder Not Otherwise Specified in DSM-III-R.

Attention-Deficit/Hyperactivity Disorder.   This integrates into one overarching category what were two categories in DSM-III-R: Attention-Deficit Hyperactivity Disorder and Undifferentiated Attention-Deficit Disorder (without hyperactivity). Literature reviews, data reanalysis, and results from the field trials suggest that this disorder is best viewed as a unitary disorder with different predominating symptom patterns. DSM-IV provides one criteria set with three subtypes (Combined Type, Predominantly Inattentive Type, Predominantly Hyperactive-Impulsive Type) that allow the clinician to note the predominance of either attention-deficit symptoms or hyperactivity-impulsivity symptoms. Criterion A organizes the items into three groupings: inattention, hyperactivity, and impulsivity. Criterion C, which requires the presence of symptoms in two or more situations (e.g., at school, work, and home), has been added to reduce false-positive diagnoses.

Conduct Disorder.   The DSM-III-R item list was modified and expanded (by adding two items: "staying out at night" and "intimidating others"). This modification is based on the field-trial results and provides a definition that includes behaviors characteristic of females with Conduct Disorder. In addition, the items are organized into thematically related groups (aggression to people and animals, destruction of property, deceitfulness or theft, serious violations of rules) to facilitate their use. New subtypes based on age at onset have been provided in DSM-IV to reflect that earlier age at onset has a worse prognosis and is more likely to be associated with aggressive behavior and with adult Antisocial Personality Disorder.

Oppositional Defiant Disorder.   Based on field-trial results, one item was deleted from Criterion A ("uses obscene language"). In addition, an impairment criterion was added to help demarcate the boundary with normality.

Feeding and Eating Disorders of Infancy or Early Childhood.   The name of this category has been changed to reflect the placement of Anorexia Nervosa and Bulimia Nervosa in a separate Eating Disorders section.

Pica.   The DSM-III-R criterion excluding this disorder in the presence of Schizophrenia or a Pervasive Developmental Disorder has been changed to allow the diagnosis in the presence of another mental disorder if the behavior is sufficiently severe to warrant independent clinical attention.

Rumination Disorder.   The criterion requiring weight loss or failure to make expected weight gain was omitted because clinically significant impairment can be present in the absence of these features and to clarify the boundary with Feeding Disorder of Infancy or Early Childhood.

Feeding Disorder of Infancy or Early Childhood.   This new category was added to provide diagnostic coverage for infants and children who fail to eat adequately and who have attendant problems in gaining or maintaining weight.

Tic Disorders.   The upper limit of age at onset has been reduced from age 21 years to age 18 years for compatibility with the ICD-10 Diagnostic Criteria for Research. A criterion that specifies that the tics cause clinically significant impairment or distress has also been added.

Encopresis.   The duration requirement has been reduced from 6 months to 3 months to reflect clinical usage and to allow for earlier case finding. The disorder is now coded based on whether or not constipation with overflow incontinence is present.

Enuresis (Not Due to a General Medical Condition).   The specified frequency and duration threshold has been raised (from twice a month to twice a week for 3 consecutive months) in an effort to reduce false-positive diagnoses. In an effort to avoid false-negative diagnoses, Criterion B also notes that the diagnosis can be made below these thresholds if there is clinically significant impairment or distress.

Separation Anxiety Disorder.   Two DSM-III-R items (8 and 9) have been combined to reduce redundancy. The duration requirement has been increased to 4 weeks for compatibility with ICD-10 Diagnostic Criteria for Research.

Selective Mutism.   Several provisions have been added to reduce false-positive identification: a duration criterion of 1 month, the exclusion of children who are quiet only during the first month of school, a criterion requiring clinically significant impairment, and a criterion requiring that the lack of speech is not better accounted for by a Communication Disorder or by lack of knowledge of the spoken language required in a social situation. In addition, the name has been changed from DSM-III-R Elective Mutism, which was less descriptive and implied motivation.

Reactive Attachment Disorder of Infancy or Early Childhood.   Subtypes that designate inhibited type versus disinhibited type have been added to allow compatibility with ICD-10 (which divides this condition into two separate disorders).

Stereotypic Movement Disorder.   The name has been changed from the DSM-III-R Stereotypy/Habit Disorder for compatibility with ICD-10. Unlike DSM-III-R, DSM-IV specifies that diagnoses of both Mental Retardation and Stereotypic Movement Disorder are only made if the stereotypic or self-injurious behavior is severe enough to become a focus of treatment. In addition, With Self-Injurious Behavior is available as a specifier.

Delirium, Dementia, and Amnestic and Other Cognitive Disorders

In DSM-III-R, these disorders were included in the Organic Mental Disorders section. The term "organic mental disorders" has been eliminated from DSM-IV because it implies that the other disorders in the manual do not have an "organic" component.

Delirium. To assist in differential diagnosis, this section includes Delirium Due to a General Medical Condition and Substance-Induced Delirium, which were listed separately in DSM-III-R, and adds a new category—Delirium Due to Multiple Etiologies. Several of the DSM-III-R criteria (reduced level of consciousness, sleep disturbance, psychomotor changes) were dropped because they often have other causes or are difficult to evaluate, particularly in a general medical/surgical population. Moreover, disorganized thinking is no longer a required criterion because it cannot be assessed in individuals who are mute.

Dementia. As in DSM-III-R, this subsection includes Dementia of the Alzheimer's Type and Vascular Dementia (which was called Multi-Infarct Dementia in DSM-III-R), but it also includes a specific listing of a variety of dementias due to general medical and neurological conditions, Substance-Induced Persisting Dementia, and Dementia Due to Multiple Etiologies. This organization is provided to assist in differential diagnosis. The definition of dementia has been reorganized and simplified to clarify that dementia is characterized by multiple cognitive deficits that must include memory impairment. Personality change, which was a diagnostic feature in DSM-III-R, has been moved to the "Associated Features and Disorders" section of the DSM-IV text because of its relative lack of specificity for dementia.

Amnestic Disorders. This section includes Amnestic Disorder Due to a General Medical Condition and Substance-Induced Persisting Amnestic Disorder, which were listed separately in DSM-III-R. This organization is provided to assist in differential diagnosis. The definition of an amnestic disorder has been simplified and the description of its essential feature (development of memory impairment) has been sharpened.

Mental Disorders Due to a General Medical Condition Not Elsewhere Classified

Catatonic Disorder Due to a General Medical Condition. This category is included because it is a frequent explanation for catatonic symptoms and is important in their differential diagnosis.

Personality Change Due to a General Medical Condition. For this disorder, called Organic Personality Disorder in DSM-III-R, subtypes including Labile, Disinhibited, Aggressive, Apathetic, and Paranoid have been added.

Substance-Related Disorders

In DSM-III-R, these disorders were located in two different sections: Psychoactive Substance Use Disorders (i.e., Dependence and Abuse) and Psychoactive Substance–Induced Organic Mental Disorders. For convenience of use, Substance Use Disorders and Substance-Induced Disorders are now contained in a single "Substance-Related Disorders" section.

Substance Dependence. The nine items included in DSM-III-R have been reduced to seven; two items tapping withdrawal in DSM-III-R have been combined and DSM-III-R Criterion 4 (i.e., failure to fulfill major role obligations) has been moved to the abuse criteria set to sharpen the distinction between Dependence and Abuse. Subtyping for physiological dependence has been provided to allow the clinician to note the presence of tolerance or withdrawal. The duration criterion was dropped for two reasons: 1) it is redundant given that the individual items require a clinically significant duration to be counted as present; and 2) a clustering criterion has been added to DSM-IV that specifies that at least three items be present during the same 12-month period. The course specifiers have been expanded and made more specific to take into account differences between early and sustained remission, partial and full remission, and whether the remission occurred while the individual was on agonist therapy or in a controlled environment.

Substance Abuse.   In DSM-III-R, Substance Abuse was a residual category without a clear conceptual framework. In DSM-IV, Substance Abuse is conceptualized as a maladaptive pattern of substance use leading to adverse consequences that occurs in the absence of Substance Dependence. The item list has been expanded from two to four items by adding "failure to fulfill major role obligations" and "recurrent substance-related legal problems."

Substance Intoxication.   The general definition of intoxication has not been changed, but some of the substance-specific intoxication criteria sets have been refined. The criteria sets for Amphetamine Intoxication and Cocaine Intoxication are now equivalent.

Alcohol Idiosyncratic Intoxication.   This has been omitted as a separate category because of lack of supporting evidence that it is distinct from Alcohol Intoxication.

Substance Withdrawal.   The general definition of withdrawal has not been changed, but some of the substance-specific withdrawal criteria sets have been refined. The criteria sets for Alcohol Withdrawal and Sedative, Hypnotic, or Anxiolytic Withdrawal are now equivalent.

Table of Substance-Induced Disorders.   DSM-III-R contained a table indicating the association between particular classes of substances and particular substance-induced syndromal presentations. Based on evidence supporting the existence and clinical relevance of some additional combinations, this table has been expanded in DSM-IV. The new categories include 1) for Alcohol—Mood, Anxiety, and Sleep Disorders and Sexual Dysfunction; 2) for Amphetamine—Mood, Anxiety, and Sleep Disorders and Sexual Dysfunction; 3) for Caffeine—Anxiety and Sleep Disorders; 4) for Cannabis—Delirium and Anxiety Disorder; 5) for Cocaine—Mood, Anxiety, and Sleep Disorders and Sexual Dysfunction; 6) for Hallucinogens—Delirium and Anxiety Disorder; 7) for Inhalants—Delirium, Persisting Dementia, and Psychotic, Mood, and Anxiety Disorders; 8) for Opioids—Delirium and Psychotic, Mood, and Sleep Disorders, and Sexual Dysfunction; 9) for Phencyclidine—Anxiety Disorder; 10) for Sedatives, Hypnotics, or Anxiolytics—Persisting Dementia, Psychotic, Mood, Anxiety, and Sleep Disorders, and Sexual Dysfunction. Specifiers are also provided to indicate whether the symptoms had their onset during intoxication or withdrawal.

Schizophrenia and Other Psychotic Disorders

This section brings together the contents of three sections in DSM-III-R: Schizophrenia, Delusional Disorder, and Psychotic Disorder Not Elsewhere Classified.

Schizophrenia.   DSM-IV increases the required duration of the active-phase symptoms from DSM-III-R's 1 week to 1 month to reduce false-positive diagnoses and to increase compatibility with ICD-10 Diagnostic Criteria for Research. The presentation of characteristic symptoms in Criterion A has been simplified. Additional negative symptoms (alogia and avolition) have been included in Criterion A. The definition of prodromal and residual phases has been simplified by eliminating the list of specific symptoms. New course specifiers have been adapted from ICD-10.

Schizoaffective Disorder.   The criteria set has been changed to focus on an uninterrupted episode of illness rather than on the lifetime pattern of symptoms.

Brief Psychotic Disorder.   The DSM-III-R construct of Brief Reactive Psychosis has been broadened by eliminating the requirement for a severe stressor (although this can be indicated by the subtype With Marked Stressor). The resulting category now includes all psychotic disturbances lasting less than 1 month that are not attributable to a mood disorder and are not due to the direct physiological effects of substance use or a general medical condition. In addition, the minimum duration of the psychotic symptoms has been increased from a few hours to 1 day.

Psychotic Disorder Due to a General Medical Condition.   The DSM-III-R terms Organic Delusional Disorder and Organic Hallucinosis were applied to substance-induced conditions and to those due to a general medical condition. DSM-IV creates two disorders based on etiology (Psychotic Disorder Due to a General Medical Condition and Substance-Induced Psychotic Disorder [see below]) but combines delusional disorder and hallucinosis into a single Psychotic Disorder. The distinction between presentations that are predominantly delusional versus those that are predominantly characterized by hallucinations is preserved in the subtyping. Psychotic Disorder Due to a General Medical Condition is included in the "Schizophrenia and Other Psychotic Disorders" section to facilitate differential diagnosis.

Substance-Induced Psychotic Disorder.   The DSM-III-R terms Organic Delusional Disorder and Organic Hallucinosis were applied to substance-induced conditions and to those due to a general medical condition. DSM-IV creates two disorders based on etiology (Psychotic Disorder Due to a General Medical Condition [see above] and Substance-Induced Psychotic Disorder) but combines delusional disorder and hallucinosis into a single Psychotic Disorder. The distinction between presentations that are predominantly delusional versus those that are predominantly characterized by hallucinations is preserved in the subtyping. Substance-Induced Psychotic Disorder is included in the "Schizophrenia and Other Psychotic Disorders" section to facilitate differential diagnosis.

Mood Disorders

Major Depressive Episode.   DSM-IV adds a Criterion C to ensure the clinical significance of the symptomatic presentation. In addition, DSM-IV includes a Criterion E that clarifies the boundary with Bereavement—that is, a Major Depressive Episode may be diagnosed if the symptoms persist for longer than 2 months after the loss of a loved one.

Manic Episode.   The DSM-III duration of 1 week (which had been dropped in DSM-III-R) has been reinstated in DSM-IV. In contrast to DSM-III-R, Manic Episodes that are clearly precipitated by antidepressant treatment are diagnosed as Substance-Induced Manic Episodes and do not count toward a diagnosis of Bipolar I Disorder.

Mixed Episode.   In DSM-III-R, Mixed Episodes did not have a separate criteria set and instead were defined as one of the subtypes of Bipolar Disorder. In DSM-IV, a separate criteria set is provided that specifies that the symptom criteria for both a Manic Episode and a Major Depressive Episode are met nearly every day for 1 week.

Hypomanic Episode.   In DSM-III-R, Hypomanic Episodes did not have a separate criteria set and instead were defined with the same criteria (except for severity) as for a Manic Episode. In DSM-IV, a separate criteria set is provided that specifies a duration of at least 4 days of mood change (distinct from the usual nondepressed mood) and an unequivocal change in functioning that is observable by others. In contrast to mania, hypomania is defined as not severe enough to cause marked impairment or to require hospitalization.

Dysthymic Disorder.   The DSM-III-R subtyping of primary versus secondary was dropped because of difficulty in applying it and lack of supportive evidence. DSM-IV adds a criterion to ensure the clinical significance of the symptomatic presentation.

Bipolar Disorders.   The organization and terminology for Bipolar Disorders has been changed in DSM-IV. Bipolar Disorders have been divided into Bipolar I Disorders and Bipolar II Disorder. Bipolar I Disorders have been divided into Single Manic Episode and Most Recent Episode Hypomanic, Manic, Mixed, Depressed, and Unspecified.

Bipolar I Disorder, Single Manic Episode.   This disorder is new for DSM-IV and has been added to increase specificity and for compatibility with ICD-10 coding requirements. A duration of 2 months without manic symptoms has been established to define recurrence.

Bipolar I Disorder, Most Recent Episode Hypomanic.   This disorder is new for DSM-IV and was added to increase specificity and coverage.

Bipolar I Disorder, Most Recent Episode Mixed.   In DSM-III-R, the mixed type included presentations of manic and depressive symptoms that were intermixed or rapidly alternating every few days, with the requirement that the depressive symptoms last at least 1 full day. This disorder has been modified in DSM-IV to require at least 1 week of both manic and major depressive symptoms, and that both of these occur nearly every day.

Bipolar I Disorder, Most Recent Episode Unspecified.   This disorder is new for DSM-IV and allows the clinician to note the onset of a new mood episode before the full duration criteria are met.

Bipolar II Disorder.   This disorder has been introduced as a separate category in DSM-IV to cover what in DSM-III-R was an example in Bipolar Disorder Not Otherwise Specified. Bipolar II Disorder describes presentations in which there is at least one Major Depressive Episode and at least one Hypomanic Episode but, unlike Bipolar I Disorder, no history of Manic Episodes. Bipolar II Disorder has been added in response to the evidence from the literature review and data reanalysis that suggested its utility and to increase diagnostic coverage.

Mood Disorder Due to a General Medical Condition.   Text and criteria for this disorder, which was called Organic Mood Disorder in DSM-III-R, are included in the "Mood Disorders" section to facilitate differential diagnosis.

Substance-Induced Mood Disorder.   Text and criteria for this disorder, which was called Organic Mood Disorder in DSM-III-R, are included in the "Mood Disorders" section to facilitate differential diagnosis.

With Catatonic Features.   This is a new specifier introduced into DSM-IV to reflect evidence that many catatonic presentations are associated with mood disorders.

With Melancholic Features.   The DSM-IV criteria set for this specifier departs from that for DSM-III-R and is essentially the same as that for DSM-III, except that it requires either loss of pleasure *or* lack of reactivity to pleasurable stimuli (rather than both). This reflects the evidence from the literature review that the DSM-III definition may have been too narrow but in other respects was superior to the definition in DSM-III-R.

With Atypical Features.   This is a new specifier introduced into DSM-IV to reflect evidence that this presentation (e.g., mood reactivity, reverse vegetative symptoms, rejection sensitivity) may have implications for treatment selection.

With Postpartum Onset.   This is a new specifier introduced into DSM-IV to reflect evidence that this presentation may have implications for prognosis and treatment selection.

Longitudinal Course Specifiers.   Course specifiers describing the lifetime pattern of Major Depressive Disorder and Bipolar I and II Disorders have been introduced into DSM-IV to allow the clinician to specify the degree of interepisode recovery. Diagrams have also been provided to illustrate various course patterns.

With Seasonal Pattern.   Several changes have been made to this specifier so that the criteria conform more closely to clinical and research usage. These changes include restricting the application of the seasonal pattern to Major Depressive Episodes only, elimination of the 60-day window for appearance of symptoms in Criterion A, and the inclusion of a more specific requirement regarding the relationship between seasonal and nonseasonal episodes.

With Rapid Cycling.   This is a new specifier introduced into DSM-IV to reflect evidence that this presentation may have implications for prognosis and treatment selection.

Anxiety Disorders

Panic Attack.   The criteria set for Panic Attack has been provided separately at the beginning of the "Anxiety Disorders" section to clarify that Panic Attacks can occur as part of the presentation of a variety of Anxiety Disorders. The DSM-III-R items and the threshold for Panic Attack were supported by the data reanalysis and field-trial results and remain the same for DSM-IV, but the order of items has been changed to reflect their frequency.

Panic Disorder Without Agoraphobia.   In response to the literature review, data reanalyses, and field-trial results, the threshold for Panic Disorder Without Agoraphobia has been revised. The DSM-IV definition requires recurrent unexpected Panic Attacks accompanied by a month or more of persistent concern about having additional attacks or about the implications of the attacks, or a significant change in behavior. This is in contrast to DSM-III-R, which required either four attacks in 4 weeks or one attack followed by a month of persistent fear of having another attack.

Panic Disorder With Agoraphobia.   The threshold for Panic Attacks in Panic Disorder With Agoraphobia has been revised in the same way as the threshold for Panic Disorder Without Agoraphobia. In addition, the definition of Agoraphobia has been modified to emphasize that agoraphobic fears typically involve a characteristic cluster of situations. Specific criteria for mild, moderate, and severe that were provided in DSM-III-R have been deleted. (The general severity specifiers provided in "Use of the Manual" can be used instead [see p. 2].)

Agoraphobia Without History of Panic Disorder.   DSM-III-R provided no guidance concerning whether avoidance associated with a general medical condition warrants this diagnosis. DSM-IV Criterion D indicates that the diagnosis might include avoidance associated with a general medical condition if the fear is clearly in excess of that usually associated with this condition.

Specific Phobia.   For compatibility with ICD-10, the name of this category has been changed from Simple Phobia to Specific Phobia. The threshold of the fear in Criterion A has been raised by requiring that it be marked and excessive or unreasonable (as well as persistent). Based on literature review and data reanalysis, subtypes are provided that describe the focus of the phobias.

Social Phobia.   This disorder now subsumes DSM-III-R Avoidant Disorder of Childhood, and criteria have been modified for childhood presentations.

Obsessive-Compulsive Disorder.   The distinction between obsessions and compulsions has been clarified. Obsessions cause marked anxiety or distress, whereas compulsions (including mental acts) prevent or reduce anxiety or distress. In recognition that insight into whether the obsessions or compulsions are unreasonable occurs on a continuum, a specifier is provided to allow the clinician to note whether the condition is of the With Poor Insight type.

Posttraumatic Stress Disorder.   Based on literature review, data reanalyses, and field-trial results, the phrase that describes the stressor in DSM-III-R Criterion A, "outside the range of normal human experience," has been deleted because it was unreliable and inaccurate (the prevalence of such stressors is not low in general populations). DSM-IV Criterion A2 instead requires that the person's response to the stressor must involve intense fear, helplessness, or horror. Physiological reactivity on exposure to cues was moved from Criterion D (increased arousal) to Criterion B (reexperiencing the trauma). A criterion requiring that the symptoms cause clinically significant distress or impairment has been included. Acute and Chronic specifiers are also provided.

Acute Stress Disorder.   This category is new in DSM-IV and was added to describe acute reactions to extreme stress (i.e., occurring within 4 weeks of the stressor and lasting from 2 days to 4 weeks). It was added for compatibility with ICD-10 and to assist early case finding, because Acute Stress Disorder may predict the later development of Posttraumatic Stress Disorder.

Generalized Anxiety Disorder.   This disorder now subsumes DSM-III-R Overanxious Disorder of Childhood. Criterion A requires excessive anxiety and worry, in contrast to DSM-III-R, which included unrealistic worries. A requirement that the person must find it difficult to control the worry has been added. Based on data reanalysis, Criterion C now has a 6-item set that is simpler, more reliable, and more coherent than the 18-item set in DSM-III-R.

Anxiety Disorder Due to a General Medical Condition.   Text and criteria for this disorder, which was called Organic Anxiety Disorder in DSM-III-R, are included in the "Anxiety Disorders" section to facilitate differential diagnosis.

Substance-Induced Anxiety Disorder.   Text and criteria for this disorder, which was called Organic Anxiety Disorder in DSM-III-R, are included in the "Anxiety Disorders" section to facilitate differential diagnosis.

Somatoform Disorders

Somatization Disorder.   Based on the literature review, data reanalysis, and field-trial results, the DSM-III-R list of 35 items has been condensed, simplified, and divided into four symptom groupings (pain, gastrointestinal, sexual, and pseudoneurological).

Conversion Disorder.   Unlike the broader definition in DSM-III-R, the presenting problem must be a symptom or deficit that affects voluntary motor or sensory functioning. Other problems that reflect a change in functioning (e.g., pseudocyesis) are listed under Somatoform Disorder Not Otherwise Specified. A subtyping scheme (Motor, Sensory, Seizure, Mixed) has been provided for increased specificity and for compatibility with ICD-10.

Pain Disorder.   The name has been changed from DSM-III-R Somatoform Pain Disorder. The definition has been broadened to include two types of pain disorder: Pain Disorder Associated With Psychological Factors and Pain Disorder Associated With Both Psychological Factors and a General Medical Condition. In addition, Acute and Chronic specifiers are provided.

Hypochondriasis.   A specifier is provided to allow the clinician to note whether the condition is of the With Poor Insight type.

Body Dysmorphic Disorder.   The DSM-III-R exclusion that the belief not be of delusional intensity was dropped so that this diagnosis can now be made concurrently with a diagnosis of Delusional Disorder.

Factitious Disorders

DSM-IV provides one set of criteria for Factitious Disorder instead of the previous two, with separate types based on the predominance of presenting signs and symptoms (Psychological, Physical, Combined).

Dissociative Disorders

Dissociative Amnesia.   The name has been changed from DSM-III-R Psychogenic Amnesia to be more descriptive and to be more compatible with ICD-10.

Dissociative Fugue.   The name has been changed from DSM-III-R Psychogenic Fugue to be more descriptive and to be more compatible with ICD-10. The requirement for assumption of a new identity has been dropped because confusion about personal identity has been found to be the predominant symptom.

Dissociative Identity Disorder.   The name has been changed from DSM-III-R Multiple Personality Disorder to be more descriptive. The DSM-III requirement that there be an inability to recall important personal information has been reinstated.

Sexual and Gender Identity Disorders

Sexual Dysfunctions.   Each of the disorders listed in this section now includes a clinical significance criterion (i.e., that the dysfunction causes marked distress or interpersonal difficulty).

Female Sexual Arousal Disorder.   DSM-IV returns to the DSM-III definition by dropping the DSM-III-R Item A2 that stated that the diagnosis could be given if there were subjective complaints without any difficulty with physiological arousal.

Male Erectile Disorder.   DSM-IV returns to the DSM-III definition by dropping DSM-III-R Item A2, which allowed the diagnosis to be given even if there were only subjective complaints without any difficulty with physiological arousal.

Female Orgasmic Disorder. The name has been changed from DSM-III-R Inhibited Female Orgasm. Criterion A has been simplified and revised to be more in accord with clinical usage.

Male Orgasmic Disorder. The name has been changed from DSM-III-R Inhibited Male Orgasm.

Sexual Dysfunction Due to a General Medical Condition. This disorder was included in the "Genitourinary System" section of ICD-9-CM, but was not included in the DSM-III-R Classification. It is included in DSM-IV to facilitate differential diagnosis.

Substance-Induced Sexual Dysfunction. This disorder was not included in DSM-III-R and is included in DSM-IV to increase coverage and to facilitate differential diagnosis.

Transvestic Fetishism. A specifier has been added for those individuals with Transvestic Fetishism who also have persistent discomfort with gender role that does not meet criteria for Gender Identity Disorder.

Gender Identity Disorder. This DSM-IV diagnosis subsumes three DSM-III-R diagnoses: Gender Identity Disorder of Childhood; Gender Identity Disorder of Adolescence or Adulthood, Nontranssexual Type (GIDAANT); and Transsexualism. It is placed in the "Sexual and Gender Identity Disorders" section rather than in the "Disorders Usually First Diagnosed in Infancy, Childhood, or Adolescence," section as in DSM-III-R. The criteria set accommodates both sexes and all ages.

Eating Disorders

Anorexia Nervosa. This disorder has been moved from the "Disorders Usually First Diagnosed in Infancy, Childhood, or Adolescence" section to the "Eating Disorders" section of the Classification. In DSM-IV, a presentation that includes binge eating and purging that occurs exclusively during Anorexia Nervosa is no longer given a separate diagnosis of Bulimia Nervosa, but rather is subsumed as a subtype under Anorexia Nervosa. The subtyping for Anorexia Nervosa now indicates the presence of binge-eating/purging versus restricting behavior.

Bulimia Nervosa. This disorder has been moved from the "Disorders Usually First Diagnosed in Infancy, Childhood, or Adolescence" section to the "Eating Disorders" section of the Classification. An exclusion criterion has been added so that the diagnosis is not given if the behavior occurs exclusively during episodes of Anorexia Nervosa. Subtypes are provided to distinguish between purging and nonpurging types.

Sleep Disorders

The organization of this section has been changed from that in DSM-III-R. The disorders are grouped into four sections based on presumed etiology (primary, related to another mental disorder, due to a general medical condition, and substance-induced), rather than on presenting symptoms. The section is compatible with the International Classification of Sleep Disorders.

Primary Insomnia. The frequency criterion of at least three times a week was dropped for DSM-IV, although the 1-month duration is retained. A clinical significance criterion has been added.

Primary Hypersomnia. Hypersomnia is no longer diagnosed if the presentation is better accounted for by insomnia. The DSM-III-R inclusion of sleep drunkenness (i.e., the prolonged transition to the fully awake state) has been deleted as a sufficient criterion for hypersomnia. A Recurrent subtype has been added for noting the presence of Kleine-Levin syndrome.

Narcolepsy. This disorder was included in the "Nervous System" section of ICD-9-CM, but was not included in DSM-III-R. It is included in the "Sleep Disorders" section of DSM-IV to assist in differential diagnosis.

Breathing-Related Sleep Disorder. This disorder was included outside the "Mental Disorders" chapter of ICD-9-CM, but was not included in DSM-III-R. It is included in the "Sleep Disorders" section of DSM-IV to assist in differential diagnosis.

Circadian Rhythm Sleep Disorder. The name has been changed from DSM-III-R Sleep-Wake Schedule Disorder. Subtyping (Delayed Sleep Phase, Jet Lag, Shift Work) has been revised to reflect clinical usage.

Nightmare Disorder. The name has been changed from DSM-III-R Dream Anxiety Disorder.

Insomnia Related to Another Mental Disorder. In DSM-IV, this diagnosis is used in addition to the related Axis I or Axis II diagnosis only when the insomnia is sufficiently severe to warrant independent clinical attention.

Hypersomnia Related to Another Mental Disorder. In DSM-IV, this diagnosis is used in addition to the related Axis I or Axis II diagnosis only when the hypersomnia is sufficiently severe to warrant independent clinical attention.

Sleep Disorder Due to a General Medical Condition. The DSM-III-R terms "Insomnia Related to a Known Organic Factor" and "Hypersomnia Related to a Known Organic Factor" were applied to both Substance-Induced Sleep Disorders and those due to a general medical condition. Two disorders based on etiology (Sleep Disorder Due to a General Medical Condition and Substance-Induced Sleep Disorder) have been created for DSM-IV. A provision to indicate insomnia, hypersomnia, parasomnia, or mixed type has been included. In contrast to DSM-III-R, in DSM-IV this diagnosis is used in addition to the general medical condition diagnosis only when the sleep disturbance is sufficiently severe to warrant independent clinical attention.

Substance-Induced Sleep Disorder. The DSM-III-R terms "Insomnia Related to a Known Organic Factor" and "Hypersomnia Related to a Known Organic Factor" were applied to both Substance-Induced Sleep Disorders and to those due to a general medical condition. Two disorders were created for DSM-IV based on etiology (Sleep Disorder Due to a General Medical Condition and Substance-Induced Sleep Disorder). A provision to indicate insomnia, hypersomnia, parasomnia, or mixed type has been included. In contrast to DSM-III-R, in DSM-IV this diagnosis is used instead of a substance use diagnosis only when the sleep disturbance is sufficiently severe to warrant independent clinical attention.

Impulse-Control Disorders

Intermittent Explosive Disorder.   The DSM-III-R criterion excluding this diagnosis in the presence of generalized impulsiveness or aggressiveness between episodes has been deleted.

Pathological Gambling.   The criteria set has been revised to increase specificity.

Adjustment Disorders

DSM-III-R had a limit of 6 months of symptoms. This criterion has been modified in DSM-IV to allow for symptoms lasting up to an additional 6 months after the termination of a chronic stressor (or its consequences). Acute and Chronic specifications have been provided to indicate presentations lasting less than 6 months and 6 months or longer, respectively. In addition, several subtypes have been deleted (physical complaints, withdrawal, work or academic inhibition).

Personality Disorders

Based on literature reviews, data reanalysis, and desire for compatibility with ICD-10 Diagnostic Criteria for Research, items have been modified to increase clarity and specificity and to reduce possible gender bias.

Antisocial Personality Disorder.   Based on the literature review, data reanalyses, and field-trial results, the criteria set has been condensed, simplified, and slightly altered: two items (irresponsible parenting and failure to sustain a monogamous relationship) have been deleted; two items tapping consistent irresponsibility (failure to sustain consistent work behavior or honor financial obligations) have been collapsed into one item; and Criterion C (specifying the relationship to Conduct Disorder) has been simplified.

Borderline Personality Disorder.   An additional item for transient, stress-related paranoid ideation or severe dissociative symptoms has been added in DSM-IV.

Passive-Aggressive Personality Disorder.   This disorder has been deleted from the Classification. A revised version has been moved to Appendix B, "Criteria Sets and Axes Provided for Further Study."

Other Conditions That May
Be a Focus of Clinical Attention

The name of this section has been changed from DSM-III-R Conditions Not Attributable to a Mental Disorder, and a number of additional conditions have been added.

Psychological Factors Affecting Medical Condition.   Because this category does not constitute a mental disorder, it has been moved into the "Other Conditions That May Be a Focus of Clinical Attention" section. The concept has been broadened to include factors that interfere with treatment and factors that constitute health risks to the individual. Subtypes are provided that allow specification of the particular type of psychological factor involved.

Medication-Induced Movement Disorders.   These disorders have been included because of their importance in treatment and differential diagnosis.

Relational Problems.   These problems are now named and grouped together. Two new relational problems have been added: Relational Problem Related to a Mental Disorder or General Medical Condition and Sibling Relational Problem.

Problems Related to Abuse or Neglect.   This category has been introduced into this section to cover physical abuse, sexual abuse, and neglect of a child and physical abuse and sexual abuse of an adult. It is included because of the clinical and public health significance of these conditions.

Age-Related Cognitive Decline.   This is a new problem added to DSM-IV to improve coverage.

Bereavement.   The name has been changed from DSM-III-R Uncomplicated Bereavement because bereavement may cause significant impairment and complications. Guidelines relating to the duration of symptoms and particular types of symptoms have been provided to sharpen the boundary between Bereavement and Major Depressive Episode.

Identity Problem.   In DSM-IV, this is listed in the "Other Conditions That May Be a Focus of Clinical Attention" section rather than being placed in the "Disorders Usually First Diagnosed in Infancy, Childhood, or Adolescence" section (as in DSM-III-R).

Religious or Spiritual Problem.   This is a new problem added to DSM-IV to improve coverage.

Acculturation Problem.   This is a new problem added to DSM-IV to improve coverage.

New Disorders Introduced Into DSM-IV (Excluding Other Conditions That May Be a Focus of Clinical Attention)

Rett's Disorder
Childhood Disintegrative Disorder
Asperger's Disorder
Feeding Disorder of Infancy or Early Childhood
Delirium Due to Multiple Etiologies
Dementia Due to Multiple Etiologies
Catatonic Disorder Due to a General Medical Condition
Bipolar II Disorder
Acute Stress Disorder
Sexual Dysfunction Due to a General Medical Condition
Substance-Induced Sexual Dysfunction
Narcolepsy
Breathing-Related Sleep Disorder

DSM-III-R Disorders Deleted From DSM-IV or Subsumed Into Other DSM-IV Categories

Cluttering
Overanxious Disorder of Childhood
Avoidant Disorder of Childhood
Undifferentiated Attention-Deficit Disorder
Identity Disorder
Transsexualism
Idiosyncratic Alcohol Intoxication
Passive-Aggressive Personality Disorder

Appendixes

Appendix A—Decision Trees for Differential Diagnosis.   The DSM-III-R decision tree for Organic Mental Disorders has been replaced by two separate decision trees: one for Mental Disorders Due to a General Medical Condition and one for Substance-Induced Disorders. Each of the other decision trees has been modified, and there is an increased emphasis throughout DSM-IV on the differential diagnosis with Mental Disorders Due to a General Medical Condition and Substance-Induced Disorders.

Appendix B—Criteria Sets and Axes Provided for Further Study.   This appendix has been greatly expanded to include a number of new proposals:

Criteria Sets and Axes Provided for Further Study

Postconcussional disorder
Mild neurocognitive disorder
Caffeine withdrawal
Alternative dimensional descriptors for Schizophrenia

Postpsychotic depressive disorder of Schizophrenia
Simple deteriorative disorder
Premenstrual dysphoric disorder
Alternative Criterion B for Dysthymic Disorder
Minor depressive disorder
Recurrent brief depressive disorder
Mixed anxiety-depressive disorder
Factitious disorder by proxy
Dissociative trance disorder
Binge-eating disorder
Depressive personality disorder
Passive-aggressive personality disorder (negativistic personality disorder)
Medication-Induced Movement Disorders
    Neuroleptic-Induced Parkinsonism
    Neuroleptic Malignant Syndrome
    Neuroleptic-Induced Acute Dystonia
    Neuroleptic-Induced Acute Akathisia
    Neuroleptic-Induced Tardive Dyskinesia
    Medication-Induced Postural Tremor
    Medication-Induced Movement Disorder Not Otherwise Specified
Defensive Functioning Scale
Global Assessment of Relational Functioning (GARF) Scale
Social and Occupational Functioning Assessment Scale (SOFAS)

Appendix C—Glossary of Technical Terms.   Existing definitions have been refined, and a number of new terms have been added.

Appendix D—Annotated Listing of Changes in DSM-IV.   This appendix has been presented in a new format to clarify the ways in which DSM-IV differs from DSM-III-R.

Appendix E—Alphabetical Listing of DSM-IV Diagnoses and Codes.   This listing of categories has been revised to include the DSM-IV disorders and conditions.

Appendix F—Numerical Listing of DSM-IV Diagnoses and Codes.   This listing of categories has been revised to include the DSM-IV disorders and conditions.

Appendix G—ICD-9-CM Codes for Selected General Medical Conditions and Medication-Induced Disorders.   This appendix is new for DSM-IV. It includes a selective index of conditions classified outside the "Mental Disorders" chapter of ICD-9-CM that are most relevant to diagnosis and care in mental health settings. In addition, the appendix contains a list of ICD-9-CM codes for selected medications that may cause Substance-Induced Disorders.

Appendix H—DSM-IV Classification With ICD-10 Codes.   At some point within the next several years, the U.S. Department of Health and Human Services will require the use of codes from the *International Statistical Classification of Diseases and Related Health Problems,* Tenth Revision (ICD-10), for reporting purposes in the United States. To facilitate this transition, this appendix lists the DSM-IV Classification with codes from the ICD-10 system.

Appendix I—Outline for Cultural Formulation and Glossary of Culture-Bound Syndromes.   This appendix is provided to assist the clinician in using DSM-IV in a multicultural environment. It is divided into two sections. The first section contains an outline for cultural formulation designed to assist the clinician in systematically evaluating and reporting the impact of the individual's cultural context. The second section provides a list of "culture-bound syndromes" that denote recurrent, locality-specific patterns of aberrant behavior and experience that may not be linked specifically to a particular DSM-IV diagnostic category.

Appendix J—DSM-IV Contributors.   This appendix contains a list of individuals who participated in the preparation of DSM-IV.

Appendix E

Alphabetical Listing of DSM-IV Diagnoses and Codes

NOS = Not Otherwise Specified.

V62.3	Academic Problem
V62.4	Acculturation Problem
308.3	Acute Stress Disorder
	Adjustment Disorders
309.9	Unspecified
309.24	With Anxiety
309.0	With Depressed Mood
309.3	With Disturbance of Conduct
309.28	With Mixed Anxiety and Depressed Mood
309.4	With Mixed Disturbance of Emotions and Conduct
V71.01	Adult Antisocial Behavior
995.2	Adverse Effects of Medication NOS
780.9	Age-Related Cognitive Decline
300.22	Agoraphobia Without History of Panic Disorder
	Alcohol
305.00	Abuse
303.90	Dependence
291.8	-Induced Anxiety Disorder
291.8	-Induced Mood Disorder
291.1	-Induced Persisting Amnestic Disorder
291.2	-Induced Persisting Dementia
	-Induced Psychotic Disorder
291.5	With Delusions
291.3	With Hallucinations
291.8	-Induced Sexual Dysfunction
291.8	-Induced Sleep Disorder

Alcohol *(continued)*

303.00	Intoxication
291.0	Intoxication Delirium
291.9	-Related Disorder NOS
291.8	Withdrawal
291.0	Withdrawal Delirium
294.0	Amnestic Disorder Due to . . . *[Indicate the General Medical Condition]*
294.8	Amnestic Disorder NOS

Amphetamine (or Amphetamine-Like)

305.70	Abuse
304.40	Dependence
292.89	-Induced Anxiety Disorder
292.84	-Induced Mood Disorder
	-Induced Psychotic Disorder
292.11	With Delusions
292.12	With Hallucinations
292.89	-Induced Sexual Dysfunction
292.89	-Induced Sleep Disorder
292.89	Intoxication
292.81	Intoxication Delirium
292.9	-Related Disorder NOS
292.0	Withdrawal
307.1	Anorexia Nervosa
301.7	Antisocial Personality Disorder
293.89	Anxiety Disorder Due to . . . *[Indicate the General Medical Condition]*
300.00	Anxiety Disorder NOS
299.80	Asperger's Disorder

Attention-Deficit/Hyperactivity Disorder

314.01	Combined Type
314.01	Predominantly Hyperactive-Impulsive Type
314.00	Predominantly Inattentive Type
314.9	Attention-Deficit/Hyperactivity Disorder NOS
299.00	Autistic Disorder
301.82	Avoidant Personality Disorder
V62.82	Bereavement
296.80	Bipolar Disorder NOS

Bipolar I Disorder, Most Recent Episode Depressed

296.56	In Full Remission
296.55	In Partial Remission
296.51	Mild
296.52	Moderate
296.53	Severe Without Psychotic Features
296.54	Severe With Psychotic Features
296.50	Unspecified
296.40	Bipolar I Disorder, Most Recent Episode Hypomanic

Bipolar I Disorder, Most Recent Episode Manic

296.46	In Full Remission
296.45	In Partial Remission
296.41	Mild

Bipolar I Disorder, Most Recent Episode Manic *(continued)*
296.42	Moderate
296.43	Severe Without Psychotic Features
296.44	Severe With Psychotic Features
296.40	Unspecified

Bipolar I Disorder, Most Recent Episode Mixed
296.66	In Full Remission
296.65	In Partial Remission
296.61	Mild
296.62	Moderate
296.63	Severe Without Psychotic Features
296.64	Severe With Psychotic Features
296.60	Unspecified
296.7	Bipolar I Disorder, Most Recent Episode Unspecified

Bipolar I Disorder, Single Manic Episode
296.06	In Full Remission
296.05	In Partial Remission
296.01	Mild
296.02	Moderate
296.03	Severe Without Psychotic Features
296.04	Severe With Psychotic Features
296.00	Unspecified
296.89	Bipolar II Disorder
300.7	Body Dysmorphic Disorder
V62.89	Borderline Intellectual Functioning
301.83	Borderline Personality Disorder
780.59	Breathing-Related Sleep Disorder
298.8	Brief Psychotic Disorder
307.51	Bulimia Nervosa

Caffeine
292.89	-Induced Anxiety Disorder
292.89	-Induced Sleep Disorder
305.90	Intoxication
292.9	-Related Disorder NOS

Cannabis
305.20	Abuse
304.30	Dependence
292.89	-Induced Anxiety Disorder
	-Induced Psychotic Disorder
292.11	With Delusions
292.12	With Hallucinations
292.89	Intoxication
292.81	Intoxication Delirium
292.9	-Related Disorder NOS
293.89	Catatonic Disorder Due to . . . *[Indicate the General Medical Condition]*
299.10	Childhood Disintegrative Disorder
V71.02	Child or Adolescent Antisocial Behavior
307.22	Chronic Motor or Vocal Tic Disorder
307.45	Circadian Rhythm Sleep Disorder

	Cocaine
305.60	Abuse
304.20	Dependence
292.89	-Induced Anxiety Disorder
292.84	-Induced Mood Disorder
	-Induced Psychotic Disorder
292.11	With Delusions
292.12	With Hallucinations
292.89	-Induced Sexual Dysfunction
292.89	-Induced Sleep Disorder
292.89	Intoxication
292.81	Intoxication Delirium
292.9	-Related Disorder NOS
292.0	Withdrawal
294.9	Cognitive Disorder NOS
307.9	Communication Disorder NOS
312.8	Conduct Disorder
300.11	Conversion Disorder
301.13	Cyclothymic Disorder
293.0	Delirium Due to . . . *[Indicate the General Medical Condition]*
780.09	Delirium NOS
297.1	Delusional Disorder
290.10	Dementia Due to Creutzfeldt-Jakob Disease
294.1	Dementia Due to Head Trauma
294.9	Dementia Due to HIV Disease
294.1	Dementia Due to Huntington's Disease
294.1	Dementia Due to Parkinson's Disease
290.10	Dementia Due to Pick's Disease
294.1	Dementia Due to . . . *[Indicate Other General Medical Condition]*
294.8	Dementia NOS
	Dementia of the Alzheimer's Type, With Early Onset
290.10	Uncomplicated
290.11	With Delirium
290.12	With Delusions
290.13	With Depressed Mood
	Dementia of the Alzheimer's Type, With Late Onset
290.0	Uncomplicated
290.3	With Delirium
290.20	With Delusions
290.21	With Depressed Mood
301.6	Dependent Personality Disorder
300.6	Depersonalization Disorder
311	Depressive Disorder NOS
315.4	Developmental Coordination Disorder
799.9	Diagnosis Deferred on Axis II
799.9	Diagnosis or Condition Deferred on Axis I
313.9	Disorder of Infancy, Childhood, or Adolescence NOS
315.2	Disorder of Written Expression
312.9	Disruptive Behavior Disorder NOS

	Inhalant
305.90	Abuse
304.60	Dependence
292.89	-Induced Anxiety Disorder
292.84	-Induced Mood Disorder
292.82	-Induced Persisting Dementia
	-Induced Psychotic Disorder
292.11	With Delusions
292.12	With Hallucinations
292.89	Intoxication
292.81	Intoxication Delirium
292.9	-Related Disorder NOS
307.42	Insomnia Related to . . . [Indicate the Axis I or Axis II Disorder]
312.34	Intermittent Explosive Disorder
312.32	Kleptomania
315.9	Learning Disorder NOS
	Major Depressive Disorder, Recurrent
296.36	In Full Remission
296.35	In Partial Remission
296.31	Mild
296.32	Moderate
296.33	Severe Without Psychotic Features
296.34	Severe With Psychotic Features
296.30	Unspecified
	Major Depressive Disorder, Single Episode
296.26	In Full Remission
296.25	In Partial Remission
296 21	Mild
296.22	Moderate
296.23	Severe Without Psychotic Features
296.24	Severe With Psychotic Features
296.20	Unspecified
608.89	Male Dyspareunia Due to . . . [Indicate the General Medical Condition]
302.72	Male Erectile Disorder
607.84	Male Erectile Disorder Due to . . . [Indicate the General Medical Condition]
608.89	Male Hypoactive Sexual Desire Disorder Due to . . . [Indicate the General Medical Condition]
302.74	Male Orgasmic Disorder
V65.2	Malingering
315.1	Mathematics Disorder
	Medication-Induced
333.90	Movement Disorder NOS
333.1	Postural Tremor
293.9	Mental Disorder NOS Due to . . . [Indicate the General Medical Condition]
319	Mental Retardation, Severity Unspecified
317	Mild Mental Retardation
315.31	Mixed Receptive-Expressive Language Disorder
318.0	Moderate Mental Retardation

293.83	Mood Disorder Due to . . . *[Indicate the General Medical Condition]*
296.90	Mood Disorder NOS
301.81	Narcissistic Personality Disorder
347	Narcolepsy
V61.21	Neglect of Child
995.5	Neglect of Child *(if focus of attention is on victim)*
	Neuroleptic-Induced
333.99	Acute Akathisia
333.7	Acute Dystonia
332.1	Parkinsonism
333.82	Tardive Dyskinesia
333.92	Neuroleptic Malignant Syndrome
	Nicotine
305.10	Dependence
292.9	-Related Disorder NOS
292.0	Withdrawal
307.47	Nightmare Disorder
V71.09	No Diagnosis on Axis II
V71.09	No Diagnosis or Condition on Axis I
V15.81	Noncompliance With Treatment
300.3	Obsessive-Compulsive Disorder
301.4	Obsessive-Compulsive Personality Disorder
V62.2	Occupational Problem
	Opioid
305.50	Abuse
304.00	Dependence
292.84	-Induced Mood Disorder
	-Induced Psychotic Disorder
292.11	With Delusions
292.12	With Hallucinations
292.89	-Induced Sexual Dysfunction
292.89	-Induced Sleep Disorder
292.89	Intoxication
292.81	Intoxication Delirium
292.9	-Related Disorder NOS
292.0	Withdrawal
313.81	Oppositional Defiant Disorder
625.8	Other Female Sexual Dysfunction Due to . . . *[Indicate the General Medical Condition]*
608.89	Other Male Sexual Dysfunction Due to . . . *[Indicate the General Medical Condition]*
	Other (or Unknown) Substance
305.90	Abuse
304.90	Dependence
292.89	–Induced Anxiety Disorder
292.81	–Induced Delirium
292.84	–Induced Mood Disorder
292.83	–Induced Persisting Amnestic Disorder
292.82	–Induced Persisting Dementia

Other (or Unknown) Substance *(continued)*
  –Induced Psychotic Disorder
292.11   With Delusions
292.12   With Hallucinations
292.89   –Induced Sexual Dysfunction
292.89   –Induced Sleep Disorder
292.89   Intoxication
292.9   –Related Disorder NOS
292.0   Withdrawal
Pain Disorder
307.89   Associated With Both Psychological Factors and a General
              Medical Condition
307.80   Associated With Psychological Factors
Panic Disorder
300.21   With Agoraphobia
300.01   Without Agoraphobia
301.0   Paranoid Personality Disorder
302.9   Paraphilia NOS
307.47 Parasomnia NOS
V61.20 Parent-Child Relational Problem
V61.1   Partner Relational Problem
312.31 Pathological Gambling
302.2   Pedophilia
310.1   Personality Change Due to . . . *[Indicate the General Medical Condition]*
301.9   Personality Disorder NOS
299.80 Pervasive Developmental Disorder NOS
V62.89 Phase of Life Problem
Phencyclidine (or Phencyclidine-Like)
305.90   Abuse
304.90   Dependence
292.89   –Induced Anxiety Disorder
292.84   –Induced Mood Disorder
             –Induced Psychotic Disorder
292.11   With Delusions
292.12   With Hallucinations
292.89   Intoxication
292.81   Intoxication Delirium
292.9   –Related Disorder NOS
315.39 Phonological Disorder
V61.1   Physical Abuse of Adult
995.81 Physical Abuse of Adult *(if focus of attention is on victim)*
V61.21 Physical Abuse of Child
995.5   Physical Abuse of Child *(if focus of attention is on victim)*
307.52 Pica
304.80 Polysubstance Dependence
309.81 Posttraumatic Stress Disorder
302.75 Premature Ejaculation
307.44 Primary Hypersomnia
307.42 Primary Insomnia

318.2	Profound Mental Retardation
316	Psychological Factors Affecting Medical Condition
	Psychotic Disorder Due to . . . *[Indicate the General Medical Condition]*
293.81	With Delusions
293.82	With Hallucinations
298.9	Psychotic Disorder NOS
312.33	Pyromania
313.89	Reactive Attachment Disorder of Infancy or Early Childhood
315.00	Reading Disorder
V62.81	Relational Problem NOS
V61.9	Relational Problem Related to a Mental Disorder or General Medical Condition
V62.89	Religious or Spiritual Problem
299.80	Rett's Disorder
307.53	Rumination Disorder
295.70	Schizoaffective Disorder
301.20	Schizoid Personality Disorder
	Schizophrenia
295.20	Catatonic Type
295.10	Disorganized Type
295.30	Paranoid Type
295.60	Residual Type
295.90	Undifferentiated Type
295.40	Schizophreniform Disorder
301.22	Schizotypal Personality Disorder
	Sedative, Hypnotic, or Anxiolytic
305.40	Abuse
304.10	Dependence
292.89	-Induced Anxiety Disorder
292.84	-Induced Mood Disorder
292.83	-Induced Persisting Amnestic Disorder
292.82	-Induced Persisting Dementia
	-Induced Psychotic Disorder
292.11	With Delusions
292.12	With Hallucinations
292.89	-Induced Sexual Dysfunction
292.89	-Induced Sleep Disorder
292.89	Intoxication
292.81	Intoxication Delirium
292.9	-Related Disorder NOS
292.0	Withdrawal
292.81	Withdrawal Delirium
313.23	Selective Mutism
309.21	Separation Anxiety Disorder
318.1	Severe Mental Retardation
V61.1	Sexual Abuse of Adult
995.81	Sexual Abuse of Adult *(if focus of attention is on victim)*
V61.21	Sexual Abuse of Child
995.5	Sexual Abuse of Child *(if focus of attention is on victim)*

302.79	Sexual Aversion Disorder
302.9	Sexual Disorder NOS
302.70	Sexual Dysfunction NOS
302.83	Sexual Masochism
302.84	Sexual Sadism
297.3	Shared Psychotic Disorder
V61.8	Sibling Relational Problem
	Sleep Disorder Due to . . . *[Indicate the General Medical Condition]*
780.54	Hypersomnia Type
780.52	Insomnia Type
780.59	Mixed Type
780.59	Parasomnia Type
307.46	Sleep Terror Disorder
307.46	Sleepwalking Disorder
300.23	Social Phobia
300.81	Somatization Disorder
300.81	Somatoform Disorder NOS
300.29	Specific Phobia
307.3	Stereotypic Movement Disorder
307.0	Stuttering
307.20	Tic Disorder NOS
307.23	Tourette's Disorder
307.21	Transient Tic Disorder
302.3	Transvestic Fetishism
312.39	Trichotillomania
300.81	Undifferentiated Somatoform Disorder
300.9	Unspecified Mental Disorder (nonpsychotic)
306.51	Vaginismus (Not Due to a General Medical Condition)
	Vascular Dementia
290.40	Uncomplicated
290.41	With Delirium
290.42	With Delusions
290.43	With Depressed Mood
302.82	Voyeurism

Appendix F

Numerical Listing of DSM-IV Diagnoses and Codes

To maintain compatibility with ICD-9-CM, some DSM-IV diagnoses share the same code numbers. These are indicated in this list by brackets.

NOS = Not Otherwise Specified.

290.0	Dementia of the Alzheimer's Type, With Late Onset, Uncomplicated
290.10	Dementia Due to Creutzfeldt-Jakob Disease
290.10	Dementia Due to Pick's Disease
290.10	Dementia of the Alzheimer's Type, With Early Onset, Uncomplicated
290.11	Dementia of the Alzheimer's Type, With Early Onset, With Delirium
290.12	Dementia of the Alzheimer's Type, With Early Onset, With Delusions
290.13	Dementia of the Alzheimer's Type, With Early Onset, With Depressed Mood
290.20	Dementia of the Alzheimer's Type, With Late Onset, With Delusions
290.21	Dementia of the Alzheimer's Type, With Late Onset, With Depressed Mood
290.3	Dementia of the Alzheimer's Type, With Late Onset, With Delirium
290.40	Vascular Dementia, Uncomplicated
290.41	Vascular Dementia, With Delirium
290.42	Vascular Dementia, With Delusions
290.43	Vascular Dementia, With Depressed Mood
291.0	Alcohol Intoxication Delirium
291.0	Alcohol Withdrawal Delirium
291.1	Alcohol-Induced Persisting Amnestic Disorder
291.2	Alcohol-Induced Persisting Dementia
291.3	Alcohol-Induced Psychotic Disorder, With Hallucinations
291.5	Alcohol-Induced Psychotic Disorder, With Delusions
291.8	Alcohol-Induced Anxiety Disorder

291.8	Alcohol-Induced Mood Disorder
291.8	Alcohol-Induced Sexual Dysfunction
291.8	Alcohol-Induced Sleep Disorder
291.8	Alcohol Withdrawal
291.9	Alcohol-Related Disorder NOS
292.0	Amphetamine Withdrawal
292.0	Cocaine Withdrawal
292.0	Nicotine Withdrawal
292.0	Opioid Withdrawal
292.0	Other (or Unknown) Substance Withdrawal
292.0	Sedative, Hypnotic, or Anxiolytic Withdrawal
292.11	Amphetamine-Induced Psychotic Disorder, With Delusions
292.11	Cannabis-Induced Psychotic Disorder, With Delusions
292.11	Cocaine-Induced Psychotic Disorder, With Delusions
292.11	Hallucinogen-Induced Psychotic Disorder, With Delusions
292.11	Inhalant-Induced Psychotic Disorder, With Delusions
292.11	Opioid-Induced Psychotic Disorder, With Delusions
292.11	Other (or Unknown) Substance–Induced Psychotic Disorder, With Delusions
292.11	Phencyclidine-Induced Psychotic Disorder, With Delusions
292.11	Sedative-, Hypnotic-, or Anxiolytic-Induced Psychotic Disorder, With Delusions
292.12	Amphetamine-Induced Psychotic Disorder, With Hallucinations
292.12	Cannabis-Induced Psychotic Disorder, With Hallucinations
292.12	Cocaine-Induced Psychotic Disorder, With Hallucinations
292.12	Hallucinogen-Induced Psychotic Disorder, With Hallucinations
292.12	Inhalant-Induced Psychotic Disorder, With Hallucinations
292.12	Opioid-Induced Psychotic Disorder, With Hallucinations
292.12	Other (or Unknown) Substance–Induced Psychotic Disorder, With Hallucinations
292.12	Phencyclidine-Induced Psychotic Disorder, With Hallucinations
292.12	Sedative-, Hypnotic-, or Anxiolytic-Induced Psychotic Disorder, With Hallucinations
292.81	Amphetamine Intoxication Delirium
292.81	Cannabis Intoxication Delirium
292.81	Cocaine Intoxication Delirium
292.81	Hallucinogen Intoxication Delirium
292.81	Inhalant Intoxication Delirium
292.81	Opioid Intoxication Delirium
292.81	Other (or Unknown) Substance–Induced Delirium
292.81	Phencyclidine Intoxication Delirium
292.81	Sedative, Hypnotic, or Anxiolytic Intoxication Delirium
292.81	Sedative, Hypnotic, or Anxiolytic Withdrawal Delirium
292.82	Inhalant-Induced Persisting Dementia
292.82	Other (or Unknown) Substance–Induced Persisting Dementia
292.82	Sedative-, Hypnotic-, or Anxiolytic-Induced Persisting Dementia
292.83	Other (or Unknown) Substance–Induced Persisting Amnestic Disorder
292.83	Sedative-, Hypnotic-, or Anxiolytic-Induced Persisting Amnestic Disorder
292.84	Amphetamine-Induced Mood Disorder

292.84	Cocaine-Induced Mood Disorder
292.84	Hallucinogen-Induced Mood Disorder
292.84	Inhalant-Induced Mood Disorder
292.84	Opioid-Induced Mood Disorder
292.84	Other (or Unknown) Substance–Induced Mood Disorder
292.84	Phencyclidine-Induced Mood Disorder
292.84	Sedative-, Hypnotic-, or Anxiolytic-Induced Mood Disorder
292.89	Amphetamine-Induced Anxiety Disorder
292.89	Amphetamine-Induced Sexual Dysfunction
292.89	Amphetamine-Induced Sleep Disorder
292.89	Amphetamine Intoxication
292.89	Caffeine-Induced Anxiety Disorder
292.89	Caffeine-Induced Sleep Disorder
292.89	Cannabis-Induced Anxiety Disorder
292.89	Cannabis Intoxication
292.89	Cocaine-Induced Anxiety Disorder
292.89	Cocaine-Induced Sexual Dysfunction
292.89	Cocaine-Induced Sleep Disorder
292.89	Cocaine Intoxication
292.89	Hallucinogen-Induced Anxiety Disorder
292.89	Hallucinogen Intoxication
292.89	Hallucinogen Persisting Perception Disorder
292.89	Inhalant-Induced Anxiety Disorder
292.89	Inhalant Intoxication
292.89	Opioid-Induced Sleep Disorder
292.89	Opioid-Induced Sexual Dysfunction
292.89	Opioid Intoxication
292.89	Other (or Unknown) Substance–Induced Anxiety Disorder
292.89	Other (or Unknown) Substance–Induced Sexual Dysfunction
292.89	Other (or Unknown) Substance–Induced Sleep Disorder
292.89	Other (or Unknown) Substance Intoxication
292.89	Phencyclidine-Induced Anxiety Disorder
292.89	Phencyclidine Intoxication
292.89	Sedative-, Hypnotic-, or Anxiolytic-Induced Anxiety Disorder
292.89	Sedative-, Hypnotic-, or Anxiolytic-Induced Sexual Dysfunction
292.89	Sedative-, Hypnotic-, or Anxiolytic-Induced Sleep Disorder
292.89	Sedative, Hypnotic, or Anxiolytic Intoxication
292.9	Amphetamine-Related Disorder NOS
292.9	Caffeine-Related Disorder NOS
292.9	Cannabis-Related Disorder NOS
292.9	Cocaine-Related Disorder NOS
292.9	Hallucinogen-Related Disorder NOS
292.9	Inhalant-Related Disorder NOS
292.9	Nicotine-Related Disorder NOS
292.9	Opioid-Related Disorder NOS
292.9	Other (or Unknown) Substance–Related Disorder NOS
292.9	Phencyclidine-Related Disorder NOS
292.9	Sedative-, Hypnotic-, or Anxiolytic-Related Disorder NOS
293.0	Delirium Due to . . . *[Indicate the General Medical Condition]*

293.81   Psychotic Disorder Due to . . . *[Indicate the General Medical Condition]*, With Delusions

293.82   Psychotic Disorder Due to . . . *[Indicate the General Medical Condition]*, With Hallucinations

293.83   Mood Disorder Due to . . . *[Indicate the General Medical Condition]*

293.89   Anxiety Disorder Due to . . . *[Indicate the General Medical Condition]*
293.89   Catatonic Disorder Due to . . . *[Indicate the General Medical Condition]*

293.9   Mental Disorder NOS Due to . . . *[Indicate the General Medical Condition]*

294.0   Amnestic Disorder Due to . . . *[Indicate the General Medical Condition]*

294.1   Dementia Due to . . . *[Indicate the General Medical Condition]*

294.8   Amnestic Disorder NOS
294.8   Dementia NOS

294.9   Cognitive Disorder NOS
294.9   Dementia Due to HIV Disease

295.10   Schizophrenia, Disorganized Type

295.20   Schizophrenia, Catatonic Type

295.30   Schizophrenia, Paranoid Type

295.40   Schizophreniform Disorder

295.60   Schizophrenia, Residual Type

295.70   Schizoaffective Disorder

295.90   Schizophrenia, Undifferentiated Type

296.00   Bipolar I Disorder, Single Manic Episode, Unspecified

296.01   Bipolar I Disorder, Single Manic Episode, Mild

296.02   Bipolar I Disorder, Single Manic Episode, Moderate

296.03   Bipolar I Disorder, Single Manic Episode, Severe Without Psychotic Features

296.04   Bipolar I Disorder, Single Manic Episode, Severe With Psychotic Features

296.05   Bipolar I Disorder, Single Manic Episode, In Partial Remission

296.06   Bipolar I Disorder, Single Manic Episode, In Full Remission

296.20   Major Depressive Disorder, Single Episode, Unspecified

296.21   Major Depressive Disorder, Single Episode, Mild

296.22   Major Depressive Disorder, Single Episode, Moderate

296.23   Major Depressive Disorder, Single Episode, Severe Without Psychotic Features

296.24   Major Depressive Disorder, Single Episode, Severe With Psychotic Features

296.25   Major Depressive Disorder, Single Episode, In Partial Remission

296.26   Major Depressive Disorder, Single Episode, In Full Remission

296.30   Major Depressive Disorder, Recurrent, Unspecified

296.31   Major Depressive Disorder, Recurrent, Mild

296.32   Major Depressive Disorder, Recurrent, Moderate

296.33   Major Depressive Disorder, Recurrent, Severe Without Psychotic Features

296.34   Major Depressive Disorder, Recurrent, Severe With Psychotic Features

296.35   Major Depressive Disorder, Recurrent, In Partial Remission

296.36   Major Depressive Disorder, Recurrent, In Full Remission

296.40   Bipolar I Disorder, Most Recent Episode Hypomanic
296.40   Bipolar I Disorder, Most Recent Episode Manic, Unspecified

296.41   Bipolar I Disorder, Most Recent Episode Manic, Mild

296.42   Bipolar I Disorder, Most Recent Episode Manic, Moderate

296.43	Bipolar I Disorder, Most Recent Episode Manic, Severe Without Psychotic Features
296.44	Bipolar I Disorder, Most Recent Episode Manic, Severe With Psychotic Features
296.45	Bipolar I Disorder, Most Recent Episode Manic, In Partial Remission
296.46	Bipolar I Disorder, Most Recent Episode Manic, In Full Remission
296.50	Bipolar I Disorder, Most Recent Episode Depressed, Unspecified
296.51	Bipolar I Disorder, Most Recent Episode Depressed, Mild
296.52	Bipolar I Disorder, Most Recent Episode Depressed, Moderate
296.53	Bipolar I Disorder, Most Recent Episode Depressed, Severe Without Psychotic Features
296.54	Bipolar I Disorder, Most Recent Episode Depressed, Severe With Psychotic Features
296.55	Bipolar I Disorder, Most Recent Episode Depressed, In Partial Remission
296.56	Bipolar I Disorder, Most Recent Episode Depressed, In Full Remission
296.60	Bipolar I Disorder, Most Recent Episode Mixed, Unspecified
296.61	Bipolar I Disorder, Most Recent Episode Mixed, Mild
296.62	Bipolar I Disorder, Most Recent Episode Mixed, Moderate
296.63	Bipolar I Disorder, Most Recent Episode Mixed, Severe Without Psychotic Features
296.64	Bipolar I Disorder, Most Recent Episode Mixed, Severe With Psychotic Features
296.65	Bipolar I Disorder, Most Recent Episode Mixed, In Partial Remission
296.66	Bipolar I Disorder, Most Recent Episode Mixed, In Full Remission
296.7	Bipolar I Disorder, Most Recent Episode Unspecified
296.80	Bipolar Disorder NOS
296.89	Bipolar II Disorder
296.90	Mood Disorder NOS
297.1	Delusional Disorder
297.3	Shared Psychotic Disorder
298.8	Brief Psychotic Disorder
298.9	Psychotic Disorder NOS
299.00	Autistic Disorder
299.10	Childhood Disintegrative Disorder
299.80	Asperger's Disorder
299.80	Pervasive Developmental Disorder NOS
299.80	Rett's Disorder
300.00	Anxiety Disorder NOS
300.01	Panic Disorder Without Agoraphobia
300.02	Generalized Anxiety Disorder
300.11	Conversion Disorder
300.12	Dissociative Amnesia
300.13	Dissociative Fugue
300.14	Dissociative Identity Disorder
300.15	Dissociative Disorder NOS
300.16	Factitious Disorder With Predominantly Psychological Signs and Symptoms
300.19	Factitious Disorder NOS

300.19	Factitious Disorder With Combined Psychological and Physical Signs and Symptoms
300.19	Factitious Disorder With Predominantly Physical Signs and Symptoms
300.21	Panic Disorder With Agoraphobia
300.22	Agoraphobia Without History of Panic Disorder
300.23	Social Phobia
300.29	Specific Phobia
300.3	Obsessive-Compulsive Disorder
300.4	Dysthymic Disorder
300.6	Depersonalization Disorder
300.7	Body Dysmorphic Disorder
300.7	Hypochondriasis
300.81	Somatization Disorder
300.81	Somatoform Disorder NOS
300.81	Undifferentiated Somatoform Disorder
300.9	Unspecified Mental Disorder (nonpsychotic)
301.0	Paranoid Personality Disorder
301.13	Cyclothymic Disorder
301.20	Schizoid Personality Disorder
301.22	Schizotypal Personality Disorder
301.4	Obsessive-Compulsive Personality Disorder
301.50	Histrionic Personality Disorder
301.6	Dependent Personality Disorder
301.7	Antisocial Personality Disorder
301.81	Narcissistic Personality Disorder
301.82	Avoidant Personality Disorder
301.83	Borderline Personality Disorder
301.9	Personality Disorder NOS
302.2	Pedophilia
302.3	Transvestic Fetishism
302.4	Exhibitionism
302.6	Gender Identity Disorder in Children
302.6	Gender Identity Disorder NOS
302.70	Sexual Dysfunction NOS
302.71	Hypoactive Sexual Desire Disorder
302.72	Female Sexual Arousal Disorder
302.72	Male Erectile Disorder
302.73	Female Orgasmic Disorder
302.74	Male Orgasmic Disorder
302.75	Premature Ejaculation
302.76	Dyspareunia (Not Due to a General Medical Condition)
302.79	Sexual Aversion Disorder
302.81	Fetishism
302.82	Voyeurism
302.83	Sexual Masochism
302.84	Sexual Sadism
302.85	Gender Identity Disorder in Adolescents or Adults
302.89	Frotteurism
302.9	Paraphilia NOS

302.9	Sexual Disorder NOS
303.00	Alcohol Intoxication
303.90	Alcohol Dependence
304.00	Opioid Dependence
304.10	Sedative, Hypnotic, or Anxiolytic Dependence
304.20	Cocaine Dependence
304.30	Cannabis Dependence
304.40	Amphetamine Dependence
304.50	Hallucinogen Dependence
304.60	Inhalant Dependence
304.80	Polysubstance Dependence
304.90	Other (or Unknown) Substance Dependence
304.90	Phencyclidine Dependence
305.00	Alcohol Abuse
305.10	Nicotine Dependence
305.20	Cannabis Abuse
305.30	Hallucinogen Abuse
305.40	Sedative, Hypnotic, or Anxiolytic Abuse
305.50	Opioid Abuse
305.60	Cocaine Abuse
305.70	Amphetamine Abuse
305.90	Caffeine Intoxication
305.90	Inhalant Abuse
305.90	Other (or Unknown) Substance Abuse
305.90	Phencyclidine Abuse
306.51	Vaginismus (Not Due to a General Medical Condition)
307.0	Stuttering
307.1	Anorexia Nervosa
307.20	Tic Disorder NOS
307.21	Transient Tic Disorder
307.22	Chronic Motor or Vocal Tic Disorder
307.23	Tourette's Disorder
307.3	Stereotypic Movement Disorder
307.42	Insomnia Related to . . . *[Indicate the Axis I or Axis II Disorder]*
307.42	Primary Insomnia
307.44	Hypersomnia Related to . . . *[Indicate the Axis I or Axis II Disorder]*
307.44	Primary Hypersomnia
307.45	Circadian Rhythm Sleep Disorder
307.46	Sleep Terror Disorder
307.46	Sleepwalking Disorder
307.47	Dyssomnia NOS
307.47	Nightmare Disorder
307.47	Parasomnia NOS
307.50	Eating Disorder NOS
307.51	Bulimia Nervosa
307.52	Pica
307.53	Rumination Disorder
307.59	Feeding Disorder of Infancy or Early Childhood
307.6	Enuresis (Not Due to a General Medical Condition)

307.7	Encopresis, Without Constipation and Overflow Incontinence
307.80	Pain Disorder Associated With Psychological Factors
307.89	Pain Disorder Associated With Both Psychological Factors and a General Medical Condition
307.9	Communication Disorder NOS
308.3	Acute Stress Disorder
309.0	Adjustment Disorder With Depressed Mood
309.21	Separation Anxiety Disorder
309.24	Adjustment Disorder With Anxiety
309.28	Adjustment Disorder With Mixed Anxiety and Depressed Mood
309.3	Adjustment Disorder With Disturbance of Conduct
309.4	Adjustment Disorder With Mixed Disturbance of Emotions and Conduct
309.81	Posttraumatic Stress Disorder
309.9	Adjustment Disorder Unspecified
310.1	Personality Change Due to . . . *[Indicate the General Medical Condition]*
311	Depressive Disorder NOS
312.30	Impulse-Control Disorder NOS
312.31	Pathological Gambling
312.32	Kleptomania
312.33	Pyromania
312.34	Intermittent Explosive Disorder
312.39	Trichotillomania
312.8	Conduct Disorder
312.9	Disruptive Behavior Disorder NOS
313.23	Selective Mutism
313.81	Oppositional Defiant Disorder
313.82	Identity Problem
313.89	Reactive Attachment Disorder of Infancy or Early Childhood
313.9	Disorder of Infancy, Childhood, or Adolescence NOS
314.00	Attention-Deficit/Hyperactivity Disorder, Predominantly Inattentive Type
⌈ 314.01	Attention-Deficit/Hyperactivity Disorder, Combined Type
⌊ 314.01	Attention-Deficit/Hyperactivity Disorder, Predominantly Hyperactive-Impulsive Type
314.9	Attention-Deficit/Hyperactivity Disorder NOS
315.00	Reading Disorder
315.1	Mathematics Disorder
315.2	Disorder of Written Expression
⌈ 315.31	Expressive Language Disorder
⌊ 315.31	Mixed Receptive-Expressive Language Disorder
315.39	Phonological Disorder
315.4	Developmental Coordination Disorder
315.9	Learning Disorder NOS
316	. . . *[Specified Psychological Factor]* Affecting . . . *[Indicate the General Medical Condition]*
317	Mild Mental Retardation
318.0	Moderate Mental Retardation
318.1	Severe Mental Retardation
318.2	Profound Mental Retardation
319	Mental Retardation, Severity Unspecified

332.1   Neuroleptic-Induced Parkinsonism
333.1   Medication-Induced Postural Tremor
333.7   Neuroleptic-Induced Acute Dystonia
333.82   Neuroleptic-Induced Tardive Dyskinesia
333.90   Medication-Induced Movement Disorder NOS
333.92   Neuroleptic Malignant Syndrome
333.99   Neuroleptic-Induced Acute Akathisia
347   Narcolepsy
607.84   Male Erectile Disorder Due to . . . *[Indicate the General Medical Condition]*
608.89   Male Dyspareunia Due to . . . *[Indicate the General Medical Condition]*
608.89   Male Hypoactive Sexual Desire Disorder Due to . . . *[Indicate the Medical Condition]*
608.89   Other Male Sexual Dysfunction Due to . . . *[Indicate the General Medical Condition]*
625.0   Female Dyspareunia Due to . . . *[Indicate the General Medical Condition]*
625.8   Female Hypoactive Sexual Desire Disorder Due to . . . *[Indicate the General Medical Condition]*
625.8   Other Female Sexual Dysfunction Due to . . . *[Indicate the General Medical Condition]*
780.09   Delirium NOS
780.52   Sleep Disorder Due to . . . *[Indicate the General Medical Condition]*, Insomnia Type
780.54   Sleep Disorder Due to . . . *[Indicate the General Medical Condition]*, Hypersomnia Type
780.59   Breathing-Related Sleep Disorder
780.59   Sleep Disorder Due to . . . *[Indicate the General Medical Condition]*, Mixed Type
780.59   Sleep Disorder Due to . . . *[Indicate the General Medical Condition]*, Parasomnia Type
780.9   Age-Related Cognitive Decline
787.6   Encopresis, With Constipation and Overflow Incontinence
799.9   Diagnosis Deferred on Axis II
799.9   Diagnosis or Condition Deferred on Axis I
995.2   Adverse Effects of Medication NOS
995.5   Neglect of Child *(if focus of attention is on victim)*
995.5   Physical Abuse of Child *(if focus of attention is on victim)*
995.5   Sexual Abuse of Child *(if focus of attention is on victim)*
995.81   Physical Abuse of Adult *(if focus of attention is on victim)*
995.81   Sexual Abuse of Adult *(if focus of attention is on victim)*
V15.81   Noncompliance With Treatment
V61.1   Partner Relational Problem
V61.1   Physical Abuse of Adult
V61.1   Sexual Abuse of Adult
V61.20   Parent-Child Relational Problem
V61.21   Neglect of Child
V61.21   Physical Abuse of Child
V61.21   Sexual Abuse of Child
V61.8   Sibling Relational Problem

V61.9	Relational Problem Related to a Mental Disorder or General Medical Condition
V62.2	Occupational Problem
V62.3	Academic Problem
V62.4	Acculturation Problem
V62.81	Relational Problem NOS
V62.82	Bereavement
V62.89	Borderline Intellectual Functioning
V62.89	Phase of Life Problem
V62.89	Religious or Spiritual Problem
V65.2	Malingering
V71.01	Adult Antisocial Behavior
V71.02	Child or Adolescent Antisocial Behavior
V71.09	No Diagnosis on Axis II
V71.09	No Diagnosis or Condition on Axis I

Appendix G

ICD-9-CM Codes for Selected General Medical Conditions and Medication-Induced Disorders

The official coding system in use as of the publication of DSM-IV is the *International Classification of Diseases,* 9th Revision, Clinical Modification (ICD-9-CM). This appendix contains two sections that are provided to facilitate ICD-9-CM coding: 1) codes for selected general medical conditions, and 2) codes for medication-induced disorders.

ICD-9-CM Codes for Selected General Medical Conditions

The codes specified for use on Axis I and Axis II of DSM-IV represent only a small fraction of the codes provided in ICD-9-CM. The conditions classified outside the "Mental Disorders" chapter of ICD-9-CM are also important for clinical diagnosis and management in mental health settings. Axis III is provided to facilitate the reporting of these conditions (see p. 27). To assist clinicians in finding the ICD-9-CM codes, this appendix provides a selective index of those ICD-9-CM codes for general medical conditions that are most relevant to diagnosis and care in mental health settings. ICD-9-CM offers diagnostic specificity beyond that reflected in many of the codes that appear in this appendix (e.g., to denote a specific anatomical site or the presence of a specific complication). In cases in which increased specificity is noted in the fifth digit of the code, the least specific code (usually "0") has been selected. For example, the code for lymphosarcoma is given as 200.10 (for unspecified site), although more specificity with regard to anatomical site can be noted in the other fifth-digit codes, for example, 200.12 lymphosarcoma, intrathoracic lymph nodes. In cases in which increased specificity is reflected in the fourth digit of the code, this appendix often provides the "unspecified" category (e.g., 555.9 is listed for regional enteritis; ICD-9-CM also includes 555.0 for enteritis involving the small intestine, 555.1 for involvement of the large intestine, and 555.2 for involvement of both). Diagnostic codes for which more specificity is available are indicated in this appendix by an asterisk (*). Clinicians interested in recording greater specificity should refer to the complete listing of codes published in the ICD-9-CM Diseases: Tabular List (Volume 1) and the ICD-9-CM Diseases: Alphabetic Index

---

(Volume 2). These documents are updated every October and are published by the U.S. Department of Health and Human Services. They are available from the Superintendent of Documents, U.S. Government Printing Office, as well as from a number of private publishers.

Note: An asterisk (*) following the ICD-9-CM code indicates that greater specificity (e.g., a specific complication or anatomical site) is available. Refer to the ICD-9-CM Diseases: Tabular List (Volume 1) entry for that code for additional information.

Diseases of the Nervous System

324.0	Abscess, intracranial
331.0	Alzheimer's disease
437.0	Atherosclerosis, cerebral
354.0	Carpal tunnel syndrome
354.4	Causalgia
334.3	Cerebellar ataxia
850.9*	Concussion
851.80*	Contusion, cerebral
359.1	Dystrophy, Duchenne's muscular
348.5	Edema, cerebral
049.9*	Encephalitis, viral
572.2	Encephalopathy, hepatic
437.2	Encephalopathy, hypertensive
348.3*	Encephalopathy, unspecified
345.10*	Epilepsy, grand mal
345.40*	Epilepsy, partial, with impairment of consciousness (temporal lobe)
345.50*	Epilepsy, partial, without impairment of consciousness (Jacksonian)
345.00*	Epilepsy, petit mal (absences)
346.20	Headache, cluster
432.0	Hemorrhage, extradural, nontraumatic
852.40*	Hemorrhage, extradural, traumatic
431	Hemorrhage, intracerebral, nontraumatic
430	Hemorrhage, subarachnoid, nontraumatic
852.00*	Hemorrhage, subarachnoid, traumatic
432.1	Hemorrhage, subdural, nontraumatic
852.20*	Hemorrhage, subdural, traumatic
333.4	Huntington's chorea
331.3	Hydrocephalus, communicating
331.4	Hydrocephalus, obstructive
435.9*	Ischemic attack, transient
046.1	Creutzfeldt-Jakob disease
046.0	Kuru
046.3	Leukoencephalopathy, progressive multifocal
330.1	Lipidosis, cerebral
320.9*	Meningitis, bacterial (due to unspecified bacterium)
321.0	Meningitis, cryptococcal
054.72	Meningitis, herpes simplex virus

053.0	Meningitis, herpes zoster
321.1*	Meningitis, other fungal
094.2	Meningitis, syphilitic
047.9*	Meningitis, viral (due to unspecified virus)
346.00*	Migraine, classical (with aura)
346.10*	Migraine, common
346.90*	Migraine, unspecified
358.0	Myasthenia gravis
350.1	Neuralgia, trigeminal
337.1	Neuropathy, peripheral autonomic
434.9*	Occlusion, cerebral artery
350.2	Pain, face, atypical
351.0	Palsy, Bell's
343.9*	Palsy, cerebral
335.23	Palsy, pseudobulbar
046.2	Panencephalitis, subacute sclerosing
094.1	Paresis, general
332.0	Parkinson's disease, primary
331.1	Pick's disease
357.9*	Polyneuropathy
348.2	Pseudotumor cerebri (benign intracranial hypertension)
335.20	Sclerosis, amyotrophic lateral
340	Sclerosis, multiple (MS)
345.3	Status, grand mal
345.2	Status, petit mal
345.70	Status, temporal lobe
433.1	Stenosis, carotid artery, without cerebral infarction
436	Stroke (CVA)
330.1	Tay-Sachs disease
333.1	Tremor, benign essential

Diseases of the Circulatory System

413.9*	Angina pectoris
424.1	Aortic valve disorder
440.9*	Atherosclerosis
414.0	Atherosclerotic heart disease
426.10*	Block, atrioventricular
426.3*	Block, left bundle branch
426.4	Block, right bundle branch
427.5	Cardiac arrest
425.5	Cardiomyopathy, alcoholic
425.4*	Cardiomyopathy, idiopathic
416.9*	Chronic pulmonary heart disease
427.9*	Dysrhythmia, cardiac, unspecified
415.1	Embolism, pulmonary
421.9*	Endocarditis, bacterial
428.0*	Failure, congestive heart

427.31   Fibrillation, atrial
427.41   Fibrillation, ventricular
427.32   Flutter, atrial
427.42   Flutter, ventricular
455.6*   Hemorrhoids
401.9*   Hypertension, essential
402.91*   Hypertensive heart disease with congestive heart failure
402.90*   Hypertensive heart disease without congestive heart failure
403.91*   Hypertensive renal disease with failure
403.90*   Hypertensive renal disease without failure
458.0   Hypotension, orthostatic
410.90*   Infarction, myocardial, acute
424.0   Mitral valve insufficiency (nonrheumatic)
424.0   Mitral valve prolapse
394.0*   Mitral valve stenosis (rheumatic)
423.9*   Pericarditis
443.9*   Peripheral vascular disease
451.9*   Phlebitis/thrombophlebitis
446.0   Polyarteritis nodosa
427.60*   Premature beats
424.3   Pulmonary valve disease (nonrheumatic)
397.1   Pulmonary valve disease, rheumatic
427.0   Tachycardia, paroxysmal supraventricular
427.2   Tachycardia, paroxysmal, unspecified
427.1   Tachycardia, ventricular (paroxysmal)
424.2   Tricuspid valve disease (nonrheumatic)
397.0   Tricuspid valve disease, rheumatic
456.0   Varices, esophageal, with bleeding
456.1   Varices, esophageal, without bleeding
454.9*   Varicose veins, lower extremities

Diseases of the Respiratory System

513.0   Abscess of lung
518.0   Atelectasis
493.20*   Asthma, chronic obstructive
493.90*   Asthma, unspecified
494   Bronchiectasis
466.0   Bronchitis, acute
491.21   Bronchitis, obstructive chronic (COPD), with acute exacerbation
491.20   Bronchitis, obstructive chronic (COPD), without acute exacerbation
277.00*   Cystic fibrosis
511.9*   Effusion, pleural
492.8*   Emphysema
518.81*   Failure, respiratory
505   Pneumoconiosis
860.4*   Pneumohemothorax, traumatic
483.0   Pneumonia, mycoplasma

482.9*	Pneumonia, unspecified bacterial
481	Pneumonia, pneumococcal
136.3	Pneumonia, pneumocystis
482.30*	Pneumonia, streptococcus
486*	Pneumonia, unspecified organism
480.9*	Pneumonia, viral
512.8*	Pneumothorax, spontaneous
860.0*	Pneumothorax, traumatic
011.9*	Tuberculosis, pulmonary

Neoplasms

ICD-9-CM diagnostic codes for neoplasms are classified in the table of neoplasms in the ICD-9-CM Alphabetic Index (Volume 2) according to site and degree of malignancy (primary, secondary, in situ, benign, uncertain, unspecified). **Note:** For patients with a personal history of malignant neoplasms that have been surgically removed or eradicated by chemotherapy or radiation therapy, codes V10.0–V10.9 should be used; for specific sites, refer to the Alphabetic Index (Volume 2) of ICD-9-CM under "History (personal) of, malignant neoplasm."

Listed below are some of the most common codes assigned for neoplasms.

228.02	Hemangioma of brain
201.90*	Hodgkin's disease
176.9*	Kaposi's sarcoma
208.01*	Leukemia, acute, in remission
208.00*	Leukemia, acute
208.11*	Leukemia, chronic, in remission
208.10*	Leukemia, chronic
200.10*	Lymphosarcoma
225.2	Meningioma (cerebral)
203.01	Multiple myeloma, in remission
203.00	Multiple myeloma
225.0	Neoplasm, benign, of brain
211.4	Neoplasm, benign, of colon
195.2	Neoplasm, malignant, abdominal cavity, primary
194.0	Neoplasm, malignant, adrenal gland, primary
188.9*	Neoplasm, malignant, bladder, primary
170.9*	Neoplasm, malignant, bone, primary
198.5	Neoplasm, malignant, bone, secondary
191.9*	Neoplasm, malignant, brain, primary
198.3	Neoplasm, malignant, brain, secondary
174.9*	Neoplasm, malignant, breast, female, primary
175.9*	Neoplasm, malignant, breast, male, primary
162.9*	Neoplasm, malignant, bronchus, primary
180.9*	Neoplasm, malignant, cervix, primary
153.9*	Neoplasm, malignant, colon, primary
197.5	Neoplasm, malignant, colon, secondary
171.9*	Neoplasm, malignant, connective tissue, primary
150.9*	Neoplasm, malignant, esophagus, primary

152.9*	Neoplasm, malignant, intestine, small, primary
189.0*	Neoplasm, malignant, kidney, primary
155.0	Neoplasm, malignant, liver, primary
197.7	Neoplasm, malignant, liver, secondary
162.9*	Neoplasm, malignant, lung, primary
197.0	Neoplasm, malignant, lung, secondary
196.9*	Neoplasm, malignant, lymph nodes, secondary
172.9*	Neoplasm, malignant, melanoma, primary
183.0*	Neoplasm, malignant, ovary, primary
157.9*	Neoplasm, malignant, pancreas, primary
185	Neoplasm, malignant, prostate, primary
154.1	Neoplasm, malignant, rectum, primary
173.9*	Neoplasm, malignant, skin, primary
151.9*	Neoplasm, malignant, stomach, site unspecified, primary
186.9*	Neoplasm, malignant, testis, primary
193	Neoplasm, malignant, thyroid, primary
179*	Neoplasm, malignant, uterus, primary
237.70*	Neurofibromatosis
227.0	Pheochromocytoma, benign
194.0	Pheochromocytoma, malignant
238.4	Polycythemia vera

Endocrine Diseases

253.0	Acromegaly
255.2	Adrenogenital disorder
259.2	Carcinoid syndrome
255.4	Corticoadrenal insufficiency
255.0	Cushing's syndrome
253.5	Diabetes insipidus
250.00*	Diabetes mellitus, type II/non-insulin-dependent
250.01*	Diabetes mellitus, type I/insulin-dependent
253.2	Dwarfism, pituitary
241.9*	Goiter, nontoxic nodular
240.9*	Goiter, simple
255.1	Hyperaldosteronism
252.0	Hyperparathyroidism
252.1	Hypoparathyroidism
244.9*	Hypothyroidism, acquired
243	Hypothyroidism, congenital
256.9*	Ovarian dysfunction
253.2	Panhypopituitarism
259.0	Sexual development and puberty, delayed
259.1	Sexual development and puberty, precocious
257.9*	Testicular dysfunction
245.9*	Thyroiditis
242.9*	Thyrotoxicosis

Nutritional Diseases

265.0	Beriberi
269.3	Calcium deficiency
266.2	Folic acid deficiency
269.3	Iodine deficiency
260	Kwashiorkor
262	Malnutrition, protein-caloric, severe
261	Nutritional marasmus
278.0	Obesity
265.2	Pellagra (niacin deficiency)
266.0	Riboflavin deficiency
264.9*	Vitamin A deficiency
266.1	Vitamin B_6 deficiency
266.2	Vitamin B_{12} deficiency
267	Vitamin C deficiency
268.9*	Vitamin D deficiency
269.1	Vitamin E deficiency
269.0	Vitamin K deficiency

Metabolic Diseases

276.2	Acidosis
276.3	Alkalosis
277.3	Amyloidosis
276.5	Depletion, volume (dehydration)
271.3	Disaccharide malabsorption (lactose intolerance)
276.9*	Electrolyte imbalance
276.6	Fluid overload/retention
274.9*	Gout
275.0	Hemochromatosis
275.4	Hypercalcemia
276.7	Hyperkalemia
276.0	Hypernatremia
275.4	Hypocalcemia
276.8	Hypokalemia
276.1	Hyponatremia
270.1	Phenylketonuria (PKU)
277.1	Porphyria
277.2	Lesch-Nyhan syndrome
275.1	Wilson's disease

Diseases of the Digestive System

540.9*	Appendicitis, acute
578.9*	Bleeding, gastrointestinal
575.0	Cholecystitis, acute
575.1	Cholecystitis, chronic
571.2	Cirrhosis, alcoholic

556   Colitis, ulcerative
564.0   Constipation
555.9*   Crohn's disease
009.2   Diarrhea, infectious
558.9*   Diarrhea, unspecified
562.10   Diverticulitis of colon, unspecified
562.12   Diverticulitis of colon, with hemorrhage
562.11   Diverticulosis of colon, unspecified
562.13   Diverticulosis of colon, with hemorrhage
535.50*   Duodenitis and gastritis
555.9*   Enteritis, regional
535.50*   Gastritis and duodenitis
558.9*   Gastroenteritis
530.1   Esophagitis
571.1   Hepatitis, alcoholic, acute
571.40*   Hepatitis, chronic
573.3*   Hepatitis, toxic (includes drug induced)
070.1*   Hepatitis, viral A
070.30*   Hepatitis, viral B
070.51*   Hepatitis, viral C
560.39*   Impaction, fecal
550.90*   Inguinal hernia
564.1   Irritable bowel syndrome
576.2   Obstruction, bile duct
560.9*   Obstruction, intestinal
577.0   Pancreatitis, acute
577.1   Pancreatitis, chronic
567.9*   Peritonitis
530.1   Reflux, esophageal
530.4   Rupture, esophageal
530.3   Stricture, esophageal
532.30*   Ulcer, duodenal, acute
532.70*   Ulcer, duodenal, chronic
531.30*   Ulcer, gastric, acute
531.70*   Ulcer, gastric, chronic

Genitourinary System Diseases

596.4   Atonic bladder
592.0   Calculus, renal
592.1   Calculus, ureter
592.9*   Calculus, urinary, unspecified
595.9*   Cystitis
625.3   Dysmenorrhea
617.9*   Endometriosis
584.9*   Failure, renal, acute
585   Failure, renal, chronic
403.91*   Failure, renal, hypertensive

586[*]	Failure, renal, unspecified
218.9[*]	Fibroid of uterus
580.9[*]	Glomerulonephritis, acute
600	Hypertrophy, prostatic, benign (BPH)
628.9[*]	Infertility, female
606.9[*]	Infertility, male
627.9[*]	Menopausal or postmenopausal disorder
626.9[*]	Menstruation, disorder of, and abnormal bleeding
625.2	Mittelschmerz
620.2[*]	Ovarian cyst
614.9[*]	Pelvic inflammatory disease (PID)
607.3	Priapism
618.9[*]	Prolapse, genital
601.9[*]	Prostatitis
593.3	Stricture, ureteral
598.9[*]	Stricture, urethral
599.0	Urinary tract infection (UTI)

Hematological Diseases

288.0	Agranulocytosis
287.0	Allergic purpura
284.9[*]	Anemia, aplastic
281.2	Anemia, folate-deficiency
283.9[*]	Anemia, hemolytic, acquired
283.11	Anemia, hemolytic-uremic syndrome
280.9[*]	Anemia, iron-deficiency
283.10	Anemia, nonautoimmune hemolytic, unspecified
283.19	Anemia, other autoimmune hemolytic
281.0	Anemia, pernicious
282.60[*]	Anemia, sickle-cell
286.9[*]	Coagulation defects
288.3	Eosinophilia
282.4	Thalassemia
287.5[*]	Thrombocytopenia

Diseases of the Eye

366.9[*]	Cataract
372.9[*]	Conjunctiva disorder
361.9[*]	Detachment, retinal
365.9[*]	Glaucoma
377.30[*]	Neuritis, optic
379.50[*]	Nystagmus
377.00[*]	Papilledema
369.9[*]	Visual loss

Diseases of the Ear, Nose, and Throat

460	Common cold
389.9*	Hearing loss
464.0	Laryngitis, acute
386.00*	Ménière's disease
382.9*	Otitis media
462	Pharyngitis, acute
477.9*	Rhinitis, allergic
461.9*	Sinusitis, acute
473.9*	Sinusitis, chronic
388.30*	Tinnitus, unspecified
463	Tonsillitis, acute

Musculoskeletal System and Connective Tissue Diseases

716.20*	Arthritis, allergic
711.90*	Arthritis, infective
714.0	Arthritis, rheumatoid
733.40*	Aseptic necrosis of bone
710.3	Dermatomyositis
722.91	Disc disorder, intervertebral, cervical
722.93	Disc disorder, intervertebral, lumbar
722.92	Disc disorder, intervertebral, thoracic
733.10*	Fracture, pathological
715.90*	Osteoarthrosis (osteoarthritis)
730.20*	Osteomyelitis
733.00*	Osteoporosis
710.1	Scleroderma (systemic sclerosis)
737.30	Scoliosis
710.2	Sjögren's disease
720.0	Spondylitis, ankylosing
710.0	Systemic lupus erythematosus

Diseases of the Skin

704.00*	Alopecia
692.9*	Dermatitis, contact
693.0*	Dermatitis, due to substance (taken internally)
682.9*	Cellulitis, unspecified site
695.1	Erythema multiforme
703.0	Ingrowing nail
701.4	Keloid scar
696.1*	Psoriasis
707.0	Ulcer, decubitus
708.0	Urticaria, allergic

Congenital Malformations, Deformations, and Chromosomal Abnormalities

749.10*	Cleft lip
749.00*	Cleft palate
758.3	Cri-du-chat syndrome (antimongolism)
758.0	Down's syndrome
760.71	Fetal alcohol syndrome
751.3	Hirschsprung's disease (congenital colon dysfunction)
742.3	Hydrocephalus, congenital
752.7	Indeterminate sex and pseudohermaphroditism
758.7	Klinefelter's syndrome
759.82	Marfan's syndrome
742.1	Microcephalus
741.90*	Spina bifida
750.5	Stenosis, congenital hypertrophic pyloric
760.71	Toxic effects of alcohol
760.75	Toxic effects of cocaine
760.73	Toxic effects of hallucinogens
760.72	Toxic effects of narcotics
760.70	Toxic effects of other substances (including medications)
759.5	Tuberous sclerosis
758.6	Turner's syndrome
752.5	Undescended testicle

Diseases of Pregnancy, Childbirth, and the Puerperium

Diagnoses associated with pregnancies can be located in the Alphabetic Index (Volume 2) of ICD-9-CM indented under "Pregnancy, complicated (by)," or "Pregnancy, management affected by." Listed below are some of the most common conditions.

642.00*	Eclampsia
643.0*	Hyperemesis gravidarum, mild
643.0*	Hyperemesis gravidarum, with metabolic disturbance
642.0*	Pre-eclampsia, mild
642.0*	Pre-eclampsia, severe

HIV Infection

Common disorders associated with human immunodeficiency virus (HIV) infection are indexed under "Human immunodeficiency virus" in the Alphabetic Index (Volume 2) of ICD-9-CM.

HIV is classified into three categories depending on the progression of the disease, as follows:

042	HIV infection associated with specified conditions
043	HIV infection causing other specified conditions
044	Other HIV infections

Each category is further subdivided into fourth-digit subclassification for greater specificity. It is customary to report one diagnostic code for the HIV disease and one code for the manifestation. Due to the complexity of the coding of HIV disease, direct reference to the Alphabetic Index (Volume 2) of ICD-9-CM is recommended.

042.0*   AIDS with specified infections
042.1*   AIDS with other specified infections
042.2*   AIDS with specified malignant neoplasms
042.9*   AIDS, unspecified
043.0*   AIDS-related complex (ARC) causing lymphadenopathy
043.1*   HIV infection affecting central nervous system
043.2*   ARC causing other disorders involving the immune mechanism
043.3*   ARC causing other specific conditions
043.9*   ARC, unspecified
044.0*   HIV infection causing specified acute infections
044.9*   HIV infections, unspecified

Infectious Diseases

The following codes represent ICD-9-CM diagnostic codes for infections from specific organisms. Traditionally, codes for organisms from the 041 category are used as secondary codes (e.g., urinary tract infection due to *Escherichia coli* would be coded as 599.0 [primary diagnosis] and 041.4 [secondary diagnosis]).

006.9*   Amebiasis
112.5   Candidiasis, disseminated
112.4   Candidiasis, lung
112.0   Candidiasis, mouth
112.2   Candidiasis, other urogenital sites
112.3   Candidiasis, skin and nails
112.9   Candidiasis, unspecified site
112.1   Candidiasis, vulva and vagina
099.41   *Chlamydia trachomatis*
001.9*   Cholera
041.83   *Clostridium perfrigens*
114.9*   Coccidioidomycosis
078.1   *Condyloma acuminatum* (viral warts)
079.2   Coxsackie virus
117.5   Cryptococcosis
041.4   *Escherichia coli (E. coli)*
007.1   Giardiasis
098.2*   Gonorrhea
041.5   *Hemophilus influenzae (H. influenzae)*
070.1*   Hepatitis, viral A
070.3*   Hepatitis, viral B
070.51   Hepatitis, viral C
054.9*   Herpes simplex
053.9*   Herpes zoster
115.9*   Histoplasmosis
036.9*   Infection, meningococcal
079.99*   Infection, viral, unspecified
487.1   Influenza, unspecified

487.0	Influenza, with pneumonia
041.3*	*Klebsiella pneumoniae*
088.81	Lyme disease
084.6*	Malaria
075	Mononucleosis
072.9*	Mumps
041.81	*Mycoplasma*
041.2	*Pneumococcus*
041.6	*Proteus*
041.7	*Pseudomonas*
071	Rabies
056.9*	Rubella
003.9*	Salmonella
135	Sarcoidosis
004.9*	Shigellosis
041.10*	*Staphylococcus*
041.00*	*Streptococcus*
097.9*	Syphilis
082.9*	Tick-borne rikettsiosis
130.9*	Toxoplasmosis
124	Trichinosis
131.9*	Trichomoniasis
002.0	Typhoid fever
081.9*	Typhus

Overdose

Additional diagnostic codes for overdose/poisoning can be located in the Alphabetic Index (Volume 2) of ICD-9-CM in the table of drugs and chemicals, listed alphabetically by drug in the "Poisoning" column.

965.4	Acetaminophen
962.0	Adrenal cortical steroids
972.4	Amyl/butyl/nitrite
962.1	Androgens and anabolic steroids
971.1	Anticholinergics
969.0	Antidepressants
967.0	Barbiturates
969.4	Benzodiazepine-based tranquilizers
969.2	Butyrophenone-based tranquilizers
967.1	Chloral hydrate
968.5	Cocaine
967.5	Glutethimide
969.6	Hallucinogens/cannabis
962.3	Insulin and antidiabetic agents
967.4	Methaqualone
968.2	Nitrous oxide
970.1	Opioid antagonists
965.00	Opioids

967.2   Paraldehyde
968.3   Phencyclidine
969.1   Phenothiazine-based tranquilizers
965.1   Salicylates
970.9   Stimulants
962.7   Thyroid and thyroid derivatives

Additional Codes for Medication-Induced Disorders

The following are the ICD-9-CM codes for selected medications that may cause Substance-Induced Disorders. They are made available for optional use by clinicians in situations in which these medications, prescribed at therapeutic dose levels, have resulted in one of the following: Substance-Induced Delirium, Substance-Induced Persisting Dementia, Substance-Induced Persisting Amnestic Disorder, Substance-Induced Psychotic Disorder, Substance-Induced Mood Disorder, Substance-Induced Anxiety Disorder, Substance-Induced Sexual Dysfunction, Substance-Induced Sleep Disorder, and Medication-Induced Movement Disorders. When used in multiaxial evaluation, the E-codes should be coded on Axis I immediately following the related disorder. It should be noted that these E-codes do not apply to poisonings or to a medication taken as an overdose.

Example: 292.39 Substance-Induced Mood Disorder, With Depressive Features
           E932.2 Oral contraceptives

Analgesics and Antipyretics

E935.4   Acetaminophen/phenacetin
E935.1   Methadone
E935.6   Nonsteroidal anti-inflammatory agents
E935.2   Other narcotics (e.g., codeine, meperidine)
E935.3   Salicylates (e.g., aspirin)

Anticonvulsants

E936.3   Carbamazepine
E936.2   Ethosuximide
E937.0   Phenobarbital
E936.1   Phenytoin
E936.3   Valproic acid

Antiparkinsonian Medications

E936.4   Amantadine
E941.1   Benztropine
E933.0   Diphenhydramine
E936.4   l-Dopa

Neuroleptic Medications

E939.2   Butyrophenone-based neuroleptics (e.g., haloperidol)
E939.3   Other neuroleptics (e.g., thiothixene)
E939.1   Phenothiazine-based neuroleptics (e.g., chlorpromazine)

Sedatives, Hypnotics, and Anxiolytics

E937.0   Barbiturates
E939.4   Benzodiazepine-based medications
E937.1   Chloral hydrate
E939.5   Hydroxyzine
E937.2   Paraldehyde

Other Psychotropic Medications

E939.0   Antidepressants
E939.6   Cannabis
E940.1   Opioid antagonists
E939.7   Stimulants (excluding central appetite depressants)

Cardiovascular Medications

E942.0   Antiarrhythmic medication (includes propranolol)
E942.2   Antilipemic and cholesterol-lowering medication
E942.1   Cardiac glycosides (e.g., digitalis)
E942.4   Coronary vasodilators (e.g., nitrates)
E942.3   Ganglion-blocking agents (pentamethonium)
E942.6   Other antihypertensive agents (e.g., clonidine, guanethidine, reserpine)
E942.5   Other vasodilators (e.g., hydralazine)

Primarily Systemic Agents

E933.0   Antiallergic and antiemetic agents (excluding phenothiazines, hydroxyzine)
E941.1   Anticholinergics (e.g., atropine) and spasmolytics
E934.2   Anticoagulants
E933.1   Antineoplastic and immunosuppressive drugs
E941.0   Cholinergics (parasympathomimetics)
E941.2   Sympathomimetics (adrenergics)
E933.5   Vitamins (excluding vitamin K)

Medications Acting on Muscles and the Respiratory System

E945.7   Antiasthmatics (aminophylline)
E945.4   Antitussives (e.g., dextromethorphan)
E945.8   Other respiratory drugs
E945.0   Oxytocic agents (ergot alkaloids, prostaglandins)

E945.2   Skeletal muscle relaxants
E945.1   Smooth muscle relaxants (metaproterenol)

Hormones and Synthetic Substitutes

E932.0   Adrenal cortical steroids
E932.1   Anabolic steroids and androgens
E932.8   Antithyroid agents
E932.2   Ovarian hormones (includes oral contraceptives)
E932.7   Thyroid replacements

Diuretics and Mineral and Uric Acid Metabolism Drugs

E944.2   Carbonic acid anhydrase inhibitors
E944.3   Chlorthiazides
E944.0   Mercurial diuretics
E944.4   Other diuretics (furosemide, ethacrynic acid)
E944.1   Purine derivative diuretics
E944.7   Uric acid metabolism drugs (probenecid)

Appendix H

DSM-IV Classification With ICD-10 Codes

As of the publication of this manual (in early 1994), the official coding system in use in the United States is the *International Classification of Diseases,* Ninth Revision, Clinical Modification (ICD-9-CM). At some point within the next several years, the U.S. Department of Health and Human Services will require for reporting purposes in the United States the use of codes from the *International Statistical Classification of Diseases and Related Health Problems,* Tenth Revision (ICD-10). To facilitate this transition process, the preparation of DSM-IV has been closely coordinated with the preparation of Chapter V, "Mental and Behavioural Disorders," of ICD-10 (developed by the World Health Organization). Consultations between the American Psychiatric Association and the World Health Organization have resulted in DSM-IV codes and terms that are fully compatible with the codes and terms in the tabular index of ICD-10. Presented below is the DSM-IV Classification with the ICD-10 codes.

NOS = Not Otherwise Specified.

An *x* appearing in a diagnostic code indicates that a specific code number is required.

An ellipsis (. . .) is used in the names of certain disorders to indicate that the name of a specific mental disorder or general medical condition should be inserted when recording the name (e.g., F05.0 Delirium Due to Hypothyroidism).

Numbers in parentheses are page numbers.

If criteria are currently met, one of the following severity specifiers may be noted after the diagnosis:
   Mild
   Moderate
   Severe

If criteria are no longer met, one of the following specifiers may be noted:
   In Partial Remission
   In Full Remission
   Prior History

Disorders Usually First Diagnosed in Infancy, Childhood, or Adolescence (37)

MENTAL RETARDATION (39)
Note: *These are coded on Axis II.*
F70.9   Mild Mental Retardation (41)
F71.9   Moderate Mental Retardation (41)
F72.9   Severe Mental Retardation (41)
F73.9   Profound Mental Retardation (41)
F79.9   Mental Retardation, Severity
         Unspecified (42)

LEARNING DISORDERS (46)
F81.0   Reading Disorder (48)
F81.2   Mathematics Disorder (50)
F81.8   Disorder of Written Expression (51)
F81.9   Learning Disorder NOS (53)

MOTOR SKILLS DISORDER
F82   Developmental Coordination
         Disorder (53)

COMMUNICATION DISORDERS (55)
F80.1   Expressive Language Disorder (55)
F80.2   Mixed Receptive-Expressive
         Language Disorder (58)
F80.0   Phonological Disorder (61)
F98.5   Stuttering (63)
F80.9   Communication Disorder NOS (65)

**PERVASIVE DEVELOPMENTAL
DISORDERS** (65)
F84.0   Autistic Disorder (66)
F84.2   Rett's Disorder (71)
F84.3   Childhood Disintegrative
         Disorder (73)
F84.5   Asperger's Disorder (75)
F84.9   Pervasive Developmental
         Disorder NOS (77)

**ATTENTION-DEFICIT AND
DISRUPTIVE BEHAVIOR
DISORDERS** (78)
——.–   Attention-Deficit/Hyperactivity
         Disorder (78)
F90.0   Combined Type
F98.8   Predominantly Inattentive
            Type
F90.0   Predominantly Hyperactive-
            Impulsive Type

F90.9   Attention-Deficit/Hyperactivity
         Disorder NOS (85)
F91.8   Conduct Disorder (85)
         Specify type: Childhood-Onset Type/
         Adolescent-Onset Type
F91.3   Oppositional Defiant Disorder (91)
F91.9   Disruptive Behavior Disorder
         NOS (94)

**FEEDING AND EATING DISORDERS
OF INFANCY OR EARLY
CHILDHOOD** (94)
F98.3   Pica (95)
F98.2   Rumination Disorder (96)
F98.2   Feeding Disorder of Infancy or
         Early Childhood (98)

TIC DISORDERS (100)
F95.2   Tourette's Disorder (101)
F95.1   Chronic Motor or Vocal Tic
         Disorder (103)
F95.0   Transient Tic Disorder (104)
         Specify if: Single Episode/Recurrent
F95.9   Tic Disorder NOS (105)

ELIMINATION DISORDERS (106)
——.–   Encopresis (106)
R15   With Constipation and
            Overflow Incontinence (*also
            code K59.0 constipation on
            Axis III*)
F98.1   Without Constipation and
            Overflow Incontinence
F98.0   Enuresis (Not Due to a General
         Medical Condition) (108)
         Specify type: Nocturnal Only/Diurnal
         Only/Nocturnal and Diurnal

**OTHER DISORDERS OF INFANCY,
CHILDHOOD, OR ADOLESCENCE**
F93.0   Separation Anxiety Disorder (110)
         Specify if: Early Onset
F94.0   Selective Mutism (114)
F94.x   Reactive Attachment Disorder of
         Infancy or Early Childhood (116)
   .1   Inhibited Type
   .2   Disinhibited Type
F98.4   Stereotypic Movement Disorder (118)
         Specify if: With Self-Injurious Behavior

F98.9   Disorder of Infancy, Childhood,
         or Adolescence NOS (121)

Delirium, Dementia, and Amnestic and Other Cognitive Disorders (123)

DELIRIUM (124)

F05.0   Delirium Due to . . . *[Indicate the General Medical Condition] (code F05.1 if superimposed on Dementia)* (127)

——.—   Substance Intoxication Delirium *(refer to Substance-Related Disorders for substance-specific codes)* (129)

——.—   Substance Withdrawal Delirium *(refer to Substance-Related Disorders for substance-specific codes)* (129)

——.—   Delirium Due to Multiple Etiologies *(code each of the specific etiologies)* (132)

F05.9   Delirium NOS (133)

DEMENTIA (133)

F00.xx   Dementia of the Alzheimer's Type, With Early Onset *(also code G30.0 Alzheimer's Disease, With Early Onset, on Axis III)* (139)

.00   Uncomplicated
.01   With Delusions
.03   With Depressed Mood
         Specify if: With Behavioral Disturbance

F00.xx   Dementia of the Alzheimer's Type, With Late Onset *(also code G30.1 Alzheimer's Disease, With Late Onset, on Axis III)* (139)

.10   Uncomplicated
.11   With Delusions
.13   With Depressed Mood
         Specify if: With Behavioral Disturbance

F01.xx   Vascular Dementia (143)
.80   Uncomplicated
.81   With Delusions
.83   With Depressed Mood
         Specify if: With Behavioral Disturbance

F02.4   Dementia Due to HIV Disease *(also code B22.0 HIV disease resulting in encephalopathy on Axis III)* (148)

F02.8   Dementia Due to Head Trauma *(also code S06.9 Intracranial injury on Axis III)* (148)

F02.3   Dementia Due to Parkinson's Disease *(also code G20 Parkinson's disease on Axis III)* (148)

F02.2   Dementia Due to Huntington's Disease *(also code G10 Huntington's disease on Axis III)* (149)

F02.0   Dementia Due to Pick's Disease *(also code G31.0 Pick's disease on Axis III)* (149)

F02.1   Dementia Due to Creutzfeldt-Jakob Disease *(also code A81.0 Creutzfeldt-Jakob disease on Axis III)* (150)

F02.8   Dementia Due to . . . *[Indicate the General Medical Condition not listed above] (also code the general medical condition on Axis III)* (151)

——.—   Substance-Induced Persisting Dementia *(refer to Substance-Related Disorders for substance-specific codes)* (152)

F02.8   Dementia Due to Multiple Etiologies *(instead code F00.2 for mixed Alzheimer's and Vascular Dementia)* (154)

F03   Dementia NOS (155)

AMNESTIC DISORDERS (156)

F04   Amnestic Disorder Due to . . . *[Indicate the General Medical Condition]* (158)
        Specify if: Transient/Chronic

——.—   Substance-Induced Persisting Amnestic Disorder *(refer to Substance-Related Disorders for substance-specific codes)* (161)

R41.3   Amnestic Disorder NOS (163)

OTHER COGNITIVE DISORDERS (163)

F06.9   Cognitive Disorder NOS (163)

Mental Disorders Due to a General Medical Condition Not Elsewhere Classified (165)

F06.1   Catatonic Disorder Due to . . . *[Indicate the General Medical Condition]* (169)

F07.0   Personality Change Due to . . . *[Indicate the General Medical Condition]* (171)
 Specify type: Labile Type/Disinhibited Type/Aggressive Type/Apathetic Type/ Paranoid Type/Other Type/Combined Type/Unspecified Type

F09   Mental Disorder NOS Due to . . . *[Indicate the General Medical Condition]* (174)

Substance-Related Disorders (175)

[a] *The following specifiers may be applied to Substance Dependence:*
 Specify if: With Physiological Dependence/ Without Physiological Dependence

Code course of Dependence in fifth character:
 0 = Early Full Remission/Early Partial Remission
 0 = Sustained Full Remission/Sustained Partial Remission
 1 = In a Controlled Environment
 2 = On Agonist Therapy
 4 = Mild/Moderate/Severe

The following specifiers apply to Substance-Induced Disorders as noted:
 [I]With Onset During Intoxication/[W]With Onset During Withdrawal

ALCOHOL-RELATED DISORDERS (194)

Alcohol Use Disorders

F10.2x   Alcohol Dependence[a] (195)

F10.1   Alcohol Abuse (196)

Alcohol-Induced Disorders

F10.00   Alcohol Intoxication (196)

F10.3   Alcohol Withdrawal (197)
 Specify if: With Perceptual Disturbances

F10.03   Alcohol Intoxication Delirium (129)

F10.4   Alcohol Withdrawal Delirium (129)

F10.73   Alcohol-Induced Persisting Dementia (152)

F10.6   Alcohol-Induced Persisting Amnestic Disorder (161)

F10.xx   Alcohol-Induced Psychotic Disorder (310)
 .51   With Delusions[I,W]
 .52   With Hallucinations[I,W]

F10.8   Alcohol-Induced Mood Disorder[I,W] (370)

F10.8   Alcohol-Induced Anxiety Disorder[I,W] (439)

F10.8   Alcohol-Induced Sexual Dysfunction[I] (519)

F10.8   Alcohol-Induced Sleep Disorder[I,W] (601)

F10.9   Alcohol-Related Disorder NOS (204)

AMPHETAMINE (OR AMPHETAMINE-LIKE)– RELATED DISORDERS (204)

Amphetamine Use Disorders

F15.2x   Amphetamine Dependence[a] (206)

F15.1   Amphetamine Abuse (206)

Amphetamine-Induced Disorders

F15.00   Amphetamine Intoxication (207)

F15.04   Amphetamine Intoxication, With Perceptual Disturbances (207)

F15.3   Amphetamine Withdrawal (208)

F15.03   Amphetamine Intoxication Delirium (129)

F15.xx   Amphetamine-Induced Psychotic Disorder (310)
 .51   With Delusions[I]
 .52   With Hallucinations[I]

F15.8   Amphetamine-Induced Mood Disorder[I,W] (370)

F15.8   Amphetamine-Induced Anxiety Disorder[I] (439)

F15.8   Amphetamine-Induced Sexual Dysfunction[I] (519)

F15.8   Amphetamine-Induced Sleep Disorder[I,W] (601)

F15.9   Amphetamine-Related Disorder NOS (211)

CAFFEINE-RELATED DISORDERS (212)

Caffeine-Induced Disorders

F15.00   Caffeine Intoxication (212)
F15.8   Caffeine-Induced Anxiety Disorder[I] (439)
F15.8   Caffeine-Induced Sleep Disorder[I] (601)

F15.9   Caffeine-Related Disorder NOS (215)

CANNABIS-RELATED DISORDERS (215)

Cannabis Use Disorders

F12.2x   Cannabis Dependence[a] (216)
F12.1   Cannabis Abuse (217)

Cannabis-Induced Disorders

F12.00   Cannabis Intoxication (217)
F12.04   Cannabis Intoxication, With Perceptual Disturbances (217)
F12.03   Cannabis Intoxication Delirium (129)
F12.xx   Cannabis-Induced Psychotic Disorder (310)
   .51   With Delusions[I]
   .52   With Hallucinations[I]
F12.8   Cannabis-Induced Anxiety Disorder[I] (439)

F12.9   Cannabis-Related Disorder NOS (221)

COCAINE-RELATED DISORDERS (221)

Cocaine Use Disorders

F14.2x   Cocaine Dependence[a] (222)
F14.1   Cocaine Abuse (223)

Cocaine-Induced Disorders

F14.00   Cocaine Intoxication (223)
F14.04   Cocaine Intoxication, With Perceptual Disturbances (223)
F14.3   Cocaine Withdrawal (225)
F14.03   Cocaine Intoxication Delirium (129)
F14.xx   Cocaine-Induced Psychotic Disorder (310)
   .51   With Delusions[I]
   .52   With Hallucinations[I]

F14.8   Cocaine-Induced Mood Disorder[I,W] (370)
F14.8   Cocaine-Induced Anxiety Disorder[I,W] (439)
F14.8   Cocaine-Induced Sexual Dysfunction[I] (519)
F14.8   Cocaine-Induced Sleep Disorder[I,W] (601)

F14.9   Cocaine-Related Disorder NOS (229)

HALLUCINOGEN-RELATED DISORDERS (229)

Hallucinogen Use Disorders

F16.2x   Hallucinogen Dependence[a] (230)
F16.1   Hallucinogen Abuse (231)

Hallucinogen-Induced Disorders

F16.00   Hallucinogen Intoxication (232)
F16.70   Hallucinogen Persisting Perception Disorder (Flashbacks) (233)
F16.03   Hallucinogen Intoxication Delirium (129)
F16.xx   Hallucinogen-Induced Psychotic Disorder (310)
   .51   With Delusions[I]
   .52   With Hallucinations[I]
F16.8   Hallucinogen-Induced Mood Disorder[I] (370)
F16.8   Hallucinogen-Induced Anxiety Disorder[I] (439)

F16.9   Hallucinogen-Related Disorder NOS (236)

INHALANT-RELATED DISORDERS (236)

Inhalant Use Disorders

F18.2x   Inhalant Dependence[a] (238)
F18.1   Inhalant Abuse (238)

Inhalant-Induced Disorders

F18.00   Inhalant Intoxication (239)
F18.03   Inhalant Intoxication Delirium (129)
F18.73   Inhalant-Induced Persisting Dementia (152)
F18.xx   Inhalant-Induced Psychotic Disorder (310)
   .51   With Delusions[I]
   .52   With Hallucinations[I]

F13.8   Sedative-, Hypnotic-, or Anxiolytic-Induced Mood Disorder[I,W] (370)

F13.8   Sedative-, Hypnotic-, or Anxiolytic-Induced Anxiety Disorder[W] (439)

F13.8   Sedative-, Hypnotic-, or Anxiolytic-Induced Sexual Dysfunction[I] (519)

F13.8   Sedative-, Hypnotic-, or Anxiolytic-Induced Sleep Disorder[I,W] (601)

F13.9   Sedative-, Hypnotic-, or Anxiolytic-Related Disorder NOS (269)

POLYSUBSTANCE-RELATED DISORDER

F19.2x   Polysubstance Dependence[a] (270)

OTHER (OR UNKNOWN) SUBSTANCE–RELATED DISORDERS (270)

Other (or Unknown) Substance Use Disorders

F19.2x   Other (or Unknown) Substance Dependence[a] (176)

F19.1   Other (or Unknown) Substance Abuse (182)

Other (or Unknown) Substance–Induced Disorders

F19.00   Other (or Unknown) Substance Intoxication (183)

F19.04   Other (or Unknown) Substance Intoxication, With Perceptual Disturbances (183)

F19.3   Other (or Unknown) Substance Withdrawal (184)
Specify if: With Perceptual Disturbances

F19.03   Other (or Unknown) Substance–Induced Delirium *(code F19.4 if onset during withdrawal)* (129)

F19.73   Other (or Unknown) Substance–Induced Persisting Dementia (152)

F19.6   Other (or Unknown) Substance–Induced Persisting Amnestic Disorder (161)

F19.xx   Other (or Unknown) Substance–Induced Psychotic Disorder (310)
.51   With Delusions[I,W]
.52   With Hallucinations[I,W]

F19.8   Other (or Unknown) Substance–Induced Mood Disorder[I,W] (370)

F19.8   Other (or Unknown) Substance– Induced Anxiety Disorder[I,W] (439)

F19.8   Other (or Unknown) Substance–Induced Sexual Dysfunction[I] (519)

F19.8   Other (or Unknown) Substance–Induced Sleep Disorder[I,W] (601)

F19.9   Other (or Unknown) Substance–Related Disorder NOS (272)

Schizophrenia and Other Psychotic Disorders (273)

F20.xx   Schizophrenia (274)
.0x   Paranoid Type (287)
.1x   Disorganized Type (287)
.2x   Catatonic Type (288)
.3x   Undifferentiated Type (289)
.5x   Residual Type (289)

Code course of Schizophrenia in fifth character:

2 = Episodic With Interepisode Residual Symptoms (*specify if:* With Prominent Negative Symptoms)
3 = Episodic With No Interepisode Residual Symptoms
0 = Continuous (*specify if:* With Prominent Negative Symptoms)
4 = Single Episode In Partial Remission (*specify if:* With Prominent Negative Symptoms)
5 = Single Episode In Full Remission
8 = Other or Unspecified Pattern
9 = Less than 1 year since onset of initial active-phase symptoms

F20.8   Schizophreniform Disorder (290)
Specify if: Without Good Prognostic Features/With Good Prognostic Features

F25.x   Schizoaffective Disorder (292)
.0   Bipolar Type
.1   Depressive Type

F22.0   Delusional Disorder (296)
Specify type: Erotomanic Type/Grandiose Type/Jealous Type/Persecutory Type/Somatic Type/Mixed Type/Unspecified Type

F23.xx   Brief Psychotic Disorder (302)
 .81   With Marked Stressor(s)
 .80   Without Marked Stressor(s)
Specify if: With Postpartum Onset

F24   Shared Psychotic Disorder (305)

F06.x   Psychotic Disorder Due to . . . *[Indicate the General Medical Condition]* (306)
 .2   With Delusions
 .0   With Hallucinations

——.–   Substance-Induced Psychotic Disorder *(refer to Substance-Related Disorders for substance-specific codes)* (310)
Specify if: With Onset During Intoxication/With Onset During Withdrawal

F29   Psychotic Disorder NOS (315)

Mood Disorders (317)

The following specifiers apply (for current or most recent episode) to Mood Disorders as noted:

[a]Severity/Psychotic/Remission Specifiers/[b]Chronic/[c]With Catatonic Features/[d]With Melancholic Features/[e]With Atypical Features/[f]With Postpartum Onset

The following specifiers apply to Mood Disorders as noted:

[g]With or Without Full Interepisode Recovery/[h]With Seasonal Pattern/[i]With Rapid Cycling

DEPRESSIVE DISORDERS (339)

F32.x   Major Depressive Disorder, Single Episode[a,b,c,d,e,f] (339)

F33.x   Major Depressive Disorder, Recurrent[a,b,c,d,e,f,g,h] (339)

Code current state of Major Depressive Episode in fourth character:

 0 = Mild
 1 = Moderate
 2 = Severe Without Psychotic Features

 3 = Severe With Psychotic Features
   Specify: Mood-Congruent Psychotic Features/Mood-Incongruent Psychotic Features
 4 = In Partial Remission
 4 = In Full Remission
 9 = Unspecified

F34.1   Dysthymic Disorder (345)
Specify if: Early Onset/Late Onset
Specify: With Atypical Features

F32.9   Depressive Disorder NOS (350)

BIPOLAR DISORDERS (350)

F30.x   Bipolar I Disorder, Single Manic Episode[a,c,f] (350)
Specify if: Mixed

Code current state of Manic Episode in fourth character:

 1 = Mild, Moderate, or Severe Without Psychotic Features
 2 = Severe With Psychotic Features
 8 = In Partial or Full Remission

F31.0   Bipolar I Disorder, Most Recent Episode Hypomanic[g,h,i] (350)

F31.x   Bipolar I Disorder, Most Recent Episode Manic[a,c,f,g,h,i] (350)

Code current state of Manic Episode in fourth character:

 1 = Mild, Moderate, or Severe Without Psychotic Features
 2 = Severe With Psychotic Features
 7 = In Partial or Full Remission

F31.6   Bipolar I Disorder, Most Recent Episode Mixed[a,c,f,g,h,i] (350)

F31.x   Bipolar I Disorder, Most Recent Episode Depressed[a,b,c,d,e,f,g,h,i] (350)

Code current state of Major Depressive Episode in fourth character:

 3 = Mild or Moderate
 4 = Severe Without Psychotic Features
 5 = Severe With Psychotic Features
 7 = In Partial or Full Remission

F31.9   Bipolar I Disorder, Most Recent Episode Unspecified[g,h,i] (350)

F31.8   Bipolar II Disorder[a,b,c,d,e,f,g,h,i] (359)
Specify (current or most recent episode): Hypomanic/Depressed

F34.0   Cyclothymic Disorder (363)

F31.9 Bipolar Disorder NOS (366)

F06.xx Mood Disorder Due to . . .
   *[Indicate the General Medical
   Condition]* (366)
   .32 With Depressive Features
   .32 With Major Depressive–Like
   Episode
   .30 With Manic Features
   .33 With Mixed Features
——.– Substance-Induced Mood Disorder
   *(refer to Substance-Related
   Disorders for substance-specific
   codes)* (370)
   Specify type: With Depressive Features/
   With Manic Features/With Mixed
   Features
   Specify if: With Onset During
   Intoxication/With Onset During
   Withdrawal

F39 Mood Disorder NOS (375)

Anxiety Disorders (393)

F41.0 Panic Disorder Without
   Agoraphobia (397)
F40.01 Panic Disorder With
   Agoraphobia (397)
F40.00 Agoraphobia Without History of
   Panic Disorder (403)
F40.2 Specific Phobia (405)
   Specify type: Animal Type/Natural
   Environment Type/Blood-Injection-
   Injury Type/Situational Type/Other Type
F40.1 Social Phobia (411)
   Specify if: Generalized
F42.8 Obsessive-Compulsive
   Disorder (417)
   Specify if: With Poor Insight
F43.1 Posttraumatic Stress Disorder (424)
   Specify if: Acute/Chronic
   Specify if: With Delayed Onset
F43.0 Acute Stress Disorder (429)
F41.1 Generalized Anxiety Disorder (432)
F06.4 Anxiety Disorder Due to . . .
   *[Indicate the General Medical
   Condition]* (436)
   Specify if: With Generalized Anxiety/
   With Panic Attacks/With Obsessive-
   Compulsive Symptoms

——.– Substance-Induced Anxiety
   Disorder *(refer to Substance-
   Related Disorders for substance-
   specific codes)* (439)
   Specify if: With Generalized
   Anxiety/With Panic Attacks/With
   Obsessive-Compulsive Symptoms/With
   Phobic Symptoms
   Specify if: With Onset During
   Intoxication/With Onset During
   Withdrawal
F41.9 Anxiety Disorder NOS (444)

Somatoform Disorders (445)

F45.0 Somatization Disorder (446)
F45.1 Undifferentiated Somatoform
   Disorder (450)
F44.x Conversion Disorder (452)
   .4 With Motor Symptom or
   Deficit
   .5 With Seizures or Convulsions
   .6 With Sensory Symptom or
   Deficit
   .7 With Mixed Presentation
F45.4 Pain Disorder (458)
   Specify type: Associated With
   Psychological Factors/Associated With
   Both Psychological Factors and a
   General Medical Condition
   Specify if: Acute/Chronic
F45.2 Hypochondriasis (462)
   Specify if: With Poor Insight
F45.2 Body Dysmorphic Disorder (466)
F45.9 Somatoform Disorder NOS (468)

Factitious Disorders (471)

F68.1 Factitious Disorder (471)
   Specify type: With Predominantly
   Psychological Signs and Symptoms/
   With Predominantly Physical Signs and
   Symptoms/With Combined
   Psychological and Physical Signs and
   Symptoms
F68.1 Factitious Disorder NOS (475)

Dissociative Disorders (477)

F44.0 Dissociative Amnesia (478)
F44.1 Dissociative Fugue (481)
F44.81 Dissociative Identity Disorder (484)

Eating Disorders (539)

F50.0   Anorexia Nervosa (539)
Specify type: Restricting Type;
Binge-Eating/Purging Type
F50.2   Bulimia Nervosa (545)
Specify type: Purging Type/
Nonpurging Type
F50.9   Eating Disorder NOS (550)

Sleep Disorders (551)

PRIMARY SLEEP DISORDERS (553)

Dyssomnias (553)
F51.0   Primary Insomnia (553)
F51.1   Primary Hypersomnia (557)
Specify if: Recurrent
G47.4   Narcolepsy (562)
G47.3   Breathing-Related Sleep
Disorder (567)
F51.2   Circadian Rhythm Sleep
Disorder (573)
Specify type: Delayed Sleep Phase
Type/Jet Lag Type/Shift Work Type/
Unspecified Type
F51.9   Dyssomnia NOS (579)

Parasomnias (579)
F51.5   Nightmare Disorder (580)
F51.4   Sleep Terror Disorder (583)
F51.3   Sleepwalking Disorder (587)
F51.8   Parasomnia NOS (592)

**SLEEP DISORDERS RELATED TO
ANOTHER MENTAL DISORDER** (592)
F51.0   Insomnia Related to . . .
*[Indicate the Axis I or Axis II
Disorder]* (592)
F51.1   Hypersomnia Related to . . .
*[Indicate the Axis I or Axis II
Disorder]* (592)

OTHER SLEEP DISORDERS
G47.x   Sleep Disorder Due to . . .
*[Indicate the General Medical
Condition]* (597)
   .0   Insomnia Type
   .1   Hypersomnia Type
   .8   Parasomnia Type
   .8   Mixed Type

——.–   Substance-Induced Sleep Disorder
*(refer to Substance-Related
Disorders for substance-specific
codes)* (601)
Specify type: Insomnia Type/
Hypersomnia Type/Parasomnia Type/
Mixed Type
Specify if: With Onset During
Intoxication/With Onset During
Withdrawal

Impulse-Control Disorders Not Elsewhere Classified (609)

F63.8   Intermittent Explosive
Disorder (609)
F63.2   Kleptomania (612)
F63.1   Pyromania (614)
F63.0   Pathological Gambling (615)
F63.3   Trichotillomania (618)
F63.9   Impulse-Control Disorder
NOS (621)

Adjustment Disorders (623)

F43.xx   Adjustment Disorder (623)
   .20   With Depressed Mood
   .28   With Anxiety
   .22   With Mixed Anxiety and
Depressed Mood
   .24   With Disturbance of Conduct
   .25   With Mixed Disturbance of
Emotions and Conduct
   .9   Unspecified
Specify if: Acute/Chronic

Personality Disorders (629)

Note: *These are coded on Axis II.*
F60.0   Paranoid Personality Disorder (634)
F60.1   Schizoid Personality Disorder (638)
F21   Schizotypal Personality
Disorder (641)
F60.2   Antisocial Personality Disorder (645)
F60.31   Borderline Personality
Disorder (650)
F60.4   Histrionic Personality Disorder (655)
F60.8   Narcissistic Personality
Disorder (658)

F60.6   Avoidant Personality Disorder (662)
F60.7   Dependent Personality
         Disorder (665)
F60.5   Obsessive-Compulsive Personality
         Disorder (669)
F60.9   Personality Disorder NOS (673)

Other Conditions That May Be a Focus of Clinical Attention (675)

PSYCHOLOGICAL FACTORS AFFECTING MEDICAL CONDITION (675)

F54   *. . . [Specified Psychological Factor] Affecting . . . [Indicate the General Medical Condition]* (675)
       Choose name based on nature of factors:
       Mental Disorder Affecting Medical
           Condition
       Psychological Symptoms Affecting
           Medical Condition
       Personality Traits or Coping Style
           Affecting Medical Condition
       Maladaptive Health Behaviors
           Affecting Medical Condition
       Stress-Related Physiological
           Response Affecting Medical
           Condition
       Other or Unspecified
           Psychological Factors
           Affecting Medical Condition

MEDICATION-INDUCED MOVEMENT DISORDERS (678)

G21.0   Neuroleptic-Induced
         Parkinsonism (679)
G21.0   Neuroleptic Malignant
         Syndrome (679)
G24.0   Neuroleptic-Induced Acute
         Dystonia (679)
G21.1   Neuroleptic-Induced Acute
         Akathisia (679)
G24.0   Neuroleptic-Induced Tardive
         Dyskinesia (679)

G25.1   Medication-Induced Postural
         Tremor (680)
G25.9   Medication-Induced Movement
         Disorder NOS (680)

OTHER MEDICATION-INDUCED DISORDER

T88.7   Adverse Effects of Medication
         NOS (680)

RELATIONAL PROBLEMS (680)

Z63.7   Relational Problem Related to a
         Mental Disorder or General
         Medical Condition (681)
Z63.8   Parent-Child Relational Problem
         *(code Z63.1 if focus of attention
         is on child)* (681)
Z63.0   Partner Relational Problem (681)
F93.3   Sibling Relational Problem (681)
Z63.9   Relational Problem NOS (681)

PROBLEMS RELATED TO ABUSE OR NEGLECT (682)

T74.1   Physical Abuse of Child (682)
T74.2   Sexual Abuse of Child (682)
T74.0   Neglect of Child (682)
T74.1   Physical Abuse of Adult (682)
T74.2   Sexual Abuse of Adult (682)

ADDITIONAL CONDITIONS THAT MAY BE A FOCUS OF CLINICAL ATTENTION (683)

Z91.1   Noncompliance With
         Treatment (683)
Z76.5   Malingering (683)
Z72.8   Adult Antisocial Behavior (683)
Z72.8   Child or Adolescent Antisocial
         Behavior (684)
R41.8   Borderline Intellectual
         Functioning (684)
R41.8   Age-Related Cognitive
         Decline (684)
Z63.4   Bereavement (684)
Z55.8   Academic Problem (685)
Z56.7   Occupational Problem (685)
F93.8   Identity Problem (685)
Z71.8   Religious or Spiritual Problem (685)
Z60.3   Acculturation Problem (685)
Z60.0   Phase of Life Problem (685)

Additional Codes

F99   Unspecified Mental Disorder
(nonpsychotic) (687)
Z03.2   No Diagnosis or Condition on
Axis I (687)

R69   Diagnosis or Condition Deferred
on Axis I (687)
Z03.2   No Diagnosis on Axis II (687)
R46.8   Diagnosis Deferred on Axis II (687)

Appendix I

Outline for Cultural Formulation and Glossary of Culture-Bound Syndromes

This appendix is divided into two sections. The first section provides an outline for cultural formulation designed to assist the clinician in systematically evaluating and reporting the impact of the individual's cultural context. The second is a glossary of culture-bound syndromes.

Outline for Cultural Formulation

The following outline for cultural formulation is meant to supplement the multiaxial diagnostic assessment and to address difficulties that may be encountered in applying DSM-IV criteria in a multicultural environment. The cultural formulation provides a systematic review of the individual's cultural background, the role of the cultural context in the expression and evaluation of symptoms and dysfunction, and the effect that cultural differences may have on the relationship between the individual and the clinician.

As indicated in the introduction to the manual (see p. xxiv), it is important that the clinician take into account the individual's ethnic and cultural context in the evaluation of each of the DSM-IV axes. In addition, the cultural formulation suggested below provides an opportunity to describe systematically the individual's cultural and social reference group and ways in which the cultural context is relevant to clinical care. The clinician may provide a narrative summary for each of the following categories:

Cultural identity of the individual.   Note the individual's ethnic or cultural reference groups. For immigrants and ethnic minorities, note separately the degree of involvement with both the culture of origin and the host culture (where applicable). Also note language abilities, use, and preference (including multilingualism).

Cultural explanations of the individual's illness.   The following may be identified: the predominant idioms of distress through which symptoms or the need for social support are communicated (e.g., "nerves," possessing spirits, somatic complaints, inexplicable misfortune), the meaning and perceived severity of the individual's symptoms in relation to norms of the cultural reference group, any local illness category used by the individual's family and community to identify the condition (see "Glossary of Culture-Bound Syndromes" below), the perceived causes or explanatory models that the individual and the reference group use to explain the illness, and current preferences for and past experiences with professional and popular sources of care.

Cultural factors related to psychosocial environment and levels of functioning. Note culturally relevant interpretations of social stressors, available social supports, and levels of functioning and disability. This would include stresses in the local social environment and the role of religion and kin networks in providing emotional, instrumental, and informational support.

Cultural elements of the relationship between the individual and the clinician. Indicate differences in culture and social status between the individual and the clinician and problems that these differences may cause in diagnosis and treatment (e.g., difficulty in communicating in the individual's first language, in eliciting symptoms or understanding their cultural significance, in negotiating an appropriate relationship or level of intimacy, in determining whether a behavior is normative or pathological).

Overall cultural assessment for diagnosis and care.   The formulation concludes with a discussion of how cultural considerations specifically influence comprehensive diagnosis and care.

Glossary of Culture-Bound Syndromes

The term *culture-bound syndrome* denotes recurrent, locality-specific patterns of aberrant behavior and troubling experience that may or may not be linked to a particular DSM-IV diagnostic category. Many of these patterns are indigenously considered to be "illnesses," or at least afflictions, and most have local names. Although presentations conforming to the major DSM-IV categories can be found throughout the world, the particular symptoms, course, and social response are very often influenced by local cultural factors. In contrast, culture-bound syndromes are generally limited to specific societies or culture areas and are localized, folk, diagnostic categories that frame coherent meanings for certain repetitive, patterned, and troubling sets of experiences and observations.

There is seldom a one-to-one equivalence of any culture-bound syndrome with a DSM diagnostic entity. Aberrant behavior that might be sorted by a diagnostician using DSM-IV into several categories may be included in a single folk category, and presentations that might be considered by a diagnostician using DSM-IV as belonging to a single category may be sorted into several by an indigenous clinician. Moreover, some conditions and disorders have been conceptualized as culture-bound syndromes specific to industrialized culture (e.g., Anorexia Nervosa, Dissociative Identity Disorder) given their apparent rarity or absence in other cultures. It should also be noted that all industrialized societies include distinctive subcultures and widely diverse immigrant groups who may present with culture-bound syndromes.

This glossary lists some of the best-studied culture-bound syndromes and idioms of distress that may be encountered in clinical practice in North America and includes relevant DSM-IV categories when data suggest that they should be considered in a diagnostic formulation.

amok   A dissociative episode characterized by a period of brooding followed by an outburst of violent, aggressive, or homicidal behavior directed at people and objects. The episode tends to be precipitated by a perceived slight or insult and seems to be prevalent only among males. The episode is often accompanied by persecutory ideas, automatism, amnesia, exhaustion, and a return to premorbid state following the episode. Some instances of amok may occur during a brief psychotic episode or constitute the onset or an exacerbation of a chronic psychotic process. The original reports that used this term were from Malaysia. A similar behavior pattern is found in Laos, Philippines, Polynesia (*cafard* or *cathard*), Papua New Guinea, and Puerto Rico (*mal de pelea*), and among the Navajo (*iich'aa*).

ataque de nervios   An idiom of distress principally reported among Latinos from the Caribbean, but recognized among many Latin American and Latin Mediterranean groups. Commonly reported symptoms include uncontrollable shouting, attacks of crying, trembling, heat in the chest rising into the head, and verbal or physical aggression. Dissociative experiences, seizurelike or fainting episodes, and suicidal gestures are prominent in some attacks but absent in others. A general feature of an ataque de nervios is a sense of being out of control. Ataques de nervios frequently occur as a direct result of a stressful event relating to the family (e.g., news of the death of a close relative, a separation or divorce from a spouse, conflicts with a spouse or children, or witnessing an accident involving a family member). People may experience amnesia for what occurred during the ataque de nervios, but they otherwise return rapidly to their usual level of functioning. Although descriptions of some ataques de nervios most closely fit with the DSM-IV description of Panic Attacks, the association of most ataques with a precipitating event and the frequent absence of the hallmark symptoms of acute fear or apprehension distinguish them from Panic Disorder. Ataques span the range from normal expressions of distress not associated with having a mental disorder to symptom presentations associated with the diagnoses of Anxiety, Mood, Dissociative, or Somatoform Disorders.

bilis and **colera** (also referred to as *muina*)   The underlying cause of these syndromes is thought to be strongly experienced anger or rage. Anger is viewed among many Latino groups as a particularly powerful emotion that can have direct effects on the body and can exacerbate existing symptoms. The major effect of anger is to disturb core body balances (which are understood as a balance between hot and cold valences in the body and between the material and spiritual aspects of the body). Symptoms can include acute nervous tension, headache, trembling, screaming, stomach disturbances, and, in more severe cases, loss of consciousness. Chronic fatigue may result from the acute episode.

bouffée delirante   A syndrome observed in West Africa and Haiti. This French term refers to a sudden outburst of agitated and aggressive behavior, marked confusion, and psychomotor excitement. It may sometimes be accompanied by visual and auditory hallucinations or paranoid ideation. These episodes may resemble an episode of Brief Psychotic Disorder.

brain fag A term initially used in West Africa to refer to a condition experienced by high school or university students in response to the challenges of schooling. Symptoms include difficulties in concentrating, remembering, and thinking. Students often state that their brains are "fatigued." Additional somatic symptoms are usually centered around the head and neck and include pain, pressure or tightness, blurring of vision, heat, or burning. "Brain tiredness" or fatigue from "too much thinking" is an idiom of distress in many cultures, and resulting syndromes can resemble certain Anxiety, Depressive, and Somatoform Disorders.

dhat A folk diagnostic term used in India to refer to severe anxiety and hypochondriacal concerns associated with the discharge of semen, whitish discoloration of the urine, and feelings of weakness and exhaustion. Similar to *jiryan* (India), *sukra prameha* (Sri Lanka), and *shen-k'uei* (China).

falling-out or **blacking out** These episodes occur primarily in southern United States and Caribbean groups. They are characterized by a sudden collapse, which sometimes occurs without warning but sometimes is preceded by feelings of dizziness or "swimming" in the head. The individual's eyes are usually open but the person claims an inability to see. The person usually hears and understands what is occurring around him or her but feels powerless to move. This may correspond to a diagnosis of Conversion Disorder or a Dissociative Disorder.

ghost sickness A preoccupation with death and the deceased (sometimes associated with witchcraft) frequently observed among members of many American Indian tribes. Various symptoms can be attributed to ghost sickness, including bad dreams, weakness, feelings of danger, loss of appetite, fainting, dizziness, fear, anxiety, hallucinations, loss of consciousness, confusion, feelings of futility, and a sense of suffocation.

hwa-byung (also known as **wool-hwa-byung**) A Korean folk syndrome literally translated into English as "anger syndrome" and attributed to the suppression of anger. The symptoms include insomnia, fatigue, panic, fear of impending death, dysphoric affect, indigestion, anorexia, dyspnea, palpitations, generalized aches and pains, and a feeling of a mass in the epigastrium.

koro A term, probably of Malaysian origin, that refers to an episode of sudden and intense anxiety that the penis (or, in females, the vulva and nipples) will recede into the body and possibly cause death. The syndrome is reported in south and east Asia, where it is known by a variety of local terms, such as *shuk yang, shook yong,* and *suo yang* (Chinese); *jinjinia bemar* (Assam); or *rok-joo* (Thailand). It is occasionally found in the West. Koro at times occurs in localized epidemic form in east Asian areas. This diagnosis is included in the *Chinese Classification of Mental Disorders,* Second Edition (CCMD-2).

latah Hypersensitivity to sudden fright, often with echopraxia, echolalia, command obedience, and dissociative or trancelike behavior. The term *latah* is of Malaysian or Indonesian origin, but the syndrome has been found in many parts of the world. Other terms for this condition are *amurakh, irkunii, ikota, olan, myriachit,* and *menkeiti* (Siberian groups); *bah tschi, bah-tsi, baah-ji* (Thailand); *imu* (Ainu, Sakhalin, Japan); and *mali-mali* and *silok* (Philippines). In Malaysia it is more frequent in middle-aged women.

locura A term used by Latinos in the United States and Latin America to refer to a severe form of chronic psychosis. The condition is attributed to an inherited vulnerability, to the effect of multiple life difficulties, or to a combination of both factors. Symptoms exhibited by persons with locura include incoherence, agitation, auditory and visual hallucinations, inability to follow rules of social interaction, unpredictability, and possible violence.

mal de ojo A concept widely found in Mediterranean cultures and elsewhere in the world. *Mal de ojo* is a Spanish phrase translated into English as "evil eye." Children are especially at risk. Symptoms include fitful sleep, crying without apparent cause, diarrhea, vomiting, and fever in a child or infant. Sometimes adults (especially females) have the condition.

nervios A common idiom of distress among Latinos in the United States and Latin America. A number of other ethnic groups have related, though often somewhat distinctive, ideas of "nerves" (such as *nevra* among Greeks in North America). Nervios refers both to a general state of vulnerability to stressful life experiences and to a syndrome brought on by difficult life circumstances. The term *nervios* includes a wide range of symptoms of emotional distress, somatic disturbance, and inability to function. Common symptoms include headaches and "brain aches," irritability, stomach disturbances, sleep difficulties, nervousness, easy tearfulness, inability to concentrate, trembling, tingling sensations, and *mareos* (dizziness with occasional vertigo-like exacerbations). Nervios tends to be an ongoing problem, although variable in the degree of disability manifested. Nervios is a very broad syndrome that spans the range from cases free of a mental disorder to presentations resembling Adjustment, Anxiety, Depressive, Dissociative, Somatoform, or Psychotic Disorders. Differential diagnosis will depend on the constellation of symptoms experienced, the kind of social events that are associated with the onset and progress of nervios, and the level of disability experienced.

pibloktoq An abrupt dissociative episode accompanied by extreme excitement of up to 30 minutes' duration and frequently followed by convulsive seizures and coma lasting up to 12 hours. This is observed primarily in arctic and subarctic Eskimo communities, although regional variations in name exist. The individual may be withdrawn or mildly irritable for a period of hours or days before the attack and will typically report complete amnesia for the attack. During the attack, the individual may tear off his or her clothing, break furniture, shout obscenities, eat feces, flee from protective shelters, or perform other irrational or dangerous acts.

qi-gong psychotic reaction A term describing an acute, time-limited episode characterized by dissociative, paranoid, or other psychotic or nonpsychotic symptoms that may occur after participation in the Chinese folk health-enhancing practice of qi-gong ("exercise of vital energy"). Especially vulnerable are individuals who become overly involved in the practice. This diagnosis is included in the *Chinese Classification of Mental Disorders,* Second Edition (CCMD-2).

rootwork A set of cultural interpretations that ascribe illness to hexing, witchcraft, sorcery, or the evil influence of another person. Symptoms may include generalized anxiety and gastrointestinal complaints (e.g., nausea, vomiting, diarrhea), weakness, dizziness, the fear of being poisoned, and sometimes fear of being killed ("voodoo death"). "Roots," "spells," or "hexes" can be "put" or placed on other persons, causing a variety of emotional and psychological problems. The "hexed" person may even fear death until the "root" has been "taken off" (eliminated), usually through the work of a "root doctor" (a healer in this tradition), who can also be called on to bewitch an enemy. "Rootwork" is found in the southern United States among both African American and European American populations and in Caribbean societies. It is also known as *mal puesto* or *brujeria* in Latino societies.

sangue dormido ("sleeping blood")   This syndrome is found among Portuguese Cape Verde Islanders (and immigrants from there to the United States) and includes pain, numbness, tremor, paralysis, convulsions, stroke, blindness, heart attack, infection, and miscarriage.

shenjing shuairuo ("neurasthenia")   In China, a condition characterized by physical and mental fatigue, dizziness, headaches, other pains, concentration difficulties, sleep disturbance, and memory loss. Other symptoms include gastrointestinal problems, sexual dysfunction, irritability, excitability, and various signs suggesting disturbance of the autonomic nervous system. In many cases, the symptoms would meet the criteria for a DSM-IV Mood or Anxiety Disorder. This diagnosis is included in the *Chinese Classification of Mental Disorders,* Second Edition (CCMD-2).

shen-k'uei (Taiwan); **shenkui** (China)   A Chinese folk label describing marked anxiety or panic symptoms with accompanying somatic complaints for which no physical cause can be demonstrated. Symptoms include dizziness, backache, fatigability, general weakness, insomnia, frequent dreams, and complaints of sexual dysfunction (such as premature ejaculation and impotence). Symptoms are attributed to excessive semen loss from frequent intercourse, masturbation, nocturnal emission, or passing of "white turbid urine" believed to contain semen. Excessive semen loss is feared because of the belief that it represents the loss of one's vital essence and can thereby be life threatening.

shin-byung   A Korean folk label for a syndrome in which initial phases are characterized by anxiety and somatic complaints (general weakness, dizziness, fear, anorexia, insomnia, gastrointestinal problems), with subsequent dissociation and possession by ancestral spirits.

spell   A trance state in which individuals "communicate" with deceased relatives or with spirits. At times this state is associated with brief periods of personality change. This culture-specific syndrome is seen among African Americans and European Americans from the southern United States. Spells are not considered to be medical events in the folk tradition, but may be misconstrued as psychotic episodes in clinical settings.

susto ("fright," or "soul loss")   A folk illness prevalent among some Latinos in the United States and among people in Mexico, Central America, and South America. Susto is also referred to as *espanto, pasmo, tripa ida, perdida del alma,* or *chibih.* Susto is an illness attributed to a frightening event that causes the soul to leave the body and results in unhappiness and sickness. Individuals with susto also experience significant strains in key social roles. Symptoms may appear any time from days to years after the fright is experienced. It is believed that in extreme cases, susto may result in death. Typical symptoms include appetite disturbances, inadequate or excessive sleep, troubled sleep or dreams, feeling of sadness, lack of motivation to do anything, and feelings of low self-worth or dirtiness. Somatic symptoms accompanying susto include muscle aches and pains, headache, stomachache, and diarrhea. Ritual healings are focused on calling the soul back to the body and cleansing the person to restore bodily and spiritual balance. Different experiences of susto may be related to Major Depressive Disorder, Posttraumatic Stress Disorder, and Somatoform Disorders. Similar etiological beliefs and symptom configurations are found in may parts of the world.

taijin kyofusho A culturally distinctive phobia in Japan, in some ways resembling Social Phobia in DSM-IV. This syndrome refers to an individual's intense fear that his or her body, its parts or its functions, displease, embarrass, or are offensive to other people in appearance, odor, facial expressions, or movements. This syndrome is included in the official Japanese diagnostic system for mental disorders.

zar A general term applied in Ethiopia, Somalia, Egypt, Sudan, Iran, and other North African and Middle Eastern societies to the experience of spirits possessing an individual. Persons possessed by a spirit may experience dissociative episodes that may include shouting, laughing, hitting the head against a wall, singing, or weeping. Individuals may show apathy and withdrawal, refusing to eat or carry out daily tasks, or may develop a long-term relationship with the possessing spirit. Such behavior is not considered pathological locally.

Appendix J

DSM-IV Contributors

Because DSM-IV is meant to be used by a diverse group of mental health professionals in a variety of settings, the Task Force on DSM-IV and the Work Groups solicited and encouraged the participation of a wide range of professionals to serve as advisers to the Task Force and individual Work Groups. Advisers included individuals from other health associations; clinical practitioners; researchers; forensic specialists; experts on gender, age, and cultural issues; and international experts. Advisory groups identified pertinent questions regarding each diagnosis; developed and critiqued literature reviews, text, and criteria; and participated in field-trial and data-reanalysis projects. The Task Force on DSM-IV and the Work Group members extend their appreciation and heartfelt thanks to the individuals and organizations who contributed so generously of their time and expertise.

Work Group Advisers

Anxiety Disorders Advisers

W. Stewart Agras, M.D.
Hagop Akiskal, M.D.
Lauren Bersh Alloy, M.D.
James Barbie, M.D.
Aaron T. Beck, M.D.
Jean Beckham, Ph.D.
Deborah C. Beidel, Ph.D.
Istvan Bitter, M.D.
Arthur S. Blank, Jr., M.D.
Thomas D. Borkovec, Ph.D.
Loretta E. Braxton, Ph.D.
Naomi Breslau, Ph.D.
Elizabeth Brett, Ph.D.
Evelyn Bromet, Ph.D.
Timothy A. Brown, Psy.D.
Allan Burstein, M.D.
David M. Clark, Ph.D.
Lee Anna Clark, Ph.D.

Deborah S. Cowley, M.D.
Michelle G. Craske, Ph.D.
Raymond R. Crowe, M.D.
George C. Curtis, M.D.
Yael Danieli, Ph.D.
Joseph A. Deltito, M.D.
Peter A. DiNardo, Ph.D.
Keith Stephen Dobson, Ph.D.
Spencer Eth, M.D.
John Fairbank, Ph.D.
Brian Fallon, M.D.
Charles Figley, Ph.D.
Stephen M. Ford, M.D.
Ellen Frank, Ph.D.
Mathew Friedman, M.D.
Kishore Gadde, M.D.
Ronald Ganellen, Ph.D.
Michael Gelder, M.D.
Earl Giller, M.D.

Wayne Goodman, M.D.
Tana Grady, M.D.
Bonnie Green, Ph.D.
Peter J. Guarnaccia, Ph.D.
Richard Heimberg, Ph.D.
John E. Helzer, M.D.
Judith Herman, M.D.
Rudolf Hoehn-Saric, M.D.
Steven Ken Hoge, M.D.
Eric Hollander, M.D.
Mardi Horowitz, M.D.
Tom Insel, M.D.
Michael Jenike, M.D.
Wayne Katon, M.D.
Heinz Katschnig, M.D.
Terrance Keane, Ph.D.
Dean Kilpatrick, Ph.D.
Laurence Kirmayer, M.D.
Donald F. Klein, M.D.
Stuart Kleinman, M.D.
Gerald L. Klerman, M.D. (deceased)
Lawrence Kolb, M.D.
Michael J. Kozak, Ph.D.
Cynthia Last, Ph.D.
Bernard Lerer, M.D.
Andrew Levin, M.D.
R. Bruce Lydiard, M.D., Ph.D.
Salvatore Mannuzza, Ph.D.
John S. March, M.D.
Andrew Mathews, Ph.D.
Matig Mavissakalian, M.D.
Alexander McFarlane, M.B., B.S. (Hons), M.D.
Richard McNally, M.D.
Charles A. Meyer, Jr., M.D.
Karla Moras, Ph.D.
Dennis Munjack, M.D.
Lars Goran Öst, Ph.D.
Howard Parad, D.S.W.
Kok Lee Peng, M.D.
Roger Pitman, M.D.
Robert Pynoos, M.D.
Ronald M. Rapee, Ph.D.
Beverley Raphael, M.D.
Steven Rasmussen, M.D.
James Reich, M.D., M.P.H.
Patricia Resnick, Ph.D.
Jeffrey C. Richards, Ph.D.
Karl Rickels, M.D.

John H. Riskind, Ph.D.
Sir Martin Roth, M.D.
Barbara Rothbaum, Ph.D.
Peter Roy-Byrne, M.D.
Philip Saigh, Ph.D.
Paul Salkovskis, Ph.D.
William C. Sanderson, Ph.D.
Franklin Schneier, M.D.
Javaid Sheikh, M.D.
Zahava Soloman, M.D.
Susan Solomon, Ph.D.
Larry H. Strasburger, M.D., Ph.D.
Suzanne Sutherland, M.D.
Richard Swinson, M.D.
Lenore Terr, M.D.
Peter Trower, Ph.D.
Samuel M. Turner, Ph.D.
Thomas Uhde, M.D.
David Watson, Ph.D.
Hans Ulrich Wittchen, Ph.D.
Patti Zetlin, M.S.W.
Richard Zinbarg, Ph.D.
Joseph Zohar, M.D.

Delirium, Dementia, and Amnestic and Other Cognitive Disorders Advisers

Frank Benson, M.D.
John Breitner, M.D.
Steve Buckingham, M.S.S.W.
Nelson Butters, Ph.D.
Steven Cohen-Cole, M.D.
Jeffrey Lee Cummings, M.D.
Horacio Fabrega, Jr., M.D.
Barry Fogel, M.D.
Robert P. Granacher, M.D., Ph.D.
Robert C. Green, M.D.
Robert Heaton, M.D.
Steven Ken Hoge, M.D.
K. Ranga Rama Krishnan, M.D.
Keh-Ming Lin, M.D.
Zbigniew Lipowski, M.D.
Alwyn Lishman, M.D.
Richard Mayeux, M.D.
Marsel Mesulam, M.D.
Vernon Neppe, M.D.
Barry Reisberg, M.D.
Sir Martin Roth, M.D.
David Rubinow, M.D.

Randy Schiffer, M.D.
Michael Taylor, M.D.
Linda Teri, Ph.D.
Allan Yozawitz, M.D.
Stuart C. Yudofsky, M.D.
Michael Zaudig, M.D.

Disorders Usually First Diagnosed During Infancy, Childhood, or Adolescence Advisers
Marc Amaya, M.D.
Lisa Amaya-Jackson, M.D.
Adrian Angold, M.B., B.S., M.R.C.Psych.
William Arroyo, M.D.
Robert F. Asarnow, Ph.D.
George Bailey, M.D.
Joseph Biederman, M.D.
Ray Blanchard, Ph.D.
Lewis M. Bloomingdale, M.D.
John Bradford, M.D.
Joel Bregman, M.D.
Glorissa Canino, Ph.D.
Ian Alberto Canino, M.D.
Iris Chagwedera, Ph.D.
Dante Cicchetti, Ph.D.
Susan Coates, Ph.D.
Patricia Cohen, Ph.D.
C. Keith Conners, Ph.D.
Jane Costello, M.D.
Charles Davenport, M.D.
Robert Delong, M.D.
Martha Denckla, M.D.
Park Elliott Dietz, M.D., Ph.D.
Craig Donnelly, M.D.
Felton Earls, M.D.
L. Erlenmeyer-Kimling, Ph.D.
Jack Fletcher, Ph.D.
Steven Forness, Ed.D.
Richard Green, M.D., J.D.
Laurence Greenhill, M.D.
Stanley Greenspan, M.D.
Richard L. Gross, M.D.
Robert Harmon, M.D.
Lily Hechtman, M.D.
Margaret Hertzig, M.D.
James J. Hudziak, M.D.
Peter Jensen, M.D.
Gloria Johnson-Powell, M.D.
Robert King, M.D.

Mindy Krotick, M.A.
Cynthia Last, Ph.D.
James Leckman, M.D.
James Lee, M.D.
Stephen Levine, M.D.
John Lochman, M.D.
Catherine Lord, Ph.D.
John S. March, M.D.
James McKinney, Ph.D.
Jon Meyer, M.D.
Heino F.L. Meyer-Bahlburg, Dr., rer., nat.
Juan Enrique Mezzich, M.D., Ph.D.
Klaus Minde, M.D.
David Mrazek, M.D.
Joy Osofsky, Ph.D.
Ira Pauly, M.D.
Gary Peterson, M.D.
Sally Provence, M.D.
Joaquim Puig-Antich, M.D. (deceased)
Kathleen May Quinn, M.D.
Steven Rasmussen, M.D.
Robert J. Reichler, M.D.
Mark A. Riddle, M.D.
Edward Ritvo, M.D.
Richard Rosner, M.D.
Byron Rourke, Ph.D.
Diane H. Schetky, M.D.
Eric Schopler, Ph.D.
Rourke Schopler, Ph.D.
Arthur Shapiro, M.D.
Theodore Shapiro, M.D.
Bennet Shaywitz, M.D.
Larry Silver, M.D.
Robert Stoller, M.D. (deceased)
Alan Stone, M.D.
Peter Szatmari, M.D.
Ludwig Szymanski, M.D.
Paula Tallal, Ph.D.
Kenneth Towbin, M.D.
Luke Tsai, M.D.
Kenneth Jay Weiss, M.D.
Myrna M. Weissman, Ph.D.
Elizabeth Weller, M.D.
Karen Wells, Ph.D.
Agnes Whittaker, M.D.
Janet B. W. Williams, D.S.W.
Ronald Winchel, M.D.
Allan Yozawitz, M.D.
Kenneth J. Zucker, Ph.D.

Barry Zuckerman, M.D.
Bernard Zuger, M.D.

Eating Disorders Advisers
W. Stewart Agras, M.D.
Arnold Anderson, M.D.
William Berman, Ph.D.
Peter Beumont, M.D.
Barton J. Blinder, M.D.
Susan Jane Blumenthal, M.D.
LCDR James M. Blunt
Harry A. Brandt, M.D.
Timothy D. Brewerton, M.D.
Kelly Brownell, Ph.D.
Gabrielle A. Carlson, M.D.
Eva Carr, M.A.
Regina Casper, M.D.
Leslie Citrome, M.D.
Peter J. Cooper, M.D.
Arthur H. Crisp, M.D.
Maria DaCosta, M.D.
Bonnie Dansky, Ph.D.
Michael Devlin, M.D.
Adam Drewnowski, Ph.D.
Elke Eckert, M.D.
Robert Edelman, M.D.
Christopher Fairburn, M.D.
Madeline Fernstrom, Ph.D.
Manfred Fichter, M.D.
Martine Flament, M.D.
Henri Flikier, A.C.S.W.
Victor Fornari, M.D.
Chris Freeman, M.D.
David M. Garner, Ph.D.
Philip W. Gold, M.D.
Harry E. Gwirtsman, M.D.
Deborah Hasin, Ph.D.
C. Peter Herman, Ph.D.
David Herzog, M.D.
Jules Hirsch, M.D.
Hans W. Hoek, M.D., Ph.D.
Steven Ken Hoge, M.D.
L.K. George Hsu, M.D.
James I. Hudson, M.D.
Laurie Humphries, M.D.
Philippe Jeammet, M.D.
David C. Jimerson, M.D.
Craig Johnson, Ph.D.
Ross S. Kalucy, M.D.

Jack L. Katz, M.D.
Walter Kaye, M.D.
Justin Kenardy, Ph.D.
Kenneth S. Kendler, M.D.
Sid Kennedy, M.D.
Dean Kilpatrick, Ph.D.
Dean D. Krahn, M.D.
Sing Lee, M.R.C.Psych.
Pierre Leichner, M.D.
Harold Leitenberg, Ph.D.
Jill Leolbonne, M.D.
Gloria Leon, Ph.D.
Katharine Loeb, B.A.
Alexander R. Lucas, M.D.
Marsha Marcus, Ph.D.
Valerie Rae McClain, B.A.
Juan Enrique Mezzich, M.D., Ph.D.
Julian Morrow, Ph.D.
Claes Norring, Dr.Med.Sc.
Patrick O'Conner, Ph.D.
Marion P. Olmstead, Ph.D.
Carol B. Peterson, Ph.D.
Karl Pirke, M.D.
Janet Polivy, Ph.D.
Harrison Pope, M.D.
Charles Portney, M.D.
Albert M. Powell, M.D.
Raymond Prince, M.D.
Richard Pyle, M.D.
Ellen Raynes, Psy.D.
Rory Richardson, M.A.
Cheryl Ritenbaugh, Ph.D., M.P.H.
Paul Robinson, M.D.
Judith Rodin, Ph.D.
Barbara J. Rolls, Ph.D.
James Rosen, Ph.D.
Gerald Russell, M.D.
Ronna Saunders, L.C.S.W.
Joseph Silverman, M.D.
Michael Strober, Ph.D.
Albert J. Stunkard, M.D.
Allan Sugarman, M.D.
George Szmukler, M.D.
Sten Theander, M.D.
Suellen Thomsen, B.A.
David Tobin, Ph.D.
Walter Vandereycken, M.D.
David Veale, M.R.C.Psych.
Kelly Bemis Vitousek, Ph.D.

Thomas Wadden, Ph.D.
David Waller, M.D.
Winny Weeda-Mannak, Ph.D.
Herbert Weiner, M.D.
Mitchel Weiss, M.D., Ph.D.
David Wheadon, M.D.
Rena Wing, M.D.
Steve Wonderlich, Ph.D.
Susan Wooley, Ph.D.
Wayne Wooley, Ph.D.
Judith Wurtman, Ph.D.
Joel Yager, M.D.
Susan Yanovski, M.D.
Preston Zucker, M.D.

Mood Disorders Advisers
Hagop Akiskal, M.D.
Jay Amsterdam, M.D.
Jules Angst, M.D.
Paul S. Appelbaum, M.D.
Marie Åsberg, M.D.
David Avery, M.D.
Aaron T. Beck, M.D.
James C. Beck, M.D.
Dan Blazer, M.D.
Charles Bowden, M.D.
Ian Brockington, M.D.
Susan B. Campbell, Ph.D.
Dennis P. Cantwell, M.D.
Bernard J. Carroll, M.D. Ph.D.
Giovanni Cassano, M.D.
Paul Chodoff, M.D.
William Coryell, M.D.
John L. Cox, D.M.
Jonathan Davidson, M.D.
John Davis, M.D.
Christine Dean, M.D.
Robert Delong, M.D.
J. Raymond DePaulo, M.D.
Jean Endicott, Ph.D.
Cecile Ernst, M.D.
Max Fink, M.D.
Leslie M. Forman, M.D.
Linda George, Ph.D.
Robert Gerner, M.D.
Elliot Gershon, M.D.
William Goldstein, M.D.
Byron Good, Ph.D.
Frederick K. Goodwin, M.D.

Thomas Gordon Gutheil, M.D.
Wilma M. Harrison, M.D.
Jonathon M. Himmelhoch, M.D.
Robert M. A. Hirschfeld, M.D.
Steven Ken Hoge, M.D.
Charles Holzer III, M.D.
Robert Howland, M.D.
Emily Hoyer, B.A.
James Jefferson, M.D.
Ira Katz, M.D.
Gabor Keitner, M.D.
Robert Kendell, M.D.
Kenneth S. Kendler, M.D.
Daniel Klein, Ph.D.
Gerald L. Klerman, M.D. (deceased)
James Kocsis, M.D.
Harold Koenig, M.D.
Ernest Kovacs, M.D.
Helena Kraemer, Ph.D.
K. Ranga Rama Krishnan, M.D.
Andrew Krystal, M.D.
David J. Kupfer, M.D.
Jacqueline LaLive, M.D.
Peter Lewinshon, Ph.D.
Wolfgang Maier, M.D.
John Mann, M.D.
Spero Manson, Ph.D.
James P. McCullough, Ph.D.
Patrick McGrath, M.D.
Julien Mendelewicz, M.D.
Kathleen Merikangas, Ph.D.
Robert Michels, M.D.
Ivan Miller, Ph.D.
Phyllis Nash, D.S.W.
Michael O'Hara, Ph.D.
David Osser, M.D.
Gordon Parker, M.D.
Barbara Parry, M.D.
Eugene Paykel, M.D.
Kok Lee Peng, M.D.
Fredrick Petty, M.D., Ph.D.
Robert M. Post, M.D.
Daniel Purdy, A.B.
Frederic Quitkin, M.D.
Judith G. Rabkin, Ph.D.
Ted Reich, M.D.
Richard Ries, M.D.
Donald Robinson, M.D.
Holly Rogers, M.D.

Jerrold F. Rosenbaum, M.D.
Norman Rosenthal, M.D.
Anthony Rothschild, M.D.
Alec Roy, M.D.
Cordelia Russell, B.A.
Alan Schatzberg, M.D.
Jan Scott, Ph.D.
Tracie Shea, Ph.D.
Anne Simmons, Ph.D.
Stuart Sotsky, M.D.
David Steffens, M.D.
Jonathan Stewart, M.D.
Larry H. Strasburger, M.D., Ph.D.
Trisha Suppes, M.D., Ph.D.
Michael Thase, M.D.
Richard Weiner, M.D.
Jan Weissenburger, M.A.
Myrna M. Weissman, Ph.D.
Kenneth Wells, M.D.
Peter C. Whybrow, M.D.
George Winokur, M.D.
Anna Wirz-Justice, Ph.D.
Hans Ulrich Wittchen, Ph.D.

Multiaxial Issues Advisers
Jonathan F. Borus, M.D.
Kathleen Buckwalter, Ph.D.
Fredric Busch, M.D.
Eric Douglas Caine, M.D.
Thomas Carli, M.D.
Arnold Cooper, M.D.
Paul Crits-Christoph, M.D.
Susan Fine, M.A.
Paul J. Fink, M.D.
Jack Froom, M.D.
Akira Fujinawa, M.D.
Daniel W. Gillette, M.D.
Robert Glick, M.D.
Byron Good, Ph.D.
Richard E. Gordon, M.D., Ph.D.
Barry Gurland, M.D.
Herta A. Guttman, M.D.
Richard Hall, M.D.
Mardi Horowitz, M.D.
Charles Hughes, Ph.D.
T. Byram Karasu, M.D.
James Karls, D.S.W.
Florence Kaslow, Ph.D.
Otto Kernberg, M.D.

Gerald L. Klerman, M.D. (deceased)
Thomas Kuhlman, Ph.D.
Powell Lawton, Ph.D.
Joshua D. Lipsitz, Ph.D.
Christine Lloyd, M.D.
Lester Luborsky, M.D.
Roger Mackinnon, M.D.
Carolyn Mazure, Ph.D.
Theodore Millon, Ph.D.
Glen Pearson, M.D.
J. Christopher Perry, M.D.
George H. Pollock, M.D.
Joseph M. Rey, Ph.D.
Lawrence Rockland, M.D.
Geoffrey Shrader, M.D.
Ronald C. Simons, M.D., M.A.
Alan Stoudemire, M.D.
James J. Strain, M.D.
John S. Strauss, M.D.
Christopher Tennant, M.D.
Mary Durand Thomas, R.N., Ph.D.
Virginia Tilden, R.N., D.N.Sc.
George Vaillant, M.D.
Holly Skodol Wilson, R.N., Ph.D.
Ronald M. Wintrob, M.D.
Lyman C. Wynne, M.D., Ph.D.

Personality Disorders Advisers
Gerald Adler, M.D.
Salman Akhtar, M.D.
Hagop Akiskal, M.D.
Norimassa Akuta, M.D.
Renato Daniel Alarcon, M.D., M.P.H.
Arthur Alterman, Ph.D.
Antonio Andreoli, M.D.
Paul S. Appelbaum, M.D.
Beng-Ake Armelius, Ph.D.
Lorna Smith Benjamin, Ph.D.
Mark Berelowitz, M.D.
Jack Brandes, M.D.
Remi Cadoret, M.D.
Paul Chodoff, M.D.
Lee Anna Clark, Ph.D.
John Clarkin, Ph.D.
C. Robert Cloninger, M.D.
Jerome Cohen, D.S.W.
Karyl Cole, M.D.
Arnold Cooper, M.D.
Paul Costa, Ph.D.

Alv A. Dahl, M.D.
Carl Eisdorfer, M.D., Ph.D., M.S.W
Edward F. Foulks, M.D., Ph.D.
John Frosch, M.D.
William Goldstein, M.D.
Seymour L. Halleck, M.D.
Robert Hare, Ph.D.
Judith Herman, M.D.
Steven Ken Hoge, M.D.
Mardi Horowitz, M.D.
Stephen W. Hurt, Ph.D.
Steven Hyler, M.D.
Karen John, M.D.
Patricia Judd, M.S.W.
Charles Kaelber, M.D.
Oren Kalus, M.D.
Kenneth S. Kendler, M.D.
Otto Kernberg, M.D.
Donald Kiesler, Ph.D.
Daniel Klein, Ph.D.
Donald F. Klein, M.D.
Arthur Kleinman, M.D., Ph.D.
Harold Koenigsberg, M.D.
Jerome Kroll, M.D.
Marsha Linehan, Ph.D.
Paul Links, M.D.
John Lion, M.D.
W. John Livesley, M.D.
Armand Loranger, Ph.D.
Spencer Lyerly, Ph.D.
Michael Lyons, Ph.D.
K. Roy MacKenzie, M.D.
Roger Mackinnon, M.D.
Nikolas Manos, M.D.
James Masterson, M.D.
Robert McCrae, Ph.D.
Thomas McGlashan, M.D.
Robert David Miller, M.D., Ph.D.
Leslie Morey, Ph.D.
Ole Mors, M.D.
Kazuhisa Nakao, M.D.
H. George Nurnberg, M.D.
John Oldham, M.D.
Yutaka Ono, M.D.
Stephen L. Oxley, Ph.D.
Joel Paris, M.D.
Gordon Parker, M.D.
Glen Pearson, M.D.
Kok Lee Peng, M.D.

J. Christopher Perry, M.D.
Ethel Person, M.D.
Katharine Anne Phillips, M.D.
Paul Pilkonis, Ph.D.
Harrison Pope, M.D.
Charles Pull, M.D.
James Reich, M.D., M.P.H.
William H. Reid, M.D.
Lee Robins, Ph.D.
Elsa Ronningstam, Ph.D.
Loren Henry Roth, M.D.
Robert Ruegg, M.D.
Pedro Ruiz, M.D.
A. John Rush, M.D.
Marvin Schwartz, M.D.
Richard Selman, M.D.
Kenneth Silk, M.D.
Bennett Simon, M.D.
Richard C. Simons, M.D.
Erik Simonsen, M.D.
Andrew Edward Skodol II, M.D.
Paul Harris Soloff, M.D.
Stephen Sternbach, M.D.
Alan Stone, M.D.
Michael Stone, M.D.
Lawrence Tancredi, M.D.
Alex Tarnopolsky, M.D.
Auke Tellegen, Ph.D.
Pekka Tienari, M.D.
Svenn Torgensen, M.D.
Joseph Triebwasser, M.D.
Robert Tringone, Ph.D.
Timothy Trull, Ph.D.
Peter Tyrer, M.D.
Lindsey Tweed, M.D.
T. Bedirhan Ustun, M.D.
Per Vaglum, M.D.
Sonya Vaglum, M.D.
George Vaillant, M.D.
Lenore B. Walker, Ed.D.
Dermot Walsh, M.B.
Jack Wiggins, Ph.D.
Jerry Wiggins, Ph.D.
Mary C. Zanarini, Ed.D.

**Premenstrual Dysphoric
Disorder Advisers**
Elissa P. Benedek, M.D.
Sarah Berga, M.D.

Susan Jane Blumenthal, M.D.
Leah Joan Dickstein, M.D.
Ellen W. Freeman, Ph.D.
Sheryl Gallant, Ph.D.
Leslie Gise, M.D.
Uriel Halbreich, M.D.
Jean Hamilton, M.D.
Michelle Harrison, M.D.
Roger F. Haskett, M.D.
Steven Ken Hoge, M.D.
Stephen W. Hurt, Ph.D.
Renee Johns, B.A.
W. Keye, Jr., M.D.
Martha Kirkpatrick, M.D.
Martha McClintock, Ph.D.
Margaret L. Moline, Ph.D.
Carol C. Nadelson, M.D.
Howard Osofsky, M.D.
Mary Brown Parlee, Ph.D.
Jeff Rausch, M.D.
Robert Reid, M.D.
R. Rhodes, M.D.
Ana Rivera-Tovar, Ph.D.
Gail Robinson, M.D.
Miriam Rosenthal, M.D.
Peter Roy-Byrne, M.D.
David Rubinow, M.D.
Paula Schnurr, Ph.D.
John Steege, M.D.
Meir Steiner, M.D., Ph.D.
Donna Stewart, M.D.
Anna Stout, M.D.
Lenore B. Walker, Ed.D.
David Youngs, M.D.

**Psychiatric Systems Interface
Disorders (Adjustment, Dissociative,
Factitious, Impulse-Control, and
Somatoform Disorders and
Psychological Factors Affecting
Medical Condition) Advisers**
Paul S. Appelbaum, M.D.
Allyson Ashley, D.S.W.
Arthur J. Barsky, M.D.
David H. Barlow, Ph.D.
Johnathon O. Beahrs, M.D.
David Bear, M.D.
Gale Beardsley, M.D.
Sidney Benjamin, M.D., M.Phil.

Kenneth Bowers, Ph.D.
John Bradford, M.D.
Bennett Braun, M.D.
Etzel Cardena, Ph.D.
James Chu, M.D.
Catherine Classen, Ph.D.
Philip Coons, M.D.
Douglas Detrick, Ph.D.
Robert H. Dworkin, Ph.D.
David Folks, M.D.
Fred Frankel, M.D.
Edward Frischholz, Ph.D.
George Fulup, M.D.
Rollin Gallagher, M.D.
Jeffrey Geller, M.D.
Daniel W. Gillette, M.D.
Michael G. Goldstein, M.D.
Veerainder Goli, M.B.
Carlos A. Gonzalez, M.D.
Junius Gonzales, M.D.
Michael I. Good, M.D.
Ezra E. H. Griffith, M.D.
Samuel B. Guze, M.D.
Seymour L. Halleck, M.D.
Abraham L. Halpern, M.D., Ph.D.
Nelson Hendler, M.S., M.D.
Ernest Hilgard, Ph.D.
Steven Ken Hoge, M.D.
Jimmie C. Holland, M.D.
Eric Hollander, M.D.
James J. Hudziak, M.D.
Janis H. Jenkins, Ph.D.
Roger Kathol, M.D.
J. David Kinzie, M.D.
Laurence Kirmayer, M.D.
Arthur Kleinman, M.D., Ph.D.
Richard Kluft, M.D.
Cheryl Koopman, Ph.D.
Donald S. Kornfeld, M.D.
K. Ranga Rama Krishnan, M.D.
John Kurtz, M.D.
Henry R. Lesieur, Ph.D.
James Levenson, M.D.
Roberto Lewis-Fernandez, M.D.
John Lion, M.D.
Zbigniew J. Lipowski, M.D.
Don R. Lipsitt, M.D.
Richard Loewenstein, M.D.
Jeffrey Mattes, M.D.

M. Eileen McNamara, M.D.
Harold Merskey, D.M.
Michael Moran, M.D.
George B. Murray, M.D.
John Nemiah, M.D.
Jeffrey Newcorn, M.D.
Raymond Niaura, Ph.D.
Perry M. Nicassio, Ph.D.
Martin Orne, M.D., Ph.D.
Kalpana Pakianathan, M.D.
Robert O. Pasnau, M.D.
Kok Lee Peng, M.D.
Samuel W. Perry III, M.D.
Gary Peterson, M.D.
John Plewes, M.D.
Stanley L. Portnow, M.D., Ph.D.
Frank Putnam, M.D.
Phillip Jacob Resnick, M.D.
Richard J. Rosenthal, M.D.
Colin A. Ross, M.D.
John Z. Sadler, M.D.
Shirley Sanders, Ph.D.
Stephen M. Saravay, M.D.
Jonathon F. Silver, M.D.
Herbert Spiegel, M.D.
Marlene Steinberg, M.D.
Robert Stewart, D.S.W.
Marvin Swartz, M.D.
Troy L. Thompson II, M.D.
Moshe Torem, M.D.
Eldon Tunks, M.D.
William L. Webb, Jr., M.D. (deceased)
Kenneth Jay Weiss, M.D.
Mitchel Weiss, M.D., Ph.D.
Lewis Jolly West, M.D.
Ronald Winchel, M.D.
Thomas Nathan Wise, M.D.
Dennis Wolf, M.D.
Derson Young, M.D.
Stuart C. Yudofsky, M.D.
Sean Yutzy, M.D.

Schizophrenia and Other Psychotic Disorders Advisers
Xavier Amador, Ph.D.
Stephan Arndt, Ph.D.
Peter Berner, M.D.
Istvan Bitter, M.D.
Donald W. Black, M.D.

Randy Borum, M.D.
Malcolm B. Bowers, Jr., M.D.
H. Stefan Bracha, M.D.
Ian Brockington, M.D.
William Carpenter, M.D.
Richard J. Castillo, Ph.D.
David Copolov, M.D.
Lawrence A. Dunn, M.D.
William Edell, Ph.D.
Akira Fujinawa, M.D.
Carlos A. Gonzalez, M.D.
Jack Gorman, M.D.
Igor Grant, M.D.
Ezra E. H. Griffith, M.D.
Gretchen Haas, Ph.D.
Martin Harrow, Ph.D.
Steven Ken Hoge, M.D.
Janis H. Jenkins, Ph.D.
Dilip V. Jeste, M.D.
Marvin Karno, M.D.
Robert Kendell, M.D.
Anthony F. Lehman, M.D., M.S.P.H.
Roberto Lewis-Fernandez, M.D.
Robert Liberman, M.D.
Jeffrey Lieberman, M.D.
Mario Maj, M.D.
Joseph P. McEvoy, M.D.
Max McGee, M.D.
Patrick McGorry, M.B.B.S.
Herbert Meltzer, M.D.
Alan Metz, M.D.
Jeffrey L. Metzner, M.D.
Mark Richard Munetz, M.D.
Alistair Munroe, M.D.
Keith Neuchterlein, Ph.D.
Yuji Okazaki, M.D.
Alfonso Ontiveros, M.D., M.Sc.
Stein Opjordsmoen, Ph.D.
Ananda K. Pandurangi, M.D.
Godfrey Pearlson, M.D.
Delbert Robinson, M.D.
Nina Schooler, Ph.D.
Larry Siever, M.D.
Samuel Siris, M.D.
John Sweeney, Ph.D.
Sally Szymanski, D.O.
Mauricio Tohen, M.D.
Ming Tso Tsuang, M.D., Ph.D.
Michael Zaudig, M.D.

Sexual Disorders Advisers
John Bradford, M.D.
Robert P. Cabaj, M.D.
Dona L. Davis, Ph.D.
Park Elliott Dietz, M.D., Ph.D.
Leslie Gise, M.D.
Abraham L. Halpern, M.D., Ph.D.
Gilbert Herdt, Ph.D.
Steven Ken Hoge, M.D.
Helen Kaplan, M.D.
Kok Lee Peng, M.D.
Anna Stout, M.D.

Sleep Disorders Advisers
Edward Bixler, M.D.
Jack Edinger, M.D.
Charles W. Erwin, M.D.
Eugene C. Fletcher, M.D.
Abraham L. Halpern, M.D., Ph.D.
Peter Hauri, Ph.D.
Anthony Kales, M.D.
Milton Kramer, M.D.
Rocco Manfredi, M.D.
Gail Marsh, M.D.
Jeffrey L. Metzner, M.D.
Harvey Moldofsky, M.D.
Timothy H. Monk, Ph.D.
Ralph Pascualy, M.D., R.N.
Howard Roffwarg, M.D.
Thomas Roth, Ph.D.
A. John Rush, M.D.
Constantin R. Soldatos, M.D.
Edward Stepanski, Ph.D.
Michael Thorpy, M.D.

Substance-Related Disorders Advisers
Henry Abraham, M.D.
Christer Allgulander, M.D.
Arthur Alterman, Ph.D.
Roland Atkinson, M.D.
Tom Babor, Ph.D.
George Bailey, M.D.
James Barbie, M.D.
Jeffrey Bedrick, M.D.
Fred K. Berger, M.D.
Jack D. Blaine, M.D.
Sheila Blume, M.D.
Richard Bonnie, J.D.

Kathleen Bucholz, Ph.D.
John Cacciola, Ph.D.
Glorissa Canino, Ph.D.
William D. Clark, M.D.
Stephen Dinwiddie, M.D.
Griffith Edwards, M.D.
Marian Fischman, Ph.D.
Richard Frances, M.D.
William Frosch, M.D.
Marc Galanter, M.D.
Frank Gawin, M.D.
Edith S. Linansky Gomberg, Ph.D.
Enoch Gordis, M.D.
David Gorelick, M.D.
Bridget Grant, Ph.D.
Marcus Grant, Ph.D.
Lester Grinspoon, M.D.
Alfred Harkley, M.D.
James Hartford, M.D.
Deborah Hasin, Ph.D.
Steven Ken Hoge, M.D.
Arthur M. Horton, Ph.D.
John R. Hughes, M.D.
Michael Irwin, M.D.
Jerome Jaffe, M.D.
Denise Kandel, Ph.D.
Edward Kaufman, M.D.
Herbert Kleber, M.D.
Thomas Kosten, M.D.
Mary Jeanne Kreek, M.D.
James Langenbucher, Ph.D.
Edward D. Levin, Ph.D.
Benjamin Liptzin, M.D.
James Maddox, M.D.
Enrique Madrigal, M.D.
Peter Martin, M.D.
Roy Mathew, M.D.
Wayne McFadden, M.D.
Thomas McLellan, Ph.D.
Jack H. Mendelsohn, M.D.
Roger Meyer, M.D.
Norman Miller, M.D.
Robert Millman, M.D.
Maristela Monteiro, M.D.
Robert M. Morse, M.D.
David F. Naftolowitz, M.D.
Paul Nagy
Charles O'Brien, M.D.
Glen Pearson, M.D.

Stanton Peele, Ph.D.
Helen Pettinatti, Ph.D.
Roy Pickens, Ph.D.
Andrzej Piotrowski, M.D.
Rumi Price, Ph.D.
Anthony Radcliffe, M.D.
Charles Riordan, M.D.
Jed Rose, Ph.D.
Bruce Rounsaville, M.D.
John Saunders, M.D.
Sidney H. Schnoll, M.D.
Charles R. Schuster, Ph.D.

Boris Segal, M.D.
Roy Stein, M.D.
Lee L. Towle, Ph.D.
John Tsuang, M.D.
Harold Urschell III, M.D.
Dermot Walsh, M.B.
Robert Weinrieb, M.D.
Joseph Westermeyer, M.D., Ph.D.,
    M.P.H.
Kenneth Winters, Ph.D.
Sheldon Zimberg, M.D.

Task Force Advisers

Advisers on Coding Issues
Andrea Albaum-Feinstein
Margaret Amatayakul, M.B.A., R.R.A.
Amy Blum, M.P.H., R.R.A.
Delray Green, R.R.A.
Deborah K. Hansen, A.R.T., C.C.S.
Robert A. Israel, M.P.H.
L. Ann Kirner, C.C.S.
Perrianne Lurie, M.D., M.P.H.
Sue Meads, R.R.A.
James W. Thompson, M.D., M.P.H.

Advisers on Cross-Cultural Issues
Juan Enrique Mezzich, M.D., Ph.D.
Arthur Kleinman, M.D., Ph.D.
Horacio Fabrega, Jr., M.D.
Delores Parron, Ph.D.
Byron Good, Ph.D.
Keh-Ming Lin, M.D.
Spero Manson, Ph.D.
Gloria Johnson-Powell, M.D.

Victor R. Adebimpe, M.D.
Renato Daniel Alarcon, M.D., M.P.H.
William Arroyo, M.D.
Morton Beiser, M.D.
James Boster, Ph.D.
Glorissa Canino, Ph.D.
Ian Alberto Canino, M.D.
Richard J. Castillo, Ph.D.
Freda Cheung, Ph.D.
Ellen Corin, Ph.D.
Dona L. Davis, Ph.D.

Armando Favazza, M.D.
Candace Fleming, Ph.D.
Edward F. Foulks, M.D., Ph.D.
Atwood Gaines, Ph.D.
Albert Gaw, M.D.
James Gibbs, Ph.D.
Carlos A. Gonzalez, M.D.
Ezra E. H. Griffith, M.D.
Peter J. Guarnaccia, Ph.D.
Gilbert Herdt, Ph.D.
Kim Hopper, Ph.D.
David Hufford, Ph.D.
Charles Hughes, Ph.D.
Janis H. Jenkins, Ph.D.
Marvin Karno, M.D.
Marianne Kastrup, M.D., Ph.D.
J. David Kinzie, M.D.
Laurence Kirmayer, M.D.
Paul Koegel, Ph.D.
Robert F. Kraus, M.D.
Tina K. Leonard-Green, M.S., R.D.
Roberto Lewis-Fernandez, M.D.
T-Y Lin, M.D.
Roland Littlewood, M.B., D.Phil.
Francis Lu, M.D.
Enrique Madrigal, M.D.
Theresa O'Nell, Ph.D.
Raymond Prince, M.D.
Juan Ramos, Ph.D.
Cheryl Ritenbaugh, Ph.D., M.P.H.
Lloyd Rogler, Ph.D.
William H. Sack, M.D.
Ihsan Salloum, M.D., M.P.H.

Norman Sartorius, M.D., Ph.D.
Catherine L. Shisslak, Ph.D.
Ronald C. Simons, M.D., M.A.
Jeanne M. Spurlock, M.D.
Nicolette Teufel, Ph.D.
James W. Thompson, M.D., M.P.H.
Wen-Shing Tseng, M.D.
Mitchel Weiss, M.D., Ph.D.
Joseph Westermeyer, M.D., Ph.D.,
    M.P.H.
Charles Wilkinson, M.D.
Ronald M. Wintrob, M.D.
Joseph Yamamoto, M.D.

**Advisers on Family/
Relational Issues**
James Alexander, Ph.D.
Arthur M. Bodin, Ph.D.
Robert Butler, M.D.
Patricia Chamberlain, Ph.D.
Dante Cichetti, Ph.D.
John Clarkin, Ph.D.
Daniel Corwin, M.D.
Mark R. Ginsberg, Ph.D.
Michael J. Goldstein, Ph.D.
Herta A. Guttman, M.D.
Michael D. Kahn, Ph.D.
Sandra Kaplan, M.D.
Florence Kaslow, Ph.D.
John F. Knutson, Ph.D.
Judy Magil, M.S.W.
David Milkowitz, Ph.D.
K. Daniel O'Leary, Ph.D.
David Olson, Ph.D.
David Pelcovitz, Ph.D.
Angus M. Strachan, Ph.D.
Terry S. Trepper, Ph.D.
Lyman C. Wynne, M.D., Ph.D.
Ramsy Yassa, M.D.

Advisers on Forensic Issues
Paul S. Appelbaum, M.D.
James C. Beck, M.D.
Lewis M. Bloomingdale, M.D.
Richard Bonnie, J.D.
Jeffrey Lee Cummings, M.D.
Jeffrey Geller, M.D.
Robert P. Granacher, M.D., Ph.D.
Thomas Gordon Gutheil, M.D.

Abraham L. Halpern, M.D., Ph.D.
Steven Ken Hoge, M.D.
Stuart Kleinman, M.D.
Jeffrey L. Metzner, M.D.
Charles A. Meyer, Jr., M.D.
Robert David Miller, M.D., Ph.D.
Mark Richard Munetz, M.D.
Stanley L. Portnow, M.D., Ph.D.
Phillip Jacob Resnick, M.D.
Richard Rosner, M.D.
Daniel W. Shuman
Larry H. Strasburger, M.D., Ph.D.
Kenneth Jay Weiss, M.D.
Howard Zonana, M.D.

**Advisers on Medication-Induced
Movement Disorders**
Gerard Addonizio, M.D.
Lenard Adler, M.D.
Burt Angrist, M.D.
Ross J. Baldessarini, M.D.
Stanley N. Caroff, M.D.
Daniel Casey, M.D.
Jeffrey Lee Cummings, M.D.
George Gardos, M.D.
Allen Gelenberg, M.D.
James Jefferson, M.D.
Dilip V. Jeste, M.D.
John M. Kane, M.D.
Paul E. Keck, M.D.
James Levenson, M.D.
Stephan C. Mann, M.D.
Ananda K. Pandurangi, M.D.
Patricia Rosebush, M.D.
Virginia Susman, M.D.
Peter Weiden, M.D.
Ramsy Yassa, M.D.

**Advisers to the Task Force
on DSM-IV**
Boris M. Astrachan, M.D.
Robert Avant, M.D.
Jeanette Bair, B.S., M.B.A.
W. Robert Beavers, M.D.
Jeffrey Bedrick, M.D.
Carl Bell, M.D.
Ellen Berman, M.D.
Eugene Broadhead, M.D., Ph.D.
Laura Brown, Ph.D.

Robert P. Cabaj, M.D.
Robert Cahan, M.D.
Robert Chiarello, M.D.
William D. Clark, M.D.
Steven Cohen-Cole, M.D.
Lee Combrinck-Graham, M.D.
Vicky Conn, R.N.
Harris Cooper, Ph.D.
Michael Crouch, M.D.
Alan Daniels
Frank deGruy, M.D.
Susan Dime-Meenan
Stacy Donovan, B.A.
Richard Dudley, M.D.
Suzanne Dworak-Peck
Bruce Emery, A.C.S.W.
Spencer Falcon, M.D.
Louis Fine, M.D.
Susan Fine, M.A.
Rita Finnegan, R.R.A.
Gerald H. Flamm, M.D.
Laurie Flynn, B.A.
Raymond D. Fowler, Ph.D.
Richard Frances, M.D.
Jack Froom, M.D.
Robert W. Gibson, M.D.
Junius Gonzales, M.D.
Raphael S. Good, M.D.
Robert C. Green, M.D.
Larry P. Griffin, M.D.
Claire Griffin-Francell, R.N.
Alfred Harkley, M.D.
Norman B. Hartstein, M.D.
Ann Hohmann, Ph.D.
Theodore Hutchison, M.D.
Dale Johnson, Ph.D.
John E. Joyner, M.D.
Harold Kaminetzky, M.D.
Ira Katz, M.D.
Jerald Kay, M.D.
Kelly Kelleher, M.D.
Helena Kraemer, Ph.D.
John J. LaFerla, M.D.
Marion Langer, Ph.D.
Martha Lasseter, R.R.A.
Philip Lavori, Ph.D.
Lawrence N. Lazarus, M.D.
Harriet Lefley, Ph.D.

James Levenson, M.D.
Frank Ling, M.D.
Mack Lipkin, M.D.
Don-David Lusterman, Ph.D.
Richard M. Magraw, M.D.
Kathryn Magruder, Ph.D., M.P.H.
Dale Matthews, M.D.
Chuck Miles, M.D.
Sheldon I. Miller, M.D.
Paul D. Mozley, M.D.
Kathi Pajer, M.D.
Joseph Palombi, M.D.
Robert C. Park, M.D.
Elaine Purpel, M.S.W.
Peter Rabins, M.D.
Anthony Radcliffe, M.D.
Richard Rahe, M.D.
Peter Rappo, M.D.
Marilyn Rosenson, M.S.W.
Marshall Rosman, Ph.D.
Donald J. Scherl, M.D.
Sidney H. Schnoll, M.D.
Diana Seebold, R.R.A.
Charles A. Shamoian, M.D., Ph.D.
Steven Sharfstein, M.D.
J. Gregory Shea
Alfred Skinner, M.D.
William W. Snavely
Janet T. Spence
Leon Speroff, M.D.
Emanuel Steindler
Melvin Stern, M.D.
James E. Strain, M.D.
Rev. Paul C. Tomlinson
Michael B. Unhjem
Jerome Vaccaro, M.D.
Jeanne Van Riper, A.R.T.
Alan J. Wabrek, M.D.
Lenore B. Walker, Ed.D.
Steven Wartman, M.D.
Robert Weinrieb, M.D.
Robert Weinstock, Ph.D.
Bryant Welch, Ph.D.
Eleanor White, Ph.D.
Robert L. Williams, M.D.
Mark Wolraich, M.D.
David Youngs, M.D.

International Advisers

The Task Force on DSM-IV sought the expertise of a wide range of international experts. The contributions of international experts helped to ensure cultural sensitivity, applicability for international mental health professionals, and greater compatibility with ICD-10. International experts advised both the Task Force and individual Work Groups.

Christer Allgulander, M.D. (Sweden)
Paulo Alterwain, M.D. (Uruguay)
Antonio Andreoli, M.D. (Switzerland)
Jules Angst, M.D. (Switzerland)
Beng-Ake Armelius, Ph.D. (Switzerland)
Marie Åsberg, M.D. (Sweden)
Tolani Asuni, M.D. (Nigeria)
Sidney Benjamin, M.D., M.Phil.
    (England)
Mark Berelowitz, M.D. (England)
Peter Berner, M.D. (Austria)
Aksel Bertelsen, M.D. (Denmark)
Peter Beumont, M.D. (Australia)
Istvan Bitter, M.D. (Hungary)
Ray Blanchard, Ph.D. (Canada)
Daniel Bobon (Belgium)
Jacek Bomba, M.D. (Poland)
Kenneth Bowers, Ph.D. (Canada)
John Bradford, M.D. (Canada)
Susan Bradley, M.D. (Canada)
Jack Brandes, M.D. (Canada)
Ian Brockington, M.D. (England)
Graham Burrows, M.D. (Australia)
Patricia Casey, M.D. (Ireland)
Giovanni Cassano, M.D. (Italy)
Doo Young Cho, M.D. (Korea)
David M. Clark, Ph.D. (England)
John E. Cooper, M.D. (England)
Peter J. Cooper, M.D. (England)
David Copolov, M.D. (Australia)
Jorge Costa e Silva, M.D. (Brazil)
Arthur H. Crisp, M.D. (England)
Stanislaw Dabrowski, M.D. (Poland)
Adrian Dafunchio, M.D. (Argentina)
Alv A. Dahl, M.D. (Norway)
Christine Dean, M.D. (England)
Horst Dilling, M.D. (Germany)
Keith Stephen Dobson, Ph.D. (Canada)
Griffith Edwards, M.D. (England)
Christopher Fairburn, M.D. (England)
Francois Ferrero, M.D. (Switzerland)

Manfred Fichter, M.D. (Germany)
Martine Flament, M.D. (France)
Chris Freeman, M.D. (Scotland)
Harold Freyberger, M.D. (Germany)
Akira Fujinawa, M.D. (Japan)
Paul Garfinkel, M.D. (Canada)
Michael Gelder, M.D. (England)
Semyon Gluzman, M.D. (former USSR)
Judith H. Gold, M.D. (Canada)
Marcus Grant, Ph.D. (Switzerland)
Herta A. Guttman, M.D. (Canada)
Heinz Hafner, M.D. (Germany)
Robert Hare, Ph.D. (Canada)
Lily Hechtman, M.D. (Canada)
Michiel W. Hengeveld, M.D., Ph.D.
    (Netherlands)
C. Peter Herman, Ph.D. (Canada)
Hans Hippius, M.D. (Germany)
Willem M. Hirs, M.D. (Netherlands)
Teo Seng Hock, M.D. (Singapore)
Hans W. Hoek, M.D., Ph.D.
    (Netherlands)
Yoshiko Ikeda, M.D. (Japan)
Assen Jablensky, M.D. (Bulgaria)
Aleksander Janca, M.D. (Switzerland)
Philippe Jeammet, M.D. (France)
Karen John, M.D. (England)
Miguel Jorge, M.D., Ph.D. (Brazil)
Ross S. Kalucy, M.D. (Australia)
Marianne Kastrup, M.D., Ph.D.
    (Denmark)
Heinz Katschnig, M.D. (Austria)
Justin Kenardy, Ph.D. (Australia)
Robert Kendell, M.D. (Scotland)
Sid Kennedy, M.D. (Canada)
Renard Knabbe, M.D. (Switzerland)
Vladimir Kovalev, M.D. (former USSR)
Evsey Krasik, M.D. (former USSR)
Yves LeCrubier, M.D. (France)
Pierre Leichner, M.D. (Canada)
Jill Leolbonne, M.D. (England)

Bernard Lerer, M.D. (Israel)
Aubrey Levin, M.D. (South Africa)
Paul Links, M.D. (Canada)
Zbigniew Lipowski, M.D. (Canada)
Alwyn Lishman, M.D. (England)
W. John Livesley, M.D. (Canada)
J. López-Ibor, Jr., M.D. (Spain)
Mario Maj, M.D. (Italy)
Felice Lieh Mak (China)
Nikolas Manos, M.D. (Greece)
Isaac Marks, M.D. (England)
Alexander C. McFarlane, M.B.B.S.
   (Hons), M.D. (Australia)
Patrick McGorry, M.B.B.S. (Australia)
Julien Mendelewicz, M.D. (Belgium)
Klaus Minde, M.D. (Canada)
Harvey Moldofsky, M.D. (Canada)
Maristela Monteiro, M.D. (Brazil)
Stuart Montgomery, M.D. (England)
Ole Mors, M.D. (Denmark)
Alistair Munroe, M.D. (Canada)
Gulam Mustafa, M.D. (Kenya)
Yoshibumi Nakane, M.D. (Japan)
W.A. Nolen (Netherlands)
Claes Norring, Dr.Med.Sc. (Sweden)
Yuri Nuller (former USSR)
Ahmed Okasha, M.D. (Egypt)
Yuji Okazaki, M.D. (Japan)
Yutaka Ono, M.D. (Japan)
Alfonso Ontiveros, M.D., M.Sc. (Mexico)
Stein Opjordsmoen, Ph.D. (Norway)
John Orley, M.D. (Switzerland)
Lars Goran Öst, Ph.D. (Sweden)
Stefano Pallanti, M.D. (Italy)
Joel Paris, M.D. (Canada)
Gordon Parker, M.D. (Australia)
Eugene Paykel, M.D. (England)
Kok Lee Peng, M.D. (Singapore)
Uwe Henrick Peters, M.D. (Germany)
Carlo Perris, M.D. (Sweden)
Pierre Pichot, M.D. (France)
Andrzej Piotrowski, M.D. (Poland)
Karl Pirke, M.D. (Germany)
Janet Polivy, Ph.D. (Canada)
Charles Pull, M.D. (Luxembourg)
Kari Pylkkanen, M.D. (Finland)
Juan Ramon de la Fuente, M.D. (Mexico)
Beverley Raphael, M.D. (Australia)
Robert Reid, M.D. (Canada)

Helmut Remschmidt (Germany)
Nils Rettersol, M.D. (Norway)
Joseph M. Rey, Ph.D. (Australia)
Jeffrey C. Richards, Ph.D. (Australia)
Antonio A. Rizzoli, M.D. (Italy)
Paul Robinson, M.D. (England)
Sir Martin Roth, M.D. (England)
Byron Rourke, Ph.D. (Canada)
Gerald Russell, M.D. (England)
Sir Michael Rutter, M.D. (England)
Javier Saavedra, M.D. (Peru)
Paul Salkovskis, Ph.D. (England)
Norman Sartorius, M.D., Ph.D.
   (Switzerland)
John Saunders, M.D. (Australia)
Aart H. Schene, M.D. (Netherlands)
Marcus Fini Schulsinger, M.D.
   (Denmark)
Jan Scott, Ph.D. (England)
Ruben Hernandez Serrano, M.D.
   (Venezuela)
Michael Shephard, M.D. (England)
Erik Simonsen, M.D. (Denmark)
Cees J. Slooff, M.D. (Netherlands)
Constantin R. Soldatos, M.D. (Greece)
Zahava Soloman, M.D. (Israel)
Marin Stancu, M.D. (Romania)
Meir Steiner, M.D., Ph.D. (Canada)
Donna Stewart, M.D. (Canada)
Eric Stromgren, M.D. (Denmark)
Peter Szatmari, M.D. (Canada)
George Szmukler, M.D. (England)
Alex Tarnopolsky, M.D. (Canada)
Christopher Tennant, M.D. (Australia)
Sten Theander, M.D. (Sweden)
Pekka Tienari, M.D. (Finland)
Svenn Torgensen, M.D. (Norway)
Peter Trower, Ph.D. (England)
Eldon Tunks, M.D. (Canada)
Peter Tyrer, M.D. (England)
T. Bedirhan Ustun, M.D. (Switzerland)
Per Vaglum, M.D. (Norway)
Walter Vandereycken, M.D. (Belgium)
Jenny Van Drimmelen-Krabbe, M.D.
   (Switzerland)
J. T. van Mens, M.D. (Netherlands)
David Veale, M.R.C.Psych. (England)
F. C. Verhulst (Netherlands)
Marcio Versiani, M.D. (Brazil)

Marten W. de Vries, M.D. (Netherlands)
Dermot Walsh, M.B. (Ireland)
Winny Weeda-Mannak, Ph.D.
    (Netherlands)
John S. Werry, M.D. (New Zealand)
Hans Ulrich Wittchen, Ph.D. (Germany)

Ramsy Yassa, M.D. (Canada)
Derson Young, M.D. (China)
Michael Zaudig, M.D. (Germany)
Joseph Zohar, M.D. (Israel)
Kenneth J. Zucker, Ph.D. (Canada)
Roberto Llanos Zuloaga, M.D. (Peru)

DSM-IV Focused Field-Trial Projects

The field-trial projects funded by the National Institute of Mental Health in collaboration with the National Institute on Drug Abuse and the National Institute on Alcohol Abuse and Alcoholism were an invaluable source of data and contributed greatly to the quality of DSM-IV. Our thanks to Darrel Regier, M.D., M.P.H., Director of the Division of Epidemiology and Services Research, and Charles Kaelber, M.D., the Project Officer, for their support and expertise. Our thanks, too, to the following field-trial participants:

Principal Investigator
Allen Frances, M.D.

Co-Principal Investigator
Harold Alan Pincus, M.D.

Field-Trial Coordinator
Myriam Kline, M.S.

Statistical Consultant
Helena Kraemer, Ph.D.

**Antisocial Personality
Disorder Field Trial**

Project Director
Thomas A. Widiger, Ph.D.

Site Coordinators
Arthur Alterman, Ph.D.
Remi J. Cadoret, M.D.
Robert Hare, Ph.D.
Lee Robins, Ph.D.
George E. Woody, M.D.
Mary C. Zanarini, Ed.D.

**Autism and Pervasive Developmental
Disorders Field Trial**

Project Director
Fred Volkmar, M.D.
    (also Site Coordinator)

Site Coordinators
Magda Campbell, M.D.
B. J. Freeman, Ph.D.
Ami Klin, Ph.D.

Catherine Lord, Ph.D.
E. Ritvo, M.D.
Sir Michael Rutter, M.D.
Eric Schopler, Ph.D.

Site Coordinators, Volunteer Sites
Joel Bregman, M.D.
Jan Buitelaar, M.D.
Soo Churl Cho, M.D.
Eric Fombonne, M.D.
Joaquin Fuentes, M.D.
Yossie Hattab, M.D.
Yoshihiko Hoshino, M.D.
J. Kerbeshian, M.D.
William Kline, Ph.D.
Katherine Loveland, Ph.D.
Bryna Siegel, Ph.D.
Wendy Stone, M.D.
Peter Szatmari, M.D.
Ludwig Szymanski, M.D.
Kenneth Towbin, M.D.
John S. Werry, M.D.

**Disruptive Behavior
Disorder Field Trial**

Project Director
Benjamin Lahey, Ph.D.
    (also Site Coordinator)

Site Coordinators
Russell Barkley, Ph.D.
Joseph Biederman, M.D.
Barry Garfinkel, M.D.

Laurence Greenhill, M.D.
George Hynd, Ed.D.
Keith McBurnett, Ph.D.
Jeffrey Newcorn, M.D.
Thomas Ollendick, Ph.D.

Site Coordinators, Volunteer Sites
Paul Frick, Ph.D.
Peter Jensen, M.D.
Lynn Kerdyk, Ph.D.
John Richters, Ph.D.

Data Coordinator
Dorcas Perez, B.A.

Major Depression, Dysthymia, and Minor Depressive Disorder Field Trial

Project Director
Martin B. Keller, M.D.
    (also Site Coordinator)

Project Co-Directors
Michael B. First, M.D.
James Kocsis, M.D.
    (also Site Coordinator)

Site Coordinators
Robert M. A. Hirschfeld, M.D.
Charles Holzer, Ph.D.
Gabor Keitner, M.D.
Daniel Klein, Ph.D.
Deborah Marin, M.D.
James P. McCullough, Ph.D.
Ivan Miller, Ph.D.
Tracie Shea, Ph.D.

Data Coordinators
Diane Hanks, M.A.
Cordelia Russell, B.A.

Mixed Anxiety-Depressive Disorder Field Trial

Project Directors
David H. Barlow, Ph.D.
    (also Site Coordinator)
Michael R. Liebowitz, M.D.
    (also Site Coordinator)
Richard Zinbarg, Ph.D.
    (also Site Coordinator)

Site Coordinators
Phil Brantley, Ph.D.

Eugene Broadhead, M.D., Ph.D.
Wayne Katon, M.D.
Jean-Pierre Lepine, M.D.
Jeffrey C. Richards, Ph.D.
Peter Roy-Byrne, M.D.
Linda Street, Ph.D.
Mardjan Teherani, Ph.D.

Obsessive-Compulsive Disorder Field Trial

Project Director
Edna Foa, Ph.D. (also Site Coordinator)

Site Coordinators
Jane Eisen, M.D.
Wayne Goodman, M.D.
Hella Hiss, Ph.D.
Eric Hollander, M.D.
Michael Jenike, M.D.
Michael J. Kozak, Ph.D.
Steven Rasmussen, M.D.
Joseph Ricciardi, Ph.D.
Peggy Richter, M.D.
Barbara Rothbaum, Ph.D.

Panic Disorder Field Trial

Project Director
Abby Fyer, M.D. (also Site Coordinator)

Project Co-Director
James C. Ballenger, M.D.
    (also Site Coordinator)

Site Coordinators
David H. Barlow, Ph.D.
Michael Hollifield, M.D.
Wayne Katon, M.D.
Richard Swinson, M.D.

Data Analysts
Tim Chapman, M.Phil.
Salvatore Mannuzza, Ph.D.

Data Coordinator
Hilary Rassnick, M.A.

Posttraumatic Stress Disorder Field Trial

Project Director
Dean Kilpatrick, Ph.D.
    (also Site Coordinator)

Bessel van der Kolk, M.D.
    (also Site Coordinator)

Site Coordinators
John Freedy, Ph.D.
Sandra Kaplan, M.D.
David Pelcovitz, Ph.D.
Patty Resick, Ph.D.
Heidi Resnick, Ph.D.
Susan Roth, Ph.D.

Schizophrenia and Related Psychotic Disorders Field Trial

Project Directors
Nancy Coover Andreasen, M.D., Ph.D.
    (also Site Coordinator)
Michael A. Flaum, M.D.
    (also Site Coordinator)

Site Coordinators
Xavier Amador, Ph.D.
H. Stefan Bracha, M.D.
William Edell, Ph.D.
Jack Gorman, M.D.
Kenneth S. Kendler, M.D.
Jeffrey Lieberman, M.D.
Thomas McGlashan, M.D.
Ananda K. Pandurangi, M.D.
Delbert Robinson, M.D.

Site Coordinators, Volunteer Sites
Patrick McGorry, M.B.B.S.
Alfonso Ontiveros, M.D., M.Sc.
Mauricio Tohen, M.D.

Sleep Disorders Field Trial

Project Directors
Daniel Buysse, M.D.
    (also Site Coordinator)
David J. Kupfer, M.D.

Charles F. Reynolds III, M.D.

Site Coordinators
Edward Bixler, M.D.
Peter Hauri, Ph.D.
Anthony Kales, M.D.
Rocco Manfredi, M.D.
Thomas Roth, Ph.D.
Edward Stepanski, Ph.D.
Michael Thorpy, M.D.

Data Coordinator
Debbie Mesiano, B.S.

Somatization Disorder Field Trial

Project Director
C. Robert Cloninger, M.D.

Site Coordinators
Samuel B. Guze, M.D.
Roger Kathol, M.D.
Ronald L. Martin, M.D.
Richard Smith, M.D.
James J. Strain, M.D.
Sean Yutzy, M.D.

Substance Use Field Trial

Project Directors
Linda Cottler, Ph.D.
    (also Site Coordinator)
John E. Helzer, M.D.
Marc Alan Schuckit, M.D.
    (also Site Coordinator)

Site Coordinators
Thomas Crowley, M.D.
John R. Hughes, M.D.
George E. Woody, M.D.

Site Coordinators, Volunteer Sites
Jean-Pierre Lepine, M.D.

MacArthur Data-Reanalysis Project

The data-reanalysis projects funded by a generous grant from the John D. and Catherine T. MacArthur Foundation provided an extensive research database. Many thanks to Dennis Prager at the Foundation for his tremendous support. Our sincere appreciation to the following individuals who conducted data-reanalysis projects:

Principal Investigator
Allen Frances, M.D.

Co-Principal Investigators
Harold Alan Pincus, M.D.
Thomas A. Widiger, Ph.D.

Anxiety Disorders
David H. Barlow, Ph.D.
Deborah C. Beidel, Ph.D.
Thomas Burton, B.A.
Michelle G. Craske, Ph.D.
George C. Curtis, M.D.
Peter A. DiNardo, Ph.D.
Abby Fyer, M.D.
Robin Garfinkel, Ph.D.
Richard Heimberg, Ph.D.
Elizabeth M. Hill, Ph.D.
Christopher D. Hornig, B.A.
Ewald Horwath, M.D., M.Sc.
James Johnson, Ph.D. (deceased)
Harlan Juster, Ph.D.
Wayne Katon, M.D.
Gerald L. Klerman, M.D. (deceased)
Karen Law, B.A.
Andrew Leon, Ph.D.
Michael R. Liebowitz, M.D.
Salvatore Mannuzza, Ph.D.
Jill Mattia, M.A.
Eryn Oberlander, M.D.
Susan Orsillo, M.A.
Peter Roy-Byrne, M.D.
Paul Salkovskis, Ph.D.
Franklin Schneier, M.D.
Samuel M. Turner, Ph.D.
Myrna M. Weissman, Ph.D.
Susan I. Wolk, M.D.
Roberto Zarate, M.A.

Delirium, Dementia, and Amnestic and Other Cognitive Disorders
Michael O. Colvin, M.D.

Marshall Folstein, M.D.
Gary Lloyd Gottlieb, M.D.
Dilip V. Jeste, M.D.
Sue Levkoff, D.Sc.
Benjamin Liptzin, M.D.
George W. Rebok, Ph.D.
David Salmon, Ph.D.
Leon Thal, M.D.

Disorders Usually First Diagnosed During Infancy, Childhood, or Adolescence
Brooks Applegate, Ph.D.
Gerald August, Ph.D.
Susan J. Bradley, M.D.
Joel Bregman, M.D.
Patricia Cohen, Ph.D.
Michael Flory, Ph.D.
Susan Folstein, M.D.
Eric Fombonne, M.D.
Barry Garfinkel, M.D.
Richard Green, M.D., J.D.
Stephanie M. Green, M.S.
Jane E. Hood, M.A.
Kate Keenan, M.S.
Benjamin Lahey, Ph.D.
Marion Leboyer, M.D.
Rolf Loeber, Ph.D.
Catherine Lord, Ph.D.
John McLennan, M.D.
Nancy Minshew, M.D.
Rhea Paul, Ph.D.
Andrew Pickles, Ph.D.
Howard M. Rebach, Ph.D.
Mary F. Russo, Ph.D.
Sir Michael Rutter, M.D.
Eric Schopler, Ph.D.
Christopher Thomas, M.D.
Fred Volkmar, M.D.
Katherine Williams, Ph.D.
Kenneth J. Zucker, Ph.D.

Eating Disorders
Arnold Anderson, M.D.
Christopher Fairburn, M.D.
Martine Flament, M.D.
Paul Garfinkel, M.D.
Dean Kilpatrick, Ph.D.
James Mitchell, M.D.
G. Terence Wilson, Ph.D.
Steven Wonderlich, M.D.

Mood Disorders
Gregory Asnis, M.D.
Mark S. Bauer, M.D.
Diane Bynum
Joseph Calabrese, M.D.
William Coryell, M.D.
David Dunner, M.D.
Ellen Frank, Ph.D.
Laszlo Gyulai, M.D.
Martin B. Keller, M.D.
James Kocsis, M.D.
Philip Lavori, Ph.D.
Yves LeCrubier, M.D.
Robert M. Post, M.D.
Samuel J. Simmens, Ph.D.
Stuart Sotsky, M.D.
Dan L. Tweed, Ph.D.
Lindsey Tweed, M.D.
Peter C. Whybrow, M.D.
Sharon Younkin

Personality Disorders
Emil F. Coccaro, M.D.
Mark Davies, M.D.
Michael B. First, M.D.
Robert Hare, Ph.D.
Theodore Millon, Ph.D.
Vivian Mitropoulou, M.A.
Leslie Morey, Ph.D.
Bruce Pfohl, M.D.
Lee Robins, Ph.D.
Larry J. Siever, M.D.
Jeremy M. Silverman, Ph.D.
Andrew Edward Skodol II, M.D.
Timothy Trull, Ph.D.
Thomas A. Widiger, Ph.D.
Mary C. Zanarini, Ed.D.

Premenstrual Dysphoric Disorder
Ellen Frank, Ph.D.
Ellen W. Freeman, Ph.D.
Leslie Gise, M.D.
Judith H. Gold, M.D.
Barbara Parry, M.D.
Paula Schnurr, Ph.D.
Sally Severino, M.D.
John Steege, M.D.
Meir Steiner, M.D., Ph.D.

Psychiatric Systems Interface Disorders (Adjustment, Dissociative, Factitious, Impulse-Control, and Somatoform Disorders and Psychological Factors Affecting Medical Condition)
Henry R. Lesieur, M.D.
Juan Enrique Mezzich, M.D., Ph.D.
Jeffrey Newcorn, M.D.
David Spiegel, M.D.
James J. Strain, M.D.

Schizophrenia and Other Psychotic Disorders
Nancy Coover Andreasen, M.D., Ph.D.
Gretchen Haas, Ph.D.
Jeffrey Lieberman, M.D.
Patrick McGorry, M.B.B.S.
Keith Neuchterlein, Ph.D.
Mauricio Tohen, M.D.

Sleep Disorders
Daniel Buysse, M.D.
Charles F. Reynolds III, M.D.

Substance-Related Disorders
John Cacciola, Ph.D.
Linda B. Cottler, Ph.D.
John E. Helzer, M.D.
Rumi Price, Ph.D.
Lee Robins, Ph.D.
Marc Alan Schuckit, M.D.
George E. Woody, M.D.

MacArthur General Reliability Field Trial

As DSM-IV is being published, an additional project sponsored by the John D. and Catherine T. MacArthur Foundation will provide further information regarding the validity of DSM-IV criteria. The ongoing videotape field-trial project is expected to be completed in 1995. Our thanks to the following individuals who participated in the project:

Principal Investigator
Allen Frances, M.D.
James W. Thompson, M.D., M.P.H.

Co-Principal Investigators
Harold Alan Pincus, M.D.
Michael B. First, M.D.
Michael A. Flaum, M.D.
Anthony F. Lehman, M.D., M.S.P.H.

Pilot Participants
Xavier Amador, Ph.D.
Nancy Coover Andreasen, M.D., Ph.D.
F. M. Baker, M.D.
Donald W. Black, M.D.
Carlos S. Castillo, M.D.
Scott C. Clark, M.D.
William Coryell, M.D.
Lisa B. Dixon, M.D.
Jack E. Downhill, Jr., M.D.
Katherine P. Duffy, M.D.
Jean Endicott, Ph.D.
Michael A. Fauman, M.D., Ph.D.

Miriam Gibbon, M.S.W.
Jack Gorman, M.D.
Paul E. Hogsten, M.D.
Michael L. Jeffries, M.D.
Douglas Langbehn, M.D.
Joseph Liberto, M.D.
David B. Mallot, M.D.
Del D. Miller, Pharm.D., M.D.
Lewis A. Opler, M.D., Ph.D.
Jill A. RachBeisel, M.D.
Robert P. Schwartz, M.D.
Andrew Edward Skodol II, M.D.
David H. Strauss, M.D.
Scott Stuart, M.D.
Janet B. W. Williams, D.S.W.
Catherine Woodman, M.D.

Project Coordinator
Jennifer Norbeck, M.S.W.

Video Consultant
Vincent Clayton, M.A.

Expert-Phase Participants

The following represents the project participants at the time that DSM-IV went to press. It is anticipated that other sites and individuals will join the project.

Jonathan Alpert, M.D.
Katherine Attala, M.D.
David Avery, M.D.
Monica Ramirez Basco, Ph.D.
Mark S. Bauer, M.D.
    (also Site Coordinator)
Thomas F. Betzler, M.D.
Melanie M. Biggs, Ph.D.
    (also Site Coordinator)
Robert J. Bishop, M.D.
Danielle Bordeau, M.D.

Malcolm B. Bowers, Jr., M.D.
Gary Bruss, Ph.D.
Peter Buckley, M.D.
Deborah S. Cowley, M.D.
Brian Cox, Ph.D.
James David, M.D.
Collette De Marneffe, Ph.D.
Judith Dogin, M.D.
Seda Ebrahimi, Ph.D.
Jane Eisen, M.D.
Maurizio Fava, M.D.

Paul Federoff, M.D.
Mark K. Fulton, M.D.
Diego Garcia-Borreguero, M.D.
Roya Ghadimi, M.D.
David S. Goldbloom, M.D.
Reed D. Goldstein, Ph.D.
(also Site Coordinator)
Micael Golinkoff, Ph.D.
Peter Goyer, M.D.
Alan M. Gruenberg, M.D.
Michael E. Henry, M.D.
Selby C. Jacobs, M.D.
J. Joel Jeffries, M.B.
(also Site Coordinator)
Sheri Johnson, Ph.D.
Kathleen Kim, M.D., M.P.H.
Carolyn M. Mazure, Ph.D.
(also Site Coordinator)
Joseph P. McEvoy, M.D.
Arnold Merrimam, M.D.
Timothy I. Mueller, M.D.
Andrew Nierenberg, M.D.
Michael Otto, Ph.D.
Michelle Pato, M.D.
Joel Pava, Ph.D.
Katharine Anne Phillips, M.D.
(also Site Coordinator)

Mark Pollack, M.D.
Horatio Preval, M.D.
David W. Preven, M.D.
(also Site Coordinator)
Richard Ries, M.D.
Robert C. Risinger, M.D.
Robert Ronis, M.D.
Jerrold F. Rosenbaum, M.D.
(also Site Coordinator)
Peter Roy-Byrne, M.D.
(also Site Coordinator)
Mark Schmidt, M.D.
(also Site Coordinator)
S. Charles Schulz, M.D.
Bruce Schwartz, M.D.
Michael Schwartz, M.D.
(also Site Coordinator)
Michael J. Sernyak, M.D.
Richard Swinson, M.D.
Madhukar H. Trivedi, M.D.
Andrea Weiss, M.D.
Kerrin White, M.D.
Lawrence Wilson, M.D.
John Worthington, M.D.
Joan Youchah, M.D.

Other Health Organizations

At the inception of the project, the Task Force on DSM-IV invited over 60 health associations to designate liaisons to the Task Force to ensure the openness of the revision process and to ensure that a variety of views would be represented. The associations listed below designated representatives who received regular communications from the Work Groups and the Task Force.

American Academy of Child and
Adolescent Psychiatry
American Academy of Family Physicians
American Academy of Pediatrics
American Academy of Psychiatrists in
Alcoholism and Addictions
American Academy of Psychiatry and
the Law
American Association for Geriatric
Psychiatry

American Association for Marriage and
Family Therapy
American Association of Chairmen of
Departments of Psychiatry
American Association of Directors of
Psychiatric Residency Training
American Association of Psychiatric
Administrators
American Board of Family Practice
American College of Obstetricians and
Gynecologists

American College of Physicians
American Group Psychotherapy
Association
American Health Information
Management Association
American Medical Society on Alcohol
and Other Drug Dependencies
American Nurses' Association
American Occupational Therapy
Association
American Psychoanalytic Association
American Psychological Association
American Psychological Society
American Psychosomatic Society, Inc.
American Society for Adolescent
Psychiatry
Association of Departments of Family
Medicine
Association of Gay and Lesbian
Psychiatrists

Association of Mental Health Clergy
Coalition for the Family
Group for the Advancement of
Psychiatry
National Alliance for the Mentally Ill
National Association of Social Workers
National Association of Veterans Affairs
Chiefs of Psychiatry
National Center for Health Statistics
National Council of Community Mental
Health Centers
National Depressive and Manic
Depressive Association
National Medical Association
National Mental Health Association
Society of General Internal Medicine
Society of Teachers of Family Medicine
World Health Organization

Index

E

O

P